THE
COMPLETE
CANADIAN
HEALTH
GUIDE

The
Complete

University of Toronto
Faculty of Medicine

Canadian Health Guide

JUNE ENGEL, Ph.D.
EDITOR, *HEALTH NEWS*

KEY PORTER BOOKS

I dedicate this book to the memory of my father,
a chemist and violinist,
who taught me to appreciate the world of science,
and
to my daughter, Stephanie, and her remarkable family

The publisher gratefully acknowledges the assistance of the Canada Council and the Ontario Arts Council.

Canadian Cataloguing in Publication Data

Engel, June
        The complete Canadian health guide

Includes index.
ISBN 1-55013-474-4

1. Medicine, Popular. 2. Family — Health and
hygiene. I. Title.

RC81.E63 1993   616.02'4   C93-093804-6

Key Porter Books Limited
70 The Esplanade
Toronto, Ontario
Canada M5E 1R2

Design: Scott Richardson
Layout: Rodney Frost, MacTrix DTP
Typesetting: MacTrix DTP
Printed and bound in Canada

93 94 95 96 6 5 4 3 2 1

The author of this book is employed as Editor of *Health News*, a publication of the Faculty of Medicine, University of
Toronto. The statements and opinions expressed are, nevertheless, those of the author and the University of Toronto does
not accept responsibility for them.

Publisher's Note: The contents of this book are not intended to be used as a substitution for consultation with your
physician. All matters pertaining to your health should be directed to a health care professional.

Contents

CHAPTER 12: PUBERTY AND ADOLESCENT CHANGES *308*

CHAPTER 13: FACING SOME MODERN ENVIRONMENTAL HEALTH HAZARDS *331*

Preface

THIS BOOK BEGAN long ago with my interest in biological science and a passionate desire to help people understand how the body works. I was forever explaining to friends, relatives and anyone who'd listen that "No! Vitamin C does *not* dissolve fat globules in the blood," or that "Antibiotics only cure bacterial illnesses, *not* those due to viruses." As a biochemist and writer — straddling the worlds of science and journalism — I tried my best to translate medical knowledge into clear, comprehensible terms, to dispel misconceptions, to help people assess medical news correctly and distinguish truth from fiction (or half-truths). My experience as a science writer showed me that, despite an avalanche of medical reporting, an escalating public interest in health matters and an avid search for reliable information, people were often confused or, worse still, misled.

In 1982, I became the editor of *Health News*, the health letter published by the University of Toronto's Faculty of Medicine to provide the public with reliable, up-to-date, in-depth health information. The response to this health bulletin, prepared in conjunction with experts at Canada's largest medical school, has been overwhelming — from both lay readers and health professionals. Our editorial office is inundated with letters and phone calls request-ing more information and expressing gratitude for the accurate, detailed reporting that helps people make wiser healthcare choices. Many medical practitioners say they use the publication to educate patients and to update themselves on topics outside their immediate area of expertise. The time, effort and enthusiasm put into *Health News*, both by our tiny editorial staff and by hundreds of faculty members, have been well rewarded by its enthusiastic reception.

The Complete Canadian Health Guide draws on and expands the accumulated material from ten years of *Health News* — amalgamating the most current knowledge of many medical specialists working in diverse fields. The book aims to give people a concise, readable source of health information, and to arm them with the practical knowledge needed to sort through the mass of conflicting health pronouncements and make sensible, informed healthcare decisions. Any medical terms or jargon used are translated into straightforward language that everyone can understand, and enough background is given to put each topic in context. Each section has been prepared with the assistance of health professionals from the University of Toronto and elsewhere, and Canadian sources are given for those seeking further information.

Rather than simply presenting an encyclopedic compendium of diseases, I have tried to focus on health promotion, disease prevention and the principles of "health management," which is ideally a collaboration between health-care consumers (patients) and the medical fraternity and should address social, emotional and psychological problems as well as physical ones. I hope the book fosters an inquiring attitude that leads people to analyze the medical information they read, hear or see. To help them evaluate medical news in the popular press, I explain how science works, why certain strategies, procedures or treatments are tried and their relative merits and drawbacks.

After discussing the general principles of promoting and maintaining health, I consider the way that lifestyle affects well-being and how people can upgrade their health. There are sections on the care of various body parts — such as skin, hair, eyes, ears and teeth — and the health problems concerning them. There is special attention to the particular health concerns of women, men and children, and to contemporary worries such as skin cancer, sexually transmitted diseases and suicide. I list the names of medications used for various conditions, with their pros and cons, so that people can make more informed choices. Where medical opinion is sharply divided, both sides of the argument are explained, so that people can discuss the issues more fully with their physicians and know what questions to ask. There's also a comprehensive section on first aid.

While *The Complete Canadian Health Guide* aims to help readers become more informed about ways to manage their health, it in no way seeks to replace physician care. Specific health concerns must still be discussed with medical advisers. But I hope to facilitate communication with medical caregivers. The better we all understand what goes on in our bodies — and its relationship to lifestyle habits and to mental, social and emotional influences — the more we can do to keep ourselves well and to recognize and deal with any problems that crop up. How can we take care of all our responsibilities in this life, if we cannot first take care of ourselves?

Acknowledgments

THIS BOOK WOULD never have happened without the wisdom, help and support of scores of medical experts at the University of Toronto's Faculty of Medicine, and in particular of the Advisory Board of *Health News*, the faculty's lay health bulletin. I would especially like to thank three consecutive chairpersons of that Advisory Board — Drs. Gerard Burrow, Fred Lowy and Mary Jane Ashley — for their warm encouragement. A special thanks also to Dr. Warren Rubenstein, Dr. John Kellen and Dr. Cornelia Baines for tirelessly helping me by checking and revising a never-ending series of health topics, and for being ruthlessly critical in the most amazingly constructive manner.

Since some of the material in the book comes from articles in *Health News*, I owe thanks to everyone who ever helped me with the publication over the past ten years and to the hundreds of medical experts who provided source material and checked what I wrote on various subjects. Special thanks to Martha Harron, for contributing to the section on complementary medicine. Thanks also to my researcher, Isolde Prince (who excels in hunting down references at a moment's notice), to Madeline Koch, a computer magician who speedily inputted my endless revisions, and to my loyal, hard-working assistants

— especially Julie Markham and Cathy McNally — who bolstered my resolve when I was almost ready to abandon the project. It was a mammoth task to get each little section of the book on different medical topics checked by the relevant specialists.

For checking and correcting specific parts of the book I'd like to express my special gratitude to the following: Dr. Margaret Baigent, Dr. Karen Binkley, Dr. Anne Biringer, Dr. Irv Broder, Dr. Andrew Bruce, Dr. Joe Bruni, Dr. Robert Buckman, Dr. Ken Cadesky, Dr. June Carroll, Dr. Bob Casper, Dr. Rosalyn Curtis, Dr. Raisa Deber, Dr. Diane Donat, Dr. Andy Duic, Dr. Robin Eastwood, Dr. John Edmeads, Dr. Richard Ellen, Dr. Roberta Ferrence, Dr. Louis Francescutti, Dr. Richard Frecker, Dr. Paul Garfinkel, Dr. Ron Gold, Dr. David Goldbloom, Dr. Anthony Graham, Dr. Paul Gully, Dr. Henry Hallam, Dr. Stephen Holzapel, Dr. Paul Hwang, Dr. Russell Joffee, Dr. Allan Kaplan, Dr. Debbie Katzman, Dr. Sid Kennedy, Dr. Anne Kenshole, Ms. Ann Kerr, Dr. Ed Keystone, Dr. Jay Keystone, Dr. Alan Knight, Dr. Anthony Lang, Dr. Joel Lexchin, Dr. Arthur Leznoff, Ms. Jane Love, Dr. David Lowy, Dr. Donald McLachlan, Dr. William Mahon, Dr. Aaron Malkin, Dr. Morton Mamelak, Dr. Rena Mendelson, Dr. Robert Murray, Dr. Tim Murray, Dr. Julien Nedzelski, Dr. Marion Olmstead, Dr. Howard Ovens, Dr. Fred Papsin, Dr. John Parker, Dr. Marion Powell, Dr. Anita Rachlis, Dr. Stan Reed, Dr. Knox Ritchie, Ms. Monika Riutort, Dr. Michael Robinette,

Dr. Miriam Rossi, Dr. Bruce Rowat, Dr. Lawrence Rubin, Dr. Jim Ruderman, Dr. John Rutka, Dr. Diane Sacks, Dr. Issac Sakinofsky, Dr. Ricky Schachter, Ms. Mary Sharpe, Dr. David Shaul, Dr. Linda Short, Dr. Ken Shulman, Dr. R. Silver, Dr. Allan Slomovic, Dr. Douglas Snell, Dr. Wilf Steinberg, Dr. Leonard Sternberg, Dr. Donna Stewart, Dr. Gordon Sussman, Dr. Donald Sutherland, Dr. Richard Swinson, Dr. William Tatton, Dr. John Trachtenberg, Dr. Joan Vale, Dr. Sarah VanderBurgh, Dr. Mladin Vranic, Dr. Philip Wade, Dr. Evelyn Wallace, Ms. Earlene Wasik, Dr. John Wherrett, Ms. Joan Wright, Dr. Trevor Young, Dr. Barry Zimmerman, Dr. Stanley Zlotkin.

Thanks also to my copy editor, Gena Gorrell, for her meticulous attention to detail, for her questioning — sometimes caustic — but always humorously phrased comments, for patiently explaining why I couldn't say this or that, and for endlessly transporting pages of edited manuscript through the snowy streets of Toronto during the frightful winter of '92.

Finally, I must thank my family and friends for their forbearance during the 18 months that I worked on the book for long hours, seven days a week, devoting too little time or attention to them.

HEALTH NEWS
Advisory Board List

What is good health all about?

What is health? • Measuring health • Changing attitudes to healthcare • How to assess health news

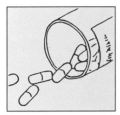

WHAT IS HEALTH?

There is no universally accepted definition of health. The meaning of health has changed through the ages and across different cultures. The term derives from the Anglo-Saxon word "haelth," meaning safe, sound or whole. In medieval times "haelthing" meant "sharing a few drinks with one's friends," having previously meant "hello" and "holiness." The term "disease" generally refers to a diagnosable physical or biochemical abnormality, while "illness" means the personal experience of sickness, the *perceived* suffering and disability due to a disorder. In other words, disease is what's diagnosed or what the doctors say you have, while illness is what you feel.

Today's public seems to have immense faith in medical technology, believing that whatever ails them will somehow be cured by modern therapeutics. Many people in Western cultures confidently expect medical expertise to provide a cure or "technological fix" for almost every ill. And people seem transfixed by the torrent of publicity accompanying every new medical announcement, no matter how equivocal the research finding, no matter how experimental the treatment. With the help of medical progress, and through personal fitness efforts, people hope to escape disease, conquer life's everyday ailments and even evade the decline of aging.

Although the health improvements seen during the last century are popularly attributed to advances in medical science, historian Thomas McKeown concluded in his 1976 study of the British population that many of the health improvements in the nineteenth and early twentieth centuries actually predated most of the major medical discoveries. Far from being due to medical progress, the improved health status of the British population was the result of smaller family size, a cleaner environment, better hygiene, water purification and improvements in food production and distribution.

From the mid-1900s onwards, medical practice has been largely based on a *biomedical* model that has focused more on curing illness than preventing it. During the past few decades, North American medical practitioners have concentrated mainly on identifying diseases and dividing them into categories — for example, targeting a "cirrhotic liver" or "ischemic heart" for treatment. This method tended to separate physical from psychological problems, which were sometimes dismissed as "all in the head" and not worthy of medical attention.

Modern views of health

Views of health and illness are now undergoing radical changes in meaning and perception. The idea of health as the "absence of disease or infirmity" is shifting to an image of an "optimal state of well-being for body and mind." The emerging *biopsychosocial* model of health

1

THE BASICS OF HEALTH

Health depends on four essentials: biology — the "genes" or body you're born with; a health-promoting environment — clean air and water, no excessive noise or other pollution; lifestyle — good diet, avoiding smoking or excess alcohol intake; and the quality and accessibility of healthcare.

Putting the WHO definition into more concrete terms, good health demands:

• enough food and shelter; adequate income;
• good hygiene — clean air and water supplies and adequate sewage disposal;
• a stable, secure and health-promoting environment;
• physical fitness;
• lifestyle factors that enhance physical fitness — adequate exercise, sound sleep, not smoking, avoiding excess alcohol and other health-harming drugs; eating a low-fat diet; avoiding needless injuries (e.g., by using seatbelts and bike helmets);
• the ability to meet crises and environmental challenges;
• self-responsibility in looking after health and dealing with illness — together with chosen health-care providers;
• emotional balance — healthy self-esteem, "feeling good" about oneself;
• mental health — the ability to cope with stress and emergencies;
• social well-being — forging intimate relationships, interacting effectively with other people;
• a nonaggravating interaction with the environment — for example, avoiding contaminants that may worsen personal ailments (such as hay fever, asthma);
• access to adequate medical care when needed.

regards mind, spirit and body as one intertwined unit and tries to treat people less mechanistically, as "whole persons," paying more attention to emotional, psychological and social factors. Health is no longer viewed as something that "just happens" by luck, fate, chance or good genes, but as a positive asset that people can work toward. Health promotion and disease prevention are today's mottos. But to achieve health, people need the information necessary to make sensible choices, and they need a supportive, health-promoting environment.

In 1948 the World Health Organization (WHO) defined health as a "state of complete physical, mental and social wellbeing, encompassing the ability to achieve full potential, deal with crises and meet environmental challenges." In other words, health — or wellness, to use a trendy term — is the capacity to respond favorably to physical effort, to live within one's own potential and carry out tasks with vigor and alertness, leaving enough energy to meet unforeseen emergencies. Although many health professionals and lay people still adhere to the "freedom from disease" concept, the WHO definition has profoundly altered views of health and healthcare. By implying that health is a positive resource that people can work toward rather than an inbuilt feature in those lucky enough to avoid disease, the new definition suggests that people have a fair measure of control over their health.

The concept of health given in the 1986 Ottawa Charter for Health Promotion goes still farther, outlining the fundamentals for health as: "Peace, shelter, education, food, income, a stable ecosystem, sustainable resources, social justice and equity" — prerequisites that go far beyond what has traditionally been considered necessary for health. For example, people can't easily remain healthy if there's a lack of food and they're starving, or if the air is polluted and low in oxygen, or during wartime when bullets are flying and they're constantly anxious about being killed. The Ottawa Charter also stressed that health is a means rather than an end in itself: "A resource for everyday life, not the objective of living." Rather than spending inordinate amounts of money on curing disorders that could be prevented, it suggested, we should allocate more funds for education and community efforts in disease-prevention.

Just being fit isn't it!

In search of good health and longevity, many contemporary North Americans devote endless time and effort to fitness. They conscientiously run, jog, attend aerobics classes, watch their weight, restrict cholesterol intake, avoid aluminum cookware and get annual medical checkups. The quest for fitness leads them to spend considerable time caring for their bodies — on exercise bicycles and rowing machines, in swimming pools, weight rooms, saunas, whirlpools and massage parlours, learning how to breathe, conquer stress, manage low back pain, eat sensibly and erase wrinkles.

In order to acquire a fashionably lean body, some slavishly follow the latest exercise or diet fads. Obsessed with the pursuit of thinness, many no longer exercise "for fun," or to enjoy the marvels of the human body. They do their workouts with grim-faced determination devoid of pleasure — not to increase cardio-vascular fitness or muscular strength — but merely to become or stay thin. Beyond any health benefits, some people seem to view fitness as a way to purify the soul and become a nobler person. Fitness — equated not only with the sought-after slender look, but also with "success" — is seen as an end in itself, so that any malaise or sign of illness seems like an affront. The slightest tinge of unwellness, even everyday aches and twinges, may seem worrisome and send people scurrying to the doctor.

Yet, as one University of Toronto expert puts it, "Just being fit isn't it!" Although physical fitness — for example, acquiring muscular strength and flexibility and maintaining desirable weight — is a prerequisite for well-being, fitness alone doesn't guarantee good health. Being physically fit when mentally unbalanced, "stressed out," socially isolated or emotionally disturbed doesn't add up to good health. And exercising obsessively not only increases the risk of sports injuries but may jeopardize family and social life.

MEASURING HEALTH

Since the WHO definition of health came out, many researchers have tried to measure its main components — namely, physical, mental and social well-being. Not surprisingly, efforts have concentrated on physical health, the dimension easiest to measure. However, even that is an elusive property. For example, some people diagnosed with a disease such as arthritis or diabetes may feel perfectly healthy and function well. Or, older people with disabilities such as osteoporosis or atherosclerosis may consider themselves in "excellent health for someone of their age" — a common viewpoint, especially among those with an optimistic outlook.

People living in various cultures perceive health and disease in various ways, tolerating different degrees of pain and discomfort. And the perception of health and illness also varies vastly from one person to another. Two different people with the same disease may experience it very differently. While one person may express agony from a small cut or splinter, another may stoically put up with a far worse wound, bruise or other ailment.

Take as examples a man who inherited a polycystic kidney disease that destroyed both kidneys by midlife. Even though he requires thrice-weekly dialysis (after two failed kidney transplants), he nonetheless enjoys a "healthy life" in which he swims three times a week, walks to work and pursues an active professional career. Similarly, a woman bank employee considers herself "healthy" even though she lost one breast to cancer 15 years ago, and suffers from arthritis and carpal tunnel syndrome (pinched wrist nerve), for which she wears a wrist splint at night. In contrast, we all know healthy people with no physical disorders who complain about every little muscle ache or transient pain.

The placebo effect

The discrepancy between objective disease and its subjective experience is well illustrated by the placebo effect, where inert substances known as placebos — "dummy drugs" — provide relief from a wide range of disorders even though they contain no biologically active ingredient against the conditions being treated. For instance, plain sugar or chalk gives relief to many people who think they are taking "real drugs" and believe in their healing powers. Medical and surgical procedures can also act as placebos, even if they have no true curative action.

Evidence from many studies indicates that about one-third of those treated with placebos obtain symptomatic relief for conditions such as postoperative discomfort, chest pain, stomach upsets and motion sickness. People treated with placebos improve because of faith in the "healer" (physician) and because they expect a pill or procedure to be effective. If it's *expected* to work, the substance will likely afford relief. An even more remarkable finding is that 10 percent of people receiving placebos report that the fake drug causes unpleasant side effects such as skin itching, diarrhea and nausea — effects similar to those found among people taking the chemically active equivalent.

Mental and social health are harder to measure than physical health, although efforts have been made to do so. Assessing "social health" is particularly controversial. One University of Toronto expert cites some of the problems in quantifying social health — such as vague concepts, lack of norms, the many interactive variables, the subjective nature of social health and the many diverse but equally satisfactory ways of functioning socially. Just as health is hard to quantify, so is sickness. At one end of the wellness spectrum are "perfectly healthy" individuals with no diagnosable diseases who have a sense of control over their lives, see change as a challenge rather than as a threat, have no significant symptoms of "disease" (unwellness) and feel energetic, satisfied with their social, spiritual, occupational and personal existence.

Elsewhere on the scale are those with recognized and diagnosed disorders. The state labeled "disease" represents conditions with detectable symptoms and abnormalities as well as "silent" diseases such as high blood pressure, which although demonstrably present may not exhibit symptoms or be felt by the sufferers. At other points on the scale are those who feel "vaguely ill" or "out of sorts" — people with a vague sense of "dis-ease" that isn't diagnosable or easily explained by conventional medicine.

Many of us are the "worried well"

Although North Americans on the whole are a remarkably healthy lot, with an increased life expectancy, many of us worry unduly about our health and want to be still "healthier." As U.S. physician Dr. Arthur Barsky writes in his book *Worried Sick*: "Our sense of physical well-being has not kept pace with the improvements in our collective health status . . . there is a pervasive atmosphere of dis-ease. The ability to appreciate good health and achieve a secure feeling of physical well-being eludes us." Dr. Barsky sees us as a society in headlong pursuit of health and medical care. "Wellness," he concludes, "has become something deliberately and consciously sought after. Good health, seen as an end in itself and not just as a means to other goals such as family and professional life, has become an imperative, a sort of supervalue that symbolizes personal achievement, self-esteem, and willpower."

Almost every aspect of daily life is scrutinized for its health implications and labeled healthful or harmful — making everyday actions into a series of "prescribed" and "forbidden" behaviors. In the name of health, foods are dubbed as "good" (life-prolonging) or "bad" (health-harming) according to the latest fad — instead of being regarded as nutrients for the body. Our society's idealization of thinness has made even people of normal weight feel fat and somehow to blame for today's natural biological tendency towards a larger body size (partly because of better nutrition in the Western world). Personal habits, diet and leisure activities are constantly modified in line with the latest publicity about what constitutes a healthy lifestyle and a desirable "look."

Hypochondriacs are illness-obsessed

Hypochondriasis is an extreme form of anxiety about health. Hypochondriacs differ from the worried well in having a distinct psychiatric disorder. They are obsessed with sickness, rather than merely worried about health. Hypochondriasis is characterized by an excessive preoccupation with minor ailments and normal bodily sensations, which are unrealistically assessed or magnified so that transient discomforts become imaginary signals of disease and harmless sensations a source of panic.

Perpetually fussing over tiny symptoms, hypochondriacs imagine that disease is about to strike even though medical investigation shows no signs of it. In contrast to the worried well, who feel better once they have been medically reassured that nothing's wrong, hypochondriacs have so unshakeable a fear of illness that neither repeated physician assurance nor negative lab tests allay the anxiety. They're convinced that a scratch will get infected, a slight stomach pain is an incipient ulcer, a freckle is melanoma or a minor arm ache signals muscle-wasting. Believing themselves to be on the brink of some deadly malady, they run to the doctor with passing ailments that most of us would ignore. For the hypochondriac, invalidism is a way of life. In some cases, early childhood experiences of illness in the family may have ingrained the sickness behavior, which requires psychotherapy. Yet most hypochondriacs adamantly reject the suggestion that nonmedical factors such as stress, emotions or psychiatric disorders underlie their anxiety.

At times of stress many of us become slightly hypochondriacal and worry unduly about our health. It is not uncommon for the recently bereaved or those undergoing a crisis to become anxious or depressed and "somatize," or translate mental and psychological distress into physical symptoms. Many of those recovering from heart attacks or major surgery are also anxious about health, monitoring every trivial sensation. The elderly, too, are liable to be hypochondriacal, their unease fueled by physical decline and its limitations, and the inevitable approach of death.

CHANGING ATTITUDES TO HEALTHCARE

Critics of our healthcare system castigate it as too technological, distant and inhumane. The older, traditional model of healthcare is therefore gradually being replaced by a broader, more humane and user-friendly model, where the authoritarian attitude is giving way to a more egalitarian approach. The restricted "absence-of-disease" concept is being replaced by a flexible, multidimensional view of health. The patient is increasingly seen as a partner in health transactions rather than as a passive recipient of treatment. Some of the responsibility and decision-making in healthcare is shifting onto the consumer or patient, instead of

USEFUL TERMS TO KNOW

- A *placebo* is an inactive substance (or procedure) given to a control group to parallel the treatment being investigated. Placebos are necessary to check the efficacy of a treatment being studied. As mentioned earlier, about one-third of test subjects react positively to any treatment, active or inactive, perhaps because of the expectation of benefit. But in time, if the drug or procedure is effective, it will outperform the placebo.
- A *clinical study* is an investigation of human beings — not animals — done to observe the effect of some kind of intervention (treatment, drug or procedure), often in a hospital.
- *Epidemiological research* is the study of the determinants and distribution of disease. It attempts to discover the risk factors for certain diseases by describing the frequency and distribution of exposures (health-related events) in human populations.
- A *control group* is a group of people used for comparison. The experimental or trial group takes the drug or has the procedure, and the control group gets either the best available current therapy, no treatment or a placebo. The results are then compared. The decision about who gets into the trial group and who gets into the control group is made randomly, not by personal choice or preference, to eliminate bias.

- A *case-control* study looks backward in time to compare past exposure to certain factors in people with the problem or disease being studied ("cases") with exposure in people without the disease ("controls"). For example, over the years many studies have found that tobacco smoking is far more common in those with lung cancer than in those without. Case-control studies do not prove anything, but indicate a possible link.
- A *clinical trial or experimental study* (experiment) is done forward in time, and with tight controls, to establish a direct cause-and-effect link — for example, to show that a new drug works better than a

currently used one.
- A *survey* examines a limited group of people. Its results can be extended to a larger population only if the sample is representative of the larger population. For example, the results of a survey of young athletes may have little application to the population at large.
- A *single-blind study* is one where the person being treated doesn't know whether he or she is receiving the test procedure under investigation, although the doctors and research team do know.
- A *double-blind study* is one where neither the participants nor the researchers know which people are in the experimental group and which are in the control group.

Double-blind studies are used to eliminate unconscious bias or other psychological effects among the researchers.
- A *triple-blind study* is one where even the person who's running the study doesn't know which patients are getting the procedure being tested.
- *Anecdotal evidence* is word-of-mouth testimony or hearsay, based on a few cases, rather than statistically significant scientific evidence. However, accumulating anecdotal evidence (such as several people alleging that "something in the office air is making my throat sore") often leads to a hypothesis or theory which can then be tested through a scientific study.

COMMON ERRORS IN EVALUATING MEDICAL NEWS:

- too much readiness to believe the popular press;
- overreliance on the competence and objectivity of the media;
- uncritical willingness to jump to unwarranted conclusions;
- belief that unchallenged information is necessarily accurate;
- too little time spent by reporters checking facts and making sure that they understand them clearly;
- too little background material provided to journalists;
- failure to realize that health stories are often cut, altered and shaped to meet media constraints;
- unawareness among the medical community of the pervasive public faith in "media messages."

being put entirely on the professional caregivers. Thus, looking after health or disease is becoming more of a collaboration between consumers and health professionals.

While some people may still opt for the quick medical fix, preferring to know little about it, many now want to be educated healthcare consumers. They prefer to understand what's wrong with them and what treatments are proposed, to weigh up the options and to participate in their own health management. Studies show that well-informed healthcare consumers who take an active role in discussing and selecting their treatment feel more in control. They generally stay healthier, and recover faster from disease and/or surgery, than those who don't share the responsibility.

In some ways, taking responsibility for one's own health is a demanding role that not everyone is prepared for or wishes to accept. In becoming part of the healthcare team, people are expected to read up on their ailments and take an active part in managing them. Some studies investigating the call for greater patient participation in the decision-making process find a duality or mixed reactions. While people want to be informed and welcome the opportunity to participate, they still look to healthcare professionals for a great deal of guidance. The call to be "better informed" and take more part in decisions also has its down side, as some health-conscious people may regard sickness as a slur on their character, something that's entirely their own fault. Yet it is absurd to think or expect that all illness will vanish or be avoided simply by one's own efforts. Just as death is inevitable, there will always be diseases that afflict us.

Many medical schools now emphasize the need for physicians to understand the impact of illness, improve their communication skills and become better listeners. Sick people are generally anxious and seek help not only for physical ills but also for social and emotional problems. Ideally, anything that produces distress and affects health — be it physical, emotional or spiritual — should be taken into consideration by the attending physician. In many centers, medical education is emphasizing care by non-hospital, community-based healthcare workers.

More and more, healthcare is moving from hospitals and other institutions to care in the home by visiting professionals — which is less expensive and often brings swifter improvement.

Consumers seeking medical attention can help to conserve healthcare dollars by learning how to access and use the system appropriately — for example, by finding a trusted family physician to look after minor and everyday health concerns, rather than using expensive emergency services for this purpose, and by altering their lifestyle to avoid illness.

HOW TO ASSESS HEALTH NEWS

Beset by medical reports of all kinds, our society is obsessed with health issues. Many of us are intensely curious about medical, health and nutritional news. Newspapers devote entire sections to lifestyle topics, and TV programs regularly cover medical issues. We are deluged with messages and services designed to make us fitter and help us stay young, ward off disease and expunge every complaint. The print and broadcast media are today's main sources of health information. With each passing month, a different disease is highly publicized to explain vague discomforts and afflictions — such as Yuppie flu (chronic fatigue syndrome), candidiasis or 20th-century allergy syndrome. Even the most preliminary research findings may be trumpeted and mislabeled as a breakthrough, spawning a press conference, torrents of publicity and sometimes, cruelly raised hopes.

All too many people bring no critical appraisal to the health news they hear, unquestioningly believing whatever they are told. They don't know how to assess medical news and easily jump to false conclusions based on phrases such as "suggests," "increases risks" or "contributes to." In fact, many pay less heed to what they're told in a doctor's office than what they read in the popular press — perhaps because it's easier to absorb information at home than in an anxiety-provoking clinical atmosphere.

Many people don't realize that, on the whole, journalists don't regard themselves as educators but as information conveyors who try to report findings as accurately as possible. Unfortunately, health news is often poorly reported and simplified to the point of distortion. The media tend to "humanize" complex medical topics with personal anecdotes or dramatized images, sometimes sacrificing accuracy. Some of those reporting on health stories have little or no background knowledge of scientific matters. Many a reporter sent to cover medical issues is diverted from a regular sports, crime or entertainment beat. Moreover, the material handed in by journalists is frequently changed by desk editors, producers and others in charge, to fit available space, to adhere to the organization's image or even to please financial backers.

Any medical study or scientific work, no matter how trivial or dubious, can make headlines if it sounds sensational enough and is picked up without critical appraisal. This is particularly true of results presented before the studies have been subjected to critical scrutiny or published in a reputable, peer-reviewed journal. Material publicized at a news conference may neglect some detail that is essential for interpreting the study, and the apparent results may be prematurely seized upon as newsworthy and disseminated before the results have been confirmed. Findings are likely to be most reliably reported when health professionals furnish the full text of their work, so that journalists have a detailed account with which to make the story more accurate and realistic.

Bridging the communication gap

For the public to evaluate health stories better, and for medical scientists to get their message across more reliably, all must consider the constraints of the communication networks. People must learn to assess medical news more critically, bearing in mind not only the quality of the information but the limits of the medium through which it's being conveyed. The trick is to use a bit of skepticism.

Working within a tight time-frame, reporters can easily distort the facts, especially when trying to render their piece interesting or to make the front page. Moreover, items handed in by the reporter may later be topped by an eye-catching headline — possibly one chosen hours before the item was even handed in. A health story may be truncated again at the last moment and key phrases or qualifying clauses chopped out for space reasons. Even the most assiduous and responsible of news reporters seldom has time to check and recheck the facts. But it's crucial not to over-sensationalize material which could be misinterpreted in the rush of getting a story out.

Health professionals should familiarize themselves with the way in which the different media put together news items, remembering the pressure under which many journalists work, with copy often processed at breakneck speed. They can help to avoid the perils of distortion by capsuling their message in the right way and rehearsing it beforehand. Many successful medical communicators use a succinct "pyramid" style, stating the key message (the discovery, advance or results) first, then explaining why the finding is useful, supporting it with relevant background material. Routinely translating complex jargon into lay terms can help to get the message right, and scientists can make themselves available for last-minute telephone checking. Articles for magazines, although prepared at a more leisurely pace with more time for checking, may also be cut or changed, often without consulting the writer who prepared the story.

BEWARE THE SLIPPERY SLOPE OF WORDS

- **"Doctor"** may mean a physician or someone with a Ph.D. in some subject other than medicine, such as chemistry, philosophy, theology or physiology.
- **"May"** does not mean **"will."**
- **"In some people"** does not mean **"in everyone."**
- **"Indicates"** does not mean **"proves"** or **"confirms."**
- **"Contributes to,"** **"is linked to"** or **"is associated with"** does not mean **"causes."**
- **"Proves"** refers to conclusions based on scientific evidence systematically amassed in several studies. (One study, taken alone, seldom proves anything.)
- A **"breakthrough"** is a rare happening — for example, the discovery of penicillin or the development of the polio vaccine are rare events.
- **"Doubles the risk"** may or may not be meaningful, depending on the risk in the first place. If the risk was one in a million and is now doubled, that's still only one in 500,000. But if the risk was one in 100 and it doubles, it's now one in 50 and a real cause for worry.
- **Studies comparing "before" and "after"** effects are not as scientifically valid as controlled studies because comparing past with present treatment introduces too many variables. Two procedures are best compared simultaneously to avoid bias and eliminate coincidental factors.

Cultivating a healthier lifestyle

Preventable illnesses • The risks of smoking • Weight control is crucial to good health • Getting enough exercise • Sleep hygiene and sleep disorders • Preventing needless injuries • Putting drug use in perspective • Tackling alcohol abuse

2

PREVENTABLE ILLNESSES

Much disability and early death stems from diseases caused by lifestyle or everyday habits. The foremost causes of death in North America today — heart disease, cancer, strokes, liver cirrhosis, diabetes, unintentional injuries and suicide — are largely self-induced. What's needed is more illness prevention, urging people not to smoke, to eat lower-fat, heart-healthy diets, to get enough exercise, to moderate alcohol intake, to steer clear of other health-harming drugs and to avoid needless injuries.

THE RISKS OF SMOKING

Tobacco smoking is known to be dangerous, yet 26 percent of Canadians still smoke and smoking tobacco remains the number-one preventable cause of death and disease in Canada. It is responsible for an estimated 30 percent of heart-disease deaths and 83 percent of deaths due to lung cancer. Tobacco smoking, branded "the chief avoidable cause of death in our society," endangers not only smokers but also nonsmokers who inhale secondhand smoke from idling cigarettes and the smoke exhaled by others.

The tragedy is that many young people are still lighting up and starting this health-harming habit, often while still in school. Surveys show

that 23 percent of students from grades 7 to 13 smoke occasionally, two-thirds of them regularly. Smoking schoolmates inspire others to try the weed. Reports show that smoking begins primarily in adolescence, and that 18 percent of Canadian adolescents aged 15 to 19 smoke (20 percent of girls, compared to 12 percent of similarly aged boys). The earlier someone starts smoking, the greater the danger of addiction and death from some tobacco-related disease. Out of every 100,000 smokers now aged 15, 18,000 will die from tobacco-related diseases by age 65.

Teenage girls and third-world populations are popular targets for ads that portray smoking as "cool" and "empowering." Girls may light up in their teens to lose weight. However, women beware! Lung cancer has now outstripped breast cancer in the United States and most Canadian provinces as the major killer of women. The children of smoking parents are much more likely to smoke than those from nonsmoking households, and those who regularly use three or more cigarettes daily are likely to become tobacco-addicted adults.

The good news is that many former smokers have given up. Faced with the undisputed reality of its many health dangers and the inescapable truth that "smoking kills," together with escalating bans on smoking, nearly half of all living North Americans who ever smoked have quit, with women lagging slightly behind men. And on another positive note, Canada is a world leader in nonsmoking policies and controls — in establishing smoke-free environments, curbing ads, restricting workplace smoking and issuing health warnings. In some parts of Canada, smokers have almost become social outcasts — forced to sneak outside and huddle with their cigarettes. They're becoming society's butts for not butting out, and for continuing a practice that's not only self-destructive but also harms others.

Shaking tobacco's addictive hold isn't easy

To anyone who's ever tried to quit smoking or watched someone else try, it's obvious that stopping is no easy task. Nicotine is a stimulant that acts on binding sites in the brain, getting into the brain more quickly and more easily than many other drugs. It crosses the blood-brain barrier as fast as heroin, or even faster.

Considering its addictive nature, it's curious that so few people view nicotine as a drug. Yet the behavior that perpetuates its use resembles that associated with any other powerful drug. The U.S. Surgeon General's 1988 report stated that "cigarettes and other forms of tobacco are just as addicting as heroin and cocaine, illegal drugs regarded by most adults with scorn and disapproval (if not outrage)." One renowned smoking expert defines addiction as "psychoactive drug use that's hard to stop, the bottom line being can you give up or not." On a more scientific note, the Royal Society of Canada Committee on Tobacco, Nicotine and Addiction calls smoking addictive, describing it as "a strongly established pattern of behaviour characterized by (1) repeated self-administration in amounts which reliably produce reinforcing psychoactive effects, and (2) great difficulty in achieving voluntary, long-term cessation even when the user is strongly motivated to stop." The urge to maintain blood levels of nicotine and stave off unpleasant withdrawal symptoms is clearly shown by those who will brave a snowstorm in the middle of the night to replenish their supplies.

Withdrawal symptoms frequently undermine quitting efforts

When someone stops smoking, the nicotine deprivation often provokes a swift physiological withdrawal effect that's a common reason for would-be quitters to light up again. While physical withdrawal symptoms, which peak at 48–96 hours, generally subside in about a week and are gone within a month, the craving and psychological dependence may linger on.

Symptoms of nicotine withdrawal include:
- a slowed heart rate;
- difficulty concentrating;
- reduced cognitive (thinking) ability;
- irritability, anger;
- anxiety ("the jitters"), restlessness, insomnia;
- tremors (nervous shaking);
- headaches;
- slight dizziness or "spaced-out" sensation;
- tingling or numbness in the arms and legs, as the smoking-impaired circulation returns to normal;
- greater hunger, especially for sweets;
- increased coughing, because smoking paralyzes the hair-like cilia that naturally clean the lungs; coughing occurs as the cilia regain their cleansing action and subsides once normal function returns;
- a strong craving for cigarettes and incessant thoughts about smoking, which, handled properly, needn't last too long. Most ex-smokers experience a craving. Half of those who relapse say they lit up again because of it. Some quitters understandably mourn as though they'd lost an old friend and source of comfort — their grief deserves sympathy!

Physiological withdrawal symptoms can be reduced by nicotine replacement with chewing gum or skin patches. But since psychological dependence may outlast nicotine's physical hold, many cessation programs focus equally on overcoming behavior and habits, helping ex-smokers develop a new, nonsmoking self-image.

Quitting tactics: "if at first you don't succeed — try, try again"

Almost 80 percent of smokers claim they'd like to stop, especially if there were an easy way to do it! Most tobacco smokers have tried to quit at some time in their lives. It's never too late to quit.

Treatment methods include self-help guides, behavioral therapy, pharmacotherapy

---

KEY STEPS TO BETTER HEALTH:

- **not smoking tobacco;**
- **maintaining a desirable weight;**
- **exercising sufficiently;**
- **getting enough sound sleep;**
- **avoiding accidental injuries;**
- **moderating alcohol use;**
- **avoiding other health-harming drugs.**

FIGHTING THE FIVE "A'S" THAT PERPETUATE SMOKING

- *Addiction.* Nicotine in tobacco is among the most powerful and rapidly absorbed psycho-active (mood-altering) substances known, at least as addictive as heroin. It is now formally listed as an addictive substance, and nicotine addiction is labeled the "Tobacco Dependence Disorder." Tragically, the incentive to quit often comes only after a heart attack or other serious tobacco-related illness. Even then, it's hard for many to stop — witness the post-bypass patient who surreptitiously escapes to light up in the visitors' room.
- *Advertising* by tobacco companies is a major contributor: a powerful campaign against good sense and good health, promoting a habit that kills millions annually. With so much bad press about smoking, tobacco companies are seeking new markets for their dangerous products, especially in developing countries, where consumption — even among children — is rising rapidly. The tobacco industry spends billions to associate tobacco with glamour, success and sophistication. In its battle to seduce recruits, the industry must strive incessantly to counter evidence that cigarette smoking is unhealthy.
- *Acceptance* of tobacco use, in contrast to other addictive drugs such as alcohol or heroin, supports the popular view of smoking as a plea-surable and tension-releasing pastime with which to "fill lonely hours," "mark occasions," "solve problems" or "be companionable." Paradoxically, while society deplores the use of illicit drugs — which kill a couple of dozen Canadians annually — it tends to ignore the 30,000-plus annual deaths from smoking.
- *Apathy* — the "I've heard it all before" or "It won't happen to me" or "I'll never manage to quit anyway" syndrome — keeps many people smoking, as does neglect by physicians in not stressing the dangers of smoking or not assisting people to quit. Many smokers don't bother to try stopping because they believe that "nothing works" and quitting is just too tough.
- The *Awareness Gap* is the persistent ignorance about what smoking does to the body. As one official from Canada's Laboratory Centre for Disease Control says: "Many smokers still remain unconvinced that inhaling tobacco smoke — either their own or that of others — harms health."

(nicotine substitution or sensitizers that make smoking taste bad) and many other methods. Most cigarette smokers who quit manage to give up with self-help methods rather than through formal programs. Repeated quitting attempts usually pay off; many smokers "give up" half a dozen times before finally managing to stop for good. Even those who attend smoke-ending programs may not succeed at first. Combined strategies generally work best, sometimes aided by less formal approaches such as acupuncture, nicotineless cigarettes, computerized behavior tracking (e.g., Lifesign) or hypnosis.

Not all smokers find it equally hard to quit. The least dependent or lightest smokers — those who smoke fewer than 10 cigarettes a day — find it easiest to abstain. About 30 percent of heavy smokers find it "fairly difficult" and 19 percent call it "very tough" to stop smoking. Those who reach for a cigarette within 10 minutes of awakening, or before getting out of bed, are usually the most addicted. They need more quitting determination and support than those who can wait until after breakfast for their first cigarette! Having once stopped, many ex-smokers relapse at times of crisis — the chances of relapse being greatest in the first few weeks after quitting.

Recognizing the dangers of smoking helps many quit

While most people are vaguely aware that smoking is bad for their health, many are ignorant of the ways in which it damages the body. Surveys reveal that close to half of all smokers are totally unaware that smoking shortens life expectancy by six to seven years and that, as well as lung cancer, it is a major cause of heart disease, stroke and emphysema, and increases risks of stomach ulcers and cancers of the colon, mouth, throat, pancreas, bladder and cervix. Nor do most people realize that some-one sharing a home with a smoker for several years faces a 30 percent increase in the risk of dying from heart disease. Women smokers often don't know that the habit can harm an unborn child and stunt its development. Few

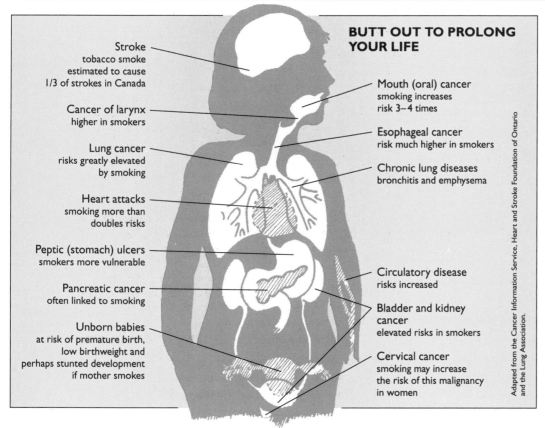

BUTT OUT TO PROLONG YOUR LIFE

Stroke
tobacco smoke
estimated to cause
1/3 of strokes in Canada

Cancer of larynx
higher in smokers

Lung cancer
risks greatly elevated
by smoking

Heart attacks
smoking more than
doubles risks

Peptic (stomach) ulcers
smokers more vulnerable

Pancreatic cancer
often linked to smoking

Unborn babies
at risk of premature birth,
low birthweight and
perhaps stunted development
if mother smokes

Mouth (oral) cancer
smoking increases
risk 3–4 times

Esophageal cancer
risk much higher in smokers

Chronic lung diseases
bronchitis and emphysema

Circulatory disease
risks increased

Bladder and kidney
cancer
elevated risks in smokers

Cervical cancer
smoking may increase
the risk of this malignancy
in women

Adapted from the Cancer Information Service, Heart and Stroke Foundation of Ontario and the Lung Association.

smokers know that secondhand smoke damages children, increases their risk of respiratory illness and encourages them to smoke later on. Surveys reveal that while healthcare professionals rank "not smoking" as the number-one step to improve health, the average person ranks it tenth, after such actions as "taking extra vitamins" or "eating oat bran."

Physicians can play a major role in assisting smokers to overcome the habit, by giving those who want to quit advice and support. But many doctors don't know much about cessation techniques, and aren't set up to help quitters or reimbursed for the time spent counseling them. Nonetheless, a scientific rundown by a healthcare professional, listing the damaging effects of smoking, carries more weight than what's heard elsewhere. The family physician can also personalize the situation by referring to the smoker's own health status, family background and medical history. Physicians can help those motivated to set a quit date and give support by supplying take-home quit guides. Doctors can also prescribe nicotine substitution, with chewing gum or the new transdermal skin patch, to help smokers through the early withdrawal stages. Anyone who really wants to stop smoking can. There is lots of assistance out there, and the new nicotine-replacement methods are a great help.

Smokers sometimes believe that changing brands will lower their health risks. But while low-tar and low-nicotine cigarettes are available, most smokers still favor medium- or high-nicotine brands. Furthermore, switching brands won't guarantee lower exposure to tobacco's dangerous toxins, because those who smoke low-nicotine or low-tar brands often unconsciously alter their smoking habits (e.g., puff harder) and absorb just as many toxins.

Each smoker must find a personal reason and travel a unique road in casting off addiction. Success in conquering tobacco requires motivation, serious commitment and the "right moment." Those who just idly think about "stopping sometime" are less likely to succeed than those who find definite reasons and fix a specific time for doing so. Finding a strong personal reason for quitting, whatever it is, is a critical first step in making the positive choice to become a nonsmoker. Those who succeed are fully aware of why they choose to stop.

BASIC QUITTING STAGES

- **contemplation —
no precise quitting
schedule, but open
to suggestion;**
- **serious intentions —
checking out pos-
sible quit aids; listing
personal reasons for
stopping;**
- **choosing a target
quit date — at a
convenient, non-
stressful time, extin-
guishing familiar
smoking cues, estab-
lishing new patterns
(like putting ciga-
rettes in less acces-
sible places);**
- **action plan — choos-
ing the quitting
strategy; recording
your own smoking
patterns and the
cues that spark the
smoking urge; iden-
tifying difficult
moments and likely
lighting-up tempta-
tions and planning to
avoid them; select-
ing "oral gratifica-
tion" replacements
such as sugarless
gum or tobaccoless
cigarettes; thinking
up ways to avoid
weight gain;**
- **recruiting support;**
- **rewarding yourself
for every nonsmok-
ing day.**

Stop "cold turkey" rather than tapering down

The ability to quit is highly individual. Some people stop "cold turkey" while others taper off slowly. Although millions have succeeded with either approach, studies indicate that withdrawal symptoms subside faster for smokers who stop completely than for those who gradually cut down. According to one researcher, "the hardest jump for any smoker is going from almost any number of cigarettes a day down to zero." By quitting cold turkey the body rids itself of nicotine in about 48 hours, so that the number, total intensity and duration of withdrawal symptoms may be less than in those who simply cut down over a period of time. But psychological dependence will continue for a while in either case.

Cutting down is often self-defeating. Studies show that those who taper off may find it extra hard to quit, and will generally change their smoking manner to get more from each drag. A Canadian study on smoking which used blood tests to measure nicotine levels before and after reducing the number of cigarettes found that participants who smoked an average of 37 cigarettes a day achieved only slightly lower blood levels of nicotine when they cut down to 10–15 cigarettes daily. Their blood-nicotine levels went down less than expected because they took more puffs from each cigarette, inhaling more deeply to compensate for the smaller number smoked. Most smokers didn't mind cutting their daily intake by about half but complained bitterly when asked to smoke less than that. The remaining cigarettes were not only more avidly smoked, but offered greater pleasure, increasing the chance of backsliding to full smoking.

Smokers who gradually reduce their blood nicotine level may live in a state of constant withdrawal. The longer the body goes without a cigarette, the lower the blood nicotine drops and the more pleasurable the next smoke becomes. After cutting down to 12 or fewer cigarettes daily, many reach a point beyond which they just can't reduce. This is why experts urge people to quit "cold turkey" once they've cut down to 12–15 cigarettes a day.

Set a target quit date

Casting off the smoking urge takes energy, attention and scheduling, plus all the support a quitter can muster. Smokers must change their habitual response to countless daily cues and plan ahead how not to smoke when having a cup of coffee, reading the paper or dealing with a crisis. Timing is critical: choose a convenient time to stop smoking, preferably during a non-stressful period. Trying to break the habit during a difficult time at work or at home will only make it harder.

Discuss the intention to quit with a sympathetic, knowledgeable person, preferably someone who's already beaten tobacco, knows the problems and wants you to succeed. Check out the resources and cessation guides beforehand. Countless aids and stop-smoking programs are now available from many health agencies and hospitals. Surveys reveal that 90 percent of smokers prefer to quit on their own — perhaps aided by pamphlets, books, guides or videos. On the appointed day, either stop altogether or cut back according to the personal agenda. It's best to think up substitute activities to replace the act of lighting up and holding a cigarette — chewing gum, doodling with a pencil or fiddling with something (perhaps a marble or an elastic?). On the big day, keep very busy — plan an outing or shopping spree, go to a movie or attend a favorite sports event.

Nicotine-substitution therapy tides many over withdrawal pangs

Substitution therapy using nicotine gum, skin patches or aerosols (still experimental and not presently available in Canada) is a recognized part of many quitting plans. Nicotine replacement reduces the craving for cigarettes, although the amount of substitute nicotine supplied by gum or a skin patch is usually lower than with cigarettes, avoiding the peak "highs." The first rule in substitution therapy is not to smoke at the same time. The gum or patch should completely replace all tobacco.

The substitute nicotine absorbed via the mouth (from gum) or skin (from a patch) into the bloodstream eases withdrawal symptoms, allowing quitters to focus on beating the psychological aspects of their addiction. Nicotine from gum or a patch is not a magic potion — smokers must still break their lighting-up habits. But used as prescribed, nicotine replacement takes addicts gently off their drug. It is best used in conjunction with support, behavioral therapy and other quit aids. Later, ex-smokers are weaned off the nicotine substitutes.

Nicotine gum may taste odd at first, but most chewers quickly get used to it. Since each chew releases a little nicotine, chewing must be slow, with pauses of a few seconds between chews. Chewers carry the nicotine gum with them at all times, perhaps keeping it where they formerly stored their cigarettes. Using the gum is far less harmful than smoking because the toxic ingredients of tobacco smoke (about 4,000 of them) are absent, reducing the risks of lung and heart disorders, cancer and other conditions. Studies show that nicotine gum is much more effective than placebo or behavioral therapy alone in aiding quitters. Side effects of the gum — a bad taste, upset stomach, hiccups and a sore mouth — are usually mild enough to allow continued use. The final quitting stage is to stop using the gum, usually after 10 to 12 weeks of use. Flavored nicorette gum is now available *without* prescription as a "behind-the-counter" product in pharmacies by request.

Patching up smokers

Nicotine skin patches overcome some of the side effects of nicotine gum and provide an easier way for some to get replacement nicotine into the bloodstream. The patches, such as the Nicoderm or Habitrol brands available in Canada, deliver nicotine through the skin. As one University of Toronto pharmacologist and smoking-cessation expert puts it: "The nicotine patch is a useful new tool in an otherwise sparse toolbox for those motivated and ready to stop smoking."

Prescribed by a physician, the nicotine patches look like square or round Band-aids. Usually prescribed for a 10–12-week course and worn on the back, chest or upper arm, the patches come in strengths of 21, 14 or 7 mg. The strongest patch achieves blood nicotine concentrations equivalent to about half that obtained by smoking a pack to a pack and a half a day. A fresh patch is applied each day to dry, hair-free skin, at a different site each time to cut down on skin irritation. Nicotine patches are used in a gradual, step-down fashion, starting with the highest strength for four to six weeks, then the 14 mg dose for a few weeks and lastly the weakest patch. Success rates improve if nicotine substitution is used together with supportive therapy.

The inner membrane or control system of the patch releases nicotine steadily into the bloodstream, avoiding the highs provided by cigarettes. The patch is worn all day for 16, sometimes 24 hours. While 24-hour use may stave off early-morning craving, some users experience insomnia, vivid dreams or nightmares, so many decide to leave it off at night. The patch may cause skin itching or burning in some, or (less often) a rash, inflammation and an occasional allergic reaction. The commonest side effects are minor skin irritation (reddening and itchiness) at the application site and insomnia for those patched overnight.

Those who still feel edgy or desperately crave a smoke may supplement with nicotine gum or an extra 7-mg patch for especially stressful occasions. For someone on one of the weaker patches, an extra 7-mg patch can safely be used in times of need. But since the patch contains a potent drug, it must be kept away from children, pets and nonusers. Always discard patches (folded up) after use, and trash safely. Report any side effects noticed.

Many studies confirm that wearing the patch diminishes the symptoms of nicotine withdrawal. It decreases the craving for tobacco and the restlessness, irritability, anxiety and loss of concentration frequent in those who quit. With the physical distress lessened, quitters can concentrate on overcoming the behavioral aspects of their addiction. The patch is not supposed to be a lifelong replacement of one form of nicotine addiction by another. Eventually, users must be entirely weaned off the drug, and ideally they will remain both smoke- and patch-free. But when users ultimately give up their patches, many "grieve" over the loss of their final nicotine fix.

Success rates for the patch are good — up to 40 percent remaining nonsmokers after three to six months. A 1992 article in the

GETTING THE MOST OUT OF NICOTINE PATCHES

- **Put the patch on every day at the same time.**
- **Put it on at quit day or the night before (as this may reduce early-morning craving).**
- **If wearing the patch for the full 24 hours causes insomnia, remove it at night.**
- **Change the site daily to avoid skin irritation.**
- **Wear the patch in the bath or shower or while swimming.**
- **Carry nicotine gum to prevent relapse in stressful situations.**
- **Remember that the patch is not suitable for people with serious heart problems, pregnant women or those with chronic skin disorders.**

RUNDOWN OF SMOKING-CESSATION AIDS

- Self-help print materials and manuals for "going it alone" provide a simple approach for the many smokers who prefer to quit on their own. For publications, consult local health units, local branches of the Lung Association, Heart and Stroke Foundation and Cancer Society, local drug-abuse services, Ontario's Addiction Research Foundation and the Non-Smokers' Rights Association.
- Formal cessation clinics, programs and classes are run by local health agencies, hospitals, work-site or other organizations — on either a profit or a nonprofit basis. Many include pre-course activities, such as charting smoking patterns, scheduling a quit date and practicing stress-coping techniques. Most cessation programs also teach behavior-modification techniques, such as cue-extinction (to avoid smoking triggers), stress management, a self-reward system and relapse-avoidance training. One example, Countdown, is run by the Ontario Lung Association.

  Group sessions vary widely in length and cost. Some groups meet only once, some weekly and others daily for a week or two. Group therapy may include temptation-avoidance tactics, stress management, homework projects and progress reports. If you don't like one group, try another. Sticking to programs offered by certified health organizations may avoid expensive (and perhaps useless) gimmicks.

  The Five-Day Plan, devised by Seventh-Day Adventists, relies on simple techniques to overcome the physiological and behavioral aspects of tobacco addiction by breaking key associations (such as "a cigarette with every cup of coffee") and building a positive nonsmoking image.
- Smoke Stoppers, run by the National (Canadian) Centre for Health Promotion, is a program designed by formerly smoking health-care professionals. Participants quit cold turkey partway through the five-week program.
- Smokenders Canada Ltd. is a six-week program to help smokers reduce their cigarette intake gradually while learning to change habits, reactions and behaviors associated with smoking.
- Acupuncture, an ancient Oriental art, may suppress the desire to smoke. Needles are put into the outer ear and left in place between treatments, to be stimulated whenever the smoking urge surfaces. Acupuncture may make cigarettes taste odd and dull the wish to smoke. Acupuncturists usually perform three to five treatments and may refuse to do more if it doesn't work.
- Laser therapy (or laser acupuncture) is a method that claims high success rates, but hasn't yet been scientifically validated. Using laser beams on acupuncture points may reduce nicotine craving.
- Hypnosis, a popular smoking-cessation aid, is sometimes called the "quick route to behavior modification." It is offered in individual or group sessions, on a once-only or repeat basis. Prices and credentials vary widely and don't necessarily correlate with expertise or success rates. Hypnotic suggestion makes smoking seem so undesirable that people develop headaches or become nauseated if they light up. Positive reinforcement helps people feel virtuous for not lighting up. Hypnosis won't help everyone but may be worth a try for those who fail with other methods. However, anybody can practice hypnosis, so get a professional referral.
- "Lifesign," a pocket computer that records the amount and frequency of smoking and gives signals for gradually stepping down the habit, helps some smokers.
- "Magic" filters are not that magical! Some cigarette filters claim to help smokers "taper down" to zero. Available in drugstores and supermarkets, kits usually cost under $20. For instance, One Step at a Time (produced by Teledyne) has four reusable filters that eliminate 20, 50, 70 and 90 percent of the tar and nicotine. The filters are used over an eight-week period. One serious flaw is that smokers may simply smoke more cigarettes or inhale more deeply to compensate for the decreased tobacco products. Studies show that many who try Teledyne filters get stuck at the fourth filter stage, unable to quit completely.
- There are also over-the-counter antismoking medicines: certain lozenges aim to make cigarettes taste bad by causing an unpleasant body reaction to nicotine. (Unlike Nicorette gum, they do not contain nicotine.) For example, silver acetate, ammonium chloride and carboxylase (an enzyme) in such products as Healthbreak lozenges or BanSmoke gum interact with nicotine to make it taste foul. Although widely promoted, none of these products has been scientifically proven effective.
- Local hotlines or buddy-calling systems can help smokers quit at low cost; hotlines give callers quitting information and a reading list. One Ontario hotline found that of callers who attempted to stop, 21 percent had quit for at least a week and were also abstinent at a six-month follow-up.

American Family Physician, reviewing ten double-blind, placebo-controlled trials, found the nicotine patch to be about twice as effective as dummy patches in helping people to quit. Quit rates varied from moderate to extraordinary — 18–77 percent of patched smokers managing to hold out for at least several months, 17 percent for one year, 12 percent for two years.

Fears of post-quitting weight gain are exaggerated

Many smokers start up or continue smoking for fear of gaining weight. This fear is a major obstacle to quitting, cited by many young women, especially adolescent girls. The desire for slimness is a powerful incentive to smoke, especially if girls view even a small weight gain as a diminution in sex appeal! Many quitters do experience a temporary rise in appetite and a desire for sweet snacks. But while smokers often weigh several kilograms or six to seven pounds less than comparable nonsmokers, studies show that post-smoking weight gain affects only a third of all quitters and usually amounts to only

a few kilograms or pounds. Weight gain after giving up tobacco is not usually a cause for relapse. To offset possible weight gain, quitters can exercise a bit more and replace fat-rich foods with less calorific items, satisfying the desire for oral satisfaction by chewing sugarless gum or carrot sticks. In any case, a bit of extra weight is far less of a health risk than smoking, and once the smoking urge is quenched and the stress of quitting is over, the added weight is usually shed within a few weeks.

The benefits of quitting start almost at once

The immediate benefits of not smoking can fortify a smoker's resolve to stop. The cardiovascular benefits begin within 30 minutes of the last smoke: the pulse rate slows down and blood pressure drops toward normal. Within hours of stopping, the blood's carbon monoxide levels go down, reviving oxygen-carrying capacity. A couple of days later, nerve endings begin to recover, revitalizing the sense of smell and taste. Within 72 hours of smoking cessation, the lung's

SOME QUIT TIPS FOR BUTTIN' OUT

- Recognize that nicotine in tobacco is addictive.
- Realize that it's difficult but not impossible to quit.
- Find a personal motive for choosing not to smoke.
- List reasons for stopping and post in a prominent spot — near phone or deskpad.
- Put cigarettes in new, inaccessible places; buy one pack at a time, preferably least-favored brands.
- Acknowledge the need for behavior modification.
- Be skeptical of those who say they gave up "completely alone"

or just "walked away from it" — a huge understatement for the complex behavior involved in combating nicotine addiction. They probably got much support from family, friends, colleagues, a persuasive physician and the rising cost of cigarettes.
- Feel good even about buying no more cigarettes or throwing out all ashtrays — a gigantic step forward.
- Congratulate yourself on the decision to liberate yourself from smoking.
- Publicize your intention to quit.
- Recruit support from

family, workmates and friends.
- Choose a definite target date and select a method that suits your needs, starting with the simplest, easiest, and cheapest — understanding that no approach is likely to be effortless.
- Celebrate each smoke-free day, week or month. Reward the accomplishment.
- Focus on the immediate benefits of butting out — improved blood circulation, reduced heart-attack risks, better exercise tolerance, sweeter smell, whiter teeth, money saved, social acceptance.

- Expect to overcome hurdles but anticipate possible relapses. Repeated tries improve coping skills and raise the odds for ultimate success.
- Practice cue-extinction to overcome smoking triggers and arm yourself in advance to cope with crisis situations that could sabotage quitting plans.
- Plan how to avoid relapses at stressful or socially tempting times — especially in the first weeks after quitting.
- Don't dwell on a single failure — rejoice for even a few smoke-free days; next time

will be easier.
- Try not to be overly judgmental or hard on yourself if goals aren't reached. Instead of saying "I failed," tell yourself "It didn't work this time around," or "I am one step nearer to success."
- Analyze the reasons why a method didn't work.
- Try any new strategy, unless it's hazardous or outrageously overpriced.
- Remember that the only real failure in smoking cessation is the failure to try again.
- Above all, keep trying!

bronchial tubes expand, enhancing exercise capacity. In the months after quitting, shortness of breath noticeably decreases. In both men and women, heart-attack risks decline markedly in the year after quitting and are largely back to nonsmoking levels two to three years later. The survival benefits of not smoking also hold true after age 65. It's worthwhile even for seniors to quit.

Where to get quitting help

A dizzying array of smoking-cessation aids, programs and guides is now available, varying from ways to make cigarettes seem undesirable to stress management, nicotine fading (using progressively stronger cigarette filters), pharmacotherapy — which includes nicotine substitution by gum or skin patch and dopamine-modulators to overcome the pleasurable stimulus — acupuncture, laser therapy and hypnosis. There are formal programs run by companies and nonprofit groups, costs varying from zero to $500; many hospitals now offer free quitting information. Although some programs allege that paying good money makes quitters try harder, cost does not predict whether or not an antismoking program will be effective. The higher price may simply attract more motivated quitters. Programs that tackle psychological as well as physical problems usually work best.

It's wise to ignore touted (often exaggerated) success rates and select a method that seems personally appealing. Cited success rates for quit programs range from 15 to 30 percent (except for programs that also use Nicorette gum or nicotine patches — which have higher success rates). In selecting a quit-smoking program, remember that anybody can claim to be an expert or offer advice. Claims that one program is better than another are best ignored. No single quitting method suits everyone. Smokers often do best with several cessation approaches. Women, for example, often prefer group therapy while men tend to opt for physician advice. If one method doesn't work, try another!

For more information, contact local branches of the Lung Association; the Canadian Cancer Society; the Heart and Stroke Foundation; the Non-Smokers' Rights Association; Physicians for a Smoke-Free Canada; Toronto's Addiction Research Foundation (ARF); The Canadian Council on Smoking and Health; the Canadian Medical Association or other health agencies.

WEIGHT CONTROL IS CRUCIAL TO GOOD HEALTH

Millions of North Americans, endlessly preoccupied with being overweight, groan in dismay each time they step on the scales. Trying to conform to the modern image of slenderness is no easy matter in a society that equates a taut, lean body with success and sex appeal, while simultaneously bombarding us with an over-abundance of fat-laden foods. Many dieters try to subsist on low-calorie, semi-starvation rations too scanty to provide the nutrients necessary for health or vigor. Since fat cells are the body's way of storing excess energy, doing more exercise as well as eating sensibly might be a better route.

According to international experts such as the late Dr. Hilde Bruch and Dr. John Garrow of Britain, we've carried our obsession with slimness to absurd extremes, forcing even stocky types or moderate fatties to aim unrealistically for a shape that's unnatural to their biological makeup. Recent studies show that the psychological stress of continual self-denial may actually involve more ill health than a few extra kilograms or pounds ever would. In the past century, improvements in hygiene and nutrition brought an upward trend in weight, and amid the social climate praising thinness, even the mildly overweight often feel they must strive for a shape that's physiologically unattain-able without cutting food intake to the point of malnutrition.

Medical experts now suggest a new approach. They urge us to overcome diet myths, to abandon the "D" word, give up the idea of dieting and replace it with sound nutrition. We should ask ourselves why we allow fashion to dictate our size rather than deciding for ourselves what weight suits us and lets us function well. Doctors advise us to live comfortably with a slight degree of excess weight rather than subject ourselves to the stress of repeated dieting, which, in the long run, may be unhealthier for us.

According to one University of Toronto expert, "Obesity remains one of the world's most intractable disorders and the difficulty of reversing it is as well known to physicians as to their discouraged patients. Records show only about five percent of the obese manage to shed unwanted pounds permanently." The rest, after intermittent tries, regain or pass their starting weights within a year or two. As Dr. Bruch said: "Heavy people should be assessed in terms of their average physiological weight, at which they feel well, not by arbitrary standards."

What weight is overweight?

People are considered medically obese if they are 20 percent or more above their "ideal" weight as stated on standard weight/height reference tables such as that published by the Metropolitan Life Insurance Group.

At birth, the body fat of a normal baby is about 12 percent of its weight, but by the mid-twenties a person's body fat has risen to an average of 25 percent. Between the ages of 25 and 30 the average North American begins to put on 0.5 kg (1 lb) a year, by eating too much of the wrong foods and taking too little exercise. But it's vital to differentiate cosmetic obesity — weight above the supposed ideal, with no associated health risks — from medical obesity — excess weight that endangers health. The health risks of obesity include a propensity to diabetes, heart disease and other ills. A person who is 30 percent above the ideal weight has a 50–70 percent elevation in heart-attack risk.

An active, lean, muscular person who exercises frequently may be overweight by ordinary standards yet carry below-average amounts of body fat, while an inactive person of the same weight, height and build may be storing excess fat. Today's weight tables have been updated to reflect the fact that people generally weigh more than they used to, thanks to improved nutrition and hygiene. However, many physicians still consider these tables unrealistic, pressuring even slightly overweight people to slim down to weights that are impossible for them to maintain.

Who needs to lose weight?

People needn't necessarily lose weight just because they are a little over an arbitrarily defined "norm." Those who are overweight may simply be carrying a few kilograms or pounds more than they wish or than is suggested by standard weight tables for their age, height and body frame, with no pressing need to lose. However, those who exceed their desirable weight by 20 percent or more and also have elevated health risks — such as diabetes, a heart problem or hyperlipidemia (excess blood fats) — should try to reduce. For those of us who are healthy but less than 20 percent above our reference-table weight, there is no medical reason to struggle with weight loss.

The ideal way to judge overweight versus obesity is by the amount of body fat, calculated by the body mass index or BMI. This is not a very easy method, but it gives a far better assessment than other methods. The specific parts of the body where fat has accumulated may also determine the need to lose. Fat over the abdomen (shown by the waist-to-hip ratio) is most likely to increase health dangers. When men put on weight, the fat accumulates largely around the trunk or belly giving an "apple shape." In women, fat stores tend to increase all over the body, and in particular on the thighs and buttocks, giving a "pear shape." A waist-to-hip ratio greater than 1.0 for men and 0.8 for women indicates increased cardiovascular risks. (This ratio can be worked out by measuring the waist at the navel and the hips at the largest circumference, then dividing waist size by hip size.) In other words, a man's waist measurement should not exceed that of his hips, and a woman's waist should be at least 20 percent narrower than her hips. Another omission in previous weight tables is their failure to take account of advancing years. With increasing age almost everyone gains weight. Although we eat the same amount, with each advancing decade the body's energy needs decline. Studies show that while either weight extreme — being too fat or too thin — increases health hazards, a slight degree of overweight in older people may actually improve well-being and extend life expectancy.

Uncovering the reasons for obesity

It used to be fashionable to blame glands for obesity but this is now "out." Hormonal or glandular causes account for barely 1 percent of all cases. Diverse factors — genetic, physiological and psychological — contribute to obesity. But whatever its origins, being overweight means that a person's energy (calorie) intake is greater than the energy (calories) burned off. When people gain excess weight, their fat cells either expand in size or multiply, or both. Many obese people have fat cells two to three times the normal size, but some forms of obesity also involve an increase in the number of fat cells, especially with lifelong or massive obesity. University of Toronto researchers speculate that something may be different from birth onward in the metabolism of the massively obese, because even when these people get thinner, their fat cells remain metabolically abnormal.

Psychological factors and childhood training also play a key part. According to Dr. Bruch, "It's now generally recognized that abnormal patterns of food intake and energy expenditure are expressions of underlying psychological disturbances." That's one major reason why weight reduction treatments have so little success. All fat people, she suggested, "are under inner stress, not coping adequately with life problems, have low feelings of self-worth, feel guilty, catastrophize and are unable to relax around food." Most don't really enjoy food because their hunger cues are out of kilter. Hunger cues, contrary to popular myth, are not wholly innate but a partly learned response. Parents who react to all their baby's cries as though they were hunger signals, and ply their child with food, ingrain the idea that food is the answer not just to hunger but to all of life's problems — cold, wet, anxiety, fear, and the need for love and attention.

Our bodies may be programmed to defend a "set weight"

In studies on prison volunteers in Vermont, where men were fed vast amounts of food (up to 10,000 calories a day), some became obese while others on the identical fare consumed four times their usual dietary intake but gained less than expected. In other words, people vary in their ability to burn off extra calories. During the overfeeding phase, metabolic rate and body-heat production went up in most of the volunteers so that they burned more energy. When normally lean individuals did become fat, they required more calories to maintain the excess weight than did the previously obese. Such experiments have spawned the "set-point" theory of obesity, suggesting that human beings are programmed for a steady weight (much as a thermostat keeps the heat in a house steady) and that our bodies try valiantly to maintain that set weight.

By the same principle, when we diet, the body reacts as if starved and promptly lowers its metabolic rate to conserve energy, while the depleted fat cells trigger a violent craving for food. If valid, the set-point idea may help explain why most dieters fail miserably in their reducing efforts as the body struggles to defend its weight plateau. Without a pressing medical reason — such as diabetes, a heart condition,

DIET THERAPISTS ADVISE A MULTIPRONGED APPROACH, INCLUDING:

- a sound food plan to meet all nutrient needs;
- development of self-management skills for changing eating behavior;
- avoiding total fasting — now considered dangerous because it alters the enzyme pathways, which catalyze and regulate fat buildup or breakdown; 70 percent of the loss through fasting is fluid, protein and muscle, which are all regained when the fast ends. Also, since fasting is a temporary measure, it does not create any lasting improvement in eating habits;
- daily planned exercise using large muscle groups (legs, arms), such as walking, cycling, skiing or swimming, to encourage weight loss and, as an added bonus, to reduce appetite;
- self-acceptance at a weight slightly above that suggested by reference tables;
- understanding that at times overeating lapses will occur, and that this is not a catastrophe;
- no pressure to reach impossible weight goals;
- a positive support system, enlisting help from physicians, relatives and friends;
- no illusions about "quick" cures that promise rapid reduction;
- rejecting the dieting concept, since this implies "going on" and therefore eventually "going off" a regime;
- recognition that the main goal is not just to lose but to keep weight off, by aiming for gradual (i.e., 0.5–1 kg, or 1–2 lb, weekly) loss with permanent changes in eating habits;
- behavior modification, whereby an eating-disorder specialist helps the person relearn eating habits and revamp lifestyles.

SOME PRACTICAL TIPS FOR WEIGHT CONTROL

- Reduce food intake (but not below 1,000–1,200 calories daily for women, and 1,200–1,600 for men and adolescents), relying on low-fat foods and emphasizing grains, fruit and vegetables. Recent studies suggest that the body transforms dietary fat into fat stores more smoothly than starches and sugars, so be especially wary of high-fat foods.
- Go for a gradual weight loss not exceeding 1 kg (2.2 lb) weekly.
- Plan an increase in daily and weekly physical activity.
- Choose a weight-loss regime that offers variety and fits your lifestyle — preferably one planned by someone with good nutritional credentials (e.g., a registered dietitian, hospital nutritionist or physician knowledgeable about eating disorders).
- Be supervised by a trained nutritionist or physician if substantially restricting your food intake.
- Aim for permanently improved eating patterns. Remember that changes must be forever — you can't revert to your old ways once the weight is lost.
- Realize that obesity is due to many factors, some biological, some psychological, each needing attention.
- Remember to eat slowly, avoid packaged fatty snacks, go easy on salad dressings and processed foods, bake or poach rather than fry foods.
- Find enjoyable treats to replace food, such as gardening, walks, movies, visits to friends.

high blood pressure or gallstones — there's little point in urging the moderately overweight to reduce.

Treatment: diet alone isn't enough

Treatments vary, but therapists and experts on eating disorders agree that diet alone — whether total fasting, calorie-restricted balanced meals or one of the modern protein-sparing regimes — won't keep weight off unless underlying psychological problems are resolved first. Most of the obese drop out of treatment; of those who persist, most don't lose enough weight and those who do ultimately regain the same amount or more. Losing weight is hard, but keeping it off is even harder, and modern therapy focuses as much on keeping weight off as on merely losing it.

Why crash diets are such dismal failures

Very low-calorie diets (below 1,000 calories a day) can be hazardous, especially if prolonged. Moreover, the dangers are greatest in those with the least need to lose — the moderately overweight, whose bodies go into a "starvation mode." No diet with an energy content less than 1,000–1,200 calories should be undertaken without medical guidance. Once crash diets are stopped, the weight regained comes back fast, perhaps exceeding the previous amount. Several factors argue against the benefits of rapid weight loss. For one thing, the initial weight loss is mostly water; also, dieters eating less than 1,200 calories a day may lose muscle (protein) before fat, thus weakening rather than thinning down their bodies. Moreover, in a crash diet the body adapts to a restricted food intake, regarding it as a crisis situation that threatens survival. The body lowers its metabolic rate and reroutes enzyme pathways to conserve energy, so that a little food goes farther. Once the diet stops, the enhanced energy-conserving pathways make weight gain faster than before. Having become used to starvation rations, the body regards the return to more ample intakes as an excess, quickly turning the extra food into fat stores. Thus the dieter becomes more obese than ever, conserving more fat than before the diet began. Those who go on and off diets — especially very low-calorie diets — suffer the "yo-yo" effect: they take progressively longer to shed the unwanted weight each time around and regain it faster than before.

Another reason for the failure of crash diets is that they set up unrealistic expectations of transformations based on extremely monotonous eating patterns that cannot be kept up. The very idea of a "diet" suggests something short-term, rather than a lifelong change toward better nutrition. Once the diet stops, bad eating patterns return, and dieting starts afresh. The exclusion principle — forbidding certain foods — also leads to diet failures: no food should be taboo or it will become irresistible. Better to have a few mouthfuls of ice cream or pie in the weekly regime than to go on a secret binge, become disgusted at your lack of willpower and dump the whole diet plan.

CASE STUDY: SUCCESS AFTER AN UPHILL DIETING BATTLE

Janet grew up as the only child of immigrant parents who were proud of her early chubbiness. Her father, survivor of a concentration camp in Poland, also tended to be stout, and as his business expanded, so did his waistline. He had little time for Janet and was often traveling, secretly resentful of his daughter, as he'd wanted a son. Janet's mother, a slim social-climber occupied with her bridge club, volunteer work and cocktail parties, plied Janet with cookies and candy to keep her quiet, giving her little real attention. As Janet grew into a moon-faced, impassive schoolchild, she seemed to pick up every cold and other minor infection around. Now 47 and a mother of three, she recalls that "food had an overwhelming power over me. I'd be sitting eating in a café with no idea how I'd got there. My stomach owned me. I felt condemned by others — as I incriminated myself — for lack of willpower, for the inability to melt away my mounds of flesh."

When Janet was ten years old and weighed 58 kg (128 lb), the family doctor convinced her parents that she should reduce under medical care. Insulted at the mention of psychiatric counseling, her parents ignored his advice and continued to tempt her with strudel and cream. The pounds crept on until finally her parents realized that the plumpness which had seemed so endearing in early childhood was now shameful. After years of pressing food upon her, they suddenly began to watch her every bite. Defiant at the sudden reversal, Janet ate more than ever, becoming a grossly obese teenager. She was humiliated by the jeers of her peers. Her mother began to drag her from doctors to beauty parlors to reducing clinics.

"She badgered me to stop eating and moaned that no man would want so ugly a creature," recalls Janet. Like nearly all the obese, Janet hid behind her fat, using it as an excuse for failure, to explain why she gave up piano and had no friends. "As long as I stayed fat," she says, "I could avoid facing deeper issues, remain blameless, steer clear of sex and avoid possible rejection. The fat hid any feminine curves I might have had, helping me rationalize that if men didn't like me it was because of my size. My fat kept them away, preventing people from getting to know or reject the real me." In a way, she felt that her fat made her more important, more like her Dad, from whom she craved approval. "I was afraid that if I got thin I'd be shown up as a sham, a nothing."

In her twenties, however, Janet tried every dieting trick. No matter how stunning the temporary losses, the weight crept back. After a briefly slimmer phase at age 24, she gained some confidence, started to make friends and married. "But even after I married — partly to spite my mother,

who'd said I'd never find a husband — the old food habits took over." Despite her happy marriage to an accountant, she still felt a complete flop, abandoning one university course after another, going from one weight-reducing strategy to the next. At age 32, she was more than 30 kg (70 lb) overweight for her 170-cm (five-foot-seven) height and delicate frame. Her husband tried to help but couldn't curb her binges. "At night," he remembers, "despite a hefty dinner, she'd have a cup of peanuts, a few cookies, a glass of milk before going to bed. That's tantamount to a second supper. She might even slip downstairs later for another snack — a slice or two of pie, a glass of milk, a couple of bananas." Janet adds, "I couldn't help myself; my stomach may not have needed it but my mouth craved food." Again and again she determined to start a diet anew, cleared the house of all high-calorie items, had a bath and began whatever fad was going, only to give up again.

As Janet once told her group reducing session, her two children, then five and seven, were mortified by her appearance but didn't dare mention it. "It took the children's disapproval for me to realize that I was in big trouble," she admits, "to see that I needed psychological help." Finally, the children's embarrassment, the aggravation of being fat, the leg chafing, the hindrance to job advancement, the need for two seats on the bus drove Janet to seek help from a sympathetic physician. Ultimately, she knew she had to tackle the deeper reasons for overeating. After a thorough medical examination, the doctor prescribed a supervised 1,000-calorie-a-day diet to bring her 96 kg (212 lb) down to manageable size, and an appetite-reducing drug (fenfluramine HCl) for a few weeks. The drug's side effect — slight dizziness — was tolerable and carefully monitored. The physician also advised counseling by a psychotherapist who helped Janet probe the childhood roots of her obesity.

Janet kept a food diary, recording every morsel eaten, along with its caloric value. Like many other dieters, she got a rude shock to discover how she'd kidded herself about the calories in that piece of cherry pie (about 400 calories) or handful of peanuts (440 calories per half cup). Her therapist cautioned her against gulping down food or compulsively clearing her own or her children's plates. "It's far better," she suggested, "to eat slowly, put less in the mouth and take time over a meal, because the brain's hunger receptors don't respond for 20 minutes or so. If someone eats slowly, they'll eventually feel full and stop before consuming too much." Janet also had to note the five W's — when, why, what, where and with whom she ate — to encourage her to eat only at mealtimes, only to satisfy hunger, only what was permitted, only in one chosen place, and preferably not alone, to avoid the tendency to gorge.

Therapy helped Janet untangle her poor childhood relationships and boosted her ego. Her now aging mother was asked to stop nagging, and the family was advised that reproaches were counterproductive. They were asked instead to emphasize her good points — her quick wit, high intelligence and cheerful nature. Janet's children were asked to help themselves to dessert rather than putting it on the table, and to prepare their own meals for a while so Janet wouldn't get the urge to nibble.

Later, Janet's diet was relaxed to ban nothing, provided that meals were nutritious and totaled no more than about 1,200 calories a day (according to her activity level). Occasional lapses, common to all dieters, weren't considered a tragedy, but she had to record her feelings at the time (anger, pleasure, rebellion) and whether it was a meal or a snack. "No need to panic," her counselor said, "nothing's blown, just get right back on the rails." Later, Janet began a supervised exercise program, starting with a daily walk or run and muscle-toning.

About six months into her reducing program, Janet returned to college. Her exercise routine expanded to include swimming and more energetic aerobics. Janet won her battle against obesity in 18 months, to plateau at 65 kg (142 lb). For a while, her body image lagged behind her weight loss — she would be amazed that there was room for someone else to sit beside her on the bus, that she could get into a size 14 dress. Her changed self-image allowed her to pursue her career. She earned her B.Sc. and, at age 37, her Ph.D. A year later she was lecturing at the university, and at age 45 she became a full professor.

Janet is still within the normal weight range for her height and build — 56–63 kg (124–139 lb) — a weight she can maintain without stress, at which she functions comfortably, can do her job without getting too tired, feels energetic and needn't censor every bite. By standard medical charts she's still considered slightly overweight, but while she'd dearly love to, she doesn't feel pressured to shed those last few kilograms or pounds.

In bringing up her own children and looking after her grandchildren, Janet took special care not to repeat her parents' mistakes. She never overstuffed them, and didn't use food as a bribe or substitute for attention. She instilled in them a sensible attitude toward food — so that they would eat when hungry, not for attention — and a love of exercise. In other words, she practiced prevention — the best obesity cure of all.

Behavior therapy is often useful

Behavior modification, in which a therapist helps the overweight person restructure eating patterns and revamp his or her lifestyle, helps many people control obesity. The approach focuses on relapse training — anticipating and coping with lapses in the reducing program. Counselors teach people how to handle occasions such as dining out, parties, anniversaries and events of special culinary temptation, and help them get back on the rails if they break the diet. The key is to avoid the "all or none" attitude that makes dieters give up if they touch a morsel of forbidden food.

Those most likely to benefit from behavior modification are people who feel a pressing medical need to reduce. Married people do better than singles, parents better than the childless, those from happy families better than those from deprived or unhappy backgrounds. Behavior therapy also helps to overcome faulty eating patterns learned in childhood. "The successful management of obesity," according to one University of Toronto specialist, "is the result of a knowledgeable sympathetic physician or therapist with the time and concern to plan therapy and set goals that are realistic and achievable."

Even under the most favorable circumstances, behavior modification is often not enough to defeat obesity. Success rates average no more than 20 percent. Psychotherapy, particularly if the obese person has been fat since infancy, is often also necessary to resolve underlying emotional problems. "Better weight regulation," asserted Dr. Hilde Bruch, "becomes possible only as a result of better adjustment. And, ultimately, it means accepting responsibility for one's own fat and the motivation to do something about it."

The obese need a great deal of support: both help in organizing and sticking to a long-term reducing plan, and reassurance that they'll manage it. Subconsciously, family, friends and peers frequently sabotage the reducer's efforts, sometimes because of rivalry, often through insensitivity. A really supportive friend or relative might reinforce the dieter's resolve by removing all food temptations or by suggesting a walk, movie or some other activity instead of dining out.

Summing up the weight-loss message

Would-be reducers must abandon fad diets. People often finally lose weight when they stop dieting, don't watch the scales, eat normally and learn to accept themselves as they are. Those who want to improve their looks can try non-dieting strategies such as a visit to the hair-dresser or barber, new makeup, a new tie or scarf — better methods than starving the body and ultimately worsening a weight problem.

Anyone who is less than 20 percent over-weight and has no known health problems from the excess poundage should not desperately try to reduce. Those who do need to lose should realize there's no magic route to slen-derness. Obesity is curable only by a lifelong commitment to correcting faulty eating pat-terns. In sum, a suitable weight-loss regime must satisfy nutrient needs, be palatable, minimize hunger and fatigue, be readily obtainable, have no "forbidden" foods, be socially workable and promote a lasting improvement in eating habits.

For help with weight reduction

Consult a family physician; seek advice from a public-health nurse, clinic or registered dietit-ian. Some hospitals now have eating-disorder clinics. Obtain guidelines from a local dietetic or nutritional association; find a reliable weight-control clinic recommended by a health profes-sional. Consult Health and Welfare Canada's Task Force Report on the Treatment of Obesity; get advice from the National Institute of Nutrition.

GETTING ENOUGH EXERCISE

Whether in pursuit of beauty, health, youth, endurance or longevity, more and more people now give exercise top priority, conscientiously toning muscles and burning energy. But a recent Canada Fitness Survey found that while increas-ing numbers of men and women say they are dedicated to exercise, many who think they're active don't exercise often or vigorously enough to benefit their hearts. Over 50 percent of Canadians are still sedentary and less fit than they imagine. Only about 25 percent of Canadian adults exercise at a level that raises the heartbeat to the target zone and keeps it there for at least 20 minutes, thrice weekly. Common reasons for not exercising

enough are "no willpower," "poor facilities," "boredom," "sheer laziness" or "lack of time."

Although activity also helps seniors stay agile, only one-third of Canadians over age 65 even take recreational walks, let alone regular exercise. Yet many an elderly person who keeps on exercising has a lower heartrate than an inactive youngster who sits eating chips in front of the TV. Age is no barrier to fitness — regular exercise can't necessarily cure ailments, but it improves mental outlook, enhances body image and makes life more enjoyable. It's never too late to start!

Aerobic exercise is the cornerstone of fitness

The purpose of aerobic exercise, which literally means exercise "with oxygen," is to enhance oxygen availability throughout the body, by cre-ating a demand on the cardiovascular system (lungs, heart and blood vessels). Aerobic exer-cise should consist of continuous, steady, rhyth-mic movements. Done at the correct pace, intensity and duration, aerobics strengthen the heart, allowing it to pump more blood with each stroke for less effort.

Among the best, most convenient and easiest of aerobic activities are brisk walking, running, jogging and cycling, done at sufficient speed and for long enough. Swimming is also highly recommended, provided it is not too leisurely. It doesn't jar the legs or abuse the feet and suits people of all ages. Less effective aer-obics are tennis, golf and volleyball, which are stop-and-start activities. Workouts involving mainly the upper body and isometrics (strength exercises) increase muscle power but have little significant effect on cardiac health because they do not work the cardiovascular system hard enough. Once aerobic muscle energy is exhausted, an anaerobic (without oxygen) enzyme pathway comes into play, allowing a short burst of extra muscular energy, as in sprints to the finish line. But after the extra endeavor — the final sprint, shoveling snow or a narrow escape — the oxygen debt must be repaid.

Throughout exercise sessions, the emphasis should be on control, not how high or how fast. It's better to exercise at half the speed, in the correct position, than flailing madly. Remember, you do not have to "burn" (a term formerly used by misinformed fitness instructors) or overuse a muscle to attain the desired toning effect. Pain is not gain for sensible exercise.

How much exercise does it take to protect the heart?

All too often, physicians vaguely tell patients to "get more exercise" without specifying how much or what type. Yet, much as medications are individually prescribed, so too exercise routines should be tailored to a person's age and lifestyle. It's wise to consult a fitness instructor about your own needs and ask for advice on how best to start. Experts tell you to begin with a medical checkup and fitness test, especially if you are over age 35 or have disorders such as dizziness, high blood pressure, diabetes, arthritis or signs of cardiovascular disease. An appropriate test may spot weaknesses in lungs, heart or blood circulation that could make over-arduous exercise dangerous. Also, you should start gradually and work up to full workouts. A sudden plunge into unaccustomed exercise invites injuries, disillusionment and dropouts.

Current medical opinion holds that for the full heart-protecting benefits, people must exercise at least three times a week, steadily for at least 20–30 minutes, with movements that involve the large muscles (arms and legs). The activity should be regular and done at the right intensity (heartrate). Ideally, never let more than four days go by without a workout. The cardiovascular system must work vigorously enough to improve the heart's pumping capacity but not so hard as to strain it. If you exercise at the right intensity, the effort will bring on a sweat and should increase your pulse to the "training range," i.e., 60–85 percent of the heart's maximum pumping capacity.

To calculate the correct training heartrate, estimate your own maximum heartrate (heartrate at exhaustion) by subtracting your age from 220. The target range for your exercise sessions is 60–85 percent of that. (Note: 220 beats per minute is the exhaustion rate of a young child.) A 50-year-old man, for example,

---

ACTIVE PEOPLE ARE HEALTHIER

The message is loud and clear: exercise benefits body and mind and should be an integral part of everyone's life. Studies on postal and transit workers found a third fewer heart-attack deaths among those who were active than among those who sat still at work. Sedentary British bus drivers had more heart disease than conductors, who moved about; Washington letter carriers suffered fewer heart attacks than sedentary postal clerks; inactive Israeli kibbutz workers had more than double the heart-attack rate of those doing physical labor. A study of over 6,000 U.S. longshoremen, aged 35–74, showed that the vigorously active (unloading boats) had half the coronary death rate of the inactive (clerks and foremen). A British study that followed the pursuits of 18,000 middle-aged civil servants showed that 30 minutes a day of physical activity in chosen sports — walking, hiking, jogging, swimming — at rates using 7.5 kcal (kilocalories) a minute, halved the risks of heart attacks. (Note: 7.5 kcal is the amount of energy used in one minute of brisk walking, at a rate that burns 450 kcals per hour.) Another study, of 1,700 Harvard alumni aged 35–70, found fewer heart attacks in those expending more than 2,000 kcal (equivalent to about 32 km, or 20 miles, of brisk walking by an average-weight man) per week. In sum, any *sustained* activity — walking, running, dancing, rowing, mountain climbing — that burns 2,000–3,500 kcal weekly will help protect the heart. Lower energy outputs probably do not protect the heart.

OVERALL HEALTH BENEFITS OF REGULAR VIGOROUS ACTIVITY:

- the pleasure of movement;
- a sense of well-being — greater vitality and zest for life;
- less fatigue;
- a healthier appearance;
- increased physical and mental efficiency;
- less need for medical care and lower medical costs;
- better weight control and body composition;
- better sleeping patterns;
- improved ability to handle stress and crisis situations;
- possible delay in the outward signs of aging;
- psychological benefits, e.g., reduction of mild anxiety. Researchers suggest that physical activity may be as good as psychotherapy or medication in relieving mild to moderate depression;
- mood elevation — a euphoric lift experienced after at least 20 minutes of steady running ("runner's high") or equivalent activity, owing to release of the body's natural, opiate-like chemicals (endorphins);
- reduced risks of osteoporosis — especially through weight-bearing activities (walking, jogging);
- possible protection against coronary heart disease;
- possible lowering of blood pressure.

THE FIVE BASIC COMPONENTS OF FITNESS

- *Cardiovascular endurance.* Also known as cardiorespiratory or aerobic endurance, cardiovascular fitness enables the heart to withstand sudden exertion — such as fast stair-climbing, jogging or snow-shoveling — that calls for an increased oxygen supply to the working muscles (and faster removal of wastes such as lactic acid and carbon dioxide). Since both oxygen and wastes are carried by the blood, the heart must pump harder and move blood faster to meet muscular demands. A fit heart, with a slower resting beat (pulse rate at rest), can pump more forcefully, expelling more blood per beat than an unfit one. Many physically fit people have resting heartrates as low as 40–50 beats per minute, making them well able to cope with sudden physical exertion.

- *Muscular (isotonic) endurance.* The ability of a large muscle group to apply repeated force over a period of time is essential in many jobs. Bricklayers and typists need good shoulder, arm and back endurance. Weight-lifting and workout machines are popular ways to increase muscular endurance. For correct muscular training techniques, consult Fitness Canada.

- *Muscular (isometric) strength.* The ability of a muscle or muscle group to exert force against resistance provides efficiency for everyday tasks.

- *Flexibility.* Flexibility depends on a full range of movement for the body's joints. Stretching exercises, each held for a minimum of 10 seconds — preferably longer — develop and retain flexibility, especially crucial to maintain mobility with advancing years and to reduce injury risks from sudden bursts of movement (such as running for a bus).

- *Body composition.* Body composition depends on the ratio of fat to lean muscle and bone. Less fat and more muscle improves overall fitness. But some body fat is essential for insulation, protecting vital organs and — in women — carrying female hormones. Women ideally have 13–18 percent body fat, men 10–13 percent by weight. The amount of body fat can be gauged by skin-fold measurements (pinching skin with calipers) — more than 2.5 cm (1 in) is too much — or more accurately by the water displacement method. (Or try the mirror test: do you like what you see?)

has a maximum heartrate of 220 − 50 = 170 beats per minute and he should exercise at 60–85 percent of that rate, which means between 102 and 144 beats per minute. And don't suppose that, if 85 percent of the maximum rate improves cardiovascular fitness, 90 percent is better. It's not necessary or even safe to exercise above that 85 percent mark. Above the cut-off level, the body's activity may become "anaerobic" — done without oxygen — and not benefit but even perhaps harm the body.

Check your heartrate during exercise. If it's below your target range, the activity isn't vigorous enough to strengthen the cardiovascular system; if it's above the range for your age, slow down. Correct pacing means that the speed of activity is geared to the person, not to nearby exercisers or the music's beat. Signs that one is exercising in the target range are audible breathing — but not wheezing or panting — the ability to speak while exercising (some say able to converse but not to sing!) and a personal perception of exerting oneself to the fullest but *not* to exhaustion.

The breathing test
Lower limit: should hear the breathing.
Upper limit: breathing should be heavy but no wheezing.

The talk test
Lower limit: can easily carry on a conversation.
Upper limit: "just" able to speak while exercising.

The Rate of Perceived Exertion (RPE) test
The most up-to-date means of gauging the intensity of an exercise routine is the Rate of Perceived Exertion (RPE), now often used together with pulse-rate checks. Within a range of 1 to 10 (1 being low intensity, 10 being exhaustion level), try to exercise within the 6–8 range. This self-evaluation method also takes into account how the body "feels" and reacts to strenuous workouts.

Use it or lose it
Regular exercise enhances the lungs' ability to absorb oxygen, increases the amount of blood

pumped by the heart with each beat, increases the number of mitochondria that keep the muscle cells working, expands the network of capillary blood vessels which carry oxygen to the muscles and raises the activity of respiratory enzymes — no mean feat! But the benefits drop precipitously once habitual exercise stops.

Some training benefits are gone after even two weeks of inactivity, and significantly more in four to ten weeks. After twelve weeks about 70 percent of the muscular strength and endurance built up by regular exercise is gone. The heart puts out less blood with each beat and the ability of the working muscles to burn fat fades. The agility and coordination needed for sports such as tennis, skiing or swimming also decline. After long abstinence from activity, former regulars may have to start training from scratch.

Unfortunately, the largest drop in cardiovascular health comes quickly: half vanishes within two to three weeks of diminished activity. The body's oxygen-absorbing capacity drops in the first month of inactivity, as does the heart's pumping capacity. The increased mitochondrial (energy-producing) activity in the muscles falls in a couple of months. The expanded blood-capillary network may persist through several months, but if it isn't put to much use, the body becomes like a railroad that's lost most of its traffic — the tracks are there but not used enough.

Don't omit warm-ups and final cooldowns

A warm-up of seven to twelve minutes is essential before starting an exercise routine — to warm up the muscles slowly and prevent injury. Warm-ups should use movements similar to the intended activity, done slowly. They should also stretch the muscles of the back and extremities, start increasing the heartbeat, raise blood pressure and body temperature, increase elasticity of tendons and joints and trigger biochemical pathways that supply energy for movement. A proper warm-up may also protect the heart from irregular beats which can occur with sudden, vigorous exercise.

A cooldown of five to ten minutes allows a slowdown of physiological activity and gradual return to resting levels. During the cooldown,

do not drop the head below the heart (to avoid dizziness). The cooldown helps to avoid the transient giddiness, lightheadedness or chills that can occur when exercise stops too abruptly. During vigorous exercise, the heart pumps blood fast to the working muscles. Stopping abruptly lessens the pressure on the valves of the leg veins so that less blood is pushed back to the heart. The blood may temporarily "pool" in the extremities, depriving the heart and brain of oxygen, producing dizziness or fainting.

FINDING YOUR PERSONAL TARGET HEARTRATE ZONE

AGE	MAX.	60%		85% (cut-off)	
		Beats/10 secs.	Beats/min.	Beats/10 secs.	Beats/min.
25	195	22	132	30	180
30	190	19	114	27	162
40	180	18	108	26	156
45	175	18	108	25	150
50	170	17	102	24	144
55	165	17	102	23	138
60	160	16	96	23	138
65	155	16	96	22	132
70	150	15	90	21	126
			or less		or less

Monitor your heartrate by taking your pulse (on wrist or neck) about five minutes into the aerobic routine, then again at peak exercise intensity, keeping the legs moving while doing so.

The easiest way to take your pulse is by placing your middle two or three fingers on the carotid artery in the neck (see diagram), but not so tightly that you suppress it! Or, take the pulse with the middle two fingers (not the thumb) on the wrist. Start at zero and take the pulse for 10 seconds, then multiply by six to obtain your heartrate per minute. Also take the pulse rate after completing the aerobic component, then assess the speed of recovery — the time taken to reach the resting heartrate.

A few precautions

Never exercise after a heavy meal. When the stomach is full, much of the blood supply is diverted to the digestive system, and exercising may compromise the blood supply. The heart and working muscles will then have less than their full oxygen supply. You could also vomit and choke.

To avoid heatstroke, don't exercise under a hot sun, or in excessive heat. Prevent dehydration by replacing fluids lost during exercise. Drink plenty of liquid — preferably water, not alcohol, which only dehydrates you further!

After exercising, avoid steam, hot saunas or

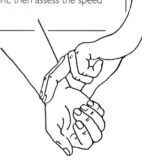

THE EXERCISE PRESCRIPTION

Frequency: **at least three times a week.**

Intensity: **in target heartrate zone (60 percent of maximum heartrate = lower limit; 85 percent = upper limit).**

Duration: **minimum of 20–30 minutes (at target heartrate).**

Type: **continuous, steady and rhythmic, using large muscle groups (legs and arms).**

Note: There is little training effect if exercise is less than three times a week or is done below 60 percent of the maximum heartrate. Listen to your body: if it tells you the time's ripe to work out more vigorously, act accordingly; if it signals a need to slow down, do so!

very hot showers until the body is well cooled down. Sudden heat makes surface blood capillaries dilate (widen) and may keep blood away from the heart.

Try not to regard recreational activity as a competition to the death. If exercise becomes obsessive, it can worsen health problems. Some grim-faced, lip-biting exercisers look more stressed out than hard-driving executives. For them, exercise is not the healthy, relaxing therapy it should be but a situation where they are pitted against themselves or others. Someone who starts each day with a pre-breakfast run — striving for a better speed each morning — then has a daily lunchtime squash game and a vigorous evening workout may be overdoing things, and increasing rather than relieving tension.

A few athletes and exercisers exhibit such a compulsive approach to their activity that it has been likened to anorexia nervosa, the condition common in adolescent girls where dieting is carried to the point of starvation. Preoccupation with diet and exercise can lead to excessive weight loss, emaciation or even death.

Although there is a transient increase in the risk of sudden cardiac arrest (heart attack) during extreme exertion, there is mounting evidence that habitual activity reduces the risks of coronary (heart) disease. Nonetheless, about a quarter of nonfatal heart attacks occur during vigorous physical activity, usually in unfavorable conditions — after a heavy meal, during extreme heat, under emotional stress or when the person is unprepared for the exertion. Despite occasional deaths on the tennis court or running track, the chances of a healthy heart stopping during a workout are far outweighed by the risks of underactivity. In almost every case, athletes

who suffered cardiac arrest while exercising had preexisting (often undiagnosed) heart disease. One University of Toronto expert estimates that "the odds of a physically healthy person, with no history of heart problems, dying during exercise are one in 5 million for men, one in 17 million for women." Nonetheless, exercisers should be familiar with the sudden signs of heart trouble.

Alerting signs of heart trouble

If you experience any or several of the following symptoms, see your physician: chest discomfort or pressure; pain down the arms (especially the left arm); swelling of ankles or hands; purple fingertips; lightheadedness; profuse sweating; anxiety.

Any suspicion of unexpected heart trouble demands urgent medical attention. If you wait to make sure, it may be too late. (For more on heart problems see the section on heart disease in chapter 16 and emergency action for heart attacks in chapter 17.)

General tips for sensible exercise

• *Plain water is the safest drink.* Caffeine and alcohol should be avoided — both are diuretics that flush out water through the kidneys. Drink two to three cups of water two or three hours before engaging in strenuous activity, another cup 15 minutes before the start and then one cup every 15–20 minutes. Take plenty of fluid after exercise to rehydrate the body. (Strongly colored urine signals dehydration and the need to replenish liquids.)

• *Alcohol should be avoided* because it impairs judgment and coordination (easily leading to mishaps such as falls overboard when boating) and gives an illusion of warmth, although it speeds up body cooling/heat loss (by allowing the blood vessels to expand, speeding up heat loss) so that body temperature drops faster. It's also a diuretic.

• *Drink plenty!* One needs ample fluids before, during and after exercising, particularly in hot weather. To maintain a safe core (inner) body temperature, the body must sweat profusely to cool the body. During strenuous exercise the body can lose up to 2 litres (0.5 gal) of water per hour, which seriously decreases the circulating blood volume. Dehydration is a major danger in ardent exercisers.

- *Drink as much in cold weather as in hot.* It's easy to become dehydrated in cold weather because of the water lost by sweating and because the cold air inhaled must be moistened as well as warmed.
- *Be extra vigilant when exercising in windy conditions.* Wind can increase or mask the onset of sunburn or hypothermia (body-chilling).
- *Make footwear comfortable and supportive.* Shop for shoes in the afternoon, when feet are hot and possibly swollen. The shoe sole should be flexible, for easy push-off, and an extra layer of shock-absorbent foam helps to protect the toes. Beware of a stiff and uncomfortable midsole. The heel should be well cushioned for shock absorption, especially in runners. A padded collar topping at the back protects the Achilles tendon. Leather is increasingly used for sport shoes, although those whose feet tend to get hot may prefer a leather and mesh mixture.

Avoiding some common sports injuries

Given the importance now attached to sport and physical fitness, the management of sports injuries has become a major subspecialty of medical science. Sports injuries range from simple bruises and strains to dislocated joints and broken bones. They can be sudden and acute (emergency) events or occur slowly due to overuse. A few, such as spine or skull fractures, heat stress, abdominal bleeding or organ rupture, can threaten life.

Key steps in managing sports injuries

Rest, ice, compression, elevation (RICE) plus controlled or limited motion are the basic tenets for managing sports injuries, whatever their causes. One University of Toronto specialist prefers the term MICE meaning "movement (limited), ice, compression and elevation" — to downplay the idea of extended rest and immobility for sports injuries. The primary goal is to reduce the inflammation that follows injury in the first 72 hours or so. The body may overreact, allowing too much fluid to collect, prolonging healing time. Once the swelling goes down, gentle controlled movement should begin, with gradual return of the injured area to full function.

General principles for sports injuries:

- *Consult a physician* about any but the mildest of sprains, strains or other injuries.
- *Never disregard pain.*
- *Wrap the injured part in ice* (well-crushed, or a package of frozen peas, wrapped in a towel or old woolen sock, to prevent frostbite) and apply for 15–20 minutes every two hours for severe injuries, every six hours for milder injuries. Deep-seated injuries will require the full 20 minutes, one to four times daily. Apply ice for briefer periods if injury is close to the skin. (Do not use ice if you have circulatory problems.)
- *Apply pressure* (compression) with an elastic bandage that's moderately tight but does not press on nerves or reduce blood circulation. Always wrap from the point farthest away from the heart toward the heart (e.g., wrist to elbow). The tensor bandage should not usually be worn at night, to prevent circulation problems. *Tip*: if the far end of the limb turns blue, the bandage is too tight!
- *Elevate the injured part* to prevent pooling of accumulated fluid in inflamed tissues. Prop legs at rest above hip level. Injured hands and forearms can be supported in a sling with hands at shoulder level. For upper-arm injuries, raise the arm above the head at regular intervals.
- *To reduce swelling/inflammation*, try ASA; for pain, take acetaminophen.
- *Begin limited gentle exercise during recovery* to regain strength and flexibility, preferably guided by a trained physiotherapist.
- *Return to full activity only when well healed* and pain-free — usually ten days to eight weeks for a sprain, depending on severity.
- *Go easy on the use of heat* (often improperly used to treat exercise-induced injuries). Never apply heat to an acute bruise, strain or soft-tissue injury. (That means no hot baths and no heating pads following such injuries.) Heat may make the injury feel better, but will also increase local inflammation and worsen the swelling. It's generally best to opt for ice. Heat should only be used, if at all, once the swelling has gone down. "Contrast baths" — alternating cold with hot water — may be useful for stimulating blood circulation to the injury, but only several days after the acute injury phase.

SAFETY SUGGESTIONS FOR SUMMER SPORTS

- *Remember that exercising in the heat* strains the heart more than similar activities done in cool conditions, so ease up in summertime. It takes two to three weeks to become acclimatized to warm-weather exercise.
- *Always warm up and cool down,* even in hot weather.
- *Avoid running or other vigorous exercise* during the hottest time of the day (11:00 a.m.–3:00 p.m.).
- *Try not to be in direct sunlight* all the time. (See chapter 17, Emergency medicine, for ways to recognize and treat heat stress/heatstroke.)
- *Use sun-protection/sunscreen* to avoid excess exposure to UV rays (see section on skin cancer in chapter 5).
- *Wear loose clothing* in a material that breathes — cotton is best in hot weather — so that air can circulate over the skin, allowing sweat to evaporate. Light colors reflect the sun's rays better than dark colors.
- *Use a well-ventilated, wide-brimmed hat* to shade the head and neck in sunny conditions.
- *Allow for water-stops* every 20 minutes or so.
- *Watch for hypothermia* (excessive body cooling) in water sports. A dangerously low body temperature can result from exposure to cold water or windy conditions, and Canadian waters rarely warm up, even at the height of summer. The main signs of hypothermia (cold injury) are: shivering (although it stops when people are overchilled), slurred speech, stumbling, weakness, confusion, drowsiness, shallow breathing, weak pulse, loss of consciousness (maybe). Treatment for hypothermia is to keep the person warm and dry, seek medical attention, never give alcoholic beverages. (See chapter 17, Emergency medicine, and following section on winter exercise.)

FOR WINDSURFING:
- *Always wear a personal flotation device* (PFD) or lifejacket (it's required by law).
- *Know your own limits* and stick within them.
- *Windsurf with a buddy* for support and assistance.
- *Have a friend ashore* who knows where you plan to go and is on the alert for rescue if necessary.
- *Check the weather forecast* before setting out — put ashore before thunderstorms hit.
- *Be on the alert for shipping hazards* — give large vessels a wide berth.
- *If a novice, avoid overchilling* from dumps into cold water.
- *Head for shore* if tired.

FOR SAILING/BOATING:
- *Learn to handle the boat*; keep rigging and equipment in good order. Know and respect your own limits and those of the crew.
- *Ensure that all boaters wear a lifejacket or PFD* — you are required by law to have one for each passenger. (About one-third of all drownings occur through people not wearing PFDs.) Approved lifejackets automatically turn people who fall overboard face up for air; PFDs only keep them afloat.

- *Take good care of your PFD* — do not use it as a cushion or fender. Dry in open air and *keep* dry.
- *Be sure children have lifejackets* of the right size. A too-small jacket will not float a child high enough to breathe, a too-large jacket can slide right off.
- *Practice capsizing*, man-overboard and self-rescue techniques.
- *Get weather forecasts*; watch for signs of impending storms. Shorten sail well ahead of time.
- *Check and obey local boating guidelines* and regulations.
- *Sail sober!* Avoid alcohol until landing safely; many boating deaths are linked to alcohol. It is illegal for *anyone* to consume alcohol on a boat unless it has overnight facilities and is moored for the night.

FOR WATER-SKIING:
- *Learn technique* from a certified instructor.
- *Check all equipment* before setting out.
- *Always have an observer* in the boat — it is the law.
- *Use common sense* if driving waterskiers: go slow for beginners.
- *Wear an approved lifejacket or PFD.*
- *Be sure that the skier, boat-driver and observer all use the same hand signals* for "go" and "stop"!
- *Stay away from docks,* boats and shallow areas; avoid swimmers.
- *If fallen into the water, lift ski* to signal position.

FOR SWIMMING:
- *Never dive into unknown waters* that could be shallow or rocky and cause a head injury/unconsciousness.
- *Don't swim too soon after eating.* Stomach cramps can lead to vomiting, even drowning. Wait half an hour to an hour after eating a full meal before swimming.
- *Take out contact lenses* before swimming — they easily get contaminated (especially soft contacts) and can get lost!
- *Stay close to shore or to a boat* if not a strong swimmer.
- *Get out of the water in thunderstorms.*

FOR BIKING:
- *Ensure that the bicycle functions properly,* especially the brakes.
- *Make sure the bike fits* the rider — many accidents happen to people on oversized bikes, especially children.
- *Obey the rules of the road,* stop at all intersections, marked or unmarked. Use the correct hand signals.
- *Never ride two abreast.* Keep hands available for the bike; carry parcels in fixed holders.
- *On long trips, carry a water bottle* — dehydration is common in summer bikers.
- *Be visible at night:* use lights on bike, or reflectors on bicycle or clothes. Children should not ride at dusk or in the dark — it's very risky.

- *Above all, wear an approved helmet*; it can significantly reduce the frequency and severity of brain damage from cycling accidents. Get a helmet approved by the CSA (Canadian Standards Association) or an equivalent one.
- *Let children choose their own helmet*; never trade safety for style, but make sure the child likes the selected model.
- *Select a bike helmet with adjustable straps* and a quick-release buckle that doesn't pinch: adjust straps for a snug fit.

FOR HIKING:
- *If hiking, always carry waterproof matches, compass, knife*, snare wire, fishhook, first-aid kit, high-calorie snacks.
- *Learn wilderness survival* if hiking in isolated areas. Don't wander aimlessly if lost — fix position relative to a hillock, lake, other landmark or the sun. Follow downhill slopes — they may lead to a recognizable trail or lake.
- *Make camp during daylight* on an elevated spot in a clearing (more visible to rescuers). If lost, build three fires in a triangle (a recognized "distress signal"), preferably on rocky ground (in order not to start a forest fire), adding green boughs for extra smoke.

FOR TENNIS:
- *Warm up beforehand*, being sure to include good calf stretches and Achilles tendon (heel) stretches to reduce risks of Achilles tendon injuries — common in tennis players.
- *Avoid incorrect arm posture* during the swing, strike and follow-through.
- *Aluminum tennis frames aren't advised for novices*; fiberglass or the newer vibration-dampening materials provide greater flexibility.
- *Beginners should take lessons* to ensure proper techniques that lessen chances of injury.
- *"Tennis elbow"* — painful swelling from racquet vibrations — arises from striking the ball too hard and from a faulty grip

that increases vibrations traveling up the arm. Treat with painkillers, perhaps anti-inflammatories, plus rest, and then learn a better technique.

FOR GOLF:
- *Do warm-ups before the game*, with special attention to stretching the lower back and hamstring muscles.
- *Lessons ensure that the body moves correctly* during swing, strike and follow-through.
- *Even golfers can suffer dehydration* and heat stress — so drink enough and be vigilant!
- *Back problems are common* among golfers, although golf seems to be a leisurely game unlikely to cause injury. Back-strengthening exercises are a good idea. And don't forget the post-golf stretch to prevent lower-back tension.

FOR ROLLER-SKATING OR ROLLER-BLADING:
- *Try not to fall on hard pavements* — a danger with any type of roller-skating.
- *Consider wearing splint-type wrist guards*, knee and elbow pads.
- *Helmets are a must*.
- *Stick to quiet, level streets* until able to stop!

AVOID "OVERUSE": PAIN IS NOT GAIN FOR SPORTS

Pain signals something wrong and should never be ignored. It's an urgent message to slow down and attend to what's causing the discomfort. If someone continues to exercise — trying to "run off" the pain — further damage will occur. The only way to combat the inflammation due to muscular overuse is to rest when there is pain and resume exercise when it subsides. Overuse injuries typically cause stress fractures and/or inflammation.

Stress fractures — hairline bone breaks — occur if repeated exercise creates such intense muscle fatigue that the muscles can no longer adequately support the skeleton. "Continuous loading" that exceeds the bone's inherent elasticity may bend the bone and eventually produce a hairline crack. The treatment of stress fractures involves rest until bone healing is complete — up to eight weeks — with limited exercise during recovery that won't aggravate the injury (try swimming or stationary bicycling for leg overuse problems).

Inflammation, the body's natural response to tissue injury, often affects muscles and tendons, especially where they attach to bone. The inflammatory pain may disappear between activity and during pre-exercise warm-ups but re-appear during or following activity. The condition is termed *tendonitis* if it affects a tendon, *bursitis* if the inflammation affects a joint bursa — the fluid-filled pouch near the joint. Treatment is simple: remove or stop the movement that causes the pain, cool with ice, elevate the painful part and follow with stretching and strengthening exercises (preferably advised by a physiotherapist).

SAFETY TIPS FOR SPECIFIC WINTER SPORTS

FOR TOBOGGANING:

- *Recognize that while tobogganing is an excellent family sport* — the best of aerobic exercise, as it entails hill climbing and carrying a load (the toboggan) — it takes a heavy injury toll.
- *Wait until the ground is covered with a thick layer of soft snow.* A thin layer often conceals logs, rocks or chunks of ice. Hitting a chunk of ice can be as dangerous as striking a hard rock.
- *Make sure the hill isn't too icy or steep.* An icy hill makes the toboggan go faster and it is harder to control.
- *Wear a helmet.* About half of all tobogganing injuries are to the head, sometimes serious.

FOR CROSS-COUNTRY SKIING:

- *Dress appropriately.* Remember that this sport requires more exertion than downhill skiing, and wear lighter clothing. But watch out for hypothermia and frostbite, which are distinct risks when out on the trail, especially when the temperature drops at day's end.
- *If skiing across a frozen lake or pond, beware of cracks* in the ice. Stay within 6 m (20 ft) of shore, and steer clear of rocks or docks where the ice may be thin.
- *Eat and drink enough before setting out* to stock up on energy and prevent dehydration.
- *Take along snacks of complex carbohydrates* (e.g., dried fruit, granola bars).
- *Stick to well-traveled trails and ski in pairs.* For maximum safety never venture alone onto isolated trails.
- *Plan the route ahead* and stick to it, calculating expected return time and leaving the information with someone who's not going out.
- *Leave enough time to get back before dusk,* unless the trails are well lit.
- *Carry a first-aid kit* and light plastic blanket — they easily fit into a backpack.
- *Fall backwards,* if you must fall!

FOR DOWNHILL SKIING:

- *Remember that there are an estimated 10 injuries per 1,000 downhill skiers per season,* half of them severe enough to need medical care, mostly the first time people venture onto their skis each year. The most frequent ski injuries are to the knees and head.
- *Get in shape beforehand,* perhaps with "ski-fit" classes. Include workouts to build strong leg muscles. (Nowadays, with the ankle locked into place, torsional forces go to the knee instead of the ankle during a fall.) Knee injuries are frequent among alpine skiers, so work the quadriceps (the muscle on the front inside of the thigh) and the calf muscles ahead of time to help avoid injuries.
- *Start each ski day with warm-up exercises.* A cold, unstretched muscle is prone to injury.
- *Increase carbohydrate intake* before a ski day to maintain stores of glycogen (for muscular effort).
- *Make sure that all equipment is in proper working order.*

Have skis checked by a reputable dealer in the fall to ensure that bindings will release when needed. Bindings must be adjusted to the skier's weight, height, age and skiing ability. (Novices may prefer looser bindings that easily release.)
- *Stop skiing before fatigue sets in.* Most downhill skiing injuries occur in the late afternoon, after enthusiasts have already been at it for several hours.
- *Dress warmly enough* in layers, as this is not a "high activity" sport. Protect the hands, legs, face and feet from the cold (the latest boots contain battery warmers!).
- *Watch for soft snow* where skis can get stuck without release of bindings.
- *Beware of ice!* The bindings may release in time, but ice is hard to fall on and an outstretched arm easily fractures.
- *Helmets are a must for speed downhill skiing.* Collision with another skier or a tree is a distinct possibility!
- *When night skiing* — an option at many resorts — recognize your limits and stop when tired or cold. After warming up by the fire with a cup of hot chocolate or soup, you can always return to the slopes!

FOR SKATING:

- *Get boots with firm ankle support and a snug fit;* for young, growing feet, softer boots are better than hard, unyielding ones.
- *Before going out on the ice,* check that the skate blades haven't become dull or rusted.
- *Many skating clubs and rinks insist that beginners and all skaters under age 16 wear helmets,* but others feel that only pair skaters need the extra protection for the twists and throws.
- *Padded pants provide protection* in a fall, but some instructors believe that wearing pads makes skaters too dependent on them, so that they never learn to fall properly.
- *If you fall, try to fall backwards!*
- *For an ankle sprain,* leave skate on to keep down the swelling (unless told otherwise by a medical authority or coach).

FOR ICE HOCKEY:

- *Make sure all equipment is in good repair.* About one-third of hockey injuries are due to equipment failure, because players wrongly consider themselves invincible in their protective gear. While hockey gear is expensive and children grow out of it fast, it is vital to replace it regularly.
- *Replace cracked shin pads or helmets* and brittle equipment where the foam is damaged.
- *Make sure helmet padding* is adequate.

FOR SNOWMOBILING:

- *Be in sufficiently good shape* to lift the machine if necessary!
- *Watch for frostbite* and other signs of excess body cooling.
- *Carry a first-aid kit.*
- *Wear a jacket with built-in flotation capacity* (e.g., Mustang type), if going over ice.

HOT TIPS FOR COOL SPORTS: SAFETY TIPS FOR WINTER EXERCISE

- *Never overdress*. A common mistake among winter exercisers is wearing not too little but too much clothing.
- *Keep clothing loose*. Tight socks, shoes or gloves can cut off the circulation, leading to frostbite.
- *Protect the head and neck*. Up to 40 percent of the body's heat can be lost from the head. The best bet is a wool or polypropylene cap or hood which also covers the ears. A balaclava or a cap with a fold-down face mask is useful on very cold days, in falling snow or gusting wind — but be sure it doesn't reduce vision or hearing.
- *Wear a scarf or neck tube* that can be put over the mouth to warm cold air before it's breathed in (carry a neck tube in your pocket — it can cover the ears, mouth and most of the face).
- *Use light, thin clothing to maintain the body's "micro-climate."* Have good ankle and wrist closures to trap the heat generated. Remove layers if too warm (tying garments around the waist or putting them in a day pack). Don them again if cold.
- *Dress in layers* to vary insulation. One should feel chilly in the first five minutes of winter exercise and comfortable after that.
- *Choose underwear — closest to the skin —* for absorption, to draw sweat away from the skin so that it keeps the body drier. Modern "thermal" underwear often has an inner layer (usually cotton or synthetic) that absorbs perspiration and "wicks" it to the outer layers, keeping moisture off the skin. (Pure cotton tends to hold in sweat and become cold and clammy.)
- *Make at least one layer wool*, either the middle or second-to-top layer — for optimal warmth. Wool retains body heat even when wet.
- *Make the top or outer layer windproof*, preferably of fabric that "breathes" so that moisture isn't trapped inside. Gore-Tex, Lycra and nylon fit the bill. Nylon provides better protection from strong winds than most woven fabrics and is also water-repellent.
- *Turtlenecks are good for cold days* to protect the back of the neck (a high heat-loss area).
- *Zip 'em up!* Jackets should be fastened in *two* ways — with both zips and buttons or Velcro —to make them fully windproof. Choose clothes for ease of removal, i.e., clothes that unzip or unbutton to let you cool off or close swiftly again if you're cold. (Tie a small loop of string or fabric to zippers so you won't have to search for the ends or remove gloves.)
- *Pants can be cotton with a nylon covering*, wool or Gore-Tex — waterproof for skiers. Use tights, leg warmers or thermal long johns underneath in really cold weather.
- *Wear goggles* to protect the eyes. Leave no area of the face exposed in severe cold.
- *To keep the hands warm, mittens are better* than gloves since they keep the fingers together, with less surface area for heat to escape. In very cold weather the warmth of mittens is worth the loss in dexterity. Mitten or glove liners are excellent for very cold days.

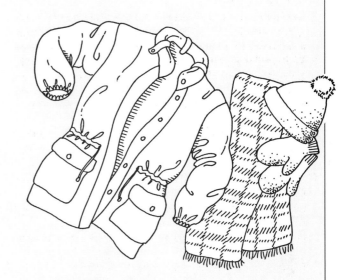

- *Protect the feet well*. Thick-soled rubber boots with lace-ups and a removable felt liner (that can be dried out) are ideal for snowy, icy or slushy conditions. They can be removed and exchanged for other footwear when getting into the car. (Snowboots can cause accidents if worn while driving!)
- *Footgear should be loose enough* to allow the toes to wiggle, and to trap warm air and allow room for an extra pair of socks.
- *Don't go out on an empty stomach*. Food provides energy to combat the cold. It may even prevent hypothermia if you are lost, stranded or injured.
- *Increase carbohydrate intake*. Choose the complex variety, avoiding too many sugary sweets. Take snacks along if planning to be out for more than an hour or two.
- *Never push yourself to exhaustion*. Overdoing it may leave the body uncoordinated and vulnerable to injury. (Don't expect to have the same stamina in winter as in summer; even a one-degree drop in temperature reduces endurance.)
- *Be on the defensive against fog, mist, twilight and darkness*. When planning a hiking or cross-country ski trip, remember that the days are much shorter in wintertime. And listen to the weather forecast!
- *Beware of ice!* While some people manage to exercise in the worst weather without injury, exercising on ice is often risky unless the pace is slowed (take smaller steps and wear footwear with good traction). For safety, carry a rope and ice awl if trekking on ice. If starting to fall through ice, throw the body forward, hands outstretched, and try to propel yourself to safety with your legs.
- *Develop an emergency or "injury action" plan*. Deal promptly with minor injuries to stop them from becoming major problems, and watch for frostbite. (See chapter 17 for frostbite and cold injury treatment.)

SUGGESTED WAYS TO PREVENT SPORTS INJURIES

GENERAL GUIDELINES

- Have a thorough physical exam by your family physician to uncover any underlying health problems that could be worsened by certain types of exercise.
- Prepare well for the chosen sport, acquiring adequate training and skills.
- Do warm-up/stretching and cooldown exercises for the sport.
- Develop balanced muscle strength to improve joint stability.
- Increase intensity and duration gradually.
- Continue conditioning in the off season.
- Rest injured areas for at least 10 days and seek professional advice about return to activity.
- Wear correct protective equipment — e.g., helmets, good athletic footwear and eye-protectors.
- Conduct frequent equipment checks, promptly replacing defective parts.
- Use correct techniques — e.g., proper grip for racquet sports, aligned gait while walking or jogging.
- Avoid hyperextension — keep joints "unlocked."
- Learn and follow the safety rules for each sport pursued.

PROTECTIVE GUIDELINES FOR PARTICULAR BODY PARTS

Neck

- Avoid rapid circular neck rotations.
- Avoid extensive hyperextension — i.e., drooping head, arched back;
- Develop strength and flexibility of all neck muscles.
- Remember, longer necks are more susceptible to strain.
- Never dive into unknown waters. Check for depth and hidden rocks or other underwater objects before diving in, and recheck at subsequent dates, as water levels may change.

Shoulders

- Avoid needless overuse of shoulder joints — e.g., multi-repetitions of overhead arm movements.
- Strengthen all muscles of the shoulder girdle.
- Ensure correct techniques when performing sports that involve excessive use of shoulder joints — e.g., tennis, swimming, weight lifting.
- Develop shoulder flexibility by exercises learned from a physiotherapist.

Elbow

- To avoid "tennis elbow," ensure that muscles around shoulder, elbow and forearm are strong and balanced; check grip size, weight of racquet, technique; regulate/limit frequency of play to avoid overuse. (Forearms can be strengthened simply by repeated squeezing of a tennis ball.) Do regular stretching routines.

Lower back

- Use correct posture when lifting — e.g., bent knees with hips and toes aligned; use leg strength, not back strength, when weight lifting.
- Strengthen the abdominal muscles to support the back.
- Develop lower-back strength and flexibility.
- Improve flexibility of the leg's hamstring muscles.
- Avoid unnecessary forward flexion, especially with a straight back and/or locked knees.
- Avoid prolonged excessive hyperextension (back arching).
- Maintain "pelvic tilt" posture throughout activity (hips tucked forward to avoid back arching).
- Use any break in activity to do "pelvic tilts" and to stretch hamstring and lower back muscles — for example, when walking to the next hole during golf or to the tennis court.

Knees

- Strengthen all muscles surrounding the knee, including hip abductors and adductors (inner and outer thighs), hamstrings (backs of leg) and especially the quadriceps or upper thigh muscles, which are often weak in comparison to their counterpart, the hamstrings. Strengthen the quadriceps by sitting on a chair and extending the lower leg slowly to the front, holding for three seconds in the horizontal but not locked position. Exercise one leg at a time increasing weight resistance gradually by adding small Velcro-fastened weight bands on the ankles.
- Check gait. Avoid excessive foot pronation or supination (rolling in or out).
- Try corrective shoes or orthotics (shoe inserts) if knees hurt.
- Avoid needless repeated jumping.
- Choose activities that transfer weight from side to side.
- Keep knee flexion to 90 degrees or more (overflexing at the knees — e.g., resting the buttocks on the heels — can place exceptional stress on the knee joint).
- As often as possible, keep knees lined up with the feet and hips, not twisted.

Lower leg

- To help prevent shin splints — a common overuse inflammation injury affecting the lower leg muscles on either side of the leg bone — keep calf muscles stretched, and evenly strengthen the muscles that surround the bone. (You can do this by dorsiflexion: that is, flexing the toes up toward the knee.) Check foot alignment and avoid unnecessary pounding. (Shin splints frequently arise from running on hard pavement.) Always stretch calf muscles before activity, especially if you wear high-heeled shoes. Wear good, supportive, cushioned shoes.

Foot

- *Plantar fascitiis,* a common overuse injury affecting the longitudinal muscles in the foot's arch, results from repeated hard impact — common in soccer players and joggers. To prevent it, check foot alignment (supination and pronation), wear supportive footwear for support and shock absorption and change direction frequently during long-distance running. If a distance runner always runs in the same direction, with the right foot on the upward side of a slanted surface, that foot will pronate (roll in) more forcibly than the left, increasing stress on the plantar fascia.

For more information, contact Participaction (416-977-7467), local health departments, family physicians, local sports medicine clinics, athletics centers, medical associations, local sports clinics, physiatrists and sports physiotherapists.

SLEEP HYGIENE AND SLEEP DISORDERS

Most adults average seven and a half to eight hours of sleep per night but need more sleep when they're stressed and less when untroubled. Some individuals can do with as little sleep as five hours nightly or less, historic examples being Napoleon, Thomas Edison and Chou En-lai. Others require nine or more hours. Studies show that bed-sharing couples sleep less than singles but couples in separate beds sleep more soundly!

Sleep requirements are greatest in infancy (16–18 hours a day), and gradually decrease. The soundest sleep is typically that of ten- to twelve-year-olds, who effortlessly slumber nine to ten hours nightly and remain fully alert all day long. During adolescence sleep patterns approach the adult average, later decreasing to about six hours a night in the elderly. Sleep patterns in older people are variable, generally more fragmented with more nocturnal awakenings, possibly due to inactivity and daytime naps.

In very young children, bedtime fears, nightmares and bedwetting are the commonest sleep problems, while adolescents typically find it hard to get up. Young adults most often complain of difficulties in falling asleep, but sleep peacefully once they have dropped off. In contrast, the elderly, who tend to turn in early and fall asleep fast, awaken often and have difficulty getting back to sleep, sometimes because of arthritic pain or other health problems. Over a third of our population complains of insomnia, and in desperate attempts to get a good night's rest many turn to alcohol, sedatives or tranquilizers.

Curiously, sleep experts report frequent discrepancies between the way people think they sleep and their actual sleep patterns, as is shown when they are wired up to EEG (electroencephalographic) machines, which record brain-wave patterns, with electrodes on the scalp. Many people who call themselves poor sleepers and complain of hardly sleeping a wink all night actually fall asleep quickly in sleep labs and slumber soundly. For some reason — often unknown — their sleep is non-restorative and fails to give them the desired freshness.

Sleep is a dynamic, rhythmic process

Sleep used to be considered an inactive state, but modern science sees it as an active, cyclic process regulated by various neurotransmitters (chemicals that affect nerve impulses). Some sleep phases are as busy and alert as wakefulness, although in different ways. Essentially, sleep begins with relaxed wakefulness, which is a drowsy period lasting a few minutes to half an hour, before people drop off. It progresses into two main states described as non–rapid-eye-movement (non-REM) and rapid-eye-movement (REM) sleep. REM sleep is thought to reflect dreaming periods. Normal sleep begins as non-REM, deep or "delta-wave" sleep, with EEG readings showing a slow wave. The first REM episode occurs some 70 to 90 minutes into sleep and lasts perhaps five minutes, with the EEG registering faster waves of brain activity. Subsequent cycles of non-REM and REM sleep continue through the night at roughly 90-minute intervals, with later REM episodes averaging 15–20 minutes. Morning naps tend to have more REM cycles and more dreams than afternoon naps.

During REM sleep there are recognizable physiological changes — an increased and variable heartrate, a rise in blood pressure and respiration, increased cerebral bloodflow and oxygen consumption, reduced body-temperature control, marked loss of postural muscle tone (prohibiting movement) and, in men, penile erections. Most of us experience three to six REM periods a night, and if we are awakened abruptly from them we recall vivid dreams that are often later forgotten or repressed. Basically we are the same personalities in dreams as during wakefulness: creative people report more creative dreams, schizophrenics experience bizarre dreams and depressed patients dream of helplessness, hopelessness and escape. Dreams emphasize aspects of our personality that may be less apparent during wakefulness.

REM sleep and dreaming are suppressed by various sedatives (such as barbiturates), antidepressants and alcohol. When deprived of REM sleep, many people become agitated and aggressive. By contrast, people deprived of non-REM sleep become very withdrawn; a few develop symptoms resembling fibrositis — now called the arthritic pain modulation disorder — with musculoskeletal tenderness and increased pain sensitivity at specific body points.

A 24-hour biological clock, or circadian rhythm, controls our wake-sleep patterns. It explains why we tend to sleep better at some times of day than others. In a cave lit only by artificial means, a normal person given plenty of food but no clock or set mealtimes will still maintain a circadian rhythm, usually somewhat over 24 hours (if not forced to adhere to 24-hour routines). Our normal sleep-wake routine, harmonized with the sun's 24-hour cycle, is reinforced by day-time checkpoints such as mealtimes, work or school timetables and regular retiring and rising times. Shift workers classically find it hard to sleep when their circadian rhythm is at odds with their work hours. At night, the biological clock "turns down" many functions that enhance daytime alertness — such as cortisone (adrenal hormone) release, certain transmitter levels and the heart rate. Studies show that workers at the start of a night-shift are slower and less efficient than usual at many tasks. That may explain why so many trucking mishaps and accidents (such as the Three Mile Island nuclear leak and the London, England, underground crash) happen between 1:00 and 4:00 a.m. at the circadian low point. Some airlines and other organizations try to arrange night shifts so that the natural circadian rhythm isn't too drastically undermined. (Jet lag is a typical case of disturbed circadian rhythm and disrupted sleep-wake cycles.) (See chapter 13 for more on shiftwork.)

Occasional sleeplessness is not unhealthy

In healthy people, even long periods of sleeplessness produce no permanent detrimental changes. People with some rare brain diseases never sleep yet survive for months. Young, healthy volunteers, kept awake for 24–48 hours or even longer, show remarkably little deterioration in task performance. Despite fatigue and mood changes, bodily reserves can rally to bring performance up to par for short periods. But as sleep deprivation continues, little "microsleeps" occur, with lapses in brain function that may cause driving errors or endanger people in other ways. Short-term sleep losses can be harmful to epileptics, in whom they trigger seizures, and to those with jobs that demand focused attention, such as air-traffic control.

Surprisingly, in some clinically depressed people a sleepless night actually elevates mood and performance for a few days. Some European medical centers use sleep-deprivation therapy in depressed patients to reset skewed circadian clocks. Its mechanism is still a mystery, but sleep loss may normalize a disturbed circadian rhythm and improve neurotransmitter balance.

Insomnia — an abnormally prolonged inability to sleep — comes from a disruption of either waking or sleep patterns. Most of us suffer the odd sleepless night when we stay awake due to excitement, worry, jet lag, overuse of caffeine or shift work. But many chronic insomniacs always sleep poorly and feel perpetually fatigued. Of the main types of insomnia, by far the commonest is situational or transient, caused by something like an impending exam, emotional stress, job worry, certain medications, overwork or pain. Sleeplessness that lasts no more than three to four weeks requires no therapy; once the stress or distress passes, so does the insomnia. Some experts recommend the brief use of a sleep remedy, perhaps one of the benzodiazepines (for example Valium, Dalmane, Halcion or Xanax), to provide much-needed rest and prevent short-term sleeplessness from becoming a chronic complaint. These anti-anxiety medications also act as sedatives and are useful for short-term use. Disorders of the sleep-wake cycle (due to abnormal circadian rhythms or biological clock dysfunction) are newly recognized sleep disorders, requiring special therapy.

Sleep medications should never be regularly taken without specific medical advice. The use of most sleep medications, especially short-acting benzodiazepines, leads to tolerance; i.e., the drug is no longer effective unless the dosage is increased. Withdrawal can lead to hangover-like symptoms, blurred vision, disorientation, daytime drowsiness and "rebound insomnia," after even brief use. Once hooked, many people need professional help to kick the habit of a nightly sedative fix. Therefore experts warn strongly against unnecessary or pro-longed use of sedating medications — particu-larly for the elderly, who should take only half the usual prescribed dose or use a shorter-acting drug. (The cumulative effects of long-acting sedatives may leave the elderly in a constantly confused state.)

The use of alcohol at bedtime is likely to be more troublesome than helpful. Although it facilitates sleep onset, it also suppresses the initial REM episode. As the alcohol breaks down, its depressant effects are followed by cerebral excitation and more REM sleep than usual, and the sleeper may be aroused fre-quently by vivid or distressing dreams. Thus, although alcohol first lulls you to sleep, as its sedating effect wears off it leaves your mind restless and disturbed.

Persistent insomnia — a vicious cycle

Emotional and psychological conflicts, as well as psychiatric disorders, often cause long-term sleeplessness. Insomnia is frequent in the introverted, who tend to mull over problems at night. Among schizophrenics and the depressed, insomnia waxes and wanes with their condition; it is often a sign of depression. Sleep difficulties can also be provoked by certain drugs, such as the blood pressure medication propranolol, which may produce vivid dreams. A self-perpetuating cycle of in-somnia can be set off by some event or illness in people who previously slept perfectly well. The sleepless nights create anxiety about insuf-ficient rest, cause fatigue and lead to more insomnia. Worry about not sleeping often lessens the ability to fall asleep. In trying to combat their insomnia, many people start taking more and more sedatives. They may also take several alcoholic drinks at bedtime, if other drugs no longer put them to sleep. As the cycle continues and drug dependence builds, desper-ation creeps in.

The management of chronic insomnia depends on uncovering the underlying reasons for it, through a thorough medical evaluation, physical exam and analysis of psychosocial, alcohol and drug history. Treatment of persis-tent nonmedical insomnia usually attempts to improve sleep habits and break the vicious cycle.

Counseling and psychotherapy may be useful, depending on the extent of anxiety. Sedative drugs may occasionally be used to carry people through an especially troubling time, but never for more than a few days each week.

Daytime sleepiness can be risky

People who sleep too much can be worse off than those who sleep too little. Although less common than sleeplessness, excessive daytime drowsiness is more dangerous. People may fall asleep on the job or at the wheel of a car and cause accidents. Excessive sleepiness, which sometimes goes undiagnosed, is heralded by dozing off without apparent cause, irresistible napping and uncontrollable bouts of sleep at inconvenient moments — while at work, making love, chatting on the phone, eating or driving. If attacks occur during potentially risky circumstances, the affected person is strongly advised to obtain treatment, and to desist from potentially hazardous activities until the condi-tion is under control.

Sleep labs may be able to pinpoint the reason for excessive sleepiness, which has three main causes: narcolepsy, sleep apnea and noc-turnal myoclonus.

Narcolepsy is a rare syndrome affecting about one in 2,500 people, which is possibly inherited and first surfaces in adolescence or young adulthood. It is defined as excessive daytime sleepiness with abnormal REM sleep patterns. Symptoms include brief, sudden loss of muscle tone with involuntary collapse of the limbs (cataplexy), eye twitching, facial immobil-ity, sleep paralysis (inability to move during sleep) and dreamlike hallucinations. Although narcoleptics appear fully alert, many remain sleepy at all times and most suffer psychological disorders due to the disability.

Narcoleptics typically fall asleep at inap-propriate times despite a full night's sleep. Intense emotions such as laughter, surprise, anger and excitement can trigger muscular col-lapse. Classic stories about narcoleptics tell of an angry mother who collapses as she swings at her child, a sergeant who falls to the ground motionless as he shouts commands, a fisherman who buckles at the knees while reeling in a fish. Narcoleptic episodes occur because the onset of REM sleep — whether at night or in daytime — occurs suddenly and unexpectedly, or at once after dozing off, instead of following a period of non-REM sleep. The result is immediate vivid dreaming, fragmented sleep and sudden loss of muscle tone.

Since narcolepsy is a lifelong condition without a cure, treatment depends on controlling its symptoms. It includes scheduled daytime naps, suitable stimulants to overcome the daytime drowsiness and antidepressants to suppress sleep paralysis. A new remedy, gammahydroxybutyrate (a natural constituent of the human brain), developed by researchers at the universities of Ottawa and Toronto, not only helps muscular control but can consolidate sleep into coherent periods. It acts as a kind of "sleep-glue" that encourages narcoleptics to sleep at night rather than in daytime snatches.

In *sleep apnea*, breathing ceases for 10–60 seconds from time to time during sleep, sometimes many times a night, momentarily cutting off the body's oxygen supply. The sleeper often remains unaware of the countless nocturnal breathing lapses, accompanied by snoring, which bed partners find unbearably disturbing. The lapses in breathing — an interval of silence followed by a mighty heave, snort or gasp and then resumed snoring — are both annoying and scary. The apneic breathing stoppages not only produce poor sleep and daytime drowsiness (perhaps dangerous for those driving or operating complex machinery) but can trigger a heart attack in adults, and may be a cause of some crib deaths (Sudden Infant Death Syndrome) in vulnerable babies. Reasons for sleep apnea include anatomical obstructions (such as a jaw abnormality, enlarged tonsils or adenoids), nasal polyps, sleeping on the back, loose dentures and flabby throat muscles (in the elderly). It is typically a condition of the obese — especially middle-aged men. Telltale features of this rare but hazardous disorder include a slowed heartrate, abnormal leg kicking and flailing movements, falls from bed and sleepwalking. Some apnea sufferers complain of choking sensations that interrupt their sleep, and report memory problems, hallucinations, irritability, mood or personality changes and waning sex drive.

Treatment of apnea includes weight loss (for the obese), decongestants, sleeping on the side (perhaps with a tennis ball fixed in the pyjama back to prevent rolling onto the back), avoidance of alcohol and medications (such as sedatives and tranquilizers) that depress breathing, mask-like devices to improve airflow and surgery to correct anatomical impediments.

In *nocturnal myoclonus*, which may accompany narcolepsy or sleep apnea or occur independently, rhythmic leg-jerking awakens the sleeper. Episodes of this twitching last from five minutes to two hours and alternate with peaceful sleep. The restless night produces extreme daytime drowsiness. The affliction appears mostly in middle-aged men and women, and is of unknown cause, but is often seen in kidney patients who are on peritoneal dialysis, and in people with fibrositis. The cause is unknown. Treatment is with drugs that

---

TIPS TO PROMOTE HEALTHY SLEEP

Avoid:
- daytime naps;
- heavy meals late at night;
- arguing or working in bed;
- alcoholic nightcaps (which fragment sleep);
- drinking too much fluid in the evenings;
- caffeine-containing products such as coffee, tea, colas, chocolate;
- evening hunger — eat a light snack, drink a glass of milk or have cereal with milk (rich in tryptophan, a natural food component conducive to sleep);
- smoking tobacco (which is a stimulant);
- regular use of tranquilizers and sedatives;
- trying too hard to go to sleep, which may

have the opposite effect (instead of lying there counting sheep, do something — read a relaxing novel or watch TV);
- self-reproach for inability to sleep: it's not an illness, a crime or even necessarily unhealthy;
- staring at the bedside clock (turn it to the wall);
- overwork or getting too exhausted.

Do:
- have a good daily exercise routine (especially in the late afternoon or early evening), to promote sleep;
- use the bedroom for sleep and sex, not for all general activities;
- provide a quiet, dark, comfortable sleep environment;

- keep the ambient temperature right — not above 75°F (24°C), which disturbs sleep, but not too cold;
- regulate your sleep and awakening times to reinforce your circadian rhythm — go to bed after about 16 hours of nonstop activity and stay there! Have a regular wake-up time;
- sleep as much as needed to feel refreshed the following day, but not more; curtailing time in bed seems to solidify sleep, while staying in bed lightens it;
- allow an hour's relaxing "wind-down time" after the day's turmoil before retiring to bed;
- seek professional assistance if needed.

suppress the leg jerks. Alcohol and caffeine should be avoided, and leg-stretching exercises are sometimes recommended.

Night terrors and sleepwalking

Predominantly a problem of the young, night terrors and sleepwalking start around age four and usually vanish by adolescence. The sleeper partly awakens from deep slumber, and is simultaneously asleep and semiconscious. In night terrors, a terrified child may sit up in bed and scream while still seemingly asleep; the episode of fear usually occurs an hour or two after bedtime, and the youngster usually cannot be awakened. Night terrors are more common when schedules are erratic or when children are stressed or overtired, so regular schedules may diminish the problem. Waking the child up to discuss the fear usually just aggravates the condition.

Sleepwalking, in which movement is clumsier than normal but still remarkably deft, also occurs in semi-arousal from deep sleep. As they roam, sleepwalkers often perform purposeful actions such as eating, toothbrushing and dressing — usually indoors, although some venture outside. Occasional sleepwalking appears in 5 to 15 percent of children (compared to night terrors in only about 5 percent). Again, stress and emotional tension increase the problem. Should sleepwalking continue into adulthood, psychotherapy may be advisable. Management includes safety measures to prevent the injuries so easily incurred by unprotected sleepwalkers. Doors and windows should be well secured and harmful instruments should be put away.

Before you imagine yourself to be a sleep-disordered person, remember that in most people sleep problems are temporary and harmless. For the small number of people with serious sleep disturbances, new research can help. And finally — sleep is as vital to health as diet and exercise and should be given enough attention.

PREVENTING NEEDLESS INJURIES

Traumatic injuries are a major and little-appreciated health problem in this country. They outrank all other fatalities in those aged one to 24 and rate fourth as a cause of all deaths in Canada, behind cardiovascular diseases, cancer and respiratory illness. Since injuries so often kill the young, they pose as serious a health problem as diseases in terms of productive life years lost.

During the 1930s, many people were crushed to death in malfunctioning elevators; children suffered terrible burns when their nightwear caught fire; infants often choked on small toy parts or were strangled in the rails of their crib. Even in the 1970s, countless Canadian deaths occurred among people who motorcycled bareheaded, drivers who didn't use seatbelts and children who rode unrestrained in cars on parents' laps. Thanks to intensive consumer lobbying, legislation, public education and engineering improvements, many dangers once considered part of life have been reduced. Killer elevators and inflammable nightwear are becoming a thing of the past, and unhelmeted motorcyclists appear suicidal to most onlookers.

Yet death from unintentional injuries still takes an appallingly heavy toll. And death is only the tip of the iceberg. For every trauma death, 45 people with injuries are admitted to hospital. Injury-related death rates in Canada exceed those in Japan, Australia, Sweden and most West European countries. Children are especially vulnerable. One University of Toronto expert notes that "during peak travel times, emergency rooms are filled with children whose injuries could have been minimized or prevented by a little good car sense." In Sweden, for example, simple measures such as introducing bike lanes and arranging routes to school through traffic-free zones have halved the injury rates among children.

"Accident" is a misnomer — most are not random

Too many of us regard injuries as random, chance events that "just happen" through fate, human nature, clumsiness or bad luck. The very term "accident" suggests something unexpected and unavoidable. The fact that the circumstances leading to injury are considered unpredictable may explain why accidents aren't generally considered a health problem.

THE SIX MAJOR CAUSES OF PREVENTABLE DEATH AND INJURY:

- traffic collisions;
- falls;
- fires/burns;
- suffocation;
- poisoning;
- drowning;

Of preventable injuries:

- **33 percent are due to traffic crashes;**
- **23 percent are sports-related;**
- **21 percent are work-related;**
- **13 percent happen at home.**
- **The rest happen for miscellaneous reasons.**

However, there has been a dramatic shift in medical thinking about so-called accidental injuries. The notion that injuries are unpredictable is now outmoded, replaced by the view that they are both predictable and preventable. The very term "accident" is being abandoned, because injuries — like diseases — arise for definite reasons. While the idea of an accident-prone personality is a myth, certain factors are closely tied to injury — particularly high childhood activity levels, risk behavior and family stresses (such as house moves, job loss or divorce).

Public-health specialists point out that, like diseases, many injuries have clear-cut causes — such as icy sidewalks, insufficient lighting or poorly timed shiftwork rotation. Car crashes may happen because of poor vision (wrong glasses) or alcohol consumption. People may fall in the shower for lack of a safety mat. Children can get hurt in countless ways: by a television falling on them when they pull on the cord, by being shut in a cupboard, through playground mishaps. It may seem unforeseeable that a preschooler would dart in front of a car and get hurt. However, as a group, five-year-olds living on busy streets are quite likely to be hit by cars, more so than a similar group living in a village. Among teenagers and adults, alcohol use and failure to use seatbelts are as clearly linked to injury as high blood cholesterol is linked to heart disease. The list is endless.

Experts stress that most injuries are predictable, can be anticipated and in many cases could be prevented. Injuries typically occur through lack of awareness, inadequate planning and society's acceptance of unsafe environments. Although there's no entirely risk-free environment, much can be done to reduce the dangers. Once the causes of injury are identified, preventive measures can be put into place — much like marketing low-fat products to combat high blood cholesterol. But unfortunately injuries rarely garner the same attention as cancer, heart disease or meningitis. A news story about one meningitis case typically gets greater coverage than a car crash that killed six teenagers the same day.

Who's most at risk?

At all ages, males have more injuries than females. Boys undertake more hazardous activities and have more injuries than girls in every category. Boys drown 14 times more often than girls; they are killed on bicycles five times more often and hit by cars three times more frequently. Injury risks peak in toddlers and in teens — both stages of life when ability and experience are mismatched.

After our highways and roads, home is another frequent site of injuries. Although thoughts of "home" conjure up images of comfort and security, home mishaps account for almost 40 percent of injury and death away from the workplace. Socioeconomic status also affects injury rates. For complex reasons, but mainly because of overcrowding and poor supervision, children of low socioeconomic status have an above-average number of injuries. There are also large variations in provincial injury rates, which are usually higher for Native than non-Native populations.

Children are especially vulnerable

Canada has introduced laws covering child car seats, childproof packaging, flame-resistant nightwear, toy labeling, fireworks and a multitude of other hazards. However, childproof packaging isn't going to work if parents don't fasten the lids properly; child car seats won't work if they aren't used. Caregivers frequently underestimate dangers to children. A recent survey found that parents were more worried about their child being kidnapped or abusing drugs than about the less dramatic but far more prevalent risk of traffic injuries. Only 6 percent of parents surveyed knew that injury is the leading cause of childhood deaths.

Childhood injuries typically happen when caregivers relax their watchful gaze, become distracted or overestimate a child's skill. They can even occur with parents or other caregivers in the next or the same room. Not everyone realizes that within seconds a child can fall off a high surface (even a bed), drown (even in the bathtub or diaper pail) or get badly burned (by a hot kettle or iron). Anticipating how and where injuries occur is the first step in avoiding them. Childproofing of the home, the car and other surroundings must be geared to each age group's ability, activity and competence levels. The greatest danger arises when activity levels exceed a child's judgment abilities.

Different dangers at different ages

Newborns can't get into much harm on their own, but safety measures include smoke detectors, cribs of safe design and infant car seats (correctly used and properly installed).

Infants/crawlers: A baby a few months old can roll over, put things in its mouth, crawl and fall from high places or get burned by hot liquids or cigarettes. Never leave an infant unattended on a high surface — don't wait until your child falls off the table to find out that it can roll over.

Toddlers and preschoolers: Injury risk increases sharply as crawlers become toddlers. As they learn to walk and climb, the home becomes increasingly unsafe. Kitchens, bathrooms, closets and drawers need to be reorganized. The risk of burns increases with toddlers — from tap water, stoves, irons and heaters. Toddler reins have not really caught on in this country, but they're a good idea to prevent small children from darting in front of cars or getting lost in crowds. Besides falls from furniture, stairs and playground equipment, drowning is a special threat at this age. Poisonings also peak in toddlers, being 10 times more frequent than in older children. Grandparents' or other visitors' purses containing medications (such as heart pills — for instance, digoxin — sleep-aids or painkillers) should be kept safely away from exploratory young fingers. It's also wise to childproof the homes of grandparents and other relatives visited.

Schoolchildren are less likely to be injured than younger age groups, but pedestrian and bicycle injuries are common at this age, when children may still lack the skill to negotiate busy streets. Up to age 10 they should not be permitted to cross busy streets unsupervised. Children must be shown (not told) how to stop and look both ways — left and right and then left again — before crossing the street. Tragically, children are sometimes killed by the family car in their own driveway. Watch for children playing behind the car, approach the driver's seat from behind the car and walk around the vehicle to do a safety check before reversing out.

Teenagers: Adolescence is the time of greatest risk, as many teenagers challenge authority, have a sense of invincibility, overestimate their abilities and show off to peers. Statistics show that access to firearms and other means of self-destruction increases risks of teenage suicide — a leading killer of adolescents. (In Quebec, for instance, suicides outdo traffic crashes as a cause of adolescent death.) One in 50 North American teenagers is involved in an auto crash. Drivers under age 21 drive faster and are less likely to wear seatbelts than older people. Substance abuse (liquor and drugs) is an added danger.

ALCOHOL AND DRUGS POSE EXTRA DANGERS

Alcohol is often a factor in injuries, especially among teenagers. Everybody knows it is dangerous as well as illegal to drink and drive. Liquor impairs judgment, coordination and balance. Surveys show that 36 percent of teenage males and 17 percent of teenage females involved in traffic fatalities have blood-alcohol levels over the legal limit. If, despite the risk, parents allow their teenage children to drive cars and motorcycles, they must teach them road safety and clearly explain the dangers of drinking and driving. Many adolescents themselves are becoming more aware of drinking-driving hazards, and peer-group organizations,

such as Students Against Drinking and Driving, are very effective in promoting responsible habits. Some authorities promote graduated driving licenses for young drivers, rather than "carte blanche" permission to drive anywhere, anytime. Thus, on first obtaining a driver's license, a teenager might be prohibited from highway driving, as well as driving late at night or with other teenagers in the car.

It's even dangerous to drink and walk. More than one-half of pedestrians over age 16 involved in fatal traffic incidents have blood-alcohol levels over the legal limit. It is equally hazardous to drink and swim or sail, and alcohol consumption is a common

factor in boating mishaps. Likewise, half of all adults who die in house fires are found to have high blood-alcohol levels. Falls, too, are often linked to alcohol ingestion. Besides alcohol, drugs — whether illicit, prescription or over-the-counter (OTC) medications — can increase injury risks. For example, some antihistamines (such as Hismanal and Chlor-Tripolon) increase drowsiness and may impair driving ability. Painkillers and sedatives also impair the ability to drive or operate machinery safely. In one University of Toronto hospital study, 75 percent of those coming in with trauma injuries had high blood levels of OTC or prescription medications.

Preventing the six major causes of injury

Traffic collisions

Automobiles are becoming safer, thanks to public campaigns. Gone are the dangerous fins and hood ornaments of the sixties; interiors are remodeled and modern cars have shatterproof windshields, headrests and other safety features. Seatbelts have been highly effective in preventing death and injury from traffic mishaps. During a car crash, safety belts protect passengers by preventing ejection from the moving car, minimizing the severity of injuries due to impact with the vehicle's hard interior. They stop people from going through the windshield if the vehicle comes to an abrupt halt — especially useful in rollovers and head-on crashes. Worn properly, lap and shoulder belts halve the chances of death in an auto crash, often allowing people to walk away from an incident that would otherwise have killed them.

In Canada, children must legally be restrained in car seats from the moment the newborn leaves hospital. Unrestrained infants held on laps or left free in cars become projectiles on impact. Yet some parents only belt in their children on long trips (even though most crashes happen at busy intersections or close to home). Child seats not only provide safety but permit children to see out of the window more easily (as they're sitting higher). Small infants should be in seats placed against the dashboard — facing the rear window — so they can see and make eye contact with the driver. Older children should be properly secured in an approved child seat, facing forward, in the back of the car. (For more on car safety and preventing childhood injuries, see chapter 11.)

Air bags that inflate on impact give added protection to front-seat passengers, preventing injuries to the face and spine in frontal, but not in side, rear or roll-over collisions. Sensors under the hood pick up the impact, producing inflation within milliseconds, so that air bags balloon out to surround the driver and front-seat passenger.

In 1992, air bags became optional on 80 vehicle models sold in Canada. According to the Canadian Automobile Association, almost half of all new vehicles now feature them as standard equipment. Air bags do *not* replace seatbelts but offer added protection to driver and front-seat passengers. At speeds under 40 km/h (25 mph), seatbelts give adequate protection, but at higher speeds the head usually strikes the dashboard or steering wheel and the brain moves forward in the skull at a swift pace. Air bags prevent the violent whiplash forces on neck and head in frontal crashes, so that the brain moves forward less forcefully against the skull and is less likely to be drastically damaged.

Being built into the car, air bags work without compliance; unlike seatbelts, worn at will, air bags are automatically inflated. They remain "at the ready," their protection not contingent upon occupant cooperation. Once all cars have air bags, it's estimated that they will reduce fatalities from motor vehicle mishaps by a further 10-15 percent over and above the 40 percent injury diminution already provided by seatbelts (if worn). Auto experts warn about the mistaken tendency to stop wearing seatbelts in cars with air bags. Air bags are *not* a substitute for seatbelts, which remain a must.

The bad press about the few injuries reported from air bags that burst (minor facial burns and eye damage due to the chemicals released) hardly detracts from their ability to prevent death and disability. There have been no permanently serious wounds or health problems from air bags.

In praise of seatbelts
- Make "buckling up" an automatic habit whenever riding in a motor vehicle — you should feel "undressed" without a seatbelt.
- Remember that seatbelts must be well tethered and correctly adjusted.
- Seatbelts keep the driver behind the wheel and in control of the car. (If there's also an air bag, the seatbelt keeps front passengers in place for air bag protection.)
- Wear the seatbelt assembly as snugly as possible without being uncomfortable.
- Always consult your doctor if you are involved in an accident, even if you seem uninjured.

Bicycle safety also reduces the traffic-injury

toll. Bicycles are often regarded as toys, but falls from bicycles can be very serious. Parents often buy a bike that is too big for the child, so he or she will grow into it. This is a mistake. Bicycles should fit the child. Because people tend to fall head first, cycling injuries are often fatal. Many such deaths could be prevented by wearing helmets. Children should wear bike helmets from the time they get their very first bike. Although bicycle helmets reduce the risk of brain injury by 85-88 percent, fewer than 4 percent of schoolchildren and even fewer adults wear them. Children in bicycle-mounted seats should also wear helmets.

Helmets work as shock absorbers. Most properly designed and manufactured bike helmets consist of an outer shell, an energy-absorbing liner, a layer of soft foam and fabric pads and a good retention system. The helmet's shell distributes the force of impact and its inner foam absorbs the blow, preventing it from crushing the skull and injuring the brain. The foam liner — the life-saving portion — is usually made of expanded polystyrene or, more costly but better, polypropylene or polyethylene; it shouldn't be too stiff, because if it doesn't bend or crush on impact, the shock isn't adequately absorbed. Models have become successively lighter and more stylish. Many now have very thin outer shells, making them more comfortable. The Canadian Standards Association (CSA) publishes a Canadian National Standard for bike helmets. Approved helmets include the older hard-shell types (with a heavy, solid plastic covering), the newer thin-shell or micro-shell models (with a thin, semi-rigid cover over the foam liner that looks like one piece but is a double layer) and the latest, lightest, no-shell types (with the foam wrapped in the thinnest of Lycra sheets).

Falls

Injuries from falls are especially common in the elderly and young children. Fatal falls often occur on stairways, or from windows, trees, roofs and steep embankments. Older people often fall from ladders or on sidewalks, slippery floors or stairs. A serious hazard in themselves, stairs become still more danger- ous if objects are left on them. Death and

---

PREVENTION IS A MUST

Injury prevention involves:
- **education, which includes anti–drink-ing-and-driving cam-paigns, bicycle-safety campaigns, home safety education;**
- **legislation, which includes seatbelt laws and compul-sory child car restraints;**
- **modification of the product or environ-ment, including mea-sures such as child-proof medicine containers, flame-resistant toys and nightwear, home smoke detectors.**

While they can reduce injury risks, none of the three methods works on its own. Safety tutoring alone will not neces-sarily alter behavior. Studies have shown over and over again that telling people what to do may not make them comply. On the other hand, passing laws aimed at an uninformed and resistant public is not likely to work either. By contrast, passive injury control (making the environment safer) can be dramatically successful. Childproof

medication containers are one example. Deaths from aspirin ingestion dropped in the United States from 144 deaths per year in 1960 to 12 per year in 1973 after childproof-packaging legislation came in. However, passive pro-tection can be expen-sive, and the public must sometimes be coerced into compli-ance. Prevention is most successful if done at the community or "grass roots" level, where everyone par-ticipates in making the environment safer.

---

serious injury from falls in baby walkers are also common; many medical experts consider baby walkers highly dangerous.

Fire hazards

Studies show that deaths from fire are far less common in homes with smoke detectors than in those without them. Being incapacitated by smoke is a major cause of death in house fires, which often start at night. The elderly and the very young are in particular danger, because they can't get out fast enough. Smoke detectors should be installed on each floor, near bed-rooms, living rooms and in the basement. They alert people before smoke levels become dan-gerous. Check smoke-detector batteries regu-larly. In addition, every family should plan and practice fire drills. In nighttime fires people are drowsy, and those who have practiced before-hand are less likely to panic. Plan to meet at a designated spot outside the house in case of fire, so that you can quickly determine who's missing or still inside.

Burns and scalds, especially from hot coffee, irons and lit cigarettes, endanger young children, who may be scalded/burned even when held on the lap by an adult drinking coffee or smoking. Children can also sustain severe burns by chewing electrical wiring. A child's skin is more sensitive than an adult's and takes less time to sustain heat injury. Electrical devices and outlets should be blocked from young fingers. Check for frayed wiring. Discourage smoking in the home. Make sure hot food is covered or out of reach.

Suffocation
Some 40 percent of all injury-related deaths under age one are due to suffocation or choking on food and toy parts. Small parts from toys and games belonging to older siblings are frequent offenders. Round things are a special danger to tiny throats — such as small balls and round foods. Avoid giving children under age four round hot dog pieces, peanuts, popcorn, hard candy and non–bite-sized pieces of food that require chewing, as well as small toys and uninflated balloons. Swallowing bits of balloon or even whole uninflated balloons has been known to choke children in minutes. Never leave a child alone in a car, as deaths from asphyxiation have occurred when children got tangled in the straps.

Poisonings
Poisoning, the second most common reason for hospitalizing children under age four, becomes a potential danger as soon as a child begins to put things in its mouth. For every poisoning death that occurs, 20,000 toxic ingestions are

GENERAL HOME SAFETY TIPS

- Wipe up spilled liquids or grease immediately — they invite disaster.
- Replace burned-out or inadequate light bulbs; have lights and light switches at both the top and bottom of stairs; install night lights in dark hallways.
- Secure scatter rugs with rubber backing or anti-skid coating, or by tacking them in place.
- Wear well-fitting, well-tied shoes or nonslip footwear when working around the house.
- Repair curled linoleum, broken or loose tiles and loose floorboards promptly.
- Install handrails or handles on the bathtub to aid getting in and out. Also use nonskid bathmats.
- Discourage use of electrical appliances in the bathroom. Be sure bathroom electrical outlets are grounded or on a ground-fault interrupter that cuts power instantly in case of need.
- Clear snow and ice promptly from stairs and porches. Sweep away water to prevent ice patches.
- Make sure that bed lamps are easily turned on and off — for getting up at night — to avoid falls.
- Install a night light in the bathroom.
- Put out grease fires by covering with a large lid. Do not use water or dump baking soda as they may cause worse spattering.
- Do not carry out a pot of grease that's on fire — a slip or trip could be fatal.
- Keep a dry-chemical fire extinguisher in an accessible location and tell everyone where it is and how to use it. Follow instructions for shaking and inspecting it regularly.

- Avoid portable home heaters, which can easily give burns.
- Keep electrical appliances away from curtains and bedding.
- Check electrical appliances for defects.
- Clean fireplace and chimney regularly.
- Equip house with smoke detectors and regularly check the batteries.
- Place firescreen around fireplace.
- Put out cigarettes in deep, flat-bottomed ashtrays and never empty them into wastebaskets or garbage until completely cooled.
- If on multiple medications, keep a diary of which was taken when or use a well-marked pillbox to avoid dosage errors.
- Read labels on household products, noting which are corrosive, toxic or inflammable. Take appropriate precautions when using.
- Work with volatile chemicals in a well-ventilated space.
- Store knives in a proper knife rack on the wall or in a drawer adapted for this purpose.
- Avoid picking up broken glass with the fingers. Sweep it up and wrap it in newspaper before discarding. Pick up small bits with wet paper toweling.
- Store power tools away from power source.
- Do not refuel gas-powered equipment when the engine is running or hot, and be extremely careful in cold weather that you do not spill gasoline on your hands — it can cause instant freezing.
- Take first-aid training.

reported to local Poison Control Centres across the country. Although medicine and poison containers are now usually childproofed, all medications and household cleaners should be stored out of a child's sight and reach. Not all poisons are obvious: perfumes, cosmetics, alcohol, paints and paint thinners can also be toxic. Keep poisons in original containers marked "poison." Never store paint thinner or similar substances in a cup or glass, even for a minute. If it's not something you'd feed a child, don't leave it within the child's reach. Keep ipecac syrup at home to induce vomiting if necessary, but call the Poison Control Centre before administering it. Keep the local Emergency and Poison Control Centre numbers near every phone.

Drowning

A residential swimming pool is considered an even more likely cause of death for a child under five than riding in the family car. Childproof fencing around swimming pools is the law in Canada, which greatly reduces drowning risks. But toddlers can drown in a small amount of water in a bathtub or a bucket, not just in pools or lakes. Teens are also at risk of water-related injuries, and must learn the rules of boating (such as wearing lifejackets), and be aware that alcohol and swimming or boating make a bad mix, regardless of TV ads suggesting the opposite. Learning how to swim does not necessarily decrease the risk of drowning. In fact, novice swimmers are among those most likely to drown, as they're apt to venture out too far, be deceived by the distance covered or energy expended and run into trouble when trying to swim back.

PUTTING DRUG USE IN PERSPECTIVE

Illegal drug use, while serious and personally devastating, is not, as is commonly believed, increasing dangerously in Canada. Rather, it is declining, especially among schoolchildren. Statistics show that only a small minority of Canadians use illegal drugs, and an even smaller proportion use drugs with any regularity. Most illicit drug users try them only experimentally or occasionally for recreation. On the other

---

TIPS FOR POOL AND WATER SAFETY

- **Do not let children run alongside pool edges, as they are wet and slippery.**
- **Have a childproof fence surrounding the swimming pool.**
- **Install a telephone near the pool and use it, so that supervising adults are not called** away. This also provides a quick way to call for help if necessary.
- **Make sure safety equipment — rings, buoys and lifejackets — is within reach and undamaged.**
- **If boating, obey the law by providing** lifejackets or personal flotation devices for all passengers.
- **Install propeller guards on motorized boats. Propellers are dangerous and a frequent source of terrible cuts and other injuries.**

---

hand, over three-quarters of the normal adult population regularly use legal, socially sanctioned caffeine, alcohol and nicotine (tobacco).

From earliest times, intoxicating substances have been popular, although their legal status has varied from culture to culture. Archaeologists have unearthed evidence of *cannabis sativa* (marijuana) use dating back 8,000 years, and cannabis is still smoked throughout the Middle East. Biblical writings frequently mention wine. Coca leaves are still chewed by many Bolivian and Peruvian Natives as a source of cocaine. East Indians chew betel nuts, which contain arecoline, a nicotine-like substance. Opium (from the poppy plant) has been used for centuries as a painkiller and inducer of euphoric drowsiness. Many medicines still contain opiates (e.g., codeine and morphine), and before 1912 opiate dependency was common throughout America, with women users outnumbering men two to one. Opium eating and smoking remains an accepted practice in many East Asian countries. Yet some groups and religions — for instance, orthodox Moslems and Mormons — rigorously forbid all drug use.

Rumors of illicit-drug epidemics create a "war-on-drugs" mentality that overlooks the extent to which drug use is a widespread social custom in Western culture. In fact, moderate responsible drug use (of alcohol and caffeine) is actually linked to an active social life, while total abstainers are sometimes regarded as "antisocial." In Canada, caffeine, alcohol and nicotine are so popular that many people don't think of them as drugs. One University of Toronto expert suggests that "instead of labeling drug use as an epidemic we should more accurately call it endemic." In other words, drug use is such an entrenched part of our modern lifestyle (as of most human societies past and present) that it is more the rule than the exception.

A 1989 Ontario survey showed that in that year, of Canadians over age 15:
• 97 percent used caffeine;
• 86 percent used alcohol;
• 26 percent smoked tobacco;
• 9–12 percent used marijuana;
• 7–10 percent used tranquilizers (e.g., benzo-diazepines like Valium);
• 8–9 percent used sleeping pills (e.g., barbiturates);
• 2–3 percent used stimulants (e.g., amphetamines, benzedrine or phenylpropanolamine);
• 1–3 percent used cocaine (although 6 percent of Ontarians reported trying cocaine at some time in their lives);
• 0.7 percent used crack (a preparation of cocaine with baking soda, which can be smoked).

The discrepancy between reality and the public perception of illicit drug use arises partly from mistakenly equating street violence, drug busts, seizures, criminal activities and hospital admissions with the extent of illicit drug use. But drug arrests and detox rates don't necessarily correlate with the amount of drug use. Drug seizures can increase while use remains the same or declines. And the number of people requiring drug-abuse treatment doesn't reflect present use because of the time lag between the development of a specific drug problem and the seeking of treatment by users.

What is a drug?

A drug is any substance other than body constituents or those needed for normal body functioning (e.g., food) which, on ingestion, alters brain and body function. Therapeutic drugs are used — often on prescription — to cure or alleviate health problems. Psychoactive or mood-altering substances — today's most popular drugs — alter the way people think, feel and act, and include most illicit drugs, as well as many legal and socially acceptable substances.

Some drugs (amphetamines, cocaine, caffeine) are stimulants, which increase alertness. Others (alcohol, barbiturates) are depressants, which dampen brain activity, reduce anxiety and seemingly calm the spirit. Still others (lysergic acid diethylamide or LSD, and phencyclidine or PCP) are hallucinogens, which produce visual and auditory hallucinations. Certain drugs occur naturally, such as psilocybin or "shrooms" (an LSD-like substance from mushrooms), mescaline (from the peyote cactus), cocaine (from coca leaves) and heroin (from poppies). Others are made from plants (e.g., alcohol, from fruit, vegetables or grains). Yet others are synthetics, manufactured legally or illegally (e.g., amphetamine or "speed" and methamphetamine or "ice").

Why people take drugs

Psychoactive substances have a great range of effects. They help people overcome shyness and encourage self-esteem, remove pain, promote joviality (at ceremonies, parties) or create an intense "high" or elation that is a goal in itself. They may be taken for private pleasure — wine with dinner, a cigarette afterwards. Some "do drugs" for fun, mind-expansion or in order to belong to the "in group," or they may be a last resort for people who are at a low point in their lives, those who want to escape from a difficult home or school situation, to rebel, to cope with distress or to alleviate a psychological disturbance such as depression.

THE USUAL EFFECTS OF DRUGS

Most mood- and mind-altering drugs have some or all of the following effects:
• tolerance — the body's adaptation to repeated consumption, with ever-higher doses needed to achieve the desired "high." With some drugs such as amphetamines, tolerance builds so fast that before long users may need 20 times the starting dose to obtain any effect. Barbiturate users may become so tolerant that the gap between the amount they need to get high and a lethal dose becomes perilously small;
• physical dependence — the body's response to the drug, which means that when it's abruptly stopped there are usually unpleasant (and sometimes drastic) withdrawal symptoms;
• psychological dependence — emotional and mental preoccupation with the drug's effects. A substance may become so central to existence that a dependent user will be unable to go for even a day without a "hit," dose or alcoholic drink. The greater the reliance on the drug's perceived benefit, the more effort the user will make to get it.

ADDICTION IS NOT PREDICTABLE

"Once an addict, always an addict" and the "addictive personality" are widely touted myths. Experts stress that there's no such thing as an addictive personality; addicts can and often do give up their substance dependency.

On the other hand, drug use does not always lead to dependence. Given conducive circumstances — the right place, time and surroundings — almost anyone might use drugs, without necessarily becoming dependent. Studies of U.S. soldiers serving in Vietnam, where use of opiates was widespread, showed that ordinary, healthy people of widely varying background became regular heroin users without becoming addicted, and then gave up the habit. The soldiers had easy access to cheap, high-grade heroin, and almost 50 percent used it regularly (once or twice weekly). But for most of them the habit was transient, triggered by heroin's ready availability and the stress of war. Once back home, most veterans easily gave up the drug and only a fraction — about 5–10 percent — lapsed into reuse. This had nothing to do with the soldiers' personalities or the amounts of heroin taken. Once they were removed from the drug-taking ambiance, most simply no longer wished to use heroin. The only significant factors linked to resumption of heroin use were a pre-Vietnam record of drug use, a low academic record and a prior criminal record.

Some people take to drugs rapidly because of sociopathic (antisocial) tendencies or simply because they mix with drug-taking companions. According to the modern biopsychosocial model, which attributes drug use to biological, psychological and social causes, people may abuse or become dependent on drugs because of a biological or metabolic predisposition, and a social reason like peer pressure and/or psychological factors (e.g., depression, anxiety).

Whatever the reasons for taking drugs and whichever drugs are used, they feed into the brain's limbic system, stimulating a "reward mechanism" that reinforces drug-taking behavior. The only common feature in the countless reasons for drug use is that the substances somehow reward the user. The same impetus (e.g., anxiety) may lead one person to alcohol, another to tranquilizers, yet another to overeating, depending on which solution seems best, easiest and most accessible.

Most of those who do drugs take several. According to Health and Welfare Canada, one in 20 Canadians has tried more than one mood-altering drug — mainly hashish (a form of marijuana) and cocaine in the young, sleeping pills and nonmedical tranquilizers (not used for the purpose prescribed) in older people. About 10 percent of separated and divorced Canadians use more than one drug; a third of tranquilizer users also take sleeping pills; nearly all cocaine users also take marijuana; and many heavy alcohol drinkers also smoke tobacco. People with a "pro-drug" mindset will likely experiment with any new substance and add it to their repertoires.

Use is not necessarily abuse

There's no sharp distinction between moderate, responsible drug use and excessive or abusive use. Rather, there is a continuum of gradual increase which may lead to dependence.

Drug abuse is defined as use "severe enough to cause health damage, social disruption, financial, workplace and family problems." If drugs become someone's main solution for every difficult situation, the habitual manner of coping, there's an abuse problem. The greater the reliance on drugs, the worse problems it creates. Whether substance use becomes abuse also depends on whether the substance is legal or illegal and on cultural and personal values. For example, LSD is nonaddictive, yet even occasional LSD-taking may be dubbed "drug abuse," because it's illegal. On the other hand, while Canadians consume a lot of caffeine, few coffee drinkers would be dubbed drug abusers. But if coffee were illegal — as it was during the Ottoman Empire, when thousands were punished for drinking the forbidden brew — caffeine consumption would be seen as drug abuse.

What is addiction?

Despite repeated efforts to define it, addiction remains poorly distinguished from habit, and the term is loosely used for any compulsion — such as being "addicted" to chocolate. The term "dependence" is now often used instead of or interchangeably with "addiction." Research suggests that drug dependence represents an abnormal response by a minority of people. The clue to dependence lies in

DRUG DEPENDENCE MAY INVOLVE:

- an overpowering preoccupation with and compulsion to get and take a substance;
- increasing use of the substance;
- development of physical dependence (withdrawal symptoms if stopped);
- the need for an "eye-opener" — a dose of the drug first thing in the morning;
- great difficulty in quitting.

FACTORS THAT ENCOURAGE SUBSTANCE DEPENDENCE

- easy availability;
- low price;
- drug-taking companions;
- looking for "kicks" (fun);
- social acceptance of
- drug use by family, peers and friends;
- ignorance of precise health dangers;
- depression, stress, a need for escape or comfort or ways
- to cope;
- genetic, biological or inherited vulnerability (possible with alcohol, opiates and perhaps some other drugs).

SIGNS OF SUBSTANCE DEPENDENCY

- a change in behavior (often the first sign) — secretiveness, unusual moodiness, unexplained absences from home, cutting classes, workplace absenteeism;
- declining or erratic school or work performance;
- an evasive, less affectionate, hostile or distant manner — no
- longer intimate with family, friends, schoolmates or workmates;
- apathy, a withdrawn demeanor;
- new companions — joining new groups and adopting their language, clothes and style;
- failure to keep curfew, remember birthdays, maintain friendships, do
- chores, attend to responsibilities;
- memory loss — concentration or learning lapses;
- change in appetite or altered eating habits;
- less or more sleep;
- an angry or defensive reaction — especially at the mention of drugs — and complaints of being "hassled."

whether the habit can be stopped — as one expert puts it: "Can you give up easily or not?" The greater the dependence, the harder it is to quit. Drug dependence includes psychological and physical dependence. The psychological aspects of addiction are at least as critical as physical dependence, and may dominate life to the exclusion of all else. According to social-learning theory, addiction is a pattern of drug use that is largely but not entirely out of the individual's control. People *can* regain control and give up the drug.

Circumstances can affect drug-taking behavior

People's attitudes can have a lot to do with their drug use. Their mindset is critical. An anxious, insecure person may react differently to a particular drug than someone who's secure, relaxed and confident. Ambitions or lifestyles may determine which drugs are used and how. For instance, an aggressive person who's eager to succeed or dominate may take stimulants (such as amphetamine or cocaine) to boost confidence and overcome inertia. Lethargic types who feel underactive may also choose stimulants but for different reasons — to heighten energy and alertness.

The place of drug-taking is also influential. Consumed in lively surroundings such as a party or a trendy bar, alcohol tends to make drinkers feel convivial, but a lonely drinker in a dingy tavern is likely to feel forlorn and depressed.

The administration route is key. Chewed or swallowed substances are absorbed slowly from the gut, diffusing into the bloodstream to produce a gradual high. Sniffing a drug gets it into the bloodstream faster, and smoking it gives a still more rapid effect. Injected into a vein, drugs enter the bloodstream immediately, producing the quickest high of all.

Rituals also play a part. The place and means of administration may have ritualistic significance, giving users heightened expectations, a sense of camaraderie or the exultation of belonging to a special fraternity.

The menace of "designer drugs"

Manufactured cheaply in clandestine laboratories from readily available chemicals, the increasingly popular "designer drugs" are designed to skirt the law through the fact that they have slightly altered chemical structures, although they achieve comparable drug effects. Designer drugs often cannot be detected by current drug tests, and hit the streets faster than regulating agencies can track or restrict them.

"Ecstasy" or MDMA (*3,4-methylenedioxymethamphetamine*), a current favorite whose effects are a cross between those of mescaline and amphetamine, is a potent hallucinogen synthesized in Germany in the early 1900s. It produces the euphoric rush of cocaine, together with mind-expanding sensations similar to those of LSD. Selling for about $10 a dose, it's been dubbed the "yuppie psychedelic." Taken orally, "ecstasy" intensifies emotions and causes slight sensory distortion. Users claim to experience greater self-insight, empathy and esthetic awareness. Its action lasts four to six hours and it's usually taken in doses of 75–150 mg, but since it is produced without quality checks, "ecstasy" can lead to fatal overdose. It can also cause serious disorientation, jaw pain, mouth stiffness, psychotic after-effects, panic attacks and even Parkinsonism (effects like those seen in Parkinson's disease) — hand tremors, drooling, rigidity and a stooped gait — due to destruction of dopamine-secreting brain cells. The U.S. Drug Enforcement Agency has put it on "Schedule One" (together with heroin and LSD) because of its dangers.

"Ice," or crystallized *methamphetamine* — named for its white crystalline look and touted as an alternative to crack — can be homemade. Purer than the formerly popular methadone — "meth" or "crank" — and now manufactured in California, "ice" came from Japan to North America via U.S. troops in the 1940s. Smoked like crack, "ice" is at least as addictive, pernicious and long-lasting. Prolonged use can cause lung and kidney disorders as well as permanent brain damage. Overdoses are often fatal. Put simply, "ice" can and does kill. Nonetheless, as it is cheaper and more potent than crack or cocaine, some fear that it may replace crack on the street.

Phencyclidine (PCP), also known as "angel dust" or "horse tranquilizer," is a white powder that's a cross between a synthetic stimulant and a "dissociative anesthetic." It produces unpredictable, sometimes violent behavior, intoxication, even delirium. A widely used street drug

TIPS FOR THOSE WISHING TO QUIT A DRUG HABIT

Pre-understanding (thinking of stopping)
- *With no precise knowledge of drug effects*, but feelings of vague concern, collect information about possible dangers.
- *Note feelings and circumstances that trigger a "trip"* or binge — e.g., stress, hostility, anxiety, anger.
- *Self-administer a Drug Abuse Screening Test* (DAST) — to determine how much is taken and how; whether able to get through a day (week) without drugs or able to cut back or stop; if ever had convulsions, tremors, flashbacks, blackouts.
- *List noticeable problems associated with drug-taking* at work, home or in public (e.g., diminished concentration, memory lapses, reduced performance, accidents, family rows).

Understanding (recognizing one's drug problem)
- *Admit possible health and other adverse effects* (possibly already evident to others).
- *Make a drug diary* — when, with whom, how and in what circumstances are drugs taken? When added up, the amount consumed may come as a surprise!
- *Devise a balance sheet of pros and cons of drug-taking:* e.g., pleasures/rewards vs. negative effects.
- *Determine whether drug consumption is already damaging health* (often sufficient to motivate a serious quitting attempt).
- *Decide that no one else is to blame:* the drug-taking is one's own decision. It can be beaten by one's own efforts.

- *Ask family doctor or other expert for advice.* Medical caregivers can often explain the risks of a particular drug, and motivate and support quitting efforts.
- *Realize that certain symptoms* (e.g., anxiety, sleeplessness, paranoia, phobias, hostility) may have been wrongly viewed as the *cause* rather than the *consequence* of drug use.
- *Check out places to get help* — experts, clinics, detox centers — and how to learn new coping skills.

Action phase — making an effort to stop (or cut back)
- *Set realistic goals for change,* e.g., short-term quit strategies — "a week without drugs," "*not* this weekend." Cut back or abstain for a day, week, month at a time.
- *Try self-help tactics* — often the preferred method — with manuals, quit guides and advice from drug-addiction-counseling agencies.
- *Plan to counter temptation* — list drug-taking "cues" and how to avoid or sidestep them.
- *Adopt an open, frank approach when seeking advice* — this is most likely to enlist maximum understanding and a frank, supportive response.
- *Anticipate relapses* — become wary of feelings, events, places that might trigger a relapse.
- *Do not regard a relapse as a failure* or loss of all that's been gained, but as a learning experience — one step on the way to doing better next time!
- *Be prepared for several tries* before breaking a drug habit.
- *Enlist cooperative support* from family and friends. The families of quitters may also need counseling.

HOW DIFFERENT DRUGS AFFECT THE BODY

	Alcohol	Amphetamines ("speed," "bennies," "black beauties," "uppers")	Cocaine ("crack")	LSD and other hallucinogens
Type of drug (chemical)	• ethyl alcohol (ethanol), a clear liquid (in beer, wine, spirits); • made from grain, fruit, vegetables or synthetically; • favored since antiquity for its relaxing, intoxicating properties; • beers contain about 5% alcohol, wines to 12% and spirits about 40%; • a sedative-hypnotic and central nervous system (CNS) depressant.	• synthetically produced: amphetamine (speed), dextro-amphetamine (Dexedrine), methylamphetamine or "ice," methylphenidate (Ritalin), etc.; • used as pills, inhaled or injected (speed); • central-nervous-system stimulants that resemble action of adrenaline (natural body hormone).	• derived from South American coca bush (still chewed in Andes to offset fatigue); • crack is mixture of cocaine and baking soda; • cocaine hydrochloride is white powder ("coke," "C," "flake," "snow"); • formerly used in many medicines (until 1920s); • stimulant action — like amphetamine — but now legally classed as a narcotic.	• derived from mushrooms (psilocybin) or cactus (mescaline) or synthetically — e.g., lysergic acid (LSD or "acid") and phencyclidine (PCP) — "hog," "angel dust"; • structures resemble catecholamines — normal brain neurotransmitters; • hallucinogens — can distort reality and produce severe delusions.
Short-term effects (after a single dose)	• effects vary with size, sex and amount of food in stomach; • initial relaxation and loss of inhibitions; • increased sociability; • impaired coordination; • slowing down of reflexes and mental processes; • attitude changes, increased risk-taking and bad judgment, danger in driving car, operating machinery; • sleepiness.	• nervous system briefly stimulated; • reduces appetite; • increases energy, offsets fatigue; • talkative restlessness, greater alertness; • faster breathing; • rise in heartrate and blood pressure (with risk of burst blood vessels and heart failure); • temperature raised, mouth dry, skin sweaty; • pupils dilated; • alleviates nose stuffiness (original medicinal use).	• short-acting, powerful central-nervous-system stimulant, also a local anesthetic; • effects vary depending on whether drug is "snorted" (inhaled), injected, put in mouth, rectum or vagina, or smoked (as crack); • transient euphoria and increased energy; • appetite loss; • rise in heartrate and breathing; • dilated pupils; • agitation, restlessness, talkativeness; • brief rise in sex drive.	• unpredictable effects — at first like amphetamine; • excitation, arousal; • temperature raised; • altered sense of smell, shape, size, color, distance; • exhilaration, "mind-expansion" or anxiety — depending on user; • rapid pulse, dilated pupils, blank stare; • exaggerated power sense with possibly violent behavior; • later — dramatic perceptual distortions; • occasionally convulsions.
With larger doses and longer use	• blackouts (memory loss); • facial flushing; slurred speech; • staggering gait, stupor; • rise in blood pressure; • pancreatitis, hepatitis, stomach ulcers, injuries (broken bones); • effects magnified by other CNS and brain depressants (e.g., opiates, barbiturates, tranquilizers, antihistamines, sleep-aids, some cold remedies); • alone or combined with other drugs, can increase accident rates; • overdose may be fatal due to respiratory distress.	• bizarre behavior, talkativeness, restlessness, tremors, excitability; • sense of power, superiority, aggression; • illusions and hallucinations; • some users become paranoid, suspicious, panicky, violent; • raised blood pressure; • insomnia.	• permanently stuffy nose (if snorted) and risk of perforated nasal septum; • brief euphoric effect followed by "crash" — depression; • anesthetic effect can depress brain function; • bizarre, erratic, perhaps violent actions; • paranoid "psychosis" (disappears if drug discontinued); • sensation of "crawling under the skin"; • convulsions, disturbed heart action, even death.	• anxiety, panic attacks, paranoid delusions, occasionally psychosis (like schizophrenia); • injury or accidents due to drug-induced delusions or distance misjudgment; • risk of fetal abnormalities; • tolerance develops rapidly but also disappears fast with renewed drug-sensitivity; • with PCP, high fever, muscle spasm, erratic behavior, psychosis lasting weeks or more.
Long-term effects (prolonged repeated use)	• harms many body organs: pancreas, gastrointestinal tract, blood circulation, heart, liver, kidneys, brain; • may produce liver cirrhosis, ulcers, memory loss, impotence; • increased risk of cancers (mouth, larynx, throat, maybe breast); • vitamin depletion; • damages fetus; • dependence frequent.	• malnutrition, emaciation (owing to appetite loss); • anxiety states; • "amphetamine-psychosis" (with schizophrenia-like hallucinations); • kidney damage; • susceptibility to infection; • sleep disorders; • psychological dependence.	• weight loss, malnutrition; • destroyed nose tissues (if sniffed); • restlessness, mood swings, insomnia, extreme excitability, suspiciousness/paranoia, delusions ("psychosis"); • depression; • impotence; • risk of heart attacks; • strong psychological dependence.	• long-term medical effects not known; • may include muscle tenseness, "flashbacks" — brief, spontaneous recurrence of prior LSD (hallucinogenic) experiences; • prolonged, profound depression; • panic attacks; • no physical dependence.
Withdrawal symptoms	• insomnia, headache; • nausea; • shakiness, tremors; • sweating, seizures.	• long sleep, chills; • ravenous hunger; • depression.	• few withdrawal effects; sleepiness; • extreme exhaustion; • possibly "cocaine blues" (depression).	• few withdrawal effects, possible "flashbacks," anxiety.

Nicotine	Caffeine	Cannabis (marijuana, "pot," "grass," hashish)	Narcotic (opioid) analgesics (painkillers)	Solvents (inhalants)
• derived from tobacco; • used medicinally in South America; • tobacco smoke contains over 4,000 chemicals but nicotine is the most addictive; • a typical cigarette contains about one mg nicotine but amount absorbed varies with smoker; • stimulates central nervous system.	• derived from tea, coffee beans, kola nuts, chocolate; • used in many medicines (e.g., painkillers, cold/cough, pain remedies, antihistamines); • average cup of coffee contains 60-75 mg caffeine, colas about 35 mg per 250 ml or 1 cup, teas 20-60 mg/cup.	• derived from cannabis sativa or hemp plant; preparations vary in potency; "hash" most potent, marijuana least; • smoked in "joints" or chewed (sometimes with food); • medicinally used for epilepsy, glaucoma, against nausea; • classed as hallucinogen.	• poppy derivatives (opium, codeine, morphine, heroin) and synthetics (Demerol, methadone, Dilaudid, Percodan); • smoked, eaten or injected; • ancient painkillers used medicinally; • deaden pain, produce euphoria and drowsiness.	• volatile organic hydrocarbons from petroleum and natural gas (e.g., gasoline, toluene, hexane, chloroform, carbon tetrachloride, nail-polish remover or acetone, lighter fluid, paint thinners, cleaning fluid, airplane cement, plastic glue); • hallucinogenic effects.
• speeds pulse; • stimulates, then reduces brain and nervous system activity; • blood-pressure rise; • sense of relaxation; • reduced urine output; • impairs cleansing action of lung's cilia (hairs); • enhances alertness and concentration abilities.	• stimulates brain, speeds nerve-cell transmission; • elevates mood and alertness; • stimulates mental activity; • speeds up breathing, metabolism; • enhances mental performance; • postpones fatigue; • shortens sleep; • more urine output; • rise in blood fats; • increases stomach acidity; • decreases appetite.	• produces dream-like euphoria, laughter, relaxation; • alters sense of space, time; • increases heartrate; • reddens eyes; • dreamy, "stoned" look; • at later stages, users quiet, reflective, sleepy; • combined with alcohol, increased effects, distorted behavior; • impairs short-term memory, thinking, and ability to drive car or perform complex tasks.	• briefly stimulate, then depress higher brain centers; • give quick pleasure surge (for few minutes), then stupor (which mutes hunger, pain, sex drive); • taken by mouth, effects slower, no initial pleasure surge; • pupils tiny, body warm, limbs heavy; • mouth dry, skin itchy; • users may "nod off," alternately awake or asleep, oblivious of surroundings.	• exhilaration, light-headedness, excitability, disorientation; • confusion, slurred speech, dizziness; • distorted perception; • visual and auditory hallucinations; • muscular control impaired; • possible nausea, increased saliva, sneezing; • reflexes dampened; • recklessness, feelings of power, invincibility.
• lung damage; • damaged blood circulation; • slowed wound-healing; • vitamin-C depletion; • shortness of breath; • increases risk of upper-respiratory infections; • cancer-formation risks.	• nervousness, hand tremors; • delays sleep onset, reduces "depth" of sleep, insomnia; • abnormally rapid heartbeat; • jitteriness; • mild delirium possible; • convulsions (rare); • suspected cancer-causing agent.	• slowed digestive (gastrointestinal) activity: • time misjudgment; • sharpened or distorted sense of color, sound; • thinking slow and confused; • apathy, loss of motivation/drive; • large doses can produce severe confusion, panic attacks; • hallucinations (even psychosis).	• extremities heavy; • permanent drowsiness; • pupils become pinpoints; • skin cold, moist, bluish; • progressively slower, depressed breathing; • supervised pain-killing doses let people remain quite clear-headed and safe; • dangers increase with alcohol intake.	• drowsiness and possible unconsciousness; • severe disorientation; • risks increase with fume concentration; • irregular heartbeat, heart action disturbed; • large doses may cause heart failure — e.g., "sudden sniffing death" (especially with spot removers or airplane cement).
• narrowed blood vessels, risk of heart attack, stroke; • bronchitis, emphysema; • raised risk of cancers of mouth, lung, larynx, throat, bladder, pancreas, possibly cervix; • stomach ulcers; • impairs fetal growth; • strong dependence.	• may raise blood cholesterol level; • risk of stomach ulcers; • suspected cancer-inducing agent; • regular coffee use (over 5 cups daily) can lead to dependence (getting "hooked" on drug).	• loss of drive, reduced energy; • regular heavy use increases risk of bronchitis, lung cancer; reduced sex hormones; impaired learning; memory loss; possible decrease in immunity; • psychological dependence.	• constipation; • moodiness; • risk of endocarditis (heart infection) and other infections (AIDS) from needle-sharing; • hormone upsets (menstrual irregularities); • liver damage; • damaged offspring; • strong dependence.	• pallor, thirst, nose, eye, mouth sores; • irritability, hostility, forgetfulness; • may damage liver, kidney and brain; • nosebleeds, impaired blood-cell formation; • depression, weight loss; • other drugs compound damage; • dependence possible.
• anxiety, jitteriness; • inability to concentrate; • increased appetite.	• severe headache; • irritability; • tiredness.	• withdrawal symptoms mild — possible nausea, insomnia, anxiety, irritability.	• striking withdrawal effects (4-5 hours after last dose), sweating, anxiety, diarrhea, "gooseflesh," shivering, tremors.	• restlessness, anxiety, irritability, headaches; • stomach upsets; • delirium (rare).

FOR MORE INFORMATION ON DRUGS, CONTACT:

- a family physician;
- community or volunteer programs;
- public-health agencies or nurses;
- crisis or intervention centers;
- drug-addiction-counseling centers/clinics or "hot lines," such as Ontario's ARF Drug Information Line: (416) 595-6111;
- Alcoholics Anonymous (AA), Toronto branch: (416) 487-5591, or Narcotics Anonymous (NA), Toronto branch: (416) 691-9519;
- the Self-Help Clearing House, Toronto branch: (416) 487-4355;
- Women for Sobriety (Toronto).

among teenagers (the groups who also use LSD, MDMA and other hallucinogens), it's often sprinkled on marijuana joints. PCP is said to alter body awareness and space perception. It impairs thinking ability and — in large amounts — can produce convulsions or coma. Several deaths (killings and suicides) have been reported from PCP overdosing or as a result of the drug's effect on behavior. Laced with or added to cocaine, it can have added dangers. PCP is often passed off as another drug, such as LSD or mescaline.

Getting off drugs

Many drug takers naturally grow out of or abandon their habit. Others decide to stop with more or less distress, depending on the degree of dependence. Those who find it hard to quit even when they realize that a substance is destroying their lives need professional help. Seeking advice is not sign of weakness, and drug dependence can be beaten. Tackling a drug problem early can reduce its toll, and there are many self-help manuals and quit guides available. It's a myth that people must "hit bottom" before quitting.

Formal treatment programs first address the addiction itself, getting the person detoxified and calmed down. Then, when they are no longer drugged, people can examine the reasons for their drug-taking and find ways to break the habit. The goal of therapy is to teach people how to alter their responses to the challenges that lead to drug use. Some treatment centers use both medication (pharmacotherapy) and counseling, while others rely mainly on drug-free therapy. Relapse rates are high, especially in people with little social support. Some need several tries before kicking a drug.

TACKLING ALCOHOL ABUSE

Legally sanctioned, socially accepted and easily obtainable, alcohol is one of our society's most destructive drugs — used more widely than all illicit drugs combined. Indeed, while overall drug use has gone down in recent years, 86 percent of Canadians over age 15 still drink alcohol at least once yearly, 10 percent using enough to qualify as problem drinkers, and 5 percent being classed as heavy drinkers ("alco-

holics"). A potent psychoactive (mind- and mood-altering) substance, alcohol is favored for its pleasurable effects and its short-term ability to alleviate anxiety. It is a particularly health-damaging drug because it harms almost every organ in the body, and tends to be consumed in large amounts. In Canada, a quarter of all medical hospital beds are occupied by people with alcohol-related illnesses.

Although the alcohol content of drinks varies from country to country, in Canada, an average drink is: one regular beer (340 ml or 12 oz, 5 percent alcohol); one glass of table wine (145 ml or 5 oz, 12 percent alcohol); or one shot of spirits (45 ml or 1.5 oz, 40 percent alcohol). Each contains about 13.6 grams of pure alcohol (ethanol).

In small amounts, alcohol is a pleasing accompaniment to meals, removing inhibitions and helping people relax. But some use alcohol as a crutch for getting through everyday difficulties or to offset anxiety, disappointment, loneliness, boredom or depression — to "forget" the unpleasantnesses of life.

How much alcohol is too much?

Most people know when their drinking is detrimental. Men who regularly consume between four and six drinks a day and women who consistently have two to three daily drinks may incur some memory loss, dulled mental capacity and impaired eye-hand coordination (all three will be reversed if drinking is reduced). Even moderate drinking may alter the pathways in the brain's *hippocampus* (learning center), *hypothalamus* (control center) and *nucleus accumbens* (reward center).

Sensible, low-risk drinking is drinking that has no negative consequences, does not involve drinking every day and doesn't disrupt daily life, work or duties. Many experts define "hazardous use" as the point at which drinkers themselves recognize the negative effects, try to set limits and make efforts to cut back. There's no unanimously agreed-upon boundary between safe and harmful drinking, but there's tenuous agreement that low-risk consumption ranges from one to four drinks per day to a maximum of twelve a week. Average intakes above six drinks a day are labeled as "heavy" or

POSSIBLE WARNING SIGNS OF PROBLEM DRINKING

- concern about alcohol intake and admission of "drinking a bit too much";
- proclaimed efforts to cut back — to drink "only on weekends" or "only after dinner";
- clear negative consequences — work problems, disrupted social relationships, loss of spouse, job, money;
- reduced interest in work, hobbies, church, friends, family;

- recognition of troubled drinking and suggestions by friends, relatives or co-workers to cut back;
- consorting mainly with other drinkers;
- memory loss or blackouts — the inability to remember anything about the night (or day) before;
- lack of concentration, dulled mental acuity;
- physical signs of impairment —

tremors, shaky grip;
- increased personal injuries (cuts, sprains, bruises, fractures) due to impaired motor coordination;
- binge drinking, especially on weekends;
- usually gulping drinks one after another;
- constantly consuming alcohol, secretly on the job or at home; hiding booze;
- desperate need for a "relief" morning drink to ward off withdrawal

symptoms;
- changed behavior — missed deadlines and appointments, lateness;
- going to work the next day with still-hazardous blood-alcohol levels (indicated by alcoholic breath);
- mistakes on the job, lowered productivity, flawed judgment, unexplained absences;
- complaints by fellow workers

about boozing;
- heavy smoking or other drug use (these often go hand in hand with chronic drinking);
- skipping meals, eating only lightly while drinking;
- belligerent, grandiose attitude;
- violent or abusive actions, starting fights;
- hostility to questions about alcohol use; refusal to discuss the topic.

"seriously harmful to health." Sensible, low-risk drinking can be defined as:

- for men — not more than two to four drinks a day, and not daily drinking;
- for women — not more than one to two drinks a day, definitely not every day;
- for a pregnant woman and her unborn child, there may be no safe level of drinking.

Note that these amounts are only averages. Someone who doesn't touch a drink all week but consumes 10–14 drinks over the weekend may become hazardously impaired and a menace on the roads.

Is alcoholism a disease?

Following Prohibition in the United States and Canada during the 1920s, alcoholism came to be viewed as a disease, with the implication that some people are biologically more susceptible than others. In 1956, the American Medical Association formally listed alcoholism as a "complex disease with a predictable course, involving biological and psychological components to be treated like other illnesses." According to this view, alcoholism is a progressive (perhaps inherited) ailment which can't be blamed on those afflicted. While Alcoholics Anonymous (AA) and many others eagerly embraced this idea, others opposed it, one University of Toronto expert calling it a "road leading nowhere that fails to address the extent and complexity of alcohol problems."

The disease model is now criticized as an outmoded, fuzzy concept, not borne out by social and behavioral studies. Describing a drug problem as a disease puts it beyond personal control, engendering the attitude "It's not my fault — I can't help it." It also emphasizes the "skid row" image of alcoholism, implying that only a minority of uncontrolled drinkers need treatment, and arbitrarily separates heavy imbibers, who supposedly "have the disease," from less severe problem drinkers, who presumably don't have it.

Can alcoholism be hereditary?

While alcohol abuse tends to run in families — children of heavy drinkers seem likelier than average to become alcoholics — experts disagree on the extent to which alcoholism is inherited. Studies in Denmark and Sweden during the 1970s showed that children of alcoholics who were adopted during infancy into nonalcoholic homes were more likely to become heavy drinkers than children of nonalcoholics. The search is on for biological markers that could pinpoint the trait for alcoholism — if it exists.

The tendency toward alcoholism seems to come mainly from the father's side. Controversial and still-debated studies on twins separated from their biological parents before six weeks of age and raised in nonrelated families suggest that children of alcoholic fathers are three to six times more likely to become alcoholics than those of nonalcoholic fathers. A 1980 report in the *British Medical Journal* claimed that 30 to 50 percent of the fathers and up to 20 percent of the mothers of alcoholic children are also alcoholic. "Given that it may take more alcohol for them to reach a high, but that the euphoria may be greater," notes one expert, "sons of alcoholic fathers may be prone to alcohol abuse because of genetic differences in their brain." The jury is still out on this topic.

Women and alcohol

Although fewer women than men are heavy drinkers, there's a slew of evidence that women are prone to health damage at lower alcohol intakes (less alcohol per body weight) than men. They are more likely to develop liver disease and mental deficiency with smaller amounts of alcohol. One expert explains that "since women's bodies contain more fat and less water than men's, they have less water with which to dilute alcohol. A woman of similar weight and height will therefore have a higher blood-alcohol content after drinking the same amount as a man."

Women also metabolize alcohol differently. They have less gastric (stomach) ADH enzyme than men, so less alcohol is broken down in the stomach, and more passes through to the bloodstream. Furthermore, a woman's liver produces more acetaldehyde, the liver-injuring product of the breakdown of alcohol.

Female hormones may also play a part. Some studies suggest that in the luteal (second) phase of the menstrual cycle, high levels of the hormone progesterone decrease smooth-muscle activity so that the stomach (which is smooth-muscled) doesn't empty as quickly. This means that alcohol sits there longer before passing into the bloodstream, and therefore blood-alcohol levels tend to be lower than in the first half of the menstrual cycle. So it may conceivably be less risky for women to drink before rather than just after a period. In post-menopausal women, alcohol provokes the conversion of androgens (male sex hormones) into estrogens (female hormones), which some studies suggest may increase breast-cancer risks. On the other hand, increased estrogens offset osteoporosis (bone thinning).

Men who drink heavily become demasculinized because alcohol lowers the level of testosterone (male hormone), diminishes sex drive and effectively castrates them, causing impotence. In men, alcohol also triggers conversion of androgens to estrogens, which may cause breast enlargement, hair growth and other effects, as well as liver damage.

It's well known that babies born to heavily drinking mothers may have *fetal alcohol syndrome* (brain damage), but very recent evidence shows that the male offspring of alcoholic mothers may *also* be demasculinized. The fetal brain of male babies is programmed for masculine behavior long before birth by exposure to testosterone from the embryonic testes. Since alcohol reduces testosterone production, male babies exposed to alcohol in a mother's womb may later fail to develop the full range of male behavior. Rats born to alcohol-fed mothers show distinct female instead of male behavior.

Advice from a physician often helps to curb alcohol intake

Paradoxically, while doctors may not ask about alcohol intake and alcohol-troubled people may not mention it for fear of being labeled "alcoholic," most welcome medical advice. Many troubled drinkers don't ask for medical help until they finally realize (or are forced to do so by family and/or employers) how drastically it's undermining their lives. People frequently haven't the faintest idea how much alcohol is damaging their health. Yet even a few words of advice from a physician about the injurious effects of alcohol can curb alcohol intake dramatically. Studies from Britain and Sweden convincingly demonstrated a substantial drop in alcohol use when doctors simply asked about drinking habits at routine medical visits, and informed people that tests showed they were consuming too much for their own good.

Getting help early increases chances of a cure

Traditional treatments for alcohol disorders focused on specialized care for the minority (5 percent) of heavily dependent drinkers with clear signs of alcoholism. The old way was inpatient clinic or hospital treatment, often with lengthy stays of three to six months. But follow-up programs show that 10 years later, 30 percent of those treated were still drinking heavily, and 18 percent in one study had died — two and a half times the rate for non-drinkers. It seemed that, because the huge numbers of mildly troubled drinkers were disregarded, people were not getting help until it was too late.

The new approach gears therapy to the whole spectrum of problem drinkers. Moderate problem drinkers who want to kick the habit can often manage with brief outpatient therapy that stresses self-help. Even minimal advice from a family doctor or other health professional, or a few sessions of outpatient sociobehavioral counseling, often helps drinkers cut back.

The decision to reduce alcohol intake is typically triggered by several bad experiences rather than one traumatic event. Drinkers come to realize that the positive aspects of alcohol are outweighed by its costs — hangovers, missed work days, interpersonal difficulties, diminished mental capacity. Among the new treatments for problem drinking, two innovative approaches have been developed at Ontario's Addiction Research Foundation (ARF).

The brief method for encouraging sensible drinking is meant for well-motivated "early stage" problem drinkers who have definite reasons to quit or reduce alcohol consumption

TIPS FOR SENSIBLE DRINKING

- Plan your drinking — decide when, where, and how much. Consider potential dangers such as driving, tiredness, health complications, medications or social pressure.
- Pace your drinking — measure the amount, count the drinks and *never* drink from the bottle!
- Make the first drink of the evening nonalcoholic, particularly if you're thirsty.
- Alternate nonalcoholic and alcoholic beverages.
- Have diluted drinks, not straight ones, or drink beverages with low or very low alcohol content (e.g., light or very light beer or dealcoholized beverages).
- Sip slowly; remember that a man's body can only handle about a half to one standard drink (8–13 g alcohol) per hour, and a woman's even less, as women are generally smaller and more sensitive to alcohol.
- Don't gulp. Put the glass down between sips.
- Don't refill the glass until it's empty and don't let others (waiters, hosts) do it either.
- Don't drink on an empty stomach — eat while drinking, but avoid salty foods, which increase thirst.
- When entertaining, always supply nonalcoholic drinks; don't buy too much booze.
- Prepare ahead by anticipating situations which may increase the pressure to drink. Plan suitable strategies and excuses such as "I'm at my limit" or "I have an early start tomorrow" or "I'm driving."
- Learn to say "no thanks" without feeling guilty or antisocial.

- Never have "one for the road" — it can easily push your blood-alcohol level above the danger (and legal) limit.
- If you regularly drink more than you want to, ask for expert help and develop activities that don't involve alcohol; find alternate interests or hobbies to take you away from your drinking.
- Don't use alcohol as a crutch for getting through tough decisions or difficult everyday situations, or to relieve boredom, loneliness, anxiety or depression, or to aid sexual activities.
- Never use alcohol as a sleep-aid (it disturbs rather than encourages sleep) or as a pain-reliever (there are far better pain medications).
- Try to be a good role model for your children by demonstrating restraint.
- Lobby for restriction of alcohol advertising and tougher drinking-and-driving laws.

Never drink:
- while swimming, boating or engaging in other water sports;
- when in a cold environment (alcohol gives a false sense of warmth);
- during domestic quarrels (because alcohol reinforces impulsive, irrational responses, rather than problem-solving techniques);
- if operating complex or dangerous machinery, or driving a vehicle;
- while on medication that interacts with alcohol, such as cough and cold remedies or codeine preparations (if in doubt consult a pharmacist).

ANTABUSE HELPS MANY STOP DRINKING

Medications such as disulfiram (Antabuse) and calcium carbimide (Temposil), used in addition to counseling, help some people stay off the bottle by causing physical discomfort if alcohol is consumed. Antabuse blocks the action of hepatic aldehyde dehydrogenase, so that drinking causes a buildup of acetaldehyde, which produces nausea, dizziness and headaches. But Antabuse works only if taken regularly. Recovering alcoholics who stop taking it risk a relapse to their old drinking habits. Some investigators have tried Antabuse implants under the skin, for a one-year effect, but blood levels of the drug were too low to be effective. (Experts don't recommend lengthy Antabuse therapy, owing to possible adverse side effects.)

and want to take responsibility for changing their drinking behavior. Treatment involves three short counseling sessions aided by self-help handouts.

The method:
- identifies their current drinking patterns to show the role of alcohol in their everyday life and the situations that trigger their urge to overdrink;
- motivates them to maintain two weeks of abstinence before deciding on the longer-term drinking goal (initial abstinence tends to improve health and thinking abilities dulled by heavy drinking);
- decides on their goal — either abstinence or sensible drinking;
- teaches strategies for maintaining the chosen goal by keeping records of daily drinking, making plans to avoid overdrinking in risky situations, not using alcohol to cope with everyday difficulties and finding constructive ways to fill time formerly spent drinking.

Women tend to do better than men with self-help methods. About 65 percent of women, compared to 30 percent of men, managed to reduce consumption to their goal. Men require more therapy sessions (typically five to six) and more "hand-holding" than women. One expert surmises that women may do twice as well as men because of their greater vulnerability: clear signals of health disturbance may strengthen women's resolve to cut back.

A longer treatment model, the guided self-management approach, is also designed for troubled drinkers willing to take responsibility for handling their problem. This program emphasizes relapse prevention and views recovery as a gradual uphill climb. The key is to see slips not as catastrophes but as minor setbacks on the path to recovery. Guided self-management draws on the drinker's inner resources, identifying weaknesses that could undermine resolve. The program includes brief counseling, relapse prevention, advice and homework to uncover personal risk situations and identification of drinking cues. The aim is to help people to analyze their drinking pattern and develop coping strategies to change it. Therapists remain on tap for more counseling if needed.

Severely dependent alcoholics may need more intensive treatment

Intensive residential treatment may still be the answer for those with entrenched alcohol dependence, and many clinics are staffed by former drinkers who have "been there" and managed to conquer their dependence. But living in (other than a brief stay) isn't necessarily best, as it's an artificial situation, with the drinker isolated from family, friends, job or studies. Acute alcohol poisoning (intoxication) and withdrawal is tackled before underlying psychological or social problems are combated. Detoxification starts by clearing all alcohol from the body. At the same time, medications such as benzodiazepines are given as needed, to ease withdrawal. A multilevel withdrawal reaction may occur, including trembling, exaggerated reflexes, sleeplessness, muscle cramps, cold, sweaty skin, nausea and insatiable thirst. Severely dependent users may experience further symptoms several days later — delirium, hallucinations, fever, blood-vessel expansion, tachycardia (racing pulse) and seizures. An alcoholic who quits too suddenly can suffer cardiac arrest (heart failure).

Once the physical aspects of alcohol dependence are under control, psychosocial therapy aims to restructure the drinker's lifestyle, social and work patterns — with the patient "unlearning" the behavior that leads to drinking and learning new coping skills. Some experts favour an *integrated* approach, using counseling combined with medication instead of older methods that use medication as a last resort. Medication is sometimes given, as one expert explains, "because in our current social climate everyone expects to get a prescription!" Concurrent counseling gives personal advice, homework and goals, and reviews risk situations.

What about AA and other support groups?

Alcoholics Anonymous (AA), Women for Sobriety and other support groups can assist drinkers to change their ways. According to the philosophy of AA, which still considers alcoholism a disease, a single drink taken by a recovering addict rekindles the craving and renews the old drinking pattern, inevitably triggering a return to heavy drinking. Hence AA's insistence on absolute abstinence. AA groups meet weekly or more often and help people stay off alcohol by getting them to talk about their problem, providing a "buddy" system to give support during difficult times. To avert a relapse to old habits, former alcoholics are encouraged to maintain contact with the support group; there is always the risk that a crisis will precipitate a return to drinking, even after several years, and keeping in touch may prevent this.

Is strict abstinence the only way?

While most therapists and detox centers call for complete abstinence in recovering alcoholics, others suggest that for many drinkers — especially early problem drinkers — moderate drinking is a more realistic goal. Some experts call the AA rule for total abstinence artificial in a society where the majority drink occasionally, and argue that treatment should simply aim to help drinkers reduce their intake. Some reformed drinkers prefer to abstain, while others do better with reduced intakes. But while some problem drinkers can learn to take an occasional drink among supportive friends, the tactic is only suitable for selected people.

In the words of one expert, "The dilemma for the future is how to curb alcohol abuse, without revoking privileges that the public expects, industry wants and to which most of us are accustomed." Strategies to reduce drinking involve taxation, penalties for drunk driving, increased awareness of alcohol as a drug and opposition to binge drinking. Other tactics include restrictions on alcohol advertising, enforced attachment of health warnings to bottles and less media portrayal of alcohol as a glamorous drink.

For more information, contact a family physician, community or volunteer programs, public-health agencies or nurses, a crisis or intervention center, Women for Sobriety (Toronto), occupational health centres, Alcoholics Anonymous: (416) 487-5591 (Toronto).

Getting medical help when it's needed

Improving patient-doctor relationships • Using medical checkups wisely • Natural, alternative or complementary medicine • Herbalism plays a key role in natural medicine

3

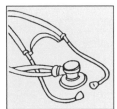

TODAY, PEOPLE IN-creasingly want to share responsibility with their physicians for looking after their own health. Many people prefer to know about their medical ailments, understand the treatment possibilities and take a more active role in decision-making. Likewise, modern healthcare professionals encourage people to become better educated, more involved healthcare consumers. Given today's increasingly complex medical technology, they prefer patients to be "informed consenters" in any tests or treatments undertaken. Looking after health or disease is becoming more of a collaboration between consumers and their medical caregivers.

IMPROVING PATIENT-DOCTOR RELATIONSHIPS

Despite the flood of new medical technologies, the patient-doctor relationship — whether with family physician, surgeon, gastroenterologist or other medical specialist — remains an intimate partnership. Trust is of the essence. Both physicians and those they care for must learn how to communicate with each other. More and more, physicians and medical schools are recognizing the need for better patient-doctor relationships.

Modern medical teaching tries to instruct upcoming doctors in the art of listening, which,

together with an empathetic manner, can draw out patient concerns and feelings. Exploratory questioning is encouraged, not just about the illness that brought the person to see the physician, but also about lifestyle and hidden concerns or anxieties. Rather than asking questions that require a curt yes-or-no answer, physicians pose open-ended questions interspersed with silences that encourage people to elaborate. Uncovering hidden worries, conflicts and family disputes helps physicians gain a more complete picture and thus propose more effective treatment. Being a competent clinician also means being an empathetic one. "Empathy is not just understanding what the person says, but also what was not said," explains one clinician. "It means bringing out the hidden agenda, things the patient is unconscious of or finds hard to discuss."

During a recent Toronto workshop on Doctor-Patient Communication, the three most common concerns found to come up in patient-doctor interviews were: fear of a serious illness, worry about being abandoned and feelings of guilt or worthlessness. From the doctor's viewpoint, a difficult patient may be someone who provokes uncomfortable feelings — such as anger, frustration or inadequacy. From the patient's perspective, a cold, uncaring doctor is one who inspires discomfort or anger (at not being taken seriously), feelings of worthlessness, and who "hurries one along" or makes one "feel stupid."

Modern medical teaching tries to help healthcare professionals understand what's behind behaviour rather than simply respond to it. This means listening carefully to comprehend the roots of an angry or abusive attitude, helping people to express their inner fears and trying to soothe them. Hostile behavior often masks anxiety. To a defensive person the medical caregiver might say, "You're being difficult," but it's friendlier to say, "I sense you're upset," taking it down a level. The physician might add: "Tell me more about this," or "Why do you feel like that?" or "What was going on at the time?" When caregivers feed back what the person fears or thinks, the patient feels better understood and the confrontational aspects of the interview may vanish.

Everyone needs a family physician for ongoing care

Everyone should have a physician for comprehensive, ongoing healthcare. Family physicians can handle most day-to-day medical problems. They know the family history, keep charts on hand and make referrals to appropriate specialists or clinics when necessary. At the turn of the century, most doctors were general practitioners who delivered babies, set broken bones and performed minor surgery — procedures now often handled by other specialists. This is partly because the information explosion makes it difficult for physicians to be experts in all areas. Today's family physicians are also trained in health promotion and illness prevention. They know how to deal with both the physical and the psychological facets of disease. An estimated 30–50 percent of all the problems that arrive at a family physician's office have a psychosocial component that requires effective interviewing and counseling skills.

Without a family physician, people may find themselves in a kind of "healthcare limbo," with no specific person to consult in times of need, and no continuity of care. Turning to specialists, walk-in clinics or hospital emergency departments for everyday health matters does not provide optimal healthcare. Specialists such as gastroenterologists or neurologists will refer patients back to their family physician for follow-up. Likewise, after post-operative checkups, surgeons usually tell patients to "see the family physician" about further problems. Similarly, those who go to hospital emergency departments for an accidental injury, bout of food poisoning or allergic reaction will be told to "report back" to their family physician later on.

Hospital emergency rooms are not geared to everyday health problems, but are set up to deal with acute situations. Whenever people visit the emergency department they are seen by different healthcare providers, who must provide treatment without access to the person's medical records. Moreover, the nurses and physicians, faced with more pressing cases, may do something to clear up the immediate problem — headache, diarrhea or other ailment — without having time to track its cause, discuss the disorder or explain how to prevent it.

How to choose a family physician

It's wise to find a family doctor who suits your own particular needs and lifestyle. Patient-doctor relationships are subtle and what satisfies one may not suit another. Ideally, a family physician should take an interest in you as a person, not just in the ailment that has brought you to the office. A good doctor considers emotional as well as physical well-being. Besides dealing with day-to-day complaints, the physician should help you to promote overall wellness, facilitate access to medical specialists when needed, and help in keeping chronic ailments (such as asthma, arthritis or diabetes) under control.

The key question, then, is how to find a family physician who meets individual and family needs. A good start is to ask trusted friends or colleagues for a recommendation. If moving to a new neighborhood, ask the neighbors, local pharmacist or public-health agencies for a good doctor. You may also ask the local medical association, nursing associations, the provincial College of Physicians and Surgeons or emergency-room nurses (who will know the physicians doing shifts there) about doctors willing to take on new patients.

It's a good idea to find a physician close to home, and preferably one who is willing to

DOCTOR CHOICE — POINTS TO DETERMINE

- Is the physician's office within easy reach of home? (Better close to home than work, as ill people usually stay home!)
- Is parking easy? Is public transportation nearby?
- Is there access for people with canes, crutches or wheelchairs?
- Are there X-ray and lab facilities in the same building or nearby?
- Is the atmosphere friendly and welcoming?
- Is the waiting room clean and neat? Are there toys for kids to play with?
- Is there up-to-date health material around to read?
- Are the office staff helpful? Do they provide useful information and answer questions?
- What are the office hours? Is the office run as a clinic or private practice? Will you always see the same physician or sometimes others in the same practice?
- Is the whole family welcome — if that's what you want?
- Are home visits made if really needed?
- Are community resources and referrals (e.g., to social workers, dietitians, therapists) appropriately arranged?
- Are phone calls promptly returned?
- Who will attend to emergency illness at night, on weekends or at other nonoffice times?
- In case of a real emergency, are you quickly fitted in and seen?
- To which hospital(s) is the physician connected?

Does he/she have admitting privileges there?
- Does the doctor listen calmly and attentively while you explain symptoms and feelings?
- Is the atmosphere relaxed?
- Does the physician seem easygoing or is he or she paternalistic and dogmatic? (Some people prefer a more authoritarian approach.)
- Does he or she give you a chance to discuss the problem in your own words or are you interrupted with a barrage of intimidating questions?
- Does the physician regularly ask about your lifestyle and counsel you about smoking, diet and alcohol/drug use, if relevant?
- Is ample time taken to explain the diagnosis and treatment choices, in understandable language?
- Are you involved in decision-making?
- Are medications and their use(s) clearly described?
- How many of the physician's services are covered by the provincial health insurance scheme? Are any extra charges (for filling in forms, phone conversations and so on) clearly explained?
- At the end of the office visit, ask yourself whether you fully understand the medical explanation(s), know what to do, understand the need for test(s) and feel free to call or go back for further clarification. Patients have the right to full disclosure about all suggested treatments or procedures and their possible effects and must give "informed consent" to any proposed treatment or tests.

provide any special services required — such as obstetric care or home visits (for appropriate situations). Some people prefer a man, others a woman; some a younger, others an older doctor. Having found a list of possible physicians, pay an exploratory visit — perhaps for a baseline checkup — to find out whether the person seems to suit your needs. Inquire about the possibility of evening or weekend visits if needed, and ask whether another physician or clinic is on call for nonoffice hours (preferably seven days a week).

The best time to look for a family physician is when you are well. Don't wait until you or someone else in the family is sick! If you've got a serious problem, it's too late to shop around. Family physicians now generally welcome people who introduce themselves as healthy individuals looking for a doctor. If the physician is not willing to discuss the philosophy of care

offered, then maybe you should keep looking.

Choose a physician with whom you can communicate freely, with whom it is easy to discuss problems ranging from a bunion to cancer to worries about weight, sex or sick parents. Find someone you like and feel comfortable with, who will discuss treatment possibilities in understandable language and involve you in the decisions. Observe the waiting room — is it neat, clean and supplied with up-to-date health information? Is the receptionist polite and helpful? Chat to others in the waiting room. Check out the ambience. Ask whether the practice will monitor pregnancies and deliver babies (if you're of childbearing age) and whether it is willing to look after the whole family, if desired.

Find out whether the doctor is affiliated with a hospital. Does he or she have admitting privileges? Studies show that physicians with hospital admitting privileges provide the most up-to-date healthcare, because they must meet prescribed standards of care, attend meetings and update their medical education. Family physicians in regular contact with specialists and the full range of hospital services can also facilitate care and arrange hospital admissions more quickly. If seeking a specialist, ask the family physician for the name of one likely to suit your particular situation. If it doesn't work out, report back and ask for another referral.

If it's what you wish, choose a physician you think is likely to tell the truth about any serious disease you or those close to you may have. Before the need arises, it is a good idea to decide how frankly you want to discuss a life-threatening disorder. Be sure all doctors involved know your wishes. You may want a "bottom-line" assessment of your own or a relative's survival chances in order to arrange affairs and power of attorney. Ask the physician to "be honest about things." While any sickness is troublesome enough, communication about a terminal illness can be tormenting. Bad news inevitably creates stress. Physicians often disagree on how much to reveal about a serious condition, but many now openly explain terminal conditions to patients and/or the family, outlining the options. The goal is to help people retain control and the best possible quality of life.

Making the most of doctor visits

Given the short time allotted per person when you finally get to see the doctor, how can you make the best of it? People don't always use their visits as well as they might. Some don't voice real worries (maybe the very problems that drove them to the doctor in the first place), not mentioning key concerns until about to leave, when they may blurt out questions about some alarming pain or lump.

It's a good idea to compile a list of concerns and questions beforehand. Jot down the points to ask, however trivial they may seem. A list serves as a memory-jogger, saves time and avoids the common mistake of forgetting or neglecting to ask key questions. People who are emotionally troubled or depressed — perhaps after some traumatic experience, such as job

PEOPLE CAN EXPECT FROM THEIR DOCTORS:

- up-to-date knowledge and skill;
- confidentiality;
- a relaxed, empathetic, nonintimidating atmosphere in which to discuss concerns;
- attentive listening;
- patience and a gentle approach for uncomfortable examinations or procedures;
- a willingness to answer questions clearly (and to acknowledge ignorance, if that's the case);
- access to personalized medical care 24 hours a day;
- prompt return of urgent phone calls;
- availability (of own physician or stand-in) when needed for emergencies;

- referral to other medical specialists if required;
- medications prescribed only if really needed — with an explanation of what each does and side effects to watch for;
- a second opinion from another physician about any suggested diagnosis or treatment, if requested;
- information on how and when test results will be divulged;
- full, appropriate disclosure in understandable language of the diagnosis, treatment options and likely prognosis;

- the right to "informed consent" — the right to give or withhold consent for a medical test or treatment after being told of its risks and benefits, without detracting from the doctor-patient relationship;
- no violation (or abuse) of the trusting relationship with the attending physician.

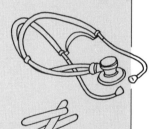

DOCTORS CAN EXPECT FROM THEIR PATIENTS:

- honest communication of all aspects of health — relaying facts about exercise, diet, smoking, alcohol, drug use, known diseases, allergies and medications taken (both prescription and over-the-counter);
- realization that physicians work within certain constraints imposed by the healthcare system and can deal with only one or two problems at any one visit;
- willingness to make special appointments

for detailed advice if needed;
- willingness to take part in their own healthcare decisions, fully discussing fears and worries;
- willingness to follow instructions (or explain why it's not possible);
- an effort to return for follow-up care when requested;
- an effort to keep appointments for tests or office visits — or to cancel reasonably well in advance;
- careful attention during doctor visits,

asking questions until what's said is fully understood;
- adherence to medication instructions, remembering that while one pill may be good, two can be harmful;
- an effort to keep track of visits, tests and treatments;
- cooperation in noting the results of treatments (for example, which therapy helped, which had an adverse effect) and to inform the physician of any problems noted.

loss or bereavement — may request a medical checkup when what they really need is supportive counseling. Many anxious or depressed people imagine they have some fatal illness and need medical reassurance as part of the healing process. Astute, sympathetic physicians watch for and give cues for airing underlying concerns, perhaps asking whether the person has "any other worries to discuss . . . ?" The physician may realize that someone needs extra time to discuss things and suggest a return visit within the next few days or weeks.

USING MEDICAL CHECKUPS WISELY

The shift in medical attitudes means that the annual physical checkup for healthy, nonpregnant adults has been dramatically revamped. The routine yearly battery of medical tests is largely being abandoned in favor of more counseling about lifestyle and health habits.

As practiced in the past few decades, the traditional medical checkup was extensive. The physician took the pulse, temperature and blood pressure, prodded the abdomen, made people stick out their tongues and say "AAAH," peered into the ears, tapped the knees with a small hammer, listened to lungs, heart and neck pulse

(carotid artery), ordered a variety of blood tests and generally gave the person a thorough going-over. Both the physician and those being examined firmly believed — given no evidence to the contrary, as the subject hadn't been much studied until 15 years ago — that finding and treating diseases at an early stage would prevent worse trouble down the road.

While some physicians still give their patients exhaustive annual examinations, and many people demand them, the old-fashioned medical checkup is slowly disappearing. In its place, more personalized versions of the periodic medical examination are coming in, together with lashings of advice, counseling and exhortations to adopt a healthier lifestyle.

During the 1970s, with the soaring costs of medical care, the Canadian and U.S. governments began to investigate the real value of annual medical exams for all. The Canadian government commissioned a task force — the Canadian Task Force on the Periodic Health Examination (CTF), made up of more than 40 scientists, clinicians and consultants, spanning a wide range of disciplines — to evaluate routine medical tests. The aim was to decide which tests should be included, which omitted and which done only for selected "at-risk"

GLOSSARY OF SPECIALISTS

Anesthesiologists decide which type of anesthesia will be used, administer it during surgery and monitor its effects.
Cardiologists specialize in diagnosing and treating abnormalities of the heart and blood vessels.
Dermatologists diagnose and treat skin disorders.
Emergency medicine specialists are trained to work in a trauma center or hospital emergency department.

Gastroenterologists diagnose and treat disorders of the digestive system and liver.
Geneticists specialize in diagnosing and predicting inherited disorders, such as cystic fibrosis, hemophilia and many other disorders.
Gynecologists — see Obstetricians.
Hematologists diagnose and treat blood disorders.
Internists specialize in the internal (but usually nonsurgical)

treatment of adults. Some internists have subspecialties, such as cardiology, gastroenterology or hematology.
Neurologists diagnose and treat disorders of the brain and nervous system, spinal cord and peripheral nerves.
Obstetricians/gynecologists specialize in the treatment of female reproductive systems. An obstetrician also specializes in pregnancy care and delivering babies.

Oncologists diagnose cancer and recommend treatment.
Pediatricians specialize in treating children and adolescents.
Physiatrists specialize in physical therapy and sports medicine.
Psychiatrists specialize in emotional problems and mental illnesses.
Radiologists administer X-rays and ultrasound. A diagnostic radiologist uses radiology to diagnose medical problems. A therapeutic radiol-

ogist uses radiation for the treatment of cancer.
Surgeons diagnose and operate on a wide range of conditions. A general surgeon may specialize further, choosing, for example, thoracic and cardiovascular, pediatric, colon and rectal, or plastic surgery.
Urologists diagnose and treat disorders of the urinary tract and, in men, problems of the reproductive tract.

WHO NEEDS WHAT MEDICAL TESTS, WHEN?

Infants need:
- thyroid function tests (in newborns within first post-birth week);
- the "startle test" to check hearing response;
- immunization at recommended intervals for diphtheria, pertussis (whooping cough), tetanus, polio, measles, mumps, rubella, Hib or Hemophilus influenza B (against infant meningitis);
- well-baby visits, paralleling the immunization schedule, at two, four, six, twelve and eighteen months, and then annually which should include:
  - measurement of child's height, weight and head circumference;
  - a check of the eyes for infection and anatomical defects;
  - a check of hearing — for example, whether an infant can locate sounds as well as would be expected and, later, whether speech is developing normally;
  - a developmental appraisal, to identify mental retardation or learning abnormalities;
  - thorough examination of hips, legs;
  - parental counseling and injury-prevention advice about fire, falls, household poisons and traffic injuries — a crucial part of the well-baby examination. Discussion of parenting problems and advice on home safety and car restraints. Parents are encouraged to ask questions about childcare at every doctor visit.

Growing children need:
- measurement of length, weight and head circumference;
- assessment of parent-child interaction;
- learning/developmental evaluation;
- eye inspection and vision tests;
- injury-prevention advice (such as encouragement to wear bicycle helmets);
- annual dental checkups, after age three, with oral-hygiene advice;
- vaccination booster shots — for diphtheria, polio, rubella (girls), tetanus;
- inquiry about educational progress.

Teens/adolescents need:
- height and weight measurement;
- vision tests;
- checks on sexual health and contraceptive advice;
- smoking-cessation counseling (if appropiate);
- risk-reduction advice.

Healthy adults aged 18–65 need:
- blood-pressure measurement at every physician visit, and at least every three to five years;
- annual dental checkups for gum disease and cavities;
- polio booster immunization (depending on whether live or inactive vaccine was previously used), tetanus booster shots every 10 years (now under debate);
- quit-smoking advice;
- counseling on alcohol use and traffic-injury prevention.

Men specifically need:
- possibly, serum (blood) cholesterol tests every five years from age 35–59 — still controversial but advised by some health agencies. Most Canadian health authorities advise regular blood-cholesterol tests only for men aged 35–59 who have one or more cardiac risk factors: smoking, extreme obesity, lack of exercise (sedentary lifestyle), high blood pressure, diabetes or close relatives who have had early heart attacks (before age 55);
- possibly, regular rectal exams for prostate cancer after age 40 (still controversial but advised by some medical authorities).

Women specifically need:
- an annual breast exam;
- mammograms every two years after age 50;
- Pap smear tests at recommended intervals;
- regular pelvic exams.

The healthy elderly (over age 65) need:
The above tests as appropriate, plus:
- blood-pressure measurement every two years;
- annual anti-influenza shots (to reduce the risk of serious complications that may follow influenza);
- once-only pneumonia immunization — advised in Health and Welfare Canada's 1989 Canadian Immunization Guide (although some authorities suggest pneumonia immunization only for high-risk groups such as those with sickle cell anemia, the institutionalized elderly and adults working or living in overcrowded conditions);
- regular dental examinations;
- hearing tests — still under debate, but recommended for those regularly exposed to loud noise;
- eye examination to test for blood-vessel disease, cataracts and glaucoma — also controversial;
- mobility checks (joint flexibility, range of motion, strength and balance);
- assessment of nutritional status (how well the senior is eating);
- a full review of all medications being taken;
- evaluation of the ability to perform the activities of daily living (dressing, bathing, toilet use, cooking, cleaning, shopping);
- cognitive (thinking) impairment tests — recommended by various U.S. health agencies, although the CTF 1991 update finds "no conclusive evidence" to indicate whether the early detection of cognitive impairment in healthy older people can lead to a net benefit (better life-management, ability to convey wishes or assign power of attorney) or net harm (feeling labeled as "unfit" and "living down"to expectations).

SOME TIPS FOR DOCTOR VISITS

- Try to schedule the appointment for a time convenient for you.
- If you need a longer consultation, ask for it ahead of time, remembering that doctors can discuss only one or two problems at any one visit. Ask for another visit to discuss less pressing or subsidiary worries.
- On the day of your appointment, phone ahead and ask whether the doctor is on schedule.
- Anticipate delays; take along a good book, work or letter-writing materials.
- Bring a short, clear list of observed symptoms, which might include: new or worsening pain, changes in bowel frequency, appetite or sex drive, or unusual stumbling — anything that may affect physical or emotional well-being.
- Record what the physician says (or, with permission, consider using a tape recorder). Note the name(s) of any disease or disorder diagnosed and any tests ordered.
- Take along all medications — both prescription and over-the-counter — currently being taken, or jot down their names.
- Perhaps bring along a trusted friend or relative — especially helpful for the elderly or those worried about a serious health problem.
- Make sure you understand what the problem or treatment is.
- Ask the physician to repeat any information not fully understood. Keep on asking until any medical jargon is quite clear.
- Remember, there's no such thing as a stupid question! It's all right to call and ask the doctor or nurse a question you left out or only thought of after leaving.

If medications are prescribed:

- Record the generic (scientific) and brand name of each medicine and inquire about side effects.
- Make sure all medications are labeled and kept in original containers to avoid errors.
- Store medicines properly. A bathroom medicine chest may not be the best place because of the high humidity. Unless specifically directed, the refrigerator also is not ideal, as cold temperatures can affect the medication. A locked cabinet in the bedroom is a good place to store medications, beyond the reach and sight of small children.
- Elderly patients or those taking multiple medications, who may have trouble seeing or remembering what medicines should be taken when, can use weekly pill dispensers loaded by a relative or nurse.
- Ask what each drug is supposed to do, how long and when to take it and what to expect in terms of relief and how soon.
- Discard unused and outdated medications; put them down the toilet or, well wrapped, into the garbage.
- Don't reuse old prescribed medication. If the same health problem redevelops, get a new prescription.
- Remind the doctor about other medications being taken — whether prescribed by the same or another physician — and inquire about possible interactions.
- Ask about side effects that may occur with a medication (e.g., drowsiness, nausea, sex-drive alterations). Will it be safe to drive a car or operate machinery? Will the drug action be affected by alcohol, food or sunlight?
- Ask what to do if an unpleasant or seemingly dangerous side effect occurs.
- Never share prescribed medications with others.

individuals. A world leader in the healthcare field, internationally recognized as the first to rigorously assess the value of routine checkups, the Canadian Task Force evaluated 78 different conditions and medical procedures, suggesting which were worth doing and for whom.

Amid broad agreement from many other health agencies, the Task Force suggested a need to tailor tests to individuals, and recommended the abandonment of many routine procedures, such as chest X-rays, electrocardiograms (recordings of heart waves), many blood tests, examination of the spleen and liver and rectal exams (although some organizations still promote annual rectal exams for men over age 40).

Physicians are urged to give far more advice on the effects of lifestyle on health — whether in the sphere of weight, diet, smoking, alcohol and other drugs, exercise or sex life. Most health authorities agree that, rather than spending a lot of time doing complex physical tests, family physicians should put more time and effort into taking a full medical history and trying to identify those predisposed to heart problems, diabetes or other diseases.

One U.S. report concludes that "the greatest promise for preventing illness lies in helping people to alter their health-endangering behavior via medical counseling and in using each and every doctor visit as an opportunity to advise people on disease prevention." Studies show that if a doctor stresses that smoking, a fatty diet or excess alcohol use already shows signs of undermining health, there's a good chance people will change their health-damaging behavior.

Agreement on the need for certain routine tests at checkups

There is wide agreement that the following procedures should be done on a routine basis:

- weight measurement (to encourage people to keep their weight within the healthy range);
- blood-pressure measurements once every two to five years and at each visit in all adults over 18 years old (treating high blood pressure in all age groups reduces the risk of stroke and heart attack);
- universal childhood immunization against many infectious diseases;
- annual influenza shots for those over age 65, daycare and health professionals and other at-risk groups (many Canadians die needlessly of influenza and its complications each year, and far too few of those who need them get annual flu shots);
- physical breast examination by a competent healthcare professional, for all women;
- mammograms (special breast X-rays) every two years for women over age 50;
- Pap tests (of the cervix), to detect premalignant or cancerous changes, for all sexually active women and/or women 18 or older. The ideal frequency of Pap tests remains in dispute, some experts suggesting that Pap smears be done only every three years if two consecutive tests show no suspicious changes. (But many physicians do them every year in all sexually active women.)

NATURAL, ALTERNATIVE OR COMPLEMENTARY MEDICINE

Many sick people don't care much about the medical principles involved in treatment, they just want to feel better as fast as possible. Fed up with today's segmented, high-tech medical system, many people are turning to alternative sources for more personal, less intimidating or more "complete" healthcare, where they're

treated as "whole persons" rather than a collection of separate organs. But it's easy to be misled or taken advantage of by unscrupulous natural-medicine practitioners. And even the most sincere and well-meaning practitioner may be wrong about the merits of his or her theories of healing. It is wise to find out what's what before accepting treatment.

Stepping into the world of alternative or "natural" medicine can be bewildering, with so many different types offered. The different branches of natural medicine include naturopathy, homeopathy, herbalism, reflexology, iridology and chiropractic, to name but a few. Most alternative healthcare practitioners, such as naturopaths and chiropractors, prefer the term "complementary," to reflect the fact that responsible therapists respect traditional medical care as the first-line approach, with alternative care as a supplementary or second choice.

Various natural-medicine therapists practice different methods. For instance, iridologists claim to assess the condition of every part of the body by looking into the eye's iris; they then suggest treatment accordingly. Reflexologists feel the soles of the feet, massaging them to break up toxic deposits elsewhere in the body. Chiropractors examine the spine and other joints, adjusting them to help restore function. Acupuncturists read the body by feeling certain key points, thereby deciding where and how to restore the body's energy flow — by twirling acupuncture needles, applying electroacupuncture, or via acupressure or moxybustion (burning herbs) at specific points.

Homeopathy, another form of natural medicine, has many followers but remains controversial. Homeopathy is based on the "law of similars," meaning that a substance that produces a certain set of symptoms in a healthy person can also cure those symptoms in a sick person suffering from them, the difference between the cause and its cure being mainly the size of the dose. Homeopaths use the smallest possible dose — micro-doses — which may mean diluting and shaking a substance and diluting it again dozens or even hundreds of times. The founder of homeopathy, Dr. Samuel Hahnemann, named his therapy after the Greek words for "similar" (homoios) and "suffering" (pathos).

It is based on the ancient Hippocratic principle that "like cures like."

Qualified naturopaths (NDs) rely on the body's innate healing qualities to combat illness with minimal medical interference. Living things have an inherent ability to repair themselves and maintain homeostasis, a state of balance sought by every cell in our bodies. Most of the time it's achieved without outside assistance, given regular supplies of oxygen, water and necessary nutrients from food. The body's own healing mechanism cures many minor injuries. Cuts heal, bruises fade, noses stop running, coughs abate, rashes disappear and temperatures return to normal. According to many naturopaths, most of the symptoms we think of as diseases are actually the body's reaction against disease or illness. Fever, inflammation, a runny nose, pain and diarrhea are reactions to imbalance, infection or unwanted toxins. Naturopaths argue that overcoming or suppressing the body's innate attempts to redress the body's normal balance, by taking medication or even using an antiperspirant, can lead to more trouble down the road. To learn more about naturopathic healing, call a local naturopathic medical association — such as the Ontario College of Naturopathic Medicine: (416) 251-5261.

Does this approach mean we should do nothing about illness except wait idly by for the body to repair itself? Of course not. Pain should never be ignored: it is a signal of something wrong that needs attention. And while sometimes nothing more than rest, an ice pack, nourishing food and tender loving care is required to help the body cure itself, at other times medical intervention is necessary.

Holistic medicine practitioners also assume that "nature knows best." The term "holistic" simply means treating people as whole "ecosystems" where everything is connected to everything else, not just as an assemblage of odd parts that can be fixed separately. Holistic practitioners believe that natural remedies, whether animal, vegetable or mineral, are more easily assimilated, with fewer side effects and better results, than man-made medications.

However, recovery by the holistic approach can take a long time, and some argue that the choice is between rapid improvement by conventional medicine and slow torture by natural methods. Holistic practitioners might reply that a "quick medical fix," although sometimes necessary to save a life or alleviate suffering, is no substitute for natural healing. For example, the holistic treatment for heart conditions might include months of taking garlic and other remedies, plus careful attention to diet, moderate exercise and stress management. Or, instead of treating an acid stomach with an antacid, the holistic approach might be to improve digestion with herbs rich in enzymes and essential oils such as papaya, ginger, mint and fennel. (Holistic practitioners might believe that while providing temporary relief, antacids would make the body react by pumping even more acid into the stomach.)

For more information on holistic medicine, call your local branch of the Canadian Holistic Medicine Association — in Toronto: (416) 485-3071.

HERBALISM PLAYS A KEY ROLE IN NATURAL MEDICINE

Herbal remedies are prepared from the whole plant, or parts of it. Many plants once considered medicinal are now viewed as weeds, a fact bemoaned by Daniel Mowrey, Ph.D., in *The Scientific Validation of Herbal Medicine*. For example, the dandelion, *Taraxacum officinale*, long considered a liver remedy, was hailed as a wonder drug when imported into North America from ancient Greece and China. Since then, tons of herbicide have been poured onto lawns and fields to get rid of dandelions.

Many Europeans remain firm believers in herbal remedies. A recent United Kingdom poll revealed that 76 percent of British family doctors now study alternative medicine after graduating. And in North America, herbalists today command a sizeable following. With a revived interest in natural healing, more and more North Americans are taking herbal agents, especially when medicine fails them. They may self-medicate with herbal remedies because of distrust of the medical system or in the belief that "natural" products are the best healers. (Thanks to the invention of the gelatin capsule, we no longer have to taste the bitter herbs we eat — and some of them are pretty foul.) Herbal remedies are readily available in health-food shops, traditional ethnic stores and from naturopaths and herbalists.

The pharmaceutical approach to medicinal herbs is to isolate and market the active ingredients. Some of our most widely used modern drugs originate from herbs, although the healing ingredients are now often chemically synthesized. The heart drug digitalis, for instance, derives from foxglove plants; morphine comes from the poppy; quinine for malaria is made from cinchona bark. Other drugs derived from herbal remedies include cocaine, colchicine, coumarin anticoagulants, curare, ephedrine, reserpine and senna. Sick animals are suspected of consuming plants for their medicinal properties. For example, Harvard anthropologists have documented chimpanzees chewing bitter Aspilia leaves, which contain active antifungal and antiparasitic agents.

Undoubtedly, much of the power of herbs — as of other medications — lies in the power of suggestion: the placebo effect; and some healing effects attributed to herbs may be coincidental. For example, arthritic pain comes and goes unpredictably, and relief attributed to anti-arthritic herbal remedies, such as Devil's Claw, may well coincide with a period of remission.

A warning note on herbal remedies

In the belief that "natural" equals "safe," some people take very concentrated herbs in large amounts. But not all herbal remedies are safe in any amount. A herbal remedy taken for medicinal purposes is still an over-the-counter medication and deserves the same cautious respect as any other drug.

People who take herbal preparations should be aware of the sparse regulations governing their use. Although widely consumed as medications, most herbal remedies are not legally permitted to be sold in Canada as health remedies, but only as foods. Being classed as foods, they require no warning labels. Some herbal products bear federal Drug Identification Numbers (DINs) on the labels approving their sale as drugs. But the long-term effects of many natural herbal healers are simply not

known, as scientific studies are sparse and the harmful reactions not reported. While traditional medicines may not have all the answers, they are at least rigorously tested before being permitted on the market, and side effects are carefully listed.

Thus, a major difference between herbal remedies and medications made by drug companies is that pharmaceuticals are "the devil you know" and have been thoroughly tested, with known dangers spelled out on the package insert.

After centuries of experience, the most highly toxic plants have been eliminated from the herbalist's stock-in-trade. Lily of the valley, daffodil, deadly nightshade, foxglove, jimsonweed and hemlock are among substances banned by Health and Welfare Canada for sale as foods or in food. But while most other herbs are harmless when used occasionally and in moderation, they too can cause adverse reactions. Many plants beneficial in tiny amounts are poisonous in larger doses.

Some adverse reports about herbal remedies are surfacing, ranging from minor to serious, from poisoning, to allergic reactions, to death. As with pharmaceutical products, the likelihood of adverse reactions from plant remedies is highest among the elderly, young children, those who are pregnant, people with chronic illnesses and those taking other medications. Occasionally, an amateur herbalist gathers a poisonous plant and mistakes it for a harmless one. In one recent case, a woman mistook oleander for eucalyptus, and died after drinking the tea. In another case, an elderly couple died within 24 hours of overdosing on digitalis, mistaking poisonous foxglove for comfrey; in yet another incident, a man who drank jimsonweed tea swiftly died of it.

Plants containing pyrrolizidine or pyrrolidine are an increasing concern. Reports of liver disease (with jaundice and cirrhosis) from consuming this substance, especially in large doses or for long periods, have now been well documented. Pyrrolizidine in Gordolobos teas, widely consumed in the southern United States for sore throats and other ailments, is no longer considered safe, as it has been blamed for widespread liver problems. Another

CONSUMER TIPS ON HERBAL REMEDIES

- Use herbal products only as directed, and only for short periods of time.
- Do not use them to replace prescribed treatment for serious conditions.
- Always tell your physician about herbal remedies being taken.
- Purchase from established and reputable suppliers. Some herbalists are knowledgeable and helpful, others less so.
- Know what you are buying: are the Latin names of herbs and their quantities listed?
- Be cautious in using concentrated oils and teas.
- Consult a physician about taking herbs if you have any chronic illnesses, are taking other medications, are pregnant or elderly, and before you consider giving them to children.
- Do not give children under age two herbal remedies.
- Familiarize yourself with the herbs you're using; inquire about side effects and potential hazards.

TOP ITEMS FOR THE MEDICINE CABINET

Stocking a medicine cabinet sensibly doesn't mean stuffing it full of remedies for every conceivable ailment, but selecting those items most likely to come in handy for everyday needs and some emergencies. In general, less is better. Any products that have lost their label or passed their expiry date should be thrown out. The following classes of over-the-counter products have been recommended by University of Toronto experts as useful for common problems that may not need medical attention, or as temporary measures to be used before consulting a physician.

- Analgesics such as ASA (acetylsalicylic acid), and acetaminophen are potent painkillers, effective against headaches, backaches and many other aches and pains. Both ASA (e.g., Aspirin) and acetaminophen (e.g., Tylenol, Tempra, Panadol) are antipyretics (fever reducers), but ASA should not be given to children because of the risk of Reye's syndrome — a dangerous liver and brain disorder. ASA (but not acetaminophen) is also an anti-inflammatory agent, able to relieve arthritis and other conditions such as inflamed muscle injuries.

- Syrup of ipecac induces vomiting and is a useful standby, especially if young children swallow a poisonous product. Syrup of ipecac can be given at any age and induces vomiting in about 10 minutes. But call the Poison Control Centre or doctor before giving the syrup, as forced vomiting may be inadvisable. Substances such as bleach or lye (Lysol) burn a second time "on the way up" and some floor waxes, kerosene and other volatile materials would be inhaled again while vomiting, possibly causing more harm. However, when a medical expert condones its use, the syrup can give fast, effective treatment and prevent the poison from being absorbed, and may even help to avoid a trip to the hospital.

- Anti-nausea pills or suppositories such as dimenhydrinate (Gravol), available in pediatric and adult strengths, quell nausea, car sickness and mild vomiting. The suppository form is useful when vomiting prevents pills from being kept down.

- Antiseptic agents keep cuts, scratches, sores and scrapes clean. While many physicians promote soap and water as a good "first choice" antiseptic to kill microorganisms, various commercial antiseptics are available: old-fashioned iodine (messy and stinging to use), Betadine (an organic iodine compound that stings less but stains like iodine), pHisoDerm (an antiseptic liquid soap), chlorhexidine solution (Hibitane) and hydrogen peroxide. Weak solutions of plain salt or, better still, Epsom salts are useful for soaking infected wounds. Antibiotic creams and ointments (such as Polysporin and Bactroban) are recommended by many physicians but are of debated usefulness in some cases.

- Oral anti-itch and anti-allergy products usually contain antihistamines of one kind or another. Individuals should select the type that works best for them. In general, the most sedating antihistamines are the most likely to relieve itchiness or allergy symptoms — e.g., chlorpheniramine (Chlor-Tripolon) or diphenhydramine (Benadryl). A note of caution: remember that alcohol used with antihistamines may cause excessive drowsiness or retard reaction times. Other medications may also enhance the impact of antihistamines. Weak hydrocortisone products (now available without prescription as creams, ointments and lotions, in 0.5 percent strength) may relieve an itchy skin but should be used with care on the face because of skin-thinning effects. Calamine lotion is a good antidote for itchiness, sunburn or a mild poison-ivy rash.

- Bowel-disorder remedies are available but should be used cautiously. Most pediatricians advise against the use of such products in children under two years of age, unless specifically prescribed. For an underactive bowel a wide range of laxatives is readily obtainable, but it's generally better to eat a well-balanced, fiber-rich diet to keep the bowel active. For specific constipated occasions, mild laxatives can be selected according to taste, such as products containing magnesia or senna, mineral oil and phenolphthalein, or bowel soothers such as Pepto-Bismol. For an overactive bowel or diarrhea, experts may recommend binding agents such as Kaopectate, or bowel-immobilizing drugs such as Imodium. But experts advise against use of Imodium in children, as it may mask the severity of symptoms. Imodium immobilizes the bowel rather than clearing up the diarrhea or its cause. Traditional remedies such as arrowroot and oat bran contain natural bowel-binding ingredients.

- For an acidic stomach or regurgitation problems, such as heartburn or indigestion, a vast array of antacid preparations (mostly aluminum and magnesium hydroxide products) is available, including Gelusil, Rolaids, Maalox, Amphojel, Tums and Riopan. Liquid forms, although messier and less portable than tablets, generally give speedier relief.

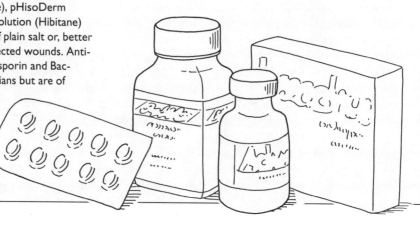

- Cold remedies, taken orally or used as nasal sprays or drops, include decongestants, painkillers and expectorants. Experts strongly recommend products containing one type of ingredient only, not those with a "mixed bag." Single-ingredient products include antipyretics (such as ASA or acetaminophen) to combat fever, analgesics for pain and decongestants against nasal stuffiness. The most effective oral decongestants are pseudoephedrine, ephedrine and phenylpropanolamine, each varying slightly in the strength, speed and duration of its effect and in its stimulating action on the brain (a side effect that may produce agitation or jitteriness). Nasal sprays usually contain similar compounds and/or oxymetazoline or xylometazoline, which have a local vasoconstricting (shrinking) effect on the nasal membranes, easing the congestion. Use of nasal sprays for more than three or four days, at specific intervals, is not recommended because of the rebound effect, which paralyzes the nasal cilia (hairs), preventing them from expelling mucus and thus increasing the stuffiness. Spray decongestants are best reserved for "must clear" occasions, such as air travel.
- A good cough medicine is useful for those kept awake by an incessant cough. The most effective cough medicines are prescription products containing codeine. Codeine suppresses coughing by acting on the brain's cough center, not on the throat, and is just as effectively absorbed from pills as from syrups, if not more so, however soothing a syrup may feel to a sore throat! A pediatrician may suggest keeping such a product at home for children with a persistent cough. Dextromethorphan (DM) is a nonprescription cough suppressant, available in single-ingredient formats (e.g., DM syrup, Delfym DM or Sucrets) or combination products (e.g., Benadryl DM, Triaminic DM or Robitussin DM). Physicians advise caution in using cough suppressants as it is not always desirable to suppress a cough. Coughing is the protective mechanism that clears the respiratory tract of mucus (phlegm).
- Skin soothers and softeners are invaluable for scaling, chapped or dry skin, rough hands or sore infant bottoms. Rough, dry skin easily becomes inflamed, and may develop cracks through which infections enter. Effective emollients (skin softeners) include petroleum (petrolatum) jelly, lanolin-based creams and products containing urea, lactic acid or phospholipids. Emollients should be applied to moist skin, to hold in water and keep the surface soft. Calamine lotion is also useful for soothing sunburned or itchy skin but is rather drying.

Safety first at all times

As a "safety first" precaution, experts suggest that even the relatively mild products listed above must be regarded with respect. Some simple rules may avert needless household tragedies or accidents:
- Don't "guess" about the possible severity of symptoms — given even the slightest doubt or uneasiness, check with a physician before using any medication.
- Throw away any product that has lost its label or passed its expiry date (prescription medication should be dated at time of purchase, preferably identifying the person and ailment for which it was bought).
- Mark all potentially poisonous substances with a clear warning sign, such as a red dot.
- Don't share prescription medication or use a medication prescribed for someone else — different people need different products.

Special precautions for children:

- Keep all medications well out of children's reach.
- Show children the symbol for toxicity, which means "Do not touch!"
- Give medicines to children rather than permitting them to self-medicate.
- Try not to let children see adults self-medicating too freely and too often or taking many combined products. Discuss the risks of drug interaction.

(For more on medications, see Appendix.)

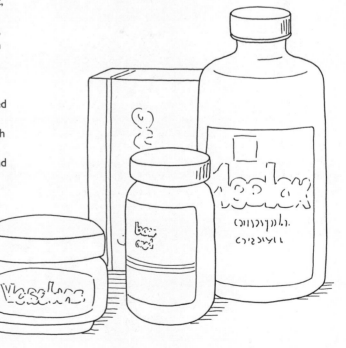

common plant containing pyrrolizidine is comfrey — a widely consumed and popular remedy, now banned in Germany and partially banned in Canada. Liver disease in Jamaica and other parts of the world has also been linked to Gordolobos or "bush" tea.

As many as 400 herbs and spices are used as herbal teas, most of unknown safety. Harmful overdoses are most likely when plants are made into strong herbal brews steeped for 10-20 minutes or more. Problems attributed to strong herbal teas include bleeding, gastro-intestinal problems and heart and nervous-system disorders. For example, liquorice contains chemicals that, taken in large quantities, can cause heart enlargement, sodium and water retention, high blood pressure and even cardiac arrest. "In general," according to one expert, "herbal medicinal teas ought not to be consumed in amounts above three or so cups a day."

Herbal remedies can also interact with prescription and nonprescription drugs, and with each other. Some plants such as tonka beans, melilot and woodruff, which increase bleeding, should not be consumed by those with circulatory disorders or those regularly taking ASA. Several herbs — such as lily of the valley, false hellebore and hawthorn — can increase the effects of the heart medication digoxin. Others such as bearberry, juniper and Saint Johnswort are diuretics, and shouldn't be taken by those on prescribed diuretics. In the final analysis, shopping for herbal products is a matter of *caveat emptor*: buyer beware!

Failure to mention herbal or other natural remedies when seeing a physician for health problems can lead to needless investigative tests and ineffective treatment. In one case, a woman with abnormal menstrual bleeding was subjected to laparoscopy and much anxiety before her excessive bleeding was linked to massive consumption of a herbal tonic containing anticoagulants.

People who turn to alternative medicine might be wise to discuss it with their physician. They should also ask the naturopath or other complementary medicine practitioner to explain what's behind the suggested remedy, being especially wary of any treatment that seems excessively costly. Those who decide to go hunting for holistic or other natural treatments will likely have to pay for it themselves. In Canada few alternative therapies are covered by private insurance and even fewer by provincial medicare. Remember that the growing "natural health industry" has its own share of incompetence, greed and charlatanism, so beware of costly miracle cures. Never pursue a course of treatment if the bill will make you sick.

Nutrition toward health

The basics of good nutrition • Nutrition for athletes • Sorting out the cholesterol puzzle • Choosing the right fat mix • The fascination of fiber • Make carbohydrates (starches) your dietary mainstay • Sugars aren't all bad • Proteins in the diet • In praise of fish • Vegetarian diets • The caffeine story • Vitamins: most people don't need supplements • Minerals in the diet • Water is also an essential dietary component

THE BASICS OF GOOD NUTRITION

In the past few decades we've been deluged with fast-changing, often unvalidated rules for good eating. Despite the information overload, many people still don't understand the simplest basics of sound nutrition. Unable to separate fads from truths, they slavishly follow eating slogans or bestseller diets. Nearly every week the announcement of some new study, not necessarily confirmed or medically accepted, sends them scurrying after the latest supposedly life-prolonging diet.

Sensible nutrition — the cornerstone of good health — is neither obscure nor hard to understand. Notwithstanding the biochemical intricacies of the body's metabolism, sound dietary principles are both simple and easy to obtain from registered dietitians and qualified nutritionists. The trick is to regard food not only as tasty and pleasurable but also as a source of fuel for the body's growth, and of *nutrients* — chemicals vital to all life processes. The food you eat is broken down into sugar (glucose), which is the energy source for all the body's cells, and into other chemical building blocks that are reassembled to form the substances needed by the body — such as digestive enzymes (catalysts), muscle-building components, immune agents, blood cells and hormones.

The main nutrient categories acquired from food are: carbohydrates (starches and sugars), proteins, fats, water, minerals and vitamins. Food must provide them all in adequate amounts. Each nutrient class performs a specific task in the body. For example, carbohydrates provide energy; fats become part of cell membranes and transport fat-soluble substances such as some vitamins and some hormones; minerals help regulate key functions such as blood production, respiration and bone and tooth formation; water is an essential part of every cell and serves as a transport medium. If food provides too little of any nutrient, the body cannot function properly. A lack of carbohydrate for fuel results in fatigue, poor mental and physical performance and ultimately starvation and death. A lack of iron may deplete supplies of hemoglobin, the red oxygen-carrying pigment in blood, resulting in iron-deficiency anemia, which causes weakness and lassitude. A deficiency of the mineral cobalt may produce another type of anemia; too little zinc may retard growth and learning; diets low in calcium shortchange growing bones and a lack of vitamin A can cause night blindness. Nutrient excesses can also undermine health. Too much vitamin A can cause nausea, headaches, irritability and skin and liver damage; excess vitamin D can damage bone, brain and liver function.

Balance is the key. Eat a widely varied diet low in fat and rich in complex carbohydrates in

4

amounts that keep you at a healthy weight. The daily diet should average 30 percent or less fat as a proportion of caloric intake and 12–15 percent protein, and over half the food eaten should be carbohydrates, preferably the complex kind (in whole grains, potatoes, pastas, rice, fruits, legumes and vegetables) rather than refined (sugars). Provided the overall meal plan is high in carbohydrates and low in fat, there's no need to avoid favorites such as an occasional milkshake, candy bar, hot dog or ice cream — just don't make them a daily habit.

Variety, balance and fun are key

The 1991 Health and Welfare Canada nutrition recommendations aim to cut through the dietary confusion and help people make better eating choices. Up to date, action-oriented and easy to read, the guidelines stress overall eating behavior and the entire dietary mix rather than giving daily meal plans. People should eat not just to prevent deficiencies but to promote health and reduce the likelihood of today's main killer illnesses: heart ailments and cancer, especially bowel and breast cancer — possibly linked to excess dietary fat.

Today's focus is on variety, the avoidance of taboos and putting the fun back into eating. To banish the view that good nutrition is boring, the federal guidelines emphasize the pleasurable aspects of food, downplaying restriction, elimination or limitation. The guidelines include the Recommended Nutrient Intakes (RNIs) —

outlining the whys and wherefores for the suggested daily amounts of all nutrients, including trace elements such as copper, chromium, cobalt and selenium.

The central nutritional messages are to reach and stay at a healthy weight, enjoy a varied diet and, above all, eat less fat. The amount of fat in the average Canadian diet is well above the recommended 30 percent level. We're among world leaders in fat consumption, only slightly behind the United States, Britain, the Netherlands, Denmark, Germany, Hungary and France. Our fat consumption remains too high even though many try to lower fat consumption by eating less butter, discarding chicken skin, choosing low-fat dairy products and other strategies. However, the chief changeover in the past few decades is in the *types* of fat eaten — from animal to vegetable types — rather than a real reduction in overall intake. There's lots of hidden fat in fast and takeout foods, salad dressings, bakery products and restaurant meals.

For growing children, the advice to lower fat intake should be followed with caution. Many experts question fat reduction for children, as it may shortchange youngsters of much-needed calories and endanger their health. Fat is a valuable source of energy for fast-growing children, and is essential for proper nerve formation and myelination (nerve coating). Parents should beware of cutting fat intakes so low in growing children that they risk a diminished growth and retarded development.

IN ESSENCE, OUR DIET SHOULD:

- provide energy consistent with maintaining body weight within the recommended range;
- include essential nutrients in amounts specified in the Recommended Nutrient Intakes;
- contain no more than 30 percent of energy as fat and no more than 10 percent of

that as saturated fat;
- provide 55 percent of energy as carbohydrates, from a variety of sources;
- contain less sodium (especially table salt);
- include no more than 5 percent of calories as alcohol (or two drinks daily, whichever is less);
- contain no more caffeine than the

equivalent of four cups of regular coffee per day;
- make sure that community water supplies contain sufficient fluoride.

In everyday language, that means we should:
- eat enough to achieve and maintain a healthy body weight, but not less than

1,800 calories a day, as lower amounts may not provide all essential nutrients. Those who want to lose weight should not go on unbalanced, intermittent or fad diets but should exercise more;
- enjoy a wide range of foods — moderation and variety are the

watchwords for a sound diet;
- consume plenty of cereals, breads, pastas, rice, grain products, vegetables and fruits;
- choose lower-fat dairy products and leaner meats, and prepare foods with little or no fat;
- moderate salt and alcohol use.

The right food for different ages

While good nutrition is important at every stage of life, the body's needs vary as people move from one decade to another. In adolescence, early adulthood and middle age, the body goes through specific changes that make special nutritional demands. As people grow older, they become more restricted in what they can comfortably eat. For women, dietary needs change during pregnancy and lactation and at the menopause. By adapting eating and exercise habits to the special needs of their age group, people can improve their vitality and their ability to withstand stress and illness.

For infants up to six months of age

Breast milk is the perfect food for infants in the first six months of life. Infants have a high metabolic rate, and their rapid growth makes nutrients and water essential, as their bodies easily lose fluid. Vitamin D and iron supplements may be recommended. Fat is essential for nerve and brain development. When weaning an infant off milk or formula, gradually add a wide assortment of solid foods, starting with cereals, progressing to nonallergenic foods (e.g., apples, carrots, bananas), and adding other items one by one to achieve a richly varied, balanced diet. Make mealtimes interesting and fun, not a struggle of wills. Never use any food as a bribe or as a reward to replace loving attention!

Childhood (age two to puberty)

Pay special attention to sufficient intake of calcium and iron for growing bones and other organs. Teach healthy eating behavior — start children on well-varied diets, offering plentiful fruits, vegetables and whole grains. Limit sugary snacks. Teach children to eat only when hungry and to stop eating when full. Ensure proper nutritional intake by offering a few choices among healthy foods, not by forcing a child to eat everything on his or her plate. (See chapter 11, "Instilling good eating habits in children.")

Adolescence (about 12-18 years)

With the body's nutritional demands at their peak, erratic meals because of today's teenage lifestyle and the advent of menstruation in young women, food must be "nutrient-dense" — providing adequate protein, vitamins and minerals for their calorie content, not just energy. Iron lost in menstrual blood needs to be replaced. Adolescents need ample protein and vitamins (notably Bs) and higher calorie intakes to cope with the huge spurt in growth (often nearly doubling the body's size). Iron and calcium tend to be too low in teen meals. Dieting, common in girls, tends to deprive teenagers of much-needed nutrients. Serious dieting can stunt teens' growth, prevent the achievement of full height, and retard the onset of menstruation in girls.

Studies by Nutrition Canada depict female adolescents as a poorly nourished group. Many adolescents ignore good nutrition, not realizing its role in health and appearance, or understanding that it lays the foundation for healthy childbearing. Embarrassed by their developing breasts and the sudden deposits of fat on hips and abdomen, many girls go on extreme diets in an effort to stay thin. Nutrition Canada reports a widespread shortage of iron and folic acid (a B vitamin) in adolescent girls, with added risks of calcium and vitamin D lack — slightly worse among the Indians and the Inuit than in the general Canadian population. In a recent evaluation of adolescent diets, a University of Toronto expert found that boys, who consume more total calories and at least get some protein by eating sandwiches, hot dogs and hamburgers, usually have more complete diets than girls, of whom 25 percent were low in iron and vitamins. Studies also show that snacks and soft drinks compose almost a third of the average adolescent's total calorie intake. While snacking was frowned on in the past, it's now acceptable provided the snacks include nutrient-rich items (fruit, low-fat yogurt, nuts, whole-grain items) rather than fat-drenched fries, cookies or chips. To ensure adequate teen nutrition, keep the fridge stocked with healthy snacks. Breakfast is an important meal for teenagers, who are often out at dinnertime. If you can persuade them to have breakfast, it should provide at least 300 calories, with some protein (e.g., from milk, cottage cheese, peanut butter). A good breakfast might include citrus fruit for vitamin C, cereal for energy and vitamin B, and 2 percent milk or yogurt for calcium and protein.

15 STEPS TOWARD HEALTHIER EATING

1. Avoid food faddism, and replace the concept of "good" versus "bad" foods with the principles of balance and moderation. Shop for nutritional value rather than fashion or trends. Ignore any nutritional news not based on scientific fact. Never shun or favor a food because of unvalidated rumors about its possible dangers. Diets that make a fetish of single foods (e.g., grapefruit, raisins or brown rice) or food groups (e.g., protein or starches) are unbalanced and can cause serious health problems, sometimes far more severe than the disorders they set out to correct.

2. Eat the right amount to maintain a healthy weight. When calories consumed do not balance energy output, the result is either obesity or malnutrition. Calorie requirements per kilogram and per pound per day for average healthy Canadians are:
   - for infants (two to four months) — 119 cals per kg (54 cals per pound)
   - for adolescents (both sexes) — 44–53 cals per kg (20–24 cals per pound)
   - for women (aged 23–50) — 36 cals per kg (16 cals per pound)
   - for men (aged 23–50) — 44 cals per kg (20 cals per pound)

   The average woman is deemed to be 162 cm and 55 kg (5 ft 4 in and 120 lb); the average man about 180 cm and 77 kg (5 ft 11 in and 170 lb).

3. Eat a wide range of foods, especially from plant sources, and an array of differently colored (red, orange, yellow, green) fruits and vegetables to get the required vitamins and minerals. Although nutritionists no longer promote the regimented idea of three "balanced" meals a day, they stress the need for overall balance with variety as the main principle, emphasizing local fresh foods when possible, rather than imported or canned goods. Frozen foods are also a good source of high-quality vegetables. Include enough orange, yellow and red fruits and vegetables rich in vitamin A. Diets high in B carotene and other natural carotenes (vitamin A), vitamin C and other antioxidants from plant foods may protect against some cancers.

4. Eat a diet high in carbohydrates, especially the "complex" variety from fruits, vegetables, grains, cereals and legumes, to make up 55 percent or more of your total calories. This means becoming more of a plant-food eater, consuming more starchy foods — cereals, breads, vegetables and fruits, rice and pastas.

5. Don't be fooled by the mistaken idea that starch is fattening. Starch, sugar and other carbohydrates have only four calories per gram, compared to fats, with nine calories per gram. The latest research suggests that starch (a complex carbohydrate) as well as the fiber in plant foods may confer health benefits (e.g., perhaps reducing the risk of colon and other cancers). While it's hard to separate the benefits of starch from those of fiber, since they're often present in the same foods, enjoying more pastas, cereals, grains, bananas, yams, rice, potatoes and legumes may promote health.

6. Don't exceed your protein needs. Protein is essential, but many eat more than they really need. Protein intake should be around 15 percent of total calories, but most Canadian diets currently exceed that amount. Protein needs vary according to age, sex and activity levels. In general, men aged 23–50, of average height and weight, need about 56 g per day, and women of the same age need about 41 g. Our protein consumption averages 83 grams per day — about 50 percent higher than the recommended level. Since protein foods tend to be expensive, it is practical as well as healthy to decrease amounts eaten. Meat or poultry need not be eaten at every meal or even every day. Proteins from fish, low-fat dairy products and plants are also good. Legumes and nuts are excellent protein sources and most whole grains, fruits and vegetables also contain some protein. But vegetarian sources must be balanced to provide complete protein (with all the necessary amino-acid components).

   About 20 g of protein are provided by: 85 g (3 oz) of cooked beef, lamb, veal, chicken or fresh fish; 150 ml (two-thirds of a cup) of canned salmon; six sardines; 105 ml (7 tbsp) of cottage cheese; two frankfurters; or 90 ml (6 tbsp) of peanut butter. Therefore, two to three servings of these foods *alone* fulfill daily protein needs — even though we also get *some* protein from other dairy products, grains and vegetables.

7. Eat enough fiber. In contrast to the Canadian Nutrition Recommendations (which specify no exact amounts for fiber intake), the World Health Organization (WHO) guidelines suggest 24–35 g (0.8–1.2 oz) of fiber a day, much of it from legumes (lentils, peas, beans), seeds, nuts and vegetables. Fiber, or roughage, a partly indigestible component of plant foods, helps to soften and expand the stool and speeds elimination, and some forms may absorb toxins that could contribute to bowel disease. Nutritionists advise us to eat more fiber-rich items such as unpeeled boiled or baked potatoes, brown rice, vegetables such as carrots, broccoli, sprouts and cabbage, and fruits like strawberries, bananas and grapefruit. Dried beans, peas and other legumes, and oat and wheat bran, are particularly valuable fiber sources which should be regularly consumed for health benefits.

8. Reduce fats to 30 percent or less of all calories consumed. Choose a sensible fat mix, low in saturated fats, but don't altogether eliminate dietary fat — it's a nutrient essential for energy and growth, especially in young children, and also crucial for the absorption of fat-soluble vitamins. Eat a mix of saturated fat (in meats, whole-milk products, butter), polyunsaturated oils (from fish and vegetables, e.g., sunflower, safflower, soya, cottonseed and some nuts, such as walnuts and pecans) and monounsaturated fats (such as olive and canola oils). It's wise to favor olive oil as it has unique health-promoting properties. It is one of the least hydrogenated and therefore healthy edible oils. Among the cooking oils, olive oil is the only one that contains natural antioxidants, which keep it stable and stop it from becoming saturated (hydrogenated) and going rancid for many years. Indeed, the health benefits of olive oil may stem more from its antioxidant levels than, as previously assumed, from its fatty-acid composition. Also favor polyunsaturates which lower blood cholesterol.

   To reduce fat to the recommended 30 percent of calories:
   - Steam, bake or poach foods. Deep-fat frying or flaming (flambéing, barbecuing) of foods produces oxidized components known to be toxic at very low concentrations.
   - Make sauces with skim, not whole milk, and use low-fat yogurt instead of cream.
   - Become a "hidden fat" detective. Watch for saturated fat often used in crackers, cookies, desserts, dressings and sauces.
   - Choose leaner cuts of meat and trim off the fat; broil or bake rather than fry. But there's no need to shun meat altogether — besides high-quality protein, it provides many other vital nutrients, such as iron, zinc and vitamins B_6 and B_{12} (to name a few).
   - Drink skim milk instead of homogenized; have a boiled egg instead of one scrambled in fat; eat fruit instead of pie or cake for dessert.

9. Shake the salt habit. Excess sodium from salt (sodium chloride) can increase the risk of high blood pressure and associated cardiovascular disease. Most people require only one or two grams per day, an amount easily supplied from a varied diet without added cooking or table salt (unless you are in a very hot climate, or exercising very vigorously and sweating profusely).

10. Eat fish two to three times weekly. Cold-water, deep-sea fish such as tuna, herring, salmon and halibut are rich in certain fatty acids which may protect the heart and cardiovascular system. Eating deep-sea fish is known to lower heart-attack risks in some Inuit populations, by reducing the blood's clotting action. Even the higher-fat fish — such as salmon, swordfish, herring and mackerel — are healthy choices. Fish also provide high-quality protein, and are generally low in cholesterol, although shellfish are somewhat higher. Canned fish is equally healthy.

11. Don't skip breakfast. A nutritious breakfast helps to improve concentration and enhance mental performance, especially in children. It should include a fruit or juice containing vitamin C, complex carbohydrates such as whole grains, and protein (milk, low-fat cheese). A good breakfast may reduce impulse eating or bingeing later in the day.

12. Eat lightly at night. People who save up all day for a large dinner at night may increase the body's conversion of food to fat. Evening snacking may provide as many calories as a second dinner. Two or three small meals a day and a light evening intake may help to maintain desirable weight levels.

13. Drink enough fluids. Water, a vital nutrient, helps regulate body temperature and acts as a solvent, transport medium and tissue lubricant. An average adult needs about 2.8 liters (3 quarts) per day from all sources, including fruit and vegetables (80 percent or more water), milk (87 percent), juices, soups, coffee, tea and other beverages. Note, however, that alcohol and the caffeine in tea, coffee and colas are diuretics that increase urine output, thus increasing the body's water needs.

14. Get your vitamins and minerals from a wholesome, varied diet of real food rather than from supplements, unless medically advised to take them. Nutrient intakes of vitamins and minerals in excess of the Recommended Nutrient Intake (RNI) aren't recommended, except for specific situations such as pregnancy (folic acid), infancy (vitamin D) and older age (when there's a risk of too little food intake).

15. Demand clear nutrition information on food labels, and become a conscientious label reader, evaluating what you read and comparing the nutrient values of foods. (Take a pocket calculator if you want, to work out fat percentages!)

Finally, relax and enjoy food! Remember that there's nothing wrong with occasional "junk" food such as chips, candy, donuts, cream cake or chocolates, provided they're not a major part of your diet.

Early adulthood (18–40 years)

Food intake should be matched to activity in order to maintain weight at the desired level. A steady balanced diet of fresh foods that supply essential nutrients in recommended amounts is the key, providing 50–60 percent of calories from carbohydrates (as in whole grains, pastas, potatoes, rice), 12–15 percent from protein and no more than 30 percent from fats (two-thirds from monounsaturated and polyunsaturated forms). Overeating leads to obesity and the accompanying health hazards of raised blood pressure, diabetes and cardiovascular disease. The calorie intake of a normally active woman should be around 1,800–2,100 calories a day, and of a man around 2,700–3,000 calories daily. Since bone density continues to build until age 35, adults need enough calcium to protect the bones from later osteoporosis. Women should also pay special attention to their iron intake. Blood loss from monthly periods can cause iron-deficiency anemia. Many young women, especially those who are pregnant or lactating, need iron supplements to meet their daily requirements. Women on birth-control pills should ask their physicians about the need for vitamin supplements. For the rest, a well-varied diet with lots of fruit and vegetables should provide all needed vitamins and minerals.

Middle age (40–65 years)

After age 40, nutritional needs change with the gradual slowing of metabolic activity. Calorie requirements drop by about 5 percent per decade. Constipation may be a problem and some drugs hinder the absorption of certain nutrients. Women's iron needs diminish when menstruation ceases, so there's less worry about getting enough of this nutrient after that time. By contrast, calcium needs rise at the menopause in women, and after age 65 in men, who also suffer osteoporosis in later life. Women approaching the menopause need to think about osteoporosis (waning bone strength) as estrogen's protective effect disappears. To offset osteoporotic bone loss, women need at least 1,000 mg of calcium per day. (See chapter 15, the section on osteoporosis, for other precautions.)

Although overall food intake should be somewhat less with advancing years, the body's actual nutrient needs remain similar or slightly increased, so it is just the total calorie count that needs to go down with each successive decade. The best strategy for the middle years is to eat healthy, nutrient-rich foods and to try to burn off extra calories by keeping up daily exercise routines. A daily walk, swim or tennis game can help to prevent "middle-aged spread."

Seniors

In the elderly, a change in dietary habits may be caused by tooth problems (which lessen the enjoyment of hard-to-chew foods), diminished taste and smell (which reduce appetite) and a sluggish digestive system (which may increase the frequency of constipation, heartburn and bloating). Low incomes and reduced shopping ability may make seniors subsist on diets that do not provide the needed nutrients. The diets of many older people, especially women, are substandard, particularly low in protein and vitamins (especially vitamin D), not even providing half the essential nutrients. As people spend less time outdoors in the sunlight, vitamin D stores can be depleted, and some seniors need a supplement. Inadequate zinc is also common because insufficient lean meat, legumes and grains/bread are being eaten. Caregivers should watch what older people keep in their kitchens and refrigerators, try to monitor what they eat, offer to shop for them and supply easy-to-eat, readymade, nutrient-rich food products, making sure they drink enough fluids to keep the kidneys working well. Avoid constipation (which in turn reduces the wish to eat properly) with fiber-rich items or yogurt. Some seniors prefer to eat frequent, smaller meals, which induce less bloating and other digestive discomforts than large ones. Less mobile seniors may request government-sponsored Meals on Wheels, which provide more nutritious meals than seniors are apt to make for themselves.

NUTRITION FOR ATHLETES

Varied diets supply the needs of most athletes, which are not very different from those of other people. Contrary to common mythology, vitamins don't build competitive strength! And sodium losses even in vigorous events are generally quite small. While the term "athlete" refers strictly to entrants in organized sports events, anyone who engages in exercise vigorous enough to challenge his or her endurance can be considered athletic. The effects of a poor diet may show up as fatigue, below-par performance and less-than-optimum achievement.

Nutrient overdoses can't improve performance

Good nutrition can maximize the body's athletic potential, but it has never been known to make an average athlete into an Olympic winner. On the other hand, poor nutrition can reduce the performance of an otherwise talented and well-trained athlete. There is a common misconception among sports enthusiasts that "more is better" — more protein, more vitamins, more minerals — but those tempted to overdose on certain nutrients should remember that doing so cannot upgrade performance and may harm the body. The physically active require enough energy from food to keep their weight at the right level; the amount required depends on individual build, height, metabolism, training level and energy expenditure. Some athletes must pay special attention to their nutrition, particularly those whose bodies are still growing and those with below-normal amounts of body fat. Women must get plenty of calcium to avoid osteoporosis (bone thinning) and enough iron to offset anemia.

Water, water and more water

Water is the ideal drink for heavy exercisers. Dehydration can occur not only during a race, but over a long heat wave or a prolonged period of training, if fluid replacement does not precede and follow each training session. Accumulated dehydration can even occur in those doing thrice-weekly vigorous workouts. It's not unusual for a runner to lose water amounting to a 225-ml (8-oz) glass every mile (or every six to eight minutes). Ideally, fluid intake should equal sweat loss, but although one could assess the actual weight loss during exercise and drink the equivalent amount of water, to do so is impractical. Experts suggest that athletes drink two to three cups of water two or three hours before engaging in strenuous activity, another

cup 15 minutes before the start and then one cup every 15–20 minutes. Also take plenty of fluid after exercise to rehydrate the body. Drinking a cup every 20 minutes is wise when competing. Paradoxically, the thirst response is blunted during and just after vigorous exercise — so don't be fooled by the fact that you don't *feel* thirsty.

Cold fluids are absorbed faster than warm drinks and also cool the body somewhat. Diluted solutions or plain water leave the stomach faster than concentrated solutions. Some studies show beneficial results with pre-hydration — drinking large amounts of water before the start of exercise, for better maintenance of blood volume and temperature control. Before adopting this tactic, it may be wise to check about easy access to washrooms during a marathon! One veteran marathoner says that when he runs he wears a cap in which he places ice cubes; he continually soaks it in water, never passing a water station without stopping and drinking two full glasses and pouring a third over his head. "Whenever there is a hose I run through the spray; and I carry a cup that I can fill with water. I purposely run 15 to 30 seconds a mile slower than my usual time." Despite such precautions, many marathoners lose 5–7 liters (1–1.5 gallons) of fluid when competing in hot weather, and end a race significantly dehydrated.

Excess protein can stress the body

Protein requirements of athletes are often wrongly assumed to be greater than those of non-athletes. Many regular exercisers continue to eat far more protein than they need, taking it in as fat-laden meats, or as protein powder, liquid or pills. Yet protein beyond the body's needs is simply stored as unnecessary fat, or converted to glucose. Protein needs may increase slightly in the early stages of training to provide increased muscle mass, enzymes and red blood cells. Although opinions vary, a liberal estimate for protein requirement during the initial phase of training is 1.2–1.5 grams per kilogram (0.5–0.7 grams per pound) of body weight per day. Once the body is accustomed to the demands of heavy exercise, protein requirements can usually be met by supplying

0.8–1.0 g/kg/day (0.4–0.5 g/lb/day). For a 70-kg (155-lb) person, this might be met by: 2 glasses of milk (8 g per 250 ml/1 cup) and two small servings of meat, poultry or fish (85 g each). The average diet provides protein in amounts that greatly exceed daily requirements. Inadequate protein intake is rarely a problem in our society. Even heavily training athletes can build muscle on the recommended protein intake as long as they also eat enough high energy (carbohydrate) foods. The excess nitrogen produced (by deaminating protein) must be excreted by the kidneys as urea, a process that requires much water. Hence an excessive protein intake may unduly burden the liver and kidneys.

Carbohydrates are good sport foods

Carbohydrates provide most of the energy for intense exercise. Much of the body's glucose is stored as glycogen, most in the liver, the rest in muscle. The supply of glucose from glycogen can be a limiting factor for long-distance or long-lasting athletic events. Any means to spare glycogen or increase its storage will help endurance athletes. When the glycogen is used up, the body switches to other less efficient mechanisms for obtaining glucose. Adequate glycogen stores depend on a diet plentiful in carbohydrates: 43 percent — the average Canadian carbohydrate intake — is too low for the physically active.

Are there merits to carbohydrate loading?

"Carbohydrate loading" has become popular among endurance competitors to increase glycogen stores. Experts emphasize that carbohydrate loading is useless for events less than 90 minutes in duration, as normal glycogen stores are sufficient to tide competitors over events lasting up to two hours. The loading process is also known as glycogen supercompensation, since it stimulates the liver to build up greater-than-normal glycogen reserves. These glycogen stores may delay marathoners from "hitting the wall" or cyclists from "bonking" (becoming confused and unable to continue). In its classic form, carbohydrate loading involves, first, a depletion bout for one day, in which the body's glycogen is used up by exercising to exhaustion;

this is followed by three days of a low-carbohydrate diet (consisting mainly of protein and fats); and concludes with three days of a carbohydrate-rich regime to supersaturate the muscles with glycogen. The strict carbohydrate loading scheme can bring discomfort to athletes. In the depletion phase, athletes accustomed to carbohydrate-rich diets frequently experience lethargy, irritability, nausea, dizziness and diarrhea, making it tough to keep on training. To overcome such problems, experts now suggest a less strenuous pre-event loading program without the depletion phase. If athletes simply reduce training somewhat for three to five days before the main event and simultaneously increase their carbohydrate intake to 70–80 percent of their total calories, they can build sufficient glycogen stores to carry them through a distance race.

SORTING OUT THE CHOLESTEROL PUZZLE

Health professionals are now pushing for more nutritional education, especially in order to lower fat intakes. Education is needed for both the public and their medical caregivers. Many health agencies now promote lower-fat diets for all of us, which would bring down blood cholesterol for the entire nation, rather than just for those whose intakes are too high. In contrast to U.S. health policies, which recommend cholesterol tests for *all* people over age 20, Canadian health agencies suggest screening only known high-risk groups.

The term "cholesterol" conjures up images of looming disaster even to those with little notion of what it is. The main reasons for the recent cholesterol scare are its link to coronary heart disease (CHD) and the fact that a high blood cholesterol level increases the risks of heart attacks. Elevated blood cholesterol is a known risk factor for atherosclerosis (artery hardening and blockage) and consequent heart disease. Studies have shown that atherosclerosis begins at younger ages and lower blood-cholesterol values than was previously assumed. Lowering the level of cholesterol in blood can save hearts. Studies by the U.S. National Heart, Lung and Blood Institute suggest that high blood cholesterol currently endangers one in four North American hearts. And more than half of Canadians over age 30 supposedly have blood cholesterols above the healthy upper limit of 5.2 millimoles per liter (mmol/l) or 200 milligrams per deciliter mg/dl (see table). However, not everyone with high blood cholesterol will develop heart disease, and, by the same token, some people with *low* blood cholesterol will have heart attacks. But many of us don't really know what "high cholesterol" means, nor can we distinguish between amounts in food and those in blood.

What exactly is cholesterol?

Cholesterol is a white waxy fat (lipid) that is a natural component of most body tissues and is found in the cells of all animals, birds and fish. It is a major constituent of cell membranes and nerve coatings and a building block for some hormones, certain vitamins and bile salts (which help to digest fat). It is found only in animal foods such as meat, eggs and dairy products. But although North Americans consume on average 400–500 mg per day, cholesterol is not a vital part of the diet; regardless of amounts eaten, the body manufactures ample quantities for its own use (mainly in the liver, at a rate around 1,000 mg of cholesterol per day).

Cholesterol is carried around the body in the blood, by special molecules, the lipoproteins — which include chylomicrons, very low-density lipoprotein (VLDL), low-density lipoprotein (LDL), high-density lipoprotein (HDL) and apolipoproteins, which also influence cholesterol levels. In general, VLDL transports triglycerides (fatty compounds that increase with the consumption of sugar and alcohol), while LDL (known as "bad" cholesterol) carries some cholesterol. LDL cholesterol is considered bad because it is taken up by large white blood cells (macrophages) and contributes to the development of heart disease. LDL cholesterol increases atherosclerosis — increased fatty deposits inside the arteries and crusty thickenings (plaque) inside the blood vessels. By contrast, HDL or "good" high-density lipoproteins help to protect against heart disease and stroke by taking cholesterol away from the arteries and delivering it to the liver, where it is converted into bile acids and excreted.

EQUIVALENT CHOLESTEROL NUMBERS

mmol/l	mg/dl	
0.9	35	
3.4	130	
4.1	160	considered "safe"
4.9	190	
5.2	200	
6.2	240	considered "high"

Cholesterol levels in blood are expressed as millimoles per liter (mmol/l) or milligrams per deciliter (mg/dl).

Although blood tests may show that someone has a high total blood cholesterol, an accurate heart-risk assessment can only be obtained by measuring the LDL level and calculating the HDL/LDL ratio through a full blood lipid (fat) analysis. Since cholesterol levels vary from day to day, a first "high" count may be unreliable. It takes several accurate blood tests to establish the real blood-cholesterol level.

Besides a high LDL cholesterol, several other features — some beyond one's control — influence heart-attack risks. For instance, being male and/or having diabetes, high blood pressure or the inherited disorder hyperlipidemia (a propensity to high blood fats) are risk factors that endanger the cardiovascular system. Self-inflicted activities that endanger the heart include smoking, obesity, lack of exercise and undue stress.

Many people wrongly assume that eating foods rich in cholesterol will invariably raise the cholesterol level in the blood. In some people, eating a cholesterol-rich diet *will* raise blood

NONLIPID RISK FACTORS FOR CORONARY HEART DISEASE AND HEART ATTACKS

Uncontrollable factors:

- male sex (just being a male)
- family history of premature heart disease
- diabetes mellitus
- genetic/inherited conditions that dramatically elevate blood lipid levels (e.g., hypercholesterolemia)

Controllable/modifiable factors:

- obesity (20 percent or more overweight); waist-to-hip ratio over 1.0 in men, over 0.8 in women
- cigarette smoking
- hypertension
- lack of exercise

FACTORS THAT RAISE LDL ("BAD") BLOOD CHOLESTEROL

- diseases such as hypothyroidism (underactive thyroid); some advanced liver and kidney ailments; ovarian failure;
- some inherited conditions such as hypercholesterolemia, where a genetic flaw

dramatically elevates blood cholesterol because faulty liver receptors can't remove it;
- certain drugs such as corticosteroids and vitamin A derivatives;
- poor dietary habits:

eating too much fat, generally overeating, drinking excess alcohol and consuming cholesterol-rich foods (in "responders," whose blood cholesterol rises in tune with amounts eaten).

levels, but not in others. And, while eating fewer eggs and less cream, liver and other cholesterol-rich foods may modestly lower blood cholesterol in some, the effect varies widely from person to person. "Responders," who react to diet changes, can dramatically lower their blood levels by eating less cholesterol. But "non-responders," whose blood cholesterol hardly varies with diet, find that lowering dietary intake has only a marginal influence. No matter how little cholesterol they eat, blood-cholesterol levels remain high in some people. More than dietary cholesterol, it is saturated or animal fat that drives up blood cholesterol. For example, the Finns and the Americans, who eat a lot of animal fats, have the highest national blood-cholesterol levels, while the Japanese, who eat more fish, have low blood-cholesterol levels. Reducing saturated fat intake is generally the best way to lower blood cholesterol rather than just avoiding cholesterol-rich foods.

So how much cholesterol is it safe to eat?

While some health authorities suggest precise limits to cholesterol intake, others oppose a "blanket rule," preferring to gear intake to a person's age, lifestyle, genetic background and individual needs. Many U.S. health agencies and the World Health Organization (WHO) suggest "restricting cholesterol intake to 250 g daily" with an "upper limit of 300 mg a day." The Canadian Heart and Stroke Foundation also suggests a limit of 300 mg per day for cholesterol intake. University of Toronto scientists estimate that reducing the average cholesterol intake from the present 500 mg per day to 300 mg might achieve no more than a modest 4 percent overall reduction in blood cholesterol.

The Canadian Scientific Review Committee for Health and Welfare Canada's Eating Guidelines set no precise limits for dietary cholesterol, suggesting only that people of all ages should "reduce consumption towards 300 mg or less" per day, provided infants and children get enough total calories and essential nutrients.

To test or not to test blood cholesterol?

Opinions vary about whether, when and whom to test for blood cholesterol. In Canada, widespread screening of people without symptoms of cardiovascular problems is suggested only for people with known coronary risk factors, such as:
- smoking;
- heart disease;
- relatives with high blood lipids (hyperlipidemia) — or relatives known to have had high blood pressure or early heart attack (a parent, brother or sister who's had a heart attack under age 50);
- other related disorders such as hypertension, diabetes, kidney failure or abdominal obesity.

How much blood cholesterol is "too high"?

Experts in the United States, Great Britain and Canada differ in their designation of "high blood cholesterol." There is no definitely known or fixed cholesterol level at which the heart is endangered, but instead a progressively rising risk with climbing levels of LDL cholesterol in blood. As LDL cholesterol goes up, so do the chances of having a heart attack or stroke. While a high LDL level doesn't necessarily spell disaster, it is a signal to take some action to bring down the risks. Experts set an arbitrary danger point for LDL readings at 160 mg/dl and over as "high risk." (Normal values are below 130 mg/dl.) Levels between 130–160 mg/dl are called "borderline risk." Individuals in the high LDL cholesterol bracket (160 mg/dl or higher) or those with one or more additional heart-risk factors should start cholesterol-lowering efforts, especially diet changes. Although it is the LDL fraction that threatens the heart, a consistently high total blood cholesterol may be a rough guide to heart risks.

To optimize the management of blood cholesterol, people can:

- ask their physician to check that the test is done by a reliable, preferably government-run laboratory with good equipment;
- avoid exercising strenuously before the cholesterol test;
- sit down for at least five minutes before the blood is drawn;
- avoid getting tested during or just after an illness;
- follow instructions about not eating for at least 12–14 hours before the test;
- request the exact reading, and if told that the result is high ask for a second, confirmatory test a month or two later (since levels fluctuate considerably). If the result still comes back high, check against the charts in this book or elsewhere to determine the probable risks. Then decide what to do about it;
- try to find out the HDL to LDL ratio. A high HDL may protect the heart, so there's little worry about a high total reading;
- adopt a lower-fat diet, even if told not to worry about a borderline reading;
- refrain from accepting cholesterol-lowering drugs to bring down levels before trying a cholesterol-lowering diet for several months.

High HDL ("helpful" or "good") blood cholesterol is no cause for worry

Total blood-cholesterol levels may be high because of an elevated HDL (good) cholesterol level — especially in those who are physically active and exercise a lot, and/or in those who consume their fats mainly in poly- or monounsaturated forms. A high HDL blood cholesterol is considered protection for the heart, perhaps even outweighing the detrimental effect of a high LDL level. In other words, a high HDL to LDL ratio exerts a heart-protecting influence. The HDL fraction often rises dramatically in athletes and those who do heavy physical work. The more the exercise, the higher the HDL — in general!

Restructuring diets to lower blood cholesterol is surprisingly easy

Dietary changes to lower blood cholesterol aren't necessarily a "big deal"; they can be achieved with small, commonsense alterations. Cutting back on saturated fats is a giant step. For starters, people can avoid all visible fat, switch from fatty, marbled cuts to leaner cuts, give up bacon and salami (obviously fat-laden), eat fish two or three times a week and use jam alone on bread instead of butter or margarine. They can buy low- or no-fat dairy products, omit cream soups, gravies, mayonnaise and potato chips and cut back on cheese — substitute cottage cheese and use yogurt instead of sour cream. Increasing the amount of soluble fiber eaten (especially oat bran, beans and other legumes) can also help to reduce blood cholesterol.

Do the "visibility" test. Look at the food on your dinner plate and try to see less meat or cheese amid a sea of vegetables and starchy foods. A little piece of meat should be nestled among attractive mounds of multicolored vegetables (peas, carrots, sprouts, tomatoes) and pasta, potatoes or rice. Some experts believe

---

NON-FAT FACTORS THAT MAY INFLUENCE BLOOD CHOLESTEROL

May lower blood-cholesterol levels:
- soluble fiber: from beans, oats, fruits and vegetables;
- polyunsaturated fats: help to lower LDL, or "bad," cholesterol. Safflower, sunflower, sesame and soybean oil are good sources;
- monounsaturated fat. Olive and canola oil are good sources;
- fatty ocean fish: certain deep-sea fish, such as mackerel, herring, salmon and tuna, contain special polyunsaturated fatty acids called omega-3s, which may lower blood cholesterol;
- aerobic exercise: although overall cholesterol remains the same, regular exercise helps increase HDL ("good") cholesterol.

May raise blood-cholesterol levels:
- excess weight: each 1 kg (2 lb) of excess weight adds, on average, one mg/dl to LDL blood cholesterol;
- foods high in saturated fat: more than any other factor, a diet high in saturated fat raises blood-cholesterol levels. Sources of saturated fat include beef, butter, whole-milk dairy products (especially cheeses), dark poultry meat, poultry skin and coconut, palm and palm-kernel oils;
- foods high in cholesterol: only animal products contain cholesterol. Eggs and organ meats are the richest sources;
- smoking: increases LDL ("bad") cholesterol and decreases HDL ("good") cholesterol.

BEWARE OF "CHOLESTEROL-FREE" LABELS

Scientists raise quizzical eyebrows at the "cholesterol-free" labels on foods that never contained any cholesterol in the first place. "Cholesterol-free" labeling has been aggressively used to market goods, and consumers should examine each claim individually. Read not just the claim but the "nutrition information" with the smaller print! Health and Welfare Canada stipulates that any low-cholesterol item must also be low in saturated fat, and the "low-cholesterol" or "cholesterol-free" label must also declare all types of fat in the product. Many cholesterol-free products (e.g., margarines) are prepared with hydrogenated vegetable oils, obliterating the benefits of the natural polyunsaturated oil. The hydrogenation process converts some polyunsaturated fats to trans fatty acids. For instance, the hydrogenation process used to stabilize vegetable oils, as in making peanut butter or margarine, not only adds hydrogen (making them more saturated) but also rearranges some of the natural chemical bonds to the unhealthy trans fatty acid form. Scientists have shown that trans fatty acids raise LDL ("bad") cholesterol in blood. Thus, food manufacturers who use hydrogenated forms of vegetable oils negate their health benefits. Processed foods containing trans fatty acids include pizza crusts, puddings, crackers, cookies, rolls, potato and corn chips, soft candy, breaded foods, french fries, frozen waffles and most margarines. Displaying the trans fatty acid content of foods on nutrition labels might help consumers make better-informed food decisions. For now, the thing to remember is to *eat less fat overall.*

that doubling the present average Canadian fiber intake (about 15–18 g a day) to a total of about 24–35 g daily, from widely varied sources, might substantially help to reduce blood cholesterol. Remember, however, that new eating habits are not emergency measures — they are a diet plan for life and it may take several months to notice much improvement.

Cholesterol-lowering drugs are a last resort

When high cholesterol levels do not respond to diet, drug therapy may be the solution. Three major drug trials have been done on middle-aged men presumed to be at cardiac risk because of high blood cholesterol. The WHO or Three Centre European Study of clofibrate, the LRC-Coronary Primary Prevention Trial (which combined a low-fat diet and the non-absorbable resin cholestyramine) and the Helsinki Heart Study (using gemfibrozil) showed that heart-attack deaths dropped when drug therapy was used to reduce blood-cholesterol levels. Unfortunately, all of the

DIETS FOR LOWERING CHOLESTEROL

Your guide to healthier eating:

- Variety and moderation are still the Golden Eating Rule — eat a wide variety of fresh foods, emphasizing those in season.
- Bring down fat intake to 30 percent or less of total calories.
- Limit saturated fats to no more than 10 percent of total calories by restricting or eliminating marbled meats, processed luncheon meats, cold cuts, cream, butter, baked goods, sauces, salad dressings and processed products made with animal fat or saturated (hydrogenated) vegetable oils (mainly palm and coconut oils).
- Choose polyunsaturated oils such as safflower, sunflower, corn, soya, walnut oils (with an upper limit of 10 percent of all fat eaten), and balance with monounsaturates (olive, canola, avocado, flax, peanut oils). A ceiling of 8 to 10 percent polyunsaturates in the diet is recommended because animal experiments suggest that eating a higher proportion of polyunsaturates could increase the risk of certain cancers.
- Use soft margarines (containing 40 to 55 percent unsaturates — preferably *nonhydrogenated*), instead of butter or block-style margarines. Watch the labels!
- When choosing margarine, select one with the maximum amount of *nonhydrogenated* (polyunsaturated) and least hydrogenated fatty acids. Watch for trans fatty acids that raise LDL (bad) cholesterol. (Calculate the amount of trans by adding up the saturated, mono- and polyunsaturated fatty

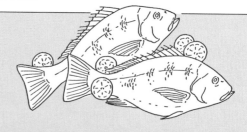

acids and subtracting from the total declared fat.)

- Make sauces with skim, not whole, milk; use yogurt instead of cream, and low-fat rather than whole-milk cheese.
- Read the labels on processed foods, particularly desserts, dressings and sauces. Desserts often contain vast amounts of concealed fat.
- Steam, poach, bake or broil instead of frying.
- Substitute fish or poultry for animal meats.
- Switch to low-fat salad dressings, or favor olive oil and plain lemon types.
- Make soups and stocks a day ahead and refrigerate, so hardened fat can be lifted off before serving.
- Eat more complex carbohydrates from fruits, vegetables and cereal grains.
- Eat fish (particularly cold-water oceanic types) two to three times weekly.
- Consume only one alcoholic drink or less per day.
- Avoid buying snacks (chips, peanuts, cookies) ahead "in case of company"; if you don't have them, you'll be less tempted!

studies also found that overall mortality did not decrease, since deaths from other causes, particularly violence and trauma, rose — the reasons for the rise have not yet been discovered. Several cholesterol-lowering drugs are available, some with considerable side effects. No completely safe, satisfactory, long-term cholesterol-lowering drug has yet been found. For this reason most physicians advise cholesterol-lowering medication only after people have tried for at least six months to get cholesterol down by diet and lifestyle changes. Anyone who does take drugs to lower blood cholesterol must be carefully monitored and should still consume a low-fat diet.

CHOOSING THE RIGHT FAT MIX

Fats — or lipids, to use the scientific term — are molecules made of a glycerol backbone with different fatty acids appended.

Depending on the types of fatty acids they contain, fats are saturated (completely hydrogenated) or unsaturated (not fully hydrogenated). Saturated fats are mainly of animal origin (butter, bacon fat), but also include tropical oils such as palm and coconut oils. Saturated fats tend to raise the levels of heart-harming LDL cholesterol and triglycerides in the blood. Polyunsaturated fats (only slightly hydrogenated) are mostly fish and vegetable oils such as corn, safflower, walnut or sunflower oil, and help to lower blood cholesterol and improve its HDL/LDL ratio — the balance of good cholesterol to bad. Monounsaturated fats such as olive oil, avocado, flax and canola (rapeseed) oils have no effect on LDL blood-cholesterol levels.

North Americans on the whole eat diets that are overloaded with saturated fats from meats, dairy products and baked goods. Hidden fats in muffins, salad dressings, soups and cheeses are a special danger as they're not as visible as bacon fat, cream or butter. People may unsuspectingly get too much saturated fat from items such as potato chips, packaged dishes, refried beans, crackers, granola cereals baked in tropical oils, crackers and cakes. Fried foods are a notorious source of saturated fat because they absorb large amounts of frying oil. Repeatedly deep frying food even in vegetable oils can trigger transformation to the trans fatty acid

CHOLESTEROL AND FAT CONTENTS
(per 90 g/3 oz, unless otherwise specified)

	Cholesterol (mg)	Total fat (g/oz)	Saturated fat (g)	Calories
Egg yolk (one large)	221	5.3	1.6	61
Cheddar cheese	92	30.0	18.0	362
Peanut butter (15 ml/1 tbsp)	0	8.0	1.5	95
Tofu/bean curd	0	4.1	0.6	65
Whipping cream (32% fat, unwhipped, 1 cup/250 ml)	290	79.0	50.0	743
Milk (2%, 250 ml/1 cup)	19	5.0	3.0	124
Butter (15 ml/1 tbsp)	32	12.0	7.0	103
Real mayonnaise (per 15 ml/1 tbsp, 65% oil)	9	12.0	1.0	112
Mayonnaise (less than 35% oil per 15 ml/1 tbsp)	4	7.3	0.5	74
Liver (calves, braised)	502	6.2	2.3	148
Liver (beef, broiled)	350	4.4	2.0	150
Fish/Seafood				
Crab (Alaskan, steamed)	48	1.0	trace	85
Steamed clams	29	3.0	0.4	90
Sole (broiled)	61	1.4	0.3	105
Cod (baked)	50	0.8	0.1	95
Trout (broiled)	66	3.9	0.6	136
Lobster (canned)	65	0.5	0	87
Shrimp (steamed)	176	1.0	0.3	90
Oysters (raw)	45	2.0	0.5	59
Tuna (light, canned, in water)	16	0.5	trace	112
Tuna (canned, in oil)	16	7.0	1.3	178
Salmon (pink, canned)	21	6.7	1.5	122
Meats & Poultry				
Beef (lean, roasted)	81	8.0	3.2	192
Veal (lean, roasted)	106	6.0	1.7	176
Pork (lean, roasted)	59	10.0	3.4	200
Lamb (leg, roasted)	78	7.0	2.3	162
Wiener, hot dog (one)	19	11.0	4.0	118
Fresh pork sausage	72	30.0	10.0	330
Chicken (with skin, roasted, light & dark meat)	75	12.2	3.4	219
Chicken breast (no skin, roasted)	70	3.0	0.9	149
Chicken (leg/thigh, no skin)	85	7.6	2.1	172
Duck (with skin)	72	24.3	8.5	303

N.B.: These are not necessarily standard serving sizes but used for comparison. Figures from Health and Welfare Canada's Nutrient File for 1991.

forms, producing as many unhealthy compounds as frying in saturated fats. Trans fatty acids act like saturated fats, also raising "bad" or LDL cholesterol in blood. Tropical oils such as palm oil (only 50 percent saturated) are more stable at high temperatures and may be a healthier alternative for frying than hydrogenated vegetable oils. (Coconut oil, although it is 90 percent saturated, may be healthier than hydrogenated vegetable oil for high-temperature cooking.)

For a healthy dietary fat consumption, scientists suggest that polyunsaturate intakes should not exceed 10 percent of the fats we eat, that the monounsaturate quota should be 10 to 12 percent, with the balance being saturated types. But these are just guidelines, as more research is needed to establish the exact health-promoting capacities of the different fatty acids in the fats we eat.

The omega-6 polyunsaturated fatty acids found in corn, safflower, sunflower, walnut (and some other nut) oils are essential nutrients and have cholesterol-lowering potential. The omega-3 polyunsaturated series from some oceanic fish and certain vegetable oils (e.g., canola, flax seed and soya) don't reduce cholesterol but bring down blood triglycerides and may prevent coronary artery disease by diminishing the blood's clotting ability and making its platelets (tiny clotting particles) less "sticky." But since the benefits of omega-3s are not fully established, more research is needed.

Monounsaturated fatty acids (mainly the omega-9 oleic acid type) found in olive, canola (rapeseed) and flax oils have not been shown to reduce LDL cholesterol and triglycerides in blood. The low heart-attack rate of some Mediterranean peoples (e.g., Italians and Greeks) who eat diets rich in olive oil has highlighted the heart-protecting benefits of monounsaturates. While neutral in their effect on blood cholesterol, monounsaturates are a good replacement for saturated fats. We should therefore eat monounsaturates such as canola, nut and olive oils as part of our daily fat quota, to help reduce blood-clotting risks. However, while olive oil, the only natural, stable, cold-pressed oil (which also contains its own antioxidant), is known to protect the blood vessels, other monounsaturates have yet to prove their heart-saving value.

SORTING OUT THE FAT FACTS

Saturated
Form: Usually solid at room temperature*
Sources: Butter, lard, vegetable shortening, coconut oil, palm oil, palm-kernel oil, hydrogenated margarines, meat, poultry, cheese, dairy products, egg yolks, chocolate

Monounsaturated
Form: Liquid at room temperature
Sources: Olive, canola, avocado oils

Polyunsaturated
Form: Liquid at room temperature
Sources: Safflower, sunflower, corn, soybean and walnut oils

THE FASCINATION OF FIBER

Under the less fashionable name of "roughage," fiber enjoyed a high level of respect among our grandparents. But its currently trendy image stems primarily from the writings of British physician Dennis Burkitt, who practiced for many years in rural Africa and noted that ailments such as gallstones, appendicitis, hernia, hemorrhoids, diabetes, diverticulitis, ulcers, varicose veins, heart disease and bowel cancer were extremely rare in that area. He became convinced that these diseases were rare because Native diets were rich in whole grains, seeds, root vegetables and nuts, and that the high incidence of bowel disorders in Western countries stemmed from the lack of fiber in modern diets. His theories were enthusiastically adopted in the 1970s as "the Bran Hypothesis." However, many scientists feel there is inadequate scientific backup for his fiber theory, since different types of fiber confer different benefits. Whatever the truth of Burkitt's observations, a spoonful of bran a day is certainly no cure for the many digestive ailments of the Western world.

What is fiber?
Traditionally, fiber was considered to be an inert part of food, passing undigested from mouth to anus and expelled intact in the stool. This view has now been amended. Fiber consists of many different substances, some of which are digested by bacteria in the bowel to form fatty acids, water and gases. The term "fiber" encompasses not just cellulose and woody plant lignins, but also pectins and various gums (guar, arabic, agar, carrageen) and psyllium. Fibers vary in their effects on the body; wheat bran, for instance, is a good stool-softener but a poor absorber of cholesterol, a function that oat bran does better.

Insoluble fiber is like a sponge that absorbs many times its weight in water, swelling up within the intestine. Insoluble fiber is found mainly in whole grains and, in the form of cellulose and lignin, on the outside of seeds, fruits, legumes and other foods. Wheat bran, which is mostly cellulose, is the outer layer of wheat grain. Being the chewiest part of food, the outer layer is often removed in food processing by milling, peeling, boiling or extracting. Hence it is wise to eat more unrefined foods to obtain insoluble fiber. High-fiber diets have now replaced former bland, mild low-residue treatments for those with bowel problems such as diverticular disease (small outpouchings of the large intestine).

Soluble fiber — which includes pectin, gums and some hemicellulose — is found in fruits, vegetables, legumes (peas, beans, lentils), some seeds, brown rice, barley, oats and oat bran. It also softens stool, but less so than insoluble forms. There is some evidence that the soluble fiber in oat bran, legumes, fruits (such as apples) and root vegetables (such as carrots) may reduce heart-disease risks by reducing the absorption of certain substances such as cholesterol into the bloodstream, thus lowering blood cholesterol. It binds bile acids, forcing the body to manufacture more from cholesterol. Soluble fiber such as guar (in dried beans of all kinds and pectins from fruit) also retards the entry of glucose into the bloodstream, which is especially useful for diabetics.

Increased fiber from varied plant foods may help to combat:

- *Constipation.* The most undisputed advantage of insoluble fiber is its ability to combat constipation by softening and expanding stool volume, leading to faster, easier and more frequent elimination. Commercial preparations such as agar (Agarol) and psyllium (Metamucil) are effective stool bulkers.
- *Diverticular bowel disease.* Fiber from whole grains such as wheat bran speeds stool transit and prevents constipation.
- *Hyperlipidemia.* Excess blood fats are possibly reduced by soluble fiber such as pectin, bean and oat gums, and the types in legumes (lentils, chick peas, navy, pinto or kidney beans).
- *Diabetes.* Soluble fiber from legumes, barley and oats can improve blood-sugar control and lower serum cholesterol in diabetics, and may lessen insulin requirements in some juvenile diabetics.

How much fiber?

Consult a physician before greatly increasing dietary fiber intake. Initially, eating large quanti-

---

SOME COMMON SOURCES OF DIETARY FIBER

Fiber source	Total g fiber per 100 g serving	Fiber source	Total g Fiber per 100 g serving
Cereals		*Fruits*	
Raw Miller's wheat bran	44.0	Pears	2.4
All Bran	26.7	Peaches	2.3
Puffed Wheat	16.2	Strawberries	2.1
Shredded Wheat	12.2	Bananas	1.8
Cornflakes	11.0	Apples	1.4
Special K	5.4	Cherries	1.2
Rice Krispies	4.5		
		Nuts	
Breads		Peanuts	9.3
Whole wheat (per slice)	8.5	Brazil nuts	7.7
White (per slice)	2.8		
Vegetables		**Sample content of a diet with**	
Peas	7.8	**20–26 g fiber per day**	
Baked Beans	7.2	4 tbsp of bran with milk	8.4 g
Carrots	3.7	1 slice of whole-wheat toast	8.5 g
Potatoes	3.2	one 50 g serving of peas or beans	3.9 g
Onions	2.1	one 100 g serving of peaches	2.3 g
Tomatoes	1.4	**Total**	**23.1 g**

---

ties of fiber may cause bloating, but this should subside in a few weeks. It is best to gradually increase amounts to the recommended level. Disorders such as ulcerative colitis, kidney disease and some symptoms of pregnancy may be aggravated by too much fiber. Large quantities of fruit containing pectin may decrease vitamin B_{12} absorption and bind some essential minerals, thus lowering blood levels of zinc, iron, calcium and other trace elements. Ensure a balanced intake and good nutritional status before making drastic alterations in your fiber consumption.

Advocates of a high-fiber diet suggest 26–35 g daily from well-varied plant sources (see fiber content chart). The current average Canadian fiber intake is 14.5 g a day, but Health and Welfare Canada suggests that Canadians should virtually double this, because of a wide range of physiological benefits. Try eating ample grains, and more unpeeled but well-washed fruit and vegetables. Be sure to include both *insoluble* fiber (in wheat bran) and *soluble* types (as in oats, legumes and root vegetables).

MAKE CARBOHYDRATES (STARCHES) YOUR DIETARY MAINSTAY

Simple carbohydrates or sugars (such as glucose, sucrose and fructose) are small molecules which we eat as refined products. They are good "pure" energy sources but provide few other nutrients. By contrast, complex carbohydrates are large molecules made up of simpler sugars that come in a vast range of foods — from potatoes, pears and pasta to cabbages, bread and popcorn — which usually provide other nutrients besides energy. For instance, 15 ml (1 tbsp) of sugar or an average soft drink provides about 50 calories, similar to one slice of wholegrain bread. But the complex carbohydrates in bread come with additional nutrients such as B vitamins, zinc, iron, calcium and valuable fiber. Although dieters trying to shed pounds traditionally considered potatoes, pasta and other carbohydrates fattening, cutting them out has been shown to work against weight loss. Carbohydrates must be included in reducing regimes for effective weight loss. In fact, carbohydrates have fewer calories per gram than fat (four per gram compared to nine per gram of fat), so that a baked potato will provide fewer calories than a piece of cheese, a burger or hot dog.

In fact, carbohydrates are less likely to be converted to body fat than dietary protein or fat, and they also have a beneficial effect on the microflora (bacterial inhabitants) of the human gut. Populations that consume a high-carbohydrate diet have lower rates of several chronic diseases, such as cancer and cardiovascular disorders.

SUGARS AREN'T ALL BAD

In recent years, sugar — known to most of us as table sugar or sucrose — has not only been accused of increasing tooth decay but has also been blamed for obesity, diabetes, hypoglycemia, depression, an alleged "Halloween effect" (obstreperous behavior following the ingestion of sweet treats), aggression and even crime and delinquency. But these claims are based largely on exaggerated reports, anecdotal information and poorly controlled studies. Rigorous scientific scrutiny shows that many of the accusations are false, and that there is no demonstrable link between sugar and most of the disorders that self-designated health experts claim for it.

Sugar is slowly gaining a better image. One University of Toronto nutrition expert explains that "the perception of sugar as a health risk is at odds with the latest scientific knowledge. Despite fears of detrimental health effects and the blame heaped on it for many disorders, average sugar consumption in Canada — at 10–12 percent of total energy — remains within safe limits."

The only valid argument against the prudent consumption of sugar is its detrimental effect on human teeth. Sugar is no more fattening than other foods, despite the widespread belief that it causes obesity. Although sugar is often blamed for the weight gained from desserts and candy, it is the fat in them rather than the sugar that's the culprit.

Tests show that sugar is *not* a proven cause of hypoglycemia, which is defined as low blood sugar and is signaled by sweating, shakiness, drowsiness and weakness lasting a few minutes to an hour. Hypoglycemic symptoms vanish soon after ingesting some sugar or injecting glucose, and this prompt relief by eating sugar distinguishes *true* hypoglycemia from conditions such as panic reactions, neurosis and anxiety. Hypoglycemia is a rare condition; contrary to the popular view that it's reaching epidemic proportions, it hardly ever occurs in response to foods eaten by healthy people. Moreover, even in the rare cases that it does occur, hypoglycemia is a sudden, debilitating condition, not the chronic lack of vigor it's rumored to be. Many physicians call sugar-induced hypoglycemia a "nondisease." Scientific evidence just doesn't support the notion that sugar causes hypoglycemia, except in extraordinary circumstances, such as ingesting vast amounts on an empty stomach together with alcohol. (Alcohol *does* cause hypoglycemia.)

Well-controlled studies demonstrate that, rather than triggering irritability, restlessness or aggression, sugar tends to be calming, possibly due to an increase in the brain transmitter serotonin, which is known to have a sedating effect. The U.S. National Institutes of Mental Health

SORTING OUT THE VARIOUS SUGARS

There are many different sugars with fancy names such as fructose, galactose (in human mother's milk), lactose (in cow's milk), maltose and glucose. Sucrose or table sugar is a molecule composed of two smaller sugar molecules strung together. It is made from sugar beet or sugar cane. Basically sugars are similar; they vary somewhat in sweetness and chemical makeup, but no one type is healthier than another.

Chemically, sugars fall into three main groups:
• monosaccharides, simple sugars such as fructose or glucose found in honey, fruits, vegetables, syrups and lactose;
• disaccharides, a chain of two simple sugars linked together — as in sucrose (table sugar);
• polysaccharides, made of many simple sugars strung together — such as starch or glycogen (energy-storage molecules).

Glucose is the form in which the body's cells use sugar for energy. Glucose is stored in the liver and muscles as glycogen and released as needed. Different foods have different effects on the rise in blood sugar that follows eating. Insulin, from the pancreas, is released in response to this sugar rise, and speeds up the absorption of glucose from the blood by the body's cells. A baked potato or white bread elevates blood sugar more than rice or corn. Legumes (peas, beans, lentils) tend to flatten the rise in blood glucose after eating owing to their soluble fiber content — an advantage for those with diabetes who want to prevent large blood-sugar swings.

tested 21 children whose behavior was said to be worsened by sugar. These children actually became less active after eating sugar compared to those taking saccharin, even in amounts equivalent to four candy bars, two ice creams or 680 ml (24 oz) of pop. Similarly, a comparison of mood changes in people taking sugar, saccharin or water found no noticeable effect after 20 minutes, but four hours later those who took sugar were less irritable than those who had had water or saccharin. In an Ottawa study, parents could not guess whether their child had been given sugar, saccharin or no sweetener during the test period. Another study found decreased activity in children receiving sucrose, compared to those on a placebo (sugar substitutes). Overall, the evidence suggests that sugar does not produce irritable behavior and that, if anything, it exerts a mildly quieting effect. No reliable studies have found that sugar causes disruptive behavior. The combined results give no support whatever to the claim that sugar worsens childhood behavior.

PROTEINS IN THE DIET

The term "protein" comes from the Greek word proteios, meaning "of first importance." Protein makes up one-fifth of the adult human weight and is the basic material of life. Muscles, hair, cartilage, skin, antibodies, some hormones and enzymes (catalysts that speed up chemical reactions in cells) are all proteins.

A protein is a chain of amino acids that can form many different configurations — like a chain of beads — and can combine with other substances. Slight differences in the amino-acid makeup and sequence of the various proteins in our bodies — in our blood, muscle and other proteins — distinguish us from one another and make us what we are. The possible amino-acid arrangements are almost infinite, and thousands of different proteins have already been identified in living creatures. Proteins are constantly broken down in our bodies, and continually built up again and replaced. Without dietary protein, growth and other bodily functions would not occur.

While plants and some bacteria can manufacture all the amino acids they need, the human body can manufacture only 13 of the 22 needed. The amino acids our bodies can manufacture are termed nonessential, while the nine we can't make must come from food,

PUTTING ENOUGH BALANCED PROTEIN INTO A MEAL

Combination	Amount	Grams of protein
Peanut butter	45 ml (3 tbsp)	12.0
Whole-wheat bread	2 slices	5.2
Lentils	250 ml (1 cup)	15.6
Brown rice	125 ml (½ cup)	2.5
Pasta (e.g., macaroni)	250 ml (1 cup)	6.5
Cheddar cheese	40 g	10.5
Whole-grain bread (or roll)	1 slice (or 1 roll)	2.2
Kasha (groats)	250 ml (1 cup)	8.0
Egg	1	6.5
Potato (baked)	1 medium	4.0
Oats (oatmeal)	250 ml (1 cup)	4.8
Skim milk	250 ml (1 cup)	9.0
Whole-wheat toast	2 slices	5.2

and are termed essential amino acids (EAAs). They are histidine, isoleucine, leucine, lysine, methionine, phenylalanine, threonine, tryptophan and valine.

Protein in food is broken down by the digestive system into its constituent amino acids, which enter the body's pool of amino acids and can be reassembled into vital body substances such as the hormone insulin, the muscle protein myoglobin, the keratin in hair, the respiratory enzymes and countless others. Each cell manufactures the proteins it needs using the building blocks available. If, however, one or more of the essential amino acids is lacking, others that may be present cannot replace them in forming crucial body proteins.

IN PRAISE OF FISH

A ration of fish or fish oil two or three times weekly may help to prevent high blood pressure and heart disease. Fish oils are also promoted to help prevent some cancers. Omega-3 fatty acids in the fish oils from deep-sea fish may benefit migraine sufferers by altering the release of the brain transmitter serotonin. They may also help arthritics and asthmatics by inhibiting leukotriene formation, which promotes inflammation and some immune dysfunctions common to these disorders. Paradoxically, the types of fish that nutritionists used to brand as "less healthful" because of their high fat contents are the very ones that contain the desirable polyunsaturated, omega-3 fatty acids now believed to have therapeutic advantages.

The protective effect of fish oils on the cardiovascular system stems from two particular omega-3 fatty acids — eicosapentanoic acid (EPA) and docosahexanoic acid (DHA) — obtainable from deep-sea fish. A diet high in omega-3s produces cells and tissues rich in compounds that alter blood platelet behavior and reduce the blood's clotting ability. Fish-eaters have far lower than average levels of blood triglycerides and somewhat less VLDL ("bad") cholesterol than meat eaters. Researchers conclude that eating one or two fish dishes a week or supplementing Western diets with certain fish oils can reduce the incidence of heart disease.

The benefits of fish oil in lowering heart-disease risks depend on the reduction in blood-clotting due to alterations in the metabolism of prostaglandins and allied compounds which play a key role in blood clotting, and the inhibition of blood-platelet stickiness or aggregation. The blood platelets encourage tiny particles to stick together along the artery walls — an early event in atherosclerosis. Consuming deep-sea fish rich in omega-3s can diminish the ability of the blood platelets to produce blood clots. Fish oils may have further effects that reduce platelet clumping, but more studies are needed to show whether enriching the average Canadian diet with omega-3s can really reduce the risk of heart disease.

Seal meat, as well as fish such as salmon, bluefish, herring, mullet and scad, which inhabit deep, cold waters, tend to have the greatest benefits. Certain shellfish such as conch, oysters and clams also have fair amounts of omega-3s. These shellfish are not — as was once believed because of imprecise measurements — particularly high in cholesterol.

Common sense suggests adherence to the advice of nutritionists, who have for years recommended the substitution of fish for meat at least twice a week as part of a balanced diet.

VEGETARIAN DIETS

Previously regarded as fads, vegetarian diets have recently gained popularity. Plant foods may offset the risk of certain diseases such as heart ailments and cancer. Many cancer, heart, diabetes and other health agencies now recommend a higher consumption of varied plant foods.

Studies show that vegetarians tend to eat less saturated fat and cholesterol and more polyunsaturated fats than the average meat-eater, although those consuming eggs, milk and cheese may still eat lots of saturated fat! A vegetarian diet rich in whole-milk products such as cheese is high in saturated fats and could endanger the heart. The Canadian Dietetic Association defines a "prudent" diet — one that offers optimal protection against a variety of diseases — as largely vegetarian, low in fat, with generous and varied quantities of plant foods. Whole grains, legumes, fruits and vegetables may provide several potentially health-

protecting substances: fiber; carotene (a precursor of vitamin A which may protect against
cancer); vitamins C and E; enzyme inhibitors;
and selenium.

Vegetarians differ
The term "vegetarianism" encompasses:
- semi-vegetarians, who eat some fish or
seafood, eggs and dairy products; they mimic
the diets of many traditional cultures which
use animal products as condiments rather
than as main dishes;
- lacto-ovo vegetarians, who eat eggs and
dairy products but no meat, poultry or
seafood;
- lacto-vegetarians, who consume dairy products but exclude eggs, meat, poultry and
seafood;
- pure (vegan) vegetarians, who exclude all
foods of animal origin.

Vegetarianism requires careful planning
Healthy vegetarianism entails more than the
haphazard avoidance of animal foods. The
body's cells don't distinguish between the
sources of nutrients, provided they arrive in
ample supply. However, getting the right nutrients in the right amounts from plants requires
more forethought than obtaining them from
animal products. A vegetarian diet, with or
without eggs and/or milk, can still provide all
essential nutrients. With a good cookbook and
the advice of a qualified dietitian, even very
strict vegetarians can produce healthy meals.
But nutritional problems are less likely with vegetarian diets that include eggs and milk. While
most essential food elements can be found in
plant foods, those on extreme vegan diets may
be short on high-quality (complete) protein,
vitamins B_{12} and D (especially when there is
little sunlight available), calcium, iron and iodine,
especially if legumes, dried fruits and iodized
salt aren't consumed.

Meeting complete protein needs is crucial
Although we talk about "eating" protein, it's
really the amino-acid components in proteins
that the body needs as building blocks. During
digestion, we break up animal and plant protein
into its constituent amino acids, which our cells

SOME TIPS TO HELP VEGETARIANS
- **Learn good mixes for complete protein:**
  - Legumes/leafy vege-tables plus cereals;
  - Soybeans plus grains (wheat, corn, rice, rye);
  - Soy/sesame produce (e.g., tofu) plus low-fat milk;
  - Nuts plus wheat, oats, corn, rice or coconut.
- **Eat some fruit and** vegetables raw, as cooking destroys some vitamin C.
- **Be vigilant about key minerals,** especially iron and calcium, which are often poorly absorbed from many vegetable foods and can be carried out of the body bound to plant phytates and oxalates.

For vegans: foods that supply the best nutrient value include fortified (check the label) soy milk; soybean products; legumes; hummus (chick peas plus sesame); green leafy vege-tables (collards, kale, turnip greens, brussels sprouts, cauliflower, spinach, cabbage, broccoli) and fruits.

---

reassemble into human proteins (e.g., hemoglobin, keratin, muscle-myoglobin, insulin) for
normal function and repair. The problem for
vegetarians (especially vegans) is not only
getting enough amino acids but getting the right
kind in the right proportion — especially of the
nine essential amino acids (EAAs) that the body
can't manufacture for itself. If even one of the
nine is low or absent, it can halt the manufacture of a vital body component, such as a particular enzyme or hormone. In contrast to most
animal foods, plants contain essential amino
acids in ratios different from those the body
requires. In other words, while eggs, milk, meat
and some fish contain "complete" protein (the
appropriate ratio and pattern of EAAs), many
plant foods lack one or more EAAs and thus
supply "incomplete" protein.

To obtain complete protein from entirely
vegetarian fare, people must combine two or
more plant proteins, preferably at each meal, e.g.,
grains with legumes, soybeans with cereals, peas
with rice, nuts with noodles, peanut butter with
whole-wheat bread, corn tortillas with beans.
Grains are low in the amino acid lysine, but combined with legumes (peas, beans), which are rich
in this amino acid, they can provide the right
quota. Soybeans, which lack methionine, combined with cereals such as rice or corn, high in
methionine, can provide complete protein.
Other good combinations for high-value protein
are nuts with noodles and peanut butter with
whole-wheat bread. Legumes such as dried
beans — pinto, kidney, garbanzo or any other —
and lentils provide protein of high biological
quality. Adding low-fat milk to cereals or legumes
will usually complete the protein value.

In practice, many traditional cultures have achieved a well-balanced protein intake. In India, for example, vegetarians stay healthy on a diet rich in lentils (dahl), chick-peas and rice. Many East Indians use animal products as just a small addition or appetizing condiment, not as a main dish. The Chinese use animal or fish products as a minor addition to beansprout, mixed vegetable, noodle, rice or soy curd dishes. Mexican corn tortillas filled with beans, Middle Eastern hummus and falafel, South American and Mexican tacos with beans and the North American peanut-butter sandwich all provide excellent complete protein.

THE CAFFEINE STORY

Throughout history, humans have ingested caffeine for either a mood lift or medicinal purposes. In earliest times it was obtained by chewing coffee plant leaves, and later by brewing them as a hot beverage. Tea was the first hot caffeinated beverage consumed, a popular drink in China some 1,600 years ago, later spreading to Japan and ultimately to Europe. Since then coffee has become one of the world's most popular drinks. Although the United States consumes three-quarters of the world's coffee beans, Canadians have a higher per-capita coffee intake. Most North Americans also ingest considerable quantities of caffeine from cola drinks and chocolate. In Canada about 60 percent of the caffeine consumed comes from coffee, another 30 percent from tea and the remainder from chocolate, soft drinks and certain medications (such as painkillers, diuretics, antihistamines and cold remedies).

On average, Canadians consume two to three cups of coffee daily, two cups of tea and a 140 ml (5 oz) serving of cola drink, which translates to an average daily caffeine intake of 230–290 mg. The intake of decaffeinated coffee, teas and colas is rising in line with escalating health concerns about caffeine. Among the young, who prefer cola drinks and herbal teas, coffee use has dramatically declined.

The current arguments over the safety of caffeine revolve around its possible contribution to heart disease, osteoporosis, cancer, birth defects, sleep disorders, stomach ulcers and nervous ailments. The 1990 Federal

Canadian Eating Guidelines advise us to "consume no more caffeine than that equivalent to four regular cups of coffee per day because of its possible link to heart disease." One University of Toronto expert, while agreeing that "it's wise to curb excessive intakes," calls the suggested restriction to four cups of coffee a day "needlessly restrictive." The federal recommendation is based on controversial evidence that coffee drinking (but not specifically caffeine) may increase coronary-heart-disease risks. Since differently brewed coffees contain varying amounts of caffeine, it's inappropriate to measure the possible health dangers in terms of cups. The amount of caffeine in coffee varies from about 65–75 mg per percolated cup (170 ml or 6 oz), to 110–180 mg in a cup of filtered coffee and 60–90 mg per cup of instant. The amount in a cup of tea ranges from 30 to 100 mg caffeine per cup and colas average 25 mg per 280 ml (10 oz) can.

How caffeine affects the body

People differ widely in their response to caffeine. In most, it enhances mental alertness. Doses of 50–200 mg (one or two cups of coffee) increase alertness and decrease drowsiness. Doses above 500 mg may produce symptoms formerly known as "caffeinism" — headaches, tremors, nervousness and irritability — in some people. While some can consume three cups of coffee plus a chocolate bar in short order with no ill effects, others feel edgy after a single cup. However, few people drink enough coffee to make themselves jittery. And everyone must individually decide whether the benefits outweigh the possible risks.

Caffeine is rapidly absorbed from the intestines, peaking in the blood after about 30 minutes, and being distributed to all tissues of the body. The speed of caffeine absorption is slower when the stomach is full. Smokers tend to metabolize caffeine much faster than nonsmokers, but they also drink more coffee — perhaps to compensate for the increased metabolism. Various other drugs, for example alcohol and cimetidine (used to treat stomach ulcers), reduce the rate of caffeine breakdown; oral contraceptives more than double the time caffeine remains in the body. Some of the variability in caffeine uptake may be inherited. Orientals, for example, appear to metabolize caffeine far more slowly than Caucasians.

Like many mood-altering substances, caffeine can be habit-forming, and the habit may lead to overconsumption. To determine whether you are dependent, simply eliminate all caffeine sources from the diet for one day. If a throbbing headache results — relieved only by a caffeine "fix" — chances are that you are suffering caffeine withdrawal.

The bottom line on caffeine

One University of Toronto expert sums it up this way: "Considering the conflicting results and smoking as a confounding variable, caffeine does not seem to cause heart rhythm disturbances nor does its long-term use raise blood pressure. There is currently inadequate evidence to link coffee or caffeine to increased risks of coronary heart disease." Moderate coffee intakes — to an upper limit of six cups a day (assuming 70–100 mg per cup) — do not seem to endanger health. Like so many lifestyle issues, sensible decisions depend on reliable information. Authorities cautiously state that, provided it's used in moderation, caffeine poses no health risk to most Canadians. However, people who consume over 650 mg daily — equivalent to six or more cups of coffee — can do themselves a favor by cutting back.

VITAMINS: MOST PEOPLE DON'T NEED SUPPLEMENTS

The easy availability of over-the-counter vitamins and the popular view of them as "natural" wonder foods able to ward off disease has made megavitamin therapy popular. Many Canadians take supplemental vitamins, occasionally in amounts 10, 50 even 250 times the recommended daily intake, often without professional advice. Although megavitamin proponents claim benefits for conditions as diverse as wound healing, poor sexual performance, premenstrual discomfort, stress and depression, no firm scientific evidence supports their claims.

What are vitamins?

Vitamins are organic chemicals that are essential to human life. They include 13 substances and some "hangers-on" classed with them (choline, folic acid, inositol, biotin) which help the body transform food into energy, aid the immune defenses, promote good eyesight, contribute to blood and tooth formation and assist many other body functions. Some vitamins (A, D, E, K) are fat-soluble and the rest (the eight different Bs and C) dissolve in water. If one or other of the vitamins is in short supply or absent, deficiency diseases may occur — such as blindness due to a lack of vitamin A, or skin problems due to B-vitamin shortages. The beneficial effect of a vitamin in preventing disease was first shown in 1753 when a Scottish surgeon proved that giving sailors daily oranges or lemons could prevent scurvy on long sea voyages. The antiscorbutic factor was later shown to be ascorbic acid — now known as vitamin C. The last vitamin to be isolated was vitamin B_{12}, in 1948.

Each vitamin performs specific tasks in the body. Vitamin A (from liver, eggs, orange and yellow fruit and vegetables) promotes vision and skin health; vitamin D (from fish, fortified milk) is vital to bone and tooth strength; vitamin C (from citrus fruits, berries, green peppers) ensures healthy skin and gums and aids wound healing; vitamin E (from nuts, vegetable oils, olives, grains) is an antioxidant that protects the body's cells against damage by oxidation; vitamin K (from cauliflower, broccoli, cabbage, soybeans) aids blood clotting; and the B vitamins (from nuts, liver, mushrooms, dairy products, eggs) assist in a host of vital functions. But we require only tiny amounts of most vitamins, easily supplied by a well-balanced diet.

Besides knowing which vitamins we need and what each does, we should also know how much of each is recommended. The RNI or Recommended Nutrient Intakes, published by Health and Welfare Canada, spell out the amounts of each vitamin required by healthy Canadians, taking into account age, sex and certain conditions such as pregnancy and lactation. Although the RNIs have been set for most vitamins, vitamin K, biotin and vitamin D are excluded, either because the RNI is not known (vitamin D) or because some (vitamin K and biotin) are synthesized in plentiful amounts in the body's alimentary system (bowel) by bacterial action.

KNOW YOUR VITAMINS

Vitamin	Good Natural Sources	Recommended Nutrient Intake (RNIs)	Toxic Dose (chronic, regular use)	Symptoms of Megadose Toxicity	Signs of Deficiency
A (Retinol Carotene)	liver, dark green and orange-yellow vegetables, milk, margarine, cantaloupe	Infants to 3 years: 400 Retinol Equivalents (RE)/day 4 years to adolescence: slow increase with weight-gain Men: 1,000 RE/day Women: 800 RE/day Lactation: 400 RE extra/day	40,000 IU (adult) 25,000 IU (child)	Headache, nausea, vomiting, double vision, ear-ringing, bone, joint, abdominal pains, hair loss, muscle pain, dry or peeling skin	Xerophthalmia (dry, crusty and inflamed eyes, infections), night blindness
D (Cholecalciferol)	fortified milk, fish-liver oils, egg yolk, butter, liver	Infants: 400 International Units (IU)/day 2–6 years: 200 IU/day 7–49 years: 100 IU/day Age 50+: 200 IU/day Pregnancy and Lactation: 200 IU/day extra	150,000 IU (adult) 10,000–30,000 IU (child)	Hypercalcemia; nausea, appetite loss, weight loss, dry skin	Rickets in children (bow legs, pigeon breast, protruding ribs, curved spine), osteomalacia in adults (bone pain in legs and back, spontaneous fractures)
E (Alpha-Tocopherol)	vegetable oils, eggs, whole-grain cereals	Infants: 3 mg/day Children 2–12 years: 4–8 mg/day Adults: 6–10 mg/day Age 50+: 5–7 mg/day Pregnancy: 2 mg extra/day Lactation: 3 mg extra/day	No toxic dose specified but probably 300–1,500 mg	No specific toxicity syndrome. Individual reactions include blurred vision, headache, nausea, fatigue, muscle weakness, slow clotting	Never seen except in premature infants
K (Menadione)	liver, leafy green vegetables, cauliflower, dairy products	Not established; part of requirement met through synthesis in the intestine	No toxic dose specified	"Spot hemorrhage" on skin, kidney damage	Very rare
B₁ (Thiamin)	pork, legumes, bran, dried yeast, oatmeal, enriched bread, peanuts, whole wheat, milk and milk products	0.40 mg/1,000 kcal/day for all age groups Pregnancy: extra 0.1 mg/day Lactation: extra 0.2 mg/day	5 mg	No known toxicity	Beri Beri (numbness in legs, muscle wasting, heart failure, scaly skin)
B₂ (Riboflavin)	milk and milk products, calf liver, other organ meats, bran flakes, brewer's yeast, pork, leafy green vegetables, enriched bread	For all age groups: 0.5 mg/1,000 kcal/day Pregnancy: extra 0.3 mg/day Lactation: extra 0.4 mg/day		No known toxicity	Ariboflavinosis (growth retardation, oral inflammation, dry and scaly skin)

Vitamin	Good Natural Sources	Recommended Nutrient Intake (RNIs)	Toxic Dose (chronic, regular use)	Symptoms of Megadose Toxicity	Signs of Deficiency
Niacin	meat, poultry, fish, enriched bread, eggs, avocados, dates, figs, prunes (milk, meats provide tryptophan, a niacin precursor)	7.2 Niacin Equivalents (NE)/ 1,000 kcal/day for all age groups. Pregnancy: 2 NE extra Lactation: 3 NE extra	100 mg	Face flushing, sweating, hand and foot tingling; liver damage (at 1–3 g/day)	Pellagra (skin rash, inflammation, diarrhea, psychosis, with severe lack)
Biotin	milk and milk products, beef liver, oatmeal, soybeans, clams, eggs, salmon, shrimp, chicken, avocado, beans, bananas, peanuts	Not established; suggested intakes: 1.5µg/kg body weight/day		No known toxicity	Not known, except in rare cases of excessive raw-egg consumption
Pantothenic acid	liver, yeast, eggs, salmon, milk, avocado, chicken, lamb leg, banana, pork, molasses, peanuts, cauliflower, oranges	Not established; suggested intakes 2–3 mg/day for children and adults	10-20 g	Diarrhea with doses greater than 10 g	Not known
Pyridoxine (B₆)	organ and muscle meats, whole-grain cereals, legumes, avocado, beer, cantaloupe, cabbage, milk, eggs	Depends on protein intake 0.015 mg/g protein eaten, averages to: Men: 1.8 mg/day Women: 1.1 mg/day	1,000–2,000 mg	Neurotoxicity with numbness and tingling in feet and hands, difficulty walking, imbalance, clumsiness	Muscle weakness, irritability, unstable gait
Cobalamin (B₁₂)	beef liver, chicken liver, clams, oysters, tuna, lamb leg, milk, eggs	Infants: 0.1 µg/day Children: graded increase Adults: 1.0 µg/day Pregnancy: 1.2 µg/day Lactation: 1.2 µg/day		No known toxicity	Pernicious anemia (burning tongue, appetite loss, abdominal pain, irritability, depression, delirium, nerve disorders)
Folacin (Folic acid)	raw spinach, romaine lettuce, liver, fish, poultry, legumes, broccoli, bananas, avocado, oranges, cooked beets, apricots	Adults: 3.1 µg/kg body weight/day Infants and children up to age 4: 4 µg/kg/day Children and teens: 3.5 µg/kg/day Pregnancy: 7 µg/kg/day Lactation: 5 µg/kg/day		No known toxicity	Megaloblastic anemia (pallor, fatigue, burning tongue); neural tube defects in fetus of folate-deficient women
C (Ascorbic acid)	citrus fruits and juices, strawberries, green leafy vegetables, green peppers, tomatoes, potatoes, melon, cauliflower	Children: requirement increases with weight from 20 mg/day– 30 mg/day (up to 15 years) 15+ years: Males: 40 mg/day; females: 30 mg/day Smokers: Males: 60 mg/day; females: 45 mg/day Pregnancy: extra 10 mg/day Lactation: extra 25 mg/day	1,000-10,000 mg	Diarrhea, intestinal cramps, skin rashes, kidney stones, nausea, vomiting, "rebound scurvy," interference with some diagnostic blood tests	Scurvy (bleeding gums, lethargy, weakness, irritability, weight loss, joint pain)

Most healthy adults do not need vitamin supplements. Vitamin deficiencies that were relatively common a few generations ago are now very rare in Canada and most developed countries, where people eat sufficiently varied diets. Modern methods of preservation, rapid food transport and a diet that includes all essential nutrients ensure that most of us are not vitamin-depleted. Moreover, in Canada, the vitamins that could be lacking in everyday diets are added to enrich some basic grocery items such as milk, cereals and refined white flour. Before taking vitamin supplements, especially greatly in excess of the RNI, consult a medical expert about possible adverse consequences.

"More vitamins" are by no means "better"

In the early 1950s, some megavitamin proponents promoted the use of various vitamins in doses much higher than recommended daily amounts to treat a wide range of disorders. The "more is better" approach has led to the overuse of vitamins, which are often promoted as medicines to combat conditions for which there is no satisfactory cure, including arthritis, senility, schizophrenia, fatigue and stress. Large doses of vitamins, dubbed "megadoses," are

DISPELLING A FEW VITAMIN MYTHS

Vitamin C (ascorbic acid) and the common cold

A carefully controlled University of Toronto study compared people given a placebo (inactive agent) to those taking vitamin C (one gram a day and four grams at the first sign of cold symptoms), and found vitamin C offered no protection against colds. Moreover, regular intake of vitamin C in amounts far exceeding the RNI (30–45 mg) can produce diarrhea, an acidic urine that favors the formation of kidney stones and (in susceptible people) excessive breakdown of red blood cells or excessive iron absorption.

Vitamin E (alpha-tocopherol): "a vitamin in search of a disease"

Vitamin E (alpha-tocopherol) is an antioxidant that prevents fat breakdown in cell membranes, but its precise physiological role is unknown. It is readily available from cooking and salad oils, and no deficiency has ever been identified in humans. In spite of this it has been promoted as a fertility aid, a fountain of youth, a booster of healing and a protector against pollution. Claims that it cures acne and atherosclerosis and has therapeutic benefit in diabetes, muscular dystrophy and cardiovascular disease are equally unproven. While it has few toxic side effects, recent research suggests that large amounts may antagonize the action of vitamin K in blood clotting, an interaction that could lead to hemorrhage in susceptible people.

Vitamin B$_3$ (niacin) and schizophrenia

Vitamin B$_3$ has proved useful in reversing the depression, memory loss, irritability, headaches, hallucinations and paranoid delusions that accompany the formerly widespread deficiency condition known as pellagra (now uncommon in the Western world). But megadoses given to relieve schizophrenia or other mental illnesses have proved useless. With doses of 3 to 10 g a day (the RNI is 13–18 mg), side effects can include liver damage, profuse sweating, flushing, itching, gout, headaches, heart-rhythm disturbances and an upset blood-sugar balance.

Vitamin B$_6$ (pyridoxine) and premenstrual syndrome

Megadoses of vitamin B$_6$ (pyridoxine) are popularly advertised to counteract the bloating, moodiness, irritability and breast tenderness of premenstrual syndrome (PMS), even though studies show inconsistent results for its efficacy in remedying this syndrome. Publicity about its usefulness in PMS has led many women to take vitamin B$_6$ indiscriminately, sometimes in huge amounts, usually without medical advice. Originally, 50–200 mg a day was the "recommended" amount of B$_6$ for PMS, but today some booklets and self-styled experts advise women to take up to 800 mg of B$_6$ a day! As might be expected with a syndrome as complex as PMS, some sufferers report improvement with B$_6$, while others don't. A recent review of the uses of vitamin B$_6$ for PMS concluded that changes in diet accompanied by B$_6$ supplements seem to alleviate PMS in some users, but there's no proof that B$_6$ is the beneficial ingredient. While doses of 80 to 200 mg of vitamin B$_6$ per day reduced PMS in some women, a mixture of B$_6$ plus evening primrose oil did even better. The researchers found a very high placebo response, with 70 percent of PMS sufferers reporting improvement on dummy drugs. Although preliminary research held out some promise that vitamin B$_6$ could alleviate PMS, the scientific evidence for its benefits is weak — and studies of its efficacy in the treatment of carpal tunnel syndrome and arthritis show similarly inconsistent results. The chief danger of B$_6$ megadosing lies not in controlled amounts prescribed by a physician who's on the alert for signs of neurological damage, but with self-administered doses taken on the assumption that it is a harmless nutrient.

Overdosing can produce numbness in hands and feet, unsteadiness and even the inability to walk without a cane. Doses as low as 250 mg a day, on a continued basis, may damage nerve function. Recovery from the nerve degeneration can take many months to years. A landmark study from New York's Albert Einstein College of Medicine, published in the 1983 *New England Journal of Medicine*, documented nerve degeneration from B$_6$ abuse as a new "megavitamin toxicity syndrome." In the unscientifically touted for many conditions but are only medically indicated for a few rare diseases. Mounting evidence shows how toxic and harmful vitamin megadosing can be.

As distinct from the limited use of vitamins to offset a deficiency, megadoses aim to saturate some of the body's biochemical pathways in the hope of accelerating certain metabolic activities to overcome disabilities. Megavitamin or "ortho-molecular" therapy might involve taking 10 to 600 times the RNI of any particular vitamin. For example, U.S. chemist Dr. Linus Pauling advised a gram or more of daily vitamin C as a remedy for the common cold; others have promoted vitamin C to speed wound-healing, enhance mental alertness and delay aging. Massive doses of niacin (vitamin B_3) have been advocated to treat schizophrenia. Megadoses of pyridoxine or vitamin B_6 were also promoted for schizophrenia and for other psychiatric disorders — to offset depression, hyperactivity, premenstrual syndrome (PMS) and behavioral problems.

In large doses, vitamins act as drugs

In megadoses, vitamins are no longer considered nutrients but "pharmacologically active substances" — drugs that, like all drugs, may produce harmful effects. They can interact with

---

study, seven adults (five women and two men) taking 2,000 to 6,000 mg of vitamin B_6 a day for periods ranging from 2 to 40 months reported an unsteady gait, loss of sensory (touch and pain) perception, numbness in the feet and hands and impaired coordination. Four of the people were self-medicating with vitamin B_6 as part of a diet; one was using it to treat premenstrual swelling on the advice of a health magazine; two were being treated for edema (fluid retention) by a gynecologist and one by an orthomolecular psychiatrist. Fortunately, the subjects slowly recovered in the months after discontinuing B_6.

Some studies have now found residual nerve dysfunction even 6 to 18 months after people stopped taking B_6 megadoses. Although the danger level was previously cited as 2,000 to 5,000 mg daily, the safe daily intake level is now thought to be about 200 mg a day. Larger doses can pose a health risk. Microscopic examination reveals deterioration of nerve fibers directly related to the doses of B_6 ingested. Excessive B_6 may also block the action of penicillamine (a drug not to be confused with the antibiotic penicillin), L-dopa and some anticonvulsants.

If you insist on extra vitamins . . .

Experts do not advise vitamin supplements for children or adults who eat a normally varied diet. If you decide to disregard this advice, take a multivitamin that includes iron and the Bs in amounts not exceeding the RNIs. For those determined to take a supplement, it makes no difference (except to the wallet) whether the vitamin preparation is synthetic or the more expensive "natural" type. The body can't tell them apart! Treat your supplement as medicine, lock it away from children and take it only with meals.

Supplements are occasionally advised

Although vitamin supplements are normally unnecessary, there are some people for whom they are valuable:

- *Pregnant women* — usually advised to take supplements of folate (folic acid), iron and calcium. Extra folic acid is also strongly recommended during lactation. In the United States, it is now recommended for all women of childbearing age to reduce the risk of neural tube defects in babies.
- *Stringent dieters or those on inadequate diets.* When dieters' calories fall below 1,000–1,200 per day it is difficult to get sufficient nutrients. Some dieters require supplements.
- *Vegetarians and their children.* Strict vegetarians who avoid eggs and milk and, especially, the nursing infants of such mothers, as well as their other children, are at real risk of deficiencies of B_{12} and other vitamins, and should take supplements.
- *The elderly,* who often have little appetite and become undernourished, may also benefit from a daily multiple vitamin-mineral supplement.
- *Frequent aspirin takers.* ASA or Aspirin interferes with the metabolism of vitamin C and folacin, so people who take aspirin regularly — arthritis sufferers, for example — should ask their physician about supplements of these vitamins.
- *Heavy drinkers.* Heavy alcohol consumption often depletes B vitamins and vitamin C in the body.
- *Smokers.* People who smoke appear to use up vitamin C at a faster rate than nonsmokers. A committee of the U.S. National Academy of Sciences recommends that the daily intake for smokers be 100 mg of vitamin C (compared to 60 mg for nonsmoking adults).
- *Breast-fed infants.* All such infants need vitamin D supplements.
- *Those on certain medications.* Medications that interfere with normal absorption of vitamins include: laxatives (chronic use, especially of mineral oil) and antibiotics such as neomycin and tetracycline. Consult your physician about supplementation if you are taking any medications on a prolonged basis.

other medications being taken. In the United States, all vitamins (except folic acid) are classed as nutrients, with no legal restrictions on the dose or potency of products marketed. But in Canada vitamin preparations are viewed as drugs and must be approved by Health and Welfare Canada's Bureau of Nonprescription Drugs before being offered for sale. When the manufacturer applies for a drug identification number (DIN), Health and Welfare Canada checks the dosage against existing legislation to make sure it's not too high. For example, the upper limit allowed by Canada's Food and Drug Act for an oral dose of vitamin B_6 is 200 mg per pill. No daily dose should exceed it. However, authorities cannot control the number of pills someone takes. One expert at the Health Protection Branch of Health and Welfare Canada suggests looking for the DIN symbol followed by a six- or eight-digit number on any vitamin preparation. If the product doesn't bear this mark it is not officially approved and can't be sold legally.

Even water-soluble vitamins can be toxic in megadoses

Whereas the dangers of megadosing with fat-soluble vitamins, especially vitamins A and D, are widely acknowledged, many vitamin advocates assume that any surplus of water-soluble vitamins will be harmlessly flushed out of the body by the kidneys, in urine. However, scientists have now shown that even some water-soluble vitamins can be harmful in large doses. Research confirms that vitamin B_6 can be neurotoxic (nerve-damaging) in amounts over 200 mg a day, leading to numbness of the limbs and an unsteady gait. Megadoses of other water-soluble vitamins, such as vitamin C, in amounts over one to one and a half grams a day may cause diarrhea, increase the risks of oxalate-type kidney stones and even lead to "rebound scurvy" (when megadosing stops, the body may falsely react as if short of vitamin C).

The key to safe vitamin-taking is to choose only preparations bearing a DIN number on their labels, and to remember that large amounts act as drugs and that both high doses taken for a short time and lower doses ingested over the longer haul may be risky. You *can* have too much of a good thing.

MINERALS IN THE DIET

Minerals are inorganic elements that occur widely in the earth's crust. Although the body's mineral content totals no more than about 4 percent of its weight, minerals play a crucial part in many body functions and are vital to growth and efficiency. Our bodies contain over 50 different minerals, and a crucial 22 are essential to our well-being. These key minerals fall into two categories:

- seven macro or major minerals required in large amounts — calcium, chloride, magnesium, phosphorus, potassium, sodium and sulphur;
- fifteen micro or trace elements, required in only trace amounts — including chromium, copper, fluorine, iodine, iron, manganese, molybdenum, selenium and zinc.

A well-balanced, varied diet supplies enough minerals for most people, although pregnant or lactating women may need supplements prescribed by their physician. Minerals regulate intricate biochemical functions such as heart action, molecular transport across cell membranes, muscle activity, water balance, nerve conduction and immune defenses. If one or another is low or missing, the body's function may be impaired. For instance, a low calcium intake hinders bone formation, too little iron can lead to anemia, a lack of iodine is linked to thyroid problems and zinc deficiency slows wound healing and diminishes the sense of taste.

The absorption and action of dietary minerals is affected by the presence of other minerals or vitamins. Copper and vitamin C, for instance, both speed iron absorption; phosphorus and vitamin D are both essential to calcium absorption in bone. Some foods bind or block the absorption of certain minerals — oxalic acid, for example, contained in rhubarb, beet greens, chard and spinach, slows calcium absorption. Phytic acid, found in fiber-rich foods such as bran, may block calcium and iron absorption. Iron, which is plentiful in vegetables, especially spinach, is more easily absorbed from animal foods such as red meat or liver. Food processing and agricultural methods may also make a difference. Some nutritionists believe that reliance on processed, convenience and fast food may lead to mineral deficiencies, particularly of iron, calcium and possibly zinc and selenium. Although it is difficult to gauge the effects of chemical fertilizers and soil depletion on the mineral balance of plants, some environmentalists suspect that plants grown in some conditions may be low in one or more of the trace elements, depending on soil conditions. One concern is the higher heart-attack rates found in areas where water treatment methods reduce magnesium levels.

Some minerals, such as phosphorus, potassium and sodium, are so plentiful in the average North American diet that excess causes health problems. For example our excessive sodium (salt) intake often contributes to high blood pressure, kidney and heart problems. Since sodium is present in almost everything we eat, there's no need to add any from the salt shaker.

As with vitamins, there's a tendency to oversell mineral power, and minerals are often touted as miracle cures for a host of ills. Some faddists promote costly "chelated" mineral products, claiming quicker absorption, although in reality once the preparation is in the stomach it's broken up and absorbed at the same rate as plain forms. Minerals taken in amounts much in excess of the recommended intake may do more harm than good. As with vitamins, the best way to ensure an adequate supply is through a varied, balanced diet. If you really think you need supplements, be sure to consult a physician or nutritionist first; it's better not to take them on your own.

Breaking the excess salt habit

Salt, one of history's prized commodities, has been valued as money (on a par with gold). Wars have been fought over it, women and children traded for it. The word "salary" is derived from the Latin *salarium*, meaning a soldier's "salt allowance." Yet in modern society salt is a cheap, dispensable item that we toss carelessly on winter roads or scatter mindlessly on our food.

Sodium regulates the amount of water in body tissues, and is crucial to the balance of acids and alkalis. It keeps the body in a balanced state and is essential to functions such as glucose absorption, fluid movements between cells, the control of blood pressure, protein metabolism

and nerve conduction. The levels of sodium in the body are controlled partly by the hormone aldosterone and partly by the kidneys. For an adult, 9 mg of sodium intake daily per kilogram (2.2 lb) of body weight is considered sufficient. Someone weighing 65 kg (145 lb) needs 585 mg of sodium a day — equivalent to about one-quarter teaspoon of salt. Growing children need about 23 mg per kg of body weight until they reach maturity. The average Canadian adult consumes 10 to 12 grams of salt a day, providing 10 times the daily requirement.

Healthy people can probably tolerate far greater amounts of dietary sodium than those prone to hypertension (high blood pressure). Some individuals are genetically so sensitive to sodium that even average amounts of salt will make their blood pressure rise, and they must restrict sodium intake. Although no direct cause-and-effect link has been proven, many researchers feel that overconsumption of sodium contributes to hypertension, which affects about 10–15 percent of the Canadian population to some degree.

WATER IS ALSO AN ESSENTIAL DIETARY COMPONENT

Rarely listed among required nutrients, water is the most vital substance to life. While human beings can survive prolonged fasts without any food, several days without water usually means death. We can tolerate a loss of half our fat or protein reserves, but even a 10-percent depletion in body fluid is serious, and a 20-percent loss can be fatal. An average adult needs about 2–2.8 liters (2.8–3 quarts) of water a day, including amounts ingested from food. Many vegetables and some fruits are 80 percent or more water; milk has 87 percent and beef 55 percent water.

Although you may consider yourself a "solid person," the human body is mostly water. Newborn babies are 75 to 85 percent water, women are 55 to 65 percent water and men 65 to 75 percent. The sex difference is due to a higher proportion of fat in a woman's body; fat holds less water than lean muscle. If the body is dehydrated, the kidneys will cut back on water lost through urine, and the urine will become dark and concentrated.

KNOW YOUR MINERALS

Macro or Major

Mineral	Function	Food Source and RNI
Calcium (Ca)	Vital to tooth and bone formation, blood clotting, nerve and muscle action. Absorption depends on sufficient intake of vitamin D and phosphorus. Deficiency causes rickets, poor growth, bone deterioration, muscle cramps. Excess may cause kidney stones, spastic muscles.	Milk products, sardines, salmon, oysters, soybean curd, broccoli, spinach, lentils, beans (dried and green). RNI: Infants: from 250–400 mg/day; 1–9 year olds: 500–700 mg/day; 10–18 year olds: 700–1,100 mg/day; Adults: men: 800 mg; women: 700 mg; up to 500 mg extra for pregnancy and lactation and after menopause. (250 ml/1 cup skim milk — 317 mg; 85 g canned red salmon — 100 mg; 125 ml/½ cup cooked spinach — 88 mg.)
Chlorine (Cl)	Essential to water balance, acid-base regulation, digestion. Deficiencies rare.	Fish; salt. RNI: not clearly established.
Magnesium (Mg)	Vital to bone structure, nerve transmission, muscle action, protein metabolism, energy production, heart action. Deficiencies common among heavy drinkers, excess sugar users, long-term diuretic takers, occasionally in people on birth-control pills or taking excess vitamin D.	Whole grains, green vegetables, bananas, apricots, milk, nuts, seafood, hard water. RNI: Infants: 20–30 mg/day; Children: 3.7 mg/kg body weight per day; Adults: 3.4 mg/kg body weight per day; pregnancy additional 45 mg/day; lactation additional 65 mg/day. (1 medium banana — 58 mg; 250 ml/1 cup 2% milk — 40 mg.)
Phosphorus (P)	Essential to bone formation, fat transport, nerve action, overall energy metabolism. Intake should balance calcium intakes (body needs same amounts). Deficiencies may cause poor growth.	Meat, liver, milk, tuna, poultry, soybeans, bran, eggs, peas, broccoli, potatoes. RNI: Infants (0–4 mo): 150 mg/day; (5–12 mo): 200 mg/day; Children: gradual increase with age; Adults: men: 1,000 mg/day; women: 850 mg/day; pregnancy and lactation: 200 mg extra/day (85 g liver — 400 mg; 250 ml/1 cup skim milk — 232 mg; 125 ml/½ cup cooked soybeans — 161 mg.)
Potassium (K)	Involved in body's water balance, acid-base regulation, protein synthesis, muscle and heart action. Deficiencies likely with prolonged diarrhea, vomiting, kidney disease, frequent diuretic use, severe dieting (water loss may flush out potassium to levels low enough to endanger heart function). Excess may also impair heart function.	Bananas, milk, oranges, tomatoes, potatoes, spinach, broccoli, fruits, whole grains. RNI: not established. (250 ml/1 cup skim milk — 428 mg; 1 medium orange — 360 mg; ½ avocado — 857 mg.)
Sodium (Na)	Regulates water balance, acid-base levels; involved in muscle action, skeletal structure and transport of materials such as glucose across cell walls. Deficiencies rare since most foods have ample amount. Imbalance upsets water retention; excess may raise blood pressure, increase cardiovascular risks.	Meat, eggs, cheese, ham, bacon, sausages, dried fish, nuts, butter, table salt, canned and processed foods, salty snacks, baking soda, antacids, bran. RNI: not established. (1 large egg — 69 mg; 30 g cheddar cheese — 186 mg; 250 ml/1 cup bran flakes — 270 mg.)
Sulfur (S)	Found in almost all body cells, a component of many amino acids (used in protein building). Deficiencies rare.	Eggs, lean beef, lentils, kidney beans. RNI: not established.

Micro or Trace

Mineral	Function	Food Source and RNI
Chromium (Cr)	Vital to body's correct insulin use. Deficiencies may increase risk of diabetes.	Scarce in most foods – amounts depend on soil conditions; some in brewer's yeast, whole wheat. RNI: not established.
Cobalt (Co)	Crucial component of vitamin B_{12}; may be lacking in strict vegetarians; extreme lack can cause pernicious anemia.	Exclusively of animal origin — liver, clams, meat. RNI: not established.
Copper (Cu)	Crucial to blood formation, skeleton, nerve action, many enzymes (body catalysts). Deficiencies (rare) cause anemia, bone damage; excess may be linked to certain mental ailments.	Oysters, lobster, liver, bran, pecans, walnuts, bananas. RNI: not established. (85 g liver — 2 mg; 250 ml/1 cup bran flakes — 0.5 mg; 1 medium banana – 0.26 mg).
Fluoride (F)	Promotes resistance to tooth decay by hardening enamel. Shortage increases tooth decay; excess mottles teeth, causes bone abnormalities.	Seafood, seaweed, tea; best source is fluoridated water. RNI: not established, but 1 mg/l water (fluoridation) advised.
Iodine (I)	Crucial part of thyroid hormone, thyroxine, which regulates body metabolism. Insufficiency causes thyroid problems such as goiter (enlargement of thyroid), poor mental and physical growth.	Iodized salt, seafood, kelp, seaweed, dairy products near the sea. Content in plants varies according to soil conditions. RNI: Infants and children: 5 µg/100 Kcal/day; adolescents and adults: 160 µg/day; pregnancy and lactation: 25 µg extra/day.
Iron (Fe)	Central core of red blood-cell pigment, hemoglobin, which carries oxygen to tissues; vital part of some enzymes. Shortages common, especially in women — lack occurs after blood loss. Deficiencies cause fatigue, weakness, iron-deficiency anemia. Absorption by body requires enough dietary copper and is improved by vitamin C.	Liver, red meat, egg yolks, poultry, leafy green vegetables, raisins. RNI: Infants (0–12 mo): 1–7 mg/day; Children (1–11 years): 6–8 mg/day; Adolescents: males: 10 mg/day; females: 13 mg/day; Adults: males: 9 mg/day; females: 3 mg/day (8 mg/day after menopause) (85 g liver — 8 mg; 85 g hamburger — 2.9 mg; 40 g raisins — 1.5 mg.)
Manganese (Mn)	Works with zinc in some metabolic actions, activates enzymes, vital to nerve transmission.	Raisins, tea, spinach, broccoli, peas. RNI: not established. (40 g raisins — 201 µg; 125 ml/½ cup cooked broccoli – 119 µg.)
Molybdenum (Mo)	Body use unclear; possibly linked to enzyme function.	Legumes, whole grains, organ meats. RNI: not established.
Selenium (Se)	Function unclear; thought to help prevent heart and cardiovascular diseases.	Meat, egg yolks, seafood, wheat germ, milk. RNI: not established.
Zinc (Zn)	Contributes to insulin action, enzyme activity, carbohydrate metabolism, blood circulation, absorption of vitamin A, wound healing; key role in child growth. Deficiencies retard physical and mental growth, impair appetite, hinder learning.	Meat, oysters, liver, wheat germ, yeast, bran. RNI: Infants (0–4 mo): 2 mg/day; Children: increasing requirements with age; Adults: women: 9 mg; men: 12 mg; more after illness; pregnancy and lactation: 6 mg extra. (85 g liver — 3.3 mg; 250 ml/1 cup bran flakes — 1.3 mg.)

Water carries nutrients and waste products to and from the body organs through the bloodstream and lymphatic system. It lubricates the joints and mucous membranes and is the solvent in which nutrients are carried, digested and absorbed. Without water, the body couldn't get rid of toxic wastes through urine and feces. Nor could it cool itself. Water regulates body temperature through sweat; the reason obese people have a harder time cooling off is because fat under the skin acts as an insulator.

Water from food and drink is released inside the body by the metabolic breakdown of proteins, carbohydrates and fats. Babies need proportionately more water than adults, and should be offered bottles of water between feedings in hot weather. Drinks containing concentrated nutrients, such as milk, sugar-sweetened soft drinks and salty tomato-based juices, count more as food than as drink since they increase the body's water needs. Contrary to widespread belief (especially among weight-conscious women), drinking water does *not* cause bloating or weight gain.

In hot weather or during workouts the amount of water lost through sweat can rise dramatically. Exercisers may lose up to two or more liters (over two quarts) of body water in one hour of vigorous exercise, resulting in extreme thirst, giddiness and a possibly dangerous rise in core body temperature. The water loss may seriously decrease the circulating blood volume and endanger the heart. That's why it's essential to drink lots of water in hot weather and during and after prolonged activity. Sports medicine specialists urge athletes to "force liquids" in the summer heat, advising them to tank up with water before as well as during and after vigorous activity.

Although some people claim warm liquids cool you faster because they increase perspiration, that's no help on humid days. Exercisers should avoid sweet drinks, because sugar slows the absorption of water into the blood and draws water from the body tissues, where they really need it. Beverages containing caffeine or alcohol are not recommended to replenish body water, because they're diuretics which increase water loss. Electrolyte drinks are not advised unless people lose more than 2.8 liters (three quarts) of water (2.5 kg, or 6 lb of weight) during prolonged activity such as marathons.

Water intoxication
a possible but rare event

Compulsive or excess water drinking has been recorded for people with certain psychiatric disorders. It has also been reported in those about to be subjected to urine drug tests in the workplace (aviation industry) or after athletic events — in an effort to dilute the urine and avoid detection. Water toxicity can occur if someone rapidly drinks a large amount of water in a few minutes or has impaired renal function where the kidney can't excrete fluid fast enough. In one recently recorded case a worker told to have a urine drug test drank a great deal and exhibited clear signs of water intoxication: confusion, slurred speech, unsteady gait, a rapid pulse and seizures due to severely diluted blood plasma and a consequently disturbed sodium balance. The excess water and diluted circulation to the brain results in cerebral dysfunction and mental confusion. A 40-year-old flight attendant who exhibited typical water toxicity was reported in California. Her body retained excess water after she was told to "drink several cups of water" for a random urine test ordered by the U.S. aviation board. Anxious and stressed in the crowded room and fearing a laboratory error, she just couldn't urinate despite the consumption of three liters (over three quarts) of tap water in two hours. Despite some vomiting, she couldn't void and was sent home, later becoming dizzy and confused, with a severe headache and suffering a seizure that necessitated emergency hospitalization.

Hyponatremia or low blood and body sodium levels may follow excess fluid ingestion. This is seen in some compulsive water drinkers — mainly psychiatric cases — who may suffer seizures and be put on drugs for years without the reason for their excess water malady being uncovered. People who drink massive amounts can weigh 9 kg (20 lb) more at night than in the morning! Sometimes compulsive water drinking is due to a fault in the brain's hypothalamic thirst regulation center.

Summing it up

As modern science learns ever more about the intricate way our bodies work, people are tempted to believe that scientists will find some "shortcut" to health, perhaps through one particular nutrient, vitamin or pharmaceutical. But people who rush from one "miracle substance" to the next are making themselves into human guinea pigs!

Although there are a few exceptions when people need specific nutrient supplements — as in pregnancy, for example, or after an illness — the nutritional road to health for most people is a moderate, well-varied diet.

Putting it all together, Health and Welfare's new Food Guide, released in the fall of 1992, emphasizes variety, moderation and a well-rounded selection. The first update since the original 1942 version — with its familiar four food groups — the "guide to healthy eating" is designed for all Canadians aged four years and older. It gives far more practical suggestions for everyday menus and food choices than its predecessor. The new food guide even includes "other" foods such as alcohol, sweets and snacks (high in calories and fat) for occasional but not regular fare, suggesting how they might fit into meal plans. The guide's key message is to choose low-fat foods often and to make high-fiber foods and complex carbohydrates (pasta, cereals, whole grains, peas, lentils and so on) a bigger part of the diet.

Copies of *Canada's Food Guide to Healthy Eating* are available free of charge, from local or community health offices, provincial health departments or from Health and Welfare Canada. Call (613) 957-1803 for information.

For further information on nutrition the following three booklets can be obtained from Health and Welfare Canada:

- *Nutrition Recommendations, The Report of the Scientific Review Committee*, 1990 ($18.95, available by mail from Canadian Government Publishing Centre, Supply and Services Canada, Ottawa, Ont. KIA 0S9);
- *Action Towards Healthy Eating, Canada's Guidelines for Healthy Eating and Recommended Strategies for Implementation* (CIC report);
- *Call For Action* (summary of SRC and CIC reports), 1990 (available by mail from Branch Publications Unit, Health Services and Promotion Branch, Health and Welfare Canada, 5th Floor, Jeanne Mance Bldg., Ottawa, Ont. KIA 1B4).

A table of the *World Health Organization Guidelines to Healthy Eating*, and a detailed diet chart for lowering cholesterol, can be obtained by calling the *Health News* office at (416) 978-5411.

Looking after the surface

Caring for your skin • Remedying dry skin problems • Help for the anguish of acne • Psoriasis control • Shingles is a pain • Help for aging skin • Avoid skin's number-one enemy • Protect yourself against skin cancers • Hair, beautiful hair • Choose hair-care products wisely • Getting rid of lice • Hand and nail care • Foot care • Banishing warts

5

CARING FOR YOUR SKIN

Pride in one's appearance starts with the skin, the body's largest, most visible organ. The skin's appearance portrays a social and sexual image to the outside world, and humans generally lavish more care on the skin of the face and neck (and perhaps also the arms and legs, in women) than on other parts of the body. Anyone who's had an unsightly pimple on the nose or chin on the night of a prom or heavy date knows how acutely embarrassing even a small facial blemish can be. By comparison, most of us pay scanty attention to the skin on parts of the body not usually displayed in public. However, far from being mere vanity, looking after the body's wrapping also improves its health.

Keeping skin clean is a good start

Skin that looks, feels and smells attractive enhances self-esteem, hence the millions spent each year on cosmetics. But steering a sensible course through the countless skin products is no easy matter. One young woman recently complained that she couldn't decide on the "right way" to clean her skin, or between the merits of soaps versus cleansing creams, because everyone offered different advice. Her esthetician warned her never to touch her face with soap, but to clean it with cleansing lotion and astringents and to apply special day and night creams, especially under the eyes. Her dermatologist told her the opposite: to wash her face with mild soap and warm water, to use creams sparingly on her oily skin and not to lather on anything under the eyes. (Eye creams can cause puffiness if left on overnight; if used at all, they're best applied for 10 minutes or so and then wiped off.) Most dermatologists consider expensive cleansing creams hardly worth the cost. Cheaper ones, or even plain mineral oil, do an equally good job for those who are not prone to acne.

Each stage of life requires a slightly different skin-cleaning routine. During childhood, adolescence and young adulthood, most dermatologists suggest washing with gentle soap and warm water — not hot or cold — and rinsing well to remove the soap. (Hot water isn't advised because it's very drying.) In young infants and the elderly, who have extra-sensitive skins, soaps should be used sparingly and washing should be less frequent. Overwashing makes the skin dry and flaky.

The right skin cleanser also depends on the skin type. One evaluation found that cleansing creams were not necessarily less drying than soaps. Any soap is fine unless you have dry skin, in which case mild, superfatted types (such as Neutrogena, Dove, Caress, Petro-phylic, Allenbury's and Lowila) are best. One University of Toronto dermatologist recommends "avoiding deodorant and antiseptic soaps unless a physician prescribes them."

Astringents containing alcohol may be useful for the oily-skinned but will further dehydrate dry skin. If used at all, astringents should be dabbed on lightly with cotton balls (not paper tissue, as it irritates the skin). Despite claims that various astringents "close the skin's pores," none fulfills this promise.

Many dermatologists suggest replacing tub baths with showers, as showers are less drying and more hygienic. The constant stream of clean water removes dirt and bacteria more efficiently. However, as a relaxant after a hard day or to soothe aching muscles, a warm (not hot and drying) bath can do wonders. A pumice stone can be used while showering or bathing to remove tough, dead skin from the soles of the feet and elbows, but rub gently to avoid harming the skin. Bubble baths and bath oils should be used sparingly. Bubble baths may appear harmless but can trigger skin irritation and may provoke urinary-tract infections in children (especially girls). While bath oils may soothe dry, itchy skin, they also make the tub slippery and increase the risk of falling. It is safer to apply creams or oils directly to damp skin after showering than to add them to the bathwater. Always use a non-slip mat in the tub, and add hand-rails to the tub or shower enclosure for seniors.

REMEDYING DRY SKIN PROBLEMS

Turning up the thermostat alleviates winter's chill, but also dries out the indoor air, making us susceptible to dry, itchy skin. This irritating problem starts off as a tight, dry feeling, but can lead to cracked, chapped, inflamed and oozing skin, known as eczema or dermatitis. The commonest causes of dry skin are centrally heated homes and workplaces, lack of room moisture, cold, dry air and too much bathing or showering. The best antidotes are to humidify the indoor surroundings well and, as one dermatologist puts it, "to moisturize, moisturize, moisturize," to trap water in the skin's surface.

John, a radio technician who lived in a small, stuffy apartment, proves the point. He rarely opened the windows and his "sealed" office was overheated. He habitually took two daily showers — one every morning, the other after his evening workout. Every year, come

STRUCTURE OF THE SKIN

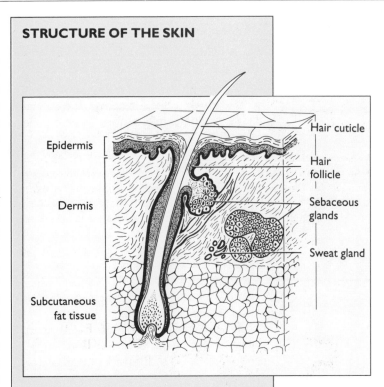

The skin basically has two layers: an outer epidermis, and an inner layer or dermis which includes the hypodermis. Men generally have thicker skins than women, but as people age the skin of both sexes becomes thinner and more fragile.

The top stratum corneum ("horny layer") of the epidermis is composed of flat, colorless cells, arranged like overlapping roof shingles, that are constantly shed and replaced by fresh cells. Anyone who has acquired a tan knows how quickly it fades as the outer epidermal layer is replaced by new cells. The epidermis is coated with an oily liquid called sebum, which gives skin its suppleness, smoothness and sheen, and helps to retain moisture. The skin's color is produced by pigment-forming cells (melanocytes) in the epidermis that produce a pigment (melanin) that protects it from sun damage by deepening its hue.

The underlying layer, or dermis, is largely composed of connective tissue, made up of collagen and elastin fibers which give skin its elasticity and firmness. The dermis contains blood vessels, which supply nutrients, as well as nerves, hair roots and nail roots, and three types of glands: the sebaceous oil glands, eccrine sweat glands and apocrine scent glands. The sebaceous glands produce sebum. Excess sebum production can backfire, causing greasy hair and plugged oil ducts, possibly contributing to acne. The amount of oil produced by the sebaceous glands determines whether a person has dry skin (underactive sebaceous glands), oily skin (overactive sebaceous glands) or normal skin (sebaceous glands working just right).

November, he'd become very itchy, particularly on his shoulders and arms, sometimes scratching until he drew blood. Finally a colleague persuaded him to see a specialist. The dermatologist took a careful history to determine whether there were any chemical irritants at work — there were none, except perhaps the photocopier fluids — and then told him to buy a humidifier for the apartment, to shower only once daily, to wash with mild, superfatted soap and to apply moisturizer to his damp skin right after showering. The dermatologist also prescribed a menthol/camphor lotion for the itchy areas. The itch soon vanished, and John keeps it at bay by repeating the same treatment when needed. Anyone with severely scaling, itchy skin should seek medical advice.

While the combination of oil and sweat normally keeps human skin soft and supple, various factors — such as lack of humidity or overexposure to water, sun, chemicals and soaps — can dehydrate it. If the skin loses water more rapidly than the deeper cells can replenish it, the upper layer dries out. Dry skin may also be linked to dermatitis (skin inflamation and irritation) or allergies and skin diseases. Characteristically, dry skin ("xerosis") starts out as small, whitish scales, possibly with some reddening and cracking. Many sufferers complain that their faces feel taut to the point of cracking. Although scratching may momentarily alleviate the irritation, the friction can lead to further breakdown.

Untreated dry skin can develop into eczema, with soreness, inflammation, and perhaps bleeding and swollen, oozing, crusty patches. Dermatologists often use the terms "dermatitis" and "eczema" interchangeably to denote badly inflamed, scaling, weepy skin. Once eczema is entrenched, it's difficult to reverse except with topical steroids such as hydrocortisone creams.

Skin itchiness can arise from innumerable causes

In tracing the causes of skin itching, physicians consider not only winter's cold and indoor dryness but allergic reactions, cosmetic acne (triggered by commercial skin products), contact and noncontact dermatitis, exposure to poison ivy or other plants, insect bites and the effect of chemical irritants, as well as certain skin diseases such as psoriasis.

Contact dermatitis is an inflammatory skin irritation, sometimes due to an allergy or to direct contact with specific substances. The irritation produces inflamed, itching, red patches, and perhaps oozing blisters — especially on prolonged exposure. Typical cases are a long-time bricklayer who suddenly developed sensitivity to the chrome in cement at age 50 and had to give up his job and take early retirement, and a hairdresser whose skin was suddenly irritated by the hair products she used on clients, forcing her into a career change. Strong irritants such as acid can blister the skin within minutes or hours; weaker irritants such as soaps or cosmetics may take some weeks to cause the dermatitis.

The skin on some parts of the body is more likely to develop dermatitis than others. The eyelids in particular are more prone to contact dermatitis than thicker-skinned areas such as the scalp, soles and palms. If the rash spreads rapidly to areas of skin not originally in contact with the irritant, it can take time to track down the causative agent. It helps if people remember the area of skin first involved as a pointer to the substance(s) causing the reaction. Sometimes the irritated patch has clear margins. It isn't always easy to distinguish allergic from other dermatitis.

A long list of substances can provoke contact dermatitis, including dyes, metals (such as mercury or nickel, in jewelry), rubber, topical medicines (such as neomycin or streptomycin creams), commercial fabric finishes, laundry products, shoe leather, perfumes, shampoos, makeup, some local anesthetics, sulfas and tars. Cosmetic ingredients, such as PPD (paraphenylenediamine) in hair dyes, preservatives (in creams), local anesthetics and lanolin, often cause dermatitis and should be avoided by those sensitive to them. Occupational dermatitis is common among hairdressers, shrimp-peelers, furniture-makers, bakers and many others daily exposed to irritating chemicals.

Ear-piercing is an often unsuspected cause of contact dermatitis, in which the itching arises due to nickel used to harden the earring metal. (Gold or stainless steel earrings usually avoid the problem.) Once the nickel allergy is entrenched, any jewelry containing nickel will irritate the skin.

For self-treatment of mild dermatitis, a 0.5 percent hydrocortisone topical ointment, cream or lotion — now available without prescription — can relieve the itching, redness and scaling. But if symptoms persist or worsen after five to seven days, a doctor should be consulted. In that case stronger cortisone preparations or oral products may be prescribed, after the cause of the dermatitis has been established and eliminated.

Atopic dermatitis, or skin itchiness is often linked to inherited allergies, but almost anything can trigger it — rapid changes in temperature, sweating, wool, polyester or nylon clothing, heavy and greasy ointments, soaps, detergents and emotional stress. In infants and children, atopic dermatitis may begin on the cheeks a few months after birth and spread to the elbows and knees, possibly provoked by crawling. During childhood, the dermatitis often moves to the creases of the arms and legs, possibly also the neck, scalp, wrists and ankles. Atopic dermatitis can be aggravated by foods given in infancy, such as eggs, milk, wheat and citrus fruits, but after two years of age, foods no longer seem to play a dominant role. The condition often clears up in adolescence, although it may continue into young adulthood.

Hives, or *urticaria* with large red patches and severe skin itchiness, can result from allergies and numerous triggers that release histamines in the body, such as drugs, chemicals, foods, inhalants, fungi, bacteria, insect stings, dust, feathers, molds, fumes, pollens, metals, heat, cold and light. The reddened, swollen skin blotches are usually evanescent — they last only a short time in the same place — but they may occur elsewhere the next day. Occasionally hives persist a month or more, a condition known as "chronic urticaria," but fortunately they too eventually burn out. Occasionally internal disorders such as thyroid disease, cancer or ulcerative colitis cause hives. Emotional stress can aggravate hives, although stress is often unfairly blamed. For instance, one dermatologist describes a woman who always broke out in itchy hives at her mother-in-law's house and attributed it to their tense rela-

tionship. The dermatologist later discovered that the parents-in-law had feather pillows that triggered the skin problem; after her in-laws changed to foam pillows, the woman no longer got hives when she visited them. Treatment of hives means avoiding the triggers or allergy-provoking substances to prevent the histamine release. Antihistamines and anti-inflammatory creams may help once the condition arises.

Impetigo is a highly contagious skin infection due to staphylococcal or streptococcal bacteria that enter the skin through small scratches. Usually seen in infants and young children, it typically starts off as small red, itchy macula (spots) that turn into blisters that soon rupture and develop thin yellow, oozy crusts. Left untreated, the sores may last for weeks, can be passed on to others and may occasionally lead to complications such as rheumatic fever and kidney disease in children. However, impetigo is usually easily managed (once the causative bacteria are pinpointed) by gently removing the crusts, washing well with an antibacterial soap, applying topical antibacterials and giving antibiotic tablets. Parents looking after children with impetigo should take precautions to avoid catching or passing on the infection — by washing the hands after touching the child and making sure each family member has a separate towel. (For impetigo in children, see chapter 11.)

Choose moisturizing skin products wisely

A cream or moisturizer's price and scientific-sounding ingredients are no guarantee of effectiveness. For good moisturizing ability, there's really no need to get any fancier than plain old petrolatum or petroleum jelly. But petroleum jelly is sticky, which makes other face products seem more appealing. However, any cream or oil that holds moisture in the skin will do. Inexpensive products such as cocoa butter, mineral oil and lanolin are as effective as expensive creams (although lanolin may cause allergies in some). One dermatologist calls the choice simple: "Never pay for the name." She adds: "Beware of the cosmetic claims! The right cream or moisturizer is a matter of cost and personal preference."

Whatever their price, moisturizers, hand and body creams, face, eye and night creams all work by trapping water and providing a protective layer on top of the skin. All are basically oil and water mixtures, with emulsifiers added to keep them well mixed, and sometimes perfumed as well. They coat the skin with oil and block evaporation of the moisture. While they can't cure dry skin, moisturizers provide protection, relieve the dry, itchy feeling and reduce the tendency to crack. Although most of the water in the cream or moisturizer evaporates, the oil stays on as a lubricant making the skin more pliable.

Despite their various forms — ointments, creams, lotions, foams, gels and oils — all moisturizers contain roughly similar ingredients: occlusives (which block the evaporation of water), humectants (which attract water) and emollients (oils such as mineral oil) that smooth the skin by filling in the spaces between dry skin flakes. The thickness of moisturizing creams varies according to their oil-water ratio. The thicker the product, the more oil it contains; the thinner the cream, the more water it contains. "Vanishing" or day creams have more water than night creams. The heavier or greasier it is, the greater the cream's lubricating qualities.

As a rule, the drier the skin, the thicker the cream to use. For dry or sensitive skins, choose any affordable moisturizer that is rich in oil. One inexpensive way to moisturize is simply to soak the skin in warm water for a few minutes, pat off the excess and apply any oil or cream of choice to the damp skin. As mentioned above, light mineral oil, cocoa butter and petroleum jelly are just as effective as costly commercial products, and because they contain no perfume or preservatives they are unlikely to irritate the skin or cause allergies. However, many dislike the texture of these plain, simple products.

Watching for allergic reactions to skincare products

Face creams rarely cause allergic reactions, but certain ingredients can act as irritants or provoke allergies, particularly perfumes, preservatives, salicylic acid, resorcinol, oxidizing agents and lanolin. Sometimes this happens because products are used on parts of the body for which they were not intended. A body cream suitable for the arms or legs may induce puffiness if used under the eyes. Skin-bleaching creams are among those most likely to cause allergic reactions. They should not be used by dark-skinned people except with medical supervision, as they often cause an inflammatory reaction and permanently lighter skin patches.

Hair products may cause skin allergies, especially those containing paraphenylene diamine or thioglycolates. Hair-removers containing barium or calcium sulphide or calcium thioglycolate can also cause allergic skin reactions. Nail polish can produce not only nail splintering and yellowing, but also allergic reactions if it touches the skin. A trace of nail polish on the eyelids can make them red and swollen, yet many of those with an allergic eyelid reaction don't realize that nail polish was to blame.

Deodorants and antiperspirants

Perspiration from the eccrine glands helps to regulate the body's temperature and cool it down after exercise or during a fever, by evaporation from the skin's surface. But if accumulated sweat stays on the skin for a few hours, especially in the body folds or on clothing, a strong body odor develops. The bacterial breakdown of sweat in the underarm or groin areas causes the most offensive odors. To counteract the smell, modern folk tend to use deodorants. Although deodorants decrease body odor, they don't reduce sweating, so many people prefer products containing both a deodorant and an antiperspirant. (Shaving off underarm hair also decreases the odor.)

The earliest deodorants were merely perfumes used to mask body odor, and were introduced by the high priests of ancient civilizations as part of their religious rituals. Only in the twentieth century did scientists discover that the bacterial breakdown of sweat is mainly to blame for body odor. Today's deodorants come as antibacterial or antiseptic-containing soaps (e.g., Dial, Irish Spring), roll-ons, sprays, sticks and creams. The antibacterial agents used in deodorants include: benzalkonium chloride, hexachlorophene and salicylanilides. Some of these can cause photosensitization, an exaggerated inflammatory response to sun exposure.

TIPS FOR PREVENTING SKIN DRYNESS AND WINTER ITCH

- Keep room temperature low but comfortable — not overheated.
- Humidify indoor air as much as possible (clean humidifiers to avoid contamination by molds).
- Keep skin clean and well moisturized.
- Use warm water for washing — not too hot or cold.
- Favour a mild soap or soap substitute, such as Dove, Petro-phylic or Neutrogena.
- Limit use of soap, detergents and solvents in wintertime.
- Favor showers and sponge baths — they are less drying than sitting in a tub of water.
- Apply moisturizers to damp skin.
- Use moisturizers recommended by University of Toronto experts, including white petroleum jelly, Dormer 211 baby oils, Nivea products, Moisturel and any personally chosen lubricants that work!
- Avoid too much friction from harsh washcloths and abrasives.
- Use lotions containing menthol, camphor or lactic acid for itchy areas, provided there's no cracking or inflammation (as it may sting); apply lotions to moist skin.
- For skin that is inflamed, red, cracked and scaling use a steroid anti-inflammatory cream or lotion such as hydrocortisone — but only with a doctor's advice and for about six weeks. Seek medical advice if skin problem persists.
- Soothe dry, itchy skin with cool compresses using Burow's solution (diluted one in 20) or Epsom salts in water — but use no menthol/camphor anti-itch products until cracks are well healed.
- Try oatmeal baths to soothe mildly inflamed skin. Place 60 ml (4 tbsp) of oatmeal in a sock and run the bathwater through.
- Try short-acting oral antihistamines (such as hydroxyzine) to relieve skin itching.

- Wear soft natural fabrics (jersey cotton, silk) next to the skin and avoid wool, nylon and polyester.
- Beware of pure lanolin skincare products, which cause allergic reactions in a few.
- Don't use paper tissues to apply oils or astringents or to remove makeup, as they are made from wood pulp and can irritate the skin; instead, use cotton balls (stored in a container to avoid contamination).
- Wear protective, cotton-lined rubber gloves when immersing hands in water or doing household tasks, and wear gloves in cold weather.
- To avoid chapped, sore lips, especially in children, apply roll-on lip balm or plain petroleum jelly (Vaseline); tell children not to lick their lips too often, and protect them from the cold.
- For severely dry, flaky scalp or dandruff (which can be fungal, due to *P. ovale* infection), try tar shampoos or get a doctor's prescription for Nizoral (ketoconazole 2 percent) or some other shampoo that reduces flakiness.
- Remove face makeup with cleansing cream or lotion (depending on skin type) or wash with mild soap and warm water; pat dry.
- Remove oil-based eye makeup with gentle oils or remover pads, and remove water-based products with water; wipe away from the eyes.
- Wash hairbrush, comb and makeup brushes at least once a week to prevent bacterial contamination.
- Always close cosmetic containers when not in use, to minimize the entry of bacteria.
- Discard old, dry, caked or dirty makeup.
- When engaging in outdoor winter activities, remember to protect the face from cold injury; cover the ears, head and neck; be alert for signs of frostbite; apply a protective face cream and a wide-spectrum sunscreen.

One safe, inexpensive deodorant recommended by a University of Toronto dermatologist is Aqueous Zephiran, or benzalkonium chloride, which is a clear, colorless, odorless liquid, easily applied with cotton balls.

Products labelled as antiperspirants must reduce normal sweating by at least 20 percent. Many contain metals, particularly aluminum, but experts suggest avoiding aluminum-containing antiperspirants for fear of adverse health effects. Some antiperspirants may also block the sweat glands and cause an irritation or rash. Antiperspirants containing perfumes, hexachlorophene and zirconium can also irritate the skin. (Those containing zirconium should be avoided because a few people develop small lumps, or granulomas, in their armpits from zirconium products.) Do not put antiperspirants on inflamed, wet or recently shaved skin as they may irritate it.

HELP FOR THE
ANGUISH OF ACNE

Acne affects many teenagers, and in severe cases leaves permanent, disfiguring scars. Although it's regarded primarily as an affliction of youth, many people continue to have acne into their thirties and forties. Acne should be treated as soon as it strikes, before it scars the skin and diminishes self-esteem. Improvement can be dramatic with modern therapies. Most people can manage their acne perfectly well once they know what to do.

Basically, acne involves a skin structure, the pilosebaceous follicle or unit, which contains tiny hair remnants, and a sebaceous gland that secretes the oily substance known as sebum. Acne varies from mild (grade one) occasional pimples to severe or cystic (grade four) eruptions. Symptoms range from a few hardly noticeable blackheads (comedones) and the occasional whitehead (pimple) to extensive, pus-filled, scarring cysts that cover the face and extend to the chest, arms and back.

Acne begins with a tiny plug (the comedo) in the sebaceous gland made of excess sebum, dead cells and keratin (a hard, tough protein). If the plug opens to the surface and darkens, it is an "open comedo" or blackhead, caused by accumulated oil and melanin pigment (not dirt). With progression to grades two and three acne, the follicles become swollen with trapped sebum, cells and bacteria, producing an inflamed red bump — the familiar acne pimple, pustule or papule. Deeper rupture of a follicle may produce the painful cysts and abscesses that typify grade-four acne, with the risk of permanent scars.

The newly developed anti-acne products tretinoin (vitamin-A acid cream) and oral 13-cis-retinoic acid (Accutane), now approved in Canada, have helped countless young people who suffer from this emotionally devastating affliction.

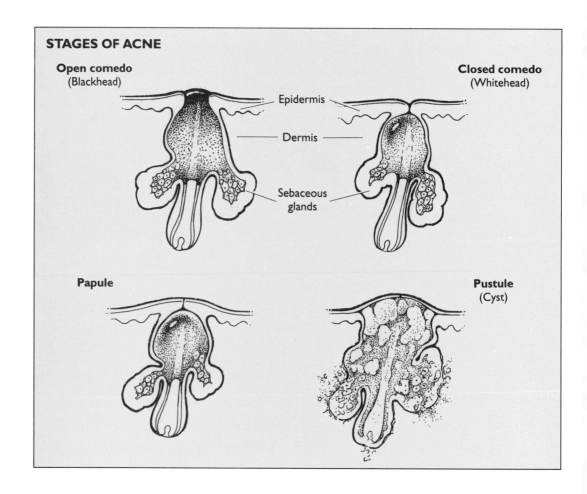

STAGES OF ACNE

Open comedo
(Blackhead)

Closed comedo
(Whitehead)

Epidermis

Dermis

Sebaceous
glands

Papule

Pustule
(Cyst)

ACNE TREATMENTS

For mild acne:

- clean the skin well to keep down oil, dirt and bacteria. Do not irritate the skin;
- wash with soap and water, and dry well;
- try to avoid stress and excess tension (acne aggravators);
- do not squeeze or pick pimples;
- shampoo the hair frequently — once a day — and keep the hair off the face;
- change washcloth, pillowcase and shirt frequently;
- drink plenty of water;
- don't use moisturizers, creams or oily cosmetics;
- apply topical tretinoin 0.01–0.05% gel (vitamin-A acid cream or Retin-A creams) if prescribed by the doctor;
- special cleansers and peeling lotions (containing salycilic acid) may be advised;
- 2.5 –20% benzoyl peroxide gel (Panoxyl, Benzac) can help mild acne;
- acne medications applied to the skin are drying and can irritate if used too much, so use them cautiously.

Further steps for papulo-pustular (grade two) acne:

- use benzoyl peroxide alternated with topical clindamycin or erythromycin (local antibiotics);
- possibly try oral antibiotics (medically prescribed);
- wear hair off the face, wash hair daily, drink plenty of water, avoid stress and get enough sleep.

Further steps for nodulo-cystic (grade three and four) acne:

- use oral antibiotics (e.g., tetracycline); if they fail, consider oral Accutane or an injection of triamcinolone (steroid);

- if using oral antibiotics, be sure to take the full dose (at least six to eight weeks) before changing treatment; watch for side effects (e.g., sun sensitivity if taking tetracycline);
- topical tretinoin in a cream or lotion can dramatically alleviate acne, either alone or in combination with other treatments. It corrects the processes that plug up the sebaceous gland channels, altering the cycle that forms blackheads and whiteheads. Tretinoin comes in three strengths: the gel, the most drying form, is for people with very oily skin; the lotion is less drying, and the cream dries the skin the least. Other than being expensive, causing some initial local redness and increasing sun (UV) sensitivity, it is a relatively innocuous remedy. Later it may be used alternately with other acne treatments (e.g., benzoyl peroxide). Topical retinoid therapy requires close supervision by a physician;
- oral anti-acne retinoids like Accutane (also called 13-cis-retinoic acid, or isotretinoin), taken by mouth as capsules, can relieve severe or cystic acne, which doesn't respond to conventional treatment. As opposed to the years often required for antibiotic treatment, a short four- to five-month course of Accutane often clears up acne, sometimes for long periods, even forever. But although considered a "breakthrough" for severe acne, this drug has some potentially serious side effects — especially the risk of birth defects and elevated blood cholesterol levels. Its use in women of childbearing age *must* be accompanied by effective birth control. It can also cause initial skin-chapping, dry lips, palms and soles, eye problems, headaches, joint pains and blood disorders. So Accutane must be taken with care under steady medical supervision.

PSORIASIS CONTROL

Psoriasis, a common skin disorder that afflicts about 3 percent of our population — an incidence similar to diabetes — ranges from mild to severe and is usually worst in winter. Although its causes remain elusive (it may have an immune-system component), new treatments can keep most psoriasis under control. Untreated psoriasis can produce disfiguring, scaling skin patches. Neither an allergy nor an infection, and not contagious, its psychological impact can be devastating. It is responsible for much personal distress, embarrassment and lost work hours. Sufferers try to hide their affliction by avoiding summer clothes and social events or refusing to go out in public. Children may find that other schoolmates refuse to hold hands, swim, attend gym classes or play with them because of the blemishes. Getting appropriate therapy and sharing the heartache of a chronic disease that's part of their lives helps sufferers come to terms with psoriasis.

TIPS FOR CONTROLLING PSORIASIS

- good skincare — patting instead of rubbing skin dry, trying not to scratch or irritate the psoriatic patches;
- basic hand care — washing only when necessary; drying well; using medicated creams on red, scaly areas (but not leaving them on too long);
- wearing cotton-lined rubber gloves when doing laundry or dishes; avoiding activities such as pottery, sanding and furniture-polishing, which involve contact with irritants; delegating jobs that chafe psoriatic areas to others;
- caring well for psoriatic feet, keeping the feet clean and dry to prevent bacterial or fungal growth, wearing cotton socks and open shoes or sandals whenever possible;
- good scalp care — avoiding injury or scratches; special shampoos and topical creams may help;
- regularly using lubricants such as hand lotion or white petroleum jelly to stop the skin from scaling;
- medicated ointments such as salicylic acid, steroid (cortisone) and tar products can be very effective;
- crude coal tar and its derivatives, an old standby for psoriasis control, often alleviates psoriasis, especially in combination with UV light therapy;
- anthralin (an alternative to tar) can be applied to affected skin for several hours at a time, but can be hard to manage, because it harms normal skin. An alternative is short-contact anthralin treatment, using a higher dose on affected spots for 5 to 15 minutes only;
- steroid creams or intralesional steroid injections help mild cases with small areas of psoriasis (cover with Saran Wrap to increase steroid absorption). However, after a while the plaques become resistant to steroids, and other treatment is needed. Systemic (oral) steroids aren't usually advised for psoriasis;
- ultraviolet light, an old and simple remedy, slows down the skin's over-rapid proliferation. But psoriatics should only expose themselves to sunlight until the skin reddens very slightly, avoiding sunburn, since it will stimulate rather than curb skin growth;
- cyclosporine is proving useful for very recalcitrant psoriasis, but needs care because of possible kidney damage;
- sulfasalazine, an inexpensive drug with few side effects, is considered for oral therapy in some patients;
- acetretin, a retinoid metabolite of Tegison, relieves psoriasis in some, but needs caution in childbearing women because of its strong fetal-deforming power;
- capsaicin is a natural chemical derived from hot pepper plants; when used topically as 0.025% cream (Zostrix), it moderates the itching often associated with psoriasis within four to six weeks. The main side effect is burning and stinging, which diminishes with continued use;
- "PUVA" therapy (psoralen pills plus UVA rays) is a new treatment that's had dramatic success (without messy creams or potentially hazardous medications) for severe psoriatics. Psoralen is a plant extract that increases skin pigmentation. Taken orally two hours before UV exposure, psoralen penetrates the skin and is activated by UVA rays. PUVA needs careful supervision, especially shielding of the eyes with special glasses that screen out the UV rays. Only about 3 to 5 percent of those treated by PUVA fail to respond; side effects include accelerated skin aging and a possibly increased susceptibility to skin cancer. However, the incidence of skin cancer (30 in 1,373) is still low enough to be considered a tolerable risk for patients with disabling psoriasis who don't do well on other treatments;
- retinoids such as etretinate (Tegison) are a great help for severe psoriasis, often bringing improvement within days to weeks. Some require longer use to keep symptoms at bay. But it cannot be used in women of childbearing age because of its fetal-deforming side effects. A new short-acting retinoid, Ro10-1670 (Etretin or Acitretin), has also proved very successful. Side effects include: lip chapping; dry nose, eyes and mouth; joint soreness; a possible rise in blood fats (needs monitoring); and altered liver function. These side effects may fade after a few weeks of therapy and vanish once the treatment stops.

Psoriasis varies widely in severity

Known since biblical times, psoriasis tends to run in families and hits people of both sexes, and all races and social classes. It can be so mild that it goes undiagnosed (a few small scaling skin patches or sore areas on the elbows or scalp), or severely disabling. It's a recurrent disease that flares up from time to time, often starting in young adulthood. The outer skin cells grow and multiply about 10 times more quickly than required — turning over every four or five days instead of every 28 days. The rapidly dividing cells produce raised, roundish, scaly patches and sometimes red, inflamed eruptions that may become cracked and sore, called plaques. Once they have formed, the plaques tend to recur again and again in the vulnerable areas.

Psoriasis typically occurs in areas of the body exposed to friction, irritation, infection or any other trauma, especially at pressure points such as elbows and knees. In the past, it was most prevalent on the knees (from praying and scrubbing postures), and it's still common there among tile-layers! Psoriasis sometimes affects areas such as the scalp (at the back of the head), where it may be confused with seborrheic dermatitis. In its mild form psoriasis is easy to miss — it may first be noticed by the barber or hairdresser. Diagnosis is by clinical appearance and skin biopsy (or sample) for lab confirmation. While the majority of sufferers have a mild form, about 10 percent of psoriatics have serious skin involvement and/or accompanying arthritis.

Psoriasis was previously thought to be just skin-deep, but it's now known that very severe psoriasis can affect the whole body. If the condition is erythrodermic (inflammatory), it may diminish the body's heat regulation, dilate blood vessels in the skin and cause heat loss and cold-sensitivity. At the extreme end of the spectrum, under 3 percent of psoriatics have severe pustular psoriasis (inflamed lesions or pustules) — a condition that may suddenly flare up, necessitating hospital treatment. Very rarely there is a general erythroderma (total body peeling and redness, with moisture loss and high fever) that can be life-threatening.

Psoriasis treatments — new and old

Physicians now treat not just the affected sites but the whole person. There is no single, effective remedy, although for many patients the plaques spontaneously fade during long periods of remission. People with psoriasis must think "control" or "management" rather than cure. For the obese, losing weight may reduce the problem; for the overbusy, relaxation may help. One doctor found that his psoriasis cleared up when he downsized his hectic practice.

Treatment usually starts with a family physician, who refers patients to a dermatologist if necessary. For mild cases, people often manage successfully by themselves. More severe cases, with ups and downs, need close professional supervision.

Dietary theories for curing psoriasis abound, although there is no evidence that food plays any role in the disease. Some health-food stores promote lecithin, vitamins or other supplements for psoriasis — substances that have not lived up to their promise. Although stress is sometimes considered to be a factor in provoking flare-ups, its precise role remains uncertain.

The best management is achieved at specific centers, such as the University of Toronto's PERC (Psoriasis Education and Research Centre), which help to educate people and keep the disease under control. This is most

---

FACTORS THAT AGGRAVATE PSORIASIS

- **Local injury (rubbing, friction, abrasion) or repeated irritation at a skin site most often sets off the problem.**
- **Environmental factors — such as pollutants, stress, emotional upsets — may exacerbate or cause psoriatic flare-ups.**
- **Infection plays a part, mostly in childhood, where streptococcal throat and other** infections may produce acute psoriasis that returns during adulthood in a different form; viral infections can also cause flare-ups.
- **Certain drugs, such as antimalarials, lithium and beta blockers (e.g. propranolol), can induce a psoriatic attack, as can withdrawal of steroid medication.**
- **Alcohol may worsen the condition, and alcoholics often fail to comply with the treatment plan.**
- **Obesity is a possible aggravating factor. While being overweight doesn't cause the condition, it makes psoriasis hard to treat because the plaques tend to "hide" within skin creases.**

---

useful for those who might otherwise need hospitalization. Such units not only teach self-care but also provide the opportunity to meet and talk to others about a common handicap.

SHINGLES IS A PAIN

Shingles, or *Herpes zoster*, is an adult reactivation of a childhood chickenpox infection. However, instead of covering large parts of the body as in chickenpox, the shingles rash appears on only a small area of skin, often in rows like shingles on a roof. A typical shingles rash is a group of reddish blisters. It follows the path of certain nerves on one side of the body only — generally on the trunk, buttocks, neck, face or scalp — usually stopping abruptly at the midline. About two-thirds of shingles cases occur in those over age 60, afflicting both sexes equally. Most people suffer only one attack, although repeat bouts occasionally occur, usually at the same site as the first eruption.

An attack of shingles generally begins with feverish discomfort (chills, headache, upset stomach). A preliminary itching or burning sensation may precede the rash by a few days (occasionally mistaken for a heart attack, lung infection or back problem). But the discomfort is more commonly felt only during and/or after the rash. Pain that persists after a shingles attack is particularly troublesome in people over 60.

The shingles rash starts as a series of raised red spots that turn into clear blisters, which

MANAGING THE SHINGLES RASH

- **Do not scratch the blisters.**
- **Apply cold compresses of Burow's solution, Betadine, other antiseptics, drying agents (cornstarch or baking soda) and bandages impregnated with petroleum jelly, with or without topical antibiotics.**
- **Try a drying lotion containing calamine, alcohol, menthol and/or phenol to speed healing.**
- **"Splinting" the area — e.g., covering it**

with cotton and wrapping with an elastic bandage — may relieve active and post-shingles pain.
- **Interferon (an extract of the natural defense substance present in all cells) helps some people.**
- **Acyclovir, given by mouth or intravenous infusion, can reduce the severity of shingles and aid healing in both normal and immunosuppressed people, and may, but does**

not necessarily, lessen post-shingles pain. Acyclovir ointment may speed healing but cannot stop the rash from spreading or prevent post-shingles pain.
- **Systemic (oral or injected) steroids are occasionally prescribed for elderly sufferers with severe or widespread shingles: given within 72 hours of its start, steroids can lessen the severity, reducing the likelihood of post-shingles pain.**

become cloudy, dry out and crust over. The spots are surrounded by a swollen area, and may bleed and become very itchy and painful. In a few people, especially those with defective immune systems, attacks are severe and the rash covers a wide area. The rash may take three to four weeks to heal and may leave whitish-silver or brown scars. Normally, once the rash fades, the area stops hurting and full recovery follows.

If shingles occurs on the face, nose, ears or cornea of the eye, it is known as *zoster keratitis*. This condition can lead to blindness if left untreated. Anyone with shingles on the upper face, no matter how mild, should see a physician at once. A tingling at the tip of the nose may herald eye involvement. When the trigeminal facial nerve and the eyes are affected, people

are more likely to experience prolonged post-shingles pain.

What causes shingles?

The *Herpes zoster* virus is responsible for both chickenpox in children and shingles in adults. This virus belongs to the same family as the *Herpes simplex* organism responsible for cold sores. Shingles occurs almost exclusively in those who had chickenpox as children and have some but not total immunity to the virus. While chickenpox is highly contagious, caught by inhaling infected droplets, shingles is not generally transmitted from one person to another. But children or adults who haven't yet had chickenpox may catch it if they touch wet shingles blisters.

About 80 percent of the Canadian population have had chickenpox, usually a mild illness, by age 10. Although childhood chickenpox almost always runs its course in a week or two, usually with full recovery, the virus may linger in the body, retreating to nerve cells and staying hidden within nerve ganglia (centers in the spinal cord). Most of us go through life maintaining an "armed truce" with zoster viruses that have remained in the body after a juvenile bout of chickenpox. If reactivated for some reason, the virus travels along affected nerves, causing a skin eruption as it goes.

There is some evidence, not proven, that shingles may be precipitated by excessive exposure to sunlight (UV radiation), stress, trauma (wounds, surgery or inflammation) and other events that lower immune resistance. Shingles is more common in older people because immune defences get weaker with progressing years. It also often afflicts AIDS patients.

REMEDIES FOR LINGERING POST-SHINGLES PAIN

- **Antidepressants (e.g., amitriptyline) help many, not because of their antidepressant effect but because the medication relieves pain (in doses lower than those normally used for depression).**
- **Transcutaneous electrical nerve stimulation (TENS) often brings relief.**
- **Opioid painkillers do not usually alleviate PHN but may be helpful if all else fails.**
- **Sympathetic nerve blockade or local**

anesthetics may be helpful. But since these methods are elaborate and expensive, and have given little evidence of long-term benefit, anesthetic remedies are not strongly supported.
- **Capsaicin, the pungent element in hot peppers (marketed as Zostrix,) can alleviate PHN. It gives considerable relief to some sufferers. Exactly how hot pepper ointments relieve post-shingles**

pain is unclear. They may deplete pain pathways of substance P (a pain transmitter), thus relieving the pain. While the hot pepper creams may relieve PHN, they also sting by stimulating nerve endings.

TO FIGHT OFF THE EXTERNAL SIGNS OF AGING SKIN, TRY TO:

- reduce sun exposure — there is no healthy tan;
- avoid certain facial expressions, such as pursing lips, arching eyebrows or grimacing, which can increase wrinkling;
- stop smoking cigarettes — young smokers often have facial wrinkles akin to those of nonsmokers in their sixties. Years of inhaling cigarette smoke give the cheeks a gaunt look, and nicotine cuts blood flow to the face, causing a leathery, gray complexion;
- avoid rapid weight loss — frequent "yo-yo" dieting can permanently wrinkle the skin;
- get an expert opinion about use of dermabrasion — with a wire wheel or other device to gently "sand" off the top skin layer (this process can leave depigmented areas);
- consider a chemical peel — "painting" an abrasive product over wrinkles near the eyes and mouth, as well as on the cheeks and chin — which slightly wounds the skin and produces a transiently smoother skin. An expert should advise you about this procedure.
- consider bovine collagen implants (injected cow's collagen) to fill in large wrinkles, such as the creases between the eyes, furrows near the nose, "marionette" lines at the corners of the mouth, vertical lines around the lips and crow's-feet around the eyes. The wrinkles will return with time, requiring a touch-up job. Be sure to get expert medical attention for the procedure. (People with auto-immune diseases such as lupus and scleroderma should *not* receive collagen implants, nor should anyone allergic to collagen);
- maybe try lipotransplantation, done under local anesthesia, which places fat from the thigh or abdomen into face wrinkles. Again, caution and expert advice are advised!

Lingering post-shingles pain is often the worst aspect of the condition, because even though the rash generally vanishes, leaving little or no discomfort, pain may continue long after the skin heals. Post-zoster pain is a continuous itching, burning sensation with bouts of stabbing and shooting or lacerating pain. It is often set off by touching the sensitive area and can last for years.

Defined as "unrelenting pain that persists for four or more weeks after the acute shingles phase," post-herpetic neuralgia (PHN) occurs in 10 percent of patients over 40 and one-half to two-thirds of those older than 60. Some find it agonizing, never letting up except perhaps during sleep, and indeed it's often bad enough to hinder sleep. Many complain of allodynia (pain on contact with certain stimuli such as the touch of clothing) and hyperpathia (prolonged, radiating pain superimposed on the continuous itch). Fortunately, the pain tends to fade with time, often vanishing in a year or so.

HELP FOR AGING SKIN

Aging skin normally becomes thinner and drier than younger skin, hence the need to moisturize extra well with advancing years. There's no way to grow older without getting some wrinkles and skin blotches, but avoidance of the sun's harmful rays and protection with good sunscreens go a long way toward preserving the skin's youthful look.

The diminution in sweating and sebum production among the elderly increases the need for regular moisturizers. A good face massage can stimulate the blood flow and reduce dryness, but without lasting benefits. Those with dry, aging skin should avoid harsh soaps, abrasive washcloths, rough towels and grainy cleansers. They should wash less often and, above all, moisturize consistently. Cleansers for the over-65s should be mild (e.g., Cetaphil, Aquanil or Dove), and without astringents. In using makeup for older skins, less is often more.

The elderly may develop discolorations such as senile angiomas (red or bluish patches on the trunk and scrotum), pruritis (itching), and rosacea, which gives a reddish and slightly bulbous look to the nose. One small advantage to aging is that sweating decreases, so there's less need for deodorants, and some conditions such as psoriasis improve. But as sweating decreases, the elderly must watch their body temperature to avoid heatstroke.

Lasers and liquid nitrogen can now lighten some unsightly skin discolorations, but so-called "rejuvenating" and hormone creams are not usually worth the cost, and can be harmful. Most products touted for "skin-renewal," such as bee-extracts, aloe vera, estrogens, mink oils and placental extracts, work no better than plain mineral oil. Exercise, however, can help by toning the muscles and increasing the circulation. For the coarse facial hair that sometimes afflicts older faces, a good electrologist can help. But be sure to choose a well-trained technician.

Retinoid (vitamin A–like) products revolutionize skin care

Retinoic acid, or Retin-A (a synthetic derivative of vitamin A), a successful acne remedy, has been found to have some antiwrinkling effects, and is now prescribed for some elderly faces. Retinoids can do marvels for skin disorders such as acne (tretinoin is used topically and Accutane is taken by mouth) and for psoriasis (through Tegison pills). (For more see entry for psoriasis.) The anti-acne products can also lighten sun-damaged skin and smooth light wrinkles. But it takes about four months of regular use to see any antiwrinkle benefits, and the products are costly, available only by prescription. Buyers must beware of imitations containing vitamin A, with deceptively similar labels. The success of synthetic retinoids has prompted manufacturers to add nonprescription vitamin A and its byproducts, such as retinyl palmitate, to moisturizers, which can easily trap the unwary into thinking these products will do the same thing. But although some announce that nonprescription vitamin A can also reduce fine skin lines, neither vitamin A nor any of its currently used derivatives has the antiwrinkling effects of the synthetic, prescription retinoids.

The wrinkle-removing benefit of retinoids was discovered at the University of Philadelphia, where dermatologists noticed that, after a few months of retinoid application for acne, many faces showed a subtle anti-aging effect. Wrinkles were smoothed and brown sunspots lightened. The anti-aging effect may be partly due to a renewed collagen buildup which provides fresh skin support. Experts stress that retinoids are pharmaceutical products which need cautious use and must be geared to individual skin types. One University of Toronto dermatologist warns that "far from offering swift wrinkle removal, retinoid creams must be diligently applied daily, for some months, before any noticeable benefits appear." The products are expensive and erase only the very fine, almost invisible wrinkles, not the crow's-feet around the eyes or mouth. Once the retinoids are stopped, the wrinkles creep back. Since retinoids exaggerate sun sensitivity, those using them must use an extra-protective sunscreen.

Apart from smoothing out some wrinkles, the retinoids herald a new era of successful treatment for several drastic skin problems, including severe acne and psoriasis. The retinoids have radically improved the outlook for those with certain skin disorders and have been hailed as a breakthrough for the treatment of disorders that involve abnormal keratinization (skin turnover). More than 1,000 different retinoids have been produced since the 1940s, and while all behave in a roughly similar manner, each has a slightly different therapeutic effect. Safe retinoid use depends on good patient-doctor communication and close supervision.

But while retinoids are recognized as a valuable treatment for several skin problems, they have come under fire owing to their deforming effects on unborn babies.

In Canada, the retinoids now available are:
• tretinoin or retinoic acid (Stieva–A or Vitamin-A acid) — in three strengths as gels, lotions or creams — used topically as creams or lotions for acne, to repair sun-damaged skin and to abolish light wrinkles. (The topical form is relatively safe and causes no fetal malformations or serious side effects, but the forms taken by mouth deflect fetal development);
• isotretinoin or 13-cis-retinoic acid (Accutane) capsules, taken by mouth, used for severe acne (with caution in younger women);
• etretinate (Tegison), taken by mouth, used mainly for severe psoriasis.

Since the oral retinoid drugs can cause serious fetal malformations, they must NOT be prescribed for, or even contemplated for, anyone who is, or may become, pregnant. Accutane, which is more rapidly excreted than Tegison, may be given to women who practice absolutely reliable, effective birth control for one month before taking the drug, while on it, and for at least one month after discontinuation. Tegison, which is cleared very slowly from the body, is generally not prescribed for any woman of childbearing age unless she's had her tubes tied. Both Accutane and Tegison can be freely prescribed for males, as the retinoids do not affect male reproductive function.

AVOID SKIN'S NUMBER-ONE ENEMY

The sun's ultraviolet rays are essential to human beings in moderate amounts for forming vitamin D by their action on the skin. But in addition, ultraviolet (UV) rays, whether from the sun, a tanning parlor or other sources, can damage and age human skin. Thus sunlight is enemy number one to human skin. Although the sun makes us feel good, it is one of the most injurious environmental agents human skin ever encounters. Solar radiation speeds up wrinkling and other external signs of aging, and can induce skin cancer and exacerbate allergies. Damage is worst with short, repeated, intense sun exposure — as with trips south when people try to soak up a year's sunshine in a brief vacation. To retain a youthful look and prevent skin cancer, protect the skin from excess sun exposure. Close inspection of a habitually tanned person's arms, legs, neck or face reveals a mass of brown spots, mottled white patches, horny bumps, finely etched lines, scaly plaques, rough (premalignant) keratoses, enlarged blood vessels and perhaps small cancerous growths.

To understand how the sun's ultraviolet rays harm human skin, think about what sunlight is: intense electromagnetic radiation emitted from the sun's inner core by the nuclear fusion of hydrogen to helium. The spectrum of emitted sunlight ranges from the long-wave radio and infrared rays through all colors of visible light to the short-wave or high-energy ultraviolet, gamma and cosmic rays. Although they make us feel hot, infrared rays do not injure human skin unless they are intense enough to burn. The brown pigment, melanin, absorbs infrared rays, which explains why black- and brown-skinned people often feel hotter than those with white skins.

The amount of skin damage from UV rays depends on cumulative lifetime exposure. The greater the UV exposure, the more the injury. The shorter the wavelength, the greater the danger. For practical purposes, dermatologists divide ultraviolet rays into three types: UVA, UVB and UVC. The longer UVA rays can penetrate glass and produce some tanning — both immediate and delayed. UVA rays were formerly considered harmless, but dermatologists now know that these rays, including those from tanning lamps, do as much damage as the shorter rays.

The UVB band, often termed the sunburn spectrum, cannot pass through glass but is the principal cause of sunburn, wrinkling and aging.

UVC rays are filtered out by the ozone layer before sunlight reaches the earth.

To counter the sun's assault, the skin's outer layer thickens and darkens. The outer cells divide to form a covering that scatters and bounces back the impinging rays. Pigmentation increases via manufacture of the brown pigment, melanin, which reduces UV penetration. People who tan easily are better protected than those who merely burn or freckle. Especially at risk of skin cancer are the Celtic races with red hair and pale, freckly complexions. Those who inherit dark, olive skins can take more sun exposure with less damage than fair-skinned types.

Sunburn: the immediate damage

When UV radiation hits human skin, some is reflected, some absorbed, some scattered. Damage may be acute (immediate and short-lived) or chronic (long-term and lasting). Sunburn may not show up at once, but peaks 15–20 hours later, when a burning, beet-red color appears. Although painful and unsightly, mild sunburn probably has no lasting consequences. But with constant exposure, even without any telltale reddening, some skin damage occurs — a few lines etched in, a little cellular degeneration. The lag between the time damage is inflicted and the point at which it shows may be 20 years. By the time obvious skin blemishes appear, much irreversible harm has already occurred. Nevertheless, it is worthwhile to prevent further sun damage at any age.

To treat sunburn, take painkillers to ease the pain and soothe the hot skin with calamine lotion. The ensuing blisters should not be broken but simply treated with cool-water compresses. A mild vinegar and water bath may make people feel cooler. A very severe sunburn may require use of topical steroid cream.

PEOPLE MOST AT RISK FOR MELANOMA

- "frecklers" — those who freckle easily, especially when young;
- children who sunburn easily and tan poorly;
- people badly sunburned in childhood;
- "moley" individuals — people with many moles (the more moles, the greater the risk of melanoma);
- redheads, blonds, blue-eyed and fair-complexioned types;
- those who've had one melanoma, or other types of skin cancer or who have family members who've had melanoma;
- people who spend much time outdoors — working or playing;
- people with "peculiar-looking" moles, dysplastic nevi, which are precursor moles quite likely to become cancerous.

PROTECT YOURSELF AGAINST SKIN CANCERS

Skin cancer is on the rise, having doubled in incidence over the past 10 years. One in seven Canadians now develops skin cancer over the course of a lifetime. If sun exposure continues, no amount of defensive action can ward off the wrinkling, color flaws and other irreversible changes that may ultimately lead to cancerous growths. Some skin flaws, seborrheic keratoses that look "stuck on," are benign and have no malignant potential. But other blemishes (actiner keratoses) may develop into premalignant horny patches and ultimately into frank malignancy. Cancerous tumors usually form in the parts that get the most sun — hands, neck, back, face and lower legs.

The danger signals of skin cancer are:
- any ulcer, sore or patch that won't heal;
- a spot that scales persistently;
- any enlarging spot or lump.

Basal cell cancer, the commonest of skin cancers, now affects 30,000–50,000 Canadians each year. It usually occurs on the face, and although it's potentially serious it almost always remains localized and is quite easily treated. Squamous cell cancer, a less common form, may spread more easily. But caught in time, these types can be removed with a 95 percent chance of total cure. People who have had one skin cancer should get regular follow-ups to check for repeats.

Melanoma — a deadly skin cancer

Malignant melanoma is the deadliest of skin cancers. It arises from melanocytes (pigment-producing cells), often from already existing moles, but also anywhere on the body, including the eyes and mouth. In contrast to other skin cancers, malignant melanoma spreads fast and dangerously if not caught early. Untreated, melanoma can kill within a few months to a couple of years. Yet early detection and removal offer an excellent chance of a cure.

Worldwide, there's a sharp rise in melanoma, especially among the fair-skinned. Melanoma rates in Canada have almost doubled since the mid-seventies, an upward shift attributed mainly to greater sun exposure, more outdoor recreation, skimpier clothing and an ardent pursuit of tanning. The much-publicized thinning of the earth's ozone layer (attributed partly to chlorfluorocarbon emissions) is also contributing to the melanoma rise. Mortality from this type of cancer is increasing faster than death from any other malignancy. If the current increase continues, experts predict, this cancer will soon be more common than breast or lung cancer. By the year 2000, an estimated one in 90 Canadians will get at least one melanoma in a lifetime. (At present about 500 Canadians die annually from it.)

Although melanoma may form in nonexposed areas, the sun's ultraviolet rays are most to blame for its development. There is no such thing as a good tan, yet too many of us link sunlight to a glamorous look, rather than to cancer! Each year's tan adds a little more damage. Short, intense recreational UV exposure, rather than steady low-level exposure, may pose the most serious threat.

RECOGNIZING THE ABCD'S OF MELANOMA

ASYMMETRY; **B**ORDER IRREGULARITY; **C**OLOR VARIATION; **D**IAMETER.

- **A**symmetry: an irregularly shaped brown spot or mole with tails and jagged edges may be cancerous; or a skin patch that changes in surface texture — that scales or oozes. A scab that keeps coming off, bleeds incessantly or becomes "velvety" may denote skin cancer and should be investigated.
- **B**order irregularity: scalloped, splayed or perhaps notched edges of a pigmented (brown) spot may be danger signals.
- **C**olor variation: uneven color is a distinct feature of melanoma. Moles may become lighter or darker or acquire black flecks or various shades of gray or pink, or pigment may spread from the mole into skin that otherwise looks normal, with color patches that are next to, but not a direct part of, the mole ("satellite pigmentation").
- **D**iameter: most melanomas exceed six mm (0.2 in) across (wider than a pencil eraser), while ordinary, benign moles are generally smaller.

THE WARNING SIGNS OF MELANOMA
How to distinguish ordinary moles or brown spots from melanomas and their precursors

	Normal moles (common nevi)	"Dyplastic" nevi: possible precursor or marker moles (Unusual-looking, bigger than average, may give rise to melanoma)	Malignant melanoma: cancerous moles/pigmented spots (Recognize by the ABCDs of change: **A**symmetry, **B**order irregularity, **C**olor variation, **D**iameter enlargement)
Color and appearance	• Uniformly tan or brown • Tend to look alike • Regular outline	• Varied mix of tans, browns, blacks, reds/pinks • May differ from each other • Sometimes look like fried egg, with central color blob and flat edges	• Possible darkening, more brown, black and bluish hues • Appearance of multiple shades of pinks, reds, blue; possible depigmentation and white patches in mole; part may vanish (although melanoma is still there)
Size (diameter)	• Usually less than 6 mm or 0.2 in (smaller than a pencil eraser)	• Often 5–10 mm (0.2–0.4 in) across or larger	• Continuing or gradual expansion over time — varies from months to years, slow or fast
Surface, shape and border	• Rounded, with sharply defined edges • Flat or elevated	• Mostly flat with some raised parts • Often merge into surrounding skin • Irregular, notched, scalloped and indistinct edges	• Development of notched, irregular margins • Surface may elevate, darken (including surrounding skin — rare) • May develop a new bump that looks like a blister
Number	• Typical adult has 10–30 scattered over body	• Wide variation; few to over 100	• Person usually develops just one at a time • If already had one, another may occur elsewhere
Age of appearance	• Infancy to fourth decade	• Childhood to old age	• Any age — 12–70 years (rare in children)
Incidence	• Most people (95–99%) have some normal moles	• In 5–10% of the population • Often run in families (may be due to inherited gene)	• 15 per 100,000 persons
Location on body	• Anywhere, but typically on sun-exposed skin • Rare on nonexposed (covered) sites	• Can occur anywhere but most frequent on back and trunk • Also occur on *unexposed* skin (e.g. scalp, breasts, buttocks)	• Any part of skin (most common on back in men and women, and on lower legs in women)
Sensation	• Not noticed (unless rubbed by garments or movement) • Do not inflame, redden or ooze	• Usually not felt or noticed	• Most are not felt or noticed • Some start to itch, hurt, ooze, inflame, ulcerate, swell, soften or crust over; bleeding a very late sign
Malignant? (Cancerous?)	• No, absolutely not	• No. But increased chance of becoming malignant	• Yes! Melanoma is a skin cancer that can spread (metastasize) to other tissues, e.g., lymphatics, liver, spleen
Malignant potential	• Ordinary moles may turn into melanomas (large congenital nevi, present since birth are especially likely to become cancerous)	• Increased, in comparison to ordinary moles	• Already cancerous

The good news is that there's a high chance of curing melanoma provided it is detected early and removed before it penetrates too deep. Pathologists predict an excellent cure rate for those less than 0.8 mm (0.03 in) thick. The deeper the tumor, the greater the likelihood it has metastasized (spread).

Moles may turn into deadly melanomas

Most experts believe that while melanomas may arise on mole-free skin, from melanocytes, some develop within the pigment cells of already existing moles. Research suggests that "moley" people are at an above-average risk for melanoma, especially from occasional excessive sun exposure. There may be a critical period in the evolution of a mole when it can be "promoted" to form melanoma (rather than regressing in the normal manner).

Congenital nevi (birthmarks) occur in 1 percent of newborns, and those bigger than a pencil eraser have a somewhat increased chance of developing into melanoma.

Giant or "garment" nevi — unusually large, hairy moles that are very conspicuous, sometimes over 20 cm (8 in) across and occupying a large area (e.g., from neck to buttocks) — unquestionably have an above-average tendency to become malignant. These moles need not necessarily be removed, but require careful watching.

Solar lentigo ("liver spots") are pigmented spots that appear late in adulthood on sun-damaged skin and are unlikely to become malignant, but a biopsy is suggested to make sure there is no malignant tendency.

"Peculiar" precursor moles may precede melanoma

Dysplastic nevi (odd-looking, multicolored notched moles) were first recognized in 1978 as possible markers or "predictors" of melanoma among 37 patients in six melanoma-prone families, and were dubbed B-K moles. Scientists have since found that dysplastic nevi are possible forerunners of melanoma. About 5 to 10 percent of the population have one or more of these strange moles. Sometimes, but not always, dysplastic moles run in families as a dominant, inherited trait. A certain number progress to malignant melanoma, and the risks are greatest in someone who's already had a confirmed melanoma or who comes from a melanoma-prone family.

When should moles be removed?

Wholesale removal of unsightly moles is impractical, unjustified and cosmetically undesirable. But moles that look suspicious or worry someone should always be removed — namely, any that are injured or irritated by movement, shaving, brushing, belts or clothing. Anyone who thinks a mole has changed color or enlarged, or who particularly dislikes a mole, should have it off. Even the best experts can miss a melanoma, and only a biopsy test can confirm one as harmless or malignant. As one University of Toronto pathologist puts it: "If in doubt, cut it out!"

Protect children from sunburn and sun exposure

Severe or frequent sunburns to a child can greatly increase melanoma risks. Studies show that fair-skinned immigrants who arrived in Australia or Israel before age 10 were far more likely to develop malignant melanoma than those who came at later ages. One bad sunburn during childhood can double the chances of developing skin cancer later in life — an avoidable risk. The message is loud and clear: protect children from sunburn.

Scan a buddy's skin for sinister spots

Self-examination and frequent checks of your loved one's moles are a great idea. The back is a place where melanoma often occurs, especially in men. So check for brown spots that are

---

DISTINGUISHING DIFFERENT MOLES

  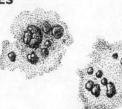

Normal Mole
(smallish, uniform roundish shape, sharp edges)

Dysplastic nevus
("pre-melanoma")
(unusual-looking, largish, varied pink, mixed colours, vague border — may merge into surrounding skin)

Frank melanoma
(cancer)
(often jagged, irregular border, large size, mix of dark and light colors)

SUNCARE TIPS

- Don't expose children under 12 months to direct sunlight.
- Protect newborns under a sun umbrella.
- Cover infant heads when in the sun.
- Wear long-sleeved shirt and pants when in strong sunlight — one can still enjoy activities on the beach or in the park.
- Remember that sheer clothing allows the sun's rays through, leaving underlying skin unprotected (apply sunscreen).
- Be especially vigilant with children with red hair and pale skins — they are at greatest risk of developing melanoma.
- Remember that UV light is reflected from sand, concrete, snow or water. Young skiers and waterlovers often sustain serious sunburns from reflected sunlight.
- Get children into good sun protection habits: teach them regular sunscreen application while outdoors. Model sun protection yourself.
- Note that baby oil is not a sunscreen — the oil intensifies the effects of sunlight and burns skin faster.
- Keep sun exposure to a minimum — especially from noon to 3:00 p.m., when sunlight is most intense.
- Beware of cool, cloudy or overcast days when 70–80 percent of the sun's UV rays still get through.
- Remember that sitting in the shade or swimming underwater does not guarantee protection (UV rays go through water).
- Use sunscreens wisely: choose SPFs of 20 and up. Most experts now recommend 20–30 SPF for good protection (unless the product contains Parsol, in which case a lower SPF may give enough protection).
- Apply sunscreen at least 30–60 minutes before going outside so that it penetrates the skin well.
- Pay special attention to sun-exposed areas — ears, face, scalp, neck, shoulders, back.
- Try different products for different occasions/activities: use a higher SPF for vigorous outdoor exertion (e.g., golfing, running), lower ones for milder exertion (e.g., walking).
- On vulnerable spots (such as nose, cheeks) consider adding a total, opaque sunblock or paste (containing titanium dioxide or zinc).
- Select a broad-spectrum sunscreen that blocks out the sun's shorter (UVB) and some of the longer (UVA) rays — such as those containing Parsol, oxybenzones or dibenzoyl methane.
- If swimming or perspiring profusely, reapply waterproof sunscreen after drying off.
- Send kids off to camp or for summer weekends with the right sunscreen in their bag!
- Be especially vigilant at high altitudes and near the equator, where solar radiation is most intense.
- Become a mole-watcher — examine the entire skin regularly for any changes in moles, freckles or discoloration.
- Get skin check-ups if there is a personal or family history of melanoma, or if you are in a known high-risk bracket.

asymmetrical, have scalloped borders, change color or become bigger. Particularly examine the back, calves of legs, upper arms, ears, and back of the neck, where skin cancers commonly form. Note the pattern of moles and freckles and look for any scaliness, change in color or shape, itching or oozing. Remember: prompt surgical excision of early melanoma offers an excellent chance of cure. If in doubt, see a dermatologist.

Choosing the best sunscreen

Everyone is advised to avoid suntanning and, when outside, to follow the SLIP, SLAP, SLOP routine: SLIP on a shirt, SLAP on a hat, SLOP on some appropriate sunscreen (SPF 20 or more, preferably waterproof). The SPF (sunburn protection factor) denotes the protection that a certain product provides. For good sun protection, the SPF number must be 20 or more. The only products that provide sun protection are those containing a specific chemical that weakens or blocks the impact of UV light. The concentration of the UV-screening compound must be high enough to protect your skin type. Ideally a sunscreen should protect against both UVB and UVA rays, but very few chemicals screen out all the UVA, so sun-sensitive people may need a total (opaque) sun block such as zinc or titanium oxide. Although many products are advertised as "sun blocks" — especially those with high SPF — most are not total sun blockers; in other words, they do let some UV rays through. Cocoa butter and oils increase the risks of sunburn and offer no protection against UV rays.

PABA (para-aminobenzoic acid) and its esters are among the most widely used sun blockers, followed by benzophenones, cinnamates, salicylates and anthranilates. Usually colorless and invisible, they are cosmetically acceptable provided they don't ruin clothes or produce adverse skin reactions. Alcoholic PABA solutions may turn clothes yellow, sting the face or occasionally cause skin irritation. Although PABA is the best of sunscreens, people cross-reactive to benzocaine and procaine (local anesthetics), some hair dyes and sulfa drugs may be allergic to it.

No chemical offers complete UVA protection, but new products, especially those containing Parsol, block some UVA rays. Broad-spectrum sunscreens containing benzophenones, oxybenzones and dibenzoyl methane also screen out some UVA as well as UVB light. Choose a product that is broad-spectrum if possible for maximum sun protection.

Sun-free tanning lotions may be the solution

Products that dye or stain the skin to give a pseudo-tan do not protect the skin from UV rays, but they enable people to attain the hue they desire, providing skin color without cancer risks. Several companies now market self-tanning milks and creams (not to be confused with tan accelerators) which on prolonged contact give a "bottle tan", turning the palest of skins a warm shade of brown — not the bright orange or pumpkin colors produced by earlier products. Two or three nighttime applications may be needed to attain the desired shade. The depth of skin color depends on the amount and frequency of application. Tan-producing chemicals such as dihydroxy acetone (DHA) stain the skin, and the color develops a few hours after application, depending on the skin type and its amino-acid content. People should do a skin (patch) test before use in case of allergies. Trial and error can show which brand is best for you. Remember that sunscreen is still needed for sun protection.

HAIR, BEAUTIFUL HAIR

The value placed on hair as a symbol of beauty, strength and sexuality is reflected in the billions spent annually on shampoos, conditioners, coloring agents, curling treatments and baldness remedies. In fact, when we meet someone, hair style and color are often the first features we notice.

Fine and transparent, human hair is a vestige of our hairier animal forebears. The adult human body averages five million hairs, of which 100,000 to 150,000 are on the scalp. Odd though it may seem to call the tangle of inert protein arising from the scalp a "healthy head of hair," our hair does reflect the overall state of the body's health. The part of the hair seen above the skin surface is a strand composed mostly of keratin — a tough, elastic protein which also makes up human fingernails, birds' beaks and mammals' hoofs. There are three basic types of human hair: *lanugo* — the very fine, transparent hair covering an unborn baby, shed by the seventh month of fetal development; *vellus hair* (from the Latin for "fleece" or "down") — short, soft, sometimes pigmented hair covering the entire body except for the soles of the feet and the palms of the hands; and *terminal hair* — the coarse, pigmented, longer hair on the human scalp, face, armpit and pubic regions.

Hair color comes from the pigment melanin, secreted by melanocytes (pigment-producing cells) near the follicle base (see diagram). The more pigment granules there are, and the more tightly packed, the darker the hair. Two kinds of melanin contribute to hair color. Eumelanin colors hair brown to black, and an iron-rich pigment, pheomelanin, colors it yellow-blond to red. Whether hair is mousy, brown, brunette or black depends on the type and amount of melanin and how densely it's distributed. For example, deep-black African hair contains closely packed melanin in the cortex. Black Japanese hair has many pigment granules in the cortex, and a few in the cuticle. Very dark European hair, quite apart from having more melanin granules than lighter or blond hair, has more melanin per granule. When the pigment-producing cells stop working hair loses its color and turns gray, the timing perhaps genetically determined.

Hair grows in cycles

A hair's growth is finite, determined by heredity and the part of the body on which it's growing. The hair follicle goes through alternating anagen (growth) and telogen (resting) phases. On a human scalp the growth phase lasts on average three to six, at most about eight, years. After growing steadily for that period the hair stops and, after a three- to four-week transition stage, the follicle goes into its resting phase. After three months or so of resting, the same follicle begins to grow a new hair, pushing out the old one, which is eventually shed. A resting hair may stay put within its follicle for a few months,

THE STRUCTURE OF A HAIR AND ITS FOLLICLES

The hair shaft has three layers: the cuticle (outer protective layer), the cortex (providing strength) and the innermost medulla, which has no known function.

The hair cuticle, made of tightly overlapping layers of flattened cells, like shingles on a roof or scales on a snake, encases the delicate cortex. If smooth and healthy, the cuticle gives hair gloss by keeping the scales non-porous and tight, preventing water loss. But the cuticle is easily damaged by heat, sun, dryness, salt water, harsh chemicals, or overtreat-
—ment (e.g., too much blow-drying, perming, or bleaching), which swells and lifts the scales, leaving the hair dry and brittle. The cortex is made up of tiny keratin fibrils twisted together like yarn, which give hair strength, bounce and elasticity — largely determining the extent of its curl.

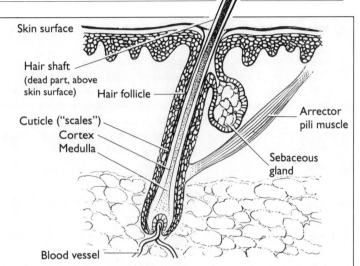

but as a fresh hair grows, the old one is shoved out to make room for its successor. At any one time, about 10 percent of the hair on our heads is in the resting stage, easily shed, while the rest (less easily tugged out) is in the growing phase. Most of us naturally shed 50 to 100 scalp hairs a day.

Given some 100,000 scalp hairs, their growth produces some 30 m (100 ft) of solid protein (keratin) each day — 11 km or seven miles per year! Hair cells are among the body's most rapidly dividing cells. Individuals who grow long hair have a long growth period of six to eight years, although their hair may not grow faster than that of those with shorter growth periods. Since healthy scalp hair grows an average of 1 cm (0.4 in) per month, it may take two years to become shoulder-length or six years for uncut female hair to reach the buttocks. (The growth phase of hair is shorter on male scalps than for females.) Scalp hair rarely exceeds a maximum of 750 cm (two and a half feet) in total length. On the eyebrows, the growing phase is only about 10 weeks, so eyebrow hairs never grow very long. Pubic and armpit hair growth rates are roughly similar, while leg hairs grow more slowly and are shorter.

Hair is kept lubricated and shiny by sebum, an oily secretion produced by small sebaceous glands near the follicles. A dog can recognize a human being by the typical scent secreted by these glands. Clusters of tiny muscles, the arrector pili, surround and move the hair follicle. Male hormones (androgens) regulate hair growth in both sexes. Pubic and armpit hair are particularly androgen-sensitive and grow at lower androgen levels than hair on the chest or legs. In boys, most pubic hair is grown by age 15, followed by the development of armpit hair two to three years later. In girls, too, an increase in androgens at puberty triggers growth of pubic and armpit hair. Scalp hair is not directly androgen-responsive, but is influenced by local amounts of a testosterone derivative, dihydrotestosterone.

Hair loss worries both men and women

Progressive hair loss begins naturally in both sexes by about age 50, accelerating in the seventies and eighties. About 40 percent of Caucasian men lose some hair by age 35. Hair shedding in males is often due to androgenetic alopecia — genetic/hormonal or "male pattern" balding. But even extensive hair-thinning rarely becomes obvious until 50 percent of the scalp hair has been lost. Many events other than male-pattern balding can make the hair shed, but only rarely do people lose more than half their hair for these other reasons. Hair may fall out because of overtight hairstyles, some illnesses, or excessive coloring and curling. Hair shedding is often noted up to six months after childbirth, following a prolonged fever, surgery, emotional upset, depression or some other traumatic event. Sudden hair loss — all over the head — can also be provoked by crash diets; thyroid, pituitary or adrenal disease; radiation or chemotherapy (for cancer); fungal or other infections; burns; habitual tugging or compulsive hair-pulling; and exposure to certain

COMMON REASONS FOR HAIR LOSS (OTHER THAN MALE BALDING)

• *Alopecia areata* (patchy baldness) is a common disorder affecting about 2 percent of the population, where hair on the scalp, eyebrows and beard comes out in oval patches, surrounded by short, broken or frayed thick-tipped club hairs. It usually occurs during childhood or early adulthood, lasting a few months. The small bald patches are sometimes tender and sore. They tend to clear up spontaneously with full hair regrowth, perhaps white or lighter in color at first, then back to the former color. Regrowth may take up to six months, and is sometimes accompanied by hair loss in another patch. Recurrences can occur, especially in those who had the condition as children, or if there are multiple patches. Occasionally the patchy shedding spreads to the hairline, eyebrows and lashes — the more serious *alopecia totalis* — or to the entire body, *alopecia universalis*.

  The reason for this patchy, circumscribed growth stoppage is unknown, but may be partly genetic (in 25 percent of cases), and probably involves an immune-system defect. *Alopecia areata* is most common in identical twins, children with Down syndrome, asthmatics, those with eczema, pernicious anemia (a vitamin B_{12} deficiency), hay fever and thyroid disease. *Alopecia areata* can be treated with liquid nitrogen (freezing), phototherapy (light), anthralin (tar), steroid lotions and intralsional steroid injections at the site of hair loss.

• *Tinea capitis*, popularly known as ringworm — a form of hair loss in children — is due to a fungus often carried by young kittens and puppies. The fungus attacks the hair shaft, causing local areas of hair loss, scalp scaling and possibly inflammation (depending on the site). A scalp sample (biopsy) may be taken to identify the parasite causing the loss, and to rule out other causes, such as psoriasis. Treatment is with antifungals such as oral griseofulvin or ketoconazole (Nizoral) for about six weeks, or a topical antifungal lotion.

• *Trichotillomania* (compulsive plucking, twisting, rubbing, pulling or tugging of the hair) is self-inflicted, transient hair loss which produces stubbly patches of short hair in children or psychiatrically disturbed adults — usually on the side of the "dominant" hand. A child may continually but unconsciously twist and pull out the hair owing to frustration or some inner tension (as with nail-biting). The relentless plucking ultimately produces visible hair loss on the scalp and occasionally eyebrows. Treatment includes reassurance for the child and, above all, the parents, and minimizing fuss.

• *Traction alopecia* results from too much physical tension on the hair, usually due to tightly pulled hairstyles such as ponytails or braids, or overtight curlers. Excessively rough or over-enthusiastic blow-drying can also produce traction hair loss at the tension points.

• *Friction alopecia* is due to hats or wigs that are overly tight, the hair literally being broken off or pulled out at the follicle by the tension.

• *Postpartum hair loss* can occur one to six months after childbirth; during pregnancy, extra anagen growth produces luxuriant hair, and when the abrupt growth spurt wanes, after delivery, the above-average numbers of resting hairs gradually fall out.

• *Some illnesses* can cause temporary hair loss, such as thyroid, adrenal and pituitary diseases; certain forms of diabetes; systemic lupus erythematosus (a connective-tissue disease that may also cause scalp scarring); certain skin disorders, — for instance scleroderma, lichen planus, shingles and herpes. If scalp scarring occurs, the hair loss is permanent.

• *Acute stress or trauma* may trigger the sudden shedding of large numbers of growing or resting hairs.

• In *anogen effluvium*, thousands of growing hairs suddenly fall out within days, for instance, following a catastrophic accident (e.g., loss of a parent or loved person), toilet training (stressful to toddlers), cancer chemotherapy or radiation therapy and fad diets (low in protein or under 1,000 calories a day). Once the cause is removed, rapid hair regrowth is the rule.

• In *telogen effluvium*, an exaggerated loss of resting hairs typically occurs when a dramatically shortened growth cycle triggers the simultaneous loss of many resting hairs — for example, a few months after a prolonged fever, a severe viral infection, blood loss, serious depression or exposure to toxic chemicals. Chemicals and drugs known to trigger exaggerated telogen hair shedding include:
  • strong bleaching agents;
  • some high blood pressure or heart medicines (e.g., propanolol);
  • some metals (e.g., arsenic, lead, mercury, thalium);
  • anticoagulants (e.g., heparin, coumarins);
  • antithyroid agents (e.g., carbimazole, thiouracil).

chemicals and drugs. Except in male balding, hair lost through injury, illness or stress usually grows back within a few months.

Male pattern baldness is widespread and distressing

While baldness isn't a disease, a cure has been avidly pursued throughout history. In the 20 centuries since Julius Caesar reportedly combed his fast-thinning hair over his bald spot, no effective baldness remedy has yet emerged. For most men, including three million or so bald-domed Canadians, losing hair is a fate to be borne with dignity.

A receding hairline reflects age, but not necessarily great age, since some men start balding quite young. With the spurt in androgen secretion at puberty, the hairline moves back a little in 96 percent of boys and 80 percent of girls. Most boys continue to shed hair as they mature. By age 35 to 40, two-thirds of Caucasian men have some signs of balding. There are several patterns of male-type baldness, but it usually follows a characteristic design, starting at the temples, often combined with a balding spot at the back of the head which gradually spreads, leaving a horseshoe-shaped fringe at the sides. The side fringe rarely disappears altogether. Male-pattern balding goes in waves punctuated by periods of stability. The loss may begin at age 20, then stop, only to start up again a few years later. Since male-pattern baldness is largely hereditary, a man can usually, although not always, predict the extent of his future baldness by examining family portraits.

The rate of male balding speeds up with advancing age, or if there is an inherited tendency to bald early or an overabundance of male hormone within the hair follicles. The hormonal link is complex. Eunuchs, who produce no testosterone, never develop male-pattern baldness — even if they inherit a baldness gene. Studies show that while balding men don't have higher-than-average circulating testosterone levels, they do possess above-average amounts of a powerful testosterone derivative, dihydrotestosterone, in the scalp. The hair follicles convert circulating testosterone into dihydrotestosterone, which produces ever weaker hairs. More and more hairs are shed, as the hairs become thinner and thinner until they are too fine to survive daily wear and tear.

People will go to almost any length to regrow thinning hair, but experts stress that, until now, inherited male-pattern balding hasn't responded to most stimulants, applications, injections or other remedies. Specific foods or vitamins don't regrow hair — although good nutrition is essential for healthy hair. A few hormonal remedies may work temporarily; systemic (oral) steroids induce hair regrowth for as long as they are taken, but the associated risks preclude their use; topical female hormones can regrow hair in balding women but have an anti-androgen effect that may feminize male bodies; spironolactone (Aldactone) may help a few men. If women have an endocrine (hormone) imbalance, vitamin-A acid lotions may have the ability to regrow hair in some.

Do any drugs reverse male-pattern baldness?

The most effective pharmaceutical baldness remedy to date is joint use of the drug minoxidil (used topically) and spironolactone (an anti-androgen, taken orally). The idea of using minoxidil for baldness arose because almost all people taking it for circulatory problems unexpectedly found increased hair growth all over the body, sometimes in embarrassing excess. Enterprising researchers ground up minoxidil tablets, put them into a cream and applied the product to balding scalps. The result was hair regrowth in some. Subsequent studies confirmed that minoxidil (marketed as Regaine or Rogaine), regularly applied in the right concentration (a 1 to 2 percent solution), stimulates hair regrowth on some bald heads. But less than 10 percent of men achieve satisfactory results. Regrowth never exceeds 4 cm (approximately an inch and a half). In about a third of the men who tried it, minoxidil produced a soft, downy fuzz; in the rest, there was no hair regrowth at all! The disadvantages of minoxidil are its high cost (not covered by health insurance schemes, as it's considered a cosmetic); the fact that it only grows hair for as long as it's applied; its unpredictable success; and the fact that it takes at least eight months of daily application to discover if one is among the lucky few whose hair will grow. Its side effects include local itching and prickling; headaches (in 40 percent of users); dizzy spells or lightheadedness; and heartbeat irregularities. Although the drug appears to be safe when rubbed into the scalp — since little is absorbed into the bloodstream — it is a vasodilator (it expands blood vessels) and is not recommended for anyone with heart disease. An initial burst of enthusiasm notwithstanding, it seems unlikely that minoxidil will improve the fate of most bald heads.

What about hair transplants?

Surgical hair transplantation with scalp reduction (scalp tightening) can be used to regrow hair in both men and women. The ideal candidates are those with thick hair at the donor site (the area from which the hair is taken). Much like shrubs that have been transplanted — roots and all — bits of growing hair transplanted to the bald parts of the scalp may grow well. Punch-graft surgery is performed in successive sessions, usually four months apart, but sometimes spread over years. The procedure is done by taking two to four mm (about 0.1 in) "plugs" of hair-bearing scalp from the still growing parts and transplanting them into small holes bored to receive them. It takes 250 to 400 plugs, with 10 to 15 hairs each, to fill a normally receding hairline. In each surgical session, only 75 to 100 plugs are transplanted, so as not to compromise the scalp's blood supply. The plugs are planted in neat rows, back to front, according to a carefully designed plan. Within a couple of weeks the hairs on the transplanted grafts fall out, but, all being well, regrow in a few months. Postoperative complications are few; pain is controlled by painkillers, bleeding is stopped by pressure and hair can be washed within about a week. It's crucial to plant the plugs in the right direction, to avoid a messy look. If done incorrectly, the transplantee may end up with hair going in all directions. One University of Toronto physician recommends that those contemplating hair replacement avoid being "scalped" by looking at pictures of those already treated by the chosen surgeon, before deciding on a hair transplant. It's wise to choose a physician who regularly does the procedure and has the required dexterity!

Women too may bald

In women, baldness is often diffuse alopecia — with hair loss all over the head, rather than just at the top and center. But it too is usually inherited, with progressive diminution in follicle size, and increasingly fine hair. One Dutch study found that 27 percent of women in their thirties and 64 percent of those between 40 and 70 showed some balding. Hair-thinning in women increases after menopause, when estrogen levels drop off, owing to hormonal imbalance. Other causes include: birth-control pills; certain drugs (e.g., danazol, cimetidine, some beta blockers, chemotherapy for cancer); adrenal or pituitary problems. Treatment for female balding includes estrogen therapy, cyproterone acetate, spironalactone, or minoxidil, and a topical solution of estradiol. But in the words of one dermatologist, "A good wig is often the best choice."

Too much hair can be as embarrassing as too little

For some women, too much hair growing in places that shouldn't be hairy can be as distressing a problem as male balding. Hirsutism (excessive hairiness), sometimes inherited, can arise from disease involving overproduction of androgens by the adrenal glands or ovaries. Excess hairiness in prepubescent children or during the menopause requires medical and hormonal assessment to rule out an underlying endocrine (glandular) abnormality. Several remedies are available for mild hair overgrowth. Dark hair can be bleached to make it less obvious. Or hair can be removed by plucking, shaving or rubbing with an abrasive such as pumice stone, without making it grow back faster or more stubbly. Waxing — applying hot wax, allowing it to cool and harden and then stripping it off together with the hair — is best done by a trained cosmetician. Depilatories — chemicals that dissolve excess hair on contact — must be used with care in order not to irritate the skin. (It's wise to test a small patch of skin first to check for sensitivity or allergy to the chemicals.) Electrolysis, the only permanent method of destroying hair follicles by an electric current, is a time-consuming procedure which may cause temporary irritation. It leaves tiny, pit-like scars, and if incompletely done results in regrowth. Newer methods using high-frequency current (electrocoagulation) give good results. A skilled operator can destroy 100 hairs in half an hour. But the process must be repeated frequently.

CHOOSE HAIR-CARE PRODUCTS WISELY

A "good" shampoo leaves hair manageable, easy to comb and glossy. It is untrue that washing hair often makes it oilier. Whether dry or greasy, hair should be washed as often as required to look good (even every day). Most experts recommend washing at least once a week to prevent dandruff. Very dry hair may be improved by massaging with a little olive or almond oil, covering and leaving on overnight, before washing next morning. Despite the exaggerated claims for countless products, studies show little difference between one shampoo and the next. Most contain the same basic ingredients with slightly more or fewer unnecessary extras (perfumes, fruit extracts, protein, herbs). Many modern hair technologists recommend acidic shampoos for all types of hair, as they don't aggravate the scalp, which is normally acidic (with a pH of 4.5 to 5.5). Acidic products help to tighten the cuticle scales, keep in moisture and enhance shine. More alkaline types (with a higher pH) that claim to suit oily hair may in fact swell the cuticle, bleach the color, and be too drying and overly harsh. Protein shampoos do not repair split ends, and although they may coat the hair shaft, making it smoother, they cannot "nourish" hair because their molecules are too large to enter the cortex.

Most modern hair conditioners contain cationic quaternary ammonium compounds, providing a positive charge that reduces static and makes hair less "fly-away." Some products, particularly those containing benzalkonium chloride as the active ingredient, are good conditioners. Those with added polymers, collagen, balsam, silicones or resins that bond with and coat the hair shaft, may provide a protective film and smooth out the cuticle, reducing snarls and tangles. Conditioners that give "extra body" may contain waxes that, when dry, make it look fuller; some contain oils/fats (e.g., lanolin, mineral oil) to smooth hair, and a few have humectants that supposedly hold in water. Price and exotic ingredients bear little or no relation to efficacy. As with shampoos, most conditioning products that claim to nourish hair do nothing of the sort, as the ingredients cannot enter the hair unless they contain transformants — molecules small enough to penetrate the cortex.

Permanent-waving solutions open up the hair shaft and rearrange the inner hair molecules, breaking and reforming the sulphur bonds by a process that gives off the familiar sulphide odor. Modern perming solutions (mostly ammonium or sodium sulphite) are more flexible, safer and more controllable than former types. They have a gentler hair-reforming action and can be used on fragile or colored hair. Wound on rollers of varying sizes, hair gets a permanent curl of the desired tightness. The extent of the wave also depends on the kind of hair (finer hair curls faster) and the time the solution stays on. To finish, a neutralizing agent or oxidizer is put on to

halt the curling process. The perming action must be stopped at the right time to avoid over-processing. A perm should never be done on hair dyed with metallic products, and only with extreme care (with gentler lotions) on hair that's recently been bleached or permanently tinted. Dual processing could disintegrate hair made porous by tinting. Perming after hair coloring requires extreme care — as any trained hairdresser well knows.

Straightening hair uses the same solutions as a perm, but is far harder on hair, as it must be constantly pulled straight during the procedure.

Combating dandruff

Although many individuals are plagued by dandruff all year round, dry, cold winter air, as well as less sunlight, worsen the problem. Dandruff results from the scalp's normal peeling process, and if it is excessive it may be a form of seborrhea. Large, dry, persistent flakes could be due to psoriasis. Medical studies suggest that dandruff may be linked to the fungus *P. ovale*, which is found on everyone's skin. In dandruff sufferers this fungus may be more abundant . While there are differing viewpoints on whether *P. ovale* is the primary cause of dandruff or merely a secondary infection, most dermatologists agree that it plays some role. Even if *P. ovale* is a cause, other factors also influence the development of dandruff. Special shampoos such as those containing selenium (e.g., Selsun) and ketoconazole (Nizoral), as well as tar shampoos can help to subdue the flaking.

GETTING RID OF LICE

Despite the best efforts of health authorities, head lice continue to plague human beings, especially school-age children. Getting rid of them is tedious, but new medications and a little understanding of louse biology go a long way in eradicating these unwelcome visitors. Anthropologists report signs of lice in most societies, recording their presence on Egyptian mummies and in ancient Greece. When Thomas à Becket was murdered in Britain's Canterbury Cathedral in 1170, a contemporary wrote that "to the horror and amusement of spectators, the lice boiled over like water in a simmering cauldron," escaping from his thick

HAIR CARE ADVICE

- avoid binding hair too often or too tightly in styles such as braids and ponytails;
- don't tease or back-comb it too much;
- comb or brush gently;
- dry at low heat or let hair dry naturally without blow-drying;
- massage scalp to enhance blood flow (unless scalp psoriasis exists, in which case never rub the scalp);
- brush hair gently away from the scalp to sweep the natural oils to the ends;
- use a brush with natural or blunt-edged bristles; jagged sharp bristles can damage the hair.

LAYING TO REST SOME LOUSY MYTHS

MYTH: Head lice attack people of poor social standing.
FACT: No! Head lice indiscriminately infest all levels of society.
MYTH: Head lice only infect unhygienic people.
FACT: No! Lice feed equally well on blood from dirty, clean, short- or long-haired human scalps.
MYTH: People often get head lice from animals.
FACT: No! Human head lice do not live on other animals — you can't catch them from a dog, cat, hamster or other pet.
MYTH: People who get head lice should have their heads shaved.
FACT: No! While shaving the head may help in getting rid of lice, it is needlessly drastic. Several medications can now safely remove head lice.
MYTH: Once treated, head lice never return.
FACT: No! Repeat infestations can occur; no available treatment prevents reinfestation.

clothing as his body cooled. Lousiness remained widespread in Europe up to the last century, with even the upper classes so notoriously louse-ridden that some observers wondered whether such a constant parasite might not benefit humankind. Not so: the human body louse carries several diseases, including epidemic typhus and trench fever.

The lice that feed on human blood include the body louse, *Pediculus humanus*; the "crab" louse, *Pediculus humanus pubis*, and the head louse, *Pediculus humanus capitis*.

Body lice live primarily on coarse body hair and hidden in the seams of clothing, especially collars — which makes them very hard to detect. But thanks to improved sanitation, frequent bathing and changing of clothes, body lice are rarely found in our society any more. When seen in Canada, body lice infest mostly the very poor, the homeless and the mentally ill.

Pubic lice (known as "crabs") are still with us, and are transmitted by sexual contact, mainly among adolescents and young adults. They may spread to the beard, mustache, eyelashes and eyebrows. If lice of the pubic variety are found on the eyelashes or eyebrows, petrolatum (petroleum) jelly may be used to suffocate them (it cuts off their oxygen supply).

Head lice, which infest the scalp and head hair, cause no serious health problems. The human head louse is a grayish-brown, bloodsucking parasite about the size of a sesame seed. Although the term "lousy" conjures up images of filth and outbreaks of lice are commonly greeted with disgust, head lice carry no diseases. Despite popular myths equating lice with uncleanliness, these insects infect clean heads as often as dirty ones. Head lice cannot survive at or below room temperatures but thrive in warm conditions — behind the ears or close to the hairline being cosy spots. A louse-ridden human head may give hospitality to about 24 lice at one time. The mature female louse lays minute, teardrop-shaped, whitish eggs close to the scalp, and they are securely attached to individual hairs by a tough, gluey cement. Popularly called "nits," louse eggs hatch in a week to 10 days, and in another week, when they reach maturity, the reproductive cycle begins again. Once a louse egg hatches, its

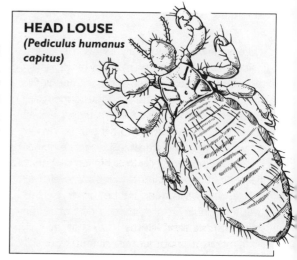

HEAD LOUSE
(Pediculus humanus capitus)

casing or "nit" is left empty. In contrast to the glistening pearly look of live eggs, nit cases are a dull gray. The duration of a louse infestation can be calculated by observing the distance of the eggs or nits from the scalp surface. Hair grows about five to six mm (0.2 in) a week so any nits found farther than that from the scalp are more than seven days old and have already hatched. Both live and hatched eggs remain so firmly attached to the hair that they're hard to remove by ordinary shampooing.

How head lice spread

Human head lice tend to spread among children crowded together in urban daycare centers and primary schools. The louse has no wings, nor can it jump from host to host. It moves by grasping a shaft of hair with its tiny front claws and swinging from hair to hair, so it can't wander far from the scalp. Lice often travel by direct head-to-head contact (as when children sit or play with their heads close together), or indirectly, via shared items such as hats, coathooks, scarves, bike helmets, headphones, hairbrushes, toys or bedding.

Head lice are more common in girls than boys, although not necessarily more common in those with long hair. Possibly girls tend to have closer physical contact with each other than boys, making it easier for lice to get around, although boys do switch baseball helmets and other gear. Why lice are uncommon among adolescent boys remains a mystery. Some experts speculate that the male hormones secreted in adolescence may be a louse "turn-off," or that boys have less close physical contact after puberty.

Most large urban schools identify a few

children with lice every year. The problem usually surfaces in the early fall when children return to school. Occasionally, a lice epidemic forces a school to close for a couple of days until all the children have been deloused. Health departments and schools are now switching from a "hands-on" head-searching policy to better lice-spotting education for teachers and parents. Each school and education authority sets its own regulations.

How to find head lice

The major sign of head lice is itchiness and scratching, particularly around the hairline and ears. As the itching only starts up a week or two after infestation, there may be no symptoms at first. Some people never feel itchy at all! But scratching may lead to secondary infections, and some louse-ridden people develop scalp scabs and enlarged neck nodes.

Confirmation of head lice means sighting a louse and/or its eggs — just visible to the naked eye. But spotting a louse and detecting the eggs isn't easy, especially on blond hair, where they hardly show up at all. Look behind the ears, close to the scalp, at the back of the neck and top of the head. Parents should check their children from time to time for lice, by parting the hair and examining it in good light, close to the scalp. The best way to see if a child has lice is to look for the eggs: tiny, white, glistening objects (or little gray hatched ones) cemented to the hair shaft, usually close to the scalp. Louse excrement looks like flecks of brown dust. In contrast to nits, dandruff or hair casts (bits of dead hair) are easily dislodged with a fingernail.

The standard treatment for head lice is an extra-thorough hair wash with a medicated, pediculicide (louse-killing) shampoo, or application of an anti-louse lotion once (and possibly again a week later). Effectiveness varies with the product and thoroughness of application. Most shampoos (except for Nix and Prioderm) will not abolish the eggs, and a repeat treatment may be needed. (Nix is a well-recommended cream rinse.) Lindane (Kwellada), an old standby used for 30 years, is primarily a louse-killer and is not as good a nit-killer — it is gradually being replaced by newer products. Some pharmacies store louse-killers behind the counter, although

PREVENTIVE ANTI-LOUSE STRATEGIES

- **Teach children not to share hats, headphones, combs, brushes or bicycle helmets, and to report any head itching.**
- **Check children's hair regularly for tell-tale signs of nits and lice, especially if a child is scratching a lot.**
- **Wash all clothing and sheets in use at the time of a louse outbreak in very hot water (above 55°C or 130°F) and dry in a hot dryer for 20 minutes at least. (Lice and their eggs are killed by high temperatures.)**
- **Since lice can't survive away from humans for more than a few days, nonwashable articles such as stuffed toys and woolens can be sealed in plastic bags for 10 days or so, or dry-cleaned.**
- **Alternatively, coats, hats and clothing can be left outside all day or overnight in winter (the cold kills lice and eggs), or put into a plastic bag and left overnight in the freezer.**
- **Soak all brushes and combs in hot water containing pediculicidal shampoo or 2 percent Lysol solution for a couple of hours.**
- **Vacuum items such as rugs, furniture, mattresses and pillows thoroughly; don't forget the car seats. Public health authorities agree that there's no need to fumigate.**
- **Certain anti-louse sprays can also be used on furniture, pillows and mattresses.**
- **Report lice in schoolchildren to the school nurse or principal.**

no prescription is needed. Once the eggs are dead, they still have to be removed, and they can't just be flicked off. A long-standing infestation with matted hair, louse discharge and a scalp infection can make a dreadful mess of hair and take ages to clean up.

"Nit-picking" is usually the worst of a lice problem. Getting rid of all the nits left after a delousing shampoo, by using a fine-toothed metal nit comb or tweezers, is a time-consuming, tedious procedure that can take hours per head, depending on the length of hair and the number of nits. Although nit combs are effective for thick hair, they are useless for the very fine hair of a young child. Each egg-bearing hair can be cut out with scissors, or one may end up using the fingernails! Some experts recommend soaking the hair in warm, diluted vinegar to make nit-picking easier — a step of no proven usefulness. A short haircut may make nit removal less time-consuming, but stigmatizes children. If someone in the family has lice, check all parts of the head on all the rest of the household members.

All household members with signs of infestation should be treated for lice at the same time. People who've had lice must be rechecked once a week for signs of lingering lice for several weeks.

HAND AND NAIL CARE TIPS:

- Use cotton-lined, vinyl gloves for wet work, but remove them frequently to let hands air out.
- Apply hand creams frequently (e.g., Aquatain, Prevex, Glyzerone, Lachydrin, urea-containing types or any chosen moisturizer) after washing.
- Try cool compresses to soothe irritated hands.
- Use steroid creams prescribed by a physician (e.g., Betnovate,

Halog) for badly cracked or inflamed hands.
- Use nail clippers to remove rough edges of nails, instead of nibbling.
- File rather than cut the nails, don't push the cuticle too far back, and use a flat wooden stick or a piece of terrycloth rather than a metal file — it's less damaging.
- When applying nail polish, keep the polish and its vapors

away from the face.
- Remove polish from nails with as little remover as possible.
- Yellowing or brittle nails may need a "polish-holiday" for a week or two.
- Try to avoid skin contact with polish or removers; use cotton swabs to remove polish; never dip the fingers into the remover.
- After using nail-polish remover, wash the nails and massage in cream.

HAND AND NAIL CARE

Dry, cracked, chapped hands are particularly common among mechanics, outdoor workers, cleaning personnel, nurses, surgeons, those who do housework and anyone whose hands are often wet and cold. Since hand irritation may be due to skin diseases such as psoriasis, herpes, contact dermatitis, impetigo or other disorders, it's wise to seek medical advice before assuming that everyday chores are to blame!

The best way to avoid chapped hands is to keep hands well dried and protected from the cold and wind, to wear pure cotton or cotton-lined vinyl gloves for wet work (rubber can cause allergies) and to frequently apply creams to moist skin. (Remove gloves often to air out the hands.) Dry, brittle nails that easily break are another common wintertime problem, but can also be due to illness, or exposure to chemicals, strong detergents or nail-polish removers. Soaking brittle nails in warm water for a few minutes and then applying olive oil or petrolatum (petroleum) jelly at night can strengthen them and make them more flexible.

Most special nail creams are no better than ordinary moisturizers. Nail hardeners will harden the nails, but may provoke a condition where the nail plate lifts from the nail bed. They can also discolor the nails or cause bleeding under them, so they should be used with caution. The adhesives used to apply artificial nails can cause allergic reactions. Contrary to folklore, gelatin usually does nothing for dry or brittle nails, unless the person is suffering from a protein deficiency, in which case it will take three to six months to get noticeable results!

FOOT CARE

Although most of us pitifully neglect our feet, those hard-working extremities deserve the very best of care. Most of us abuse these precious appendages that support and propel us, allow us to jump, dance and play sports, and, in an average lifetime, carry us some 160,000 km or 100,000 miles, or several times around the world.

Beautiful is not an apt word for most feet, which are often better described as knobbly, gnarled, callused or deformed. The deformities could be avoided by better attention to a good shoe fit! Despite their importance to our everyday movement, few of us lavish on our feet the care we give our face and hands. One doctor notes wryly that when asked to undress for an examination many "remove everything except their shoes and socks!" Taking their feet for granted, or being ashamed of them, people imagine they need no attention. Similarly, some physicians ignore foot problems and omit foot examinations during a checkup visit. However, even a seemingly insignificant foot ailment — an ingrown nail, an infected corn — can completely immobilize someone!

Foot problems arise from inherited tendencies, biomechanical factors, infections and systemic (general) diseases. The more vigorously feet are used, the greater the likelihood of foot problems. Athletes, soldiers and dancers are among those with the worst foot trouble. "Ballet dancers have the world's worst feet," comments one foot doctor. "Their feet take an awful beating with bruises, toe fractures, tarsal inflammation and soft corns."

The penalties of ill-fitting shoes and foot fetishism

Although many foot deformities are due to an inherited predisposition, they are greatly aggravated by ill-fitting shoes. Many shoes not only fail to provide enough support but disfigure feet by deforming toe joints and distorting the gait. Most of us pay too little heed to shoe buying. Even with today's emphasis on fitness, and the helpful acceptance of "running shoes for every occasion," many female shoe fashions seem tailor-made for foot torture.

Shoe fetishism and foot-eroticism are still with us. Women who want to look "smart" may wear strappy, tight, uncomfortable, narrow, dangerously high-heeled contraptions in leather, canvas and lucite created neither for comfort nor for sensible walking.

The most mutilating of foot fashions was Chinese footbinding, which stunted a baby girl's foot by bending the bones, to produce a woman with tiny "lily feet" barely able to hobble. This ancient custom supposedly started with a Chinese empress who had been born club-footed. To disguise the royal impediment, the court ladies bandaged their feet, establishing a norm for upper-caste Chinese women. And the practice, which lasted almost into this century, guaranteed they wouldn't marry below their class, as they couldn't walk without the help of servants. Although her toes might be hideously bent, a Chinese bride's tiny shoe was exhibited as proof of her worth. Foot fetishism also exists in other cultures. Ancient Jewish dress included heavy ankle bells that forced women to take tiny, mincing steps; the tinkle of bells beneath bulky skirts was supposed to act as a powerful male aphrodisiac. The wives of some African chiefs are still laden with iron leg chains reducing their gait to a slow waddle.

The high-heeled pump, most damaging of today's styles, was introduced by King Louis XIV's cobbler as an ingenious ploy to make the short monarch look taller. Foot doctors call high-heeled shoes "human leg corruptors" — forcing women to take twice the normal number of steps and teeter precariously rather than walk as nature intended them to. High-heeled shoes, especially those that are too short or have pointed toes, push the big toe toward the other toes, creating excess pressure on the joint that joins the big toe to the foot — perhaps even dislocating it — with a consequent buildup of tissue and fluid to produce bunions. A very pointed shoe warps and bends the toes into the shape of

---

FOOT SPECIALISTS

Family physicians can advise on or treat most foot problems, but for more complex disorders, specialists are needed. The providers of specialized foot care in Canada are orthopedic surgeons, dermatologists, chiropodists and podiatrists. Any major foot surgery comes under the domain of orthopedic surgeons, who specialize in bone and joint problems. For serious skin problems of the feet a dermatologist should be consulted. Podiatrists are excellent for general foot care. They are not physicians but DPMs, holding degrees in podiatric medicine, with several years of specialized training in a podiatry school. Using modern biomechanical analysis, podiatrists can identify specific foot faults and design tailor-made orthotic devices and supports that go inside shoes. Orthotics counteract underlying foot or postural faults and can compensate for a deformity, keeping people as mobile as possible. Although regulations vary, podiatrists in the United States and some parts of Canada are not only licenced to treat all foot ailments but also to do minor surgery, such as correcting a hammer toe, or some bunion removals, under local anesthesia. Podiatrists' fees are partly covered by many health insurance plans. Good podiatric care is especially helpful for looking after seniors' feet.

Chiropodists have less extensive training — two to three years — and usually help with foot care in hospitals and clinics, interacting with physicians, orthopedic surgeons and rheumatologists. Referral by a physician is not necessary to see a chiropodist, but the fees are not usually covered by health insurance plans.

---

a claw, deforming them into "hammer toes." The vamp (top) of a high-heeled shoe may irritate and inflame tissues; a too-shallow heel can create pump bumps — bony outgrowths at the heel. The posture produced by high-heeled shoes can overarch the spine, contributing to back problems. But the greatest strain in high-heeled footwear is taken by the ankles, which thicken, and by the calf muscles, which shorten. Continual wearing of high heels can alter the calf muscle so much that some women no longer feel comfortable in flat-heeled shoes. Women accustomed to high heels should not change abruptly to flats — this can strain the leg muscles.

How to buy shoes wisely
The cardinal rule in shoe-buying is to sacrifice fashion for foot health whenever possible. Shoes should be wide enough in front not to cramp the toes, with room for air to circulate, and long enough. Some experts suggest that shoes should be a thumb-width longer than the big toe (to give adequate room and prevent

toes banging the end of shoes). Test new shoes by walking around for five to ten minutes in the store before buying to be sure the fit is right. The best time to buy shoes is in the afternoon, when feet may have swelled up — even by half a size — from the day's activities. Most people have one foot larger than the other, so get both feet measured while standing, and choose a size that fits the larger foot. As to material — leather is great; calfskin is pliable and keeps its shape well so it's probably the best shoe leather. Kid stretches, and pigskin cracks when wetted and then dried. Rubber or plastic shoes are not porous and are apt to cause perspiration — which may foster maceration (wet, irritated skin). It's essential to change shoes (and socks) frequently.

Aging feet need vigilant care

Older people, who are more prone to circulatory problems and infections, should take good care of their feet and have foot problems checked by a professional. Nails, corns and calluses may best be trimmed by a specialist. Foot problems in the elderly cause much discomfort and immobility. The skin may be thin and sensitive and need cushioning in fleecy slippers. Nails may become dry and thick, requiring good moisturizing and specialized trimming. The elderly may find footcare difficult owing to arthritis, frailty or other infirmities. People with diseases such as arthritis, gout and circulatory problems must be particularly watchful about good foot care and look after their feet well. Proper shoe fitting and frequent changes of footwear and stockings are essential.

Diabetics must practice special foot care, and avoid shoes that irritate pressure points. Foot problems that would be minor in nondiabetics can quickly become dangerous in diabetics, so they should always consider getting professional foot care. A loss of nerve sensation may desensitize diabetic feet, allowing them to be injured without this being noticed. A foot ulcer or infected sore can develop without being felt, so diabetics should examine their feet every day for signs of trouble. Restricted blood circulation makes diabetic feet prone to ulcers that could be catastrophic if they develop gangrene. Because of reduced sensitivity to hot and cold, diabetics should avoid overheated baths, not sit too close to fires or heaters, switch off bed heaters on retiring, use no bedsocks unless loose and dry their feet well before putting on socks and shoes. (See also chapter 16, section on diabetes.)

BANISHING WARTS

Warts are due to transmissible viruses. They can occur at any age but are especially prevalent among children aged 12 to 16 — perhaps because of their intimacy and the frequency of open scrapes and scratches through which wart infections gain entry. One British study found that about 16 percent of teenagers had warts on the hands, feet or face. These somewhat distasteful, flesh-colored skin protrusions appear on the fingers, face, feet or other parts of the body, including the genitals (where they may be tiny, flat and almost invisible). Some warts persist for years but should nonetheless be investigated as they can spread, even if not especially uncomfortable or unsightly.

While most warts are harmless and reasonably inconspicuous, some become exceptionally big, growing several centimeters (an inch or so) across. On a prominent part of the body such as the face, they present a cosmetic problem. On the soles of the feet, warts can make walking painful. Venereal or genital warts may lead to cervical cancer in women. They should be removed in either sex, and the sex partner should also be checked for warts.

Viruses cause warts —
so most are contagious

Warts are due to viruses known as papilloma viruses. About 50 different subtypes of the human papilloma virus (HPV) family have now been identified, and are responsible for warts at specific body sites. Quite contagious, these viruses can be transferred from one body part to another — say, from hands to feet or face — or from person to person. One can pick up wart viruses from damp towels touched by an infected person or from the floors of changing rooms or showers. Genital warts are spread by sexual contact. Nasal wart viruses can be passed among cocaine users who snort the drug through shared holders.

A RUNDOWN OF SOME COMMON WARTS

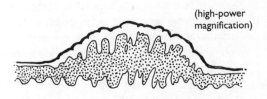

(high-power magnification)

Common warts occur on hands, fingers, face.

Common warts (Verruca vulgaris)

These solitary, raised, "spiky" bumps may grow larger over a few weeks, developing deep, scaly furrows of keratin (a hard protein). They bleed in pinpoint spots when pared or cut. Common warts may occur singly or in groups anywhere on the body, especially on hands, fingers and face — typically on children's hands. Regular treatment with over-the-counter peeling agents (such as salicylic acid and lactic acid in a collodion base) often succeeds in removing common warts, especially if applied after a good wash with soap and water and gentle abrasion with an emery board or callus-file (see "Modern wart treatments").

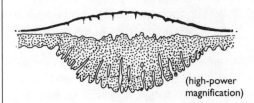

(high-power magnification)

Plantar warts occur on sole (plantar region).

Plantar warts

These foot warts are more common in adults than children. They are stubborn, long-living, deep-rooted, sometimes painful warts on the soles (plantar regions) of the feet. Under the constant pressure of walking they tend to flatten out or be pushed inwards into the foot, becoming very difficult to eradicate. Mosaic plantar warts are made up of several warts amalgamated together, producing large warts that are hard to eradicate. To distinguish an ordinary foot callus (skin thickening) from a plantar wart, the medical test is what happens on cutting or paring the skin: a wart has tiny bleeding points, a callus doesn't usually bleed.

Treatment of plantar warts is usually with a salicylic acid paint, cryotherapy (liquid nitrogen freezing) or lasers. Surgery, X-ray therapy and electrocautery (burning) are not recommended

for foot warts, particularly if they occur on weight-bearing surfaces, because of the danger of scarring and permanent discomfort. Gentle planing with an emery board may be all that's needed until they disappear on their own. Foot warts are better left alone than treated harshly, which may irritate the walking surface. A scar on the foot due to rough treatment can end up being a lifetime nuisance — more painful than the wart it was meant to eradicate.

Plane or flat warts

Plane or flat warts

Affecting adults and children, these tiny, flat, flesh-colored or brownish warts usually appear on the face, arms, hands or neck, or occasionally around the eyes. Localized, single flat warts are probably best left alone. Strong wart remedies should never be used on the face as they can cause lasting scars. Multiple severe, flat warts often respond to liquid nitrogen freezing or use of prescribed vitamin A (retinoid) creams that cause superficial peeling. Treatment may trigger the immune system into action by releasing a little wart antigen.

Genital warts:
On females: occur on vulva, cervix, anus
On males: occur on penis and anus

Genital warts (Condyloma acuminata)

The former Greek term for wart, *condyloma*, is now reserved exclusively for genital warts, which occur around the anus and on the penis, vagina, vulva and cervix. They are increasingly common in Canada, both in women and in men. These warts, spread by sexual contact, are often flat, tiny and difficult to spot and diagnose. About two-thirds of women and one-third of men with genital warts also have signs of other sexually transmitted diseases such as chlamydia, gonorrhea or syphilis. There is mounting evidence that certain genital warts may trigger cancer of the cervix in women and, although rare, cancer of the penis in men. (See also chapter 8, section on cervical cancer.)

There may be a time lag or "incubation period" of two to three months between the time of exposure, when the viruses enter the skin, and the time the wart is seen on the skin. Most warts are small, but get larger over a few weeks to months, sometimes becoming flecked with little black spots. If scraped, they may bleed in pinpoint flecks. The wart virus concentration in an infected area is greatest 6 to 12 months after infection, gradually declining thereafter, so that warts usually disappear on their own after a few months to a couple of years.

Many wart "cures" claim to take 12 weeks — a time span within which some warts would disappear without any treatment. But warts can persist stubbornly despite all efforts to obliterate them. How and why some warts regress but others don't isn't known. Possibly the body's immune defenses fight off the infection. Some wart treatments work by irritating the warts slightly so that they release wart antigen (active ingredient) into the blood, stimulating an immune response.

Wart cures old and new

Warts often persist because of low immune defenses. The variety of wart remedies demonstrates the difficulty of ridding the body of this stubborn viral nuisance. Wart cures, charms, incantations and spells date back to antiquity — "I ficky ficky thee" is one ancient charm — and some cures promoted magical transference of the wart to something or someone else. For instance, Sir Francis Bacon, the sixteenth-century scientist, rubbed warts with pork fat which he then hung out in the sun, hoping that his warts would disappear as the fat melted. In some parts of Britain, warts are still said to be removed by applying cow dung or rubbing the wart with a fresh potato and then throwing it away. In the western United States, folklore promotes rubbing warts with a coin and then throwing away the coin. In other parts of the world, warts are said to be abolished by rubbing them onto the father of an illegitimate child. The reputed success of some bizarre wart cures may rest more on the tendency of warts to clear up on their own rather than on any real efficacy.

Modern wart treatments

- *Salicylic acid* is the first line of attack, successful in 80 percent of common warts. Used regularly, salicylic acid will often cure common warts on the hands and feet within 10 to 12 weeks. It can eradicate flat warts, and small foot warts. Salicylic acid is marketed in a collodion base that hardens and covers the area to be peeled. As a solution or paste it is applied nightly from a dropper, or as a plaster (a stronger form). Since these solutions can not only destroy the wart but also damage the surrounding skin, they must not be overlavishly splashed on, but put strictly on the wart, with a toothpick, match or cuticle stick (many supplied applicators are too large). Wart paints are most effective if applied after the wart has been soaked in water and gently rubbed with a pumice stone or emery board to remove the loose top skin layer, allowing the solution better entry. If the skin gets rough, cracked or painful, salicylic acid treatment should be stopped for a day or two until the skin heals.
- *Cryotherapy* or freezing (with liquid nitrogen) is done over a period of weeks to months, with the freezing being repeated every one to three weeks. If too long a gap intervenes between freezings, the warts may regenerate. Done correctly it should not leave scars. It is often the treatment of choice and can be safely used during pregnancy.
- *Cantharidin*, available only by prescription, is a mitochondrial cell poison that causes cell membranes to break down and form blisters, getting rid of some especially resistant warts around the nail and other areas, usually without scarring. It should be used with extreme caution, especially in children, and not on the face as it can damage the delicate membranes of nose, mouth and eyes.
- *Enucleation* (blunt paring) to remove bulk may be useful for resistant plantar (foot) and other warts, to get rid of a big wart, but needs great care on pressure-bearing surfaces and remains a controversial method.
- *Interferon* and other immune-system stimulants, given systematically, have been tried for difficult warts with good reported cure

rates. However, the cost and the risk of skin reactions and other side effects limit their usefulness.

- *Electrocautery* is sometimes used, under local anesthetic, to burn off large warts — but never on the feet. It has had poor results.
- *Laser treatment* is highly successful in eradicating genital and common warts, sometimes as an adjunct to other wart remedies — but not on weight-bearing surfaces, as it can produce a painful scar.
- *Surgery* isn't encouraged for treating warts, particularly since the wart virus may spread around the cutting area, leading to recurrence. Surgery may leave a lasting scar or painful lump, particularly uncomfortable on the foot. It's not safe to pare off warts with a razor!
- *New approaches* include the use of retinoid (vitamin A) creams and inosine pranobex, chemicals only suitable for a selected few, used under medical surveillance.

Genital warts can be removed by:

- *Podophyllin*, a natural extract of plants such as the wild flower may apple, arrests cell division and is used in a 25–50 percent solution. Petroleum jelly is put onto the surrounding skin to protect it from the solution, which is precisely painted onto the wart once a week, left on two to six hours, then washed off. As treatment proceeds, podophylllin solution may be left on for progressively longer periods, but some blistering may occur and occasionally severe swelling and inflammation if too much is used. Podophyllin should not be used in pregnant women because it affects fetal development; nor should it be put on the vagina because it can be absorbed into the bloodstream causing vomiting and nausea. Self-treatment is not recommended. If four to six podophyllin treatments fail to get rid of genital warts, other methods such as freezing with liquid nitrogen, laser treatment or electrocautery may be tried.

HOME WART TREATMENTS REQUIRE CAUTION

Self-treating warts needs patience and at least 12 weeks of steady perseverance and adaptation to alternative remedies. They often fail because people give up too soon. Physicians warn that the wart treatment should never be worse than the problem itself. Since warts are generally harmless, treatment should be gentle and relatively painless, without creating excessive blisters or irritation. Wart removers available as over-the-counter products usually contain salicylic acid, and used properly they can cure 70–80 percent of common warts and 80–90 percent of plantar foot warts. But great care must be taken not to overirritate or inflame the area, and to apply the wart paint just to the warts, not to the healthy surrounding skin.

A couple of wart cures, recently reported in medical literature, claim high success rates without harmful effects:

- *Taping.* Completely cover the wart and surrounding skin by binding it (but not so tightly that it cuts off circulation) with plain surgical adhesive tape. Leave the tape on for seven days in all, removing it after the first 12 hours, and then rebinding for a further six days. This process can be repeated until the wart disappears. The method supposedly works well for finger warts.
- *The banana cure.* Cut pieces of fresh banana skin no bigger than the wart and secure with surgical tape. Apply fresh banana skin every morning. After a few weeks to three months, the wart should vanish.

(A biopsy is recommended before starting treatment to check for cancer-causing viral strains.) New forms can be applied by patients themselves.

- *Trichloracetic acid treatment* may help to remove genital warts.
- *Cryotherapy or freezing* is a popular, easy way to remove genital warts. Multiple freezing sessions may be needed, and there is occasionally some local discomfort, although the genital area generally heals easily and fast.
- *Electrocautery* can be useful in removing large areas of genital wart infection, leaving little or no scarring in this area.
- *Laser treatment* is increasingly used to remove genital warts that resist other treatment.
- *Fluorouracil cream* (containing an anti-cancer drug which blocks cell division) is a "last-ditch" method occasionally used for widespread, stubborn genital warts in women, but requires great care.

Eye, ear and tooth care

Eye care • Ear care • Ear infections • Tooth and gum care

6

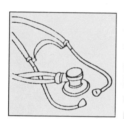

EYE CARE

The eyes, said to be "the windows of the soul," can relay clear or blurred images; they may be sparkling or dull, perhaps discolored, red, itchy, squinting or teary, thereby sometimes being a "window on disease." Eyes are sensory organs that give human beings vital information about the world around them. They need to be kept clean and in good working order. Any vision blurring, soreness, redness or other eye problems should receive prompt medical attention in order not to damage these most precious windows on the world.

Eye tests: for whom, when?

Routine eye tests should start in childhood. Every child needs an eye examination within the first year of life for conditions such as strabismus (lazy eye), again at age two or three and another upon entering school, at age six or seven. The eyes should be rechecked at age ten or eleven, and again in older teenagers, then periodically through adulthood and annually

ANATOMY OF THE HEALTHY EYE

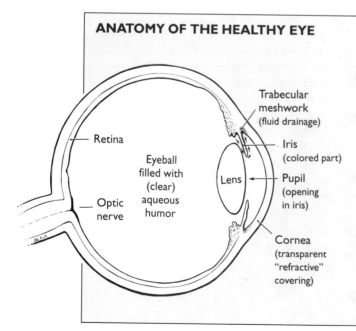

Retina

Eyeball filled with (clear) aqueous humor

Optic nerve

Lens

Trabecular meshwork (fluid drainage)

Iris (colored part)

Pupil (opening in iris)

Cornea (transparent "refractive" covering)

The eye functions like a camera. The front is covered by transparent tissue, the cornea. The colored iris opens and closes, like the diaphragm of a camera, controlling the amount of light that enters through the pupil (opening). The lens focuses light onto the retina, which registers images, much like the film in a camera. The retina also contains cells that are sensitive to color. The visual messages go from the retina via the optic nerve to the brain, where they are interpreted.

The front part of the eyeball is full of liquid, the aqueous humor, which carries nutrients to the eye tissues. The aqueous humor has been called "clear blood" — a transparent transport medium. (Obviously it wouldn't be useful to have an eye full of obscuring red blood.) In order for the nerves and other fragile structures within the eye to function properly, the aqueous humor is kept fresh and at constant pressure by fluid inflow from the ciliary body and constant outflow or drainage through the trabecular meshwork.

after age 65. The eyes need protection from foreign objects, infection and sunlight (which can cause cataracts).

Vision is tested by the familiar Snellen chart, with the big E at the top and increasingly small letters below, measuring the ability to see at a distance. A visual acuity of 20/20 means someone can see at 20 feet (6 m) what others with normal vision also see at 20 feet; 20/50 vision is less acute — the ability to see at 20 feet what those with normal sight can see at 50 feet (15 m) — and so on. Other tests assess visual field (side vision), eye-muscle function, intraocular (eyeball) pressure, and the condition of the lens and retina (using an ophthalmoscope) and the cornea (using a slit lamp).

Children who require eyeglasses are encouraged to wear them consistently — not leave them unused in a drawer! Many a school record is marred by a child's seeing the teacher or blackboard as a distant blur.

Some diseases that are not ordinarily associated with eye problems do endanger the eyes. For example, 50 percent of diabetics are at risk of eye disorders such as cataracts, glaucoma and retinopathy (retina damaged by flawed blood vessels). People with high blood pressure are also at risk for retinopathy. Rheumatoid arthritis sufferers often develop "dry eye," and people with thyroid disease may have that too, and other ocular symptoms.

Eye-focusing problems

The most common eye trouble that plagues people is faulty eye focusing — refractive errors that occur because light entering the eye isn't precisely focused on the retina by the optic lens and cornea.

In myopia (nearsightedness) nearby objects appear clear and distant ones look fuzzy or blurred. With hyperopia (farsightedness), close-up vision is hazy and distant objects are more clearly seen. Astigmatism is a distortion in the curvature of the cornea or lens. Presbyopia is an impaired ability to focus up close — a problem common in older people. Fortunately, most eye focusing problems can be remedied simply with corrective lenses, which are worn by about half the North American population, as either eyeglasses or contact lenses.

Contact lenses

Contact lenses are thin plastic (or occasionally silicone) discs, made to prescription, that float on the tears on top of the cornea — the eye's transparent outer covering. The surface layer of oil and tears holds them in place. A good contact lens allows the cornea to breathe (get oxygen) by gas exchange under the lens, or through gas-permeable material (as with soft contact lenses). Contact lenses require more care than ordinary eyeglasses because they touch the eyes and transfer onto them whatever is on them — such as pollen, dust or bacteria — possibly causing an infection. Contacts must be kept scrupulously clean with the recommended disinfectant fluids. They are particularly suitable for myopic (nearsighted) eyes. Many people find contacts comfortable, unobtrusive and infinitely preferable to glasses. But not everyone can wear them. Some eyes become irritated by contact lenses. Even satisfied everyday contact lens wearers need a pair of prescription glasses as a standby in case of eye irritation, or when suffering from a head cold.

Contact lenses now come as soft or rigid (gas-permeable) types, both available as either disposable or extended-wear forms (that can be left in overnight, some even up to a week). Hard contact lenses, the first type on the market, have been replaced by gas-permeable contact lenses with superior oxygen permeability. Gas-permeable forms provide better correction for astigmatism than soft contacts, and generally provide better vision-correction than soft lenses. But it takes an adjustment period of a few weeks to get used to them, and they can irritate the eye, so they are usually removed after 12 hours of use and at night.

Soft contact lenses, made of water-absorbing plastics, let oxygen through and are usually comfortable to wear and nonirritating from day one. They are easier to adapt to than rigid lenses, and unlikely to be dislodged when playing sports. However, they are less durable than rigid types, must be removed at night and rip easily (perhaps irritating the eye). They require meticulous cleaning, as their high water content makes them prone to bacterial contamination. Soft contacts need overnight disinfectant soaks and are ruined if allowed to dry out.

EYE-CARE SPECIALISTS

Ophthalmologists are physicians who specialize in medical and surgical eye care. In addition to testing vision and prescribing corrective glasses, they diagnose and treat eye disorders, also doing eye surgery for eye disorders when needed.
Optometrists diagnose, manage, and treat some eye conditions and are licensed to do vision tests, prescribe corrective lenses and fit contact lenses. Although not medically qualified, they have completed a three-year university science course plus a four-year program in optometry.
Opticians are technicians who fill prescriptions for eyeglasses or contact lenses; they are not permitted to test vision or treat eye problems.

EYEDROPS — CAUTION NEEDED

Most topical eyedrops or ointments tend to concentrate in the eye without getting into the bloodstream and causing side effects. However, some drops affect parts of the body far from the eyes — such as glaucoma medications, which can alter the heart rate and aggravate asthma. Always report any symptoms to the doctor, even if they don't seem related to the eye medication; also report any eye drops used when being medically checked for other problems.

SIGNS AND SYMPTOMS OF EYE TROUBLE

- eye dryness (grittiness, feeling of "something in the eye");
- red or painful eyes;
- photophobia (discomfort in bright light);
- sudden change(s) in visual function (such as blurriness, decreased side vision);
- excess eye secretions, a sticky discharge;
- eye swelling and itchiness.

Disposable soft contact lenses are worn for two weeks, then discarded and replaced by a new pair. They are very thin and comfortable to wear, reduce the risks of infection and need no special cleaning other than being kept in disinfectant fluid when not worn.

Extended-wear soft contact lenses can be worn overnight and even left in for up to a week before being removed for cleaning, but they're rather fragile and tricky to look after.

Contact lens care takes time, and it means stocking up on the necessary cleaning solutions and being sure to wash the hands before putting in or removing the lens and before applying eye cosmetics. Wearers shouldn't use old — likely contaminated — eye makeup, or share eye makeup. (Eye makeup is best applied after the contacts are inserted.) All contact lens wearers should have a backup pair of regular, up-to-date prescription eyeglasses to wear in case of eye infection or fatigue, and when suffering from a cold, as the contact lens can get coated with infected secretions, increasing risks of infection and corneal ulceration.

Sunglasses

Sunglasses are not mere fashion accessories. They prevent eye damage from excess UV light, block glare and are especially helpful when driving, boating, skiing or on the beach. Those who use prescription glasses should have one pair with good-quality tinted lenses. The darkest glasses are not necessarily the best UV blockers. Unless they have a coating that blocks out blue light (in the 290–400 nanometer range), UV rays can still penetrate and harm the eyes. Good dark lenses cut out 75–90 percent of visible and a fair proportion of UV light. They are usually amber or brown, not purple or gray. Check the labels on sunglasses; look for the proportion of UV-blockage provided. General-purpose dark glasses should screen out 95 percent of UVB (short-wave ultraviolet rays) and 60 percent of UVA (longer-wave UV), and are fine for recreation such as tennis, hiking, skating or everyday boating. Special-purpose sunglasses, recommended for bright situations such as skiing, mountain-climbing and sunny beaches, block 99 percent of UVB and at least 70 percent of

UVA, as well as 70 percent of visible light. If the UV-blocking capacity is not marked on the glasses, check with the manufacturer to see how much protection is provided. Never wear dark glasses at night as they compromise vision. Make sure all eyeglasses, dark or clear, are made of impact-resistant material that won't shatter easily.

Pay attention to aging eyes

As the eyes age, they undergo normal changes in structure and function that reduce their efficiency. For example, with age the lens loses flexibility, making it harder to focus on nearby objects. By age 65 most people have to wear reading glasses for close work. The muscles that dilate the pupil also weaken with age, and the pupil becomes smaller, so that older people require brighter light than the young for doing similar tasks. Older people may also have trouble adapting from bright to darker places, and increased sensitivity to glare because of reflection in the eye. "Accommodation difficulties" are also common, with a delay in changing focus from distant to nearby objects, such as from the traffic to the instrument panel while driving. Peripheral vision (the ability to see things at the edges of the visual field) and night vision may also diminish because of age-related retinal changes. Such vision changes may make driving and crossing streets hazardous for seniors, who should be aware of the dangers.

Age-related macular degeneration

This disorder, a common cause of vision blurring which affects about 20 percent of those over 65, occurs because of damage to the macula (from the Latin meaning "spot"), in the retina's central area. Small blood vessels grow into the macular region, harming the retinal cells that control central vision. Developing gradually and painlessly, often in both eyes (either simultaneously or one after the other), macular degeneration distorts images — producing central blurring or dimming while the surrounding vision remains clear. Straight lines or telephone poles may appear wavy or seem to have a missing segment. Because the macula

A RUNDOWN ON SOME COMMON EYE DISORDERS

Dry eye Related to the withering of the lacrimal (tear) glands, this condition predisposes the eyes to infection. True dry eye, or Sjögrens syndrome, is an autoimmune disease — also accompanied by an unpleasantly dry mouth and dry mucous membranes. Lubricating fluids and "artificial tears" can relieve the condition.

Allergies Sensitivity to grass, pollen, animal hair, pollutants or smoke may cause red, burning, tearing, itchy, swollen eyes and eyelids. In addition many soaps, shampoos, perfumes and preservatives, even some contact lens solutions (notably thimerosal), can cause eye sensitivity. To relieve the problem, try cold compresses and/or decongestants and antihistamine eyedrops. Cromolyn sodium is an alternative eyedrop which, although immediately effective for some, may take days to weeks to work in others. (Remember that eyedrops themselves may cause allergies.)

Eyelid problems Infection of the eyelash follicle is called a sty. A tender lump within the eyelid is called a chalazion. Hot compresses applied several times daily usually relieve the condition. Sometimes a painful or recurrent chalazion requires minor corrective surgery.

Blepharitis (eyelid inflammation) This condition, which is most common in the light-haired or people with ultra-sensitive skin, involves itchy, scaly flakes on the lid and lashes. Ulcerative blepharitis is an oozing inflammation. Treatment means careful cleansing of the eyelid margins twice daily.

Conjunctivitis or pinkeye A common infection of the eye's thin mucous membrane (conjunctiva), it produces red, sore eyes and a gritty feeling. The eyelashes are often stuck together in the morning. Antibiotic drops are the usual remedy, along with warm saline rinsing. Pinkeye is highly contagious and handwashing is essential to prevent its spread. (See chapter 11, "Childhood problems.")

Conjunctival hemorrhage and episcleritis Conjunctival hemorrhage sounds bad and looks awful but is a harmless, painless red spot on the white of the eye, sometimes brought on by exertion — coughing, or straining at stool or childbirth, for instance — or by bleeding in those taking ASA. The spot usually goes away by itself. Conjunctival hemorrhage occasionally occurs in those with high blood pressure. Episcleritis is a recurring sore or pinkish-red patch on the white of the eye, of unknown cause, possibly associated with rheumatoid arthritis, *Herpes zoster* (shingles) or tuberculosis. Treatment is with topical corticosteroids.

Corneal scratches Occasionally produced by contact lenses, a fingernail or a bit of grit in the eye, they are extremely painful, with teariness and photophobia (light-aversion). Antibiotics are given, along with eyedrops which temporarily dilate the pupil and paralyze the ciliary muscles of the iris. An eyepatch may be worn for a few days.

Corneal ulcers Resulting from damage to the cornea from an abrasion, or due to diseases such as Bell's palsy (facial paralysis) or infections (such as *Herpes simplex*), they can lead to corneal ulcers that threaten vision. Treatment is with special eyedrops, or if severe, corneal transplants.

Uveitis An inflammation of the iris (colored part of the eye) and its surrounding area, it causes dull pain, sensitivity to light, teariness and blurred vision. It's not always clear why it arises, but uveitis is serious as it can lead to pupil blockage or glaucoma. Treatment is with topical steroids and special eyedrops.

Retinal disorders Damage to the retina includes hypertensive retinopathy — a complication of high blood pressure (with blurred vision), diabetic retinopathy in long-term diabetics and macular degeneration. Retinal problems are now often treated with lasers.

is also responsible for perceiving color, hues may look faded. If only one eye is affected, early changes may go undetected.

People with macular degeneration often find it hard to read small print, do close work or navigate stairs. But since side vision remains untouched, they can still walk about and even cross streets unaided, albeit with care and circumspection. Macular degeneration is more common in women than men, partly because women tend to live longer. Heredity plays a role: approximately 15 percent of people with a

family history of macular degeneration will develop it. Light-eyed people tend to be more commonly afflicted than the dark-eyed. If the condition is diagnosed when central vision is still reasonably intact and before new blood vessels invade the macula, laser treatment may reduce or slow the visual loss.

The unusual "wet" or fast-progressing form of the disease is due to swift growth of abnormal blood vessels that distort the retina and make it bulge, eventually forming scars that destroy central vision. Argon laser surgery, the only treatment for "wet" macular degeneration, can seal leaking blood vessels before the macula is too badly scarred.

Unfortunately, laser surgery doesn't work in everyone. Its effectiveness depends on the exact location of the damage. For people who cannot benefit from argon laser therapy, vision can sometimes be improved with magnifying lenses and other aids.

Use of vitamin and mineral supplements for macular degeneration is a much-argued therapy, based on a study showing that people who took zinc tablets had significantly less visual loss than those on placebo. There is no proof that zinc supplements can impede the progress of macular degeneration.

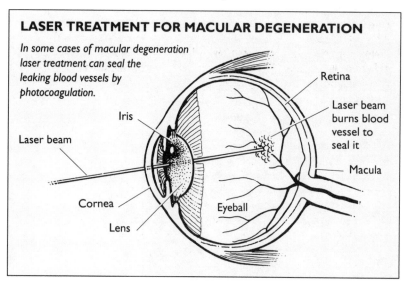

LASER TREATMENT FOR MACULAR DEGENERATION

In some cases of macular degeneration laser treatment can seal the leaking blood vessels by photocoagulation.

Retina

Iris

Laser beam burns blood vessel to seal it

Laser beam

Macula

Cornea

Lens

Eyeball

Glaucoma

Glaucoma is the third-commonest cause of blindness in North Americans over age 50. Left untreated, it inevitably leads to vision loss and possibly blindness. The problem is that glaucoma develops slowly and painlessly, often giving no hint of its presence until it has reached an advanced stage when much sight may already have been lost. Everyone should have regular eye exams after ages 40–45 — even those with no vision complaints.

Glaucoma generally affects both eyes, advancing at varying rates and to different degrees. Most forms of glaucoma progress almost imperceptibly, although some develop quickly. The disorder generally involves a rise in

intraocular pressure (IOP) because of drainage or outflow problems in the aqueous humor, the watery fluid that bathes the eye. Normally, the aqueous humor exits freely through a meshwork of small pores, the trabecular meshwork — situated where the iris meets the cornea. But if fluid outflow is hindered, pressure rises and can damage the optic nerve.

Open or wide-angle glaucoma, by far the commonest form, has been dubbed a "silent blinder" or "thief in the night" because it creeps up stealthily to rob people of their sight. Intraocular pressure builds slowly, producing gradual optic nerve deterioration. Peripheral (side) vision goes first. Tiny blind spots appear at the edges of the visual field, slowly getting larger and spreading. Many people think that the rising intraocular pressure will noticeably swell the eyes. But this isn't so. The visual impairment may only become apparent because of a car accident or some other event, or may be discovered at a routine eye examination, in people with no inkling of its presence. In serious cases, peripheral vision is altogether wiped out, leaving only central or "tunnel" vision. If this vision also disappears, the result is total blindness. Those with relatives who have glaucoma are at above-average risk, as are diabetics, hypertensives (with high blood pressure) and the strongly myopic (shortsighted).

Whereas, in the past, diagnosis of glaucoma depended primarily on the degree of eye-pressure elevation, IOP is no longer the only criterion. Not everyone with high IOP has the disorder, and glaucoma can exist in people with normal eye pressure. Eye-pressure elevation is now considered a risk factor but not proof of glaucoma. (About 8 percent of Canadians have high intraocular pressure but only one in 10 of these develops glaucoma.) Measurement of changes to the optic disc (around the optic nerve) and visual field defects also helps to establish diagnosis.

The classic "triad" signaling open-angle glaucoma:

- raised intraocular pressure;
- optic disc changes/abnormality;
- measurable visual field defects (blind spots, peripheral sight loss, "tunnel" vision).

THE MAIN MEDICATIONS FOR OPEN-ANGLE GLAUCOMA

• *Beta blockers* (such as timolol, levobunolol and betaxolol) given as eyedrops decrease fluid production and reduce pressure. Generally safe, they can be absorbed via tear ducts and nasal passages, causing bronchospasm (lung problems) — mainly in asthmatics. They may also lower heart-rate and blood pressure, possibly leading to heart failure and sometimes inducing nervous-system changes such as light-headedness, memory loss, lowered sex drive and impotence. Because of possible cardiovascular effects, these drops should not be used in people with heart problems without specific medical advice and supervision.

• *Miotics* (such as pilocarpine and carbachol) and longer-acting forms (such as phospholine iodide) constrict the pupil, increasing fluid drainage. They may cause headaches and nervous-system changes (sweating, gastrointestinal upsets) if taken in large doses. Pilocarpine can also cause eye burning and vision blurring, reduce night vision (especially in anyone with cataracts), increase myopia, disturb digestion and cause diarrhea and/ or appetite loss — mostly a problem in elderly patients.

• *Sympathomimetics* (such as epinephrine, dipivefrin) reduce aqueous inflow and enhance outflow, but can also produce blood-pressure elevation, eye redness and vision blurring. Epinephrine can increase the heart-rate and cause heartbeat irregularities. High doses may produce sweating and restlessness as well as blurred vision and teariness. It shouldn't be used in people with heart rhythm problems or after a heart attack. (Propine, a modern, low-dose form, produces fewer side effects.)

• *Carbonic anhydrase inhibitors* (such as acetazolamide, methazolamide) suppress the eye's fluid production but are less popular than other anti-glaucoma drugs because of severe side effects — nausea, depression, diuresis (frequent urination) and anemia, and possibly also numbness of the fingers and toes and stomach acidity (acidosis). They should not be used with ASA because of the increased risk of ulcers.

Treatment of open-angle glaucoma aims to lower eye pressure, relieve optic nerve compression and halt sight loss. Therapy usually starts when there's detectable optic nerve damage or dangerously elevated IOP. Most "glaucoma suspects," in whom a pressure rise is the *only* abnormal finding, with no detectable vision loss or damage to the optic nerve, are closely watched for further deterioration. But high-risk groups — such as hypertensives, diabetics and those with relatives who have glaucoma — are treated as soon as eye pressure creeps above normal. Medications (such as eyedrops or tablets) are tried first. If they don't work or are irritating, or if vision worsens, laser or conventional surgery may be advised.

Eyedrops, the commonest glaucoma treatment, may decrease eye-fluid production or increase drainage. Some glaucoma sufferers take several kinds of eyedrops as well as anti-glaucoma pills. Glaucoma medications may constrict the eye pupil or cause headaches or other minor discomforts, but most learn to tolerate them well. Glaucoma medications should be taken as prescribed, not skipped or neglected, because any vision loss that's already occurred can't be restored. Once started, glaucoma therapy is generally lifelong. Yet it's often hard to persuade people with no obvious symptoms to go on taking their medication — especially the elderly, who may be on several other drugs. People should tell any medical caregivers about their glaucoma medications, as some produce considerable side effects, and some should not be used with other medicines.

Many people don't realize that eyedrops can affect the whole body, as they are absorbed into the bloodstream. Although generally safe, glaucoma drugs drain through the tear ducts and nasal passages and can cause nonocular effects. Those taking them should watch for side effects, which can often be minimized by preventing the medication from getting into the tear ducts — for example, by pressing on the side of the nose near the eyelid with a finger, or squeezing the eye closed for a few minutes after inserting the drops.

Since eyedrops and antiglaucoma pills can be bothersome, laser treatment is increasingly popular. Laser trabeculoplasty, in which laser heating of the eye's drainage system allows fluid to flow out, is now a common surgical procedure for glaucoma. It's done in about 15 minutes, and people go home the same day.

THE EYE WITH CATARACT FORMING

Types of Cataracts

Nuclear sclerosis

Cuneiform (spokes)

Posterior subcapsular

Cornea
Anterior chamber
Iris
Posterior chamber
Retina
Lens with posterior subcapsular cataract forming
Sclera
Optic nerve
Choroid

A cataract is a clouding and/or yellowing of the eye's normally clear, crystalline lens due to protein aggregation that makes it too turbid (opaque) to see through clearly. Cataract formation is a gradual process that, in most people, ultimately affects both eyes, although not necessarily at the same time. Some cataracts (nuclear sclerosis or "hard" type) form in the middle of the lens and tend to scatter light rays, producing glare and dimming but not totally obscuring vision. Cuneiform cataracts form as "spokes," affecting only peripheral vision. The type most common with advancing age — "posterior subcapsular" — forms at the back of the lens as an overgrowth of cells, and usually develops quite quickly. Once a cataract begins in a particular part of the lens, it may remain static, but usually spreads. Regardless of type or position, it may require surgery. When a cataract completely obscures vision it is said to be "ripe."

large lenses are at increased risk of closed-angle glaucoma — for instance, the Inuit, with their often small, farsighted eyes. (Before emergency services improved, closed-angle glaucoma posed a serious threat of blindness among Inuit communities.) Rare forms of closed-angle glaucoma arise from eye inflammation, a tumor or mechanical damage.

Precipitating factors for acute glaucoma — in those prone to it — include anything that makes the eye pupil dilate or widen, even emotional events such as weddings, funerals or heart-thumping movies. Acute glaucoma is always an emergency and must be treated quickly. To alleviate the pressure and prevent sight loss, prompt medical treatment and laser surgery are required. Laser iridotomy is a simple, safe, highly effective procedure that relieves closed-angle glaucoma by puncturing a hole in the iris, enabling the fluid to escape. Once someone has had closed-angle glaucoma in one eye, the other is also at grave risk and is often treated preventively at the same time (or at a later date). In cases of known risk, both eyes may get prophylactic (preventive) laser treatment to avoid the onset of acute glaucoma.

But laser surgery doesn't always permanently alleviate the problem. In half the cases, eyeball pressure may rise again in two years or so, necessitating repeat laser or alternative treatment. Lasers are often used when drops give insufficient control of glaucoma, in the hope of avoiding surgery.

Acute (swift-onset) glaucoma

Fast-progressing but infrequent, the acute or closed-angle form of glaucoma comes on without warning, and accounts for 6 to 10 percent of cases. It occurs when the angle between the iris and the cornea becomes too narrow or closes up, blocking fluid drainage. It often hits suddenly, with blurred vision, eye pain, headache, nausea and vomiting — symptoms sometimes mistaken for migraine, a digestive attack, stroke or uveitis (eye inflammation). Unlike open-angle glaucoma, which is related to myopia or shortsightedness, this type is linked to farsightedness. Those with small eyes and/or

Cataracts: new treatments can save sight

Cataracts cloud the eye's transparent lens, diminishing and distorting eyesight. While cataracts can occur at any age, they are most prevalent in people over age 60. Almost half the men and women aged 75 and over develop them. Occasionally young people get cataracts, sometimes because of an inherited predisposition.

Cataracts can arise because of:
- metabolic lens changes with advancing years;
- hereditary predisposition (family tendency);
- injuries or blows to the eye ("traumatic cataracts") from, for instance, bicycling falls, hockey injuries or boxing blows;
- excess exposure to X-rays or infrared radiation (which can cause "glass-blower's cataracts" from the thermal effects) — hazards avoided by wearing protective goggles. Although the eye's natural lens blocks some UV light, many experts suggest

that anyone frequently exposed to bright sunlight should wear special dark glasses;

- microwave radiation in high doses (if insufficiently shielded);
- exposure to toxic chemicals, such as naphthalene or paradichlorobenzene;
- certain diseases such as hypoparathyroidism (underactivity of the parathyroid gland), diabetes, atopic dermatitis (a skin disease), retinal detachment or prolonged eye inflammation;
- certain medications (such as cortisone).

How to know if you have cataracts

The main alerting sign of cataracts is double vision in one eye, vision blurring and perhaps a disturbing glare, especially in bright light (as when facing oncoming headlights). At first the subtle haziness may be hardly noticeable — colors may dull a little, vision may blur when reading with one eye giving a brighter image than the other. As one eye clouds, eyesight seems better with the bad eye closed, but corrective lenses don't seem to improve the foggy vision.

Only the cataract sufferer can say how much the visual loss impedes everyday life — whether it affects work, recreation, reading or driving. Some find even slightly fogged vision — a 20 to 30 percent diminution in visual clarity — a distinct handicap, while others scarcely notice it. While a cataract does not usually endanger health, the visual blurring may arise from another disorder; careful investigation is needed to exclude other possible reasons for hazy vision. In the presence of an unhealthy macula, even the most technically perfect cataract operation cannot uncloud hazy vision. (See "Macular degeneration.")

Cataracts used to be removed only when they were "ripe." But today surgery is scheduled when the person and his or her surgeon agree that the time, not the cataract, is ripe! Since most cataracts progress slowly and they rarely impair eye health, the timing of surgery is flexible. Often, an early cataract that doesn't interfere with work, reading or driving isn't removed but just periodically checked. Most cataracts are removed when people find their normal activities restricted. Someone in a demanding job might request cataract removal

THREE OPTIONS FOR REPLACEMENT LENSES

Removal of a cataract leaves the eye very farsighted and in need of a lens or strong spectacles to focus light onto the retina. Today's cataract spectacles are less bulky, contacts are easier to handle than earlier models, and the plastic lens implant is an enormous improvement.

- **Aphakic cataract spectacles**, now lighter and more delicate than they used to be, are the oldest and safest way to achieve vision after eye-lens removal, especially for those who are unable to tolerate contact lenses or who do not qualify for an implant. After a cataract operation in one eye only, a corrective lens may be worn either for that eye or for the unoperated eye to improve vision. Cataract spectacles provide good vision while seated — watching TV, reading and sewing — but not for walking or driving because of poor side vision, abnormal magnification and spatial distortion.

- **Contact lenses** (soft or gas-permeable, daily or extended-wear) can provide more natural perception, giving binocular vision with full central and side vision. But some older patients find even soft contacts difficult to put in, and fragile to handle. Those unduly annoyed by the magnification of a cataract contact lens may also require one in the unoperated eye (to overcome the image disparity). New extended-wear contact lenses can be left in for three months to a year, but must occasionally be taken out and cleaned.

- **The intraocular lens (IOL)** or plastic implant was first tested by a British surgeon in 1979. The plastic implants are made of PMMA (polymethylmethacrylate) because Royal Air Force crews in World War Two did not experience any rejection symptoms to bits of this material that entered their eyes from shattered aircraft parts. Many of the early problems of these plastic lens implants — such as poor fastening and slippage — have now been overcome, and they have the great advantage of producing vision that's not distorted and that requires no manual dexterity (and no maintenance). In the 30 years since their introduction, implants have been refined to the point where they're now used in up to 95 percent of modern cataract operations.

Each IOL is carefully made, and its focusing power is individually selected according to eyeball length and corneal curvature, which determine the lens power of the implant. Provided the measurements are accurate, an implant can provide almost normal postoperative vision using regular, weak spectacles. Most people with implants need glasses for reading and/or distance vision. If the other eye is also scheduled for later cataract surgery, the implants can sometimes provide normal (even 20/20) vision, provided the eyes are otherwise healthy.

VARIOUS CATARACT OPERATIONS USED

- *Intracapsular surgery* — the only method used until about a decade ago — is still done for about 5 percent of Canadian cataract removals. It consists of extracting the whole lens and all of its covering.
- *Extracapsular surgery* — the more recent method, now used for 95 percent of cataract removals — takes out only the cataract, leaving intact the posterior holding capsule. The advantages of extracapsular cataract extraction are: a smaller incision; better support for the lens implant from the remaining (hind) portion of the capsule; fewer postoperative retinal detachments. Its disadvantage is possible post-capsular clouding after surgery, requiring laser treatment to clear vision in approximately 20 percent of patients within two or three

years of extracapsular surgery. High-energy lasers are used to open a post-operatively clouded posterior capsule, rapidly restoring vision with a painless five- to ten-minute outpatient procedure.
- *Phacoemulsification* is a form of extracapsular cataract removal that suits some cases, especially those due to trauma or in young persons who have softer eye lenses than the elderly. In this technique, the surgeon sucks out the cataract with a hollow needle after it has been fragmented (liquefied) by ultrasound. Popular because of the tiny incision required, it has benefits that may be offset by later corneal complications. Anesthesia for modern cataract surgery may be general or local. A general anesthetic may be given to

a very young or apprehensive patient, but more commonly the anesthetic is a local "freezing" that numbs sensation (as in dental procedures). Sometimes, to avert anxiety, the patient is briefly sedated by an IV infusion while the local anesthetic is injected under the eye. The anesthetic requires ten minutes to "take" and the person stays awake for the rest of the procedure. There is no worry about blinking during the operation because the injected medication stops all eye and eyelid movement. The surgery takes about 45 to 60 minutes, including lens removal and eye bandaging. Most patients can get up and walk around within three to twelve hours after surgery. During this time, they can gradually sit up, watch TV and go to the bathroom if they wish. Complete healing takes up to three months.

person depends on the cataract's form and size and whether or not other eye diseases are also present. Cataract surgery has been dramatically refined by better microscopes that allow precise surgery with less trauma; a new irrigation/aspiration cutter that "squirts" and "sucks" as it cuts, giving the surgeon unhindered movements; use of finer nylon or polypropylene sutures (stitches) — thinner than a single hair — which allow a leak-proof scar; and, above all, intraocular plastic implants inserted during surgery that almost miraculously restore clear vision.

After the cataract operation

After a cataract operation, there is a little discomfort or pain, and that can be allayed with a mild painkiller (such as Tylenol or codeine). There may be some nausea, usually relieved by one or two antinausea tablets. The affected eye usually stays patched for a day or two after surgery. Some doctors advise their patients to wear a shield taped over the eye at night for a few weeks. The eye may remain irritated for a few weeks, as the incision can be felt upon blinking and moving the eye. Some sutures need removal, but absorbable ones avoid the need.

Postoperative care is usually minimal, the wound generally being sufficiently healed within three to eight weeks for contact lenses or glasses to be fitted. Strenuous activity must be avoided during recovery and it's imperative to avoid any rubbing, injury or direct blow to the eye. Eyedrops containing an antibiotic and anti-inflammatory agent are generally used. Vision returns quickly in some, but it's more usual for vision to improve slowly as the eye recovers. Most people can shop, watch television, play cards and socialize within a few days. (Provided the unoperated eye has good vision, driving can also be resumed quite soon.) Most people resume everyday activities within a month or two of the surgery.

No surgical procedure is entirely risk-free, and complications occur in about 5 percent of cataract removals — for example, infection, hemorrhage, retinal detachment, wound breakdown and shifting of an intraocular implant. Warning signs of trouble following cataract surgery are a sudden decrease in vision or in comfort of the eye after a seemingly steady

much earlier than a retired person with a less taxing lifestyle.

About 95 percent of those with cataracts now have plastic lens implants inserted by eye surgery. Thanks to various surgical advances, lens replacement is a relatively simple, painless procedure that can be done at any age with a 90 percent success rate. A natural eye lens clouded by cataracts can be removed and replaced with a plastic lens on a "same day" basis, with only a small percentage of sufferers requiring hospitalization.

The type of operation suitable for a given

recovery. Such changes should immediately be reported to the surgeon.

Cataract surgery is now one of the most frequent and successful of operations, bringing untold joy to those who might formerly have ended their days with hazy vision or total blindness.

EAR CARE

The ear is a remarkably precise and versatile piece of sound-receiving and balance-coordinating equipment. It can hear the faintest of sounds and — when one is young — picks up frequencies from 16 to 20,000 cycles per second. However, the ear's capacity to hear and maintain balance often deteriorates with age or exposure to noise or because of certain diseases.

Hearing impairment is an invisible handicap affecting one in ten North Americans. An estimated 50 percent of the population over age 65 experience some degree of hearing impairment. Recent studies by the Canadian Hearing Society noted that over 80 percent of people tested in nursing homes were hearing-impaired. Deafness is disabling more and more people in modern society, not only because of the aging population but also because of widespread noise pollution. Few outsiders realize the impact of hearing loss on someone's everyday life. Besides making conversation difficult, deafness produces isolation and anxiety. The hearing-impaired themselves often don't recognize the problem or take steps to get and use a hearing aid, to help them stay in the mainstream of social intercourse.

Ears don't need washing: they clean themselves

Many people wrongly imagine that ears need regular cleaning to get rid of wax and dirt. In fact, ears need no special washing, cleaning or drying. They have their own inbuilt cleaning mechanism. The external ear canal is lined with thick skin containing sebaceous (oil) glands and ceruminous (modified sweat). Wax or cerumen, composed of glandular secretions, plus dead

THE STRUCTURE OF THE EAR

The ear is divided into three main parts: the external, middle and inner ear. Sound vibrations travel down the external ear canal or eustachian tube and strike the ear drum, making it vibrate. The air pressure on either side of the ear drum is equalized with every third or fourth swallow (unless the eustachian tube is blocked by a cold, when flying or by large adenoids). Sound vibrations are transmitted across the air-filled middle ear by three tiny, linked bones or ossicles — the hammer, anvil and stapes — then via the foot of the stapes and oval window to the cochlea in the fluid-bathed inner ear. About 3 cm long, the coiled cochlea contains thousands of hair cells that act as sound receptors. As the vibrations hit them, electrical impulses are set up and travel, via the auditory nerve to the brain's hearing center. The inner ear also controls the body's equilibrium — balance related to gravity — via three lymph-filled semicircular canals in the inner ear (which are "acceleration detectors" that monitor movement) and the utricle and sacule (static gravity receptors) that relay information about the position of the head at rest. Sensory hairs in these canals orient the body's position in space.

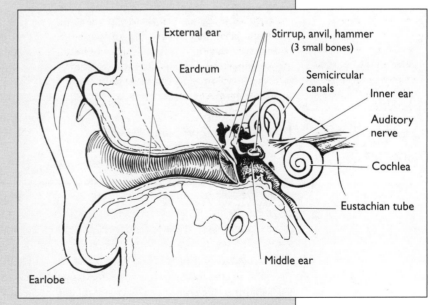

skin and other debris, forms in the outer part of the ear canal as a natural protection for the ears. But it is often impacted by persistent probing of the ear with fingers, Q-tips (cotton-tipped cleaning rods) or assorted instruments — in the mistaken name of cleanliness.

Contrary to popular misperception, ear wax isn't "dirty." It is a protective barrier that prevents contaminants from penetrating the ear canal's skin and producing infection. Enzymes in the wax help to prevent infection. All that's required is gentle washing with a finger in a wet washcloth. Over-vigorous efforts to remove water or dirt from the ears interfere with the body's self-cleansing mechanism, driving dirt farther in. Compulsive ear cleaners who poke their fingers into the ear or roughly or carelessly cleanse it with cleaning devices such as Q-tips not only remove the enzymes but can damage the delicate skin lining the ear, permitting bacteria to enter and produce itchiness, irritation and infection. Q-tips should never be used in the ears. To remove water from the ears it's best simply to tip the head well from side to side and shake gently, or mop with a washcloth.

As one hearing specialist says, "It is unfortunately very common to see people develop itchy ears, or even lose their hearing, due to cleansing of the ears with objects such as matchsticks or Q-tips that pierce the eardrum and traumatize the ear. I implore people not to clean or dry their ears. There is no need to put drops in the ear or to syringe the ears. If, for anatomical reasons, the ear does not take care of itself, please let your physician take care of it."

How about ear care when flying?

If air pressure inside the middle ear isn't balanced or if fluid accumulates, the ear can sometimes "pop," causing intense pain — as happens during an airplane descent, when scuba diving or going up fast in an elevator. Even though most modern aircraft cabins are pressurized, it is impossible to maintain exactly the same pressure in flight as on earth. During ascent, as the surrounding atmospheric pressure decreases, the air in the middle ear is at higher pressure and automatically finds its way out of the eustachian tube into the back of the nose, automatically equalizing pressure on either side of

SOME COMMON EAR PROBLEMS

Hearing loss

Hearing loss can be conductive (faulty transmission of sound waves via the eardrum or failure to transmit sound via the ossicles) or sensorineural (failure in sound reception by nerve cells), or both. Common causes of conductive hearing loss are wax blocking the ear, a perforated eardrum or fluid in the middle ear. Common reasons for nerve or sensorineural deafness are age-related changes (presbycusis), noise exposure, and ototoxic (ear-damaging) drugs. Mixed hearing losses can occur in people with chronic ear disease, who may have conductive hearing loss due to a damaged eardrum and/or injury to the little ear bones as well as infection of the inner ear.

The main causes of hearing loss:
Congenital (present at birth)
- genetic (hereditary);
- environmental causes:
  - prenatal rubella (German measles);
  - infections during pregnancy (which damage the fetus;
  - premature birth;
  - perinatal anoxia (oxygen lack), newborn jaundice, Rh (blood) disease.
Acquired hearing loss
- progressive familial (hereditary) sensorineural hearing loss — usually noted in childhood or adolescence, gradually progressing to severe or profound loss;

the eardrum. Going down, however, is not quite that easy! As air pressure increases upon descent, pressure will be greater outside the eardrum than inside, producing a blocked sensation in the ears. Air cannot enter the middle ear to equalize the pressure, unless the passenger actively swallows or blows the nose. Occasionally, excess pressure can rupture the eardrum, with a bloody discharge.

When one has a cold, the lining of the eustachian tube, like the lining of the nose and sinuses, may be swollen and block the passage of air, making pressure equalization impossible. If one must fly with a head cold, it's wise to reduce nasal congestion with decongestant tablets. In addition, a topical nasal decongestant spray such as Otrivin or Dristan should be used liberally when the plane starts its descent. For those who are "stuffed up" with an allergy, antihistamines alone or a combination of

Other causes
- presbycusis — age-related hearing loss;
- noise-induced hearing loss;
- ototoxicity (due to drugs that harm the ear);
- head injuries;
- infectious diseases affecting the middle and inner ear.

Some signs of hearing loss in adults:
- trouble understanding conversation in crowded situations or noisy rooms;
- turning the TV or radio up so loud that others are uncomfortable;
- frequently asking for repetition of words and phrases; ignoring people;
- hearing speech but finding the words unclear.

Hearing problems in children
About 4 percent of children have some degree of hearing impairment, which is sometimes mistaken for slow learning or mental retardation. Children should have hearing tests at six months of age, at school entry and again at age ten or eleven.

Normal babies startle, stir or awaken at a loud noise (a dog barking or a jet close overhead). By the age of six months or so, infants will turn their heads toward a familiar voice, even if the speaker is out of sight. By two years, most children can mimic sounds and react to simple commands. Parents should watch for hearing problems.

About one in 1,500 babies is born with a severe hearing defect. By age five, 4 percent of children will have some degree of hearing loss. A recent study showed that in 50 percent of cases there were serious delays in detecting and diagnosing a child's hearing loss. Children suspected of defective hearing need testing and prompt remedial action, particularly since the loss can have a significant effect on the child's language acquisition and learning and social skills.

Children born with normal hearing may lose it through childhood illnesses such as measles or meningitis, or because of certain drugs. Upper respiratory infections often result in middle-ear infections that need prompt attention to avoid chronic hearing loss.

Some signs of hearing loss in children:
- a newborn baby who does not jump or blink at a sudden loud noise;
- an infant aged three to six months who does not stop crying or stop moving at the sound of a voice or a strange sound;
- a child of nine to twelve months who does not turn toward a speaker;
- a two-year-old who doesn't yet use short sentences.

Parents should talk to their physician about such symptoms and request referral to an otolaryngologist (ear, nose and throat specialist) or to an audiologist for further investigation.

decongestant and antihistamine is recommended. Also, because ears tend to block on descent, air should be blown into the middle ear by holding the nose and closing the mouth and forcibly building up internal pressure (Valsalva maneuver). This can be done repeatedly as the plane lands.

If able to sleep on the plane, ask the flight attendant to awaken you upon descent. Even without a cold, your ears can be blocked if you are asleep or lying down when landing. That goes for babies, too. Wake them up and feed them to cause swallowing, which helps relieve the pressure. As a last resort, force the baby to cry if it won't feed.

Anyone who dives even a few feet underwater experiences a similar increase in pressure on the outside of the eardrum. Scuba divers are taught a simple procedure to equalize or "pop" their ears, but sometimes suffer barotrauma or even ruptured eardrums through carelessness or through diving with a head cold or allergies. Diving on decongestants is *not* recommended, as the medications may impair the diver's ability, or wear off during the dive. Non-divers who want to snorkel might ask the staff who supply the equipment to show them how to "pop" their ears, to avoid discomfort and possible damage.

Ear pain or persistent hearing loss necessitates a visit to the doctor or ear specialist. Any earache or pain, dizzy spells, imbalance, strange ringing in the ears, ear discharge, redness, swelling, or reduced or muffled hearing should always receive prompt medical attention. Treatment with decongestants for two to three weeks may be all that is required. On occasion, however, it may be necessary to lance the eardrum under local anesthetic with the aid of a microscope, to equalize the pressure and reduce discomfort.

SUDDEN SENSORINEURAL DEAFNESS

This condition, in which people suddenly (within days) go deaf, is a rare disorder affecting about 5–20 people per 100,000 per year. It may be mild and temporary or permanent and profound, and may affect one or both ears, sometimes for elusive reasons. Some people aren't aware of a sudden hearing loss in one ear until they go to answer a phone or can't hear a dinner guest on one side. Mumps, measles, influenza or mononucleosis are thought to be possible causes. Sudden deafness can also follow rupture of the eardrum due to a dramatic change in the surrounding air pressure (for instance when diving) or overly strenuous physical exertion. Drugs such as certain antibiotics, diuretics and ASA can affect hearing (in both ears equally) — although with ASA the loss is reversible. Anybody with a sudden hearing problem should consult a physician at once.

Age-related hearing loss

Aging is often accompanied by sensorineural deafness. Presbycusis — literally, "old hearing" — is the term for age-related hearing loss, which affects 50 percent of those over 65 in North America. The hearing tends to become progressively worse with advancing years. Those with presbycusis often complain not only of hearing loss (usually in both ears), but sometimes also of tinnitus (ringing in the ears). It takes only a little hearing loss to make life difficult because, although conversation is audible at low frequencies, it's not easy to hear the high frequencies that go first. Thus, the elderly may have trouble hearing the phone ring. It can also be difficult to distinguish consonants. The problem becomes particularly acute when there's a lot of background noise, as on a bus or at the dinner table. Seniors often accuse others of mumbling! They may say, "I can hear you but I don't understand what you're saying." Conversationalists can help by articulating clearly, keeping the face up so lips can be read and asking if the person has understood.

When hearing loss in the elderly begins, the hard-of-hearing are advised to get immediate counseling about use of a hearing aid, to keep them from becoming socially isolated. Increased hearing difficulties can make a person feel lonely and anxious. Such everyday activities as shopping, banking, attending group gatherings or obtaining simple information can become exercises in frustration, not only for those who have the hearing loss, but also for those who interact with them. Worse yet, hearing loss is often mistaken for senility in the elderly. Anyone who suspects they have some hearing loss should see their family physician and ask to be referred to the appropriate health professional. Given today's sophisticated technology, there is no need for anyone to do without an assistive listening device (hearing aid).

Modern hearing aids

Hearing aids work by amplifying sound, and are most effective in a quiet room with no background noise. The aids are best for one-to-one conversations, watching TV or listening to the radio. Hearing aids are highly individual and are chosen according to the type and severity of

hearing loss, the state of the ear canal and the person's ability to manipulate the hearing aid. Hearing aids that don't seem to work properly should be rechecked because many problems are correctable. For instance, some people may have an imperfectly fitted device, while others may need two hearing aids or a different brand.

Today's hearing aids are better, smaller and more efficient than yesteryear's and, appropriately chosen and fitted, can greatly improve the quality of life for the hearing-impaired. Unfortunately, they have a bad reputation. Many people remember problems their parents had, expect their hearing aids not to work well and give up too easily. Yet those who don't have hearing aids or who leave them unused in their bureau drawers may benefit from modern advice and a new fitting. In one 1991 London, Ontario, study of 115 elderly patients in a family practice clinic, 30 percent failed a hearing test and most needed hearing aids, yet none had asked for one. Even among those who have hearing aids, many don't make the best use of them. In the same study, ten of eleven elderly who had hearing aids needed to have them updated, replaced or adjusted.

The clumsy old-fashioned hearing aid, worn in a shirt pocket with a long cord to an ear mold, is not often used today except in near-complete deafness. Nowadays, hearing aids can fit inside the ear or even entirely within the ear canal. One type is worn behind the ear.

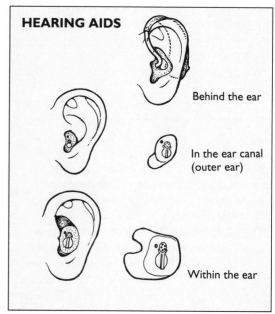

HEARING AIDS

Behind the ear

In the ear canal (outer ear)

Within the ear

NOISE-INDUCED HEARING LOSS IS ALL TOO COMMON

We are all painfully aware of the increased noise in modern urban life: sirens, rush-hour traffic, jack-hammers, subways. Many of us, attempting to find an escape, walk or drive through the city jacking up the volume on our personal headsets or car radios, compounding problems for the delicate inner ear.

Noise-induced hearing loss is a common cause of tinnitus (ringing in the ears) and of male deafness (more men are occupationally exposed to noise than women). Exposure to continuous industrial noise, snowmobiles, airplanes, power tools and rock concerts may produce temporary partial loss of hearing for a number of hours, called temporary threshold shift (TTS) — a transitory increase in the level sound has to reach to be perceived. Unfortunately, continuous noise over prolonged periods of time may gradually convert TTS into a permanent loss of hearing.

Sound is measured in decibels. A whisper or a quiet countryside averages 30 dB, normal speech 50–55 dB (about 1 m or 3.3 ft away from the source), a vacuum cleaner about 70 dB, the inside of a diesel bus 75 dB, city traffic 80 dB (just under the "hazardous" limit) and a subway 90 dB. A lawn-mower, at 90 decibels, is at the "annoyance" level (where regular eight-hour-a-day exposure will cause hearing loss). Acute discomfort is noticeable at about 95 decibels — roughly the sound of an average rock concert, nearby jet plane, chain saw or pneumatic drill. 110 decibels is the danger limit — a level at which even five minutes of steady, unremitting exposure can lead to some hearing loss, the loss increasing if exposure continues for an extended time. At 170 dB, sound can literally blow you off your feet.

Hearing loss builds up at noise exposures above 85 decibels, if experienced daily for an eight-hour day — not an uncommon noise level in many workplaces. Typically, the ability to hear high sounds — birds or women's voices — goes first, followed by loss of low-tone perception. To tell whether your environment is noisy enough to harm your ears, check whether you have to shout to make yourself heard, or whether, when you leave a noisy environment, sound seems muffled. If yes, the noise level is too high and injuring your ears. Excessively noisy environments are night-clubs, bars, busy restaurants and nearby chainsaws, motorboats, motorcycles.

According to the U.S. National Institutes of Health, 20 million North Americans are at risk of hearing loss from noisy work situations, especially farmers, truck drivers, construction workers, policemen and musicians (including classical musi-cians — playing second bass in the symphony can be an awfully noisy job). The trouble with noise-induced hearing loss is that, while entirely prevent-able, it's no more curable than other types of deafness. Poor sound perception is compounded when the listener is also exposed to background noise, e.g., a cocktail party or traffic outside an open window.

Those in noisy jobs should wear personal hearing protectors (earplugs, ear protectors) — and turn the volume down during recreational activities! The currently suggested level where hearing protection should begin (on a voluntary basis, no laws about it) is 85 dB, and according to hearing experts, ear protection should be manda-tory at 90 dB. It may seem ironic to try to enforce the use of ear protection for industrial work at 85 dB while condoning a 90 dB or higher level for pleasure from discos, rock bands and personal stereos.

If your hearing loss is traceable to work conditions, it may be worthwhile to contact the Workers' Compensation Board to see if you are eligible for a pension or at least rehabilitation with hearing aids. However, workers must have at least a 25-decibel hearing loss in each ear before the Workers' Compensation Board will even consider the case. Presently the board awards a pension of up to 2 percent to those with continuous tinnitus for more than two years, as long as there is a hear-ing loss of at least 25 percent associated with it.

The message is loud and clear: the more noise we hear today, the less we'll hear tomorrow. Protect your ears from excess noise as much as possible by:

• turning down the volume on radios, TVs and portable sound systems;
• playing personal headsets at lower volumes (not above the halfway setting);
• lodging formal complaints about environmental noise such as too much construction or traffic noise;
• wearing hearing protection when using loud equipment or household appliances;
• avoiding too many noisy concerts, movies, restaurants and lounges (better still, mounting a campaign to have these places turn down the volume);
• keeping noisy toys away from babies and young children.

Sophisticated hearing aids are now digitally controlled and programmable (tuning out the hum of low-frequency sounds such as car noises or air conditioners), making them better in noisy situations. Future hearing aids will be even more technologically advanced.

Surgically implantable hearing aids are now being tried. One type for conductive hearing loss has an internal component, a titanium screw implanted behind the ear that fuses with the bone, and an external part, a sound processor with a microphone that picks up sound waves and converts them into vibrations transmitted via the skull and processed by the auditory nerve. More and more types of implant are being investigated.

Ringing in the ears

Tinnitus, an annoying buzzing or ringing sound in the ears, is experienced momentarily by almost everyone at some time — perhaps from a loud, sudden bang near the ear or after a blow to the head. Tinnitus, from the Latin "to tinkle," often accompanies hearing loss. Sometimes it sounds more like a popping noise than a ring. It can be very irritating, even debilitating. Ancient Egyptian and Mesopotamian cures for so-called "bewitched ears" were frankincense and special oils. Modern treatments generally try to improve hearing with assistive devices or use of masking strategies.

Tinnitus is a sign of something amiss in the ear, possibly just wax buildup, or damage due to injury, noise or aging. Tinnitus can be subjective or objective. Subjective tinnitus is heard exclusively by the person afflicted. In objective tinnitus the sound can be heard by others. While a nuisance to those who have it, the ear-ringing does not usually signal some dread disease such as a brain tumor or cancer.

Tinnitus can stem from middle-ear infections, multiple sclerosis, injuries such as a bad whiplash, migraines, epilepsy, muscle spasms and exposure to loud noise. People regularly exposed to excessive noise, such as airport employees, often report an unpleasant buzz in the ears. When linked to vertigo (spinning dizziness) and fluctuating, low-tone hearing loss, tinnitus is likely due to an inner-ear disorder such as Ménière's disease.

Tinnitus fluctuates in intensity. It's usually most disturbing at night, and may be worsened by stress or anxiety. A vicious circle can result, where the ear hiss causes annoyance and the irritability in turn worsens the stress and aggravates the tinnitus. Learning to relax and avoid stress may decrease the problem.

Improved hearing through a hearing aid often reduces the annoyance. Special maskers — instruments that produce other sounds of similar frequency to mask the tinnitus — are now available, some combined with hearing aids. However, many people report greater irritation from the maskers than from the tinnitus itself. A humidifier or radio turned on low at night can just as well mute the ear-ringing. Biofeedback helps some, by producing carefully monitored relaxation with the help of a therapist.

Medications tried for tinnitus include oral anticonvulsants, which reduce the intensity of tinnitus in some. But these drugs have potentially serious side effects, such as bone-marrow suppression and kidney damage, which limit their usefulness. Antidepressants help some to live with the condition. Despite vast strides in medicine, tinnitus remains a perplexing disorder that's remarkably hard to get rid of.

Ménière's disease

This curious disorder, affecting two to six out of 1,000 people, takes its name from Prosper Ménière, a former physician-in-chief at the Imperial Institute for Deaf Mutes in Paris. In 1861 he proposed that a common triad of symptoms — vertigo, tinnitus and mild hearing loss — be designated a definite inner-ear disorder. Contrary to the prevailing view, which ascribed such symptoms to brain disease, Ménière attributed them to dysfunction in the inner ear's balancing system. Unfortunately, Ménière died before seeing his theory proved true and his name given to the disease he'd so accurately described.

The disorder generally strikes in mid-adulthood, with a slight preponderance in males. It classically begins with one or more bouts of vertigo. A typical case is Boris, a radio engineer in his mid-thirties, who suddenly felt the room begin to circle dramatically. Nauseated and faint, he sat down, gripping the chair to steady himself.

DIZZINESS

Dizziness has many different causes, ranging from trivial to more serious. It quite often accompanies hearing loss, and can arise from a transient or permanent disturbance of inner-ear function. However, dizziness from inner ear problems *must* be distinguished from that due to other conditions such as anemia, hypoglycemia (low blood sugar), cardiovascular ailments, neurological disorders (such as multiple sclerosis) and psychosomatic problems such as anxiety disorders. Dizziness accompanied by blackouts, numbness down one side or difficulty swallowing may indicate a serious nervous system disorder, or stroke.

Dizziness attacks that last only seconds are commonly due to standing up too fast after lying down, or a dysfunction in the inner ear, known as benign paroxysmal vertigo — a problem that usually vanishes spontaneously in a matter of weeks (but may recur). Among those prone to it, paroxysmal vertigo can happen, disconcertingly, several times a day. Simple head exercises can bring complete remission.

Dizziness arising from inner-ear disorders or disturbance of the balance mechanism is true vertigo — with a giddy sensation that the world is "spinning around" or that one is somersaulting helplessly through space — frequently accompanied by nausea. Dizziness lasting from half an hour to a few hours, associated with room-spinning vertigo, ringing in the ear, a feeling of pressure or fullness in the same ear and some hearing loss, is likely due to Ménière's disease (see above). Dizziness without hearing loss lasting from days to weeks may arise from vestibular neuronitis, a viral infection of the inner ear that may permanently injure the balance mechanism.

Once the vertigo subsided, he noticed a persistent roaring in his left ear and felt somewhat hard of hearing in that ear. Boris "slept off" the attack and was back at work the next day, but was rather apprehensive because the buzzing in his ear went on for about two weeks. When the same thing happened twice more within the year, he began to worry that he had a brain tumor or some other serious illness. Obsessed and fearful that an attack would start at some awkward moment, perhaps even endanger his life, he became an anxious, overwrought person, quite different from his former confident self.

This case illustrates the hallmarks of Ménière's disease:
- episodic vertigo — typically one or more attacks a year, singly or in clusters, lasting minutes to hours, possibly disabling enough to force the person to lie down;
- tinnitus — an incessant hiss or roaring in one ear, that may persist, change or disappear;
- fluctuating hearing loss — improving between attacks, but often worsening over time. The hearing loss typically distorts music and voices. The good news is that Ménière's hearing loss may worsen but is never total;
- headaches, sweating, pallor, a slow pulse, nausea and vomiting may accompany acute Ménière's spells, leading the unwary to suspect a stomach upset — until they get to know their illness.

Although the disorder generally includes vertigo, ear-ringing and hearing loss, all three symptoms are not necessarily present together. Between bouts, the disorder usually leaves few or no signs of its presence and hearing often returns to near-normal. Remissions can last for years or, rarely, forever.

The vertigo in Ménière's is distinguished by:
- sudden onset, out of the blue;
- a rotatory sensation with whirling surroundings. On lying down with eyes closed, the person feels as if tossed on a bouncing ship;
- a tendency to stagger from side to side;
- occasionally, vertigo violent enough to throw the person to the ground — known as drop attacks, urticular crises or Tumarkin spells.

The most obvious abnormality seen in Ménière's disease is increased fluid in the inner ear. Known as endolymphatic hydrops, the fluid buildup ruptures a bit of membrane from time to time, allowing the endolymph (fluid rich in potassium) to mix with the outside bathing fluid or perilymph (poor in potassium). This mixing of fluids leads to a biochemical alteration that transiently paralyzes the inner ear's balance (vestibular) system, producing the vertigo. Once the fluid balance normalizes, the vertigo passes.

Ménière's disease tends to engender tremendous anxiety because the vertigo strikes so unpredictably. Sufferers constantly fear

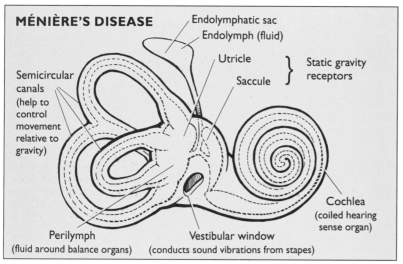

MÉNIÈRE'S DISEASE

Endolymphatic sac
Endolymph (fluid)
Utricle
Saccule
} Static gravity receptors

Semicircular canals (help to control movement relative to gravity)

Cochlea (coiled hearing sense organ)

Perilymph (fluid around balance organs)

Vestibular window (conducts sound vibrations from stapes)

another attack, making them afraid to continue activities such as driving a car or operating machinery. Reassurance and support are an essential part of therapy, encouraging the sufferers to live, work and drive as normal between episodes. (Although attacks come on unexpectedly, there is usually enough warning to allow sufferers to stop driving or put down a dangerous instrument.)

While nothing reliably stalls an attack, prevents future bouts or slows the progress of this affliction, therapies range from acupuncture and herbal remedies to diuretics, low-salt diets, vasodilators and electrical stimulation. There are various options to consider besides medical therapy, surgery being a last resort for the small number where medical management fails.

Medical therapy reduces symptoms in 80 to 90 percent of cases.

For acute spells, treatment is:
- antinauseants or anti-emetics, e.g., dimenhydrinate (Gravol), or meclizine (Bonamine), as suppositories;
- vasodilators (to widen peripheral vessels and draw fluid from the head);
- sedatives/tranquilizers, to reduce anxiety;
- diuretics (e.g., hydrochlorothiazide) with potassium replacement, to flush fluid from the body;
- dietary salt (sodium) restriction, to reduce fluid retention;
- tinnitus maskers (external sound devices), placed behind the ear. "Masking" distractions, such as listening to the radio or tapes, can minimize the tinnitus.

Surgical remedies, contemplated only if medical treatment brings no relief, have varying success rates:
- labyrinthectomy cures vertigo but also abolishes hearing in the operated ear;
- inserting a "shunt" or plastic drainage tube that lessens fluid buildup is of doubtful value;
- microsurgery to cut the vestibular (balance) nerve removes vertigo but leaves tinnitus untouched, and risks damage to nearby structures (if improperly done).

Chemical strategies include:
- parenteral streptomycin, which may abolish vertigo but leaves varying degrees of imbalance, because it selectively destroys the ear's balancing or vestibular function;
- destruction of the balance/vestibular inner-ear compartment by instilling gentamicin is an effective treatment which destroys some sensory hearing cells, with a usually acceptable risk of some hearing loss.

While Ménière's disease is a most distressing disorder, the remissions afford some relief, often for extended periods, and it tends to wane with increasing age.

EAR INFECTIONS

External-ear infections

Skin infections of the outer ear canal, popularly dubbed swimmer's ear or tropical ear and medically termed "external otitis," are often due to moisture buildup in the outer ear canal. Dampness trapped in the outer ear sets the stage for infection via small abrasions, cuts or scratches in the skin. Although swimmers are particularly likely to get it, the water need not necessarily come from swimming — showering can do it. Cleaning too vigorously often causes the infection because it scratches the skin and allows bacteria to penetrate the ear canal's protective layer of epidermal cells and wax. Dirty fingernails or abrasion with a towel or Q-tip are likelier offenders than swimming in dirty water.

The first sign of external otitis is usually an itching, burning sensation. The ear may be unbearably tender to touch or to the slightest pressure and the outer canal may look swollen and crusty. Movements such as chewing can be agonizing. A foul-smelling, clear or puslike discharge may seep out. Occasionally, the glands behind the ear and in the neck also swell. Fever or generalized body involvement is extremely rare with external-ear infections. However, people should seek medical advice for any earache, as the ears are near to the brain, which could be threatened by spreading infection.

The usual treatment for swimmer's ear is locally applied drops containing a mixture of antibiotics and steroids (to kill the bacteria and suppress inflammation). An acidic rinse of dilute aluminum acetate or Burow's solution (which contains aluminum acetate) may help reduce the swelling. To facilitate entry into a swollen ear canal, the acidic solution can be inserted on a cotton wick, adding more liquid as needed, to trickle down the canal. Painkillers can ease the discomfort.

Most cases heal up after four to five days. Sometimes, the debris must be completely removed by an ear specialist with special cleaning or irrigation, and very occasionally, if an outer-ear infection fails to diminish or shows signs of spreading, drugs are given intravenously in hospital.

Middle-ear infections

Middle-ear infections are almost as frequent as common colds during childhood. Most children have had at least one bout of bacterial middle-ear infection — otitis media — by the time they are three years old. The disorder is more common in boys than girls and most prevalent in winter. The infection usually follows a cold or a bacterial infection. Acute otitis media causes excruciating discomfort, but usually vanishes quickly with the sudden release of pus from the ear.

In middle-ear infections the eustachian tube becomes plugged, air cannot enter and the middle ear fills up with fluid — either clear (serous) or infectious (purulent). Serous otitis media, popularly called "glue ear," is a serious cause of hearing loss in children, typically those aged five to eight. Fluid replacing air in the middle ear deadens sound and can cause hearing loss in one or both ears, perhaps retarding learning in school-age children. Many cases of glue ear resolve on their own or assisted by antibiotics and other drugs. If it does not clear up in three months, ventilating tubes may have to be inserted.

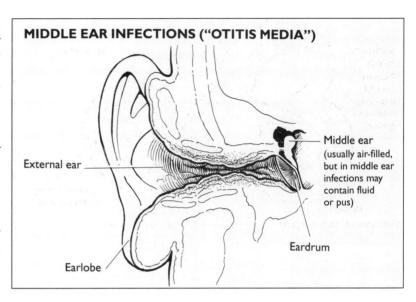

MIDDLE EAR INFECTIONS ("OTITIS MEDIA")

External ear

Middle ear (usually air-filled, but in middle ear infections may contain fluid or pus)

Eardrum

Earlobe

Acute otitis media typically follows a common cold, with symptoms such as sudden pain in the ear, sometimes severe, often starting at night, when a child may awaken howling and pulling at the ears. Or the discomfort may build gradually over 12 to 24 hours. There may also be fever, appetite loss, vomiting and diarrhea. However, some children with otitis media hardly seem sick at all, although the feeling of fullness in the ears (from the fluid) may make them tug at their ears. Since untreated middle-ear infections can also cause other serious complications, such as mastoiditis (infection of the mastoid bone behind the ear) or meningitis,

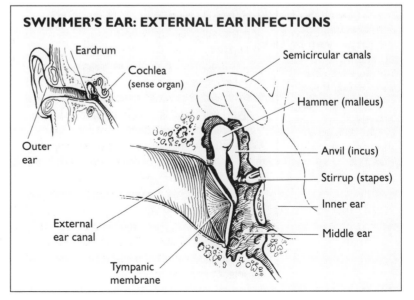

SWIMMER'S EAR: EXTERNAL EAR INFECTIONS

Eardrum

Cochlea (sense organ)

Semicircular canals

Hammer (malleus)

Anvil (incus)

Stirrup (stapes)

Inner ear

Middle ear

Outer ear

External ear canal

Tympanic membrane

THINGS PARENTS CAN DO FOR CHILD-HOOD EAR INFECTIONS

• **If you suspect your child has a middle-ear infection, contact your physician, who will examine the child's ears.**
• **Although ear infections usually get better fast with antibiotics, remember to take all the medication prescribed.**
• **Call the physician if a child shows any of the following:**
  • **a worsening earache despite treatment;**
  • **a high fever over 39°C (102°F) in spite of treatment, or one that lasts more than three days;**
  • **excessive sleepiness, crankiness or fussiness;**
  • **a skin rash;**
  • **rapid, shallow or difficult breathing;**
  • **noticeable hearing loss (doesn't clearly hear noises, tape machine or what's said).**

For more information, contact the Canadian Hearing Society, 271 Spadina Road, Toronto, Ontario M5R 2V3, (416) 964-9595.

even mild cases need prompt medical attention.

Physicians generally diagnose otitis media by looking at the eardrum with an otoscope (lighted ear-examining instrument). Sometimes it's necessary to remove wax from the outer ear canal in order to see the eardrum clearly.

If the eardrum ruptures, an exudate seeps out, and the fluid release usually gives prompt relief. But even when the symptoms of acute infection are gone, fluid may linger in the ear, sometimes for several weeks ("serous otitis media") even though it's not suspected until some hearing loss or behavioral problem alerts parents to it. Children may adapt to the slight hearing loss and parents, being unaware of it, may attribute the youngster's slow responses to stubbornness. The first hint of fluid in the ear may be lack of attention in school because a child can't hear clearly or keep up with peers. A child's inexplicable crankiness and fatigue — owing to the emotional toll of not hearing properly — may eventually drive parents to seek medical attention.

The treatment of otitis media is controversial. Many ear, nose and throat (ENT) specialists believe that the condition is self-limiting, that the fluid will be released from the middle ear and the eustachian tube will once more be properly ventilated, with or without medical treatment. Nonetheless, since there is a risk of complications as well as learning problems, most doctors treat the condition with antibiotics and painkillers. Antibiotics often make children feel better in a few days, but to eradicate the infection the whole course must be completed.

The doctor's dilemma in treating middle-ear infections is that most cases clear up in three to six weeks with or without antibiotics, using general remedies (such as fever reduction, fluids, bed rest and decongestants). By 10 weeks after a middle-ear infection, approximately 90 percent of children are better without medical therapy. Yet even with antibiotics, some children drag on and on with fluid in the ears. Of those who clear up quickly after a first infection, many get recurrences. ENT specialists stress the need for frequent checkups and hearing tests in children prone to middle-ear infections.

Myringotomy (putting a small hole in the drum) to drain off the middle-ear fluid may be tried for persistent cases that last three months or more. For children old enough to cooperate, myringotomy can be done under a local anesthetic, but those under age 15 usually need general anesthesia. Some specialists promote myringotomy in the acute phase, since it is a relatively simple procedure, perhaps preferable to continued long-term antibiotics.

Tympanotomy — insertion of small plastic ventilating tubes or grommits — is promoted by some specialists for children with persistent serous otitis media. The tubes are put into the blocked ear under general anesthesia, reventilating the middle ear and preventing or minimizing hearing loss. But "to tube or not to tube" is a much-debated question. Those who favor tubes argue that, although middle-ear infections generally heal without them, tubing helps to avoid a possible developmental lag in learning due to hearing loss. This is particularly critical from age 18 months to three years, when language develops. Missing the critical period may permanently undermine learning ability.

Those against tubing say that time alone (usually three months) makes most children better without any residual hearing loss. They cite surveys showing that with or without tubes, although 20 percent of children still have fluid in their ears and some hearing loss one month after a bout of otitis media, by two months only 9 percent and by the third month only 6 percent are still not back to normal. Opposition to ear tubes is increasing because, although insertion carries no greater surgical risks than average, it is still an operation done under general anesthesia, the tubes often need reinsertion and are a nuisance, as the need to avoid getting water in their ears restricts children's sport activities.

One controversial alternative is continuous low-dose preventive antibiotic therapy given throughout the winter for otitis-prone children whose middle ears predictably flare up at the end of each cold. Use of antibiotics may prevent ear infection. The overall message is to check hearing regularly in all children with chronic or recurrent middle-ear infections.

TOOTH AND GUM CARE

Gum disease, or, to give the condition its correct name, periodontal disease (from the Greek *peri,* around, and *odontos,* tooth), is popularly regarded as an inevitable part of aging, associated with bad breath and lengthy dental treatments. Yet periodontal disease does not need to accompany normal aging. One of the commonest causes of adult tooth loss, periodontal disease is an almost entirely preventable condition. It can usually be avoided or reversed by good oral hygiene and regular dental visits. However, left untreated, the condition will damage the tooth-supporting tissues and may ultimately lead to loss of teeth.

About nine out of ten Canadians experience occasional gum inflammation (inflamed gingival tissues), but the modern approach is to regard periodontal disease as an avoidable infection that can be prevented or kept well under control by good home mouth care and regular, professional cleaning by a dentist or dental hygienist.

Thorough tooth-brushing and, more important, between-the-teeth cleaning (by flossing or other means) go a long way in preventing periodontal disease and helping us keep our teeth to a ripe old age. But estimates show that many Canadians fail to practice even the minimum amount of daily mouth care, and less than half of all Canadians regularly visit a dentist. People are particularly negligent about daily between-the-teeth cleansing/flossing — although periodontal disease usually starts between the teeth.

Bacteria in plaque are largely to blame for gum disease

When the 17th-century Dutch microscopist Antony van Leeuwenhoek examined the whitish matter scraped from the surface of his own teeth under his microscope, he was amazed to see hundreds of tiny creatures, which he described as "small living animalcules that moved very prettily." The substance van Leeuwenhoek had dislodged was dental plaque, and the animalcules were mobile bacteria teeming in it. As we know today, bacteria in plaque are the primary cause of periodontal disease.

Plaque is the soft, gummy deposit that accumulates overnight on teeth, dentures and fillings and makes them feel unpleasantly furry in the morning. Plaque consists of many different bacteria, their nutrients and waste products. Scientists estimate that one gram (0.035 oz) of adult human plaque contains no fewer than 170,000,000,000 (1.7×10^{11}) organisms, of a few hundred different species. Plaque starts to form minutes after the teeth are brushed, and within twelve hours of even the most thorough tooth cleansing, gluey, organized bacterial colonies begin to coat the teeth. After 24 hours the bacteria in plaque already adhere tenaciously to the tooth surfaces — which explains why it's wise to clean the teeth thoroughly more than once a day!

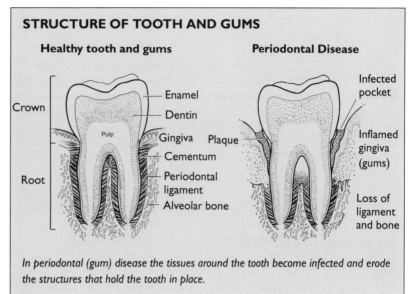

STRUCTURE OF TOOTH AND GUMS

Healthy tooth and gums   **Periodontal Disease**

Crown
Root
Pulp
Enamel
Dentin
Gingiva   Plaque
Cementum
Periodontal ligament
Alveolar bone

Infected pocket
Inflamed gingiva (gums)
Loss of ligament and bone

In periodontal (gum) disease the tissues around the tooth become infected and erode the structures that hold the tooth in place.

COMMON ERRORS IN MOUTH CARE INCLUDE:

- brushing wrongly, not thoroughly enough, not up to the gum line, too fast and not for the recommended time — some say three-minute sessions — morning, night and after meals;
- insufficient or no interdental (between-teeth) cleaning — i.e., flossing or using other between-teeth cleaning aids such as rubber-tipped stimulators, toothpicks or stim-u-dents (wooden between-teeth cleaners). Only about 15 percent of Canadians regularly use floss or other interdental cleaning devices;
- overlooking red or bleeding gums — the first signs of periodontal disease;
- waiting until it hurts — seeking dental attention only when a tooth or the gums become painful;
- neglecting regular dentist visits;
- smoking — known to be a strong factor linked to periodontal disease;
- not using fluoride to prevent tooth decay.

The greater the amount of plaque, the greater the chance of irritating the gingival (gum) tissues. Besides its quantity, the types of bacteria in plaque influence the kind and extent of periodontal disease. While some types of bacteria in plaque live in harmony with the mouth, others are pathogenic (health-damaging) strains that injure the teeth and tissues around them. As plaque accumulates, it gradually acquires more and more destructive bacteria that, together with their toxic metabolic byproducts, attack the oral tissues and trigger the body's inflammatory response. The inflammation can be locally damaging and cause bone resorption (loss). In addition, some bacteria in plaque produce volatile sulphur compounds that smell like rotting eggs, which is why some people with periodontal disease have bad breath.

Calculus, or mineralized plaque — popularly known as tartar — is plaque crystallized into hard, discolored deposits. Like coral in the ocean, calculus provides a rough surface on which bacteria can proliferate. It requires professional scaling (cleaning) by a dentist or dental hygienist.

The two main categories of periodontal disease

Gingivitis (from the Latin *gingiva*, gums) is a relatively common, reversible gum inflammation that affects many, producing at worst no more than a little bleeding, swelling and redness around the gum line. Gingivitis often arises during adolescence, when tooth-cleaning tends to be sloppy, but is usually a disease in name only, causing little "dis-ease" — little pain and discomfort (except for the form once called trench mouth). At present, it's impossible to predict in whom the mere redness and tissue puffiness of gingivitis will progress to the more serious periodontitis. Since there's no easy way to identify those at greatest risk, everyone is encouraged to practice prevention, clean their teeth well to remove plaque, avoid smoking and seek regular dental care.

Periodontitis, a less common but more persistent bacterial infection, affects about 40 percent of adults, ranges from mild to severe and extends deep into the tissues that support

---

WARNING SIGNS OF GINGIVITIS ARE:

- **gums that bleed when brushed or flossed;**
- **puffiness at the margins of the teeth;**
- **reddened, shiny, sensitive or itchy gums;**
- **red "halos" on the gums around the teeth;**
- **discharge from the gums/gingival tissues.**

Healthy gums are firm and resilient, with a snug fit around the teeth, and are light coral-pink or a darker color — depending on race.

RATING MOUTH-CARE PRODUCTS

- Plaque removal is best done mechanically by scraping or scrubbing. Meticulous tooth-brushing and flossing should get rid of most of the bacterial film above the gum line.
- Teeth should be brushed at least twice a day, morning and night, and preferably also after meals! The brushing should be thorough and should start young — as soon as the teeth appear (at age two or three). At first, parents can wipe and polish a child's teeth with a washcloth to remove plaque (up to age four or so); later they can supervise brushing until the child becomes adept enough to clean the teeth properly. Tooth-brushing should reach all teeth with short strokes and a gentle rotary motion. (The best way to learn to brush teeth properly is to get a dental professional to show you how.)
- Dental flossing, or between-teeth cleaning, although a bore to many who don't bother, is a must because it is between the teeth that plaque does the most harm. Many dental experts consider between-teeth cleaning or flossing even more important than brushing. It should be done at least once daily, with a gentle scraping motion. Never floss too vigorously or saw at the gums because this can bruise and damage these delicate tissues. Dentists recommend unwaxed or lightly waxed dental floss (waxed frays less). Those who cannot manage floss can use special toothpicks, rubber-tipped devices or interdented toothbrushes.
- The recommended toothbrush is soft, with three to four rows of tufted, polished rounded nylon bristles and a slightly rounded or flat surface. Overly hard toothbrushes can damage the gums. The brush should be changed every three to four months as bristles tend to splay and get dirty.
- Professional scaling should be done regularly (depending on individual needs), as it is not plaque above the gum line but deeper bacterial colonies that cause periodontitis. Only dental instruments used by skilled professionals can remove calculus properly.
- A new generation of power brushes claims superior plaque removal. These are recommended for those whose limited dexterity precludes efficient brushing with conventional brushes.
- Irrigators, or water-spray devices, shoot jets of water between the teeth, which may dislodge food particles and dilute bacterial products but do not remove plaque thoroughly. They are useful

adjuncts for people with braces and bridges.
- Toothpastes and mouthwashes are sold with a barrage of anti-tartar, anti-cavity claims. Which toothpaste is best? Does it make any difference? As far as periodontal disease goes, it doesn't matter. Toothpaste is not even essential. Provided the teeth are brushed properly, any toothpaste is as good as any other, although those endorsed by the Canadian Dental Association (CDA) are more likely to provide optimal results. Since toothpaste contains abrasives, it may be a little more effective at removing plaque than tap water alone, but only marginally. Most toothpastes contain about one-fifth to one-third water, a humectant (which keeps it from drying out), binding agents, foaming agents (which make it spread evenly and dissolve in water), abrasives, flavoring and perhaps artificial sweetener. Fluoride-containing toothpastes are highly recommended for fighting tooth decay.
- Claims for antiplaque and antitartar toothpaste and mouthwash abound, and some products contain active ingredients said to fight tartar (calculus). But any antitartar product can only combat calculus buildup after a thorough professional cleaning, and only above the gum line. It cannot remove old deposits but can only block the formation of new calculus. In general, the CDA approval of many products is based more on their fluoride content than on "anti-tartar" claims.
- Among the antibacterials, the more promising ones include *chlorhexidine* (in some prescription mouthwashes), essential oils (in Listerine mouthwash) and *sanguinarine* (in Viadent products).

Sorting out the anti-plaque claims

Whatever a toothpaste or mouthwash promises regarding plaque prevention, it cannot claim to be effective against the diseases of gingivitis and periodontitis, because before any product can make legitimate claims about disease prevention it must undergo rigorous testing. The CDA has recently developed a list of criteria concerning gingivitis control which toothpaste and mouthwash manufacturers must meet before being given the CDA's stamp of approval. So far no commercial product has qualified for approval (the standards are very new), although the American Dental Association has approved Listerine (an over-the-counter agent) and the prescription mouthwash Peridex for controlling gingivitis.

- **Chlorhexidine**, is an antibacterial substance used in the United States in Procter and Gamble's Peridex and in a number of other mouthwash and gel preparations in other countries. In Canada, some chlorhexidine products can be sold by the manufacturer to dentists for their office use, and dentists can prescribe chlorhexidine formulations that can be dispensed by pharmacists. Chlorhexidine binds readily to the oral tissues, stays in the mouth for some time after rinsing and is the most effective agent in controlling plaque and gingivitis. Over the long term it may transiently stain the teeth and fillings and cause some aberrations in taste sensation. Some acute allergic responses have been reported among hypersensitive individuals.
- **Essential oils** (the active ingredients in Listerine) are germicidal agents. Studies show that rinsing for 30 seconds with full-strength Listerine twice a day can decrease plaque buildup on the teeth.
- **Sanguinarine**, extracted from the roots of the bloodroot (a wild North American flowering plant), has been shown in some studies to reduce plaque buildup and gingivitis. However, the evidence is conflicting — it has not yet been proved to reduce gingivitis over the long haul, although long-term trials are just nearing completion. Viadent, both a toothpaste and mouthwash containing sanguinaria extract, have to be used in combination to achieve the therapeutic effect of the other mouth rinses alone.
- **A mouthwash called Plax**, containing sodium benzoate, sodium lauryl sulphate and sodium salicylate, has also been claimed by manufacturers to reduce plaque. Recent independent research has not substantiated this claim. Outside North America, Plax has recently been taken over by Colgate, and its formula has changed. Its efficacy is still being investigated.

The problem with all these agents is that they do not stay in the mouth long, even the longer-lasting chlorhexidine, so any effect is likely to be transitory, necessitating continued use over extended periods. Furthermore, they do not reach plaque in the pocket below the gingival margin, which is where bacteria do the most damage. Whether these mouthwashes and toothpastes will prove useful at controlling gingivitis in the long run remains to be seen. No study has shown them to be effective in preventing periodontitis.

the teeth. Advanced periodontitis, which affects about 10 percent of the North American population, can have lasting consequences — including eventual tooth loss. Some forms of periodontitis are rapidly progressive, leading to significant tissue destruction in a few years — especially a type called "juvenile-onset periodontitis," which begins in adolescence and may be hereditary.

The advance of periodontal disease — from a mild inflammatory condition to a deep gum infection — often has few signs until some bone loss in the jaw has occurred, with considerable tooth loosening. Periodontitis advances little by little, down the root of the tooth, taking hold if pathogenic bacteria penetrate deep under the gum tissues (sometimes down to the bone). As the infection progresses, the tissues recede and detach from the tooth surfaces, forming deep pockets (see diagram). With weakened attachment, the teeth feel jiggly or loose. Dentists use radiographs and a periodontal probe marked off in millimetres to determine the extent of bone loss.

The bacteria responsible for periodontitis cannot be removed by normal tooth cleaning. Severe cases need professional attention to remove the plaque and calculus, a procedure called scaling and root-planing. Together with meticulous home mouth care, this may be all that's needed. But unfortunately, about 15 percent of cases resist such treatment, and should be seen by specialists. For unresponsive cases, finding the right antibiotic would be an invaluable adjunct to therapy.

The modern approach is to try to identify the specific bacteria responsible and to reduce or eradicate them with appropriate antibiotics. There are now a few special commercial laboratories in the United States that use DNA probes to assist dentists in determining the bacteria in the colonizing areas of periodontal decay so that patients may be treated more accurately. The University of Toronto Department of Periodontics runs a consulting service, including limited microbiology, for patients plagued by severe, recurrent periodontal problems who are referred by dentists or specialists.

As in some medical infections, surgery may be needed for extensive periodontal disease, to gain better access for debridement (scraping) to reduce the extent of periodontal pockets and to impede bacterial colonization. Known as flap surgery, the procedure exposes the tooth root for rigorous cleaning and the bone for minor contouring or placement of grafting materials. New forms of periodontal surgery include "guided tissue regeneration," which tries to stimulate new growth of cells over the previously exposed and diseased parts. The true efficacy of such regeneration treatment is still being investigated.

Regular dental visits should start when a child's primary teeth come in, between the ages of two and three, and continue for life (ideally once or twice a year).

Sexual health

Developing healthy sexual attitudes • Tracing the steps in gender-role development • The development of sexual behaviour • Masturbation • Sexual dysfunction • Sex therapy • Sexually transmitted diseases • Recent trends in birth control

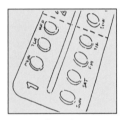

LEARNING TO BE-come a sexual person is a gradual evolution that starts at birth and continues through childhood and puberty with the gradual establishment of one's own personal sexual identity and orientation. The term "sex" is popularly used to mean intercourse or to denote male or female gender, the terms "sex" and "gender" often being used interchangeably. However, each has a slightly different meaning, sex usually referring to biological features while gender refers to male/female behaviour patterns.

DEVELOPING HEALTHY SEXUAL ATTITUDES

Sexual health depends on a positive self-image, which means feeling comfortable with one's body, knowing one's genital anatomy and function, understanding the human sexual response, being able to communicate sexual thoughts, fantasies and anxieties, feeling free to discuss and negotiate sexual wishes.

The roots of our sexual behaviour and orientation are grounded in influences received during fetal life and in early childhood. Healthy "sexual scripting" is a complex process that starts with pre-birth forces (the chromosomes and genes received at conception), is influenced by the fetal environment and is later molded by parental, societal and cultural attitudes.

Is the script for sexual behaviour mainly biological (written in the genes) or due to social conditioning? "The answer," says John Money, one of America's foremost gender experts and a medical psychologist at Johns Hopkins University, "is both together, neither alone. The only certainty is that men impregnate, women menstruate, gestate and lactate . . . beyond these basic functions, nothing sexual is immutably ordained." According to John Money, "we're born male or female, but we're made masculine or feminine."

The core *gender identity* — the internalized sense of being a boy or girl, man or woman — is jointly molded by biological forces and postnatal rearing influences. It is the "private experience" of our sexual selves, our own personal feeling as a male or female. Childhood messages about our bodies and gender-appropriate behaviour are quickly absorbed. The way that parents communicate thoughts about the genitals and eroticism profoundly influences future sexual health. In countless verbal and nonverbal ways, parents and others communicate values that affect sexual identity, sending subtle minute-by-minute messages telling infants, "You are a boy — you do this," or "You're a girl — you do that." By age two, a child can distinguish between Mummy and Daddy, and identify with the same-sex parent, siblings and others. By age three, most children have already developed a definite gender identity — a sense of belonging to one or the other sex.

7

By contrast, gender or sex role, solidified at puberty, is the *public* expression of our sexual selves, depicting to the world how we want to be viewed as men or women. Gender role, which displays to others our sense of masculinity, femininity or ambiguity, may or may not coincide with the inner gender identity. For instance, a woman may project an outwardly feminine image, yet inwardly feel ambivalent about her female sexuality. A man may privately feel effeminate, yet exhibit a strong "macho" line.

Gender identity formation begins at conception and is greatly influenced from day one after birth, by the way parents hold, feed, dress and respond to their baby. Gender roles are also influenced by what a particular society deems sex-appropriate behavior. The best insurance for a healthy sex life is to help the child base his or her gender identity firmly on biological or genital differences, leaving nonreproductive roles flexible. As long as the reproductive roles are clear, it doesn't matter who cooks the dinner, changes diapers, walks the dog or earns the bread. Rigid sex-role typing can lead to hard, unyielding personality types, people afraid to exhibit behaviors associated with the opposite sex. If male and female roles are strictly delineated, designating certain activities as "feminine" or "masculine," people can get locked into gender stereotypes that conform strictly to society's rules, making them feel limited in the jobs and other activities they can choose. For example, until recently, elementary-school books typically depicted Johnny with toy guns, trucks or footballs while Jane was shown cooking, sewing or playing with dolls.

Strict gender-role stereotyping has been much criticized of late, and the stereotyping is decreasing somewhat as Western society becomes aware of its restrictive impact on the full range of sexual expression. Yet sexism remains all too evident in present-day North America. In advertising, on TV and in many other facets of modern life, the "macho" stereotypes that dominated the culture for centuries still predominate. In North American cultural folklore, men still tend to be considered the empirical, mechanical conceptualizers and women the vague, intuitive, verbal cataloguers.

Is there any truth to the idea that sex differences in behavior and ability are wired into human brains? Modern research reveals some gender-specific differences in the rates of development of the brain's two cerebral hemispheres, and small anatomical sex differences in certain brain areas.

According to Harvard psychologists Eleanor Maccoby and Ruth Jacklin, the only well-founded intellectual sex differences are that girls outstrip boys in verbal skills, and that boys are undeniably more aggressive, and excel at math and visual-spatial ability. According to these psychologists, parental attitudes may reinforce or narrow the gap in mental development between the sexes. For instance, they suggest that overprotection may foster intellectual ability in boys, while girls seem to do best when urged to be independent. The details of brain differences in human males and females, and how they arise, is just being elucidated. (See later in this chapter for more on sex differences in the brain.)

The human brain develops in a different uterine environment according to the sex hormones released by a male or female fetus. Given the subtle differences in this fetal environment, it is no surprise that there may be subtle brain differences between the sexes. However, the impact of culture and socialization — the way people respond to male or female babies — has an overpowering influence on sexual behavior and orientation. Most sex experts believe that "nurture overrides nature in shaping sexual behavior and attitudes."

Sexual orientation — the type of person we fall in love with and desire as sex partner — depends largely on early sexual scripting. Gender dilemmas and ambiguity can arise for many reasons. For instance, if the infant's first parental role models give contradictory cues — if *he* smiles while *she* frowns — the child can't tell where it stands. To get his sexual circuits right, a boy must regard his penis as a proud part of his future manhood; a girl must know and value her breasts, vagina and vulva. Undercover messages that the genitals are displeasing or disgusting may make an anxious infant wish away the offending parts and perhaps impede later sexual enjoyment.

Nature's basic mammalian plan is female

Through evolution, natural selection has made it easier for mammalian (including human) fetuses to become female than male. All human fetuses start out basically similar, able to develop either male or female sexual anatomy. In fact, the basic mammalian mold is female. The fetus receives two sex chromosomes at conception, and while one chromosome is always an X, the other can be either another X, or a Y. To become a man, the fetus requires the Y (male) sex chromosome and the outpouring of fetal testosterone at the right moment in embryonic life. Thus the human fetus develops male or female reproductive systems depending on the sex chromosomes received at conception: XX makes a female, with female genitals, and XY makes a male. Without a Y chromosome, a human fetus will develop a female anatomy. In other words, although male and female human embryos start out with the same set of primitive tissues, males must be *made* male while the female form develops automatically. This is why U.S. sexologist Mary Jane Sherfey asserted that "in the beginning we were all created female."

To create a man's body, the primordial female mold must be subdued by male genetic and hormonal factors. The production of a human male requires a gamut of extras at critical stages of fetal growth. The timing of each stage is exquisitely precise. Unless the Y chromosome exerts its influence at the correct time to produce a fetal testis (and fetal testosterone), female human anatomy will automatically develop. (Even with a single X sex chromososome, as in XO girls with Turner's syndrome, a female body forms.)

Fetal testosterone, a male hormone, plays a key role in making a man. Hormones are powerful chemical agents, released into the bloodstream, which regulate many activities. Overriding the female plan, fetal testosterone diverts the developing baby's anatomy toward a male format. Another hormone, the Müllerian Inhibiting Hormone (MIH), simultaneously blocks female development, defeminizing the fetus, causing degeneration of those parts which would otherwise form a vagina, uterus and fallopian tubes.

If mammalian (rat, mouse or monkey) testes are removed from an XY (male) fetus at a developmental stage, the offspring develop female bodies and behavior despite their male sex-chromosome pattern, showing typical female running habits, turning-away or backside-presenting poses and female mating behavior.

TRACING THE STEPS IN GENDER-ROLE DEVELOPMENT

The steps toward sexual health can be regarded as critical stages or "gates" through which we pass *en route* to becoming sexually active men and women. Some take place before birth, some during childhood and adolescence. After a fetus takes the first steps toward female or male anatomy, it passes through further gender-forming gates. As each clicks shut, we are locked ever more firmly into male or female gender roles, behavior and attitudes.

Gate 1: Parental assumptions about the child

Is the pregnancy planned or not? Does the couple want a boy or girl? Could their expectations color the way they respond to and raise the child? Conflict, tension and stress during pregnancy can cause hormone changes in the mother that may affect the baby's future sexuality. In one study, extreme stress in mother rats produced male babies with shriveled testicles: they grew into undersexed adults with abnormal mating behavior.

Gate 2: The chromosomes and genes received at conception

The second gate in human psychosexual development occurs at fertilization, when the chromosomes of egg and sperm unite. The sex chromosome pair (XX for a female, XY for a male) differ in size and the information in their genes. Although embryos with XY sex chromosomes normally develop into males and those with an XX pair continue on the female route, the genes are a flexible blueprint, not a rigid plan, and their full expression depends upon prenatal influences in the uterus and those after birth in the outside world. Some genetic messages can be overridden by psychosocial influences.

Gate 3: Reproductive organs shape fetal progress

During the second month of fetal life, human embryos develop a pair of gonads (reproductive organs), not yet distinguished as male testes or female ovaries. Although the embryo is already genetically male or female (possessing XX or XY chromosomes), it is not yet *anatomically* male or female. Normally, a human embryo with a Y chromosome will develop a testis at six to eight weeks of gestation, whereas XX embryos develop ovaries later, at about 12 weeks after conception. The path toward male or female reproductive architecture is well under way by the third month of pregnancy, with the establishment of functioning testes or ovaries.

Gate 4: Prenatal hormones prime brain circuits

The next step in gender development depends on the presence and amount of fetal testosterone. As one expert puts it, "not only the male body, but also the foundations of the male mind are created in the womb. Male fetal hormones establish the future male pattern of acyclic hormone release, also priming brain pathways for male behavior." (We still do not know whether fetal female hormones or those from the mother's ovaries or placenta alter brain pathways.)

New research reaffirms that brain development may be influenced by the ratio of sex hormones in early fetal life, especially testosterone from the fetal testes, which circulates in the bloodstream, reaching the brain and affecting certain "target" nerve cells. In different brain areas, the male sex hormone or its metabolites may have specific effects. There is already clear evidence of gender differences in the brain for the hormonal control of reproduction. The hypothalamus, in the floor of the brain, is encoded with a *cyclic* hormone pattern in females — essential for monthly ovulation (egg release) and menstruation. Men, by contrast, do not have cyclic hormonal patterns, but instead relatively constant, noncyclic sex hormone production from puberty to death (although it may decline somewhat in old age). Thus the male brain's basic plan is primed by

fetal testosterone for acyclic release of sex hormones. Evidence also suggests that human males develop brain networks that make them more easily sexually aroused by visual stimuli, while women are more responsive to touch or words. This may underlie the common assumption that in men "sex leads to love" while in women "love leads to sex."

Gate 5: Internal anatomy: male and female ducts and organs

In the male (XY) human fetus, the Müllerian (female) ducts wither, while other — Wolffian — ducts form sperm ducts (vasa deferentia) and internal male structures. The balance and amount of fetal hormones are critical in pushing the fetus to become a male.

In female (XX) fetuses, the ovaries develop later, and the brain is encoded for cyclic female hormone production. Female anatomy develops whether or not fetal estrogens are present.

Gate 6: Birth: baby's gender assignment

When a baby is born, it is significant that everyone's first look is not at the face but at the crotch. (Monkeys too inspect their newborn offspring's genitals.) The three little words "It's a girl!" or "It's a boy!" label the newborn as a boy or girl. Sex assignment is a major turning point, regarded by many gender experts such as John Money and Robert Francoeur, a renowned American embryologist and theologian, as "paramount in forming gender role and sexual behavior." It opens the door to the powerful sway of social and cultural influences. After a quick peep at the naked baby's genitals, it's swaddled in pink or blue. And out come a raft of notions, facts, myths and fallacies about how the infant should be treated.

Gate 7: Childhood gender-scripting

Parents, siblings, relatives and friends respond to gender assignment by invoking many expectations for the newborn, already starting to script it for behavior considered suitable to its gender. Parents and other caregivers tend to treat infant girls and boys differently in North America. Baby girls are handled more gently, held, touched, cuddled and sung to more than baby boys. Baby boys are bounced around in a more physical way and are usually less pampered than baby girls — maybe because cuddling is commonly held to make a boy "wimpy," or "not manly." Boys typically get more intense pressure of all kinds, more sanctions against unmanly or "sissy" conduct, more discipline, more encouragement and praise for success. People use more baby talk with infant girls than they do with baby boys — conditioning which adds up to complex gender-scripting that may last a lifetime.

Throughout childhood, gender identity and sexual orientation are reinforced in countless ways, both verbal and non-verbal. By their expressions and gestures, parents and other caregivers communicate attitudes about the child's body, genitals and sexuality. Parents provide living examples of love, family and work relationships. The way they express (or don't express) emotions teaches a child to be expressive or reserved in later relationships.

Parental reactions to childhood eroticism strongly influence future sexual relationships. Children spontaneously explore their genitals as a natural part of growing up, and childhood play helps to shape adult sex roles. Even when discouraged, as often happens in our culture, children are intensely curious about differences between boys and girls.

Monkey studies confirm that all primates spend much time exploring their own and others' genitals, rehearsing adult sex behavior. Yet in North American culture, preadolescent sex play can evoke anxiety in adult caregivers, who easily communicate disapproval. Negative messages about the genitals — for instance, about the penis, vagina, menstruation or masturbation — influence early gender-scripting. Those who grimace if children touch their genitals may bring up sexually inhibited children who become adults with problems in establishing happy sexual relationships.

Gate 8: Pubertal development of secondary sex characteristics
A rising surge of sex hormones moves teenagers quickly through puberty and the last gates in psychosexual development. A spurt

of testosterone in boys and estrogen in girls triggers development of the secondary sex characteristics — beard, erections and wet dreams in men, periods, breasts and the potential for childbearing in women. Dating begins, romance blossoms and sex becomes a driving force. The risks of pregnancy and sexually transmitted diseases become a concern. In adolescence, people consolidate the sexual scripts developed in childhood for their erotic preferences and activities — whether, for instance, they are turned on by tall or short, trim or heavyset, large- or small-breasted, same-sex or opposite-sex partners.

Sexual scripting forms a value system that determines adult sexual attitudes. Scripting theory emphasizes the impact of learning and social influences, implying that sexual behaviour is based more on "nurture" (rearing) than on "nature" (biology). According to John Money, the sexual script completed during adolescence is a "lovemap" of the kind of erotic activities we might like and engage in. Lovemaps are "as personalized and unique as fingerprints, each containing innate courtship patterns common to all humans (because of our shared ancestry), also incorporating specific individual influences acquired during fetal development and early childhood."

Depending on our unique lovemap, each of us chooses a certain partner and reacts differently to erotic stimuli, replaying a sexual script written in childhood, based on the messages received about touching, intimacy, sensuality, erotic play, relationships and connectedness. No amount of later post-adolescent exposure to personal experiences, ads, TV or pornography will alter the basic gender script.

Since sexual "turn-ons" become apparent only in adolescence, it's often assumed that they're instilled by a first love, a homosexual or locker-room encounter, pornography, movies or some influential older friend. But in reality, adolescence is more a time of revelation than a turning point. As one eminent therapist points out, "however profound and influential the psychosocial experiences at puberty, earlier forces imprinted during infancy determine sexual health and are responsible for most sexual disturbances, anomalies and ambiguities. The roots of our sexual triggers and fantasies lie far back in our childhood biographies." Each person's sex script, formed by early influences, is consolidated at puberty, substantiated and replayed through life. This may explain why a second spouse so often resembles the first, or why a homosexual or transsexual stays that way.

Some researchers suggest that the earlier onset of puberty in girls gives the female brain less time to specialize its two hemispheres — perhaps explaining so-called female intuition, as the closer connection between the two cerebral hemispheres in women may facilitate rapid interpretation of nuances. Males, by contrast, with later puberty and more specialized cerebral hemispheres, may more easily trace logical pathways and zero in on relevant details, excluding extraneous signals. Or so the current story goes!

Gate 9: Adult gender role and sexual orientation

The sexual scripts or lovemaps engraved through childhood and consolidated at puberty determine sex-partner choice. The lovemap encoded in the brain may or may not fit what society, culture, religion and family deem acceptable. It can become distorted or perverted if, for instance, a child is sexually abused or receives disturbing sex signals. A distorted sex script may result in *paraphilias*; unconventional sexual expressions, perversions or illegal behavior such as pedophilia (sexual desire for children).

Evidence suggests that it's women who generally initiate courtship, with subtle signals, while men use more overt courtship styles. In one study asking college men and women how they flirted, researchers found that women recognized and responded to very early stages of courtship, while the young men often seemed insensitive or oblivious to the early flirtatious moves made by women. Men pegged the start of courtship at the first physical contact, women at subtle glances. As one gender expert puts it: "It is as if men are unconsciously blind — or have been blinded by defeminization — to initial courtship moves."

THE DEVELOPMENT OF SEXUAL BEHAVIOR

Researchers contend that young children learn and enjoy erotic arousal and that early sexual stimulation contributes to normal physical and psychosexual development. Current evidence suggests that most childhood sexual experiences are positive and growth-promoting, unless they involve force or abuse, or trigger negative reactions. By age two, children naturally respond to each other affectionately by touching, hugging and kissing. Whether or not such behavior is erotic varies. By age three, children casually examine each other's genitals. Games of "Doctor," "House," "You show me yours and I'll show you mine," or "Mummy and Daddy" usually involve nothing more than undressing with some touching, and lying side by side or on top of one another. Left alone, most children would naturally develop what Canadian sex researcher Bill Fisher and colleagues call "erotophilia" — natural enjoyment of erotic/tactile behavior.

Parents and society can disturb natural childhood responses by negative messages implying that certain sexual feelings or behaviors are taboo and possibly sinful, sometimes building a wall of guilt and shame around sexual activity. If parents punish a child for some sexual expression or behavior, they may script the child for erotophobia, fear of things sexual. Those who themselves received childhood messages of guilt and shame about sex may become erotophobic adults, who tend to be limited in the sexual behavior they're willing to try. They may abhor pornography and erotica, suppress sexual fantasies and avoid sexual exploration. Such attitudes may profoundly affect the way their children view sexuality.

When two or more children close in age grow up together, there may be many opportunities for sociosexual exploration, especially if they sleep in the same room. Sexual exploration between a young brother and sister, two brothers or two sisters might, strictly speaking, be labeled incest or homosexual activity, but most experts would not apply the terms "incest" and "homosexual" to childhood sexuality. However, with siblings wide apart in age, where there's no or little privacy, childhood games may more closely mimic adult behavior and include mutual masturbation, oro-genital (mouth-genital) contact and even attempts at intercourse. Dividing childhood play into male- or female-appropriate games can perhaps condition boys to believe in male toughness and girls to believe in compliance. According to many sex experts, violence, aggression, winning and being masterful and dominant are still part of the current Western "macho" script, classically suppressing "feminine" traits such as tenderness and sensitivity in men.

Psychologists stress that hugs and loving touches in childhood reaffirm a positive body image and play a vital role in the ability to forge healthy adult sex relationships. Yet, according to U.S. sexologist John Gagnon, even before the recent focus on child abuse, American parents tended to back off hugging their children after age six or so. James Prescott's studies on child-rearing customs in 49 cultures around the world, including America, revealed a clear link between the capacity for sexual intimacy and early childhood nurturance and rearing practices. Children who received lots of body contact and frequent caresses, or those in families where teenage sex was accepted, became well-adapted, peaceful adults. But children deprived of warmth and close nurturing or those given negative messages about their bodies and genitals grew into adults with a tendency to be violent, to glorify war and use drugs and/or alcohol. These findings confirm what American researchers Harry and Margaret Harlow demonstrated about the distorted behavior of infant monkeys reared with wire mesh or fur dolls instead of live monkey mothers. Young monkeys deprived of warmth and mother love grew up hostile and antisocial, uninterested in usual primate sex play and unable to mate normally.

Some sexologists fear that our recent concern about childhood sex abuse may reinforce a nontactile, distant approach to child-rearing. Many parents, as well as teachers and daycare professionals, may avoid touching children for fear their actions will be misunderstood, depriving youngsters of much-needed hugs. A few sex therapists even predict that, 20 to 30 years from now, "we may see women who, having internalized negative messages about their bodies from 'street-wising,' sexuality and self-defence courses, have troubled sex lives." To counter what she calls the "current paranoia" over childhood sex abuse, sexologist Margaret Dwyer suggests we "talk about appropriate and inappropriate touches, instead of good or bad touches."

MASTURBATION

Since sexual intimacy and erotic play are pleasurable, one would expect children to enjoy masturbating and other sexual exploration. The reflex response that produces erections in boys and men may appear as early as 17 weeks of fetal life. Ultrasound pictures reveal erections in the tiny penises of male fetuses. One study of boys 3 to 20 weeks after birth found that seven out of nine had erections as many as 5 to 40 times a day. Girls under a year old have been observed having what to all appearances seems to be a reflexive orgasm induced by pressure on the genitals. The reflexes that result in infant erections and vaginal lubrication are much like the knee jerk and other reflexes, except for the accompanying smiles suggestive of enjoyment.

Sooner or later, most children learn the pleasures of stimulating their genitals. Two-thirds of the males in one of Dr. Kinsey's early studies reported hearing about masturbation from other boys in their prepubescent or early adolescent years, before trying it themselves. Fewer than one in three males reported rediscovering masturbation entirely on their own. Two out of three females in one sample learned about masturbation by accident, sometimes not until after they were married. Some women reported they had masturbated for some time before they realized what they were doing.

Masturbation is a normal activity that will not harm those doing it, provided that the individual (or couple) does it in private without disturbing others, and that it's not accompanied by anxiety. But if masturbation generates fears of abnormality, disease (such as "warts on the fingers"), punishment (perhaps because of religious beliefs) or harsh criticism from caregivers

SEX AND AGING

With advancing years, many a man anxiously wonders whether his potency will decrease or vanish. The answer is sometimes yes, often no. Many men give up intercourse as they grow older, especially if they encounter occasional impotence or orgasmic problems. But given today's more liberal attitudes, many older men (and women) seek and expect sexual stimulation. In one study of U.S. retirement communities, 20 percent of men and women in their eighties were still sexually active, although their sexual practices were primarily touching/caressing, followed by self-pleasuring to "finish off." Those most sexually active in their younger days were likeliest to remain so as seniors. Unless health problems intervene, people can remain sexually active to a ripe old age. However, a Michigan study found 35 percent of married men over age 60 reported erectile dysfunction, rising to 64 percent by age 80. Curiously, the Michigan study found that drinking coffee increased sexual potency! Men who didn't drink coffee had a less active sex life than coffee imbibers. The authors of the study were puzzled about this link to caffeine — a central-nervous-system stimulant — wondering whether coffee is an aphrodisiac or whether coffee drinkers in general are more "liberal" in their sexual attitudes. The answer remains elusive.

who consider it "wicked" or inappropriate, it can engender acute anxiety and cause more harm than good. Occasionally, masturbation is so excessive or even compulsive a preoccupation that it symbolizes some deep anxiety or other psychological problem that needs medical attention and counseling.

SEXUAL DYSFUNCTION

Almost everyone who is sexually active sooner or later experiences some sexual difficulties. These are often resolved by communicating wishes, sharing likes or dislikes, discussing problems and finding ways to become more intimate. While sex problems arise for many reasons — for example, negative parental attitudes to sex, childhood abuse, a bad sex encounter, fear of intimacy — the same roots may produce different sex problems in different people.

Sexual dysfunction may involve recurrent problems with the desire, arousal or orgasmic phases of the human sexual response. Sex problems can be occasional and transient or long-term, depending on their origins. While many sexual disorders arise from some organic cause, most also have psychological dimensions.

Sexual difficulties are remarkably common. One study found that although the majority of North American couples reported "satisfying sex lives," 40 percent of the men reported occasional impotence or erectile dysfunction and 63 percent of the women had some arousal or orgasmic problems. In addition, 50 percent of the men and 77 percent of the women reported difficulties that were not strictly dysfunctional, such as lack of interest in sex, too little time for it or an inability to relax during intercourse. Another survey found that over half of all North American couples reported some sexual dissatisfaction, such as "lack of enjoyment," "inability to become aroused" or "boring sex lives."

Some couples feel inadequate if they enjoy mutual sexual pleasuring but one or the other doesn't reach orgasm. Many define a rewarding sexual encounter solely in terms of vaginal penetration. Orgasm through intercourse may be the supreme goal, but this is labeled by one therapist as "an obsessive and unrealistic aim when there are so many other ways of enjoying sex."

Failure to live up to expectations (their own or their partner's) may produce profound anxiety. Despite today's more flexible sexual attitudes, some men equate good sex with "scoring," "conquering" or "going all the way," while women may equate sexual adequacy with the ability to lubricate well and reach vaginal orgasm. Some couples who achieve orgasm by manual or oral stimulation, or with a vibrator, think there may be "something wrong" with them. It's a common myth that everyone should be able to become aroused and perform on demand. Many factors influence the human sexual response. Some people experience good sex in a bad relationship, others have bad sex in a good relationship.

Sexual adequacy is defined as "the ability of two people to relate with each other sexually in ways that satisfy and reward both partners." But for many people this simple definition is colored by unrealistic expectations. We are often misled by our own and others' expectations, or by the idealized or distorted media portrayal of sexual relationships. Failure to live up to expectations can create or exacerbate sexual difficulties.

Low sex drive and lack of interest in sex, among the commonest of today's sex problems, is popularly dubbed the "sex problem of the nineties." It may result from a fast-paced lifestyle where overscheduled people don't have the time or inclination to relax and enjoy sex. Feeling "burned out," couples complain of low sex drive and waning sexual interest. Sex and relationship therapy may help to restore sexual health in such cases.

Sex aversion — an extreme and rare form of sexual lack of interest — may involve fear of any sexual intimacy. It usually has deep-seated psychological origins, often requiring intensive therapy. People with the sexual aversion syndrome shun all activities that might lead to intercourse, including petting and kissing. A couple may be in a relationship with no physical contact, and any hint of sexual involvement may trigger strong feelings of disgust or fear in one or the other partner, perhaps violent enough to cause panic. Sexual aversion may stem from a traumatic sexual experience, such as rape or sexual abuse. Therapy plus relaxation techniques may help to eliminate the sex phobia.

Sexual dysfunction in the desire phase of the human sexual response can arise for religious, moral, physical, emotional, marital or occupational reasons. Sexual desire depends on adequate hormone levels and the correct functioning of specific brain circuits. Even when everything is working properly, psychological factors can inhibit or shut down sexual desire. Strong negative messages about sex from parents, family, friends or church, guilt, or fear of pregnancy or infection may quench sexual desire. A recent survey found that 31 percent of couples seeking sex therapy complained of a discrepancy or conflict in their desire for sex. Lack of communication can also undermine sexual desire. Woody Allen's movie *Annie Hall* offers a classic example of different perceptions. When the therapist asks the woman how often they have sex, she answers, "All the time — three times a week." To the same question, the man replies, "Hardly ever — three times a week!"

Occasional low points in sexual desire are natural, but if the indifference persists or becomes troublesome, professional counseling may be the answer.

Sexual dysfunction in the arousal phase means the inability to become sexually aroused. Sexual arousal is swayed by atmosphere, mood, interpersonal conflicts and negative emotions, especially anger. It may be inhibited because of off-putting parental messages about sex, an unpleasant sexual experience, sex abuse, misinformation or performance pressure. Women may be unable to become sexually aroused because the excitement level isn't enough to produce or maintain vaginal lubrication. (The old terms "frigidity" and "impotence" are no longer used because of their negative connotations.) Most healthy men and women experience occasional difficulty in becoming sexually aroused, but if it is a persistent or recurrent problem, sex therapy may be the solution.

Inhibited orgasm can also afflict men and women, and is defined as the inability to achieve orgasm and/or ejaculation during intercourse. Men may manage to ejaculate and reach orgasm by masturbation but not with vaginal intercourse, and women too may not reach orgasm during intercourse but may do so with masturbation. Some therapists believe orgasmic problems often stem from fear of intercourse, an unwillingness to perform on demand and anxiety about not satisfying a partner. Therapy often reverses the problem.

(For more on specific sex problems in women, see chapter 8; for specific sex problems in men, see chapter 9.)

SEX THERAPY

Sexual dysfunction often vanishes or improves with proficient counseling, usually involving both partners. Sex counselors are trained professionals such as physicians, social workers, psychologists, nurses and psychiatrists skilled in the art of helping people work through the emotions, guilts, hang-ups, worries, anger, myths and misconceptions that bedevil our sex lives. If the sex problem is due to an organic disorder, therapy can still help people accept and adjust to it.

Sex therapy is particularly useful for

dysfunctions that involve anxiety, performance fears, stress, ignorance, negative childhood conditioning, relationship conflicts and "spectatoring" (observing oneself and one's responses rather than participating in the event).

A non-directed "sensate focus," in which the goal is sensuous pleasure rather than intercourse, is one sex therapy method that helps couples overcome conflicts around mistimed or mismatched sexual desire or a lack of "connectedness." The couple learns to approach sexual intimacy as mutual pleasuring without anticipating intercourse or orgasm. By concentrating on sensual play — neither partner being pressured or expected to become aroused — the sensate focus exercises can often override performance anxieties and dispel problems due to poor body image, negative sex messages or communication hurdles. The couple learns to relax and playfully explore what gives the other pleasure. Each shows the other what kinds of touching he or she enjoys, where the most erotic places are, communicating verbally or by directing the partner's hand. The exercises work equally well for gay, lesbian or straight couples. Even couples with no sexual difficulties occasionally use the method to enrich their sex lives.

The PLISSIT model of sex therapy, developed about 20 years ago by Dr. Annon, is based on the premise that many people benefit from the very simplest of counseling — even just being permitted to talk about their problems. Reassurance, support and information are often enough to reverse a sex problem without intensive or lengthy psychotherapy. Using a "filter model," sex counselors distinguish people with simple sexual difficulties — who can profit from simple advice — from those requiring more intensive therapy.

The acronym "PLISSIT" refers to four basic stages:

Permission-Giving — permitting people to talk about their sex troubles, fantasies, fears or wishes;

Limited Information — often used together with permission-giving, providing some basic information (perhaps about erotic zones and genital anatomy) but no specific advice;

Specific Suggestions — given for specific sex problems; for instance, telling a man with premature ejaculation what might slow things down or suggesting how and where a woman afraid of pregnancy can get contraceptive advice;

Intensive Therapy — required by the relatively few with deeply rooted psychological problems who need longer-term psychotherapy.

The first steps, permission-giving and limited information, are often enough to resolve a sex problem — especially one due to anxiety or misinformation. Many of us occasionally get the feeling that what we are doing sexually, or would like to do, is perverted, deviant or wrong. All we may need is reassurance or someone to say, "If you are comfortable with it, carry on." Once a sex problem has been pinpointed, its solution may be obvious to those versed in human sexual behavior. For instance, a couple in a college dormitory experiencing an orgasmic problem may just be put off by the lack of privacy. One suggestion might be to find a more relaxing place for lovemaking, perhaps a friend's apartment or a nearby motel. Or, for a boy worried that masturbation will give him warts, it may be enough to say that masturbation is harmless and normal. Such specific suggestions may seem simplistic, but many sexual problems are in fact relatively simple, superficial and easily remedied.

Unfortunately, there have been cases of irresponsibility and even exploitation among people calling themselves sex therapists. Be sure anyone you consult comes well recommended. A sex therapist should never ask you to take off your clothes, unless for a medical examination; or to engage in any type of sexual activity with or without your partner in the therapist's presence.

If you feel you need a sex therapist, consult your family physician; the Ontario Association of Marriage and Family Therapy, (416) 841-6465 or (toll-free) 1-800-267-2638; local medical associations; BESTCO (Board Examiners in Sex Therapy and Counselling in Ontario), SIECAN: the Sex Information and Education Council of Canada, (416) 466-5304; or psychological associations.

SEXUALLY TRANSMITTED DISEASES

Originally termed "venereal" diseases, in reference to Venus, the goddess of love, sexually transmitted diseases (STDs) encompass various infections caused by different microorganisms. Some STDs such as syphilis and gonorrhea have been recorded since antiquity. However, many of the 50-plus viruses, bacteria, protozoa and other microorganisms now known to be sexually transmitted have only been identified in this century. Despite the advent of antibiotics, STDs still pose a serious health threat, especially to adolescents and young adults.

Teens, especially girls, are at particular risk of STDs

While gonorrhea is decreasing among the population at large, the proportion among Canadian adolescents is increasing. The spread of chlamydia — its aftereffects include sterility and risks of ectopic (outside the womb) pregnancy — continues unabated, mainly among young women. As one University of Toronto expert puts it, "teens are moving into the forefront of the STD epidemic. Girls aged 15–19 are gaining on men in their twenties for the highest incidence of gonorrhea, herpes, chlamydia and genital wart infections." The increase is explained partly by the early onset of unprotected sexual activity, the high "pool" of STD infection among young people, plus the fact that STDs so often produce no symptoms. The Canada Youth and AIDS Study (CYAS) found that 48 percent of boys and 46 percent of girls in Grade 11 were already sexually active around age 16. Moreover, teenagers tend to change sex partners frequently (every four to six months in many cases), may not be prepared for sexual intercourse, don't discriminate in their choice of partners and are likely to be "caught off guard." To add to the risks for teenage girls, the adolescent genital tract — not yet fully matured — is extra vulnerable to invading microorganisms.

Yet teens disdain condoms as "unesthetic" or "premeditated," and fail to realize how easy it is to contract an infection or get pregnant even at the first sexual encounter. The CYAS survey found strong reluctance or negative attitudes towards condom use among adolescents, whether or not they'd had sexual intercourse. In fact, youngsters with the most sexual experience were the least likely to use condoms. The survey also indicated that 22 percent of sexually active female first-year college students and 18 percent of sexually active male students had had anal intercourse at least once. Yet anal sex is high-risk behavior for transmitting AIDS and other STDs.

Untreated STDs can have devastating consequences — especially for women

STDs are sometimes called "sexist," as women usually face far more drastic health consequences than men. For anatomical reasons, women are likelier to have "hidden" STDs, for example, internal sores or a cervical discharge, in their internal reproductive organs. These are less obvious and harder to detect. Health complications from STDs are also generally more destructive in women. They include pelvic inflammatory disease (PID), sterility, ectopic pregnancy and cervical cancer which is now linked to human papilloma virus (genital wart) infections. Women should take as much care to protect themselves from STDs as to avoid unwanted pregnancy.

Some types of sex are riskier than others

Sexually transmitted infections don't respect class or race. They strike men and women of every type, rich or poor, gay, heterosexual or bisexual. Any sexually active person who doesn't take proper precautions is vulnerable to STD infection. But on the STD danger scale, some sexual practices are riskier than others. Anal sex is the riskiest, vaginal sex less so and oral sex the least likely to transmit an STD. (But that doesn't mean oral sex is "safe" — it can still transmit infections, including AIDS.) While one encounter is enough to catch a sexually transmitted disease, the risks increase with the number of lovers one has — particularly if they are chosen from groups at high risk of STDs. Epidemiologists have identified certain groups with behaviors that increase this risk — such as adolescents (who often don't take precautions);

WHEN TO GET CHECKED FOR A POSSIBLE STD:

- if you know or suspect your sex partner is infected;
- if changing sex partners often (wait about four weeks, until the infection can be detected, then get tested);
- if there are signs of:
  - a vaginal or penile discharge ("the drip");
  - rash, warty growths, pimples, itchiness or sores on the genitals;
  - persistent lower abdominal pain;
  - pain when urinating;
  - changes in menstrual flow, unusual bleeding (in women).

N.B.: Women should get regular Pap smear tests to detect and treat early signs of cervical cancer.

those with many sex partners; injection-drug users; male homosexuals; bisexuals; anyone who practices unprotected anal sex (especially with multiple partners); those who have unprotected sex with "sex-trade workers" (prostitutes); and those who use nonbarrier contraceptives such as the IUD or "the Pill," unless they also use a condom. Young children can get STDs as a result of sexual abuse.

Carriers often unknowingly spread STDs

One reason for the rampant spread of STDs is their ability to "hide" in symptomless carriers. Many men and women don't know they have a bacterial, viral or parasitic STD because they are asymptomatic, with no sign of infection. Having no symptoms, they don't go to be checked and aren't treated, and if they continue to have sex without condoms they spread the disease. For example, up to 50 percent of men and women with gonorrhea and/or chlamydia may be asymptomatic, although the disease is injuring their reproductive systems. Weeks, months or years may elapse before the serious (and possibly irreversible) complications of an untreated STD become apparent. Moreover, some STDs, such as human papilloma virus (genital warts), AIDS, hepatitis B and herpes infections, aren't curable.

Whether or not they have symptoms, carriers can infect their partners or unborn children. Depending on the particular infection, children born to mothers with some STDs — hepatitis B, serious forms of syphilis, herpes or HIV (AIDS) infection — may be endangered by pneumonia or conjunctivitis (eye inflammation — perhaps producing blindness).

Ways to practice "safer" sex

The only sensible approach to sexually transmitted diseases is prevention. STDs can be avoided by abstaining from sex, and for some, saying no may be right for a time. Those who do decide to have sex should choose safer options, such as selecting a faithful, noninfected partner (hard to determine) or consistently using condoms. Men and women should carry a packet of good latex condoms to use "just in case." Condoms provide a reasonable barrier against gonorrhea, syphilis, chlamydia, hepatitis

B and HIV (AIDS), but not against herpes or genital wart (HPV) infections, because condoms may not cover the open sores.

Unfortunately, many women feel embarrassed about condoms, and don't insist that their sex partners wear them, and men may use them inconsistently or incorrectly. Nevertheless, the risk of STD infection should far outweigh minor aversion. Women are urged to take a more "empowering" approach and to insist that male sex partners wear condoms. Or they could try the new "female condom" or vaginal pouch. Women and men both need to know that anal sex is particularly dangerous because the delicate anal canal is more easily damaged than the tougher vaginal wall, allowing easier access to microorganisms and exposure to blood. (A woman's risk of STD infection is twice as high by anal as by vaginal intercourse.)

A rundown of some common STDs

Gonorrhea: popularly known as the "clap," gonorrhea is caused by the bacteria *Neisseria gonorrhoeae*. Although decreasing among the population at large, its proportion is increasing among Canadian youth. Up to 50 percent of men and women with gonorrhea show no symptoms of infection, although they can pass the disease to their sex partners. If any symptoms do occur (usually about one week after exposure) they may include:

In men:
- thick yellowish-green penile discharge;
- sore throat (from oral sex);
- pain on voiding and frequency of urination;
- lower abdominal pain.

In women:
- thick vaginal discharge;
- sore throat (from oral sex);
- lower abdominal pain;
- urinary frequency and pain when urinating;
- increased or painful menstrual periods.

Gonorrhea coexists with chlamydia in up to 50 percent of cases. Untreated, it can result in pelvic inflammatory disease, tubal scarring, infertility and ectopic pregnancy. The gonococcal organism can be passed to newborns, causing a severe eye infection that can lead to blindness. To prevent eye disorders from gonorrhea (or chlamydia), newborns are usually

---

METHODS *NOT* EFFECTIVE IN PREVENTING STDS:

- **washing or urinating immediately after intercourse;**
- **douching;**
- **using nonbarrier birth-control methods, such as the IUD or "the Pill."**

given eyedrops containing silver nitrate or erythromycin.

Gonorrhea is curable with antibiotics but some strains have become resistant to penicillin and tetracycline. Therefore health authorities now recommend other antibiotics such as cefixime, ceftriaxone or ciprofloxacin as first-line treatment. (Since gonorrhea may coexist with chlamydia, doxycycline or tetracycline is given at the same time.) Those with gonorrhea should inform current and past sex partners, who may have been infected without knowing it.

Chlamydia: three to five times more common than gonorrhea and more frequently detected in women than men, this STD is a serious bacterial infection due to *Chlamydia trachomatis*. It is now the most prevalent sexually transmitted disease in Canada. Surveillance data (probably an underestimate) put its overall incidence at 315 cases per 100,000, but far higher (1,550 per 100,000) among adolescent girls aged 15–19. Chlamydia has been dubbed "the silent epidemic" because it so rarely produces any symptoms; half of the men and women infected show no symptoms. If symptoms do occur, they resemble those of gonorrhea but are usually milder — a discharge, pain on urination, perhaps lower abdominal pain.

The consequences of chlamydia can be devastating for women, in whom it may penetrate the whole reproductive tract, causing pelvic inflammatory disease (see below). In newborns, chlamydia can cause conjunctivitis (eye inflammation) and pneumonia. In men, it can lead to urethritis (urinary tract inflammation). Early treatment with antibiotics such as tetracycline and doxycycline can avert these consequences.

Syphilis: caused by the spirochete *Treponema pallidum*, syphilis has been the scourge of many famous people, including King Henry VIII, Oscar Wilde, Van Gogh, Napoleon and Franz Schubert. Although less common than gonorrhea or chlamydia, syphilis is still surprisingly prevalent, with rates rising in some parts of North America. It is passed on via sexual contact and may facilitate AIDS transmission. Untreated syphilis remains contagious for at least one year, and possibly up to four.

Syphilis develops in three stages, over

PELVIC INFLAMMATORY DISEASE

Pelvic inflammatory disease (PID) is a very serious health threat for women, 17,000 being hospitalized in Canada each year with the condition. But PID is probably far more common than statistics indicate. It affects mainly women under age 25. PID usually results from gonorrheal or chlamydial infections that have paved the way for other invading microorganisms that damage the female genital tract. If an infection ascends from the vagina or cervix, past the endometrium (uterine lining) to the fallopian tubes, pelvic inflammation ensues. PID can cause severe lower abdominal pain, fever, vaginal discharge, bleeding, nausea, pelvic abscess and peritonitis (general abdominal infection). But many PID sufferers have no symptoms other than consequent infertility. About 10 to 20 percent of those with PID become sterile through tubal scarring. Ectopic (outside the womb) pregnancy, another consequence of PID, causes death of the fetus and can seriously endanger the mother. In Canada there are about 6,000 ectopic pregnancies a year, the majority due to PID. Recent studies suggest that douching is an added risk factor for PID as it spreads the infection. So sexually active women are advised to avoid douching. Early treatment of PID is essential to prevent complications. Antibiotics can eradicate the infecting organisms, but may not reverse the infertility. Women with severe PID need hospital treatment.

---

many years. Stage one, primary syphilis, is a painless red sore or chancre, usually on the man's penis or rectal area, on the woman's cervix, or in the mouth of either sex. This heals in about two weeks, even without treatment. Stage two, or secondary syphilis, occurs one to three months later, with a non-itchy rash often on the palms of the hands or soles of the feet, and sometimes also fever, muscle aches and swollen lymph nodes. Symptoms disappear without treatment. During stages one or two, syphilis can be cured with antibiotics, preventing progress to stage three, tertiary syphilis, which is rare today. However, tertiary syphilis can occur up to 30 years later, damaging heart, bones and brain. Since syphilis can cause fetal defects or be passed on at birth, expectant mothers are screened by blood tests and treated with antibiotics if necessary.

Genital herpes: very common, affecting one in six or more Canadians. The symptoms may hardly be noticed or may cause an intense burning or tingling sensation, pain on urination, swollen lymph glands and small blisters anywhere in the groin area (including penis, foreskin, buttocks, vulva, cervix or anus). Herpes is most contagious when the sores are visible, but transmission is still possible (although less likely)

WHY STDS SPREAD

- more permissive sexual attitudes accompanying wide availability of the birth-control pill;
- earlier onset of sexual activity among adolescents;
- multiple sex partners;
- complacency about STDs because of the past success of penicillin and other antibiotics in curing some of them;
- the misconception that STDs affect only "high-risk" groups — giving others a false sense of security, as they imagine that they are immune to infection;
- lack of knowledge about STD symptoms, and reluctance to be tested by a physician or STD clinic even if infection is suspected;
- the insidious nature of STDs, many of which have few or no symptoms;
- asymptomatic STD carriers who have

no symptoms but continue to have sex and spread the infection(s);
- denial of sexual desire by many adolescents and a resulting unwillingness to "prepare ahead" for possible intercourse;
- the teenage belief that "it'll never happen to me," and similar parental beliefs that STDs can't strike their son or daughter;
- a "macho" attitude among men, many of whom refuse condoms despite the knowledge that they reduce STD risks;
- inadequate medical-school training in the recognition and treatment of STDs;
- old habits that "die hard" — the failure of healthcare professionals who regularly give women Pap smears to "think STDs," do relevant tests, recognize STDs or give appro-

priate treatment — perhaps because some don't keep up with medical advances (e.g., they may still use penicillin for drug-resistant gonorrhea);
- too little effort put into preventive STD education, especially for teenagers;
- school boards and teachers who don't discuss sexuality, STDs or contraception adequately, for fear of "promoting promiscuity" or "triggering parental protests";
- a hypocritical society willing to condone explicit sex in movies, on TV and in magazines, but downplaying or ignoring risks of unwanted pregnancy and STDs;
- a moralistic view that says: "You play, you pay!" and regards STDs as proper punishment for sexuality.

after the sores have healed. The herpes virus may lie dormant within nerve tracts, causing flare-ups which usually last about 10 days.

Treatment of herpes symptoms is with warm sitz baths, good hygiene, wearing loose cotton underwear, and possibly acyclovir pills to shorten the length of the illness. Condoms help to reduce its spread. Although a distressing nuisance to sufferers and contagious to others, herpes does not cause serious health problems unless it affects newborns. Over half the newborns infected at birth develop neurological problems.

Trichomonas vaginalis or "trich": this very common, sexually transmitted protozoan infection may produce few symptoms, and both sexes can carry the organism for years without knowing it, transmitting it to sex partners. In some women "trich" causes vaginitis — an irritated or itchy vulva, a malodorous, frothy discharge and perhaps pain on urination. While mainly passed on through sexual contact, trichomonas is hardier than gonorrhea, HIV or syphilis, and can survive on wet towels, washcloths or douching equipment. The infection is treated with oral metronidazole (Flagyl). Partners of infected individuals are also treated, as "ping-pong" reinfection is common. (See also chapter 8, section on vaginitis.)

Chancroid: relatively rare in Canada, this STD remains common in the southern United States and developing countries, where it has been identified as a co-factor for AIDS. Chancroid produces painful red sores, although they may produce no symptoms if on a woman's cervix. It is treated with erythromycin, ciprofloxacin or a single shot of ceftriaxone.

Human papilloma virus (HPV): these viruses cause genital warts — small, flat, pink or greyish growths, usually painless but sometimes irritated if on vagina, cervix or penis. The warts, which may not be visible to the naked eye, usually appear two to three months after contact, so anyone who has a sex partner infected with HPV or genital warts should be checked for infection. HPV viruses are easily passed on between sex partners and are strongly linked to cervical cancer in women. Therefore regular Pap smears are a must for women — especially those with male partners who have warts. For these women colposcopy (cervical scraping) may also be advisable. Men are at small risk of developing penile cancer from HPV wart viruses. Condoms may help to curb transmission. The warts are removed by podophyllin or trichloroacetic acid, cryotherapy (freezing with liquid nitrogen), cautery (burning) or lasers.

Hepatitis B: passed on mainly by sexual contact, this serious liver infection is also acquired via shared household items such as razors or toothbrushes, or from infected blood products and dirty injection needles. About 10 percent of those infected become lifetime carriers with greatly increased risks of

COMPARING SEXUALLY TRANSMITTED DISEASES

Disease	Symptoms and outlook	Complications	Diagnosis and treatment
Syphilis (the "pox") Spirochete infection. Curable in early stages. Affects mainly those in their twenties. Transmitted by oral, genital, anal contact. After a decline, case numbers rising again in North America, mainly related to drug use or exchange of sex for drugs.	Painless sore (chancre) appears 3–6 weeks after infection on genitals, mouth or rectal area, most obvious in men, hardly noticed if vaginal. Heals without scarring. About 4–10 weeks later, second stage: fever, rash, which disappears but may reappear.	If untreated, chronic, occasionally fatal. Third stage appears up to 30 years later with brain and spinal-cord damage, blindness, insanity. Untreated, can cause miscarriage and birth defects; infants of infected mother may be born with syphilis (congenital syphilis).	Even if no symptoms seen, can diagnose by simple blood test; test results usually positive by the time chancre (ulcer) appears. Antibiotics, taken as prescribed, a dependable cure in early stages (stage one and two).
Gonorrhea (the "clap") Bacterial infection, transmitted by oral, vaginal or anal sex. Prevalent in young women, teens. Untreated, can result in PID and infertility. Up to 50% of infected women and men have no symptoms.	Symptoms (if any) within 7 days of contact: painful urination, thick vaginal or penile discharge, bleeding between periods, sore throat (if contracted via oral sex), rectal pain or discharge (if through anal sex).	May lead to tubal scarring, pelvic inflammatory disease (PID), ectopic pregnancy (outside womb, dangerous for mother). Can cause permanent sterility in both sexes. Eye infection and possible blindness in infected newborns.	Diagnosed by slide-smear and lab culture. Antibiotics a reliable cure but some strains now resistant to standard antibiotics (e.g., penicillin) so require cefixime, cefriaxone or other new drugs.
Herpes Viral infection due to herpes virus types I or II. Spreads via oral, vaginal or anal sex, kissing. Can spread silently, via asymptomatic people. Most easily transmitted by direct contact with active sores or genital secretions.	Symptoms within 10 days; slight fever, tingling, shooting pains, swollen lymph glands, then painful blisters, anywhere on genitals — mainly penis, vulva or anal areas. Subsides without treatment, but can recur. First outbreak usually worst, but sometimes unnoticed.	Virus remains permanently in nerves, stays dormant for months or years. Newborns may get herpes during birth, resulting in central-nervous-system damage or death. Cesarean delivery may be advised for babies of infected mothers.	Diagnosis from blisters (scraping or culture). Acyclovir tablets, not a cure, ease symptoms and reduce length of attack and its severity. Herpes support groups helpful in combating psychological problems.
Chlamydia Bacterial infection — very common in teens, 60–80% without symptoms. Spreads via anal, vaginal or oral sex with infected partners. Often occurs together with gonorrhea.	Like gonorrhea; painful urination, vaginal or penile discharge, abdominal pain, genital itching. But often mild, unnoticed in carriers, can disappear without treatment.	In women, leading cause of PID, ectopic pregnancy, infertility. In men, can produce urinary-tract diseases and prostatitis. Babies of infected mothers prone to eye infections, pneumonia.	Diagnosis by culture or other tests. Antibiotic treatment a reliable cure if caught early.
Genital warts (condylomata) Caused by human papilloma virus (HPV). Highly contagious, spread by intimate bodily contact, especially sexual activity, often accompanies other STDs.	Warts — tiny flat growths on and around genitals — possibly itchy; pinkish, flat, irregularly surfaced, may increase in size. Often undetectable in women in vagina or on cervix, except by physician.	Certain HPV strains linked to cervical cancer in women (and possibly penile cancer in men). Infants born to mothers with HPV may develop warts.	Removal advised — chemically, by freezing with lasers. Women should have regular Pap smears to detect HPV infection and early cervical cancer changes in time for preventive treatment.
Trichomonas Protozoal infection; most frequent in those with many sex partners; often accompanies other STDs.	Few symptoms: possibly irritated, tender vulva; burning on urination; perhaps copious, possibly foul-smelling yellowish green, frothy, foamy discharge.	Frequent "ping-pong" reinfection of sex partners. Both need treatment.	Swab/slide examination may reveal twitchy-tailed organisms. Treatment is oral metronidazole (Flagyl) — also for sex partner(s). During pregnancy, use clotrimazole instead.
Hepatitis B Virus passed on via blood, semen, vaginal secretions, saliva, needles, razors, toothbrushes. Can go from mother to infant at birth. Groups most at risk: those practicing anal sex, those with many sex partners, injection-drug users, babies of infected mothers.	Usually subclinical with few or no symptoms. Possibly flu-like malaise, fever, fatigue typically lasting 6 weeks, perhaps jaundice/skin and eye-white yellowing. May linger in body unnoticed. Many of the infected become permanent "carriers."	60–90% of infected children and 10% infected as adults become lifelong carriers, at risk of cirrhosis and liver cancer. Unsuspecting carriers can infect others. Fulminant, rapidly fatal form in one per 100 cases.	Detected by blood tests for viral markers. No cure. Effective, safe vaccine recommended for all at risk — especially healthcare workers and those living with or close to known hepatitis B carriers.

developing liver cirrhosis and cancer. Carrier mothers can pass the disease to their babies at birth. Since there is a very effective vaccine for hepatitis B, all those at risk should get immunized. Pregnant mothers should get a blood test for hepatitis B, and babies are immunized at birth if necessary. Infected people should not have sex until their partners are safely vaccinated against hepatitis B.

How to curb the spread of STDs

While many people relegate STD education to health professionals and educators, studies suggest that this is hardly enough. Surveys show that Grade 11 students would like to receive sex-related information from their parents but perceive parental knowledge of AIDS and other STDs as "inadequate." Yet many adolescents don't know where else to turn for advice. Parents and educators need to discuss sexuality and STDs candidly and explicitly with youngsters well before they reach adolescence. Teens need advice on both pregnancy avoidance and STD prevention. Physicians can play a major role in helping to prevent STDs by giving teenagers the facts at medical checkups, while taking care to respect their natural urge to explore sexuality. A nonjudgmental approach works best.

Adolescents need to know that they are not alone in having to adopt new sexual practices in the age of AIDS. Today the challenge facing many is how to decline sex while respecting the other person's feelings. Although not an indefinite option for most young people, abstinence from intercourse is increasingly considered an acceptable choice for some.

For more information, contact your local health department; an STD clinic; your family physician; the Ontario STD treatment guidelines available from the Ontario government, (416) 327-4327; the revised Canadian "Guidelines for the Prevention, Diagnosis, Management and Treatment of Sexually Transmitted Diseases in Neonates, Children, Adolescents and Adults" — available from Health and Welfare Canada's Division of STD control at the Laboratory Centre for Disease Control, Ottawa.

TIPS FOR PREVENTING STDs (INCLUDING AIDS)

- Always use a condom for sexual intercourse to prevent infection until sure your partner is free of STDs — it's hard to know. Use only recommended latex (not lambskin) condoms. And use them correctly!
- Be selective about sexual partner(s), avoid one-night stands, casual pickups and sexual intimacy with people you hardly know.
- Get to know your sex partner as well as possible.
- Never let sex become a power struggle where one "wins" and the other "loses" (and risks getting an STD).
- Don't assume that STDs can't infect married people, those from "nice" families or seemingly committed sex partners.
- Remember that avowed commitment to a sex partner does not mean freedom from infection and should not engender false security or excuse failure to use condoms.
- Teens might consider postponing intercourse until they feel ready for it — to avoid both unwanted pregnancy and STDs.
- If on the Pill or using an IUD, also use a condom to combat STDs, including AIDS.
- Watch for symptoms of STDs: genital sores, rash, discharge, pain on urinating, low abdominal pain. Seek advice.
- Don't be afraid, ashamed or embarrassed to seek medical attention if you suspect you may have an STD. Get tested as soon as possible. If the test is positive, get prompt treatment, tell any sex partner(s) and refrain from sex until cured.

- Avoid sex with anyone who has obvious genital or anal sores.
- Avoid kissing, oral or genital sex when herpes sores are present.
- Remember that past (cured) STDs are no guarantee of protection from reinfection.
- Never engage in anal intercourse without "double bagging," using two condoms and ample lubrication. But remember that even this is not foolproof, as condoms tear easily with the friction of anal sex. Since spermicide irritates the rectum, its use for anal sex is controversial and many now advise against it.
- If using lubricant with condoms for anal sex, choose only water-based types (e.g., K-Y jelly), not petroleum-based products (e.g., Vaseline), which weaken the condom.
- Women should consider refusing anal intercourse; it is very risky for them, as the anal lining is thinner in women.
- Avoid oral-anal contact, which can increase the risk of STDs and other infections.
- Since STDs can be transmitted by fellatio (penile-oral sex) and cunnilingus (oral stimulation of female genitals), avoid these practices with an infected partner.
- If sexually active with more than one partner, request and get regular STD checkups.

(For detailed section on AIDS, see chapter 16.)

RECENT TRENDS IN BIRTH CONTROL

People generally choose different methods of birth control at different ages and stages of their sexual lives, but they continue to demand more of birth-control techniques than of any other drug or device. A good contraceptive must be easily acquired, reliable, safe, morally and physically acceptable and convenient to use.

Since "the Pill" revolutionized birth control in the sixties, few significant innovations have appeared on the contraceptive scene. Birth control remains a choice of "second-bests." While the inability to conceive is a searing disappointment to those who want a child, preventing conception remains one of the world's great problems. Of course, we've advanced somewhat since the days when women used sea sponges, crocodile dung or half a lemon over the cervix to prevent pregnancy. But since the advent of the hormone pill 30 years ago, contraceptive research has focused mainly on refining existing methods rather than developing new ones.

When talking about birth control, many people automatically think of the Pill, although in the United States and Canada sterilization is now the leading form of fertility control among married people over 30. During the late seventies many women shunned the Pill, fearful of its much-publicized cardiovascular side effects (e.g., heart attacks and strokes). However, the new low-dose preparations are far safer and the Pill remains a favored contraceptive for young, sexually active women. The IUD, or intrauterine device, has lost favor because one particular type — the ill-designed Dalkon Shield — created many problems and discouraged women from using IUDs. Nonetheless, many healthy women still find the IUD a simple, effective contraceptive. In Canada, about 8–10 percent of contraceptive users choose the IUD as their preferred method.

Women now have a greater variety of long-acting contraceptives to choose from, with fewer side effects and less chance of forgetting to use them than with the daily birth-control pill. The new long-term hormonal contraceptives work much like oral contraceptives — by impeding ovulation — but are given by injection, implant or intravaginally, reliably rendering women infertile for months or years. The new injectable preparations include medroxyprogesterone acetate (Depo-Provera) — injected every three months — and a new form, cyclofen, containing progesterone and estrogen (estradiol valerate), with better menstrual cycle control.

For those wanting to invest minimal time and effort, barrier methods (e.g., diaphragm, condom, cervical cap or sponge) remain popular, especially in Eastern Europe and Japan. Condoms have made a comeback, often as a second method (to accompany the Pill, diaphragm or IUD), to protect against AIDS and other sexually transmitted infections. Male condoms are the best currently available safeguard against HIV infection or AIDS. The recently available female condom is a viable alternative for some, although it is somewhat cumbersome to use.

Teens are still not well educated about birth control

Unfortunately, and with predictable results, a large percentage of sexually active teenagers and young couples use little or no birth control. According to recent estimates, although almost 40 percent of Canadian teenagers are sexually active by ages 14–18 (many before age 15), only a third of them use any birth control at first intercourse. Of those who do use birth control, many rely on withdrawal (removal of the penis before ejaculation) or spermicide alone when first having sex. But withdrawal is notoriously unreliable, as the sperm may leak out before orgasm or the man may not withdraw in time, and spermicidals (foams, gels or creams) are not enough to prevent pregnancy or STDs. In one survey, of the teen couples who used birth control at first intercourse, about 18 percent tried withdrawal, 29 percent used a condom and 30 percent were on the Pill, the rest relying vaguely on rhythm methods. Some said they engaged in anal sex "from time to time" (presumably as an alternative way to avoid pregnancy). Curiously, of the teenage girls who were on the Pill, most said their mothers knew about it, but not their boyfriends. When asked

UNFOUNDED FEARS ABOUT THE PILL

- There is no link between the Pill and infertility. After going off the Pill some women have scanty or absent periods for a few months, but in over 75 percent of them, ovulation resumes within about three months. It can take months of unprotected intercourse

for anyone — a former Pill user or nonuser alike — to conceive. The few women who have persistent amenorrhea (absent periods) for over six months after going off the Pill might have deveoped irregular periods even if they'd never gone on the Pill.
- There is no valid reason for Pill "holidays," periodic breaks from oral contraceptives — and they may lead to unwanted pregnancy.
- Contrary to misconceptions that the Pill causes cancer, evidence suggests that only cervical cancer risks might possibly be affected by Pill use. However, the link between

hormonal OCs and cervical cancer remains uncertain. Three studies have found an alleged link between long-term (10-year) Pill use and cervical cancer (a risk about double the average). An annual Pap smear, which would detect cervical cell abnormalities at an early, curable stage, is a wise safeguard for Pill takers. Ovarian and endometrial (uterine lining) cancers are reduced in Pill users. Many studies find no overall increase in breast cancer in Pill users, but a few studies suggest higher breast-cancer risks among long-term Pill users aged 20–34.

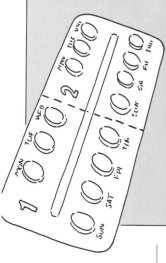

about Pill use, many thought that it protected against pregnancy "from the moment the first pill was taken" (although protection may not be effective for a couple of weeks, or even a month), and most didn't know what to do if they missed one pill.

Adolescents tend to shun birth control because of its "premeditated" nature, a reluctance to acknowledge sexual activity, a lack of confidence in themselves, a mistrust about confidentiality, and ignorance or embarrassment in getting supplies. Some feel it's okay to be sexually "swept away" but not to plan for it. One teenage girl who got AIDS said she didn't know her boyfriend "well enough" to discuss safe sex. Yet about 80 percent of women under 30 who use no birth control become pregnant within the first year of becoming sexually active. Many teen pregnancies and STDs occur just after a breakup, when each partner experiments with or establishes a new sexual relationship, using no or inadequate protection.

Any contraceptive method is safer to health than unwanted pregnancy

Many people don't realize that any method of birth control is safer than none. Women aged 15 to 40 are far more likely to be disabled or to die from pregnancy than from the Pill or other contraceptives. For example, based on studies with the older Pill formulations, the risk of Pill-related death (due to a stroke, heart attack or lung clot) in a healthy, nonsmoking woman under age 35 was 0.6 per 100,000. Compare this to the current average risk of maternal mortality from pregnancy in Canada of 5 deaths per 100,000 live births for women of any age. Maternal deaths directly or indirectly due to pregnancy can arise from conditions such as eclampsia or toxemia of pregnancy (with elevated blood pressure), a ruptured ectopic pregnancy (outside the uterus) or a lung clot.

The Pill: modern low-dose forms are far safer

The first hormonal oral contraceptive (OC), developed in the 1950s, triggered a revolution in birth control. For the first time women had access to a reliable, inexpensive way of avoiding unwanted conception. The Pill allowed women to space their babies for better health and family life; gave them control over their own bodies; permitted them to decide whether and when to have a baby; and extended many female lives by reducing the toll of unavoidable childbearing. The combination Pill, containing two different female hormones — estrogen and a progestin — is one of the best-studied drugs ever produced, and provides effective, reversible birth control. It can be safely used by most healthy women up to age 35, including teenagers whose periods have begun. The Pill stops an egg from maturing and prevents its release from the ovary. In women on the Pill, menstruation occurs because of "progesterone withdrawal," not true ovarian cycling. Used consistently and on schedule, OCs seldom fail. But although the Pill is 99 percent effective, many woman stop using it or forget to take it regularly. Also, some medications such as antibiotics and anticonvulsants reduce its effectiveness.

Multiphasic contraceptive pills, introduced

WEIGHING RISKS VERSUS BENEFITS OF THE PILL

Possibly serious risks

- blood-pressure elevation. Blood pressure normalizes once the Pill is stopped, unless there are other underlying reasons for the hypertension;
- possibly increased cardiovascular risks, especially among older users. But the elevated danger of strokes, lung clots and heart attacks is rated as very slight in healthy, nonsmoking women under age 35 with normal blood pressure. All studies to date on OC cardiovascular risk were done with the older high-dose Pill. And although cardiovascular risks of the new low-dose forms aren't yet known — because long-term follow-up studies haven't been completed — the low-dose multiphasics are expected to pose minimal cardiovascular dangers, since they have less impact on fat metabolism than previous types;
- smoking and the Pill are an undoubtedly dangerous duo. A woman who takes the Pill and smokes faces elevated risks of a fatal heart attack with advancing age; the risks become more significant over age 30 and with the amount smoked;
- nonmalignant liver tumors (hepatic adenomas), although very rare, have been linked to Pill use of more than seven years. Liver function reverts to normal once Pill use stops;
- interaction with other medications can be a risk. Pill action is altered by barbiturates (such as phenobarbital); other sedatives (e.g., chloral hydrate, meprobamate); phenylbutazone (Butazolidin), an anti-inflammatory drug; most anticonvulsants (e.g., phenytoin or Dilantin), which enhance liver enzyme action, lowering the body's level of Pill hormones, and various antibiotics (e.g., ampicillin, penicillin, neomycin, tetracycline, rifampin) that speed up the body's clearance of OCs. In addition, antacids decrease the absorption of Pill progestins; and OCs may alter insulin requirements, so they should be used cautiously by diabetics. Pill hormones reduce the efficacy of some blood-pressure pills and decrease the impact of anticoagulants, certain tranquilizers and corticoids. OCs can also alter the effectiveness of ASA, and some antidepressants.

Pill benefits

- 99.5 percent effective (if always used correctly);
- no interruption of lovemaking;
- light, regular periods, with few or no menstrual cramps;
- decreased risk of pelvic inflammatory disease;
- less danger of ectopic pregnancy, except for those on the progestin-only or mini-Pill;
- reduced incidence of ovarian cysts;
- reduced danger of ovarian and endometrial cancer (of uterine lining). Pill users have a 60 percent lower chance of developing ovarian cancer and 50 percent less risk of endometrial cancer than nonusers — a protective effect that increases with the duration of Pill use and may last up to 10 or more years after Pill discontinuation;
- possible prevention of breast cysts and reduced incidence of benign breast disease (less breast lumpiness);
- possibly lowered risk of developing uterine cancer.

in the late 1980s, have low estrogen contents and fewer side effects than earlier forms, and are increasingly prescribed for first-time Pill users. The multiphasics or triphasics generally have a steady estrogen content but a varying amount of progestin through the cycle. Many women who couldn't tolerate the side effects of former high-estrogen forms find this type of Pill acceptable. Experts stress that many reported Pill dangers were due to the earlier high-dose formulations, (which contained 80 to 150 micrograms of estrogen and 10 milligrams of progestin); the new lower-dose formulations contain 35 micrograms of estrogen or less.

Risks are minimal with the new OCs. Having eliminated or reduced many of the hazards due to the original high estrogen content (e.g., hypertension and blood clots), manufacturers are now developing different progestins with fewer side effects.

New IUDs are supposedly safer

IUDs (intrauterine devices) are still favored by about 10 percent of female contraceptive users in North America. An IUD is fundamentally an offshoot of the ancient method of putting pebbles into a camel's uterus to prevent pregnancy. Inserted through the cervix into the uterus by a trained health professional, IUDs come in various shapes, sizes, forms and materials. The "Lippes loop" of the 1960s — a plastic, polyethylene device — has been succeeded by newer IUDs, some of them medicated, that gradually release copper or hormones. In Canada, the Nova T (with copper over a silver core, left in for five years) and the Gyne-T 380 Slimline or TCu-380A (with copper wire on the arms and stem, left in for several years) are currently available. The Progestasert (a hormone-impregnated form replaced annually) can also be obtained.

IUDs can be inserted at any time into a gynecologically normal woman of childbearing age with no medical contraindications, but are usually put in at the end of or just after a period to avoid unwitting insertion into a pregnant woman. IUD insertion is often recommended right after childbirth (as soon as the placenta is

IMPROVEMENTS IN BIRTH CONTROL

- introduction of safer, low-dose, better-tolerated, multiphasic Pill formulations with estrogen content reduced to 35 micrograms or less, and progestins decreased by 25 to 40 percent;
- discovery of several unexpected Pill benefits (such as protection against ovarian cancer);
- greater awareness of and allowances made for Pill interaction with other medications (e.g., some antibiotics, anticonvulsants, anticoagulants);
- development of safer IUDs, especially medicated types that continuously release minute amounts of copper or female hormones, and designs that permit easier insertion with less risk of expulsion or slippage;
- clearer guidelines for IUD insertion and for choosing suitable candidates;
- the cervical cap, now available at many centers across Canada;
- nonprescription spermicidal sponges, easily inserted into the vagina and discarded after use, that provide a barrier to sperm and inactivate them;
- hormone injectables and implants for extended birth control — not yet approved in Canada but some already approved in the United States and many other countries — with fewer lipid-elevating and cardiovascular side effects: for example, capsules inserted under the skin in the arm, such as Norplant, giving five years of reliable contraception;
- long-acting, hormone-impregnated intra-vaginal rings that release hormones (progesterone) steadily, providing effective birth control for three to six months (or for three weeks at a time: one week out for menstruation). Inserted by the woman herself, the hormone acts locally on the cervical mucus and uterine lining. The ring can be removed at will to restore fertility;
- refinement of sterilization techniques to make them simpler and safer;
- a levonorgestrel-releasing intracervical device — being researched in Finland — that may in future provide highly effective hormonal contraception without most IUD and Pill disadvantages.

Under investigation:
- immunological contraceptives (e.g., an anti-pregnancy vaccine) that prevent embryonic development and render women infertile for about one year by triggering antibodies that inactivate human chorionic gonadotropin (HCG) — essential for implantation;
- male fertility regulators, including compounds that suppress sperm production, such as gossypol (from cottonseed oil), cyproterone acetate, sulfasalazine, and a new compound, an extract of the thunder-god vine, being tested in China.

expelled) or after elective pregnancy termination, since medical expertise is then on tap.

No one knows exactly how the IUD works. It somehow alters the uterine environment, rendering it hostile to implantation of the fertilized egg. The latest research suggests it may also prevent fertilization by injuring sperm or impeding their movement. Hormone-releasing IUDs work by their impact on the uterine lining or cervical mucus.

IUDs are considered most suitable for women who have a mutually monogamous sex life, have completed childbearing or are spacing their families, and do not have dysmenorrhea (painful periods) or medical reasons against their use. The IUD is useful for breastfeeders as it doesn't affect the quality of breastmilk. Once inserted, an IUD may give no hint of its presence and requires only a monthly check after each period to make sure the string is still hanging there. Should the string not be felt, the

IUD may have slipped or been expelled and a medical checkup is needed. IUDs are 98 to 99 percent effective in preventing pregnancy.

During the 1970s many women became disenchanted with IUDs because of problems they either experienced personally or heard about, especially heavy periods and pelvic inflammatory disease (PID). The bad press arose over one particular IUD — the Dalkon Shield — which greatly increased PID risks, producing infertility and a dramatic rise in mid-trimester abortions. Investigation showed the Dalkon Shield to be of poor design, allowing bacteria easy access to the uterus. It was taken off the U.S. market in 1975, and an avalanche of lawsuits made the manufacturer declare bankruptcy. While copper-bearing IUDs remained available in Canada and elsewhere, by January 1986 only the progesterone-releasing IUD, Progestasert, was left on the U.S. market.

Barrier contraceptives

Barrier contraceptives are devices to stop sperm from getting through the cervix (opening of womb). The barrier contraceptive may be put over the penis (as with male condoms) or placed into the vagina to block sperm entry (as with the diaphragm or sponge). Barrier contraceptives not only block sperm from getting through the cervix but may also decrease the risks of STD infection.

• *Condoms plus spermicide* Obtainable without prescription, condoms are thin sheaths of latex rubber or cecum (lamb intestines) put onto the erect penis before genital contact. People allergic to latex can try wearing a lambskin condom *under* a latex one. (Although lambskin condoms block sperm, viruses can enter, so they do not protect against STDs and they are not recommended.)

Most condoms have a reservoir tip to catch the ejaculate (semen) and prevent it from entering the vagina. One Japanese company manufactures an ultra-thin brand (0.03 mm or 0.0012 in thick), which may partly explain why so many Japanese couples favour condoms. For full effectiveness, condoms must be used with spermicide and checked for tears after removal. Effectiveness varies from 98 to 80 percent or less. Condoms are only effective if used correctly for every coital act and put on before any genital touching takes place. Besides preventing pregnancy, latex condoms protect against many STDs, such as syphilis, gonorrhea, genital herpes, HIV and hepatitis B, but not necessarily against HPV (wart) viruses, which may permeate the whole genital area.

Remove the condom from its individual sealed wrapper only when ready to use. If it looks dried out or discolored, discard it. Stored in a cool, dark, dry place, condoms can last three to five years. Latex deteriorates faster when exposed to light, heat, humidity and air pollution. Auto glove compartments and hip pockets are *not* good storage places. Most brands now bear expiry dates, and it's best to purchase them at a busy, reputable pharmacy, where the stock is likely to be fresh.

Adequate lubrication helps to lessen the

BENEFITS VERSUS RISKS OF IUD USE

Main disadvantages of IUDs

• **Menstrual flow and pain can increase. Most women using IUDs experience heavier periods, especially with unmedicated devices.**
• **IUD users have elevated risks of pelvic inflammatory disease with possible tubal damage and consequent infertility.**
• **An IUD can be partly or completely dislodged — usually within three to six months of insertion — without the woman noticing it, negating its effectiveness.**
• **Miscarriage affects about half of all pregnancies that unintentionally**

happen with an IUD left in place; about 25 percent of users miscarry if the IUD is removed when the woman is pregnant.
• **Ectopic pregnancy (outside the uterus) is an increased risk in IUD users.**
• **Infrequently, the IUD may puncture the uterine wall (about one per 2,500 insertions), possibly requiring surgical removal.**

Main benefits of IUDs

• **98.5 percent effective if used correctly;**
• **long-lasting and inexpensive;**
• **convenient, with no interference with lovemaking;**
• **no daily equipment needed;**
• **requires no continual**

attention after insertion — there's nothing to do except check the string and watch for possible infection;
• **protection is continuous;**
• **no interference with breastfeeding;**
• **easily removed and reinserted if necessary.**

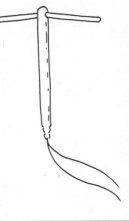

---

chance of condom breakage. Use a *water-based* lubricant, such as K-Y jelly or the newer Astroglide, but not oil-based products such as petroleum jelly (Vaseline), mineral oil, cold cream, or hand lotion, which can destroy latex within 60 seconds. (Remember, "water-soluble" isn't necessarily "water-based." The package should say that the lubricant is safe for use on latex.)

• *Spermicides* — acidic, surface-active chemicals that inactivate or destroy sperm — are essential with most barrier methods. They come as foams, gels, tablets or suppositories and are inserted high in the vagina just before intercourse. (Vaginal douching should be avoided for six hours afterwards.) Many studies confirm that currently available spermicides do not cause fetal malformation (birth defects). Studies also show that nonoxynol-9, the most effective and widely used form, destroys sperm and also kills the organisms responsible for many

HOW TO USE A CONDOM

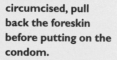

- Use a new condom for every sex act.
- Put the condom on before the penis touches the partner's body; don't wait until the last minute.
- Roll the condom onto the erect penis; leave a half-inch space at the top and unroll it all the way to the base. If not circumcised, pull back the foreskin before putting on the condom.
- If using spermicide, apply it outside the condom.
- Use lubricants for anal sex, but only water-based brands (e.g., K-Y jelly), not greasy types (e.g., petroleum jelly or Vaseline), which weaken the latex. (Some condoms are prelubricated with silicone gel.)
- If the condom breaks during intercourse, stop immediately and withdraw. Do not continue until a new condom is on and, if using spermicide, apply more.
- After ejaculation and before the penis gets soft, grip the rim of the condom and carefully withdraw. Gently pull the condom off the penis, being careful not to spill any semen. Always remove the condom before the penis becomes flaccid so that it won't slip off and leak.
- Handle the condom by the rim.
- Wrap used condom in a tissue and throw it in the trash. Because condoms may cause problems in sewers, don't flush them down the toilet.

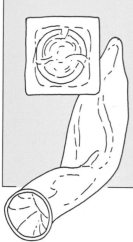

STDs — gonorrhea, syphilis, genital warts, herpes, chlamydia, trichomonas and AIDS. Since premedicated condoms contain only small amounts of the compound, use extra spermicide containing nonoxynol-9 for added protection.

Barrier methods for women

- *Diaphragm plus spermicide* The diaphragm, a round or domed, flexible rubber cap ranging in size from 60 to 90 mm (2.4–3.5 in), is prescribed and sized by a physician. It is used with spermicide and can be inserted into the vagina up to six hours before intercourse. If intercourse is repeated, more spermicide should be inserted into the vagina. The diaphragm should be left in place for six to eight hours after intercourse, and then removed to minimize risks of toxic shock — an infection (generally caused by bacteria called staphylococcii) — involving high fever, low blood pressure and skin inflammation. After pregnancy, a woman must have her diaphragm resized.

Used consistently, according to instructions, diaphragms can be up to 98 percent effective. They may also protect against the human papilloma (wart) virus transmitted from the penis, which can cause cancerous changes of the cervix. A diaphragm plus spermicide also offers some protection against STDs (gonorrhea and chlamydia, but not herpes or the HIV virus that causes AIDS). A diaphragm may elevate risks of urinary-tract infections, and a few women are allergic to the spermicide, for which a brand change may be the solution. Diaphragms are not advised for anyone with a history of toxic shock.

- *Cervical cap* Already used worldwide for over 60 years, and becoming more popular, cervical caps are thimble-sized, cup-shaped rubber devices, prescribed by a physician or nurse, that fit snugly over the cervix. A cervical cap can be inserted by a woman any time before intercourse and is left in for at least six and up to 48 hours after lovemaking. Like the diaphragm, the cervical cap prevents sperm from entering the cervix, but it is less messy and doesn't require more spermicide for repeat intercourse. Since the cervical cap is smaller, some women find it more comfortable than a diaphragm, but harder to put in and remove. Cervical caps are only prescribed for women with normal Pap smears, and a Pap test should be repeated three months after first use.

- *The vaginal sponge* comes in packets of three, available at drug stores. It is a non-prescription, polyurethane device, impregnated with nonoxynol-9 spermicide, discarded after use. Moistened with water, it is inserted deep into the vagina before intercourse. One size (50 mm or 2-in diameter) fits all, but because this may be small for some vaginas, barrier blockage may be imperfect. The sponge must be left in place for at least six hours following intercourse and can be left in up to 24 hours afterwards; it remains effective if intercourse is repeated.

Sponges are not very reliable (with 17 to 24 pregnancies per 100 users), and failure rates are especially high in women who have had children. A small percentage of users experience allergic reactions and some report trouble removing the sponge because it may fragment in the vagina. There have been a few alleged cases of toxic-shock syndrome — one case per three million sponges used — but studies fail to support these allegations, as the spermicide in the sponge would kill the bacteria responsible for toxic shock. Women can minimize this already low risk by careful adherence to directions.

• *New: a condom for women* Known as the vaginal shield or Femshield in Britain and the Reality or WPC-333 in the United States, this disposable device is inserted into the vagina just before intercourse. Available in a small envelope, the vaginal shield is an 18-cm (seven-inch), loosely fitting pouch made of soft, thin polyurethane. It's held in place by tiny, flexible anchoring rings, like an "inverted condom," and is pushed in by the thrusting penis, catching the sperm and also protecting against most STDs. At its closed end is one flexible ring, inserted much like a diaphragm, that covers the cervix. At the open end of the pouch is another flexible ring, which rests against the vulva and holds the pouch in place. It comes with a cream lubricant and can also be used with spermicide. Being made of a thicker material than a condom, it is less likely to tear.

While it is cumbersome and may not suit some couples, the female condom gives women an easy-to-use protection method against conception and most STDs. It is not foolproof against herpes or genital warts (if the sores or warts aren't covered). Health authorities have approved the new device in the United States and Canada, but so far it is not readily available. If you're having trouble finding it, consult your pharmacist.

Morning-after emergency measures

Morning-after methods of contraception range from ancient treatments — such as steaming the genitals or herbal baths — to modern post-coital remedies such as steroid hormones (in Canada), PC4 (in Britain), Tetraganon (in Germany) and RU-486 in France. Taken promptly — usually within three days of unprotected intercourse — these drugs forestall pregnancy by preventing implantation of a fertilized egg.

Post-coital methods currently used in Canada include high-dose estrogens, progestins or both — usually a mixture of ethynyl estradiol with the progestin dl-norgestrel — or a triple dose of any monophasic birth-control pill (two at night and two in the morning for two days after unprotected intercourse). These post-coital hormones are prescribed at a doctor's discretion for emergency purposes after an act of unprotected or inadequately protected intercourse — for instance, a slipped diaphragm or a torn condom — and must be taken within 72 hours. Side effects of the morning-after pill(s) may include headache, nausea and some breast tenderness for a day or two.

Injection of the new post-coital drug RU-486 is a very effective morning-after remedy, available in Europe but not yet in the United States or Canada. A copper IUD — inserted five to seven days after unprotected sex — is another post-coital measure that prevents pregnancy. The IUD may be removed after the next menstrual cycle.

Sterilization: considered a permanent contraceptive

For couples who want no more children, permanent sterilization of one partner or the other is a preferred means of birth control. The procedure involves closing off either the vas deferens (through which the sperm travel) or the fallopian tubes (through which the eggs travel). Female sterilization outnumbers vasectomy by seven to five.

Sterilization of women ("having the tubes tied") is done by blocking the fallopian tubes, i.e., tying, burning or mechanically closing (occluding) them with clips or bands. The procedure is normally done as "day surgery" in hospital. Quite often it is done right after childbirth (once a family is completed), or following abortion. After sterilization the average woman is back to normal activities in a few days. The failure rate is less than 0.5 percent.

Sterilization of men is a 20-minute procedure (vasectomy) that involves tying or cutting

COMPARING BIRTH CONTROL METHODS

Method	How It Works	Suitability	Main Advantages
The Pill Combination low-dose hormone formulation of estrogens plus progestin	Estrogen prevents egg maturation and progestin stops lining of uterus from thickening and preparing to receive egg; cervical plug may impede sperm penetration.	Good for women under age 35 (some say under 40). Not for smokers, especially if over 30, nor for women with high blood pressure, heart problems, diabetes, high cholesterol/blood fats, liver, kidney or gall-bladder disease, epilepsy or jaundice. (See product package list of contraindications.) Does *not* protect against STDs.	• Most effective, reversible method for preventing pregnancy if directions followed; • easy to use; lighter, more regular periods; fewer menstrual cramps; • lower risk of PID (pelvic inflammatory disease) and ovarian cysts; • protects against cancer of the ovaries and uterine lining; • may lessen benign lumpy breast disease; • does not impair fertility; • may reduce risk of ectopic pregnancy (outside uterus).
IUD Intrauterine device	Mechanism unclear, but foreign body in uterus triggers collection of white blood cells (which kill sperm) and hostile uterine environment impedes implantation of fertilized egg. May prevent fertilization by harming sperm.	Good for monogamous women not exposed to STDs; not suitable for women at risk of STDs; teenagers; women with multiple sex partners; often best suits women who have had all desired children or not allowed for some reason to take the Pill. Does *not* protect against STDs.	• Highly effective; inexpensive; • once fitted, usually unfelt/unnoticed; • needs replacing only once every 2½ years; • convenient, long-lasting; • easily removed and reinserted if necessary; • doesn't generally disturb intercourse; • no daily equipment needed; • no effect on breastfeeding.
Diaphragm with spermicide	Round, flexible rubber cap, smeared with spermicidal foam or jelly, inserted into vagina before intercourse, blocks entry of sperm into cervix (mouth of uterus).	Suitable for women comfortable with touching own genitals; requires expert fitting and instructions for use; not fully reliable for those (e.g., teens) who don't know how, or are likely to use incorrectly. Regular checkups advised; refitting/resizing necessary following pregnancy.	• No health risks; • may help protect against sexually transmitted diseases; • may protect against cervical cancer; • no hormonal additives to body; • needn't disturb intercourse (if put in ahead); • no effect on breastfeeding.
Vaginal Sponge	Traps and absorbs sperm, blocks entry of sperm into cervix and chemically kills sperm. Can be worn for up to 30 hours and must be left in for six hours after intercourse. An attached loop facilitates removal.	Suitable for women comfortable with touching own genitals; good for nursing mothers; not fully reliable for women who don't use it consistently and correctly (e.g., teens). NOT suitable for anyone who's had toxic shock syndrome; possibly less effective in women who have already had children (poorer muscle tone).	• One size fits all — no special fitting or prescription needed, available over the counter in most pharmacies; • no hormonal additives to body; • may help prevent sexually transmitted diseases; • inserted hours before intercourse; permits spontaneous, repeated intercourse up to 24 hours after insertion.
Condom with spermicide	Thin sheath over erect penis traps sperm, prevents entry into cervix so egg can't be fertilized. Best used with spermicide; newer spermicide-impregnated brands still need water-based sperm-killing foam or jelly (NOT Vaseline or petroleum jelly).	Helps to protect against STDs. Often first method tried by teenagers; good if can incorporate as regular part of lovemaking; not fully reliable for people who are likely to use incorrectly or inconsistently.	• Easy availability in many stores and pharmacies without prescription; • latex brands help protect against sexually transmitted diseases (e.g., AIDS, gonorrhea); • gives men an active role in birth control; • offers good protection if used consistently and carefully; • lambskin types not recommended.
Female Sterilization Tubal ligation	Fallopian tubes occluded (clipped), cauterized (burned), or cut to prevent egg from reaching uterus.	Good for women who have completed childbearing; not suitable for those with doubts about future desire for childbearing or fear of infertility.	• Highly effective; one-time, relatively simple procedure, with few complications; • done as "day"/outpatient or in-hospital procedure; • back to work in a few days; • covered by medical insurance.
Male Sterilization Vasectomy	Sperm-conducting tubes (vas deferens) cut, clipped or tied to prevent sperm getting through penis into vagina.	Good for men who have fulfilled desire for paternity; not suitable if anxious about sex life, potency or virility.	• Highly effective; one-time, simple outpatient office procedure, done in 20 minutes; • done under local anesthetic; • less risky than female sterilization; • covered by medical insurance.
Natural Family Planning or **Body Awareness Method**	Requires abstinence from sexual intercourse during female's fertile time. Chart by symptothermal method, recording temperature and changes in vaginal mucus (flow and consistency) to pinpoint day of egg release.	Suitable for stable women, willing to monitor cycles, keep accurate records, and abstain from intercourse for several days each month; instruction course advised; unsuitable for uncommitted women, those with irregular cycles or those who are often ill, do shift work or are unable to keep records.	• Condoned by various religions; • no use of chemicals or devices if used as sole birth-control method; • educates couples about fertility; • can be useful in achieving pregnancy when desired; • enhances body awareness.

Main Drawbacks and Precautions	Convenience, Availability and Cost	Estimated Failure Rate: Among average users:	Among reliable consistent users:
• Nuisance side effects in 10-12% of users: nausea, headaches, weight gain, reaction with other drugs, e.g., antibiotics; and breakthrough bleeding which may call for brand change. • Missed pill requires back-up contraception for rest of month; • slight risk of blood-pressure elevation and possible rise in blood-lipid (fat) levels; • possible rise in cardio- and cerebrovascular risks — far greater with smoking Pill-users; • may aggravate diabetes and epilepsy; • may increase risk of cervical cancer and (rarely) non-malignant liver tumors.	Easy to use for women with regular lifestyle; requires daily pill swallowing, whether or not having regular intercourse. Periodic medical checkups advised while on it. Available by prescription. Discuss benefits vs. drawbacks and drug interaction with physician. Cost: $150-$175 per year.	2–2.5%	0.5%
• Chance of unnoticed slippage or expulsion; • must regularly feel for string to check placement; • increased risk of PID, possibly with resultant infertility (especially in women with many partners); • may increase menstrual bleeding and cramping; • rare chance of uterine perforation during insertion; • possibly higher risk of ectopic pregnancy (outside uterus), miscarriage and septic abortion if conception accidentally occurs with IUD in place.	Inserted by physician. Once in place can remain for 2 1/2 years, often without trouble. Available from physician or family planning clinic. Cost: $25-$50 per insertion, may average $10-$20 per year.	4%	1.5%
• Occasional allergic reactions (to spermicide or latex in diaphragm); • somewhat messy and annoying to insert or remove; • can be dislodged during intercourse; • very rare risk of toxic shock syndrome (less than three per million).	Requires forethought; prescribed and sized by physician or family-planning expert; user must learn correct placement; most reliable for organized, monogamous steady couples; must be left in place six hours after intercourse. Available at pharmacies, family-planning clinics. Cost: $25 each; averaging $8-$10 per year, plus spermicide.	10% with spermicide	2% with spermicide
• Occasional itching, irritation or allergic reactions (to spermicide or polyurethane); • chance of being dislodged during intercourse; • very rare risk of toxic shock syndrome; • possibly annoying to insert and/or to remove; • may contribute to risk of yeast infections; • need water in order to wet the sponge prior to insertion; • a bowel movement or other internal straining may cause the sponge to move, be dislodged, or fall out; • occasional tearing on removal.	Must learn to use correctly (consult physician or family-planning expert before starting use); condoms should be used as well as sponge for first few months (added protection); must be left in place for at least six hours after intercourse. Cost: about $6 for three; might average about $300 a year for three sponges weekly.	14%	10%
• Inhibits spontaneous lovemaking; • unesthetic; may reduce pleasurable (erotic) sensation; • possible allergy to latex or other condom material and/or spermicide; • can break (1–3 tears per 100 untested brands); • may slip off; • requires care on removal to avoid spills.	Readily obtained in many stores and any pharmacy; must be put on before any genital contact; shop around for best brand; must use with spermicide. Advice available from family-planning centres, family doctor. Cost: around $5 for three (including spermicide); might average $250 yearly for thrice-weekly sex.	14% +	2–8%
• Usual risks of surgery and anesthetic (very few); • irreversible in most cases.	Minor operation done by physician in hospital, often as "day surgery"; woman usually back to work (fully active) in a few days. Cost: $150, covered by medical insurance.	Very low: 0.015%–0.04%	Very low: 0.015%–0.04%
• Some post-operative pain; • occasionally infection (cleared by antibiotics); • usually irreversible; • sometimes (unwarranted) fears of post-vasectomy impotence.	Minor operation done by physician on request; usually in doctor's office or as hospital "outpatient." Cost: about $100, covered by medical insurance.	Very low: 0.15%	Very low: 0.15%
• Uncertain method if periods irregular, or menstrual cycles easily upset; • requires motivated dedication; • disturbs natural sex life; • may cause tension, stress, worry; • requires abstinence from sex for more than a week each month; • high rate of failure if improperly used; • effectiveness dependent on body awareness and knowledgeable use, tracking signs of ovulation.	Reliable only in well-instructed, motivated women; requires cooperation and commitment; advice available from family-planning centres. Cost: computerized cervical thermometers: about $150 each; regular ovulation thermometer: about $15; charting materials: $20 yearly.	20%–40%	2–8%

the vas deferens. A few men have unfounded anxieties about impotence and post-vasectomy complications. The failure rate for male sterilization is the same as for females — under 0.5 percent — so it's essential to be tested later, to be sure the procedure was effective.

Counseling is important for men and women considering sterilization, to discuss all options and decide which partner should undergo the surgery. Despite increasing requests for reversal because of the three "D's" — death of a spouse, divorce or disaster (losing children) — sterilization is usually difficult to undo. Since about 5 percent of men and 10 percent of women suffer post-sterilization regrets, it's wise to get advice beforehand.

Periodic abstinence

Couples who opt for periodic abstinence, popularly called the "rhythm method," "natural family planning" or "fertility awareness," must limit intercourse to days when conception is deemed unlikely. To be successful, couples must precisely identify a woman's fertile days and avoid intercourse a week before and a few days afterwards. Since sperm can survive for five days or longer in the female genital tract, the "safe" or infertile time is hard to predict. Ovulation generally occurs 12 to 16 days before the onset of menstruation. To distinguish fertile from infertile days, the "symptothermal" method employs three techniques: daily temperature charting, body awareness and observation of mucus flow. Daily temperature charting relies on the peak usually observed just before ovulation. The mucus-watching (or "Billings method") depends on changes in the cervical mucus, which becomes more copious and slippery at ovulation; sexual abstinence is necessary for at least three days after the slippery "show." Intercourse is considered safest immediately after a period, on "dry days" when there's no vaginal dampness. Failure rates vary widely, ranging from 6 to 35 percent. Experts warn that female cycles can be disrupted by emotional upsets, illness or extreme diets. For women not having regular intercourse, the stimulation of a new sexual encounter may itself trigger ovulation outside the normal fertile time.

Injectable, long-term hormonal contraception

Injectable hormones such as medroxyprogesterone acetate (Depo-Provera) are now popular worldwide; they are already used by millions of women and were recently approved in the United States, but not yet in Canada. Given every three months, the intramuscular injection blocks egg release for as long as the hormone levels remain high in the body, eliminating the need for daily pill swallowing. Many health agencies consider them very useful. The hormone shots may cause irregular bleeding at first, and after a year or so periods cease altogether — a bonus to some women. Restoration of ovulation can be delayed for up to a year after the last injection wears off. Women planning to get contraceptive injections should first have their blood fat and cholesterol levels evaluated, and have them monitored periodically, as the injected hormones may elevate them. The reluctance to approve Depo-Provera for widespread contraception in North America has stemmed largely from a few animal studies suggesting a link to benign breast lumps and the elevation of blood lipids such as cholesterol.

Hormonal implants

Hormonal implants (subdermal patches), biodegradable or nonbiodegradable, are approved in many European countries and some developing areas. They are tiny cylinders containing progestins, inserted under the skin (usually the underarm) by a physician. Steadily releasing small amounts of hormone, contraceptive implants provide reliable contraception for 18 months to five years. The well-researched Norplant capsule containing levonorgestrel offers reliable contraception for five years. Fertility seems to return to normal once the implant is removed. Side effects include spotting between periods, menstrual irregularities in about a quarter of the women who try it, amenorrhea (absent periods) and occasional headaches. Long-term safety has not yet been established.

For more information consult family planning clinics (often attached to local public health units), family physicians, community-based health experts or Planned Parenthood Associations.

Women's special health concerns

Menstruation and menstrual problems • Vaginitis • Vaginal yeast infections or candidiasis • Endometriosis • Cervical cancer is a sexually transmitted disease • Menopause • The pros and cons of estrogen-replacement therapy • Sex problems in women • Breast cancer

WOMEN'S PARTICU-lar health concerns vary according to their age and stage in life. However, with today's worship of thinness, weight preoccupation is an almost universal problem among women in modern Western society. Many diet throughout their adult lives, some foisting the habit onto their children at an early age. And sad as it may be, some weight-obsessed mothers will neglect their children in the name of fitness or attending exercise classes. Among adolescents and young women, stringent dieting makes many verge on malnutrition and become near-anorexics, not to speak of the 3–5 percent who develop full-blown eating disorders such as anorexia nervosa and bulimia. Many women eat diet foods and exercise to lose weight rather than to have fun or stay healthy. Those who start dieting in their teens often fight obesity in midlife.

In adolescent females, apart from dieting and body-image problems, the main health concerns involve the stress of coping with same-sex and dating friendships, sexual activity, avoiding unwanted pregnancy, STD-prevention, smoking, alcohol use and risk-taking (due to the teen's frequent sense of invincibility). About 22 percent of young women still smoke, typically starting at age 12–14, and many drink alcohol — often "because of low self-esteem and to gain peer admiration, rather than because they like it." As one psychologist puts it: "The challenge for today's young women is to cope with a culture still largely based on male power and violence. Building self-esteem is a key issue for adolescent girls. Those with a poor self-image are likely to have low career or job aspirations, shaky marriages and a risk of family breakdown." The 1991 Premier's Council on Health Strategies identified self-esteem as a key determinant of good health. Suicide is another risk in adolescents, 23 percent of young women reporting that they had "had suicidal thoughts at some point in their lives." (See also chapter 12, on adolescent health issues.)

A 1989 nationwide survey of Canadian health practices showed that young women aged 17–24 often neglect their health. They may ignore even the basics of good health-care, perhaps in the name of acquiring a slim figure or catering to a boyfriend, spouse or to young children. Many eat diets too low in iron and calcium or don't get regular Pap smears or adequate advice about birth control, pregnancy and prevention of sexually transmitted diseases (STDs).

For women in their thirties to forties, sexual concerns, fitness, pregnancy- and child-care are predominant health issues. Weight preoccupation often continues. Self-esteem problems may carry over, and those who disliked or disapproved of themselves as teenagers may retain a poor self-image.

8

In midlife — between ages 40 and 65 — stress-related problems tend to be the serious health concerns since women often fulfill multiple roles — as wage-earner, homemaker, mother, wife and caregiver to aging or disabled relatives. Over 60 percent of adult Canadian women have jobs, many also looking after family members. "Full-time homemakers may feel stressed," notes one psychiatrist, "because sexist prejudices make them feel at the bottom of the power heap, and because of monotony, boredom and social isolation." At menopause, women must adapt to hormonal changes as well as other challenges — such as children leaving home and husbands nearing retirement. "Many middle-aged women are in need of psychological counselling," adds the psychiatrist, "but are handed prescriptions for sleep-aids and tranquilizers instead of being given time to air their worries or (being) referred to a counselor."

In old age, women have health problems that may relate to societal prejudices and agism which popularly hold that "men mature" while "women age." The health problems of elderly women include osteoporosis, increasing risks of breast cancer and nutritional deficiencies — due to poverty, waning appetite, disability, difficulties in going out to shop for food, or isolation ("no one to cook for"). Over one million of Canada's unattached elderly women live below the poverty line — at risk of malnourishment, isolation, rejection and understimulation.

Today, many health centers and clinics specially geared to women's health concerns are opening up across the country. Staffed by health professionals from various disciplines — including nurse practitioners, dietitians, gynecologists, psychiatrists and other specialists — they are ideal places for women to obtain health advice. Some women's healthcare centers offer Pap tests, colposcopy (cervical scraping), birth-control advice and pregnancy care, all conveniently under one roof.

MENSTRUATION AND MENSTRUAL PROBLEMS

Many cultures surround the onset of menstruation with taboos, rituals and myths. Some societies consider menstruating women "unclean," think they might turn food bad or damage crops, and isolate women for the first three to five days of menstrual flow each month. While Western society ignores those myths, modern folklore still perpetuates the idea that women should avoid showering, abstain from intercourse or refrain from swimming while menstruating. While there are no absolute medical indications against it, some studies show increased risks of endometriosis, PID and STDs in women who have sex while menstruating.

The normal menstrual cycle

The age at which menstruation starts ranges from 9 to 16.5 years, but it usually begins by age 14. With improved nutritional standards in Western society, the average age of menarche (onset of menstruation) has become progressively younger (three months earlier per decade) than in previous generations, although it has plateaued in the last decade. In North America today the average age of menarche is 12.8 years. The onset of menstruation marks the official entry to womanhood, the beginning of the ability to bear children.

The basis of a woman's reproductive capacity — the ovaries and their supply of eggs — is set aside way before birth, in the developing female embryo. The ova (eggs) destined for fertilization and the production of future human beings are already laid down 20 weeks after conception in the tiny fetal ovaries. The miniature ovaries start out with five to seven million immature ova each but by birth only about two million eggs remain in the newborn girl's ovaries. More eggs disintegrate during childhood, leaving only about 300,000 eggs by the time monthly menstruation begins. More eggs disintegrate and die during the childbearing years, before ever ripening, let alone being fertilized.

After the menarche, one egg a month normally ripens inside one of the ovaries, within an ovarian follicle (sac), under the influence of female hormones. The ovum is released and travels down the fallopian tube to the uterus. If it's not fertilized, menstruation ensues, the uterine lining and egg are sloughed off and the cycle begins over. The normal menstrual cycle varies from short (21 days) to long (35 days), the norm being 28 days, with blood losses averaging 30–60 ml (2–4 tbsp), sometimes more with a heavy period.

Very heavy periods should not be ignored; they need to be medically checked out. Excessively heavy periods can be due to fibroid growths in the uterus, endometriosis, hormonal abnormalities (low progesterone levels), dysfunctional uterine bleeding or possibly cancer. If menstrual bleeding is frequently heavy, or has clots in it, women may become anemic and need an iron supplement. Menstruating women should pay attention to iron in their diet and eat enough meat, liver, eggs, raisins or iron-rich vegetables.

Some women experience painful periods, known as dysmenorrhea, which can be spasmodic (sharp pelvic cramps at the start of menstrual flow) or congestive (with a deep, dull ache); either type requires consultation with a gynecologist. Hormone supplements may be advised, or other remedies according to the cause.

Amenorrhea

Amenorrhea, the cessation, absence or irregularity of periods, can be primary (if a girl gets to age 17–18 without starting her periods) or secondary (if periods stop after having once begun). Periods may cease or become irregular because of dysfunctional uterine bleeding, fibroid growths, thyroid disorders, blood problems such as thrombocytopenia (low blood platelets), infection, stress, emotional upsets, severe dieting, sudden weight loss or excessive exercise.

In young girls, as the hormonal balance becomes established, periods are often irregular and easily disturbed. According to one U.S. report, women entering the military academy in West Point found the stress of army training rigorous enough to disturb menstrual patterns. Among the 1976 class of normally menstruating women, 73 percent ceased to menstruate within two months of starting their army training, although six months later only 42 percent remained amenorrheic. After 18 months all but 7 percent had resumed normal cycles. A British private girls' school reported a similar stress effect, with many girls experiencing irregular

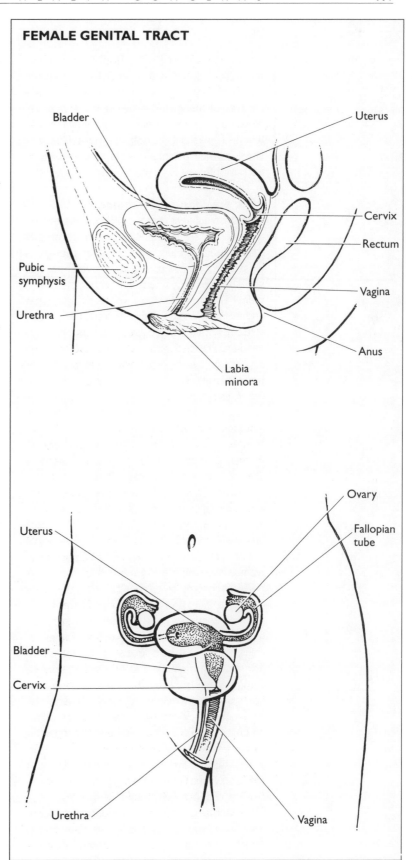

FEMALE GENITAL TRACT

Bladder

Uterus

Cervix

Rectum

Pubic symphysis

Vagina

Urethra

Anus

Labia minora

Ovary

Fallopian tube

Uterus

Bladder

Cervix

Urethra

Vagina

periods on entering the school, but returning to regular cycles once the regime became familiar. One intriguing aspect of the hormonal control of menstrual cycles is the synchrony often observed in girls' boarding schools, where those sharing a dormitory gradually synchronize their periods to about the same time each month!

PMS: premenstrual syndrome

Premenstrual syndrome, or PMS, has become a popular, largely self-diagnosed complaint that's attracted much publicity even though its existence, duration, onset, prevalence and severity remain scientifically hazy. PMS is defined as a cyclical set of complaints that come on a few days before the start of a menstrual period, typified by symptoms such as headache, breast tenderness, backache, bloating, irritability, depression and fatigue, sometimes debilitating enough to disrupt work and other activities.

Unfortunately, PMS remains poorly defined, although it is blamed for much distress. Recent studies show that less than 50 percent of women who complain of PMS have a diagnosable sequence of mood changes. Using the American Psychiatric Association's guidelines for mood changes in the five days before menstruation, only 6 percent of all women in the childbearing years are actually found to have PMS. Studies indicate that of the almost 90 percent of women who report PMS, less than 8 percent have symptoms severe enough to seriously upset their lives and qualify as the disorder.

A few studies have linked PMS symptoms to a premenstrual rise in serotonin (a neurotransmitter) and high levels of the hormone progesterone just before menstruation, but without corroboration. To date, no consistent hormonal abnormality has been detected in PMS sufferers. Well-conducted research offers no proof that PMS is consistently accompanied by aggression, violence or psychiatric changes, and no support for the notion of a link between PMS and crime, accidents or family rows. Some experts propose psychological explanations for PMS, such as underlying depression or anxiety disorders. One specialist suggests that PMS is "much over-diagnosed and sometimes not even

linked to the menstrual cycle. It may be a learned response or reflect some underlying mood instability." In fact, careful surveys show that some women even report *positive* changes, such as more energy and improved concentration, just before menstruation. While PMS is hard to manage, other than with sympathy, stress-reduction and a healthy diet, many of the problems that masquerade as the complaint can be successfully treated once their true cause is uncovered.

Good nutrition, regular exercise and reassurance that nothing is wrong generally help to allay PMS. Treatments such as progesterone, vitamin B$_6$, diuretics, oil of primrose, gammalinoleic acid and bromocriptine aren't generally helpful and studies show them to be no better than placebos (dummy remedies). The general management of PMS includes a thorough history, checking menstrual regularity, ovulation and hormonal fluctuations, and also looking for possible underlying psychiatric disorders. If PMS appears to be severe, support and understanding are a first step, as is a full explanation of the normal female hormone cycle.

"Taking charge of one's life," notes one gynecologist, "seems to be a generally recommended relief strategy for PMS sufferers." Changes that give women more control over their lives often relieve the problem — for instance, changes in lifestyle: improved diet, more regular exercise and extra time for recreation.

Medications that may alleviate PMS include:
- mefenamic acid, started 10–12 days before the menstrual period, can bring relief but is not advisable for those who plan pregnancy or suspect they might be pregnant;
- alprazolam (Xanax) — an anti-anxiety drug — taken daily for a week before the period, then tapered off, may relieve premenstrual depression and jitteriness;
- low-dose danazol (Cyclomen) — which opposes ovulation — is offered if no pregnancy is anticipated or desired;
- Gonadotropin-releasing hormone (GnRH) agonists, as a spray or patch, can be helpful — again, if no pregnancy is wanted — to reduce ovarian estrogen release.

VITAMIN B₆ IS OF DUBIOUS HELP FOR PMS

Megadoses of vitamin B₆ are widely advertised in popular publications as an antidote to the bloating, irritability and breast tenderness of PMS. Publicity about its efficacy has led many women to take the vitamin indiscriminately, sometimes in huge amounts, often without medical advice. While 50–200 mg a day is the recommended daily limit for vitamin B₆, some self-styled experts advise women to take up to 1,000 mg or more daily!

Although preliminary research held out some promise that vitamin B₆ could alleviate PMS, the scientific evidence for its benefits is weak to nonexistent. As might be expected with a syndrome as complex as PMS, some sufferers report improvement with B₆, while others do not. Mixtures of B₆ plus evening primrose oil, or the oil alone, do as well as or better than the vitamin alone. Researchers find high placebo responses, with 70 percent of PMS sufferers reporting the same improvement with dummy drugs as with B₆. A recent review of the use of vitamin B₆ for PMS concluded that "changes in diet together with B₆ supplements seem to alleviate PMS in some users, but there's no proof that B₆ is the beneficial ingredient."

There are considerable risks in B₆ megadosing. A landmark study from New York's Albert Einstein College of Medicine called excess ingestion a "megavitamin toxicity syndrome" because the researchers documented neuropathy (nerve degeneration) from B₆ megadoses, with unsteady gait, loss of sensory (touch and pain) perception, numbness in the feet and hands and clumsy movements. Later studies revealed cases where B₆-induced nerve damage persisted for years.

Large doses act as a toxic drug, and excess B₆ can be damaging at lower levels than hitherto suspected. Individual responses to B₆ overdosing vary widely — perhaps because of different inbuilt sensitivities. The signs of B₆ vitamin-induced nerve impairment include bone pains, muscle weakness, pricking in the limbs, an inability to walk without a cane, reduced touch perception and even speech problems. Women with PMS should not resort to this vitamin to cure their discomfort. (For more on B₆ and other vitamins, see chapter 4.)

For severe PMS, physicians may offer hormonal agents to halt ovulation and periods, provided pregnancy isn't planned.

Excessive exercise disturbs menstrual cycles

In ever-growing numbers, women swell the ranks of morning joggers and take up competitive sports formerly regarded as all-male domains. They participate in marathons with endurance levels at least as high as men's, and a third of all North American high school athletes are now girls. Some women who exercise ardently experience menstrual problems — most of which are no cause for alarm. But strenuous training can halt ovulation and stop menstruation.

Typically, excessive exercise leads to a delayed onset of periods, oligomenorrhea (few periods) or amenorrhea (cessation of periods). For the most part, the menstrual disturbances are transient and totally reversible by reduced training levels and upgraded diet. Exercise-linked menstrual troubles are most frequent in women who commence the intense regime before the menarche.

Although arduous exercise upsets menstrual rhythms, physical exertion is not usually the sole reason. Accompanying factors, such as stress, anxiety, energy drain and reduced body fat also play a part. The dividing line appears to be at 64–80 km (40–50 miles) of running per week, or equivalent exertion. Almost all women who run over 80 km (50 miles) weekly have menstrual irregularities. A large University of New Mexico study showed 12 percent of women athletes to be menstrually irregular compared to only 3 percent of nonexercisers. All runners covering 90 km (55 miles) or more per week were amenorrheic. The American College of Sports Medicine reports that a third of female long-distance runners have menstrual disturbances.

The exact hormonal mechanism whereby exercise alters menstrual rhythms isn't known. Vigorous activity may affect the brain's hypothalamic regulation of hormone outputs and increase levels of prolactin, growth hormone, androgens and beta-endorphins. One study of female athletes and runners found them amazingly adept at timing their menstruation by controlling body weight, knowing that below a definite point on the scales, periods would surely stop. The hormonal disturbances caused by excess exercise may produce early-onset osteoporosis, with consequent stress fractures in the bones.

Older women, whose periods are already well established when they take up strenuous exercise, are less likely to have menstrual upsets. In fact, older female marathoners often have increased menstrual flow. Women who had menstrual irregularities before going in for exercise may find the disturbances magnified.

Ballet dancers are also often beset by menstrual upsets. Studies show that the age at which ballet dancers start menstruating averages 15.4 years — well behind the norm of 12.8 years. Classical ballet ranks second only to football in terms of physical demand, stress and energy costs, with figure skating and gymnastics coming close behind. Current ideals demand that ballerinas be light and easy to lift, fit the costumes and have the right "look." Some dancers try deliberately to delay their menarche by stringent dieting in the hope of retaining a slim, prepubescent shape. The same applies to gymnasts.

On a warning note, it's a fallacy to assume that all gynecological problems in physically active women stem from their sport. Other possible reasons, such as endocrine diseases or anatomical defects, must also be considered. If it is the sport that has triggered the problems, a less vigorous training schedule may be all that's needed for normal periods to return. A gain in body fat and suitable hormone therapy (for instance, estrogen replacement) can also help restore ovulation and fertility.

Many sportswomen with menstrual difficulties have subsequently had successful pregnancies. Women with reproductive cycles altered by exercise can rest assured that normal ovulation will likely recur once exercise is reduced, body fat regained and stress minimized. It's also high time to lay to rest the old notion that women cannot or should not exercise during their menses — belied by the many Olympic records set by menstruating athletes. Sports physicians assure women that, unless they are deterred by menstrual cramping, there is no reason to stop exercising or avoid gym classes during a period.

VAGINITIS: COMMON AND ANNOYING, BUT CURABLE

Although rarely serious, vaginitis afflicts women of all ages, even young girls and babies. The term "vaginitis" lumps together several conditions that inflame and irritate the lower female genital tract.

Basically, vaginitis is due to a disturbance in the vagina's internal balance. Most adult women have some vaginal discharge, which fluctuates with age, monthly cycle, sexual activity and

DISTINGUISHING THE DIFFERENT FORMS OF INFECTIOUS VAGINITIS

- A strong, fishy odor signals infection with "mixed" bacteria. Vaginal infection due to nonspecific or *Gardnerella* microorganisms produces a milky-gray, runny discharge with a foul odor (worst at midcycle and right after intercourse). The "whiff test" (adding potassium hydroxide to a sample of the vaginal discharge) intensifies the fishy odor and helps diagnosis.

The standard treatment for this form of vaginitis is metronidazole (Flagyl), taken for seven days. Together with alcohol this antibiotic causes nausea and vomiting, so those on it should avoid alcoholic drinks until 24 hours after the last dose. The medication should not be used during pregnancy (amoxicillin is an alternative). Occasional douching with dilute vinegar may help to acidify the vagina and get rid of the infection.

- Trichomoniasis vaginalis (nicknamed "trich") is due to a tiny, almond-shaped, unicellular parasite that often produces infection with little or no discomfort and may be discovered only during a routine gynecological examination. Sometimes, however, trich causes vulvar irritation (less bothersome than with candidiasis), and a watery, greenish-yellow, sometimes frothy, bad-smelling discharge that may feel as if one has "wet the pants." Urination may be painful. Trich infections are generally sexually transmitted, with frequent reinfection between partners. But trich protozoa can survive outside the body for up to three hours and may also spread in bubble baths, hot tubs, whirlpools and via wet towels or facecloths.

A look down the microscope at a discharge sample reveals the whip-tailed trich parasites. Treatment is a single or seven-day course of metronidazole — for the woman and any sexual partner(s). Treating the sex partner(s) is crucial to avoid reinfection. Pregnant women need alternative medication.

stress. The normal discharge varies from clear and slippery to thick and sticky, sometimes staining the underpants yellow. Some women have a profuse vaginal flow just before and during ovulation, but many who complain of a copious discharge simply have an above-average but perfectly normal amount.

Changes in vaginal discharge reflect alterations in the vagina's ecosystem — the balance of microorganisms that normally inhabit its folds. Within the vagina's ridged lining, many bacteria and other organisms dwell in friendly coexistence, or symbiosis. The relative numbers of vaginal microinhabitants fluctuate according to estrogen and other hormone levels; varying amounts of glycogen (a storage carbohydrate); and use of oral contraceptives and other drugs, especially antibiotics.

The healthy vagina is usually kept slightly acidic by harmless lactobacilli — acid-producing bacteria — that live in harmony with most other vaginal microorganisms, and keep harmful organisms in check. But in the absence of sufficient lactobacilli, other infectious microorganisms can flourish and irritate the vagina. Symptoms of vaginitis include:

- a change in odor and consistency of vaginal discharge; the discharge may increase, change color, smell foul or become blood-tinged;
- vaginal inflammation and soreness, and possibly painful urination;
- vaginal itch, and spreading discomfort if the inflammation reaches the vulva (inner and outer folds of the external female genitals).

Tracking down the causes of vaginitis

The main causes of vaginitis are atrophy or vaginal thinning, dryness (as happens in older women), infection and, rarely, mechanical problems (foreign objects in the vagina). Some women have such delicately balanced vaginal ecosystems that even small, temporary changes in acidity can upset them. For instance, semen makes the vagina briefly alkaline for a few hours after intercourse, generally not long enough to cause symptoms, but a few women complain of vaginitis after each coital act. The vagina's inner environment can also be upset by douching, bits of tampon accidentally left in or small objects pushed in by exploratory young girls.

VAGINITIS: AN INFECTION THAT ATTACKS THE VAGINA AND CERVIX

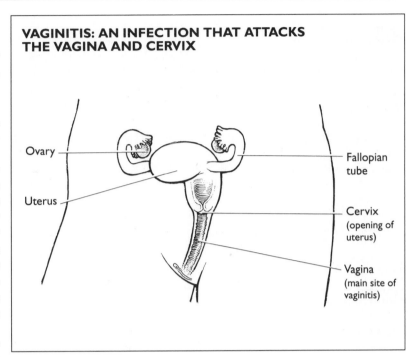

Infectious vaginitis is usually due to one of three microorganisms: mixed bacteria (including *Gardnerella*); yeasts (*Candida albicans*); and *Trichomonas vaginalis*, "trich," a protozoan. Each type of vaginitis has distinct features, but the three infections may coexist. Occasionally, symptoms similar to vaginitis arise from sexually transmitted diseases such as gonorrhea or chlamydia. Joan is a case in point. She came back from a yachting trip with her boyfriend suffering from a genital itchiness and acute soreness when urinating. A visit to her family physician — who took a vaginal swab and looked at it through his microscope — confirmed the diagnosis: she had picked up a gonorrheal infection, probably from having unprotected sex with her boyfriend.

Accurate diagnosis is the key to curing vaginitis

To diagnose the cause of vaginitis, doctors must examine the vaginal discharge with a "whiff" (smell) test and, in many cases, culture (growth) of the organism in a lab. Very often, a quick look down the microscope at the discharge ("smear") on a slide, plus a simple acidity test is enough to tell what's causing the vaginitis. For instance, women with yeasts, or candidiasis, have thick acidic vaginal secretions; those with "trich" and/or mixed bacteria have an alkaline

PREVENTIVE MEASURES AGAINST YEAST INFECTIONS

- **daily washing of the genital area with mild, unperfumed soap, especially after intercourse (preferably minimizing use of soap);**
- **rinsing with a 10 percent solution of baking soda or diluted vinegar;**
- **wiping with toilet paper from front to back (this may help avoid fecal contamination);**
- **not staying in wet swimsuits or tight-fitting clothes for long spells;**
- **cutting back on prolonged antibiotic use, if possible and medically advised;**
- **wearing pantyhose with a cotton crotch-liner, or all-cotton undergarments;**
- **avoiding excessively long, hot, bubble baths (children too!);**
- **not using vaginal douches unless medically recommended;**
- **avoiding "feminine deodorant" products and perfumed soaps;**
- **taking care to remove tampons in their entirety;**
- **avoidance of sexual intercourse during treatment;**
- **ensuring that all things entering the vagina — penises, diaphragms, tampons — are scrupulously clean!**
- **taking medication as instructed.**

discharge. Treatment is chosen according to the examination results, with follow-up to make sure the chosen medication was correct, and to adjust it if necessary. Cure of vaginitis may include treatment of any sexual partner(s), to avoid "ping-pong" reinfection.

However, because vaginitis is often poorly managed, it may keep recurring. Some physicians prescribe "shotgun" therapy based on vaguely described symptoms, without doing a thorough physical examination. Treatment may even be prescribed over the phone! A recent survey found that only one-third of the women given medication for a presumed vaginal yeast infection were ever examined. Physicians frequently didn't take smears or send samples for lab analysis, neglecting the easy office tests that could have pinpointed the cause.

Noninfectious vaginitis

Vaginitis may also arise from mechanical irritation, especially if childhood curiosity leads young girls to insert small objects into their vaginas. Doctors have removed items ranging from toothpicks and matches to paper clips and stones. In preadolescents, atrophic vaginitis may occur because of low estrogen levels. In postmenopausal women, a thinning vaginal lining may crack, bleed and become mildly infected. An estrogen cream, applied locally, can offset postmenopausal vaginal thinning.

VAGINAL YEAST INFECTIONS OR CANDIDIASIS

The yeast *Candida albicans* is a fungus that often inhabits human intestines and vaginas. As early as 400 B.C., Hippocrates noted yeast infections, or "thrush," as whitish patches on the gums and tongue. Over 50 percent of adult women suffer at least one attack of candida vaginitis, and some have repeat episodes. Ordinarily harmless, candida yeasts produce symptoms if the vaginal ecosystem is disturbed. The less acidic the vagina, the more prone it is to yeasts. Candidiasis occurs most often in young women, less postmenopausally (except in those on estrogen-replacement therapy).

The usual signs of vaginal yeast infections are intense genital itching (often severe enough

to hinder sleep); sore, swollen, possibly reddened labia; and a thick, white, curdy, cottage-cheese-like discharge. A few women with candidiasis detect a yeasty odor like fermenting dough! There's often also painful urination, and discomfort during sex.

Susceptibility to yeast infections increases during pregnancy and with prolonged use of antibiotics or, sometimes, birth-control pills. Wearing tights or jeans traps the candida organisms against the vulva, exacerbating the infection, and poor ventilation in the genital area may also increase or perpetuate (but not cause) yeast infections. Other predisposing factors include postmenopausal thinning of the vaginal wall; diabetes; cuts or abrasions in the genital area; too much douching, poor hygiene and soiled underwear (which transfer yeasts from feces to the vagina); and an immune system weakened by HIV/AIDS or other disorders. Eating too much sugar or having a defect in milk sugar (lactose) metabolism may predispose some women to yeast infections. For them, eliminating dairy products from the diet and cutting down on sugar may get rid of the yeasts.

Effective treatment for candidiasis combines antifungal drugs with scrupulous hygiene. Wearing loose cotton underwear may combat but not prevent a yeast infection.

- Antifungals such as miconazole (Monistat), clotrimazole (Canesten) and Terazol (a new antifungal) — as tablets, creams or suppositories — halt yeast growth. But since many women stop taking the antifungals once symptoms disappear, although the yeasts may linger on, a single-shot clotrimazole injection may be advised.
- A more recent antifungal, oral ketoconazole (Nizoral), is 90 percent effective against severe candidiasis, but symptoms often return once it's discontinued and this drug requires close medical care as it can damage the liver. It should never be used during pregnancy or when conception could occur.
- A trusted older remedy — gentian violet — may still be worth a try, although it can produce allergies and is a bit messy!
- Betadine douches are sometimes prescribed for mild cases.

- Sexual intercourse and tampons are discouraged while trying to clear up yeast vaginitis.
- Some women get repeat yeast infections that resist all therapy. Although antifungals clear up 90 percent of vaginal yeast proliferation, despite efforts to eliminate all possible predisposing factors (such as antibiotics or oral contraceptives), the infection comes back again and again. Recurrent candidiasis is sometimes ascribed to self-reinfection, poor hygiene or anal sex — although no scientific studies have proved this transmission route. Applying antifungals to the entire genital area can minimize recurrence.

Very occasionally, yeasts invade other organs besides the vagina, seriously threatening health. But the widely propagated claims that attribute a host of illnesses to yeast invasions are unsubstantiated. Allegations that candidiasis has reached epidemic proportions owing to carbohydrate-rich diets, birth-control pills, pollution and repressed immune systems do not stand up to scientific scrutiny. The unspecific complaints blamed on yeasts could arise from many other causes. One book, *The Yeast Connection,* has been strongly attacked by organizations such as the American Academy of Allergy and Immunology as "sheer speculation, without a shred of evidence."

Home remedies for candidiasis are generally considered of dubious help, but one "natural" therapy — inserting yogurt into the vagina — often works, perhaps because yogurt contains lactobacilli that reestablish the vagina's normal acidity and deter growth of harmful organisms. Although messy and of no proven benefit, local yogurt insertion isn't harmful! But excess vaginal douching does more harm than good for yeast flare-ups.

ENDOMETRIOSIS

Endometriosis is a common, sometimes incapacitating gynecological problem of menstruating women. It affects mostly women in their twenties and thirties, less frequently teenagers, rarely postmenopausal women. The disorder can lead to much needless suffering because of underdiagnosis — failure to recognize and treat the condition correctly. But the past decade has seen great strides in the

---

THE MAIN SYMPTOMS OF ENDOMETRIOSIS

- *premenstrual spotting,* menstrual irregularity;
- *pain* — with a period, when urinating, with a bowel movement or during intercourse. The pain typical of endometriosis often starts a few days before a period (when the islands of abnormal tissue swell and release chemicals such as prostaglandins), but it may continue throughout the menstrual period. The amount of pain by no means correlates with the extent of endometriosis, which can occur with little or no discomfort;
- *dyspareunia,* or pain during intercourse, sometimes relieved by a change of position during lovemaking. The pain is most likely with deep penetration, and worst just before a period;
- *low back pain,* if the abnormally situated endometrial tissue attaches to or presses on nerves in the lower back;
- *infertility,* because of the inflammation and adhesions around the uterus and tubes — frequent among women with endometriosis. But not all infertile women have endometriosis.

---

understanding and treatment of this disorder.

Endometriosis currently strikes 6 to 15 percent of North American women in their childbearing years. It occurs if bits of the endometrium (tissue lining the uterus) spread to and lodge in other sites — most frequently the ovaries or fallopian tubes, but sometimes also more distant sites in the pelvic cavity such as the bladder, colon and appendix. Uterine cells found at remote sites probably reached them via the lymphatic system or bloodstream. Since endometrial tissue depends on estrogen and progesterone for growth, the problem is mainly confined to menstruating women and

ENDOMETRIOSIS SITES

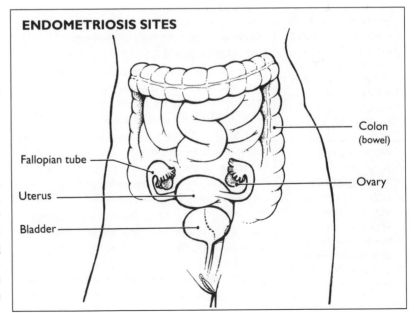

Fallopian tube

Uterus

Bladder

Colon (bowel)

Ovary

CAUSES OF ENDOMETRIOSIS REMAIN ELUSIVE

Endometriosis is an enigmatic disorder, and why only some women get it remains a mystery. In part, the disorder may be linked to menstrual cycle length and flow. It can also occur after abortions and after laparoscopic procedures. The condition may also be genetic — passed on from mother to daughter.

Women who have had several pregnancies or have been on low-dose oral contraceptives for a long time appear to have reduced risks of endometriosis. It has little cancer-forming potential. Some gynecologists believe that the more exercise a woman engages in and the earlier she starts ath-letics, the less the chance of developing endometriosis. (Vigorous exercise can diminish or abolish ovulation and menstrual periods.) One study suggested that women who exercise more than seven hours a week have one-fifth the usual risks of endometriosis, but only if regular workouts began before age 25.

tends to disappear after menopause. For severe cases ovary and uterus removal may be the only sure cure.

How endometriosis arises

In most women, small amounts of menstrual fluid flow backward into the fallopian tubes and thence into the abdominal cavity, carrying uterine lining cells that may become attached to other organs. These cells may persist and grow as displaced patches of endometrial tissue. Just as the lining of the uterus expands cyclically and is shed each month during menstruation, endometrial tissue outside the uterus also proliferates and bleeds in tune with monthly hormone cycles. But waste material from the abnormally situated endometrial tissue outside the uterus cannot escape. It accumulates and may form adhesions and scar tissue, with accompanying inflammation, pelvic pain, dysmenorrhea (painful menstruation) and other complications. The adhesions can interfere with normal function — for example, impeding fertility by displacing the fallopian tube(s). The abnormal endometrial tissue may also form cysts on the ovary which slowly fill with blood — known as "chocolate cysts" because of their brown color — or larger masses that infiltrate various organs.

The symptoms of endometriosis vary according to the sites affected, ranging from hardly noticeable — many women with the disorder being asymptomatic — to severe and debilitating. Even if painful, the condition often goes unrecognized, as the discomfort may be mistaken for menstrual cramps. Sometimes

endometriosis is only detected when women try to become pregnant but can't, and tests reveal adhesions around the fallopian tubes or other parts of the reproductive tract. On discovering they have endometriosis, many women panic, think their childbearing potential is forever blighted and rush into efforts to conceive. Yet many women with endometriosis manage to become pregnant and carry babies to term.

How is endometriosis diagnosed?

The family physician or a gynecologist may detect masses (lumps) or nodules during a routine examination, or a vaginal, pelvic or rectal exam may reveal tender spots. Occasionally endometriosis is discovered by ultrasound exams, but chiefly it's by laparoscopy — looking into the pelvic area with a fiber-optic viewing tube. The laparoscope, inserted via a tiny incision near the navel, allows physicians to see organs inside the pelvis. Analysis of biopsy (tissue) samples taken from suspicious areas confirms endometriosis by identifying it as glandular uterine-lining tissue.

For laparoscopic investigation, carbon dioxide is pumped into the abdomen, providing a cushion of gas that separates the organs and makes them clearly visible. Although it requires general anesthesia, laparoscopy doesn't usually necessitate an overnight hospital stay. Through the laparoscope, endometriosis is often seen as purple, blue, raspberry-red or brownish spots on the pelvic organs. In very severe cases, there may be many scars, adhesions and abnormal thickenings. But the amount of discoloration and scarring does not necessarily indicate the severity of endometriosis. What's actually seen may be no more than the "tip of the iceberg." Up to 15 percent of women who have endometriosis look normal during laparoscopy, although even small endometrial implants can cause discomfort. Physicians are getting better at detecting and mapping the disorder, but the condition is still often missed. Considerable effort has gone into developing noninvasive tests for endometriosis — such as ultrasound and magnetic resonance imaging — but so far none is accurate or sensitive enough. Blood tests for specific immune markers released by endometrial tissue also haven't proved very useful as yet.

Modern management of endometriosis

A frank discussion with sufferers can often put to rest the accompanying anxiety and insecurity. One University of Toronto expert explains that "a key step in treatment is to reassure women and de-dramatize the effects of this progressive but essentially benign disorder." Treatment is tailored to age, childbearing potential or plans and the desire for pregnancy. It may involve minimal intervention and a "wait-and-see" approach.

The pain may be relieved with painkillers (ASA or acetaminophen). For those with mild endometriosis, medications often diminish the symptoms to tolerable levels, so no further intervention is required. Relief at knowing what the problem is often minimizes the pain. Therapy with anti-estrogen preparations may be the next step. Alternatively, laparoscopic surgery may be recommended, where the physician removes as much of the abnormal tissue as possible. Endometrial patches on the ovaries or tubes can be vaporized off with carbon-dioxide lasers or cauterized electrically. Laser techniques lessen damage to adjacent tissue, allowing swifter recovery than with traditional surgery. But large endometrial lesions may still need surgical excision. For women with persistent disabling endometriosis, hysterectomy (removal of uterus and ovaries) may be the best solution.

Medications used for endometriosis:

Anti-estrogens used for endometriosis include low-dose birth-control pills, danazol and GnRH agonists (e.g., Synarel). They all work by suppressing gonadotropin secretion from the pituitary gland, thereby reducing ovarian estrogen release.

- *Oral contraceptives* (OCs), especially forms high in progestin, can often shrink endometrial patches. They prevent estrogen accumulation in blood platelets, thereby helping to suppress endometriosis. But while OCs may relieve symptoms and prevent the spread of minimal endometriosis, they are not a cure; they only relieve the symptoms.

- *Danazol* (Cyclomen), a male hormone derivative, given by mouth, turns off ovarian estrogen production by suppressing gonadotropin release. Since endometrial tissue is estrogen-dependent, blocking estrogen release can shrink the abnormal patches and relieve the pain. Danazol also has some anti-inflammatory benefits. But there are some masculinizing side effects including worsening acne, hirsutism (excess body hair), skin oiliness, breakthrough (between periods) bleeding and altered fat metabolism. Side effects are usually well tolerated, especially at low doses — but sometimes enough to make women reluctant to use danazol.

- *Gonadotropin-releasing hormone (GnRH) agonists* — also known as luteinizing hormone-releasing hormone (LHRH) agonists — are the newest weapons in the fight against endometriosis. These agents can reduce the size and number of endometrial lesions, often relieving the pain. Given by nasal spray (self-administered), injection or implants, they inhibit estrogen production, temporarily producing a near-menopausal state. These drugs also produce side effects, particularly insomnia, altered bone metabolism (leading to osteoporosis), and menopausal symptoms such as hot flashes, sweats and vaginal dryness. Although several GnRH agonists have been developed, only nafarelin (Synarel) and leuprolide (Lupron) are so far approved by the Canadian Health Protection Branch of Health and Welfare Canada for treating endometriosis.

- *Combination therapy with danazol* plus *GnRH agonists* is also sometimes tried. Comparative studies between GnRH agonists and danazol have shown the two equally effective in suppressing endometriosis, but both are costly and unsuitable for prolonged therapy because of side effects: bone loss with GnRH analogues, and male-type androgenic effects with danazol. However, side effects can be minimized with dose-reduction for danazol. One advantage of GnRH agonists is that long-term use (even for several years) can now be safely accomplished by adding back a low dose of estrogen and progestin when endometriosis symptoms abate. So-called

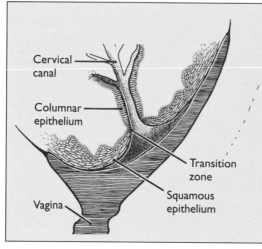

DETECTING CERVICAL CHANGES EARLY TO AVOID CANCER

The cervix, or neck of the uterus, is one of the body's most easily accessible internal organs. The columnar epithelium, which lines the canal leading from the inside of the uterus, changes to the squamous (skin-like) epithelium of the vagina, and this junction between the two types of cells is the transition zone where most cervical cancers begin. Many cervical cell abnormalities subside and vanish on their own, without treatment, never becoming a cancer. And the few that do go on to become cancer usually take five, ten, fifteen or more years to do so. The simple Pap or cervical smear test can detect abnormal changes in this transition zone at a precancerous stage.

add-back therapy can also stop hot flashes and prevent bone loss, without reactivating endometriosis.

While anti-estrogen hormone therapy relieves symptoms, how long it can be safely used in endometriosis is not clear and its merits have still to be compared with surgical methods. Anti-estrogens don't necessarily achieve a cure, since symptoms tend to recur once treatment stops. As endometriosis is a chronic disease, counseling, education and other supportive measures are generally recommended. Women who are well informed about their disease usually respond best to therapy.

CERVICAL CANCER IS A SEXUALLY TRANSMITTED DISEASE

Next to breast cancer, cancer of the cervix (uterine opening) is the second leading cause of cancer deaths worldwide among women aged 25–39. Yet it is easily prevented if abnormal changes at the mouth of the cervix are found and treated early. Tragically, many women who develop cancer of the cervix have never had the simple Pap test, which easily detects such changes in time to prevent cancer. Modern laser and other treatments make this type of cancer eminently preventable if caught in time.

A study by British Columbia's Cancer Control Agency found that cervical *carcinoma in situ* (localized precancerous changes) in women aged 20 to 29 years has doubled since the 1970s. The upswing is ascribed to greater sexual permissiveness and the younger age at which girls now begin their sex lives. There is a clear link between cervical cancer, teenage onset of sexual activity and the number of sex partners a woman has. Cigarette smoking also increases the risk of cervical cancer.

Cervical cancer usually takes several years to develop, progressing from slightly abnormal precancerous changes, or dysplasia ("dys" meaning abnormal), at the mouth of the cervix to more serious but still noncancerous stages, to early and then full invasive cancer. Before becoming invasive, the localized, noncancerous changes on the surface of the cervix can easily be located and destroyed. Left untreated, they may go on to become invasive cancer, penetrate through the lining of the cervix and invade nearby organs.

The latest scientific thinking incriminates genital wart viruses, often transmitted from the penis during sexual intercourse, as the triggering cause of cervical cancer. Take the case of a recently married woman in her early thirties who was told after her annual Pap smear test that she had some small warts on the rim of her cervix. The gynecologist said they should be removed to stop cancer from developing. He advised laser treatment and told her not to have sex with her husband until the genital warts had been cured. Her initial panic and the discomforting thought of being "unclean" were quickly replaced by a flood of relief at having found the condition in time to prevent cancer. A quick, painless office laser treatment removed the genital warts. Apart from a few days of vaginal soreness and the need for sexual abstinence while healing, the episode was soon forgotten. However, the message was remembered: get regular Pap tests and gynecological pelvic exams.

Sex and cervical cancer

Cervical cancer is very rare in women who don't have sex, and the more male partners a woman has, the greater her risk. Wives and lovers of promiscuous men are also at high risk. For over 150 years, scientists puzzled over the link between sexual intercourse and cervical cancer, especially in women with many sex partners. The suspicion that a transmissible agent might trigger this cancer arose as early as 1842, when a physician reported that the nuns in an Italian convent never developed cervical cancer, a disease then very common among married Italian women. These findings were later confirmed by a Canadian study of 13,000 Quebec nuns, among whom cervical cancer was also conspicuously absent. Today the genital warts virus, or human papilloma virus (HPV), which can be transmitted during sex, is the suspected cause of cervical cancer. Any woman who is or has ever been sexually active — even with one man — is at risk and should get regular gynecological checkups.

Regular Pap tests can save lives

Named for its inventor, an American-Greek physician, Dr. George Papanicolaou, the Pap smear is a quick, simple, painless test used to pick up precancerous and early malignant cervical changes. A little surface tissue is gently scraped from the cervix with a blunt scraper, smeared onto a glass slide and examined under the microscope. Cellular abnormalities can be seen, evaluated and graded. (Abnormal cells have larger nuclei that take up more stain and look darker than normal ones.) Women going for a Pap test should avoid douching, use of tampons and vaginal creams for a day or so beforehand.

If a Pap test result comes back positive — showing precancerous changes — more tests are done. Using special stains and a magnifying colposcope (a large viewing lens), the physician examines the cervix more closely and evaluates the extent of suspicious changes. A biopsy (removal of some abnormal cells) will be done to rule out the existence of cancer.

> ## RATING CERVICAL CANCER RISKS
>
> *Highest risk*
> - any woman who has ever been sexually active and had intercourse with men;
> - those who start having sex as teenagers;
> - those with multiple sex partners;
> - those with HPV or genital-wart infections (and possibly genital herpes);
> - cigarette smokers and those substantially exposed to secondhand smoke;
> - those with low immune defenses (e.g., transplant patients and others on immunosuppressants);
> - those whose male sex partners have HPV-caused penile warts, multiple sex partners or ex-partners with cervical cancer;
> - those who have had a previous positive Pap smear.
>
> *Lowest risk*
> - women who have never had sexual intercourse;
> - women over age 60 whose Pap smears have always been negative.

When told of a positive Pap result, many women panic and think they have cancer. But a few abnormal cells in the cervical smear don't necessarily herald cancer or even an elevated risk of cancer. Modern technology offers simple, quick ways to remove the patch of abnormal cervical cells, by cryotherapy (freezing), electrocautery (burning) or laser vaporization.

The benefits of Pap tests have been repeatedly shown in Canada — a recognized leader in Pap screening. (British Columbia's program, which administers annual Pap tests to some 80 percent of its female population, is an international model.) In addition to revealing precancerous and early cancerous changes, giving plenty of time in which to eradicate them, Pap tests are useful for picking up other gynecological infections (e.g., a yeast invasion) and cervical inflammation, which has nothing to do with cancer.

So why are 400 Canadian women a year still dying of cervical cancer? The main reason is that too many women at high risk don't bother to get regular Pap tests. Also, although all agree that well-conducted Pap screening saves lives, experts disagree about how often to do the test. Those who favor annual screening argue that a longer gap between Pap tests would allow women with rare fast-developing cancers — which may become invasive in less than three years — to slip through the screening net. Proponents of less frequent screening (every three years) argue that the Pap test picks up insignificant abnormalities that would vanish spontaneously on their own, causing needless worry.

> ## WHO NEEDS PAP SMEARS AND HOW OFTEN?
>
> All sexually active women in Canada are advised to get a Pap test and gynecological exam once a year from age 15 to 35, and then every two to three years until age 60, when they can ask their physicians how often they need testing. But many gynecologists prefer to continue yearly Pap tests for all sexually active women, even those in older age groups — especially as it brings women into the office for a general exam that may detect other health problems.

The genital-warts link in cervical cancer

Through the years, many agents have come under fire as suspects in causing cervical cancer, only to be acquitted. At first trichomonas was suspected, then smegma (collected debris under the foreskin) — both were subsequently cleared of suspicion — and later genital *herpes simplex II* (the cold-sore virus) became the prime suspect. But while genital herpes may play a part in cervical cancer, suspicion has now shifted to the human papilloma virus (HPV, or genital-wart virus) as the main culprit.

Many women who have cervical cancer are found to carry certain HPV virus strains. Genital-wart viruses are easily passed between sex partners. Although the warts themselves — tiny, flat, almost invisible growths — are hard to see, mild acetic acid (vinegar) put on the penises of men or the genitals of women makes them visible under a magnifying glass. The modern technique of "viral fingerprinting" (analyzing molecules within cells) can identify which HPV strains are in the genital warts. Estimates suggest that the number of people infected with HPV in Canada has doubled in the past ten years and is on the rise, posing a serious health problem.

Prenatal exposure to diethylstilbesterol (DES), previously given to avert miscarriage, is another high-risk factor for specific forms of cervical cancer. The American College of Obstetricians and Gynecologists strongly recommends that all women exposed to DES before birth should have frequent gynecological checkups, starting at age 14.

Removal of genital warts is encouraged in both men and women

According to the latest medical wisdom, genital warts should be removed whenever detected. The trouble is that removing them doesn't always rid the body of HPV viruses, because the viruses may have infiltrated the whole genital region. However, most physicians now promote removal of genital warts in both men and women. If concerned about genital warts, consult a family physician, dermatologist or gynecologist, who may first try painting them with a wart-remover such as podophyllin or trichloroacetic acid. If that doesn't work, warts can be removed by freezing, cautery (burning) or laser vaporization. While barrier contraceptives (such as condoms) prevent transmission of AIDS and other STDs, they don't fully protect against HPV, because the viruses can permeate the entire genital area and occur on normal-looking genital skin. Nonetheless, getting rid of genital warts reduces the virus load and lessens infectivity.

In men, long-term HPV infection and subclinical (hard-to-see) genital warts may produce dome-shaped, glistening "Bowenoid papules," spots that look and test like precancerous lesions but are usually considered harmless. Since these spots contain HPV viruses which could endanger any sex partner, they're best removed.

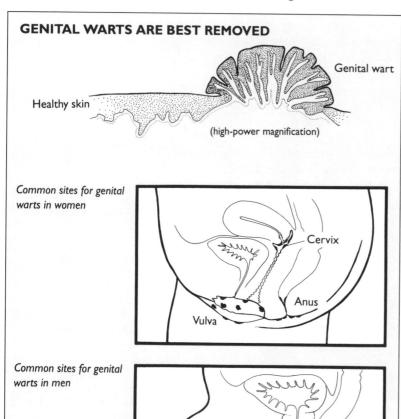

GENITAL WARTS ARE BEST REMOVED

Genital wart

Healthy skin

(high-power magnification)

Common sites for genital warts in women

Cervix

Anus

Vulva

Common sites for genital warts in men

Penis

Anus

MENOPAUSE: THERE IS LIFE AFTER 51.4 YEARS!

In contrast to the formerly prevalent view of postmenopausal women as "over the hill," "no longer sexy," or "finished," in modern times menopause — the cessation of menstruation — marks a new phase for many women, a time when they welcome freedom from periods, contraception and baby care, and look ahead to some independent years of health and vigor. For many women today, the age of 51.4 years (the average age of menopause) means a fresh start — perhaps a career change or renewed studies. Whereas formerly the average life span of a woman (worn out by years of childbearing) may have been about 27 (in Roman times) or 45 (in the Victorian era), the present average life expectancy for women in Canada is 83 years. The increased longevity means 30 years or more of active existence after the loss of childbearing ability and the drop in estrogen levels that signify menopause. As a reminder of the creative capacity of postmenopausal women, recall Golda Meir, Georgia O'Keeffe, or, in Canada, Doris Anderson, June Callwood, Pauline Jewett, Margaret Laurence, Flora Mac-Donald and Pauline McGibbon.

Menopause is not an illness or a sudden event that occurs at some preprogrammed moment. The name comes from two Greek words: *menos,* "month," and *pausis,* "halt." Some medical experts call menopause a "biologically unnatural state of estrogen deprivation." About four million Canadian women are presently in that condition — with a remaining life expectancy seven and a half years longer than men of similar birth dates.

Menopause isn't nearly as bad as it's made out to be

Although most women experience some discomfort when passing through menopause, some hardly notice it. Many who dreaded it beforehand find the experience not nearly as bad as they'd anticipated. Menopause is an intensely personal event, greatly influenced by cultural and social attitudes. Since lack of knowledge easily produces anxiety, many women claim that, in retrospect, the worst part of the menopause was "not knowing what to expect." Better understanding of the hormonal events and effective relief methods help women transcend this transition phase. Group sessions sharing experiences of menopause can make symptoms seem more acceptable, even "less troublesome." Mature Women's Clinics — such as those recently inaugurated at the University of Toronto — can help to inform women and banish menopausal myths. After the event, many postmenopausal women say they've "never felt better, more energetic and relaxed."

The menopause is a specific set of changes that take place during the climacteric, a biological epoch that spans the ages of 40–60 years. A simple Pap smear or hormone (estrogen) test can reveal how close a woman is to menopause. Periods slowly cease over two to three years, gradually becoming less regular as estrogen levels decline. When menopause begins, periods become sporadic, with one or two occasionally missed. Bleeding may be spotty, irregular, occasionally heavy. The periods eventually come to a complete halt. A woman who hasn't menstruated in twelve months has gone through menopause. Menopause is a *fait accompli.*

Menopause can be called an "estrogen deficiency state." The slower the fall in estrogen levels, the less severe menopausal symptoms are likely to be. Chubby women who store some estrogens in their fat tissues often find menopause less troublesome than thin women.

The age of menopause varies from country to country and from decade to decade, having shifted in North America from an average of 46 years to between the ages of 48 and 55, with an average of about age 52. But menstruation can cease naturally as early as age 38 or as late as age 60, and women can become menopausal at an even earlier age because of surgery, ovary removal or illness.

No need for postmenopausal women to give up sex or fun

A pervasive misconception in our society holds that sex is mainly for the young, and that the old and middle-aged inevitably abandon all interest in sexual activity. Such attitudes lead some older women who feel inadequate because of a dry vagina or a few skin wrinkles to give up sex.

THE FIRST OBVIOUS SYMPTOMS OF MENOPAUSE MIGHT BE:

- a hot flash or night sweat;
- a more frequent need to urinate;
- vaginal dryness (noticed as discomfort during intercourse).

N.B.: irregular bleeding or changes in menstrual flow can have other causes and should be investigated.

The usual accompanying signs of menopause are:

- *Hot flashes* — transient fluctuations in body-temperature control, affecting about 70 percent of menopausals women. Although unpleasant, flashes are not life-threatening. They arise from temporary vasomotor instability (overreactive blood vessels). Blood vessels in the skin suddenly dilate, sending blood rushing to the surface and creating a deep blush, mostly on neck, face and upper chest. About 10–15 percent of menopausal women have flashes severe enough to disrupt their usual activities. In those who do experience them, severe hot flashes can be embarrassing — as when a teacher suddenly turns beet-red and drips sweat in front of a class. Flashes usually last three to four minutes and may continue for years, but in time gradually decrease. Many modern remedies can minimize their severity, especially estrogen-replacement therapy (ERT).
- *Night sweats* — simply nighttime flashes that disturb sleep.
- *Sleeplessness* can be a serious problem and may occur because — for reasons yet unclear — estrogen lack alters certain brain-transmitter levels and affects sleep patterns.
- *Other vasomotor symptoms* may include dizziness and heart palpitations, also due to overreactivity of blood vessels.
- *Urinary tract problems and bladder weakness.* The menopausal drop in estrogen weakens the lining of the urethra (urinary tube) so it becomes more prone to infection. Tissue thinning also leads to more frequent urination, and possibly some urine loss when laughing or coughing.
- *Vaginal dryness.* Also due to the estrogen decline, the vagina becomes less elastic, perhaps dry and itchy, even cracked, so that some women find intercourse uncomfortable. An active sex life helps maintain vaginal suppleness. (Vaginal estrogen creams are a great help.)

In a survey that asked older women how menopause affected their sexuality, 65 percent maintained that there was "no noticeable effect"; others said sexual activity became "less important." But some reported that sexual relations were "more enjoyable" because fear of pregnancy was gone. Not all that long ago, women were raised to believe that they were nonsensuous beings not really meant to enjoy sex, and that intercourse was solely for procreation. With changing attitudes, many women today admit they feel just as sexually alive after menopause, or even more so. Many retirement homes find older people quite interested in sex!

In one recent European survey, when asked whether "menopause means the end of sexual attractiveness," 85 percent of British women said no, but only 64 percent of the French did. The discrepancy suggests that culture plays a powerful role in the way we perceive menopause. A study conducted by the Boston Women's Health Collective found that 90 percent of American women felt either "neutral" or "positive" about menopausal changes. Most were more concerned about "looking older," "losing a husband" or "getting cancer" than about menopause. Emotional responses ranged from weepiness, nervousness and sadness to delight at being able to have sex without birth control. Among the Rajput caste of Northern India, a woman who no longer menstruates can finally leave "purdah" (confinement to the home) and socialize outside, gaining status.

Menopause is often unjustly blamed for depression

The complex feelings of middle age — emptiness, depression, anxiety and nervousness — can be due as much to family and social upheavals as hormone changes. Middle age is a time when parents see children leave the nest and women have to face aging with its accompanying fears about fading sex appeal (just as men fear failing potency). The knowledge that reproductive capacity has ended or that career or personal goals may never be met can trigger regret. Yet menopausal women are not more depressed than those of other ages. Young adulthood is in fact the time of greatest depression, especially among teenage girls. Studies show that psychological problems, psychiatric

MANY REMEDIES ALLEVIATE MENOPAUSAL DISCOMFORTS

Knowledge about the hormone changes of menopause, preparedness and an upbeat approach can help women pass calmly through it.

To alleviate hot flashes women can try:
- a cold drink at the first sign, and for night sweats, a thermos of ice water or an ice pack kept near the bed;
- a strong room fan in summer or winter;
- a cool shower;
- cotton lingerie and sheets that permit perspiration to escape;
- a layered look that allows clothes to be peeled off discreetly;
- avoidance, if possible, of situations that produce hot flashes — unpleasant encounters, overly vigorous exercise, hot-weather sunning, spicy food, gulping meals or alcoholic beverages (especially wine);
- medications — non-hormonal drugs such as belladonna derivatives (Bellergal) — an antispasmodic — and clonidine (Dixarit) that may diminish the frequency of flashes; these drugs tone the blood vessels and may keep them from dilating.

To offset osteoporosis (bone-thinning) and the post-menopausal rise in heart attack risks:
- estrogen-replacement therapy (ERT) is now promoted by many healthcare providers around the world (see section on ERT later in this chapter).

To counter vaginal dryness in those not on ERT:
- many excellent hormone creams are perfectly safe to use; vaginally applied creams (Premarin or Dienestriol), used about twice a week, can increase vaginal elasticity and moisture. The hormone (estrogen) is also absorbed into the bloodstream;
- discomfort during intercourse can also be lessened by over-the-counter water-based lubricants such as K-Y jelly or the newer Astroglide. Gynecologists caution against petroleum-based gels (such as Vaseline) because many women are allergic to the petroleum base.

To help control urine leakage:
- Kegel (pelvic) exercises can help strengthen a woman's bladder control.

ailments and mental impairment are not peculiar to menopausal women. After age 60, men and women have equal rates of depression. There is no direct link between an estrogen deficit and job performance, memory or mood. Nonetheless, chronic fatigue due to frequent awakenings with night sweats can affect memory and concentration.

Ignorance about menopausal changes can exacerbate emotional problems that exist for other reasons. For example, when a 53-year-old office manager whose children can't find jobs, whose husband faces retirement and whose mother is dying of cancer is kept awake by night sweats, she understandably appears less able to cope than before. The problem cannot be blamed solely on menopause but on multiple factors.

Women who remain active, exercise, take enough calcium and seek medical advice when needed have a good chance of getting through menopause with little trouble. Those who work, help others or find interests outside the home often cope most successfully.

For many women the menopause heralds a profound sense of liberation which may lead to an increased interest in all aspects of life, including sex — what anthropologist Margaret Mead has termed PMZ, or Post Menopausal Zest.

THE PROS AND CONS OF ESTROGEN-REPLACEMENT THERAPY

With so many years of life ahead of them, many postmenopausal women wonder about the wisdom of taking postmenopausal estrogen supplements. This is a question best discussed with a trusted healthcare provider. In general, the medical establishment encourages postmenopausal hormone replacement except in cases where it's contraindicated (such as women who've had breast cancer, or have high blood pressure or blood-clotting problems).

A complete understanding is crucial to those considering postmenopausal estrogen replacement therapy (ERT), since it's a controversial, much-debated issue. Medical experts who support postmenopausal ERT favor its use to reduce menopausal discomforts, offset osteoporotic bone loss, lower women's heart-attack rates (which equal those of men after age 65), retain vaginal elasticity and combat urinary-tract slackness. Those who oppose ERT argue that menopause is a natural event that shouldn't be tampered with, and that it's best dealt with by continuing a good exercise regime, eating a cholesterol-lowering diet and using other remedies to lessen the discomforts.

One study that pointed out the benefits of

ERT was the Harvard University Medical School or Boston Nurses' Health Study, which claimed that estrogen supplementation markedly reduced the risk of coronary heart disease. It followed more than 48,000 postmenopausal women, reporting that those on ERT had half the number of fatal heart attacks. Estrogen seems to cut heart-disease risks by direct expansion of blood vessels, and by altering the blood's lipid (fat) profile — lowering levels of "bad" (LDL) and raising levels of "good" (HDL) cholesterol. However, some experts question the validity of the Nurses' Study results, because the subjects tended to be wealthier and in better shape than the average woman, and some of the effects attributed to estrogen might just be due to a healthier lifestyle.

Doubts about ERT stem from the possibility that unopposed estrogen therapy (without added progestins) — used for several years — can increase the risk of endometrial cancer (of the uterine lining). Adding the second female hormone, progesterone, counterbalances the cancer-promoting impact of estrogen. On the down side, adding progesterone or progestin causes periods to continue or resume. And although progestins blunt estrogen's cancer-promoting effects, they also lessen its benefits for the heart. Also, the long-term side effects of synthetic progestins (much newer drugs than synthetic estrogens) have yet to be established.

Another worry about ERT is its possible connection to breast cancer. The Boston Nurses' Health Study, and Swedish studies, suggested that women on ERT for many years (15 or more) have an increased risk of breast cancer compared to those not taking estrogens. But while one Swedish study found that combined estrogen-progestin therapy increased breast-cancer risks, other studies find no increased cancer risk in estrogen users. The unconfirmed link is under intense investigation.

While some physicians favor long-term ERT use, others think it should be used for only six months to two years at most, then tapered off. Some recommend ERT to all women as soon as they enter the menopause; others more cautiously reserve it for those with disturbing menopausal symptoms. Those physicians who view the menopause as a "deficiency state" are most likely to prescribe ERT — perhaps indefinitely. Those who regard menopause as a normal but troubling event are less likely to recommend ERT, especially for any significant length of time.

In sum, ERT reduces osteoporotic bone loss (and consequent bone breaks), protects against heart attack and maintains urinary-tract buoyancy and vaginal lubrication. That adds up to a big plus! It probably saves more lives than it costs, hence the shift in medical opinion toward its use. But women on ERT need to be vigilant, and to get regular breast examinations and mammograms every two years to check for early signs of breast cancer.

For ERT to achieve its full heart- and bone-protecting effects, it must be continued for several years. Currently, only 20 percent of Canadian postmenopausal women take estrogen supplements, half of them discontinuing after a year or so, some not even bothering to fill their prescriptions. The usual reasons given for not taking or discontinuing ERT are reappearance of menstrual periods and fear of bad side effects. Many worry about the unsubstantiated but widely publicized link to breast and endometrial cancer.

Women should jointly decide with their physicians whether to have ERT and for how long, bearing in mind that, to obtain the full benefits, hormone replacement should start at or soon after menopause.

Today's estrogen-replacement therapy is safer than before because:
• Doses of estrogen are now far lower than those used in the 1970s.
• Estrogen is usually prescribed in small doses, with progesterone added for a variable treatment period to counteract side effects. Women who have had their uteruses surgically removed can take estrogen alone with little risk unless there are other factors against it.
• Periodic endometrial (uterine) biopsy (looking for abnormal cells) ensures that the uterine lining isn't excessively thickened by ERT. Newer cell-sampling techniques make the procedure more accurate, thus lowering possible risks of uterine cancer from ERT.

• A transdermal skin patch can deliver the hormones directly into the bloodstream, by female passing the liver, and enabling even women with gallbladder or cholesterol problems to take ERT if they want it.

Women who should *not* have ERT include: those with active or past breast cancer, women with a strong family history of breast cancer and those with blood-clotting problems or liver disease.

SEX PROBLEMS IN WOMEN

Women, like men, may experience sexual dysfunction in the desire, arousal or orgasmic phase of the human sexual response — sometimes owing to sex-negative messages received in childhood. Some women are conditioned to think they must always "please the man," ignoring or repressing their own sexual desires, which sometimes leads to profound sexual dysfunction.

Sex problems in women include:

• *inhibited sexual desire*, which may arise because one or both partners are over-scheduled, or because the couple's mismatched timetables rarely allow them to spend time together in a relaxed fashion conducive to sexual activity.

• *sex arousal problems* such as an inability to become excited, hence poor lubrication — often for lack of pleasurable foreplay or tactile stimulation of the right kind. Poor lubrication can easily be remedied (see below), and once comfortable intercourse resumes, natural lubrication may be restored.

• *dyspareunia,* or painful intercourse, second only to anorgasmia (inability to have orgasm) among women's sex problems; many women experience it at some time or other. But it is a more obvious problem than anorgasmia, and one that can't easily be concealed. Dyspareunia can be primary (starting at the very first intercourse) or secondary (following a time of pain-free intercourse). It may be complete (occurring at all times) or situational (only with certain partners and in some lovemaking positions), superficial (with pain only at the *introitus* or vaginal entrance) or deep (with pain in the vagina, especially on deep penetration). Pelvic pain may continue after intercourse. Dyspareunia may have anatomical, pathological or psychosomatic causes. It may arise because of endometriosis, PID, birthing scars, a dry vagina, insufficient arousal or other causes.

Since many women are willing to put up with some pain or discomfort during intercourse, mistakenly considering it an unavoidable part of the sex act, there are few reliable statistics on the incidence of dyspareunia. Recent studies suggest it is far more prevalent among women of all ages than hitherto suspected. When reported, it often turns out to be due to an easily treated condition such as a vaginal infection, irritation from contraceptive foam or a dry vagina (too little lubrication). Vaginal dryness alone rarely accounts for painful intercourse, and if it is the reason it can be remedied with good lubricants such as K-Y jelly, Lubafax, Astroglide or even vegetable oils (but not Vaseline, which forms a painful crust), or with vaginal estrogen creams. If medical examination reveals no physical cause, the dyspareunia is attributed to psychological reasons — perhaps due to sex-disapproving parents, or a very orthodox upbringing implying that "sex is sinful." Interpersonal conflicts or an unpleasant sexual experience (such as incest or date rape) can trigger involuntary vaginal constriction and "turn off" the mechanism for vaginal lubrication. Although many women who experience painful intercourse discuss it with their sex partners, they may not mention it to medical caregivers, who might find a solution. (And physicians frequently fail to ask about a woman's sex life.)

Treatment for dyspareunia lies in medication, surgery or psychotherapy, or a combination, depending on the cause. Anatomical problems such as persistent hymenal tags (remnants), vulval lesions and other small obstructions are easily removed. Lubricants can reduce the discomfort. Sex therapy and special exercises can help to eliminate dyspareunia due to intercourse fears or phobias. The woman can dilate the vagina gently with her finger until it feels comfortable, allowing her partner to participate when she is ready.

- *vaginismus* — vaginal muscle spasms that interfere with intercourse. These may arise because of relationship problems, a sex-negative upbringing, a painful pelvic exam, a post-birth episiotomy scar or an unpleasant sexual experience. A history of sexual abuse is frequently found. A woman may be so fearful of having sex that her nervous system automatically causes involuntary vaginal spasms, preventing penile insertion. Therapy is with Kegel exercises (to strengthen the vaginal muscles) and using dilators of increasing size to flex the vagina and overcome insertion fears.

- *anorgasmia*, the commonest of female sex problems — is the apparent inability to achieve orgasm. This problem has sparked much debate about what really constitutes female "orgasm." Is a woman sexually dysfunctional if she can't reach orgasm through intercourse but enjoys it when her clitoris is manually stimulated by her partner (or herself)? Women clearly experience different degrees of orgasm at different times, with different sex partners, and grading or defining the subjective sensations is very difficult. Many women who get neither a superficial nor deep orgasm during intercourse nonetheless enjoy sexual intimacy with a man, although some find it hard to convince their partners that they're "sexually satisfied" — usually because the man is worried about not "performing well." (Women may fake orgasm in order to soothe the male ego, a practice deplored by sex therapists.)

Arguments around the female orgasm center on its variations. There is the "Big O," or vaginal orgasm, said to occur in less than 20 percent of women during intercourse, but quite common through masturbation by the woman or a partner. There is also the "deep orgasm" triggered as the penis hits the pelvic floor — interestingly, the response that most women obtain, but so mild that it often goes unnoticed. Finally, there is the orgasm achieved by stimulating the elusive "G spot," a recently discovered area on the anterior vaginal wall described by Dr. Graflenberg and said to swell and produce an intense orgasmic response. Although the spot has never been

precisely located, a partner's search for it can be very enjoyable, especially if a woman previously found the time devoted to foreplay rather skimpy.

Orgasmic failure in women is usually psychological in origin, but can also arise from organic disorders such as multiple sclerosis and other neurological conditions, circulatory diseases (which impair vaginal circulation) and hormonal imbalances as in Addison's disease (adrenal gland malfunction).

Short-term sex therapy can often help women with inhibited orgasm. Most women heave a sigh of relief when told that the overall incidence of so-called "deep" vaginal orgasm is only about 20 percent. Successful therapy may include some basic education about female anatomy and human sexuality, teaching women how to stimulate themselves to discover what they find erotically pleasing. Counseling to build trust with the partner and group therapy can also be helpful. Couples may be encouraged to share erotic fantasy trips, do sensate focus exercises (pleasuring each other without expecting intercourse) or use a vibrator to increase stimulation. The "tease technique" is often helpful: slow thrusts of the penis until arousal increases, then halting and starting again, in a stop-and-go stimulation that can sometimes overcome female anorgasmia.

(For more detail on sex therapy, see chapter 7.)

BREAST CANCER

Information overload about breast cancer, often inaccurate and needlessly scary, has aroused intense anxiety in today's women. Apprehension and the crossfire of differing medical opinions may deter those who find a breast lump from seeking medical advice, and prevent women at risk from getting breast checkups. Yet, caught in time, breast cancer can be treated in a manner that maximizes survival.

Breast cancer *isn't* a death warrant. There are thousands of women leading perfectly normal lives 10, 20 or even more years after removal of a malignant breast tumor. Survival can be long-term, provided the cancer is detected and treated before it spreads. To lessen the risks, women should have their breasts regularly examined and practice breast self-examination, and those over age 50 should have mammograms (breast X-rays) every one to two years.

Who needs regular mammographic screening?

There's no longer any argument about the fact that regular X-ray mammography for women can detect small breast tumors before they can be felt clinically, or that mammograms are excellent diagnostic tools for confirming malignancy. But experts disagree about the age at which routine mammography should begin, and about its benefits over expert physical examination by a skilled technician.

To understand the breast-screening controversy, it's vital to understand what screening is. Screening mammography is *not* the same as diagnostic mammography. Screening is done to detect unrecognized disease in otherwise healthy women who have no sign of breast cancer. Diagnostic mammograms are done to determine whether noticeable lumps or other breast abnormalities are in fact cancerous.

While most experts agree that periodic screening by mammography plus physical examination can cut down deaths from breast cancer in women over age 50, there's no agreement about its benefits in younger women. Some American health agencies promote regular mammograms for all women over age 40, but most Canadian health agencies discourage routine mammography for women under age 50. At present, screening mammography is advised in Canada only for women aged 50 and up. Alberta, Ontario and Saskatchewan already screen women aged 50–69 years; Manitoba, Quebec and Nova Scotia plan to do the same. The average cut-off age for breast cancer screening is 70.

Well-conducted mammography is now safe and reliable

The radiation received during a breast mammogram with modern, well-maintained equipment is no more than during a routine lung X-ray. But women having a mammogram can check with their doctors (if possible) to make sure that the equipment used is thoroughly up

REGULAR CLINICAL/PHYSICAL BREAST EXAMINATIONS ARE NEEDED FOR EARLY CANCER DETECTION

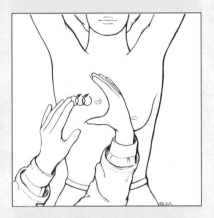

The breast examination should be done in a consistent manner by a trained professional.

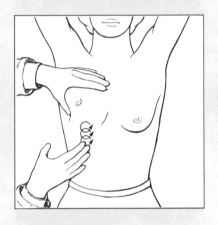

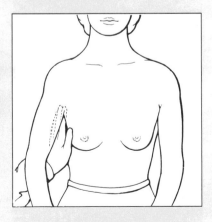

SOME KEY FACTS AND FIGURES ABOUT BREAST CANCER

- Breast cancer affects one woman in 10 in Canada during a normal life span of 80 or more years, and is the leading cause of cancer deaths in women.
- It is a chronic, potentially fatal disease of varying type and severity, ranging from tiny changes detectable only by X-ray to large, easily felt tumors that

may be invasive and spread to other areas. A breast cancer can grow quite large without causing any pain or other symptoms.
- Most breast cancers occur in women over age 50. The older the woman, the greater the risk — especially after age 70.
- The majority of breast cancers are

still discovered by women themselves — the average size at discovery being 2 cm (less than an inch).
- Men get it too — about 1 percent of all breast cancers occur in males, with an incidence around one per 1,000.
- There's no need to panic simply because a biopsy (tissue sampling) is suggested.

Most breast lumps turn out to be benign (harmless).
- If breast cancers are removed when less than 1 cm (0.4 in) across and no cancer cells are found in the underarm lymph nodes, survival chances are excellent.
- Mammographic screening in women over age 50 can reduce the death

toll from breast cancer by up to 40 per cent.
- The best way to check for breast cancer is to get regular physical examinations by a competent health-care professional, practice well-taught breast self-examination and have mammograms every one to two years after age 50.

to date and delivers the least possible radiation. Having mammography at special breast-screening centers or clinics helps to ensure that the equipment is safe and the mammograms are accurately interpreted. Apart from some discomfort, there's no need to fear mammograms these days. The brief X-ray examination may save a breast, even a life.

The advantages of mammography:
- mammograms can detect breast cancers two

years or more before they can be felt by physical examination;
- early mammographic detection can reduce breast-cancer deaths by 40 percent in women over age 50.

The disadvantages of mammography:
- it may give a "false positive" result, suggesting that a harmless (benign) lump is cancerous, leading to needless anxiety, surgical biopsy and a subsequent scar. But the same holds

THOSE AT INCREASED RISK OF BREAST CANCER

- women with close relatives who have had breast cancer, especially a mother and/or sisters, and particularly if both mother and sisters had it before the menopause and if the cancer affected both breasts;
- women who've already had cancer in one breast;
- childless women and late childbearers with their first full-term pregnancy after age 30–35;
- women who have an early menarche (start of menstruation before age 12) and/or a late menopause;
- possibly those who eat high-fat diets, although the precise diet-cancer links remain unclear. High-fat diets are known to promote breast and bowel cancer in animals, but some researchers blame too many overall calories for elevated breast-cancer rates in humans, rather than too much fat;
- women who use estrogen-containing birth-control pills for many years, especially before a first full-term pregnancy. They may be at slightly increased risk, although studies on the link between contraceptive pills and breast cancer are inconsistent. Amid the controversy, the World Health Organization reports no increased risk for breast cancer from taking the birth-control Pill and advises no change in

current contraceptive strategies;
- those taking long-term, post-menopausal estrogen-replacement therapy (ERT). Again, the link remains questionable, but long-term ERT during or after menopause may slightly elevate breast-cancer risks, so women in high-risk groups should be wary. One University of Toronto expert warns women and their medical caregivers "not to ignore the possibly increased risk of breast cancer from estrogen therapy." (See section on estrogen replacement for more detail.)
- women with atypical hyperplasia (an unusual condition normally found only on biopsy — in 2 percent of benign breast biopsies), especially if first-degree relatives have had breast cancer. However, other types of benign breast disorders such as cystic proliferation do not predispose to the development of breast cancer.

Contrary to well-publicized rumors, breast-cancer incidence does *not* seem to be increased by cigarette smoking or coffee drinking.

N.B.: Most breast cancers appear in women with few or none of these risk factors.

true for physical breast examinations;

- there may be "false negatives" indicating no cancer when a tumor is present but doesn't show up on the X-ray. In Canada's National Breast Screening Study, 23 percent of cancers clinically felt didn't appear on the mammograms in women aged 40–49, and mammography missed 12 percent of cancers in women aged 50 and over;
- it may produce a false sense of security, leading women to ignore symptoms of fast-growing cancers that didn't show up on the X-ray but grow in the interval between mammograms;
- it's less accurate in the dense breasts of young women — although, as X-ray sensitivity improves, cancers become easier to spot.

Mammography alone isn't enough. Regular physical breast examinations, performed every year or two, in a thorough, consistent manner by a competent expert, are also crucial. Even if a mammogram is negative, suspicious lumps felt on physical examination usually need to be taken out and checked.

The value of breast self-examination

Many lumps are still discovered by women themselves — 30 percent in one study, 80 percent in others. Breast self-examination (BSE) may pick up fast-growing cancers that develop between routine screenings. And since many women don't get regular mammograms or physical checkups, BSE is a valuable detection aid. But BSE is often incorrectly done and may even lead to a false sense of security and failure to get adequate checkups. It is best learned by a "hands-on" lesson from a trained health professional and should be done at the same time every month — preferably a few days after a period ends. Postmenopausal women can do BSE on the first or last day of each calendar month. One study found that even half an hour's BSE training greatly improved the skill of women in detecting small cancers (1–4 cm or 0.5–1.5 inches in size). The monthly examination gives many women a sense of mastery over their bodies. BSE dropouts say they forget, do it erratically, find it a hassle or are afraid of finding a lump. Some women hesitate to do BSE because they don't know what they're looking

BREAST SELF-EXAMINATION

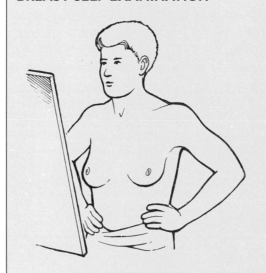

Examine breasts in mirror for any changes in shape, symmetry, nipple color or dimpling.

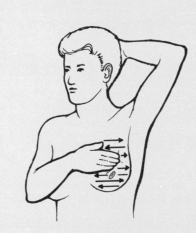

Use crosswise motion with fingers, pressing first lightly, then down to ribs, to feel any unusual lumps or thickening, while seated or standing.

Use similar movements across the chest while lying down, to feel anything unusual or something "asymmetrical" (present on one side but not on the other).

for. But its great advantage is that women get to know what the breasts normally feel like, so that changes will be noticed and can be promptly reported and evaluated.

What happens when a suspicious breast change or lump is found?

If a woman (or her partner) feels a lump, nodule or thickening in either breast, she should report it to her family physician or go to the nearest women's health clinic or breast-screening center for a thorough checkup. If there's any suspicion of cancer, a mammogram will be done. A biopsy will be ordered if either the physical exam or the mammogram suggests the possibility of cancer.

If the examination indicates a cyst, the liquid may be drawn out by fine needle aspiration, a swift, painless procedure done in a physician's office. Cysts are virtually always benign, but the fluid is sent for laboratory testing.

When the X-ray and other tests suggest the presence of breast cancer, the first step is to remove the suspicious area and examine it for malignancy.

Surgical biopsy — the removal of the whole lump or part of it — is essential to confirm the diagnosis of breast cancer. Most surgeons prefer to take out the whole lump for examination, especially if the area is small or difficult to locate. This is usually done as minor one-day surgery at a special clinic/center or hospital operating room. Local or general anes-

thesia may be used, depending on the size and depth of the lump. The material obtained can be frozen for immediate examination on the spot by a pathologist, or sent away for more accurate examination, which takes a few days. There is no danger in awaiting the lab results, nor is it necessary to proceed at once to further surgery. Only a small proportion of "suspicious lesions" biopsied will be cancer. Many women have several biopsies over a lifetime, without any of them being malignant. But even after a negative biopsy, women over 50 need regular screening, as they remain at high risk of breast cancer.

Breast surgery is now often done as a gentler "two-step" procedure

Previously, a woman with a suspicious breast lump or mammographic abnormalities was told that the area would be cut out and scanned for malignancy while she remained asleep on the operating table. If the lump was found to be cancerous, the whole breast would probably be removed. This one-step procedure meant that women would often be "put under" not knowing whether they'd awaken from the anesthetic with a small biopsy scar or with their entire breast gone. Nowadays things are different. The woman has the biopsy, awaits results and then decides together with her medical caregivers on the course of action. Instead of quick frozen sections being examined while the woman lies anesthetized, the suspicious tissue is removed and

DIFFERENT TYPES OF BREAST CANCER DEVELOP DIFFERENTLY

Breast cancer covers a wide spectrum of disease, in which some tumors metastasize (spread) fast, while others grow slowly. Some breast cancers rapidly penetrate nearby tissues — sometimes within months, especially in young women — while others take 10, 20 or more years to become invasive, or never

spread. (The term "invasive" doesn't necessarily mean that the cancer has already spread to other tissues, just that it's penetrated through the basement membrane of the breast cells.) And although many equate smallness with early cancer, small is not the same as early. A 1-cm (0.4-in) breast cancer has usually

been growing for several years before detection. Even a 0.5-cm (0.2-in) tumor, just detectable on a mammogram, has already doubled its cell numbers about 30 times, and scientists know that spreading can occur within the first 20 doublings of tumor cells. However, the risk of spread is generally less for

small tumors.

Experts stage breast cancers by size, the presence or absence of affected underarm nodes and biochemical markers that help to distinguish quick and aggressive from milder, slow-growing cancers. The growth of some breast cancers is supported by female hormones; that of others is not.

Very early, premalignant breast changes often appear in mammograms as tiny calcifications which, left alone, might become cancerous, but if removed in time may prevent cancer from ever developing. The early changes are termed carcinoma in situ — meaning "in place" and not invading adjacent tissue.

analyzed by "permanent section" analysis, which permits better evaluation. The tissue is analyzed for biochemical "markers" such as hormone receptors and other features that predict the possibility of recurrences, and help determine the best treatment. Delaying treatment by a few days does not worsen the outcome, and the two-step process gives women time to think over and discuss treatment options, and decide on the preferred therapy.

If the biopsy reveals cancer, further surgery may be needed to excise more tissue and remove the axillary (underarm) nodes to test them for malignancy. Additional postoperative treatment — which can include radiation of the breast to reduce local recurrences and systemic (whole body) chemotherapy — may also be advised.

When the mammogram, physical exam and needle biopsy all point to cancer, the surgery may still sometimes be done in one step, with the woman's fully informed consent.

Negative nodes are a good sign

Besides cutting out the cancer, surgeons dissect out the axillary (underarm) lymph nodes to look for signs of cancer. Modern experts prefer to do the axillary removal as a separate procedure after sewing up the first incision, for a better cosmetic result. If the underarm nodes test negative, showing no signs of malignancy, the chances are good for long, disease-free survival. Statistics show about 85 percent of node-negative patients alive and well five years after removal of a cancerous breast lump, and 70 percent doing well 10 years later. That's why it's essential for women to have their breasts regularly examined by professionals skilled in the art of cancer detection.

On the other hand, if some of the lymph nodes show positive signs of cancer, there is a higher risk of breast-cancer recurrence. Women who have had breast cancer aren't really free of recurrence risks for 15 or 20 years or more. Nonetheless, some women with ominous nodes at biopsy do survive for many decades.

Modern breast-cancer treatment choices

Modern breast-sparing operations are far less drastic than the traditional, radical or Halsted mastectomy, which removed the entire breast and a large section of underlying muscle, leaving the chest sunken and the arm possibly swollen and weakened. Today's cancer operations include:

- *"extended simple"* or *"modified radical"* mastectomy — removing the whole breast and some underarm lymph nodes, but no underlying muscle;
- *"simple total mastectomy"* — removing breast only (but no underarm nodes);
- *"partial"* mastectomy or lumpectomy — removing just the tumor and its surrounding margins; lumpectomy, with removal of underarm nodes, followed by post-surgical radiation, is now increasingly the norm.

The choice depends on the size and type of tumor, the breast's shape and size, the stage of the cancer and its position in the breast.

Today's breast-cancer therapy employs a two-pronged attack:

- *first*, local control by surgery, removing either the lump alone or the whole breast; either operation is usually accompanied by removal of underarm lymph nodes, with radiation to the operated breast after lumpectomy;
- *second*, systemic (bodily) control with chemotherapy and/or hormones to destroy any cancer cells that may have escaped from the breast to other parts of the body.

Survival rates are the same for lumpectomy and mastectomy

Recent studies show no difference in survival times between total breast removal and lump removal only, for very early cancers. Lumpectomy is considered just as effective and is now increasingly replacing mastectomy, with radiation to the operated breast afterward to minimize local recurrences.

Dissection to remove some axillary or underarm lymph nodes and test them for cancer usually accompanies all forms of breast-cancer surgery. The axillary operation is generally done via a separate incision for a neater look. Once there are signs of malignancy in the underarm lymph nodes, there's a strong likelihood that tumor cells have also reached other parts of the body, requiring drug treatment to kill any escaped cancer cells (as well

---

POSSIBLE WAYS TO REDUCE THE RISK OF DYING FROM BREAST CANCER

- **Report any visible changes in the size, contour or shape of the breast to a health professional; report any changes in the color or texture of the nipple(s), also any oozing or discharge and any new skin dimpling.**
- **Have regular physical breast examinations by qualified health professionals, perhaps at a breast diagnostic center.**
- **If over age 50, get regular mammograms.**
- **Learn from a qualified expert and practice BSE if comfortable with it.**
- **Maintain normal body weight and exercise regularly, starting before adolescence.**
- **Breastfeed your babies — which may reduce risks if done for at least two cumulative years (and is good for the baby).**
- **Remember that, while having breast cancer may be bad, it's worse to have it unidentified and growing bigger without knowing about it.**

as local treatment such as surgery and/or breast radiation).

After surgery, women are often referred for further advice to a medical oncologist (cancer specialist) and/or a radiation oncologist, or to a specialized cancer center. A thorough discussion determines the most suitable follow-up. Since treatment strategies vary from center to center, women with breast cancer should seek advice from the most knowledgeable, up-to-date experts around, and above all from someone they trust. If not satisfied, get a second opinion.

Whatever breast operation is done, the threat of recurrence hangs like the Sword of Damocles over all women who've ever had the disease. The chief problem in breast cancer is not local recurrence but distant spread. That's why breast cancer is now regarded as a potentially systemic disease that can affect the whole body and must be treated accordingly. Since only systemic therapy can stop distant cancer cells from growing into tumors, postoperative drug therapy is now increasingly used. Many women with breast cancer can thus expect to get chemotherapy to kill distant cancer cells.

Postoperative drug treatment, formerly reserved for advanced metastatic disease, is now routinely offered to all node-positive women with breast cancer, and sometimes also to node-negative cases. A recent alert from the U.S. National Cancer Institute recommends that node-negative women with breast cancer also consider the possibility of chemotherapy or hormone treatment.

Although the diagnosis of breast cancer is a devastating experience, most women face up to it well, and cope with it. In fact, studies show that many respond with renewed enjoyment of life and stronger interpersonal ties. There's an inevitable period of adjustment, but it's usually improved by knowing as much as possible about the disease. British studies have shown that the more accurate information women are given, in a supportive manner, the better they can face and adapt to this condition, and the better able they are to make acceptable decisions with which they can live. Women given sparse information in a curt, abrupt manner, who don't partake as much in the decision-

making, are less able to deal with what happens than those given ample information.

Postoperative treatments: who needs what?

- *Radiation* is now usual in women who have lumpectomies, generally five days a week for three to five weeks. Each session lasts a few minutes, with an initial planning session to determine the suitable site and dose of radiation. Radiation implants, inserted during surgery and left in for a few days, are an alternative. There are few aftereffects of radiation apart from a little skin redness (like a sunburn) and possible fatigue toward the end of the course.
- *Chemotherapy* uses various cytotoxic (cancer-killing) agents in an attempt to eradicate cancer cells that have spread. Since anti-cancer drugs also affect not only nearby healthy tissue but also the whole body, side effects may include transient nausea, hair loss, insomnia, sexual disturbances, fatigue, a lowered white-blood-cell count and, understandably, anxiety. Newer drugs produce fewer side effects. Many women can go on working and exercising through their chemotherapy course.
- *Hormonal therapy* has been tried for many years to impede the growth of certain breast cancers. Strategies include removal of the ovaries, adrenals and/or pituitary glands as well as administration of competitive anti-hormonal agents or anti-estrogens, such as LHRH (luteinizing hormone-releasing hormones) analogues and anti-progestins (e.g., RU-486).
- *Tamoxifen,* a powerful weapon against breast cancer, is now the mainstay of hormonal therapy. It's a well-tolerated, synthetic anti-estrogen with few side effects, increasingly used even for node-negative cases. Over 30 studies have convincingly shown that tamoxifen can improve disease-free and/or overall survival in postmenopausal women with hormone-sensitive tumors. Although its exact mechanism isn't clear, tamoxifen seems to act as both a weak female hormone and an anti-estrogen, blocking the hormone's cancer-promoting effects.

Support by family and friends is a key element in helping those with breast cancer, the influence being strongest with support from friends, colleagues and health professionals. "Above all," advises one specialist, "women should ask many questions, select medical advisors they trust and be prepared to seek a second opinion, as therapy varies from place to place." Participation in clinical trials is also encouraged. Ideally, women should enter clinical trials rather than be treated on an *ad hoc* basis, to help define the best possible future treatment.

Breast reconstruction

Breast reconstruction, using either a woman's own tissues or synthetic silicone implants, has become increasingly popular for life after mastectomy. Breast restoration can even be done many years after mastectomy. Any woman contemplating breast replacement should have a full, frank discussion about its merits, including a complete rundown of the techniques available, their failings and advantages, and should recognize that the results aren't predictable. While some surgeons do breast removal and reconstruction at the same time, others rebuild the breast after a delay of six months to two years following mastectomy. The interval allows the incision to heal well, gives time to complete any postoperative radiation or drug therapy and permits any local recurrences to be more easily detected. One University of Toronto surgeon notes that in his experience, "after the recommended wait, about half the women contemplating breast reconstruction decide against it, having come to terms with their disease, gotten used to living without a breast, feeling good about themselves and unwilling to face more surgery. Many women learn to live happily with only one or half a breast, feeling quite at ease with a removable form worn under their clothing."

Women vary widely in their wish for breast reconstruction. Some women, knowing the many drawbacks of post-mastectomy implants (those still on the market!), refuse to buy into the myth equating beauty with breasts. After weighing up the odds they decide against reconstruction. They may find that the brush with mortality clarifies their priorities, diminishes the

---

THE CHIEF WORRIES ABOUT SILICONE BREAST IMPLANTS

- **They may hinder detection of recurrent cancer in the reconstructed breast, a diminishing risk as detection methods improve.**
- **Smooth types may harden and give discomfort and a deformed look, requiring one or more corrective operations.**
- **Breakage and/or fluid leakage from the implant which necessitates repeat surgery or removal (to prevent problems** from the gel inside the implant).
- **None has the erotic sensitivity of normal breast tissue.**
- **The covering of foam-covered types may fragment and release harmful chemicals that could cause cancer.**

   The introduction of a polyurethane foam coating on silicone implants in the 1970s helped to overcome the hardening and frequent need for repeat surgery so common with smooth-walled implants. But foam-covered implants have possible ill effects, are more difficult to insert and remove in case of need than smooth types and are currently banned pending further research. At present, all gel-filled silicone breast implants are banned, except under special circumstances. Saline-filled implants are still available.

---

importance of superficial appearances and heightens the awareness that a woman's attractiveness stems not so much from breasts as from innate qualities. However, other women urgently desire breast replacement. The loss of a breast may trigger feelings of being "less than whole" and despair at having to wear a prosthesis — a depression known as the post-mastectomy syndrome. Some women consider themselves less sexually attractive without an intact breast. For them, breast reconstruction reinstates their body image, immensely improving their lives.

One increasingly popular restoration technique, which overcomes the many drawbacks of silicone implants, uses solely the woman's own tissue to fashion a new breast from muscle and skin taken from the chest wall, buttocks, or, more usually, from the lower abdomen — by the "tummy tuck" or abdominal flap operation. A flap is removed from the abdominal wall (from the "roll" often seen when seated) and placed into the defective chest area, providing the skin, fat and muscle to model a new breast. A new nipple may later be created using tissue from the unoperated side (or other skin flaps) and tattoo dyes to get the right look. Very lean women, smokers and those with chronic lung or heart ailments aren't suitable candidates for this type of operation.

Men's special health concerns

Trouble with the prostate • Prostate cancer • Infertility • Remedying sex problems • The circumcision controversy

9

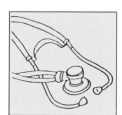

MEN'S HEALTH PROBlems tend to get less publicity than women's, but are equally worrisome to those afflicted. Men are often less well informed about health issues than women, who have traditionally been the "custodians" of family health. Men tend to find it very difficult to admit health problems — particularly those associated with sex or reproduction — to family or friends (or sometimes even to doctors). Perhaps this is because their sexual potency has popularly been seen as the foundation of "manhood." It may also be that — unlike women, who routinely deal with menstruation and all the concerns and procedures of childbirth — they just don't expect anything to "go wrong." Yet early recognition of problems and open discussion of them with health professionals are essential for prompt and effective treatment.

TROUBLE WITH THE PROSTATE

Of men's health concerns, prostate troubles are among the least known but most common. In fact, prostate troubles may be almost as prevalent and aggravating to older men as male balding, although less innocuous. Prostate enlargement causes urination difficulties in 80 percent of men over age 60, and prostate cancer is now the second leading cause of cancer deaths (after lung cancer) in Canadian men.

Unfortunately, despite rising prostate-cancer rates, many physicians don't routinely check for nodules and lumps in the prostate — done with a gloved finger through the rectum. And men may not welcome or suggest the examination. Most men may hardly even know where their prostate is, remaining barely aware of its presence until it becomes painfully inflamed or enlarged, and obstructs urination or causes other problems.

Found only in males, the prostate gland is a walnut-sized organ situated like a collar under the bladder, directly above the scrotum. The gland surrounds the urethra — the tube that carries urine from the bladder out of the body — and can be beset by three disorders: prostatitis — inflammation and/or infection; prostatic hyperplasia — overgrowth or enlargement; and cancer.

The chief known function of the human prostate is its contribution to seminal fluid; it produces enzymes that help to liquefy semen and keep sperm moist, mobile and healthy. It also secretes antibacterials such as zinc spermine and spermidine, which give seminal fluid its characteristic odor.

Prostatitis — usually a young man's complaint

Often of unknown origin, prostatitis (prostate inflammation) affects about 50 percent of men at least once in a lifetime. It can occur at any age, but usually afflicts men aged 19 to 40. Myths about prostatitis abound. The condition was once blamed on celibacy and dubbed the "priest's disease." Sexual activity was, and often still is, falsely viewed as an antidote that "prevents semen from stagnating." In fact, the disorder strikes sexually active and inactive men alike. While scientific proof is lacking, prostate inflammation has also been linked to prolonged inactivity, long periods of sitting, and too much alcohol and coffee.

Although prostatitis is occasionally due to a bacterial infection, 95 percent of cases are nonbacterial (sterile) inflammations with no traceable cause, making the condition hard to treat. Diagnosis involves analysis and culture of a midstream urine sample containing some semen (obtained by stroking or massaging the prostate via the rectum to release some into the bladder).

Men with nonbacterial prostatitis have vague discomfort in the groin, ejaculatory pain, erectile problems and perhaps abdominal pain and backache. Complaints are often voiced as "a pain down there" or "crotch ache." Sufferers report burning on urination, a need to urinate often — especially at night — and occasionally a discharge. (The discharge frequently sends men to see their physician.) On examination, the prostate may be slightly sore. Although there's no identifiable infection, men with this ailment are understandably worried about their potency, sex life and fertility. The trouble is that nonbacterial prostatitis may linger on for long periods. Some experts suggest this is because of low zinc levels, but zinc supplements do not alleviate the condition. Although laboratory tests and cystoscopy (looking into the bladder with an instrument put through the penis) find no infective source, some men may be "silent" carriers of chlamydia, yeasts or other undetected infections (for more information on these, see chapter 7). Others may have mechanical

MALE REPRODUCTIVE ORGANS

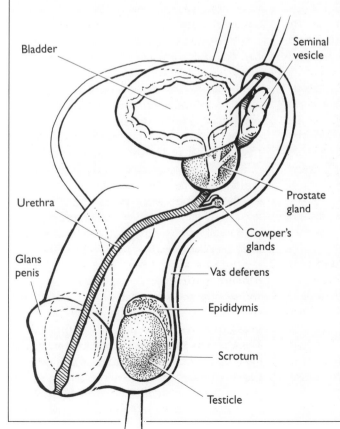

Bladder

Seminal vesicle

Urethra

Prostate gland

Cowper's glands

Glans penis

Vas deferens

Epididymis

Scrotum

Testicle

The urethra, a single tube running from the bladder through the penis, conveys both urine and semen out of the body, but not at the same time! When semen is ejaculated, the muscles surrounding the bladder contract and close off its opening so that urine cannot escape during intercourse (or masturbation).

The testes inside the testicles produce sperm, but it takes time for the sperm to mature through several complex processes. Mature sperm gather in the epididymis (tubes located behind the testicles in the scrotum that are amazingly long about 6 m (20 ft) in length each, but twisted into a small area). Sperm cells take several weeks to work their way through the epididymis, traveling into the vas deferens — one for each testicle — and from there to the seminal vesicles for storage. Small ejaculatory ducts, running through the prostate gland into the urethra, carry sperm out of the body during ejaculation.

The prostate gland surrounds the urethra and produces some seminal fluid.

The paired, sac-like seminal vesicles behind the prostate produce 70 percent of the seminal fluid or semen, which contains sugars that supply the energy that allows sperm to swim through the female reproductive tract. Both the seminal vesicles and the prostate gland continuously secrete fluid into the ejaculatory duct, but more is produced during intercourse. Scientists believe that semen contains other chemicals that help sperm swim vigorously.

Cowper's glands, a pair of pea-sized glands at the base of the penis, secrete some clear, alkaline fluid into the urethra during sexual arousal to neutralize the acidic environment of the female genital tract, which can harm sperm. (Even without vaginal penetration, secretions from Cowper's glands may leak from a partially erect penis, carrying enough sperm to cause pregnancy if the secretions touch the vagina or moist vulva.)

bladder dysfunction, perhaps a reflux of seminal fluid back into the prostate. Some may have "psychogenic" prostatitis caused by stress, anxiety or depression.

Given no specific cause, there is little physicians can do other than suggest warm sitz baths, and provide reassurance. The condition may vanish on its own, respond to antibiotics or return time and again. Nonbacterial prostatitis is harmless and usually "burns itself out," the only real danger being antibiotic overuse. Even though no infective agent is found, most cases are treated with antibiotics, usually tetracycline, doxycycline or trimethoprim-sulfamethoxazole (Septra or Bactrim), which may inexplicably clear it up. If the problem returns, antibiotics plus lots of reassurance may again succeed.

Acute bacterial prostatitis can be prostrating!

While rare, this type of prostatitis is easy to diagnose and treat. Proliferation of bacteria in the bladder or urethra leads to dramatic flu-like symptoms and sepsis (blood infection). Swelling, heat and pain in the prostate are its hallmarks. The pain may radiate up from the base of the penis, perhaps with burning on urination. There is usually a fever, possibly high. A cloudy discharge or uncontrollable drip from the penis and murky urine are typical. On rectal examination, the prostate is excruciatingly sensitive. The condition can lead to an abscess and the formation of small, gravelly stones if left untreated. Once identified, the invading bacteria can usually be eliminated with antibiotics. A catheter (voiding tube) may be inserted to assist bladder emptying.

A recurrent or lingering prostate infection, typified by urination difficulties — frequency, urgency and sometimes low backache — is a rare but hard-to-eradicate disorder. Even when the bacteria have been identified, their complete elimination often requires special antibiotics.

Prostate enlargement is very common with aging

Prostate growth depends on male hormones, mainly testosterone. When testosterone levels are low, during childhood, a boy's prostate remains small — a weight of about one gram (0.04 oz). But with the increased release of testosterone at puberty, the prostate gland enlarges. By age 20 it normally weighs about 15 grams (0.53 oz), staying that size until middle age. After age 45 to 50, the prostate often undergoes a growth spurt and swells to three times its previous size — sometimes even becoming lemon-sized. By age 50, almost 20 percent of men have an expanded prostate; by age 70 the figure is 50 percent, and by age 80 enlargement is almost universal. However, some prostates become extra big — even the size of a grapefruit. About 20 percent of men over age 65 require prostate treatment at some point .

Prostate enlargement (prostatic hyperplasia) doesn't inevitably spell trouble, but it can cause problems because the gland is located in an anatomically vulnerable spot — just where the urethra leaves the bladder. A bulky, enlarged or inflamed prostate can obstruct urination. Some urine may remain in the bladder, creating a stagnant buildup that predisposes the bladder to infection and may lead to incontinence. If urine accumulates, it may affect the kidneys, producing temporary malfunction and, in extreme cases, renal (kidney) failure. Occasionally, complete obstruction halts all urination. Known as acute retention, this is a painful emergency situation that requires immediate hospital attention and catheterization (removal of urine with a tube). Prostate expansion can also cause cystitis (bladder infection), requiring antibiotic treatment matched to the bacteria responsible.

Prostate enlargement is detected by a digital (finger) rectal examination, X-rays, ultrasound and blood and urine tests. If no difficulties occur, the condition may be left untreated, but still carefully monitored for obstruction, cancer or urinary backflow.

Modern methods to shrink enlarged prostates

Until recently, surgery was the only known way to relieve problems due to an enlarged prostate. The standard treatment for prostatic enlargement used to be simple: cut away the excess tissue. Although prostate surgery remains a leading operation among older men, an array of alternative treatments is now available to shrink the prostate, including radiation, drugs, balloons and even microwaves. New drugs can shrink the prostate and avoid surgery for some.

The course of prostate enlargement is unpredictable; some men with very enlarged prostates have few or no symptoms, while others with smaller glands have severe urination difficulties. In the absence of troubling symptoms it's probably best to take a wait-and-see approach, and carefully watch the condition with your physician.

If surgery is needed, it can now often be done through the urethra itself by transurethral prostatectomy (TURP) — a method that removes the obstruction but not the entire gland. This surgery is not trivial, although it is usually quick and carries no undue risks. A thin tube with a telescopic viewer is passed through the urethra to the prostate and a cauterizer (attachment for burning tissue) removes pieces of the obtruding prostate. This procedure, now employed for over 90 percent of enlarged prostates, spares men the trauma of a full surgical incision, allowing swift recovery. A desk-worker may be back at the job within a week.

However, there are some drawbacks to TURP — namely, postoperative infection and erectile failure (in about 5–10 percent of men operated on) and sterility, a frequent postoperative complication. Another postoperative complication is incontinence, in 1 percent of cases. While prostate reduction or removal often makes men sterile, it need not make them impotent, since the nerves that regulate erections can remain untouched. Potency generally returns within a few weeks or months. But even if the operation does not touch the mechanism responsible for erection, some men find their sex lives unsatisfactory after prostate surgery — probably because of anxiety or emotional problems, which may be reversible with the help of a good sex therapist .

The older method of major surgery for prostate removal (retropubic prostatectomy) is now reserved for greatly enlarged glands.

Alternative hormonal methods to shrink the prostate are being developed. In the prostate, the male hormone testosterone is converted to dihydrotestosterone, a more

THE ALERTING SIGNS OF PROSTATE ENLARGEMENT

- urgency (an urgent, intense need to urinate);
- increased frequency (need to urinate often);
- nocturia — a need to urinate at night;
- a weak, sluggish urine stream;
- difficulty in getting urination started;
- "stuttering" — a dribble of urine that starts and stops;
- residual leakage and/or dribbling;
- reduced ability to hold urine (incontinence);
- buildup of urine in the bladder, which may harbor bacteria;
- cystitis (bladder infection);
- acute urinary retention (if urethra is completely blocked);
- formation of calcium stones in the bladder;
- kidney problems due to the backup of urine, with possible renal (kidney) damage.

powerful hormone that regulates the gland's growth. A new drug called finasteride (Proscar) blocks this metabolic process without affecting testosterone levels, and can actually shrink the prostate. Another drug, an alpha blocker called terazosin (Hytrin), "relaxes" the prostate and can improve urinary flow. Either drug is taken once daily, perhaps for life, as symptoms return if the drugs are stopped. But the drugs don't suffice in men with severely enlarged prostates. About a third of those with prostate enlargement still need surgery.

Castration — removing the testes to eliminate testosterone — used to be done to shrink the prostate. A more recent method is to use leuprolide acetate (Lupron), given by daily injection for six months, which can shrink the prostate considerably by blocking the release of pituitary LH (luteinizing hormone), which triggers testosterone production. Half the men on Lupron experience symptom relief, but the sexually active may lose erectile capacity during treatment. Erections return once the drug is discontinued.

PROSTATE CANCER

Prostate cancer currently affects 8 percent of Canadian men — somewhat behind breast cancer in women — and causes 2,000 deaths a year. The risks of this cancer increase with advancing years, especially after age 50.

The good news is that prostate cancer usually grows very slowly and, as one eminent clinician puts it, "many more men die with prostate cancer than of it." Autopsy studies

DETECTION METHODS FOR PROSTATE CANCER

- Digital (finger) rectal examination (DRE) with a gloved finger, the oldest, easiest and quickest test, is painless and takes just a minute. Although it's still the main detection tool, DRE misses about a third to a half of prostate cancers because they are beyond the finger's reach. Only about one-third of suspicious prostate nodules or thickenings prove to be cancerous on biopsy, giving a high "false positive" rate for DRE. One Swedish study showed that although prostate cancer was suspected in 45 of 1,163 men aged 50–69, it was confirmed only in 13.
- Ultrasound prostate exams are done abdominally, via the urethra, or by trans-rectal ultrasound (TRUS) with a small probe. Improved ultrasound can now find some small tumors not felt digitally, but ultrasound detects only about 75 percent of cases, still missing a quarter of the prostate cancers felt by physicians' fingers. The Canadian Task Force on Periodic Health Examination considers ultrasound too unreliable and false results too frequent to make it a good routine test in symptom-free men.
- Blood tests for prostate-specific tumor markers include an older, less sensitive one for prostatic acid phosphatase (PAP) and a more accurate prostate-specific-antigen (PSA) test developed in 1979. However, as PSA levels may be elevated even with a non-cancerous enlarged prostate, most experts consider this marker too inaccurate for routine screening in symptom-free men. But combined with other tests, PSA levels do help to establish the diagnosis.
- Combined screening tests, using all three methods, are more efficient than any one test alone. If the rectal exam is positive there's a 30–50 percent chance of prostate cancer being present, but if both rectal and blood tests are positive, there's a 70 percent chance of prostate cancer. If all three tests — rectal, blood (PSA) and ultrasound — are abnormal, there's a high likelihood of cancer. Therefore some health agencies suggest sequential screening — routinely doing rectal and blood PSA tests, which are quick, easy and cheap, followed by ultrasound if either comes out abnormal. If all three tests are positive, a biopsy follows. One University of Toronto expert points out that "many urologists believe in screening all men over age 50 at routine visits with rectal and PSA blood tests, followed by ultrasound if either of these two is positive. Even if the ultrasound exam shows nothing (as happens in 20 percent of men with prostate cancer) but the blood PSA is up, some urologists suggest a biopsy."
- Biopsy — the "gold standard" test — takes a core of cells from the suspicious area of the prostate via the rectum or urethra. Biopsy is simplified by new techniques such as fine-needle aspiration, a spring-driven biopsy gun, and transrectal testing (removing tissue through the rectum) — a painless office procedure done without anesthetic.

reveal that latent (unsuspected) prostate cancer (producing no symptoms or detrimental health effects) exists at death in about 50 percent of men over 70 years old and 40 percent of men over age 60. Risks also increase for those with close male relatives who had prostate cancer — double if one close family member had it, and ten times higher if two close relatives suffered from it.

Symptoms of prostate cancer
Prostate cancer produces no symptoms in about a third of those who have it, and may be accidentally discovered (felt as a hard nodule) during a routine rectal examination or when treating prostate enlargement. Prostate cancer varies greatly in its progression and aggressivity, rarely producing symptoms in its early stages. If any symptoms do appear, they resemble those of benign prostate enlargement: urination difficulties, perhaps blood in the urine. By the time it is found, prostate cancer has often spread to the lymph nodes, bones or other areas, and bone pain, typically in the back or legs, may be its first alerting sign. But since prostate cancer often remains dormant, it often needs no more than observation. For example, early prostate cancer in a 78-year-old man with an estimated eight-year life expectancy may not warrant the distress of surgery, while a similar cancer found in a younger man, say at age 65, would likely be removed to prolong survival.

Treatment choices for prostate cancer
No treatment but a "watch-and-wait" approach is usually suggested for elderly men with small tumors and a life expectancy under 10 years. Younger men with cancer confined to the

prostate may be given a choice of no treatment (just observation), surgical removal, radiation (usually daily, on an outpatient basis, for five to six weeks) or combination therapy using anti-hormonal agents. Most authorities consider radical prostatectomy (complete prostate removal) and radiation the most effective form of treatment for tumors limited to the prostate. Provided the cancer has not yet invaded other areas, removing the prostate is the usual strategy for those who are not too old, too sick or too frail to tolerate surgery.

Prostate cancer treatment remains controversial. Prostate removal doesn't guarantee a cure if tumors have already metastasized (spread); cancers that have not spread may never do so. Surgery carries some risks, as well as possible post-surgical consequences: bladder weakness, incontinence and impotence. Improved surgical techniques now manage to avoid postoperative erectile problems by saving the nerve that controls erection in about 60 percent of cases. And if the cancer is caught early enough, survival rates are good.

Hormone treatments for prostate cancer that has spread used to involve high doses of female hormones, a method largely going out of fashion because of its feminizing effects. New synthetic anti-androgens with less drastic side effects include:

• LHRH analogues such as goserelin (Zoladex) given as monthly injections. LHRH analogues have few side effects other than a slightly diminished sex drive, but only shrink androgen-dependent tumors;

• nonsteroidal anti-androgens, some of which don't terminate potency, are being tried, with varying success.

Therapies that offer promise for prostate cancer but have yet to be evaluated include laser and light therapy, high energy shock-wave treatment and microwave coagulation of the tumor (still purely experimental).

INFERTILITY

Spermatogenesis (sperm production) occurs in the testes by a process not yet fully understood, although it's known that sperm take about six weeks to mature fully. Sperm maturation is controlled by hormones from the brain's *hypothalamus* and pituitary gland (similar to ovulation control in women) and by testicular secretions and the male hormone testosterone. Pituitary FSH (follicle-stimulating hormone) stimulates sperm formation while ICSH (interstitial-cell-stimulating hormone) promotes testosterone production — vital to sperm health, male potency and successful ejaculation.

The path from penis to fallopian tube is a perilous one for sperm, and millions of sperm per ejaculate (average volume — three to five ml, or less than a teaspoon) are required to achieve fertilization, because so many perish *en route* and so many are needed to assist one sperm in penetrating the egg's tough outer barrier. They must traverse the vagina — inhospitable because it's acidic, and sperm prefer an alkaline environment — and then go from the vagina through the cervix and uterus and up to the fallopian tube, where the egg is on its way down the tube to the uterus. Conception can take place in the tubes or in the uterus, but generally occurs in the lower part of the fallopian tube or just inside the uterus. Only one sperm will usually pierce and fertilize the egg. Any sperm that has the slightest imperfection usually falls by the wayside.

The main causes of infertility in men

Other than anatomical abnormalities, the main causes of infertility in men are insufficient or poor quality sperm. The Canadian Fertility Society estimates that sperm counts vary from 60 to 300 million sperm per ejaculate. (Sperm banks require a minimum sperm count of 100 million sperm per ml [about one-quarter teaspoon], but that is because the freezing process destroys some.) A sperm count below 20 million per ml is considered unlikely to achieve fertilization. But even though they have too low a sperm count to count as "fertile," there are isolated cases on record of men with only two to five million sperm per ejaculate siring babies.

A low sperm count or sperm of inferior quality may arise because of problems in the testes. If excretory ducts are blocked, damaged or absent there may be plenty of sperm, but they may not be delivered to the woman's vagina. Sometimes the problem is premature ejaculation. All too often the roots of male infertility remain a mystery.

Various factors may aggravate infertility in men who are marginally subfertile:

- excess alcohol consumption;
- post-pubertal mumps (if there is orchitis — painful testicular inflammation);
- undescended testes;
- overheating of the genitals due to tight clothing, long spells of sitting, too many saunas or hot baths (a cool temperature favors sperm survival);
- drugs that diminish sperm count, such as anti-hypertensives (blood pressure drugs) or

marijuana (which distorts sperm and reduces their quality).

REMEDYING SEX PROBLEMS

Sexual dysfunction in men may involve transient or recurrent problems with the desire, arousal, erectile or orgasmic phase of the human sexual response. Sex problems can be occasional or long term, depending on their origins. While many sex disorders in men may start with an organic cause, most also have psychological dimensions. An array of new drugs and devices, together with counseling, can often overcome sexual difficulties.

Alcohol and sex

Although alcohol may relax a man and put him "in the mood" for sex, at the same time it can make him unable to have or sustain an erection; as Shakespeare noted in *Macbeth*, drink "provokes the desire, but it takes away the performance." The problem may become circular — fearing some permanent disability or organic disease, the man may undergo intense anxiety, and may be afraid to attempt intercourse without the reassurance of the alcohol which is causing the problem!

Chronic alcohol use may be associated with even more persistent problems. People who down large volumes of liquor, or come home from work to pour themselves several drinks and collapse into the comfort of mental and physical detumescence, may not be able to develop stable sexual relationships. Other characteristics associated with problem drinking — such as bellicose behavior and hangovers — will also make long-term relationships very difficult. If alcohol is suspected as the cause of erectile problems, alcohol counseling should be sought without delay, followed by sex therapy.

Tests for erectile capacity

For men who can't achieve or keep an erection, the first priority is a complete medical exam and tests to rule out hormone deficiencies, treatable diseases, alcoholism or the influence of medications. In trying to distinguish organic from psychological reasons, physicians also do a psychological work-up insofar as is possible. They ask whether the erectile difficulty

BLOOD SUPPLY TO THE PENIS

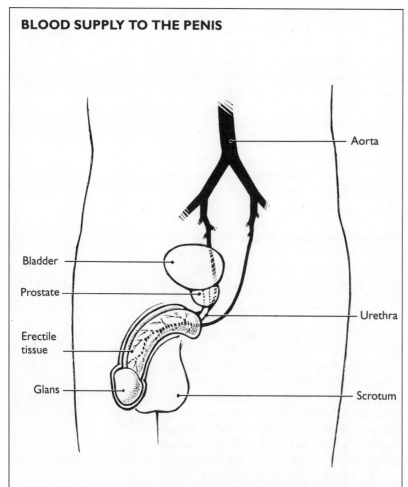

In order for a penis to attain and maintain erection, its arteries, veins and nerves must be in good working order and able to engorge the penis with blood. Psychoerotic or physical stimulation acting on the brain will increase blood flow in the penis, making its spongy (corporal) tissues fill with blood and expand into an erection.

came on suddenly (suggesting psychological factors) or gradually (suggesting physical reasons), whether it is always a problem or only sometimes, whether it occurs with masturbation too, only during waking hours or also at night. Specialized tests can determine whether or not a man is capable of having an erection. (If he can get an erection when intercourse is not the purpose, the problem is likely psychological.)

SOME SEXUAL DISORDERS IN MEN

- *Sex problems in the desire stage* mean an inability to become sexually interested in a partner, sometimes because busy, overscheduled men don't have the time or occasion to relax and enjoy sex. Sex aversion — an extreme form of sexual disinterest — may involve fear of any sexual intimacy, usually with deep-seated psychological origins, often requiring intensive psychotherapy.

- *Sexual dysfunction in the arousal or excitement phase* is the inability to become aroused, perhaps because of negative parental attitudes to sex, an unpleasant early sexual experience, sex abuse, an off-putting relationship, misinformation or performance pressure. Sex therapy is usually the solution.

- *Dyspareunia* — genital pain before, during and/or after intercourse — may be due to penile vascular problems or a tight foreskin that won't retract during intercourse. It can also arise for psychological reasons. The problem needs medical attention and is often easily remediable.

- *Early or premature ejaculation*, afflicting 30 percent of men at some time or other, is an orgasmic disorder where men ejaculate sooner than they wish to. It arises from inadequate control over the precise timing of ejaculation and the responses that trigger it, or because of infrequent ejaculation — if the man hasn't had sex for a while. One sex therapist explains that it often happens if men "lose touch" with their orgasmic sensations: "Timing ejaculation at will is a learned art and takes practice." The disorder is often remedied by more frequent ejaculation (whether by intercourse or masturbation) and appropriate individual or couple therapy.

- *Inhibited male orgasm* (IMO) is the inability to achieve orgasm during intercourse. Men with IMO often manage to ejaculate and reach orgasm by masturbation but not with vaginal intercourse. Some therapists believe IMO stems from fear of intercourse, an unwillingness to perform on demand or anxiety about not satisfying a partner. A man may find his orgasm inhibited because he fears loss of control during intercourse, because he's put off by a woman's touch or, in some instances, because he does not want to have sex with one particular woman. This type of sexual dysfunction is more difficult to treat than premature ejaculation, often requiring intensive psychotherapy.

- *Erectile dysfunction* — previously called impotence — is defined as the "inability or waning ability to achieve and sustain an erection for the purpose of sexual intercourse," and afflicts many men at some time or other. (The term "impotence" has now been dropped because of its pejorative connotations.) Accurate statistics on male erectile troubles are elusive. One study reports that as many as 16 percent (another says 34 percent) of healthy young men in their prime have occasional erectile failure. Manufacturing companies who supply erectile devices estimate that one in ten men has erectile difficulties at some point. An array of new drugs, devices and surgical procedures can now help to overcome the problem of achieving an erection.

  Once thought to be "all in the head" or, as Sigmund Freud put it, of "psychic origin," erectile dysfunction is no longer considered to be purely psychological. But while organic reasons underlie some types of erectile dysfunction, the problem usually also has psychological overtones. In older men, well over half of the erectile difficulties experienced have contributory physical causes — such as diabetes, atherosclerosis, hormone imbalance, smoking, alcohol consumption, obesity or the use of certain medications (particularly blood-pressure pills). But since sexuality is complex, erectile competence too is complicated. Failure to achieve erection because of a physical cause is often worsened by anxiety. Sometimes what starts out as a sporadic organic dysfunction develops into a psychological hang-up owing to performance fears, and may tip the scales into non-erection. For example, a man with atherosclerotic buildup ("hardening") in his penile arteries may experience occasional erectile failure, which in turn leads to anxiety about nonperformance, exacerbating the problem.

REASONS FOR ERECTILE FAILURE

Physical or organic reasons:

- medical disorders such as kidney impairment, liver cirrhosis, prostate disorders, alcoholism, Peyronie's disease (curvature of the penis), Parkinson's disease, multiple sclerosis and diabetes (many young diabetics experience erectile problems);
- endocrine (hormonal) imbalances such as low testosterone output, thyroid disorders, hyperprolactinemia (excess prolactin hormone), Cushing's syndrome and other adrenal-gland disorders;
- neurological problems such as spinal-cord injury;
- surgery for the prostate gland, bladder or rectum, which may damage the nerves responsible for erection;
- blood vessel disorders that restrict penile blood flow, such as artery-narrowing due to atherosclerosis, or veins that don't clamp off properly to maintain erection (penile veins that don't close off allow blood to drain out and cause penile collapse — a condition sometimes reparable by surgery);
- smoking tobacco — a major reason for erectile failure — because nicotine causes spasms in small penile arteries and also leads to atherosclerosis;
- alcohol — another major cause — because it affects blood flow and acts on brain centers with effects that impede the ability to hold an erection. In addition, alcohol has a "feminizing" effect on the male hormone system so that long-term use may destroy erectile capacity. Heavy drinking lowers testerone levels, diminishes male sex drive and effectively "castrates" men, causing erectile dysfunction. Alcohol also triggers conversion of androgens (male sex hormones) to estrogens (female sex hormones) sometimes causing hair loss and breast enlargement. Excess alcohol may eventually cause atrophy (shrinkage) of the testes and impair the mechanism that shunts blood into the penis (see "Alcohol and sex," above).
- a long list of medications including antihistamines, antipsychotics, antidepressants, marijuana, minor tranquilizers, anticancer drugs, cimetidine (a stomach-ulcer drug), muscle relaxants and especially antihypertensives (blood-pressure medications). As many as 40 percent of men on diuretics and other blood-pressure pills have erectile problems. They should consult their family physician; perhaps other drugs can be prescribed instead. Switching the medication often reverses the problem.

Psychological reasons:

- depression, anger, stress, fatigue, guilt, performance anxiety, job loss or impending exams;
- childhood experiences of parental conflict, sex abuse or disapproving, unjoyful attitudes to sex;
- a negative sex encounter that leaves a man full of self-doubts even though he may be perfectly capable of attaining an erection; feelings of inadequacy may make him hesitate to attempt intercourse. The longer such anxiety lingers, the greater the chance of a persistent sex problem;
- lack of privacy (at home or in student quarters);
- poor communication with a partner, lack of intimacy, fear of causing pregnancy, divergent views on what constitutes a happy sex life and varying perceptions of "normality."

- *The nocturnal penile tumescence* test is a recent innovation that avoids the need for hospital investigation. It tests the occurrence and frequency of nighttime erections. Most men normally have several erections nightly, related to different sleep stages. The nocturnal penile tumescence test simply consists of wrapping a bit of tape with small string binders around the penis while the man sleeps. If the tiny strings holding the tape together break at night, the man is clearly capable of erection, ruling out an organic cause.
- *Measuring penile activity in men watching erotic videos*, with devices attached to the penis, can demonstrate erectile competence. If an erection occurs, it suggests that the man is dysfunctional only in certain situations, and likely has a psychological problem.
- *Injecting papaverine* is another test for erectile capacity; the drug is injected into the erectile tissue of the penis. In men with normal blood flow, papaverine dilates the blood vessels and induces erection. Its failure to do so may indicate a penile blood vessel disorder. Almost any man capable of erection responds to this drug.
- *Tests for penile blood vessel disorders* and restricted blood flow — an increasingly recognized cause of erectile failure — can be done with ultrasound, arteriography (X-rays used in conjuction with injected dye) and cavernostomy (with saline solution infused into the penis) to examine tissue expansion capacity.

Treatment of erectile dysfunction

If the erectile problem is physical, drugs, hormones or mechanical devices may be the answer. If it's psychological, sex therapy and counseling may help. If it can't be traced to a definite reason, the man may be offered therapy with drugs, devices and counseling. There are now many ingenious methods available to help men regain erectile power. For some men, a device or drug can restore enough confidence that after a while erections can be sustained without such aids. Since drugs and devices won't overcome emotional or intimacy problems, sex or relationship therapy is often also advised. For a variety of reasons, a couple should usually get counseling together. Exercise, yoga, relaxation and a change of environment may also help.

In the days before psychological reasons for sex problems were known, aphrodisiacs were considered the answer. For example, North American Indians ate raspberry leaves when too tired for sex; others chewed ginseng roots or yohimbine bark. Dong quai roots were used in the Orient to enhance sexual desire.

Mechanical erection-producing devices

Penile prostheses of various kinds can now restore erectile capacity without disturbing libido, ejaculation or orgasm, although they don't enlarge the penis beyond its natural erect size.

Vacuum devices (such as ErectAid), made of silicone rubber and placed on the penis, have a side arm that withdraws air, creating a vacuum around the penis which increases blood flow into the penis. The basic model contains a soft plastic tube that fits over the flaccid penis, and a hand-held pump. A rubber band is wrapped around the bottom of the penis to stop blood flowing out. The cylinder is removed during intercourse and the blood drawn into the penis keeps it erect. "A man can get a good enough erection for penetration, but it's not rock hard," says one University of Toronto expert. "Some love the vacuum devices and others hate them, but many willingly accept them. However, it takes practice to use them deftly." Most are available on prescription for varying sums — some as costly as $500. They are rather cumbersome and may dim sensation, which detracts somewhat from their popularity. The obvious

drawback is interference with sexual spontaneity. Also men must not fall asleep with the rubber band in place.

Permanent penile implants come in inflatable models, or uninflatable models that are semi-rigid (giving a permanent erection). They can be bent down to seem more natural when not in use. One uninflatable model, composed of two silicone rods, is surgically implanted into the penis, providing a natural-looking erection.

Inflatable models — inflated for sex, then deflated afterwards — are the more popular type, and operate more like the "real thing." One model is composed of two inflatable tubes put into the shaft of the penis with a fluid reservoir in the abdomen and a pump in the

---

MEDICAL METHODS AND DRUGS TO OVERCOME ERECTILE FAILURE

- **Testosterone-replacement therapy,** GnRH analogues or other drugs can correct some hormone deficiencies.
- **Corrective surgery** for venous leaks and arterial blockage can sometimes restore erectile ability.
- **Yohimbine,** a plant derivative that stimulates the parasympathetic nervous system and decreases blood outflow from penile tissue, helps about 30 percent of men with mild impotence — which make it about as successful as sex counseling. Side effects of the drug include facial flushing, tachycardia (racing heart), occasional panic attacks, low blood pressure and tremors.
- **Minoxidil,** a vasodilator drug sprayed

onto the penis, may achieve erection in some.
- **Papaverine,** a self-injectable drug used since 1983, is a smooth-muscle relaxant that increases arterial blood flow in the penis and restricts venous outflow. Injected directly into the side of the penis just before intercourse, it produces an erection in 5–10 minutes, without disturbing ejaculation or orgasm. While some men dislike the idea of needles or drugs, many are enthusiastic about this method and it is gaining popularity. Possible side effects include dizziness, cardiac complications and a painful, prolonged erection lasting several hours

— which requires medical relief measures. The effectiveness of papaverine may diminish with repeated injections and occasionally produces scarring. Papaverine is now often used in combination with phentolamine, and sometimes also prostaglandin E_1 — as "triple therapy" — with greater efficacy, smaller doses of each drug and fewer side effects. However, some initial enthusiasts discontinue the method after a while and resort to penile implants.
- **Newer drugs** such as prostaglandin E_1 can be as effective as papaverine or may be combined with it, although in some men prostaglandin E_1 produces local discomfort.

THE ARGUMENTS FOR AND AGAINST CIRCUMCISION

Medical opinion in North America has flip-flopped on the issue of circumcision for many years. Earlier this century, when circumcision was almost the norm among middle-class boys, most medical experts supported the practice. But in 1975 the American Academy of Pediatrics published a statement saying that "there is no valid medical indication for routine circumcision of the neonate," a sentiment echoed by the Canadian Pediatric Society. These pronouncements were followed by a downturn in numbers circumcised.

Nonetheless, health experts continued to point out the need for penile cleansing in uncircumcised boys as a preventive against infection — as with any other body part. Only about 4 percent of boys have a retractable foreskin at birth, 15 percent at six months, and 50 percent at one year. Although many parents think they should retract the foreskin when bathing baby boys, one University of Toronto expert says, "leave it alone — it takes care of itself at that age!" By three years of age, the foreskin can be retracted in 90 percent of uncircumcised boys.

Modern research has shown that circumcision helps to prevent or reduce certain penile infections and phimosis (inability to retract the foreskin) and reduces the risk of urinary-tract infections in infancy. It may also lessen the risks of acquiring sexually transmitted diseases such as AIDS. A proportion of boys not circumcised as newborns later require the procedure for treatment of conditions such as phimosis and balanoposthitis (inflammation of the glans). Pediatric organizations have therefore now adopted a different stance. The U.S. Academy of Pediatrics' 1989 statement outlines the medical benefits of circumcision, recommending that parents be told about the pros and cons to help them decide whether or not to have their infants circumcised. Canada's Pediatric Society is in the process of reviewing its position, neither promoting nor discouraging the practice.

Infants who should *not* be circumcised include those who are ill or have genito-urinary malformation or a known family history of bleeding problems.

implants. The risks include infection — requiring removal — swelling and pain.

Summing up, one urologist notes that "Erection does not equate with good lovemaking, sensuality or happiness," and "There are many other ways to give and enjoy sexual pleasure." Sex or relationship therapy for both partners together is usually recommended, along with any methods that aim to restore erectile capacity or overcome other male sex problems. (See chapter 7 for details of sex therapy and how to find a sex therapist.)

THE CIRCUMCISION CONTROVERSY

A bystander to the circumcision debate might feel somewhat bewildered by the intense controversy over this tiny scrap of newborn skin. Critics argue that circumcision is barbaric, ritualistic and of no proven medical benefit. By contrast, proponents of circumcision point to the accumulating scientific evidence suggesting that, from a health viewpoint, boys may be better off circumcised. Recent research confirms that circumcision cuts down the risks of penile and urinary-tract infections, and possibly also reduces risks of penile cancer.

What exactly is circumcision?

Circumcision is a minor surgical procedure that removes the foreskin that hoods the end of the penis, thereby exposing its tip, the glans. The operation is usually done within days of birth, preferably before age two months, with or without local anesthetic. Some surgeons give painkillers such as acetaminophen (Tylenol); others use neither painkillers nor any anesthetic. After circumcision, the scar is protected with gauze and petroleum jelly (Vaseline). Overall, circumcision is a safe, low-risk procedure provided the operator is well trained and experienced.

While circumcision is routinely done among certain religious groups, notably Moslems, Jews and some Africans, many of the world's peoples have never practiced it. Circumcision was introduced in the nineteenth century in the English-speaking world for hygienic reasons, and as a possible "cure" for masturbation. Widespread during the 1940s and 1950s, the practice has been declining. Many North American hospitals no longer circumcise babies

scrotum. Squeezing the pump moves fluid from the reservoir into the penis.

Penile implants are a last resort, as surgical insertion destroys some erectile tissue and the devices tend to break down. The more complex the mechanical device, the more likely it is to malfunction. Advanced models are more reliable, but many still need to be replaced or repaired. A candidate requesting an implant must be in good health, and have a high sex drive, and good penile sensitivity; if he has a regular sex partner, the partner must favor the idea. It is imperative that the couple be assessed for suitability and well informed about the benefits and risks of unless specifically requested, and many young physicians prefer not to do it. The British, Americans and New Zealanders no longer routinely circumcise boys and the custom is also waning in Canada; Quebec and Newfoundland do little routine circumcision, but in other parts of Canada 40–60 percent of newborn boys are still circumcised. In the United States, circumcision figures approach 70 percent.

Arguments against circumcision

Against the benefits of circumcision are its possible complications, which include excessive bleeding, postoperative infection and scarring. Such misadventures are rare, occurring in less than 1 percent of boys, but mishaps do happen. Every year one or two baby boys die from the operation in North America. On the other hand, death from meningitis and renal failure — resulting from infant urinary-tract infections — can be largely prevented by circumcision.

Those against circumcision allege that in order to justify so "cruel" a medical procedure on so many healthy infants, the benefits must greatly outweigh the risks. Infant urinary-tract infections, they claim, are still rare — about 1 to 4 percent — and deaths or complications from them unusual. They argue that the number of boys who would have to be circumcised in order to prevent one serious case of urinary-tract infection hardly justifies the cost or complications of the procedure. Some go so far as to call the practice cruel, mutilating and a cause of "castration anxiety."

The anticircumcision lobby in the United States, which includes such organizations as the National Organization of Circumcision Resource Centers, maintains that, given high enough standards of hygiene, penile cancer is no problem. They argue that introducing a surgical procedure to prevent a condition that can be avoided simply with soap and water amounts to "overkill." To this the pro-circumcision group retorts that, even if soap and water can prevent penile cancer, it is irrelevant since little boys are not very clean. (Studies on British schoolboys showed three-quarters of them to be very sloppy penile washers.)

Finally, some anticircumcision groups allege that the practice reduces sexual sensitivity and pleasure. One U.S. doctor writes that "Not only are there complications from penile surgery, such as bleeding, but the uncovered glans is uncomfortably exposed to ammonia and other harmful chemicals from urine, as well as the abrading influence of toilet paper and clothing. After years of rubbing against underwear and jeans, the penile skin loses its sensitivity, reducing pleasure and the intensity of sensations experienced in intercourse." With the loss of his foreskin, a man loses the natural gliding mechanism that helps with the sex act. With a foreskin it is possible for the shaft to move back and forth within the loose outer skin. Others counter that sexual pleasure remains unmarred in circumcised men!

All agree on the need for good penile hygiene

Amid the controversy, all agree that the decision not to circumcise must be accompanied by a lifetime commitment to genital hygiene. Health-care providers must teach penile care and show uncircumcised boys how to wash their penises by gently retracting the foreskin until resistance is met (full retraction is not achieved until about age three), washing well with soap and water. Good hygiene may help to prevent conditions such as phimosis (unretractable foreskin), balanoposthitis (inflammation of the glans) and posthitis (inflammation of the foreskin), which often necessitate circumcision later in life.

THE USUAL REASONS FOR CIRCUMCISION

- **for religious beliefs;**
- **so the child looks like the father (or the brothers, if the father isn't circumcised);**
- **to resemble friends at school (in the shower);**
- **for cleanliness — it's hard to keep an uncircumcised penis scrupulously clean no matter how it's washed;**
- **to avoid the need for future circumcision.**

THE MEDICAL BENEFITS OF CIRCUMCISION

- **prevention of infant urinary-tract infections, reduced risks of penile inflammation and possibly lowered risks of penile cancer;**
- **better penile hygiene (little boys often forget to wash under foreskins);**
- **possible avoidance of some sexually transmitted diseases. Several** reports suggest lower risks of contracting gonorrhea, herpes, candidiasis and HIV infection (AIDS) among circumcised men. Studies from Africa show that uncircumcised men are more likely to become HIV-positive after exposure to the HIV virus. But better-controlled studies are needed to confirm the benefits of circumcision in preventing STDs.

  Those who favor circumcision also point out that foreskin removal has not been shown to cause psychosexual problems, and that charges of mutilation are grossly exaggerated.

CIRCUMCISION REDUCES RISKS OF INFANT URINARY-TRACT INFECTIONS

The strongest medical argument in favor of circumcision is its ability to prevent childhood urinary-tract infections. Several large U.S. studies have found that uncircumcised boys aged one week to eight months were 10–20 times likelier to have urinary-tract infections than those circumcised. Childhood urinary-tract infections may necessitate hospitalization and can scar fragile young kidneys or even lead to kidney failure. Urinary-tract infections can also lead to meningitis and generalized blood sepsis (sometimes fatal). Recent evidence suggests that uncircumcised adult men also suffer more urinary-tract infections than the circumcised.

A newly found link between intact foreskins and penile cancer gives circumcision another boost. In the United States, the incidence of penile cancer is 2.2 per 100,000 in the uncircumcised, but only three isolated cases have been reported in circumcised men in the past 20 years. While only 750–1,000 cases are reported yearly in U.S. men, circumcision proponents calculate that this number could rise to 3,000 per year if the whole U.S. male population were uncircumcised.

Statistics vary on the number of men who eventually require circumcision for medical reasons. One U.S. study found that 12–15 percent of uncircumcised men eventually sought circumcision as adults, but a Finnish study found that only 6 per 100,000 men were later circumcised. Cultural variables probably play a role. Since foreskins are considered expendable in the United States, they would be cut off at the first sign of trouble. But in Finland, where foreskins are the norm, any infection or other problem may be differently handled. Done after infancy, circumcision requires a general anesthetic and can be painful afterwards.

In conclusion

When deciding whether or not to circumcise their infant boys, parents must weigh the pros and cons. There are tiny risks involved in having a foreskin and equally tiny risks in having it cut off. Individual decisions about circumcision are rarely rational, usually being based more on cultural, religious, emotional or esthetic values. One University of Toronto clinician sums it up this way: "Parents must be given adequate counseling, with the potential risks and benefits of the procedure fully explained. The procedure should certainly be performed by a competent operator. Given adequate counseling and an experienced physician, parents who elect to have their son circumcised can rest assured of full support from the medical profession."

Producing the healthiest possible baby

Preconception preparation • Fertilization and conception • Reversing infertility • Pregnancy in the over-thirties • Modern "windows" into the womb • The course and care of pregnancy • Choice of birthplace • The role of midwives • Changes in the mother's body during pregnancy • Charting fetal progress • Nutrition in pregnancy • Exercise in pregnancy • Spotting high-risk pregnancies • The three stages of labor • From fetus to newborn • Cesarean birth • Newborn child-parent bonding • Breast is still best

BIRTH IS A UNIVERSAL journey we've all taken — from the shelter of our mother's body out into the exterior world. But in the past few decades, attitudes to childbirth have changed dramatically.

As late as the mid-1700s, theorists like the French philosopher Descartes viewed the unborn child as a miniature, preformed adult, curled up inside the womb with all its tiny organs already intact. Biologists claimed to have seen minuscule, preformed chicks, horses, pigs and humans inside an egg or sperm.

With the development of microscopes, the discovery of bacteria and Louis Pasteur's refutation of the "spontaneous generation of life," unborn babies came to be regarded as tadpole-like creatures, their brains a "blank slate" upon which rearing and experience would engrave personality and other features. Today's research opposes such overemphasis on "nurture" — the influence of home, environment and education — proposing that biology (genes) and the environment *jointly* mold human development.

The quest for a "superbaby"

Only in recent years have scientists recognized the many influences — such as nutrition, smoking, alcohol, and medications — on fetal development. Modern obstetric care aims to prevent avoidable handicaps and help mothers bear babies that can develop their genetic potential to the fullest. The goal is to produce the healthiest possible babies through prenatal care and education, good nutrition, closely monitored fetal progress, and referral of high-risk pregnancies to specialized centers for labor and birth whenever necessary. Since time immemorial parents have always wished for a perfect baby, and the first question at birth is still an anxious "is my baby normal?" But while everyone wants the healthiest baby possible, there's still considerable argument about how best to achieve it.

In the early part of this century, medical care for pregnancy and childbirth was minimal. By the 1940s, physicians had become more involved in the process of childbirth and pregnancy monitoring, largely supplanting midwives in North America. Birthing began to move out of homes and into hospitals, becoming more "medicalized." The accompanying fall in infant and maternal death rates was attributed to better medical care, even though better overall health and nutrition, fewer pregnancies and smaller family size also played a role.

Studies in the 1960s and 1970s reinforced the belief in medicalized birthing, showing that women who received antenatal care from physicians and gave birth in hospital were most likely to deliver healthy babies. Not surprisingly, this led to even more medical involvement, with the introduction of obstetric specialists, prenatal tests and high-tech birthing

10

procedures, along with authoritarian pronouncements on diet, exercise, sex and birth positions. Many a baby today has had a "medical checkup" long before emerging from the womb. Sophisticated genetic screening and high-definition ultrasound may have determined the baby's sex and diagnosed some imperfections before birth. Ultrasound screening may show up physical defects such as a missing limb or brain and heart flaws; analysis of a little amniotic fluid surrounding the fetus or of cord blood may reveal some chromosome and other genetic faults. On discovering fetal imperfections, parents may choose to terminate a pregnancy or carry it to term and prepare for a less-than-perfect child.

Nowadays, biochemical tests can also detect parents carrying certain genetic flaws before conception and assess their chances of having a defective child. For example, a simple "mouthwash" test to analyze buccal cells (from the mouth) can determine whether one or both parents carry the gene for cystic fibrosis (a serious defect affecting the lungs and digestive system), and predict the risks of bearing an affected child (one in four if both parents carry the cystic-fibrosis gene). The knowledge may influence their decision to start a family. Should they decide to risk it, pre-birth tests on the fetus can determine whether it carries the faulty gene, giving them the option of terminating the pregnancy.

There is now considerable debate over the extent to which medical techniques can improve a potentially bad birth outcome — for example, in a mother who is malnourished or smokes — and how far medical interventions (such as electronic monitoring of the fetal heart during labor) are desirable or can produce fewer deaths and complications.

Identifying and treating maternal high blood pressure is one intervention that can prevent low-birthweight babies and the adverse consequences. Prenatal rubella immunization and genetic counseling are other examples by which malformations can be prevented, as is persuading women not to smoke, take drugs or drink alcohol while pregnant. Detecting a fetus with a kidney or heart ailment can lead to arrangements for birth in a special

unit with facilities to operate on the newborn and correct or minimize the defect.

However, many medical approaches practiced in the past 20 years are being reassessed for their efficacy, their cost to the healthcare system and their possible adverse effects. For example, there's a recent trend in some centers against intervention for normal, low-risk births, with fewer medical procedures. And the dogma of "once a Cesarean always a Cesarean" is being overturned. Many women who've already had one Cesarean are encouraged to try a vaginal birth for the next baby; physicians are also relearning how to manage breech (buttocks first) births instead of automatically doing a Cesarean. The practice of episiotomy (cutting tissue in the area between vagina and anus to widen the passage) — almost routine in many North American delivery rooms — is now under attack, as studies suggest it may be causing the very problems (such as incontinence and more tearing) that it's supposed to prevent. Use of low forceps to assist delivery of the baby's head is also now less common. (Vacuum suctioning to ease delivery is now sometimes used instead.) Routine electronic monitoring of the fetal heartbeat during labor is now also being questioned from many quarters, as it has not been shown to improve fetal outcomes.

The quest to bear a "perfect" baby also raises ethical dilemmas. Some health professionals anticipate possible problems from the technology that tells parents in advance the sex of their child and some of the abnormalities it may have. In future, as more and more genes are identified and pinpointed, it may be possible to test for a wider range of defects. Some fear that genetic tests may promote eugenic or "quality" control and lead to a mentality where parents select for birth only "designer" babies — perhaps only males — and where even marginally handicapped children may be castigated or blamed for not having been "terminated."

New emphasis on caring
Pregnancy and childbirth procedures are now moving from high tech to lower tech, as women demand more control over their bodies. Driven

by those who consider pregnancy a natural, healthy life event rather than a "disease," and under increasing pressure from nonspecialists, family practitioners, nurses, midwife lobbyists and women themselves, pregnancy management has moved away from the "intensive care" concept to the "family-centered" or "birthing-center" concept.

Although the basics of the medical model remain, with their emphasis on detecting and managing pregnancy risks (such as hypertension, gestational diabetes and retarded fetal growth), a supportive medical caregiver — whether physician, nurse or midwife — is emerging as the most crucial element in pregnancy care. In fact, obstetrics is now called "care in pregnancy and childbirth," and, as one London, Ontario, family practitioner emphasizes, "We need to see women as inherently gifted in bearing children," rather than as "defective incubators, reliant on medical professionals to deliver their babies." Or, as a Toronto family doctor puts it, "Babies are *born*, not delivered."

Caregivers looking after pregnant women are beginning to take on more supportive and educational roles. Counseling on matters involving lifestyle and family dynamics are considered at least as important as strict medical care, perhaps more so. And women prefer a personalized, supportive and educative approach.

Childbirth is becoming more of a family affair

Not only is the pregnant woman receiving more care, but the well-being of the whole family, especially the father, is beginning to get greater attention. For example, a woman's relationship to her partner is seen as crucial to successful childbirth and parenting. Several new studies have shown that stress and anxiety in pregnancy are related to poor obstetric outcomes, and women with satisfying relationships have fewer adverse symptoms in pregnancy and are better adapted to parenthood one year after birth. In other words, happy women make happier mothers and healthier babies.

One University of Toronto family physician explains that "a family-oriented approach helps couples make room for and adjust to the new baby and give it optimal care." There are also fewer pregnancy problems — less anxiety, apprehension and denial — in couples who are well prepared for parenting and jointly supervise the pregnancy. Alerting signs of "unpreparedness for parenthood" may include: the mother's ambivalent feelings about the pregnancy, insecurity about parenting skills, no plans made for the baby, a feeling that "pregnancy interferes with my lifestyle," expectation that the newborn will "be a friend," fears of the new role alignment and a father who doesn't attend at doctor-visits or delivery. Noticing such attitudes at prenatal visits, the caregiver may make more effort to involve the father in pregnancy care and provide extra counseling for the couple.

Support systems — the father, grandparents, siblings, friends and extended family — are seen as vitally important to the successful outcome of pregnancy. Experts in family-centered pregnancy care now include the father of baby-to-be in discussions, counseling and education, as well as in prenatal classes. "Family-centered care," explains one physician at the McMaster Medical Centre, "recognizes birth as a primal life event rather than a medical procedure, encourages the presence of fathers, siblings, even grandparents, doing everything possible to make it a family event, letting them share the exhaustion, exhilaration and wonder of a new baby."

Since close contact in the post-birth period may strengthen parent-child ties, maternity staff encourage parents to have some private time with their new baby. They encourage a mother to put the newborn against her body, as skin-to-skin touching makes many mothers fondle their infants more and may elicit behaviors not seen with blanket-wrapped babies. An added advantage is that putting the baby to the breast soon after delivery speeds uterine contraction, expels blood-clots, establishes the baby's sucking reflex (strong right after birth), speeds the arrival of mother's milk and gets things off to a good start. Family-centered care has now been largely accepted across Canada, although some maternity caregivers say "It's more lip service than reality." (A few hospitals still don't allow partners — especially those of single mothers — to be present at the birthing.)

Fathers play a crucial role in childbirth
Fathers play an important part in helping their partners with pregnancy, birth and early motherhood, giving them confidence and establishing a family environment at the birthing scene. Yet fathers too may feel insecure and ambivalent about the pregnancy, find it hard to accept (even deny it), be reluctant to attend prenatal visits and have trouble committing to the parenting role. However, family-centered caregivers actively encourage fathers-to-be to attend doctor visits, be present at the ultrasound exam (where the baby may be seen moving), take part in discussions about labor, birth positions, breast-feeding and postpartum help — and handle the newborn in the delivery room.

Fathers of sick or premature babies (whose mothers may be hospitalized elsewhere) can help with frequent visits. A Canadian study showed that fathers of pre-term infants held them longer and took more part in their upbringing than those of full-term babies, the concern for their children overcoming any effects of separation due to initial frailty. However, the absence of the father is not necessarily a lasting or negative influence on children.

PRECONCEPTION PREPARATION

Pregnancy should be regarded not as an illness but as a natural process or continuum that starts with conception and continues through nine months of fetal development inside the uterus to infant life outside it. Birth is just *one* step — albeit a crucial one — along the way. By the time a baby is born, it has already gone through nine critical months of development.

Ideally, pregnancy care starts before conception, by assessing fitness for childbearing. It might help if future parents find out as much as possible beforehand, so they can make informed choices on pregnancy care and birthing of their child. Testing for disorders such as hepatitis B, syphilis, gonorrhea and other conditions that could endanger the baby may be done, so that steps can be taken to lessen the risk. Preconception testing for antibodies to rubella (German measles) in the mother is *vital*, as this infection during pregnancy can seriously deform the fetus. Women without rubella antibodies should be immunized and then avoid conception for three months afterwards.

Genetic counseling is advised for couples who know of inherited diseases in the family — such as phenylketonuria, (a protein-digesting flaw), Tay-Sachs disease (nerve degeneration, invariably fatal by age four), cystic fibrosis (a digestive and lung disorder), hemophilia (failure of blood to clot), sickle cell anemia (with abnormal hemoglobin leading to oxygen lack), muscular dystrophy (muscle-wasting) and others. Blood tests can now detect parent-carriers of many such inherited defects.

Sensible lifestyle habits — balanced nutrition, regular exercise, avoidance of tobacco, alcohol and drugs (unless medically advised) — should ideally begin before conception. Giving up tobacco smoking before and during pregnancy is a wise precaution. Most of the tissues destined to form vital organs are laid down

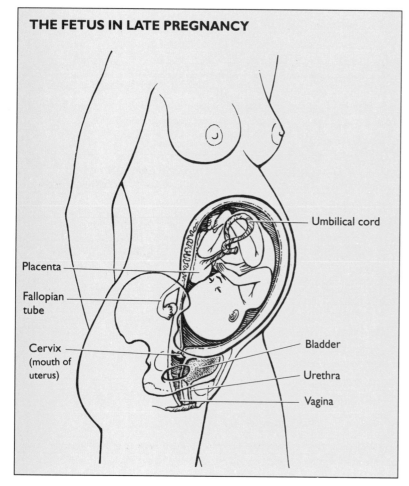

THE FETUS IN LATE PREGNANCY

Umbilical cord

Placenta

Fallopian tube

Cervix (mouth of uterus)

Bladder

Urethra

Vagina

during the first 12 weeks of embryonic development, when a woman may not even know she's pregnant. It is precisely during this early stage that the unborn child is most vulnerable to environmental toxins and insults from infections, medications, alcohol and malnutrition.

Good nutritional status of mothers-to-be at or near conception, and in early pregnancy, is crucial for bearing healthy babies. One University of Toronto expert explains that "malnourishment or early nutrient deprivation is hard to make up later in pregnancy (especially after the 12th to 14th week). Mal-fed fetuses may not reach their normal growth curve, remaining underweight until birth and after." One British researcher points to the fact that many women don't realize how nutritionally deprived their bodies are. Specific nutrient deficiencies can lead to specific infant damage. For example, a shortage of *folic acid* (one of the B vitamins) can lead to neural tube disorders — with an incomplete spine or brain. So women are now advised to make sure they have enough folic acid in their diets (or take supplements) to help avoid these congenital faults in their babies. Many experts think that folic acid supplementation should ideally start *before* conception.

FERTILIZATION AND CONCEPTION
Fertilization is normally achieved by sexual intercourse. A woman need not reach orgasm to procreate. All that's required for successful fertilization is the union of one egg with one sperm. But normally it's a random rendezvous; chance decides which egg in which ovary is released and penetrated by which viable sperm.

Requisites for fertility
For conception, a sperm must fertilize an egg within 24 hours of ejaculation and ovulation, because both sperm and egg soon deteriorate, even though they may still be able to unite for another day or two. Although they may remain alive for as long as four days, sperm survival time is highly variable. Ejaculated sperm lodge at the top of the vagina, then travel to meet the egg. The path from penis to fallopian tube (where the egg waits) is perilous. Sperm must traverse the vagina — inhospitable because it's

acidic, and sperm prefer an alkaline environment — go through the uterus and up to the fallopian tube. Millions of sperm per ejaculate are required because many perish *en route* to the egg and others fail to penetrate the egg's tough outer membrane. If enough sperm have survived the journey, conception generally occurs in the lower part of the fallopian tube or upper part of the uterus. Sperm that have the slightest imperfections (being slow swimmers or short-tailed, for instance) generally fall by the wayside.

The Canadian Fertility Society estimates that sperm counts vary from 60 to 300 million sperm per ejaculate (averaging three to five ml). For unknown reasons, up to 40 percent of men on occasion have sperm counts lower than the 20 million per ejaculate usually needed for fertilization. A sperm count below 20 million per ml is unlikely to achieve fertilization. Even though

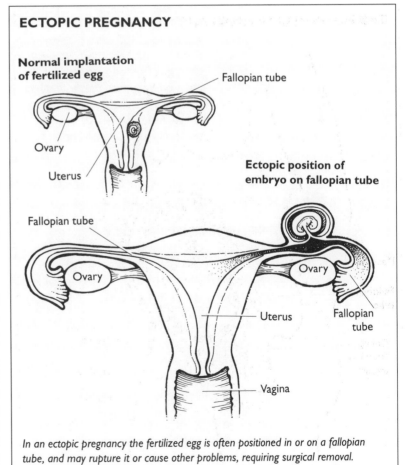

ECTOPIC PREGNANCY

Normal implantation of fertilized egg

Fallopian tube

Ovary

Uterus

Fallopian tube

Ovary

Ectopic position of embryo on fallopian tube

Ovary

Uterus

Fallopian tube

Vagina

In an ectopic pregnancy the fertilized egg is often positioned in or on a fallopian tube, and may rupture it or cause other problems, requiring surgical removal.

CAUSES OF INFERTILITY

In women:
- absence of or irregular ovulation;
- surgical or radiation treatments that destroy the ovaries;
- obstruction or damage to fallopian tubes due to causes such as sexually transmitted diseases;
- pelvic inflammatory disease (PID) due to an IUD or sexually transmitted disease (often symptomless);
- a ruptured appendix or previous surgery;
- congenitally absent ovaries (e.g., in Turner's syndrome);
- endometriosis (where the uterine lining grows outside the uterus and blocks or damages the tubes);
- hostile cervical mucus;
- antibodies to sperm, which may explain why conception fails in the "normal infertile" couple.

In men:
- insufficient sperm or poor sperm quality;
- in men who are marginally subfertile, various factors may aggravate the infertility, such as:
  - premature ejaculation;
  - excess alcohol consumption;
  - postpubertal mumps (if there is *orchitis* — painful testicular inflammation);
  - testes that have not descended;
  - overheating of the genitals (due to tight clothing, long spells of sitting, too many saunas or hot baths) — since a cool temperature favors sperm survival;
  - certain drugs that diminish sperm count (such as marijuana).

The causes of infertility in men are often harder to pinpoint than in women, and, if found, harder to treat. In about 85 percent of male infertility the reason remains unknown. Incidentally, sterility in men — inability to fertilize an egg — should *not* be confused with impotence, which is the inability to sustain an erection.

Although sperm numbers are critical, sperm quality — motility, speed, vigor, size and shape — also play a vital role. It's difficult to upgrade a low sperm count — certain drugs (such as clomiphene) and hormones (which are rarely effective) may be tried.

they may have too low a sperm count to be classed as "fertile," there are isolated cases of men with only 2 to 5 million sperm per ejaculate siring babies. But sperm banks, which usually prefer youngish men as donors, require a minimum sperm count of 100 million sperm per ml, since the freezing process destroys some.

Once the egg is fertilized, an immediate chemical reaction on its surface prevents other sperm from entering it. Fertilization also triggers division of the egg into two cells, to become a zygote. Six or seven days later, having gone through many cell divisions, the hollow ball of cells becomes a blastocyst that burrows into the spongy, blood-rich wall of the uterus. This process of implantation is the start of pregnancy.

REVERSING INFERTILITY

Infertility fluctuates from place to place and decade to decade. It is increasing in Canada, possibly due to delayed childbearing (older women being less fertile) and an increase in sexually transmitted diseases (such as chlamydia and gonorrhea) that can cause sterility. About 15 percent of Canadian couples are infertile and another 10 percent have fewer offspring than they want. On a global scale, unwanted fertility poses a drastic population problem; but on an individual level, when a couple cannot conceive a child, it is a personal tragedy. Fortunately, new methods now help many infertile couples conceive and bear babies.

Officially, infertility is defined as "the inability of a couple to conceive after a year of unprotected regular coitus (without contraception)." In many couples who cannot conceive, neither partner is really infertile — and with a different partner each might manage to conceive. In a small number, 10 percent or less, of such involuntarily childless couples, both partners appear normal but cannot jointly conceive a child. Such a couple is termed "normally infertile" with infertility "of no apparent cause."

About a third of all infertility is due to a female disorder, another third is caused by male problems, the remainder arising from combined incompatibility. In some cases, mistimed intercourse is the only reason for infertility. The odds of being able to conceive can sometimes be improved by explicit information, better coital mechanics (change of lovemaking position) and precise timing to the day of ovulation. About 25 percent of infertile couples become pregnant once they seek medical help, sometimes with no treatment other than general sex and intercourse counseling. Another 30 percent respond to appropriate treatment for the man, woman or both.

Infertility can come as an unexpected shock. Take as an example a couple who finally decide, in their late thirties, to start a family. She goes off the Pill; they have well-timed intercourse and assume conception will occur. When it does not, they consult the family doctor. The advice may be to "relax and try again." But if there's no conception, tension, anger and disappointment often ensue. Sex life loses spontaneity and becomes joyless. With parenting ambitions thwarted, both partners become bitter, often directing hostility at each other, the physician or both.

The discovery of infertility, almost invariably traumatic, sets up a vicious circle of recrimination and worry and an obsession with sex roles. The time-consuming, tedious and costly fertility tests seem demeaning; both partners feel victimized, sensing a loss of control over their bodies. All too often infertile people suffer silently, finding their inadequacy too shameful to share with others, particularly since so many are apt to confuse fertility with their sexual identity.

Test-tube or in vitro fertilization (IVF)

Since the birth of the first test-tube babies, Louise Brown in Britain and Candice Reed in Australia, many infants have been successfully born by IVF worldwide. But the success rate remains incredibly low.

In vitro fertilization (the Latin means "in glass") entails the fertilization of an egg or several eggs with ejaculated sperm in a glass dish. The eggs, artificially ripened by hormonal agents taken by the woman, are removed surgically from her ovaries.

After being incubated and fertilized, then grown in a dish for 48–72 hours, the tiny fertilized eggs — now embryos — are put back into the mother's uterus in the hope that at least one will develop into a full-term baby. IVF is most often successful if four fertilized eggs are inserted into the uterus; however, implanting several embryos increases the chance of twins and multiple births, should gestation of more than one proceed to term.

The best outlook is for women who have had previous pregnancies (even an "ectopic" one, outside the womb), because it proves that conception can occur.

Before entering an IVF program women must undergo a "scout laparoscopy" — the ovaries are examined (via a viewing tube inserted through a tiny cut in the umbilicus) to make sure that eggs can easily be harvested. If for any reason the ovaries are inaccessible, the couple is refused entry into the IVF program. While some centers limit the number of tries at test-tube fertilization to five times per couple, others allow unlimited attempts. One couple achieved a birth on the twentieth attempt!

For more information contact the Canadian Fertility Society or any infertility clinic or IVF center.

PREGNANCY IN THE OVER-THIRTIES

The number of women having a first baby after age 30 has been steadily climbing in Western nations. Some studies suggest that older women are at above-average risk of problems such as miscarriage, premature birth or low-birthweight babies. Others find few extra risks related to age or because of delaying pregnancy until age 30–35 or later. Some risks may be due to pre-existing disorders such as high blood pressure or a tendency to diabetes. New reports find reassuringly little evidence of increased risks of low-birthweight or premature

---

MODERN METHODS HELP SOME INFERTILE COUPLES

Many new centers within large hospitals specialize in treating infertility with a variety of methods:

- **Ovulation may be induced by means of hormonal agents such as clomiphene, Pergonal and others.**
- **Tubal microsurgery — performed under a special operating microscope, sometimes with lasers to vaporize scar tissue and adhesions — may clear or repair blocked or injured fallopian tubes. Surgery on fallopian tubes, which are as fine as Saran wrap, is laborious, often requiring repeat** operations.
- **Artificial insemination (AI) uses a syringe to insert the habitual mate's seminal fluid (or that of a donor) near to the woman's cervix at ovulation time.**
- **Intrauterine insemination (IUI), an offshoot of AI, uses washed, concentrated sperm — from the habitual mate or an anonymous donor — inserted right into the uterine cavity. Sperm-cleansing methods can improve sperm numbers and quality by repeated washing and centrifuging to sift out dead and defective** sperm, concentrating the "best of a bad lot" for artificial insemination or in vitro fertilization.
- **Surrogate motherhood — rarely done through infertility clinics — involves insemination of a fertile woman other than the habitual partner with the chosen man's sperm, or transplantation of a test-tube-fertilized embryo into her womb. This surrogate (substitute) mother then carries the baby to term (a procedure fraught with ethical dilemmas and possible parenthood disputes!).**

babies in women who start a family after age 30. One study from New York's Mount Sinai School of Medicine, which followed almost 4,000 first-time pregnancies, found mothers over age 30 no likelier to deliver prematurely or have a stillbirth than younger first-time mothers. Mothers over age 35 had only slightly higher risks of producing low-birthweight or premature babies.

Nonetheless, while mothers-to-be in their thirties are usually readier for responsibility and more health-conscious than younger mothers, they face above-average risks of bearing congenitally defective babies. The risks of bearing a baby with a chromosomal aberration (especially Down syndrome) increase dramatically after age 35. For a Down syndrome baby, the risk at age 20 is one in 1,000, rising at age 30 to one in 500 and to one in 300 at age 35, and one in 60 by age 40.

Overall, healthy women attempting a first pregnancy after age 30 have an excellent chance of producing a healthy baby. Even women in their early forties can still bear healthy babies, provided they take some simple precautions, seek professional advice and get regular pregnancy care. But it's wise to embark on pregnancy before age 40, since fertility declines quickly thereafter and the chance of fetal abnormalities increases. Childbearers of advancing years might consider being tested to see whether the fetus they are carrying has Down syndrome or other congenital problems. The tests are done by ultrasound, amniocentesis, chorionic villus (placenta blood) sampling and other methods (described below).

MODERN "WINDOWS" INTO THE WOMB

In the past few decades, advances such as ultrasound and fetoscopy (use of a miniature waterproof camera) have allowed scientists to peer into the uterine world to see the unborn child and check whether it has certain defects.

Ultrasound monitoring is now done almost routinely by many pregnancy caregivers — at around 16–18 weeks of gestation — although many medical authorities criticize its routine use. Ultrasound techniques bounce high-frequency sound waves off tissues in the mother's abdomen to produce an image on a TV screen that reveals the baby's shape, size and movements. Ultrasound can also detect certain abnormalities, such as retarded intrauterine growth (shown by a disproportionately small body size when growth is delayed), extra digits, missing limbs, a cleft palate, certain heart flaws, an incomplete skull (anencephaly), perhaps also other neural tube disorders such as an unfused spine (spina bifida) and new markers for Down syndrome. In fact, ultrasound promises to be the future noninvasive method for detecting Down syndrome. It also shows the baby's position — correctly head first (vertex), feet or buttocks first (breech) or sideways across the womb (transverse lie). Ultrasound also gives clues to fetal age, helps to estimate the due date and identifies multiple pregnancies.

Besides giving the clinician some valuable information, the ultrasound exam can reassure parents (as is mostly the case) that the baby's major parts and organs are developing normally. (But nonetheless, ultrasound doesn't pick up minor abnormalities.) Glimpsing their baby on the ultrasound screen, watching it kick and even suck its thumb, months before birth, sometimes gives parents an added sense of reality about the expected child. It can also persuade the smoking mother of a growth-retarded fetus to quit.

However, given that ultrasound is expensive and that although there are no known risks at present, fetal risks are unknown, there is disagreement about its use for routine screening of normal, low-risk pregnancies. In September 1992, the Canadian Task Force on the Periodic Health Examination reported "fair evidence" — reasonable but not strong evidence — in favor of a single ultrasound test during the second trimester. It can lead to increased-birthweight babies and reduced perinatal death rates — perhaps by detecting congenital abnormalities that lead to elective abortion, meaning that fewer babies are born defective, and maybe also because smoking or undernourished women whose infants are found by ultrasound to be underweight may quit smoking or eat better. The task force did not recommend routine, serial, repeat ultrasound examinations for all pregnant women, as the evidence of its benefits is not indisputably clear.

Amniocentesis may be done at 13 to 16 weeks of gestation (16–19 weeks post-conception). It is increasingly done earlier (around 14 weeks of gestation) to permit early termination of pregnancy, should an abnormality be detected. Also, doing the test earlier reduces the time spent worrying about the pregnancy outcome. The procedure can detect abnormalities such as spina bifida, Down syndrome ("trisomy 21"), and hundreds of chromosome and genetic defects such as cystic fibrosis, or sickle cell anemia. In this test, a little amniotic fluid is withdrawn via the abdomen from around the fetus by a fine hypodermic needle (guided by ultrasound), usually under local anesthetic. The fluid is analyzed for biochemical levels of substances such as alphafetoprotein (which may indicate a baby with neural tube defects such as spina bifida) and the fetal cells in it are examined for chromosome flaws. The test may be done again later if there's a risk of Rh sensitization and a possible blood incompatibility between fetus and mother.

Since the test carries some risks (a one in 200 risk of miscarriage), only women at above-average danger of fetal anomalies are usually offered it. Besides women over age 35, these might include women who have formerly had an affected baby, one with Down syndrome or those with known genetic defects in the family. (The test results take about 3–4 weeks.)

A blood test in the mother for alphafetoprotein (AFP) is done at 16 weeks into gestation: high values may be correlated with neural tube defects in the fetus. If high, an amniocentesis is advised to check further. In future, a "triple test" on the mother's blood will not only check AFP levels, but also measure estratriol and human chorionic gonadotrophin to check for neural tube defects with greater accuracy and specificity.

Chorionic villus sampling (CVS), a somewhat newer and more specialized technique for detecting chromosomal, gene and other fetal defects, is done at 9–12 weeks into gestation. It involves taking small blood and tissue samples from the fetal side of the placenta — the chorionic villi — by means of a tiny instrument inserted via a laparoscope (viewing tube) put through the abdomen or cervix, often near the vagina, guided by ultrasound. It is offered to women over age 37. Test results take about three weeks, so that if obtained early enough, a pregnancy can be terminated earlier in case fetal defects are discovered. Risks of abortion with CVS are double those with amniocentesis.

Mothers-to-be can help to check fetal vigor by counting the baby's kicks in the last trimester, for instance noting the usual 4–6 kicks per hour after supper. Although controversial, the method may help to monitor fetal well-being. Should the fetal activity diminish, expectant mothers can alert the physician. Pregnant women should also report any noticed changes in themselves — especially possible danger signs such as dizziness, blackouts, headaches, severe back pain, unusual swelling, early rupture of the bag of waters or bleeding.

THE COURSE AND CARE OF PREGNANCY

Normal human gestation (growth of a baby within the uterus) lasts about 266 days (nine months or 39 weeks) from conception. During the embryonic stage, spanning the first eight weeks, most miniature organ systems are laid down, including brain, heart, liver, lungs, limbs and digestive tract. In the fetal stage which follows and lasts until birth, the development of organs is completed in preparation for life outside the mother's uterus. While birth can happen at any point during fetal life, it is safest at or near term, after nine full months of development have made the baby ready to face the outside world and obtain oxygen by breathing air, rather than absorbing it from the mother's blood supply. While a fetus may survive if born prematurely or at below-average weight, "preemies" and low-birthweight babies do not usually thrive as well as full-term, full-weight newborns.

Pregnancy is traditionally divided into three trimesters, each roughly three months. The expected time of birth, or "due date," can be calculated from the last menstrual period using various formulae. It's generally estimated as 280 days from the first day of the mother's last menstrual period or 266 days from the day of fertilization (assuming normal menstrual cycles with mid-cycle ovulation). Another strategy is adding one year and 7 days to the date when the last menstrual period began and subtracting three months from the total. But due dates are notoriously misjudged. Although 90 percent of babies are born within 10 to 15 days of the estimated date, many arrive earlier or later.

A woman with a first pregnancy is called a primigravida, those with subsequent pregnancies multigravida. The risks of toxemia of pregnancy (a metabolic disturbance with symptoms such as face swelling, swollen limbs and raised blood pressure) — now often called "eclampsia" — are highest in first pregnancies and those of very young (especially teen) mothers. Bleeding problems tend to increase after three or more pregnancies, or in women over age 35. Miscarriages or spontaneous abortions may occur for no known reason among fetuses below 500 g (18 oz), and are more frequent among older women than among women aged 20 to 30. In fact, according to some specialists, many fetuses are naturally lost because of faulty chromosomes or other flaws within the first two months after conception, often without a woman ever suspecting she has conceived.

Choosing "caregivers" for pregnancy and birth

Pregnant women become prey to all sorts of fears, from "Will eating tomatoes cause birthmarks?" (it won't) to other food worries, distrust of environmental chemicals, apprehension over the pain of childbirth or the use of anesthetics, ambivalence over the pregnancy, fears of being an incapable parent, apprehension about coping with the stress of pregnancy and a new baby — the list goes on and on.

Therefore, the pregnant woman is well advised to seek a really empathetic caregiver for support during pregnancy and birth — the family physician, nurse, midwife or obstetrician who can best reassure and help her and her partner cope with the changes of pregnancy, both physical and emotional. It is best to choose a caregiver who welcomes questions and encourages her to express concerns, and with whom she feels free to discuss any worries, no matter how trivial or bizarre — from heartburn

to backache to fears of infanticide. Trusting relationships and good communication with the pregnancy-care team can help to achieve a safe and satisfying pregnancy and birth experience.

Prenatal care

The best present parents can give their baby is their own good health. As one expert puts it, "What women want during pregnancy, birth and lactation is not intensive care but an intensely caring situation." Woman need all the support and encouragement they can get at this time. Until a few decades ago, neither expectant mothers nor their caregivers paid much attention to the pre-birth period. The fetus was not monitored or checked and no one thought much about its development inside the uterus, all eyes being focused on the birth itself. Today, care of *both* mother and developing fetus is considered crucial in anticipating and forestalling risks. "Windows into the womb" (such as ultrasound and amniotic fluid sampling) can help parents-to-be and their caregivers chart the unborn baby's progress and detect some abnormalities. But all the tests women now undergo can instill anxiety and worry while awaiting the results. All the more reason why they need reassurance and support.

A "birth plan" suits many

A "birth plan" agreed on ahead of time with the pregnancy care team can help a couple get the conditions they want for labor and birth. "It's not a contract or a written declaration of expected rights," says a maternity care specialist at the McMaster Medical Centre, "but a flexible plan, worked out together with the support team, stating preferences for the atmosphere and conduct a couple would like for the birth of their baby. Informed decisions are the basis of good maternity care, and health professionals should share their knowledge with parents-to-be, so they can make wise choices."

Obstetricians at the McMaster Medical Centre suggest that women "interview their intended physician(s) or other caregivers, enquire tactfully about their attitudes to weight gain, childbirth education and birthing procedures (pre-birth shaves, enemas, inductions or whatever else concerns them)." They might ask how many Cesareans the physician or clinic performs, whether they encourage vaginal births after Cesareans, how much they promote breastfeeding and so on. They can also inquire about the birthing-room or ward and nursery policies and ask whether the father (or another relative or friend) can be present at delivery.

Valmai Elkins, a Montreal physiotherapist, childbirth educator and author of *The Rights of the Pregnant Parent*, suggests that women state their wishes well ahead of labor to make sure they won't be "promised one type of birth but be given another." She also advises a pre-birth tour of the hospital facilities (now routine in many centers) to become familiar with the setting and avoid being intimidated later on. The birthing attendant, whether family doctor, nurse, obstetrician or midwife, should be someone the mother-to-be likes, trusts and can communicate comfortably with, and someone who takes the time to impart information clearly. Since the ability to communicate wishes to the support team is critical for an enjoyable birthing, the chosen caregiver should not only agree with the birth plans but be an empathetic adviser.

Monitoring the pregnancy
Monitoring pregnancy means regular prenatal visits to keep tabs on mother's and baby's progress. Ideally, every woman should be seen within the first 12 weeks of pregnancy to thoroughly evaluate her condition and compare it with later changes. Women with normal pregnancies are seen every 4–6 weeks, then fortnightly and weekly toward the end of gestation.

"The first prenatal visit," notes one University of Toronto obstetrician, "helps to date the baby's age, vital for correct care, and allows testing for any disorders present in the mother." At the first visit, the caregiver notes the woman's feelings and observations about her pregnancy, takes a detailed history about background, any illnesses in the mother and previous pregnancies. Tests are done for hemoglobin levels (to check for anemia and iron status), urinary-tract and other infections such as hepatitis B, syphilis, HIV, gonorrhea, chlamydia, and others. Some infections — such as rubella, syphilis, HIV, and toxoplasmosis — can seriously endanger the baby and call for protective

measures or perhaps a Cesarean birth (as for women with active genital herpes). To avoid the risks of toxoplasmosis — an infection due to organisms often carried in cat feces and raw meat that can cause fetal malformation — women are advised not to change the cat litter or eat underdone meat.

At subsequent prenatal visits, the caregiver evaluates fetal growth by assessing uterus size, felt by hand and measured with a tape. At each visit, weight is checked, blood pressure taken and urine tested for protein and glucose. Besides physical evaluation of the mother and baby, the parent's emotional and psychological well-being are discussed.

Blood samples are usually examined at the first visit and again at weeks 16 and 26–28 to screen for gestational diabetes, anemia and Rh blood problems. Samples are sometimes also examined in between, for example, to check for maternal alphafetoprotein (AFP), which may suggest the presence of neural tube abnormalities. (Neural tube defects are higher in those with a previously affected child or relatives who had the disorder, and in women with insulin-dependent diabetes.)

CHOICE OF BIRTHPLACE AND BIRTH ASSISTANT
The choice of birthplace in Canada is limited, but there are now proposals for free-standing birthing centers with a less clinical atmosphere than hospitals, but with all emergency procedures available in case of need. Some women still opt for a home birth attended by a midwife and physician, but most physicians prefer hospital delivery because of back-up in case of unforeseeable complications, such as sudden hemorrhage or "failure to progress" (a sluggish labor). Nonetheless, those who opt for home birth can rest assured that midwives carry emergency equipment and will arrange transfer to hospital in case of need.

Even in hospital nowadays, it's becoming possible to have a more "humanized," less medicalized birthing. Some hospitals have set up birth units that simulate a home environment — with cosy decor, soft music, even a rocking chair — and the full range of emergency technology available close by. In many hospitals, childbirth positions are now optional. The flat-on-the-back delivery position is uncomfortable — with the mother working to push the baby out uphill, against gravity. Mothers are encouraged to give birth in any position they like — sitting, squatting or lying sideways — as in many primitive societies. Walk-abouts during first-stage labor — another aid to uterine contractions — are promoted in most birth units, routine pubic-hair shaves are only done in some; intravenous systems (for medication or feeding if needed) are no longer routinely set up. Mothers are given mirrors to let them view the birth. Hospitals are also beginning to respect the desire for a quiet birth, with lights dimmed to a level where child and parent(s) can comfortably greet each other. Breastfeeding is greatly encouraged, and babies are often kept beside the mother around the clock to facilitate it.

"At McMaster," says one associate professor, "nurses do much of the first-stage maternity labor care. The same nurse looks after mother and baby. We've long ago stopped routine enemas, shaves and the use of stirrups (except in problem births). Women deliver in any chosen position — squatting, sitting, standing — with the father symbolically allowed to cut the cord (if he wants to), and 80 percent of mothers leave as breastfeeders." Women are now being discharged as early as 12 to 48 hours after birth, if all goes well, from many centers. Shorter maternity stays reduce the risks of hospital infection, enhance family closeness and are also cheaper.

The debate over home vs. hospital births

Home birth remains an emotional and controversial issue, discouraged by the Canadian Medical Association, the Canadian Society of Obstetrics and Gynecology and equivalent agencies in many other countries. The argument against home birth is that it may subject mother and/or baby to avoidable risks and that even in a seemingly healthy, normal pregnancy things can go wrong at the last minute, necessitating a Cesarean section or other medical procedure. However, research shows that most emergency birthing situations can be predicted ahead and that a well-trained birth assistant can handle most emergencies at home or transfer to hospital in ample time to avoid risks to baby or mother.

Since the 1930s, home births have dwindled in most industrialized countries and "safety" has become almost synonymous with hospital birth. Statistics show that in Canada only 0.9 percent of women gave birth at home in 1989 (some unplanned), compared with virtually none in the United States, 35.5 percent in Holland and 1.7 percent in Britain. (However, in the United States there are many free-standing birth centers for women, as an alternative to hospital deliveries.) Home births in Canada were attended almost solely by midwives and a handful of physicians willing to assist. In Canada, many branches of the College of Physicians and Surgeons forbid physicians to attend home births because of "unnecessary risks to mother and infant." The success of the Dutch model, in which healthy, nonrisk mothers can opt for either home or hospital birth, depends critically on a view of birth as a normal physiological process which goes at its own pace and requires as little interference as possible. But it requires scrupulous prenatal screening and careful selection of women who are suitable for home birth.

The debate on home versus hospital births still centers on safety issues — especially as a number of women with low-risk pregnancies who opt for home birth have to be transferred to hospital because of unforeseen emergencies such as hemorrhage, unsuspected breech position, abnormal fetal heartbeat, prolonged or nonprogressing second-stage labor or a retained placenta.

One study of over 1,000 planned home births in Toronto between 1983 and 1988 found that 83 percent proceeded normally, 17 percent required transfer to hospital and two infants died. These figures are similar to those found in hospital births. The study found the transfer rate of planned home births to hospital three times higher in first-time (primipara) pregnancies than in subsequent ones. Several other studies report that home births result in fewer medical interventions — such as forceps deliveries, episiotomies, induced labor or Cesareans — than hospital births. It also appears that there are no more life-threatening emergencies than in hospital for normal, low-risk pregnancies. (More research is needed into the real risks.)

At a pregnancy-care conference in England during the late 1980s, a statistician from Nottingham University declared that "in Britain, for the 90 percent of normal uncomplicated labors, large hospitals are the least safe places of birth, with an increased incidence of jaundice, forceps deliveries and asphyxia (from labor drugs like Demerol), and certainly less safe than small maternity units staffed by general practitioners and midwives." Another British survey concluded that the setting, environment and type of obstetric care greatly influence birth outcomes and that the "spillover of medical knowledge to the home setting may be the best situation for normal pregnancies at no anticipated risk, while hospital delivery best suits pregnancies at known risk."

Although midwives may go into hospital with a laboring woman, many believe that normal, low-risk, pregnant women should also be free to choose the option of home births. The recent move to reinstate midwives in some provinces as active partners in maternity healthcare is a welcome step. In 1991, for instance, a report by the government of Alberta concluded that low-risk women may safely be allowed to give birth at home, accompanied by the midwife, and perhaps also the physician. With the comeback of midwives in Canada, home births may become a better-regulated and safer option in Canada, and some health authorities are considering the possibility of making arrangements for quicker transfer to hospital of endangered home-birth babies or mothers in case of need.

THE ROLE OF MIDWIVES
Midwives have an ancient tradition of providing consistent prenatal care through pregnancy, offering education and training for labor, assisting at the birth (in former times often without a physician's help) and coming in afterward to help the mother and newborn for up to six weeks. But in Canada, the United States and many other Western nations, midwives have been largely displaced by

physicians, and are given a variable welcome in delivery rooms. Most industrialized countries, including the United States, Britain, Holland and Sweden, still train and license midwives to practice and conduct deliveries on their own responsibility. In Canada, however, with the increasing medicalization of birth procedures, independent community midwives largely went out of practice earlier in this century and had no official status or legal place in the healthcare system. Today there are fewer than 100 midwives in this country, affiliated with provincial organizations, half of them in Ontario — represented by the Association of Ontario Midwives.

Midwifery making a comeback in Canada
Midwives are nonetheless now achieving official status for pregnancy care in many parts of Canada. Prompted by the efforts of midwives themselves and by public interest, several provinces, including Quebec, Ontario, Alberta and British Columbia, are initiating legislation to bring midwives under formal regulation and designate them as primary caregivers in maternity care. New government of Ontario legislation allows Canada's first group of *registered* midwives — comprising 70 women (and one man) — all of whom have already been practicing midwives, to be licensed by late 1993. This group, the new Ontario College of Midwives, will regulate and organize the training of future midwives. In August 1992, Alberta passed legislation designating midwifery a "profession."

The philosophy behind midwifery is that pregnancy and childbirth are natural, healthy processes that can be facilitated by a midwife's skills, and that women have a right to make choices about how and where they give birth. As defined by the World Health Organization, midwives are qualified to provide the necessary care and advice throughout pregnancy, labor and the *puerperium* (immediate post-birth period) and to conduct normal, healthy, low-risk deliveries on their own. Midwives aim to help women and their families enjoy the safest possible birth with as little intervention as possible. Their approach is client-centered and nonauthoritarian. A key part of their job is to spot warning signs and identify women who might develop problems (such as those who are obese, have high blood pressure or have had difficult deliveries in the past) and refer them for further consultation with a physician or at a specialized obstetric unit .

Essentially, midwives can give the necessary supervision, care and support to women during pregnancy, labor and the postpartum period, can conduct deliveries on their own at home or in hospital, and care for the newborn. They provide continuing, personalized care, giving information and emotional support to the woman and her family throughout pregnancy and labor. Their care includes the detection of abnormal conditions in mother and child, the procurement of medical assistance if needed and the execution of emergency measures in the absence of medical help. Midwives themselves have emergency equipment on hand for use if necessary, and will rapidly transfer to hospital in case of need, continuing the care there together with other health professionals.

Midwives may practice in hospitals, clinics, domiciliary conditions or in any other service and can attend births in hospital, birth centers (or units) or in homes, according to the woman's choice and risk status. They provide hospital care in cooperation with other members of the healthcare team. A woman who chooses midwifery care will thus be seen by her midwife for prenatal visits, and the midwife will arrange for laboratory testing and consultation with specialists if needed.

TRACKING FETAL GROWTH AND DEVELOPMENT

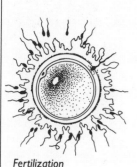

Fertilization (Conception)

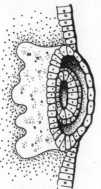

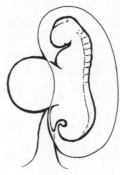

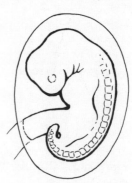

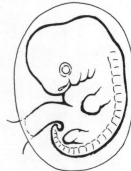

— EMBRYONIC STAGE —

WEEK 1
• fertilized egg moves along fallopian tube towards uterus, dividing as it goes
• 46 chromosomes are copied into every new cell (except the future egg and sperm cells), giving the future child its inherited characteristics

WEEK 2
• fertilized egg attaches to uterine wall
• placenta begins to form

WEEK 3
• blood system laid down
• membranes and bag of waters begins to form around embryo

WEEK 4
• placenta formed
• heart begins beating
• backbone, spinal cord and brain forming
• digestive system forming

WEEKS 5–7
• testes form in males and start to secrete testosterone (male hormone); future sperm ("germ") cells set aside with chromosome number halved (to 23 per sperm)
• limb-buds being shaped and muscles forming by week 6
• four chambers formed in heart by week 7

NOTE: Normal human gestation (growth of fetus in the uterus) lasts about 266 days (39–40 weeks) from conception. The "due date" is 266 days from the day of fertilization (or 280 days from the first day of the mother's last period). About 90 percent of babies are born within 10–14 days of the estimated due date but some are "premature" (born before 36 weeks gestation), some are "postmature" (born after 42 weeks gestation).

Spontaneous (normal) vaginal birth can be attended by the midwife, who will examine the newborn and provide care for up to six weeks postpartum for baby and mother.

CHANGES IN THE MOTHER'S BODY DURING PREGNANCY

Female hormones maintain the conditions needed for the developing fetus. Progesterone is first secreted by the ovary, later in large quantities by the placenta. Hormones stimulate development of the mammary glands: breasts swell, the areolae (nipple areas) increase in size and nipples protrude. Some troublesome symptoms are common at the start of pregnancy — morning sickness, heartburn, dizziness and weariness — but these tend to disappear by the fourth month. After that, many pregnant women feel amazingly energetic, often right up to the start of labor.

The cardiovascular system changes in response to the call for a larger blood supply with an increase in blood volume. Blood pressure usually decreases during the first two trimesters of pregnancy, returning to normal during the third. Varicose veins are quite common because of hormonal effects on blood-vessel walls, and because the expanded uterus depresses the venous blood return. As diaphragm movement is somewhat restricted, the ribcage tends to flare out, not always returning to its normal position after the birth. Late in pregnancy, breathing may become shallower and more frequent as the lungs become somewhat restricted.

The muscles of the gastrointestinal tract

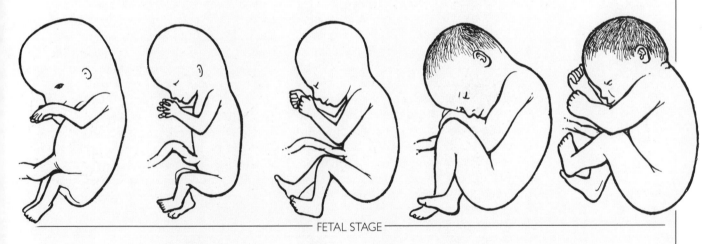

— FETAL STAGE —

WEEK 8
• facial features and teeth forming
• limbs taking shape
• fingers and toes forming
• long bones and internal organs developing

WEEK 12
• fetal heartbeat may be heard
• eyes almost fully developed; ears ready
• tooth buds forming
• nails present
• ovaries forming in females and future "eggs" set aside with half chromosome number (23) per egg

WEEK 16
• most bones formed
• muscles active
• facial features better defined
• external genitalia formed in males and females
• "quickening" — fetal movements may first be noticed around week 18–20

WEEKS 20–36
• survival possible outside womb after 24–26 weeks
• baby can be clearly felt moving
• head proportions more balanced
• bones and limbs elongate
• lungs still immature, lacking surfactant

WEEKS 37–40
• baby moves down into birth position (usually head down)
• baby gains weight fast as fat deposits accumulate
• lungs mature
• hair soft and downy
• "full-term" birth is at 37 or more weeks, "premature" before 36 weeks gestation

tend to become less contractile, with slow stomach emptying, sometimes resulting in heartburn and constipation. Urination becomes more frequent as the enlarging uterus presses on the bladder.

Other changes may include increased pigmentation on the face, known as chloasma; stretch marks on the abdomen; changes in posture that may cause leg and back pain.

As the neck of the uterus softens — an early sign of pregnancy which may be detected by the examining physician — and as the uterus expands, it also rises, reaching the level of the navel about the middle of the fourth month. By the end of the pregnancy, the uterus has expanded to about 36 cm (15 in) above the pubis.

Fetal activity may begin as early as the 10th week of gestation, but it's not usually noticed until 18–20 weeks into pregnancy (even later with firstborns). By that time, the developing fetus is a lively little entity that moves around in its increasingly confined space and responds to loud sounds. "Quickening," the first sign of fetal movement, is usually felt around the fifth month — and often described as being like "the fluttering of a tiny bird." It's sometimes so faint that a mother wonders whether her unborn baby really moved. Unborn babies have rest periods alternating with times of vigorous action when arms flail, legs kick, the body bends and arches. The movements are more discernible when the mother is relaxed. The fetal kicks continue on and off throughout the rest of pregnancy. If they diminish markedly in late pregnancy, it may be a sign of fetal trouble, and should be reported to the caregivers.

CHARTING FETAL PROGRESS
About four weeks after conception, when the embryo is only 4 mm (⅙ of an inch) long, the tubelike heart begins to beat. At five to six weeks postconception, arms and legs are mere fingerless buds, becoming paws around the eighth week. By twelve weeks, the fingers can grasp objects, and the fetus can suck its toes, grimace, frown and press its lips together. By this time it's also swallowing and urinating amniotic fluid. The "hairy ape" stage of fetal development refers to a stage when the unborn's

body is temporarily covered with hair. Strangely, the very first fetal hair grows in as coarse bristles, particularly on the eyebrows, lips and even the palms of the hands and soles of the feet. This primary hair is soon replaced by a soft down all over the body, called lanugo, shed just before term. Most newborns have scanty hair, although some premature babies may still be downy all over. The fetal body is also covered with vernix, a thick, waxy coat — especially thick on the scalp and eyebrows — that protects the delicate skin from being chapped by the salty amniotic waters.

By the fourth to fifth month of pregnancy, the fetus wriggles within its cramped quarters, turns somersaults, and flexes and stretches its limbs — movements that feel like butterfly wings within the mother's belly. It reacts to the mother's movements and outside sounds — perhaps remaining inactive while gently rocked, and jerking sharply in response to loud bangs. Its responses to sound are measurable by changes in heartrate and body movements. A microphone inserted into the uterus shows the dominant sounds to be the mother's digestive noises and the steady beat of her heart; no doubt this is why some mothers report that holding an infant over the left breast calms it. Machines that mimic a human heartbeat (at about 60–80 beats a minute), or the tick of a grandfather clock, can also soothe fussy babies, and some hospital baby-care units use heartbeat machines to comfort preemies. But while some parents believe that reciting Blake or playing Mozart to an unborn child can shape its personality, most experts consider this a far-fetched notion.

At 22 to 26 weeks of growth the fetus is wrinkled, because the skin lacks fat under its surface layer. At this stage the genes that regulate liver function, respiration and digestion may not yet be fully "turned on," one crucial reason why babies born before 26 weeks have a tough time surviving. By 29 weeks, fat, an enormous safeguard for newborn well-being, is laid down. Fetal fat stores nourish the newborn during its critical transition from the womb to the exterior world. Brown adipose fat, a unique fetal feature, is deposited around the kidneys and in the neck. A rapid heat-producer, brown fat warms the tiny newborn body, which cannot yet shiver to create heat.

Most babies are born at "term" — between 39 to 41 weeks of gestation — but some are born prematurely (before completing 37 weeks of development) and some late, after 42 weeks of gestation, as "post-term" or "post-mature" babies.

NUTRITION IN PREGNANCY

While no one can choose a baby's eye or hair color, eating well and gaining adequate weight can increase the chances of giving birth to a healthy, full-weight baby. An infant's birthweight is often linked to the mother's weight gain during pregnancy. In general, heavier newborns thrive better, are more resistant to infection and have fewer risks of illness than small newborns (who weigh under six pounds at birth). Maternal weight gain in pregnancy is very variable and should ideally be 11–16 kg (25–35 lb), ideally producing a baby weighing seven and a half to eight pounds. "Yet," comments one health consultant at Toronto's Department of Public Health, "many women still worry about gaining too much and go on diets that could harm their babies." An overweight woman should wait until after the birth to reduce, since dieting during pregnancy may release toxins that could harm the fetus. Those who are underweight at the start of pregnancy may need to put on as much as 18 kg (40 lb). Pregnant teenagers, still growing themselves, have particular nutrient needs.

Expectant mothers may gain weight steadily, but caregivers must be alert to any sudden spurts, which may herald unhealthy fluid retention or the onset of pre-eclampsia (characterized by elevated blood pressure and swelling of the face, hands and feet). The rate of gain varies from woman to woman, and is about 0.9–1.8 kg (2–4 lb) in the first 12 weeks of gestation, then roughly 0.5 kg (1 lb) a week to about 4.5 kg (10 lb) extra by the 20th week of gestation, 9 kg (20 lb) by 30 weeks, to a total of 11–16 kg (25–35 lb) by term (39 to 40 weeks). At first, the weight gain is mostly in the mother's body — putting on extra fat, more breast tissue, increasing maternal blood volume, enlarging the uterus and filling it with fluid. The later weight gain is largely in the unborn child and the placenta.

A well-balanced diet of fresh foods that includes enough protein and overall calories (about 1,800–2,500 a day by mid-pregnancy) and adequate vitamins and minerals, with special attention to iron, salt and calcium, is advised. Protein is a crucial nutrient for healthy fetal development, and is also needed for the mother's increased blood volume. About 75 to 80 grams of protein a day is recommended, an increase of about 50 percent above average intakes, or one extra 30-gram serving of protein in the form of meat, fish, poultry, eggs, cheeses, nuts or legumes.

Iron is essential to both mother and baby for the manufacture of hemoglobin (the red pigment in blood that carries oxygen to tissues). Liver, red meat and dried beans are good natural iron sources. While most women in developed countries who eat a well-balanced diet get ample iron, many physicians recommend a daily iron supplement from mid-pregnancy on, especially for women who are anemic.

A diet that includes meat contains enough natural salt (sodium) without adding any when cooking or at the table. But salt should not be excluded from the diet except on medical advice, since sodium is vital for the growing baby and the mother's extra blood volume.

Calcium is essential for the developing baby's bones and tooth buds, and for efficient nerve and muscle function. A low-calcium diet may permit calcium to leach out of the mother's bones. Three or four cups of milk a day — or the equivalent in other dairy products (yogurt, cottage cheese) — should provide the needed daily 1.2 grams. Nondairy sources of calcium are broccoli, dried beans, canned salmon and some grains.

Vitamin supplements aren't necessary, given a good diet, but folic acid, one of the B vitamins — essential to blood-cell formation — is sometimes low in a pregnant woman. This can lead to a certain type of anemia in the mother, and folate deficiency has been linked to congenital neural tube defects (such as spina bifida). To avoid the risk of neural tube defects, many physicians now recommend folic acid supplements of 50 to 100 micrograms daily.

SOME DIETARY TIPS DURING PREGNANCY

- Shun junk foods — they contain calories but few valuable nutrients.
- Avoid alcohol, known to produce fetal deformities; malformations due to alcohol absorbed from the mother arise mostly during the first trimester of pregnancy, so alcohol is best avoided in the first half of pregnancy, and restricted to an "occasional" drink for the rest.

- Avoid all medications before conception and during pregnancy. Check with your doctor or other caregiver about use of any over-the-counter medications, such as antihistamines, painkillers, cough medicines and so on during pregnancy, as some can harm the developing fetus.
- If constipated, don't take laxatives without medical

advice (Metamucil is considered safe). Having 15 ml (1 tbsp) of wheat bran a day may overcome the problem.
- If nauseated with "morning sickness," try some plain dry crackers and sips of water before getting out of bed. Eat smaller meals more often throughout the day, rather than a few large ones. If nausea persists, seek medical advice.

Natural sources of folate are green leafy vegetables, mushrooms, organ meats and cantaloupe melon.

Vitamin A, the rest of the B's, C, D and E will probably be ample in a varied diet containing fresh fruits, vegetables and fortified milk products. But pregnant vegetarians are at risk of nutritional deficiencies — especially of iron, calcium and protein — because of the sheer bulk of plant foods needed to supply adequate nutrients. Vegetarian mothers-to-be may need advice on vitamin and mineral supplements.

Medications, smoking and alcohol

Medications during pregnancy may deflect normal fetal development and produce various deformities, according to the type of medication and the amount absorbed. Many substances that get into the mother's bloodstream also cross the placenta and reach the developing baby. Once regarded as a "magic barrier," the placenta was termed a "bloody sieve" by the late Virginia Apgar, the anesthesiologist who originated the Apgar score for rating newborn well-being. For each fetal organ — eyes, lungs, heart — there's a specific critical period when its growth can be distorted by chemicals and drugs. Some medications can be safely taken in pregnancy, and for others a substitute may be available. But many seemingly innocent medications, such as anticonvulsants, antinauseants, laxatives and cold remedies, may harm unborn

babies. The greatest danger of malformation for most organs occurs during their most rapid period of growth, usually in the first 12–14 weeks of pregnancy. If prescription drugs are essential to control a disorder such as epilepsy or diabetes, a couple should seek medical advice before conceiving.

Smoking tobacco increases the risk of placental insufficiency and premature birth, often resulting in underweight babies. Studies show that babies born to smoking mothers are shorter than those of nonsmokers, weigh less and are more susceptible to respiratory infections after birth. There is some evidence that babies born to smoking mothers may also be more prone to hyperactivity, suffer more crib deaths (Sudden Infant Death Syndrome) and be slow learners.

Alcohol consumption, now on the rise among women, is alleged by the director of the U.S. National Institute of Alcohol Abuse and Alcoholism to be "the third leading cause of mental retardation and neurological problems in infants, also causing a roster of malformations in heart, limbs . . . skull, head and brain." Collectively termed Fetal Alcohol Syndrome (FAS), the greatest fetal dangers from alcohol occur in the first three months of pregnancy. Some go so far as to claim that "the only known safe limit for alcohol in pregnancy is none." Others say that, late in pregnancy, an occasional glass of wine or beer does no harm.

Saunas are considered a "no, no" during pregnancy, and hot tub soaks are also not advised (unless the belly isn't immersed), as the heat may raise the mother's "core" temperature, alter blood flow to the fetus and possibly cause fetal damage.

EXERCISE IN PREGNANCY

Many women, on becoming pregnant (particularly for the first time), wonder whether they should carry on with their exercise programs or usual sports. Provided the pregnancy is progressing without complications, normal activities need not be curtailed. Women accustomed to sporting activities can continue them. Exercise should be done regularly to tone the muscles — including pelvic-floor or Kegel exercises — to prepare for labor. Activities such as tennis, swimming, jogging or cycling may be continued, but moderated in late pregnancy. Some caregivers might discourage the exertion of sports such as downhill skiing, water skiing and horse riding, and heavy lifting is obviously best avoided. Scuba diving is *not* recommended, as the effects of underwater pressure on the fetus have not been determined.

SPOTTING HIGH-RISK PREGNANCIES

"Risk scoring" is a technique used to evaluate the progress of pregnancy with parameters that help to determine whether mother or baby is in a risk bracket that necessitates referral to a specialized unit for safer birthing. A prenatal score chart is used to plot maternal changes as they appear. According to a pediatrician at the University of Western Ontario, the method can "significantly reduce risks of physical or mental handicaps in the baby. Different risks may surface as pregnancy progresses."

Overall, about 10 percent of all pregnancies pose some danger to mother, fetus or both at labor or birth, and 70–80 percent of these are predictable in advance. The rest happen unexpectedly, due to unanticipated problems, such as a cervix that is sluggish and won't dilate (open), baby in an awkward position, the cord wrapped around the baby's neck, maternal hemorrhage, failure to progress, the placenta blocking the baby's passage or the baby becoming distressed by oxygen shortage. Such unexpected problems underlie the modern rationale for giving birth in specialized obstetric units or hospitals, where medical help is instantly on hand. But most problems can be spotted in plenty of time to avoid mishaps, correct them or transfer to hospital if need be.

Risk factors that are obvious ahead of time include maternal obesity, narrow pelvis, incomplete cervix, drug use, poor nutrition, previous miscarriage, previous problem labors, diabetes or other medical disorders. Additional risks may surface at different times as pregnancy advances — such as eclampsia, bleeding (perhaps from a loosening placenta), retarded fetal growth, early membrane rupture ("waters breaking") and — most feared of complications — a very premature labor.

Prematurity and low birthweight bring risks

Although premature or low-birthweight babies are more vulnerable than full-term ones, and some may have to spend time in a neonatal unit (sometimes in incubators), many survive. However, prematurity is still a leading cause of infant mortality, and a number of the preemie or low-birthweight survivors have above-average risks of health and learning problems. At present, 5–10 percent of live births in North America are premature, and pre-term babies have less ability to withstand temperature changes, respiratory problems and infection. "Prematurity" is defined as birth occurring before 36 weeks of gestation and "low birthweight" as newborn weight less than 2.5 kg (5½ lb). The more premature or underweight the newborn, the greater the risks of illness and disability. Factors that predispose to prematurity are multiple births (e.g., twins), placental failure and excess amniotic fluid.

A premature or pre-term birth whether spontaneous, or engineered by induction or early Cesarean section, removes an unfinished fetus from the womb, possibly converting it into an endangered infant. The body may not have enough fat stores to bridge the gap. Fat reserves are critical to survival until the mother's milk comes in, a few days after birth. Premature babies who lack brown adipose stores have more trouble regulating their body temperature than full-term babies. The digestive system is immature and the lungs may not yet be ready to breathe air. Nevertheless, perinatal units can now save smaller and smaller babies — the cut-off point for survival currently being about 24 weeks after the last menstrual period (or 22 weeks after conception). If newborns cannot feed and swallow they may have to be fed intravenously, and if unable to control body temperature will be kept in an incubator.

Many very premature infants die of infections, respiratory distress or other problems. In one Canadian study, of 260 infants born between 23–28 weeks of (gestational) age, one-third couldn't survive. Those that did survive had above-average risks of physical and mental disabilities. In another study on surviving preemies born at 24–29 weeks of gestational development, 80 percent developed normally without handicaps, about 5 percent suffered severe disabilities (such as cerebral palsy and learning problems) and 16 percent had mild disabilities. Other studies find that 14–15 percent of babies born earlier than 29 weeks gestation end up mildly to severely disabled. Efforts made to avert a premature birth include bedrest and certain medications. If it can't be stopped, the mother may be given medications that stimulate rapid maturation of the fetal lungs, to facilitate newborn breathing.

Low birthweight (being "small for dates" or small for a given developmental stage) — not the same as prematurity — also puts newborns at risk of health problems. Babies that weigh 2.5 kg (5.5 lb) or less at birth — even if full-term — have fewer than average reserves with which to face life outside the uterus. The World Health Organization defines low birthweight as below 2,500 g (less than 5.5 lb) at delivery; very low birthweight as less than 1,500 g (3.3 lb). Very-low-birthweight babies are at still greater risk of infection, also of hearing and vision problems, and possibly learning difficulties.

SOME PREGNANCY AND BIRTH COMPLICATIONS

- *Placenta previa* — where a fetus sits high up in the uterine wall and the growing placenta partly or completely blocks the uterine outlet, hindering safe delivery, possibly necessitating premature induction of labor or a Cesarean.
- *Abruptio placenta* — premature detachment from the uterine wall of a normal placenta — associated with intense pain and jeopardizing fetal well-being, necessitating a Cesarean to save a distressed fetus.

- *Pre-eclampsia and eclampsia* (formerly called "toxemia") — a still poorly understood condition, most common in young women with a first pregnancy and in those with diabetes and/or multiple pregnancies (e.g., twins). It is signalled by rising blood pressure, swelling of feet, legs, hands and face, and protein in the urine. If not halted, pre-eclampsia may lead to full eclampsia, which threatens mother and fetus, possibly necessitating

early delivery. The treatment is bedrest and blood-pressure medications while watching for kidney and other problems.
- *Multiple birth (e.g., twins)*, either "identical" (with identical genes, from one egg, fertilized by one sperm) or "fraternal (nonidentical), where two separate eggs are fertilized by two separate sperm and the twins are not necessarily "same sex" or in any way similar. About two-thirds of twins are fraternal, one-third identical.

PRENATAL CLASSES: PREPARING FOR LABOR

Prenatal education classes, given by childbirth educators, help women make choices and prepare for labor. They include lectures and films as well as discussion and maybe physiotherapy sessions. Prenatal childbirth classes are offered in most hospitals for parents-to-be and include training in breathing, relaxation and muscle control (or pelvic-floor exercises) for an easier labor and birth.

The Lamaze system, a well-known prenatal birth-preparation system, named after Dr. Fernand Lamaze, a French obstetrician, adapted Russian conditioning tactics to lessen labor discomfort. The four basic principles of Lamaze training are: replacement of the word "pain" with contraction (building an image of controllable labor); replacement of myths by detailed facts (to allay fears and build confidence); diversion of pain signals (by focusing on a known object brought into hospital); reliance on a supportive coach (partner, relative or other helper) to time contractions, give gentle massage and encouragement. This method is not guaranteed to be painless, or to allow childbirth without anesthetic; rather, medication is regarded as a tool to use if needed. Lamaze birthing has been shown to be both pleasant and safe. Lamaze-trained childbearers tend to be relaxed, take few drugs and have fewer than usual Cesareans, forceps deliveries or episiotomies. If there is a vaginal tear, it is often less serious than with unprepared birthers.

Leboyer's "nonviolent childbirth" aims to ease newborn transit with low lights, hushed voices, delayed cord-cutting (after the blood stops pulsating — deemed dangerous by some experts because it could artificially increase newborn blood volume), gentle skin massage and placing the newborn in a warm bath at once. Some aspects of Leboyer's birthing method have now been incorporated into some obstetric units, which dim the lights, place the baby on the mother's abdomen immediately after birth (even before cord-cutting) and generally soften the birthing atmosphere.

Modern childbirth-preparation methods discuss pregnancy care and childbirth choices, support from caregivers, how to facilitate the birth, ambulation during labor, the right to privacy and rooming-in. Most amalgamate some Lamazian principles with other ideas, like those of British anthropologist and childbirth educator Sheila Kitzinger, who takes a psychosexual approach to labor. She views birth as a "keenly sensual, vaginal pleasure — especially in the final stage of labor, as the head descends — in which women trust their body, and work *with*, not against, its rhythms and see it not as a suffering vehicle, but as something over which they have control." She warns women to expect at least a half-hour of "extreme discomfort during transition" (from first to second, or pushing, stage of labor), and calls for "pain relief to be on hand when requested or needed."

THE THREE STAGES OF LABOR

The process by which labor starts is not fully understood. The first stage begins as the cervix, or neck of the womb, begins to open and the mucus plug that fills it is dislodged. This "show," a small pinkish blob, often heralds the start of labor. There's a progressive increase in frequency, strength and duration of uterine contractions which dilate the cervix, ultimately to 10 cm (4 in) — usually wide enough to let through the baby's head.

Breathing exercises help the mother to relax and cope more easily with the discomfort. Typically, the sac that holds the water bulges in front of the baby's head and ruptures at or before full dilation of the cervix, at the end of the first stage (but it often breaks sooner, even before contractions begin). The first stage usually lasts about 12–16 or more hours in first-time mothers, and less — perhaps only 4–6 or fewer hours — in subsequent births. The baby's heartrate is checked regularly (babies at risk may be electronically monitored throughout labor), and the mother may be occasionally examined internally to see how labor is progressing. When the cervix is fully dilated, at the end of first-stage labor, the mother often feels a tremendous pressure and an urge to "push" — in transition to the second stage.

The second stage of labor begins once the cervix is fully dilated. The mother may feel an irresistible urge to push. As the baby passes through the birth canal the mother bears

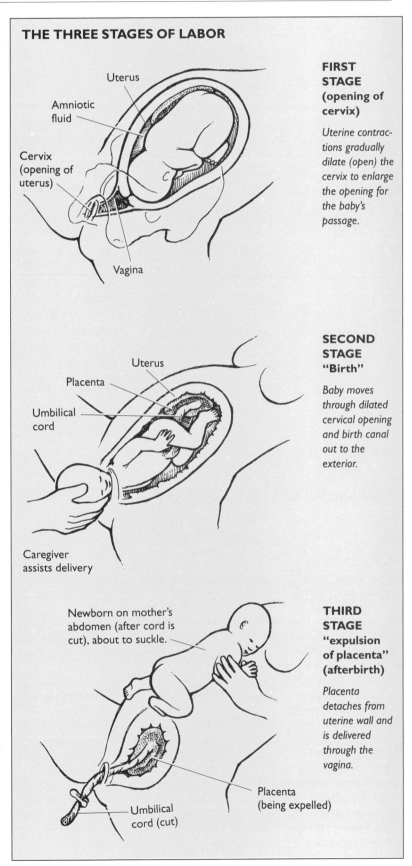

THE THREE STAGES OF LABOR

Uterus
Amniotic fluid
Cervix (opening of uterus)
Vagina

FIRST STAGE (opening of cervix)

Uterine contractions gradually dilate (open) the cervix to enlarge the opening for the baby's passage.

Uterus
Placenta
Umbilical cord
Caregiver assists delivery

SECOND STAGE "Birth"

Baby moves through dilated cervical opening and birth canal out to the exterior.

Newborn on mother's abdomen (after cord is cut), about to suckle.
Placenta (being expelled)
Umbilical cord (cut)

THIRD STAGE "expulsion of placenta" (afterbirth)

Placenta detaches from uterine wall and is delivered through the vagina.

down, taking deep breaths. Relaxation between contractions is usually blissfully painless, as the baby's head pushes against the cervix and anesthetizes the nerve endings! No one who's seen the transcendental euphoria on a woman's face can doubt the magical impact of the birthing moment.

The third stage of labor is expulsion of the placenta, or "afterbirth," which may take place in a few minutes or up to half an hour later. Sometimes it's expelled more quickly if the baby is immediately placed on the mother's abdomen, before the cord is cut, and allowed to suckle. The sucking action stimulates release of the hormone *oxytocin*, which contracts and closes up the uterus, forcing out the placenta.

Painkillers and/or anesthetics are used by about half of Canadian women in hospital deliveries, according to one survey. "Labor medications," states one specialist, "are still a source of some perinatal breathing problems — with possibly subtle changes in babies' brains." Another expert adds that "we now have antidotes that can reverse some drug effects in newborns, but all medicated labors need extra vigilance." The epidural (spinal block by hypodermic injection) is a popular way to ease the pain without affecting the baby's breathing. And use of the harmless pain-reliever nitrous oxide, better known as "laughing gas," can help.

Electronic fetal monitoring of the baby's heartbeat during labor is almost routine in many North American hospitals and birthing units. A belt is strapped over the mother's abdomen to record the baby's heart pattern, which is displayed on a screen. The fetal heart can also be monitored with a small electrode placed on the baby's head. As so often happens, practice lags behind research, and routine electronic monitoring is now roundly criticized by many experts. They allege that unless it's done "in conjunction with fetal scalp blood tests (for fetal oxygen levels) it does not improve fetal safety or health and is no better than regular monitoring with a stethoscope." (But often there are too few nurses to do regular stethoscope monitoring.) Many experts thus consider electronic fetal monitoring unreliable without the biochemical backup of blood-oxygen levels — taken by fetal scalp sampling to measure the blood's pH (acidity level). And even with fetal blood sampling, electronic monitoring of the fetal heart has *not* been definitely shown to improve birth outcomes. One specialist at the University of Western Ontario says: "Fetal heart patterns and reactions are often interpreted by inexperienced staff, producing false alarms of fetal distress in perfectly healthy babies, resulting in much needless Cesarean surgery." Fetal distress can also be detected not only by stethoscope checks but also by a decreasing volume of amniotic fluid and other signs.

Induction of labor — inducing the uterus to start contracting with hormones such as oxytocin and prostaglandin E (to soften the cervix), or by breaking the bag of waters (or both) — is done in 15 percent of Canadian births, compared to 3 to 5 percent in many

BREECH BABIES

The term "presentation" refers to the position of the fetal head relative to the cervix (mouth of the uterus). As birth begins, most full-term babies present head down (in the vertex position — from the Latin for "top of the head"). In this position, the largest part of the baby, its head, pushes down and dilates the cervix sufficiently to allow the rest of the body to slip through. But 3 percent of babies present in a breech position (from the Anglo-Saxon term for britches), where the baby's bottom or feet press down first, and may not dilate the cervix enough to allow the head through — creating an emergency situation.

Breech babies may present as:
• a frank breech, with the buttocks presenting first and fetal heels up around the ears, a position usually manageable by vaginal birth;
• a complete breech, where both buttocks and feet present with foot soles showing through (riskier but sometimes manageable by vaginal birth);
• a footling breech, where feet appear first, a position rare at term but common with premature breech babies, which is very risky and demands a Cesarean.

The recent Canadian Consensus Report advocated vaginal delivery for fully developed frank or complete breech babies with an estimated birth weight of 2,500 to 4,000 g (five to 9 lb). For less mature babies, 31 to 35 weeks old, they suggested a planned vaginal birth. Both U.S. and Canadian experts require the attending physician to be experienced in doing vaginal breech births.

PRODUCING THE HEALTHIEST POSSIBLE BABY

European centers, where the practice is frowned upon. Usual reasons for induction include a distressed baby, a mother in trouble (e.g., with eclampsia, diabetes or a blood incompatibility) and an overdue or post-mature baby. Induction of labor, however, has some disadvantages. When done by breaking the bag of waters, it allows the sterile buffering fluid to leave the uterus, which may increase risks of infection. The induction method using oxytocin may also produce overly strong contractions. And overly strong contractions may loosen the placenta. Thus caution is urged for the artificial induction of labor. The induction of labor, like other birthing practices, is being reassessed at present for its validity and usefulness.

About 10 percent of pregnancies go well beyond the due date. Those that last two or more weeks past the due date (or 42 weeks) are considered "post-due" — perhaps because something fails to trigger labor. Problems can then arise, such as fetal oxygen lack or a baby too big to pass through the woman's pelvis. In the past 30 years or so, post-term pregnancies have been managed either by inducing labor or by awaiting spontaneous labor while carefully monitoring fetal well-being, and inducing labor at any hint of fetal distress.

Episiotomies — making a cut in the vaginal wall to ease the baby's passage and then sewing it up again — used to be almost routine in North American deliveries, but is now done less often in most hospitals, as its usefulness is in many cases contested. Studies show that cutting the vaginal wall may increase the tearing, cause laxity in the pelvic floor, incontinence and lead to dyspareunia (pain on intercourse), so the practice is now declining. Recent British studies show a dramatic drop in British episiotomy rates with *no* change in birth outcomes.

FROM FETUS TO NEWBORN: A LEAP INTO THE UNKNOWN

By the time a fetus is ready to be born, the volume of amniotic fluid has been reduced to about a quart (the "waters" that break when labor begins). At term, the average baby is about 50 cm (20 in) long and weighs about 3,500 g (7.5 lb). Babies that weigh less than 2,500 g (5.5 lb) are labeled "low birthweight," but not all low-birthweight newborns are premature, some are just "small-for-dates" babies.

Human infants are born somewhat immature compared to most other animals, requiring a long period of parental nurturing before they become independent. In most full-term newborns, the body is plump, most biochemical systems and enzymes are ready for action, the tiny lungs are coated with surfactant (a substance vital to lung expansion) and the chest is able to take that crucial first gasp of air.

The passage through a heaving birth canal out through the cervix into the bright, harsh exterior brings immense changes for the fetus. Within minutes, it must change from being an aquatic creature, cushioned in a warm, dark, sterile bag of waters, obtaining oxygen and food from the mother's bloodstream, to being a self-sustaining, air-breathing creature. A newborn must start breathing with the lungs — a new exercise, albeit already rehearsed in the womb by full-term babies. (The labor contractions often help to get the lungs working.) The lungs of premature infants may be imperfectly prepared for air-breathing, one of the factors that imperils their survival. Obstetricians and pediatricians will do everything in their power to keep pre-term babies safely inside the uterus (perhaps hospitalizing a mother in danger of premature labor) rather than let a frail fetus with immature lungs out to attempt air-breathing.

The immediate post-birth period

Baby care immediately after birth includes examination of baby and placenta (afterbirth) for signs of infection or abnormality, weight and length measurements and rating the baby's well-being on the Apgar scale at one and five minutes after delivery. The ten-point Apgar scale allots zero to two points each for:
• heartrate;
• skin color;
• muscle tone;
• reflexes;
• respiration.

In Canadian hospitals, silver-nitrate drops or erythromycin ointment are routinely given

ASSESSING NEWBORN HEALTH

Newborn reflexes checked include:
- **The rooting reflex — the turn of a baby's head when its cheek is touched — nature's way of ensuring that a newborn will turn to the nipple, be nourished, grow and thrive. (Right from the first moments after birth an infant will search with its mouth and turn its head to try to find the breast.)**
- **The grasp reflex — newborns hang on to an adult finger so tightly that they can often be pulled upright.**
- **The "doll's eye" reflex — eyes pointing in a fixed direction as the head turns.**
- **The startle or "Moro" reflex — dipping of the head and stretching, then flexing of arms and legs (as if surprised, but it's not real shock, just a transient reflex!).**
- **The stepping reflex — a one-day-old infant will "step out" as if walking when held upright on the examining table (a dramatic reflex that disappears by a few weeks after birth).**

    Another system of measurement, Brazelton's Neonatal Scale, evaluates neonatal behavior with more sophisticated ratings of mental, social and temperamental capacities. The method measures infant reactions to sound, light and other stimuli, distinguishing time spent awake, semiconscious or asleep and amounts of crying, gazing, kicking or looking, assessing 26 different behaviors.

to newborns to forestall possible blindness due to maternal gonorrhea. Vitamin K is usually also administered to newborns to help with blood-clotting and minimize bleeding at birth, as the immature liver doesn't yet produce this vital substance.

Caring for sick or premature babies

Health professionals now encourage parents to spend time with premature or sick newborns — even those in incubators. Neonatal units support parents in trying to feed ailing newborns, and some even encourage siblings to visit, to promote family ties. Parents can briefly hold and touch sick newborns in intensive care or neonatal units. And preemie nurseries encourage parents to see and handle their infant, even if it simply means putting a hand into the incubator to stroke the baby. This handling stimulates the infants, keeps them alert and assists respiration.

Mothers are encouraged to come in and breastfeed, and learn to express their breastmilk and store it in sterile refrigerated bottles for later feedings, not only for its nutritional value, but to make breastfeeding easier when the baby arrives home. In some birth centers, parents also get psychophysiological instruction and support from the baby-care team in handling their vulnerable preemies. New research suggests that newborns are more resilient and adaptable than we used to believe.

A vast new field of infant psychiatry identifies communication problems and can assist parent-infant interaction and reinforce parental feelings of competence.

CESAREAN BIRTH: TIME FOR REAPPRAISAL

Once a rare and often fatal operation — previously considered an "obstetric defeat" — Cesarean surgery is currently done more often to deliver a distressed fetus and avoid damage in difficult birth situations. In fact, it is now the manner of birth for nearly one in five Canadian babies. (Rates have climbed from 5.2 percent in 1970 to 18.6 percent in 1982 and almost 20 percent of all births in 1991, giving Canada one of the highest Cesarean rates in the world.) As Cesareans have become safer, the decision to operate has likewise become easier. Rather than using Cesareans as a "last-ditch" measure, physicians have begun to favor surgery over any difficult or manipulative birth. The dramatic rise in North American Cesareans has been paralleled by an equally sharp decline in perinatal mortality (babies dying after 28 weeks of development or at 1 kg (2 lb) in weight, or up to a week after birth). But tempting though it may be to link the drop in perinatal deaths to the rise in Cesareans, studies disprove the connection. In reality, perinatal mortality dropped *before* the rise in Cesareans.

Alarmed at the escalating rates of Cesareans, many obstetricians, health officials and consumers claim that Cesareans are no longer done just for accepted medical reasons — such as a breech position, a large baby in a small pelvis or a prematurely separated placenta — but because the operation gives physicians more control and avoids the potentially serious complications of a difficult vaginal birth. But while medical advances have made Cesarean birth safer, it's still not as safe as an uncomplicated vaginal birth. Borderline cases (such as a long labor that doesn't necessarily threaten the mother or infant) raise many doubts about current practices in doing Cesareans.

What is a Cesarean section?

The origin of the term "Cesarean section" is obscure. Legend has it that Julius Caesar was born by cutting open his mother's abdomen and extracting the baby, but since Caesar's mother survived the operation (then invariably fatal for the mother) the theory is open to doubt! The procedure more probably got its name from the Latin *caedere*: "to cut." In a Cesarean operation the surgeon cuts through ("sections") the abdominal skin and muscle and lifts the baby out of the uterus. Although the dangers have been greatly reduced, it is nonetheless abdominal surgery, with all its usual risks. The classic vertical incision in the uterus has now been largely replaced by a horizontal incision in the uterus and also a horizontal cut in the abdomen when possible (as it's more cosmetically pleasing). In an emergency situation the surgeon may still make a vertical cut in the abdomen (because it's quicker and easier), but will still do a transverse uterine incision whenever possible, because it is stronger than the vertical, less likely to bleed profusely and far less likely to rupture in subsequent labor. General anesthesia may be employed, but the surgery is usually conducted with regional (epidural) anesthesia, which permits the mother to see her newborn immediately and avoids the slower recuperation after a general anesthetic.

Risks of the Cesarean

Newborn health can suffer from a Cesarean birth, especially if a premature baby is taken out too soon. Also, Cesarean babies tend to have a slightly greater risk of Respiratory Distress Syndrome (RDS), owing to the lack of stimulation obtained during normal vaginal birth — which squeezes the fetal lungs, or because the lungs lack the surfactant coating vital to their expansion — particularly if the Cesarean is done electively (by choice) and the baby's calculated due date is wrong, leading to premature birth.

Maternal illness or complications following Cesareans now average 11 to 18 percent, the risks being greater for those who are obese or anemic, or who have emergency surgery after a difficult labor. Infection of the wound site, uterine lining, urinary tract or pelvis is the commonest complication in the mother. (But infection can likewise occur after a long or difficult vaginal birth.) Fortunately, antibiotics greatly reduce the dangers of post-Cesarean infection. Complications are fewer in those who choose a repeat Cesarean than in those done as emergency operations. (The Society of Obstetricians and Gynecologists of Canada quotes a mortality figure for emergency Cesareans of 9.9 per 100,000 births, which is twice that for elective repeats and about two to four times that for modern vaginal births.)

The psychological impact of unexpected Cesarean surgery in a couple that anticipated a natural vaginal birth can be devastating if they aren't adequately prepared and made comfortable with the decision. Prenatal classes educate women to value participation in labor and natural childbirth, and so a mother who unexpectedly needs a Cesarean to save a distressed baby may have strong feelings of inadequacy and failure. Including the mother (and her supporters) in the decision-making, plus reassurance and counseling can allay this feeling, as can the father's presence in the delivery room and keeping the newborn close to the mother after birth. Of course, some women actually welcome a Cesarean as deliverance from what they call the "painful, terrifying experience" of vaginal birth.

Vaginal birth after Cesarean (VBAC)

Well-documented studies show that, in thousands of women, trial of labor (TOL) — attempting vaginal labor after a Cesarean — is a safe, often successful, even beneficial procedure for childbirth. The risks of uterine rupture with the new lower-segment transverse Cesarean scar are minimal. In a study of 10,000 women giving birth vaginally with a transverse scar, there were no maternal deaths. Even if a transverse incision opens a little before or during an ensuing labor, there is very little risk of complications, and it usually heals easily without further attention. In fact, dangers may be lower with a VBAC than with a planned repeat Cesarean.

REASONS FOR CESAREAN SECTION

- **failure of labor to progress normally;**
- **fetal distress possibly seen on the electronic heart monitor (due to lack of oxygen);**
- **fetal malposition (such as breech — buttocks first — or a transverse lie, baby lying horizontally and unable to emerge);**
- **cephalopelvic disproportion — a woman with a pelvis too narrow for the baby's transit;**
- ***abruptio placenta* — a placenta that separates too soon and endangers the baby through lack of oxygen and the mother through hemorrhage;**
- ***placenta previa* — one that implants in an unusual position and blocks the baby's passage, with risk of hemorrhage during labor;**
- **a previous Cesarean.**

THE BENEFITS OF VBAC INCLUDE:

- faster post-birth recovery;
- greater parental satisfaction;
- less risk of post-birth complications such as infection in the mother;
- less risk of respiratory problems in the newborn;
- reduced healthcare costs;
- shorter hospital stay.

Many centers now promote normal labor as a safe option for women after a Cesarean birth, provided they fulfill certain criteria. Yet, despite its advantages, acceptance of VBAC has been slow and parents-to-be may have to search for a physician and center which are willing to encourage it.

The odds for succeeding in VBAC are about 70 percent. Although theoretically any woman (except someone with a classic uterine incision) can try for VBAC, some women are likelier to succeed than others. The outcome depends partly on the reason the first Cesarean was performed, since some problems tend to recur. Breech presentation, fetal distress, *abruptio placenta, placenta previa* and accidental cord prolapse are not likely to recur. In essence, the latest advice is that VBAC be treated like any other natural labor, except that a very long second-stage labor is discouraged in case of any uterine weakness.

NEWBORN CHILD-PARENT BONDING

Newborn/parent bonding is a concept introduced by Marshall Klaus, an Ohio pediatrician who showed that, contrary to former ideas of the newborn as an inert blob, it has an innate urge to look around and respond before falling into its first neonatal sleep. To promote parent/infant contact in the sensitive post-birth period, many maternity units now encourage parents to spend time alone with their new baby right after birth.

Immediately after birth, most normal, full-term newborns have a period of "quiet alertness," possibly due to the stimulation of birth and the release of adrenal hormones during labor. In this phase, with eyes wide open, newborns stare at faces and scan their surroundings. Seeing their infant gazing at them, parents may "bond" instantly to the new arrival. After this the babies usually doze off into a long, deep sleep.

The newborn bonding concept has recently come under fire, since the idea of a "critical period" right after birth does not hold up as a universal phenomenon. While some parents enjoy immediate contact with their newborn, others take longer to form emotional ties. Although many studies show more interaction (more face-to-face gazing, stroking, chatting and patting) after early parent-baby contact, none has found any long-term differences in closeness, or proof that the initial bonding advantages persist into later relationships. The publicity about early bonding may create a false belief that if this experience is missed, parents can never make it up. In fact, for all of those who cannot bond at once — because of medical intervention during birth (such as Cesarean section) or problems with the infant's health (such as anoxia or premature birth) — professionals stress that there are countless other bonding times. As one University of Toronto research psychiatrist puts it: "popularization of the bonding idea has led to the distorted view that the first hours after birth are critical and if missed may impair parental nurturing abilities — an inflexible concept now questioned by many experts." Bonding isn't irretrievably blighted because a magical moment in time is lost; parents can establish just as meaningful, close relationships later on with their babies.

Rooming-in — with babies remaining in their mothers' rooms rather than returning to the nursery between feedings — is not yet a universal practice, although it is now very common, to encourage bonding and breastfeeding. Experiments show that mothers who keep their babies rooming-in beside them exhibit greater maternal behavior — looking, soothing, cuddling, chatting and feeding — than parents of babies in a central nursery. But mothers who need time to rest before holding their baby should not feel abnormal or unmotherly. If a mother doesn't want to keep the baby in her room all the time — perhaps after a long and difficult birth — she should be encouraged to feel comfortable with her decision, and other family members can help in baby-care at first. According to many researchers, when fathers also have extended early contact with their babies, they spend more time holding them, playing and chatting with them, and also continue to spend more time in child care later on.

The amazing abilities of newborns

Parents often attribute to their babies perceptions that could not yet be present. For example, although a newborn recognizes its mother's smell and voice, it may not feel anything special about her until several weeks later. Even the first "social smile," at around six weeks of age, is not uniquely directed at parents but at anyone who coos to the infant. So while parents may "bond" at once to their infant, the child may take months to become truly attached to them. But by six to eight months of age, an infant generally shows a clear preference for its parents over strangers, and has separation anxiety if removed from them.

Even so, the German term *Wunderkind* (wonderchild) — coined for Mozart and his amazing abilities as a child prodigy — might well be applied to full-term newborns, who show an amazing aptitude for adapting to their chaotic environment. Within minutes of birth they can respond appropriately to their unfamiliar surroundings. A newborn can turn its head toward a sound, may recognize and respond to its mother's voice, can suck milk and cry. But the stimulus to which it is most responsive — which it apparently finds most intriguing — is the human face.

Recent research shows that the newborn possesses a perceptual apparatus that enables it to respond effectively to its new world and, more important, to shape the behavior of its parents and caregivers. Helpless as they seem, newborns come well equipped to signal their needs. Harvard pediatrician T. Berry Brazelton noted two survival mechanisms: the ability to pick out and respond appropriately to stimuli that enhance well-being, and the capacity to "tune out" disturbing stimuli (such as loud noises or bright lights), which allows the infant to avoid sensory overload. For example, a full-term newborn turns toward a rattle while a premature one turns away, not yet ready to deal with that stimulus. Newborn crying — tearless, because tear-ducts are not yet working — produces parental comforting and feeding, which causes the crying to cease, allowing caregivers to gain confidence, which encourages more nurturing.

Until recently, it was popularly believed that newborns could not see clearly. Research now shows that they not only see in three dimensions, but show distinct visual prefer-

ences. Being nearsighted, they focus best at about eight to ten inches, roughly the distance of a baby's mouth from its mother's face while nursing. Research also shows that even day-old babies prefer the human face and black-and-white or outlined pictures of it to abstract or blurred images. They can follow moving objects and will turn their heads to see a human face. Infants look longer at a slow-moving object than at a static one, and soon after birth most babies demonstrate a greater ability to follow a diagrammatic outline of a normal face than one with scrambled features.

Newborns hear well, showing a distinct preference for the human voice, for women's voices over men's, and for high-pitched sounds to low-pitched ones. This may explain the human tendency to address infants with high-pitched baby-talk or songs. In studying the response to human voices, Brazelton and his Harvard colleagues found that about 68 percent of newborns turned toward a human voice, some actively searching for its source. Such complex, coordinated behavior involves many auditory pathways. As one researcher puts it: "A remarkable feat for an organism that until recently was given no credit for hearing, seeing or feeling."

A baby's sense of smell is sufficiently sensitive within a few days of birth to recognize its mother's odor, even that of a pad soaked in her milk. Presented with a pad soaked in their mother's breastmilk, infants will ignore all other stimuli and turn to it. Touch is also sensitively developed in newborns. Skin-to-skin contact is not only soothing to parents and baby, but has various health advantages — especially in colonizing the baby's system with the mother's (rather than alien) bacteria. Skin-to-skin contact often makes parents massage and stroke their babies extensively, which is less frequent with clothed contact.

New evidence about innate newborn personality may help to remove the guilt often felt by parents of extra-demanding, fussy or colicky babies, or those who fear they missed the post-birth bonding boat. Some babies are simply more "difficult" and less responsive than others — more unpredictable, irritable and easily upset. U.S. child psychologists Stella Chess and

Alexander Thomas label parental anxieties over nurturing skills as the *mal de mère* syndrome, ("sick mother" syndrome), typified by the fear that any innocent act, word or gesture may irreparably harm a child. This type of parent may be afraid to criticize or punish an infant for fear of lowering its self-esteem, and dare not praise it or show affection in case of "spoiling" it. Yet parents who respond promptly to their infant's cries generate warmth and confidence; attentiveness and loving care build trust, which makes youngsters secure and less likely to demand excess attention.

There's no evidence that any one child-rearing method inevitably creates this or that type of child. For instance, domineering, authoritarian treatment may make one infant submissive, another defiant. Much depends upon the child's individual coping mechanisms. Even when parents are obviously abusive, there's no absolute or predictable outcome. Some children who grow up under horrendous conditions — with psychotic, alcoholic or violent caretakers — develop into balanced, competent human beings. Over the long haul, neglect damages children, but by the same token a day's irritation or momentary burst of anger is not disastrous, provided there's a steady undercurrent of tender affection.

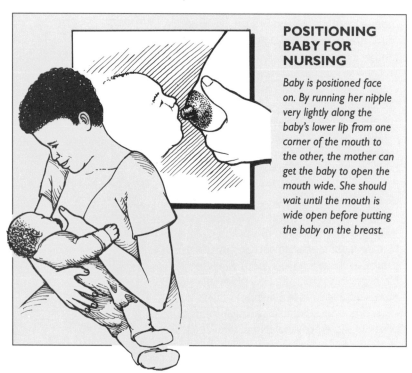

POSITIONING BABY FOR NURSING

Baby is positioned face on. By running her nipple very lightly along the baby's lower lip from one corner of the mouth to the other, the mother can get the baby to open the mouth wide. She should wait until the mouth is wide open before putting the baby on the breast.

BREAST IS STILL BEST

Breastmilk, specifically tailored to human development by the long process of evolution, supplies all the nutrients necessary for optimal infant development in the first few months after birth. Despite increasing public awareness and scientific validation of the enormous benefits of breastmilk for infants, many mothers who begin nursing quit too soon for lack of know-how, assistance and emotional support. While three-quarters of new mothers in Canada start off breastfeeding, a quarter give up within a month or so, usually sooner than intended, and only a third are still breastfeeding by the time their babies are three to four months old. When deciding whether or not to breastfeed their baby, new parents need accurate information in order to wend their way through the wealth of conflicting data.

For all its apparent simplicity, breastfeeding is not a reflex action or an instinct that comes naturally, but an art that must be taught and practiced. Although the sucking reflex is instinctive, women must learn how to position the newborn and latch it correctly to the breast. Good positioning is all-important. There are some infants who must learn to suck properly as well! Knowledge about breastfeeding was formerly passed on from mothers to daughters — a vanishing experience in today's culture. The best way to succeed is to learn ahead about the science of lactation and watch others nursing. Successful nursing involves tenacity, confidence and freedom from emotional tension, and requires constructive help at critical moments. Given some basic information during the first weeks of lactation, and helpful support, most women have an excellent chance of success.

Although practices such as rooming-in and family-centered birth units encourage breastfeeding, shorter postpartum hospitalization is now the rule, and many mothers leave hospital within a day or two — before their milk comes in (generally on the third post-birth day). The shorter hospital stay gives little time for instruction in breastfeeding techniques. And not all hospitals have an atmosphere that encourages breastfeeding; some healthcare attendants have an inbuilt prejudice against nudity or don't regard the breast as a nurturant part of the body, valuing it mainly for its sexual appeal. While most health experts today recognize the benefits of breastfeeding, few may actually have watched a mother nurse her baby! Whether verbally or nonverbally expressed, such attitudes may subtly undermine a new mother's confidence. What nursing mothers need is plenty of practical advice and support to persevere, particularly as the inability to nurse a firstborn can be a bitter disappointment and may engender guilt feelings.

Tips for nursing mothers

Following a few simple steps and anticipating possible deterrents may help to get nursing off to a good start .

- *Obtain competent breastfeeding instruction* before the baby's birth, ideally during prenatal classes. Classes generally include details of breast anatomy, the mechanism of milk production, the stimulative effect of sucking, the benefits of demand feeding, a physical nipple examination and preparation of inverted or small nipples if necessary.
- *Have baby room-in* (request it ahead) and feed on demand whenever possible, *not by the clock*. One University of Toronto expert reminds nursing mothers that "new babies with easily famished bodies need food every two hours or less." Newborns should be beside the mother from birth onwards if possible and suckle whenever hungry (not when the clock says it's time to feed). The more a baby sucks, the more the milk comes in. Contrary to the supposition that scheduled feedings reduce demands on the hospital staff's time and attention, one British study found that babies kept beside the mother's bed (not taken away even for diaper changes) and fed on demand exerted a far smaller load on the nursing staff, gained weight faster, caused fewer problems (such as nipple soreness or breast engorgement) and were easier to handle. On this basis, some hospitals have abolished scheduled feeds as a waste of nurses' time and a hindrance to successful lactation.
- *Feed the newborn immediately* after delivery. The sucking reflex is strongest in the first half-

---

SOME REASONS WHY WOMEN ABANDON BREASTFEEDING

- insufficient knowledge of its benefits;
- inadequate prenatal instruction;
- failure to get off to a good start;
- too little expert help for starters, in dealing with small but common problems;
- poor positioning of the baby at the breast;
- a delay of several hours in newborn nursing (thwarting the strong post-birth sucking reflex);
- separation of newborn and mother rather than "rooming-in";
- feeding by schedule instead of on demand;
- omitting night feedings;
- early fluid supplements (which undermine the baby's breast-sucking urge);
- need or desire to go back to job after 8–12 weeks (but even this amount of breastfeeding is worthwhile);
- conscious or uncon-
- scious reinforcement of mother's (unwarranted) fears about inadequate milk;
- derogatory comments or attitudes about the probable difficulties or messiness of breastfeeding, which communicate a negative attitude to insecure mothers;
- exhaustion or frustration from the need to be on 24-hour call (compared to bottle feeders, who can share the load).

---

hour after birth, fading somewhat thereafter, before it reappears at full force some 40 hours later. And the baby's sucking action stimulates release of the hormone oxytocin, which hastens milk secretion and also helps to expel the placenta and contract the mother's uterus, lessening the risk of hemorrhage. (Some obstetricians put a healthy, full-term baby to the breast instantly, even before the cord is cut.)

- *Remember that the pre-milk fluid, colostrum, is a valuable first nourishment.* Even the few drops of this clear, yellowish secretion obtained at an initial feeding provide some protein, minerals and vitamins, as well as maternal IgA antibodies, with concentrations many times above those found in breastmilk a few days later, providing protection against infections. As an extra bonus, the laxative effect of colostrum encourages the evacuation of the sludgy meconium (which fills the newborn's bowel), making the infant hungrier and more likely to nurse vigorously, thereby bringing in the mother's milk sooner. Finally, immediate postnatal feeding and early bowel clearance reduce the absorption of bilirubin (from red-blood-cell debris), diminishing the chance of newborn jaundice.
- *Be sure to position the baby correctly.* For a good sucking position, the whole nipple and

as much as is comfortable of its surrounding areola (colored part) should be well grasped in the baby's mouth

- *Avoid too-frequent post-feed weight checks.* While weekly tracking of newborn weight is essential, test-weighing after feeds to see how much milk has been swallowed creates undue anxiety. A demand-fed baby sometimes takes a snack, at other times a full meal. Some weight loss is common after birth, and it may take babies 10 to 14 days or so to regain their birthweight.
- *Assess the adequacy of the milk supply* through natural signs and infant habits. Many a woman needlessly abandons nursing for fear of scanty or poor milk. But milk adequacy can be evaluated by hearing the steady slurp of the baby swallowing, seeing a trickle of milk from its mouth, noting the many wet diapers. A mother can rest assured that she has enough milk if the infant settles down after satisfying nursings every few hours, has a steady weekly weight gain of 120–210 g (4–7 oz), six to twelve wet (colorless) diapers a day and frequent soft, seedy, yellow stools. A need to nurse frequently may just mean that the baby is seeking comfort or undergoing a growth spurt; frequent hunger pangs are natural, since breastmilk digests easily and leaves the stomach quickly. Leaky breasts and fussy periods are also normal and do not indicate too little milk.

Overcoming some common pitfalls in breastfeeding

- *Don't skip night feedings.* Leaving a newborn unfed for several hours — perhaps to give the mother some uninterrupted sleep — may diminish the milk supply, cause breast engorgement and hinder nursing. (The mother has a right to participate in the decision-making process, and should know that around-the-clock access and more sucking increases milk production.)
- *Request or insist that hospital birthing staff avoid fluid supplements* from rubber-nippled bottles during the first few post-birth days. No studies document a regular need for water supplements in the first few days of life, and most babies do fine without a lot of fluid

in the first day or two. However, many institutions still give supplemental sugared or plain water by bottle (often to allow the mother some rest, to "top off" a feed, avoid dehydration, facilitate mucus-swallowing or line up hospital schedules). Some experts claim that even one or two bottles given soon after birth can subtly disrupt the complex natural sucking urge.

- *Avoid "nipple confusion" or "bottle spoiling."* The early introduction to a rubber nipple, with its different sucking style, can make newborns suck poorly at the breast. Bottle nipples give an immediate reward — different from the kind of sucking needed to extract milk from the human breast — and a baby who's known the ease of a bottle nipple may fight the breast, refuse it or just fall asleep after a few token sucks. Ineffective sucking fails to stimulate milk production and, through no fault of the mother or baby, is a common cause of "failure-to-thrive" (insufficient weight gain) and a frequent reason for abandoning nursing. If the real root of the trouble (early introduction to rubber nipples) isn't spotted, the problem may be ascribed to irrelevant causes such as "a lazy baby" or "flat nipples."
- *Realize that colic or excessive crying fits are not necessarily reasons to stop nursing.* Colicky babies often do better if fed at one breast only at each feeding, for 30 minutes or so. (After the initial adjustment period, experts often advise mothers to nurse routinely at alternate breasts to empty each completely.)
- *Learn how to cope with excess milk ejection.* Occasionally the milk "let-down" or ejection is so strong that the nursing infant draws back, unable to suck and unsatisfied. The problem is easily handled by a brief burping session, expressing a little milk first, and by nursing the baby at one breast only per feeding so that both the watery foremilk and richer hindmilk (last drops) are obtained. The problem fades as mother and baby adapt to each other. Lying down while feeding may ease the flow. Feeding the baby before it is fully awake, rather than waiting for a ravenous infant, may also help to avoid a sudden gush.

• *Anticipate and learn to deal with engorgement* (uncomfortably full, hard breasts). Breast engorgement, due to increased vascularity (blood supply) and milk accumulation, produces an overfull breast difficult for the baby to grasp. Severe engorgement can lead to plugged milk ducts and mastitis (inflammation of the breast), inhibiting lactation. Frequent nursing at the breasts will minimize the problem, and some milk can be expressed manually or with a pump before feedings to soften the areola so that the baby can latch on better. If engorgement occurs, hot towels or breast massage in the shower before a feeding may help. Between feedings, ice-packs can be soothing.

• *Realize that infant jaundice* is a frequently cited but usually invalid reason to abandon the breast. If a baby's eyes look yellow and its skin sallow, it may be due to a high level of bilirubin (blood-breakdown product), which peaks in the first week after birth. This was once regarded as a reason to stop nursing, but the latest research shows just the opposite. In most cases, frequent and continued breastfeeding is the best way to get rid of the bilirubin that causes physiological newborn jaundice. (The jaundice of newborns is usually harmless and gone in a few days.)

Avoiding sore nipples

Sore nipples can often be prevented by prenatal preparation for breastfeeding, avoiding harsh soaps (which dry and harden the skin), exposing the nipples to air whenever possible and making sure the bra doesn't irritate them. To assist flat or inverted nipples, women can wear a breast shield designed to draw the nipples out during pregnancy and between nursing times. Since sore nipples are easier to prevent than to treat, it is important to remember that nipples usually become sore (and then cracked) if the baby isn't well positioned and sucking properly.

The cure for sore nipples is not less nursing but good baby positioning, nursing first on the less sore side (to satisfy the ravenous hunger) and air-drying nipples after feeds.

Should soreness occur, it can be minimized by bathing with plain water (breastmilk has enough antiseptic properties) and air-drying nipples for 20 minutes after feedings whenever possible. Clothes and bra-liners that trap moisture and increase wetness should be avoided. Breast shells (shields) can be worn between feedings — to help air circulate. Rubber nipple shields should *not* be worn while nursing as they reduce the baby's sucking power and drastically diminish the milk supply. Heat, ultraviolet lamps and hair-dryers may soothe the soreness. Creams and ointments only loosen the baby's grasp and make it slip off, so must be rinsed off before a feed. (Most nipple creams are not recommended by experts, especially those containing steroids, antibiotics or other drugs.) With feeding position corrected, sore nipples usually improve within days. A fungal thrush infection on the breast or in the baby's mouth can be cured by gentian violet or antifungal drugs.

New lactation aids can overcome nipple soreness. Mothers with breast-rejecting babies, who don't latch properly onto the breast, can be helped by temporary lactation aids. These provide extra calories from formula (without a bottle) by trickling a little through a long tube into the baby's mouth, rewarding it as it feeds at the breast, thus reviving its interest in nursing. The system, which requires patience, often manages to correct the suckle. The aid is also helpful in dealing with newborn jaundice due to inadequate milk intake.

Help is available

The La Leche League (LLL), founded about 30 years ago by a small volunteer band of nursing mothers, has now expanded to become an international authority on breastfeeding with branches across Canada; the telephone number is listed under La Leche League and "Breastfeeding Help." Lactation experts and breastfeeding clinics such as the one at the University of Toronto Hospital for Sick Children can also help in breastfeeding, or ask your local health department for a public-health nurse.

Helping children grow up healthy

Breastfeeding • Instilling good eating habits • Toilet training • Building in self-esteem • Preventing avoidable injuries • Preventing childhood choking • Recognizing and managing childhood disorders • Vaccines save young lives • Understanding childhood fever • Allergies • Asthma • Autism • Birthmarks • Cerebral Palsy • Chickenpox • Colic • Common colds • Croup • Juvenile, Type I or "insulin-dependent" diabetes • Diarrhea • Diphtheria • Down syndrome • Ear infections • Eczema • Enuresis (bedwetting) • Epiglottitis • Epilepsy (seizure disorder) • Fifth disease (Erythema infectiosum) • Foot disorders • Giardiasis • Haemophilus influenzae type b infections • Hepatitis A • Hepatitis B • Impetigo • Left-handedness • Measles • Meningitis • Mumps • Pinkeye (conjunctivitis) • Polio (poliomyelitis) • Rheumatic fever • Roseola • Rubella (German measles) • Scabies • Sore throats • Sudden Infant Death Syndrome • Teething • Tetanus (lockjaw) • Thrush or candida (yeast) diaper rash • Tonsillitis • Whooping cough (pertussis) • Worms

11

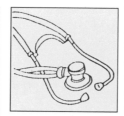

THIS CHAPTER CONsiders some general health topics related to children, and then describes (in alphabetical order) a number of specific ailments and conditions that may affect children.

Among the many influences on child health, pediatricians stress the need to breastfeed for the first six months if possible; to wean wisely in order to establish good lifelong eating habits; to refrain from smoking in the home, as cigarette smoke increases risks of pneumonia and other childhood chest infections; to ingrain self-esteem at every opportunity; to prevent needless injuries and to know the basics for recognizing and handling childhood illnesses.

BREASTFEEDING

Despite increasing public awareness and scientific validation of the benefits of breastmilk as the only food for infants in the first few months, many mothers who begin nursing quit too soon. When deciding whether to breastfeed their baby, new parents need accurate information to wend their way through the conflicting data — and they need support in persisting. Breastmilk is biologically tailored to human development. It not only supplies all the nutrients necessary for optimal infant development, but also contains antibodies and living cells (such as white blood cells) that can protect newborns against

bacteria, viruses, fungi and parasites. Formula manufacturers have not yet managed to duplicate the many complex properties of human milk, a living fluid. Furthermore breastmilk is "on tap" at the right temperature, requiring no addition of (possibly unclean) water, no mixing, no warming or night trips to the fridge. Breastfed babies seem to have stronger teeth, better facial structure and fewer dental problems than bottlefeds because of the way their tiny jaws work to get food. They are also less prone to allergies than those fed formula.

In addition to providing optimal nutrition, breastfeeding is also a dynamic, personal relationship between mother and infant that may enhance emotional bonding. Since breastfed babies tend to feed more frequently than bottlefed babies, they often spend more time interacting with the world around them, and some pediatricians believe that the extra stimulation makes them livelier, with swifter eye-hand coordination — due to the interaction with the mother's body, the movement from one breast to the other and the "rooting" reflex (searching for her breast). And the mother may receive a boost in morale from the knowledge that she's providing the best possible food for her child. In addition, a nursing mother often slims down faster after delivery, because the suckling baby consumes 500 or more calories a day.

While breastfeeding is the optimal nutrition in the first few postbirth months, this doesn't mean that babies fed modern, scientifically researched, meticulously produced and carefully selected formula are nutritionally deprived. However, parents should get enough information beforehand to make an informed choice about the best way to feed their infants. If, for whatever reason, a woman cannot or does not want to nurse her baby — perhaps because of job commitments or an illness (such as hepatitis B), or because she must take certain drugs — she needn't feel less competent as a mother. Better to bottlefeed than to be perpetually worried or uncomfortable about nursing.

(See chapter 10 for more on breastfeeding and ways to successful nursing.)

INSTILLING GOOD EATING HABITS

Lifelong eating patterns, are often set in infancy — when a child is weaned from milk to solids. It's best to introduce a wide variety of different foods one by one, keeping a lookout for allergic reactions.

Teach children to eat only when hungry and to stop when full. Offer small servings of individual foods and remove them after 20 minutes. Try to stay calm and relaxed when feeding young children; anxious parents can make children refuse food as an attention-seeking gimmick. Accept some mess and expect day-to-day appetite swings. Try not to coax, force-feed or insist on children "cleaning

THE MANY BENEFITS OF BREASTMILK

- always ready to serve, at the right temperature; no mixing needed;
- portable and affordable;
- easily digested — its composition produces smaller, softer curds than formula;
- laxative effects help to clear bowels quickly;
- promotes good facial structure (by the breast-sucking action of the infant jaws);
- encourages interaction with mother, enhances bonding and provides lots of environmental stimulation;
- contains growth and other factors that promote infant metabolism;

Main nutritional advantages:
- biochemical blend right for human babies (different from cow's-milk formula); calcium and zinc in particular are more readily absorbed from breastmilk than from formula;
- nutrients more "bio-available" (easily utilized) than those in formula;
- protein and salt content lower than formula, so less burden on infant kidneys;
- protein and amino-acid composition well balanced for human brain and nerve development. The proportions of whey and casein protein in breastmilk favor human metabolism, and are less allergy-provoking than cow's-milk formula;
- contains taurine — a component of neonatal bile salts — that may enhance iron absorption in breastfeds;
- contains human milk fats of the right type, with lipase enzymes that make it more digestible than formula fat;
- higher in valuable polyunsaturates;
- cholesterol content (absent in formula) may

induce enzyme action that promotes better cholesterol metabolism, possibly avoiding some health problems later in life;
- the increase in fat content at the end of a feeding (in the "hindmilk") may provide a "fullness" signal that prevents overfeeding;
- good iron absorption supplies stores sufficient for first six months, provided mother is not anemic and the baby's not premature (in which case iron stores may run out sooner). Formula-feds should have iron-enriched brands, but some formulas have excess iron (which may interfere with zinc absorption);
- contains more vitamin C than formula, and all other vitamins in ample amounts, except vitamin D.

Main anti-infective benefits:
- high lactoferrin content favors growth of lacto-bacilli bacteria in the infant's gut, ousting harmful microorganisms, and by binding to iron, lactoferrin impedes the growth of *E. coli* (diarrhea-causing) and other bacteria;
- immunological benefits from antiviral agents, white blood cells (e.g., macrophages and lympho-cytes) and immunoglobulins (antibodies) that protect against infective agents — such as *E. coli*, salmonella, *staphylococci, streptococci* and micro-organisms that cause giardiasis, polio, shigellosis, meningitis and pneumonia. The combined immuno-logical properties of breastmilk help newborns resist infection, reducing the incidence of diar-rhea, gastric, respiratory and other illnesses.

Note that there are two maternal conditions in which breastfeeding is *not* advisable: acute or chronic hepatitis B and HIV (AIDS) infection.

their plate" — forcing them to eat more than they want only leads to later eating disorders. If they consistently refuse to eat at mealtimes, offer water rather than juice between meals. If they keep up a "hunger strike" for days on end, remember that they rarely starve themselves.

Parents who react to all their baby's cries as though they were hunger signals and ply a youngster with tasty morsels may make the child regard food as the answer not only to hunger but to all life's discomforts — cold, wet, anxiety and stress. Similarly, it's best not to use food as a reward or bribe, which gives the impression that food equals love, attention or approval. Using food for bribes can make children (and adults) turn to favorite goodies for solace or to counter every moment of sadness.

Family and cultural attitudes to food have a tremendous impact on eating styles. Since children learn by watching other family members, parents should try to display good dietary habits themselves and avoid food faddism. For instance, if Dad refuses all vegetables or Mother turns her nose up at liver, the child will likely acquire food aversions. For children who reject vegetables, caregivers can set a good example by pleasurably eating the proffered vegetable themselves before coaxing a child to eat it. Helping to prepare the vegetables may also encourage a child to eat them!

Generally, how much and how a child eats depends on his or her individual makeup. Respect true dislikes but encourage the child to sample as many different foods as possible, to instill the idea of well-varied nutrition. Children usually eat as much food as they need to keep them going, even if the amount seems too small. Childhood appetites vary with the weather, illness and growth spurts.

Tips for developing good eating habits
- When weaning from breast or bottle, start with bland, nonallergenic foods: rice cereal, puréed carrots, squash, potatoes, bananas, apples and pears.
- Use sound dietary information when introducing new foods, and provide amounts required at different stages.
- Watch for signs that the child is full, such as turning the head away from the spoon,

clamping the mouth shut and other obvious gestures.
- Never force or bribe a child to eat: children know when they're no longer hungry.
- Offer only small amounts of food and fluids at a time. There's always more. Children get overwhelmed by large amounts, and there is less to clean up when spills occur.
- Serve well-balanced meals that include a wide range of tastes and textures, so that your child learns about enjoyable variety.
- Watch for allergic reactions (hives, throat or tongue swelling: See "Childhood food intolerances and food allergies," below.)
- Use unbreakable dishes. Try a cup with a lid or straw for children who are first using a cup (six to eight months old), since both mimic sucking actions.
- Examine your own attitudes and those of other family members toward eating to determine how they might influence the child. A stress-free atmosphere promotes self-feeding skills and good lifetime food attitudes. Remember that your mood will influence the child.
- Make mealtimes enjoyable. Mealtimes are not just times to eat but also opportunities for socializing. ("The family that eats together stays together!")
- Settle your child comfortably and maintain a slow, relaxed pace.
- Don't "hurry along" meals.
- Try not to force-feed, if possible.
- With very young children, allow time for play and experimentation but stop the meal before the play and mess become too bothersome.
- Ignore food throwing or messiness at first; it's part of normal development. Children "drop" things in order to learn the "letting go" reflex, and where better to practice than dumping bits of food from a highchair? Cleanup may be made easier by putting newspaper or plastic sheeting under the highchair. Once children acquire the skill of letting go and spilling, it's just a game that shouldn't be rewarded by continually picking up the dropped food. Instead, after the third or fourth throw, remove all food — the child is likely full.
- Encourage a child who bolts food to slow

down by talking between spoonfuls. It also helps if adults eat slowly. Put small amounts of food on the plate and use gentle reminders to chew well before swallowing.

- Encourage independence. Children need time to practice eating skills. Success helps them feel good about themselves.

- Promote choice and responsibility in food selection and respect the child's decisions. For example, let the child choose between two vegetables, and once the child has chosen, express pleasure that your child is eating a vegetable. Providing limited and realistic choices encourages children to think independently and exercise some control. For example, "Would you like a few carrots or a lot of carrots?" Allowing choices makes children feel like people!

- For children who dislike vegetables, try calling them something descriptive and fun. For example, if the child likes colours, call peas "green balls" and carrots "orange circles." Let children hand-pick them from a bowl of mixed vegetables. If the child is interested in numbers, count the number of peas or carrots in a spoonful before offering it.

- Let toddlers pick food from the family serving plate, so that they feel free to decide what and how much to eat. This helps reduce frustration during the "no" stage. Offer some foods to eat with a spoon at each meal (to teach the child how to handle utensils) but allow some finger foods to make the transition easier.

- Don't hover expectantly while a child eats, monitoring each mouthful, and avoid talking about food too much, as though it were the "be all and end all"! Food is for health, not for obsession.

- Teach children to snack sensibly. A snack between meals may be necessary for enough childhood energy, and nutritious snacking establishes the foundation for later healthy eating habits. However, older children should be discouraged from snacking throughout the day. It can lead to tooth decay and makes for bad eating patterns later on.

Childhood food intolerances and food allergies

Certain common foods disagree with some children. Food intolerances differ from food allergies, which are identifiable immunological reactions to a specific food ingredient, with definite symptoms such as hives, wheezing, and swelling of the tongue and throat. By contrast, a food intolerance may produce bloating, loose stools, gas or vomiting but not immune-system symptoms. Some children are lactose-intolerant owing to the lack of an enzyme called lactase, normally present in the bowel wall, which digests lactose (milk sugar). A child with lactase deficiency develops gastric discomfort after ingesting lactose-containing foods such as milk, butter and yogurt. This food intolerance can be managed by feeding milk-free substitutes, such as soy formula, for a short time. In older children, milk intake may be limited, or they can be given special low-lactose or lactose-free milk products.

As distinct from food intolerances, food allergies involve an immune system reaction with the formation of antibodies in response to eating a specific food ingredient. The allergic reaction may become noticeable only the second or third time the food is eaten. Once the child is "sensitized" to a particular allergen — such as egg yolk, nuts, strawberries, shellfish, wheat — a possibly severe reaction can occur on ingesting even traces of the allergy-provoking food. The symptoms — hives (a weal or rash), tongue-swelling, wheezing, difficulty breathing, faintness — may come on suddenly and can be very serious, even life-threatening. A severe reaction, called anaphylactic shock, is a medical emergency that requires immediate attention. Milder allergic reactions may appear more slowly, with a delay of hours or even a day or two after eating the allergy-triggering food.

(See chapters 13 and 17 for more on allergic reactions, their avoidance and treatment.)

TOILET TRAINING

Learning to go to the toilet is part of natural human development and should start only when the child is ready — usually between two and three years of age. But each child's physical progress differs: a child may be ready earlier or later than a sibling, other people's offspring or daycare friends. Let the child set the pace.

SIGNS OF READINESS FOR TOILET TRAINING

- **child stays dry for longer periods;**
- **child recognizes and mentions wet or soiled diapers;**
- **child uses words or gestures to communicate need to urinate or defecate;**
- **child demonstrates interest in the toilet;**
- **child goes to the potty and sits on it;**
- **child can pull own pants down.**

Patience, support and understanding are essential. A child may show signs of readiness but not yet be really ready — for example, when in the "no's" stage, having temper tantrums or going through a stressful or disruptive period (perhaps because of a move to a new home or a divorce). "Accidents" will happen. From time to time even toilet-trained children may revert to diapers because of stress — perhaps a new baby in the family, a parent's absence or some illness. This is common and usually does not last long.

Children are emotionally prepared to use the toilet when:
- they tell you about the urge to urinate or have a bowel movement;
- they know what is expected when on the toilet;
- they are willing to urinate or have a bowel movement in the toilet instead of in a diaper.

Children are physically prepared to use the toilet when:
- they can control their bladders (when they can hold enough fluid in);
- they can control the sphincter (anal) muscles that hold in stool.

Tips for toilet training

- Use the same words and routines for toilet learning at home as in childcare programs. Give encouragement and verbal praise as positive support.
- Use potty chairs — they are less intimidating than toilets.
- Make toilets feel safer with a special seat, and/or secure a stool or box under the feet for children sitting on the toilet.
- Never force a child to use a potty; it only sets up a power struggle and negative feelings toward it.
- Encourage a child to sit for short periods of time, and be sure to try at key times — i.e., soon after meals, before naps and after waking up dry from a nap (once the child is comfortably awake).
- With growing success, start leaving off diapers for a short period. Encourage the child to do this by himself or herself. Leave the potty in the same area for the child to use periodically.

- Don't reward children with food or candy (it puts the wrong connotation on food, equating it with approval).
- Try removing diapers all day once the child gets the hang of things. Most children will stay dry during the day well before they can be out of diapers at night.
- Watching older brothers and sisters or parents use the toilet provides positive role modeling.
- Praise the child for getting to the toilet on time, but don't get angry if there's an accident. Instead, reassure the child that accidents do happen, and that they're "no big deal."
- In order to teach proper personal hygiene, always wash the child's hands and your own hands after changing soiled diapers or after a child uses the toilet; when the child is old enough, teach him or her to consistently wash the hands after toilet use.

BUILDING IN SELF-ESTEEM

The critical importance to childhood health of ingraining self-worth is becoming ever more clear. From day one after birth, by everything they say and do and by verbal and nonverbal actions, parents, teachers and siblings communicate approval or disapproval, likes or dislikes, which profoundly influence the way children view themselves. Displaying disapproval by a facial expression or hunched shoulders can be just as influential as open criticism. A disgusted grimace while changing diapers makes a baby feel "dirty" or "ashamed" of his or her body.

To bolster childhood self-esteem, parents and caregivers should express respect, acceptance and love to children, regardless of their behavior. Children need to be unconditionally valued as worthwhile people even when their behavior is not acceptable. While expressing disapproval for bad or unacceptable behavior, do not reject the child as a whole. Make children feel accepted for what they are, and emphasize the positive rather than the negative sides of their character and abilities. Make children feel loved for their own unique qualities: "I like your sturdy legs"; "You have the silkiest cheeks imaginable"; "Your drawings are great." In depressed or low times, children will remember these comments and feel better about themselves.

Always remember to acknowledge good childhood actions or progress. Relatives visiting young nieces, nephews or grandchildren can help by making each child feel "special." Instead of giving a blanket greeting — "Hi kids!" — they can single out each child for separate attention. "Hello, Andrea, how is your new school?" or "Tell me, Jeremy, are you still playing the guitar? Give me a tune." For frazzled parents, the extra attention given to children by others can be a great help, while the children gain self-esteem by relating separately to other relatives, friends and teachers.

Children who don't feel accepted may think they're all bad and therefore unable to control or change their actions, instead of believing that they are okay and can change the way they behave. Child guidance should be positive, with a sympathetic but firm approach. Consider the child's viewpoint before handing out punishment. Be clear and direct in explaining what you disapprove of and why; don't just be cold or withdrawn. It's better for children to know why you are displeased than to guess they've done something far worse; better to be told that you're angry about "the lie told" or "skipping class" than to feel utterly worthless.

Showing respect for children and helping them to build self-esteem means:
• valuing the child's feelings and thoughts;
• accepting the child's ideas and contributions;
• being honest with the child;
• understanding the child's point of view;
• telling children, including infants, what to expect from you, so that any reprimand or disapproval is understood and not taken as total rejection;
• listening attentively and picking up cues from children's unique communication modes — for example, the particular way an infant coos, smiles, cries or moves; its preferred toys; how a toddler gestures or tries out words; the way an older child communicates ideas;
• demanding realistic rather than perfect behavior and setting realistic limits;
• offering choices to foster independence: "Would you like your medicine now or in 10 minutes?" or "It's bedtime – would you like your teddy or doggie to cuddle?"

• communicating with "I" messages or personal statements about how undesirable behavior affects you. "I" messages help children see the immediate effects of their behavior; for example, "When you throw blocks, I worry that you may hurt someone or break a window even if you don't mean to." This beats saying, "Naughty boy, that's a bad thing to do!" Such scolding provides only negative, character-deprecating information, giving the child no positive direction. Allow children to make mistakes and then remain neutral so that the child learns by his or her own errors. Children need time to find their own solutions. They also learn by having to repair the consequences of their behavior — for example, wiping up spilled juice.

PREVENTING AVOIDABLE INJURIES
Injury tops the list for causes of death and permanent disability among children in Canada. Over half the deaths in people under age 24 are due to unintentional injuries. (In infants under one year old, however, although injury rates are high, they are the sixth cause of deaths, after birth problems, inherited defects, Sudden Infant Death Syndrome, infections and heart flaws.) Apart from death, accidents take an immense toll in needless injury. And Canada is a global leader in childhood injury, with rates higher than Australia, Japan and most of Western Europe.

(See also chapter 2, the section on injury-prevention.)

Knowing how injuries are likely to happen and at which ages, and planning to avoid them, can prevent much tragedy. Many needless

LEADING CAUSES OF FATAL CHILDHOOD INJURIES
• **motor vehicle crashes (often because of failure to wear appropriate restraints);**
• **falls — from beds, table tops, shelves, ledges, stairs or play equipment;**
• **burns (due to no smoke detectors, or carelessness with** fireplaces, matches, lighters, stoves);
• **drownings (in bathtubs, sinks, diaper pails, laundry pails, pools and ponds);**
• **suffocation, choking (on small toys, nuts, balloons, combs, candy, plastic bags of all kinds);**
• **poisoning from medicines, cleaning products and other chemicals (very frequent);**
• **being struck by heavy or sharp falling objects (bookcase, TV set, anything that can easily topple if pulled by tiny hands).**

deaths result from auto crashes (where children weren't wearing car restraints), drownings (because of unsupervised water play or baths), fires (no smoke detectors in the house) and bicycle accidents (children not wearing helmets). Other injuries, generally somewhat less serious, result from children being struck or pierced by objects, and from sports. Children have been killed or badly hurt because a TV fell on them when they pulled the cord, because they were accidentally shut in a fridge or freezer, because they roller-bladed without a helmet and in countless other home and playground mishaps. One two-year-old recently drowned in a garden pond; a one-year-old suffocated when caught between her mother's bed and the wall; a five-year-old died when struck by a falling bookcase.

Canada has introduced laws covering child car restraint seats, childproof packaging, flame-resistant nightwear and toy labeling, as well as fireworks and a multitude of other hazards. However, childproof packaging isn't going to work if parents don't fasten the lids properly; child car seats won't work if they aren't used. Caregivers frequently underestimate dangers to children — for instance, when crossing streets or bicycling, both common causes of childhood deaths. A recent survey found that parents were more worried about their child being kidnapped or abusing drugs than about the less dramatic but far more prevalent risk of traffic injuries. Only 6 percent of parents surveyed knew that injury is the main cause of childhood deaths.

How "accidents" happen

Injuries typically happen when caregivers relax their watchful gaze or overestimate a child's skills. They can occur with parents or other caregivers in the next room — or even in the same room. Not everyone realizes that within seconds a child can fall off a high surface (even a bed), drown or get badly burned. Anticipating how and where injuries may occur is the first step in avoiding them. The childproofing of the home, car and surroundings must be geared to each age group and the youngsters' activity levels. The greatest danger arises when children's activity levels exceed their judgment.

Once babies can reach and grasp (around age three to four months), they're at risk of burns from pulling or toppling hot coffee pots, toasters or kettles, or of choking on objects reached and put in the mouth (such as beads, small parts of toys, peanuts, popcorn, candy, plastic bags).

In toddlers, the most frequent causes of injury or death are drownings, traffic accidents and poisonings. In preschoolers up to about age five, falls, burns, choking, auto accidents and poisonings are the most frequent causes. In schoolchildren, cycling and pedestrian mishaps top the list, and in adolescents, the causes are car passenger deaths (often due to careless or drunken driving), suicide, substance abuse and homicide.

PREVENTING CHILDHOOD CHOKING

(For how to handle a choking emergency, see "Choking" in chapter 17. Do *not* slap the choker on the back. Call for emergency help *at once*, if a choking victim becomes limp, blue or unconscious.) Choking is the second most common cause of death in children under age five. It can occur from awkwardly sized bits of food, eating too fast, not chewing well, running with food in the mouth or swallowing small objects. Foods liable to cause choking and considered unsafe until chewing is mastered

PROTECTING CHILDREN FROM INJURY

As primary safety measures for infants unable to protect themselves, install household smoke detectors, ensure safe cribs (remember the secondhand, older models may not conform to modern standards) and make sure any play equipment (swings, slides, seesaws, dollhouses, ladders) is in safe working order, has no sharp edges or nails sticking out, meets Canadian Standards Association (CSA) standards and bears the CSA seal of approval. Be sure to use age-appropriate, properly installed car restraints. (In one study, unrestrained children were 11 times likelier to die in auto crashes than those properly secured.)

Once children can move about and explore their surroundings, store all sharp objects, medications and household chemicals well out of reach, up and away out of sight. Drowning is a particular threat to toddlers if a child is momentarily left alone. (One child recently drowned in a small puddle of water on top of a swimming pool cover!) Burns from over-hot tap water are another hazard; keep maximum water temperature below 48°C (120°F).

TIPS FOR REDUCING CHILDHOOD INJURIES

- Reorganize and child-proof all rooms to which young children have access.
- Store all sharp objects and household chemicals well out of reach of tiny explorers.
- Make sure play equipment (swings, slides, seesaws, dollhouses, ladders) is in good working order.
- Ensure that electrical cords don't dangle over counter edges. They can get caught in a cupboard door or drawer, or be pulled by a child. Unplug cords from electrical outlets when not in use.
- Don't carry hot foods or liquids when children are nearby.
- Turn pot handles toward the back of the stove.
- Store unopened glass pop bottles in a locked cupboard. Pressurized pop bottles easily shatter

or explode, and the shattered glass can cause serious injuries.
- Safety-proof stairs: put handrails on both sides of the staircase and don't leave clutter on steps. Put a safety gate at the top and bottom of stairs.
- Keep cleaning products in their original containers or ensure that they are properly labeled, and store them safely beyond children's reach.
- Use special latches, locks or other safety devices to make storage areas inaccessible to children.
- Since plastic bags of all kinds present a suffocation hazard, don't keep them loose — instead, tie in several knots and discard, or use alternative packaging.
- Don't let small children play with balloons inflated or

uninflated (in the last few years, several children have perished by choking on them).
- Don't allow children to sit on window ledges; never leave them unattended on a balcony.
- Never leave "crawlers" unattended on high surfaces (even a bed).
- Don't let children play in or around cars.
- Forbid playing with matches, lighters and cigarettes.

Tips for safer childhood car travel:
- Fasten luggage below seatback level (especially in the back of station wagons or "hatchbacks"), as a sudden stop can make it fly forward. Never put items of any weight in the back window — in a sudden stop they become dangerous projectiles.
- Make sure all children

are secured in car restraints approved by the Canadian Standards Association (CSA).
- Place small infants in rear-facing child car seats that conform with the Motor Vehicle Safety Act — either portable infant carriers or convertible seats — fastening the infant well by the harness straps, and making sure the seat is securely tethered.
- Seat toddlers (9–18 kg or 20–40 lb) in child car seats behind the driver conforming to the Children's Car Seats and Harness Regulations (set by the Hazardous Products Act). This can be a convertible or a special child seat in a forward-facing position with a tether strap to prevent the seat from flying forward. The harness straps must be

securely fastened.
- Teach older children to fasten seat belts at all times, before the car is started.
- Avoid looking at children in a rear seat — removing your attention from the road for even a few seconds can easily lead to a collision.
- If the child requires care, don't do it while driving — park the car first.
- Walk around your car before backing out of the garage or driveway to be sure it is clear of children, toys, bicycles and other obstructions.
- Many car-rental companies offer car seats. Check for this option and their safety when renting.
- Have a first-aid kit on hand for minor injuries. Even if seemingly unhurt after a car crash, have a checkup by a physician or local hospital.

(around age four) include peanuts, popcorn, hard candy and hot dogs.

Tips to prevent choking in children
Practice and teach children safe eating habits:
- Take small bites, chew thoroughly and swallow *before* taking another bite.
- Don't eat while talking or laughing.
- Sit still during meals; don't run or play, or eat and drink simultaneously.
- Cut food into small enough pieces.
- Don't eat lying down.
- If something is difficult to swallow, spit it out!
- Don't discourage a child from coughing food up — it could save a life.
- Never force a drowsy child to eat.
- Minimize distractions while eating.

- Don't reswallow what's coughed up; spit it into a napkin instead.
- Never take off or completely push in pop can tabs, which can cause choking if swallowed.
- Babies have a strong cough reflex — encourage them to cough if choking.
- If a child begins to choke, don't pound him or her on the back; it may make the obstruction worse; don't give bread either — it causes a bigger blockage.

- *Be aware of items that easily cause choking in children,* for instance:
  - Do not give children under five years of age peanuts (which easily get stuck), peanut butter or soft cheese products (except spread thinly), soft bread, hard

candy, popcorn, unpeeled apples, carrots, celery or grapes. (Peanuts and similar foods aren't really considered safe until around age five to six.)
- To avoid trouble, grate carrots and remove pits from fruit. Note that hot dogs can cause choking because a youngster's airway is about the size of an average hot dog. To avoid trouble, skin hot dogs and either dice them or cut them lengthwise, not in coin shapes.

- Children have choked on small balls, buttons, batteries, coins, crayon pieces, marbles, tiny toys, balloons, pieces of a plant or even bits of plastic from a disposable diaper.
- Make sure children's toys can stand up to rough play and are in good repair, with no broken or loose parts that could stick in the throat. Keep older children's toys, which may have small detachable parts, away from young children.
- Keep children's sleep and play areas free of small objects such as marbles that could be inhaled or swallowed.
- Note that *balloons are especially dangerous* to children. One expert tells of a child who bit a balloon on his first birthday, choked on it and died. The balloon's adhesive quality makes it very difficult to dislodge.
- Do not prop a baby under the age of nine months with a bottle while lying down, as it may choke on the liquid.

Preparing yourself for a choking emergency

Choking is a very serious emergency because lack of oxygen may lead to permanent brain damage even before the ambulance arrives. There are simple techniques that are highly effective for dealing with choking, but a life-and-death crisis is not the ideal time to learn them!

Anyone who expects to be responsible for an infant or child should spend a few hours of an evening or weekend learning to prevent and deal with this and other breathing emergencies. There are even special courses for babysitters. For more information, call your local branch of the Red Cross, St. John Ambulance, or the Heart and Stroke Foundation. (See chapter 17 for more on choking.)

RECOGNIZING AND MANAGING CHILDHOOD DISORDERS

The most common childhood disorders seen by family practitioners are coughs and colds, sore throats (including tonsillitis), ear infections, roseola, chickenpox and various cuts, bruises and unintentional injuries. In the modern world, vaccination can save children from many infectious diseases that formerly killed countless youngsters. But parents still

SOME EARLY SIGNS OF ILLNESS IN CHILDREN

- **Unusual fussiness, irritability or altered behavior is a significant sign. The greater the change in a child's behavior, the greater the likelihood of serious illness. Children who remain active, hungry and playful aren't usually too ill. But those who seem unusually sleepy, dozy, irritable, lethargic or unresponsive may be harboring some serious disorder.**
- **A runny nose may signify infection. The commonest causes of a runny nose in young children are viral infections — for example, the common cold. Allergies and chemical irritation are other causes. The color change of a nasal discharge is not significant, but if it persists for more than a week, the child should be medically checked.**
- **Coughing can be triggered by infection and or irritation anywhere in the respiratory tract, from the nose to the lungs, or may be due to allergies, asthma, chemical irritation, cystic fibrosis, an inhaled object or a child's psychological state (anxiety). A cough often long outlasts a runny nose. If it's persistent, see a physician about it.**
- **Wheezing when breathing out — due to air-passage narrowing and/or excess mucus in the airways (tubes) of the lungs — is often due to a viral infection or asthma. Rapid shallow breathing needs medical attention.**
- **Vomiting is much more frequent in children than in adults, and produces much less discomfort; it may be due to the general effects of an infection rather than a specific stomach irritation. Vomiting in itself isn't dangerous unless the** child chokes on inhaled vomitus, or vomits frequently enough to become dehydrated.
- **Diarrhea with frequent, watery or unformed stools can be a risk if the amount of water lost surpasses the amount taken in, leading to dehydration. Dehydration can be serious because it impairs the blood circulation, and occurs much more rapidly in infants than in older children or adults. If children vomit as well as having diarrhea, the danger of dehydration increases and medical attention is needed.**
- **A suddenly pale complexion, or yellowing of the whites of the eyes, may signify acute illness that needs prompt medical attention.**
- **For fever, see "Understanding childhood fever" later in this chapter.**

need to watch for and know how to treat childhood ailments, and when to get medical advice.

VACCINES SAVE YOUNG LIVES

Immunization against communicable diseases is one of the most cost-effective and life-saving health measures of our time. Widespread vaccination programs in the Western world have dramatically curtailed some previously ravaging infectious diseases such as diphtheria and smallpox. The medical advances in vaccine production have led many people to regard themselves as invulnerable to infectious diseases, and to believe they can all be avoided by immunization or antibiotics. Yet antibiotics work only against bacterial infections, not against viruses. And despite vigorous immunization campaigns, some vaccine-preventable diseases still occur in Canada, and remain major killers around the world. In some developing countries, epidemics of infectious diseases now rare in Canada — such as diphtheria, polio and tetanus (lockjaw) — still claim thousands of lives each year.

Even in Canada, children and adults need protection against vaccine-preventable illnesses. The "Canadian Immunization Guide" put out by Health and Welfare Canada outlines the routine schedule for childhood immunization against diphtheria, tetanus, polio, rubella and

IMMUNIZATION TAKES TWO FORMS

- **Live, attenuated vaccines (e.g., measles, rubella, mumps and oral Sabin polio vaccines) contain whole, live but greatly weakened agents which trigger an immune reaction without causing illness.**
- **Inactivated vaccines** (e.g., Hib meningitis, tetanus, diphtheria, pertussis, influenza and Salk polio vaccine) contain killed, totally inactivated particles of the infective organisms or their toxins (infective components), sufficiently potent to evoke immunity. Some (e.g., hepatitis B vaccine) are now made by genetic engineering. Broader hepatitis B vaccination — possibly for all children — is now being strongly promoted.

measles, also giving guidelines for hepatitis B vaccination and use of the new antimeningitis (Hib) vaccine for young infants.

Antimeningitis vaccine can now protect infants

In infants and toddlers aged three months to about five years, 60–70 percent of bacterially caused meningitis (inflammation of the brain and spinal-cord membranes) used to be due to *Haemophilus influenzae type b* (Hib) bacteria. Hib also causes other illnesses, such as epiglottitis (a life-threatening infection that can obstruct breathing), pneumonia and septic joint inflammation. A new, safe and effective vaccine

SOME SENSIBLE PRECAUTIONS ABOUT VACCINATION

While adverse reactions to vaccines are rare, there are certain people and some conditions that warrant caution:

- **People allergic to eggs and specific chemicals must be cautious about receiving vaccines that contain traces of egg-protein (in measles, mumps, influenza and yellow-fever vaccines), or such substances as thimerosal (a mercurial preservative in most inactivated vaccines) and antibiotics (such as neomycin, in some polio vaccines).**
- **Live viral vaccines are unsuitable for some. Measles, rubella, mumps, yellow-fever and oral polio vaccines all contain weakened but live microorganisms. While there is no solid proof that live virus vaccines can harm the fetus, it is safer to err on the side of caution and avoid them while pregnant.**
- **People who have a** moderate or severe illness should wait until they're better to be immunized (although a minor infection such as a head cold, with or without fever, need not prevent vaccination).
- **People with immune-deficiency diseases, those on immunosuppressants and children with leukemia should not receive live virus immunization, although those infected with HIV may do so.**
- **Those living with an immunosuppressed person should not take live (oral) polio vaccine, as the virus can be passed on. No problem exists with other live vaccines.**
- **The pertussis component of the DPT vaccine is generally blamed for postvaccination discomforts: fever, redness and swelling at the injection site, and fussiness, drowsiness and appetite loss experienced in about 50 percent of inoculated babies. These reactions, which are usually short-lived, mild and no cause for alarm, are easily minimized by giving fretful children acetaminophen (Children's Tylenol, Tempra, Atasol, Panadol), perhaps at the time of injection and again a few hours later. A tiny proportion get further adverse reactions to the pertussis vaccine, though far less so with newer vaccines. Severe reactions are rare.**

ROUTINE CHILDHOOD IMMUNIZATION SCHEDULE

Immunization done as suggested in these schedules will provide basic protection against the disease listed.

Age	Immunization(s) against:
2 months	DPT (combined diphtheria, pertussis, tetanus vaccine) + polio (OPV or IPV)*
4 months	DPT, polio
6 months	DPT, polio (if IPV inactivated form used; not necessary for OPV live form)
12 months	MMR (measles, mumps, rubella) – combined live vaccine
18 months	DPT, polio and Hib (Haemophilus influenzae b vaccine) against meningitis and other forms of this infection**
4–6 years	DPT, polio
14–16 years	Td (tetanus, diphtheria) boosters and polio (if IPV used)
Every 10 years thereafter	Diphtheria, tetanus, polio* boosters (if IPV used).

*   POLIO: both live and inactivated polio vaccines are used in Canada with equal efficacy. (P.E.I. uses both.)
        IPV: inactivated (Salk) polio vaccine is given by injection in Ont., N.S. and Nfld. Improved IPV now being tested.
        OPV: oral live but attenuated or weakened (Sabin) polio vaccine given in Que., Man., Alta., Sask., N.B., B.C. and the Territories and throughout U.S., requires no postpuberty boosters, is cheaper, gives lifelong immunity and is easier to administer; live polio vaccine indirectly spreads protection to others in community (as small amounts of live virus absorbed by the nonimmunized may make them immune).

**   *Haemophilus influenzae b* (Hib) conjugate vaccine should be given to all children aged 2–4 months at the same times as the DPT shots, to protect them against meningitis and other Hib infections.

against Hib infection can protect infants as young as two months old. The Canadian Pediatric Society and the National Advisory Committee on Immunization advocate giving Hib vaccine to all children at the same time as the routine diphtheria-pertussis-tetanus (DPT) immunization. The cost of vaccination is covered by all provincial health-insurance plans. The benefits are already clear: Hib is no longer the prime cause of childhood meningitis, and other forms of Hib disease, such as epiglottitis, have also become uncommon.

UNDERSTANDING CHILDHOOD FEVER

Children seem to get fevers from almost everything — except, contrary to popular folklore, teething. Colds, sore throats, middle-ear, gastric and many other infections cause a child's temperature to climb. The degree of fever in itself generally poses no danger. The child's behavior is usually a more telling clue to the severity of an illness. But in those under two months of age, fevers that would be no cause for alarm in older children may signal a serious problem that requires urgent medical care.

Medication isn't always needed for feverish children. When recommended, acetaminophen, every four hours, is given. ASA (acetylsalicylic acid, such as Aspirin) should *never* be given to a feverish child or teenager because, should the fever be due to some infection such as influenza or chickenpox, taking ASA can increase the risks of Reye's syndrome — a serious disorder that often leads to severe liver and brain damage, sometimes death.

Fever in itself is no danger

Both the public at large and health professionals tend to overestimate the dangers of fever. Unrealistic fears, sometimes dubbed "fever-phobia," may lead to exaggeratedly vigorous efforts to bring down the child's temperature. While caregivers may worry about fever, many small children are not particularly bothered by it. However, it's not always easy to know when to call the doctor. Whether or not fever needs immediate medical attention depends largely on the age of the child and his or her general appearance.

Saying that a child is "running a fever" or "has a temperature" means that the body temperature is elevated above the level considered "normal." Human body temperature fluctuates slightly·during the day and is usually lower in the morning and higher in the afternoon and evening. When an infection or some other disease process sets in, substances may be released which elevate body temperature. Fever does *not* harm the body and may in fact assist the immune defenses. While its exact mechanism remains unclear, recent medical evidence shows that fever may actually help the body fight disease by increasing the activity of the immune system and the white-blood-cell defense activity. Thus, lowering the fever may make sufferers more comfortable, but does not necessarily assist the body in combating disease.

Children generally run higher temperatures than adults without being as ill. For instance, a two-year-old with an ear infection can easily have a temperature of 40°C (104°F), while such high fevers are rarely seen in older children. If a child has a fever higher than 39°C (102.2°F) it's generally time to consult a physician. But fever alone isn't dangerous as long as it is not excessively high (over 41.5°C or 106.7°F), and provided fluid intake replaces the body water lost.

The definition of a "significant" temperature varies but is generally considered to be one that's over 38.5°C (101.4°F). A temperature higher than 40°C (104°F) is regarded as high, but even that won't cause brain damage or permanently threaten health.

Causes of childhood fever vary with age

- At all ages, viral infections are a much more common cause of fever than bacterial infections.
- In newborns (birth to one month), fever is often due to infection — sometimes bacterial, occasionally serious. Dehydration, overdressing or an overheated environment may also cause a mild temperature rise.
- In infants (one month to a year), fever is primarily due to upper-respiratory viral infections, often complicated by an ear infection.
- In toddlers (aged one to four) and preschoolers (aged four to six), the most common fever-causing conditions are infections such

---

NORMAL BODY TEMPERATURE IS:

in the armpit:	36.4°C (97.5°F) – 37°C (98.6°F)
in the mouth:	37°C (98.6°F)
in the rectum:	37.5°C (99.5°F)

A child has a fever if the temperature is:

in the armpit:	38°C (100.4°F) or higher (although armpit temperatures are not very accurate and have a wide range)
in the mouth:	38°C (100.4°F) or higher
in the rectum:	38.5°C (101.4°F) or higher

---

as upper-respiratory viral infections, bacterial pharyngitis (sore or "strep" throat), tonsillitis, ear infections and bronchitis. Other causes are digestive- and urinary-tract infections.
- In schoolchildren (aged six to 12 years), respiratory infections top the list of fever-causing problems, as well as urinary-tract infections, especially in girls.

Measuring fever

Temperatures are taken by mouth or rectum, in the axilla (armpit) or in the ear. Thermometer scales are marked in degrees Celsius (centigrade), Fahrenheit or both. Commonly used fever thermometers are glass or digital and both work well. Digital thermometers are more sensitive than glass ones and may be used for oral, rectal or armpit measurement. The heat-sensitive tapes or forehead strips that change color on contact with the skin are considered very inaccurate. An excellent new technique, used in some hospitals and perhaps soon to become popular for doctors' offices, employs a tiny temperature-recording instrument put into the ear which registers a very accurate reading within a few seconds. Ear measurement is easier than taking rectal temperatures in tiny babies. Rectal or armpit readings are best for home measurement in children under five years old, as a glass thermometer can easily break. Rectal readings are usually about one-half to one degree higher than those in the mouth, while underarm temperatures read lower. By age five, most children can hold a thermometer safely in their mouths.
- When taking a rectal reading, some suggest placing the child on the stomach across your knees and cuddling him or her to keep quiet, while others prefer laying the baby face up

---

CENTIGRADE – FAHRENHEIT CONVERSION CHART

37°C	=	**98.6°F**
37.2°C	=	**99.0°F**
37.5°C	=	**99.5°F**
37.8°C	=	**100°F**
38°C	=	**100.4°F**
38.5°C	=	**101.4°F**
39°C	=	**102.2°F**
39.5°C	=	**103°F**
40°C	=	**104°F**
40.5°C	=	**105°F**
41°C	=	**105.8°F**

N.B. To convert Celsius readings to Fahrenheit, double the degrees C, subtract 10 percent, then add 32. (E.g., 40°C x 2 – 10% + 32 = 104°F.)

and, lifting the legs — meanwhile smiling reassuringly! The thermometer is held about 2.5 cm (1 in) from the tip, lubricated (e.g., with Vaseline) and inserted about 2.5 cm (1 in) into the rectum — up to the point at which it's being held.

- To clean a digital thermometer, wash only the tip with soap and warm (not hot) water and wipe off with alcohol after use. Dry well. To clean a glass thermometer, wash in lukewarm soapy water and rinse with alcohol.

Fever in newborns always needs medical attention

Any fever in newborns up to about eight weeks of age should immediately be reported to the physician. The fever itself is not the danger but the underlying cause may be serious at this young age. Fever is often the *only* sign of infection in young infants, who give fewer alerting clues than older children to illnesses they may be harboring. It is difficult to know when babies feel below par. Since very young infants cannot localize and fight infection as well as older children, they are at greater risk for bacteremia (a spreading bacterial infection) and meningitis (inflammation of the brain and spinal-cord coverings).

The challenge for doctors is to distinguish mild viral from serious bacterial infections. Because of the risk, many physicians automatically hospitalize newborns with fevers in order to observe them closely and start treatment, possibly giving them antibiotics while awaiting the results of laboratory tests. If the lab culture results are negative and the infant quickly returns to normal feeding and activity, the hospital stay will be short.

Once past the newborn period, at two to three months of age, fever is less worrisome. The illness may then be handled at home with close observation and follow-up. In infants aged three months to two years, a fever over 38.5°C (101.4°F) for 24 hours merits a call to the doctor. In children aged three to six, a fever that lasts 48 hours needs medical attention, even if the child looks well and has a good appetite.

In schoolchildren, the same fever may be left for 72 hours before calling the doctor, provided the child doesn't seem ill and is lively, feeding and behaving normally. As children grow, the symptoms of illness become easier to identify because the child can explain what's wrong. Also, parents get better at assessing the gravity of their child's condition.

TIPS FOR COOLING FEVERISH CHILDREN

Do's
- **Keep the child lightly dressed indoors, unless he or she is uncomfortable.**
- **Give plenty of cool, clear liquids to replace lost body fluid. Popsicles, ice water or carbonated beverages help to cool a feverish child.**
- **Give acetaminophen (e.g., Children's Tylenol, Atasol, Tempra or Panadol) at a dose of 10–15 mg/kg (5–7 mg per lb) every four hours, if needed to reduce** discomfort, remembering that it may not bring their temperature right down to normal. Since most children don't feel too uncomfortable until the temperature reaches 39.5°C (103°F), fever-reducers are unnecessary unless the child feels miserable.
- **Consider lukewarm sponge baths or sitting the child in a lukewarm bath — a strategy which, although controversial, is recommended** by some physicians, especially for a high fever. Although some doubt its efficacy, it may be worth sponging an uncomfortably feverish child for 15 minutes — not immersing him or her completely but leaving most of the body exposed to speed evaporation. But sponge baths should be used only if medically recommended, and children should never be left alone in the bathtub (for safety reasons).

If sponging makes a feverish child chilled, shivery or unhappy, forget it!

Don'ts
- **Don't overdress or cover a feverish child with heavy bedding. Bundling up a child for fear of "getting a chill" is a common mistake.**
- **Don't overheat the room; keep it no warmer than 20–21°C (68–70°F). Turn off the heat or open a window slightly, if necessary.**

Use a fan or an air conditioner in hot weather.
- **Don't cover the child with wet towels or wet sheets — it is uncomfortable.**
- **Don't use alcohol sponging because alcohol can be absorbed through the skin.**
- **Do not give ASA because of the link to Reye's syndrome in the presence of certain viral illnesses such as influenza and chickenpox.**

Appearance and behavior are more critical indicators

Do not regard the height of the thermometer reading as the only measure of childhood illness: how a child looks and behaves are more important. A mild viral infection can cause a fever as high as 40°C (104°F), while a severely ill child with meningitis may have a lower fever around 38.5°C (101.4°F). In general, the child's behavior tells more about the severity of the illness than does the degree of fever. When judging a child's condition and deciding whether or not to call the doctor, caregivers should be guided not by fever alone but also by how sick the child seems.

Caregivers should assess whether the child is:
- lively and alert or droopy, apathetic and unusually listless;
- eating well or has a diminished appetite;
- playing normally or ignoring toys;
- gazing around curiously or uninterested;
- smiling at familiar caregivers or unresponsive;
- able to be comforted or inconsolably cranky;
- a normal pink color or pale and looks ashen;
- breathing normally or taking rapid breaths (more than 40 a minute)
- "dry" or "wet" in the mucous membranes (nose, eyes);
- showing obvious signs of pain or discomfort, such as pulling at the ears, holding the head or indicating pain on swallowing;

Watch particularly for such signs of serious illness as a stiff neck; a pale complexion; listless behavior; *petechiae* (purple spots) on the body — all indicative of meningococcal infection (meningitis).

Seizures occasionally occur in feverish children

A few children have seizures (convulsions) at temperatures above a certain level, often when the fever starts to rise. Such seizures never cause brain damage, and the tendency usually fades as children grow, often vanishing around the time a child reaches first grade. The doctor should be called at once the first time a child has a febrile seizure, as it could be due to an infection such as meningitis. But once it's clear that the child is seizure-prone, and once

---

WHEN TO CALL THE DOCTOR ABOUT FEVER

Call immediately if the child:
- is under 12 weeks old;
- has fever over 40.5°C (105°F);
- acts or looks very sick;
- is crying inconsolably, hard to awaken, delirious or confused;
- has trouble breathing;
- has known medical risk factors (such as leukemia, or sickle cell anemia) or is on immunosuppressants;
- has a stiff neck;
- has febrile convulsions (twitching or shaking) for the first time;
- has purple spots (petechiae) anywhere on the skin;
- has burning or pain with urination.

Call during office hours if:
- the temperature is over 38.5°C (101.4°F) for 24 hours or more;
- the fever runs for more than three days (no matter how mild, or what age the child);
- the behavior of the child is particularly fussy or cranky, or unusually quiet;
- you are anxious about the child's appearance and/or behavior.

---

parents know how to handle the situation, it's no longer an emergency. Fever-induced convulsions often run in families. Antipyretic (fever-reducing) medication such as acetaminophen, given every four hours for the duration of the fever, may prevent further seizures. (Some experts suggest calling the doctor about any seizure, even in children prone to them, for reassurance and to make sure there is no serious illness causing it.)

ALLERGIES

Allergies typically produce wheezing, coughing, shortness of breath, tongue and/or throat swelling, hives (skin redness or weals), itching and perhaps difficulty swallowing. They arise through exposure to particular substances (allergens) — such as dust mites, pollen, food ingredients, pollutants, insect stings and certain medications — which sensitize the body and cause a buildup of antibodies that set off an allergic response. Since allergic reactions can come on rapidly and in some cases may be life-threatening, people must watch for and respect them.

It usually takes more than one exposure to build up sensitivity to a particular substance. For example, the first time a child eats peanut butter, there may be no sign of an allergic reaction. But if peanut sensitivity develops, the next peanut-butter sandwich or cookie may trigger an immunological response with breathing difficulty or even anaphylactic shock.

Anaphylactic shock is an emergency, a severe allergic reaction with symptoms such as swelling of the eyes, tongue and face, hives on many parts of the body, low blood pressure, vomiting, diarrhea and possibly loss of consciousness. Once someone is "sensitized," symptoms can develop within minutes. Severe allergic reactions require prompt adrenalin (epinephrine) administration, by inhaler or injection. Allergy kits are available from pharmacies, and include full instructions. The best strategy, though, is to identify the allergy-triggering item(s) and avoid them if possible. Mild allergies are treated with antihistamines. Medicated sprays, including steroids, may be used during the ragweed or hay-fever season (August to September) for hay-fever sufferers.

(See chapter 13 for more on allergies.)

ASTHMA

About one in eight children develops asthma between ages three to six — sometimes as early as six months — and continues to have episodes up to age ten or even later. But many children "grow out of" their asthma. The telltale clues to asthma are labored breathing and wheezing. A child prone to frequent chest colds, a dry cough (especially at night) and/or troubled breathing may well have asthma.

Specialized advice generally helps to achieve enough control to allow young asthmatics to attend school and enjoy usual childhood activities. Counseling can help to remove any stigma due to the breathing problems. As with adults, there's now greater emphasis on treating asthma as primarily an inflammatory disorder, with more use of anti-inflammatory agents. Therapy aims for freedom from wheeze, no sleep disturbances and regular school and sports attendance.

One University of Toronto specialist defines childhood asthma as "recurrent (three or more) episodes of wheezing and shortness of breath unless other causes are found." About 75 percent of childhood asthma is mild, with sporadic wheezing and/or coughing, usually well controlled by no more than twice-daily puffs of bronchodilating medication from a small "ventilator" device. But asthma in children is likelier to involve severe attacks that develop rapidly, in a few days or hours — sometimes with no prior warning — possibly triggered by a viral infection. Attacks tend to increase at night ("nocturnal asthma"), especially in the predawn hours ("morning dipping"). Like everyone else, asthmatics have a daily or circadian rhythm in their

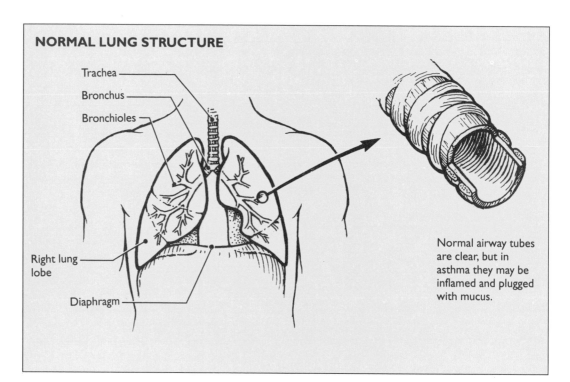

NORMAL LUNG STRUCTURE

Trachea
Bronchus
Bronchioles
Right lung lobe
Diaphragm

Normal airway tubes are clear, but in asthma they may be inflamed and plugged with mucus.

breathing, and even normal airways tend to be narrowest between four and five a.m. — when body temperature and certain hormone levels are at their lowest.

About 20 percent of asthmatic children have moderate disease, with episodes every four to six weeks — for these, inhaled cromoglycate or ketotifen (Zaditen) tablets or syrup are usually advised. Additional treatment is needed during attacks or for children who wheeze with exercise, or on exposure to cold, dust mites (in house dust), animal dander or other triggers. If the medication doesn't keep symptoms down after a few weeks, an inhaled corticosteroid may be suggested. The 5 percent or so of asthmatic children who have severe problems, with troubled breathing on most days (serious enough to interfere with school and sleep), need regularly inhaled corticosteroids plus bronchodilators for "breakthrough" wheezing. Studies show few or no toxic side effects from regular, low-dose inhaled corticosteroids in children. (See chapter 16 for more on asthma.)

AUTISM
Autism is a disorder where children can't relate normally to others, but escape into their own inner world, unable to bear too much sensory "input" or stimulation. Occasionally, the term Pervasive Development Disorder (PDD) is used to describe autism and its distorted perception, sense of reality and movement. Autistic children are not just delayed, they are very different. About 4 per 10,000 children (one in 2,500) is autistic.

Typically, autistic children display:
• an inability to form social relationships;
• disordered speech;
• obsessive repetition of phrases, activities and habits;
• resistance to the smallest changes in familiar surroundings;
• an impaired ability to form abstract concepts.

Children who exhibit only one or two of these characteristics for a short time are not autistic. Children with autism have the problem for many years. The causes of autism are not known, but it may stem from problems in brain function. Because many autistic children have difficult behavior, special management is a major part of the treatment. Most children with autism enter special schools, but some with good cognitive ability can be integrated into regular grade school systems.

BIRTHMARKS
Almost one in three children is born with a pink, red or brown skin spot, popularly called a birthmark, the vast majority of which are small and inconspicuous. But a few birthmarks need treatment because they're disfiguring or endanger health. Although parents may despair for children born with them, most birthmarks are harmless and many fade with time, some disappearing around age eight.

A birthmark is loosely defined as any spot, stain, swelling or other mark obvious within two weeks of birth on a baby's skin, including vascular (blood-filled) lesions such as strawberry marks that show up a bit later. Most birthmarks appear on the face, neck, ears or buttocks. While the vast majority are harmless, occasionally the presence of many birthmarks, possibly along with other symptoms, may point to underlying disease.

No one knows exactly what causes birthmarks, but they are generally considered remnants from fetal life. Most are not hereditary, although some occur more frequently in specific races. Certainly they are not of dietary origin: babies do not, as some used to believe, have red birthmarks because their mothers ate tomatoes or beets while pregnant! Nor do they result from shock or exposure to environmental toxins. Nonetheless, myths abound. Red birthmarks (which look like bloodstains) have long been regarded as signs of a violent character. According to European folklore, birthmarks often arose from a mother's strong feelings during pregnancy; if she became excessively disturbed or frightened in pregnancy, it was thought, her distress might forever "mark" the child in her womb. Another common misconception was that if women were denied some especially craved food during pregnancy, their babies would be born blemished. Accordingly, in France a birthmark is called *envie* (desire), and in Italy it's termed a *voglia* (wish or craving).

SOME COMMON BIRTHMARKS

Stork bites, also popularly known as *salmon marks*, are reddish-pink marks at the nape of the neck or on the forehead, seen in 30–40 percent of white-skinned newborns. If the stain shows up on the neck or eyelids, it's called an *angel's kiss*. This harmless little mark is a collection of surface blood vessels that dilate and cause redness. It almost always fades during the first year, although faint signs may remain forever. Those on the eyelids or middle of the head usually disappear by nine months — if not, they may need laser treatment.

Mongolian spots, more a bluish smudge than a spot, are due to a collection of pigment-producing cells, and occur mostly on the lower back or buttocks. The name is a misnomer because the spot is by no means exclusive to (or common in) Mongols (babies with Down syndrome) or among Mongolian races, but is most frequent among blacks, Orientals and Jews of Spanish or Portuguese origin. There are no reliable figures on its incidence, but one survey found the Mongolian spot in 50 percent of black infants. This harmless birthmark, which fades with time, was first recorded by the Japanese as a "bluespot," supposedly representing a mark made by Kami-Sama, the goddess of childbirth. It has been attributed to rubbing of the fetal back against the placenta.

Café-au-lait patches are light brown stains made up of pigment-producing cells, seen in about 10 percent of Caucasian newborns. These birthmarks appear mainly on the trunk and can be any size. Being inconspicuous, they rarely pose a cosmetic problem although they can last a lifetime. More than five café-au-lait spots on a child may signal the presence of an underlying disease, neurofibromatosis (disfiguring, sometimes progressive formation of tumors on the skin or nerves).

Spider angiomas are small, red, wispy spots on the face with networks of fine blood vessels radiating outwards, somewhat like a spider's web. Not strictly defined as birthmarks, they often don't appear until the age of two to three years and usually fade by puberty. They also sometimes develop in women during pregnancy or in older people, and are occasionally left behind after strawberry birthmarks have faded. They are generally harmless, but large numbers of them may signal liver problems or an unsuspected vitamin B deficiency. Some can now be treated with electrical therapy or lightened by tunable dye laser treatment.

Port wine stains are present at birth, affect 0.3 percent of all babies and come in many shapes and sizes, ranging from small and inconspicuous to large and obvious, on any part of the body, but mostly on the face or neck. Usually permanent, a port wine stain (*nevus flammeus*) is a malformation of blood vessels just under the skin. It usually starts off pale pink but gradually darkens, until by middle age it is a deep reddish purple, possibly with some wart-like skin changes. The chief complication of port wine stains is the psychological burden of feeling "marked," and the resulting feelings of embarrassment may require supportive counseling to boost self-esteem.

In a minority of cases, a port wine stain affects the underlying tissues. Some children with port wine stains on the face have accompanying abnormalities of certain blood vessels in the brain, a congenital condition known as the Sturge-Weber syndrome. In its more serious manifestations, this syndrome can lead to seizures or glaucoma (increased eye pressure). When a port wine stain is large and covers both the cheek and forehead there is a 50 percent risk of glaucoma. And since about a quarter of infants with port wine stains on the face have symptomless Sturge-Weber syndrome, experts advise that all such children have a brain CT (X-ray) scan and an eye test before the age of five or six months.

Over the decades, many treatments have been tried to erase port wine stains, most meeting with little success. Excision and replacement with a skin graft from another part of the body usually gives a cosmetically poor match, with the added risk of scarring. Such treatments as carbon dioxide freezing, electrocautery, X-ray therapy or camouflage by tattooing with flesh-colored dyes were generally unsatisfactory, sometimes dangerous and often painful, almost always leaving scars. Today, laser therapy has dramatically improved the treatment of port wine stains. Properly performed on adults, argon laser treatment is considered good to excellent, with effective lightening in about 70–80 percent of cases, although it may leave scars. In children, use of flashlamp-pulsed tunable dye lasers can give excellent results even at ages as young as three months. (The best time to treat port wine stains is in early childhood, to avoid the hardship of disfigurement in the school years.)

Strawberry mark is the popular name for a

bright red or pink, clearly demarcated, raised or domed, spongy, blood-filled skin tumor seen in 4 to 10 percent of babies. It purportedly arises because of the arrested embryonic development of a small part of the blood system. About 55 percent are obvious at birth; another 25 percent show up within a week and the rest up to a month after birth. The strawberry mark usually appears on the head, face or neck, sometimes on the lip, nose or eyelid, less often on the trunk. It can be tiny, but most average two to five cm (an inch or two) and a few cover a larger area. Strawberry marks affect twice as many girls as boys. They generally grow rapidly until the child is about 9 to 12 months of age and then stop expanding and gradually lighten, usually vanishing or fading to a cosmetically acceptable shade by the time a child starts school; the earliest sign of their disappearance is the development of central gray spots. About 50 percent disappear by age five, 70 percent by the age of seven and 90 percent by the time a child is nine.

Most experts recommend no treatment for strawberry marks. Parents are advised to "watch and wait" for them to fade or disappear. (Seeing "before" and "after" photos of strawberry marks that have faded by themselves can encourage patience.) The long wait can be worrisome, and many parents are upset by the blemish, especially a large or disfiguring one — but when surgeons are persuaded to operate rather than wait for the fading, the result is often lifelong scars.

A small proportion of strawberry marks fail to lighten or get smaller, leaving some residual skin wrinkling or a pinkish tinge. Very rarely, complications arise from strawberry marks that become infected or ulcerated, bleed or cause irreversible facial distortion. Strawberry marks near the mouth may impede feeding, those on the eyelid may obscure vision. Large marks on the eyelid or in the ear can lead to medical problems. In such cases, steroid therapy — taking prednisone for a short time — may be the solution. But because of its potential side effects in young children (slowed growth and possible immune-system suppression) only those at serious risk are given steroid therapy. Almost all strawberry marks on the lip that don't regress on their own by age six or so need some form of therapy, usually surgery. Still in its experimental stages, laser therapy is now considered for some cases.

Corrective makeups can hide birthmarks

Those with birthmarks who cannot or do not wish to undergo laser therapy or other treatment can use dermatological makeups (such as Dermablend or Covermark) containing titanium dioxide, which conceals birthmarks better than ordinary cosmetics. Dermablend, for example, comes in a wide range of shades, suitable for any skin. The product is waterproof and fragrance-free, and can be worn for days, even through baths or in bed.

CEREBRAL PALSY

Cerebral palsy (CP) is a disorder often acquired because of an injury to the brain during pregnancy or birth, resulting in impaired movement and posture. About one case in 10 develops after birth as a result of, for example, a motor-vehicle crash or violent child abuse. Some, but not all, children with CP have perfectly normal intellectual abilities. However, others have hearing problems, seizures, visual difficulties and language problems, which may lead people to assume that they are mentally handicapped when they are not. The amount of brain damage doesn't increase over time, but as children with CP grow older the movement problems may change.

The type of CP depends on the part of the brain damaged and can be:
* *spastic* — weak or jerky muscles;
* *choreoathetotic or extrapyramidal* — difficulty coordinating movement;
* *diplegic* —affecting the two lower limbs;
* *quadriplegic* — affecting all four limbs;
* *hemiplegic* — where one half of the body (left or right) is affected.

The types of CP range from merely an awkward walk or arm movements to impairment bad enough to necessitate a wheelchair. Occasionally, a teacher is the first to suspect CP — for example, if a child has difficulty achieving age-appropriate learning milestones.

Treatment (for instance, regular physical therapy) aims to improve the child's skills before the problem interferes too much with function. Those who have difficulty speaking may need technical aids. Caregivers can consult the attending physician or the Canadian Cerebral Palsy Association.

WHAT TO DO FOR CHICKENPOX

• If a child comes down with chickenpox, watch other children for signs of it during the next two to three weeks. If your child develops chickenpox, make sure you tell the school, and contact your physician.

• Keep children with chickenpox out of school and daycare facilities for five days after the rash begins or until all blisters have crusted, whichever is shorter.

• Do not give acetylsalicylic acid (ASA or Aspirin), or any products containing it, to children with chickenpox. ASA increases the risk of Reye's syndrome (a severe illness that damages the liver and brain). Instead, use acetaminophen products to control fever.

• A new medication, acyclovir, is now available to treat the complications of chickenpox. Many authorities recommend giving it immediately to all adolescents and adults with chickenpox. It has far less benefit in children, but may be given to those at high risk — for instance, children with leukemia or the immunosuppressed.

CHICKENPOX

Since there's no vaccine yet available in Canada or the United States, chickenpox is still a very common childhood infection, caused by the *varicella-zoster* virus. Usually mild in children, chickenpox begins with a fever, followed by a characteristic rash in a day or two. The rash starts as little red spots, and these turn into fluid-filled blisters that crust over in a few days. The illness is usually mild, but may be accompanied by a high fever and severe rash in some. Complications include pneumonia, secondary bacterial infection of the pox rash and encephalitis (inflammation of the brain) — quite rare. Fortunately, provided children don't scratch, even the most awesome-looking chickenpox rash usually fades without leaving pockmarks.

In adults, chickenpox can be dangerous. Pregnant women who get chickenpox are at increased risk of pneumonia and, in addition, the virus may infect the unborn or newborn baby, causing severe illness. People with immune deficiencies — such as leukemia or those on steroid medication — are also at risk of severe illness if they get chickenpox.

Chickenpox viruses spread through air or via direct contact with the blisters. People remain infectious until the last blister has crusted or five days after the rash first appeared, whichever is shorter. The only way to stop the spread of the virus is to prevent infected people from sharing the same room or house — not very practical! The chickenpox virus can survive for many years in the body and may later be reactivated as shingles or zoster. (For more on shingles, see chapter 5.) Since the same virus causes both chickenpox and shingles, someone who never had chickenpox can catch it from a person with shingles.

COLIC

A colicky baby is one who cries often and long enough to aggravate parents and caregivers. Also known as "three-month colic" or "periodic irritability," the condition generally disappears by the age of three to four months. While most infants fuss now and then — typically for one to four hours at suppertime — colicky babies cry for hours on end, despite cuddling, feeding, burping or changing. They supposedly have some "tummy discomfort," but no one really knows what causes colic. Nothing is definitely wrong with the bowels of most colicky infants, nor is there generally excess gas or wind, or any identified food allergy. However, excessive crying makes infants swallow air, which they burp up or pass as wind. The straining and tightening of the stomach muscles during crying also forces air out of the rectum so that these babies seem "windy."

Parents often feel stressed by the endless crying, and it may reassure them to know that this behavior during the first three or four post-birth months does not predict future irritability or health problems. While all possible efforts should be made to comfort colicky babies, their regular sleep and feeding schedule needn't be disrupted by excessive comforting attempts. The best bet is to wrap them up snugly, cradle them soothingly and handle them gently.

WHAT TO DO FOR COMMON COLDS

• Wash your own and children's hands often — especially before preparing or eating food.

• Give plenty of fluids.

• Give acetaminophen (if necessary) to bring down fever and relieve aches and pains, and decongestants (on the physician's advice) to lessen nasal stuffiness. Although these medications may make people feel better, they don't alter or shorten the course of infection.

• Contact the physician if a child with a cold has:
  • earache;
  • fever higher than 39°C (102°F);
  • unusual sleepiness;
  • excessive crankiness or fussiness;
  • rapid breathing or difficulty breathing;
  • persistent coughing.

(See also section on common cold in chapter 16.)

Reducing noise and dimming lights may help. Steady, smooth vibrations such as those from a rocking chair or car ride often quiets them. The long crying spells generally stop by age three months or so, and whatever care was given at the moment usually gets the credit!

COMMON COLDS

The common cold is a viral infection that usually lasts a week, slightly longer in young children. Most children have several colds a year, sometimes being quite sick (with a high fever, lack of energy and loss of appetite), at other times hardly ill at all. Occasionally, a cold can lead to complications, such as ear infections and pneumonia. Children with colds usually have runny noses, coughs and fever. Being due to viruses, colds cannot be treated with antibiotics.

Cold viruses spread from person to person mainly by:
- direct contact, whenever a child with a cold touches his or her saliva or runny nose and then touches another child or object;
- indirect contact, whenever a child with a cold rubs his or her saliva or runny nose and then touches an object, such as a toy or furniture, contaminating it with the cold viruses (which are quite tough and can survive for hours on surfaces such as eating utensils, counters, towels). People catch the cold by touching the contaminated object, picking up the virus on their hands and then rubbing their eyes or nose.

CROUP

A viral infection of the throat and vocal cords (larynx), croup is a severe respiratory condition in children under age five, called laryngitis in older children. Croup often begins as a cough with some evident breathing difficulty. The lining of the throat and larynx become red and swollen, producing a hoarse voice and a bark-like cough. The passage below the vocal cords may also be inflamed, making it difficult for the child to move air in or out. Breathing can become rapid and noisy, but croup mostly sounds worse than it is. However, children may become tired through the labored breathing and in rare, very severe cases, breathing can be obstructed. A few children are sick enough

to need hospital treatment. Antibiotics do not work on croup because it's a viral infection.

JUVENILE, TYPE I OR "INSULIN-DEPENDENT" DIABETES

Diabetes occurs when the pancreas does not produce enough of the hormone insulin to keep blood-sugar levels within safe limits. Insulin is a hormone that helps the body store and use glucose (sugar) — the body's main fuel for energy. Without enough insulin, the body cannot survive, because the cells cannot absorb enough glucose from the blood.

One in 600 to 700 children has early-onset or type I diabetes. While the condition is largely hereditary, triggers in the environment (such as a virus or toxin) can start it off or destroy the insulin-producing pancreas cells. Children with diabetes should be encouraged to participate fully in school and suitable sports.

Type I or juvenile diabetes is controlled by:
- insulin injections;
- carefully regulated diet;
- monitored exercise.

Those with early-onset type I diabetes need insulin injections for a lifetime — usually twice daily, to keep blood glucose at near-normal levels. The insulin doses are tailored to fluctuating blood-glucose levels, determined by testing a finger-prick drop of blood with a small portable kit. The blood droplet is put on a paper strip and its color change shows the glucose reading. The required insulin dose is then calculated and given by injection just under the skin, in the arm, leg, abdomen or buttocks, usually before breakfast and supper.

People with type I need a carefully regulated diet to provide sufficient calories for growth, best divided into three balanced meals and three snacks to distribute the energy evenly through the day. Youngsters must eat their entire carbohydrate (starch/sugar) content, or its equivalent, at each meal to ensure a steady sugar intake and avoid *hypo* (low) or *hyper* (high) blood-sugar swings.

What to do about juvenile diabetes
- Follow doctor's orders.
- Get enough exercise to lower blood sugar by

SIGNS AND SYMPTOMS OF UNTREATED DIABETES

- **tiredness, weakness;**
- **excessive, frequent urination;**
- **a raging thirst;**
- **vision blurring;**
- **weight loss.**

WHAT TO DO FOR CROUP

- **If a child has suspected croup, contact a physician.**
- **To relieve the harsh, dry cough, humidify the air well.**
- **Try putting the child in the bathroom and running the hot water taps to get up a good steam.**
- **Follow directions for any prescribed medication.**
- **Should any or all of the following appear, immediately take the child to see a physician or to the hospital emergency department:**
  - **fever higher than 39°C (102°F);**
  - **rapid or difficult breathing;**
  - **new or increased drooling;**
  - **severe sore throat — refusal to swallow;**
  - **extreme discomfort when lying down.**

WHAT TO DO FOR CHILDHOOD DIARRHEA

- Ignore the old adage of "starving out the diarrhea" and continue light meals — unless the child is vomiting. Contrary to the former idea of "fluids only," the modern approach is to continue eating a normal diet after the first 12–24 hours of diarrhea, and above all to keep on drinking enough water or other fluids to avoid dehydration.
- Contact a physician if the child has symptoms suggesting dehydration or worsening infection:
  - has a fever higher than 39°C (102°F);
  - refuses to drink;
  - vomits repeatedly;
  - has very large, watery stools or several stools in a day;
  - has less than the usual number of daily wet diapers (or urinates less);
  - has a sunken fontanel (soft spot on top of the head in infants);
  - has sunken eyes;
  - is listless;
  - has rapid breathing;
  - has bloody stools.

As protective measures and to manage the diarrhea:
- Make sure that all household members wash their hands after changing diapers or going to the toilet, and before eating or handling food.
- Do not share toothbrushes, cups or eating utensils.
- If the child with diarrhea is on milk formula, do not boil, concentrate or thicken it, because this may worsen dehydration.
- Follow the new guidelines for feeding children with diarrhea:
  - For breastfed children under six months old breastfeeding can continue, but also give extra water.
  - For infants on formula, replace the formula for 12 to 24 hours with oral rehydration solution (ORS), as advised by a physician. Make up for lost fluids by offering the infant 30 to 60 ml (1 to 2 oz) of ORS every half to one hour when awake, or after each loose stool, more if tolerated. The ORS, marketed as Gastrolyte, Pedialyte or Riceolyte, can be bought at any pharmacy or grocery store. If juice is given, it should be diluted (half water, half juice). Avoid plain water, as it's not nourishing enough. Always consult the doctor if the diarrhea is severe.
- Do not give only ORS for longer than 24 hours. This could deprive the child of valuable nutrients. ORS is not given to stop diarrhea, but to replace lost fluids and electrolytes.
- Infants can also have rice cereal, bananas, potatoes and other lactose-free, carbohydrate-rich (starchy) foods. When juices are given, continue to dilute with water. Give a variety of juices.
- For older children, regular diet can continue after giving fluids for only 12 hours or so. Children over six months of age can eat a regular diet, although the child may not feel much like eating. However, he or she should drink as much as possible.
- After one day of diarrhea, feed older infants and children such foods as:
  - Jello;
  - frozen Popsicles;
  - noncarbonated soft drinks;
  - whole-wheat noodles;
  - cereals (especially rice cereals);
  - light meats (fish, chicken);
  - bananas;
  - potatoes.
- Consult a physician or pediatrician if you still have any questions about feeding a child with diarrhea.
- Do not give the child medication unless medically advised. Antibiotics cure only bacterial, not viral, diarrhea.
- Keep the child at home until bowel movements normalize or until you are told the child can return to school or daycare.

making the body burn more glucose. Both diet and insulin dosage in diabetics must be tailored to the amount of physical activity. With more exercise, more carbohydrate-rich food must be eaten beforehand.

(See also "Diabetes" in chapter 16.)

DIARRHEA

Diarrhea is a common childhood problem that's generally harmless and brief, but occasionally severe, especially in infants. Its hallmarks are unusually frequent bowel movements with unformed, watery stools. A child with diarrhea may also vomit, and have fever, loss of appetite, nausea, stomach cramps and blood and/or mucus in the stool. Diarrhea-causing microbes spread easily from person to person, especially among children who don't yet use the toilet. Most diarrhea is due to viral infections that cannot be cured with antibiotics, although some forms are caused by food-borne bacteria, such as *Campylobacter, Shigella* and *E. coli,* and may be cured with antibiotics. Spread can be curbed through scrupulous hand-washing after every diaper change and before preparing and eating food.

DIPHTHERIA

Diphtheria is a very severe, contagious, bacterial throat infection, easily spread by coughs and sneezes, which can lead to heart failure and nerve damage; one in 10 cases is fatal. Symptoms include fever, rapid pulse, swollen neck glands, a thick yellow discharge from the nose and — most distinctively — a grayish membrane on the throat and tonsils. Diphtheria can totally block breathing and may cause skin or ear infections. It is now rare in Canada, because almost all children are immunized, but is still common in many parts of the world. Diphtheria vaccine, usually given in combination with pertussis and tetanus vaccines (DPT), protects most of those immunized. In some provinces/ territories, DPT is also combined with polio and Hib (antimeningitis) vaccine. Adult diphtheria vaccine boosters are required every 10 years to sustain protection. If you do suspect diphtheria, call your physician at once.

DOWN SYNDROME

Down syndrome (before known as Down's syndrome) which affects the brain, head, heart, hands and feet, was first described by Dr. Down in 1866. It was formerly called mongolism because of the slanted eyes often seen with the disorder. It afflicts one in 600 children and is now known to be associated with a specific chromosome flaw or extra number 21 chromosome (known as "trisomy 21"). The extra chromosome 21 usually arises by a quirk of nature before birth (sometimes because of faulty cell division). Occasionally the flaw is passed from parent to child. The risk of bearing children with Down syndrome increases as women get older — approaching one in 200 at age 35, and more with advancing years.

Almost all children with Down syndrome have impaired mental development. However, some, especially in preschool years, show only mildly delayed mental development. Most have impaired language skills. Children with Down syndrome tend to be more "loose" or floppy (hypotonic) than average, often with odd movements known as atlantoaxial instability due to looseness of the spinal vertebrae. They are prone to respiratory-tract and middle-ear infections and tend to be nearsighted (myopic), requiring glasses at a young age.

EAR INFECTIONS

Most children will have had at least one bout of middle-ear infection — *otitis media* — by the time they reach the age of three. Middle-ear infections are almost as frequent in children as the common cold, though far less frequent in adults.

Otitis media — from *oto* for ear, *itis* for inflammation, *media* for middle — is more common in boys than girls, most prevalent in winter and often follows a cold. When young children have a cold or other respiratory infection, or sometimes an allergy, the eustachian tube (which connects the throat to the middle ear) is likely to get blocked, allowing bacteria to flourish and reach the middle ear. If the eustachian tube becomes plugged, air cannot enter the middle ear and it fills up with fluid — either clear (serous) or infectious (purulent). The fluid presses against the eardrum, causing pain, even sometimes perforating it by creating a small hole.

Fluid replacing air in the middle ear deadens sound and can cause transient hearing loss in one or both ears. Since untreated middle-ear infections can spread to surrounding areas and cause serious complications, even mild cases need prompt medical attention.

Symptoms of middle-ear infection are pain, sometimes severe, typically starting at night, when a child awakens howling with pain, pulling at the ears. There may also be fever, appetite loss, vomiting and diarrhea. Yet some children with *otitis media* hardly seem sick at all, although

MIDDLE-EAR INFECTIONS IN CHILDREN

The middle ear contains three tiny bones or ossicles — the hammer, anvil and stirrup — that conduct sound from the eardrum to the inner ear. Normally, a little air enters the middle ear with each swallow, equalizing pressure on either side of the eardrum. But in young children the eustachian tube is narrow, short and angled so that it easily gets blocked. As children grow older, the eustachian tube lengthens and otitis media becomes less frequent.

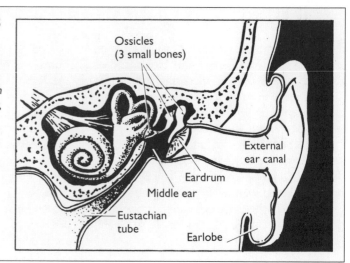

the feeling of fullness in the ears (from the fluid) may make them tug at their ears.

Physicians generally diagnose *otitis media* by looking at the eardrum with an otoscope (lighted ear-examining instrument) and with a device to detect fluid in the middle ear (known as a tympanometer or reflectometer). Sometimes it's necessary to remove wax from the outer ear canal in order to see the eardrum clearly.

Antibiotics are the usual treatment and generally make children better in a few days (but to eradicate the infection, the whole antibiotic course must be completed). Middle-ear infections may also resolve spontaneously within seven to ten days without any treatment. The eardrum often ruptures, letting out an exudate, usually giving prompt relief.

The trouble is that many children get recurrent middle-ear infections. And even when the infection is gone, fluid may linger on in the ear for months— perhaps not suspected until some hearing loss or behavioral problem alerts parents to it. Children may adapt to the slight hearing loss without noticing it and parents may remain equally unaware, attributing the youngster's slow responses to stubbornness. A child's inexplicable crankiness — owing to the emotional toll of not hearing properly — may eventually drive parents to seek medical attention. Or the teacher may notice a lack of attention at school because of a child's inability to hear clearly or keep up with peers.

The doctor's dilemma in treating childhood fluid in the ear is that most cases clear up in three to six weeks with or without antibiotics or any other treatment. By 12 weeks after a middle-ear infection, approximately 90 percent of children are better without antibiotics. Yet despite antibiotic therapy, some children drag on and on with fluid in the ears, which often leads to some loss of hearing. Experts stress the need for frequent checkups and hearing tests for children prone to middle-ear infections.

Myringotomy (putting a small hole in the eardrum) to drain off middle-ear fluid may be tried for persistent cases. For children old enough to cooperate, myringotomy can be done under a local anesthetic, but those under age eight usually need general anesthesia.

Tympanotomy — insertion of ventilating tubes or "grommits" into the eardrum of the blocked ear (under general anesthesia) to let air into the middle ear — is often done to

WHAT PARENTS CAN DO FOR CHILDHOOD EAR INFECTIONS

- If you suspect your child has a middle-ear infection, contact your physician, who will examine the child's ears.
- Ear infections usually get better with antibiotics, but it is important to take all of the medication prescribed. Call the

physician if the child shows any of the following:
- a worsening earache despite treatment;
- a high fever over 39°C (102°F) in spite of treatment, or one that lasts more than three days;

- excessive sleepiness, crankiness or fussiness;
- a skin rash;
- rapid or difficult breathing;
- noticeable hearing loss (can't clearly hear noises, tapes or what's being said).

prevent or minimize hearing loss. But to tube or not to tube children's ears is a much-debated question. Some experts oppose ear tubes because their benefits are transient and time alone (about three months) makes most children better with no residual hearing loss. Tests show that with or without antibiotics, with or without tubes, 20 percent of children still have fluid in their ears and some hearing loss one month after a bout of *otitis media*, but by two months only 9 percent and by the third month only 6 percent are still not back to normal. There's increasing opposition to tubing because, although it carries no greater surgical risks than average, it is still an operation done under general anesthesia, the tubes tend to need reinsertion and there's an increased risk of scars of the eardrum after tubing. Moreover, they're a nuisance because children with tubes must not get water in the ear.

Those who favor tubing argue that although middle-ear infections generally heal without them, tubes help to avoid a possible developmental lag in learning due to hearing loss from fluid in the ears. Avoiding hearing loss is particularly critical between the ages of 18 months and three years, when language develops. But it has not been proven that the temporary hearing loss due to middle-ear infections has any long-term effects on language development or learning ability

The alternative is to give continuous low-dose preventive antibiotics throughout the winter for *otitis*-prone children. However, "breakthrough" infections can occur. For kids whose middle ears predictably flare up at the end of each cold, early use of antibiotics may prevent ear infection. Also, recent experimental use of steroids seems to help.

ECZEMA

Eczema is one of the most troublesome infant rashes — on the face, body and in any skin creases. In older children, it tends to be localized on elbows, knees, necks and behind the ears. The itchy rash may be moist and weepy or dry and scaly. The eczema rash is usually red, patchy and scaly, with flareups that look oozy, weeping and "angry." Most children with eczema have very itchy skin, worsened by

---

WHAT TO DO FOR CHILDREN WITH ECZEMA

- **Avoid known triggers, and use anti-inflammatory steroid creams, moisturizers, anti-itch medication and possibly antibiotics (if the eczema is infected).**
- **Dress in cotton clothing.**
- **Avoid anything that** might irritate the skin or increase sweating.
- **Don't overdress infants.**
- **Avoid wool — particularly irritating to the skin of those prone to eczema — and also steer clear of synthetics such as nylon because they** do not allow the skin to "breathe."
- **Use bland hypoallergenic soaps for washing.**
- **Avoid bubble baths and excessive bathing, which may worsen eczema.**
- **Specific anti-inflammatory ointments may help.**

---

scratching. Eczema is not dangerous unless the rash becomes infected. In some cases, eczema is an allergic reaction to cow's milk protein in formula, citrus fruits, chocolate, eggs or other foods. While it is usually a long-term condition, 50 percent of children outgrow eczema by the age of 21. It may be linked to conditions such as asthma or other allergies. Eczema is often confused with impetigo because the rashes look alike, but eczema is not infectious.

ENURESIS (BEDWETTING)

Parents eagerly look forward to the time when their offspring can make it through the night without wetting the bed and tiresome diapers can be discarded. Yet, although most children are dry by age four or five, many go on wetting at night for several more years. About 15 percent of children are still nighttime bedwetters by the time they start school, 3 percent by age 10, and although almost all are dry by age 11 without any treatment, 1 to 2 percent go on wetting into adolescence — to their own and their parents' embarrassment. (One study even

---

BEDWETTING NOT DUE TO NAUGHTINESS, REBELLION OR POOR PARENTING

While disruptive to a family, and upsetting and uncomfortable for the child, bedwetting must be kept in perspective. For the most part, it is more a housekeeping annoyance than a medical abnormality. Nocturnal bedwetters are not misbehaving.

If undertaken at all, treatment should include reassurance, perhaps gentle attempts to increase bladder holding or possibly an alarm system. Nightly charts may encourage progress, and some drugs are worth considering. In some cases, medication helps to dry up the urine flow for special occasions (a weekend away, a holiday or going to camp).

WHAT TO DO FOR BEDWETTING

- Seek professional advice if :
  - the child is still wetting after age five or six;
  - half the nights per week are wet;
  - the child has persistent daytime wetting after age four to five or for several months;
  - the child has been dry at night for six months or more and suddenly starts wetting again.
- Remember that most bedwetting eventually vanishes, given time and patience (provided there's no organic abnormality).
- Since the overwhelming majority of bedwetters do not have organic or psychological problems, refrain from scolding children for an involuntary problem.
- Try charting "wet" nights to sharpen the child's bladder consciousness and speed up the drying-out process.
- Make bedwetters change and launder soiled linen; it may do the trick.
- For the wetter's bed, try small cot sheets, single bed sheets folded in half or bits of old woolen blankets under the bottom sheet to limit urine spread.
- Consider alarm systems to stop the wetting. Urinary alarm systems, powered by batteries, attach to the child's pyjamas near the urine outlet (urethra); the first drops of wetness set off the alarm, and the child's bladder muscles automatically contract, squeezing off the urine flow. The slumbering child awakens, goes to the toilet and reattaches the device before going back to sleep. Alarms can take up to 16 weeks to become effective. According to learning theory, alarms change the innate signal "urinate" into its opposite, "don't urinate" (unless awake and at the toilet!). For an alarm to work, the child must be old enough, want to do something about the problem and be willing to go through the necessary steps. The most suitable candidates are older children (aged 10 or more) who are greatly bothered by wetting. The decision to use an alarm should be made only with a child's full consent.

- Ask about medications against bedwetting:
- Imipramine (Tofranil), an antidepressant, can suppress nocturnal enuresis. Taken regularly, it makes about 50 percent of bedwetters permanently dry. But when it is stopped, bedwetting often returns. Common side effects include irritability, lethargy and mild gastrointestinal problems — symptoms that disappear once the drug is withdrawn. Since Tofranil is a dangerous drug when taken in overdose, it must be kept well out of children's reach and safely locked up, which explains why many parents prefer not to give it to children.
- Desmopressin, an antidiuretic hormone, shows great promise for nighttime enuresis. Used as an aerosol spray (squirted into the nose), it concentrates urine, reduces flow and decreases the amount held in the bladder. This drug helps up to 40 percent or more of bedwetting children, who become completely dry as long as they're on it. Some relapse on discontinuation, and about 30 percent fail to respond. It's very useful as a short-term "fix" for children going to camp or on an overnight stay.
- Antispasmodic drugs such as oxybutynin chloride (Ditropan) can be useful for daytime wetting by reducing the frequency of bladder contractions, delaying the urge to urinate. These drugs are especially useful for wetters for whom every tiny bladder squeeze sends them running.
- As a final ploy, buy a book called *Sammy the Elephant and Mr. Camel*, written by two psychologists (Joyce C. Mills and Richard J. Crowly). The story describes an elephant unable to carry a trunkful of water like other elephants, and who is guided by Mr. Camel to gain self-control and self-esteem. In the end the elephant puts out a fire with a trunkful of water. Children don't mind the somewhat weak plot, and the book is a "healing metaphor" whereby the child subconsciously goes through the steps with Sammy the elephant until able to hold in urine.

found that 2 percent of U.S. soldiers were occasional nighttime wetters!)

Enuresis or bedwetting is defined as "the involuntary voiding of urine, at least twice a month, in children aged four to six years, and once monthly (or more) in older children." It is usually due to slow maturation of the bladder's complex urine-voiding system. If there are no other symptoms or abnormalities, bedwetting is considered a variant of normal development. Male bedwetters outnumber girls by two to one up to age 11, after which the sexes even out.

Despite the popular myth that bedwetting stems mainly from psychological reasons or bad parenting, it is not the child's fault or due to

poor upbringing. Current medical wisdom advises worried parents not to scold but to let "the tincture of time" help children outgrow the annoyance. Yet although the vast majority naturally grow out of this harmless condition, children have been beaten, bled, blistered, fed nauseating concoctions, given electric shocks and otherwise tormented in efforts to make them dry. Among the many attempted remedies, incontinent children have been treated with juniper berries and beer, or given boiled mice (the ancient Roman strategy for strengthening weak bladders). Other treatments involved bandaging penises, burning leaves between a bedwetter's legs or tying a toad to

SOME "DO'S" AND "DON'TS" FOR BEDWETTING

"Do's"

- Recognize that bedwetting is quite common in girls up to age five and in boys up to age eight, ten or even older.
- Give reassurance: it's crucial for bedwetters and their caregivers to realize that enuresis is a normal condition and nothing to worry about, remembering that many of a child's classmates probably also suffer from it. A matter-of-fact attitude, dismissing it as "nothing out of the ordinary," is best.
- Banish feelings of guilt or shame: it's not the child's fault.
- A night light in the bathroom is useful to help children go to the toilet or change bedwear.
- Try using absorbent bed pads or a folded blanket under the bottom sheet to limit urine spread; placing absorbent pads between bottom sheet and mattress minimizes the dampness and reduces the cleanup operation.
- A reward or positive-reinforcement system can help — praising dry nights, giving the child a small reward or a star on a chart for every dry night — or bigger rewards for several dry nights in a row.
- Encouraging a child to help change and wash the wet bed sheets is a sound idea — not as a punishment but as a practical aid, to engender a sense of responsibility and the pride of "lending a hand." It should be requested in a nonjudgmental, good-humoured style.
- Behaviour modification may be tried, with guidelines given by a family physician or pediatrician (or just plain common sense).
- Slow, steady training to go to the bathroom before bed can increase bladder consciousness.
- Cleanliness is essential. Be sure the bedwetter has a shower or bath before going to school; the smell of urine clings.
- For children who wet during the day, bladder retraining may work. It teaches "bladder awareness" and how to control bladder capacity by drinking fluids, then holding urine in with the sphincter muscles and releasing it at will. Regular, timed trips to the washroom, with gradually longer times between emptyings, can help.

"Don'ts"

- Don't scold or shame a bedwetting child, even if you're angry: disapproval only compounds the problem.
- Don't curb fluids. Many parents and caregivers restrict fluids in bedwetting children after supper, in the vain hope that they'll stay dry — a strategy that sounds reasonable but rarely works. Whether or not any liquid is taken, some fluid will accumulate in the bladder, and a child with poor bladder mastery will wet the bed whether there's a little or a lot in the bladder. Since caffeine (in tea, coffee, chocolate, or some soft drinks) stimulates the bladder directly, it should not be given to wetters near bedtime.
- Don't awaken the child and take him or her to the toilet at your own bedtime. While this strategy works for some bedwetters, it isn't foolproof, and since it disturbs the child's sleep, many pediatricians consider the practice disruptive and think it may interfere with natural bladder control, stopping the child from learning to respond to the body's own signals. (Some experts dispute this, saying that if nighttime lifting works, it is unreasonable to tell parents to stop.)
- Don't put bedwetters to bed in diapers or training (padded) pants — this is strongly discouraged by most pediatricians. Despite the possible convenience to parents, continuing to wear diapers after age five may be demeaning to a growing youngster and could "infantalize" the child, encourage immature behavior and undermine security. In older children it can produce skin irritation.
- Don't be tempted by intensive "dry bed" training — "psyching" the child to get heavily involved in beating incontinence by getting up every hour at night, for example, plus other steps to persuade the child to work toward dryness. The method is controversial and advised against by most experts.

the penis (on the assumption that it would croak as urine was passed).

Three main types of childhood bedwetting

- *Primary nocturnal enuresis* — nighttime bedwetting in a child who's never been dry and still wets past age four to five — is often hereditary, and without psychological undertones. A child with primary nocturnal enuresis requires a thorough physical examination and urine tests to rule out infection or structural causes.
- *Diurnal enuresis* — daytime as well as nighttime wetting — can stem from underlying anatomical disorders or emotional problems.

Most children can stay dry during the day, with occasional lapses, by age three to four. Those who consistently wet during the day after age four should have a full medical workup because, although it could be due to a developmental lag, diurnal incontinence is the type most likely to arise from an underlying abnormality (infection, sickle cell anemia, diabetes or structural defects). A small number of daytime wetters have psychological problems that require special counseling.

- *Secondary enuresis* (the least common form of bedwetting) starts up after children have already been persistently dry for six months

EPILEPSY TRIGGERS MAY INCLUDE:

• infections;
• a rapidly rising fever;
• flashing or blinking lights (such as camera flashes);
• fatigue;
• a scary amusement ride (such as a roller coaster);
• certain sounds or odors.

N.B.: Seizures due to high fever are not epilepsy. (See also "Understanding childhood fever," above, and section on epilepsy in chapter 16.)

TREATMENT OF EPILEPSY

To prevent seizures, children often need daily anticonvulsant medication such as:

• phenobarbital;
• phenytoin (Dilantin);
• valproic acid (Depakene);
• carbamazepine (Tegretol).

Side effects of anticonvulsant drugs may include: lack of coordination, behavior changes, headaches, drowsiness, dizziness, rash, increased gum size, baldness, anemia, gastrointestinal upset, liver abnormalities, double vision, blood abnormalities.

to a year. It may be nocturnal or diurnal, and calls for a thorough medical examination. The reappearance of wetting in a previously dry child could arise from a urinary-tract infection but is often due to emotional distress — perhaps difficulties at home or school, often signaling some underlying anxiety.

Tracing the reasons for bedwetting

In the early 1900s, bedwetting was regarded as a childhood neurosis, even a masturbation substitute. But today it's considered a normal variation in the speed of bladder development and, except in rare cases, not a psychological disorder or a form of rebellion. Bedwetters don't do it on purpose. Enuresis does not lead to kidney failure or permanent disability.

• Organic causes include diabetes mellitus, kidney problems, epilepsy, sickle cell anemia and urinary-tract infections.
• Extra deep sleep is no longer blamed for night-time wetting. Formerly, bedwetting was thought to occur in children who sleep so deeply that they don't respond to the bladder-emptying urge when the bladder is full. But many parents notice that even when they awaken a bedwetting child to go to the toilet, another wetting episode occurs within an hour of voiding, with a half-empty bladder. The latest research shows no link between deep slumber and bedwetting. The claim that night-time enuresis is a dream disorder has also never been scientifically proved. Although enuretics often describe dreams of wetting the bed — after which they wake up in a puddle — it's likely that the child first passed urine and then dreamed about it.
• Some nightly wetters are deficient in an antidiuretic hormone, vasopressin, which regulates urine flow from kidney to bladder. Adults usually produce more vasopressin at night, suppressing urinary flow. Children who continue bedwetting past the usual age may be slow to produce the hormone. (Giving the drug desmopressin acetate, which mimics the body hormone, can cut back urine production and halt bedwetting until the child's system is mature.)
• If both parents were bedwetters, there is a 77 percent chance that their offspring will also be

bedwetters. If only one parent was enuretic, there is a 40 percent chance. Recognizing the inherited roots of bedwetting may deter parents from scolding or inflicting "cures" for a problem that will vanish with time. (It may also reassure bedwetting children to know that their parents also wet their beds!)

EPIGLOTTITIS

Epiglottitis is a very severe, life-threatening infection of the epiglottis, a flap of tissue at the back of the throat that closes over the vocal cords (larynx or voicebox) when a person swallows. If a child with epiglottitis isn't immediately treated, the swelling can become severe enough to block the airway within hours and lead to sudden death by suffocation. Early signs resemble croup, but with epiglottitis the child becomes rapidly ill, with high fever, severe sore throat, drooling and difficulty breathing. Epiglottitis is always an emergency. It's almost always due to *Haemophilus influenzae type b* (Hib) bacteria (not related to influenza viruses). Fortunately, epiglottitis has become very uncommon through infant immunization with the new Hib vaccine.

What to do for a child with suspected epiglottitis

• Call the doctor at once.
• Keep the child upright (sitting).
• Take the child at once to an emergency room if:
  • fever is 39°C (102°F) or more;
  • breathing is rapid or difficult;
  • there's much drooling;
  • the child won't or can't swallow.

EPILEPSY (SEIZURE DISORDER)

Epilepsy (now called "seizure disorder") involves sporadic seizures (convulsions) that occur because of a temporary, unusually high level of electrical activity in the brain. During a seizure, the body loses control of its sensory systems (such as hearing), as well as breathing, body temperature and/or blood-pressure regulation. Overall, 1 to 2 percent of all children have seizure disorders, but less than one in 100 preschoolers. The disorder may be inherited, but the cause is largely unknown. Children with underlying brain damage such as

WHAT TO DO FOR GENERALIZED (GRAND MAL) SEIZURES

- Most important, remain calm.
- If possible, place the child on the floor — on the side or stomach, not on the back — to prevent choking on saliva.
- Remove any object that could injure the child (such as toys and chairs), and move the child away from other potential dangers such as stairwells.
- Loosen tight clothing around the child's neck and remove eyeglasses.
- If possible, put something flat and soft under the head.
- Do not put anything in the mouth. Do not try to open the child's mouth (people do *not* swallow their tongues during epileptic seizures).
- Do not try to restrain the jerky movements: it could injure the child. Children who are having a seizure are unaware of what they are doing and their body movements are very powerful.
- Do not attempt artificial respiration unless the child fails to start breathing again once the seizure stops. If this happens, begin artificial respiration (see chapter 17) and call an ambulance.
- Allow the seizure to stop on its own. If it lasts more than five minutes, or if the first seizure is followed by a second one, call for medical help. Once a seizure has started, it can be stopped only by special medication.
- When the seizure is over, place the child in the "recovery position" (see chapter 17). This will keep the airway open and prevent the possibility of breathing vomitus or saliva into the lungs.
- After a seizure, children will be sleepy for some time. Stay close by and reassure the child as soon as he or she awakens.
- Do not give food or drink until the child is fully awake.
- During a seizure, it is not uncommon for the child to urinate or have a bowel movement. Depending on the child's age, this can be very embarrassing, and should be handled discreetly when the child awakens.
- Record the seizure's duration, any injuries and how the child felt afterwards.
- If possible, prevent other children from witnessing a grand mal seizure, which can be very frightening.

cerebral palsy may be especially prone to seizures. For some children, certain triggers bring on the seizures.

Signs and symptoms of:
- ***mild (epileptic) seizures***
  - drowsiness;
  - rolling of eyes;
  - inattention and fading awareness.

- ***"Grand mal," generalized epileptic seizures***

Grand mal or "tonic-clonic" seizures may affect just one part of the body, but more often the whole body shakes and trembles, even violently. The child may drool at the mouth and/or bite the lips, cheeks or tongue, falling down unconscious, possibly also losing control over bladder and bowel movements. Tonic-clonic seizures usually last only a few minutes. Although frightening to onlookers, they generally pass without complications for the child. A deep sleep often follows the seizure. (See also chapter 16.)

- ***"Petit mal" or absence seizures***

Absence seizures are usually very short in duration, often just a few seconds. The child may simply appear momentarily blank and inattentive, as though daydreaming. However, unlike daydreaming, the child cannot be aroused. Some children have many of these brief seizures during the course of a day. If you suspect a child of having seizures, always consult a physician.

(For more on epilepsy, see chapter 16.)

FIFTH DISEASE (ERYTHEMA INFECTIOSUM)

Fifth disease is an infection of the respiratory system caused by the parvovirus B_{19}, which spreads as the common cold does, i.e.,
- from the hands of someone with the infection;
- from something touched by the infected person;
- through the air.

The infection produces a very red rash on the cheeks, as if they've been slapped. By the time the rash develops, the child is no longer infectious. One to four days later, a lace-like rash appears on the arms and the rest of the body, lasting from one to three weeks, possibly accompanied by fever. The illness is often mild and the child may not feel at all sick. (Adults usually get a more severe case, with fever and painful joints, but at least 50 percent of adults have had fifth disease in childhood and will not get it again.) Outbreaks of the disease can occur in school-age children. There is no vaccine to prevent it and no medication to treat it.

WHAT TO DO FOR FIFTH DISEASE
- Watch a child for signs of it if a school chum has it.
- Contact a physician if you are pregnant and exposed to this disease, as it can (rarely) affect the fetus.

FOOT DISORDERS

- *Club foot*: an inherited or congenital anomaly frequently detected in newborn infants. Children may need casts and/or corrective surgery, plus orthopedic care by a physician.
- *Flat feet*: a common childhood problem for which children must wear shoes with special arch supports to allow normal foot growth and reduce discomfort.
- *In-toeing*: an inward-pointing or "pigeon-toed" forefoot (metatarsus varus) often detected in newborns and corrected with a cast. Other, rare forms of in-toeing require treatment with special shoes, braces or surgery. Most children will improve at least slightly as they grow older. Frequently, children with this problem appear clumsy and require patience.
- *Out-toeing*: walking in a slightly out-pointing manner; this usually improves with time.
- *Limping*: a sign that something is wrong, possibly a cut, wart, infection, bone disease or just uncomfortable shoes. A child with a constant or sudden, unexplained limp should be seen by a physician.
- *Toe-walking*: usually just a bad habit, but the heel cord may be abnormally tight because of underlying cerebral palsy or spinal-cord problems. The child should be seen by a physician.

GIARDIASIS

Giardiasis is a bowel infection due to a parasite, and is quite common in daycare centers, especially where children are still in diapers. The *Giardia* parasites are often present in a child's stool without causing any illness. They spread from the hands of someone who has changed diapers or used the toilet, and their spread can be prevented by carefully washing hands after changing diapers or going to the toilet, and before preparing and eating food. Routine hand-washing is crucial to prevent the spread of the disease, even when no one has diarrhea.

Although giardiasis produces few or no symptoms, in some it may cause:
- diarrhea or mushy bowel movements (with a bad smell);
- gas, abdominal pain;
- poor appetite and weight loss.

The infection can be cleared up by medication.

HAEMOPHILUS INFLUENZAE TYPE B INFECTIONS

Haemophilus influenzae type b (Hib) bacteria frequently infect young children, but rarely adults. They can cause serious illnesses, including:
- meningitis (infection of the brain's covering membranes);
- epiglottitis (infection of the windpipe);
- cellulitis (deep skin infection);
- pneumonia;
- joint and bone infections;
- bacterial tracheitis (croupy cough).

Before widespread infant immunization with the Hib vaccine, one child in 200 came down with a serious Hib illness before age five, children under two years of age being most endangered. A major consequence of Hib infection, bacterial meningitis, spreads fast among those crowded together in close quarters. Therefore parents and caregivers of an infected child should be vigilant about the possibility of transmission. The spread of Hib infections can often be prevented by immediately treating all household, childcare or school contacts with an antibiotic. Intravenous antibiotics are given to prevent complications in those with Hib illness, and to their close contacts.

Fortunately, the new and effective Hib vaccine can prevent the disease. It is given as three injections starting at two months of age, usually at the same time as the diphtheria-pertussis-tetanus shots, plus a booster at 15 to 18 months of age.

HEPATITIS A

Hepatitis A is a viral liver infection, often with few or no symptoms, but possibly accompanied by yellowing of the skin and whites of the eyes (jaundice), fever, appetite loss, nausea and "feeling sick all over." It is usually a mild illness and rarely produces permanent liver damage. Many infants and children infected with hepatitis A have no sign of illness, but it can be more severe in adults. The hepatitis A virus is acquired via infected stool and through contaminated food or water, and it spreads easily if people do not wash their hands after changing

---

WHAT TO DO FOR GIARDIASIS

- **Watch the child for signs of diarrhea, if others have it.**
- **Contact a physician if you think your child has a *Giardia* infection. Stool samples may be taken to confirm the diagnosis.**
- **Ensure that all household members wash their hands after changing a diaper or using the toilet, and before preparing or eating food.**

diapers or having a bowel movement. For those known to have been exposed, infection can be prevented by an injection of immune (gamma) globulin. There is no medication to treat the disease, but a new vaccine is very effective in preventing it, and is used mainly for travelers to infected areas and to prevent outbreaks. (See "Hepatitis A" in chapter 16.)

HEPATITIS B

Hepatitis B is a dangerous, potentially fatal liver infection, caused by a virus different from that responsible for hepatitis A, and is transmitted via blood and body fluids. Like AIDS, it is transmitted primarily by sexual contact and via blood products or contaminated IV needles. In Canada, at least half a million people are hepatitis B carriers; they show no symptoms themselves, but can spread the infection to others. Young children are less than adults likely to have symptoms of illness. Some children develop lifelong hepatitis B infection and become permanent "carriers" of the virus. Newborns of mothers with hepatitis B are often infected.

Pregnant women can pass on hepatitis B to their developing fetus or to newborns during delivery, which can result in serious disease at a young age, even though no signs may show at birth, with a high risk of later developing liver cancer. Therefore all pregnant women are given a simple blood test for hepatitis B. Endangered babies can be protected by hepatitis B immune globulin (HBIG), given as soon as possible after birth, followed by vaccination. Older children of hepatitis B carriers should also be vaccinated. Indeed, immunization has now been recommended for all children in Canada. The program will likely start by immunizing preteens, at 10–12 years of age, and vaccination could be accompanied by "safer sex" education.

IMPETIGO

Impetigo is a common childhood skin infection caused by *Streptococcus* (strep) and *Staphylococcus* (staph) bacteria that enter via scrapes, cuts and insect bites. Some people mistakenly think that only unclean children get impetigo — however, the condition does not arise from too

---

WHAT TO DO FOR HIB INFECTION

- Contact your physician immediately if a sick child has:
- high fever;
- excessive sleepiness, or unusual crankiness or fussiness;
- a stiff neck (unwillingness to move the head up and down);
- vomiting;
- rapid or difficult breathing;
- new or increased drooling;
- a sore throat;
- pain on swallowing or refusal to swallow.
- Check your child's immunization record. A child aged two months to five years who has not been immunized should be given Hib vaccine. The vaccine is not a substitute for antibiotics in treating Hib disease or preventing it in those already exposed.

WHAT TO DO FOR HEPATITIS A

- Watch for signs of hepatitis A if someone else in your household has it, or a child's playmate.
- Be sure that all household members wash their hands after going to the toilet or changing a diaper, and before preparing or eating food.
- Ask whether immune globulin injections can be obtained to prevent infection.

WHAT TO DO FOR HEPATITIS B

- Be vaccinated if in a risk category.
- If pregnant, have a blood test to determine whether or not you are carrying hepatitis B, so the baby can be immunized at birth if necessary.
- Note that health authorities now urge hepatitis B immunization for everyone, probably before adolescence. (See "Hepatitis B" in chapter 16.)

---

little washing. The impetigo skin rash is a cluster of blisters or red bumps that ooze and may form honey-colored crusts. The rash usually appears around the nose, mouth and parts of the skin not covered by clothes. It spreads when someone touches an impetigo spot, and can be prevented by washing hands after touching infected skin.

Treatment of impetigo with antibiotics helps to prevent its spread. Antibiotics are given by mouth or applied on the skin as an ointment.

WHAT TO DO FOR IMPETIGO

- If you think your child has impetigo, contact your physician.
- Make sure that all household members wash their hands thoroughly with soap and running water after touching infected skin.
- Don't share facecloths or hand and bath towels.
- Take all the antibiotics prescribed, even after the impetigo rash has cleared. (See also section on impetigo in chapter 5.)

LEFT-HANDEDNESS

There is no agreed, simple, scientific explanation of why some children prefer the left to the right hand for skilled activities such as writing, toothbrushing and drawing. A steady minority of about 10–15 percent, a quarter more males than females, fall into this category. Left-handedness is more common in twins than in "singletons."

Researchers have long argued about whether left-handedness is inherited or learned, normal or pathological behavior, variously attributing it to genes (heredity), social programming (mimicking other lefties), brain damage (due to pregnancy or birth problems) and, more recently, to fetal sex hormones (prenatal testosterone levels).

While some studies have suggested an unusually high proportion of developmental problems and immune disorders among lefties, left-handedness is also conspicuous among the most gifted of humans — individuals such as Paul McCartney and Johann Sebastian Bach; Pablo Picasso and Michelangelo; Harpo Marx and Charlie Chaplin; Babe Ruth and Martina Navratilova; Leonardo da Vinci and Albert Einstein.

Since the middle of this century, reports have trickled in suggesting a preponderance of prolonged labor, prematurity, low birth weight and multiple births among the left-handed. Such claims have prompted speculation that left-handedness may result from slight anoxia (oxygen lack) in the brain during pregnancy or at birth. However, scientific research has now eradicated the myth of left-handers as inept, abnormal or devious. Left-handers are not necessarily more prone to accidents or immune disorders, nor is there any proof that they have a shorter life span.

The fact that there has always been a steady minority of lefties points strongly to an inherited tendency. Historic records — ancient cave drawings, Egyptian hieroglyphics and Babylonian friezes — reveal an unchanging proportion of about 10 percent of left-handers through the ages. Experts argue that if it were deleterious, the trait would have been weeded out through evolution. As summed up by one eminent scientist, "the condemnation of an entire group of humans on the basis of hand preference alone amounts to the attempted suppression of what researchers now think is a basic biological trait."

One renowned Michigan State University child psychologist (a left-hander himself) points out that "although sinistrals have been considered inordinately abundant among the less fortunate, they are also overrepresented at the gifted end of the scale. Many lefties are unusually talented in mathematics, music, art, spatial ability, engineering, architecture, creative originality and elaborate thinking — a benefit to any social group." Modern studies show no differences between the mental powers of right- and left-handers. Left- or mixed-handedness occurs more frequently than average in those who excel in modern confrontation sports. In fact, in baseball, left-handers are often used to great advantage!

The latest scientific findings discredit the notion that left-handedness usually stems from birth or prenatal stress. Only a tiny subset (perhaps 1 percent) of children become left-handed because of problem births or pregnancies. In the same way, a few natural lefties may be forced into right-handedness by marginal birth injury! Studies also discount any link between left-handedness and childhood disabilities such as autism, dyslexia or stuttering.

Many experts now believe there is a genetic or family tendency toward handedness. Lefties are more likely than others to produce left-handed children, although many dextral (right-handed) parents have sinistral (left-handed) children. Recent studies show that about 9 percent of children with two right-handed parents are left-handed compared to 19 percent of those with *one* left-handed parent and 26 percent of those with *two* left-handed parents.

Combining the many divergent theories, there seem to be two or more subgroups of left-handers. Most left-handedness is genetic or biologically based but a small subset may become left-handed because something goes wrong during pregnancy or birth. Whatever the cause, students of the left hand argue that if left-handedness and mathematical or artistic genius originate from the same mechanism, then curing left-handedness might also "cure" or remove much human talent!

If left-handedness *were* to carry with it an added risk of immune disorders, developmental handicaps, accidents and other unlucky events, would it be desirable to try and "correct" it (a difficult task)? Modern psychologists say no. Correction is only successful in the very young, and only about a third of the time. Forcing leftie children to switch hands usually only works for a targeted activity such as writing or drawing; it can cause stress and may lead to stuttering and other stress-related disorders. Finally, the child may lose dexterity in both hands and never be able to manage fine eye-hand coordination with either hand. It is also possible that imposing right-handed patterns on a left-handed person's activities might make the person more accident-prone.

MEASLES

Although often considered a trivial disease, "red" measles, or rubeola, is one of the most serious of common childhood illnesses. One in 10 children with measles gets an ear infection or pneumonia, and adults with measles are usually very sick.

Alerting symptoms of measles include fever (38.3°C, or 101°F, or higher), runny nose, red eyes, cough, white spots inside the mouth (hard to see, and lasting one to three days), followed by a red rash that spreads from the face to the rest of the body, lasting three or more days. Some children are so ill they need to be hospitalized. Measles continues to have a mortality rate of about one in 1,000, and encephalitis (brain inflammation) is also a complication in one per 1,000 cases, sometimes producing deafness and mental retardation. Once people have had red measles they become immune and are very unlikely to catch it again.

The measles virus spreads easily from person to person through the air, and is infectious from about three to five days before the rash appears and up to four days after that. Almost everyone exposed to the virus who has not been immunized or already had it will get measles. In exposed children who haven't been immunized, the infection can be prevented with an immediate injection of immune

WHAT TO DO FOR MEASLES

- Parents who suspect their child has measles should call their physician.
- Since measles is very contagious and outbreaks can be magnified by infected children passing on the virus to others in doctors' and hospital waiting rooms, special arrangements may be made to have the child examined.
- If you suspect you have measles, you should stay well away from people who may be susceptible.
- Those exposed can ask about eligibility for a protective immune (gamma) globulin shot.

(gamma) globulin. Measles vaccination within three days of exposure can usually prevent the illness from developing, and may even be considered for infants as young as six months (although they need revaccination soon after their first birthday).

The modern measles vaccine is highly effective in preventing the disease among those immunized on schedule. Measles has become less common in Canada, since vaccination reduced large outbreaks, especially in provinces with compulsory measles immunization. The standard immunization procedure is one shot of live vaccine at (or as soon as possible after) a child's first birthday. A second shot is now advised for all children at school entry, around four to six years of age. The National Advisory Committee on Immunization of Health and Welfare Canada considers the elimination of measles in Canada a top priority. Recent outbreaks highlight the pressing need for more widespread immunization, especially among schoolchildren.

Vaccination side effects are rare, other than transient swelling and redness at the injection site and fever in 15 percent of vaccine recipients. Some centers, schools and daycare facilities require documented proof of immunity for all children on entry.

N.B.: People hypersensitive (allergic) to eggs should not receive measles vaccine, as it contains traces of egg products.

MENINGITIS

Meningitis, which arises from many different causes, can be a very serious, possibly fatal illness, affecting mainly children and teenagers. Despite treatment, it may leave survivors with

THE MAIN ALERTING SYMPTOMS OF MENINGITIS

- fever;
- irritability;
- extreme drowsiness;
- intense headache;
- stiff neck;
- nausea, vomiting;
- confusion;
- a pink or purplish, pinpoint rash (in some forms);
- eye sensitivity or light aversion (photophobia);
- seizures (in later stages).

WHAT TO DO FOR MENINGITIS

- **Watch for the main alerting symptoms: fever, unusual fussiness, irritability (in infants), extreme drowsiness, intense headache, stiff neck.**
- **Have infants vaccinated against the form due to Hib bacteria. A safe and effective vaccine against Hib-caused meningitis is now licensed to protect all children from two months to five years. (For more on Hib vaccine see section on vaccination earlier in this chapter.) The Hib vaccine is not useful for people over age five, since meningitis is usually due to different bacteria in older age groups.**

permanent brain damage, but fortunately antibiotics and safe vaccines can reduce the danger.

Meningitis is an umbrella term meaning inflammation of the meninges — the membranes covering the brain and spinal cord. Meningitis can arise from a variety of viral infections or bacterial *meningococci*. It can be mild and self-limiting or life-threatening, depending on the cause and the degree of inflammation. Any inflammation around or in the brain and spinal cord — no matter what the reason — can have serious consequences.

The warning signs of meningitis can come on slowly or suddenly. Since the early signs — fever, irritability and headache — mimic those of less serious ailments, such as respiratory infections (e.g., flu or a feverish cold), parents or physicians may not recognize meningitis at first. It is wise to become familiar with the symptoms and potential seriousness of meningitis.

In infants, meningitis can begin with rather nonspecific symptoms — irritability and poor feeding, extreme drowsiness and lethargy.

In toddlers and young children, meningitis usually starts off with fever, drowsiness and irritability — sometimes preceded by a common cold. Some children also vomit and find light disturbing. But the most telling feature of meningitis is a stiff neck that makes it painful to move the head up or down (looking at the ceiling or floor); sufferers tend to lie still with their necks straight, as the slightest neck movement hurts the inflamed nerve roots.

Older children and adults may complain first of a searing headache and, later, of a stiff neck. They may also develop a strange purplish rash (petechial rash) that gives meningitis its nickname of "spotted fever."

Sorting out the different types of meningitis

Viral meningitis (the "aseptic" form) is by far the most usual and least serious variety, sometimes arising as a complication of other viral infections, such as mumps, polio, measles and chickenpox. Viral meningitis is rarely fatal. Recovery from this form is usually complete except for rare cases (such as meningitis due to *herpes simplex*).

Bacterial meningitis, although less common, is more serious and can cause permanent neurological injury or death. The bacteria responsible include *streptococci*, *Haemophilus influenzae type b* or Hib (nothing to do with influenza!), *Neisseria meningitidis* and *tuberculosis*. The bacterial infection often begins in the nose and/or throat, later invading the bloodstream and spreading to the meninges and cerebrospinal fluid.

The type often called meningococcal meningitis is caused by various strains or "serogroups" of *Neisseria meningitidis* bacteria (mostly types B and C in Canada). The bacteria often inhabit the throat and nose without causing any illness, or the infection can become invasive and spread via the bloodstream throughout the body. If the meningococcal bacteria invade parts of the body that are normally sterile (free of infective agents) — such as the blood or fluid around the brain and spinal cord — they can produce a fulminant (rapid) invasive infection. Galloping or fulminating cases can progress to septic shock collapse and death in six to 10 hours.

While bacterial meningitis can strike at any age, three-quarters of those affected are children. Whether or not a child will come down with meningitis depends largely upon the level of natural immunity.

Meningococcal bacteria are transmitted from person to person in nasal droplets, but the infection is not highly contagious and requires close contact for transmission. It spreads most rapidly among people in confined quarters — such as schools, households and daycare centers. In North America, most of the population acquires natural immunity by early adulthood; about 80 percent of those over age 20 are immune. But even immune persons can harbor the bacteria in their noses and throats, passing it on without being ill themselves. During epidemics many people may carry and transmit the bacteria without being unwell. The incubation period for the development of bacterial meningitis is two to 10 days, and about half of those who develop the illness do so within a few days of contact with an infected person.

At present, Canada averages one case of meningococcal meningitis per 100,000 people of all ages — totalling 300–400 cases a year — with little change during the past 40 years. Since the major meningitis epidemic in North America during the early 1940s, no nationwide epidemics of this illness have occurred in Canada, although mini-outbreaks occur from time to time, a few clusters surfacing here and there. In the 1991/92 outbreak, there were 300 cases Canada-wide, and 19 deaths. The proportion of cases among school-age children was higher than usual, the outbreak involving a particularly virulent strain of type C meningococcal bacteria that affects mainly teenagers.

Luckily the available vaccine prevented the disease's spread. But meningococcal vaccines are not universally available, and none protects against all currently circulating forms. Recent outbreaks in Canada have been mostly due to *Neisseria meningitidis*, strains B and C. The vaccines available in Canada are only against strains A, C, Y and W-135, not B, and the vaccines give protection for only about four years.

If detected in time, bacterial meningitis can be treated by antibiotics. Close contacts of people with Hib or meningococcal meningitis may be given the antibiotic rifampicin (rifampin) to prevent the illness. Taken within 48 hours of contact, the antibiotic can forestall illness. Rifampin may also be used during outbreaks in daycare centers or nursery schools but is not usually given as a large-scale preventive except during serious epidemics — for fear of facilitating the emergence of drug-resistant strains. Antibiotics are not effective against viral forms of meningitis, but anti-viral agents may help.

In newborns (under three months of age), meningitis may stem from bacterial organisms that are rarely the cause in the general population, such as *E. coli*, *streptococci* and *Listeria*. In older infants and toddlers, aged three months to five years, 70 percent of bacterially caused meningitis was formerly due to *Haemophilus influenzae type b* bacteria. But immunization of infants with Hib vaccine has significantly reduced the frequency of this infection, and once all children have been vaccinated, Hib meningitis will become a rare disease.

MUMPS

A serious viral disease affecting mainly children aged five to 10, mumps can be prevented by vaccination at one year of age. The main symptoms of mumps are fever, headache, swollen neck glands, stiff jaw, swollen cheeks, and possibly swollen testes in boys. Deafness, meningitis and sterility are rare complications. These days, mumps is usually a mild illness in children, sometimes not even producing swollen glands. The infection can be more severe in adults. A blood test confirms the diagnosis.

Mumps spreads from person to person through the air up to seven days before the glands start to swell and as long as nine days later. The incubation period is two to three weeks — i.e., it takes that long to come down with mumps after exposure. There is no treatment beyond time, bed rest and other comforts. Since the infection is caused by a virus, antibiotics have no effect.

PINKEYE (CONJUNCTIVITIS)

Pinkeye is an infection of the eyeball covering, usually due to a virus, but sometimes bacterial. It can also be caused by an allergy or rubbing the eyes excessively. Pinkeye turns the whites of the eyes pink or red, causes a scratchy feeling or pain in the eyes and may produce tears and pus. By morning, the pus or discharge often makes the eyelids stick together.

Pinkeye is spread when:
- an infected person touches the discharge and then touches another person or object;
- an uninfected child touches an infected child's eye discharge and then his or her own eyes;
- an adult wipes an infected child's eyes and then touches his or her own eyes, or someone else's.

WHAT TO DO FOR MUMPS

- **Check your child's immunization record to see if he or she has had the mumps or MMR (measles, mumps, rubella) vaccine.**
- **If your child is in contact with mumps and has not had the vaccine, and is one year of age or older, contact your physician or the local public health agency to arrange vaccination as soon as possible.**
- **Contact your physician if you think your child has mumps.**

WHAT TO DO FOR PINKEYE

- **Get medical advice; it is not easy to tell whether the infection is caused by bacteria or viruses. Bacterial pinkeye can be cured with antibiotics, which** also stop the infection from spreading. There is no treatment for viral pinkeye other than hot compresses.
- **Try not to rub the eye; if you do rub it,** wash your hands.
- **Wash your hands carefully after touching infected eyes.**
- **Do not share towels or washcloths with anyone else (it spreads infection).**

POLIO (POLIOMYELITIS)

Poliomyelitis, now rare in Canada thanks to widespread immunization, remains common in many parts of the world. (Travelers to endemic areas should be sure their vaccination boosters are up to date.) Polio is caused by a virus that enters via the mouth and can produce permanent paralysis by damaging nerve cells in the spinal cord.

Although poliomyelitis is a rare disease in Canada today, some who had it in the past are now suffering post-polio syndrome, which requires special exercise therapy.

Two forms of polio vaccine are used in Canada: an inactivated form, given by injection, which requires a booster every 10 years; and a live, weakened virus vaccine, given by mouth (sometimes on a lump of sugar), that confers lifetime immunity. For details see section on vaccination, earlier in this chapter.

RHEUMATIC FEVER

Rheumatic fever, now rare in Canada and the United States, is still a serious illness, and a continuing danger in many developing areas. The illness arises from strep-throat infections. Rheumatic fever is characterized by inflammation of the heart (carditis) and joints (arthritis), "St. Vitus dance" (nerve impairment producing involuntary jerky movements) and painful nodules under the skin. While most of these complications leave few or no lasting traces, the cardiac inflammation can permanently injure the heart valves. Anyone known to have rheumatic fever stays on penicillin for life (or at least up to age 18), to prevent recurrence of an illness which might further injure a heart already damaged by one bout of carditis. Despite the rarity of rheumatic fever in the Western world, concern lingers about the possibility of lasting heart defects following a strep throat.

Rheumatic fever can be prevented by antibiotics that eradicate a streptococcal throat infection before serious complications set in. (For signs of a strep throat, see "Sore throats," later in this chapter.) In the developed world, antibiotics have dramatically reduced the toll of rheumatic fever, a decline that, for unknown reasons, began before the widespread use of these drugs. Currently, in Canada, rheumatic fever affects only two to five people per million per year. Nonetheless, physicians warn against complacency in treating strep throats, particularly since there has been a slight upswing in U.S. rheumatic-fever cases.

ROSEOLA

Roseola, a common viral infection caused by human herpes virus number 6, can produce a high fever in young children — as high as 40.5°C (105°F) — generally with no other symptoms until the third day, when a rash of small red spots appears, mainly on the face, abdomen and extremities. Typically, comments one pediatrician, "when the rash comes, the fever goes!" The telltale clue to this disorder, as against more serious conditions, is that, despite high fever, children with roseola do not seem particularly ill, although a few may have seizures (convulsions) caused by the fever. Roseola gets better without any treatment, and complications are rare. But it's hard to diagnose until the rash appears, and since fever may arise from more severe illnesses, a doctor should be contacted. The infection is very common in children aged six to 24 months, and rare in older children.

RUBELLA (GERMAN MEASLES)

Rubella is a mild viral infection, now rare because a very good vaccine given at one year of age prevents most cases. Rubella causes a low-grade fever, swollen glands in the neck and behind the ears, and a rash with small red spots. The rubella virus spreads through air or by touch, and is infectious for a few days before the rash appears and up to five to seven days afterwards. Children with rubella usually show few signs of illness. Antibiotics and other medicines can't cure the disease.

The infection may also be very mild in adults, but it can create serious problems for pregnant women. If a woman gets rubella in the first three months of pregnancy, there is a high chance that the unborn child will die or develop serious defects, including malformations of the brain, eyes, heart and/or other organs. Vaccination is important to prevent rubella in children and adults, so it will not spread to any pregnant women.

SCABIES

Scabies is caused by tiny insects called mites that burrow into skin and cause a very itchy rash that looks like curvy white threads, tiny red bumps or scratches. It can appear anywhere on the body, but is usually between the fingers or around wrists or elbows. On an infant, it can affect the head, face, neck and body. Scabies spreads by contact with clothing or other contaminated items. The mites can live on clothing, other objects and skin for up to four days, dying after that if the clothes are not worn. Washing clothes in hot water and putting them in a hot dryer gets rid of the mites. But a child may remain itchy for weeks after treatment, because of reaction to the mites, even though the treatment already got rid of them.

SORE THROATS

A sore throat is one of the commonest complaints seen by family physicians. Throats can become sore from prolonged overuse of the voice, swallowing a sharp object, cigarette smoke, seasonal allergies or eating spicy food. But a sore throat often heralds an oncoming illness such as measles, influenza or a common cold. Generally, as the measles, flu or cold takes hold and its identifying symptoms — such as a rash, cough or runny nose — appear, the throat becomes less sore.

The term "pharyngitis" describes an inflammation of the pharynx (throat) and surrounding tissues, including the larynx, adenoids and tonsils — if they haven't been removed. Pharyngitis is the chief symptom of unusual diseases such as infectious mononucleosis, caused by the Epstein-Barr virus. The sore throat may persist for weeks after other discomforts vanish. The ravaging sore throat due to diphtheria — which inflames the larynx — rarely occurs any more in immunized communities. However, although often associated with other illnesses, a sore throat can be a viral (less commonly a bacterial) infection in its own right — if it persists without other symptoms.

Viral pharyngitis tends to cure itself spontaneously within five to seven days, generally requiring no treatment other than topical painkillers to ease the soreness, antipyretics to bring down any fever and soothing warm drinks.

Bacterial pharyngitis, less usual but more dangerous, may also vanish within a few days with or without treatment. But streptococcal pharyngitis (a strep throat) needs prompt medical attention because it may lead to a number of complications.

Signs and symptoms of strep throat :
- fever over 38°C (100°F);
- fiery red, inflamed tonsils;
- a painfully sore/raw throat;

WHAT TO DO FOR SCABIES

- **Treat scabies with prescribed medication as recommended.**
- **If any child has scabies, all household members need antiscabies medication as per instructions on the bottle.**
- **If a child has scabies, wash the child's bed linen, towels and clothes in hot water and dry in a dryer at the hottest setting.**
- **The child with scabies should not return to daycare or school until treated.**

GENERAL STRUCTURE OF THROAT

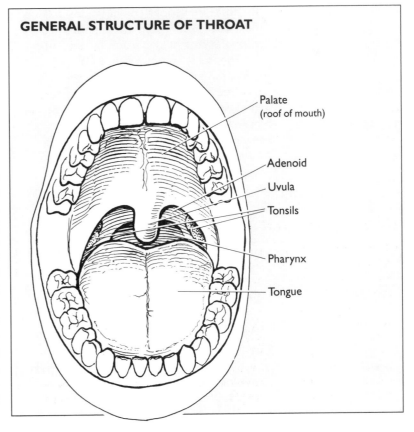

Palate (roof of mouth)

Adenoid

Uvula

Tonsils

Pharynx

Tongue

WHAT TO DO FOR SORE THROATS

- The problem with sore throats is knowing when to consult a doctor. A mild sore throat, without fever, perhaps accompanied by a runny nose, may be no more than a common cold needing no medical help. But any sore throat accompanied by a fever merits medical attention.
- The best relief for sore throats is rest, warm fluids, gentle gargling and perhaps painkillers.
- Fever-reducers such as acetaminophen (Children's Tylenol, Tempra, Panadol, Atasol) can bring down the temperature and reduce the pain, but not reduce the risk of complications. ASA (such as Aspirin) should never be used to relieve fever in children or teens because of the risk of Reye's syndrome.
- Antibiotics are prescribed for bacterial throat infections (usually penicillin or erythromycin), but are useless against viral sore throats.
- The many over-the-counter remedies — antiseptic gargles, lozenges, sprays and throat rinses, avidly sought by sore-throat sufferers — achieve no better results than those obtained with a warm saltwater gargle, a hot cup of tea or your favourite "toddy."

- enlarged, tender neck glands (lymph nodes);
- a yellowish fluid on the tonsils;
- a generally sick, listless state;
- occasionally, a scarlet-fever-like rash all over the body.

In the absence of complications, streptococcal pharyngitis subsides in a few days, all symptoms usually being gone within a week. The modern medical approach is to ease the symptoms and check the throat for signs of bacterial infection, especially by *streptococci*. The condition needs watching, as a strep throat may lead to middle-ear infections, sinusitis and more serious complications such as rheumatic fever or glomerulonephritis (kidney inflammation, not prevented by antibiotics).

Physicians suspect a streptococcal throat infection when they see a feverish patient with fiery red tonsils coated by an exudate and enlarged neck nodes. But while many doctors think they can identify a strep throat on sight, studies show they may be wrong in a mere visual assessment. Surveys comparing office diagnosis against throat culture (bacterial growth) laboratory tests showed that physicians can correctly spot a bacterial throat infection only 50 percent of the time. Therefore, experts recommend taking a throat swab for lab analysis from every inflamed throat that brings someone to the physician.

Antibiotic treatment can shorten the duration of a strep throat and prevent serious consequences. But since antibiotics may be needlessly prescribed for viral pharyngitis, many experts advocate waiting out the few hours needed to get back the lab results, before prescribing drugs. The American Heart Association strongly recommends treatment based strictly on test results. The brief delay does not increase risks, for studies show that even a few days after the onset of strep pharyngitis, antibiotics can prevent rheumatic fever. In everyday practice, the proffered advice is often ignored and antibiotics are frequently prescribed for what looks streptococcal before the culture results are in.

SUDDEN INFANT DEATH SYNDROME

Also known as "crib death," Sudden Infant Death Syndrome (SIDS) is the unexpected death of a seemingly healthy infant, usually during sleep. Infants who die of SIDS show no outward signs of distress or struggle: they simply stop breathing. SIDS shatters parents and bewilders doctors. It's the leading cause of death in Canadian babies aged two weeks to one year, affecting one to two per 1,000 infants. Despite various clues and suspected triggers, the cause(s) of SIDS deaths remains unexplained even after thorough postmortem investigation.

A century ago, "crib deaths" were attributed to carelessness or to drunken mothers who rolled onto their children and smothered them while asleep. Later, when separate beds for babies became popular but brought no reduction in crib deaths, these infants were believed to have suffocated in their bedding or choked on their vomit. Only in the 1940s did investigators stop accusing parents of misconduct and explore other reasons for these deaths.

Recent evidence suggests that, despite the outward appearance of perfectly good health before death, SIDS babies probably have "something wrong" — some as yet unidentified abnormality — that predisposes them to sudden death. The definition of SIDS has therefore been updated to discard the idea of these babies as "perfectly normal."

The new definition of SIDS excludes identifiable reasons for sudden infant death, numbering as SIDS cases only those where exhaustive investigation turns up no known reason for death. Infant deaths due to food poisoning, allergies (for instance to cow's milk or dust mites), child neglect or infanticide — formerly blamed for crib death — do not qualify as SIDS. Nor do babies who suffocate on bedding or have inborn errors of metabolism (metabolic abnormalities), or any cases not thoroughly investigated. About 10 percent of cases suspected as SIDS before autopsy later turn out to stem from other conditions that are easily confused with SIDS, such as fulminant (galloping) meningitis, encephalitis and overlooked congenital flaws.

Most SIDS deaths occur under six months of age, usually in those aged one to four months and more commonly in males (about 60 percent) than females. There is also a seasonal link: two-thirds of SIDS deaths occur in winter. Some experts link the seasonality of SIDS to overswaddling and overheating of vulnerable babies. Poor infant temperature control is believed to be one possible contributor.

The fact that SIDS babies die during sleep has prompted speculation that these infants have some flaw in the mechanism that fine-tunes breathing control. Although SIDS isn't yet traceable to any specific disorder, research at the University of Toronto's Hospital for Sick Children indicates that they may be born with borderline breathing abnormalities that delay maturation of those parts of the nervous system which control respiratory rhythms.

There's no known way to prevent SIDS. The majority of SIDS infants don't have any noticeable breathing difficulties or warning signs of impending catastrophe. However, premature and low-birth-weight babies and those with slower than normal growth rates are at above-average risk. There is *no evidence* that vaccination causes or increases SIDS risks. In fact, babies who die of SIDS are less likely than average to have been recently immunized.

Profiles of the mothers of SIDS infants support the notion that problems during pregnancy may predispose these babies to unexpected death. For example, women who smoke, are anemic, undernourished, or prone to bladder infections, and very young mothers (especially teenagers) are at above-average risk of having SIDS babies. Such women often receive scanty prenatal health care, which could disturb fetal health. One Florida study showed a SIDS risk of 3.2 per 1,000 for mothers under age 19 compared with 1 per 1,000 for mothers aged 25 to 29. However, babies of any parents can die of SIDS.

Sleeping position recently blamed for SIDS

Recent evidence, given much media attention, suggests that some crib deaths may be related to sleeping prone (face down, on the stomach). Several studies, particularly those from Australia (Tasmania) and New Zealand, have linked this position to elevated SIDS risks. Based on the evaluation of numerous studies, the American Academy of Pediatrics and the Canadian Pediatric Society both issued 1992 recommendations that "normal infants be put to bed on their sides or backs rather than on their stomachs" — a change from the currently popular North American position.

WHAT TO DO TO HELP PREVENT SIDS

- **Have good medical care and adequate nutrition during pregnancy.**
- **Keep baby in smoke-free surroundings (smoking by either parent, as well as secondhand smoke, is clearly linked to SIDS).**
- **Put baby to sleep on a firm mattress.**
- **Breastfeed if possible.**
- **If apnea, breathing stoppage or "blue spells" are noticed in the infant, get prompt medical advice.**
- **If a breathing lapse is noticed, awaken the infant with a small jolt or stimulus — a flick of the finger on the feet — which may set the baby breathing again. If that doesn't do the trick, the next step is vigorous stimulation — perhaps a hard pinch. If that doesn't work, the parent should begin mouth-to-mouth resuscitation. (See "The ABCs of AR and CPR" in chapter 17.) (Never shake the baby hard, as it could** cause a head injury, even death.)
- **Try not to let the baby get too hot (don't overswaddle).**
- **Never have the infant's face covered by bedclothes.**
- **Avoid thick blankets, pillows or bumpers in the crib.**
- **Try not to let the infant sleep on his or her stomach. Put the baby to sleep on his or her side or back (a rolled-up towel along the back will help to keep the baby on his or her side).**

European studies have also consistently linked the prone sleeping position to higher SIDS rates. For example, in Holland during the 1970s — when infant sleeping positions were changed from the back to the stomach on the advice of pediatricians — there was a rise in SIDS deaths. But when the advice switched back to a recommendation for babies to sleep on their sides or backs, Dutch SIDS cases declined dramatically. In Britain, a change in baby sleeping position from prone to supine (on the back) was also associated with a 50 percent decrease in crib deaths.

On a cautionary note, one University of Toronto expert warns against "placing too much faith in sleeping positions until more results come in." SIDS has low prevalence rates in the United States, where so many babies sleep on their stomachs. And some argue that the sleep-position studies done in Australia and New Zealand didn't allow for the popular Antipodean habit of putting babies to sleep on sheepskin bedding to keep them warm in the absence of central heating; the high SIDS rate may have gone down when infants slept on their backs because they no longer breathed in bits of sheepskin.

Apnea, a momentary halt in breathing, has also been blamed as a possible forerunner of SIDS. Tiny infants often stop breathing for a few seconds, especially after a deep sigh. Breathing stoppage lasting less than 20 seconds is not considered hazardous, but if the lapses last more than 20 seconds they may signal danger. Such Apparent Life-Threatening Episodes (ALTEs) — to give them their scientific name — often happen in the same age range as SIDS, also more commonly in males than females, and 1 to 2 per cent of infants who suffer ALTEs eventually die.

Home apnea monitors that trigger an alarm if the child's heartbeat becomes too fast or slow, or if the baby stops breathing for more than 20 seconds, haven't been too successful. Their use was explored as a way to prevent SIDS in babies at higher than average risk of breathing stoppage. The best monitors have an inbuilt "memory" that can relay what happened before the alarm sounded — whether and how long breathing ceased, and how fast or slow the heartrate was. But no studies have shown that monitoring prevents SIDS. And while, a few years back, infants thought to be at risk of SIDS might automatically be put on monitors, their use is declining because of frequent false alarms, and since babies wearing them have died of SIDS anyway.

The mysterious death of a seemingly healthy infant can cause immense grief, self-blame and anxiety. Parents and other caregivers may mull endlessly over the events leading up to the death. Guilt may worsen the usual anger, denial and intense sense of bereavement, even though no known measures could have prevented the infant death. Counseling for families after crib death aims to reassure them that nobody was to blame. Medical experts explain the importance of autopsy results. The police investigation of sudden infant deaths — while initially distressing — ultimately serves to lighten the burden. Parents also need reassurance that SIDS wasn't the doctor's fault. Marriages can become strained and siblings understandably distressed after a SIDS death; the siblings must be encouraged to express their sadness, self-doubts and confusion. Some may not show their grief directly but "act it out" by renewed bedwetting, naughtiness or poor schoolwork. Expert counseling and sharing experiences with others who've been through similar situations can be a help.

TEETHING

In the vast majority of healthy children, the incisor teeth (the front four on the top and the front four on the bottom) come through painlessly. Discomfort is sometimes experienced with the molars and canine teeth, which erupt at between 12 and 36 months of age. However, teething, like growing, is mostly painless. Occasionally, when a tooth is about to break through, the gum may become tender and look obviously swollen, with a purplish bulge over the site of the new tooth, and the area may be painful when touched. The discomfort is usually short-lived. Medications are rarely necessary and should be avoided as much as possible.

If a fever, cold or diarrhea develops, it is probably due to an infection, not teething. It is a mistake, and can even be dangerous, to

WHAT TO DO FOR TEETHING

• Give painkillers (acetaminophen, not ASA) to relieve discomfort, but only if really necessary.
• Be patient — it's all over by about age three, once the canines are through.
• If there's any fever, lethargy or diarrhea, don't automatically dismiss it as "just teething"; it is more likely due to an infection that needs medical attention. (Teething doesn't cause fever or stomach upsets.)

assume that teething is the cause of any change in the infant's behavior. Teething does not cause fever. The fact that infants want to suck their hands does not mean they are teething but simply that infants find sucking pleasurable. Teething goes on continuously throughout the first two years of life, and the hand-sucking is a coincidence, not the result.

TETANUS (LOCKJAW)

Tetanus is a disease that results if bacteria from soil, rust, manure or animal dirt enter cuts, scratches, wounds or grazes in people who have not been immunized. The infection kills 6 out of every 10 people who get it, but vaccination effectively prevents this lethal infection. Tetanus is rare in Canada today because most people are vaccinated, but they must remember to get their vaccination boosters every 10 years. (Each year about 20 to 30 people are hospitalized with tetanus in Canada, and there are a few deaths from it.) Tetanus remains very common in parts of the world where the vaccine is not used. Tetanus vaccine — usually given in combination with diphtheria toxoid and pertussis vaccine (DPT) during childhood — protects almost everyone immunized with the recommended three shots.

THRUSH OR CANDIDA (YEAST) DIAPER RASH

Candida is a fungus or yeast that infects the skin, mouth or throat. If it's in the throat or mouth, it's called thrush. The candida fungus is present in the intestines of many people without causing any illness and is common among youngsters still in diapers. It may also occur after prolonged treatment with antibiotics for other infections. Thrush appears as a tough, whitish-gray coating on the tongue and insides of the cheeks and gums that's hard to wipe off. Over-vigorous attempts to remove it may leave a bleeding, raw surface. In severe cases, the mouth may be so sore that the infant finds it painful to suck. Most infants do not get complications from thrush.

Candida diaper rash tends to settle in the creases of groin and buttocks, as a rash that can be very red, with a clearly defined border and small red spots close to larger patches. Candida

infections can be cured with prescribed antifungals, such as pills, lotions or ointment.

TONSILLITIS

Throat infections that affect the tonsils — known as tonsillitis — were a serious threat before the advent of antibiotics. Infected tonsils were routinely removed to prevent complications such as middle-ear infections, glomerulonephritis (kidney inflammation) and rheumatic fever. Tonsillectomy (tonsil removal) usually was, and often still is, done in combination with adenoid removal.

However, once antibiotics became available in the 1950s, physicians took a more conservative "wait-and-see" approach, resorting to surgery only in extreme cases. The pendulum is now swinging back as it's becoming clear that a few children benefit from tonsil and/or adenoid removal, especially if sleep and breathing problems result from the enlarged tonsils or adenoids. Currently, about 15 percent of children have their tonsils and/or adenoids removed, with about two adenoidectomies for every ten tonsillectomies plus adenoid removals.

The first step with tonsillar infections is antibiotic therapy (penicillin being the drug of first choice). The antibiotic must be taken for the full period prescribed, even if the person feels well sooner, in order to completely eradicate the infective organisms. A throat swab is usually sent to a lab in order to identify the microorganism responsible for tonsillitis. While awaiting the lab results (which may take 24–48 hours), nonallergic patients are often put on penicillin. The current policy is to treat bacterial sore throats and inflamed tonsils or adenoids with antibiotic therapy to prevent spread to the ears or other organs.

WHAT TO DO ABOUT TETANUS

- For any cut or puncture or animal bite, wash thoroughly and disinfect.
- Make sure that tetanus immunization is up to date. Booster shots are needed every 10 years to ensure continuing protection. (Many adults, especially the elderly, neglect to get their required booster shots. But provided tetanus boosters have been given, the vaccine isn't necessary for every little cut or injury.)

WHAT TO DO FOR A CANDIDA (YEAST) INFECTION

- If you suspect your child has a yeast infection, contact your physician.
- Make sure you follow directions for any prescribed anti-thrush medication.
- For babies with

mouth thrush: regularly sanitize the bottle nipples and soothers by boiling them for ten minutes.
- For babies with diaper rash: when changing diapers, wash the child's

buttocks and genitals with mild soap and warm water. Rinse, dry and apply prescribed ointment.
- Wash your own and your child's hands carefully after changing diapers.

Reasons for tonsil removal include:

- "kissing tonsils" — enlarged tonsils that meet in the middle and cause breathing problems, particularly at night. It's generally accepted that any child who is a persistent mouth breather (in the absence of a cold or respiratory infection) should have the tonsils out;
- Obstructive Sleep syndrome, or sleep apnea, a serious condition due to obstructed airways that cause heavy snoring, daytime sleepiness and night sweats. Owing to poor nighttime rest, youngsters may be tired and lazy throughout the day. Adults too sometimes have disturbed sleep patterns due to tonsil enlargement, a newly recognized problem. Enlarged tonsils that cause sleep or breathing difficulties must come out at any age;
- quinsy (abscess) — an unusual but serious infection in and around the tonsils which makes it difficult to swallow; tonsil removal is done once the abscess heals;
- recurrent middle-ear infections accompanied by tonsillitis — three to four times yearly;
- an "adenoidal" or elongated face associated with mouth breathing due to swollen tonsils and/or adenoids.

Less common indicators for tonsil removal include:
- increasing unilateral (one-sided) tonsil enlargement;
- recurrent bleeding from an infected ulcer on the tonsil;
- diphtheria (now rare in Canada);
- halitosis (bad breath) in teenagers or adults, due to decaying food caught on the tonsils.

WHOOPING COUGH (PERTUSSIS)

Whooping cough (pertussis) is a very contagious bacterial infection that affects all ages and is preventable by a safe, effective vaccine. Most usual in children under age seven (and very dangerous in youngsters under age two), whooping cough usually begins with a runny nose and racking cough which gets more frequent and severe, with a prolonged spasm ("whoop") when breathing in. During attacks, the child may become blue in the face, perhaps vomit, have convulsions and appear very weak. The temporary bouts of oxygen shortage can damage the brain. It takes children a long time to recover from whooping cough, up to 10 weeks.

The disease is most severe in infants under one year old, many of whom are so ill they must be cared for in hospital. The illness can be fatal in young children. If an unvaccinated child catches the infection, antibiotics can treat it — but vaccination is far safer. Fever, crying, sleepiness, and pain or swelling at the injection site may briefly follow vaccination, but the risk of dangerous complications from the disease in infants is much greater than the vaccine risks.

Whooping cough spreads easily, through the air or by touch, until up to three weeks after the coughing attacks start. It takes from 7 to 10 days to come down with whooping cough after exposure to the pertussis microbes. Although complications are rare beyond the age of two, whooping cough is still quite common among adolescents and adults. About 20–25 percent of adults with a cough lasting longer than 7–10 days have whooping cough — even though they may not know it and rarely whoop!

WORMS

Pinworms are tiny, white thread-like worms that live in the intestines; they crawl out of the anus at night and lay their eggs on nearby skin. Most children with pinworms have no symptoms, although some get very itchy around the anus and vagina. Pinworms are a nuisance rather than a disease. They are very common and spread easily among children and staff in child-care facilities, especially when those infected scratch the itchy area and get pinworm eggs on the fingers or under the fingernails and then touch someone or something else. Uninfected people can pick up pinworm eggs from infected clothes, pyjamas, sheets or surroundings. (The eggs can survive for several weeks outside the body.)

Ringworm is a fungal skin infection — not a worm at all — which causes a ring-shaped rash, with a raised edge, that is usually quite itchy and flaky. When the scalp is infected, there is often a bald patch; ringworm on the feet is usually very itchy with cracking between the toes. Ringworm spreads from person to person by touch. When someone with ringworm touches or scratches the rash, the fungus sticks to the

---

WHAT TO DO FOR WHOOPING COUGH (PERTUSSIS)

- **Check your child's immunization record to see if he or she has been vaccinated against pertussis. (Note that the vaccine is given together with diphtheria and tetanus (DPT) shots.)**
- **See a physician at the earliest hint of possible whooping cough.**

fingers or gets under the fingernails. Ringworm on the scalp can spread via combs and hairbrushes. It can be cured with medication, taken by mouth or as ointments or creams put on infected areas.

Roundworms (*Ascaris*) are a common but harmless affliction in young children, with large worms (up to 20 cm or 8 inches long) that may emerge from the anus or even the nostrils. The sign of infestation is itching in the anal area. Mostly innocuous, the worms may occasionally cause a mild form of pneumonia. Treatment is with effective medication, taken for three days. (A different form of roundworm, much smaller in size, can be picked up from the feces of infected cats and other pets. It also requires special medication.)

For more information on childhood illnesses, contact your family physician, pediatrician or local children's hospital.

Consult *Well Beings* — a very comprehensive book funded by Health and Welfare Canada, endorsed by the Canadian Pediatric Society.

WHAT TO DO ABOUT PINWORMS

- **To halt the spread, stop children from scratching.**
- **Ensure that all household members wash their hands carefully after going** to the toilet or changing diapers, and before preparing or eating food.
- **Ask your physician whether all household members** should also be treated with medication.
- **Inform school or daycare staff that the child has pinworms.**

WHAT TO DO ABOUT RINGWORM

- **To prevent the spread, check your child for signs of a typical "circular rash" on the head, skin or feet.**
- **Call the doctor if you think your child** has ringworm.
- **Ensure that the hands are washed after touching the infected skin.**
- **If a child has ringworm on the scalp, make sure that no one else uses the** same comb, hairbrush, facecloths or towels.
- **Don't let children with ringworm return to school or daycare until after treatment has started.**

WHAT TO DO ABOUT ROUNDWORMS

- **Contact your physician if you notice that a child is scratching the anal** area, or if you see a worm emerge.
- **Inform the school or daycare authorities.**
- **Give the prescribed medication as instructed.**

Puberty and adolescent changes

The stages of adolescence • The physical changes of puberty • Body-image concerns • The tragic pursuit of thinness: Anorexia nervosa and bulimia• Psychosocial development in adolescence • Helping adolescents through the transition • Medical checkups for adolescents • School problems • Adolescent sexuality • Risk-taking behavior • The heavy toll of adolescent suicide • Teenage and student drug use

12

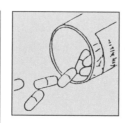

DURING THE LONG plateau of childhood, girls and boys look and behave much alike, but from ages 10 and 11 and onward, each gender develops different sex-specific changes as hormonal triggers initiate puberty and the development of secondary sex characteristics — changes that signify the transition from boy or girl into man or woman.

Adolescence is a biopsychosocial process that involves intense physical, emotional and psychological changes, with a huge variation of what's considered "normal." Each teenager reacts somewhat differently to the demands of growing up. Rather than being a sudden event, adolescence is a gradual transition with many social and emotional demands both on teenagers and their parents. But while it has been described as a period of "extreme instability," or "normal psychosis," most adolescents remain relatively unruffled by the process, cope well with the transition and survive with no lasting difficulties. "In reality," says one University of Toronto pediatrician, "about 30 percent have an easy growth process, 40 percent have periods of calm intermingled with turbulent times and 30 percent have a tumultuous adolescence marked by storm and stress."

Adolescents eagerly seek greater control of their lives, but although no longer children, they're not yet fully equipped — or allowed — to take on adult roles or responsibilities. Despite the outward trappings of bravado, many feel deeply unsure about their changing looks and ability to cope with things ahead. It is normal for adolescents to feel uncertain — young and unsure — one minute, mature and confident the next.

The primary tasks of adolescence are separation from parents and the establishment of a new personal identity. In achieving them, adolescents must accept their new body image, adopt peer codes, establish a sexual ego, plan vocational goals and formulate their own opinions — no mean feat! Some feel overwhelmed by the sudden body changes and the pressure to look after appearance, worry about weight, keep up with schoolwork and conform to peer values. During this period, psychological conflicts from early childhood may resurface and cause additional turmoil as adolescents work through and resolve them.

The emergence of a new physical, cognitive and social self may result in a person with values different from (and sometimes contradictory to) parental expectations. Parents and other caring adults can ease children through the process by knowing what to expect, being tolerant and explaining to teenagers what's ahead — for example the many emotional, cognitive and relationship changes, as well as physical maturation — with developing breasts and menstruation in daughters, "breaking" voice and nocturnal emissions in sons.

THE STAGES OF ADOLESCENCE

Some experts divide the period into early adolescence (the junior-high years); middle adolescence (the high-school years); and late adolescence (the university years or early employment years). These three stages overlap, but by the time they're completed most adolescents have gained autonomy, attained a psychosexual identity and begun to support themselves emotionally and financially.

Early adolescence
(approximately ages 12–14)

This phase is marked by rapid physical growth, the emergence of secondary sexual characteristics, a focus on the changing body and a wish to "belong" to peer groups.

- Rapid physical changes lead to intense "self-centeredness" — concerns about being normal, preoccupation with body image, uncertainty about appearance, interest in sexual anatomy, anxieties about breasts and periods in girls, about wet dreams and penis size in boys.
- The tendency to "size themselves up" leads adolescents to compare themselves (often with despair) against their peers.
- Along with the rapid, somewhat discomfiting physical changes comes a testing of new strength in sex-appeal and opinion-forming skills.
- In forming close, intense (possibly idealized) friendships with same-sex chums, boys may swear "eternal comradeship" and girls may develop a "crush" on another (sometimes older) female.
- The social world appears to early adolescents as a place in which to explore their burgeoning potential and practice adult-like behavior — even though they are still far from having a stable identity.
- An independence struggle may begin, with a shift from reliance on parents to greater peer-group involvement — turning to friends as a source of advice and comfort.
- Cognitive abilities rapidly develop, with increased capacities for abstract reasoning.
- A tendency to daydream and build a fantasy world is a normal component of identity development (not a "waste of time").

- A sense of being constantly "on stage," scrutinized and evaluated by others, is accompanied by a tendency to magnify personal problems or events.
- Testing authority is commonplace as teens try to define themselves and their powers — behavior that may create friction within the family.
- Journal writing is common; feelings and thoughts are expressed.
- The inability to control impulses may lead to dangerous risk-taking.

Middle adolescence
(approximately ages 15–17)

This stage is typified by still more rapid growth of cognitive skills, the ability to conceptualize and operate according to abstract thought, increased intensity of feelings, further separation from parents and greater reliance on peer groups. Peer relationships play a key role in the development of personal identity, their support and advice replacing that of parents.

- Body-image concerns wane as most start to feel more comfortable in their new body, spending more time on making it look attractive.
- With the distancing of family ties, peers set the going standards, helping to compensate for the frustrations of everyday life or "not being understood" by adults.
- Middle adolescents live almost entirely in the present, swaying with whatever peers decide to do, annoyingly unable to state or stick to plans, never knowing what they're going to do the same evening, let alone next day.
- They avidly seek more privacy and many complain about the lack of personal space and a place of their own to meet in, preferably devoid of adults.
- Family conflicts may become more frequent with the adolescent's declining interest in parental wishes; new "powerlines" are forged.
- In addition to peer attachments, middle adolescents often ally themselves emotionally with adults *outside* the home, perhaps as idols, mentors or "hero" figures — attachments that can profoundly influence ideas, career and the future course in life.

- Many start dating, testing their newfound sex roles.
- Some claim to be "stressed out" by the concurrent demands of school, extracurricular activities, home duties and maintaining same-sex as well as "dating" relationships.
- Identity development bounds ahead, with an enhanced ability to express feelings and explore those of others.
- A sense of omnipotence frequently increases risk-taking behavior, accidents, alcohol use and other dangers.
- The still-limited economic independence of middle adolescents curbs their activities — many don't have the money or opportunity to explore as fully as they would like.

Late adolescence
(approximately ages 18–21)
In this last phase of the quest for independence, if all has gone well, the young person will be well on the way to handling the tasks and responsibilities of adulthood. Having successfully separated from the family, the late adolescent often comes to reappreciate parental values and support.

- Parental advice may once more be sought and a new, positive relationship with the family often emerges. (However, some late adolescents are still struggling with independence issues.)
- The perfected adult body of late adolescence has acquired a self-image to go with it and a clear sexual identity.
- Peer-group attachments become less important as the adolescent becomes secure in his or her own values.
- Late adolescents develop more of a "conscience," a sense of perspective, the ability to delay gratification and to compromise, with a refinement of religious, moral and sexual values.
- Relationships become less exploitative and more reciprocal, the focus being on enjoyable

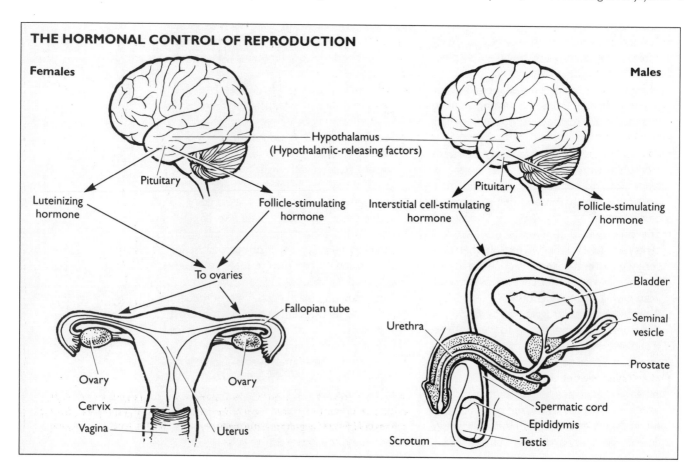

THE HORMONAL CONTROL OF REPRODUCTION

Females

Males

Hypothalamus (Hypothalamic-releasing factors)

Pituitary

Luteinizing hormone

Follicle-stimulating hormone

Interstitial cell-stimulating hormone

Follicle-stimulating hormone

To ovaries

Fallopian tube

Bladder

Seminal vesicle

Urethra

Prostate

Ovary

Ovary

Cervix

Spermatic cord

Vagina

Uterus

Epididymis

Scrotum

Testis

companionship rather than peer adherence. More sustained friendships are forged, involving tenderness and responsibility.

• The late adolescent thinks in more concrete terms about career, job and plans for the future, can organize time better and plan a productive lifestyle.

THE PHYSICAL CHANGES OF PUBERTY

Girls usually begin puberty between ages nine and twelve, boys two to three years later. The changes in height, weight and sexual development encompass a wide range of normal. The fastest growth in height occurs around ages 12 or 13 in girls and 14 to 16 in boys. Growth tends to be greatest in spring and summer. Muscle strength in girls increases up to ages 15 or 16, then tapers off, but increases steadily in boys up to ages 16 to 18 or beyond.

The secondary sexual changes of puberty are triggered by hormones from the *hypothalamus* and *pituitary* glands in the brain. The hypothalamus produces gonadotropin-releasing hormones (GRH), which cause the pea-sized pituitary gland at the base of the brain (just behind the eyes), to produce two hormones: follicle-stimulating hormone (FSH) and luteinizing hormone (LH), which in turn trigger production of sex hormones by the male testes and female ovaries.

• FSH stimulates sperm maturation in males, ovarian follicle development in females;
• LH stimulates testosterone output in males, ovulation and progesterone production in females;
• estradiol increases bone growth in boys, and in girls it triggers the development of breasts, labia, vagina and uterus;
• testosterone accelerates growth and stimulates in boys development of penis, scrotum, muscle mass, pubic and underarm hair, larynx size (and voice-deepening), and in girls the development of pubic and underarm hair.

The onset of menstruation

Menarche, the first menstrual period, is a memorable — sometimes unexpected, occasionally unnerving — event. The normal age of menarche ranges from 9 to 16 years,

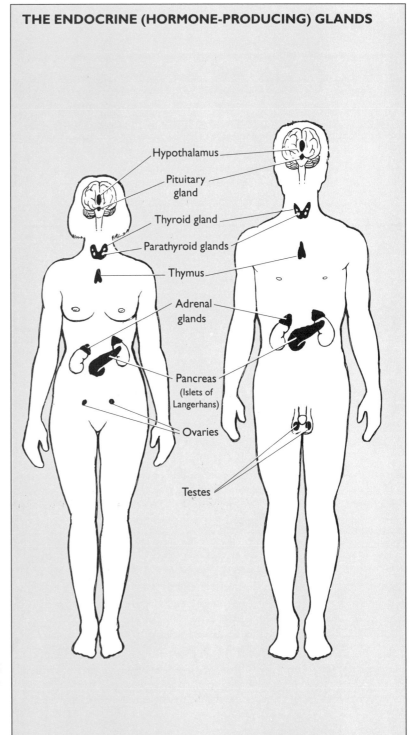

THE ENDOCRINE (HORMONE-PRODUCING) GLANDS

Hypothalamus
Pituitary gland
Thyroid gland
Parathyroid glands
Thymus
Adrenal glands
Pancreas (Islets of Langerhans)
Ovaries
Testes

The endocrine glands are the same in both sexes except for the gonads: men have testes and women have ovaries. Most of the pancreas makes digestive juices, but the specialized islets of Langerhans make the hormone insulin. The brain, stomach and intestines also make and release hormones.

averaging 12.4 years in North America today.

Once menstrual periods begin, a girl can get pregnant any time, even at her very first sexual encounter. Some mothers do not bother to tell their daughters much about menstruation, assuming they will learn about it in school. But schools do not always do a thorough job of sex education, often failing to explain adequately the meaning of menstruation and also giving too little information about birth control and sexually transmitted diseases. Yet if parents prepare a daughter well ahead for her first menstrual period, the event can be celebrated in a positive manner. It can also be used as an opportunity to discuss birth control, sexuality and parenthood.

Body fat plays a key role in the onset of periods

For menstrual periods to begin, a girl's body must have about 22–24 percent of body fat. (At maturity, the average girl's body has 24–28 percent body fat, compared to about 14 percent fat in boys.) Results from many countries confirm that menstrual periods become irregular or cease when body fat dwindles below 22 percent in women of average height. Halted ovulation may be a protective biological mechanism that prevents pregnancy when a woman has insufficient energy stores to nourish a developing fetus or breastfeed a newborn.

Changes of puberty in boys

For most boys, the first hint of imminent manhood is growth of the testicles and penis, and the development of pubic hair, which gradually becomes darker and more abundant, with hair also appearing under the arms and on the legs and perhaps on the chest and back. Later, usually between ages 13 and 18, the beard starts to appear and the voice deepens. Although boys generally start growing later than girls, they go on growing for several years after most girls have stopped, often reaching full height between ages 16 and 18.

Wet dreams and penis fantasies

Wet dreams — nocturnal emissions or the ejaculation of semen while asleep — are common during puberty. But the first nocturnal emission can be very upsetting, even though it's an involuntary response to erotic thoughts or dreams. Nocturnal emissions are a normal part of adolescence, and parents usually understand better than boys think they will! Some boys also have involuntary erections at awkward times during the day. There is not much that can be done about such erections, but it may help to remember that this happens to most boys, diminishing with maturity. Boys naturally tend to compare penis size and some hold contests to see who can ejaculate or urinate the furthest. Penis size has nothing to do with potency, sex drive or fertility, nor does it make any difference to the ability to conceive children. Similarly it has nothing to do with the capacity to give sexual pleasure. An erect penis of even 7 to 10 cm (3 to 4 in) can stimulate the vaginal nerves and give ample pleasure. (While the vagina's entire length is erotically sensitive, the outer third is most sensitive, especially to tactile stimulation.) Yet macho myths often lead men to equate masculinity with penis size — just as women can be led to believe that sex appeal has to do with the size of their breasts. Such unfounded notions only exacerbate natural adolescent uncertainties.

BODY-IMAGE CONCERNS

Dissatisfaction with body shape and size is almost a rite of passage for teens, and in one survey 54 percent of adolescent girls and 33 percent of boys reported "dissatisfaction" with their bodies. Other surveys reveal that 90 percent of young women and a growing number of young men in Western society dislike their bodies and are preoccupied with weight and shape, sometimes for life.

The wish to acquire a fashionably thin body makes many adolescents resort to unhealthy practices such as dieting, fluid deprivation, or overuse of saunas or weight-lifting equipment. Dieting, fasting, "binge and purge" behavior, and abuse of laxatives and diuretics (water-loss pills) are widespread among adolescents — especially females — sometimes leading to malnutrition. "Since weight concerns are almost universal," notes one U.S. nutrition expert, "we should no longer consider them pathological but an adaptive response to growing up in a society obsessed with thinness." Given that the media and fashion industry portray successful women as thin and asexual, adolescent girls tend to regard a naturally soft or buxom female shape as undesirable.

Basing self-esteem more on outward appearance and body shape than on other assets — such as musical, artistic, creative, scholastic, nurturing or other abilities — many of today's adolescent girls have an appallingly low sense of self-worth, poor views of their value to society and often less confidence than boys of similar age. One Canadian survey found that while 60 percent of girls aged eight to nine report they are "happy with the way they are," by the time they reach 16, only 29 percent of girls are content and confident about themselves, compared to 48 percent of similarly aged boys.

Dieting and nutritional deficiencies

In trying to conform to the media portrayal of a desirably thin body, many adolescents — girls in particular — adopt unhealthy practices such as smoking (to curb appetite) and very restricted diets. Efforts to acquire a lean, svelte shape lead many of today's young women to consume too few (and/or the wrong) calories. They may select "lite" foods for the wrong reason — not as part of a healthy eating regimen, but because they don't like themselves the way they are.

Believing that "mind over matter" should allow them to achieve a skinny look — despite today's biological tendency to be larger and heavier — many young women feel guilty for being even slightly overweight or less slender than TV or magazine models. And if they fail to adhere to the self-proclaimed diet, they feel ashamed, further lowering self-esteem.

One reason for the dieting mania is the current view of female beauty, which equates a slim body with success and desirability. As one specialist puts it, "today's images tell women that thinness equals power and confidence, leading to an unhealthy preoccupation with weight, shape and dieting." Struggling to reduce or maintain their weight, many young women restrict their food choices and limit calories to 1,000 or less a day — generally too little to supply the needed nutrients. Yet most women can never achieve the idealized slim shape —

no matter how rigorously they diet — because of the body's biological tendency to maintain a "set-point" and to put back the weight lost as soon as a diet ends. (For more on the pitfalls of dieting, see chapter 2.)

According to some experts, "weight preoccupation has become a way in which people, especially women, express control, and for some weight control is a substitute for gaining mastery over other aspects of their lives." Focusing on weight may be a coping strategy to avoid dealing with painful emotions or experiences such as sex abuse. Those with low self-esteem may hope to gain approval through being thin, precariously relying on body-image as tangible proof of worthiness rather than on more substantial qualities, achievements and attributes. Becoming or staying thin may become a primary goal in life, overshadowing attention to family, career and friendships. Weight preoccupation and eating disorders are basically an expression of "dissatisfaction with oneself." They fall on a continuum with inveterate dieters at one end and those diagnosed with anorexia nervosa and bulimia at the other.

The massive preoccupation with dieting, which often starts in the primary grades, gives adolescent females the nutritional challenge of obtaining enough nutrients while restricting calories to avoid weight gain. Surveys reveal that the challenge is often unmet and that many women aged 15 to 24 are malnourished and consume less than the recommended daily intakes of key nutrients such as calcium, iron, zinc, magnesium, some B vitamins and vitamin D. Health problems arising from the nutrient lack include fatigue, an inability to learn properly, disturbed (or halted) menstrual cycles, anemia (from lack of iron), depleted bone density (from shortage of calcium), and — in extreme cases — dangerous illnesses such as anorexia nervosa and bulimia. The disordered eating habits may last a lifetime and the tragedy is that the yo-yo dieting spiral which starts in the teenage years may lead to obesity later on.

Society needs to set new values to help young people get out of the dieting trap, overcome the idolization of thinness, and base their self-worth on assets other than appearance or body shape.

THE TRAGIC PURSUIT OF THINNESS: ANOREXIA NERVOSA AND BULIMIA

Western society's idealization of thinness is producing an alarming increase in eating disorders, especially among young women. The never-ending efforts to lose weight and conform to the media image of an "ideal" shape are leading more and more young people to diet at the cost of health. Weight-preoccupation is now widespread in our society, affecting people of all ages, classes, occupations and ethnic backgrounds.

There's a steadily rising incidence of anorexia nervosa and bulimia nervosa, which can cause devastating health problems, even death. Over 300,000 Canadians suffer from these eating disorders, which may coexist, overlap or occur separately. Anorexia nervosa involves the pursuit of thinness to the point of starvation, seriously endangering health. Bulimia nervosa also involves weight-obsession, but with frequent binge eating followed by vomiting and purging sessions, to counteract the effects of overeating.

Besides those actually diagnosed with anorexia nervosa and bulimia, countless others — an estimated 10–20 percent of all North American women — are weight-obsessed and engage in many of the self-harming behaviors associated with these eating disorders. Many who are not strictly anorexic or bulimic nonetheless share some characteristics of these illnesses — such as relentless dieting and an intense fear of weight gain. Girls and women make up about 95 percent of those struggling with severe eating problems, boys and men the rest. Studies find a high rate of depression and other psychiatric disturbances (including sex abuse) among those diagnosed with serious eating problems.

Anorexia nervosa

Anorexia nervosa (AN) affects about 1 percent of young females aged 14–25 (and some males), of whom 15 percent are in danger of dying from the disorder. The disorder afflicts primarily adolescents and young women, who starve themselves in the relentless pursuit of a slender figure. The term anorexia nervosa, barely heard of 30 years ago, has now become a familiar household word. But "anorexia nervosa," meaning a nervous loss of appetite, is a misnomer, since appetite loss usually appears, if at all, late in the disease. While the disorder was previously confined mainly to girls from affluent families, it has now spread to all social classes and ethnic groups.

An English doctor first described a case of anorexia nervosa in the 1800s as a "skeleton clad only in skin" — a woman who stubbornly refused to eat, "giving no reason for her obstinacy." Typically, people with anorexia nervosa have an unshakable preoccupation with dieting and are at least 15 percent below their normal weight. Many feel fat despite their emaciated appearance and are socially withdrawn. Some subsist on as little as 300 calories a day. They refuse to acknowledge normal hunger pangs, seeing resistance as a sign of self-discipline. AN can result in many metabolic, hormonal and physical disturbances. Sufferers may finally seek medical advice because of fatigue, bloating, brittle nails, a yellowing skin and other characteristic signs of starvation.

The causes of AN are multifactorial and include biological, family, psychological and societal influences, including a history of sex abuse.

CHARACTERISTICS OF ANOREXIA NERVOSA

- **Increasingly desperate pursuit of thinness.**
- **Terror of becoming fat or "losing control."**
- **Misperception of inner sensations such as fatigue, anger.**
- **Low sense of self-worth — dependent on external looks.**
- **Feelings of helplessness (lack of initiative, failure to gain autonomy, being overly tied to family).**
- **Denial of illness, refusal to acknowledge "anything wrong."**
- **Fear of growing up.**
- **Lack of trust in self** and others.
- **Perfectionist tendencies — excessive desire to perform well.**
- **Withdrawal from social or sexual contacts, increasing isolation; avoidance of occasions that involve eating.**
- **Compulsive weighing and measuring of body size, all activities being regulated by "what the scales say."**
- **Compulsive exercise (even standing all day to hasten weight loss).**
- **Intense preoccupation with food —** collection of menus, recipes, cookbooks, utensils.
- **Subterfuges to avoid eating (giving food to dog, throwing it in garbage); peculiar patterns of handling food (e.g., hoarding but not eating it; preparing meals for others but not eating themselves).**
- **Undivided attention to meals — hours taken to consume even tiny amounts.**
- **Reproductive changes: amenorrhea in women, impotence in men.**
- **Osteoporosis (bone loss).**

Some blame its prevalence on our society's excessive weight-consciousness. Scientists are debating whether chronic dieters and compulsive exercisers differ from those with full-blown anorexia nervosa only in degree — with AN representing an extreme consequence of dieting — or also qualitatively. (Mild anorectic symptoms occur in many compulsive exercisers and obsessive dieters.)

Most medical specialists regard anorexia nervosa as a psychiatric illness. As defined by the American Psychiatric Association's Diagnostic and Statistical Manual of Mental Disorders its hallmarks are: a relentless pursuit of thinness; body weight 15 percent or more below desirable weight; intense fear of being fat or putting on a gram or ounce; misperception about inner sensations (such as anger, disappointment); absence of at least three consecutive menstrual cycles and a distorted image of body size and shape (viewing an emaciated body as fat). The outwardly defiant and stubborn demeanor of those with AN often hides an extreme vulnerability and lack of self-esteem.

The disorder may delay sexual development if it starts young. Female anorexics typically become amenorrheic (menstrual periods cease), their breasts diminish, fat dwindles, feminine curves vanish, osteoporosis (bone loss) occurs, the body may become covered with fine hair (lanugo) and many medical disorders appear — such as pancreatitis, anemia, low blood pressure, cold-intolerance (blue extremities), heart irregularities and liver ailments. Social life is forfeited in pursuing weight-loss to the exclusion of all else. Many anorexics also exercise compulsively — perhaps walking or swimming great distances each day — to the point of utter exhaustion, in order to "burn calories" rather than for fun or good health.

The symptoms of AN may start imperceptibly, with a narrowing of food choices, preference for low-calorie diet foods, counting calories, omitting meats, eating primarily fiber-rich foods, a refusal to dine with the family, excuses of "eating later" and withdrawal from social occasions.

Self-starvation may be a drive for control

While the bizarre eating patterns may seem to come out of the blue, they often result from childhood experiences, overly strict upbringing, neglect or abuse, all of which produce an extremely low sense of self-worth. Recent research reveals that 65 percent of those with anorexia and other severe eating disorders have experienced some form of abuse, whether physical, sexual, verbal or emotional, or have witnessed violence between parents. The abuse can leave children with feelings of revulsion, shame, guilt and powerlessness, leading them to think that they can't control their bodies. These feelings may translate into an extreme need to control or "punish" the body through self-starvation. The focus on weight and the maintenance of a thin, childlike form may help women to avoid growing up and thinking about victimization or unpleasant experiences.

The family of someone with AN is often restrictive and overprotective. The child's needs may be denied, communication may be restrained and family members may avoid conflict only by suppressing emotions and feelings. While outwardly harmonious, the family may discourage independent opinions or actions, expecting total obedience. Although AN is labeled an eating disorder, many believe it might more aptly be called a disorder of control, since most anorexics have a profound feeling of inadequacy in directing their lives. The weight preoccupation may deflect their thoughts and stop them from dwelling on an intolerable situation.

The underpinnings of AN are apprehension about maturing and an overwhelming sense of ineffectiveness. Some experts view the disorder as a push for autonomy and a way to escape or rebel against stifling domination. The relentless drive for thinness and its attainment proves mastery over *at least one area* — their own bodies. Typically, anorexics base their self-worth entirely on external appearance and the approval of others.

The pre-illness personality of anorexics is often described by parents, teachers and peers as being that of a "perfect little girl," someone who has always complied with the wishes of others. Such children tend to be obliging, industrious and academically bright, with a desperate wish to succeed but no clear self-identity. Long

---

USUAL EFFECTS SEEN IN STARVING PEOPLE (PRESENT BUT NOT UNIQUE TO ANOREXIA)

- sleep disturbances — insomnia, restlessness;
- hair loss (on head) but growth of downy hair (lanugo) on body;
- dry skin, brittle nails;
- cold extremities — bluish hands and feet;
- altered cardiovascular function — lowered or irregular heartbeat;
- potassium depletion (which can cause cardiac arrest);
- bloating — even if fasting;
- unabated ravenous sensation on eating;
- mood swings: irritability, poor concentration, apathy;
- nail-biting and gum-chewing (food substitutes).

before the illness manifests itself, these children are obedient and reluctant to test their own capacities. Anorexia nervosa is now spreading to a broader range of adolescents who are less compliant, industrious and achievement-oriented.

Precipitating events

The triggering events that may start someone on the anorectic dieting spiral often seem no different from those facing many women in our slimness-obsessed society. The dieting may be set off by a teasing remark about being chubby, a dieting parent or friend or some stressful circumstance such as going to camp, starting university or doubts about dating.

Alerting signs may be excessive weight concern, a diet with repeatedly lowered weight goals, avoidance of foods considered "fattening," eating smaller and smaller portions, leaving meals to go to the bathroom, worries about imagined flabbiness, loss of hair, complaints of feeling cold, expressions of self-loathing, wearing oversized clothes and withdrawal from social life.

By the time anorexics come to medical attention there are usually clear signs of starvation. A typical case might be a quiet, studious girl who continues a more and more restricted diet until she consumes a daily ration of one grapefruit, two slices of melba toast, a morsel of cheese and plain tea. The reduced food intake may create great distress among family and friends, who urge her to eat normally, but denial of sickness is typical. Anorexics may consider their bodies obese no matter how thin, failing to recognize that the emaciated body is neither beautiful nor healthy.

Family background may set the stage

Although no single home scenario predetermines anorexia nervosa, there are recognizable family dynamics and risk factors — particularly authoritarian rules, overprotection, an emphasis on appearance and scholastic grades rather than on other attributes, and "over-enmeshment" — where actions and achievements are valued in terms of the family, not the individual. Predisposing influences include parents who discourage independence, and expect the child to subordinate her wishes to those of the family.

A stifling, overprotective attitude may retard the development of a child's identity in families that try at all costs to keep up appearances, never allowing any argument or disagreement to surface. One expert describes a typical anorexic's family as "too involved with each other — unwittingly preventing the teenager from gaining independence or coping skills." When all activities are dictated by the parents' concept of what is right, the child grows up with a deficient sense of self and poor decision-making skills. Some have deep fears of maturity and the responsibilities of growing up — sometimes labeled "phobic avoidance" of the demands of adolescence. By bringing back an immature, unthreatening body contour and stopping menstruation, weight loss delays the need to face adult womanhood.

Treatment of anorexia nervosa

Although food avoidance is the overt feature of anorexia nervosa, any other underlying psychiatric problems or mental illnesses — such as depression, anxiety and obsessive-compulsive disorders — must also be assessed and tackled.

Support and guidance can come from a trusted friend, relative, co-worker, teacher or counselor. In helping anorexics it is crucial to maintain a nonjudgmental attitude, to listen without trying to exert control and to guide them to professional therapy. Therapy may take the form of individual or group sessions, sometimes best in a hospital setting — on an outpatient or inpatient basis — and may involve medication as well as psychotherapy. Hospital admission is mandatory for some anorexics, because of severe starvation and accompanying health hazards. Bed rest and a reasonable goal for weight-gain reinforce the idea of anoxeria as an illness that needs nursing, and permit close monitoring of mealtimes. Antidepressants may be tried, as well as zinc supplements — said to help some cases but still under debate.

Since anorexia is such a complex problem, recovery too is complex and may take several years. About 30 to 50 percent of anorexics recover fully within a few years, either spontaneously (on their own) or with correct therapy.

Those in whom the eating disorder continues untreated face complications such as osteoporosis, metabolic disorders, cardiovascular and other illnesses. The outlook is best if treatment starts before weight loss is too extreme and if the family dynamics are not too distorted.

The top priority is to reverse the weight loss and save a desperately unhappy, ill person. For successful treatment, a good psychiatric assessment is essential, with cognitive and behavioral therapy as well as refeeding. Treatment includes reeducating the family, to improve relationships and to correct the anorexic's eating habits, with clear information about the hazards of starvation, including its effects on thinking and behavior. In the past, some experts recommended that the topic of eating be avoided, focusing on psychological factors. Today this is not considered useful; issues of weight and food *must* be addressed. The goal is not control of the anorexic, but relief of suffering and cognitive therapy to reverse the individual's poor self-image.

The family is advised to participate in therapy — especially if the anorexic is still living at home — even though many resist involvement, regarding the illness as the "child's problem" or denying it to save face. Some blame the adolescent for not eating, saying, "If only she'd eat properly we'd all be happy again." The physician's insistence on family involvement may arouse strong parental feelings of guilt or recrimination that must be faced for treatment to succeed. Some parents of anorexics ignore their offspring's plight, feel ashamed or won't devote time to their ailing teenager, preferring to leave treatment to medical experts — an attitude not likely to help the anorexic as the problem is aggravated by the family dynamics. The family members must be taught to see themselves as helpers, not "scapegoats," and as an integral part of the treatment plan.

The most basic elements in refeeding anorexics are getting them to trust the medical caregivers and to stick to a meal plan with enough calories. Clinicians try to establish an empathetic relationship by discussing the anorexic's feelings, going beyond weight gain to deeper worries. Anorexics generally respond well to frank information about the cultural, familial and biological roots of their condition and how their behavior arose. Sufferers often express amazement at their misconceptions about nutrition and family influences.

Bulimia nervosa

Once considered just a subclass of anorexia nervosa, bulimia nervosa is now recognized as a dangerous disorder in its own right, occurring mainly in women aged 16 to 25, especially prevalent among high school and college students. Bulimia nervosa afflicts an estimated 2–4 percent of Canadian females aged 12 to 25 (and some adolescent males). Like anorexia nervosa, it too involves extreme weight-preoccupation, but with alternate bouts of bingeing and fasting, vomiting and purging being commonplace after binges. Predisposing factors include a family history of alcoholism and depression.

There's been a dramatic upsurge in numbers of cases of bulimia in recent years, and again, this is blamed on society's worship of thinness in the face of increasing average body weights for women. Adolescent anorexics may later become bulimics. Sadly, many remain eating-disordered and dissatisfied with themselves for life. Bulimics share the anorexic's fear of losing control, are similarly obsessed with weight loss, and also have a high incidence of depression and other psychiatric disorders. Like those with anorexia, bulimics embark upon restricted diets but can't stick to them, and engage in cycles of restricted eating, bingeing and self-inflicted vomiting and purging — with excessive use of laxatives, diuretics and perhaps ipecac syrup (to induce vomiting). When their dietary restraint breaks down, bulimics binge on vast amounts of food — cakes, desserts, hotdogs, whatever — then vomit it all up to avoid weight-gain. Since hunger returns after vomiting, bulimics are constantly tempted to binge again, and face dangerous medical consequences. The binge-and-purge pattern allows many bulimics to keep a normal or slightly below normal weight so that their disordered eating may remain hidden from all but close family members. Bulimia, however, can occur with any body weight.

Bulimics often use laxatives in vast quantities, on the false premise that they reduce calorie absorption, when in fact they only cause dehydration. The purging doesn't rid the body of unwanted calories, as laxatives work on the large intestine *after* the calories have been absorbed (higher up, in the small intestine). Self-imposed vomiting, which may take hours per session, gets rid of only a few calories and is extremely hard on the digestive system, throat and heart. Diuretics or water pills rid the body of some water — as well as valuable minerals. Loss of potassium can seriously disturb the heart rhythm.

The diagnostic criteria for bulimia nervosa are: persistent over-concern about body weight, a morbid fear of being fat, recurrent episodes of binge eating (rapid consumption of vast amounts of food in a short period) — averaging at least two binge-and-purge sessions per week for three or more months, and behavior that aims to offset the overeating, such as regular self-induced vomiting, overuse of laxatives and diuretics, together with feelings of shame and "loss of control." Alerting signs may be a chipmunk-like face — with swollen cheeks (from enlarged parotid or salivary glands) — and dental problems from teeth eroded by the acidity of frequent vomiting. Many bulimics seek medical advice because of constipation, fatigue, rectal bleeding and Russel's sign — callused hands, rubbed by being stuck down the throat to induce vomiting. Laxative abuse may produce alternating diarrhea and constipation or rebound water retention. Diuretics, used to eliminate body water, compound the health risks. Other complications of bulimia nervosa include stomach bleeds, kidney disorders and electrolyte imbalance — possibly producing serious, sometimes fatal, heartbeat irregularities.

Bulimics may need hospitalization, but less often than anorexics. Treatment means understanding and accepting the diagnosis, offering cognitive and behavioral therapy — to modify the disturbed body-image, overcome feelings of shame, perhaps to deal with previous sexual abuse and improve social and family interaction. Group therapy may be particularly successful. Antidepressants (such as imipramine, fluoxetine and others) may also help to reduce binge eating or stabilize a depressed mood. Recovery takes a variable time and relapse rates average 30 to 40 percent.

PSYCHOSOCIAL DEVELOPMENT IN ADOLESCENCE

The teenager's world, filled with new experiences and the acquisition of new skills, may produce a jumble of emotions which many find hard to articulate. What seems important to the adolescent may seem trivial to the adult. Parents may deplore the adolescent's erratic schedule or tendency to daydream, not realizing that these are normal aspects of development.

Adolescence also provides a "window" or an interval of time when psychological difficulties or struggles of early childhood — for example separation anxiety, desolation over a divorce, fears of going to daycare, sibling

---

TIPS FOR BUILDING SELF-ESTEEM AND IMPROVING BODY IMAGE

For the person with low self-esteem

- Think about how you treat your body and the way it works for you — by carrying you around, bending and stretching, housing your thoughts — and focus on parts you like or consider okay. Enjoy being in your own body.
- List the things you do well and the things you like about yourself — ask friends and school- or workmates what they appreciate most about you.
- Ask whether you are good to yourself and your body or always depriving it. Reward yourself for things well done — a drawing, helping a friend, writing an essay. Give yourself

non-food treats, whether taking a bubble bath, going to a movie or renting a favorite video.
- Find ways to express painful feelings or memories — write them down, draw or paint them, share the feelings with a friend or even with a pet.

For family and friends

- Avoid making comments about weight or looks — they'll only perpetuate the obsession with body image and weight.
- Do not try to tempt with or engage in a power struggle around food — those with eating disorders have deep psychological reasons for the behavior and need to be in control

of their eating.
- Be available to give support, advice and to listen, to provide information and suggest treatment choices for the anorexic, while leaving the decision to her.
- If close to or trying to help someone with disordered eating, examine *your* own attitudes to dieting, size and appearance so that you don't convey any prejudices or exacerbate the weight preoccupation. Don't unwittingly reinforce or pass on society's harmful idolization of thinness.

For more information contact the National Eating Disorders Information Centre: (416) 340-4156.

rivalries — may be reworked, sometimes with "acting out" behavior and rebellious conduct. Parents who are perturbed by what seem to be exaggeratedly emotional or hostile attitudes might note that the teenager is likely working through deep-rooted psychological problems from earlier years. They may be encouraged to bear in mind that it's only a transient stage in growing up.

In the teenage years, the values and mores of peers begin to supersede those of parents. Suddenly the parents — who previously seemed all-knowing — are revealed as ordinary people with normal human flaws, which sometimes come as a revelation to adolescents. In developing independence and their own opinions, teens may discover a gulf between their views and those of their parents, which can engender conflicts. It takes a deft parental touch to set limits that permit teenagers the freedom and exploration needed to foster self-esteem, while protecting them from danger. Adolescents need rules and guidance, though they may stridently oppose them.

HELPING ADOLESCENTS THROUGH THE TRANSITION

Parents, confronted by their children's emergent, sometimes flamboyant, independence, also face major adjustments as their offspring pass through puberty. Some parents find it hard to accept teens as sexual persons and shun casual or dinner-time chat on the subject, perhaps limiting discussion of sex to occasional advice about birth control and sexually transmitted diseases.

Mother-daughter discussions about sex are far more frequent and wide-ranging than mother-son discussions. Few boys receive (or seek) sex education from parents. Fathers often don't fill the communication gap. Yet parents can help adolescents formulate their ideas by using TV shows, news headlines or magazine articles as an opening to discuss sex, relationships, violence and other issues.

Some parents become reticent about physically showing affection to adolescents, just when these young people need reassurance about still being wanted. Parents who frequently cuddled their children when young may be uncomfortable about hugging a teenager, or

---

THE CHIEF DEVELOPMENTAL TASKS OF ADOLESCENCE:

- developing an identity distinct from that within the family;
- overcoming worry about body changes and physical appearance; accepting a new body image and forging fresh self-esteem to match it;
- forming intimate relationships with same-sex and opposite-sex peers outside the home;
- understanding and gaining control over sexual urges;
- developing an adult role that fits (or doesn't) the sex-specific behavior patterns expected by society;
- gaining a sense of "self," believing in personal opinions, knowing who one is;
- perfecting a personal value system and vocational ambitions — developing a world view — and sorting out which values will form a guiding principle for one's life and behavior;
- creating a perspective of the future — setting goals that seem worthwhile, realistic and attainable;
- making study/employment decisions: deciding what one wants to accomplish or must learn;
- developing marriage thoughts or plans: ideas of what one's partner might be like;
- assuming responsibility for personal decisions and actions — learning to run one's own life.

COMPARING PARENTAL AND ADOLESCENT CONCERNS

Typical concerns of parents include:
- rebellion — common in early and middle adolescence (severe rebellion needs professional attention);
- daydreaming — a normal part of adolescent development;
- excessive risk-taking — best handled by family discussions,

limit-setting, evaluation of unmet adolescent needs or wishes;
- rudeness and hostility;
- reluctance to adhere to the limits set;
- violent mood swings — which require assessment to check for depression, bipolar disorder (manic-depression)

or other psychiatric disorders;
- school problems — which call for evaluation of type and frequency;
- sexual interests — possibly intercourse, risks of pregnancy and STDs (especially AIDS). Sexuality needs frank discussion and information

about birth control and STD avoidance.

Typical teenager concerns include:
- family conflicts, limits, arguments over curfew, friends, privacy;
- peer relationships, dating;
- school — academic record, popularity,

teachers, changing schools;
- identity: who am I? body image, shyness, loneliness;
- medical/health worries — am I normal? too short? too fat? beset by acne; psychosomatic problems (such as headaches, stomach aches, insomnia);
- mild depression.

COMPARING ADOLESCENT AND PARENTAL DEVELOPMENT TASKS

Adolescent task	Parental task
Accept physical changes of puberty.	• Accept that adolescent is no longer a child, and treat as an emerging adult; • recognize that behavior and mood are affected by hormonal changes of puberty.
Develop new self-image.	• Be content with less intimacy; • allow privacy but maintain enough contact to affirm love and concern.
Build independence from family.	• Determine what behavior is desirable or unacceptable (set clear rules); • determine, communicate and negotiate limits (boundaries), and penalties for exceeding them or transgressing agreed limits; • adapt to changing needs of adolescent; • teach adolescent how to make decisions by role-modeling.
Develop stable role identity.	• Encourage self-esteem-enhancing activities to boost adolescent's sense of self-worth; • recognize parental influence in identity problems; • maintain long-term view of process rather than arguing over minor infringements.
Develop adult thinking skills.	• Differentiate between egocentrism, self-evolution and selfishness; • recognize adolescence as a transitional and developmental stage.

fathers and sons may avoid physical contact because it seems "unmanly." Sometimes barriers to parent-child affection are raised by adolescents themselves because of stories heard about sex abuse or molestation by family members. Yet adolescent boys and girls need reassurance more than ever. Although they may appear offhand and independent, most teens desperately need positive feedback. If physical affection is withdrawn, this may be taken as rejection and breed resentment and feelings of no longer being desirable.

It's salutory to remember that most teenagers have deep concerns about their self-worth and sometimes feel uncomfortable with themselves. They may have ambivalent feelings about the roles of family and friendship, about school performance, employment possibilities,

their future. Such feelings of inadequacy are compounded if parents unconsciously reinforce a teenager's self-doubts by avoiding the closeness of physical touch. Withholding expressions of affection can impede intimacy and create relationship problems later in life.

One 16-year-old girl beset by self-doubts described how her mother stopped stroking or kissing her once she entered puberty, making her feel totally rejected. The feeling was luckily offset by her aunt, who boosted her self-esteem and — sometimes to the girl's embarrassment — continued to hug her, repeatedly telling her how attractive, creative and intelligent she was.

As adolescents strive to consolidate personal values it's worth remembering the hurdles they face, especially when one is exasperated by their untidiness, erratic mealtimes or other provocations. The best bet for parents is to open the lines of communication, make sure that their teenager stays in touch, avoid a judgmental attitude and see that the teenager still feels wanted and valued.

By the same token, parents have a right to expect a modicum of responsibility and should negotiate "fines" or removal of privileges if the agreed rules are transgressed or duties left undone. Teenagers still need firm guidelines and empathy even though their behavior may be annoying. It may help to remember that other parents probably face similarly erratic behavior. However hard it may be to accept, detachment from parents and family is an inevitable part of growing up. Adolescents must be encouraged to develop their own opinions, values and friends. It happens in each generation!

MEDICAL CHECKUPS FOR ADOLESCENTS

Teenagers should be medically assessed in early and middle adolescence. Physicians generally prefer to see the adolescent alone, chat informally, listen to concerns and treat comments seriously. They try to build confidence, establish rapport and ideally act as the teenager's advocate.

The doctor takes a full medical and psychosocial history, asks about home, family relationships, friends, hobbies, drug and alcohol use, dating and sexual activity. The medical evaluation will also screen for psychological/mental health and assess risk behaviors, giving physicians a chance to spot adolescent anxieties about physical maturation, allowing discussion of breast and penis size, acne, skin and hair care, exercise and diet. It also offers an excellent opportunity to check on school pressures and discuss family conflicts, social isolation, loneliness, and anxiety or depression. Physicians may counsel on accident-prevention and are often the first to spot substance abuse.

A skilled physician listens for any "hidden agenda" that may reveal inner worries. For instance, a teenager who visits a physician about stomach pains or a headache may really be worried about family conflicts or becoming pregnant. Open-ended questions — for example, "Tell me more about it" — often bring out the adolescent's true concerns. Providing the youngsters with the doctor's telephone number allows them to go for advice on their own if they wish.

The checkup generally includes measurements of height, weight, blood pressure and pulse rate; evaluation of vision, hearing, teeth and gums, neck (thyroid), abdomen and pelvis, as well as immunization status — with booster shots being given if needed. Since myopia (short-sightedness) tends to worsen in puberty, this may be the time to suggest glasses or contact lenses (usually soft, replaceable types that need minimal cleaning and care). Pubertal progress is evaluated by examining the external genitals — testes and pubic hair in boys, breast development, pubic hair and menstrual regularity in girls.

The physician will likely inquire about sexual activity, knowledge of STDs and how to prevent them. It is a good opportunity to provide counseling on birth control and to instruct teenagers in contraceptive choices and their correct use. Nutritional status is assessed, with discussion of diet, weight-maintenance and any eating disorders possibly present. Some teenagers may feel awkward and worry about confidentiality if discussing worries with a doctor who has seen them through childhood and who may also look after the rest of the family. Sensing this, a physician may recommend a colleague.

SCHOOL PROBLEMS

Scholastic problems frequently appear in adolescence, partly because of the many competing demands, hormonal changes and new friendships. School grades may fall short of parental expectations, and the expressed "disappointment" can engender a sense of failure,

---

TIPS ON COMMUNICATING BETTER WITH TEENS

- Listen attentively.
- Be sensitive to teenage feelings and a "hidden agenda" of worries.
- Treat problems seriously, do not scoff at or minimize them.
- Avoid power struggles.
- Show interest and concern, but express trust.
- Acknowledge the adolescent's maturity by offering choices and exploring them.
- Be open and honest — adolescents

quickly pick up on deceit.
- Use an interactive rather than an interrogative style, progress from neutral to more sensitive topics and try a third-person, objective approach to delicate subjects.
- Maintain nonjudgmental frankness.
- Assure confidentiality. Be mindful that intimate teen disclosures are delicate matters. Having promised confiden-

tiality, stick to it!
- Use and explain the proper terms, avoiding slang. "Do you know exactly what's meant by sexual intercourse?" "Do you know what STDs are and what they can lead to?" "Do you know why it's dangerous to drink and drive and what to do about it?"
- Don't lecture, moralize or be self-righteous: instead try to stand back and gently help in the

decision-making.
- Be firm and don't condone risky behavior.
- Avoid barriers to communication such as:
  - comparison with other teens;
  - minimizing a problem;
  - excessive talking;
  - "taking over" an adolescent's problem;
  - using phrases such as "The trouble with you is . . . ," "How could you

do this to me?", "In my day . . . ," "Is that all?", "You're all wrong . . . ," "How can you think like that?", "That's a dumb thing to say," "I'm busy right now . . . "
- Make resources, advice and expert help easily available.
- Let the adolescent know that if he or she indicates an intention to pursue illegal activities, you may need to inform the authorities.

perhaps depression — even if the teenager is really doing fine. Academic failure, particularly in high-achieving families, is a recognized factor in teen suicides. Parents should avoid creating needless stress at this sensitive age and remember that an academic shortfall is often made up later on. It may help if concerned adults outside the family give teens a chance to air their anxieties. If concerned, contact the teacher, school principal, guidance counselor or the physical education staff.

ADOLESCENT SEXUALITY

Making the decision to have or not have sexual intercourse is serious business for teenagers. And the fact that adolescents now attain reproductive capacity at an earlier age has widened the gap between physical maturity and economic independence. Caught between peer and parental values and media images of sexuality, adolescents often have hazy notions of realistic sexual relationships. Current North American culture gives young people conflicting messages about sex, sometimes showing it as a "sign of maturity," and other times disapproving of teenage sexuality. Parents may say one thing, friends or favorite TV programs the opposite. On the one hand, young people are told to refrain, and on the other, they are bombarded by TV shows that implicitly encourage them to be sexually active. Adolescents are understandably confused about what's right or wrong, and some claim to be formidably pressured to have sex before they feel ready for it.

Since many high school students spend a lot of time glued to the TV, it should come as no surprise that many get much of their sex education from what sociologists call "alternative sources." In one year of prime-time TV viewing, a typical teen will see an estimated 20,000 scenes of sexual behavior or innuendo. But what the media shows about sexuality is often exploitive, with too little emphasis on tenderness and responsibility, too much on violence.

Sexual violence is a distinct risk among young people. One study found that more than 10 percent of students had been involved in one or more abusive relationships, beginning around age 15. Acquaintance-assault is common. Because of their immaturity, vulnerable teenagers may feel compelled to act as though they can handle any situation. Their inexperience in sexual situations makes them easy victims, and they may minimize or even deny an assault, blaming themselves or fearing that no one will believe them.

Many young females allegedly also feel "put down" by males and may put up with exploitive, even violent, behavior, in the belief that they somehow provoked the undesirable action, whether date rape or other abusive behavior.

In one survey, over 90 percent of teenagers cited TV shows that pressured them toward early sex. Four out of five teens mentioned at least one popular TV program that portrays casual sex, depicting it as "power, not love." A 1986 poll conducted for the U.S. Parenthood Federation ranked peer pressure first as the incentive to have sex, curiosity second, the idea that "everyone does it" third, sexually excited boys pressuring girls fourth and the wish for sexual gratification last.

Although sexual activity is rare in Canada before age 13, statistics show that, by Grade 11, 41 percent of girls and 49 percent of boys have had intercourse at least once. By the time they leave high school, over half have tried intercourse. However, despite the prevailing myth that "everyone does it," these statistics reveal that only *half* of all Canadians actually have had sex before ages 18 to 20. Surveys also reveal that the first sexual encounter(s) in adolescents are unexpected and frequently unprotected by birth control or measures to reduce risks of sexually transmitted infections. Adolescents frequently act on impulse, and are completely unprepared at first intercourse — despite the seeming plethora of information and the push for safer sex.

Studies show that one in three Canadian teenagers currently uses no birth control at the first sexual encounter. The teenage sense of immortality may make them disregard the risks. Some teens say they consider condoms unesthetic or too open an admission of the intention to "do it." They thus start their sex lives in a manner that's quite likely to give them a sexually transmitted disease (including AIDS) and/or an unwanted pregnancy. Many teenagers commonly wait over a year after first intercourse before receiving reliable contraceptives or STD-prevention advice. Main reasons given for the delay are fear that parents will find out, aversion to a pelvic exam and mistaken beliefs about the side effects of contraception.

Adolescents need much guidance in coping with sexuality and strong support for the decision to postpone sexual involvement until they feel ready for it. They need reinforcement in believing that their body is their own private possession and that no one — including relatives and friends — has the right to touch it sexually if not wanted. Saying no to sex is every person's option, no matter who they are or what someone else says, and teenagers need to know that it's perfectly normal to do so.

Sex education is still far too scanty

Parents and educators need to candidly discuss sexuality, well before youngsters reach adolescence, with explicit information on both pregnancy avoidance and STD prevention. Adolescents should recognize the similarities and differences between male and female roles, how values affect decisions, the importance of self-confidence in one's own choice, the need to respect the choices of others and that prompt treatment of an STD can prevent serious health impairment. And they need to know how to say no to sex and feel comfortable with the decision.

Yet many teenagers don't know where to get *precise* advice on sexuality and ways to avoid unwanted pregnancy or protect themselves against STDs. School sex-education courses tend to be short and factual, emphasizing reproductive function rather than sexual choices, emotions or decision-making skills. While many parents relegate sex education to health professionals and educators, studies suggest that that is hardly enough. And parents don't fill the gap. Surveys show that high school students would like to receive sex-related information from parents but perceive parental knowledge as "inadequate." Numerous studies report that two-thirds or more of adolescents can't communicate with their parents about sex, and many parents wrongly assume that

---

FOR HEALTHIER, SAFER SEX, ADOLESCENTS MUST :

- clearly understand male and female reproductive roles and functions;
- be well informed about sexuality and intercourse, its pleasures, risks and health consequences;
- feel proud and comfortable about their bodies;
- have a strong sense of self;
- be aware of sexual feelings;
- realize that sexuality is natural and normal;
- be able to share and discuss sexual wishes or aversions;
- know about birth control and how to avoid unwanted pregnancy;
- know about the different sexually transmitted diseases, how they're contracted, what the signs and effects are and what to do about them;
- know where to get information, advice and help (e.g., from family physicians, school nurses, guidance counselors, planned parenthood organizations or STD clinics).

---

their children don't wish to, even though in fact they'd like to talk to parents about it.

Contrary to popular opinion, sex education is not part of everyday schooling. According to one Planned Parenthood Association, while Canadian national guidelines for sex education are underway, at present education given in schools is haphazard and hampered by controversy and lack of trained leadership. "In fact," states one counselor, "between grades 8 and 13, most teens may encounter one non-mandatory unit on sexuality in one required physical health and safety course (if they are not off doing an alternative project or team practice or skipping class). Sexual health is just not a number-one priority for harassed educators."

In talking to teenagers about sexuality it's wise to be matter-of-fact and nonjudgmental, steering away from joking about a matter they take very seriously. Parents can admit to embarrassment or discomfort (if that's the case) — teenagers respect honesty. It's essential to honor the adolescent's privacy and not to pry about things they don't want to talk about. And it's useful to provide detailed, practical, up-to-date pamphlets, books and other materials answering questions about sex, and to suggest easily accessible, neutral sources for reliable advice — such as family-planning units, STD clinics, pediatricians, family doctors and local health units.

Physicians can play a major role in helping to prevent unwanted adolescent pregnancy and

STDs by encouraging questions, giving explicit information and making it clear that adolescents are responsible for their own sexual health but that adults can and will arm them with knowledge. Although teens ultimately decide for themselves when, how and with whom to have sex, it may help to suggest that they talk to each other about the use of condoms and other safer ways to have sex.

Adolescents need to know that they are not alone in having to practice safer sex in the age of AIDS. Although not a long-term option for most young people, abstinence from intercourse is increasingly considered an acceptable choice. (And it's still all right to say no even if you're not a virgin.) "Calls for abstinence are probably less effective," says one University of Toronto pediatrician, "than suggesting postponement of sexual intercourse until ready." Abstinence can be defined as refraining from intercourse rather than restraint from all sexual activity. Teenagers can be encouraged to choose nonpenetrative yet pleasurable intimacy (or "outercourse") rather than intercourse — in short, "everything but." Kissing and mutual massage are safer, noninsertive ways to enjoy sexual contact, provided there is no exchange of body fluids. Giving valid scientific reasons can strengthen the argument: the sexual health of teenage girls is enhanced by postponing intercourse because the immature cervix is easily invaded by the human papilloma virus, chlamydia, gonorrhea and other infective organisms.

RISK-TAKING BEHAVIOR

Embarking on the road to emancipation and self-determination, adolescents may participate in potentially destructive activities. Experimenting with a vast variety of new experiences, many take inordinate risks — sometimes unaware of or stridently denying the possible consequences.

Parents may be dumbfounded by the adolescent's urge to practice dangerous behavior, often with an air of invincibility that belies the uncertainty beneath. The gap between the teenager's abilities and the adult view of them frequently leads to arguments. The failure of adults to appreciate and encourage developing teenage capacities can increase reliance upon peer groups which may encourage further risk-taking, where teenagers participate for the badge of "belonging."

Risk behaviors are usually exacerbated by alcohol or drug use and early sexual activity. Although most adolescents don't lie when questioned about their actions, they are unlikely to volunteer such information. Often, knowledge of friends and a glance around the teenager's room — which typically contains the adolescent's entire worldly belongings — may reveal risk-taking tendencies. Discarded games and stuffed animals are jumbled together with objects portraying new interests — posters, books, audio, video and computer equipment. Parents may be alerted to sexual activity or drug use by the discovery of injection and other paraphernalia left lying around, or by the types of books and magazines.

Runaway behavior

Defined as "unauthorized absence from home," the behavior is tried by many adolescents, typically those aged 15 to 17, mostly from white, suburban families. The average stay away from home is less than three days (72 percent of runaways), with about 15 percent staying away up to two weeks and only 13 percent leaving home for longer. The return home is a personal decision in over half the adolescent runaways, and prompted by parental or peer influence in the rest. About 6 percent never return home.

Reasons given for running away range from school failure or lack of communication with parents to revenge for some disciplinary action or peer imitation. Family rows may trigger the action. It's often a declaration that things at home have become unbearable due to excessive "tightening of the reins" — or a statement of autonomy perhaps because of a lack of trust, or the family's refusal to grant independence. One out of four runaways is labeled a "throwaway" — forced to go or excluded from the family rather than running by choice. In some parts of the United States, an estimated one in eight teenagers runs away at least once. Sometimes the adolescent's strengthening peer relationships and shifting loyalties lead the family either to try to bind closer ("enmesh") or to unwittingly "expel" the youngster. Family dynamics that may predispose adolescent runaways include emotional arguments, overly strict rules, lack of interest or adult alcohol and drug use.

Peers can play a strong role in runaway behavior. As one psychiatrist puts it, "having a friend who's not liked or sanctioned by the parents might force a choice between family and friend. With disrupted family ties or frequent conflicts at home, the teen will likely opt for the disfavored friend or peer group (which promises acceptance and support)." But running away may endanger the teen, who gives up a caring, concerned environment for uncertain shelter and security. The result can be a disastrous chain reaction with reduced opportunities, inadequate nutrition, poor hygiene, lack of support, loss of the sense of "belonging" and increasing isolation. Separating from the family before they have forged a clear identity of their own puts runaway adolescents at high risk.

THE HEAVY TOLL OF ADOLESCENT SUICIDE

The intentional self-destruction of a life is an almost incomprehensible tragedy. Yet suicide is now a leading cause of death among Canadian men aged 15 to 24, the rate having tripled in the last 30 years, especially among teenagers. With about 3,500 completed suicides a year, Canada supposedly has one of the world's highest suicide rates, males greatly outnumbering females as suicide "completers," although females outnumber males as "attempters."

Statistics for 1990–91 show a suicide rate in Canada of 13 per 100,000, with four times more men than women completing the act but more women attempting it. For children under age 14, the suicide rate is very low, rising at ages 14 to 19 to 11–13 per 100,000 for males and 1–3 per 100,000 for females. (The rate is highest between ages 20 and 29.) Of those who try to kill themselves, one in 50 to one in 100 succeeds, and there are repeat tries in 6 to 16 percent of suicide attempters. Of methods used in Canada, firearms top the list for males, followed by suffocation (hanging, drowning), piercing with a sharp instrument and poisonings. In females, poisonings are the most frequent method, followed by

hanging, jumping from heights and suffocation, only a few trying firearms.

Suicides are especially common among aboriginal (Native) populations. Death by suicide among Canada's Native populations is almost four times higher than for the rest of Canada, half the suicides being in the 15–24 age range, often occurring in clusters. One suicide often sets the stage for more — perhaps by making it appear to be "permissible" behavior. Contributing factors are the loss of traditional values, religion and culture, alcoholism, dysfunctional families, poor adult role models and media publicity about suicides.

Adolescence is an especially vulnerable period

Adolescence is a particular danger time for suicide, as it's a period of change and challenge. One U.S. study found that 10–20 percent of 15–19-year-olds had "some suicidal thoughts and intentions"; a French study of 13–16-year-olds living outside Paris found that one in 20 boys and one in 10 girls frequently "thought about suicide." In an Ontario survey, the prevalence of suicidal behavior or thoughts was 5–10 percent in boys, 10–20 percent among girls. A suicide attempt may be a call for help or may represent a final gesture of hopelessness. For the family, suicide imposes grief at the loss, rage at the act, a sense of waste and guilt for having failed as parents.

Factors commonly linked to suicide

Conditions thought to play a role in suicide include: unemployment, broken homes, low morale, social chaos and mental illness. Suicides

---

THOSE MOST AT RISK FOR COMMITTING SUICIDE:

- **Native populations, such as Indians, Métis and the Inuit (with suicide rates four times that in the rest of Canada);**
- **the bereaved — those who have suffered the recent loss of a close family member, friend or** other loved one;
- **alcohol abusers — alcohol impairs judgment and may induce someone to "finish the job";**
- **people from dysfunctional homes with a disrupted family life or hostile family relationships;**
- **persons with a history of previous suicide attempts;**
- **people with relatives who committed suicide;**
- **isolated individuals, with no social support network (family, friends, church group).**

FACTORS AND EVENTS THAT MAY TRIGGER SUICIDE:

- loss or death of a "significant" person;
- break-up of an intimate relationship with a friend, relative, girlfriend or boyfriend;
- alienation from family and friends;
- low self-esteem;
- feelings of failure;
- divorce or separation of parents;
- too few rules or guidelines within the family;
- overly high parental expectations;
- obsessive perfectionism and teenage

- anxiety about falling short of expectations (their own or those of parents);
- reduced school performance — an inability to achieve or maintain a valued position in school or to get good grades;
- truancy, running away, theft;
- inability to cope with stress;
- disciplinary incidents at school or at home;
- a family history of major depression or alcoholism;
- family turmoil,

- quarrels or disputes;
- physical or sexual abuse/assault;
- publicity about suicide in others — inducing a chain reaction (especially common in Native peoples);
- a chronic or debilitating physical illness;
- mental illnesses (e.g., anxiety disorders, schizophrenia, manic-depression, obsessive-compulsive disorder);
- a previous suicide attempt.

are especially prevalent among the mentally disordered. Retrospective studies show that up to 80 to 90 percent of suicides had definable psychiatric problems, such as major depression (not just sadness), bipolar disorder (manic-depression), anxiety disorders or schizophrenia. Someone may also be predisposed to suicide if there's a family history of depression or manic-depression. Substance abuse, especially of alcohol, may contribute by undermining personal functioning and social relationships and by encouraging impulsive, self-destructive acts.

Social factors also count. Isolated individuals without a network of supportive friends are at much the highest risk. Among adolescents, low self-esteem and anxiety arising from the changes they experience often lead to thoughts of self-destruction. Given their inexperience, young people may not realize that disappointments and setbacks are part of everyday life and can be overcome. Poor job prospects, marriage breakdown, moving house, family violence and sexual abuse are also known to fuel a sense of hopelessness and increase suicide risks. Besides stressful life events and emotional fluctuations, having the means of self-destruction — such as firearms or dangerous medications — close at hand increases suicide rates.

Repeated or sensationalized media stories of suicide have a greater impact in precipitating more suicides than a single report about the incident. Media publicity about suicide is often followed by a "rash" or cluster of teen suicides — maybe because this seems to condone the behavior, persuading vulnerable youngsters to mimic it. Schools and communities need to be aware of the dangers and implement preventive strategies.

Depression may play a role in suicide

Depression is more common during adolescence than hitherto recognized and a frequent reason for suicide attempts. Although its extent is unknown, most specialists believe that childhood depression can be as severe as in adults, but identifying it can be difficult. It may be hard to recognize the depth of despondency felt by some young people because their apparent "coolness" or air of invincibility hides the inner despair. Tragically, parents and other adults may overlook it because they *expect* adolescence to be a time of turmoil.

Depression in adolescents is still poorly understood and may vary from mood swings or short-lived episodes to chronic recurrent feelings of worthlessness, helplessness and hopelessness. Depressed adolescents often "act out" their despondency with out-of-control behavior and a rebellious attitude that hides the underlying dejection. The alerting signs of adolescent depression include withdrawal from the family, noncommunication, loss of interest in usual activities and changes in sleep and eating patterns.

Warning signs or markers for suicide

Talk of suicide is often a plea for help and should never be taken lightly. Studies reveal that two-thirds of successful suicides had hinted at their intention before carrying it out. Yet parents often remain oblivious to their youngster's suicidal thoughts, far less aware of their dejected feelings than peers. Physicians, families and teachers should be on the alert for possible signs of suicidal intent — sadness, hopelessness, emptiness, lack of energy, loss of interest in friends, school or hobbies, irritability, conduct disorders (such as truancy), emotional disturbances and mood swings.

Some experts call suicide a "deficiency disease" — a lack of close friendships and social connections. There is a growing recognition that even children aged five to six can already harbor suicidal ideas. In many teens who attempt suicide, a vulnerability already present in childhood, is exacerbated by the demands of adolescence and by family conflicts (if the parents fail to deal adequately with the teenager's developmental process). However, many suicide attempters (and completers) are not "social misfits," but ordinary, anxious teenagers. They may feel increasingly distanced from their family, friends and society, becoming outsiders or loners. The final triggering event may be a failed exam, loss of a boyfriend or girlfriend, pregnancy or a family quarrel. Family cohesion appears to be a protective influence.

Any expressed wish to end life must be taken seriously and never dismissed as an idle threat. Far from being impulsive or "spur-of-the-moment" actions, most suicides are carefully planned. It's crucial to be available to comfort the distressed person and get him or her into treatment promptly if possible. Be particularly suspicious when someone's previously gloomy mood suddenly changes to cheerfulness without sufficient reason. This is often a sign that the person has finally resolved to commit suicide and is relieved that the decision is made.

The easiest way to ferret out suicidal thoughts is to ask whether the teenager has ever thought of "ending it all." Don't be afraid to raise the question for fear of putting ideas into the person's head. Teenagers may come

---

FACTORS IN AND SIGNS OF ADOLESCENT DEPRESSION:

- decreased sense of self-worth; achievements falling short of aspirations;
- significant loss — death of a loved relative or boyfriend/girlfriend;
- separation or divorce of parents;
- loss of boundaries and guidelines within the family;
- inability to cope with developmental tasks of adolescence;
- parental substance abuse;
- family conflicts or poor communication;
- problems with peer relationships; real or imaginary rejection by peers, which

can tip an insecure adolescent into depression;
- a perpetually sad or worried expression;
- loss of interest or pleasure in all activities;
- refusal to go to school, participate in peer activities;
- poor concentration;
- low energy all day long, every day;
- declining schoolwork;
- glum outlook, bleak view of future and own relationship to it;
- excessive self-criticism
- poor stress-coping skills — which may make the slightest challenge seem overwhelming;

- rapid mood swings, irritability, angry outbursts;
- "acting-out behavior" — truancy, running away, sexual promiscuity;
- substance abuse;
- a wish to be "left alone."

Physiological changes (psychosomatic clues):
- constant fatigue;
- insomnia or excessive need for sleep;
- anorexia and weight loss, or significant weight gain or loss even if not dieting;
- menstrual irregularities;
- headaches;
- abdominal pain.

---

right out and confess suicidal intent, and most will talk about other forms of distress. Allow adolescents to open up and speak about what's troubling them. Try questions such as:
- Have you ever felt that life is not worth living?
- Is the feeling urgent?
- How long has the feeling been there?
- Is it increasing in intensity?
- Have you formed any specific plans for killing yourself?

Although each suicide try is different,

POSSIBLE HINTS OF SUICIDAL INTENTION:

- mention of death wishes, or "being a burden," which may remain unvoiced unless someone inquires;
- suicidal letters, quotes, poems, allusions;
- references to death or suicide,

even in jest;
- sense of hopelessness;
- a bleak view of the future;
- aggressive or antisocial conduct;
- irritability, angry outbursts, hostility directed at self or others;
- "acting out" —

conduct disorders, truancy, running away;
- boredom, loss of interest in usual activities;
- understated or vague allusions to suicide or of "being better off dead," possibly revealed in letters,

diaries or essays;
- excessive guilt and expressions of unworthiness;
- expressed fears of becoming insane, losing control, hurting others;
- giving away cherished possessions for no apparent

reason;
- inappropriate preoccupation with making a will;
- a sudden tranquillity or cheery mood in the formerly depressed — indicating that death has been accepted.

many adolescent cases have a pattern that falls into three stages. First, there's a deficiency of close social connections — few family ties, frequent quarrels and no intimate friendships, creating an underlying vulnerability. The background scenario may include alcoholic or abusive parents, unwanted stepparents, divorce or death of a cherished person. In the second or "escalation phase," insecurity is magnified because of family conflict, isolation and again, lack of close friendships. The final event that caps the despair and precipitates the suicide may be the loss of a girl- or boyfriend, a broken friendship, an inability to surmount hurdles, a family quarrel, peer rejection, school failure or some other disappointment.

Access to firearms greatly increases suicide risks

Access to means of suicide, especially firearms, will endanger those at risk and can help them to succeed in killing themselves. Owners of firearms should weigh their reasons for keeping a gun at home against the possibility that it might some day be used for the suicide of their children. Attempts at suicide are a warning sign of future tries — the risk being higher with someone who attempted suicide in a remote site with little chance of discovery. For such instances, family and school should be especially vigilant and try to restrict means of self-destruction.

Suicide-proofing: preventive measures

The best preventive strategy is to promote the mental health and self-esteem of adolescents, to try and identify troubled youngsters at home or in school and to make counseling and mental-health care available to them via teen clinics and mental-healthcare providers. There's a crying need for more suicide-proofing. "Rather than taking a blunderbuss approach to all schoolchildren," says one educationalist, "we must make efforts to screen for and identify vulnerable adolescents, specifically counseling those at risk. This means training parents and high school educators to identify mentally ill youngsters who are at particular risk, such as those suffering from depression, anxiety disorders, schizophrenia and other psychiatric problems."

It's also vital to curb excessive publicity about teen suicides. In order to forestall a copycat rash of suicides, the press might be persuaded to act responsibly and restrict themselves to single, rather than multiple and sensationalized, statements about suicide, preferably not putting them on the front page or at prime viewing time — and refraining from casting the suicide in a heroic or flattering light.

Schools and communities might have a preventive contingency plan in case of a suicide cluster, rather than taking a "wait-and-see" approach. Families can help by showing concern, interest and empathy. There's often a tendency by parents and teachers to brush aside the possible danger of suicide, a reluctance to intervene or say anything in case of worsening the problem. Anyone who is worried about a youngster's suicidal intent should face the possibility and take or guide the adolescent to professional assistance.

If an adolescent talks or even hints of suicide or shows other warning signs, it's imperative to seek professional help so that the risks can be assessed and real intent separated from fleeting thoughts. A thorough examination by a child psychiatrist, psychologist or mental-health team can determine if an adolescent is truly depressed and suicidal. Handling suicidal people deftly depends on familiarity with the person, a good psychiatric assessment and supportive therapy. People who admit that they have definite plans to commit suicide should *not* be left alone and in many cases, are best admitted to hospital. Follow-up of suicide attempts is essential — with counseling and attention to improving school and family relationships. Help for despondent teens is available via pediatricians, psychiatrists, school counselors and telephone hotlines. Make sure the numbers are posted and accessible.

Indigenous or aboriginal Native populations — among whom suicide rates are particularly high — are in special need of suicide-prevention strategies. Because of poverty, poor education and unemployment, many have a low sense of self-worth and try to escape via alcohol use and/or suicide tries. They

ARE YOUR KIDS ON ILLICIT DRUGS?

Signs of excess alcohol/drug use in teenagers:
• suddenly become less affectionate, more irritable, secretive, hostile, depressed, apathetic, withdrawn, unable to sleep or sleeping too much;
• behave less responsibly, neglect chores, don't keep curfew, forget family birthdays or occasions, don't do homework, cut classes;
• drop old friends and adopt new ones, acquiring the habits and language of the new friends, lose interest in school and hobbies;
• become uncommunicative or aggressive, defensive when drugs are mentioned, and voice approval of or concern for friends who use drugs;
• complain of parents "hassling" or "trampling their rights";
• disordered thinking, memory lapses, difficulty with concentration; increased or decreased appetite, heightened sensitivity to taste, touch or smell.

Tips for dealing with drug-taking adolescents
• Don't jump to unwarranted conclusions.
• Respect the adolescent's privacy — searching through belongings will only erode mutual trust and respect.
• Talk with another trusted adult to put things into proper perspective before going to the adolescent.
• When you confront your son or daughter, don't assume he or she is immature, or a drug addict.

The first time you discuss drugs (or alcohol) is very important — how parents react can put an end to the whole matter, or make it worse and drive it underground.
• Handle the problem objectively; face the reality of drug use.
• Avoid moralizing, saying things like "How could you do this?" or "Think of your dismal future."
• Dwell on the person's positive attributes and avoid showing resentment.
• Be honest, empathetic, firm, even-tempered and avoid personal attack on the adolescent's character.
• Express concern about health, explain that you feel worried, hurt.
• Try to stay calm. Reaffirm your continuing love while expressing disapproval of drug use.
• Say what action you intend to take, then follow through.
• If professional help is needed, don't be afraid to seek it.

Many people find parents' support groups invaluable. For example, Parents Against Drugs, an Ontario nonprofit organization, has several chapters across the province, operates a phone-in support line and holds regular seminars for parents, teenagers and teachers, helping kids to say no to drugs. The Addiction Research Foundation in Toronto and other substance-abuse research units across the country can also furnish help and information.

---

need Native-run crisis centers, special training schemes and education in traditional practices that can promote self-esteem, enhance self-awareness and help redefine an individual's "purpose in life."

Suicide-prevention strategies might also include efforts to make lethal methods — such as firearms, poisonous gases and medications less available — by stricter gun laws, detoxification of car exhaust and restricted access to subway lines.

Boosting adolescent self-esteem is crucial

Boosting self-esteem is the key to preventing suicide. Every decision made by young people is influenced by the way they feel about themselves. To prevent suicide, we must promote self-confidence among adolescents so they can better avail themselves of openings and opportunities. Instead of the common tendency to dismiss youth as "callow," "superficial," "self-indulgent" or "lazy," we should value their abundant energy and creative potential, explore their thought styles and try to understand the current teen culture. We must do all we can to make youth feel respected — listening to their opinions and treating them as valued members of society. Young people can be encouraged to participate in the decision-making at home, in school, at work and in the community. A positive step is to signal to teens that their innovative and questioning attitudes offer an invaluable counterpoint to adult perspectives.

Communities should provide recreational

facilities and gathering places where young people can meet, enjoy and define themselves freely, without adults present. Many teenagers complain of a lack of privacy, no place to be on their own, away from the ever-watchful gaze of adults. Teenagers typically say they feel as though they're constantly under scrutiny, being observed, and not trusted or allowed to develop autonomy. We should tap young people's amazing energy, originality and enthusiasm to run their own peer counseling and support groups. Every positive action or contribution by adolescents should be recognized and praised by relatives, teachers, workmates and health professionals.

TEENAGE AND STUDENT DRUG USE

Drug use increased rapidly among high school and college students during the 1960s when many experimented with alternative lifestyles. It peaked in the late 1970s and has declined dramatically since then. The good news is that among both American and Canadian students drug use is less fashionable than in past decades, perhaps because of rising health concerns.

Experimenting with drugs doesn't inevitably lead to addiction. Many young people sample drugs at school or college, for fun or to go along with their peer group, trying whatever is the "in" thing. Alcohol, tobacco and marijuana remain the most popular teen drugs and, being an illicit substance, marijuana may act as a "gateway" to use of other illicit drugs. If drug use begins in adolescence, it's more likely to occur in adult life, although most young people who do drugs try them out of curiosity once or twice and then abandon them.

The teenagers most likely to try illicit drugs are those with companions who can procure them. Those who do use drugs may use several. Adolescents who use drugs just to go along with the group are less likely to continue beyond their twenties than those who take them up for personal enjoyment or because of underlying psychological factors. Teenage use of alcohol is also a matter of concern. Having experimented with many illegal drugs, young people today seem to prefer legal, easily obtainable alcohol.

If illicit drug use does continue, however, new associations and new companions may be woven into everyday life, making the pattern hard to break. The story of a young Montreal art student is typical. As a shy teenager, low in self-esteem, she smoked marijuana at school to please her peers, gradually becoming a regular user. Later she tried heroin too, mainly to alleviate depression after her boyfriend left her. After that she took marijuana daily and heroin several times a week, neglecting her studies. Her finances were depleted by her drug habit, which finally led her to a therapist for help. Explaining the powerful grip of heroin on her life, she told a therapy group that "at first I only took a little at weekend parties but then I bought my own supplies, because even if my body didn't physically desire the drug, inside my head I was terrified I'd run out when I needed it. Now I haven't had 'smack' [heroin] or marijuana for over six weeks, and I think I'm going to kick it." (See also chapter 2, the section on drug and alcohol use.)

Modern environmental health hazards

Allergies • Hay fever • Insect allergies • Food allergies • "Total allergy syndrome" • Tight-building syndrome • How safe is our drinking water? • Getting the lead out • Coping with temperature extremes • Staying fit on the job • Toward healthier global travel

ENVIRONMENTAL pollution is an unavoidable by-product of modern industrialized society. Our consumer-driven culture provides us with a high standard of living but also exposes us to ever-increasing contaminants in the air we breathe, the water we drink, the food we eat and our workplaces. We know that certain substances (such as PCBs and dioxins) cause cancer, that workplace chemicals (such as cereal dusts and soldering fumes) worsen asthma and that heavy metals (such as lead) can cause learning problems. While we can't protect ourselves from all environmental risks, being aware of them and minimizing our exposure to some of them can help us to reduce their health-harming effects.

For example:
- Running the water in older homes with lead pipes for three minutes each morning before drinking it can reduce risks of lead poisoning.
- Avoiding the midday sun and consistently using sunscreens can reduce skin-cancer risks.
- Breastfeeding an infant born to allergy-prone parents can delay the onset and possibly reduce the likelihood of allergic reactions (such as hay fever or asthma) in that child.
- Wearing protective clothing (long sleeves and long pants) and using insect repellents can lessen the danger of insect bites and the disorders they spread — such as encephalitis (from

mosquitoes) and Lyme disease (from ticks).
- Keeping the house dust-free can reduce asthmatic attacks in those sensitive to dust mites.
- Regularly cleaning air conditioners and humidifiers can minimize the risk of infections from the microorganisms they harbor.
- Not smoking in the home reduces risks of childhood respiratory illnesses.

ALLERGIES

An estimated 15 to 20 percent of North Americans have allergies, and they tend to run in families. A child with one allergic parent has a one-in-four chance of developing allergies. If both parents are allergy-prone, there's a two-in-three chance.

The tendency to regard all pollutants as allergy-provokers is a false generalization, as some merely cause irritation — such as a cough, sore throat or skin irritation — rather than a true allergic reaction.

Allergies are definite immunological reactions

A true allergic reaction is an inflammatory or immune-system response, with observable skin, breathing and/or other changes, brought on in certain people by repeated exposure to specific substances.

The allergy-provoking agents — known as allergens — include biologicals (such as pollens or other plant components), pharmaceuticals (such as sulfa drugs or penicillin), foods (such as

13

components in eggs or nuts) and synthetics (such as toluene dyes or isocyanates in furnishings). The most common and annoying allergens include inhalants — such as animal dander, pollens and molds. More dangerous allergens include insect venoms and specific foods such as peanuts (which are not really nuts but legumes), seeds, nuts (for example, walnuts) and shellfish (such as lobster, crab and shrimp).

An allergic response results from the body's remarkable ability to distinguish "self" from "nonself" or "foreign" substances, and its attempt to fend off those that are "nonself." In sensitive individuals, the offending substance or allergen — which is harmless to most people — causes overreaction of the body's immune system. Whether inhaled, ingested, injected or absorbed through the skin, the allergen provokes the manufacture of specific antibodies known as IgE (immunoglobin type E) antibodies. The IgE antibodies bind to special mast cells and are carried around the body by the bloodstream.

The reaction between the allergen and IgE antibodies on the mast cells triggers the release of a powerful cocktail of vasoactive (from the Latin *vas*, meaning "vessel") mediators. These substances, such as leukotrienes, histamines and others, make blood vessels leak and cause swelling and congestion, producing a sometimes violent inflammation — with hives (a red weal or spreading rash), swelling of the tongue and throat, weepy eyes and other reactions.

Scientists speculate that the allergic response arose as a protective evolutionary strategy to ward off parasites. Nonallergic people also produce some antibodies to common allergens, but their central control mechanism suppresses an unnecessarily large immune response. The explosive response of allergy-prone people to relatively harmless allergens amounts to overkill.

Specificity is the hallmark of the allergic response: it's a specific immunological reaction. For example, someone allergic to plicatic acid, found in western red cedar dust, will form IgE antibodies on inhaling this chemical, reacting with throat swelling, wheezing and other symptoms. Those sensitive to the allergen (protein) in cat dander form IgE antibodies and react with wheezing, hives, skin itching and other symptoms. Thus, while the "foreign" substances that cause allergies vary widely, the reactions they set off are specific, identifiable and predictable.

The symptoms typical of an allergic reaction include wheezing, coughing, skin itching, hives, perhaps also shortness of breath, vomiting and — in severe cases — weakness, collapse, even death. A rare but severe *generalized* allergic response that affects the whole body can put it into anaphylactic shock — a life-endangering condition with some or all of the above, as well as flushing, swelling of the eyelids, mouth and throat (which threatens breathing), confusion and perhaps a sense of impending doom. Blood pressure may drop precipitously, depriving the heart and brain of oxygen — leading to blue lips (cyanosis) and unconsciousness, and possibly death within minutes unless immediate medical relief is available. (See "Allergic shock" in chapter 17 for emergency treatment.)

Delayed allergic reactions are less common but may occur in some instances, starting four, six or more hours after exposure to the allergen, peaking at around 48 hours. Delayed reactions, which may be a result of IgE or other types of antibodies, are also very distressing and the major factor in allergic asthma.

It takes more than one exposure to sensitize someone to a particular allergen. As a rule, on the first encounter nothing happens. It may even take several exposures to get the manufacture of IgE antibodies going. But once the

DIAGNOSING ALLERGIES

Allergists try their best to pinpoint the offending allergen(s) so that people can avoid them, but that's not always easy. Sometimes the culprit is obvious — a family pet or eating eggs — but often it's hard to discover exactly what sets off the allergic reaction. Accurate diagnosis depends on detailed history-taking and sometimes a series of tests.

Skin or "prick" tests, although not very specific, are commonly used as a cheap, easy way to identify allergens. Tiny amounts of suspected allergens are inserted into a series of shallow punctures (scratches) in the skin of the arm or back. An allergic person responds within about 15 minutes with hista-mine release and the development of a local red weal and flare where the allergen was inserted.

The RAST (radio-allergosorbent test) analyzes a small sample of blood for the presence of specific IgE antibodies. It is more complex, less reliable, less sensitive, more expensive and more time-consuming than skin-testing.

body is fully sensitized to a specific allergen, the IgE antibodies are produced whenever it enters the body, setting off the reactions.

A typical case is a 40-year-old man, sensitized to penicillin (which he'd received for an infected leg wound in his teens), who went into allergic shock when he was again injected with the drug after a car accident. In his case, the emergency crew recognized the reaction, guessed he was allergic to penicillin and immediately administered a life-saving adrenaline shot. Sometimes allergic shock goes unrecognized, and a sudden death may be mistakenly attributed to a heart attack or some other disorder.

Avoiding allergens is the best bet

There are three main ways to manage your allergy: remove or avoid the causative agent; reduce the inflammation with drugs; or (possibly) decrease sensitivity with allergic immunotherapy.

Allergy treatment includes:

- steroids — either topically (in a cream) or by mouth or via an inhaler — to mute the inflammatory response;
- antihistamines — with a wide range to choose from, the newer ones being less sedating;
- eyedrops or nasal spray of disodium cromoglycate to help prevent attacks;
- immunotherapy — allergy injections to prevent the reaction — a final resort for those with hay fever but essential for people with severe bee and wasp allergies. (This method is only partially successful for most other allergies.) Gradually increasing doses of the allergen are given, starting with dilute amounts at short intervals, increasing the dose over a period of two to five years.

For anaphylactic shock, the first step is to inject adrenaline (epinephrine) to constrict the small blood vessels and raise the blood pressure. This may be followed by injection of antihistamines and/or steroids, plus use of life-support systems in hospital.

People who know they are susceptible to acute reactions should wear a medical identification bracelet mentioning their particular allergy, and carry a pocket emergency kit — such as the EpiPen, a spring-loaded syringe containing adrenaline that's very easy to use,

and available by prescription. Should no improvement show within 15 minutes of the adrenaline injection, waste no time in getting to the nearest hospital. Always seek medical advice after an allergic attack.

HAY FEVER CAN RUIN LIFE'S PLEASURES

Hay fever is a popular misnomer for allergic rhinitis — it's *not* usually due to hay. Afflicting 15 percent of Canadians, it's a seasonal irritation of the nose, eyes, throat and lungs in response to lightweight, wind-carried pollens. Said to be a modern epidemic, this condition now affects millions around the world.

In Canada, the pollens that cause hay fever come from trees during early spring; in June and July the villains are grass pollens; and in late summer and fall, weeds, particularly ragweed, are the culprits. (Heavier, sticky pollens of plants such as goldenrod, dandelion and most garden flowers do not trigger this type of allergy.) Allergies provoked by other allergens typically occur at different times. House-dust allergies, for example, are usually worst in fall when windows are closed and the furnace starts up.

The all-too-familiar symptoms of hay fever

The first sign of hay fever is often a smarting, burning sensation in the nose and eyes. The nose becomes red from constant blowing. Children often develop an "allergic salute" — an upward nose-rubbing action to alleviate the

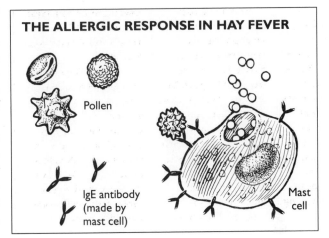

THE ALLERGIC RESPONSE IN HAY FEVER

Pollen

IgE antibody
(made by
mast cell)

Mast
cell

MEDICAL HAY-FEVER REMEDIES

• Topical corticosteroids such as beclomethasone (Beconase), flunisolide (Rhinolon) and budenoside (Rhinocort) — the mainstay of allergy treatments — are the agents of choice for hay fever. Used as a nasal spray and inhaled daily during the hay-fever season, they are about 90 percent effective in relieving nasal symptoms with no major side effects.

• Antihistamines — whatever type suits you best — can help to control symptoms. However, antihistamines can have side effects — especially drowsiness and fatigue — which may interfere with driving, work and other activities. (They should not be taken with alcohol, as the two make a dangerous mix.) The new, nondrowsy varieties suit some hay-fever sufferers. The longer-acting types include astemizole (Hismanal), terfenadine (Seldane) and loratadine (Claritin). Hismanal is designed for regular preventive use and takes time to work. However, the stated dose shouldn't be exceeded, as an excess can cause heart palpitations and other adverse reactions in some people. Both astemizole and terfenadine reportedly can cause cardiovascular effects when used in excess, or with the antibiotic erythromycin or the antifungal drug ketoconazole.

• Topical (local) nasal decongestants can be used very occasionally, but never regularly, or they may cause "rebound" congestion. In the long run, decongestant nose sprays exacerbate rather than halt hay-fever symptoms and are best reserved for situations of extreme nasal stuffiness such as at night when sleep is hampered.

allergic itch. As the nasal passages get swollen and obstructed, sneezing fits ensue and the nose discharges a clear, thin fluid unlike the thick, colored drip of a typical cold. The eyes get watery — eyelashes of hay fever sufferers are typically wet and silky, the eyes often encircled with dark "allergic shiners" caused by the engorged blood vessels around them. The voice becomes husky as the irritation spreads to throat and lungs. Hay fever can start up within 10 minutes of pollen grains entering the body, and tissues become more responsive with continued aggravation, giving almost constant misery. Once the triggering pollens have left the scene, usually after the first fall frost, the symptoms vanish.

Much seasonal discomfort can be prevented if hay-fever sufferers take a few simple measures:

• Avoid treks through woods and fields.
• Air-condition the home or at least the bedroom, and keep the windows shut; keep the vent on the air conditioner closed to prevent the inflow of pollens.
• Use bedding made of synthetic fibers, as it's easily washed. Consider covering mattresses with plastic or other impervious covers, sealed with a zipper. Wash bed sheets weekly, and blankets regularly, on the hot-water cycle.
• Allow no pets in the bedroom and remove all carpets from the bedroom.
• Try lingering in the morning shower, while breathing deeply, to clear the sinuses.
• Take exercise indoors in pollen season.
• Discard mildewed or damp objects which may harbor molds.
• Keep the basement clean and dry.
• Steer clear of nonspecific irritants that may aggravate hay fever — cigarette smoke, dust, drafts, alcohol (which is a histamine-releaser) and even contact lenses (which may aggravate the eye irritation).

INSECT ALLERGIES: WHAT BIT OR STUNG YOU?

Insect secretions can produce reactions ranging from a barely perceptible itch to a life-threatening allergic response. The first documented insect-allergy death was King Menes of Egypt, who, according to the hieroglyphics on his tomb, died of a wasp or hornet sting in 2621 B.C. No one knows exactly how many fatalities occur each year from insect allergies but the real number may be far greater than records suggest, since some such deaths may be misattributed to heat stroke or heart attacks.

Specific insect venoms can cause an immediate response or a delayed reaction — hours or even days after an encounter. The faster the allergic response, the more serious it usually is. In some allergy-prone individuals, insect venoms can not only trigger production of IgE antibodies, but sometimes cause a massive histamine release that rapidly affects the entire body.

Insect allergens can penetrate the body via a piercing bite or a sting from the insect's rear, or by inhalation of wind-blown hairs, spines or other insect parts. Most of these insects either bite or sting, but a few, such as some ants, are both biters and stingers. Bites normally cause milder symptoms than stings because less venom is injected.

Biting insects — such as blackflies, horseflies and deerflies, bedbugs, lice, fleas, mosquitoes and ants — attack humans mainly in search of blood. In order to obtain the blood, biters release enzymes that soften the skin and dilate the blood vessels. These salivary secretions can trigger an immediate or delayed allergic response.

Stinging insects — such as the honeybee and other bees, hornets, yellow jackets and wasps — attack either in self-defense or to subdue prey. Their stingers inject venom, a potent substance that can cause severe allergies, even sudden death. Insect venom is a remarkably powerful toxic substance — mostly protein — in some instances able to totally paralyze prey by a neuromuscular block. Although some experts reserve the term "venom" exclusively for insect-sting chemicals, the scientific definition is "any poisonous matter that animals secrete and insert into other animals by biting or stinging."

Those allergic to insects are usually sensitive to just one species, although there can be cross-reactivity: for example, people allergic to hornets may also react to yellow-jacket stings. The most frequent insect allergies arise from

ALLERGIC REACTIONS TO INSECT STINGS OR BITES MAY BE:

- a moderate local reaction with swelling and itchy redness appearing within about 20 minutes, lasting a few hours and fading without serious consequences;
- an extensive local reaction with a huge, hot swelling — reaching maybe from wrist to shoulder, or ankle to thigh — that is very bothersome but still more or less around the attack site;
- a generalized systemic reaction, occurring within minutes or (rarely) seconds, involving many other areas of the body, with itchy hands and feet, widespread hives, chest tightness, wheezing, abdominal cramps, diarrhea and faintness. These symptoms may occur without much local discomfort at the actual sting or bite site and require prompt medical assistance. (See above and in chapter 17, under "Allergic shock.")

yellow-jacket stings, followed by wasps, hornets and bees. Children tend to grow out of their insect allergies. By contrast, those never previously allergic to insects may become so in later life. If someone has had a generalized body reaction to insects, even a mild one, skin tests should be done to determine the type and extent of the allergy, and preventive steps should be taken.

A FEW CAUTIONARY TIPS ABOUT INSECT STINGS OR BITES

- Avoid insect attractants such as cooking smells, outdoor picnics, messy garbage, pet food, perfumes and cosmetics.
- Don't wear bright or shiny objects or clothes, as these attract most daytime insects, especially stingers (although mosquitoes like dark colors). White, light green and khaki seem least attractive

to insects.
- If you know you're severely allergic to insects, try not to be alone outdoors, so that others are around in case of need.
- Behave calmly around insects. Sudden movements and flailing arms frighten them into self-defensive action.
- Be especially vigilant when it's humid, as some

insects are angrier in wet weather.
- Garden cautiously. Take care not to disturb a nest or a bunch of wasps feeding on garbage; avoid use of clippers on hanging plants or places that may conceal insects or their nests.
- Be on the lookout for hidden nests — often under eaves, decks, fallen logs, compost heaps, hanging vines.

- Should a hazardous insect enter your vehicle, don't attempt to drive. Pull off the road and swish it out carefully.
- Try using insect repellent containing diethyl-m-toluamide (DEET), for instance, Muskol. Products containing citronella oil, ethyl hexanediol and dimethyl phthalate may also repel some insects. Put repellents on the skin

(avoiding the eyes) or spray on clothes.
- Immunotherapy or desensitizing shots are recommended for those allergic to honeybees, yellow jackets, hornets and certain wasps. Appropriate skin testing with very dilute amounts of pure venom can pinpoint the allergy and indicate who's a suitable candidate for immunotherapy.

What to do about insect attacks

If stung or bitten, gently flick off the offending insect. Don't run but walk (overheating increases toxin absorption); a dip in cold water or a nearby lake may minimize the reaction by constricting blood vessels, and by stimulating a natural adrenaline release through the shock of hitting cold water.

If stung by a bee, which leaves its stinger in its victim, flick or scrape off the stinger. Never squeeze the stinger as it only injects more venom.

For mild local symptoms such as redness, swelling and itching, wash the attack site, perhaps swabbing with antiseptic. Use an ice pack or cold compress and elevate the leg, arm or other part, if possible. Try antihistamines to reduce itchiness. Apply a steroid or combined steroid-antibiotic cream to reduce inflammation and prevent infection. The absorption can be enhanced by rubbing the cream in and covering the area with plastic wrap secured with cellulose tape.

For a severe local response, seek medical attention. As first aid for a sting on a limb, put a tourniquet between the attack site and the heart, to prevent the spread of venom — releasing after 60 seconds. The physician may prescribe steroid tablets (such as prednisone).

For an ensuing infection at the bite site consult a physician.

Be alert to the possibility of spread to the rest of the body, and get to hospital quickly at the first hint of anaphylactic shock (see above and chapter 17, "Allergic shock" and "Bites and stings.")

Beware of insects that carry diseases

Blackflies, common day-biters in northern U.S. and Canadian cottage country (particularly in May and June), are tiny, stout-bodied insects, sometimes visible in swarms. Their razor-sharp mouth parts can bore a hole in you silently and swiftly, producing a large, red weal three to four centimeters (an inch or more) across. Although blackflies are more a nuisance than a danger in Canada, in West Africa and some parts of South America they carry small nematode worms responsible for river blindness.

Sand flies, known as gnats or "no-see-ums" because of their tiny size, get through some screens and can cause extensive local allergies, but while one person itches madly, another remains untouched!

Mosquitoes, known as the "king of disease-carriers," are the most medically devastating of insects, owing to the various disease organisms they carry — the protozoa responsible for malaria, tiny nematode worms that cause elephantiasis and, in Canada, western equine encephalitis. This viral illness — a sporadic problem in the western provinces, especially in a heavy mosquito year — attacks the nervous system, hitting more children than adults (about 5–15 cases a year) and sometimes inflicting permanent paralysis, deafness and mental disability.

Fleas are blood-eaters that carry no diseases in Canada, but are renowned elsewhere for spreading bubonic plague. Fleas prefer other animals (especially rodents) and only jump onto humans when pets die or go away.

Fire ants, named after their fiery bite, are not a hazard here but are a fearsome pest in many parts of the United States, particularly Florida. Residual scarring and severe allergic reactions can occur from fire-ant venom.

Spiders, universally feared owing to the superstitions surrounding them, are usually harmless, but some, such as the tarantula and black widow, can inflict lethal injury on humans. Another type common in North America, the brown recluse spider, causes considerable aggravation, with nasty, spreading blisters that can leave unsightly scars.

FOOD ALLERGIES: ONE PERSON'S MEAT IS ANOTHER'S POISON

Although virtually any food can trigger an allergy in a susceptible person, some of the most common allergens are in eggs, cow's milk, peanuts, nuts, seafood (especially shrimp, oysters and lobster), wheat, celery and certain seeds. People can be allergic not only to natural food ingredients but also occasionally to preservatives and "fresheners" (such as sulfiting agents).

Someone who reacts to one food may also have an allergic response to other similar foods. For example, those sensitive to peanuts may also react to soy products. Those allergic to tree pollens may react with an itchy mouth to certain fruits (such as apples, plums, pears,

POISON IVY

The poison-ivy plant, toxicodendron, is a common weed of the cashew family that grows from coast to coast in North America. (There are several related plants, and names vary from place to place — "poison ivy," "poison oak," "poison sumac" — but the term "poison ivy" will be used here to cover all of them.) Contact with the leaves or oil of poison ivy causes a nasty skin eruption or allergic contact dermatitis in about 70 percent of people. All parts of this plant — leaves, roots and stem — contain the chemical urushiol, responsible for the skin reaction, which ranges from mild to severe.

Poison ivy causes a delayed hypersensitivity reaction which, in contrast to hay fever and most food allergies, involves not IgE antibodies but sensitized T-cells. An initial exposure is necessary to "sensitize" the person, after which subsequent exposures result in the typical poison-ivy rash — a red, itchy, weepy eruption with fluid-filled blisters. The rash may occur in streaks where the plant or its oil touched the skin, usually develops within 24–48 hours of contact and may last for days or weeks.

Washing immediately may prevent the itchy rash from developing, but unfortunately many people are unaware that they have encountered this noxious plant or its oils until the streaky, red, itchy rash appears.

Poison ivy or its oil can cause a rash even if someone touches the dead plant in winter, or if it gets onto a sensitive person's clothes from the smoke of burning plants or if oil is touched on the fur of pets. Most commonly, though, the oil is released onto the skin when the plant is trodden on or broken, and spread by touch. People can suffer a repeat outbreak if they later don contaminated clothing. The rash itself is not contagious and doesn't spread from person to person once the oil is washed off the skin.

The problem is usually worst in those with other skin problems, such as psoriasis or acne. If someone is very sensitive or allergic to the urushiol, a severe reaction can occur that requires immediate medical attention.

The best remedy is prevention — learning to recognize the plant and avoid touching it. If it grows in your neighborhood, post a color photo of the plant where children (and guests) will see it. Next best is to remove the oil from the skin as soon as possible. If the oil has been on the skin for less than two to six hours, thorough washing with ordinary soap (not forgetting to clean under the fingernails) will often prevent or lessen the reaction. If the oil is removed within five to ten minutes of contact, a rash may be avoided. Alcohol-based cleansing tissues, available in pre-packaged form (such as Alco-wipe), are effective. Rubbing alcohol on a washcloth is even better. Clothing should be washed separately in hot water and detergent. Also wash a pet suspected of contact.

The best treatment for mild local cases is a topical corticosteroid cream (such as Cortone, Cortaid or betamethasone valerate), and for severe cases or generalized rashes a seven- to ten-day course of oral corticosteroids (such as prednisone). Antihistamines such as Benadryl, or less sedating types like terfenadine (Seldane) or astemizole (Hismanal), may help to reduce the itching. Always see a physician for a severe poison-ivy rash.

Once the rash appears, keep the blisters clean and dry. Cool compresses, ice packs or aluminum acetate (Burow's) solution applied for 20–30 minutes every few hours helps to dry out the blisters and soothe the itching. Bathing in tepid water with colloidal oatmeal (Aveenol) may also help. Soothing calamine lotion may be applied to the affected skin. Beware of other over-the-counter preparations that could worsen the condition — especially those containing benzocaine.

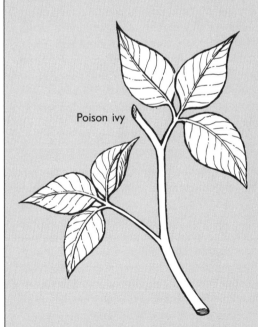

Poison ivy

The identifying features of poison ivy are its three (and sometimes more) shiny, toothed or lobed leaves, the middle leaf being larger than the two side ones. It grows as a droopy vine or shrub, and its flowers and berries are greenish to white.

TIPS FOR SAFER FOOD HANDLING AND PREPARATION

- *Buy perishables and frozen foods last at the supermarket;* get them home and into the refrigerator promptly. Check "best before" dates on perishable items. If expired, report to the store manager.
- *To avoid botulism, take great care in home bottling,* don't buy foods in cracked jars, swollen or dented cans and don't eat canned goods that have a milky instead of the usually clear liquid around them. Never taste suspect goods — discard, well-wrapped in plastic. ("When in doubt, throw it out"!)
- *Freeze meat, fish and poultry as soon as possible after purchasing.* Freeze in freezer bags to prevent "freezer burn," which makes meat tough when cooked. Date the frozen packages. In general, fresh meats can be kept safely frozen for six to 12 months, hamburgers for three to four months, ham for two months, bacon for only one. Fish shouldn't be kept frozen for more than four months.
- *Refrigerate raw poultry, fish, ground meat and liver* for no longer than two days and other uncooked meats no more than five days. Keep cooked meat dishes refrigerated for at most three to four days.
- *Refrigerate cooked leftovers* promptly, dividing into small portions for fast chilling. Make sure that the warm food doesn't touch cold, already refrigerated products.
- *Defrost or thaw foods inside the refrigerator or in a microwave* oven rather than on the kitchen counter. Cook soon after thawing.
- *Carefully follow package instructions* for store-bought frozen foods (e.g., frozen dinners which state "do not thaw before cooking").
- *Eat hot foods hot, cold foods really cold,* not lukewarm.
- *Keep food at safe temperatures* — at 0°–5°C (32°–40°F) for cold foods, over 60°C (140°F) for hot foods.
- *Do not keep prepared dishes at room temperature for longer* than an hour before cooking and two hours afterwards.
- *Consider all raw meat and poultry contaminated.* Rinse well before cutting or cooking. Never let other foods touch them because microorganisms can "jump ship." Also rinse the sink well after washing poultry and meats. Never serve cooked meats or poultry on the same plate that held the raw meat or chicken.
- *Marinate meats inside the fridge* and never use the marinade for gravy without boiling for several minutes.
- *Cook meat, poultry and fish really well;* hamburger and poultry in particular must never be pinkish in the middle.
- *Use a meat thermometer.* Beef, veal, poultry and lamb should be well cooked — to temperatures of at least 74°C (165°F).

cherries). Some foods are less allergenic if cooked. A few specific allergens have been isolated from the foods that contain them, such as those from codfish (antigen "m"), shrimp (antigen II), milk (betaglobulin), soybeans (trypsin-inhibitor) and peanuts (antigen I). But many others aren't yet identified.

Sometimes, exercise aggravates a food allergy. In one instance, a young man always became nauseated and broke out in hives when he exercised within two hours of eating celery — to which he was slightly allergic — but had no reaction if he ate it without exercising.

As with other allergies, the reaction results because the body mistakes a harmless nutrient for a dangerous substance and reacts with IgE antibody production. Also as with other allergies, a reaction doesn't usually appear until a second or subsequent exposure to the food allergen. Once the allergy-prone person is sensitized, future exposure can elicit symptoms within minutes or hours of eating the offending morsel.

Some food allergies cause delayed symptoms that come on hours later. About 40 percent of those known to have a food allergy suffer nausea, cramps, vomiting and diarrhea. Many also have hives or, in children, eczema (on the face in infants; behind the ears and on arms, neck and legs in older children). Occasionally the allergic reaction spreads to the entire body, causing life-threatening anaphylactic shock (see earlier in chapter).

Someone sensitive to a certain food component may react from merely inhaling or touching the ingredient. One woman allergic to oysters collapsed at an oyster-shucking party after just inhaling the sensitizing ingredient; she had neither eaten nor touched them! (An adrenaline shot revived her.) A boy allergic to peanuts collapsed and died within minutes of eating a sandwich prepared with a knife previously contaminated with a tiny amount of peanut butter. For this reason it's vital to take allergies seriously. *Never* assume that someone just "doesn't like" a food, and won't notice a small amount — the results could be tragic.

Young children are particularly vulnerable to food allergies, especially if the first solids given on weaning are cow's milk or meat

- When *barbecuing* a whole chicken or roast, preferably precook or premicrowave it. After barbecuing, meat often stays raw on the inside.
- If *stuffing poultry*, insert stuffing immediately before roasting or preferably cook separately and then insert.
- When *buying and cooking fish*, choose one with the head still on; nonsunken, glossy eyes; shiny, tight scales and pink gills.
- To *increase egg safety*, buy government-inspected, grade A eggs (washed before marketing), throw out obviously cracked eggs, cook eggs well and do not cool hard-boiled eggs by plunging into cold water (which may create air pockets where bacteria can grow).
- *Drink only pasteurized milk*; if buying from farms, shun unpasteurized milk (not legally sold in Canada).
- *Wash fresh fruit and vegetables carefully* to remove dirt, soil and bacteria; also wash the tops of cans and jars before opening.
- *Wash all utensils, dishes, sponges, cloths, cutting boards* and counters with hot soapy water (not just rinse water) after use, perhaps also rinsing with bleach. Remember that cutting boards may harbour harmful bacteria in crevices.
- *Cut foods to be eaten raw* (such as salad) on a clean board with a clean knife. If using the same board for both meat and other foods, maximize safety by shredding other items before cutting meat.
- When *packing lunches*, allow time to chill items containing meat. Tell children to keep lunches as cool as possible. At work, refrigerate your lunch.
- *Chill picnic perishables* well before packing and carry in a cooler. Use insulated containers to keep hot foods hot and cold foods cold. Preheat or precool them for extra safety.
- When *microwaving*, rotate foods for even heating. (Although microwaving heats food fast, it heats unevenly.) Cover foods with plastic to create steam that heats the food surface.
- When *eating out*, make sure that food is served well cooked and hot — if not, send it back.
- Note that, *contrary to popular belief, commercial mayonnaise does not usually cause food poisoning*. The lemon juice or other acid in mayonnaise usually thwarts bacterial growth.
- *Wash hands and clean fingernails*, using soap, before and after handling food, especially raw meat, poultry, fish and shellfish.
- When *on kitchen duty*, wear clean clothing and don't touch the face or hair while preparing food.
- *Never prepare food if you have boils, sores or other skin infections*: if no alternative, use extra precautions.

proteins. Breastfeeding for as long as possible may help to delay and possibly reduce the risk of food allergies and is encouraged for offspring of allergy-prone parents. Starting solid foods one by one at intervals of two or three weeks, and watching for adverse reactions, can also help to detect and minimize childhood allergies. (See chapter 11 for more on childhood allergies.)

Warning signs of food allergies
- swelling of tongue and throat;
- stomach and intestinal upsets;
- eczema on the hands or cheeks;
- hives (weal or rash) anywhere on the body;
- a sudden drop in blood pressure with weakness, perhaps oncoming unconsciousness — requiring emergency medical aid.

Treatment of food allergies is simple: avoid any foods known to bring on the distress, and exclude all foods containing even traces of the identified allergen. Allergy-prone people must become careful label readers and food watchers. When dinner invitations are accepted, the host can be tactfully advised that a certain food is a problem. People going to a party where unknown foods may be served can take an antihistamine an hour or so beforehand to moderate the allergy (although it won't block it). Those known to have severe food allergies can carry an emergency EpiPen (described above).

Distinguishing food allergies from food intolerance
It's a common mistake to confuse a food allergy with food intolerance. For example, having a headache, being fatigued or feeling nauseated after eating something (such as chocolate or strawberries) is not necessarily an allergic reaction. As discussed above, allergies are immune system changes that cause an inflammatory response with hives, wheezing or other specific symptoms. In contrast, a food intolerance, irritation or food poisoning is not an allergic response. For instance, the phenylethylamine in chocolate may make people "hyper" (excitable or edgy) but not necessarily cause an allergy. Red wine contains tyramine, which dilates blood vessels and may produce a headache, but that's not an allergic reaction either. Bacteria in

underdone hamburger meat may cause diarrhea and nausea — but that too is not an allergic response.

Here are some common nonallergic food reactions:

Lactose intolerance is an inherited lack of the enzyme lactase, required to break down lactose (milk sugar). The disorder may mimic a milk allergy and is prevalent in groups whose ancestors weren't exposed to milk from domesticated cattle (most common in Aborigines, American blacks and Indians, Bantus, Chinese and Finns). Symptoms include vomiting, diarrhea and bloating.

Celiac disease, which affects one in 3,000 people, is a delayed hypersensitivity response in those who lack the metabolic ability to handle gluten from cereals such as oats, wheat, barley and rye. In children, symptoms may be serious diarrhea, bloating and cramps.

Hemolysis (red-blood-cell destruction) — or favism — is a reaction to broad (fava) beans in those deficient in a particular enzyme, leading to fever, headache, anemia and coma.

Tyramine, an amino acid commonly found in red wine, aged cheeses, canned fish and yeast fermentation products may cause headaches, nausea and other symptoms.

Monosodium glutamate (MSG), a flavoring used in Chinese cooking and some prepared foods and seasonings, can cause headaches, palpitations, weakness and numbness.

Metabisulfite, a preservative used in red wine and on many foods such as potatoes, apples, restaurant salads, dips and beer, may trigger asthma and hives.

Food poisoning — not a food allergy
An estimated one in six Canadians suffers at least one bout of food poisoning in any given year, usually contracted from cafeteria meals or goodies eaten at a catered gathering. Foods likely to harbor health-harming microorganisms include undercooked meat and poultry, rice dishes, custards, cream, unpasteurized milk, shellfish and commercially prepared foods. Food poisoning in North America has been traced to such unsuspected sources as Belgian chocolates, low-calorie ice cream, commercially prepared garlic in oil, grilled onions and baked potatoes.

The alerting signs of food poisoning are primarily diarrhea, nausea, perhaps also chills, fever and vomiting. But often the only indication of a foodborne infection is diarrhea. The discomfort may begin within a few hours of consuming the contaminated food or only appear days later, when it no longer seems linked to a particular food and may be self-diagnosed as stomach flu. Food poisoning usually causes no more discomfort than a stomachache and transient diarrhea, but it can be severe, even fatal — especially in the elderly, children, pregnant women, diabetics, alcoholics and the immune-deficient.

What to do about food poisoning
- Never let your dinner or sandwich become a "microclimate" for bacteria. Remember that bacteria do best in warm, moist, protein-rich surroundings such as meaty broths, gravies, soups, mayonnaise mixtures and custards, where they can multiply by the million.
- To reduce risks of food poisoning, keep hot foods really hot and cold foods really cold; reheat leftovers thoroughly. Heat food to 74°–100°C (165°–212°F), or cool it to 0°–5°C (32°–41°F). Never leave spoilable food like meat, fish or eggs at room temperature for more than two to three hours raw or cooked.
- Don't let raw meat and poultry or their juices contaminate other foods, especially those that will not have further cooking — for example, don't let raw meat touch delicatessen meat or salads.
- When barbecuing meat, cook it well and place cooked barbecued food on a clean plate, not the one that held the raw meat.
- Avoid stuffing a raw bird with a warm cooked dressing; cool the dressing well first.
- Always wash the hands well with soap before and after handling food. Cross-contamination via dirty fingers and unclean cooking utensils is frequent.
- In case of food poisoning, give plenty of clear fluids, preferably water or flat ginger ale.
- If a foodborne infection is suspected, report it to the family physician (it's a reportable disease in some provinces).
- See a physician if symptoms are severe,

there's persistent diarrhea and/or vomiting, and/or there is a high or persistent fever.

• Don't take antidiarrheals without medical advice.

• If the sufferer is an infant, continue breast-feeding.

• If you believe the food was already tainted when you bought it from a store or restaurant, advise your local public-health department.

"TOTAL ALLERGY SYNDROME": TWENTIETH-CENTURY DISEASE

"Total allergy syndrome" and "twentieth-century disease" are terms used to describe a condition where people believe they are so ultrasensitive to elements (mostly synthetic) in the environment that they're rendered incapable of functioning in the modern world. People with total allergy syndrome ascribe any or all of their symptoms to a sensitivity to a wide range of foods, electromagnetic fields and materials such as paint, perfume, automobile exhaust, furniture glue, detergent, ammonia, cigarette smoke and other products with distinct smells. They feel so disabled that they must withdraw to a pollution-free "haven."

Although people with so-called twentieth-century disease see themselves as victims of multiple-chemical sensitivity, their vague complaints lack the hallmarks of real allergic (immunological) reactions (described above). "Total allergy" sufferers typically report light-headedness, headaches, migraine, poor concentration, dizziness, a sense of tightness in the throat (although on physical exam the throat looks normal), an inability to get air into the chest (but no wheezing), abdominal distention, gastric upsets, "pins and needles" and confusion.

While the ailment has attracted much media attention, there is so far little scientific backup for its existence. "People claiming to have total allergy syndrome," argues one University of Toronto allergist, "often have a long history of poorly defined complaints and an overconcern about environmental toxins. They tend to doctor-shop, seeing family physicians and various specialists." Prick and patch tests, blood tests and other investigations usually show no sign of elevated IgE antibodies, inflam-

mation, other immune-system changes or organic disease.

The allergist explains that "no matter how carefully these people are investigated, it is hard to demonstrate immunologic abnormalities linked to multiple sensitizing agents. Their sensitivity reactions don't have the features characteristic of an allergic response. Physical examination is nearly always normal. Scientific tests show no evidence of widespread allergies: there are no rashes, no asthma, no biochemical changes in liver, kidney or bladder function. Pulmonary function and immune tests are normal."

Failing to obtain satisfactory treatment from conventional medical practitioners, many seek help from so-called clinical ecologists and self-styled specialists in environmental medicine, sometimes traveling to distant clinics. They may undergo costly, unorthodox and unproven therapies, perhaps being advised to drink only triply distilled water, administer sublingual "neutralizing drops" at the onset of symptoms and isolate themselves in special "environmentally safe" havens.

Although skeptical about the existence of twentieth-century disease, health professionals find the condition hard to manage. "Most total allergy sufferers," notes one University of Toronto psychiatrist, "are bright, see many doctors for their complaints and are hard to treat." In many cases, they have entirely withdrawn from society, cannot work because colleagues smoke or wear perfume, and spend all or most of the time at home – permitting only a few select visitors free of all scents and pollutants. Of one total-allergy patient group seen in a teaching hospital, most believed themselves to be seriously disabled — only 34 percent expected to be employed again, and none expected to return to their previous jobs. They clearly viewed themselves as very unwell, despite a healthy outward appearance and normal physical and laboratory findings. In cases where a specific industrial insult is the alleged trigger for the disease, compensation claims often total thousands of dollars.

The pattern of seclusion and withdrawal from society is typical of the anxiety disorder known as "agoraphobia" — fear of open or

SYMPTOMS TYPICAL OF TIGHT-BUILDING SYNDROME

- extreme fatigue and lethargy (especially in the afternoons);
- mucous membrane (throat and nose) irritation;
- eye soreness;
- dry, itchy skin (redness and irritation);
- decreased performance and concentration;
- headaches;
- respiratory infections and wheezing;
- allergic reactions with no allergen pinpointed;
- exacerbation of asthmatic symptoms;
- nausea and dizziness;
- flu-like chills, fever;
- mental confusion.

public places. But despite the fact that many symptoms of twentieth-century disease are characteristic of psychiatric disorders, sufferers tend to deny this explanation, and vigorously resist psychiatric help.

"Yet when one considers this constellation of behavior," continues the psychiatrist, "it becomes obvious that the person probably has some psychological problem such as an anxiety disorder that would likely respond well to appropriate treatment." In one study, most patients presenting with total allergy syndrome were found to have underlying psychiatric disturbances such as depression, phobias or obsessive-compulsive disorder.

But rather than admit to a psychiatric problem they prefer to blame their discomfort on allergies. As the psychiatrist explains, "they *somatize* or translate their psychological distress into physical symptoms, expressing mental upsets as physical ailments for which they seek medical assistance. Their denial of obvious problems is sometimes startling; they view psychological difficulties as weaknesses and feel demeaned by a psychiatric diagnosis, while physical problems are considered beyond control and therefore a more legitimate reason for being ill. Clearly, media publicity about such nonspecific, poorly documented pseudo-illnesses meets a public need, leading one to speculate that there are probably many people with vague symptoms in search of a diagnosis."

A typical case is a 42-year-old woman complaining of shortness of breath, headache, fatigue and dizziness. She attributed her malaise to office cleaning materials and had consulted many physicians, none of whom could diagnose or relieve her condition. Finally, a clinical ecologist in the United States said she had twentieth-century allergy disease, recommending a "rotary diet" with a limited number of "safe" foods eaten in rotation. He told her to stay in an "environmentally safe place" within her home. Consequently, she seldom left the house, and never without an oxygen tank and mask, as well as neutralizing solutions to be put under her tongue if she had "a spell." Ultimately consulting a psychiatrist, she showed typical characteristics of agoraphobia, with fear of subways, small spaces and closed windows. The

psychiatrist diagnosed her condition and the woman improved with the help of modern antianxiety drugs and psychotherapy, which allowed her to resume a relatively normal life.

In conclusion: since no consistent immune flaws, organic dysfunction or antibody abnormalities are found in those with twentieth-century disease/total allergy syndrome, most scientists believe it to be primarily psychiatric in origin.

For more information on dealing with allergies consult your family physician, an immunologist or allergist, or a local Allergy Information Association.

TIGHT-BUILDING SYNDROME

The health complaints designated as "tight-building syndrome" first surfaced during the energy crunch of the 1970s, when many buildings were tightly sealed and heavily insulated in an effort to cut energy consumption and fuel costs. (The syndrome is also dubbed "stuffy-building," "sick-building" and "sealed-building" syndrome.)

Tight-building syndrome (TBS) is generally defined as a set of nonspecific, environmentally caused discomforts reported among a significant number (at least 20 percent, sometimes up to 40 or 50 percent) of occupants in buildings such as schools, offices, and retail and residential structures. Sufferers generally feel dramatically better when they leave the building, even on a lunch break, but worse again on reentry. Health complaints are most frequent after the ventilation system has been shut down over a weekend, the malaise typically appearing at the start of the work week and gradually worsening during the working day.

Experts use the term "tight-building syndrome" to describe vague discomforts — such as fatigue and mild nasal irritation — reported when there are no physical or medical findings to support the complaint. They reserve the name "building-related illness" for the less common allergic reactions and fevers (such as humidifier fever) identifiable by laboratory tests.

Sometimes, TBS complaints are restricted to people in certain parts of a building. Very often, the sickness is too vague to warrant sick leave. But among any group of employees,

TRACKING DOWN THE ELUSIVE CAUSES OF TIGHT-BUILDING SYNDROME

- Physical and mechanical ventilation problems (blamed for 50 to 70 percent of discomforts) include temperature and humidity imbalances, a lack of fresh air with adequate oxygen, and poor maintenance.
- Chemical irritants (blamed for roughly 15 percent of TBS symptoms), include:
- outdoor contaminants — such as carbon monoxide, nitrogen oxide and other compounds drawn in from parking garages, storage sites or loading docks (which account for about 10 percent of cases);
- chemicals emitted indoors — such as tobacco smoke, and emissions from office furniture, equipment, carpets, drapes, cleaning materials and other sources (responsible for about 5 percent of cases);
- biological (microbial) contaminants that accumulate in the moist slime of uncleaned HVAC systems.
- "People-pollutants" — such as perfumes, aerosol sprays and personal odors — may also add to the problem.
- Mass hysteria and group suggestibility are sometimes cited as contributors to TBS, but this is widely considered implausible by experts, particularly as hysteria tends to appear and disappear suddenly, while TBS symptoms are remarkably consistent and persistent.
- Job stress and work demands may be a factor. A British study suggests that stress owing to lack of control over the indoor environment underlies some tight-building problems — especially among clerical workers "stuck in one place" all day long. This study found more than twice as many cases of nasal stuffiness, headaches and other symptoms among people in mechanically ventilated offices as among workers in naturally ventilated buildings where fresh air could be let in through windows.

N.B.: These factors may act, in combination, to produce cumulative effects.

there will be a few hypersensitive individuals who are severely affected by even small changes in temperature and airflow, or tiny concentrations of chemicals, far below the amounts that would bother most.

TBS may be roughly divided into subsets, with people having:
- mild discomforts — e.g., sore eyes, dry skin, fatigue — with no distinct physical/or medical signs;
- allergic-type reactions — e.g., allergic rhinitis — with runny nose, sinus congestion (with measurable physical changes);
- a flu-like reaction — with fever, muscle aches and chills (triggered by microorganisms).

Poor indoor air quality is largely to blame
In the past, odors and air pollution could quickly be flushed out of buildings by opening windows. But in modern structures with sealed outer envelopes and complex air-handling systems, reports of TBS have mushroomed. Air quality is worsened by interior surfaces made of synthetic materials — which often emit chemicals — and by the fact that space is often partitioned into sections smaller than was envisaged by the original building planners. The main sources of indoor air pollution are volatile organic chemicals (VOCs) given off by furnishings and building materials, and biological contaminants (bacteria and fungi).

Buildings where TBS complaints arise often have ventilation systems based on a variable air volume — which can be varied to lower costs — where fresh air makes up only part of the total circulating air. In the name of economy, the HVAC (heating, ventilation and air-conditioning) systems allow incoming air to be reduced or shut off, so that predominantly stale air recirculates through all or parts of a building. On very cold or hot days, the proportion of fresh air coming in may fall to zero. HVAC systems are often poorly maintained and inadequately cleaned. In addition, occupants can tamper with the system and upset the airflow by closing or blocking vents. Better ventilation and a ductwork cleanup often banish complaints and reduce absenteeism.

Microorganisms can cause serious problems
Stagnant water and moisture in humidifiers, filters, condensers, drip pans, cooling towers, ducts, coils and pumps provide the damp, dark, warm conditions ideal for breeding microorganisms such as bacteria, fungi, algae, amoebae and mites. If dispersed within contaminated droplets and inhaled by people and

SOME SUSPECTED INDOOR AIR CONTAMINANTS AND THEIR EFFECT ON HEALTH

Substance/irritant	Some major sources and entry paths	Possible health effects	Suggested control measures
Volatile organic compounds (VOCs) — organic chemicals that easily evaporate into indoor air at room temperature — e.g., solvents, benzene products, adhesives, plastic polymers, combustion products.	Paints, plastics, tiles, pesticides, sealants, wood substitutes, synthetic furnishings, liquid-process photocopiers, foam fillings, insulation, upholstery. N.B.: indoor concentrations may be 5–10 times above those outdoors.	Eye, mucous-membrane or skin irritation, dizziness, nausea, respiratory impairment, depressed brain function. Benzene products may increase cancer risks.	"Bake off" gases before occupying a new building; substitute less volatile compounds; use charcoal filters; ventilate well. Although U.S. and Canadian guidelines set upper limits for permissible amounts of certain chemicals in indoor air, none are yet established for VOCs.
Formaldehyde, a VOC (an aldehyde) with a potent smell, has been a much-publicized TBS problem in modern buildings.	Building materials; urea-foam insulation; pressed-wood products (plywood, particle board); carpets, upholstery foams and fabrics; adhesives, household waxes, wallboard, dyes, plastics, combustion products, preservatives.	Eye, nose, throat irritation; skin rashes; headaches; memory lapses; allergy-provoking (sensitization). May increase cancer risks (not proven).	Select materials carefully when furnishing home or office, avoiding synthetics and glued products whenever possible.
Phenols — organic compounds, antiseptics, also called carbolic acid.	Disinfectants, plastic resins, wood preservatives, tobacco smoke, household cleaners, air fresheners, polishes, glues.	Skin sensitization, nausea, breathing difficulties in those who are susceptible.	If sensitive, select phenol-free household products (look at labels).
Nitrogen dioxide — strong-smelling toxic gas (the brown haze in city smog).	Combustion byproducts, furnaces, wood stoves, cigarette smoke, car exhaust; portable kerosene heaters and gas ranges.	Eye-burning and watering, throat irritation, lightheadedness. Lung damage at high exposures.	Ventilate combustion appliances well. Supply enough outside air; minimize back-drafting of flues.
Carbon monoxide (CO) — a toxic, colorless, odorless gas.	Incomplete combustion from indoor heat sources, automobile exhaust.	Headaches; combines with blood-hemoglobin, displacing oxygen, reducing its supply to body tissues. Fatal in large amounts. Symptoms of CO poisoning include dizziness, vision blurring, nausea, loss of consciousness.	Watch for exposure to car exhaust or other incomplete-combustion products.
Ozone (O_3) — a colorless, unstable gas, irritating even in tiny amounts to those with respiratory problems. Traces in "natural" air are usually higher outside than indoors.	High electrical discharges, action of sunlight on "smog," photocopiers, dirty electronic air cleaners. (Concentrations of 0.001 parts per million are normal indoors; levels 40 times higher may cause symptoms.)	Nose, throat, sinus, lung irritation (perhaps burning sensation), eye watering, blurred vision.	Ventilate well if ozone sources are present. Change or clean electrostatic filters regularly; run only with fan on.
Airborne or aerosolized micro-organisms — bacteria, viruses, fungi, protozoa and other microbes that grow in dark, damp conditions, e.g., inside air conditioners, vaporizers, humidifiers.	Live on dirt; thrive in damp conditions and poorly maintained HVAC systems.	Can cause allergic reactions or flu-like illnesses such as Humidifier fever, Pontiac fever, Legionnaire's disease.	Reduce humidity below 50%. Discard damp furnishings. Check that HVAC systems work as designed. Clean well, maintain properly to prevent sludge (microbial buildup). Use humidistat control of ventilation fans.

pets, these microbes can cause illness. Microbial contamination of indoor air arises from poor maintenance and infrequent or nonexistent cleaning of air-conditioning and humidifying systems, not only due to negligence but also because design flaws may hinder access.

Even dirty home air conditioners and humidifiers may harbor biological contaminants. Fungi that accumulate in dirty drip pans are particularly tough to dislodge once colonies form, and their resistant spores are a well-known cause of allergic reactions. Some fungi produce mycotoxins (poisons) that can seriously endanger human health, and these forms should be at zero-level.

TBS health problems due to microorganisms include:

- *Allergic rhinitis,* a sinus and nose irritation that strikes susceptible people soon after they enter a contaminated building.
- *Asthma,* which may be triggered or exacerbated by microorganisms, especially fungal spores.
- *Hypersensitivity pneumonitis,* also known as allergic alveolitis, a lung impairment due to allergic sensitization to organic dusts, aerosols or fungal spores disseminated through dirty HVAC systems. One of the more serious tight-building sicknesses, its symptoms include chills, coughing, breathing difficulties and diminished lung function.
- *Humidifier fever,* a noncontagious, mild, flu-like infection that results from microorganisms dispersed in fine airborne droplets from contaminated HVAC systems. Although the specific microbes responsible remain obscure, certain bacteria and protozoan amoebae (or their components) are under suspicion. The infection typically develops a few hours into a workshift, following a weekend or vacation. This illness, which primarily affects industrial workers (particularly in grain and cotton works), is signaled by fever, chills and coughing (normally without lung involvement). Attacks may last a day or two, and be few or frequent, and mild or severe enough to necessitate sick leave. Recovery is usually rapid.
- *Pontiac fever,* named for an outbreak in Pontiac, Michigan, when 95 of 100 hospital employees were struck by chills, fever, headache and muscle pains due to bacterial contamination of air conditioners. This mild, self-limiting, flu-like condition is sometimes called "Monday fever." It typically starts on return to work, lasts three to five days, and carries no risk of pneumonia.
- *Legionnaire's disease,* a life-threatening bacterial pneumonia, usually spreads through air-conditioning systems.

SOME TIPS AND SOLUTIONS FOR TIGHT-BUILDING SYNDROME

- Ensure that building managers meet air-quality guidelines and introduce sufficient outside "makeup" air.
- Check that temperatures remain at 20–23°C (68–73°F) in winter, and 23–27°C (73–81°F) in summer.
- Maintain humidity around 30–60 percent for optimal comfort and minimal microbial growth.
- Change air-conditioning filters as often as recommended, and make sure filters fit properly.
- Ensure that HVAC systems are adequately maintained, cleaned and periodically checked (metal ducts and fans are easier to keep clean than fiberglass, which attracts moisture).
- Adopt a nonsmoking policy, or at least arrange separately ventilated areas for smokers.
- Do not partition space in a way that impedes airflow.
- Avoid cool-mist and ultrasonic humidifiers or vaporizers; if not well cleaned, they breed microorganisms (the steam type is preferable).
- Discard or remove for cleaning water-damaged items — e.g., porous materials, carpets, drapes, upholstery, moldy ceiling tiles. Promptly repair all internal leaks.
- Wash smooth surfaces well with bleach to keep down microbe levels.
- Make the indoor climate as health-promoting as possible by substituting nonirritating, natural materials for synthetics when feasible (especially at home) — e.g., use cotton instead of synthetics; wood instead of vinyl; avoid particle-board (which emits VOCs); avoid carpet and other glues or use no carpets; cut down on solvents when possible.
- "Bake out" new buildings (freshly laid carpet and furnishings emit volatile organics) by turning up the heat and then the ventilation, to vaporize and flush out volatile fumes before people move in.
- Restart ventilating systems in work premises before the work week begins.
- Urge building owners to attend promptly to occupant health complaints by calling in experts to examine HVAC systems.

Home humidifiers can be a health hazard

Home humidifiers can also cause ill health and symptoms similar to those discussed above if not kept clean. Steam or evaporative humidifiers are less likely to contaminate the air with microorganisms than cool-mist types. Whatever you choose, keep it scrupulously clean. Wash the tank thoroughly according to the manufacturer's instructions. Any standing water (even a pan on the radiator) can quickly become contaminated by molds and bacteria. Vinegar or hydrogen peroxide will kill molds; chlorine bleach kills bacteria.

In conclusion

Experts called in to investigate TBS complaints generally find the indoor air quality within accepted guidelines. Levels of formaldehyde, ozone and carbon monoxide are not usually present in amounts considered a health hazard. However, managers and building owners are strongly advised to take health complaints seriously, attend to them promptly and ask for expert advice.

HOW SAFE IS OUR DRINKING WATER?

Given today's sophisticated water-purification methods, Canadians can rest assured that their municipal supplies are relatively free of disease-causing organisms. Thanks to chlorination and other water-treatment processes, we no longer suffer the previously prevalent epidemics of waterborne diseases such as cholera, typhoid and dysentery. Universal provision of drinkable water, virtually free of health-damaging microbes, is a major twentieth-century accomplishment in Western countries.

While wide-scale outbreaks of waterborne infections have become a rarity here, there's still a need for vigilance. A recent U.S. outbreak of cryptosporidosis — a severe diarrheal illness due to protozoan organisms — is a dramatic reminder of the need to be on the lookout for waterborne microbes. (The probable cause of the U.S. outbreak was a sewage spill containing the protozoa or their eggs, which came from infected cattle feces.)

The U.S. Centers for Disease Control (CDC) still report sporadic cases of illness from waterborne pathogens such as *Giardia* and *Campylobacter* from public or private water supplies. While Canada is spared the worst of such microbial illnesses by virtue of location — because the main pathogens thrive in hotter climates — giardiasis ("Beaver fever") is still common in the lakes and rivers of northern Canada. Campers, hikers and travelers who drink unboiled and untreated stream or lake water can get serious diarrheal infections from these microorganisms!

Increasing worries about chemical contamination

Largely free of waterborne diseases, Canadians have now shifted their concerns about drinking water to chemical pollutants. Such fears have made increasing numbers turn to bottled water, some shunning tap water altogether, even for making coffee or tea.

Since World War II, through improper waste disposal, global waters have become contaminated by a steady buildup of chemicals, including:

- industrial and synthetic chemicals;
- chlorinated and other compounds formed during water-chlorination and -treatment processes;
- naturally occurring chemicals, such as arsenic;
- natural and industrial radioactive materials, such as radon;
- substances such as lead that leach in from water-conducting pipes.

Among the most potentially health-harming contaminants in Canadian drinking water are the chlorinated compounds — formed by water disinfection with chlorine and coming from chlorinated industrial byproducts such as PCBs (polychlorinated biphenyls), dioxins, cyclodiene pesticides (e.g., aldrin, chlordane, lindane, heptachlor), trichloroethylene and carbon tetrachloride. Being fat-soluble, these chlorinated hydrocarbons endanger fish and other marine life by being absorbed into their fatty tissues, and are then perhaps consumed by humans and other animals.

Industrial, agricultural and household chemicals enter ground and surface waters via a few main routes, namely:

- sewage-treatment plants;

METALS IN DRINKING WATER THAT COULD INJURE HEALTH

- **Aluminum** — a component of a material used in purifying water — is not easily absorbed by the body. Suspected of being linked to Alzheimer's disease, aluminum is a nerve toxin and endangers those with kidney failure. In countries such as Canada, Norway and Sweden, with a big acid-rain problem — i.e., where large amounts of aluminum are released into the water — authorities set strict limits on concentrations.
- **Arsenic** — widely found in the earth's crust, and present in trace amounts in food — is a poison that may damage bone marrow, and also a human carcinogen; the ideal level is zero.
- **Barium** can harm the heart, circulation and nerves, so authorities recommend strict controls.
- **Cadmium** — a metal highly toxic even at low concentrations — occurs naturally and leaches into soil and water from vehicular exhaust and industrial wastes.
- **Mercury** — known to damage human nerves — may be present at danger levels in large fish such as lake trout, whitefish and swordfish. Eating them may pose a health risk far greater than mercury absorption from drinking water!
- **Lead** can damage the developing brains, blood systems and bones of unborn and young children. Currently, both U.S. and Canadian health agencies strictly limit lead levels in household water, calling for still lower allowable levels. Household tap water is likely to contain lead if it is carried by lead, lead-soldered or brass pipes. U.S. regulations ban the use of lead pipes, lead solder or flux in the installation or repair of public water systems, and Canada is doing likewise.

- direct industrial discharge or industrial spills;
- surface runoff of pesticides, herbicides and fertilizers;
- improper disposal of hazardous chemicals (some of them from households);
- storage-tank leaks;
- garbage- and dump-site seepage.

The "dirty dozen" water contaminants

About 400 chemicals, 360 of them synthetics, have already been identified in the Great Lakes, which provide drinking water for millions of people. The number is hardly surprising, since there are 164 toxic-waste sites along the U.S. side of the Niagara River alone. Twelve of these chemicals, popularly called the "dirty dozen" — among them the dioxins, toxophenes, PCBs, DDT, benzo (alpha) pyrene and hexachlorobenzene — are known to endanger health. Some of them cause birth defects; others are cell deformers.

To the best of their ability, health officials keep tabs on the levels of these compounds in drinking water, and their long-term effects. Most chemical contaminants are present in such tiny amounts that the health hazard, if any, will creep up slowly, becoming noticeable only after years or decades of exposure. In our search for clean water, we may forget that the possible dangers from food contaminants far outweigh those from drinking water. It is estimated that eating a single fish contaminated with PCBs, or filling up just once at a leaky gas pump and breathing in benzene, could endanger health more than a lifetime of drinking municipal tap water in most parts of Canada.

Is our tap water safe?

So far there's little evidence to suggest that Canadian drinking water is generally unsafe. A 30-month survey of Great Lakes drinking water suggested that it poses negligible health hazards. However, environmentalists remain concerned about contamination. Technological advances provide ever-more-sensitive measuring methods, so that each year chemicals can be detected at levels far below those detectable before. Trace levels in parts per billion, trillion or quadrillion can now be measured, though scientists do not yet know the impact of such low levels on human health.

The big question remains: what is a "safe level" of contamination? How do we know that a lifetime's exposure, even to trace levels of industrial and agricultural chemicals in water, will not produce birth defects, cancer or chronic illnesses? The answer is that, while there is good reason for concern, there's no cause for alarm. Experts assure us that the trace levels of most chemicals currently present in drinking water are not a health risk.

The good news for now is that Canadian

THE CHIEF POSSIBLE CONTAMINANTS IN DRINKING WATER

Metals
Water naturally contains dissolved metals and their ions (charged forms), some of which, such as zinc, copper, cobalt, magnesium, molybdenum and manganese, are essential in trace amounts to human life. Current research indicates that the health risks of exposure to other metals in drinking water are generally low, and that in the small amounts present most do not harm human health, although some have potentially injurious effects.

Asbestos
Asbestos fibers can get into drinking water from naturally occurring rock deposits and industrial uses. Although we may inadvertently consume a little asbestos through drinking water, studies to date find no link between asbestos absorbed from tap water and cancer or any other diseases.

Nitrates
Nitrates occur naturally and also seep into drinking water from sewage, fertilizer and septic tank runoffs, as well as from feedlot wastes. Although the health risks of current intakes from tap water remain unclear, there are concerns that quite low nitrate levels may increase risks of stomach cancer. High concentrations (more than 10 mg/l of water) can cause a rare blood disease in young children — infantile methemoglobinemia — in which nitrates (reduced to nitrites in the stomach) disrupt the blood's oxygen-carrying ability. Authorities remind us that nitrates abound even in natural foods such as fiber-rich vegetables, and if eaten in great excess could endanger the health of those who are vulnerable.

Organic chemicals
Organic chemicals comprise a vast array of substances both natural and synthetic — pesticides, herbicides and petroleum products. Some synthetic organics, which in high doses promote cancer, can pose a health risk by accumulating in meat, poultry, milk or fish. Animal studies show that in high doses, these substances produce sterility, impair the nervous system and damage the heart. Drinking-water levels of synthetic organics — such as dioxins, aldrin, chlordane, DDT, PCBs and furan — are therefore kept as low as possible. While their trace-level danger is hard to evaluate, tiny daily doses of such organic contaminants could have cumulative health effects.

Salt
In areas where salt (sodium chloride) is used as a de-icing agent, sodium can seep into water supplies, and high sodium levels may threaten the health of people with high blood pressure. Commercial water softeners, which replace calcium with sodium salts, may also exacerbate high blood pressure and increase the risk of heart problems. However, for most people, the amount of sodium obtained in drinking water is negligible compared to the quantity ingested in food.

Dissolved radon gas
Radon, a radioactive gas (a decay product of uranium), can dissolve in water from uranium ore, granite, shale, phosphate and pitchblende or, more infrequently, through uranium-contaminated buildings. Radon is one of several naturally occurring radioactive elements in drinking water. It can enter household air from basements and, along with radon from other sources, contribute to lung-cancer risks. Water from lakes, rivers and reservoirs generally contains very little (one picocurie or less per liter), but underground water may contain more. Public utilities usually monitor the total radioactivity of their water, but not radon levels specifically. Even drinking water from high-radon sources often remains in reservoirs long enough for the dissolved gas to dissipate. But if radon-rich water is drawn from wells and goes straight into the home, it may later emit radioactivity in a bathtub or teakettle.

Fluoride
An ever-increasing number of countries and cities around the globe fluoridate their water to prevent tooth decay in children, a practice that may also diminish osteoporosis risks in later life. Many experts believe that adding fluoride to drinking water is a wise health measure.
Note: On balance, drinking water provides more benefits than health hazards.

---

drinking water provides a safe beverage that poses a far lesser danger than smoking tobacco or eating too much animal fat. The bad news is that there may be as-yet-unrecognized health risks from daily exposure to trace contaminants that will endanger future generations.

Are bottled waters any safer?
Many health-conscious consumers have turned to bottled water; annual sales doubled to 5 l (1.1 gallons) per capita in Canada from 1982 to 1990. Some people prefer the taste of bottled water (and there's no disputing tastes), but it's not necessarily safer than tap water. Bottled water simply comes out of some alternative water source — like an artesian well or a natural spring — but can contain contaminants in amounts that are well above the guidelines set for tap water. The label "natural" means only that its mineral content hasn't been altered, not that it is healthy.

Although tap-water quality may be open to question, it is at least rigorously tested for 100 or more substances. Only three contaminant levels must be checked in bottled waters: bacteria and coliform organisms; fluoride levels; and TDS (Total Dissolved Solids such as magnesium, iron and sodium). Labels need only identify the source of the bottled water and state the amount of fluoride and TDS. (Quebec has tighter bottled-water regulations calling for the analysis and listing of eleven substances — requirements not necessarily observed!)

In Canada, bottled spring water must, by law, come from underground springs, but there is no law dictating that it must be pure. Even waters advertised as "impeccably purified" may be less pure than consumers expect. American consumer studies have detected several contaminants in commercially bottled water, including acetaldehyde and toluene (possibly carcinogenic), arsenic (toxic), high sodium, a range of industrial solvents and traces of plastics. One Canadian consumer study found that some bottled water contained arsenic in amounts well above those allowable in tap water, lead in quantities above proposed guidelines and barium. Other bottled waters were unacceptably high in sodium. Some bottled waters have more fluoride than allowed for tap water (one brand contained four times the maximum allowable concentration), but most bottled waters contain none. A child who drinks only bottled water, without taking fluoride supplements, may therefore be at risk of tooth decay and osteoporosis!

Being ozonized but not chlorinated, bottled water doesn't smell of chlorine or contain any of the potentially health-harming chlorinated chemicals. More critical from a health standpoint, however, unchlorinated water may be contaminated at the bottling plant by bacteria and other microbes. Once the bottles are opened, any microorganism present begins to proliferate. In one study, researchers analyzed the microbiological content of bottled water sold in stores across Canada; of 114 lots, both domestic and imported, 46 percent were bacterially contaminated and 12 lots were "grossly contaminated" — to the point of threatening health. Another study found 25 percent of bottled water to be ordinary tap water! Whatever concerns there may be about drinking water, bottled water has not proved to be the answer.

Hard versus soft water

Water with a level of calcium carbonate over 80–100 mg per liter is considered "hard." Water with less than 100 mg per liter is generally labeled "soft." Ground and well water (particularly in limestone areas) is usually hard, surface (lake or river) water usually soft. Since they are in a limestone basin, the Great Lakes have relatively hard water, while lakes in the Canadian Shield (e.g., Lake Muskoka) are soft.

Hard drinking water may promote health. A large-scale 1986 study found that inhabitants living in cities served by hard water (Kitchener and Toronto) tended to live longer than those in areas with soft water (northern Ontario, Newfoundland). Although several studies suggest a heart-protecting effect from hard water, the matter remains controversial.

What about home water-treatment devices?

Probably cheaper in the long run than buying bottled water are home water-purification devices, attached to the faucet or under the sink, or used in a jug of water. However, experts warn that such systems, used in homes served by municipal treatment plants, may end up supplying water more contaminated than that straight from the tap. Eventually any filter becomes saturated and ineffective, but it is not possible to know by merely looking at it when this point is reached, as it may occur well before the expiry date. A dirty filter becomes a breeding ground for bacteria.

Checking out home drinking-water quality

Your local branch of Environment Canada should be able to answer general queries about water safety, but questions about specific drinking-water sources should be directed to local water suppliers and/or local departments of public health.

People can have their private well water tested (free of charge in some cases) for nitrate, fluoride, sodium and hardness levels, and for bacterial content. What's needed, according to one University of Toronto expert, "is a program enabling private well-owners and tap water drinkers with justified concerns to

WATER-TREATMENT DEVICES

• Activated carbon filters are the most popular type: water from the tap is flushed through or stays in contact with a carbon filter that traps impurities. Large below-sink units containing granular activated charcoal are the most efficient of these devices. They remove bad tastes and smells caused by impurities and in addition, when new, filter out many organic chemicals (such as chloroform and pesticides). The activated carbon binds some, but not necessarily all, organic compounds. However, once the filter becomes saturated, it may actually release impurities into the water rather than removing them. Users must be aware that:
• carbon filters should be used only with water disinfected according to microbiological limits;
• filters need to be changed regularly — at least every three to six months;
• taps should run for thirty seconds before the water is used, to flush out the filter.

• Reverse-osmosis devices — originally used to convert salt water to fresh — attach under the sink. The tap water goes through a semipermeable membrane that traps impurities. These appliances can remove inorganics but are not very good at eliminating organics, particularly chloroform. The membrane requires changing every two to four years, and it can rupture, allowing concentrated chemicals and bacteria to pass into the water. Users must be aware that:
• high water pressure is needed with reverse-osmosis devices;
• devices should only be used with disinfected water that meets present guidelines.

• Distillation devices distill water by boiling, steaming and then condensing it into a holding tank, a method which disinfects the water and precipitates out some metal salts and organic chemicals. Since distillation may concentrate volatile organics which evaporate with the distilled water, most distilling units incorporate some other method, such as a vent, to discard the first distillate collected. Users must be aware that:
• maintenance and thorough cleaning are essential;
• distillation uses a fair amount of electricity;
• the water tastes flat!

request additional tests for contaminants such as lead and PCBs, for a minimal fee, by local environment or health departments." At present, it can cost several hundred dollars to check 20 or more chemicals.

• Turbid drinking water is usually a sign that excess particulate impurities are present, which may encourage the growth of bacteria and other microorganisms. Turbidity-causing material also interferes with chlorine disinfection. Home owners should consult local health authorities.

• If radon levels are known to be high in the neighborhood, householders can ask to have an atmospheric test done by local Environment Canada or health-department officials, and if airborne radon is high and the house depends on well water, it should be checked for radioactivity.

• Ask to have lead levels in tap water checked in houses built before World War II (when lead pipes were commonly used), particularly if there are small children in the household.

• People drinking water from private or shared wells should — as a rule of thumb — have a once-only test for lead, petrochemicals (if a gas tank is located nearby), and specific pesticides or herbicides used in the area. In some areas testing of wells is advised two to three times a year, during spring runoff and periods of drought/dry spells thereafter, which can be done by local Environment Canada officials if health concerns are legitimate.

Two simple measures to improve drinking-water quality

• Before using water for drinking or food preparation, first thing in the morning or if the water has been unused for several hours, run the cold tap until the water is as cold as possible, to get rid of metals such as lead. Never consume water from the hot tap (hot water dissolves lead and other metals more easily than cold).

• Let water sit overnight in the fridge in an uncapped container, to get rid of the chlorine smell.

N.B.: Water Analysis and Evaluation Kits that test for 92 substances are available from The Consumers' Association of Canada, Box 9300, Ottawa, Ont. KIG 3T9 Tel. (613) 723-0187.

GETTING THE LEAD OUT

Lead is everywhere — the metal occurs naturally in rocks, and industry transfers it into the air, snow and rain, whence it is deposited back onto land and into rivers, lakes and seas. And it can seriously damage health. Severe lead poisoning leads to coma and death; smaller amounts have subtler effects, and may damage learning ability in children and bone strength in adults.

One legendary theory attributes the downfall of Ancient Rome partly to mental deterioration and infertility caused by absorption of this toxic metal from plumbing, water cisterns, lead-glazed dishes and, above all, wine sweetened with lead acetate ("sugar of lead"). A recent archeological find in Canada uncovered three members of Sir John Franklin's 1845 expedition to the North Pole who reportedly died of lead poisoning — perhaps from defective tin cans — judging by the large amounts discovered in their bones.

Getting the lead out of our lives is no easy matter. A global increase in lead pollution took place during the Industrial Revolution, and another when tetraethyl lead was added to gasoline as an antiknock agent. Even in the mid-Atlantic, lead levels are now 40 times above presumed prehistoric levels. Lead enters the body from food, as small particles inhaled from the air, via the ingestion of lead-laden dirt, and to a small extent from drinking water and other beverages. Most of the lead in our bodies comes from lead-contaminated food. Plants pick up lead from the soil, and are consumed by animals, and human beings — at the top of the food chain — eat the contaminated livestock as well as plants. Thus our entire food supply is contaminated, but since lead concentration diminishes on its way up the food chain, animal products contain less than plants.

Drinking water poses a minimal lead hazard in most cases, and any lead in tap water can be largely eliminated by flushing the pipes for a few minutes before taking a drink or using water for cooking. Schools in some areas have been advised to let their drinking taps and fountains run for a minimum of five minutes before permitting children to drink.

Over the past couple of decades, "safe" levels of lead in the blood have progressively gone down. The U.S. Centers for Disease Control in Atlanta pronounced 30 μg/dL (micrograms per decilitre) as the upper limit for health safety in 1978, but lowered this figure to 25 μg/dL in 1985 and to 10 μg/dL in 1991. This is the "action" level that should trigger active steps to find the source of exposure and reduce or avoid it. Canadian public-health authorities have set similar but slightly higher action levels, varying slightly from province to province.

However, many health authorities consider today's "safe" level of lead not safe enough. Recent studies show childhood brain and neurological impairment can occur at lead levels well below those previously accepted as safe. Below the "action" level of blood lead, there is a "concern" level that may adversely affect health and behavior (especially in children), but is not considered bad enough to warrant active steps for lead removal.

According to one Health and Welfare Canada official, the real level at which health damage could occur is 5–10 μg/dL, or even lower in groups at particular risk — such as young children and the fetus. Many experts also argue that, for the sake of reproductive safety, permissible lead levels for women in the child-bearing years should be set as low as for young children — although this could bar them from certain types of employment.

Aided by the phase-down of lead in gasoline, average blood-lead levels in Canadians have declined, but worries remain about people living in lead-polluted residential areas and those who live close to industrial lead-emitters.

HOW LEAD ENDANGERS HEALTH

- raises blood pressure (perhaps even at currently permissible blood-lead levels), with possibly increased risk of strokes and heart attacks;
- impairs the nervous system — which may cause learning problems and stunted growth in children;
- is linked to gastrointestinal problems, e.g., colic;
- may trigger gout;
- causes kidney damage (usually at high toxic levels);
- disrupts red-blood-cell function and interferes with the action of enzymes needed for hemoglobin formation, possibly causing anemia;
- possibly impairs male sperm;
- may damage the fetus, as lead in the mother's blood is transferred across the placenta to the developing baby; miscarriage is a risk if the maternal blood lead is high;
- possibly damages bone, leading to osteoporosis and other ills.

Tracing the lead in household sources

- *Paint* — in many countries, including Canada, lead-containing paint is forbidden for use indoors or on children's toys, pencils and other items. Canadian children living in older homes (pre-1940s) still face a possible but rare risk of lead poisoning, even from indoor paint, if bits from old layers of lead-based paint are inhaled or swallowed. Lead-containing paint for outdoor use must bear warning labels on the can.
- *Food cans soldered with lead* — recognizable by their dark inner seams — are a known source of lead contamination; in the past, heavy consumers of canned goods often spooned lead into their bodies along with the food. Modern welded cans and molded plastic ones (recognizable by their rounded bottoms) are gradually replacing older leaded types.

- *Dishes, ceramics, lead-glazed earthenware, crystal decanters and pottery* can leach lead into their contents, especially if the contents are acidic. Lead-glazed ceramics pose a greater health danger if the coating is cracked or when in contact with acidic liquids — for instance, citrus juices, wine or vinegar — that attack the lead-containing glaze or glass, leaching the metal into food or drink. One Montrealer who regularly used a cracked ceramic jug for his morning orange juice suffered acute lead poisoning. Imported earthenware (and imported paints) may sometimes slip through Canadian regulations. Recently, U.S. researchers reported that wine kept for four or more months in crystal decanters contained up to 200 times the level of lead deemed hazardous.
- *People who work with ceramics* run the risk of lead poisoning from lead-containing glazes and paints, whether the craft is pursued as a job or a hobby. Arts councils strongly advise against the use of lead glazes.
- *Antiques* such as old pewter mugs (pewter being a mixture of lead and tin) and *lead seals* on wine bottles (now being phased out) are other possible sources of lead poisoning.
- *Colored comics* — which may contain lead-containing pigments — are occasionally chewed by children.
- *Firearms ammunition* — many cases of lead poisoning have been reported among gun-club members using poorly ventilated indoor firing ranges. Ducks and other waterfowl with drooping necks have been found to have lead poisoning from eating lead shot and nibbling fishing weights!
- *Renovations and home construction* — although dozens of countries banned the interior use of lead paint in the early 1900s, North America did so only in the late 1970s. Many homes still have lead-based paint on their walls. Home renovators may thus inhale lead dust while sanding off old paint or tearing down painted wood and steel structures. Oxyacetylene torches used for cutting and burning lead paint can create dangerous lead fumes. A recent example of lead poisoning occurred among construction workers on Toronto Island who were using torches to

HOW TO GET THE LEAD OUT OF YOUR LIFE

- **Never drink water that's been standing overnight in household lead plumbing.**
- **Run water from the cold tap for a few minutes — until it runs very cold — before drawing water for drinking or cooking.**
- **Never use water from the hot water tap in food or drink, and especially not for baby's formula, because hot water may dissolve more lead than cold water does.**
- **Practice good hygiene — wash hands before eating or snacking, and after playing outside or handling pets.**
- **Wash children's hands well after they've played**

outside; discourage them from swallowing soil, dirt or paint chips.
- **Avoid burning colored newsprint, comics, magazines or wrapping paper in the barbecue pit or fireplace — they may give off lead-laden fumes.**
- **Wash leafy vegetables well and discard outer leaves.**
- **Peel root vegetables, especially if grown in lead-rich areas.**
- **Keep home as dust-free as possible.**
- **Avoid food from lead-soldered cans.**
- **Have any paint chips from old buildings checked for lead by local health authorities.**
- **If renovating, avoid using a heat gun on leaded paint; wear a**

mask and coveralls; wash workclothes separately from the family wash.
- **Eat well away from any renovating area.**
- **If using an old electric kettle (which may contain lead solder), empty stale water and replace with fresh before boiling.**
- **Grow vegetables as far as possible from roads and highways.**
- **Don't preserve foods in glazed pots that may contain lead.**
- **Don't store acidic food or drink in lead crystal or lead-glazed containers.**
- **If your home has lead pipes, consider having the water tested by the local board of Environment Canada.**

demolish old lead-painted water tanks inside a building. Proper ventilation and cleanliness are essential when renovating, and special care must be taken not to contaminate young children.

- *Soil near a metal refinery*, smelter or heavily traveled highway may be far higher in lead than in most urban areas. Above the 500 ppm (parts per million) mark, residents of some provinces can ask to have their soil retested by local authorities, to see whether replacement should be considered. There is, however, no strong scientific evidence that soil replacement is the solution in all situations. On a cautionary note, environmentalists remind us that the discarded lead-rich soil would create a disposal problem.

- *Vegetables grown* in soil containing over 500 ppm should probably be regarded as toxic. Turnips, potatoes and onions are those most likely to absorb lead. As a safeguard, people are advised to wash hands well before preparing food, discard the outer leaves of leafy vegetables (such as cabbages and lettuces) and peel root vegetables grown in lead-rich areas.

Treatment to rid the body of lead

In most cases, all that's required to lower blood-lead levels is to get away from the lead contaminator(s). Chelation therapy (using substances that bind to lead so that it can be extracted) may be used in severe cases to get rid of lead already in the body. But chelation carries the disadvantage of pulling lead in the bone out into the bloodstream, producing transiently high levels that may endanger the kidneys.

COPING WITH TEMPERATURE EXTREMES

Many animals — like fish and reptiles — have to function at the temperatures they find themselves in, adapting their behavior to whatever their bodies are capable of in the warm or the cold. But humans (like other mammals) are warm-blooded — our bodies expect to be maintained within a very narrow temperature range (at least for the body's core) and cannot work for long outside that range. We have developed complex mechanisms — such as shivering, sweating, and constriction and dilation of blood vessels — to protect our bodies from losing or gaining too much heat. When these mechanisms are overwhelmed by excessive or prolonged heat or cold, our body functions can be severely affected. Thus, anticipating climatic changes, and being prepared for them, can easily become a matter of survival.

Avoiding heat illness (hyperthermia)

Heat stress, or heat-related illness, ranges from mild to severe. The start of heat stress often goes unnoticed — perhaps producing only irritability and somewhat slowed reaction times. But a severe rise in the core body temperature impairs coordination and hinders the ability to focus or think clearly. Hot, confused people may further endanger themselves by failing to don hats, losing sunglasses, forgetting to take off

---

TIPS TO BEAT THE HEAT

- **Minimize physical activities and outdoor exposure during the hottest parts of the day (11:00 a.m.–3:00 p.m.).**
- **Drink plenty of liquids (preferably a gallon a day!); thirst is quenched long before lost fluids are really replenished. Vigorous exercisers are advised to drink at least 15–20 ounces (two cups, or half a liter) of water before working out or starting a race.**
- **If running a long race or exercising vigorously, replace fluids with plain water. While some people favor *iso-molar* solutions (balanced electrolyte drinks) like Gatorade, plain water is the best drink in hot weather** and immediately before and during vigorous exercise, because it dilutes and counteracts the rise in plasma (blood) potassium that can occur in these circumstances.
- **Limit alcoholic beverages and caffeinated drinks (such as tea, coffee and colas) as they are diuretics, and increase fluid loss.**
- **Wear a hat (wide-brimmed if possible) or use an umbrella or sunshade, and wear loose, lightweight, light-colored garments (preferably cotton).**
- **Acclimatize the body gradually by increasing heat exposure slowly.**
- **Walk on the shady side of the street.**
- **Spend as much time as possible in air-conditioned rooms or buildings, set air-conditioners at 24°C (75°F) or place large fans in windows to draw heat outdoors.**
- **Park vehicles in the shade and open car windows and doors before entering a parked vehicle.**
- **Take frequent cool showers or baths.**
- **Slightly increase dietary salt intake during hot summers or if regularly exercising hard — by adding a little to cooked food or salads. (Do not take salt tablets unless medically advised to do so.)**
- **Omit heavy, fatty foods, desserts, gravies and sauces.**
- **Cook during the cooler part of the day.**

excess clothes or not drinking enough fluids.

If heat buildup outstrips the body's ability to lose it by sweating and evaporation from the skin, the body's normal heat-regulating mechanism can fail, leading to the cessation of sweating — a dangerous situation where the brain's hypothalamic temperature-regulating center loses control. Huge swings in blood volume and pressure may produce sudden collapse, even death.

Anyone who succumbs to heat stress must be rapidly cooled off to avoid damaging the brain and other organs. Since there's all too often a lack of water, ice and medical expertise on hand to treat those affected by heat, prevention is definitely best. (See chapter 17 for first aid measures against heat illness.)

Avoiding cold injury (hypothermia)

Hypothermia — dangerous body cooling — can occur if normal body temperature falls by even two degrees. Mild hypothermia occurs if body temperature drops to 33–35°C

(91–95°F); below 30°C (86°F), hypothermia is life-threatening.

As the body loses heat, metabolism and heartrate slow down. With mild to moderate hypothermia, shivering — the body's way of building heat by muscular activity — remains violent but the person may stagger as if intoxicated and speech may be slurred. Hypothermic people become quiet, may refuse food and drink and become sluggish, fatigued and drowsy. The skin may be deceptively pink even though icy cold. The pulse is slow and weak, and breathing is shallow. As body cooling progresses, shivering lessens; the person appears weary, withdrawn, confused and irritable and may act strangely — perhaps undressing despite the cold — due to a deceptively warm sensation. With severe hypothermia, shivering stops; people hallucinate, stare with fixed pupils and may lose consciousness. The pulse, heartbeat and breathing may seem imperceptible — as if the person is already dead.

The treatment for mild hypothermia — for someone still shivering and coherent — is to prevent further heat loss, find shelter and rewarm the casualty by adding extra clothes (preferably woolen), covering with blankets, cuddling against others or sharing a sleeping bag. Contrary to popular folklore, alcohol does *not* warm people up. On the contrary, it dilates blood vessels and gives them a false sense of warmth.

If hypothermia is more severe — if the person is no longer shivering — get medical help as soon as possible. Severe hypothermia is a medical emergency; the casualty needs expert rewarming to prevent further damage and avoid endangering the heart. (See chapter 17 for details of emergency first aid for hypothermia.)

STAYING FIT ON THE JOB

Although the benefits of a healthy lifestyle are not yet fully documented, fitness clearly pays off in not only individual but also corporate terms. A healthy employee has fewer accidents, takes fewer sick days, uses less health-insurance benefits, is more productive and costs less than an ailing worker. Accordingly, many companies are now introducing fitness and lifestyle programs to decrease absenteeism, reduce staff turnover,

---

TIPS TO BEAT THE COLD

- Dress appropriately, in layers (for details, see section on winter sport tips in chapter 2).
- If stranded or very cold, find or build any kind of shelter (under a tree, in a hollow or cave) and stay out of the wind.
- Try to remain dry. Dampness against the skin increases heat loss. However, it's not always advantageous to change damp or wet garments. In very cold air, changing clothes may produce extra heat loss, so use your discretion. It may be better simply to cover up the damp clothes with more clothes on top.
- Avoid exercise that makes you sweat. Although movement creates body heat, the resulting perspiration may wet clothes and enhance heat loss. Move slowly and methodically rather than quickly.
- Put on extra clothes or blankets if possible, or wrap up in plastic.
- Keep head, neck and hands covered. As much as 40 percent of the body's heat loss occurs through the neck and head, and up to 20 percent via the hands. Covering the head, mouth and nose lightly with a cap or scarf creates a heat flow that allows you to breathe warmer air.
- Stay awake at all costs. The body's metabolism and heat production diminish even more during sleep.
- Don't sit or lie directly on the cold ground. Insulate yourself with objects such as branches, leaves, dry, loose soil, backpacks, shoes.
- Huddle close to others in a group.
- Remain with others; do not wander off alone.
- Don't eat snow. It doesn't satisfy thirst and wastes precious body heat.

improve productivity and boost morale. Classes range from regular aerobics to lifestyle-improvement workshops in nutrition, smoking cessation, and so on.

Fit employees feel and work better and are cheaper to maintain. One study, conducted by the University of Toronto together with two life-insurance companies, showed the cost-effectiveness of a worker-fitness program. Over 1,000 employees participated. Half of the test-employees at the Canada Life Assurance Company exercised regularly, and they were compared to a control group of nonexercisers in another insurance company. The Canada Life classes included graded exercise routines as well as seminars on nutrition and weight control. A monthly newsletter gave practical tips on diet, hypertension, smoking and other health matters.

The results were gratifying. The programs attracted 35 percent of all employees (as many clerical as managerial staff), and after six months participants were doing regular 17-minute aerobic sessions, compared to no work-place exercise in the control group. Employee turnover during the ten-month study went down from 15 percent to 1.5 percent among exercising employees. Absenteeism in this group declined by 22 percent, and they used the medical system less often than the seden-tary group. The life-insurance company calcu-lated a potential overall saving of $150,000 annually if just 28 percent of employees parti-cipated in the health-promotion program — a saving of 1 percent of the payroll. Needless to say, even after the study ended, the company retained the health program.

In general, about 30 percent of employees will take up a regular workplace fitness and lifestyle program, but half are likely to defect over the first 6 to 18 months. Dropout rates are greatest among older people; the unpunc-tual; the obese; smokers; blue-collar workers; those with high blood pressure, angina, heart pain or arthritis; people with unsupportive partners; those who consider the instructor "uncaring" or "inattentive."

A recent University of Toronto study found that those adhering to fitness programs perceived them as fun, worthwhile, healthy or

---

BENEFITS OF A SUCCESSFUL WORKPLACE FITNESS PROGRAM

- convenient and easy to attend;
- no need to com-mute or find parking space;
- better morale and productivity due to less illness and less staff turnover, and greater concentra-tion on tasks;
- boosted self-esteem, owing to fitter self-image and the feeling that the employer cares about employee well-being;
- solidarity and group spirit, from the shared camaraderie;
- reduced healthcare costs;
- lowered life-insur-ance costs — some insurance companies offer reduced premi-ums to individuals who practice healthy lifestyles;
- better public image of organization; a health-promotion program improves corporate image at local and national levels.

"tension-relieving." Noncompliers, on the other hand, saw no link between exercise and good health, and many reported that they got enough exercise anyway — a false conviction common among nonexercisers.

The ABC's of a worksite fitness and lifestyle program

Programs range from simple exercise classes to full-scale health clubs with gymnasiums, swim-ming pools, running tracks and badminton or squash courts. Besides basic exercise facilities, comprehensive programs offer workshops on smoking cessation, back care, nutrition, weight control and stress management. To achieve its aims, a fitness program must be lively, safe and enjoyable — conveniently located, effectively led and attractively packaged. As a minimum effort, a company could offer a running track or an exercise room..

- *Creative planning* should include collaboration with employees. A fitness committee, with a director, proposes a budget, obtains funds, discusses how and where classes should be held.
- *A preliminary questionnaire* measures employee eagerness, exercise preferences (aerobics, swimming, jogging) and willingness to pay minimum fees to defray costs and maintain participation.
- *Involving upper management* is a key to success; if superiors take part in exercise classes, workers are encouraged to join in.
- *No universal blueprint* works for all; the

SHIFT WORK AND CIRCADIAN RHYTHMS

Companies can also improve productivity and employee health by careful scheduling of shift work. Since many jobs are now done around the clock, some workers are exposed to "occupational jet lag." Many shift-work schemes are arranged for convenience and economic expediency and ignore the body's natural circadian rhythm (biological clock), possibly wreaking havoc with worker health and efficiency.

While about a third of shift workers say they enjoy the changing schedules, citing the advantages of more free time, and days off that give them a chance to shop, bank and share family activities, others dislike it and feel unwell. Individuals vary in their susceptibility to health problems from shift work (gastrointestinal upsets, fatigue from lack of sleep). Those who are "owls" and adapt to changing sleep times may be more suited to shift work than "larks" who like set sleep and wake-up times. As their biological clocks struggle to adapt at the start of a shift change, most workers complain of discomforts such as headaches, mood swings and stress. An accumulated sleep debt may cause lapses in concentration and vigilance. Also the inner biological clock may keep body temperature and hormone levels low just when they should be high for optimal efficiency. Well-documented studies from many countries indicate a performance dip, with diminished attention, between 2:00 and 4:00 a.m. — with a parallel increase in errors, performance failures and mishaps among train drivers, truckers, pilots, healthcare workers and others.

There is much debate about the best way to overcome these problems. One-week shifts are considered the most disrupting to physical, social and psychological health. It takes about a week for sleep-wake rhythms to adapt, and they're no sooner adjusted than a new shift begins and circadian rhythms must change afresh.

Although it's not always feasible, many experts suggest that shift-work rotations should be every three weeks instead of every week, to give the biological clock more time to adjust. While many North American companies now favor 21-day shifts, Europeans prefer shifts that change every two or three days, which don't disturb the circadian sleep-wake rhythm as much and avoid forcing the biological clock to adapt. This system also proves less disturbing to family and social life, as workers return to normal every third day.

program must be geared to target participants, whether clerical or sales staff, executives or laborers.

- *A preliminary fitness test* for participants is wise, and is best done in conjunction with the company's health department, to assess safe limits for exercising.
- *Showers* are an absolute requirement.
- *The program should attract 20–30 percent* of employees as regular adherents. It may also draw in the unfit and nonexercisers, not just the already converted. In Canadian companies, less than 5 percent of employees are usually committed to vigorous physical activity; hence, a fitness program that attracts even 20 percent is enhancing the health of at least 15 percent more.
- *Limiting initial enrollment,* far from deterring participation, often creates interest.
- *Set realistic goals* that don't raise false hopes for a magic route to guaranteed health.
- *Broad-based, varied programs* work best — with graded exercise classes and varied activities (as seasons permit), including lifestyle-improvement seminars.

- *Skilled, well-trained, enthusiastic leadership* is crucial. An invigorating, creative and credible fitness instructor, who can explain things clearly and individualize exercise prescriptions, is a top priority, and well worth the cost entailed.
- *The fitness instructor should be qualified in first aid* and CPR; if not, other employees with these skills should be on call.
- *Classes should be convenient and accessible,* preferably conducted at the worksite.
- *Good facilities* improve adherence, and are more important than expensive equipment in making classes a success.
- *Flextime is best,* allowing various exercise times.
- *The approach should be lighthearted,* nonjudgmental and sociable. Participants will broadcast the success of an enjoyable program.

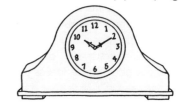

TOWARD HEALTHIER GLOBAL TRAVEL

As tourists increasingly venture off the beaten track, they become more susceptible to infections such as traveler's diarrhea and rare diseases such as Lassa and Dengue fever. It's wise to obtain health advice from reliable sources such as travel clinics before you leave home. If you get sick during or after your travels, be sure to tell the doctor where you have been and ask whether the problem could be travel-related.

Travel to most parts of North America and Europe (including the former Soviet Union) and the Caribbean requires fewer precautions than going to Asia, Africa or South America. Staying in clean, air-conditioned hotels poses fewer health risks than camping, going to less traveled places or renting a local room. The well-nourished are less apt to become ill than the poorly fed. Remaining in disease-ridden areas for lengthy stays obviously brings greater risks than a short vacation.

Tips to keep adventurous trippers healthier:

- *Travel tip #1*

  See your physician before departure, especially to exotic places. Get advice on sensible precautions, what to take in a medicine kit and where and when to get any needed immunizations. Take a medical kit containing bandages, adhesive plaster, antiseptic and antibiotic creams, antinauseants, antimalarial tablets (if needed), antihistamines, painkillers, antidiarrheal agents, tablets for purifying water, insect repellents, antibiotic pills (to treat traveler's diarrhea), any special prescription medications and needles plus syringes in a commercial kit (with a physician's letter explaining why you're carrying them, i.e., to have a clean, non-AIDS-contaminated set in case of need). Keep records of any drugs used. Take spare eyeglasses. One University of Toronto travel expert suggests including condoms because, as he rhymes it: "a tisket, a tasket, a condom or a casket." If appropriate, wear a Medic-Alert bracelet documenting allergies and special individual health problems.

- *Travel tip #2*

  Review your inoculation status and seek advice about any immunization boosters needed against diphtheria, polio, tetanus, measles, rubella and mumps. Get your required shots in good time. Immunization requirements vary from country to country. (See "Immunization schedule" in chapter 10.) Inoculations against some diseases rare in North America, such as yellow fever and cholera, are regulated by the World Health Organization (WHO). Since vaccination requirements and travel risks change, travelers should check with a travel clinic, officer of health or Health and Welfare Canada to see what is advised for the areas you plan to visit.

- *Tetanus vaccination* is essential for all non-immunized travelers. Tetanus is caused by a bacterium that exists in the soil, and is found throughout the world but is more prevalent in damp, warm climates. Tetanus vaccine gives effective protection, but booster shots are needed every 10 years.

- *Diphtheria reimmunization* may be needed (every 10 years) because, although diphtheria is uncommon in Canada, it's still widespread elsewhere.

- *Rubella* (German measles) is a relatively mild and innocuous infection in adults, but can drastically malform unborn babies; all women of childbearing age should ensure they have the necessary booster shots.

Travelers may also need vaccination for the following less common diseases:

- *Yellow fever*, a viral disease transmitted by mosquitoes. WHO requires inoculation (which lasts 10 years) at designated yellow-fever centers for anyone entering or passing through an infected zone. Some countries demand yellow-fever vaccination for all entering visitors, others only for those from certain areas.

- *Cholera*, a bacterial illness transmitted through water, is still rampant in Asia, Africa and the Middle East and has recently broken out in South America. Cholera is not much of a danger to travelers provided they drink safe water and don't eat unpeeled fruit or uncooked shellfish. Since existing vaccines give little protection, cholera inoculation is no longer recommended. For countries that still require vaccination certificates, some Canadian doctors issue exemption certificates or give one dose of cholera vaccine to satisfy foreign authorities.

- *Typhoid fever*, a worldwide febrile disease transmitted via food and water, is prevalent wherever there's poor sanitation and hygiene. The currently available typhoid vaccines (including the new oral Vivotif Berna and the injectable Typhin-V) offer partial — about 75 percent — protection.

- *Meningococcal disease* (meningitis) can occur in epidemic proportions — as happened recently in Kenya and Tanzania. Vaccines are available against strains A, C, Y and W-135 and are advised for those staying two weeks or more in areas where the disease is a major problem — for instance, in Central Africa, Egypt, Chad, Ethiopia, Morocco and parts of India.

- *Hepatitis*, a viral liver infection, is acquired from fecally contaminated food and water or the blood and secretions of carriers. The various forms of viral hepatitis (A, B, C and D) are caused by different viruses. There's now an effective vaccine against hepatitis B (which is especially prevalent in South East Asia and Africa). Those traveling to areas where hepatitis B is epidemic should be immunized against it, as it has a 1 percent mortality rate and leads to liver cancer. Although less dangerous than hepatitis B, the A form is more frequently encountered by travelers. Hepatitis A can be prevented by a shot of immune serum globulin (gamma globulin), which gives protection for three to six months. (For more on hepatitis, see chapters 11 and 16.)

- *Japanese B encephalitis* vaccine is suggested for travelers to rural South East Asia, especially in summer and fall. This mosquito-borne disease is prevalent in rice-growing areas of China, Nepal, Thailand, Vietnam, Taiwan, Korea and the Philippines. Three doses of the Biken vaccine, one week apart, are recommended — if it's available.

- *Rabies* is a worldwide viral disease spread by wild and domestic animals such as foxes, raccoons and dogs. Those likely to come into intimate contact with wildlife and those staying for a long time in rabies-ridden areas of the developing world should be immunized.

- *Travel tip #3*
Protect yourself from malaria if traversing mosquito-infested areas. Malaria is still one of the greatest health threats to travelers abroad. It's a protozoal infection spread by mosquitoes that feed on human blood, usually biting between dusk and dawn. The main risk areas are: tropical parts of Africa, Asia, Mexico, South and Central America, Haiti, South East Asia and some Pacific islands. At present, malaria is on the upswing, partly owing to the cutback of insecticide spraying for environmental and other reasons. Although malaria can be transmitted from mother to unborn baby, and (rarely) via a contaminated blood transfusion, it is usually acquired from the bite of an infected female *anopheles* mosquito. The incubation period is 10–60 days but can be longer. The parasites enter the liver where they multiply, then break out, reenter the bloodstream and cause fever, chills, headache, muscle aches, fatigue, perhaps also vomiting and a cough. The illness can be fatal.

Even though malaria infects over 300 million people a year, and causes about two million deaths annually, it is still regarded by some as a rare and exotic affliction. Yet not so long ago malaria was quite common in Canada. Canada still reports about 250 cases a year, mainly among immigrants and those returning from trips to South America, Asia and Africa. For instance, on their return to Montreal and Vancouver from a trip to Africa, two students fell ill with flu-like symptoms. A teacher familiar with the tropics suspected that the Montreal student might have malaria and suggested treatment in hospital. The diagnosis confirmed, antimalaria treatment was promptly begun and the student swiftly recovered. His travel companion from Vancouver was less fortunate; his malaria wasn't diagnosed, but just taken for flu, and he died of the illness soon after getting home.

A killer strain of malaria, not treatable by

the main antimalarial drug, chloroquine phosphate, has now emerged in many tropical areas. Of the four types of malarial infection in humans, *Plasmodium falciparum* is the most lethal, and those going to risk areas need special preventive drugs. None of the drugs currently available guarantees complete protection, but mefloquine is now the drug of choice for travel to areas with chloroquine-resistant malaria.

As a preventive, get and take antimalarials, cover yourself well, sleep under mosquito nets and use insect repellent. New, light, portable mosquito nets, with bamboo frames are a good idea. (Bear in mind that the mosquitoes that carry Dengue fever may even bite during the day.)

Treatment of malaria must be swift and appropriate, to prevent respiratory failure and even death. A fever in any traveler coming from a malarial area should be considered a medical emergency. Since some forms of malaria linger in the body (even in those who have been conscientiously taking antimalarials), people who have visited a danger zone and develop a fever or chills within two years of their travels — especially within the first few months — should suspect malaria and seek prompt treatment.

To protect yourself from malaria:
- Reduce time spent outdoors from dusk to dawn, and wear protective clothing, covering legs and arms.
- Apply a nonaerosol insect repellent to all exposed skin, the most effective being 30-percent or higher-strength *diethyl-m-toluamide* or DEET (a chemical found in Muskol, Off, Deep Woods and other preparations). This product should not be used in excess on children, or put on wounded or irritated skin.
- Sleep in screened lodgings or under mosquito nets.
- Take antimalarial drugs at least 24 hours before (ideally a week or two before) entering a danger zone; continue regularly throughout your stay and for four weeks after returning.
- Watch for and report any adverse side

effects from antimalarial drugs — such as itchiness, swelling, nausea or a skin rash. Although antimalarial drugs do not prevent the mosquito from infecting you, they usually stop the symptoms from appearing.
- *Travel tip # 4*
Avoid or learn to treat "traveler's diarrhea," also known as turista, Montezuma's Revenge, the Hong Kong dog, Delhi belly, Casablanca crud, the Rangoon runs and the Aztec two-step. Traveler's diarrhea, due to bacterial organisms, affects up to 80 percent of unwary vacationers to areas such as Mexico, Southern Asia and the Caribbean. Typically, it causes one or more short episodes of watery stools, often starting one to five days after arrival or five days after leaving an endemic area. It is due to bacterial contamination of food or water. The diarrhea may be accompanied by abdominal cramps, vomiting, chills, fever and appetite loss. Blood and mucus are not usually present in the diarrheal stool; if they are, get immediate medical advice. Self-remedies are fine for mild to moderate diarrhea but severe bouts need medical attention — because of the risk of more serious problems.

Drink clear fluids such as broth, bottled carbonated drinks and clear tea (no milk) until the diarrhea stops. Stick to rice, noodles, puréed cooked foods (carrots, apples, potatoes) until better, and resume full diet gradually. Add milk products last. Don't take medications such as Enterovioform or those containing chloramphenicol (a bone-marrow depressant). Use medications that slow diarrhea, such as Lomotil, Imodium or paregorics, sparingly. (Imodium and Lomotil can also be used in children: they work by slowing the bowel spasms.) Do not use even these drugs when there is high fever, chills or persistent (bloody) diarrhea. In such cases consult a doctor.

To avoid or manage traveler's diarrhea, don't eat undercooked or uncooked food, avoid leftovers, unpasteurized milk or milk products and raw shellfish, and eat only peelable fruit. Remember that fruits and vegetables in some countries are washed in impure, fecally contaminated water. Always wash fruit and vegetables with previously boiled or bottled water. If food can't be washed or peeled, boil or bake it well. Drink only beverages made with purified or commercially bottled water. For fluid replacement one travel expert recommends Gastrolyte as "ideal for children or adults."

To clear up traveler's diarrhea, take 28g (2 tbsp) or two tablets of Pepto-Bismol every half-hour. Eight doses often clear up traveler's diarrhea. Some travel advisors suggest carrying self-treatment antibiotics such as norfloxacin, ciprofloxacin or trimethoprim sulfamethoxazole, to be taken when the diarrhea starts; the dose for moderate to severe diarrhea is one tablet twice daily for three days. These same antibiotics, or Pepto-Bismol, can be taken as preventives for traveler's diarrhea, but are usually so advised only for high-risk travelers (with health problems). Physicians warn against the routine use of antibiotics such as trimethoprim (Septra,

Bactrim) as a preventive because they may cause sun-sensitivity, allergies, super-infections and drug-resistant infection.

- *Travel tip # 5*
Drink only "safe" water, or purify it. Water (including ice cubes) in most tropical countries is contaminated because of poor sewage disposal and improperly treated water supplies. Animals and humans may defecate in the water supply. Filtration alone isn't enough. Even staying at first-class hotels doesn't guarantee pure water.

Safe drinks include:
- beverages (such as tea and coffee) made with boiled water;
- canned or commercially bottled carbonated beverages, including bottled water, soft drinks, beer and wine. Wipe obviously dirty bottles or cans before drinking;
- coconut juice directly from the shell;
- water you have purified yourself.

To purify water, add chlorine bleach (two drops per liter or quart) until the chlorine smell is just detectable after mixing, or add 2 percent tincture of iodine (five drops per liter or quart), or boil the water — bringing it to a boil is usually sufficient. The Water-Tech portable purifiers are lightweight and ideal for short-term trips, work well and last a long time. They can purify more than 455 liters (100 gal) of water.

To make water safe for tooth brushing, collect the hottest water possible from the tap in a clean glass and let it cool.
- *Travel tip # 6*
Do not wander barefoot in unknown places. Protect the feet against cuts, abrasions, snakebites, insects (sand fleas and ticks) and parasites such as hookworms and threadworms. Several parasites and worms can burrow through the foot's unbroken skin. (See also below, tip # 9.)
- *Travel tip # 7*
Be aware of a few rare but potentially deadly infections that may afflict travelers to exotic places:
- *Lassa fever*, first described in Nigeria in 1969, is one of the most dangerous viral illnesses. It is transmitted by an arenavirus

HINTS FOR AVOIDING TRAVELER'S DIARRHEA

- **Avoid salads and raw vegetables (often contaminated by nightsoil — excrement used as fertilizer) and dressings such as mayonnaise. Eat only freshly cooked, hot vegetables.**
- **Wash all fruit and vegetables with soap and water before peeling and eating.**
- **Tomatoes should also be washed, and should be unbruised.**
- **Eat no leftovers.**
- **Don't use food from bent or dented cans.**
- **Avoid buffets or a "chef's special table," particularly if food is outdoors and exposed to flies. Cold meats provide an excellent milieu for infective organisms, particularly in**

tropical heat and humidity. Stick to well-cooked meats, served hot. (Even in Canada, eaters of raw sushi risk infection.)
- **Stay away from unpasteurized ice-cream and other dairy foods. Tuberculosis and brucellosis may be passed on from infected cow's milk, and contaminated water may be added to milk to make it go farther! Consume only dairy products labeled as "pasteurized."**
- **Avoid ice cubes. Freezing water does not kill organisms, nor does the alcohol in a drink (although strong liquor does reduce bacterial**

numbers).
- **Don't swim, wade or wash in unfamiliar fresh or sea water, only in chlorinated pools. Swimming in the ocean is safe only if the beach is far from the mouth of a river or sewage outlet.**
- **Remember that besides traveler's diarrhea, which is usually mild and self-limiting, other diseases with diarrhea as a symptom — such as typhoid, cholera, hepatitis and parasitic infections — can be acquired from contaminated food and drink producing bloody stool, fever and other symptoms besides diarrhea.**

found in the urine of rodents in rural areas of West Africa, producing high fever and prostration.

- *Dengue fever*, generally mild and short-lived, is transmitted by day-biting mosquitoes and is common in the Caribbean, South East Asia, Central America, the South Pacific and Africa. It comes in various forms and characteristically produces a sudden high fever, sore throat, severe joint and muscle aches and a rash on the torso and face — rather like measles.

- *Encephalitis*, a viral infection of the nervous system spread by mosquitoes and ticks, occurs in rural areas of Europe, the former Soviet Union and the Orient, especially during summer months. General anti-insect precautions should be taken — wear long-sleeved shirts and long pants, use DEET insecticide.

- *Sleeping sickness (trypanosomiasis)* is a rare, insect-borne disease that causes acute fever and can strike visitors to African game reserves. The African variety is carried by tsetse flies. South American trypanosomiasis (also called Chagas' disease) is transmitted by bugs that live in the mud cracks of adobe huts and in thatched roofs.

- *Leishmaniasis*, transmitted by sand flies, has an incubation period of months to years and results in skin sores and a rarely serious febrile illness. It occurs mainly in India, Asia and some Mediterranean areas.

- *Travel tip # 8*
Acclimatize yourself and combat "jet lag." Maintain adequate fluids and get enough rest to avoid stress, heatstroke and immune-system problems. Wear loose-fitting clothes in hot climates, bathe often and dry well afterwards. If you have high blood pressure and go to a hot climate, minimize blood-pressure problems due to the heat by seeking air-conditioned rest places.

In adapting to a warm climate, your body must adjust to sweating without undue loss of salt, and to working in the heat. Pretravel preparation, suitable clothing, sunglasses, sun lotions and adequate fluid intake assist acclimatization, which is especially tough for the old, the obese and those who are in poor health

or have chronic ailments such as diabetes.

Reduce stress on the body by taking two suitcases instead of one massive, heavy one. Take an inflatable neck pillow for comfort while traveling. Since acclimatization takes several days, travelers should rest after arrival, particularly if their flight has taken them through several time zones. Take along a few candy bars, dried fruit or other energy foods in case altered schedules lead to long delays without food. (Diabetics in particular should prepare for this contingency.)

Avoid jet lag by paying attention to your biological clock, which automatically regulates temperature, hormone secretion and many other body functions in a 24-hour rhythm. For a westward time shift, the biological (circadian) system requires about two days to readjust the sleep-wake cycle, five for body temperature, and eight days or more for other rhythms. Jet lag lasts longer and is more troublesome going east than west. Diabetics and heart patients must keep accurate track of time to take their medication as needed. People with angina or other heart trouble should beware of high altitudes and bring plenty of their prescribed medication. (Bring twice the usual amount in case the stay is extended.)

- *Travel tip # 9*
Do not swim, wade or even dabble in unknown, untreated fresh waters (chlorinated swimming pools are fine). Many water-dwelling parasites in hot climates can enter the skin, including schistosomiasis. Schistosomas are blood flukes that go from snails to humans and then back again from human feces to snails. The schistosome parasites are released by snails into the water (river, stream or pond) and infect people by penetrating the skin. Once inside the body, they travel through the bloodstream and damage the large intestine, bladder, liver and lungs. Schistosomiasis, also known as bilharzia, is prevalent in all African fresh waters, the Middle East, the Caribbean, parts of South America and South East Asia. Ask about contamination before wading, swimming or plunging into foreign waters. If accidentally wet, dry off as fast as possible.

- *Travel tip #10*

  Be wary of your means of transportation in foreign places. Next to heart disease and cancer, the next major cause of death among vacationers is motor-vehicle accidents. Travelers should avoid overcrowded public vehicles and especially motorcycles (the number-one killer abroad). Rural travel should never be attempted at night. Taxi drivers who are reckless or drive too fast should be cautioned. Always buckle up — if there's a seatbelt! Know your blood type. If you need a transfusion and have time, locate blood that's been tested and shown free of HIV (AIDS) and hepatitis B viruses, and call your embassy (or other official representation).

Home again — what to do on your return

Since infections can remain latent in your body for a long time before erupting, it's a good idea to be on the lookout for their signs and symptoms during and after distant travels. See your physician if you feel at all unwell, feverish or overly tired, or if you have persistent diarrhea. Report any unusual swelling, skin rash, sore or itch. Tell your physician where you have been, and about any medical complaints or treatments while you were away. And be sure to keep on taking your antimalarial drugs for the full four weeks after you are back.

For more travel health information, contact public-health units, travel clinics (where they exist) in hospitals — such as those in Toronto at the Toronto Hospital (tel.: 416-595-3670) or St. Michael's Hospital (tel.: 416-360-4000); your family physician; Health and Welfare Canada offices; CATMAT (The Committee to Advise on Tropical Medicine and Travel) — established by Health and Welfare Canada. Or consult Missionary Health Institute International Travel Services, at 4000 Leslie Street, Willowdale, Ontario M2K 2R9 (tel.: 416-494-7512). Consult MMWR (Morbidity and Mortality Weekly Report from the U.S. Centers for Disease Control), which has a supplement called "Health Advice for International Travel" providing updates on current recommendations and infectious-disease outbreaks around the world — the travel expert's "bible." Read "Don't Drink the Water," published by the Canadian Society for International Health and the Canadian Public Health Association. See the Canadian "Recommendations for Preventing and Treating Malaria among International Travellers," published by CATMAT, or contact the International Association for Medical Assistance to Travelers (IAMAT); in Ontario call 416-652-0137.

Coping with mental and emotional problems

Where does stress come from? • Coping with stress • Depression • Postpartum depression • Holiday blues • Manic depression • Chronic fatigue syndrome • The disabling effects of anxiety disorders • Schizophrenia • Finding therapy for mental and emotional problems

HEALTH SURVEYS consistently reveal that 15 percent or more of North Americans have emotional or mental disturbances severe enough to require professional help. Mental health problems range from stress-related discomforts to anxiety disorders and phobias, and — at the far end of the scale — mental illnesses such as schizophrenia. Since anxiety, depression and other mental disorders may express themselves in physical terms, it's not always easy for physicians to discern the underlying problem.

According to one University of Toronto professor of psychiatry, "Mental and emotional disorders often masquerade or 'somatize' as physical ailments. In fact, more than 50 percent of people with psychosocial distress first present to doctors with physical complaints, such as muscle aches, headache, back pain, dizziness, nervousness, digestive upsets, sleeplessness and fatigue." Somatization is defined as "a tendency to express emotional or mental disturbances in physical terms, especially common in those with anxiety disorders or depression." The psychiatrist explains that "Somatizers typically find it difficult to acknowledge emotional upsets, personal feelings, losses or conflict. They may view mental or emotional disturbances as a weakness, preferring to assume the sick role because of organic ailments — such as allergy or

fatigue syndromes — which are regarded as beyond control and not one's fault." In other words, somatization helps people unconsciously disguise the reasons for the distress and so avoid the stigma of mental illness. According to psychiatrists, some chronic somatizers will embrace each "newly discovered, poorly defined, fashionable ailment," such as candidiasis (bodily yeast invasion), 'Yuppie flu' or twentieth-century allergy disease, to explain undiagnosed complaints of unwellness — a maladaptive way to deal with an underlying mental disorder.

WHERE DOES STRESS COME FROM?

Stress, which is the demand placed upon the body's physical and mental reserves, is essential to human productivity. Without it we become passive and wither — as sometimes happens when people are bored or unoccupied, or retire without planning ahead. A little stress acts as a human motivator and mobilizer, making us more alert and "on the ball." Students, for example, often do best with the pressure of exams; athletes may excel under the tension of a race; actors deliver their best lines before an audience rather than during rehearsal.

While stress can improve performance, too much is counterproductive. Everyone is exposed to some everyday stress, but how much is too much? In one evaluation, the stress levels of various events were rated comparatively. Ranked in order of highest to lowest stress-producers were: death of a spouse or

14

SOME SIGNS OF MENTAL OR EMOTIONAL DISTURBANCE

- a pervasive sense of helplessness;
- inability to function normally;
- unexplained anxiety;
- irrational fears;
- incapacitating fatigue;
- sleep disturbances — unusual difficulty falling asleep, frequent nighttime awakening;
- diminished concentration powers,

- wandering attention;
- nervous restlessness;
- unmerited guilt feelings;
- obsessional behavior (e.g., checking endlessly to see if the stove's turned off or the toothpaste cap is in place);
- unshakable thought preoccupation (overriding usual interests and social interaction);

- lack of interest in family, friends; neglect of usual companions;
- dismal outlook, negative thoughts, crumbling defense mechanisms — a feeling of nothing working out "as it should";
- diminished sense of self-worth (a frequent sign of depression).

other loved one, divorce, jail term, robberies/hold-ups, personal injury, being fired, getting married, retirement, illness of a relative, moving house, changing schools, children leaving home, trouble with in-laws, mortgage foreclosure, workplace conflicts, holidays (especially Christmas).

What is stress?

There is no universally accepted definition of stress. Some psychologists define it as "a reaction to an observable event (stressor) that influences the person in a harmful way." Others call stress "a situation where the internal or external demands exceed the person's coping skills." Stress is harmful only if the events or situations causing it are *perceived* as burdensome, and if the body cannot adapt to the demands made upon it. Failure to adapt to stress may ultimately damage health.

Scientifically, stress is a "state of arousal" in which psychological, physiological and biochemical changes are provoked by specific stressors. A stressor is any force, change or event that calls upon a person's coping skills and inner resources. Stressors may be positive or negative. For instance, a job promotion or marriage, although a welcome change, nonetheless produces stress by necessitating change. A negative stressor, such as a loved one's death or losing a job, brings disturbing stress.

Stressors may be acute (such as nuclear accidents, divorce, bereavement), developmental (such as marriage, adolescence, a job promotion), or ongoing (such as poverty or an alcoholic parent). Workplace stressors include job overload or underload, time pressures, role ambiguity (uncertainty about lines of responsibility), role conflict (simultaneously trying to please those above and under oneself), fear of making mistakes, thwarted career plans, lack of promotion, shift work, an aggravating work environment (noise pollution, cigarette smoke, inadequate safety precautions).

Certain workplace stressors may be an integral part of the job. Telephone operators, for example, undergo stress from being constantly monitored for their voice and client approach, while also being bombarded with consumer questions they can't answer — about weather conditions, road reports, hospitals, restaurants and movies. Bus drivers too are plagued by job stress, pressured by the simultaneous need to meet schedules, be polite to passengers and deal with traffic. Worldwide, bus drivers suffer more than most employees from stress-related gastrointestinal disorders and hypertension (high blood pressure). Teachers also experience high stress levels; after idealistically setting out to enlighten the young, they may find themselves burdened with administrative chores, meal duties, budget cuts and uninterested or obstreperous pupils.

Tracing the stress pathway

Evolution marvelously prepared human beings to react to danger through the "fight-or-flight" response. In the immediate, alarm stage of this reaction, the adrenal glands release stimulatory hormones, the heart races to send oxygen faster around the body, extra glucose is supplied for energy, the hair "stands on end" (a throwback to the days when our heavy body-hair made us look larger), blood is diverted from the gut to the working muscles, and other changes make the body stronger and swifter. But this fight-or-flight response — very apt for fighting or fleeing tigers — hardly equips us to face most stressors of modern urban life.

Continued or frequent stress results in profound physical, emotional and psychological

STRESS PATHWAY

Stressor	⇨	Perception	⇨	Response	⇨	Outcomes
A change, event or situation that calls upon inner resources to adapt to or neutralize it.		How the stressor — event, situation or change — is perceived; e.g., as a threat or as a challenge that might promote growth.		**Short-term** Alarm/fight-or-flight reaction. Rise in adrenal medulla hormones, increased heartrate, blood sugar.		

		Response		Outcomes
Long-term				
Physical:	Increased corticoid hormones		Changes in blood lipids (fats)	
	Exhaustion		Peptic ulcers	
	Elevated blood pressure		Reduced immune defenses	
	Gastrointestinal upsets			
	Appetite changes			
Emotional:	Shock		Depression	
	Denial		Burnout	
	Anxiety			
Cognitive and Behavioral:	Self-medication		Chronic alcoholism/drug addiction	
	Refusal to face situation		Hide and give up	
	or		or	
	Rational problem solving		Rise to challenge and develop more coping skills	

N.B.: At each arrow, many individual factors influence the reaction.

---

changes. Skyrocketing levels of corticoid (adrenal gland) hormones and other biochemical changes can lead to extreme exhaustion; physical ailments such as chronic muscle aches, headaches and back pain; anxiety disorders; poor concentration; insomnia; social isolation; depression; burnout; high blood pressure; heart disease; weakened immune defenses (with increased risks of infection); and escape into alcohol and/or other drug abuse.

One person's challenge is another's threat

The amount of stress people can handle depends on genetic makeup, upbringing, coping mechanisms and social support. Reactions to a stressor also vary depending on the way we perceive it. While the outcome of stress can be very damaging, what one person finds devastating may stimulate another. In some people a stressful challenge even leads to personal growth and better coping mechanisms. Compare one widow who, unable to face her loss, never ventured out and became clinically depressed, to another who, after mourning her husband's death, took up a career and found satisfaction in new relationships.

These individual differences explain why — faced with events such as war, hijacking, job demotion or relocation — people react differently. The same situation can seem challenging ("the spice of life") or terrifying ("the kiss of death"), depending on how it's interpreted. Thus, a new supervisor, added duties or office computerization may present an intriguing challenge to some, while in others it provokes terror. Or a noon-hour fitness class may relieve tension in some but prove stressful to others who, perhaps, dislike group activities or hate wearing shorts. Jumping out of an airplane would daunt most of us, but is exhilarating to those who choose it as a personal challenge.

It's a fallacy to think that only high-level occupations or positions induce stress. Although executives, bureau chiefs and medical officers do bear heavy burdens — for looking after money, human beings and resources — they also possess the authority to carry through their aims. Bosses who "run

THE OUTCOME OF STRESS IS INFLUENCED BY:

- family background — for instance, whether there is a predisposition to depression, heart ailments or alcoholism;
- learned behavior and upbringing — someone who was taught problem-solving skills and acquired self-esteem at a parent's knee is likely to cope better with stress than a child of more punitive or authoritarian parents;
- mindset — individual cognitive (thinking) styles. A flexible, constructive, "problem-solving" mode in the face of difficulties, rather than panic, improves stress management;
- social support — having close relatives and friends to share problems with;
- a sense of "belonging" to a religious, national, ethnic or other group;
- solidarity with compatible colleagues and fellow workers who can give practical advice and "cover" when asked. A study of air-traffic controllers showed that those with close confidantes suffered fewer headaches, sleep disturbances, anxiety and other signs of stress.

the ship" tend to be less stressed than subordinates who shoulder responsibility but have little overall control. Assistants, secretaries and nurses, who often bear front-line responsibility for making things run smoothly but lack the authority to make decisions, are highly prone to stress. Traditionally, middle managers suffer the most stress.

People who let others make all their decisions can also suffer great stress, particularly if suddenly forced by circumstances (perhaps a death or separation from a spouse) to abandon the dependent role and take on responsibility. The change may precipitate extreme anxiety, leading to an "adjustment disorder" because of unmet dependency needs and lack of coping skills.

The three C's that lessen stress

People who feel in control of their own actions and on top of circumstances tend to deal more effectively with stress than those who see themselves as helpless victims buffeted by adverse circumstances. A recent study of executives showed that under prolonged stress some (but not others) developed hypertension and heart disease. Those who successfully withstood long-term stress not only felt "in command" but also had a so-called hardy personality, exemplified by the three C's: Control, Commitment and Challenge.

Effective stress-copers were *confidently* in control — with faith in their own abilities; were *committed* to any task in hand; and welcomed *challenge*. They tended to be involved in many activities — whether work, family or social — and viewed change, even if stressful, as part of life, not something aimed personally at them. Being curious and confident, they sought new ways to overcome setbacks and surmount hurdles.

COPING WITH STRESS

Stress-managing skills include the ability to communicate and share feelings, thoughts and problems — dialoguing with others at work or at home — and to put expectations in line with reality. Gaining control and learning to take charge of one's life is another powerful stress-coping strategy. Regular exercise helps to reduce tension. However, experts warn against regarding exercise, jogging or other sports as a panacea for stress reduction, since overachievers often take the same compulsive attitude to exercise programs as to the rest of life, and become stressed by activities undertaken for relaxation!

Stress-management courses may help

A flood of stress-management courses and programs has emerged, to help people change the way they perceive and respond to stress-inducing situations. They may focus on relaxation

BASIC STEPS IN COPING WITH STRESS

- **Sort out the stressors and assess which are avoidable, which not; avoid the avoidable.**
- **Think of ways to alter stress-provoking situations.**
- **Step back and appraise reality.**
- **Get rid of unrealistic expectations of yourself and others.**
- **Assess expectations and their achievability, admitting that no** one can always be perfect.
- **Don't condemn yourself for failure. Try to adopt a more self-accepting attitude.**
- **Adopt a philosophy of uncertainty to replace rigid anticipation.**
- **Take stock of priorities — decide what's a "must" and what can be deferred.**
- **Gain control over areas that** cause stress.
- **Emphasize strengths rather than weaknesses.**
- **Learn to say "Yes . . . but no," or "Sorry, I would love to, but I just can't help . . . stand in . . . cooperate this time."**
- **Incorporate rest periods into everyday schedules, making time for yourself.**
- **Be good to yourself at least once a day.**

techniques, deep-breathing routines, "sound health" or music therapy and biofeedback. Above all, such courses try to improve the personal sense of control. Therapists range from medically trained psychiatrists to social workers, psychologists, relaxation therapists, massage therapists and company Employee Assistance Program counselors.

Occupational burnout

"Burnout" — a popular but misapplied catchword — is often used to mean "stressed out" or exhausted by job-related activities. The term has become part of our vocabulary, loosely used for anyone who devotes too much time and energy to specific activities. There is considerable debate about the validity of this label applied to the complex, psychobiological outcomes of stress.

The term "burnout" was coined during the 1970s as street slang for excessive drug use, and later adopted to denote stress among healthcare personnel such as nurses, social workers and physicians, especially those working in pediatric wards, and intensive-care and psychiatric units. Nurses caring for sick infants frequently became emotionally attached to their tiny patients, suffering stress for those who later died. Health professionals in such units complained of irritability, anxiety, apathy, exhaustion and an inability to carry on. Psychologists attributed the syndrome to the relentless stress of daily exposure to conditions that were physically and emotionally taxing, and often worsened by budget cuts and staff shortages.

The concept of occupational burnout has since spread to people in many occupations, such as teachers, homemakers, air-traffic controllers, transit workers, administrators, dentists and lawyers (particularly those dealing with low-income clients). Experts emphasize, however, that burnout is a complex interaction between the job and people who tend to overinvest in their work.

A classic case of burnout is that of an intensive-care nurse who, having entered her career with idealistic hopes, found that, despite her dedication and best efforts, many patients — including tiny children — failed to recover. Case loads were excessive, overtime was frequent

and too little time was provided to comfort patients or relatives. Few thanks were given. Disappointed at her inability to save everyone, the lack of gratitude and the frustrations of the job, she would come home angry and "dump" on her husband, with uncontrollable crying fits. She finally lost all interest in both her patients and her household. The only solution was a complete break from nursing and a new career. (She went back to school, with the financial support of her spouse, and became a librarian!)

STRESS-MANAGEMENT COURSES GENERALLY OFFER:

- relaxation techniques, which may include special tricks such as "power naps," taking 10 minutes off for an exercise bout or visualizing a soothing activity to attain tranquillity;
- deep-breathing methods to improve muscle relaxation;
- exercise and fitness programs;
- advice on nutrition;
- self-help manuals; group therapy;
- training toward a positive outlook and improved self-image;
- mind-focusing strategies, repetition of personally meaningful words or phrases that help people calm down;
- altering thinking styles and positive "visualization";
- music therapy, special sound tapes and soothing imagery;
- training in meditation skills;
- advice on managing leisure time and vacations — perhaps taking several small holidays rather than one long one (which may bring its own stresses).

COPING SKILLS TO HANDLE OR REDUCE BURNOUT

- Step back, relax and appraise reality.
- Evaluate hopes and job expectations.
- Dissect and analyze the work situation — its demands and benefits.
- Improve time-management. Space and pace work better. Parcel tasks into smaller portions — don't try to do everything at once.
- Don't condemn yourself for occasional lapses, mistakes or failure to achieve aims.
- Recognize that work alone can rarely provide all life's rewards and satisfactions.
- Banish the idea that only job success is worthwhile.
- Diversify interests — cultivate hobbies.
- Become less of a perfectionist; tolerate flaws in yourself and others.
- Bolster self-esteem by rewarding yourself for tasks well done.
- Discuss problems with colleagues; share thoughts.
- Build social supports;
- nurture relationships.
- Practice "detached concern" rather than overinvolvement.
- Don't take work home too often — make a cut-off between work and home life. Have a "defuse" time between work and home, perhaps a walk or an exercise workout.
- Try to turn stress into a positive challenge.
- Attend stress-management courses. Learn relaxation techniques.

STAGES AND SIGNS OF BURNOUT

Stage 1: *The "eager beaver"*
- Overly high expectations of self and job.
- Feeling of omnipotence, perfectionism: "I can do anything"; "I will conquer all"; "I will never make mistakes."
- Idealistic, single-minded attitude.
- Unrealistic concept that job should be 100 percent satisfying.
- Expectation of continual praise and approval.
- Inability to detach from work situation.

Stage 2: *Disillusionment*
- Job not measuring up to expectations or fulfilling hopes.
- Guilt if any time taken off for self.
- Trying even harder; striving and pushing more.
- Dissatisfaction with own performance.
- Progressive loss of self-confidence.
- Reduced enthusiasm and creativity; disenchantment.
- Disappointment in co-workers.
- Sense of being unappreciated.
- Becoming impatient and argumentative.

Stage 3: *Frustration*
- Increasing fatigue, irritability, angry outbursts.
- Lowered job performance and morale; inappropriate reactions to people or situations, bitter remarks.
- Repetitive accidents, unfinished tasks.
- Spending more time achieving less.

- Finding fault with everyone and everything.
- Callous, detached attitude.
- Hostility toward formerly revered supervisors or well-liked colleagues.
- Denial of emotions, feelings; not sharing or discussing thoughts.
- Restless search for risky diversions (e.g., parachuting, deep-sea diving).
- Boredom, bouts of absenteeism.

Stage 4: *Despair and apathy*
- Negative self-image; sense of failure.
- Apathy, loss of energy, resignation.
- Helplessness, sense of drowning.
- Alienation, emptiness, refusal to see friends.
- Conflict-laden dreams.
- Neglected personal appearance.
- Extreme cynicism: the former workaholic, having lost all devotion to the cause, becomes increasingly bitter.
- Forgetting appointments, deadlines.
- Losing possessions.
- Rash of minor physical ailments — headaches, stomach upsets, bowel problems, colds, backaches.
- Morbid fear of death.
- Mental, physical and emotional exhaustion — spiritual malaise
- The endpoint of burnout — inability to continue daily activities.

Job-person mismatch is usually to blame

The job environment alone is rarely responsible for occupational burnout; there's no such thing as a job that's equally taxing for all. Job stress arises not just from the specific task but from the *interaction* of the person and the job. If the demands of a position exceed someone's abilities, or if an employee lacks the mental agility needed, that position will prove stressful for that individual. For example, a job that requires typing at 80 words per minute will pressure someone who can do only 40 words per minute. A job that requires knowledge of math will prove stressful to someone who dropped it in grade 9. Working in an air-control tower may seem extremely stressful, but given the necessary expertise, together with a personality that thrives on a hectic pace, it may in fact be exciting.

Occupational stress is likely to produce burnout in people with unrealistic notions about their own capacities and what the job can offer. It is common in those who devote their "all" to work and little to outside interests.

IT'S NOT JUST THE INDIVIDUAL'S PROBLEM

Since the reasons for job stress stem jointly from the organization and the individual, minimizing it should also be a shared venture. Healthy organizational approaches could include the following:
- Allowing workers to participate in decisions that affect their jobs.

- Job rotation to give periodic relief from front-line positions — perhaps by temporary transfer to an administrative, training or research position.
- Organizational attempts to foster peer support networks, either through team-building or by allotting time to discussion of staff stress.
- Feedback about performance; praise for tasks well done.
- Flexible schedules.
- Fitness programs to enhance well-being.
- Helping people channel stress, which is an integral part of existence, toward enhanced productivity.

Burnout is often seen in "type-A" overachievers. The type-A personality is said to have free-floating hostility and overaggressive competitiveness — typified by a confrontational approach, a tendency to shout, abuse and blame others and "hurry-sickness" — an exaggerated sense of urgency, and a compulsion to do everything in a rush rather than ponder actions. Others who fall prey to job stress may have striven too hard to reach their goal, or may have exaggerated expectations.

Those to whom job success is critical for self-esteem are more likely to suffer burnout than those whose self-worth derives from non-work sources such as family, children, friends and hobbies. People with a poor self-image may succumb to burnout because they view all failures as their own fault rather than as a common workplace problem. For example, people with work overload may believe they should be able to "accomplish everything," rather than admitting it would be too much for anyone. Some suffer burnout owing to a lack of appreciation and a feeling of inadequacy; they need constant approval to feel worthwhile.

Experts warn against jumping to the conclusion that someone is "burned out" when the symptoms may stem from another disorder. Burnout must be differentiated from depression and other mental illnesses before diagnosis is made. Signs of depression often mimic those of burnout — namely, changes in sleep patterns (typically early awakening), diminished appetite, diurnal mood swings (feeling low in the morning, more cheerful as the day progresses), muscular fatigue (as if "walking through molasses"), a dry mouth.

DEPRESSION: MORE THAN JUST TRANSIENT BLUES

Occasionally feeling glum and discouraged is a normal response to the strains and stresses of everyday life; sporadic bouts of the blues may arise for no obvious reason. But although such spells are colloquially described as "depression," the term also refers to a clinical mood disturbance that needs professional help. Effective treatment is now available and in most cases can do much to alleviate the misery of true depression, even though, to those submerged by it, recovery often seems impossible.

Health professionals subdivide depressive illnesses into unipolar and bipolar forms. If depression is the only mood (or "affective") disturbance, the disorder has one "pole" and is called *unipolar depressive disorder*. If there are alternating phases of depression and mania (exaggerated elation), with mood swings at two extreme poles, the condition is termed *bipolar disorder* — also known as manic-depressive disorder, or "la folie circulaire" (circular insanity).

Clinical depression (unipolar disorder)

Depression ranges from a mild bout of the "blues," to a deeper dejection in which people can still function and work, to a severe clinical condition where depressives lose touch with reality and can barely summon up the will to eat, drink or move. This condition — "clinical depression" — is a definite psychiatric illness. Once viewed as a spiritual malady, depression is now considered a disorder of body, mind and spirit, involving physical, biochemical and mental changes.

Depression respects no boundaries, affecting kings and ordinary folk alike. One account of depression is the Old Testament story of King Saul, whose episodes of guilt and despair were relieved only when David, the Bethlehem shepherd boy, played his harp. As his illness progressed, the king's black moods became less and less amenable to the shepherd's music, and ultimately Saul killed himself.

Renaissance writers frequently mention "melancholia" — a trait sometimes considered a mark of refinement. The word "melancholy" describes the bleak outlook typical of real depressives. Many great figures reportedly suffered from depression, among them George Washington, Charles Darwin, Lord Byron, Abraham Lincoln and Winston Churchill — who referred to his depression as a "black dog." The British poet John Milton frequently referred to his "moping melancholy," Shakespeare refers to that "sad companion, dull-eyed melancholy," Samuel Johnson described depression as a malady that made him "arise earlier than desired," filling him with a "constant dread of insanity," and Sigmund Freud, who wrote extensively about depression as "separation loss," self-treated his depressive episodes with opium.

Depressive illness affects 3 to 20 percent of North Americans at least once in their lifetime, regardless of race, nationality, religion or culture. Sickness, death and suicide rates are high among the severely depressed. The average age of onset is midlife, but about a third of those who experience a major depressive episode suffer it only once. Depression may be precipitated by hormonal changes, loss or stressful events (e.g., financial worries, job loss). Estimates suggest that less than 10–25 percent of depressives seek or receive medical treatment. Married people and those with an intimate companion apparently suffer less depressive illness than the widowed, divorced and lonely. Curiously, men, but not necessarily women, are protected against depression by marriage.

Depression is a common psychiatric illness among the elderly. However, some signs of depression — appetite loss, sleep problems, delusional thoughts — are often mistakenly attributed to normal aging or some medical problem, and therefore not given proper attention. Correct treatment of depression in seniors can bring remarkable improvement in outlook and function, and avoid suicide attempts, so common among seniors, especially men.

In children and adolescents, depression is often hard to recognize. In young children it frequently reveals itself by a constant woefulness despite a reluctance to cry, or in school by behavioral or learning problems, withdrawal, antisocial actions, slow speech, reading difficulties, a refusal to attend class and poor eating habits.

During adolescence, depression may show itself by antisocial or aggressive behavior, perhaps accompanied by grouchiness, withdrawal from family closeness, irritability and inexplicably worsening school grades. It can lead to suicide attempts, and parents who notice such changes should keep an eye on their teenager and have the behavior investigated. (See also the section on teenage suicide in chapter 12.)

In every culture, women are allegedly twice as likely as men to suffer clinical depression. Some experts question the sex discrepancy, suggesting that women only *appear* to suffer more depression than men because they more easily admit to mental problems and seek therapy, while men escape into alcohol, drugs and suicide. Dispute not withstanding, women in lower income brackets and those divorced and widowed seem to be most likely to suffer. Studies show that young, unemployed women, especially those living alone with dependent children, are the group most vulnerable to depressive illness.

How to recognize clinical depression

Typically, depression shows a diurnal or night-and-day variation — most depressed people feel worse in the morning, with a gradual mood lift as the day wears on. Major depressive episodes are usually self-limiting and ultimately pass, but left untreated they may last six to nine months or more.

In adults, clinical depression may be marked by slowed thoughts and sluggish actions, a tendency to fidget restlessly with the hands and feet, self-devaluation, magnification of past failures and exaggeratedly despondent feelings that surpass the bounds of normal. The hallmark of depression is *anhedonia* — a loss of pleasure pervasive enough to color all of life with inescapable gloom.

Although highly variable, the mood changes in depression often have a peculiar quality described as "feeling strange" or "a loss of all feeling" — no longer "caring about anything or anyone." Some sufferers describe the descent of "a black cloud of doom." The classic depressive is a Hamlet-like figure: a self-critical brooder, interminably mulling over minor shortcomings and perceived guilts, convinced the malady is deserved and incurable, obsessed with suicide — indecisively agonizing whether "to be or not to be."

The American Psychiatric Association defines clinical depression as a major affective disorder with emotional, cognitive (thinking), behavioral and vegetative (physical) distortions. The mood becomes joyless; thought patterns are negativistic and actions slow down as if burdened by a heavy weight. The dysphoric (pleasureless) mood is accompanied by at least four of about 15 symptoms. Sleep patterns are altered, appetite wanes; vague aches and pains are frequent; bowel and bladder function can be disturbed. The depressed may hallucinate, perhaps

SIGNS AND SYMPTOMS OF CLINICAL DEPRESSION

Criteria that identify a major depressive episode

A major depressive syndrome is characterized by a pervasive loss of pleasure and at least four of the following symptoms:
- poor appetite and weight loss (or increased appetite and weight gain)
- energy diminution
- fatigue and weakness
- sleeping poorly or oversleeping (altered sleep rhythm)
- slowed movements or restless agitation
- anxiety, helplessness, despair
- loss of interest in usual activities
- reduced sex drive
- slowed, confused thinking, inability to concentrate
- unusual indecisiveness
- self-reproach, feelings of worthlessness
- inappropriate guilts
- crying spells, recurrent brooding, suicidal thoughts

N.B.: Symptoms must be present almost every day for two or more weeks, occur without other medical conditions (disease), and not be preceded by other psychiatric disorders (such as schizophrenia). In children under six, at least three of the first four symptoms should be present for at least two weeks, nearly every day (with a constantly sad expression and inability to cry).

Note: Depression often accompanies diseases certain as lung, pancreatic and other cancers, hypothyroidism and drug/alcohol abuse; it can be induced by certain medications, such as anti-hypertensives and steroids.

In fact, depression may be the first indicator of certain physical diseases, requiring treatment both for depressive and disease symptoms.

Common signs and symptoms by which to recognize clinical depression:

1. PHYSICAL (VEGETATIVE) CHANGES:
- *Appetite and weight disturbances.* Waning appetite and weight loss, a bad taste or a dry mouth and altered bowel habits may signal depression; the depressed person may become thin and haggard. Paradoxically, a few depressives overeat and rapidly gain weight.
- *Sleep and circadian rhythm alterations.* Many depressives have distorted circadian rhythms (biological clocks), with disturbed sleep patterns. Typically, depressives awaken early in the morning and lie awake brooding. Trouble falling asleep and night-insomnia can occur but are more characteristic of anxiety. Many depressed people sleep less than usual, awaken in the middle of the night, perhaps weeping inconsolably. Hypersomnia (oversleeping), where the depressed sleep as much as 12 to 14 hours nightly, can occur, but is less

common. Rapid eye movement (REM) sleep (with dreaming) tends to be more frequent, the dream state coming on more abruptly and vividly than normal, although the total amount of dream-time may be below normal.
- *Slowed movement.* The depressed seem to droop, sag and walk slowly — as though laboring under a great weight. But psychomotor agitation can also occur, with twitchy restlessness. Depressives may find it hard to sit still; they may pace up and down, wring their hands, pull at their hair or twist objects interminably in their hands.
- *Waning sex drive.*
- *Loss of energy, weakness and extreme fatigue.* No "get up and go," a reluctance to dress, go to work or do tiny chores (which appear as monumental tasks).

2. EMOTIONAL FACTORS:
- *Lack of interest, feelings, merriment and inability to have fun.* The most universal sign of depression is an absence of pleasure in activities which normally give satisfaction. An expressionless, blank face, reduced eye-scanning, a downcast look or a slow, monotonous voice can signal mood change. Severely depressed patients may become unable to move, eat or talk, all willpower seemingly gone.
- *Anxiety.* Some 60–70 percent of depressives feel anxious with impaired autonomic (involuntary) nervous system control (resulting in increased heart rate, blood pressure and respiration).
- *Irritability and unusual hostility.* The depressed may appear abnormally upset by minor unpleasant events.

3. COGNITIVE (THINKING) DISTORTIONS:
- *Loss of concentration and decision-making ability.* Impeded performance can magnify feelings of self-doubt and failure, especially in perfectionists who recognize their reduced mental prowess; the simplest decisions — such as writing a letter or beginning a meal — may take hours.
- *A sense of worthlessness.* Rumination about faults and failures, either real or imaginary, is common. Plagued by remorse, depressives blame themselves for their illness, insisting they have let others down — a disturbed judgment about which it is usually impossible to reason.
- *A hopelessly bleak outlook.* All goals — including recovery — seem unattainable.
- *Hypochondriacal preoccupation about health.* Exaggerated, unfounded fears of nonexistent madness or impending death are common.
- *Suicidal thoughts and death wishes.* The unendurable prospect of continued misery often involves amazingly well-constructed plans that may be hinted at and, unless picked up and dealt with, may lead to a successful suicide or repeated attempts to terminate life.

hear voices condemning them as "bad" or have delusions linked to feelings of worthlessness — perhaps imagining themselves solely responsible for the Vietnam War or for crimes they didn't commit.

Depression can be difficult to diagnose and assess

Masquerading in a number of disguises, depression can easily go unrecognized. The depressed often "doctor shop" for help, visiting one physician after another. People who mask their depression may have grown up in families where psychological or mental problems were considered shameful, and hence channel their despair into more acceptable physical signs. Some of the severely depressed appear deceptively cheerful, revealing no outward sign of their inner despondency ("masked depression").

The first sign of clinical depression is often not a doleful mood, but physical symptoms such as weakness, fatigue, chest tightness, stomach upsets, constipation, neckaches or backaches and diminished libido. This "somatization" may make unwary physicians miss the underlying depression. Misled by the vehemence of physical complaints, they may order many needless medical tests, or prescribe remedies that cannot relieve the symptoms because the psychiatric problem hasn't been pinpointed.

It can be tough not only to diagnose clinical depression but also to assess its severity. Certain tests such as the *dexamethasone suppression test (DST)* have been investigated as a means of detecting the hormonal (cortisol) changes frequently present in severe depression. Other tests that assess changes in certain neurotransmitters or check circadian rhythm and sleep cycles offer some promise as diagnostic tools. But at present there's no reliable biochemical test for depression. Diagnosis relies on careful history-taking, symptoms reported by the depressed person, clinically observed signs and psychiatric evaluation.

Many influences contribute to depression

Most experts believe that depression stems from a variety of factors, sometimes mainly biological in origin, at other times more psychological. In adults, a tendency to depression usually arises from a biological vulnerability coupled with early predisposing factors such as childhood abuse, deprivation or the loss of a loved caregiver. According to one University of Toronto expert, "in and of itself neither a biological, genetic or biochemical predisposition alone, nor environmental events, nor purely psychological reasons explain clinical depression." Depression often follows or accompanies a physical illness such as arthritis, hypothyroidism, Parkinson's disease or heart attacks.

The biological roots of depression

Modern evidence points to changes or an imbalance in neurotransmitters or chemical messengers in the brain of the amine type, specifically serotonin and norepinephrine, in many cases of depression. Researchers believe that one or both of these transmitters may malfunction, or be depleted or ineffective, during depressive episodes. This theory gains validity from the effect of antidepressant medications that increase the transmitters' availability. Yet despite the various biochemical abnormalities linked to depression, no clear cause-and-effect link has yet emerged. Nonetheless, drug treatment can help to redress the neurotransmitter imbalance.

The psychological roots of depression

Parental death or absence, feelings of abandonment, a disapproving or withdrawn parent, lack of intimacy and loving care during childhood, feelings of rejection and lengthy hospitalizations — before about age six — can predispose someone to depression in later life. But the depression may also be triggered by some stressful experience — a career failure, job loss or house move. Without other contributing reasons, childhood losses alone are unlikely to produce depressive illness.

Depression-prone individuals are sometimes described as dependent, insecure and introverted people — perfectionists with obsessional traits and low stress tolerance. And although the theory is controversial, some experts say depressives tend to depend on the external approval of others for self-esteem rather than relying upon inner qualities.

The genetic connection

Clinical depression tends to run in families. Those with siblings, parents or other relatives who are or have been depressed are at above-average risk; among the Amish in Pennsylvania, of the 26 suicides that occurred in a 100-year span, all belonged to four extended families prone to depression. A recent report from Toronto's Clarke Institute of Psychiatry suggests the existence of a specific gene for depression, but this remains unproven. Although a genetic influence may predispose someone to depression, several twin studies show that biological reasons alone do not necessarily produce the condition, but do so only in combination with other forces.

The risk of suicide is high

Suicide is 30 times higher among those with clinical depression than in the rest of the population. Although women attempt suicide more often than men, men are twice as likely to succeed, using more effective methods such as guns, knives, hanging and fatal jumps. Suicide is now the second leading cause of death among men aged 15 to 30, especially in Native populations. Talk of suicide is often a plea for help and should *never* be taken as a joke; studies reveal that two-thirds of successful suicides voiced or hinted at their intention before carrying it out. Physicians, families and teachers can be on the alert for possible signs of suicidal intent, and seek counseling if necessary. (See also the section on adolescent suicide in chapter 12.)

Modern multipronged treatment can lift depression

Before the advent of modern antidepressants, the treatment for depression used to be opium, rest, bloodletting and ice-cold baths. Patients were sometimes whipped and often relegated to mental asylums. Today we have many more humane and effective therapies.

Modern therapy can alleviate mild as well as severe depression, and even those who think they're not ill enough to need medical attention may benefit from treatment. But the depressed need encouragement to seek therapy because the very nature of their malady makes them imagine that their suffering is "justified," and that treatment is futile. Friends and relatives can help by encouraging the depressed to seek and stick with treatment, never accusing them of "faking it" or telling them to "snap out of it," or making them feel guilty. It's helpful to express compassion, interest and a willingness to listen.

In the grip of debilitating torment, self-loathing depressives often feel too "down" — physically and emotionally — to bother with medical advice. Many resist help, and family and friends can assist by persuading the depressed person to seek help. Anyone whose depressed humor lasts over two weeks should seek professional help. The family doctor is the first person to consult, and will, if necessary, refer the depressive to a psychiatrist. For suicidal people, the emergency department of any large hospital usually offers assistance around the clock.

Psychotherapy, especially cognitive therapy — which corrects the depressed thinking mode rather than the actual mood — can be extremely successful. Cognitive therapy helps the depressed "think through" their situation and understand why they feel so low. It helps to correct distorted or negative ideas and engender a more optimistic outlook. Even if the black humor doesn't lift entirely, depressives can manage to cope better, set achievable goals and carry on with life.

Antidepressant medications combined with psychotherapy can make treatment very effective. Among the most effective drugs in medical use today, the impact of antidepressants can be dramatic. For example, after a mere month on a new antidepressant medication — sertraline (Zoloft) — a severely depressed woman, frustrated in her career, vexed with her husband and disappointed with her new house, changed her viewpoint and reported that her job was "stimulating," her husband "okay" and the house "really quite nice." But it's essential that people on antidepressants be closely monitored, as reactions vary. Those who experience unpleasant side effects from one type have many others to choose from.

Antidepressant drugs include:

• *serotonin-reuptake-inhibitors* (SRIs), such as fluoxetine (Prozac), sertraline (Zoloft) and fluoxamine (Fluvox) — now usually the first-line and safest drugs for depression;

- *tricyclics and heterocyclics,* such as the older amitryptiline and the newer desipramine and nortriptyline — are also very effective antidepressants with few side effects;

- *monoamine oxidase inhibitors* (MAOIs) such as phenelzine (Nardil), are still used for atypical depression, especially if accompanied by much anxiety, but becoming less popular, mainly owing to side effects and the dietary restrictions (a high-blood-pressure crisis may occur if MAOIs are taken with foods containing tyramine, such as red wine, ripe cheese and smoked meat);

- *reversible MAOIs (RIMAs)* such as moclomebe-mide (Manerix) are now often used as a replacement for MAOIs, as they have fewer side effects and no dietary restrictions.

Current research is developing ever newer types of antidepressants aimed at influencing certain brain transmitters, with fewer side effects and greater specificity.

Antidepressants usually take at least two to three weeks to work at full dosage, and people should persevere during the lag time. Since different types suit different depressives, they are individually prescribed and continued for long enough (usually 3 to 12 months) to quench symptoms completely. If side effects are severe, or if the medication fails to work after several weeks or the dose is wrong, it is corrected or another drug is substituted. The addition of thyroxine (thyroid hormone) or lithium carbonate may enhance the effect in people who do not respond at first.

Lithium carbonate is used mostly as a mood stabilizer in manic-depressive disorders and, to a lesser degree, in depression. Lithium carbonate requires several weeks to work and must be carefully regulated to reach the therapeutic range without toxicity. Used correctly, lithium is a potent weapon in controlling depressive illness.

How about electroconvulsive shock therapy?

Despite its bad press (much of it due to misinformation), electroconvulsive therapy (ECT) remains the most effective remedy for severe depressives who are suicidal or don't respond to other treatment. ECT is done with premedication by muscle relaxants and short-acting, general anesthesia. Electrodes on the head painlessly apply an electric current for half a second. Treatments are usually given two or three times weekly, for 6 to 12 sessions. The main side effect is temporary memory loss, usually only with successive treatments. The psychiatric associations of Canada, the United States and Britain advocate selective, judicious use of ECT for severe depression, where it is often 80–88 percent effective.

Sleep deprivation therapy is sometimes helpful

Manipulating sleep cycles by partial or complete sleep deprivation, or by advancing bedtimes (going to bed a few hours earlier), is used experimentally in some centers (especially European ones) to normalize circadian rhythm and sleep patterns. In some cases this therapy brings striking improvement, but such manipulations often give only temporary relief, unless accompanied by antidepressant medication.

Depressive variants

Dysthymia is a chronic form of mild depression where the perpetually negative outlook and discontent continue with mild symptoms that never seem to lift completely.

In *seasonal affective disorder*, the depressive symptoms (such as lethargy and weight gain) vary with the amount of daylight — worsening in fall or winter, and occasionally being relieved by a trip south! This type of depression may be a separate disorder, possibly related to levels of melatonin (a hormone secreted by the pineal gland). Daily phototherapy using exposure to full-spectrum bright light sometimes rapidly alleviates this type of seasonal depression, but it must be professionally supervised.

For help or information about depression, contact your family physician, a local branch of any psychiatric association or, in some centers, self-help groups (in Toronto, the Manic-Depressive Association, tel.: 416-486-8045; in Montreal, Depressives Anonymous, tel.: 514-842-7557).

POSTPARTUM DEPRESSION

Psychiatric disturbances related to childbirth — including major depression — can occur within six months of delivery, even in women who were never previously depressive. Such disturbances range in severity from a transient attack of the blues, to modest depression, to severe psychosis that may last several weeks. Most women adjust well to the postbirth situation, but about 10 percent experience postpartum depression — usually of moderate intensity — probably triggered by sensitivity to the postbirth hormonal fluctuations.

Certain features are unique and specific to severe postpartum depression, notably the extremely good recovery rates and an unusual mix of symptoms — confusion, perplexity, both manic and depressive episodes, as well as schizophrenic-like symptoms. Severe postpartum depression is marginally more common with first babies. Hospitalization is usually necessary, the baby being admitted along with the mother, or being taken in for visits. About 95 percent of women improve within two to three months, although some have persisting depression. About 20–40 percent suffer another episode after subsequent deliveries. Since the medications may enter breast milk and damage the newborn, those on antidepressants or major tranquilizers are usually encouraged to bottle-feed rather than nurse their babies.

HOLIDAY BLUES

Holidays — especially the yuletide season — are traditionally a time of generosity, love and fulfillment, yet few survive the festive period without some disappointment and conflict. As our society has come to observe them, holiday times promise fun and enjoyment. Christmas in particular dangles the lure of boundless warmth and material wishes magically granted by sugar-plum fairies. Western society goes berserk at this time, exaggerating the occasion beyond its original meaning with media hype and an orgy of commercialization, and the season intensifies the contrast between fantasy and reality, the difference between the way we wish our lives to be and the way they really are.

Most people manage to have a satisfying time at Christmas, family rifts being glossed over and assuaged by the pleasures of eating, drinking, togetherness, hearing from old friends, phoning distant relatives, visiting the elderly and generally taking stock before another year begins. However, because of the high expectations, the time for reflection and the comparison with others, disappointments are inevitable. The term "holiday blues syndrome" has been coined by psychiatrists to describe the downside, which brings fatigue, irritability, bitter nostalgia for lost youth, awareness of mortality, regrets about failed ambitions and relationships, coupled with a strong hope for magical solutions. As many of us struggle with unspoken anxieties or conflicts, stress starts to take its toll — shown by the higher rates of people seeking psychiatric advice at Christmas time.

Everyone goes to such lengths to have a merry Christmas that the failure to enjoy the holiday can create unbearable stress. People who usually manage to maintain their equilibrium may break down because of inner loneliness, boredom, removal of the usual routine and the image of everyone else apparently having a great time.

Holiday times are especially hard on those who feel abandoned. The lonely, isolated, sick and recently bereaved often feel private despair in the face of holiday activities. For people who cope with isolation year round, feelings of loss are exaggerated. By no means are feelings of loneliness confined to those who are truly alone. Even in the midst of their families, some feel desperately lonely, surrounded by people they don't really care for, who fail to live up to their expectations. To those with incipient psychiatric problems, holidays can prove stressful enough to precipitate a breakdown.

People who are troubled by the holiday season can take solace in the fact that Christmas is but one week out of 52, and try to make the annual event as pleasant as possible. Coping strategies may include setting realistic goals, not expecting too much of yourself or others, examining your expectations, planning ahead, assigning and parcelling out specific tasks to others willing to help, and sharing responsibilities. It's particularly important to avoid excessive drinking — a difficult temptation at this time of year — as it will only increase the sense of misery and depression. Instead, go for a brisk walk, or plan an excursion that gets you out of the house — and out of yourself — for a few hours.

Those who do enjoy Christmas might take a moment to remember that others find the time very difficult. Someone who avoids Christmas celebrations, or deliberately arranges to work through the festivities, may need extra consideration and kindliness.

MANIC DEPRESSION

Manic depression (bipolar disorder), a mood disorder with alternating episodes of depression and mania, is a serious illness with sometimes devastating effects on the sufferer and his or her family. Fortunately, in most cases, modern medications can stop or diminish the emotional rollercoaster.

A manic depressive's mood swings from one emotional pole to its opposite — bouts of mania alternating with glum depression. However, in many cases the depressive episodes greatly outnumber the manic ones. The depression in bipolar disorder is identical to that of major clinical depressions, and it is therefore the *manic* episodes that identify the condition.

Mania seldom occurs on its own, without depression. However, some bipolar patients experience mainly depression with only a few bouts of mild mania — "hypomania" rather than full mania. The cycles of depression and mania may not be predictable or regular. In certain cases, known as "rapid cycling," the manic and depressive stages may alternate rapidly — a condition that can be hard to control or treat.

As in clinical depression, suicide is a serious danger in manic depressives. About 15 percent of bipolar patients commit suicide during the depressed phase. (For more on suicide, see earlier in this chapter, and the section on adolescent suicide risks in chapter 12.)

The manic phase identifies bipolar disorder

Usually, the mania appears quite suddenly — within days to weeks — often, but not always, emerging from a period of deep depression. At first, before they have had the experience of living with a manic person, family and friends may be delighted at the mood elevation, welcoming the increased energy, cheerfulness and sociability. However, it soon becomes apparent that the "hyper" mood and the person's actions are odd, with rapid speech, disconnected, racing thoughts, decreased sleep needs, exaggerated self-praise, grandiose notions and irritability. Sometimes extreme irritability is the most prominent mood alteration in the manic stage.

Mania tends to distort thinking and judgment. About 60 percent of manic people have omnipotent thoughts in their "up" mood, perhaps thinking they're God, the queen or a rock star. Some have hallucinations, and hear voices or see visions. Fueled by their mania, some bipolar patients behave dangerously and foolishly. For example, while in a manic state they may spend money recklessly and embark on crazy schemes that bankrupt themselves and their families, or they may become angry, sometimes paranoid and even violent. Some become hypersexual, with openly promiscuous behavior. "Young manic males are among the

RECOGNIZING THE HALLMARKS OF THE MANIC PHASE

In differing degrees, the following symptoms define mania:
• indefatigable restlessness — always on the go;
• increasingly less sleep — sometimes only a few hours nightly;
• cheerfulness and optimism, verging on euphoria — as if perpetually "high";
• lack of judgment;
• loud, rapid, pressured speech, full of jokes and puns, that's hard to interrupt;
• jumping from idea to idea — completely unintelligible in the severely manic;

• irritable, suspicious outbursts.
In diagnosing manic depression, doctors must rule out other possible causes of mania such as:
• *endocrine and metabolic disorders* — for instance, adrenal diseases (such as Addison's disease or Cushing's syndrome), liver ailments, hyperthyroidism (excess thyroid function), porphyria (a metabolic disorder) and vitamin B$_{12}$ deficiency;
• *hemodialysis* (kidney failure);
• *neurological problems* — for instance, Hunt-

ington's disease, brain tumors, encephalitis, multiple sclerosis, Wilson's disease, consequences of AIDS, temporal-lobe lesions;
• *certain medications* — e.g., the antianxiety drug alprazolam, cimetidine and ranitidine (stomach-ulcer drugs), corticoids, levodopa (for Parkinson's disease), some psychostimulants (such as amphetamine) and antidepressants;
• *drug abuse* — of alcohol, cocaine, phencyclidine.

most difficult patients we encounter," says one University of Toronto psychiatrist. "They may exhibit an extraordinary increase in muscle strength, which combined with a lack of judgment and sense of invincibility, can be a formidable challenge." The manic episodes can last for months, long enough for sufferers to wreck their lives, lose their jobs, or break up their marriages — good reasons why mania should be treated as soon as it's discovered. A few manic depressives exhibit bursts of productivity or creativity during their elated phase.

Diagnosing manic depression

The diagnosis of bipolar disorder can be confirmed only after identifying a manic episode, which ranges from mild to severe and typically first appears in adolescence or between ages 20 and 30 — although the disorder is increasingly seen in people over age 50. In contrast to clinical depression — which affects more women than men — manic depression afflicts both sexes equally.

Treatment of manic depression

Persuading those in a manic state to get treatment can be difficult, as they often not only don't feel sick, but in fact may say they feel great — although most manics find the experience is distressing and show signs of irritability. Since it is hard to reason with manic people, most receive treatment in hospital, usually with drugs and perhaps also with psychotherapy. Before treatment, tests are done to rule out kidney ailments, thyroid abnormalities (especially important for those with frequent rapid cycles) and other possible causes. Routine tests include electrolyte measures, blood counts and electrocardiograms.

Lithium salts are the backbone of therapy for manic-depression. How lithium manages to modify both manic and depressive mood swings isn't known, but it is an effective mood stabilizer in 50–60 percent of manic depressives. Lithium may be combined with an antipsychotic drug such as haloperidol or, increasingly, with antiepileptic drugs such as carbamazepine or valproic acid. Combined medication using lithium plus haloperidol is frequently prescribed at first, because lithium

CRITERIA FOR DIAGNOSIS OF MANIC EPISODES

A. A distinct period of abnormally and persistently elevated, expansive or irritable mood.

B. During the mood disturbance, at least three of the following symptoms (four if the mood disturbance was mainly irritable):
- inflated self-esteem, grandiosity;
- decreased need for sleep, e.g., awake after only three hours of sleep;
- more talkative than usual;
- flight of ideas or "racing" thoughts;
- distractibility, e.g., attention too easily drawn to unimportant or irrelevant stimuli;
- increase in goal-directed activity either socially, at work, at school or sexually;
- excessive involvement in risky activities — e.g., unrestrained buying sprees, sexual indiscretions or foolish business investments.

C. A mood disturbance severe enough to damage job or social functioning or relationships with others, or requiring hospitalization to prevent harm to others or self.

D. Hallucinations or delusions.

E. Not superimposed by other psychiatric illness, such as schizophrenia.

F. Not caused by an organic disturbance or drug (see list above).

takes about 14 days to work and several weeks to become fully effective.

Since there is a narrow range between the therapeutic and toxic levels of lithium, periodic monitoring of blood levels is essential. Symptoms of lithium toxicity include hand tremors, nausea and decreased coordination. Annoying but usually tolerable side effects include frequent urination, thirst, mild nausea, diarrhea and weight gain — a very troublesome side effect that often leads to noncompliance and relapses.

Long-term lithium therapy makes it possible for many manic depressives to live productive, normal lives. The therapy may have to be lifelong, as stopping it is a major reason for relapses. The burden is therefore on sufferers to understand why they need the medication. A trusted physician who is sensitive to individual problems can help in minimizing side effects and persuading the sufferer to stick with the therapy. Earlier fears that lithium can damage the kidneys have not been realized, and today, after 40 years of lithium use, renal failure is not considered a danger. But those on lithium must be aware of fluctuations in its level (with fluid intake) and of interaction with other drugs. Fevers, excessive dieting, diarrhea, non-steroidal anti-inflammatory drugs (including ASA) and chlorothiazide may increase blood lithium levels.

Alternative medications for those who don't respond well to lithium — for example, rapid cyclers — include anticonvulsants alone, or antidepressants together with lithium for episodes of severe depression.

CHRONIC FATIGUE SYNDROME
Known by many popular names, chronic fatigue syndrome (CFS) hits mainly achievement-oriented young adults. For over a century, reports from many countries have described a perplexing ailment typified by prolonged fatigue, feverishness, sore throat, tender neck nodes and decreased concentration powers. Unrelieved by normal rest, the persistent tiredness is enough to stop people from working, exercising and having fun.

During the past century, fashionable complaints involving overpowering lassitude bore exotic names such as chlorosis ("the green sickness," attributed to iron-deficiency anemia), epidemic neuromyasthenia (nerve-and-muscle weakness) and neurasthenia (described by one famous U.S. physician as "a lightheaded nervous exhaustion, inability to concentrate, and exquisite intolerance to coffee and alcohol").

Similar symptoms have been ascribed to other poorly defined diseases, such as twentieth-century disease (total allergy syndrome), hypoglycemia (low blood sugar), severe vitamin-mineral deficiencies and the "Royal Free disease" (a cluster of unmitigated fatigue cases among nurses at Britain's Royal Free Hospital in 1955 — ascribed by some to mass hysteria). Similar outbreaks in Britain were labeled myalgic encephalomyelitis (muscle and brain inflammation), with many sufferers blaming their exhausted condition on the fast pace of life.

For some time, the prevailing chronic fatigue problems were attributed to Epstein-Barr virus (the virus responsible for mononucleosis), which is accompanied by pervasive fatigue. But the link to the Epstein-Barr virus (EBV) remains unproven. The most recent nickname for the inexplicable fatigue is "Yuppie flu," the name deriving from the flu-like symptoms and the prevalence of the condition among ambitious young professionals. Reaching near-epidemic proportions on both sides of the Atlantic, its hallmarks are constant, lingering exhaustion — sometimes debilitating enough to ruin a career and family life. Many people today blame it for their low energy and "lack of wellness." Publicity about the ailment, frequently inaccurate, has encouraged many to think they have it, often with a remarkable absence of abnormal findings and no medical foundation. Although Yuppie flu was originally suspected of being a viral infection, recent evidence finds no consistent link to infectious agents, and experts suggest this syndrome may be the physical expression of underlying psychological dissatisfaction, depression or a need to "opt out."

Fatigue syndrome is commonest among hard-driving young adults
Prime candidates for chronic fatigue syndrome are career-oriented professionals, especially unmarried, well-educated overachievers aged 25 to 40. About one-quarter of sufferers are healthcare workers (doctors, nurses, therapists), and it affects twice as many women as men. Those afflicted tend to be perfectionists who strive to excel in all areas — job, sports, looks — and many are ardent exercisers, working out strenuously several times a week. The syndrome's impact on these overscheduled sufferers can be devastating, especially if pervasive fatigue forces them to give up part or all of their activities.

Frequently cited complaints
The fatigue syndrome typically produces unmitigated exhaustion, a niggling sore throat, muscular weakness and a general malaise sufficient to prevent usual activities. Sufferers frequently report peculiar headaches, tender, swollen lymph nodes, joint pains, disrupted sleep, chills, night sweats and feverishness. Some also experience light aversion, an inability to abide the slightest noise, nausea, appetite changes and bladder problems. Many report a shortened attention span and a decline in normally sharp thinking processes. There may be some memory loss, confusion and slurred speech. Often severe enough to diminish the mental

acuity needed for job performance, the illness leads to lengthy sick leave and numerous disability claims. The least exertion greatly exaggerates the weariness. Symptoms may be severe enough to halt all activity, with sufferers spending hours each day in bed. The average duration of the disorder is two years, but many improve in a few weeks to months. The disorder tends to return at times of emotional and/or physical stress.

The good news is that, despite the distressing impact of the disorder, most sufferers gradually recover at least 80 percent of their former capacities when it wanes. Perhaps guided in part by the "wisdom of their bodies," once they recover, many don't resume their previously unrealistic, overextended, action-packed lives, instead reevaluating their priorities and choosing a slower pace.

A typical case

Jane, a 27-year-old, ambitious female physician, capably handled a heavy workload, including evening lecturing and regular aerobics classes. She suddenly developed a flu-like illness just after moving to a new office (an added stress). Unable to shake off the incessant fatigue, Jane felt "wiped out" by the muscle weakness and constant sore throat. She could no longer focus her thoughts and felt too disabled to carry on. Since even a mild bout of exercise worsened the weariness, she gave up aerobics, reduced her caseload and rested frequently. Even working at half-pace, she was perpetually tired. None of the numerous medical specialists she consulted could pinpoint the reason for her fatigue.

Despite her malaise, Jane looked surprisingly well, always impeccably groomed. Her healthy appearance belied any grave physical disorder. One medical advisor suggested she might have chronic Epstein-Barr mononucleosis, but an endless battery of tests didn't show the presence of Epstein-Barr or any other infection, and found no physical abnormalities or other medical reason for her fatigue. Finally, having seen many physicians and tried various medications — tranquilizers, antibiotics, anti-inflammatories and antidepressants — none of which seemed to work, she attended a stress-management program and obtained psychiatric counseling. After a year, the lethargy lifted, Jane's energy returned as inexplicably as it had vanished and she went back to work. Although fearful that she wouldn't be able to function properly, she slowly returned to full capacity.

Chronic fatigue syndrome is now more precisely defined

In 1988 the Centers for Disease Control (CDC) in Atlanta officially named the perplexing ailment chronic fatigue syndrome (CFS), with a restricted set of identifying symptoms. Lacking evidence of any link to the Epstein-Barr virus, the Epstein-Barr tag has been dropped. To qualify for diagnosis of CFS, a person must have endured at least six months of newly acquired, constant or recurrent tiredness, enough to reduce normal activities by half, with a minimum number of designated symptoms. The CDC guidelines help physicians avoid confusing CFS with other frequent causes of fatigue, such as depression, TB, diabetes, fibrositis, cancer, underactive thyroid function, hormonal disturbances and anemia.

However, the roots of this enigmatic disorder remain controversial. Some medical experts view CFS as a lingering infection, while others believe it stems from psychiatric disorders that masquerade with physical symptoms.

No consistent infection found in CFS

Reliable medical and laboratory tests have failed to reveal a consistent link between CFS and any infection. Most patients who "felt feverish" actually had normal temperatures. The CDC cautions that in this illness, with its "wide-ranging, nonspecific symptoms, the connection to Epstein-Barr is tenuous and unproven." Well-controlled studies also found no correlation between CFS and a high antibody level, or evidence of any consistent immune-system flaw. Many of the chronically fatigued actually had *less* suppressed immune systems than healthy, nonfatigued control subjects. None of the reported immune-system abnormalities correlates with the severity of CFS or the improvement noted during therapy.

BASIS FOR DIAGNOSING CHRONIC FATIGUE SYNDROME (CFS)
(recognizing that there may be several joint causes)

Common signs and symptoms of chronic fatigue syndrome: a designated number must be present to confirm the diagnosis

To be confirmed as having CFS a person must have:

• New onset of persistent or recurrent fatigue lasting over six months (not resolved by rest) severe enough to reduce average daily activities by 50 percent.
• Reliable, thorough medical and laboratory tests to exclude other, treatable, clinical diseases and conditions that could cause the fatigue, such as:
  • psychiatric diseases (e.g., depression, anxiety, somatization disorders);
  • diabetes;
  • endocrine/hormonal disturbances (e.g., thyroid or adrenal disorders);
  • heart, kidney, blood diseases;
  • anemia;
  • cancer;
  • infection by bacteria (e.g., TB);
  • parasitic diseases (e.g., toxoplasmosis);
  • fungal invasions (e.g., histoplasmosis);
  • chronic hepatitis;
  • street-drug or medication side effects.

Subjective symptoms experienced:

• extreme prolonged fatigue (lasting over 6 months);
• chills, feverishness;
• nighttime sweats;
• sore throat;
• tender, swollen lymph nodes in neck and/or armpits;
• headaches;
• unexplained muscle weakness;
• muscle aches;
• joint pains that come and go;
• sleep disturbances;
• difficulty concentrating;
• memory loss;
• mood changes;
• visual changes;
• stomach (abdominal) cramps;
• appetite change;
• weight loss or gain;
• irritable bladder;
• dizziness;
• lightheadedness;
• "blue" spells, crying fits;
• rapid pulse.

Laboratory and medical or physical findings*

• low-grade fever (37.6°–38.6°C, or 99.7°–101.5°F)
• pharyngitis (red, inflamed throat);
• swollen lymph nodes;
• minor immune-system changes (in 30% of sufferers), such as:
  • elevated antibodies to some viruses, e.g., Epstein-Barr virus, measles, Coxsackie, herpes;
  • low gamma globulin;
  • increased synthetase enzymes;
  • decreased "killer cell" activity (lowered immune defenses).

Other syndromes/illnesses sometimes mistaken for CFS

• depression, anxiety
• infections, e.g., AIDS, Coxsackie virus, Epstein-Barr, brucellosis;
• fibrositis (arthritic syndrome/fibromyalgia)
• sleep apnea
• diabetes
• hypothyroidism (underactive thyroid)
• anemia
• cancer
• Addison's disease

* to be documented by a physician.

Psychological factors usually play a major role in CFS

Since researchers find no credibility for a consistent organic cause in CFS, they look to mental disturbance as an explanation — the more so because the severity of symptoms seems to ebb and flow in harmony with mood and emotional states. According to recent research, a high proportion of the ceaselessly fatigued (over 60 percent in some studies) have had one or more past episodes of psychiatric disturbance, such as depression, panic attacks or phobias. In addition, many CFS sufferers admit to having blamed other well-publicized "diseases of the year" (which they heard about through the media) for their malaise. Experts speculate that in those prone to mental disturbances, CFS represents a maladaptive response to physical and mental pressure. A stressful event — moving house, changing jobs, marriage, divorce — often precipitates it.

Many psychiatrists believe that CFS emanates largely from a propensity to mental and emotional disturbances which express themselves in the guise of fatigue and other physical symptoms. One University of Toronto specialist found that 67 percent of CFS sufferers in her practice "had episodes of depression and other psychiatric disorders, several years before the onset of their debilitating fatigue." One U.S. study from the National Institutes of Health (NIH) in Maryland found that 75 percent of CFS sufferers "warranted a psychiatric diagnosis of anxiety disorder, affective (mood) disorder, substance abuse or antisocial personality problems." The NIH expert reached the inescapable conclusion that "psychoneurosis contributes significantly to the syndrome, represented as physical symptoms."

The combined evidence shows that two-thirds of those with CFS meet the criteria for psychiatric illness, usually depression. Depression bears distinct similarities to the syndrome, being also accompanied by extreme fatigue, headaches, muscle pain, weakness, dizziness, dysuria (bladder dysfunction) and gastrointestinal upsets — all cardinal symptoms of CFS.

However, many CFS sufferers object to being labeled as "psychiatrically ill" and deny psychological problems (for which they might feel guilty), preferring to pin their discomfort on an organic condition. But whether its roots are organic or psychological, the syndrome is equally distressing. The dearth of medical evidence for anything organically wrong does not diminish the very real pain and frustration of those with CFS.

Treatment: life must go on

Key points in handling CFS are a thorough medical evaluation, investigation of lifestyle issues, laboratory tests and psychiatric assessment to exclude treatable physical or mental disorders.

Since psychiatric disturbances may underlie the disorder, they must be considered in recommending treatment. The best therapy is rest, supportive counseling, a graduated program of physical activity, avoidance of a "catastrophic" attitude and symptomatic drug therapy with painkillers, antihistamines, and antidepressants. Accurate scientific information helps to dispel misconceptions and lessen the frustration felt by CFS sufferers. They are not malingering — they really feel ill — but they can be encouraged to feel better. The key is to help them accept some discomfort as a normal part of life.

As for medications, anti-inflammatories, antibiotics and tranquilizers don't offer a cure or even much relief for CFS, but many sufferers do improve on one or other of the newer antidepressant drugs, especially types that act as both mood-lifters and pain-relievers — if they can be persuaded to take them. Low doses of doxepin (Sinequan), nortriptyline, desipramine and fluoxetine (Prozac) help many. Their mood-elevating properties heighten concentration and increase vigor, allowing sufferers to carry on more normal lives. But close monitoring is crucial.

Activity, modeled on rehabilitation programs, with gradually increasing energy levels, is strongly encouraged. It helps to reduce anxiety, affirms the ability to move and avoids anticipation of prolonged bed rest and disability. Since many people feel most energetic in the morning, wearying as the day progresses, exercise is best planned for the early hours. Rewards are given for increased activity.

Treatment may also include cognitive therapy to stop CFS sufferers from "catastrophizing" — believing they will never again be fully active — giving reassurance that the illness isn't lethal and will likely diminish and vanish with time. Sufferers are taught to attribute the symptoms to real reasons — perhaps just "work overload," a bad day or staying up late. They are encouraged to take it easy, but not to stay in bed — to "continue with their lives" while awaiting recovery. Psychotherapy can help if anxiety, depression or a somatization disorder is present.

THE DISABLING EFFECTS OF ANXIETY DISORDERS

Anxiety disorders are a group of different conditions with anxiety as their common core. Recent studies have exposed the surprising prevalence of anxiety disorders in modern society, a hidden epidemic now known to affect over 10 percent of North Americans at some point in their lives. The word "anxiety" comes from the Greek "to strangle," capturing the strong physical sensations of tightness or choking prominent in these disorders.

Distinguishing normal anxiety from true anxiety syndromes

There is a profound difference between normal anxiety, which is a protective human response, and anxiety as a debilitating psychiatric disorder. Fear is a biologically adaptive reaction to real danger. By contrast, unfounded or unrealistic anxiety — a vague fear of hostility, of "danger at every turn" (even when there's no real threat), is destructive. Fear arouses the body's autonomic (involuntary) nervous system, evoking the fight-or-flight response and triggering production of the hormone norepinephrine (adrenaline), which puts all senses on the alert, speeds the heartbeat, dilates the pupils and diverts blood to the working muscles.

In anxiety disorders, a similar but uncalled-for fight-or-flight response releases norepinephrine when there's nothing to fight or flee. Human beings cannot endure intense anxiety for long without feeling ill or developing a "phobic" avoidance of the fear-arousing situation(s). Unresolved anxiety problems may lead to clinical depression, alcoholism and suicidal tendencies. If anxiety destroys the ability to function normally, it requires professional help.

Anxiety disorders include:
- simple phobia;
- social phobia;
- panic disorder;
- agoraphobia;
- generalized anxiety disorder (GAD);
- post-traumatic stress disorder (PTSD);
- obsessive-compulsive disorder (OCD).

Although each anxiety disorder is distinct, with its own set of symptoms, different forms can coexist.

Anxiety disorders are more disabling than hitherto recognized

Since all of us fret to some extent about everyday problems, anxiety disorders tend to be trivialized; they often go undiagnosed, and are considered less troublesome than other psychiatric conditions. A recent University of Toronto study showed that many who suffer from anxiety syndromes are misdiagnosed, and get extensive cardiac, neurological and other medical workups and perhaps even faulty treatment, because an anxiety disorder that might have responded to simple therapy has gone unrecognized. Yet true anxiety disorders are far from trivial. They can destroy careers, families and friendships. The life of someone with post-traumatic stress disorder (following a life-threatening assault) or of an obsessive-compulsive may be almost as disrupted as that of a schizophrenic.

A 1988 National Institute of Mental Health survey of more than 18,000 people in five U.S. cities astonished the psychiatric community by revealing that anxiety disorders are now the most prevalent psychiatric illness in North America. The largest survey of psychiatric problems ever undertaken, it found the rate of anxiety disorders among the population over a period of six months to be 7.3 percent, with 14 percent of respondents reporting transient anxiety problems at some time in their lives. (By contrast, the level of alcohol and drug abuse was 3.8 percent, schizophrenia 0.6 percent and depression 2.2 percent.)

Anxiety symptoms mimic those of medical conditions, such as shortness of breath (as in asthma), chest pain (as in heart disease), diarrhea (as in bowel disorders) — an added reason for incorrect diagnosis. Also, anxiety may accompany other illnesses, such as thyroid disease, asthma, heart ailments and gastric problems. Some drugs, licit and illicit — for instance, caffeine, cocaine, bronchodilators and amphetamines — provoke anxiety-like symptoms. Surveys show that many patients in family-practice units (one-quarter of patients, according to some studies) have transient panic attacks in certain situations or due to drugs such as marijuana or cocaine. Occasional panic attacks or those linked to drug use are not true anxiety disorders.

General treatment for anxiety disorders

Whatever the cause(s) of anxiety disorders, treatment usually entails psychological counseling, behavior or cognitive therapy and sometimes medication. A good therapist assesses the reasons for the anxiety, traces events that might have triggered it and evaluates its impact on everyday activities. The link between the underlying anxiety and physical symptoms such as chest pain and gastrointestinal upsets is pointed out to the anxious person.

For many, the most frightening part is the dread that some terrible disease is causing these symptoms. Many people seem to cope once they get a clear explanation of the condition, and know there's no incipient heart failure

UNDERSTANDING HOW ANXIETY BUILDS

Anxiety disorders usually first appear in adolescence or early adulthood, and often persist for life. They were once ascribed to "separation anxiety" (being separated from parents), castration anxiety, punitive parenting or conflict. Nowadays, experts believe that biochemical plus psychological, cognitive, behavioral, social and cultural factors jointly produce these disorders. Many researchers lean toward a biological explanation for anxiety disorders, with an overactive nervous system and specific abnormalities or imbalances in the brain's neurotransmitters.

Finding the trigger(s) for anxiety problems is not easy, but in about half the cases therapists can piece together a scenario that at least partly accounts for the disorder. Many sufferers can point to stressors such as a family loss or conflict with an "important other" that precipitated the problem.

or other illness about to strike. Those whose anxiety is related to only a few situations can often get by without much professional aid. For example, someone who is afraid of public speaking faces no anxiety problem unless forced to address large groups; a woman who's afraid of dogs will be fine unless she is a veterinarian or marries someone who adores dogs. However, obsessive hand-washers who peel off their skin, or agoraphobics too afraid to leave the house, need intensive therapy. Fortunately, specific behavior therapy is often very effective.

Exposure therapy, which is becoming increasingly popular, will quickly relieve some anxiety disorders, especially phobias. It helps people to confront the fear-evoking situation(s), enabling them to develop coping mechanisms. For example, an arachnophobic may be asked first to look at pictures of spiders, then to keep a spider in a cage at home, then in the bedroom, until the discomfort subsides. An agoraphobic may be taken on subway rides, exposed to busy streets or asked to spend hours in a shopping mall. For social phobics, the therapist may role-play the fear-arousing situation (e.g., dating or speaking at a wedding) to build strength. Exposure therapy may abolish the anxiety swiftly; or it may take several sessions, each lasting a few hours.

Cognitive therapy means helping sufferers to understand the reason(s) for anxiety and to rationally reappraise the beliefs that make them feel defenceless and "forced to flee." The fearful thought mode — expectation of dreadful things that might happen — is replaced by logical patterns to break the cycle.

Pharmacotherapy employs anxiety-relieving medications (anxiolytics), for instance, the benzodiazepines, such as alprazolam, clonazepam or lorazepam. Many anxious people are reluctant to take such drugs for fear of dependence or addiction, but addiction is very unusual in those taking benzodiazepines for anxiety. The benzodiazepines are usually given for two to six months, not generally for long-term therapy — unless severe symptoms warrant continued use. Withdrawal symptoms of rebound anxiety, insomnia and tremors can be a problem when discontinuing benzodiazepines, so it's best to taper down dosages gradually. Other useful antianxiety medications include the antidepressants (such as imipramine or desipramine) and fluoxetine, often used for longer-term therapy.

Panic disorder in particular

The word "panic" comes from the Greek god Pan, who used to jump at passersby as a practical joke. But panic disorder is no laughing matter. Panic attacks often begin in the teens or early adulthood, and may come out of the blue, as episodes of terror that hit for no discernible reason. Previously mislabeled "housewives' disease" or "soldier's heart," panic attacks can immobilize people from all walks of life. Panic-ridden people may think they're having a heart attack or some other crisis; the typical symptoms — chest pain, shortness of breath and a sense of choking — send many rushing to the hospital emergency department with the first few episodes. But the chest tightness is due to the anxiety, and is not a cardiac problem. Other symptoms include palpitations, flushing, chills, sweating, difficulty swallowing, dizziness, unsteadiness, feelings of unreality and a sense of incapacity. During an attack, many people feel strangely disconnected from their surroundings. Some think they are going to die or go mad. If the attacks continue, they begin to wonder whether they're crazy. Comments one University of Toronto specialist, "They may imagine it's due to something they did or that there is something about the situation during which the attacks happen that somehow triggered them. In trying to come up with answers, many misattribute the cause of panic attacks to the context in which they arose." For example, someone who had an attack while driving a car may believe there is something about driving or the destination that caused the panic. Panickers who link attacks with the situations in which they occur may avoid more and more places, developing an increasingly constricted lifestyle and sometimes becoming completely housebound. Yet those beset by panic attacks may not seem outwardly agitated. A U.S. National Institutes of Health report notes that many anxious patients see 10 or more doctors before their condition is accurately pinpointed and properly treated.

AGORAPHOBIA — OFTEN LINKED TO PANIC ATTACKS

Agoraphobia is the terror of being away from a safe place, or being somewhere from which escape is difficult. Agoraphobics typically develop a fear of driving, tunnels, bridges, shopping malls and subways. "What underlies the fear," says one expert, "is being in a place or situation where they can't get immediate help in case of a sudden panic attack. At its most extreme, agoraphobics won't even leave the house because of the terror expected."

Agoraphobia is often linked to or follows panic attacks, but it may also arise independently. The agoraphobic fear may relate to specific places: if a woman was in the laundromat when she first experienced panic, she may be reluctant to go into any laundromat. Treatment for agoraphobia is similar to that for panic disorder — psychotherapy, reassurance and perhaps the newer anxiolytic drugs, e.g., clonazepam (Rivotril). Tricyclic antidepressants, monoamine oxidase inhibitors (MAOIs), beta blockers and fluoxetine can also relieve the condition.

Panic attacks may start during major life changes, and in some cases therapists can piece together a psychosocial picture of what triggered the attacks — such as a divorce, a death in the family, stress or excess work. Some people function all right during the stressful event(s) and then panic when things calm down. Some have panic attacks mostly at night, others more in the daytime. Some experience several attacks a day — very unnerving. A typical panic attack lasts for two to 10 minutes, sometimes up to an hour. Even when the attack is over, anxiety can linger on for hours or days.

The diagnostic manual of the American Psychiatric Association defines panic disorder as "one or more panic attacks per week for four weeks or one or more, followed by persistent fears of panic." To qualify as panic disorder, some attacks must be spontaneous and unexpected, not triggered by a definite event such as an exam or sighting a snake. Since alcohol may relieve the panic, it's not surprising that some panickers (about a third) become alcoholics. Panic disorders may also result in depression and suicide.

Treatment for panic attacks is the same as for most anxiety problems — behavior therapy, knowledge of what's going on in the person's life and reassurance that disease or death isn't imminent. Many panickers calm down once they know that the condition likely stems from a biochemical transmitter imbalance in the brain.

Simple phobia

Simple phobias, among the commonest of anxiety disorders, entail persistent, irrational fears (sometimes amounting to panic) of circumscribed events or situations. Among the countless specific phobias, the most frequent fears are of animals (such as dogs, snakes, mice), heights, blood, crowds, enclosed spaces, lightning or air travel. More unusual phobias include arachnophobia (fear of spiders), photophobia (fear of light), sarcophagophobia (fear of being buried alive) and apiphobia (fear of bees). Phobias are more common in women than in men. They often begin around ages seven to nine, but may persist through life. Many phobic people prefer to hide their phobias, just avoiding the triggers, but if circumstances force them to be in repeated contact with the feared situation — as with politicians afraid of air travel — therapy may be sought.

Treatment is with exposure therapy (see above), which often works well; sometimes a single session lasting a few hours eradicates the phobia. For example, one woman terrified of cats was confronted with a small cat in her therapy session, stood trembling by the door for 40 minutes, gradually came nearer, touched the cat on the therapist's lap and, at the end of a four-hour session, ended up with the cat on her lap, the phobia gone.

Social phobia

More common in men than women, social phobia is the fear of performing, of being scrutinized by peers or by the public, of "not being liked." Fearing evaluation, the social phobic blushes, trembles, feels faint and may be totally unable to perform. Social phobias typically revolve around speaking in public, going to restaurants, using public washrooms or signing one's name in front of a bank teller (for fear of a trembling hand and wobbly signature!). Often beginning in adolescence, social phobias affect about 2 percent of the population. The inhibition or shyness can cripple social and professional life, possibly resulting in alcoholism and depression. For example, an eight-year-old who can't speak up in class may skip school; a lawyer unable to address the jury without trembling may change careers; an advertising creator, afraid to present ideas, may turn to writing copy for others; or someone asked to join the head table at a banquet may refuse for fear others will see his or her inability to swallow.

Therapy may include MAOI antidepressants (e.g., phenelzine, tranylcypromine). For those with stage fright, beta blockers or benzodiazepines taken just before a performance may reduce the anxiety.

Generalized anxiety disorder (GAD)

Although less debilitating than panic disorder, generalized anxiety disorder (GAD) is a distressing complaint, with free-floating anxiety and jitteriness that are not usually crystallized into discrete panic episodes. General anxiety often manifests itself as physical symptoms with no anatomical or identifiable basis — such as tension (trembling, twitching, restlessness), gastric upsets, urinary problems, chest pain, headaches, autonomic system overactivity (dizziness, sweating, palpitations) and hypervigilance (being perpetually keyed up). GAD sufferers often report pervasive fatigue, insomnia and an inability to fall asleep. To qualify as GAD, symptoms must be prominent for six months or longer. GAD affects 2 to 5 percent of the population, striking more women than men. The disorder resembles panic, but people with GAD get worried about far less severe symptoms than true panickers, often consulting physicians not only about physical ailments, but to discuss unrealistic worries such as fussing over a perfectly well child's health, anxiety about money when there are no financial problems or fear of losing a job when there is no cause for concern.

Treatment for generalized anxiety disorder is psychotherapy and medication plus reassurance that it's not a deadly disease. GAD sufferers often recover once they realize that the physical manifestations stem from underlying anxiety and that lifestyle changes may solve the problem — for example, more rest periods, exercise and holidays. Buspirone, a new medication with few side effects and less habit-forming potential than other anxiety-reducing medications, is useful.

Post-traumatic stress disorder (PTSD)

This anxiety condition arises after some overwhelming trauma such as rape, assault, car accidents, plane crashes, war, torture, imprisonment or natural disasters such as earthquakes or floods. Its prevalence and severity are often underestimated. "Shell shock" was the expression used for the World War I veterans in whom post-traumatic stress disorder was first documented. It is frequent among U.S. Vietnam combat veterans, as many as 50 percent of those who engaged in heavy combat apparently suffering from it. A University of Toronto study showed that 50 years later, many World War II concentration camp survivors, especially those from Auschwitz, still suffer severe PTSD. Its striking features are recurrent nightmares, flashbacks of the traumatic event and intense anxiety on exposure to any reminders — such as helicopters for Vietnam veterans, and news bulletins or anti-Israeli propaganda for Nazi concentration-camp survivors. Those with PTSD may have numbing emotional detachment, recurrent insomnia, an exaggerated startle response (jumpiness) and profound guilt over having survived when others perished. The prevalence of post-traumatic disorder in the overall North American population is 1 percent.

Treatment for PTSD is psychotherapy to dispel the terrifying flashbacks, plus tricyclic antidepressants (such as imipramine) or MAOI antidepressants. But despite treatment, many with PTSD continue to suffer great distress.

Obsessive-compulsive disorder

Once regarded as a psychiatric curiosity, obsessive-compulsive disorder or OCD is now proving to be very common, affecting as many as one in 50 North Americans. After a flurry of media interest, evoked by 1980s television talk shows publicizing the usefulness of the drug buspirone for treating OCD, many people revealed their strange, sometimes bizarre, often secret behaviors. Obsessive-compulsives whose problem had nearly wrecked their lives told fellow sufferers how therapy had helped them. When columnist Ann Landers wrote about OCD, she was deluged with 8,000 letters in one week.

Many with OCD try to hide their behavior even from family and close friends. Sigmund Freud noted that obsessives were adept at concealment because, having devoted several hours to their "secret doings," they functioned well for the rest of the day. The secret doings that Freud referred to were rituals performed to relieve the anxiety caused by obsessive thoughts. A person who touches every lamppost, chews every mouthful hundreds of times, must brush the hair 200 times, spends hours opening and closing cupboards or is afraid to use the toilet for fear of germs may resemble a schizophrenic. But unlike psychotics, who believe their thoughts come from outside sources — from aliens or devils — obsessives know that their thoughts are their own. Neither are they neurotics; they know their actions are pointless, struggle to resist them, describe their behavior as "dumb," but are convinced that if they don't continue the rituals something bad will befall them or others. A well-known journalist feels compelled to check 10 times that her front door is closed every morning before going work. An internist calls the lab a dozen times to make sure the test results are right, noting that his compulsion seems senseless, but still feeling obliged to call. Some OCD sufferers stretch a routine activity like dressing from minutes to hours. Some feel compelled to go from the car to the front door in a certain way — four steps forward, two back, or singing "Yankee Doodle Dandy" (to the despair of their families and the possible amusement of neighbors).

It should be noted that mild "obsessions" can simply be rigid ways of doing things. For example, some ultra-neat people can't sleep until every dinner dish has been cleared, all ashtrays emptied or crooked paintings straightened. Such eccentrics do *not* necessarily have OCD.

The American Psychiatric Association describes OCD as an illness with recurrent obsessions or compulsions, or both, severe enough to cause marked distress, be time-consuming (over one hour a day) or interfere significantly with normal routine. The obsessive thoughts are deeply disturbing, not pleasurable. In severe cases, the thoughts become so tormenting that the person sacrifices relationships, work, school and basic comfort to escape them. In some instances obsessives do nothing all day except attend to their rituals.

OCD tends to emerge in adolescence through to the mid-thirties, although it can start in childhood. Fear of contamination is a common theme, many obsessives being afraid to shake hands or touch doorknobs because of possible dirt, or to eat for fear of poisoning. Others fear loss of control — they are afraid of strangling their children or killing a dog. Some have disturbing sexual thoughts, tormenting fantasies, blasphemous images, pathological doubts or concerns about sin or hell. Families often worry that the person with OCD may act out hostile obsessions, but obsessives want to avoid their thoughts, not derive pleasure from them. OCD patients very rarely put violent thoughts into action.

Common types of obsessives

- *Cleaners* (85 percent of those with OCD) have a fear of contagion that compels many to spend hours in the shower, or to wash their hands 50 or 60 times a day, often with harsh soaps, until the hands are raw. Although the obsessive knows that the dread of filth is irrational, the thoughts create such psychic distress that they must be relieved by constant cleansing. Washing eases the tension, but the distress soon builds up again until the cleaning must start over.
- *Checkers* (doubters) are compelled to continually recheck their actions — for instance, to make sure they have turned off the stove or locked the door. Some repeatedly visit the scene of an imagined accident to be certain they haven't run over a child on the way home. "They are reassurance addicts," comments one therapist, "constantly checking to make sure nothing's amiss."
- *Hoarders* may save every piece of mail they've ever received, every scrap of paper, even Christmas trees from past years — for fear that they'll throw out something valuable.

Common obsessions:
- fear of contamination: "Everything I touch is full of germs";
- doubt: "Did I hit that dog with my car?";
- orderliness: "I can't attend class until everything in my room is in perfect order";
- fear of aggression toward oneself or others —"If I had a knife, I might lose control and

stab my mother" — necessitating compulsive acts to make sure the violence cannot happen (e.g., throwing out all sharp objects).

OCD was traditionally viewed as a psychological disorder, attributed to restrictive parenting, early toilet training (causing an unhealthy obsession with cleanliness) or anxiety over sexual urges. But modern scientists believe it to be caused by a biological abnormality, probably an imbalance in one or more neurotransmitters (chemicals that act as messengers between nerve cells) — particularly serotonin, which modulates repetitive actions, sleep, aggression and grooming behavior. There may be too little serotonin in some areas of OCD brains, causing grooming behavior to go out of control. The fact that one-third of OCD cases improve with serotoninergic drugs (which raise serotonin levels) emphasizes this possibility.

Treatment for obsessive-compulsive disorder is with psychotherapy, antidepressants, buspirone and new serotonin-activating drugs such as clomipramine (Anafranil), fluoxetine (Prozac) and fluvoxamine (Luvox). Hailed as a breakthrough, these agents may take six to ten weeks to become effective. Since the medications suppress symptoms rather than curing the illness, the disorder may reemerge if the drugs are discontinued. In serious cases, several drugs may be needed. However, OCD is a complex disorder, and therapy is not a matter of handing out a few pills and expecting lifelong horrors to vanish overnight. Many OCD sufferers have devoted hours each day to their obsessions for years, and it takes a great deal of psychotherapy to eradicate such deep-rooted behavior.

Behavior therapy employs "exposure" and "response prevention," exposing patients to the feared situations to reduce the rituals. In some studies, these methods are as effective as medication. Behavioral techniques provide relief to about 50–70 percent of patients. The therapist guides sufferers to confront the situation being avoided, such as touching door handles, shaking hands or eating certain foods, helping them to refrain from the ritualistic practices. Someone who detests dirt, for instance, will be asked to rub dirt on the hands and abstain from handwashing for a while. Alternatively, the person might be encouraged to visualize the anticipated catastrophe, such as running over a cat, become accustomed to the thought and extinguish the anxiety. In the most severe cases, when OCD makes life unlivable, brain surgery may be a last resort.

For further information or help, contact anxiety-disorder clinics (e.g., at Toronto's Clarke Institute) or the Freedom from Fear Foundation, tel. 416-761-6006.

SCHIZOPHRENIA

Schizophrenia is a serious, often lifelong psychiatric illness that usually starts in young adulthood. Among historic figures thought to be schizophrenics, Louis Riel and the painter Hieronymus Bosch are two of the better known. Schizophrenia is a common illness. Many of us probably know someone who is a schizophrenic. Regardless of race, culture, sex or social class, everyone stands a one-in-a-hundred chance of developing schizophrenia. That's 10 times the risk of having multiple sclerosis or muscular dystrophy. The tragedy of schizophrenia is that it often comes as a bitter and unexpected blow, during or soon after the difficult teenage years, just when a youngster seems about to fulfill the promise of his or her childhood.

There is a genetic element — not yet fully understood — to schizophrenia. If one or other parent is a schizophrenic, the chance of a child having the illness rises to 10 percent. Should both parents be afflicted, the risk for their offspring is 40 percent. Although males and females are equally at risk, schizophrenia tends to show up earlier in males — in the late teens and early twenties — while in females the first schizophrenic crisis usually hits between age 25 and 30. Traditionally, schizophrenics have been feared as violent criminal types — a myth to be dispelled, since the rate of violence among schizophrenics is no higher than among the rest of the population.

Defining schizophrenia

Still imperfectly understood, schizophrenia is a brain disorder now controllable by various drugs. The term "schizophrenia" originates from the Greek schizo and phren, meaning split mind, a term formerly used to describe the disorder's more common symptoms such as disconnected ideas, the hearing of voices and an inability to comprehend reality. Until recently, much confusion surrounded the definition of this and other mental illnesses, which were often indiscriminately lumped together.

A new diagnostic rigor has clarified the definition of schizophrenia as a "thought disorder." By the currently accepted definition, schizophrenia is an illness with psychotic episodes, heralded by an initial, acute (active) phase occurring before age 45, often in adolescence, with continuous, intense symptoms (such as delusions and disordered thoughts) lasting at least six months. Its minor features may creep up slowly (before the onset of an obvious breakdown) and seem little different from the ordinary ups and downs of adolescence. In others, the illness hits like a bolt from the blue, with a full-blown, acute psychotic attack. Before schizophrenia is diagnosed, other possible causes of the symptoms — such as drug abuse, epilepsy, a brain tumor, or metabolic disturbances — must be ruled out, and the condition must be clearly differentiated from affective (mood) disorders. The use of standardized, well-structured interviews has made the diagnosis of schizophrenia more accurate.

Some schizoid symptoms are hard to handle

The illness is signaled by a number of features, none of which is unique, but which together confirm and characterize schizophrenia. The most usual signs of an acute phase are the so-called positive (although detrimental) behavior changes:

- Disturbed thought processes — incoherent and illogical reasoning — shown by fragmented speech, jumbled or "nonsense" talk and use of idiosyncratic, sometimes unusually concrete phrases, often with a fixation on body parts.
- Perceptual problems, in which schizophrenics think their thoughts are being deciphered or broadcast aloud, or that they can read the thoughts of others.
- Hallucinations — typical of the illness — in which those affected hear voices inside their heads telling them what to do, or behave

strangely in response to such instructions.
- Delusions — false convictions of grandeur, power or persecution, during the psychotic stage. Classic examples are a schizophrenic who imagines that he is Jesus or that an accidental bump in the subway is an assassination plot. Such convictions are tenaciously held against all reason.
- Paranoid suspicions — where an innocent smile, remark or joke is misconstrued as being directed solely against the schizophrenic, perhaps with malicious intent.
- Intense and prolonged spiritual and other preoccupation; schizophrenics may become lost in ideas which, if communicated, seem bizarre to others.
- Inability to distinguish fantasy from fact; a belief that daydreams are true.

The reappearance of some of these symptoms during a quiescent phase of the illness should alert the schizophrenic, caregivers and family to the possibility of a repeat breakdown.

Apathetic inactivity awaits many with schizophrenia

Alternating with psychotic interludes in schizophrenia are calmer intervals when the person is not really back to normal, but exhibits "negative" aspects of the condition — not easily amenable to drugs or psychiatric treatment. These include extreme apathy (often mistaken for laziness), passivity or a tendency to shun social contact, slow and impoverished thinking, sluggish movement, incongruous emotions (such as laughing at a sad event), ritualistic behavior and isolation. There may be an inability to complete even small jobs or to organize and plan daily living. Poor hygiene, sloppy dressing and social withdrawal make it difficult for the schizophrenic to cope with jobs, friendships and dating.

The apathetic state continues — sometimes for a lifetime — with occasional psychotic flare-ups which can be triggered by stress or excitement. Some people with schizophrenia find the quiescent stage of their illness dull, empty and harder to bear than its hallucinatory highs. A few may try — by quitting medication or seeking tense situations — to reawaken the acute phase and lose themselves in delusions of grandeur rather than face the reality of an unsatisfying existence.

Research probes the causes of schizophrenia

The causes of schizophrenia remain obscure, but increasing evidence points to a biochemical imbalance in the brain. Although the exact nature of the malfunction is unknown, neurochemists believe that it probably involves an imbalance in dopamine, a brain transmitter, and speculate that the disorder may stem from an abnormal reactivity to dopamine. In certain areas of some schizophrenic brains, an excess of dopamine-sensitive receptors has been found. The drugs used for the illness work by suppressing dopamine action. Some studies suggest alternative causes of schizophrenia, such as early viral infection, birth injuries that deprive brain cells of oxygen, and anatomical brain abnormalities — shown by CAT scans (special brain X-rays).

The knowledge that schizophrenia arises from some organic or biochemical dysfunction, rather than from faulty upbringing or psychological influences, comforts many parents who might otherwise feel responsible for bringing about their child's disorder.

Treatment with drugs can usually control symptoms

Thanks to psychotherapy, a broad range of neuroleptic (antipsychotic) drugs and a more tolerant public attitude toward mental illness, those with schizophrenia are no longer shamefully shunted off to psychiatric institutions. Many now live and work within the community. Brief admissions to hospital may be necessary for relapses when symptoms flare, but hospital treatment, although a crucial element, is no longer the only therapy. Like diabetes, schizophrenia is a chronic complaint that needs regular attention. Some people suffer only one attack, but most require lifelong drug treatment to suppress the difficult symptoms. Regular use of neuroleptics can prevent psychotic attacks.

The main neuroleptic drugs used for schizophrenia include chlorpromazine (Largactil), trifluoperazine (Apotex, Stelazine) and haloperidol (Haldol). These drugs block dopamine receptors at nerve endings in the brain, cutting down the excess dopamine action thought to be involved in the disorder. Long-acting injections are sometimes better than tablets, which many forget or neglect to take.

Short-term side effects of the neuroleptics include a restless desire to move and pace about, vision disturbances, weight gain, muscle tremors (like those in Parkinson's disease), a mask-like expression and sleepiness. A late-onset, long-term side effect of the antipsychotic drugs is tardive dyskinesia — largely involuntary movements of fingers, jaws and tongue which produce strange gestures, of which schizophrenics are unaware but which may disconcert others. Some of the side effects can be reduced by counteractive medication.

A newly approved, antipsychotic medication called risperidone (Risperdal) has an advantage over previously available agents for treating schizophrenia, in combating not only the delusions, hallucinations and suspicion common in this malady, but also in relieving its "negative" features such as withdrawal, apathy and dampened emotions. Moreover, risperidone has far fewer adverse side effects and produces none of the tics and twitches common with other antischizophrenia drugs. Instead of targeting just the dopamine neurotransmitter pathway, risperidone evidently also acts on the disturbed serotonin system, rebalancing the brain's biochemical/bioelectrical balance.

In general, schizophrenics are maintained on a steady low dose of medication to suppress the most unpleasant psychotic symptoms of their illness, with temporarily higher doses when a breakdown is imminent. Full recovery, relatively uncommon, depends on the severity of the illness. If it occurs, it usually comes within the first two years; it's rare after five years of the disease. However, a degree of social recovery — the ability to function outside the hospital — does occur. With time, each schizophrenic learns his or her limits and realizes the usefulness of the medication. After the age of 40 life with schizophrenia often becomes less distressing — psychotic episodes diminish, maintenance drugs can be minimal and the quality of life improves.

A FEW GUIDELINES FOR FAMILY AND FRIENDS OF THOSE WITH SCHIZOPHRENIA

- Above all, persuade sufferers to stay on their prescribed medication regime and keep doctors' appointments.
- Provide a calm, supportive, unstressful atmosphere.
- Explain clearly at all times what you're doing and why; speak precisely.
- Be realistic in your expectations.
- Avoid being too inquisitive or probing thoughts too deeply, while still inviting schizophrenics to share ideas and experiences.
- Arguing or calling schizoid delusions irrational only leads to mistrust and anger. A better response to a sufferer's belief that he or she is Jesus would be "I guess you feel special and different today. Let's try a low-key routine for the next few days."
- Encourage a struc-tured lifestyle with a regular routine and small tasks, praised if well done; include sanctions and rewards as suitable.
- Remember that motor actions — such as cooking, carpentry, drawing and other mechanical tasks — may be easier than verbal efforts (although this varies according to former ability); most will attempt whatever activities they did before becoming ill.
- Enlist help in volunteer jobs, such as making cookies or helping the blind, provided it's within the abilities of the individual patient.
- Remember that, depending on the severity of the illness and previous abilities, each person with schizophrenia can tackle different challenges.
- Coax the sufferer to engage in gentle social interaction, but avoid large parties or big family gatherings.
- Since schizophrenics are shy people and find intimate and sexual relationships difficult, don't push them unduly.
- If in doubt about what to do, consult the patient's therapist, and consider joining a friends' and relatives' discussion group.

Skipping medication is a big problem

Often, those with schizophrenia feel so well on the neuroleptic medication that they go off their drugs, risking relapse. Many patients quit because of the false illusion that they're cured, in denial of their illness or because of discomfort from side effects. They miss medical appointments and often move — even out of town — to avoid supervision. Some heap abuse on their caretakers, venting the frustration of their illness on others. Quitting or skipping medication usually produces a slow deterioration, a return of acute symptoms and rehospitalization, so people looking after schizophrenics should aim to be viewed as aides rather than adversaries. Treatment programs should be flexible and nonjudgmental and help patients remain in treatment.

Rehabilitation is an uphill battle

Since this illness strikes the young, their lives are often interrupted during the formative years by repeated hospital stays. They therefore have little schooling or job skills. Owing to unemployment, apathy and neglect, many schizophrenics are malnourished and poor, forced to live in hardship and deprivation. A few rehabilitation programs are available to help them learn new job skills, and to teach them to look after themselves, manage their illness and avoid relapses. For lack of alternatives, many schizophrenics use emergency departments of hospitals as primary care (medical help) facilities.

Some schizophrenics ultimately manage to live alone and hold a job — a situation that not only lessens the burden on the family but also helps raise self-esteem. Others live in group homes, which provide a range of supervision from round the clock to once a week or so. Families can join support groups and share their worries with other families of schizophrenics.

Schizophrenia is no longer the bleak illness portrayed in older texts. Whereas, in the past, a schizophrenic who recovered was often rediagnosed as having had some other illness, today we recognize that many do well on medication and a few even recover completely.

Various organizations have sprung up to help schizophrenics and their families and helpers, such as The Canadian Friends of Schizophrenics, 95 Barber Greene Road, Suite 309, Don Mills, Ontario M3C 3E9, tel. 416-445-8204. A book published by the University of Toronto Press — *Living and Working with Schizophrenia* — and a videotape by the same name produced by the University of Toronto Medical Faculty, IMS department — call 416-978-6302 — may also be helpful.

FINDING THERAPY FOR MENTAL AND EMOTIONAL PROBLEMS

In deciding where to find help for mental, emotional and psychological disorders, people are often confused by the multitude of different therapists out there — ranging from psychiatrists and psychologists to social workers, marital counselors and behaviorists. It's wise to find out what's what in the world of psychosocial counseling, and distinguish between "stress-related distress" (which may stem from work or lifestyle habits), remedied by simple relaxation therapy, and deeper problems that need the attention of a psychologist or psychiatrist. Mentally troubled or disturbed people have to decide whether they need advice from a psychiatrist (who has a medical degree, with fees usually covered by provincial healthcare plans) or nonmedical therapy from a clinical psychologist, social worker or other counselor.

In general, psychiatrists are best equipped to handle a mental illness such as schizophrenia, phobias or depression. If the symptoms seem to be purely emotional or stress-related, with no other problems (such as anxiety, phobias), talking to a nonmedical therapist about worries and feelings may be as good as or better than psychiatric treatment. But if there are signs of more profound mental disturbances — such as panic attacks, obsessionality or excessive thought preoccupation — psychiatric help may be best.

The way to start is by discussing the problem with your family physician, who can help in advising you where to turn and give you an appropriate referral. Friends and colleagues at work are also good people to ask for advice on where to get help. Nonmedical therapists vary from clinical experts to research-oriented therapists to behavioral counselors. The plethora of different therapists can be confusing, as it's difficult to know who does what! There is no licensing body for psychotherapists,

---

THE CHOICE OF THERAPISTS FOR EMOTIONAL AND PSYCHIATRIC PROBLEMS INCLUDES:

- **medically trained psychiatrists (fees covered by health-care plans);**
- **psychologists, who practice various forms of psycho-therapy and may be research-oriented or clinical (giving practical advice);**
- **psychoanalysts, who have no medical degree but have themselves under-gone some kind of rigorous analysis (Jungian, Freudian, Adlerian, Reichian,** Gestalt, whatever) and now administer similarly oriented psychotherapy to others;
- **social workers, who may provide individual or group psychological and lifestyle counseling, or do mainly community or organizational social work. Clinical social workers generally provide therapy in the context of family, marital, work, lifestyle and other problems;**
- **pastoral counselors** (excellent for those with religious affiliations);
- **relaxation therapists;**
- **various types of sex-counseling services;**
- **child- and family-service associations for marital and child-care counseling;**
- **workplace employee-assistance programs, often an excellent place to get advice and therapy;**
- **group therapists;**
- **self-help agencies, which are increasingly popular.**

---

and so anyone can hang up a sign as a "therapist." To distinguish one therapist from another, ask for credentials and inquire about the therapist's training and background. Does he or she belong to a licensed body or association? Does he or she have a special license to practice?

Overcoming the stigma of mental illness

Discrimination against those with psychiatric illnesses has a long, dark history. Even today the stigma remains, and people with manic depressive disorder, depression or other psychiatric illnesses often hesitate to seek help because of it. Millions who suffer from psychiatric disorders, which respond well to modern treatment, do not obtain professional care and suffer needlessly. In recent years, efforts have been made to heighten the awareness of mental illness as a major health problem. Many employers have developed employee-assistance programs (EAPs) through which people can get confidential help for mental or emotional problems that disrupt their family and work lives.

Keeping up the quality of life with advancing years

The aging brain • Caring for well elderly relatives • Incontinence • Parkinson's disease • Osteoporosis • Alzheimer's disease

15

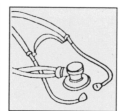

AGING IS NOT A disease. Mental ability and intelligence do not inevitably dwindle as we age. While there's some loss of brain cells and non-disease-related loss of memory as people age, other mental functions such as wisdom, knowledge and judgment often improve with advancing years. Seniors vary widely in their retention of mental capacities. Well-known people who made valuable contributions to society long past the time when most of us retire include Picasso, Verdi, Michelangelo, Edison, Golda Meir, Winston Churchill, Dr. Robert McClure (active until age 91), Northrop Frye (who wrote and lectured into his eighties) and Oliver Wendell Holmes (who remained on the U.S. Supreme Court until he was 90). But one needn't be a Picasso or a Verdi to function into old age — most of us know interesting people who have retained their capacities well into their eighties and nineties.

The vast majority of older people are the "well" elderly, who remain healthy into their later years, often needing little or no help. Given safe household organization, social involvement and an active lifestyle, many can go on living at home to a ripe old age.

THE AGING BRAIN

Contrary to earlier beliefs, the brain remains open to learning even in the very old, provided it's not diseased. Crystalline intelligence, which uses past experience and verbal ability, may actually increase with advancing years, provided there are no serious health problems and the person continues to use the brain by reading,

---

LAYING TO REST SOME COMMON MYTHS ABOUT AGING

- *Myth:* The elderly are all alike.
  Fact: People over age 65 are more unlike one another than members of any other age group. Immune-system function and mental agility differ more widely in the elderly than at other ages, and personality too seems to differentiate more with advancing years. As the saying goes, "People remain themselves, only more so."
- *Myth:* Aging means degenerative diseases and disorders.
  Fact: Few diseases are directly due to aging. While conditions such as atherosclerosis (artery blockage) and arthritis (joint stiffness) are more common in old age, they are not just a consequence of advancing years. Similarly, many disorders such as cataracts, hearing loss, depression and incontinence are not a normal or inevitable part of aging. Old age is not a disease!
- *Myth:* Younger people don't really think about old age.
  Fact: Modern society has an obsessive fear of both growing old and the ultimate, common, human destiny of death.
- *Myth:* It's too late to start healthy habits in old age.
  Fact: The elderly benefit as much as other age groups from good nutrition, regular exercise and other health-promoting activities.

socializing, game playing and taking on new interests. Cognitive decline in aging humans may increase with boredom, depression or loss of interest. The popular saying "Use it or lose it" may be trite but is likely quite apt.

The exact nature of the brain's cognitive (thinking) changes with increasing age remains controversial. While some experts argue that functions such as memory and reasoning tend to diminish, others suggest that such apparent changes may be a matter of prejudice and perception, or may stem from a lack of stimulation or too little motivation to do well on mental function tests. In many of those who do poorly on such tests, the failure stems from physical illness, depression or medications taken, rather than old age.

Modern research shows the brain to be far more adaptable than hitherto imagined. Scientists have recently discovered that one type of neuron (nerve cell) abundant in adulthood is preserved in the healthy elderly, perhaps contributing to their wisdom. Recent research also suggests that while many brain cells do die off and cannot be replaced, the decay of synapses (nerve connections) is not necessarily irreversible. The growth of new nerve connections is the brain's way of sculpting quicker pathways. Many experts now think that the brain possesses more neuroplasticity and restructuring ability than formerly believed, and that new nerve pathways replace old ones after injury or cell death.

Normal versus abnormal mental changes

There is generally some slowing of reaction times with advancing years, but recent studies show that the healthy elderly are only fractionally slower than younger people. For example, a 70-year-old may take one quarter of a second more time to identify a familiar object or read a speedometer than a 30-year-old. In practical terms, reaction times slowed by even a fraction of a second can be dangerous when quick reflexes are essential — as in crossing the street or driving a car; however, the greater experience and caution of older people may compensate for their slightly slower reactions.

Memory declines with advancing years, but memory problems are complex, related to

---

USUAL CHANGES OF THE NERVOUS SYSTEM WITH AGE

The average brain of a 75-year-old man weighs 45 percent less than that of a 30-year-old. Cerebral blood flow, oxygen and glucose metabolism decline with age. These changes produce various sensory, perceptual and behaviour alterations, but the effects of these changes can be minimized or accommodated.

- **Diminished heat and cold regulation** Elderly people are less adaptable to temperature extremes and feel the heat and cold more than the young. A reduction in sweating makes them more susceptible to heat exhaustion, and an impaired ability to increase the core body temperature makes them more vulnerable to the cold.
- **Dulled taste and smell** Starting in middle age, many people experience diminished taste sensitivity, due to a loss of taste buds. A combined loss of taste and smell may make older people more vulnerable to appetite disorders and malnutrition.
- **Hearing changes** Hearing may begin to deteriorate starting at age 30, and it becomes progressively harder to hear high frequencies. Speech processing too becomes more difficult, and many elderly people can't distinguish among certain sounds (in particular c, t, s). Speaking clearly when addressing the elderly and facilitating lip-reading by keeping one's face in the light can ease communication.
- **Eye and vision alterations** Changes in both the structure and the function of the eyes mean that many people come to need reading glasses. With advancing age, they find it harder to adapt from a bright environment to a darker one, and they need brighter lights for reading. Most of these changes (as opposed to disease-related disorders) can be accommodated — for example, using sunglasses in bright light, night lights in the dark or large-print books. Peripheral vision (being able to see at the edges of the visual field) may also become impaired. The elderly may have difficulty focusing on near objects (such as the speedometer) after looking at distant objects, and many find glare a problem — which can increase the hazards of driving a car or crossing the street. (Seniors must beware of driving at night, especially in vehicles with tinted windows.)

---

both storing and retrieving facts. The retrieval of recent knowledge when wanted, at a particular moment in time, is often difficult for the elderly, but the information frequently surfaces later — not really amounting to memory loss. So-called memory-pills such as Gerovital, Ribaminol, lecithin, and various vitamin and dietary supplements have *not* been shown to be efficacious, and experimental drugs such as cognitive and metabolic enhancers — ergoloid mesylates (Hydergine), physigimine and tetrahydroaminoacridine — which target certain neurotransmitter systems, have only limited (if any) benefits. At present, there are no effective memory drugs.

Although old age is commonly equated with senility and dementia (a decline in intellectual abilities such as language and abstract thought), less than 30 percent of the population ever suffers from any form of dementia, including Alzheimer's disease. On the other hand, such disorders cannot at present be prevented, even with early detection. A 1991 update from the Canadian Task Force on Periodic Health Exams finds "no conclusive evidence to show that the early detection of cognitive impairment in healthy older people leads to either a net benefit (better life-management, ability to convey wishes or assign power of attorney) or net harm (feeling labeled as 'unfit')." Problems such as wandering, hostility, aggression, failure to recognize relatives, memory loss, physical neglect and psychotic episodes — which may indicate illness — require medical assessment. Arrangements for care, relocation, power of attorney and other necessities should be made before mental competence declines too far.

CARING FOR WELL ELDERLY RELATIVES

One of contemporary society's challenges is care of an increasing elderly population. In Canada, as elsewhere, family members — mostly women — are the primary caregivers of aging relatives. Their support is critical in keeping older people out of institutions. Yet, with growing numbers of women in the workforce, these added responsibilities may cause considerable strain. The goal is to give enough help while not "taking over," letting elders retain as much independence as possible for as long as possible, while at the same time ensuring that caregivers don't abandon or neglect their own interests. While the population of the "frail elderly" (over age 85) grows, the number of children aged 14 and under is steadily declining. Even at present, the elderly use more healthcare services than any other segment of the population.

According to experts from the University of Toronto's Centre for Studies on Aging, the job of keeping "frail older people out of institutions rests mainly on the backs of informal caregivers — relatives and friends — who provide about 80 percent of needed assistance to the elderly." Those looking after the unwell or fragile elderly can enlist varied services — home-support agencies, visiting nurses, aides, physiotherapists, social workers, homemakers, social clubs and Meals on Wheels — which help to maintain a senior's independence. But even though many cheerfully accept their role as caregivers for older people, the task can be exhausting, leading to physical and emotional stress, reduced coping abilities and time constraints that undermine the caregiver's health, employment and personal relationships. Caregivers need respite!

Maintain elderly independence as long as possible

Surveys show that seniors fear the loss of independence and admission into long-term care facilities above all else. The specter of reliance on others is upsetting; even losses such as no longer driving a car can be hard to accept, and may be resisted long after it is unsafe for the driver to be on the road. Anyone looking after older people must recognize this intense anxiety and respect their wish for continued independence. The average age of entry into geriatric institutions in Canada is 82, but we tend to overinstitutionalize our old people. About 7 percent of elderly citizens in Canada reside in long-term care institutions (excluding senior citizens' apartments and retirement homes), compared to only 5 percent in the United States and United Kingdom, and 4 percent in West Germany.

Geriatricians see an urgent need for more varied living arrangements that suit seniors, especially since premature institutionalization may accelerate a decline in functions such as memory and walking ability. Supported housing (with centralized care available), retirement homes, or innovative boarding arrangements (e.g., a live-in student who gives assistance in return for a room) can help seniors to remain independent. Accessory apartments, garden suites or other residential options may help families care for aging relatives. High- and low-tech devices can prolong the ability of frail seniors to stay at home — for instance, vital-function monitors, surveillance devices for wanderers, or emergency alarm systems — but they are not publicized enough, readily available or easily affordable.

When the condition of an older person deteriorates to the point that home caregivers can no longer cope, full investigation of all possible institutional options and a thorough discussion of the choices are advised. This will help to reduce and possibly eliminate resistance from the elderly relative, and relieve the caregiver's inevitable feelings of guilt and doubt. When the time comes, institutional care will be more pleasant if close ties are maintained, making sure seniors still feel part of the family by taking them on outings, sharing a meal, sending letters and gifts and providing clean and pressed laundry or suitable clothes.

Moving in with family members

While most older people prefer to go on living in their own homes, there are several other choices — for example, housing plans or "continuing-care" retirement communities that offer residential and healthcare facilities under one roof.

People who decide to live with their children should plan the transition thoughtfully, express feelings openly, anticipate how the arrangement might work and ask themselves a few key questions:

- Do I really want to live with this son or daughter?
- Can I adapt to my offspring's habits and lifestyle?
- How good a relationship do I have with my children? Is it comfortable and easy? Stressed and strained?
- Would I feel like a "constant visitor"?
- Could I still pursue my personal hobbies and interests?
- How much space and privacy would there be?
- Are there stairs to climb? How convenient are the toilet and bathroom?
- How about the financial arrangements; would I share household expenses?

Use all available support and community services

Caregivers should investigate and use all the supplemental support services they need or can afford from community, government, non-profit and private home-support services. It's wise to enlist simultaneous help from several organizations, such as seniors' health centers, day hospitals, outpatient and in-patient medical and psychiatric services, hospital-based home care, geriatric day centers, community and social clubs (e.g., Second Mile or Senior Link in Toronto).

- *For housekeeping help*: visiting homemakers will clean the house, prepare meals, shop and do laundry. Cost is usually geared to income, and provinces and municipalities may subsidize services.
- *For personal hygiene*: a private or nonprofit trained helper, suggested by a physician or other healthcare professional, may come in to assist an elderly person with bathing, dressing, eating and some homemaking activities.
- *For safety*: to alleviate anxiety and summon emergency help if needed, telephone security checks may be organized. A volunteer, friend or neighbor may telephone seniors each day and, if there's no answer, initiate emergency procedures. Many hospitals and private organizations supply electronic devices such as beepers that alert emergency medical units if seniors need help.
- *For social needs*: many clubs and senior day programs offer companionship and rehabilitative activities. Studies show that social support benefits health — even support as simple as someone to chat with, to share the occasional meal with, to provide companionship or facilitate attendance at religious services.
- *For food:* Meals on Wheels (or other agencies) may deliver hot meals several times a week.
- *For medical disorders:* some healthcare services provide multidisciplinary assessment teams (of nurses, social workers, physical and occupational therapists, recreation experts, physicians, dentists, audiologists, dietitians, respirologists, speech therapists and others) to offer advice and help. Therapeutic, educational, social and recreation programs may be provided, with

CARE OF THE ELDERLY SHOULD:

- **provide support while preserving independence and the best possible quality of life;**
- **identify and ameliorate physical and psychiatric disorders;**
- **help organize living arrangements to promote independence — especially by preventing possible falls, monitoring medications taken, ensuring adequate nutrition and encouraging activity;**
- **find supported housing when needed;**
- **counsel those facing serious or terminal illnesses;**
- **ease the burden on caregivers — giving them periodic respite as well as physical and psychological support.**

costs sometimes covered by provincial health-care plans. Home-care visits may be arranged for those who qualify under Ministry of Health guidelines. Geriatric daycare or home-care programs (sometimes funded by provincial agencies) have many advantages over hospital stays. Pioneering efforts include New Brunswick's Extra-Mural Hospital or "Hospital without Walls," which provides hospital care at home, British Columbia's Quick Response Team (in Victoria) and the Regional Geriatric Program of Metro Toronto (affiliated with the University of Toronto).

- *For relieving caregivers:* some nursing homes provide temporary (vacation or respite) admittance for a day or week, or a relief caregiver may come into the house for a few hours weekly. Geriatric daycare, short stays in an institutional setting and even round-the-clock in-home services for a limited time can ease the caregiver's burden.

Encourage exercise: it can make people act and feel younger

Although regular exercise can make one feel (and even look) younger, many seniors are slow to don sneakers. Reduced cardiovascular function, muscle wasting and bone loss are no longer considered a natural part of aging, but a result of inactivity. Yet only about one-fifth of the current elderly population is physically active at a level that upgrades heart health. Studies confirm that the elderly can greatly improve their quality of life, and perhaps ward off osteoporosis, by regular weight-bearing exercise. A brisk walk gives a good workout, provided it's done at the right pace and for at least 20–30 minutes, three times a week. (Getting a dog often gives seniors an extra incentive to walk!) For those who can't walk, swimming and stationary bicycles give a good workout. One University of Toronto expert says that "even in their seventies, some people can push their functional ages back by as much as 20 years by regular exercise, the gains showing up as more efficient cardiovascular function (heart able to pump blood with less effort). Exercise also enhances the ability to cope with stress, offsets depression, facilitates sleep and enhances appetite." Recent studies show that exercise may even help to keep the brain in shape. A 1989 study comparing cognitive scores in a group of elderly people who exercised with scores of those who did not found both mind and body performances better in exercisers than in the inactive.

Promote good nutrition

Nutritional requirements in old age roughly parallel those for other adults, although after

WAYS TO AVOID INSTITUTIONALIZATION

- **Granny flats (zoning requirements permitting)** are self-contained, portable units temporarily installed on the property of relatives with single-family homes. (They are not very successful — nobody seems to want them and the elderly won't stay in them.) One expert says, "Either take them into your home as 24-hour members of the family or find another solution."
- **Accessory apartments** are part of a family member's home, or an added room converted to create a small, self-contained unit.
- **In group homes** people share the expenses, staff and management of a property and communal rooms such as the kitchen and living room, while retaining their own bedrooms and possibly bathrooms.

Jointly hired staff can help with or provide cooking and maintenance. (Consult local health departments for contacts.)
- **Foster care** suits elderly people who cannot live alone; they move in with an unrelated family that provides meals and personal care for an arranged fee.
- **In home-sharing,** elderly home owners with extra space take in tenants who give housekeeping help in exchange for reduced rent.
- **Supported housing** refers to residences within a neighborhood or a section of an apartment building, or specially designed multiple-unit buildings, which provide elderly people with self-contained units connected to a central administration area by a call system. Residents usually come together for some meals and social activities.

To find help, consult the local Ministry of Health, Ministry of Community and Social Services, provincial offices for seniors' affairs (some of which have a toll-free 800 line) and municipal health departments, which provide information on local homes for the aged, seniors' apartments and social clubs.

age 50 fewer and fewer calories are required. But some of the elderly are malnourished because of poverty, physical disabilities, multiple medications, social isolation and a natural decline in smell and taste which reduces appetite. Widowed or single people often lose interest in preparing meals for themselves, and their food choices may be restricted by poverty. Difficulties in mobility, seeing and chewing may make it burdensome to prepare and eat food. In particular, older people must remember to eat high-quality, easily digestible protein such as fish, chicken and eggs. Getting enough calcium is also essential, to reduce the risks of osteoporosis. Besides milk, good sources of calcium are canned salmon (eaten with mashed bones), milk products such as yogurt and cottage cheese and other soft cheeses and some green vegetables such as broccoli. Since chewing can be difficult for some, especially those with ill-fitting dentures, they may prefer soft foods and puréed fruit or vegetables. But they should choose meat, vegetables and fruit rather than pre-prepared combination dinners or soups. Be sure to round out the meal with starches such as pasta, potatoes and rice. Dehydration is another risk for the elderly, who should remember to drink enough fluids. Vitamin and/or mineral supplements may occasionally be prescribed for older people, but only after a thorough medical assessment.

Avoiding falls is a top priority

Bone and soft-tissue injuries from falls are the sixth major cause of death among over-65s. For those 80 years old and over who suffer hip fractures, the six-month mortality rate exceeds 20 percent, because of postoperative complications. The chance of falling in a given year increases from 25 percent at age 70 to 40 percent after age 75, and half of those who fall do so repeatedly — acquiring a fear of falling and severely curtailing their activities. Until age 75 women outdo men in falls, but after that the sexes even out. Besides broken bones, other injuries (bleeding, sprains, joint dislocations) contribute to the toll of falls. Repeated falls are a major reason for institutionalizing the elderly, and for the reduction in activity that can cause further deterioration.

KEEP TABS ON ALL MEDICATIONS

Overmedication, inappropriate prescribing (doses not properly geared to the elderly) and harmfully interacting drug combinations can compound the disabilities of aging. Most drugs are tested in young and middle-aged adults and standard drug doses may endanger older people, who metabolize the same drugs differently. The World Health Organization (WHO) and other agencies have issued guidelines for prescribing drugs to the elderly.

WHO drug guidelines for the elderly:
- **No drug should be used if there is an effective and reasonable nonpharmaceutical alternative (e.g., exercise, physiotherapy or behavior therapy).**
- **A medication should not be prescribed if it is only marginally useful and has possible adverse effects.**
- **Pharmacists should be consulted to avoid drug interactions between substances prescribed for different conditions. (Fill prescriptions at the same pharmacy to aid monitoring.)**
- **Prescribing practices that contradict these principles should be questioned.**

Thorough medical checkups are advisable

Successful care of the elderly means distinguishing the so-called "normal" changes of aging from those due to underlying diseases that can be treated. Besides ongoing therapy for chronic, long-term conditions (such as diabetes and arthritis), medical exams permit early detection of newly developing conditions (such as low thyroid function or vision loss). During medical visits, the elderly shouldn't remain passive but should discuss any worries about their health or treatment. Make a list

---

REGULAR MEDICAL CHECKUPS FOR SENIORS MAY INCLUDE:

- **an eye examination to check for glaucoma, cataracts, retinal degeneration and other problems;**
- **a yearly dental examination;**
- **ear and hearing tests;**
- **monitoring of ongoing conditions such as diabetes, arthritis, high blood cholesterol or hypertension, and disorders prone to complications;**
- **breast examination;**
- **encouragement to get recommended immunizations — yearly flu shots, a once-only antipneumonia shot, tetanus boosters.**

Other examinations, if warranted, are:
- **mobility checks (joint flexibility, range of motion, strength);**
- **a full review of all medications being taken;**
- **evaluation of the ability to perform the activities of daily living (dressing, bathing, toilet use, cooking, cleaning, shopping);**
- **mental status assessment for mood, memory, cognition and depression;**
- **review of the use of aids and support services such as wheelchairs, canes, visiting healthcare helpers and homemakers.**

SENSIBLE TIPS FOR THE ELDERLY AND THOSE LOOKING AFTER THEM

Ensure adequate nutrition

- *Watch for signs of malnutrition* such as weight loss, low energy, mental confusion. Act early to correct poor eating habits.
- *Eat enough high-quality protein* (e.g., fish, chicken, eggs).
- *Prepare and freeze small portions* — for reheating in boiling water or a microwave oven.
- *If chewing is a problem*, choose nourishing puréed foods.
- *Avoid sudden or drastic weight-reduction programs*; there is always a trade-off between the fun of eating and diets that undermine health.
- *Caregivers can provide transportation to the supermarket*, do the shopping, carry heavy parcels or ask volunteers from a home support service to help.
- *Consider Meals on Wheels.*

Get enough exercise/activity

- *Activity should continue* within personal limits.
- *Promote weight-bearing activity*, which helps to ward off osteo-porosis — especially walking, which can build bone strength. Wear nonslip shoes with good support. Try balance exercises.
- *Check out the YMCA/YWCA and other community organizations* for seniors' exercise programs.

Monitor medications

- *Assist the elderly person to check* on the drugs being taken from time to time.
- *Discuss whether medications are taken correctly*; use clocks, notes and phone calls as reminders.
- *Label containers VERY clearly.*
- *Check expiry dates*, throw out and appropriately replace expired items.
- *Ask the physician and/or pharmacist about adverse side effects* and possible complications of prescribed medications; try to use the same pharmacist for all prescriptions to establish a personal relationship and systematic file.
- *Ask the physician if there are nondrug alternatives* to prescribed medicines (especially if falling is frequent).

Prevent falls and accidents (a top priority)

- *Watch for causes and risks of falls* such as: waning muscle strength; weak hand grip; acute illnesses (e.g., influenza, food poisoning); vision disturbances (cataracts, glaucoma, macular degeneration); arthritis (stiffened joints); previous strokes; gait disturbances and multiple medications (especially sedat-ing, tranquilizing and blood-pressure drugs).
- *Periodically review all drugs taken*, making sure instructions are followed. Inquire about medication side effects. Some drug combinations, such as tranquilizers, antihistamines, sedatives and antidepressants, increase the risk of falls. Decreasing doses can reduce the danger.
- *Encourage the elderly person to get vision checks* and obtain proper eyeglasses.
- *Get the right walking aids*, ensure good footwear (with enough support and nonslip soles).
- *Eliminate obvious* home hazards: e.g., loose rugs, high-pile carpeting, slippery or polished floors, obstacles, stairs without rails.

- *Put handrails on each side of stairs*; identify the edge of each step with paint or tape in a contrasting color. Carpet the stairs with low-pile material.
- *Simplify the furniture layout.* Use contrasting colors on floors, stairs and walls to clearly demarcate stairs and obstacles.
- *Improve lighting* and minimize glare.
- *Use nonslip mats in the bath*, install grab bars for bathtubs, showers.
- *Keep a night-light on* in the hall and bathroom.
- *Have snow and ice removed from walkways.*
- *Check safety aids* such as canes for wear and tear (the rubber tip on a cane can become slippery when worn thin).
- *Consider a personal "emergency response system"* (worn at home around the neck or wrist) that summons help at the push of a button.
- *In the kitchen*, use safety devices such as kettles with an automatic turnoff when boiling.
- *Remember to turn off the stove.* A microwave might be a safer alternative.
- *Use smoke detectors to warn of fire*, and carbon-monoxide detectors to signal gas dangers.

Promote good personal hygiene

- *Help to maintain cleanliness* and an attractive appearance, even if the elderly person has lost interest.
- *Keep up oral hygiene* and get regular dental care.

Combat loneliness, anxiety and depression

- *Discuss grief at loss* of friends and family.
- *Watch for signs of depression.* Frequent signs include appetite or weight loss, agitated behavior, fitful sleep, early morning awakening, reduced energy, lack of pleasure in things previ-ously enjoyed.
- *Watch for evidence of alcoholism* or excess drug use.

Encourage social interaction and stimulation

- *Investigate community programs* that augment the support provided by family and friends. Explore church and other group activities, daycare for seniors, community-care organizations, geriatric or seniors' centers, the "Y" and so on.
- *Consider a pet* for those fond of animals. A cat, dog or bird can help to keep up or rekindle an elderly person's interest in life.
- *Promote as much mental and social stimulation as possible* — integrate into family activities, take on outings; visit often; try to keep seniors involved, wanted and useful.

Investigate aids for the disabled

- *Look into aids for independent living*, e.g., Velcro closings on clothing, nonskid dishes, special utensils to overcome arthritic stiffness.
- *Bell Canada has a "Special Needs Centre"* to serve visually and hearing impaired customers. See your phone book for the toll-free number.
- *Use memory aids*, routines, clocks, notes, oral and written reminders about medications, appointments and mealtimes.

beforehand and report any abnormal occurrences, pain or discomfort. Even a seemingly small or meaningless symptom may give clues to some underlying disorder. Caregivers can act as affirmers or advocates, helping to overcome language difficulties and explain things, but should never assume the role of "parent" or exclude the elder from the discussion. The elderly person and caregivers should disclose any and all symptoms and bring along all medications being taken. Inquire about the medications prescribed — what they do, how they act, whether they have side effects, and about possible nondrug alternatives. Those worried about an aged person's ability to live alone or the extent and appropriateness of medication can ask the physician how best to manage the situation. Referral for specialized geriatric evaluation helps to reveal the overall picture. Geriatricians stress the need for house calls by family physicians, particularly for the frail elderly, to permit assessment in the home surroundings. A home visit may reveal hazards such as an unsafe bathroom, a poorly lit staircase, unopened pill containers (suggesting failure to take prescribed medication), a hidden whisky bottle or the inability of a seemingly competent 80-year-old to use the telephone (perhaps revealing memory loss due to Alzheimer's disease).

For further information on care of the elderly contact the National Advisory Council on Aging (NACA); senior-care, services; regional geriatric programs; makers of special alert devices; the Parkinson Foundation of Canada, Toronto, tel. (416) 964-1155; the Alzheimer Society of Canada, tel. (416) 925-3552. Meals on Wheels; visiting homemaker associations; local Ministry of Community and Social Services. In Ontario: the Baycrest Centre for Geriatric Care, 3560 Bathurst St., North York, Ontario M6A 2E1, tel. (416) 789-5131; Senior Care, tel. (416) 635-9492; the Regional Geriatric Program of Metropolitan Toronto, tel. (416) 785-2488. Read *Planning Your Retirement*, by Blossom Wigdor; *Old Enough to Feel Better* and *An Ounce of Prevention: The Canadian Guide to Healthy and Successful Retirement*, by Michael Gordon.

INCONTINENCE

Previously considered an unmentionable subject, the elderly and not-so-elderly leaky bladder is now taken more seriously. Incontinence is the involuntary loss of urine to a degree that causes social and/or health problems. It plagues many people, old and young, and is often the final event that puts the elderly into chronic-care institutions when the family can no longer cope. Recent studies reveal not only that incontinence is amazingly common, but that it can often be completely cured or dramatically relieved.

Too much needless suffering

Untreated incontinence can lead to poor hygiene, urinary-tract infections, rashes and other skin disorders. In rushing to the washroom the incontinent often suffer falls and fractures. Fears of being far from a restroom and of unpleasant odors can cause sufferers to avoid outings, friends and family gatherings, leading to isolation and depression. Many give up their sex lives for fear of leaking, and, as the last straw that sends them into chronic-care institutions, the problem can cost seniors their independence. A recent consensus conference of the National Institutes of Health (NIH) in the United States concluded that millions suffer in silence due to embarrassment, failure to seek advice and lack of proper treatment. The shroud of secrecy and the myth of inevitability are perpetuated by adult diaper manufacturers, many of whom wrongly imply that urinary incontinence is a normal result of aging and that diapers are the best remedy. Believing incontinence to be incurable, only a fraction of sufferers seek medical help, turning prematurely to pads without ever having a proper diagnosis. Yet incontinence can almost always be relieved once its cause is pinpointed. It requires a thorough medical examination and laboratory workup, and specific treatment, not diapers.

According to the NIH and other studies, only one in five of the incontinent gets properly evaluated for this much-neglected health problem, and only about one in three physicians treats it properly. Many physicians don't ask the right questions and some don't even know how to evaluate it. When the popular newspaper column "Dear Abby" discussed incontinence in 1983 and recommended the American information organization Help for Incontinent People, the association was deluged with over 50,000 letters in three weeks.

About 5 to 10 percent of the population is incontinent at some time or other (some during childhood), increasing to 15 to 20 percent in older people — more in women than in men, although after age 70 the two sexes even out. An astonishing 37 percent of women over age 65 and 50 percent of nursing-home residents suffer from incontinence, partly explaining why the condition costs billions. (In 1989, the United States spent 15 billion dollars on incontinence — far outstripping the amounts spent on AIDS, heart surgery or kidney dialysis.) Incontinence will likely become an even greater health-care burden as the proportion of the population over age 65 increases from 11 percent in the 1980s to an estimated 20 percent by 2021.

More common in women than in men

Although getting older does not in itself *cause* incontinence, normal changes in the genito-urinary tract make the condition more common in the elderly, and far more prevalent in women than in men. With advancing age most people void more frequently than when young — especially at night, as the kidneys produce more nighttime urine. The elderly are also more likely to have detrusor instability (bladder spasms or uninhibited bladder contractions), producing a sudden, uncontrollable urge to urinate. As people age, their bladder capacity declines, the urethra (urine-conducting tube) becomes less elastic and the bladder base may sag. Childbirth in women and an enlarged prostate or prostate surgery in men can damage the urinogenital muscles and lead to incontinence. The common ailments that afflict the elderly (such as arthritis, failing eyesight, strokes, Parkinsonism) and the many medications they take, compounded with difficulties in reaching the toilet, can increase bladder problems and tip a borderline case into full incontinence.

Identifying the cause of incontinence is a top priority

Finding the cause of incontinence often suggests the cure. A good medical workup will establish whether it's nocturnal (only at night) or diurnal (both during the day and at night); whether it's continuous, intermittent, severe or mild; how much urine is lost and what triggers it. A list of medications taken (both prescription and over-the-counter), assessment of the person's mental state plus instructions for keeping a micturition or voiding diary (recording fluid intake and urine output) help to establish the reason(s) for the incontinence. Testing for leakage on coughing or bending may indicate stress incontinence. Measuring how well the bladder empties may pinpoint an overflow problem. Occasionally, more extensive bladder testing may be required. Once the pattern of incontinence is determined, appropriate therapy can be started.

Treatment for incontinence

For the most part, incontinence can be successfully relieved. Clearly, if some medication or disease is behind the problem, the disease should be treated or the drugs discontinued if possible. If the cause is basically irreversible, as with Alzheimer's disease or dementia, the patient can be made more comfortable with absorbent undergarments, by use of bedpans, or intermittent use of catheters (flexible voiding tubes) — a last resort, since catheterized patients are prone to infection. The idea is to start with the least invasive strategies, such as behavior therapy and toilet habit improvement. If that doesn't work, the physician may move on to drugs or surgery. Treating incontinence also depends on the personality of the sufferer — for instance, a confused older person with severe, long-standing incontinence is less likely to manage pelvic-floor exercises than a younger person with mild stress incontinence. Overflow incontinence is often treated surgically — for example, by reducing an enlarged prostate or with intermittent catheter voiding. Surgery doesn't help urge incontinence due to detrusor instability — it's generally best managed with medication.

• Exercises often help. Many experts suggest

TYPES AND CAUSES OF INCONTINENCE

Transient, reversible or acute forms

Reversible incontinence accounts for as much as one-third of all cases and can be triggered by other disorders. A sudden bout of incontinence calls for prompt medical attention. Common reasons for transient incontinence include urinary-tract infections, medications (especially sleeping pills, tranquilizers, and antidepressants), illnesses that limit movement or cause confusion, such as hip fractures or high fever.

One physician has proposed the acronym DIAPPERS to list the reasons for transient incontinence (mainly in the elderly):

- D for delirium. Someone who's confused may be unaware that the bladder is emptying without control.
- I for infection. Urinary-tract infections often cause urgency, but are treatable with antibiotics.
- A for atrophic urethritis or vaginitis. Thinning of pelvic and urinary-tract tissues in women after the menopause (when estrogen levels drop) can produce symptoms similar to urinary-tract infections, treatable with hormones or other medication.
- P for pharmacologic — over-the-counter and prescription medications that contribute to incontinence include:
  - diuretics (which increase urine output);
  - sedative hypnotics or sleep-aids (which relax the bladder muscle);
  - anticholinergics (e.g., anti-Parkinson drugs), which cause urine retention;
  - antipsychotics and antidepressants (sedating and accident-causing);
  - blood-pressure medications (e.g., beta blockers such as propranolol) or other drugs (e.g., prazosin, clonidine, methyldopa, reserpine) that induce urine retention;
  - antihistamines and anti-inflammatories (e.g., nonsteroidal anti-inflamatory drugs), decongestants and cold remedies (e.g., ephedrine, chlorpheniramine).
- P for psychological problems such as depression or anxiety;
- E for endocrine or hormonal reasons, such as diabetes and hypercalcemia;
- R for restricted mobility, which makes it hard for people to get to the toilet;
- S for stool impaction, where constipation allows the bowel to press on the bladder.

Chronic, persistent or long-term incontinence

- *Genuine stress incontinence* — the commonest type — arises from a sudden increase in abdominal pressure, for example when coughing, lifting, sneezing or laughing. If severe, just standing up may release a dribble. It's thought to arise from weakened urethral muscles, which control bladder outflow. Smoking, obesity, constipation and respiratory problems can precipitate stress incontinence. It can occur at any age but is most often seen in middle-aged and older women, sometimes following childbirth. It is less common in men, except when the urination muscles are damaged by prostate surgery. Pelvic exercises and medications often cure it. If due to postmenopausal tissue thinning in the urinary or genital tract, estrogens may help by building up the lining tissues.
- *Urge incontinence* — the second-commonest type — is due to uncontrollable bladder spasms, called *detrusor instability*. Most frequent in older adults, urge incontinence may produce a sudden need to pass urine before a toilet can be reached. Accidents occur while hurrying to the bathroom or on rising from a chair. The condition can appear spontaneously or may stem from a urinary-tract infection or problems such as strokes and spinal-cord disorders. In *reflex urge incontinence* (common with some spinal-cord disorders), accidents happen without any warning — the unsuppressed voiding occurs without any sense of urgency.
- *Overflow incontinence* — which involves frequent, almost constant urinary leakage — occurs when a full bladder doesn't empty properly and becomes permanently overdistended. Although there may be no identifiable cause, this form is more common in men and may be related to prostate problems. It can also arise because of anatomical obstructions such as a tumor, diseases that impair the bladder's normal contractions, certain back problems (e.g., spinal stenosis), strokes and other neurological disorders, or from medications.
- *Functional incontinence* develops when someone becomes unable or unwilling to use the bathroom, perhaps because of an illness that restricts movement or some psychiatric condition.

N.B.: Different types of incontinence may occur together.

Kegel (pelvic-floor) exercises as the first remedy for stress and urge incontinence. Some will benefit, some will not. Exercises are now recommended not only for women with moderate stress incontinence, but also increasingly for men. Contracting the pelvic floor muscles also tightens the loop of muscle around the urethra (the one that holds back gas or bowel movements) and strengthens the muscles that support the bladder. To benefit from Kegel exercises, it is vital to first identify the right muscle; a physician or nurse can demonstrate how to squeeze the muscle around a gloved finger inserted into the vagina (or rectum in men). Once people figure out which muscles to exercise, the usual regime is to squeeze the muscles for five seconds, release for five seconds, and repeat this cycle for five minutes at least three to four times a day. Doing the exercises at specific times or accompanying certain activities can help the patient to remember them. Kegel exercises must be done *regularly and consistently.* Properly done, they can be highly successful in strengthening the bladder outlet, although noticeable improvement takes weeks to months. (Kegel exercises should not be done while sitting on the toilet trying to void, as this only promotes incomplete emptying.)

- Bladder or behavior training, using breathing and relaxation to suppress the urge to urinate, is another effective therapy for those with urge or stress incontinence. People are taught to "hold on" for increasing times and learn to void at regular, scheduled intervals, the interval being gradually extended over the weeks and months of training to the normal three- to four-hour lapse between voidings. The retraining scheme teaches people to resist urgency, postpone voiding and urinate by the clock rather than because of the urge. The cure rate is around 10–15 percent, with marked improvement in 75 percent of cases.
- Combined bladder training, Kegel exercises and variations on these strategies help many to overcome incontinence. These remedies are sometimes also combined with hypnosis, biofeedback and other behavioral therapies.

But the training requires a high level of commitment, and is generally best for younger or middle-aged groups.
- Medications include muscle calmants for urge incontinence and estrogens for the stress type — the latter build up the uro-genital tract's lining tissues. Some drugs work by dampening bladder contractions or increasing bladder capacity. Self-medicating with over-the-counter products is strongly discouraged.
- For detrusor instability or urge incontinence the best medication is oxybutynin chloride (Ditropan) — an antispasmodic, helpful even for the very old, that increases bladder storage and dampens bladder spasms, delaying the urge to void. (One side effect is a dry, bad-tasting mouth.) Flavoxate (Urispas) and dicyclomine (Bentylol) are similar drugs.
- Calcium channel blockers, which are widely used heart drugs, the tricyclic antidepressant imipramine or the drug desmopressin can be useful for drying out a leaky bladder, but may cause undesirable urinary retention, and are therefore not yet widely used.
- For nocturnal enuresis (nighttime bedwetting) a small dose of desmopressin may resolve the problem.
- Bladder surgery can be 90 percent successful in women with severe stress incontinence. The "vaginal sling" operation creates a "hammock" under the urethra to give support; several other operations can also be used. More complicated surgical procedures include implantation of an artificial sphincter — a cuff that can be inflated to squeeze the urethra, impeding urine flow.
- Contigen injection, using a type of collagen injected into the urethral lining, is a promising new treatment for stress incontinence. Types of Teflon have also been tried. The advantage of contigen injections is that they can be done as a rapid office procedure under local rather than general anesthetic. Preliminary results are encouraging: studies show a success rate of 60 percent in men and 96 percent in women. The procedure is already offered in certain specialist centers across Canada.

TIPS FOR MANAGING INCONTINENCE

- Take steps to avoid increasing intra-abdominal pressure (e.g., weight reduction, avoiding coughing if possible).
- Don't consume foods that increase urination or irritate the bladder (e.g., parsley, coffee, tea, alcohol), and avoid smoking.
- If constipation is troublesome, increase fiber and fluid intake.
- If urinating too frequently, try bladder training — consciously extending the interval between voidings by 15–30 minutes, aiming for three- to four-hour gaps.
- Quench the urgent need to void by remaining still, relaxing and then moving slowly to the toilet.
- When urinating, empty the bladder completely, and after it seems totally empty, always give an extra push to get out the last drops of urine — "double voiding."
- Drink plenty of fluids during the day but nothing for two to three hours before going to bed.
- Use absorbent pads, inserts, belts or adult diapers as a last resort. They are not generally encouraged because people who use them tend not to get correct treatment. However, those who must use these garments can find a wider variety at a health-supply house than in a pharmacy. Search the Yellow Pages under "Hospital Equipment and Supplies." (Delivery is often available.)

Incontinent patients must be their own advocates

Often, physicians don't know what to do about their incontinent patients. If your doctor doesn't understand or is unsympathetic to the problem, demand referral to a urologist, gynecologist or incontinence expert. There's no reason to live with untreated incontinence.

For further information write to the Simon Foundation, P.O. Box 264, Station E, Toronto, Ontario M6H 4E2.

PARKINSON'S DISEASE

Parkinson's disease is a neurological disorder, clinically defined as a "movement disorder," usually of unknown origin, while "parkinsonism" refers to similar symptoms that mimic those of Parkinson's disease, resulting from other brain disorders or injuries. Parkinson's disease occurs mostly in middle and old age, and can be ameliorated (but not cured) by various drugs used alone or in combination. Named for the British physician Dr. James Parkinson, who first described it in his 1817 essay "The Shaking Palsy," the disease affects about 1 percent of Canadians over age 60 and 2 percent over age 70. It occurs slightly more often in men than in women, and in whites more often than in blacks. Although about three-quarters of those afflicted develop the disease between ages 50 and 65, it occasionally strikes younger people. There may be a mild genetic predisposition to Parkinson's disease, and those exposed to specific environmental toxins and some drugs may develop signs of parkinsonism.

After a global pandemic of *encephalitis lethargica*, or sleeping sickness, following World War I, many people developed parkinsonism up to 30 years later — attributed by some experts to the high fever, by others to contaminants in the rubbing alcohol used to cool feverish brows. Current research is uncovering the mechanism that causes parkinsonism and may ultimately lead to ways to prevent it.

What happens in Parkinson's disease?

Parkinson's disease is a central nervous system disorder involving a lack of the neurotransmitter dopamine, caused by the accelerated death of a group of dopamine-producing brain cells deep within a cerebral region known as the *substantia nigra*. The brain needs dopamine to send correct signals to the muscles. Symptoms of Parkinson's disease appear when 60–80 percent of these dopamine-producing cells are gone, no matter how they are destroyed. As people age, some dopamine-producing cells die off naturally, but it's not clear whether or not normal aging processes contribute to Parkinson's disease or parkinsonism. There's some evidence that age-related cell loss in the *substantia nigra* differs from the changes found in parkinsonism. In any case, the shortage of dopamine leads to neurotransmission failure in pathways that normally regulate muscular skills such as standing, sitting and walking, gradually producing movement disorders including an involuntary tremor and a stooped shuffle.

Although scientists now know which areas of parkinsonian brains die off and which neurotransmitter is lacking, they do not yet know what leads to the dopamine depletion. While many cases of Parkinson's have no known cause, studies reveal that certain environmental agents can destroy dopamine-producing brain cells. Together, the normal neuronal losses of aging plus possible environmental brain damage will cause parkinsonism when 60–80 percent of the brain's dopamine-producing cells have gone.

Clues to the mechanism of Parkinson's disease came from the observation that the substance known as *methylphenyltetrahydropyridine* (MPTP) causes parkinsonian effects. The link between MPTP and parkinsonism surfaced when a young drug-user who was trying illegally to make a kitchen-brewed version of the narcotic meperidine (a morphine substitute known as Demerol) accidentally produced and took MPTP. Within days he developed a "frozen" parkinsonian pose. (He was subsequently "unfrozen" by the drug L-dopa, commonly used to treat Parkinson's.)

Scientists at the U.S. National Institutes of Health showed that MPTP, a chemical similar to some herbicides (such as paraquat), can kill dopamine-producing brain cells in the *substantia nigra*. Since then, experiments with monkeys have demonstrated that MPTP induces permanent parkinsonism similar to that in humans, a discovery that gave scientists an animal model in which to investigate Parkinson's disease.

Exposure to other toxins may also produce parkinsonian disabilities. Parkinsonism has appeared among some inhabitants of Guam who, in times of famine, make flour from sago palm seeds, which contain a toxin (cycasin) that produces extensive nerve degeneration decades later. (But the role of the cycad plant is still somewhat controversial.)

Neuroleptics (antipsychotic drugs) such as haloperidol and phenothiazines and a few anti-nauseants can also produce parkinsonism, by temporarily blocking the action of dopamine at receptor sites in the brain.

Scientists think that environmental toxins, such as MPTP, that easily enter the brain may damage glial (binding) and other cells by blocking the action of their mitochondria (energy-producing particles), thereby damaging brain cells and causing them to die. In addition, there may be some link to excess iron, as the nerve cells that die seem to have accumulated iron.

Treatment benefits many with Parkinson's disease

The big breakthrough in managing parkinsonism came when a Canadian researcher developed the drug *levodopa* (L-dopa) in 1967 to help restore the brain's flagging dopamine production. Although this and other antiparkinsonian medications can partly replenish or compensate for the lost dopamine, most drugs are disappointing because they work only for a while, and can't reverse or arrest the disease. After about five to 10 years, problems arise with L-dopa therapy.

Medications to alleviate parkinsonism

- Anticholinergic drugs (e.g., Artane, Cogentin and Kemadrin) inhibit the activity of acetylcholine, a neurotransmitter relatively plentiful in the brain. These drugs may reduce some parkinsonian symptoms, particularly tremors and drooling in the early stages.
- Antiviral agents (e.g., amantadine or Symmetrel) may help to increase dopamine release in the brain.
- Antidepressants can relieve depression.
- Levodopa (L-dopa), now the mainstay of treatment, is taken by mouth several times a day. Once inside the brain, L-dopa is

SOME POSSIBLE CAUSES OF PARKINSON'S DISEASE

- *previous encephalitis* infection;
- *damage by toxins* or environmental poisons: e.g., manganese dust, carbon monoxide; MPTP (a "designer" street drug that resembles Demerol);
- *certain medications*; such as neuroleptics or antipsychotics, that are dopamine-

depleters (e.g., reserpine, haloperidol), phenothiazines such as fluphenazine, chlorpromazine (Largactil), trifluoperazine (Stelazine) and some antiemetic drugs (such as benzamides — Maxeran or metoclopramide);
- *trauma/injury to head*;
- *other neurodegenerative disease*: e.g.,

Wilson's disease; Huntington's chorea (juvenile representations); Creutzfeldt-Jakob disease; Steele-Richardson-Olszewski disease (progressive supranuclear palsy), which mimics Parkinson's but involves degeneration of different brain regions and rarely includes tremor.

THE HALLMARKS OF PARKINSON'S DISEASE

Parkinson's, or the "shaking palsy," produces progressive rigidity, tremor and slowed movement. As Dr. Parkinson himself put it, "the disorder may first show itself by an involuntary tremulous motion, with lessened muscular power, in parts not in action and even when unsupported, with a propensity to bend the trunk forward, and to pass from a walking to a running pace." Parkinson's typically starts with some muscle stiffness, an altered gait and limb shaking in repose. The very first signs may seem insignificant — slightly clumsy fingers, a little trouble placing one foot before the other, a bit of a shuffle, the hint of a stoop, an almost imperceptible hand-trembling. A few sufferers deteriorate quickly, but many can carry on their usual lives with mild symptoms for years. Some never become significantly disabled.

The various parkinsonian symptoms appear at different rates, in any order, with varying intensity. They include vague symptoms that often go undiagnosed for months or years and may be shrugged off as mere aging, namely:
• a slow, heavy feeling;
• unusually easy tiring;
• a hand that trembles ever so slightly.

Later signs include:
• stiffness of the limbs;
• involuntary trembling;
• walking with a shuffling, stooped gait;
• reduced facial animation;
• soft, monotone voice;
• the parkinsonian tremor — not necessarily the first but often the clearest sign of Parkinson's, and one of its more annoying signs. At first an intermittent "tapping" of the hand (when hands are resting or supported on the lap), the shaking usually subsides when hands are moved or during sleep, but increases with stress. Later — often years later — the tremor may spread to legs and lips;
• bradykinesia — acute difficulty in movements such as rising from the table, reaching for objects or getting out of bed;
• akinesia — loss of automatic initiation of movement; loss of spontaneous movement, which diminishes ability to carry out movements such as arm-swinging while walking; reduced emotional expressiveness (it may create a somewhat stony stare with infrequent blinking);
• a shuffling gait — "festination" — the inability to walk slowly and a tendency to take increasingly tiny, fast steps;
• rigidity (often disabling), muscle stiffness which in advanced stages "freezes" patients in place;
• depression, which may need treatment as urgently as the physical problems;
• intellectual impairment, which can include reduced problem-solving ability, visuospatial abnormalities and slow thought;
• parkinsonian dementia in later stages;
• diminutive handwriting (micrographia);
• increased body secretions (saliva, perspiration and skin oil); muscle cramps; leg swelling;
• susceptibility to bladder and chest infections (partly due to immobility).

converted to dopamine, replenishing neurotransmitter supplies and giving temporary relief of symptoms. About 80–90 percent of Parkinsonians respond well to L-dopa therapy, but a small percentage cannot tolerate the side effects, such as hypotension (low blood pressure), cardiac irregularity, insomnia, nausea, weakness, sweating, confusion, hallucinations and emotional changes. Some experts believe L-dopa should be delayed as long as possible; others advise giving it as soon as the diagnosis is made.
• Decarboxylase inhibitors, such as carbidopa and benserazide, prevent L-dopa breakdown in peripheral tissues, and are usually added to L-dopa so it won't disintegrate before reaching the brain. (L-dopa with carbidopa is Sinemet; with benserazide it's Prolopa).
• Dopamine agonists potentiate or imitate L-dopa effects, and may accompany L-dopa therapy. They can complement its effectiveness by direct stimulation of the brain receptors where dopamine acts. Dopamine agonists (stimulants) alone may alleviate some parkinsonian rigidity and tremor, permitting lower L-dopa dosage with fewer side effects. But they too can have unpleasant side effects (primarily nausea, hypotension and psychotic effects). In general, a combination of an agonist plus L-dopa achieves good control. (Parlodel or bromocriptine and pergolide are the only dopamine agonists available in Canada.)
• Selegiline, or Eldepryl (also known as deprenyl) — a drug similar to MAOI antidepressants — usually given early in the disease, often delays the onset of disabling parkinsonian symptoms by 13 to 24 months and puts off the need for L-dopa. The recently completed DATATOP (Deprenyl and Tocopherol Antioxidant Therapy of Parkinsonism) study — combining research at 28 medical centers, including the University of Toronto — showed a marked slowing of cell death and a delay in disabling symptoms among those with early Parkinson's

disease. The tocopherol (vitamin E) had no beneficial effect. How deprenyl retards the progress of the disease isn't clear, but one University of Toronto researcher believes deprenyl "rescues" damaged brain cells rather than protecting the cells from harm.

- In animals, transplantation of adrenal medulla cells (which produce dopamine) from the adrenal gland into the brain can reverse some parkinsonian symptoms. Transplanted adrenal tissue may replace damaged neurons, or in some way partly restore dopamine secretion. The results of adrenal medullary grafts in humans have so far been disappointing.
- Experimental implantation of fetal embryonic tissues (which manufacture dopamine) into the brain — tried in Sweden and other centers — restored some dopamine-producing capacity in animal experiments. Preliminary studies in humans show promising results.
- Insertion of neurotrophic nerve growth factors (NGF) may someday help to promote the recovery of dopamine-producing brain cells. Experiments are underway with genetically engineered NGF in animals.
- Physiotherapy and exercise (especially swimming and walking) can help maintain fitness and muscle tone in parkinsonian patients, helping them to stay mobile.

Some complications of long-term drug treatment

Parkinsonians can continue on a levodopa drug regime for five or more years, without bad effects, but unfortunately, after extended therapy, involuntary movements and rigidity become increasingly troublesome. Drug side effects may become worse than the symptoms they're meant to suppress.

- *Dyskinesia*, which involves bizarre, involuntary, jerky movements of head, tongue and extremities, is a particularly troublesome side effect of L-dopa. The abnormal movements can gradually become incapacitating unless the dosage is reduced.
- "Freezing" episodes, especially when starting to walk, turn or change direction, are frequent as the drug wears off.

- *End-of-dose deterioration* means that, as each dose of medication wears off, symptoms may return, with varying "good" and "bad" times through the day. More frequent L-dopa doses, sometimes together with bromocriptine, may help.
- *The "on-off" phenomenon* refers to sudden spells of immobility, apparently unrelated to drug doses, which may occur several times a day and last from minutes to hours. Drugs do not help this type of parkinsonian immobility, but lowering L-dopa dosage (and perhaps adding bromocriptine) may be useful.
- *Psychiatric side effects* may occur, especially in elderly patients or those with underlying cognitive decline. Often the dose of medication has to be lowered, with the result that parkinsonian symptoms increase.

For further information, consult your family physician, a neurologist or the neurology unit at your local hospital, or the local chapter of the Parkinson Foundation of Canada.

OSTEOPOROSIS

Osteoporosis is a common and disabling ailment in which both the amount and the quality of bone tissue diminishes, leading to a weakened skeleton that easily fractures. It afflicts men and women of all ages but is most prevalent in postmenopausal women, especially those who are thin, small and Caucasian. Approximately one in four North American women past the menopause suffers fractures of bones made fragile by osteoporosis, breaks of the spine, wrist and hip being most typical. Starting in mid-adulthood (at age 35 or so), there is some bone loss in both sexes, but women lose bone faster than men of the same age for about five to eight years after the onset of menopause. Between ages 70 and 75, male and female bone loss evens out. Since osteoporotic bone loss can't be restored, prevention is by far the best bet — by ensuring adequate calcium and vitamin D intake, doing enough weight-bearing exercise and not smoking.

What is osteoporosis?

Basically, osteoporosis stems from an imbalance in the body's bone-building mechanism,

BONE STRUCTURE

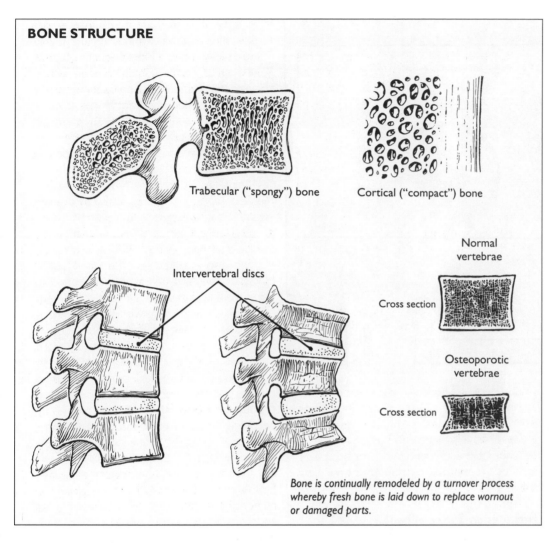

Trabecular ("spongy") bone

Cortical ("compact") bone

Intervertebral discs

Normal vertebrae

Cross section

Osteoporotic vertebrae

Cross section

Bone is continually remodeled by a turnover process whereby fresh bone is laid down to replace wornout or damaged parts.

whereby bone loss exceeds the amount of bone re-formed. In some cases there is also an initial bone deficit (perhaps because of a long-term lack of calcium in the diet).

There are two main types of osteoporosis:
- *primary osteoporosis* — of which type I, seen mainly in postmenopausal women aged 55–65, affects the trabecular (spongy) part of bone, and type II (previously called "senile osteoporosis"), which is age-related and affects both sexes over age 75 equally, and involves cortical (compact) bone;
- *secondary osteoporosis* — affecting young and middle-aged persons — which is often of unknown cause but is sometimes due to an inflammatory condition, anorexia nervosa (extreme dieting and malnourishment) or

excessive exercise in women (which disturbs menstrual function, halts periods and diminishes estrogen output).

Bone consists primarily of minerals (largely calcium phosphate), together with collagen, proteins and other components. It undergoes a continual, dynamic turnover with a process that repairs minor damage and brittle areas, replacing them with new bone. The process of "resorption" chews up the damaged parts of bone, allowing it to be "remodeled" by the laying down of fresh tissue. The remodeling cycle takes about 100 days and is influenced by hormone output (for example, levels of insulin, estrogen and parathyroid hormones) and by calcium and vitamin D intake. After a certain age, around 30–35 years, there is normally a

HIP FRACTURES A COMMON PROBLEM IN THE ELDERLY

Hip fractures are now often repaired with the help of metal screws which allow an earlier return of mobility.

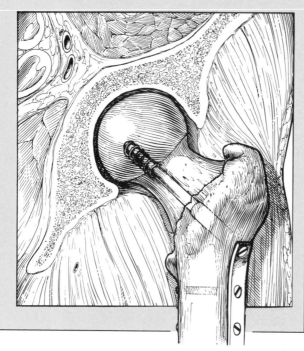

fifties and sixties, they are only nuisance fractures, as most heal well without surgery. But hip fractures — which are more frequent after age 75, in men as well as women — often require surgery. And although the operation is usually successful, the elderly do not always tolerate major surgery well, and may require lengthy convalescence. Many never regain their former agility, finding their daily activities seriously handicapped.

Spinal "crush" fractures — where the vertebrae collapse or become greatly compressed — are a particularly painful result of osteoporosis. A single vertebral fracture that's just a hairline crack hardly visible by X-ray may not be noticed and may cause little or no pain. However, several vertebral crush fractures can be extremely disabling. If every movement hurts, as it may in those with severely osteoporotic backs, daily activities can be burdensome. Successive vertebral fractures — more a crumbling of bone than a clear break — can be very painful and lead to years of deformed posture and restricted activity, although some produce no pain at all, the person only becoming aware of them through lost height and a bent back. If several back vertebrae are injured by crush fractures, the spinal compression noticeably diminishes height — sometimes by 10 to 20 cm (4 to 8 in) — giving the humped look. With the reduced height, the abdominal cavity becomes compressed, making those afflicted feel bloated after eating even small meals.

Estrogen drop at menopause is a key cause

In women, bone loss is greatly accelerated at and for a few years after the menopause. Whereas in premenstrual women the annual bone loss averages 0.25 to 1 percent, it rises to 2 to 3 percent during the first 3 to 7 years after menopause begins. The accelerated bone loss stems from estrogen deficiency, as the ovaries stop producing this hormone and the gap between bone resorption and bone remodeling increases. Changes in the output of parathyroid hormone and in vitamin D metabolism may also aggravate the bone loss.

Female athletes, especially distance

gradual decline in bone density — attributed to an imbalance in the remodeling process whereby bone resorption outpaces its buildup. However, bone strength and fracture resistance depend not only on bone mass, but also on its architecture and the distribution of minerals within it.

Fractures are the chief health problem in osteoporosis

Health problems from osteoporosis arise not so much from the bone loss, which in itself poses no real difficulties, but from multiple fractures. All bones will snap under enough force, but with bones made brittle by osteoporosis, fractures can occur with hardly any impact at all. In severe cases, breaks can occur from the mere wear and tear of daily life — even while resting in bed. In advanced stages, osteoporotic bones become so fragile that a mere hug, a stumble or the slightest pressure can cause a fracture. But until bones break, many remain unaware that they have the disease.

The main sites for osteoporotic fractures are the hip, wrist, arm and spinal vertebrae, less often the ribs. While broken wrists are common for postmenopausal women in their runners, and young women with anorexia nervosa (self-inflicted starvation) may experience early-onset osteoporosis because of disturbed menstrual cycles. The drop in estrogens sometimes causes a loss of bone mass even greater than that usually seen in postmenopausal women.

Who's at greatest risk of osteoporosis?

Most at risk for osteoporosis are thin, small, Caucasian people, those with relatives who have had multiple senile fractures, people on certain medications or with diseases known to exacerbate bone loss, and some under-exercised, inadequately fed individuals.

The risk of osteoporosis is increased by certain lifestyle habits, such as smoking, excessive alcohol intake and lack of exercise, and some disorders, such as diabetes mellitus, hyperthyroidism (overproduction of thyroid

RISK FACTORS FOR OSTEOPOROSIS

- advancing age;
- being female;
- lack of regular weight-bearing exercise;
- Caucasian (white) race;
- being petite or thin;
- family history of osteoporosis;
- smoking cigarettes;
- heavy alcohol consumption;
- diet low in calcium (especially during adolescence and early adulthood) or lacking vitamin D;
- medical disorders such as diabetes, hyperthyroidism, anorexia nervosa;
- use of certain medications (e.g., aluminum-containing antacids, cortisone-type drugs).

hormone), parathyroid hormone disturbances, excess corticosteroid output (from the adrenal gland), anorexia nervosa and some sex-hormone deficiencies. Medications such as cortisone derivatives (e.g., prednisone), tranquilizers, heparin (a blood thinner), some anti-cancer medications and antacids (which affect calcium absorption), as well as radiation, can increase risks.

OSTEOPOROTIC SPINAL "CRUSH" FRACTURES SHORTEN BACKS

Successive crush fractures of the vertebrae may deform the back and cause loss of height and a severely bent posture.

Crush fractures

Severely bent osteoporotic spine

M. B. MACKAY 82 ©

Lack of weight-bearing exercise is a major cause

Skeletal strength and health depend on the mechanical stresses and daily forces exerted on the bones by physical activity. Regular weight-bearing exercise such as walking, jogging or dancing (but not swimming) can help to offset osteoporosis. The few studies done to date on the relationship between exercise and osteoporosis show that people who stay active, such as athletes and dancers, have denser bones than sedentary types. One study showed that women enrolled in a regular exercise program lost less bone than a similar group of nonexercisers.

The inevitable reduction in activity as we age contributes to osteoporotic bone loss. Any further immobility, through fear of injury or actual confinement to bed, compounds the problem. It is well known that anyone immobilized for an extended period — as with a limb cast, paralysis or a prolonged illness — quickly loses bone mass, as much as 30–40 percent disappearing after six months of immobility. The lost bone may or may not come back. Curiously, astronauts floating weightlessly in space lost bone despite vigorous exercise routines. Metabolic studies on one Skylab crew revealed a bone diminution analogous to that seen with prolonged confinement in bed.

One cautionary note: osteoporotics who have already had fractures, or have weakened backs, should take great care about the type of exercise they do so they don't cause further injury, but they should still do recommended exercises.

Nutrition also plays a key role

People of all ages, including children and adolescents, need to eat enough calcium as an investment to prevent or minimize later bone loss. A lack of dietary calcium contributes to osteoporosis even if it occurs at an early age. Most Canadians consume enough calcium for daily needs but not necessarily enough to prevent bone loss later in life.

The recommended daily dietary intake of calcium is 800 mg, but some researchers suggest a need for yet more — about a gram a day premenopausally (the amount in a liter or quart of 2 percent milk). After the menopause, as much as a gram and a half of calcium a day may be necessary to preserve bone strength in women. Yet studies show that the middle-aged and elderly, as well as many adolescents (especially girls watching their weight), fall short of the recommended intake. Some of the elderly consume no more than 400 mg calcium a day.

Both vitamins D and C are also essential to a healthy skeleton, but megadoses should be avoided — particularly of vitamin D, which can be toxic in excess. The skin can synthesize vitamin D, but only if it receives adequate sunlight; in a country like Canada, which has limited sunlight for many months of the year, people may be short of vitamin D, especially if their diet is low in the vitamin-D-supplemented foods, such as milk products. In age-related osteoporosis type II, there are also changes in vitamin D metabolism, so the elderly should be extra sure to get enough vitamin D. Up to an extra 800 units a day of vitamin D may be advised if sun exposure is low and dietary sources are insufficient. Foods rich in vitamin D include fortified milk, eggs, canned sardines (in oil), canned salmon and eels. (See chapter 4 for recommended vitamin and mineral intakes.)

The obese are somewhat protected against osteoporosis, possibly because adrenal hormones convert to estrogen in fat tissues.

Diagnosing osteoporosis

Early warning signs may include a stab of pain in the back while doing routine chores, coughing, sneezing, laughing or even standing still! But all too often the disease creeps up with few premonitory signs, and is discovered only after multiple fractures have occurred.

The first step in diagnosing it is a thorough medical investigation to rule out causes such as the diseases and drugs known to increase bone loss. Examination may include blood and urine tests for hormone function, assessment of calcium and vitamin D intake and perhaps X-rays. But diagnosing osteoporosis before fractures occur is difficult; X-rays indicate osteoporotic loss only after a 25–35 percent diminution in bone density, and bone mass alone does not predict the likelihood of fractures. Modern bone scans using special techniques can now more accurately measure bone mass at specific sites.

Managing osteoporosis

So far, there's no safe and effective way to add new, strong, fracture-resistant bone to an osteoporotic skeleton. Today's treatment relies mainly on preventing further bone loss by a few strategies, such as ensuring sufficient calcium and vitamin D intake, increasing weight-bearing exercise and using treatments such as estrogen replacement therapy (ERT) and agents that alter bone modeling — for example, biphosphonates, calcitonin and sodium fluoride.

The present advice for those prone to osteoporosis is to stop smoking, moderate alcoholic intake and consume enough dairy products and other high-calcium foods (such as sardines, canned salmon and broccoli), with calcium tablets if needed to meet the requirement. People also should get enough — but not excessive — vitamins D and C. Many physicians now prescribe estrogen-replacement therapy (with added progesterone) for all menopausal women, particularly those most at risk, unless there are reasons against it. But estrogen replacement isn't enough — even women who take estrogens ultimately start losing bone again after a while. Although today's therapy may halt or slow the bone-resorption process, no known method can reliably put back bone that's already been lost. Sodium fluoride treatment can stimulate bone formation but has not lived up to its early promise; not everyone responds to it, the rebuilt bone is weaker than normal (and may even fracture more easily) and there are side effects. New bone-building drugs are being investigated and may help future osteoporotics.

Current treatments for osteoporosis

• *Estrogen-replacement therapy* (ERT) with conjugated estrogens and another female hormone (progestin), started around or just after the menopause, can diminish bone mass depletion but only at and for a few years after menopause. It does no more than delay the bone loss for the time that ERT is continued; whenever the therapy stops, the inevitable skeletal thinning takes place. The downside of ERT is a return of menstrual bleeding due to stimulation of the uterus by the female hormones. However, periods are generally light.

Once a woman is 15 or so years past her menopause, the benefits of estrogen become less certain. Health professionals rarely advise taking estrogen supplements indefinitely, owing to possible adverse side effects with increasing years of use.

• *Sodium fluoride treatment*, first tried in 1961 for osteoporosis, can stimulate new bone growth in up to 80 percent of those who take it. But although fluoride can stimulate the regrowth of *trabecular* bone, found in the vertebrae and ends of the long bones, it has no demonstrable fracture-reducing effect in *cortical* bone — the compact long bones in the arms and legs.

Given at the correct, individualized dose, with supplemental calcium, fluoride can put back some spinal bone lost through osteoporosis at a rate of 3 to 6 percent per year. Within two years, fluoride-treated patients generally have significantly fewer crush fractures than those not treated. However, fluoride therapy is controversial, and only hesitantly accepted by the medical profession. The new bone is not as strong as hoped for; there's a narrow line between the therapeutic and toxic dose, and excess fluoride can pose a health threat. Fluoride toxicity, or *fluorosis*, is known in regions of India, China and South Africa where water is naturally high in fluoride, and occupational exposure is a recognized health problem in industries such as smelting, ceramics, battery-manufacture, brick production and metalworks; fluorine emissions can produce skeletal deformities. It was the observation that people exposed to high levels of fluoride developed dense bone that sparked the idea of using it to replace bone lost through osteoporosis.

The optimal length of fluoride treatment depends on the amount of bone already lost, but should not be less than two or longer than five years, as studies of longer use have not been made. Those likely to benefit most are people with spinal osteoporosis and many fractures, regardless of age. It is especially useful for those who don't respond to other therapies. Supplementation with calcium (about a gram a day) is essential during fluoride treatment, and enough vitamin D is also needed. Side effects include digestive upsets (such as nausea and vomiting) in about 10 to 40 percent of patients — mostly transient, mild and easily diminished by taking the fluoride with, or right after, meals. Joint and limb pain — like "growing pains" — in the ankles, feet and knees is also felt by 10 to 50 percent of those treated, due to active bone reformation. Once fluoride intake stops, some of the regrown bone may disappear. Fluoride treatment is not advised for people with kidney disorders, osteomalacia (a bone mineralization disorder), peptic ulcers or previous hip or wrist fractures.

• *Calcitonin*, a hormone made by the thyroid gland, can — in large doses — inhibit bone resorption, and may help preserve bone mass in postmenopausal osteoporotics, although its antifracture efficacy has not yet been demonstrated. It is given by injection twice weekly, a therapy that may be continued for a year or so. Bothersome side effects include nausea and flushing .

• *Synthetic parathyroid hormone (PTH)* is a calcium-regulating agent that can stabilize bone mineral for as long as it's taken; it is believed to stimulate bone remodeling.

• *Biphosphonates* such as etidronate, the latest weapon in the fight against osteoporosis, not only slow resorptive bone loss but also reduce fracture rates. They may be given in combination with other medications.

• *Combination or coherence therapy* attempts to rebuild bone at many sites by manipulating the remodeling process via a sequential drug regime known as ADFR, which first tries to **A**ctivate bone formation (perhaps with parathyroid hormone), then to retain the rebuilt bone by **D**epressing its resorption with biphosphonates, followed by a **F**ree period (no drugs except calcium supplements), followed by a **R**estart of the drug cycle. ADFR has yet to prove itself.

• *Strengthening exercises* are highly recommended for osteoporotics, and are suitable even for the elderly, who can participate in special classes. Many 70-year-olds and even 80-year-olds are surprised at their agility once

they get going under expert guidance. The aim of exercises is not only to stop bone loss but to improve posture, prevent spinal deformity and impart a sense of well-being. Even a short-term (9 to 12 months) regime of weight-bearing exercise may enhance bone density in older people, and relieve back pain. Recommended exercises include:
  • muscle strengthening, with weights on the limbs;
  • low-impact aerobics, e.g., walking, slow dancing.

• *Preventing falls* is another top priority in managing osteoporosis, as falls are a prime reason for hip fractures in the elderly, with a risk of permanent disability, or even death from complications following the injury.

As always, prevention is best

The main strategies in preventing osteoporosis are to maintain bone strength by consuming adequate calcium throughout life, doing regular weight-bearing exercise and avoiding smoking and alcohol abuse. At menopause, women can consider taking estrogen supplements to retard bone loss. The elderly should do all they can to avoid falls by checking for loose steps or tiles, installing good lighting, wearing nonslip footwear, making sure eyesight is corrected, limiting use of balance-disturbing drugs, removing scatter rugs and installing safety rails on the stairs and in the bathroom. (See earlier in this chapter and Chapter 2 for more on home safety.)

For more information, contact the Osteoporosis Society of Canada, 79 St. Clair Avenue West, Suite 502, Toronto, Ontario M4V 1N2, tel. (416) 922-1358.

ALZHEIMER'S DISEASE

Senile dementia, including that due to Alzheimer's disease, is already of great concern and is likely to be the greatest public health problem of coming decades.

Alzheimer's disease (AD) accounts for about 20 percent of severe elderly dementia and affects 5 percent of the over-65s. Its prevalence rises steeply with advancing years, and it affects 20–25 percent of those over age 80. The disease is marked by a decline in judgment, memory and thought processes, usually ending in death 5 to 10 years after its onset. It exacts a devastating toll on human emotions, family relationships and the healthcare system.

What exactly is Alzheimer's disease?

Alzheimer's disease (AD) is a progressive degenerative disease of the central nervous system which can be definitively diagnosed only after death, by an autopsy examination of the brain. Named after the German psychiatrist Alois Alzheimer, who first described the condition as a "disease entity" in 1907, it involves a gradual loss of motor ability and a general decline in intellect. Originally, Alzheimer's disease was defined as presenile dementia, or "intellectual decline starting before age 65," but today — despite some disagreement — most experts believe AD is the same disease at whatever age it strikes. Unlike other dementing conditions, such as vascular dementia or dementia due to strokes, AD has nothing directly to do with faulty arteries or poor circulation. It results from massive brain-cell death involving abnormal tangles, plaques and a buildup of protein within nerve cells.

Its slow, insidious onset allows those affected to adopt compensating strategies that may mask its early stages. Sometimes a sudden stress, such as a move, an illness or the loss of spouse, can precipitate signs of the illness, such as carelessness about one's appearance, forgetfulness of time, mental confusion and wanderings. Knowledge acquired from learning and memories of past experiences are gradually destroyed, until the AD sufferer has no real existence in the past or present.

There are stable periods or plateaus when AD's destructive path seems to slow down or improve. But despite these "good" times, which may last a few hours, days or weeks, intellectual deterioration inevitably sets in again.

Diagnosis of Alzheimer's disease

As confirmation of Alzheimer's disease is only possible after death (by examination of brain tissue), a diagnosis of AD is given after excluding other possible reasons for the symptoms, such as strokes, malnutrition, infection, depression, drug reactions, anxiety, blood-vessel

---

THE STAGES OF ALZHEIMER'S DISEASE

- **The first stage is a slow, subtle loss of short-term memory — an inability to remember what happened an hour or a week ago — irritability and an aversion to new situations.**
- **The second stage is increasing forgetfulness — perhaps an inability to remem-** ber grandchildren's names — neurological and spatial distortion, impaired speech and loss of coordination. Alterations in personality — from a previously trusting person to one who is constantly suspicious, easily upset, even hostile — are typical.
- **The third or terminal** stage is profound deterioration in motor and mental function, sometimes with seizures, limb twitches and loss of bladder and bowel control, necessitating around-the-clock nursing. There may be an almost total absence of response to people or activities.

---

disease, head injury, thyroid disturbances, brain tumors and drug intoxication.

Descriptions by friends and relatives in situations where they can talk freely without embarrassing the sufferer are key elements in diagnosing Alzheimer's disease — especially in its early stages, when sufferers tend to deny their memory loss and gloss over deficits with excuses about absentmindedness, fatigue or anxiety. The accounts given by a relative or friend often contradict those of the patient, revealing the inability to continue usual tasks such as shopping, going to work or getting clothes cleaned. To the casual observer, someone moderately affected by Alzheimer's disease may appear totally normal — well groomed, polite, pleasant and competent — whereas a more penetrating analysis reveals conspicuous errors of reasoning. The chief hints of oncoming AD are repeated lapses of memory and an inability to do usual tasks, lasting at least one year.

Recently, researchers have found a substance known as glutamine synthetase that's elevated in the spinal fluid of those identified with AD and may provide a marker for the disease. Others have found antibodies to the beta-amyloid protein found in Alzheimer's sufferers' plaques that may some day provide a diagnostic tool. Ultimately a genetic test may determine those at risk and possibly allow early intervention.

Strong evidence for a genetic link in AD

Amid conflicting data, studies show that one in 10 cases has some family or genetic connection,

---

CHARACTERISTIC SIGNS OF AD REVEALED AT AUTOPSY

- shrinkage of brain mass, due to loss of neurons (nerve cells) in regions crucial to learning, memory and thinking;
- death of brain cells at above-average rates in specific brain regions;
- twisted neurofibrillary tangles within the neurons of the brain's cerebral

cortex. While most aging brains have some tangles and plaques within brain cells, they occur in vastly greater amounts in AD brains;
- abnormal "senile plaques" (clusters);
- enlargement of the brain's ventricles or cavities;
- lack of the neuro-

transmitter acetylcholine, due to reduced amounts of choline acetyl transferase, the enzyme needed to make this neurotransmitter (essential for learning and memory);
- clumps of abnormal beta-amyloid protein in and around brain cells and within senile plaques.

---

suggesting a genetic predisposition. In fact, genes related to Alzheimer's disease have already been located on chromosomes 21, 14 and 19, and a dozen families have surfaced around the world with a dominant genetic mutation linked to the beta-amyloid protein buildup — a hallmark of the disease. Those carrying the dominant gene all develop AD in their forties or fifties, with abnormal deposition of beta-amyloid protein. (The abnormal production and accumulation of beta-amyloid proteins found in the plaques within Alzeimer brains is under intense investigation.) The genetic model gains support from the fact that nearly all people with Down syndrome, or trisomy-21 (where individuals have an extra chromosome 21 in their cells) develop Alzheimer's disease if they reach age 40 or over.

Precise risk factors remain elusive
Of some 40 possible causes and risk factors explored since Alzheimer's disease was first defined, only two are relatively uncontroversial: old age and family history. Risks of Alzheimer's disease definitely increase with age. After age 65, the risks double every five years, until by age 85, 20 percent of people suffer Alzheimer's dementia. But neuroscientists are mystified by the triggers that set it off.

The various suspected triggers of AD include:
- an unusual or slow-acting transmissible agent, perhaps a slow virus akin to those responsible for kuru (a disease transmitted in cannibals who eat human brains) and

Creutzfeldt-Jakob disease (a rare transmissible dementia) — but evidence for a viral cause remains scanty. AD is not currently considered to be transmissible.
- environmental agents leading to the degenerative brain changes — aluminum, in particular, is strongly under suspicion. Many studies find elevated amounts of aluminum in Alzheimer brains, at levels known to be lethal in animals. Researchers are investigating whether aluminum (a known neurotoxin or nerve poison), widespread in the earth's crust and in many foods, medicines and drinking water, could be a participating factor.

The aluminum-Alzheimer connection
Among the possible causes of Alzheimer's disease, aluminum has aroused considerable interest. When examined after death, brains of those with Alzheimer's disease often contain above-normal amounts of aluminum. Although aluminum isn't a cause of AD, in excess it's known to damage brain cells.

Reports from Britain, Norway, France, Canada and the United States of unusually large amounts of aluminum in Alzheimer brains led researchers to surmise that the neurotoxic effects of this metal may be related to the development of AD. University of Toronto researchers — leading proponents of the aluminum-Alzheimer theory — repeatedly detected high levels of aluminum in the tangled plaques of brain cells of people who had died of AD (at levels two to five times that in normal brains).

The third most abundant element in the earth's crust, aluminum is everywhere — in soil, air, water, plant and animal tissues. Aluminum salts are added to drinking water in many purification plants to clarify discolored water. Aluminum is also a common ingredient in baked and processed foods (e.g., from baking powder and table salt), in beer, in nonlacquered aluminum cans, in muffins (those containing aluminum maltolates) and in teas, medications (e.g., some antacids or buffered ASA) and cosmetics (e.g., antiperspirants). More than 50 percent of all cookware is aluminum.

Fortunately, evolution has to some extent protected humans from this potentially toxic

GUIDELINES FOR FAMILY AND FRIENDS OF PEOPLE WITH ALZHEIMER'S DISEASE

Symptom, behavior or personality change	Suggested coping strategy
• Memory loss and repetitious behavior; inability to remember things said minutes earlier; names of friends and objects forgotten; inability to find possessions; lost interest in personal hygiene.	Tell friends to expect less responsiveness; place items in visible accessible places; ignore repetitious actions or questions; supervise daily dressing and washing routines.
• Missed appointments and skipped meals.	Give constant reminders with calendars, schedules, clocks, notes, lists, diagrams and repeated instructions.
• Depression, frustration, anger and despondency.	Be understanding, give reassurance with messages of continued affection; discussion of illness may or may not help.
• Loss of judgment and sensory feedback about climate, time of day and behavior, with inappropriate dressing, wandering about inadequately clothed and spilling of food, etc.	Provide nighttime supervision; give patient assistance in dressing; try to be a cheery "cleaner-upper."
• Sudden mood swings — from sadness (with crying) to laughing euphoria (a passing phase).	Reassure, support and avoid disapproval or rejection.
• Spatial disorientation — inability to find own room, familiar places; attempts to board bus on wrong side; getting lost; risk of injury.	Avoid radical changes of surroundings, moving furniture; accompany on outings; beware of scatter rugs, sharp-edged furniture, loose objects.
• Pacing and aimless wandering, especially at night.	Get a hard-to-open door lock to restrict excursions; supply an ID bracelet.
• Sleep problems and insomnia, nighttime fears.	Encourage sufficient daily exercise (within individual limits) to facilitate sleep; use a night-light to reduce anxiety; arouse slowly if asleep.
• Increasing apprehension and anxiety in line with increasing inability to do simple tasks.	Provide greater reassurance with a touch, a hug, a smile and a calm attitude.
• Irritability and aggression — with temper outbursts.	Try to stay cool, avoid arguments or attempts at logic; if possible don't raise the voice but be soothing.
• Decreased social skills with diminished responses and avoidance of eye contact.	Maintain eye contact, talk facing the person; when possible, continue social and group activities as usual, helping others to realize that avoidance doesn't mean rejection; help with telephoning and letter writing.
• Slowed motion and coordination.	Employ only for sheltered tasks; allow daytime rests, flexible routines.
• Speech and language deterioriation with diminished comprehension.	Continue to communicate; repeat questions phrased for yes or no answers; don't talk down or condescend but speak clearly, expressing one idea at a time; lower voice pitch rather than talking loudly.
• Increased safety hazards due to disabilities.	Prevent driving, cooking, smoking, use of appliances and other risk situations; adjust hot water heater to a safe temperature, store medicines out of reach.
• Loss of bladder control.	Discreetly remind about toileting; help clean up; curtail evening liquids; use pads and protective bedding.
• Inability to move or feed self.	Need attending team to move from bed to chair and assist in feeding, bathing and other functions.
• Increasing isolation.	Try to keep up efforts to encourage visitors, remembering that seeming unresponsiveness may not mean total lack of interest.
• More physical dysfunction with seizures, loss of sphincter control, weight loss, increased susceptibility to infection.	Adopt medical treatment with doctor and nurse in team; discuss possibility of death openly, allowing for honest discussion. Make sure caregivers get adequate respite and time off so they don't get sick. Inform doctors of any noticeable changes

element via the "blood-brain" barrier — which prevents the influx of certain chemicals into the brain. Normally, only about half the aluminum consumed in food and drink gets into the bloodstream, and most cannot enter the brain. However, under some circumstances aluminum can get through the blood-brain barrier and reach toxic levels. Theory has it that excess aluminum may tip the scales and push preclinical or incipient AD into full disease.

Some studies in Europe and North America have linked high levels of aluminum in drinking water to an increase in AD cases, but the results await confirmation. One 1989 British study found that in those regions where aluminum concentrations in water were high (110 parts per billion) there was a 50 percent increase in Alzheimer's disease, compared to areas with levels below 10 parts per billion. Other studies in Norway, France and Sweden report similar findings but have been criticized for poor methodology. Moreover, certain factors — such as the water's fluoride and silicic-acid contents — may protect against the damaging effects of aluminum by binding the metal.

There's another puzzle in the aluminum story: people who habitually consume large amounts of aluminum, such as tea drinkers, or antacid users (who consume as much as 1,000 mg of aluminum a day), don't have a higher-than-average incidence of Alzheimer's disease. Antacid users, in fact, have been found to have somewhat below-usual rates of AD. Furthermore, people generally consume far more aluminum from food than from drinking water.

To sum up the evidence to date, the role of aluminum in Alzheimer's disease remains highly controversial and so far there is a suggestion but no proof of a link.

Treatment: no cure, but some helpful strategies

A central dilemma in coping with Alzheimer's disease is that it creeps up in such a gradual fashion that it's hard for the afflicted person and family to acknowledge that anything is wrong. Support and understanding can be slow in coming. Sharing knowledge may help caregivers to cope with patients, who are often the last to recognize their illness. The frustration of trying

to help someone who often seems bent on defeating every effort may drive caregivers to the limits of self-control and beyond. Caregivers need respite, and physicians should recommend it. One University of Toronto expert speaks of "a crying need for other forms of support for those looking after people with dementia, many of whom demand around-the-clock, 24-hour supervision."

Treatment of Alzheimer's disease means managing the declining memory and gradually worsening behavioral symptoms with medications such as anticonvulsants, tranquilizers, antidepressants, mood stabilizers, sleep-aids, antianxiety drugs and psychiatric counseling (for both patient and caregivers).

Finding a drug that gives some, albeit transient, relief of symptoms is a tricky trial-and-error process. Of some two dozen drugs tested for AD, many of which aim to replace the brain's depleted acetylcholine (neurotransmitter) supplies, some show promise. For example, tetrahydroaminoacridine (Tacrine) has received much publicity, but the slight mental improvement achieved must be weighed against liver toxicity, and it is not yet approved for use. Deprenyl, also known as selegiline and already used in Parkinson's disease, shows some promise in halting (but not reversing) the mental decline in AD and perhaps an ability to "rescue" damaged nerve cells. Other drugs being tested include cerebral vasodilators, nerve-growth factors and dopamine-releasers. Lecithin (which helps the body produce acetylcholine) has been tested but, despite encouraging initial reports, the overall results are disappointing. Naloxone (which inhibits brain chemicals thought to be excessive in this disease) has also not proved useful.

At present, no available medication can halt or reverse the progressive intellectual impairment of Alzheimer's disease.

Coping with Alzheimer's disease is an agonizing challenge

For many patients and caregivers this fatal aging disease brings untold turmoil, guilt and almost insurmountable challenges. Aggressive behavior, night wandering, obstinacy, paranoia and an inability to understand what's happening make the disease especially difficult. Yet despite the great emotional toll, many families try to care for afflicted relatives at home. In handling someone who was once a source of support but is now a totally dependent, mentally impaired and, eventually, immobile person, caregivers must tread a fine line between assisting sufferers in doing what they can still do and recognizing what's impossible. Home visits by health professionals can greatly ease the burden. Several University of Toronto hospitals have instituted a home-care plan that takes psychiatrists, nurses, occupational therapists and other health professionals into the homes of Alzheimer patients. Of most help in the foreseeable future will be better support systems for AD sufferers and the heroic caregivers who manage them at home. "What's critically needed," notes one specialist, "is a comprehensive and coordinated system for delivering community, institutional and residential help to those in need."

For more information, contact the Alzheimer Society in your community or write to the Alzheimer Society of Canada, 491 Lawrence Avenue West, Suite 501, Toronto, Ontario M5M 1C7, tel. (416) 789-0503.

Some specific diseases and disorders

AIDS • Arthritis • Asthma • Back problems • Bowel problems • Carpal tunnel syndrome • Common cold • Cystic fibrosis • Diabetes • Epilepsy • Gallbladder problems • Headaches • Heart disease • Heart murmurs • Heartburn • Hemorrhoids • Hepatitis • Hernias • Hypertension • Influenza • Kidney stones • Knee problems • Liver cirrhosis • Lyme disease • Peptic ulcers • Strokes • Thyroid disorders • Urinary tract infections • Zoonoses: diseases from pets

16

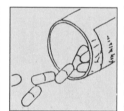

THIS CHAPTER DOES not attempt to catalogue all human diseases in an encyclopedic manner, but deals with conditions of special concern in North America today, and a few newly emergent disorders of particular interest. The topics are arranged in alphabetical order. Some of the subjects are also discussed, in other contexts, in other chapters.

AIDS

AIDS is an insidious fatal illness thought to be caused by the slow-acting, human immunodeficiency virus (HIV), which invades white blood cells — especially the immune system's *CD4-lymphocytes* or *T-helper cells* — and certain other body cells, including the brain. Like other viruses, HIV is basically a tiny package of genes. But as a retrovirus it has the rare capacity to insert its genes right into the molecules of a human cell's chromosomes (DNA). Inside a human cell, the retrovirus uses its own enzyme, reverse transcriptase, to copy and incorporate its genetic code into the host's cell. Thus HIV becomes an integral part of the person's own body, and the viral DNA may sit hidden like a genetic parasite for years. Biologists have studied the HIV virus in detail and mapped its genes, yet we still do not understand exactly how it causes disease, which hampers the design of drugs and vaccines.

According to Canada's Laboratory Centre for Disease Control, the dormant HIV virus seems to be "triggered" into replicating itself 3 to 18 years, or more, after first invading human cells. The latent (incubation) period averages 10–12 years. During this long period, HIV carriers with no sign of infection may unknowingly infect others. Once the virus is "switched on," its replication may speed along, producing new HIV viruses that destroy fresh lymphocytes. As viral multiplication progresses, it virtually sabotages the immune system, producing the condition known as AIDS. Thus the HIV virus does not kill people, it merely renders the immune system defenseless against "opportunistic" infections such as yeast, toxoplasmosis and cytomegalovirus infections, tuberculosis, cancers such as Kaposi's sarcoma and lymphoma and a devastating form of pneumonia (*Pneumocystis*

OF THE AIDS CASES IN CANADA (IN 1992):

- **78 percent are known homosexuals or bisexuals, but not injection-drug users;**
- **2 percent are heterosexual injection-drug users (both male and female);**
- **4 percent are both homosexuals or bisexuals *and* injec-**
- **tion-drug users;**
- **2 percent are recipients of blood transfusions;**
- **2 percent are recipients of blood products;**
- **4 percent are heterosexuals with sex partners in known risk groups;**
- **4 percent originate**
- **from countries where AIDS is widespread (mostly acquired by heterosexual contact);**
- **4 percent have no identified risk factors;**
- **one isolated case has resulted from occupational exposure to infected blood.**

SOME DEVELOPMENTS IN OUR KNOWLEDGE AND TREATMENT OF AIDS

- Confirmation that AIDS is not spread by casual contact.
- Proof that other STDs such as herpes, chancroid and syphilis facilitate HIV transmission (partly because open sores allow the viruses easier entry).
- Clarification that, while at the start of the AIDS epidemic the infection was thought to spread mainly via small scratches, cuts or sores, there is evidence that it can also pass through intact membranes lining the mouth, vagina and rectum. Thus any unprotected sex act with a possibly

infected partner is risky behavior.
- Evidence that AIDS is spreading to heterosexuals in North America. Women are the fastest-growing subgroup infected with HIV.
- HIV tests advised for anyone with other STDs.
- Recommendation (in the 1992 update of the Canadian Task Force on the Periodic Health Examination) that physicians obtain a full sexual history at medical checkups, with counseling and AIDS tests offered to anyone at risk, particularly those with other STDs.

- Wider availability of drugs that slow down the progress of AIDS, in particular azidothymidine (AZT), which blocks the action of HIV's enzyme (reverse transcriptase), halting viral replication. Early AZT treatment of HIV-positive people who don't yet have signs of AIDS can delay the onset of illness for a limited time. But AZT has side effects such as diarrhea, headaches, muscle-wasting, bone-marrow damage and anemia. (Using lower doses or starting treatment sooner reduces bone-

marrow suppression.) As HIV frequently mutates after about six months to produce AZT-resistant strains, other drugs may be added, if immune-cell (CD4) counts are low.
- Drugs with mechanisms similar to AZT now licensed in Canada, including didanosine or dideoxyinosine (DDI) and dideocytidine (DDC), both useful for AZT-resistant patients and those intolerant to AZT.
- Various drug combinations being tried by researchers, because two or more together may delay

the development of resistant viral strains.
- Alternative drugs such as protease inhibitors, which prevent HIV from multiplying, are also being investigated.
- Aerosol pentamidine given to HIV carriers with low immune-cell (CD4) counts, as a prophylactic to reduce risks of the virulent pneumonia that endangers those with AIDS. The U.S. Centers for Disease Control (CDC) recommends either aerosol pentamidine or trimethoprim-sulfamethoxazole for preventing pneumonia in HIV-positive people.

carinii), the killer in half of all AIDS patients.

AIDS is not spread by sharing household items, or by mosquitoes or bedbugs. It is a less contagious disease than measles, chickenpox or herpes. While AIDS is predominantly sexually transmitted, it can also spread via contaminated blood, breastmilk and shared injection equipment. Small amounts of HIV have been isolated from urine, tears, saliva, cerebrospinal and amniotic fluid, but since the concentration of virus is highest in semen, the most common transmission routes are anal or vaginal intercourse. Female HIV carriers can infect male sex partners and vice versa. There are reported cases of heterosexually acquired AIDS from a single unprotected sex encounter. Worldwide, an estimated 75 percent of cases were acquired by heterosexual contact, often closely linked to other sexually transmitted diseases. Current evidence implicates only semen, blood and vaginal secretions in HIV transmission; although the HIV virus is found in saliva, there is no evidence that kissing has ever infected anyone with HIV. However, cuts

in the mouth or bleeding gums will expose sex partners to blood which may be infected. Pregnant mothers can pass the infection to their babies, and infant mortality from AIDS is rising. Breastfeeding is a rare transmission route, but North American health officials suggest that mothers who have tested HIV positive bottlefeed their babies.

Routine blood tests can detect antibodies to the HIV organism, but since those infected may show no signs of antibody production for many months, a negative test result at a first screening may be falsely reassuring. A second test some months later is advised for those who think they may be at risk. Another reliable HIV test detects an antigen (viral protein), but is not yet routinely used.

The global picture
The World Health Organization (WHO) estimates that already 5–6 million men and 3–4 million women around the world are HIV-infected. In some central African cities, one in three adults tests positive for HIV infection.

By the year 2000, WHO estimates global numbers will be 30–40 million men, women and children HIV-infected, with 12–18 million reported AIDS cases.

In North America, AIDS continues to affect mainly bisexual and homosexual men, but there is evidence of spread to heterosexual women. In Canada an estimated 35,000 people were HIV-infected and 6,560 AIDS cases had been reported by July 1992 to the Canadian Laboratory Centre for Disease Control, 4,112 (63 percent) already having died. (These estimates include adjustments for under-reporting and/or delayed reporting.)

A safe, effective vaccine against AIDS may be decades away, mainly because of the variability of the viral agent. Like the influenza virus, HIV mutates (changes structure) quickly, producing different strains. Not only does the virus infecting one person diverge to form different strains, but different individuals may carry different HIV strains. A vaccine effective against one strain may not protect against another.

Because the HIV virus can lie dormant for so long, to be certain a sex partner doesn't carry AIDS one must either insist on a test, or know that he or she has not been exposed for at least 12, perhaps 15 to 18 years! And who can be sure on this delicate subject? Therein lies the dilemma of our times — how to choose a "safe" sex partner in the age of AIDS.

For more information or help regarding AIDS call local AIDS committees or public-health departments; AIDS hotlines (e.g., 1-800-392-2437); local STD clinics; Laboratory Centre for Disease Control, Ottawa.

ARTHRITIS

Arthritis is an umbrella term encompassing 116 different disorders formerly called "rheumatic" complaints. One of the commonest chronic disorders, it afflicts one in seven Canadians, half in the prime of life (aged 30 to 50). Arthritic disorders may be inflammatory in nature — such as rheumatoid arthritis; metabolic — as with gout and pseudogout; or degenerative — like osteoarthritis. Some affect primarily the joints; others are associated with inflammation and damage to other body organs. For instance, *lupus erythematosus* may present with a facial rash but often spreads to other organs including the joints, kidneys and lungs; *scleroderma* not only produces skin thickening but also harms many parts of the body such as the blood vessels, kidneys and lungs.

Although the roots of many arthritic diseases remain unknown, scientists believe that inflammatory forms may be triggered by bacterial or viral infections along with a flaw in the body's immune system, setting the stage for an immune response that turns against and destroys the sufferer's own tissues. Heredity plays a part in some forms of arthritis. An example is *ankylosing spondylitis*, where many people carry a specific genetic marker. The genetics of other forms are less well understood, but hereditary mechanisms have been demonstrated in rheumatoid arthritis and others.

Symptoms and warning signs of the more severe forms of arthritis may include persistent, unexplained soreness; pain; redness; early morning stiffness; swelling and loss of movement in the fingers and toes, wrists, knees and hips; and lower back pain.

Among the myriad forms, five main types account for more than half of all arthritic diseases diagnosed in North America.
- *Osteoarthritis (OA)*, the commonest form, affects more than one million Canadians, particularly people over age 60. In this degenerative condition the joint cartilage wears away, leaving bone ends to rub painfully together, but giving little discomfort

SYMPTOMS OF HIV INFECTION, INCLUDING FULL-BLOWN AIDS:

- unexplained weight loss or wasting;
- unexplained profound fatigue;
- persistent fever or night sweats;
- unexplained diarrhea for more than one month;
- new persistent skin lesions consistent with Kaposi's sarcoma (skin cancer);
- chronic or subacute cough or shortness of breath;
- headache, mental changes, or neck stiffness;
- chronic oral or anal lesions;
- chest pain on swallowing;
- impaired vision (retinitis);
- persistent lym-phadenopathy (lymph nodes greater than one cm or 0.4 in in diameter) involving two or more extrainguinal (non-groin) sites;
- dementia;
- oral candidiasis.

Note: An additional symptom in infants is unexplained failure to thrive and develop.

until its more advanced stages. OA may be primary, developing spontaneously for no apparent reason, or secondary, where the joint damage or degeneration results from trauma, surgery or injury to the weight-bearing surfaces, or is caused by other forms of arthritis (such as rheumatoid arthritis). OA may follow bone fractures that damage the cartilaginous joint surfaces by releasing inflammatory substances, explaining why many ex-athletes suffer from it. Overall, OA occurs equally in both sexes, but under age 45 it is more prevalent in men.

In OA's earliest stages, the cartilage covering bone ends begins to break, producing irregularities and loss of "shock absorption." With time, larger sections of cartilage wear away, leaving the bone totally unprotected. In severe cases, fragments of bone and cartilage can float freely in the joint capsule, aggravating its covering membrane and producing inflammation. Cartilage has no nerve endings, so the osteoarthritic pain sensation arises from other parts of the joint — bone, muscle, ligament or tendon — due to distension or inflammation, typically after activity. Joint pain from OA is relieved by rest. As the disease progresses, the soreness becomes more frequent, continuing at night, often with a few minutes of morning stiffness. OA sufferers often try to stop using the afflicted joint because of the pain, but inaction can lead to wasted joint muscles, worsening the condition.

Treatment is with anti-inflammatory medications and/or painkillers. Acetaminophen or coated ASA — the usual arthritis remedies — are often effective. Rest is the next line of defense, followed by physiotherapy to regain muscle strength and full range of movement. In those severely disabled by OA, surgery may help, to clean out the joint sac or replace the joint with an artificial or real substitute.

- *Rheumatoid arthritis (RA),* better known but less common than osteoarthritis, strikes about one per 100 persons, more women than men. It typically starts in the fingers and toes on both sides of the body, progressing to other joints (including knuckles, wrists, elbows and knee joints). The disease usually strikes between ages 30 and 50, but can start

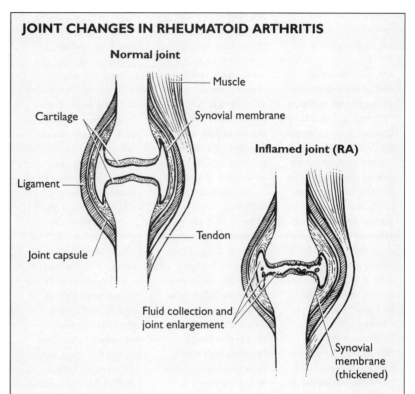

JOINT CHANGES IN RHEUMATOID ARTHRITIS

Normal joint

Muscle

Cartilage

Synovial membrane

Inflamed joint (RA)

Ligament

Tendon

Joint capsule

Fluid collection and joint enlargement

Synovial membrane (thickened)

Joints, which are hinges that enable the skeleton to bend and move, are subjected to a great deal of pressure, particularly weight-bearing joints like the knees and hips. They require lubrication and mechanisms to absorb the shock of movement or they would wear away. Cartilage, a tough elastic coating covering the ends of bones, performs both of these functions. The high water content of cartilage gives it a cushioning effect. When weight is put on a joint, the water is squeezed out and the cartilage flattens like a sponge being squeezed; when the weight is removed, the water moves back in and the cartilage expands. Every joint is encapsulated in a sac-like structure, which stops the water from escaping. Lining the sac is a membrane called the synovium, which supplies nourishment to the cartilage. Each type of arthritis affects the joints in different ways: the cartilage can be worn away; the cartilage and synovium can be inflamed; or gritty substances floating free in the joint sac can get in between the layers of cartilage.

at any time, even in young children aged 2–5. It may begin suddenly with a severe attack or come on gradually. Symptoms generally linger on, although more commonly there are extended times of remission without pain. The pain is caused by an inflamed and thickened *synovium,* or joint lining. Fluid also builds up in the joint cavity, causing swelling and more pain. Surrounding tissues, such as the ligaments or muscles, can also swell, making the whole joint and surrounding area painful

GENERAL MANAGEMENT OF ARTHRITIS

There's no cure for most forms of arthritis, so the goal of treatment is to reduce the inflammation and pain by lifestyle changes and exercise regimes tailored to the disease. Early diagnosis is crucial for good control; attention to the warning signs can help to prevent disability, frustration and disfigurement. Many types of arthritis are managed by the family physician in consultation with rheumatologists, orthopedists, and physiatrists — as needed.

Treatment includes ice (for acute inflammation), heat (for relief, once inflammation subsides), specific medications, physiotherapy and psychological and occupational counseling with attention to social life and family dynamics. A new product, Capsaicin (from hot peppers), may relieve the local pain and hotness of arthritic joints if applied directly to the skin.

Medications for arthritis, either local or systemic, are generally used in a "stepped" manner. ASA is the first line of defense and one of the most powerful anti-inflammatory agents known, but only if its concentration in the blood remains high enough (at a level prescribed by the healthcare provider). NSAIDs, which include over 20 modern medications, are used when ASA fails, followed by disease-retarding, second-line anti-arthritic agents. Nowadays, the second-line drugs (such as gold salts, hydroxychloroquine and other agents) are given earlier in the course of disease, as the anti-inflammatories don't prevent deformity and joint destruction. The failure of NSAIDs to achieve improvement in 2–4 months calls for the introduction of second-line drugs, often first trying hydroxychloroquine, followed by gold salts or methotrexate if needed. Use of second-line drugs must be medically monitored.

to touch and move. If pain becomes severe, the surrounding muscles contract in spasm and become stiff due to inactivity. Over time, the muscles weaken and the joint becomes increasingly difficult to move. Rheumatoid arthritis sufferers may be constantly fatigued by the pain and general systemic effects of the illness.

Treatment for rheumatoid arthritis is rest, therapeutic exercise and a range of medications, first anti-inflammatory drugs (e.g., ASA and other, nonsteroidal anti-inflammatories) and second, a range of disease-modifying antirheumatic agents which include hydroxychloroquine, methotrexate, low-dose corticosteroids, sulfasalazine (Azulfidine), penicillamine (Cuprimine), immuno-modulators such as Imuran and gold salts. These drugs, unlike ASA, offer no pain relief, but may delay the progression of arthritis. Self-help devices like long-handled combs and brushes help sufferers perform everyday tasks. Replacement of severely damaged joints, once the inflammation has subsided, is now an option.

- *Gout and pseudogout*, classified as "crystal-associated" arthritis, involve crystal deposits within the joints. The symptoms of both are acute joint inflammation, swelling, heat, redness and pain, but the causes differ.

Gout occurs from the accumulation of uric acid, a waste product from the breakdown of food and drink. The excess uric acid forms sodium urate crystals that collect in many tissues, including the joint linings, producing inflammation. A gout attack is extremely painful, generally lasting 7 to 10 days, sometimes up to three weeks. The first attack may start in the big toe, but the ankles, knees, elbows and fingers can all be affected. Over 80 percent of gout sufferers are men; women rarely suffer gout before the menopause. There is much evidence that primary gout is genetic, but it can also be precipitated by excessive alcohol consumption, obesity and conditions where large amounts of tissue are suddenly broken down. Renal (kidney) failure may also be linked to high uric-acid levels. Sufferers have a tendency to high blood pressure and elevated blood-lipid (fat) levels. Since the buildup of uric acid is due to metabolic causes, the popular image of the gout-ridden person as one who overindulges in food and drink may be somewhat exaggerated.

Treatment for a first attack of gout includes nonsteroidal anti-inflammatories (NSAIDs) *other than* ASA and then steroid injections to control inflammation. (ASA is not advisable as it affects the manner in which the kidneys handle uric acid, and may lead to kidney stones.) If attacks recur and uric-acid levels stay high, patients are usually put on a lifetime regime of allopurinol, a uric-acid-synthesis inhibitor. For those allergic to allopurinol, an alternative (but less effective) medication is sulfinpyrazone .

Pseudogout involves excess calcium pyrophosphate crystals in the joints. The attacks come on suddenly, with acute pain and inflammation lasting from days to weeks — often indistinguishable from gout. The acute form most commonly affects the knee, while the chronic form can attack several joints — such as wrists and knees — at the same time. Those who develop pseudogout are generally 65 or over, and equal numbers of men and women are affected. There is a possible link between pseudogout crystals and diseases such as hyperparathyroidism and diabetes. People with pseudogout often have "gouty associates" — high blood pressure, kidney stones, arteriosclerosis (artery hardening) and hyperlipidemia (high blood fats).

Pseudogout is best treated with rest, special exercises and NSAIDs. In severe cases, the joint may be aspirated and steroids (cortisone) injected for rapid relief.

• *Ankylosing spondylitis,* which affects one in 1,000 persons, attacks the joints of the spine, causing inflammation and eventual stiffening as bony overgrowths fuse the vertebrae. Vertebral ligaments may also be overgrown by bone, giving a rigid spine. Until recently sci-entists believed the disorder affected only men; however, it is now clear that both sexes can suffer from it, although it is seemingly less severe in women. The first symptoms are a dull ache in the buttocks, possibly extending down to the knees, and/or mid-spine pain. It strikes mainly young people aged 18–30. The pain can be noticed when turning over in bed, and may awaken sufferers, who may dismiss it as just "stiffness." Later symptoms include morning stiffness in the mid and lower back, which is often relieved by hot showers and activity. But eventually the pain can move all the way up the spine, affecting the chest and neck, as well as larger joints such as hips and shoulders.

Treatment for ankylosing spondylitis is mainly exercise and postural training. NSAIDs are given to reduce inflammation and help improve exercise performance. Surgery is recommended only when hips or knees are badly damaged.

ARTHRITIS REMEDIES INCLUDE:

• *acetaminophen* (e.g., Tylenol);
• *anti-inflammatory medications,* which include ASA (e.g., Aspirin) and other nonsteroidal anti-inflammatories (NSAIDs). Recent studies indicate that, although the medication may stop further joint degeneration, half of all rheumatoid arthritis sufferers don't take their medications as prescribed. Yet long-term pain relief depends on keeping medications at the correct concentration;
• *diet.* Despite some people's faith in its healing properties, diet doesn't usually alleviate or cure arthritis, but well-balanced nutrition will help keep the body at its strongest. Research shows no link between dietary changes and the progress of arthritis, except for gout, where eliminating foods such as liver, kidneys and other organ meats (which produce uric acid) may help to forestall attacks;
• *gold salts* (an old standby for arthritis). Gold salts given by injection or as tablets are potent drugs used to combat rheumatoid arthritis; how and why they work is unclear. They somehow reduce the progress of the disease, but efficacy varies from person to person and it can take months before benefits are noticed. Side effects of gold salts include a skin rash, nausea and (rarely) anemia;
• *chloroquine and hydroxychloroquine* (antimalarial drugs), which may alleviate rheumatoid arthritis but must be taken for at least two months before any improvement appears. Serious side effects are rare, but may include skin and bone-marrow problems;
• *solozopyrine,* which is a recent addition to the therapeutic arsenal; like chloroquine, it is best used early in the disease to prevent or reduce joint deformity;
• *penicillamine* (Depen, Cuprimine) can be an effective anti-rheumatoid drug, but adverse effects (e.g., rash, ulcers, blood disorders) limit its usefulness;
• *immunosuppressives* (such as Imuran), given to arthritics who fail to respond to other treatments or have serious complications. These drugs also weaken the body's natural defenses, leaving it open to infection. Regular blood tests are required to ensure that bone-marrow cells are not being damaged;
• *methotrexate,* a mild immunosuppressant and anticancer drug, increasingly tried early in arthritis therapy; its effect is seen within 6–8 weeks of treatment. It is usually well tolerated and an effective antiarthritic drug, although it can cause stomach upsets, abdominal cramps and coughing when first taken. Its use must be carefully monitored to avoid liver problems;
• *sulfasalazine* — a drug long used for bowel disease — may also alleviate rheumatoid arthritis, with few adverse effects, although some patients are allergic to it.

Caution is required with NSAIDs

The need for care in those taking NSAIDs cannot be overstated. These anti-inflammatory medications can have serious side effects such as dizziness, drowsiness, tinnitus (ringing in the ears), kidney problems and *in particular* gastrointestinal bleeding, which may damage the stomach lining and cause ulcers. Although some may tolerate other NSAIDs better than ASA (e.g., Aspirin), their effects may cause problems. The most serious risk of NSAIDs is an increased risk of peptic (stomach) ulcers, which can cause fatal bleeding, and are particularly dangerous in the elderly and people with impaired liver and/or kidney function, or in those with previous or current stomach ulcers. (See also "Peptic ulcers" later in this chapter.) Some NSAIDs are now marketed in combination with agents that protect against peptic ulcers — such as misoprostol (Cytotec), ranitidine (Zantac) or omeprazole (Losec). All people taking NSAIDs need careful medical supervision. Protection by antacid medication and agents that coat the stomach is recommended for high-risk patients.

For more information about arthritis, contact the Arthritis Society of Canada (Ontario address: 920 Yonge Street, Suite 420, Toronto, Ontario M4W 3J7; tel. (416) 967-1414).

ASTHMA

The word "asthma" comes from the Greek *asthmatos*, meaning shortness of breath. Asthma is a lung disorder in which breathing becomes labored due to narrowing and inflammation of the airway. Asthma affects about 4 percent of the population, or over a million Canadians. It is a common childhood disease, but many "grow out of it." On the other hand, some people first experience it as adults —

about 10 percent of asthmatics first develop symptoms after age 40. However, good management and proper medical supervision allow most asthmatics to lead active lives.

In normal breathing, air is drawn into the trachea (large air tube in the throat) and then into the bronchi (passages leading to the lungs). The bronchi branch into tiny tubes (bronchioles), each ending in a tiny balloon-like sac (alveolus) where oxygen is absorbed into the bloodstream and carbon-dioxide waste is expelled. While normal shortness of breath during exertion quickly subsides once exercise stops, asthmatic shortness of breath (not necessarily related to exercise) can last longer — for days, weeks or months, even though lung function often returns to normal between bouts. Asthmatic airways are obstructed by inflammatory changes, with collected fluid, damaged cells, and debris that hinder the movement of air in and out of the lungs. Blocked airway passages prevent asthmatic lungs from pushing stale air out efficiently, or from taking in new air, producing oxygen shortage. Paradoxically, in its struggle to speed up breathing and take in more oxygen, the brain drives the breathing muscles to ever greater efforts, making asthmatics feel even more breathless. If the increased ventilatory drive persists long enough, the muscles tire; a very severe asthma attack with serious oxygen shortage can be fatal without immediate medical attention.

Baffling rise in asthma deaths

Yesterday's generation considered asthma a relatively mild disorder, afflicting mainly young children like "Piggy" in *Lord of the Flies*. This viewpoint is swiftly vanishing as more people develop asthma in their adult years. Not only are more people being diagnosed with asthma, but complacency about its "harmless" nature has been shattered by a steep rise in hospital admissions and deaths. Yet asthma deaths are almost always preventable. Those who die have often had ample warning of problems to come: previous life-threatening episodes, recent hospitalizations for a severe attack or poorly controlled symptoms.

Nobody knows exactly why more people

SEEK IMMEDIATE EMERGENCY HELP IF:

- symptoms are severe and not relieved by usual medication;
- medication is needed more than six times in 24 hours;
- usual daytime activities can't be carried on because of asthma symptoms;
- asthmatic is kept awake by the condition for several nights;
- asthmatic can't say a complete sentence without gasping for air.

are dying of asthma in many countries despite more available medications, although it is possible that they're wrongly used. Suggested reasons are the failure of physicians to recognize the disease early, failure of asthmatics to follow the prescribed treatment, overreliance on certain drugs (airway-widening bronchodilators) and undertreatment with others (anti-inflammatories). Many asthmatics go to the emergency department only hours after self-administering large amounts of their usual quick-relief bronchodilator, hoping that what works for a mild attack will ease a severe one.

Another possible reason for increased fatalities is failure by healthcare personnel to recognize the inflammatory condition and assess the severity of an attack; they may not give enough anti-inflammatories (steroids) quickly enough, or may discharge asthmatics too soon without proper medicines and instruction. Relapses often occur shortly after a bad attack that hasn't been adequately treated.

New emphasis on airway inflammation

Asthma is now regarded primarily as a persistent inflammatory condition, even in newly diagnosed or mild cases. While bronchodilators (airway-widening) drugs are still essential, modern experts promote earlier and greater use of anti-inflammatory medications (as well as bronchodilators) to suppress the underlying inflammation. They also stress diligent monitoring of the air-passage obstruction.

Until recently, bronchodilators were routinely prescribed for asthma, but experts now recommend their use only when symptoms occur. The initial, transient airway narrowing, due to bronchial muscle contraction responds rapidly (within minutes) to an inhaled bronchodilator, but the long-term, underlying airway inflammation — which takes some hours to develop — may also need urgent attention. It may linger for weeks, even though obvious symptoms are gone and the person feels better. Untreated, the inflamed, swollen and "hyper-responsive" airway remains prone to serious obstruction. Many specialists now believe that all asthmatics who experience regular (daily) symptoms should be treated with inhaled corticosteroids (beclomethasone

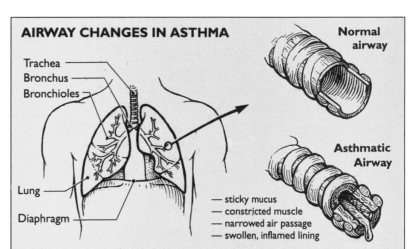

AIRWAY CHANGES IN ASTHMA

Trachea
Bronchus
Bronchioles

Normal airway

Asthmatic Airway

Lung
Diaphragm

— sticky mucus
— constricted muscle
— narrowed air passage
— swollen, inflamed lining

Bronchial (airway) narrowing in asthma follows a complex chain of events that may occur spontaneously or be provoked by certain triggers. It involves contraction of the muscles encircling the air passages, inflammation and thickening of the airway linings (walls) and increased mucus secretion. With obstructed breathing tubes, asthmatics find it hard to move air in and out of their lungs, which makes them feel short of breath. Breathing through clogged airways leads to the characteristic wheezing sound sometimes made by asthmatics on exhaling.

or budesonide) as well as bronchodilators. Overuse of bronchodilators (more than twice a day) may mask worsening symptoms without ameliorating the underlying disease.

However, not all physicians use anti-inflammatories soon enough, and asthmatics may need reassurance about the safety of corticosteroids because of bad press about their side

---

WAYS TO IMPROVE ASTHMA CONTROL

- **Heed warning signs of increasing severity (e.g., interrupted sleep, increasing cough or need for more bronchodilator puffs).**
- **Avoid overreliance on bronchodilators.**
- **Know when to call the physician and what to do if a physician is unavailable (e.g., take steroid pills or go to the nearest emergency); never delay seeking**

medical help.
- **As changing airflow rates reveal increasing severity, invest in a cheap, portable, home-measuring flow meter.**
- **On holidays, know where to go for help if needed.**
- **Watch for nocturnal asthma (increasing nighttime or early morning symptoms), which signal worsening asthma. Nocturnal asthma is a**

signal to get in touch with your physician.
- **Remember that viral respiratory infections increase the risk of serious asthma attacks — take precautions.**
- **Get an annual flu shot — recommended for all asthmatic adults not allergic to eggs.**
- **Have regular follow-up medical visits.**

A LOOK AT SOME FAMILIAR ANTIASTHMA DRUGS

Antiasthma medications are divided into three main groups, sometimes used together:
- *bronchodilators* that ease breathing but don't influence inflammation;
- *nonsteroidal anti-inflammatory agents* that dampen airway inflammation;
- *steroidal compounds* (corticosteroids) that reduce airway inflammation.

Bronchodilator ("quick-relief") medications

- Inhaled beta-2-adrenergics such as salbutamol (Ventolin), terbutaline (Bricanyl), fenoterol (Berotec) and procaterol (Pro-Air) relieve breathing within minutes of being inhaled. Beta-2-adrenergics are best used "as needed" to ease breathing, *not* on a routine basis. It's wise to keep tabs on the number of bronchodilator puffs used daily to tell whether the asthma is well controlled. If needed more than prescribed — usually two to four times a day — control is inadequate. It's time to seek further medical advice.

  Side effects of beta-2-adrenergic inhalers are uncommon but may include tremors, rapid pulse and cardiac palpitations, which usually wear off with a continued or reduced dose. If side effects are annoying, consult your physician or an asthma clinic.
- Ipratropium bromide (Atrovent) — another inhaled bronchodilator — may enhance airway widening when used in combination with a beta-2-adrenergic agent. Quite often, Atrovent is given together with Ventolin.
- Theophylline bronchodilators (e.g., Uniphyl, Theo-Dur) taken as pills are also airway dilators, but are now used less often for asthma. The effects of theophylline vary greatly with the use of other drugs and various illnesses, such as viral infections, cardiac and liver diseases, antibiotics and ulcer medications (e.g., cimetidine), which increase theophylline blood levels. Smoking, phenobarbital, high-protein diets and eating charbroiled beef decrease blood-theophylline levels. Side effects are a frequent problem.

Nonsteroidal anti-inflammatory medications

- Cromoglycate or cromolyn (Intal), one of the safest asthma drugs, is used as a preventive rather than for short-term breathing relief — especially in children with mild asthma. But unfortunately it's not effective in all asthmatics. A trial run of six weeks can determine whether someone will respond to the drug.
- Inhaled nedocromil sodium (Tilade) works like cromoglycate in reducing symptoms, although it takes time to see improvement. Again, it doesn't work in all asthmatics.
- Oral ketotifen (Zaditen) is a user-friendly anti-inflammatory agent, useful for children, especially infants.

Steroidal compounds

- Inhaled corticosteroids such as beclomethasone (Beclovent, Becloforte), budesonide (Pulmicort) and flunisolide (Bronalide) are increasingly used to reduce and prevent airway inflammation. Patients may start out on 8 to 12 puffs a day to bring their asthma under control, later tapering to less — two to four puffs daily. Steroids often help asthmatics attain a peaceful night's sleep and improve their exercise tolerance.

  Unwarranted anxiety about possible side effects from inhaled corticosteroids has made both asthmatics and their caregivers wary of using steroids. While corticosteroids taken by mouth over long periods may cause side effects such as weight gain, fluid retention, hypertension, osteoporosis, diabetes and cataracts, *inhaled* corticosteroids taken in moderate doses have few ill effects and are considered safe, although they may produce local effects, such as a transient burning sensation, oral thrush (yeast or candida overgrowth) and hoarseness. Rinsing the mouth after inhaler use decreases adverse effects. However, long-term, steady use of steroid inhalers may produce some adrenal (immune system) suppression, which needs attention. In children, long-term use may retard growth, but this effect is still being debated.
- Oral steroids (such as prednisone) are required for poorly managed or severe asthma and emergency situations, and are now given more promptly and to more asthmatics than before. Some keep steroid tablets on hand in case of need — for instance, when a cough, cold, flu, sinusitis or bronchitis worsens the asthma — perhaps using them as well as the usual steroid puffer, but stopping when symptoms abate.

The future will likely see many more medications introduced, including long-acting inhaled beta-agonists, different anti-inflammatories and possibly antagonists (antidotes) to the airway chemicals and mediators that aggravate asthma.

effects. Since the inhaled steroids used in asthma act locally on the airway tubes, hardly any are absorbed into the bloodstream, producing negligible side effects at usual doses.

Even the mildest of asthma can become severe under certain circumstances. Asthmatics must learn the signs of worsening asthma and know "what to do if . . ." An asthma crisis plan suggested by Toronto's Asthma Centre is a three-step process. First, on noticing worsening symptoms, the asthmatic doubles, triples or quadruples the usual dose of inhaled corticosteroid. Second, if there's no relief from inhaled corticosteroids, a tapering course of oral steroids may be advised. (Asthmatics prone to troublesome episodes should keep steroid pills on hand for times of crisis — accompanied, of course, by a phone call to the physician.) Third, if symptoms worsen, asthmatics should go at once to the nearest hospital emergency service.

Asthma is best managed by physician–patient partnership

Treatment usually works best when doctor and asthmatic jointly assume symptom management. The development of new inhaler delivery systems makes antiasthma drugs easier to use.

There is now a wide range of inhalers to choose from, including spacers and aerosol-holding chambers (Aerochambers) and breath-activated "powder-puffers" (e.g., the Turbuhaler, Rotahaler, Spin and Dischaler) that spray in powder. The aim is to put as much of the drug as possible into the airway, leaving as little as possible in the mouth and throat. Spacers avoid the need to activate the inhaler and breathe in simultaneously; the drug is released into a holding chamber, giving extra time to coordinate inhalation. Since breathing needn't be as carefully timed, people who have difficulty with standard inhalers (mainly the very young and the old) can use their drugs more effectively. Inhalers that use dry powder instead of aerosol products are an advance, requiring just a small click to release the drug before it is breathed in.

For more information, contact your family doctor; the Lung Association; the Asthma Society of Canada; or your local respiratory-disease unit, hospital or specialist.

BACK PROBLEMS

Almost 90 percent of Canadians aged 29 to 65 have back pain at some time. In fact, sore backs follow the common cold as the most frequent reason for doctor visits. Ordinary backache varies from mild and gradual to the sudden, excruciating pain (hexenschuss or "witch's blow") brought on by a single acute stress. Fortunately, even without medical aid, 90 percent of back pain improves or is gone within four to eight weeks. But as backache tends to recur,

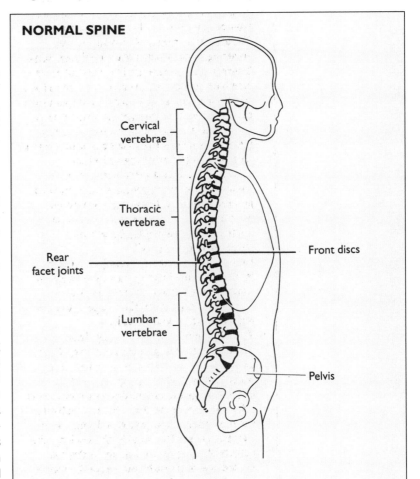

NORMAL SPINE

Cervical vertebrae

Thoracic vertebrae

Rear facet joints

Front discs

Lumbar vertebrae

Pelvis

Viewed from the side, the spine is a column with three gentle "curves" — the cervical, thoracic and lumbar regions. The back's bony elements are 33 flat-surfaced, circular bones (the vertebrae), stacked on top of each other, separated by discs (little oval pads made of fibrous tissue) that act as shock absorbers. The vertebrae articulate with each other by means of knuckle-sized facet joints at the rear, and connect via the cushioning discs in front. The discs allow smooth motion without bone rubbing abrasively on bone. Somewhat like truck tires, the discs have a tough, fibrous outer coating (the annulus) and a soft, inner, jelly-like portion, the nucleus pulposus.

COMMON REASONS FOR BACKACHE

- *Muscle spasm* from irritation or damage to the spinal nerves. Back muscles go into spasm to immobilize the back and protect it from injury. Since pain from a muscle spasm in the back may travel down to the buttocks and legs, it's often difficult to pinpoint the exact location of the problem.

- *Worn facet (spinal) joints* can cause a stab of pain after some minor exertion or twisting motion such as picking up a golf ball. Pain may be immediate or worsen a day or two later. Leaning backward accentuates facet joint pain, while bending forward usually eases it. Common symptoms are: an inability to roll over or get out of bed easily; difficulty getting out of a chair or car; trouble walking erect. While felt mainly in the lower back, facet-joint pain may radiate into the buttocks and down the back of one or both thighs, typically with one hurting more than the other (possibly mimicking sciatic pain — radiating down the leg). With rest, facet-joint pain usually recedes within 4 to 14 days. It may return a few times a year, or never recur.

- *Disc trouble* (discogenic back pain) is due to bulging discs that irritate spinal nerves. With advancing age, discs lose water and elasticity wanes. They may then develop thin spots through which the soft inner material protrudes and presses on a nerve, producing back pain. Disc pain often escalates from mild to severe over a couple of days, and although it usually recedes in a week or two, it can linger on as a nagging ache. When a disc's inner portion bulges but doesn't actually protrude through the outer shell, it causes a dullish ache rather than a sharp pain. Disc pain usually worsens on bending forward; hence, disc sufferers prefer to stand erect and avoid bending.

  Those with short, acute attacks alternating with longer bouts of backache, and pain on bending both forward and backward, could have *both* worn facet joints and thinning discs. Thinning discs can throw the facet joints out of kilter, making them more prone to strain; reduce the back's suppleness, lessening its range of motion; bulge and pinch a nerve sufficiently to cause sciatic leg pain.

- A *herniated, prolapsed or ruptured disc* occurs when part of the inner pulp bursts through the tough, outer coat and irritates the spinal nerve(s) to produce persisting back and leg pain. Herniated discs tend to be a problem in younger age-groups (in the thirties and forties), most often in those who spend more than half their time sitting, such as truckers, and those who make repeated twisting movements. The sign of a truly herniated disc is intense sciatic pain down the leg, reaching the foot (in contrast to other disc problems that generally don't cause pain below the knee). Pain from a ruptured disc often worsens on coughing, sneezing and certain movements; it may be accompanied by muscle weakness, numbness and, if serious, bowel and bladder problems. Disc rupture is confirmed by CAT scans, a myelogram (X-ray pictures taken after dye injection) and other tests. If diagnosis is reasonably certain and conservative management (rest, heat and painkillers) fails, surgery or chymopapain (enzyme) dissolution may be advised.

- *Sciatica* (leg pain), which arises from a pinched spinal nerve compressed by a protruding disc or bone spur, usually builds up over a day or two and may last for two to six weeks. It tends to worsen with movement, especially bending forward, and frequently runs past the knees to the feet, sometimes accompanied by tingling or numbness. Sciatic leg pain may exceed the backache and shouldn't be ignored, since, with sufficient nerve pressure, muscular weakness and even bowel and bladder dysfunction may result. If not relieved by conservative treatment, sciatica may call for surgery to remove the nerve-pinching part.

- *Bone spurs* (osteophytes) may jut out from vertebrae and compress nerves. Fortunately they're sometimes self-limiting and tend to fuse spontaneously after about age 60. Once the bones are immobilized ("rusted stiff"), they no longer cause pain, although the tradeoff is diminished suppleness.

- *Spinal stenosis* arises when the canal that houses the spinal cord becomes narrowed — usually by encroaching bone spurs — causing a diminished nutrient and oxygen supply to the nerves. If minor, spinal stenosis poses little threat; but in the few cases where it is severe and accompanied by symptoms such as numbness and reduced mobility, a CAT scan may be used to assess the need for surgery.

TYPICAL BACKACHE: CASE STUDIES

Dave, a tall, 38-year-old construction worker with recurrent backaches, had poor lifting techniques, a beer belly and a habit of slumping in front of the television each evening. Told in incomprehensible medical jargon that he had "degenerating disc disease" (DDD) and some "encroaching osteophytes," Dave worried about injury, job loss and permanent dependency. His terror mounted each time his back "went out" and, seeing no solution, he began to drink to drown his anxiety. Both Dave's back problem and his incipient alcoholism might have been improved by reassurance, in understandable language, that his back pain was simply due to worn discs — a normal result of aging. A few lessons in proper lifting techniques would have greatly reduced his discomfort and boosted his confidence. Amazingly, however, Dave's backache vanished around his 58th birthday. (With aging, bone spurs may fuse spontaneously, stabilizing spinal joints and relieving the pain.)

Anne, a housewife with habitually poor posture, suddenly "froze" one day while lifting her youngest child. After the event, she found that the simplest activities — bending forward to the stove, reaching down to her children, brushing her teeth, getting out of a car, or even sneezing — sent excruciating pain down her spine and into her buttocks. Too "busy" to seek proper medical help, Anne tried numerous painkillers and tranquilizers and, following the advice of a well-meaning neighbor, applied mustard plasters and slept on her stomach (the worst possible position, because it arches the spine). Deciding in a panic that she had a "slipped" disc, Anne consulted, in turn, a masseuse, an acupuncturist, a herbal specialist, a chiropractor (who provided transient relief) and, finally, her family physician, who found her caught in a vicious cycle of pain and anxiety. Earlier medical advice could have comforted Anne with the knowledge that she had a temporarily painful, but not diseased, spinal disc that was bulging, not "slipping," and she might have been referred to a physiotherapist to learn correct posture.

Mary, a 29-year-old, rather overweight, under-exercised executive secretary, fared better. She received expert medical assistance and tuition in ways to overcome her job-related back problem — she had spent her days hunched over a computer in a nonsupportive chair. Initially Mary's physician prescribed muscle relaxants but no preventive training. However, a second attack prompted her to see an orthopedic specialist, who diagnosed her condition as a minor facet-joint problem, explained clearly why her back hurt, told her the pain would fade with rest and taught her how to avoid stressing her back. With some weight loss, a physiotherapy program, exercises to strengthen the abdominal muscles, plus a sensible chair at work, Mary's back seldom aches any more. She does daily back exercises to minimize recurrences and knows what to do should the pain return.

early diagnosis, prompt treatment and education to prevent recurrence are essential. Most common backache is not a disease but stems from a combination of aging, wear and tear and poor posture, much of it preventable. Holding objects near the body rather than at arm's length and making legs do the work eases spinal stress. Learning to stand, sit, lift and bend correctly, plus a few daily exercises to strengthen the abdominal muscles, can relieve or eliminate a vast amount of back pain. Less than 5 percent of back sufferers need surgery.

Diagnostic findings may not match pain felt

Paradoxically, the intensity of back pain, which is highly individual, correlates poorly with X-rays or myelograms, which may show seemingly serious back damage when the patient reports little or no pain. Nonetheless, X-rays must be taken for severe back pain to rule out serious conditions such as a tumor, infection

SOME POPULAR MISCONCEPTIONS ABOUT BACKACHE

- Discs don't "slip," "disintegrate" or "turn to dust," although they may bulge, touch a nerve and cause pain.
- Backs don't "go out," but spinal joints can be strained in the same way as other joints if overextended.

- Sitting is far harder on backs than standing, and much unnecessary backache occurs because of poor body posture when seated, as well as faulty lifting and bending techniques.
- Backs aren't ultra-sensitive. Although they get a bit worn

from daily wear and tear, they are quite strong.
- Back pain isn't usually due to disease; it hurts but rarely harms. In less than 1 percent of cases does back pain stem from a serious underlying disease.

TREATING LOW BACK PAIN

- Treat the whole body, not just the spine. Most back pain tends to diminish or disappear on its own within six weeks.
- Relieve the initial, acute pain with anti-inflammatories, painkillers (such as ASA or acetaminophen) and a cold pack.
- After the initial phase (about one week), try heat (perhaps a hot bath twice a day) as well as painkillers and

muscle relaxants. (Heat should *not* be used in the initial phase as it may aggravate inflamed tissue.)
- Rest and immobilization should last only a few days (five days maximum) followed by a gradual return to mobility.
- Learn back-strengthening exercises and do them regularly, plus 15 minutes daily of slow, static stretch exercises.

- Regular walking, cycling or swimming strengthens the back without strain.
- Consult a physiotherapist about back care and self-management, including how to move, stand, work and lift.
- Try TENS (transcutaneous electrical stimulation).
- Massage helps some, provided it's done by a registered practitioner.

- Consider back manipulation by a physician or chiropractor. Manipulation of the spinal vertebrae often brings speedier improvement than standard medical approaches alone; it's not a cure, but it provides relief for certain types of low back pain such as facet-joint problems and sacroiliac irritation.
- Surgery is a last

resort for back conditions that result in nerve deterioration severe enough to weaken the legs, or produce long-lasting sciatica or loss of bowel or bladder function. Spinal-bone fusion is still occasionally recommended for discogenic problems that remain incapacitating despite several months of nonsurgical treatment.

HOW ABOUT "FAILED BACK" PROBLEMS?

The term "failed back syndrome" is used for backs that have undergone repeated surgery or been subjected to multiple interventions such as manipulation and chymopapain injections. "Failed

back" problems following surgery usually result from one or more of three possible "wrongs": the wrong (i.e., intractable) back problem, the wrong diagnosis or the wrong surgeon. One

University of Toronto specialist points out that "about 15 to 20 years ago there was an epidemic of back operations when surgeons operated on almost any kind of back problem. Pain clinics

are now dealing with the aftermath." The pain may persist because, in a back stabilized by surgical fusion, other parts of the spine become burdened by the extra load, which may make

them degenerate faster. Another problem is that repeated back surgery may lead to scarring of the epidural nerve roots. The new credo is "Avoid back surgery if possible!"

or nerve injury. Many experts claim that using a battery of tests, some of which (like the myelogram) are invasive, may lead to further, often needless, tests, and is only warranted when the pain is disabling, is felt right down the leg or lasts long enough for surgery to be contemplated.

Mobility is better than inactivity
Most back problems are manageable by simple corrective measures, posture improvement and daily exercise routines. It is now recognized that surgery, bed rest and other traditional methods have failed to help the vast majority of people with low back pain. Surgery benefits only about 1 percent of sufferers — for example, those with proven spinal instability, *spondylolisthesis*

(misaligned vertebrae) or persistent nerve compression. Countless studies confirm that prolonged inactivity harmfully debilitates the muscles, leads to bone loss, increases risks of a blood clot, induces depression and delays the return to normal activities. Therefore, physicians now prescribe only a short rest period, painkillers and anti-inflammatories while the back pain is acute, followed by exercise geared to the specific disorder and efforts to improve fitness. Provided it's done correctly, movement does not aggravate back pain, and brisk walking, cycling and swimming are particularly good forms of exercise for those with bad backs.

For more information contact an orthopedic surgeon, or the Back Association of Canada.

BOWEL PROBLEMS

The undigested remains of food enter the bowel from the intestines, which, in an adult, measure up to 6 m (20 ft), about half of that making up the small intestine, the rest the large intestine or colon. The intestines extract essential nutrients, fluid and electrolytes (such as sodium and potassium) from food and dispose of undigested waste. Undigested food may remain in the descending colon for days, while fluids and electrolytes (salts) are reabsorbed into the bloodstream. One to two liters (quarts) of fluid pass through the colon every day, much of it absorbed in its ascending and transverse sections. The bowel contents are gradually moved along by wave-like muscular movements. The unabsorbed food is evacuated as a semisolid called feces or stool, by a bowel movement.

Constipation

Most healthy adults have a bowel movement three times daily to three times weekly with soft, watery (but not too watery) stools. Provided bowel habits don't alter drastically, and given well-formed stool eliminated almost daily, people needn't worry much about bowel function. Constipation, however, is a frequent North American complaint, more common in women than men, especially frequent in the elderly. There are two main types of constipation: one due to delayed movement of stool through the colon (large intestine), the other involving a blockage at the colon outlet, perhaps with faulty defecation. Drinking more fluid and eating more dietary fiber (for example from bran, cereals, vegetables) often relieves constipation. Overuse of laxatives is strongly discouraged. Over three million North Americans regularly use laxatives, often overstimulating their bowels into sluggish inactivity.

Constipation can be defined as the passage of hard stools fewer than three times a week, possibly accompanied by gas and discomfort. It may result from poor diet (low in fiber), bowel disorders and/or the use of certain drugs (such as aluminum-containing antacids and medicines containing codeine) that prolong stool transit time or alter the amount of water absorbed.

STRUCTURE OF THE BOWEL OR LARGE INTESTINE

The medical name for the large intestine or "large bowel" is "colon" — describing the looped part of the large intestine extending from the end of the small intestine, the cecum (near the appendix), to the anus (exit point). The lower portions of the colon or bowel are called the sigmoid colon and rectum.

Diverticulitis

Outpouchings of the colon, affecting almost one-third of the Western population over age 50, produce the condition known as diverticulosis. It usually causes no discomfort, but in about 15 percent of cases the outpouchings become inflamed — producing diverticular disease, or diverticulitis — signaled by crampy pain, abdominal tenderness on the left side, fever, low appetite, nausea and perhaps vomiting.

HOW TO PREVENT CONSTIPATION

- **Eat plenty of fiber (about 20–26 g/7–9 oz a day) from fruit, vegetables, wheat bran, high-fiber cereals and breads.**
- **Drink enough fluids — six to ten glasses daily (including soups, juices, water, tea and other drinks), remembering that** alcohol and coffee and other caffeinated products are diuretics that increase the body's fluid losses.
- **Develop regular bowel habits — don't delay emptying:**
  - **don't strain or push at stool;**
  - **don't read on the toilet;**
- **don't overuse laxatives.**
- **If stool evacuation is infrequent and fiber intake is low, try other bulk-formers or stool softeners (e.g., Surfak, Colace, Metamucil), along with enough fluids.**

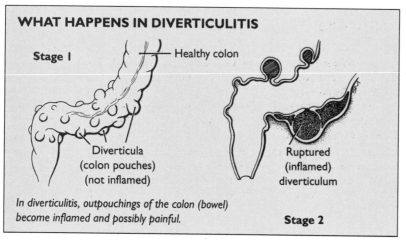

WHAT HAPPENS IN DIVERTICULITIS

Stage 1

Healthy colon

Diverticula
(colon pouches)
(not inflamed)

Ruptured
(inflamed)
diverticulum

*In diverticulitis, outpouchings of the colon (bowel)
become inflamed and possibly painful.*

Stage 2

afflicts 20 percent of Canadians at some time in their lives, women twice as often as men, and whites more often than nonwhites. Although a source of much embarrassment and annoyance, IBS is not a disease or a forerunner of serious disorders. It's an aggravation that many ignore or learn to live with, few considering it distressing enough to merit medical attention. The problem is often relieved by eating more fiber.

The hallmarks of IBS are pain-relief after bowel movements, and loose stools when the pain occurs. IBS is diagnosed "negatively," by excluding other bowel diseases as the cause of the discomfort. Symptoms that do *not* usually signify IBS and *do* require medical attention include rectal bleeding, continuous (non-crampy) pain, weight loss and nighttime discomfort. IBS symptoms generally fade at night, not disturbing sleep, whereas serious conditions (such as colitis) continue or worsen at night.

The elusive reasons for IBS

What is frequently found — or at least suspected — in IBS is an unusual pattern of intestinal movement, where the colon's normal wave-like activity is particularly sensitive and the muscles of the colon undergo abnormal contractions that sometimes show up on a routine bowel exam (with X-rays or sigmoidoscopy — looking up the colon with a special instrument). The exaggerated movements may produce bowel spasms that accelerate or delay the movement of the bowel contents, causing diarrhea or constipation. Delayed stool passage may prolong the mucosal contact with the intestinal wall, which allows further absorption of water and aggravates the problem.

Many experts think IBS is closely linked to feelings of uncertainty, tension, anxiety and/or depression. Since the colon is controlled by cerebral nerve pathways (influenced by emotions), stress can stimulate abnormal colonic movements. Many sufferers first notice their bowel problem after some distressing or upsetting event. And although recent studies on IBS have focused on colon motility rather than psychological factors, many people with the disorder have underlying psychiatric disturbances that may show up as intestinal symptoms. Two

While most attacks of diverticulitis are mild and need no treatment, severe forms (possibly accompanied by infection and an abscess or diverticular rupture) may require surgery. Occasionally the condition causes painless bleeding (which usually stops on its own), but heavy bleeding — an uncommon occurrence — may require surgical management. A new treatment is to inject remedial materials right into the bleeding bowel vessel through a hollow tube, under X-ray guidance.

As with other bowel trouble, eating more fiber may help to prevent the condition.

Irritable bowel syndrome

Irritable bowel syndrome, or IBS — also known as spastic colon, nervous bowel, mucous colitis or functional bowel disorder — is an annoying malady characterized by bloating, gas, abdominal cramps and erratic bowel habits: sufferers experience episodes of constipation interspersed with explosive diarrhea, sometimes many times a day. Irritable bowel syndrome

THE VARIABLE SYMPTOMS OF IBS:

- constipation alternating with diarrhea (changing from day to day or week to week), lasting many months;
- abdominal bloating (gas), seemingly relieved only by defecation;
- constant urge to defecate;

- mucus in the stool;
- cramping pain beginning about one hour after eating, usually in the lower left abdomen (above the sigmoid colon), perhaps radiating to other abdominal regions;
- pain eased after bowel movement;

- possibly abnormal intestinal motility (contractions);
- spasm of the colon (may "feel hard");
- occasional pain around the anus at defecation;
- emotional or psychological stress/instability — frequently present.

TREATMENTS FOR IRRITABLE BOWEL SYNDROME

- Reassurance about its harmless nature, alleviating fears of colitis, cancer or other serious disorders. Counseling and perhaps psychotherapy. Recognition of the link between anxiety and an irritable bowel helps to overcome the problem. Brief use of tranquilizers may be suggested.
- Stress-reduction classes.
- Hypnosis and relaxation techniques.
- Dietary changes, especially the addition of fiber — much promoted. Many IBS sufferers do well just by adding 60 ml (2 tbsp) of bran a day to their food — the less refined the bran the better, wheat bran being best — adding fiber to the diet up to a level of about 26 g (9 oz) a day (more could increase symptoms). The added bulk keeps the colon mildly distended, preventing pockets of high pressure that may cause pain. (Abdominal cramping and gas may worsen for a short while after adding bulk but usually subside after a month or so.)
- Small, non-fatty meals.

MEDICATIONS FOR SHORT-TERM USE IN IBS

- *Antispasmodics* (such as Buscopan and Levsin) may reduce colonic spasms and may be advised for short-term use. (Side effects include mouth dryness, a hesitant or sluggish bladder, vision blurring and slow bowel function.)
- *Carminatives* (such as peppermint oil) — smooth-muscle relaxants — are sometimes recommended.
- *Trimebutine* (Modulon) may alter stool transit time and relieve IBS, especially in those with both diarrhea and constipation.
- *Stool softeners* such as docusate sodium (e.g., Colace) are useful for excessively hard stools that are uncomfortable to pass, although more fluid intake and bulking agents do much the same and are preferable.
- *Cholestyramine* (Questran) — a resin that binds bile salts — may be worth a try for those with continuous diarrhea.
- *Loperamide* (Imodium) may lessen crampy pain and prevent severe, explosive diarrhea, but can also worsen constipation in the long run.
- *Maxeran, Motilium* and other drugs that alter gut motility may accelerate transit time and help sufferers whose symptoms arise from slow stomach emptying.
- Periodic use of tranquilizers such as *benzodiazepines* for stressful times can calm the gut, but should not be taken for more than one or two months.
- *Antidepressants* may help IBS sufferers with underlying depression. Besides elevating mood, they also have antispasmodic properties that reduce bowel spasms.

U.S. studies found that approximately 50 percent of those reporting IBS suffered from psychiatric illnesses such as anxiety disorders. By comparison, only one-fifth of people with organic gastrointestinal diseases (such as colitis) have accompanying anxiety syndromes. While not all IBS sufferers are psychologically disturbed, they share certain characteristics:
- a tendency to be hypochondriacal;
- frequent doctor visits;
- a history of being pampered as children, given treats when sick and allowed to stay home from school more often than others;
- other family members with IBS — suggesting "learned illness behavior."

Inflammatory bowel disease (IBD)
Although lumped together under the umbrella term "inflammatory bowel disease" (IBD), ulcerative colitis and Crohn's disease are two distinct disorders: Crohn's disease can attack any part of the digestive tract from mouth to anus, but most often affects the small intestine. Ulcerative colitis is confined to the colon (large intestine). Inflammatory bowel disease can arise at any age, even during infancy, but usually appears between the ages of 15 and 25, affecting males and females equally.

Symptoms of both include severe diarrhea, abdominal cramps, waning appetite, weight loss. Of the many possible complications of IBD, the most serious are weight loss, weakness and fatigue, anemia, kidney stones, arthritic complaints, rash, eye disorders, and

MEDICATIONS FOR IBS ARE CONTROVERSIAL

No drugs tried for IBS have been shown to be consistently superior to placebos. Treatment failures may reflect the difficulty of curing a subjective disorder that worsens and improves without rhyme or reason. The best therapy for irritable bowel syndrome is education, nutritional changes and adding bulk-forming agents to the diet rather than turning to drugs. A mild laxative (e.g., lactulose) may help to soften hard stools before the high-fiber regime is begun.

growth retardation and delayed sexual maturation (in children). Some of these conditions arise directly from the disease itself (nutrient deprivation); others, such as arthritis, are related to mechanisms not yet fully understood. Neither surgery nor drugs can cure Crohn's, but removal of the colon will permanently eliminate ulcerative colitis.

Possible causes of inflammatory bowel disease

- *Infections* — bacterial or viral triggers.
- *Altered immunological responses.* An immune response mounted against the body's own cells is now considered largely responsible.
- *Diet.* Studies implicating such foods as sugar and cornflakes in IBD have been largely discredited. There is some evidence that lack of fiber is a cause, but the jury is still out.
- *Genetic makeup.* Between 20 and 40 percent of people with IBD have one or more relatives with the disease.

It is no longer believed that psychological problems trigger IBD, although IBD can certainly cause psychological problems. People ill from IBD may experience a sense of hopelessness which may lead to depression as a consequence rather than a cause of IBD.

Dietary treatment of IBD

Nutrition is crucial in IBD, but the exact role of diet is controversial. Experts have tried low-sugar, high-carbohydrate diets, exclusion diets and low-fiber diets with inconclusive results. The response of IBD sufferers to food varies widely. Ulcerative colitis sufferers are often lactose intolerant and must avoid milk products. Some with bowel stricture (narrowing) do best by avoiding bulky high-fiber foods. One study on Crohn's patients who had undergone surgery found that the most troublesome foods were corn, nuts, fizzy drinks, raw fruits, shellfish, lettuce, pickles, alcohol and tomatoes. Least likely to cause problems were chicken,

RECENT STRIDES IN IBD MANAGEMENT

- **Corticosteroid drugs reduce bowel inflammation in moderate to severe ulcerative colitis and Crohn's flare-ups. Besides relieving symptoms, corticosteroids increase appetite and help people to regain lost weight. Unfortunately they have undesirable side effects — headaches, face flushing, facial puffiness, increased body fat especially around the trunk and fluid retention (particularly around the ankles) — and also more serious side effects such as osteoporosis, blood-pressure elevation and reduced immune resistance. New corticosteroid** preparations, now in clinical trials, promise fewer side effects.
- **Sulfasalazine — a mixture of sulfapyridine (an antibacterial) and 5-amino-salicylate (5-ASA), a relative of ASA — is widely used to prevent flare-ups and alleviate mild to moderate ulcerative colitis, and also for Crohn's disease confined to the colon. Side effects are common in the first few weeks of use (headaches, nausea, loss of appetite) but minimized by taking the medication on a full stomach or as coated pills. Some people are allergic to sulfasalazine, devel-** oping a rash or hives.
- **Use of 5-ASA in a variety of forms is a big advance in managing ulcerative colitis. Since most side effects of sulfasalazine stem from the sulfa component, use of 5-ASA on its own, without sulfapyridine, as daily enemas, suppositories or by mouth, may avoid problems. Various coated tablets can deliver the medication right to the affected part of the intestine. Enemas of 5-ASA now achieve remission in 80–90 percent of ulcerative colitis (confined to the left side of the colon), although, to maintain remission,** sufferers may also need oral drugs (e.g., Asacol, Pentasa, Salofalk, Mesasal, Dipentum) or need to continue thrice-weekly enemas.
- **Metronidazole, an antibiotic, is increasingly used for Crohn's sufferers, especially to alleviate anal complications.**
- **Immunosuppressants (6-mercaptopurine and azathioprine) may be helpful in Crohn's disease by reducing the required dosage of corticosteroids and healing fistulas, or for cases that don't respond to corticosteroids. Cyclosporine — an immunosuppressant widely used for trans-** plants — is also being tried for IBD.
- **The new pelvic pouch surgery — used for ulcerative colitis (not Crohn's) — avoids the need for an external stool-collecting bag. The operation removes the colon and rectum, leaving intact the muscles of the anus, connecting the small intestine to them. A "pouch" made out of the small intestine serves as a surrogate colon. Although it doesn't permit completely normal bowel movements, the operation reduces the inconvenience of frequent defecation without disturbing daily life.**

A COMPARISON CHART OF ULCERATIVE COLITIS AND CROHN'S DISEASE

Ulcerative colitis

- First described in 1875, ulcerative colitis is an inflammation of the colon's inner lining, sometimes extending to the rectum. Once thought to be restricted to North America and Europe, ulcerative colitis is now increasingly reported in Japan, India, Thailand and many other parts of the world. It afflicts young adults, three-quarters of the cases developing before age 30, although it occasionally affects children and older people. It's especially common among Jewish people.
- Ulcerative colitis may be restricted to one side of the colon (often the left) or spread to the whole large intestine (pancolitis).
- Symptoms are severe bloody diarrhea, weight loss, poor appetite, mild fever, anemia and loss of body fluids.
- Attacks vary in frequency and severity. Ulcerative colitis is mild in 60 percent of cases, moderate in 25 percent, severe in 15 percent. Some people have one attack, then none for years; others suffer frequent relapses. The disease is unpredictable. Mild disease may suddenly erupt into a severe form or go into remission for years. Flare-ups can occur for no identifiable reason.
- Complications include blood loss or, rarely, toxic megacolon (dilation of the colon) or colonic perforation — a medical emergency.
- The risks of colon cancer increase with ulcerative colitis, especialy if it lasts 10 or more years and if most of the colon is affected.
- Treatment must correct malnutrition, restore disturbed fluid and electrolyte imbalance (resulting from diarrhea), control inflammation and reduce the risk of ulcers.
- Medications include sulfasalazine, 5-amino ASA products (e.g., Asacol), used as enemas, suppositories or tablets, steroids (hydrocortisone, prednisone or new forms) and cyclosporine (experimental).
- Some must stay on maintenance medication to prevent flare-ups.
- Surgery, reserved for those who don't improve with other treatment, entails removal of the colon and rectum and perhaps an ileostomy (artificial opening to which the small intestine is attached, allowing feces to empty into a small, disposable bag). The removal of the (entire) colon cures ulcerative colitis, since, unlike Crohn's, the disease affects only this part of the digestive tract. Such surgery may seem drastic, but many colitis sufferers prefer it to a debilitating illness.
- The new pelvic pouch operation or ileo-anal anastomosis — connecting the ileum to the anal canal — avoids an ileostomy (external bag), and makes bowel surgery easier for those who need it. More people with ulcerative colitis now opt for surgery earlier in the course of the disease, based on an informed decision taken jointly by patient and physician.
- Regular follow-up and checkups are advisable. After 10 years or so, people with ulcerative colitis should undergo yearly colonoscopy (fiber-optic visualization of the colon) to detect incipient cancers.

Crohn's disease

- Named after the physician who first described it, Crohn's disease has increased dramatically since World War II in Europe and North America but remains rare in the developing world. It is most frequent among Europeans, especially Jews. The reason for the sudden rise in Crohn's disease in the Western world remains a mystery. It's not traceable to any specific features of modern urban life, such as stress, diet, infant-feeding practices, toxins or infectious agents.
- Crohn's disease can attack any part of the digestive tract but typically affects the lower portion of the small intestine and the colon, with thickening and inflammation of the intestinal wall.
- Symptoms, depending on the areas affected, are usually diarrhea, abdominal pain, diminished appetite, weight loss, weakness and fatigue. By the time it's diagnosed, people with Crohn's may be quite ill, partly due to malnutrition from inadequate food intake. Symptoms may also include, nausea and vomiting (stomach affected), mouth ulcers, heartburn (esophageal involvement), hemorrhoids (anal disease) and infection. In some, mild symptoms drag on for years. Others have single attacks followed by long remissions.
- Major complications are bowel obstruction, fistulas (abnormal channels between intestinal loops) and mild bleeding.
- Although the risk of colon cancer in those with long-standing Crohn's is marginally increased, it is not clear how much likelier than average they are to develop colon cancer.
- Treatment aims to restore good nutrition, control inflammation and delay relapses. Since many Crohn's sufferers are malnourished by the time of diagnosis, the first step is to restore nutritional well-being with fluid, electrolyte and vitamin replacement. Many new feeding methods can help.
- Medications include: corticosteroids, sulfasalazine (for disease confined to the colon) and antibiotics such as metronidazole.
- New steroids with fewer side effects are bringing relief to some (e.g., budesonide) — still experimental.
- Intravenous feeding or *total parenteral nutrition* (TPN) often achieves remission, obviating the need for surgery. At first it was thought that TPN gave the bowels a rest. However, recent research suggests that "resting" the bowel may not be the main benefit. Merely restoring nutritional status, whether by intravenous or normal feeding (together with appropriate medication), produces great improvement in many Crohn's sufferers. An "elemental" diet of basic nutrients helps some.
- Strictureplasty, a new procedure, shows promise in alleviating the obstruction due to bowel scarring by a technique that widens the bowel and relieves the stricture. The great advantage is that strictureplasty can be done without removing any bowel sections — especially useful for those with widespread disease.
- Surgery cannot permanently cure Crohn's disease, as it may recur in other parts of the digestive tract and call for repeat surgery.

white bread, rice and potatoes. Each IBD sufferer must identify the foods that aggravate symptoms and avoid them, remembering that regular, well-balanced meals are essential for good nutrition. One recent approach being investigated by a University of Toronto team is an "elemental diet" of nutrients in their basic format, fed through a tube, used without any medications or surgery, which helps many Crohn's sufferers. Pioneered as a diet for space travelers, it contains premixed amino acids, fats, carbohydrates and other essential nutrients, producing minimal digestive activity and little stool formation.

For more information, contact the IBD Clinic at the University of Toronto's Mount Sinai Hospital, or the Canadian Foundation for Ileitis and Colitis.

Bowel cancer

Bowel cancer follows lung cancer as the commonest form of malignancy in men, ranking third in women after breast and lung cancer. The incidence of bowel cancer among Canadians is about 45 per 100,000 males per year, slightly less for women. People with close relatives who have had bowel cancer have a greater than average risk of getting the disease. Certain families with an uncommon condition known as familial polyposis have a propensity to develop many — even thousands of — bowel polyps before age 30, with a high risk of developing cancer if the entire bowel isn't removed. Individuals with long-standing ulcerative colitis involving the left side of the colon, are also more at risk than the general population. (See preceding section, "Inflammatory bowel disease.")

POSSIBLE SIGNS OF BOWEL CANCER

About 10 percent of persons with bowel cancer have no warning symptoms at all. However, most observe some signs:

- Visible red blood in or on the stool (perhaps as a red streak), which occurs if the polyp bleeds. The color of the blood may be bright or dark red according to the polyp's position in the colon. However, most rectal bleeding arises from hemorrhoids, and is characteristically not mixed into the stool but on top of it or just on the toilet paper.
- Occult (hidden) blood in the stool, which may be present at an early stage and is detectable by a simple test which, although not entirely reliable, is a useful marker of bowel cancer.
- A change in bowel habits persisting more than two weeks.
- Abdominal pain.

- If the growth is large enough, bowel obstruction and severe abdominal pain, perhaps nausea and vomiting (uncommon) and a sense of incomplete defecation.
- Iron-deficiency anemia (from intestinal bleeding).

Anyone who notices these changes should see a physician at once, for investigation and treatment if necessary. Experts stress that although the vast majority of rectal bleeding is due to hemorrhoids, the possibility of colon cancer warrants medical investigation when rectal blood is noticed.

TESTS FOR COLON (BOWEL) CANCER INCLUDE:

- a digital palpation (with a gloved finger inserted up the rectum), which allows clinicians to feel growths in the rectal area and assess their size but not whether they are malignant. A thorough digital exam detects roughly 10 percent of all bowel tumors;

- sigmoidoscopy — with a flexible sigmoidoscope (illuminated, metal, fiberoptic tube) inserted through the rectum that allows visualization about 35–40 cm (14–15 in) up the colon, revealing growths in the rectum, sigmoid, even lower descending colon;

- colonoscopy — direct fiber-optic visualization using a colonoscope, a 7.8-m (6-ft), flexible tube that allows clinicians to peer into every nook and cranny of the intestine and at the same time to snip off small growths for biopsy (cell sampling). During colonoscopy all but the smallest of polyps are usually removed, however innocent they appear, and tested for cancer. Colonoscopy is done without anesthetic, but Valium and other drugs are given to mute pain;

- an air-contrast barium enema X-ray is still a key diagnostic tool for bowel growths. After liquid barium solution is instilled in the rectum, X-rays detect unusual lumps, bumps, elevations, polyps or tumors along the colon. But X-ray pictures do not reveal whether growths are malignant, and may miss subtle changes that show up better with colonoscopy.

SCREENING FOR BOWEL CANCER

The U.S. Cancer Society recommends that everyone over 40 be screened for bowel cancer by an annual rectal exam, tests for occult blood in the stool and a flexible sigmoidoscopy every two to three years. Canadian health experts disagree, pointing to the risks involved in invasive investigation and the frequency of false-positive and false-negative results. They suggest screening only those known to be at high risk — people who have already had bowel polyps or cancers, those with ulcerative colitis or other predisposing conditions and people with a family history of bowel disease.

Benign bowel polyps may become malignant

There is increasing evidence that people who develop bowel (colorectal) cancer have previously had harmless growths (polyps) in the bowel wall. Opinions differ, but many believe that certain bowel polyps can become malignant — especially adenomatous polyps, with fingerlike fronds. With bowel polyps smaller than one cm (less than half an inch) in diameter, cancer is rare; from 1 to 2 cm (0.4 to 0.8 in), risk increases to one in 10, and with polyps over 2 cm (0.8 in) there is almost a 50 percent chance of malignancy. Why some polyps become malignant while others don't remains a mystery. In Canada and the United States, the majority of bowel polyps and cancers arise in the lower (sigmoid) part of the colon and the rectal area.

Treatment of bowel cancer

Fortunately, many bowel growths can now be removed via colonoscopy, obviating the need for major surgery. If the cancer has invaded the bowel's inner lining, surgical excision (resection) with lymph node removal is still advised, depending on the person's overall well-being. These days, surgical excision of a piece of bowel requires less drastic techniques than formerly, with rapid recovery for most people. Only infrequently is a *colostomy* (removal of the rectum, requiring an external feces-collection bag) necessary.

The dietary link to bowel cancer

Since most populations with high fiber intakes have low rates of bowel cancer, many experts now suspect low fiber, high-fat diets as a prime cause. The high fat content of red meat is one food component closely linked to bowel disease. Argentina, with its penchant for meat consumption, has very high bowel cancer rates. While eating more fiber may protect against bowel cancer, study results are inconsistent, and claims that vitamins A and C protect against bowel cancer remain unproven. American and Canadian cancer societies recommend that, in an effort to reduce bowel-cancer risks, we should all cut down fat consumption (both saturated and unsaturated kinds) and increase our fiber intake.

CARPAL TUNNEL SYNDROME

Carpal tunnel syndrome (CTS) is an easily treatable wrist and hand disorder, more frequent in women than in men. The problem arises through compression of the median (arm) nerve in its narrow passageway through the wrist, often starts up in mid-life to old age and generally affects both hands, the dominant (most-used) one more severely. CTS can arise from certain jobs or hobbies where repeated movements or vibrations inflame the wrist tissues — for instance, knitting, computer keyboard work, driving or operating certain hand-held power tools such as drills, hammers, chain saws. The disorder is frequently seen among miners, roadmenders and others whose jobs involve use of hand-held tools that vibrate.

The first hint of CTS is a sensation of numbness or pain, usually on first awakening — as if parts of the hand had "gone to sleep" — typically felt in the thumb and index finger, but sometimes all the fingers tingle. The tingling sensation worsens on flexing or extension of the wrist, subsiding when the hand is bent inwards or at rest (in a "neutral" position).

Numbness from carpal tunnel syndrome may appear after any movement that keeps the wrist overextended for long periods: stitching,

CARPAL TUNNEL SYNDROME

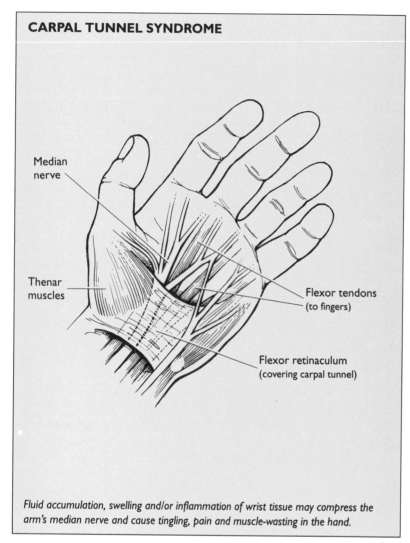

Median nerve

Thenar muscles

Flexor tendons (to fingers)

Flexor retinaculum (covering carpal tunnel)

Fluid accumulation, swelling and/or inflammation of wrist tissue may compress the arm's median nerve and cause tingling, pain and muscle-wasting in the hand.

typical nighttime or early-morning hand tingling, use of Phalen's test (flexing the hands at a 90-degree angle to see if and when tingling occurs) and Tinel's test (tapping the median nerve at the wrist to see if and how strongly it produces tingling). The sooner the tingling appears, the more serious the condition. Confirmation is with a nerve-conduction study and electromyogram (EMG), in which small electric shocks are applied at different spots along the median nerve and the muscle twitch is charted to show whether, and to what extent, the hand muscle has retained or lost its nerve supply.

Treatment for carpal tunnel syndrome can be conservative: wearing a light plastic wrist-splint at night, taking anti-inflammatory medications by mouth or injected into the wrist, altering sleep positions and avoiding movements that worsen the disorder. With correct therapy, time and patience, the loss of nerve conduction can often be reversed. Sometimes operating tools in a better, more neutral wrist position helps to alleviate the problem. Modern designers are working on vibration dampeners, shock absorbers and other ways to lessen the damaging vibrations of hand-held tools.

If other methods fail to correct CTS, surgery to decompress the nerve may be suggested — a simple procedure done under general or local anesthetic that frees the trapped nerve and usually provides rapid relief. After a few days, stitches are removed, but splinting may be needed until the wound heals.

COMMON COLD

The common cold is an upper-respiratory-tract viral infection which, being due to viruses, cannot be cured by antibiotics. Colds are self-limiting infections, generally fought off by the body's immune defenses within a week. The first sign of a cold — usually a sore throat — appears after an incubation period of two to three days, and symptoms usually peak on the third day. The sore throat is followed by swelling of the nasal membranes and a discharge that starts out clear but later becomes turbid. To date, no one has improved upon Sir William Osler's classic description of the common cold as "an acute inflammation of the upper air passages, whereby the patient sneezes

painting, doing manicures or giving a massage. Besides being annoying, the sensory loss may lead to burns (due to lessened sensation of heat, pain, pressure), and the muscle-wasting can make wrist movements clumsy. As CTS progresses, wrist and thumb strength may seriously decline. The reduced grip may make it difficult to grasp even light objects.

The tingling can be set off or worsened by anything that makes the wrist tissues swell and compress the median nerve. Fluid accumulation during pregnancy or before a menstrual period, a Colles' (wrist-bone) fracture, gout, rheumatic (arthritic) swelling, and adrenal or thyroid diseases are typical causes.

Diagnosis of CTS is relatively easy by the

frequently, feels indisposed, perhaps chilly, with a slight headache — rarely (adults) having a fever more than a degree above normal." If the virus invades the larynx (voice box) and inflames the vocal cords, laryngitis may also occur, with a husky, muted or silenced voice for a few days.

Colds afflict young children more than adults, and schoolchildren often bring colds into the home. The average preschooler has five to ten colds annually and spends almost three months of the year with a runny nose. Fortunately, the number of yearly colds dwindles to about three to six by age 10 to 14, and decreases with advancing age. Children with colds may have a fever and an upset stomach, but no runny nose.

Catching a cold is a contact sport

Cold viruses are transmitted by direct contact with infected nasal secretions, typically picked up from the hands or from some other object, transferred to the virus-permeable membranes of eyes or nose. Cold viruses can survive for hours on hard surfaces (dishes, counters) but not as long on porous items such as disposable tissues. When fingers contaminated with cold viruses touch or rub the eyes or nose, the viruses enter and multiply in the nasal passages. The mucous membranes of the mouth are quite resistant to cold viruses, so it may be easier to catch a cold from a handshake than a kiss!

No scientific data support the notion that a cold, despite its name, is actually caused by chilly conditions, scanty clothes or damp weather, but being cold can lessen the body's defenses. Arctic explorers, continually cold and damp, are *less* rather than more likely to catch colds, because they are isolated. Volunteers infected with cold viruses who spent days sitting in damp, chilly rooms clad only in their underwear did not develop more colds than warmly dressed controls. Nonetheless, in northern climates, colds occur with higher frequency in fall and winter because of more time spent indoors, with people herded close together.

Despite the popular belief that colds settle in the chest and cause pneumonia, this doesn't usually happen, although they are sometimes followed by bacterial infections of the sinuses or, especially in children, of the middle ear. Staying indoors doesn't necessarily help. Some people, especially children, feel better outdoors.

Are there ways to prevent a cold?

Scrupulous handwashing and avoiding crowded places may help to reduce the spread of cold viruses. Hopes for a preventive vaccine have dimmed with the isolation of over 100 subtypes of the common cold rhinovirus. But researchers are experimenting with virus-destroying solutions, "killer Kleenex" (saturated with chemicals that destroy the viruses) and antiviral drugs. New antiviral agents such as interferon (produced naturally by human cells) and enviroxine (a synthetic drug) offer some hope of prevention. Now produced by genetic engineering, interferon, given as a nosewash or spray, prevents rhinovirus replication but won't stop a cold once it has started. Side effects from interferon, which appear after a couple of weeks (e.g., nasal bleeding), reduce its usefulness, but interferon is of value for high-risk groups such as the elderly.

Beware of multi-ingredient cold remedies

Cold remedies typically clutter our medicine cabinets, but experts warn against *combination* remedies that contain multiple ingredients — for example, remedies containing antihistamines, caffeine (to counteract sedating effects), decongestants, painkillers, cough suppressants, vitamin C, and sometimes even antacids. Combined cold-relief products, especially those overloaded with antihistamines and short on

---

CALL THE DOCTOR ABOUT A COLD IF YOU:

- **have symptoms lasting for a week or more;**
- **are short of breath;**
- **have persistent wheezing;**
- **have a high fever (over 39°C or 102°F) lasting more than 48 hours;**
- **cough up thick green or yellow sputum and/or blood;**
- **feel more ill than you usually do with a cold.**

TREATING THE COMMON COLD

There is no drug — certainly no antibiotic — that kills cold viruses, but symptoms can be moderated by:
- **bed rest and a little pampering, to make the sniffles more tolerable;**

- **drinking fluids to offset dehydration due to sweating or fever (rare with the common cold);**
- **steam or cool mists to help liquefy nasal secretions;**
- **hot chicken soup — that classic remedy,**

much studied by scientists — shown to alleviate symptoms through its rising vapor or by some aromatic ingredient which seemingly clears nasal congestion better than steam alone.

RATING THE COLD REMEDIES: EXPERTS PROMOTE SINGLE-DRUG, NOT COMBINED PRODUCTS

- **Topical decongestants** (such as Otrivin, Privine or Afrin) come as drops or sprays — sprays being somewhat superior to drops. Although not much supported by physicians, most shrink the nasal membranes by constricting blood vessels, thus lessening congestion and drying out the sinuses. Their effects last from 4 to 10 hours, depending on the type. Topical decongestants should be used only for a *maximum of four days*, strictly as directed, to prevent rebound congestion (increased stuffiness) — which can surface even after short use. Topical sprays are best reserved for "must clear" occasions (e.g., air travel).

- **Oral decongestants** (such as pseudoephedrine or Sudafed) come as short-acting or sustained-release products that act more slowly than sprays, but are not habit-forming or likely to cause rebound stuffiness. Hypertensives should use oral decongestants cautiously as most raise blood pressure.

- **Antihistamines** (such as Chlor-Tripolon, Actifed) have only a marginal impact on colds, but are useful for allergy-related nasal stuffiness. Most cold remedies contain too much and too many antihistamines. Largely sedative in their effect, antihistamines may be helpful at night.

- **Cough suppressants (antitussives)** often contain codeine (as in Tylenol No. 1 or Veganin), dextromethorphan or DM (as in Benadryl DM, Triaminic DM or Robitussin DM) or hydrocodone, a stronger cough suppressant. Available without prescription, dextromethorphan is almost as good a cough suppressant as codeine, with fewer side effects. These agents suppress coughing by acting on the brain's cough center, *not* on the throat, and are just as, if not more, effectively absorbed from pills than syrups — however soothing a syrup may feel to a sore throat! Some physicians advise caution in using cough suppressants, as it is not always desirable

to suppress a cough, the protective mechanism that clears the respiratory tract of mucus (phlegm). However, a dry, hacking cough that hampers work or sleep may call for control with cough medicines, which generally do no harm.

- **Expectorants** (e.g., guaifenesin), said to loosen and help expel secretions and enhance a productive cough, are considered useless by most experts. (Pure steam is better.)

- **Vitamin C**, widely promoted in small doses (about 250 mg daily) to prevent colds, and in massive doses (up to 10 g) to stop a cold at the first hint of symptoms, has not lived up to its promise. No anticold claims for vitamin C have been scientifically validated, although millions still consume it against colds. While a little vitamin C won't hurt, no long-term studies prove that massive doses are safe.

- **Zinc gluconate lozenges**, which have an unpleasant taste, have recently been shown capable of shortening some colds by a day or two, because zinc ions may reduce rhinovirus replication.

- **Analgesics and fever reducers** such as ASA (Aspirin) or acetaminophen (Tylenol) are useless against most common-cold symptoms, but can combat headaches, reduce muscle aches or fever — typical of flu but rare with mere colds. (Suitable adult doses are stated on the product package.)

NOTE: Children with fever from an apparent cold should not be given ASA (Aspirin) because the symptoms may resemble a mild case of flu. Together with ASA, influenza viruses can produce Reye's syndrome (a dangerous liver and brain complication). To avoid the risks of Reye's syndrome, fever in young sufferers can be reduced with acetaminophen products (e.g., Tylenol or Tempra).

N.B: Antibiotics are no use against any viruses, cold or other types.

decongestants, do nothing for most colds. Decongestants alone are best to clear a stuffy nose. The U.S. Food and Drug Administration finds "no justification for the large number of combined ingredients in a single blunderbuss anti-cold product." Some ingredients, such as cough stimulants, cough suppressants or laxatives, are frankly irrational; some act against each other; some (e.g., phenylpropanolamine) are toxic in excess. Single-ingredient products are best: analgesics for pain; antipyretics to combat fever; antihistamines for some nasal drying; decongestants against nasal or sinus stuffiness; cough suppressants to reduce a tiring cough. There is no point in treating symptoms that you *don't* have!

CYSTIC FIBROSIS

Cystic fibrosis (CF) is the commonest potentially fatal inherited disease among Caucasians, especially those of North European descent. In North America, about one in 2,500 children is born with cystic fibrosis.

Until about 10 years ago, all that was known of CF was the fact that it causes chronic lung and digestive problems linked to abnormal salt transport, and its classic inheritance pattern as a single-gene, recessive disorder. (If both parents carry the CF gene, each child they bear has a one in four chance of being born with the disease.)

About one in 25 persons in North America and Europe carries the flawed gene, usually without knowing it and without any signs of the illness. Hence, the parents of an affected child may be unable to understand why their baby has the disease. They need to understand that CF is not due to diet, stress or any problems during pregnancy, nor can it be passed from one child to another; it's entirely due to genes inherited from both parents.

While the exact mechanism behind cystic fibrosis remains unknown, the good news is that the recent discovery and cloning of the CF gene has enabled scientists to identify and analyze the structure of the abnormal protein involved in the disease, and locate its site in affected cells — knowledge that will ultimately lead to more effective treatment of this devastating disease, and perhaps also a cure.

What is cystic fibrosis?

Cystic fibrosis involves an inability to move salt (sodium chloride, particularly the chloride part) and water through the channels in the cells that line certain organs. The flawed chloride transport and consequent dryness of cell surfaces produces abnormally thick secretions that hamper the normal function of organs such as the lungs, sweat glands, intestines and pancreas. CF strikes with varying degrees of severity.

The first detailed report of the disease, in 1936, described it as "cystic fibrosis of the pancreas" because of the thick mucus that blocks the flow of secretions and causes fibrosis (scarring) of the pancreas. However, the pancreatic problem isn't usually the most dangerous aspect of CF, nor is the pancreas always seriously affected. It's the thick, sticky mucus in the lungs that usually poses the greatest danger and leads to frequent respiratory infections. Many CF sufferers find life a constant battle against infection.

Digestion may also be impeded, because thick secretions slow the flow and deplete the supply of pancreatic enzymes, hindering food absorption, perhaps leading to malnutrition. In afflicted males, reproductive-tract blockages often lead to sterility. The sweat of CF sufferers is unusually salty. The "sweat test," which detects the elevated salt content, has become the standard diagnostic tool for CF.

Treatment has gradually improved, prolonging survival so that some CF sufferers now live well into their forties. And many of those who reach adulthood lead near-normal lives. However, most need lifelong medication to combat lung infections and assist digestion.

The inheritance pattern in cystic fibrosis

Cystic fibrosis is a single-gene recessive disorder, so a child must receive a flawed gene from each parent to have the disease. Someone with one faulty and one normal gene will be a carrier but will not have CF. A child with one carrier parent and one non-carrier parent may or may not be a carrier (depending on which genes are transmitted) but will not have CF. However, if both mother and father are CF carriers, there's a one in four chance that a child will receive the defective gene from both sides, and therefore have the disease. It's purely a matter of chance. The risk remains one in four for each further child conceived.

How is cystic fibrosis detected?

Cystic fibrosis may show itself soon after birth — with bowel obstruction or abnormally fatty stools, and the failure to grow normally. But although present at birth, the disease is sometimes not detected until puberty or early adulthood, because if no sweat test is done, the symptoms — such as breathing difficulties — may be blamed on other causes, such as asthma or bronchitis. About half of all CF cases are detected in infancy or childhood because of

SIGNS OF CYSTIC FIBROSIS:

- intestinal (bowel) blockage in infancy, which causes abdominal swelling, vomiting and dehydration, often requiring surgery;
- unusually salty taste of baby's skin when kissed;
- inability of the pancreas to deliver necessary digestive enzymes, and failure to gain weight despite a normal or unusually large appetite;
- fatty stools (greasy, flecked with fat);
- frequent respiratory infections;
- finger clubbing (abnormal fingernail growth) — also seen in other chronic illnesses;
- sinusitis or nasal polyps;
- delayed puberty, possible reproductive abnormalities — especially male sterility (over 90 percent of males with CF are infertile).

lung infections; 10 percent are discovered through bowel obstruction right after birth or even before (by ultrasound tests); and another 30–40 percent are diagnosed later due to pancreatic insufficiency and failure to thrive.

Managing a devastating disease

Since there's no cure at present, therapy must usually be continued throughout life — a demanding regime for CF sufferers, parents and doctors alike. Besides medical care, patients generally require psychological, occupational, social and genetic counseling.

Medical care for CF means primarily managing the lung and digestive problems. Treatment for lung congestion includes exercises to drain fluid, methods to assist in clearing mucus and antibiotics to combat recurrent bacterial infections. While not all CF sufferers have pancreatic insufficiency, most have some degree of abnormality in the production and supply of pancreatic enzymes and many need pills to make up the deficit. Children with CF may improve so markedly with supplements, achieving excellent school records and participation in sports, that parents wonder whether their youngster really has CF. A child's response depends largely on the severity of the illness when first detected.

Gene discovery brings fresh hope of cure

A stunning piece of collaborative research done by scientists at the universities of Toronto and Michigan has located the gene responsible for CF, worked out its genetic code and defined many of the mutations that produce the disorder. Knowing the gene's chemical (base) sequence, scientists deduced the structure of the protein controlled by the gene — a protein now named CFTR (TR stands for "transmembrane conductance regulator"). This gene-product, CFTR, resides in the cell membrane and seemingly assists in regulating the transport of chloride (and perhaps other substances) through cell surfaces.

A combined effort of 80 research teams in 20 countries has found 60 different mutations in the same CF gene. Of these, one specific mutation accounts for 70 percent of CF in North America, about 85 percent in northern Europe, 40–60 percent in southern Europe (for instance, Italy and Spain) and 30-40 percent in Middle Eastern countries (such as Israel and Turkey). Some of the less common mutations occur only in isolated populations.

Until the precise flaw (exactly how salt regulating goes wrong) is known, treatment can slow down but cannot halt the disease. However, the discovery of the CF-causing gene and its protein-product opens up the chance of developing drugs to correct the abnormal salt movement.

Gene therapy may soon provide a cure for this disease. Inserting a normal gene into CF cells to replace the defective one could overcome cystic fibrosis. The first step has already been achieved — transferring a normal version of the gene into defective pancreatic cells in a culture dish, thereby regularizing chloride/water transport.

Carrier screening and prenatal diagnosis are now possible

The discovery of the CF gene has set the stage for carrier tests. Before the discovery, parents were alerted to the possibility of having a child with CF only if they'd already had an affected child. Now, carriers can be detected with reasonable accuracy before they bear children. And genetic tests on unborn babies (examining cells removed from the amniotic fluid around the fetus) permit prenatal diagnosis as early as two months after conception. If the flawed gene is found, the fetus has CF and the parents can decide whether to terminate the pregnancy.

There is, however, a vigorous debate as to whether widespread, universal screening for CF should be performed before all existing mutations are known. Since the mutations reported to date add up to only 85 percent of the possible gene errors, mass screening done now would miss some carriers. And while the benefit of identifying carriers is clear, most experts oppose widescale screening until at least 95 percent of the possible CF mutations are in. Once all the main variants of the mutant gene are known, routine screening of the population will identify nearly all CF carriers. (Nonetheless, some biotechnology companies have already developed CF-carrier test kits and are prepared to start commercial testing.)

Many ethical dilemmas remain

Even when carrier screening tests become generally available, they will raise social, financial and ethical dilemmas. For instance, how and by whom should the tests be done? When should they be administered? Should they be given to teenagers — risking possible hardship or stigma if a youngster turns out to be a CF carrier? Or should the test be offered to couples contemplating marriage, or at a woman's first obstetric visit? If a genetic test shows that a fetus has CF, is that sufficient grounds for terminating a pregnancy? Such difficult questions have no simple answers. But pilot studies done in Britain and Canada among students and young people brought an overwhelming "yes" in favor of CF screening, even though the test would miss some carriers.

For more information contact the Canadian Cystic Fibrosis Foundation.

DIABETES

Over the past couple of decades, much has been learned about the causes and complications of diabetes, but there's no cure yet for this widespread disease. It still ranks as a major killer because of the damage done to the heart, kidneys, eyes, brain and other organs. Diabetes affects 3 to 5 percent of people living in the Western world, including a million Canadians, both adults and children. Almost a quarter of those diagnosed require daily insulin injections. Yet many who have the disease remain unaware of it until major complications appear.

Understanding diabetes

Diabetes is a disease where the body's cells cannot use glucose (sugar) properly for lack of or resistance to the hormone *insulin*, produced by the pancreas. In severe, untreated diabetes the body's cells are starved of the "fuel" needed for energy, and the tissues may "melt away" in a state resembling severe malnutrition.

Normally, insulin keeps blood levels of glucose within safe limits, ranging from 4–7 mmol/L. But in people with diabetes who have too little or no insulin, blood glucose may reach dangerously high levels, and if left untreated it can lead to dehydration, coma, and possible brain damage. Some of the excess blood sugar may spill out into the urine — "sweet urine" is a telltale sign of the disease.

The most immediate danger in diabetes is *hyperglycemia* (high blood sugar), which can lead to *ketoacidosis*, with a buildup of ketone bodies in the blood and possible diabetic coma, even death. But persistently raised levels of blood sugar may lead to long-term complications such as blindness, kidney failure, nerve degeneration, stroke and heart disease.

The modern management of diabetes emphasizes good nutrition, adherence to diet, regular exercise and medications to keep blood sugar in the desirable range and offset its worst consequences. Experts advise those with diabetes to eat at regular times and exercise at the same time each day if possible.

Different types of diabetes

There are (at least) three distinct types of diabetes — types I and II, and gestational diabetes (which arises in pregnancy) — each with different causes and mechanisms, requiring different therapy. About 80 percent of those diagnosed have Type II or non–insulin-dependent diabetes mellitus (NIDDM), which usually develops in middle age, most often in the obese and underexercised. This form usually responds to weight loss and dietary management, rarely requiring insulin shots. The remaining 10 percent of those with diabetes have Type I — formerly called "juvenile" diabetes, but now termed insulin-dependent diabetes mellitus (IDDM). Fortunately, these people can now be kept alive by lifelong use of insulin — first isolated by the historic Banting and Best research team at the University of Toronto physiology department in 1921.

The insulin connection

The body normally regulates the absorption of glucose into cells and controls its level in blood with the help of insulin, a hormone produced by an area of the pancreas known as the *Islets of Langerhans*. The pancreatic beta cells secrete insulin into the blood as needed — especially after meals.

Glucose is vital to life, but it cannot get into cells without insulin, which assists in transporting

---

SYMPTOMS OF DIABETES INCLUDE:

- unusual tiredness;
- increased thirst;
- frequent urination, day and night;
- changes in appetite, unexplained weight loss;

- blurred vision;
- itchy skin, slow healing of cuts and wounds;
- abdominal pain, nausea;
- curiously "sweet-smelling" breath;

- tingling in the limbs. Anyone with these symptoms — including people known to have diabetes — should promptly consult a physician.

---

it across cell membranes. Once in the blood, this hormone signals liver, muscle, fat and other tissues to take up glucose. Insulin also encourages the removal of fat from the blood. If the pancreatic beta cells make too little insulin (as in Type I diabetes), or if the body's cells can't respond to it (as in Type II diabetes), the tissues will be short of their essential fuel and will draw on protein and fat stores to make up for the lack. The classic symptoms of diabetes are: blurred vision, frequent urination (polyuria), excessive thirst (polydipsia) and weight loss.

Diabetes is usually diagnosed by a blood test done after fasting for 12 hours — the fasting glucose test. A high blood sugar reading confirms the presence of diabetes.

In poorly controlled diabetes, alternate fuel stores are used to the point where the person may lose weight and feel tired most of the time. If blood sugar levels remain out of control, the body can suffer lasting abuse, resulting in complications such as kidney failure, stroke, heart disease, nerve damage and eye problems. Diabetes is a leading cause of blindness in North America and a frequent reason for people to go on dialysis or require kidney transplants.

Type I or insulin-dependent diabetes mellitus (IDDM)

Type I diabetes, which was formerly called "juvenile" and is now known as insulin-dependent diabetes mellitus (IDDM), affects one in 600 North Americans, mostly children, often showing up in adolescence.

Type I diabetes or IDDM is now viewed as a progressive autoimmune disorder where antibodies form and attack the the body's own insulin-producing beta cells, resulting in insulin deficiency. At diagnosis, 70–90 percent of those

with IDDM have identifiable anti-insulin and anti-islet antibodies. The triggers that lead to the autoimmune destruction aren't fully understood, but may include genetic and environmental factors. Researchers have identified some genetic markers (HLA or *human leukocyte antigens*) that occur more frequently than usual in people with Type I diabetes, and they are searching for other markers that may identify those at greatest risk.

Studies of identical twins show that if one has Type I diabetes there is a 50 percent chance that the other twin will also develop the disorder. But the unpredictability suggests that although the susceptibility to IDDM is inherited, unknown triggers — possibly a virus, toxin or some dietary ingredient — "trip" the autoimmune process into action. Most cases of IDDM occur without a family history of diabetes.

The symptoms of Type I diabetes — frequent urination, blurred vision, unusual thirst, extreme hunger, easy tiring, irritability and nausea — may come on suddenly. Deprived of their own natural insulin, people with Type I diabetes rely on lifelong insulin replacement by injection. The more consistent and regular the timing of insulin injections, the better the control and the easier it is to balance insulin action to activity and diet. People with Type I diabetes must learn to be consistent in their food intake, exercise regularly and self-administer insulin shots as needed, in correct doses. Those with diabetes are nonetheless encouraged to lead normal lives — to play, work, study, see friends, go on trips and enjoy family life.

Treatment aims to mimic or duplicate as closely as possible the body's normal control of blood sugar, with insulin doses geared to prevent fluctuations in blood sugar. Very recent studies confirm that intensive therapy to keep blood sugar levels as normal as possible *markedly* lowers the risk of diabetic complications such as eye and kidney problems. "These results," notes one researcher, "show that more frequent insulin injections, better monitoring and stricter diets can halve the rate of major complications, including blindness, kidney failure and nerve damage."

Insulin is available in short-, medium- or

long-acting forms. Thanks to recombinant engineering, besides beef (cow) and pork (pig) insulin, there is now also a human variety that causes fewer skin and allergy problems, although it's shorter-acting. However, human insulin is more expensive than animal-based products and provides neither better control nor fewer serious complications. The action of different insulins peaks at varying times after injection, and mixtures can be geared to individual diet, activity and lifestyle.

Many people with diabetes achieve the best control by using a mixture of fast- and intermediate-acting forms, prescribed to their particular needs. Insulin requirements increase at times of stress, illness or extra activity and during pregnancy. The injection site should be rotated, and experts caution about the need to watch for nighttime dips or peaks in insulin action, to avoid problems while asleep. As low blood sugar levels (hypoglycemia) can occur during sleep and go unrecognized, it is wise to check nighttime blood sugar from time to time.

Taking care of Type I diabetes is a daily ritual, not so different (time-wise) from brushing one's teeth twice daily. To get a handle on how well insulin injections are keeping blood sugar at safe levels throughout the day and night, blood must be regularly tested (before and after meals, before and after exercise) for its sugar content. This means using simple test kits, most of which register a colour change according to the amount of sugar in a drop of blood. People with Type I diabetes must also know how when and why to test for the presence of ketones in urine. (If the ketone reading is high, a doctor should always be consulted.)

New methods facilitate insulin therapy
Fortunately, insulin injections are now more tolerable, as modern devices have very fine needles that are more comfortable to use. There are also advances in ways to monitor blood glucose, easier calculation of the needed insulin dose and simpler injection devices. Keeping tabs on blood glucose levels with regular tests is now simpler and more convenient. As the traditional urine test gives only an indirect measure of blood sugar it has limited usefulness. Measuring blood sugar directly gives better control.

Modern easy-to-use home blood glucose monitors have essentially replaced the older dipstick urine tests. Blood glucose monitoring was introduced for home use in the late 1970s. Self-monitoring of blood glucose on a finger prick sample can be done with a visually read paper strip (Chemstrip) or with a small, portable meter — a major advance in diabetic management. Some people with diabetes test once a day at a specific time, others more often.

Portable meters can now read the chemical strips and show exact blood sugar levels. Most blood glucose monitors (e.g., Glucometer, Glucosan, Accucheck, One-touch, EXACTECA) are small enough to fit in a purse or a pocket and can be used almost anywhere. Some contain an electronic memory, and more advanced models even have built-in modems for transmitting the test results directly to the physician. It is wise to check the home monitor's accuracy from time to time, by doing a self-test on a blood sample that's also sent for laboratory evaluation.

There are now many innovative self-injection methods, with increasingly simpler devices. Especially popular are the new preloaded insulin-injecting "pens," about the size of a large fountain pen, which combine the needle, syringe and a vial of insulin all in one and can be carried in the pocket. The small, lightweight insulin pens (e.g., Novolin Pen and B-D Pen) are plastic devices with a screw mechanism that dials up the necessary dose and injects the needed insulin through the skin with a simple click. The pens are especially useful for intensive control requiring frequent insulin shots. (Their disadvantage is that pens are costlier and, being preloaded, they don't allow for individual mixing or adjustment of slow- and fast-acting insulins.)

Other new ways to administer insulin include small pumps that infuse a steady supply or doses at regular times, either implanted or worn on the belt or inside the clothes, which suit some people but give no better control than multiple daily injections.

Type II or non–insulin-dependent diabetes mellitus (NIDDM)
Once called "maturity" or "adult-onset" diabetes but now labeled non–insulin-dependent

diabetes mellitus (NIDDM), this form tends to develop gradually in later life. By age 65, it affects 10 percent of the North American population, much of it going undiagnosed. Many people with Type II diabetes have none of the usual symptoms (frequent urination, vision problems, tingling of arms, legs or feet and slow healing) and therefore remain oblivious to the problem for years, until complications begin to appear. Owing to the diuretic effect produced by elevated blood glucose, frequent urination may be an alerting symptom, but the condition is usually diagnosed by a routine blood test. A high reading of a fasting blood sugar test confirms the diagnosis. In women, elevated circulating glucose often leads to recurrent vaginal yeast infections.

The strongest factors predisposing people to NIDDM are a family history of diabetes and obesity, the risks being almost directly proportional to body weight. In North America, 80 percent of those diagnosed are overweight (but the condition can also develop in lean individuals).

About a third of those with Type II diabetes control the disease by weight loss and diet alone, but others need medication. Oral medications work for another third with Type II, who have a pancreas that still manufactures some insulin — by "whipping" it into producing more. Oral medications for Type II diabetes include the *sulfonylureas* (such as DiaBeta, Glyburide), which stimulate the pancreas to make more insulin, and the *biguanides* (such as Metformin), which increase insulin sensitivity and induce the body's cells to take up glucose faster. The medication prescribed depends on the person's blood sugar levels, weight and exercise habits. After a while, oral antidiabetic agents often lose their effectiveness and insulin injections may be needed.

It's a mistake to think of Type II as "mild" diabetes just because routine insulin injections aren't needed to sustain life. Some people with NIDDM suffer devastating complications similar to those with insulin-dependent diabetes — increased risks of heart attack, stroke, peripheral vascular disease and amputation.

Gestational diabetes (in pregnancy)

Gestational diabetes affects 2 to 5 percent of pregnancies and in Canada pregnant women are advised to have screening tests — especially those who are obese, have a family history of diabetes, or are of advancing age — for the condition during weeks 24–28 of gestation. In some pregnant women, diabetes develops for the first (and only) time and seems to differ somewhat from types I and II. In pregnancy, two things may trigger diabetes: first, weight gain, second, the production of certain hormones (such as cortisol and placental lactogen) in quantities that alter the way insulin works, making blood sugar levels rise and perhaps tipping a predisposed woman into a transient diabetic state. Older, overweight diabetic women are at greater risk of producing *macrosomic* (large but immature) infants. A baby born to a diabetic mother, although very large (4.5 kg or 10 lb), may have immature organs and suffer the complications of prematurity.

Gestational diabetes demands close attention to diet, fetal surveillance, careful monitoring of blood sugar and, if all else fails, insulin therapy. If blood sugar levels cannot be normalized (and occasionally even if they are), complications may arise during pregnancy. New research suggests that the condition is due to enhanced resistance to insulin rather than to full-fledged diabetes and that the fetal risks may have been overestimated. Gestational diabetes may vanish after delivery but recur in subsequent pregnancies. Statistics from the Canadian Diabetes Association show that, after giving birth, about 30–40 percent of women with gestational diabetes eventually develop Type II diabetes.

Women who already have diabetes and wish to become pregnant should get preconception counseling, plan their pregnancy carefully and make sure to get their diabetes well under control first. With adequate control of blood sugar, they have as good a chance of successful pregnancy outcomes as nondiabetics.

The many possible complications of diabetes

The main risk of diabetes lies in the long-term complications such as retinopathy (eye damage), joint alterations, growth failure in children, kidney disease, nerve degeneration, hypertension (high blood pressure), elevated cholesterol levels, heart disease and peripheral vascular (blood vessel) problems, especially in the feet.

Eye problems in diabetes arise because of bleeding from burst blood vessels in the retina, known as *diabetic retinopathy,* which can occur without warning — so those affected should have regular eye checkups. If caught in time the blood vessel may be sealed with laser treatment. The vision blurring that happens from time to time is *not* related to retinal blood flow problems, and may vanish on its own with better blood glucose control. Strict attention to blood sugar levels is believed to reduce the danger of eye damage.

The arterial blood vessel changes that commonly accompany diabetes occur for unknown reasons, possibly because high levels of circulating glucose damage the walls of large blood vessels, which develop weak spots that balloon out or build atherosclerotic plaque.

Nephropathy (kidney disease) is another complication of poorly controlled diabetes, resulting in leakage of protein into the urine, buildup of waste products in blood and blood vessel problems. Signs of kidney damage may include protein in the urine and swelling of hands and feet.

Neuropathy (nerve damage) is also a possible complication, perhaps signaled by shooting pains in the legs or feet, or by tingling (numbness) in the limbs and a diminished ability to feel pain — especially in the feet — necessitating meticulous foot care.

Treatment of diabetes

Treatment aims to keep blood sugar within acceptable limits through careful attention to diet, exercise and, when needed, through use of medications. Diabetes management includes education about the disease, attention to diet, regulated meal plans, weight control, adequate exercise, adherence to insulin or other medication regimes and help in adjusting to the disorder. Nurse educators, dietitians and other health professionals work closely with diabetics to improve good management.

One primary goal in managing diabetes is to limit blood sugar swings — preventing either hyperglycemia (high blood sugar) or transient hypoglycemia (low blood sugar). In those taking medications for diabetes, there is always a chance that an occasional excess of insulin or antidiabetic agent will cause "hyperinsulinism" and transient hypoglycemia with symptoms that may include: irritability, trembling, faintness, clammy hands, blurred vision, mood swings, personality changes, sweating, ravenous hunger (especially for sweets), headache, dizziness, nausea, as well as a staggering gait, slurred speech and drowsiness. The condition is swiftly remedied by consuming something rich in sugar, such as a couple of sugar cubes, a glass of juice, a candy or a spoonful of honey. If the hypoglycemic episodes happen often, see a physician about adjusting doses of insulin or other medications.

When a meal is unavoidably delayed, those on insulin should plan ahead and compensate by "borrowing" from the next meal or snack (perhaps nibbling some cheese and crackers). They must always be prepared for bouts of low blood sugar and carry quickly absorbed sugary snacks. As delays in restaurants are common, those with diabetes are advised to "have a little something" at home first when eating out. If blood sugar seems low, start the meal with juice as an appetizer.

When traveling, people with diabetes may need to compensate with more frequent insulin shots for the extra stress and activity, and going through time zones requires vigilance in timing meals and medication. It's wise to keep food on hand for emergencies (e.g., small cans of juice, crackers, dried fruit) to avoid low blood sugar.

Diet plays a key role in managing diabetes

Diet is critical in managing diabetes and is best prescribed by a qualified dietitian. It entails not just losing weight (for those who are overweight), but also knowing which foods to eat and when. But there's considerable debate over the best diabetic diet. Some experts feel that provided meals are regular it doesn't much matter what is eaten, while others suggest that saturated fats should be radically reduced with an accompanying increase in the intake of complex carbohydrates — to "flatten out" the post-meal rise in blood sugar.

Many specialists argue that diets low in fats and high in complex carbohydrates — once forbidden for diabetics — reduce the levels of LDL ("bad") cholesterol, moderate the post-meal rise in blood sugar and improve glucose tolerance. The latest theory is that complex carbohydrates may have beneficial effects in flattening the rise in blood sugar and/or increased sensitivity to insulin (so that smaller amounts of insulin are more effective). The Canadian Diabetes Association recommends that carbohydrates be eaten primarily in the form of legumes, grains, breads and pastas. Fibrous foods such as oat bran, lentils, beans, peas and whole and cracked wheat also retard the rise in blood sugar.

Normally the beta cells secrete insulin after each meal to encourage the entry of blood glucose into body cells so that glucose levels tend to decline between meals. But as injected insulin cannot mimic the precise and exquisite pancreatic control, the body is alternately flooded with and starved of insulin, resulting in fluctuating blood glucose levels. Missing a meal or delaying it too long may result in a dangerously low blood sugar level.

It has recently been shown that good lifelong blood glucose control can help to prevent the many diabetes-linked complications. Therefore, people with diabetes must learn to eat at regular times, with regular snacks, without overeating or skipping meals. It's a difficult regime, and many, especially teenagers, need professional counseling and careful dietary planning. Teachers should be alerted to the disorder and equipped with food and the knowledge to deal with potential problems (especially episodes of low blood sugar).

Overall, the current dogma for those with diabetes is to eat what everybody else is supposed to eat — a "heart-healthy" diet comprising 55–60 percent complex carbohydrates, about 12–25 percent protein, 30 percent or less of the total calories as fat (only 10 percent of the fat quota being the saturated type, 10 percent polyunsaturated forms, the rest monounsaturated fats) and no more than 300 mg cholesterol a day. Sucrose (refined sugar) should be kept to a prescribed minimum (usually around 50 g a day). Of the artificial sweeteners, noncalorific aspartame is considered safe, even in generous amounts. To keep this regime it's a good idea to get practical advice from a dietitian.

Exercise also crucial for good control of diabetes

Physical activity promotes the sensitivity of tissues to both insulin and other antidiabetic agents, and regular exercise can guard against or combat Type II (obesity-linked) diabetes — which accounts for three-quarters of all cases.

PRECAUTIONS FOR EXERCISING (WITH DIABETES)

- **Try to fit regular exercise into the daily routine at about the same time each day.**
- **Check blood sugar before and after exercising to determine the effect of activity.**
- **Ideally, exercise when blood glucose is within acceptable limits, because when the level is either too high or too low vigorous activity can cause problems.**

- **A sensible time to exercise is 30 minutes after a meal, when blood sugar is rising.**
- **Never exercise if blood sugar is above a certain prescribed level, or if ketones are present in blood or urine.**
- **Avoid exercising during the peak insulin action, as this is the time of greatest risk for hypoglycemia.**

- **Inject insulin into muscles that won't be worked (e.g., if cycling, inject into the abdomen rather than the thigh). Injecting insulin into or near a hardworking muscle speeds its absorption and may cause hypoglycemia.**
- **Note any signs of low blood glucose during and after exercise — for instance, dizziness, confusion or hunger.**

- **Compensate with extra food for extra activity, especially if it's strenuous (for instance, playing hockey, speed-swimming or running) — perhaps adding one fruit choice per hour of vigorous activity. Get advice on the best way to compensate for blood-sugar use while exercising.**
- **Take extra fluids or skip exercise on par-**

ticularly warm days to avoid the risk of dehydration.
- **Carry sugary snacks — such as hard candies, glucose tablets or some other readily absorbed form of carbohydrate — to use if signs of low blood glucose appear.**
- **Wear a medical alert card or bracelet to identify yourself as having diabetes.**

Exercise brings about a short-term improvement in insulin sensitivity — an improvement that disappears within a few days of discontinuing an exercise program. Exercise also helps those who are obese to lose weight, improves the blood lipid (fat) profile and may reduce the risks of cardiovascular disease — a major cause of increased mortality in those with either Type I or Type II diabetes.

The past decade has seen the publication of several large studies linking a sedentary lifestyle to NIDDM, indicating that vigorous exercise (such as running or swimming) may have a stronger protective effect than walking and other more moderate activities. Provocative evidence has emerged suggesting that the incidence of the disease tends to increase if people become markedly less active. Studies of populations in Western Samoa and the South Pacific showed a lower rate of Type II diabetes in rural islanders who led strenuous lives than in those who moved to urban areas and became less active. Harvard investigators found Type II to be less common among women who had been athletes in college than among nonathletic alumnae.

A research team at Stanford University that followed nearly 6,000 men over a period of 14 years found that those who regularly played a sport, walked or otherwise kept physically active were less likely than their sedentary counterparts to develop diabetes. Their study also showed that the risk fell by 6 percent for every 500 kilocalories of energy expended each week — approximately the energy used by a man of average size in jogging or swimming for an hour, or in walking 8 km (5 miles). Although the exact mechanism at work is unclear, exercise helps to control blood sugar levels and reduces the amount of insulin needed.

U.S. and Canadian diabetes associations urge people with diabetes to exercise regularly. But as strenuous exercise can aggravate pre-existing health problems (for example, by precipitating episodes of arrhythmia in someone with heart disease or by damaging arthritic knees), a thorough medical examination is advised before embarking on a fitness program. Proper footwear is mandatory, as diabetes can

---

FOOT CARE FOR THOSE WITH DIABETES MEANS:

- **avoiding injury by not going barefoot;**
- **washing feet daily and drying well;**
- **preventing dry skin by use of moisturizing creams;**
- **wearing clean socks daily;**
- **changing footwear often;**
- **checking inside shoes** for sharp bits or bulges;
- **avoiding thongs** (which may irritate the foot);
- **doing a daily "foot check"** for sores, blisters, scratches or any other injury;
- **filing or cutting nails straight across,** taking care to avoid nicks (if unable to see well, get someone else to keep your nails short);
- **removing calluses gently with pumice or emery boards;**
- **consulting a physician about any foot sores, pain or redness.**

---

reduce the circulation and sensation in the feet. People with diabetes must wear well-fitting shoes and inspect their feet daily for injury after exercising. Blood sugar levels must also be monitored when planning an exercise routine. Taking a few precautions can make regular physical activity a valuable component of diabetic care and help in managing the disease.

Good foot care is essential for those with diabetes

Neuropathy — nerve degeneration — puts the feet in jeopardy due to reduced circulation, increased risks of infection and loss of sensation, which obscures pain so that blisters, sores and other foot injuries don't hurt. People with diabetes must take special care of their feet, shake the shoes before donning them to remove foreign objects and do a daily inspection of the toes, heels, soles, nails and between the toes for sores, cuts, broken skin and any injuries. Many wear specially made shoes to help prevent foot problems. Rotating the shoes — not wearing the same pair all the time — is a good idea so that one part of the foot doesn't get constantly rubbed or sore.

Some recent developments

Despite an intensive search for ways to eliminate the need for insulin injections, daily insulin shots continue to be the rule for many with insulin-dependent, Type I diabetes. And if diet and drugs don't work, insulin injections may also be needed for Type II diabetes. Oral insulin is out of the question, as stomach acids destroy the hormone. Several imaginative attempts have been made to develop insulin suppositories, vaginal and anal forms, nose drops and so on, but so far without great success. For blood sugar monitoring, a machine is being developed to detect glucose levels through the skin, avoiding the need for finger pricking.

Immunosuppressants have been tried for Type I diabetes. The autoimmune process resulting in the destruction of beta cells takes several years to appear and suggests that immunosuppressive drugs given early in the disease might halt or at least slow its progress. Cyclosporin (an immunosuppressant widely used in transplant operations), started early in diabetes, can induce remission in 10 to 20 percent of young sufferers. Unfortunately, its potential side effects (kidney damage, for instance) detract from its usefulness.

The ideal situation for those with insulin-dependent diabetes would be to throw away the syringes and acquire transplanted, insulin-producing cells. Since rejection is the major problem with pancreas transplants, researchers are working on ways to protect the transplanted cells by surrounding them with a coating or microencapsulation, to protect them from the host's attacking cells. In one University of Toronto study, the cells are enclosed in a protective capsule of alginate, an extract from seaweed, and a protein called polylysine. The membrane formed by the alginate and polylysine allows free passage of nutrients and hormones, including insulin, but keeps out components of the body's immune system which could reject the cell. Encapsulated cells are injected into the liver and begin producing insulin which is released into the blood and reaches peripheral areas, in much the same way as in people without the disease.

Managing diabetes mellitus and living *with* it and not *for* it is an art, not a science, and happily even many with "poor" control remain well decades after diagnosis. By contrast, others may develop complications while maintaining "good" control. Genes (heredity) play a role in the way people respond to the disorder. Most manage to live productive lives despite the disease.

For more information contact the Canadian Diabetes Association.

EPILEPSY

Anyone who has witnessed someone having an epileptic seizure can understand why the ancients thought that it represented "a visit from the gods." It's high time to set the record straight and replace superstition with science. In fact, epilepsy is a common neurological (brain) disorder, characterized by recurrent seizures, that usually has no impact on intelligence, character or ability. It affects about one in 100 people, equal numbers of males and females, three-quarters of whom develop the condition in childhood. Most people with epilepsy manage to carry on normal, productive lives, but it can be a difficult condition for people of all ages to manage — especially for adolescents, who are simultaneously undergoing hormonal changes and struggling with emerging independence. The management of epilepsy includes correct diagnosis, evaluation and medication, as well as dealing with any associated psychosocial problems.

Understanding epilepsy

Once called the "falling sickness," the term "epilepsy" takes its name from the Greek *lepsis* meaning "a seizure" — and that's just what the disorder is: a tendency to have recurrent seizures. Epilepsy — sometimes called "seizure disorder" — is a neurological condition that predisposes the brain (or parts of it) to bursts or *paroxysms* of abnormal electrical activity.

Brain cells usually communicate in an orderly manner by means of electrochemical signals, mediated by neurochemicals which inhibit some messages, selectively allowing others through, to avoid "cross-talk" or nerve-message overload. But occasionally a group of brain cells simultaneously "fires" or discharges excess electrical signals that produce a temporary rise in electrical activity in certain parts of the brain. A seizure is thus due to a burst of electrical energy that temporarily disturbs normal brain function and may disrupt consciousness and muscular action — much as a lightning storm can disturb the electrical power supply.

The type of seizure reflects the brain areas affected by the electrical paroxysm, and the seizure may spread throughout the brain. A person with epilepsy can have more than one type of seizure. During a seizure, the body sometimes loses control of sensory systems (such as sight and hearing), breathing, body temperature and/or blood-pressure regulation, possibly also bowel and bladder action.

The causes of epilepsy

In many cases there is no identifiable cause for epileptic seizures and the condition is termed "idiopathic epilepsy." There may be a familial or genetic link: the prevalence of idiopathic epilepsy in close relatives of epileptics is about three to four times above that in the general population. (Preliminary research suggests a flaw in the short arm of chromosome number six in some cases.)

When physicians can identify a reason for the disorder, it's called "symptomatic epilepsy," and the reasons include:
- head injury;
- birth trauma (e.g., lack of oxygen, forceps delivery);
- an excess of certain drugs or toxic substances — e.g., lead or theophylline bronchodilators (used for asthma), and illicit drugs (such as cocaine);
- stroke, brain tumors and other conditions that interrupt cerebral blood flow;
- low blood sugar (hypoglycemia);
- diseases that alter the balance of blood or its chemical constituents or those that damage brain cells (such as Tay-Sachs disease, multiple sclerosis);
- high fever in infancy (a rare cause);
- serious infections of the brain (such as encephalitis, meningitis, herpes).

Not all seizures add up to epilepsy

One seizure alone does not an epileptic make. Having had one or two seizures does not mean someone has epilepsy. Eight to 10 percent of people have isolated seizures, usually in infancy or old age. For example, a very high fever will provoke seizures in 2 to 5 percent of children aged six months to five years. While childhood seizures understandably frighten parents, and may — in a few cases — go on to become epilepsy, a seizure associated with fever does not usually signal epilepsy and does not harm the child. Almost any injury or condition that affects the brain can trigger a seizure — for example, fetal injuries, birth mishaps, newborn infections, anoxia (lack of oxygen). Certain metabolic diseases such as phenylketonuria are also accompanied by seizures. Other seizures not classed as epilepsy are those due to alcohol, drug withdrawal or a result of illnesses such as meningitis or encephalitis.

In contrast to isolated seizures, epilepsy involves *recurrent* seizures, varying from infrequent — occurring once or twice a year or less — to once a month or even several times daily. In some people, certain stimulants or triggers — such as flickering lights or excitement — bring on a seizure.

An "aura" or warning sign may herald a seizure

People with epilepsy often report curious sensations before a seizure. These vary from person to person and can take many forms, including strange smells, abdominal flutters, hallucinations, illusions (distorted perception), musical sounds, a sense of dread, feelings of tension or anxiety. The type of aura may help to pinpoint the abnormally reacting brain site. Odd smells may indicate that the medial temporal lobe is involved; strange sounds may indicate injury to the hearing area of the brain and so on.

The aura may occur far enough in advance to give the person time to lie down, thereby avoiding possible injury. An aura can occur without a seizure following, which may in some cases constitute a simple partial seizure.

Diagnosing epilepsy

Correct diagnosis and evaluation are imperative for the treatment of seizures. Disorders commonly mistaken for epilepsy include hysterical outbursts (psychogenic seizures), transient ischemic attacks (ministrokes) and migraine headaches. Studies show that one-fifth of those referred to epilepsy clinics have pseudoseizures — not true epilepsy. Correct diagnosis depends on careful history-taking — preferably with a description of the seizure by someone who witnessed it — blood tests, neurological and electroencephalogram (EEG) exams to detect

---

STAGES OF AN EPILEPTIC SEIZURE:

- the prodome, or altered sensations occurring minutes to hours before a seizure (a rare experience);
- the aura — altered sensations or other early signs of a seizure, occurring before consciousness fades, usually seconds before a seizure (often suggesting focal onset);
- the ictus — the seizure itself;
- the postictal state — often with confusion and lethargy — following a seizure.

AN AURA MAY BE ACCOMPANIED BY:

- distorted perception ("hallucinations") of sound, sight, smell and taste;
- dreamlike experiences, floating sensation;
- distortion of time, space, memory ("*déjà vu*" experiences);
- a curious taste in the mouth, hand tingling and other sensations.

SORTING OUT THE SEIZURES

- *Simple partial seizures* (formerly known as "focal seizures") may involve strange or unusual sensations, including sudden, jerky movements of one body part, distortions in hearing or sight, stomach upsets or a sudden sense of fear. Consciousness is not impaired. If no seizure follows, these sensations may simply be called an aura.

- *Complex partial seizures* (formerly called "psychomotor" or "temporal lobe" epilepsy) are most common in adults, but can occur at any age. They are characterized by complicated "automaton-like" actions and altered consciousness. Complex partial seizures are so termed because they affect complex cerebral functions rather than just muscular actions. In this type of seizure, memory usually fades, there's a loss of awareness and some impairment of learning and perception, but no drop attacks or falling episodes. Typically, the person seems dazed and confused, appears irritable and edgy, with glassy eyes

and ceaseless fidgeting, often performing purposeless actions such as random walking, mumbling, head turning or pulling at clothing. During the seizure some experience numbness of hands or feet, a choking sensation, sweating, strange, "*déjà vu*" dreams or visions. In some people, this seizure may consist merely of staring and a little lip-smacking and can be confused with absence seizures. After the episode, the person often has no memory of it and is usually sleepy.

Although not violent, someone with complex partial epilepsy may struggle or fight if impeded during a seizure. This type of epilepsy is renowned because of its use as a defense ploy by some people accused of criminal actions: since the person supposedly had no awareness of what happened, the defense may argue that he or she bears no responsibility for the crime. However, most people with this form of epilepsy are not violent and during a seizure can

not perform complicated actions such as robbing, hitting or killing others.

- *Absence (formerly called "petit mal") seizures* are characterized by 5- to 10-second lapses in consciousness, during which the person stares mindlessly into space with the eyes rolling upwards. Most common in children aged 4 to 12, the seizure has a loss of consciousness, but no aura, no falls or drop attacks, just a lack of awareness during the attack. A child may simply appear momentarily blank, with blinking eyes, facial twitching, odd finger movements, confusion and inattention — as though daydreaming. However, unlike a daydreamer, the child *cannot* be aroused. Some children have several such brief seizures during the course of a day, without knowing it, with total amnesia (forgetfulness) afterwards. One-third of childhood absence seizures stop in adolescence.

- *Tonic-clonic (formerly "grand mal") seizures*, in which the brain is swamped with "elec-

trical overload," involve two phases. In the tonic phase, the individual loses consciousness, goes stiff and falls. The muscles go into spasm and the body becomes rigid. In the clonic stage, the limbs jerk repeatedly and twitch. Tonic-clonic seizures may just affect part of the body, but more often the entire body goes rigid, shakes and trembles. In this most dramatic of seizures, the person may cry out (not in fear or pain but as a reflex reaction when air is forced out of the lungs), contort the face, lose consciousness and fall to the ground. The person may briefly stop breathing and go blue. There may be some drooling, biting of cheeks or tongue and possibly loss of bladder and bowel control. Tonic-clonic seizures that begin locally (with a partial seizure) are usually preceded by an aura. Tonic-clonic seizures rarely last longer than a minute (averaging 40 seconds) and, although frightening to watch, generally pass without inflicting any harm —

unless the head is hit, the seizure happens while swimming or driving, for example, and leads to some other injury, or if the person chokes on vomit. After the seizure, consciousness slowly returns and the person may become limp and confused, usually falling into a deep sleep.

- *Status epilepticus* represents serial seizures — one after another — without recovery in between, the person coming partly out of one seizure and going into another. This is an emergency situation that risks permanent brain injury or death, and the person must promptly receive medical attention.

Besides these main types of epileptic seizure, other subtypes include atonic or "drop attacks," procursive epilepsy (a complex-partial form with a curious, swift running behavior), photogenic epilepsy (triggered by flickering lights such as strobe lights, television or video games) and musicogenic epilepsy (set off by certain types of music).

patterns of increased brain activity. (The EEG procedure samples brain-wave activity via small electrodes placed on the scalp.) Additional tools for diagnosis include brain imaging with CAT (computerized axial tomography) scans, magnetic resonance imaging, single photon emission, computerized tomography and positron emission tomography.

New classification of seizures

The frequency and form of seizure vary greatly from person to person. Because there are so many nuances in epilepsy and so many different kinds of seizure (over 30 types), a new classification system has been established by the International League against Epilepsy (ILAE), which aims to replace outdated seizure terminology such as "grand mal" and "petit mal."

According to the new classification, there are two basic types of epilepsy:

- *generalized epilepsy* — where the seizure activity spreads throughout the brain, disabling large areas of consciousness, even if the attack begins as a focal (local) burst of abnormal electrical activity;
- *partial epilepsy* — where specific, localized areas of the brain are affected and the abnormal electrical activity is confined to a small area — a condition possibly arising from a head blow or injury, birth complications, meningitis, encephalitis, central-nervous-system infection or other identifiable causes.

The distinction between "partial" and "generalized" seizures is the key to the new classification. In focal or partial seizures, the most frequently encountered type, the electrical overstimulation is confined to a small brain area without any loss of consciousness. But if the seizure activity involves centers of consciousness on both sides of the brain, with loss of consciousness, it is said to be generalized. But even a generalized seizure may produce so minor a change in function that the person having the seizure is unaware of anything wrong, as happens in "absence" (formerly called "petit mal") seizures.

Treatment of epilepsy

Treatment is primarily with anticonvulsant medications that aim to control the seizures and help the person to carry on a normal life — participating in usual activities, including most sports. Many different anticonvulsants are now available. The medications dampen the hyper-excitable areas of the brain, mute nerve conductivity and lessen the frequency and likelihood of seizures. They allow many people to achieve prolonged remission — sometimes just with one medication. (Remission is defined as "freedom from seizures for two to five years.") In 50–60 percent of those with epilepsy, correct medication eliminates all seizures, and another 30 percent obtain enough control to work and live normally. The chances that epilepsy will vanish or go into remission are greatest during the first few years after diagnosis. If the seizures have not diminished or disappeared after five years, chances of complete remission fade.

Those who have problems with one anti-seizure medication can try another. Finding the right medication and its dosage can take some time. The medication should be taken as prescribed and never stopped abruptly. Typical side effects depend on the drug used and may include unsteadiness, sleepiness/drowsiness, skin rashes and poor concentration. Other side effects, which lessen over time and vary from one medication to another, may include tremor, weight gain and nausea. Side effects may also include vision blurring and dizziness — calling for a change of dose and/or a different drug. About 20 percent of cases of epilepsy resist medication.

People with seizure disorders often need lifelong medication. But neurologists believe that anticonvulsant drugs can be stopped if seizures have vanished and the EEG is normal. If someone goes for about two years without a seizure, the medications may be slowly tapered off. But epilepsy drugs should never be suddenly stopped, as this may prompt a series of seizures that could be fatal.

Unfortunately, about a third of those who stop their medication will have repeat seizures during withdrawal, requiring reinstatement of drug therapy. Once the pills are stopped, 30 percent ultimately experience recurrent seizures and must go back on the medication. Emotional stress, drugs, alcohol and lack of sleep can provoke repeat seizures. If medication is stopped and seizures are allowed to continue unhalted, the condition may worsen. New anticonvulsant drugs are appearing all the time, and research has recently produced 17 new medications currently being tested.

EPILEPSY MEDICATIONS INCLUDE:

- phenobarbital (Luminal);
- ethosuximide (Zarontin);
- primidone (Mysoline);
- phenytoin (Dilantin);
- valproic acid (Depakene or Epival);
- carbamazepine (Tegretol);
- clobazam (Frisium);
- clonazepam (Rivotril).

FIRST AID — WHAT TO DO FOR SEIZURES

For tonic-clonic ("grand mal") seizures:
- Remain calm.
- Let the seizure run its course. You cannot stop a seizure once it has started. Do not try to revive or restrain the person. People having seizures don't know what they're doing and their body movements can be very powerful.
- Ease the person to the ground; loosen tight clothing.
- Remove glasses.
- Turn the head to one side to allow saliva to drain out. Do *not* put anything into the person's mouth.
- Remove any hard, sharp or hot objects that might injure the person. If the casualty is in a dangerous position (for example, at the top of a flight of stairs), you may be able to drag him or her a few feet away by the clothing, but be careful.
- After the seizure, allow the person to rest or sleep.
- After resting, most people can carry on as before. If the person is not at home and still seems groggy, weak or confused, it may be best to accompany him or her home.
- If a child has a seizure, contact the parents or guardian; if they are not available, be sure they are notified later.
- Allow the seizure to stop on its own. If it lasts more than five or ten minutes, call for emergency medical services (dial 9-1-1).
- If the person starts to bleed from the mouth, do not panic. He or she has probably bitten the tongue and is not bleeding internally.
- Do not be frightened if the person appears to stop breathing for a few seconds only. This is to be expected.
- If the person undergoes a series of seizures, with each new one occurring before consciousness is regained, immediately seek emergency medical assistance.
- Do not attempt resuscitation unless the person fails to start breathing again once the seizure stops. If this happens, begin artificial respiration and call an ambulance.
- When the seizure is over (if not possible before), place the person in the "recovery position" (see chapter 17) to keep the airway open and prevent the possibility of breathing vomitus or saliva into the lungs.
- After a tonic-clonic ("grand mal") seizure, the person should be checked by a physician so that any injuries may be detected or necessary adjustments made in the medication.
- After the seizure, stay close by and reassure the person once he or she is awake.
- Do not give food or drink until fully awake.
- Record the seizure's duration.

For complex partial ("psychomotor") seizures:
- Do *not* restrain. Protect from injury by moving away sharp or hot objects.
- If wandering occurs, stay with the person and talk quietly and reassuringly.

For simple partial (focal) seizures:
- No first aid required.

For absence ("petit mal") seizures:
- No first aid required.

Brain surgery may be advised for some

Pioneered largely at Montreal's Neurological Institute in the 1930s, brain surgery for focal epilepsy can in certain cases remove the damaged area and alleviate seizures. But surgery is tried only when medication fails to control seizures, and only in certain cases where the injured brain tissue causing seizures is confined to a small area (usually with partial-complex seizures originating in the temporal lobe) and can be safely removed without damaging personality or function. Those most suitable are people in whom the damaged area is easily pinpointed. For the 20 percent of those with partial epilepsy who don't improve with medication, surgery can be a savior, and significantly improve the quality of life. Many neurologists believe that the technique is underused, especially as advances in epilepsy-monitoring and imaging techniques have greatly improved the chances of surgical success by more accurately locating the "hot-spots" responsible for seizures. Many neurological centers report that about 50 percent of those who undergo surgery for epilepsy are seizure-free after the operation and another 25–30 percent show significant improvement. Neurological problems following epilepsy-relieving surgery are uncommon — occurring in about 1 percent of cases.

Women with epilepsy contemplating pregnancy need counseling

Women with epilepsy who want to have babies must achieve good seizure-control. Provided this is done, risks can be minimized. They should discuss the risks with their physician before conception and may require careful monitoring during gestation. A change in medication may be advised; taking anticonvulsants during pregnancy may put the fetus at slightly higher risk of malformation, due either to the epilepsy itself or to the anticonvulsant medications. (The danger isn't excessive — it is a 6 to 10 percent risk of fetal malformation compared to the usual 2 percent risk.) As a rule, the fewer anticonvulsant medications used while pregnant the better.

Living with seizures

Although medication allows most people with epilepsy to lead normal lives, common sense suggests a few precautions. For example, activities such as contact sports may be risky if there's a chance of hitting the head. Those prone to sudden seizures without warning must be wary while cooking (burns are common in these cases). People with epilepsy must also take care in baths, boating or swimming, as deaths by drowning are a distinct risk. (Many experts promote showers as safer than baths for those with seizure disorder.) Of the many annual bathtub drownings in North America, almost half the victims have a history of seizure disorder. Wearing a lifejacket while boating is a wise precaution for those who have seizures, as for everyone. Driving regulations vary from place to place but have been largely standardized in Canada: people who have been seizure-free for 12 months or more and are under good medical supervision are usually licensed. Physicians are legally required to report individuals with seizures if driving poses a hazard. Licenses may be suspended until the seizure recurrences subside, and reinstated after 12 seizure-free months.

People with epilepsy are barred from some activities (such as airplane piloting) and may be well advised to avoid occupations that necessitate the use of dangerous machinery or put themselves or others at risk. But employers should remember that people with seizure disorders do *not* necessarily have more accidents than others on the job, nor do they take more time off work. Hiring those with epilepsy has no effect on the assessment rates charged to employers for Workers' Compensation. Those who believe they have been victimized by employment discrimination should seek legal advice.

While epilepsy is a medical problem, someone with seizures must also make a number of emotional adjustments, primarily accepting the diagnosis and sticking with the medication prescribed. Initially, people diagnosed with epilepsy (and their families) may experience shock or denial. Anger, fear and depression are common. However, given information and support, people with epilepsy can understand the condition and develop coping skills. Family and friends may be overprotective or impose needless restrictions, making the person lose confidence and feel useless. It is important to remember that most people with epilepsy can and do live full, productive lives. Open discussion with friends, family and professional counselors can help people overcome hurdles. Epilepsy sufferers can also take heart from the burgeoning research on new treatments and the many new seizure-control drugs appearing on the horizon. The more medications available, the greater the chance that one will control the seizures.

For further information on epilepsy, contact your local Epilepsy Association or the neurology department of a local hospital.

CARE OF ADOLESCENTS WITH SEIZURE DISORDERS

- Eliminate myths about epilepsy.
- Reassure the teenager that:
  - the condition is not contagious;
  - the seizures may disappear or become less frequent with age;
  - most seizures can be controlled with medication;
  - epilepsy does not lower intelligence;
  - it's still possible to participate in most activities;
  - there is no need for special schooling.
- Keep an accurate record of seizures.
- Know what to do for a seizure.

For further information on epilepsy, contact your local Epilepsy Association or the neurology department of a local hospital.

GALLBLADDER PROBLEMS

A normally functioning gallbladder stores bile (digestive juice) produced by the liver; after a meal, the pear-shaped gallbladder contracts to move the bile through the common bile duct into the small intestine, where it mixes with food to help digest fat. Gallbladders can become diseased, resulting in gallstones, which occur in 20 percent of women and 10 percent of men by age 60. The tendency to form gallstones is partly inherited and is more common in the obese or those who lose weight rapidly through extreme diets (which release a flood of fat and cholesterol into the bloodstream). In many people gallstones remain "silent" and undetected, but if the gallstones move into the smaller, funnel-like end of the gallbladder or enter the narrow bile duct, they can block the flow of bile and cause severe pain.

When gallstones need treatment

If the gallbladder contracts against a stone, it causes biliary colic, a characteristic, severe pain in the upper abdomen or under the breastbone which may radiate to the right upper abdomen and into the back. Biliary colic is the only specific symptom of uncomplicated gallstones. It often occurs after eating fatty foods and typically awakens people in the middle of the night. While "silent gallstones" are best left alone, even a single episode of biliary colic indicates a stone that may cause complications and must be treated. If a gallstone becomes lodged in the narrow bile duct, the flow of bile from the liver may be blocked, causing jaundice, liver infection or inflammation of the pancreas — illnesses that can occasionally be life-threatening.

The most effective remedy for gallstones is removal of the gallbladder (cholecystectomy). While traditional open surgery is highly successful with minimal risks, most people dread the discomfort of a large abdominal incision, the six-day hospital stay and the six-week recuperation period, and so the newer, less invasive laparoscopic cholecystectomy is more popular. This new technology permits a return home the day after surgery, and, in most cases, return to work in one to two weeks. The financial benefits are also considerable: about $2,000 less than an open gallbladder operation.

Very few people with gallstones are now considered unsuitable for laparoscopic surgery, but one condition that still makes the operation inadvisable is cholangitis (stones in the bile duct causing inflammation). In some cases, however, stones lodged in the duct can be removed with an endoscope and the gallbladder taken out via laparoscope a day or two later. Open surgery remains the favored choice for people who have more than one of the following: previous abdominal surgery, gallbladder inflammation, disorders that hinder distention of the abdomen, certain liver diseases and portal hypertension (high blood pressure within the liver).

Other treatment options

Other new treatments available for gallstones include dissolution therapy (using drugs) and shock-wave lithotripsy (shock waves that smash the gallstones so that they can be naturally excreted or dissolved with drugs). However, dissolution therapies have not been as

---

GALLBLADDER OPERATIONS NOW SIMPLER

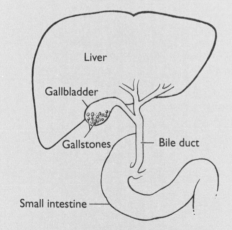

First reported in June 1988, the surgical technique of laparoscopic cholecystectomy is now the surgical procedure of choice for gallbladder removals, since it requires only four small incisions. Fine tubes are inserted into the abdomen, permitting the surgeon to view the gallbladder and surrounding internal structures without opening up the belly. The abdomen is inflated with carbon-dioxide gas to form a hollow cavity, and the laparoscope, fitted with a light and camera, is inserted through the tube at the navel. The camera, connected to a video monitor, gives the surgeon a superb magnified view that is actually more detailed than that in open surgery. The operating instruments dissect tissues, clip off the cystic artery and duct, cauterize (burn away) the tissue holding the gallbladder in place and then remove it via the opening near the navel.

successful as hoped, since, if the gallbladder remains, stones often recur. Only 15 to 20 percent of patients have the type of gallstones that qualify for shock-wave lithotripsy — usually a single, small stone 1–2 cm (half a inch to an inch) in diameter. Possible complications of the treatment include recurrent pain, and infection and/or inflammation of the pancreas, gallbladder and bile ducts caused by residual fragments.

HEADACHES

Most headaches are transient annoyances that disappear by themselves or with the help of mild painkillers such as ASA (e.g., Aspirin) or acetaminophen (e.g.,Tylenol). But for one person in 10, a headache is an excruciating experience, and in a few rare cases a headache may herald some serious disorder. About 15 percent of the population has headaches severe or frequent enough to consult a physician. Even children get headaches, some well before the age of 10. Before puberty, headaches are more common in boys. But in adults, headaches are four times more prevalent in women and often linked to menstrual fluctuations. In both sexes the severity and frequency of headaches decline with advancing years. Although many of us call any headache a "migraine," only about a quarter of all headaches are true migraines.

While the vast majority of headaches don't signal serious diseases, some do require prompt medical investigation.

Tension headaches afflict most of us occasionally, particularly when we're overtired, rushed, anxious, emotionally upset or harassed. Tension contracts the muscles of scalp, jaw, neck, shoulder and face, possibly causing the headache. Generally described as pressure or a "dull ache" — usually all over rather than on one side of the head — tension headaches are said to occur in "uptight" people with "uptight" muscles. They can also stem from undue fatigue, eyestrain or sitting for prolonged periods in one position, such as over a computer or behind a steering wheel.

Tension headaches typically appear in the late teens or early twenties, and in contrast to migraines are not hereditary, are not usually one-sided and have no clear-cut onset or

HEADACHES THAT DEMAND MEDICAL ATTENTION
• those that come on suddenly in middle age;
• those that strike like a "bolt from the blue" with unbearable intensity;
• those accompanied by seizures, loss of consciousness, mental confusion;
• those accompanied by fever and/or a stiff neck (which could signal meningitis);
• recurrent headaches;
• those that relentlessly worsen over days or weeks;
• those localized to one spot — ears, eye or one side of the head;
• those accompanied by impaired function such as imbalance or double vision (which could signify a stroke);
• those at the back of the head;
• those worst early in the morning and lightening during the day (could be due to high blood pressure).

ending, one headache merging imperceptibly into the next. Tension headaches are typically worst at the end of the day. Since the reason for them is often obvious, self-treatment — avoiding or eliminating the stressful situation, taking some over-the-counter remedy, relaxing, exercising — usually suffices. But if they continue or worsen, medical help is needed.

Sinus headaches usually occur with or following nasal congestion and disappear once the sinusitis is cleared up with antibiotics or other treatment.

"Cluster headaches," an uncommon acute form, far more prevalent in men than women, come on and vanish very quickly. They are typically accompanied by a stuffy nose, tearing eyes, almost unbearable pain but no nausea. They tend to occur in clusters — over a few days, weeks or months — are nonhereditary and not stress-related, and are often triggered by alcohol. They respond poorly to most medication, although lithium, methysergide and calcium channel blockers help some cases.

"Ice pick" headaches, of unknown cause, are sudden severe headaches that hit at a small, localized spot.

Migraine is no ordinary headache
Migraine, which ranges from mild to severe, often occurs as one-sided head pain but sometimes on both sides, even in those who usually have it on just one side. Its location, intensity and duration vary widely, not only from person to person, but also within each individual. Migraine is no recent affliction — Hippocrates was one of the first to describe it. Many famous people, such as Karl Marx,

DIFFERENT HEADACHES HAVE DIFFERENT FEATURES

	Muscle-contraction headache	Common migraine	Classic migraine	Cluster headache
Incidence	very common	common	not common	uncommon
Age of onset	15–40	19–30		20–40
Sex	more females	more females		mostly males
Family history of headache	frequent	very frequent		infrequent
Headache frequency	variable, can be daily	variable, but "never" daily		daily during cluster
Possible triggers	stress or fatigue	stress, fatigue, menstruation, oral contraceptives, certain foods, alcohol, weather changes, bright lights, odors		alcohol if taken during cluster
Exacerbating factors	stress or fatigue	movement, head jarring, low head position		none
Onset during sleep	extremely rare	not uncommon		typical
Warning signs	none	none	visual or sensory aura	none
Location	bilateral (both sides of head)	often unilateral (one side of head), sometimes bilateral		unilateral
Severity	mild to moderate	moderate to severe		extremely severe
Accompaniments	none	nausea, sometimes vomiting, light and noise aversion		redness and tearing in one eye, stuffiness and dripping in one nostril, on same side as affected eye
Duration	hours to days	hours to all day — seldom more than two days		20–90 minutes

Charles Darwin and Sigmund Freud, were "migraineurs." About 10 to 12 percent of the population suffers from migraine, half developing it before age 20, some during early childhood. Migraine headaches afflict more women than men, often occurring just before or during menstrual periods and usually waning after the menopause. In about 75 percent of those afflicted there is a clear family connection — parents, siblings, children or other relatives being fellow-sufferers. In fact, a family history of migraine is often the most telling clue to its diagnosis.

Some suffer only the occasional migraine; others have it as often as twice a month or more. Migraine is typically experienced as a pulsating pain on one side of the head, commonly accompanied by other symptoms such as nausea, vomiting and possibly visual disturbances. Each episode lasts 2 to 72 hours —averaging 12–18 hours — and may be incapacitating enough to disrupt daily activities. Some people retire to rest in a dark room until it's over.

During a migraine attack the body may swell with retained fluid, and appetite wanes. Sufferers feel wretched and often have a strong aversion to noise, light and certain smells. The end of an attack is marked by a rewarming of the limbs and return of appetite. There are seldom any aftereffects.

Recent investigations have linked migraine to fluctuations in a brain neurotransmitter called serotonin. Other research suggests that many migraineurs also have below-normal amounts of endorphin — the body's natural painkiller — making them ultra-sensitive to pain.

Despite the misery of migraine and the new drugs available to relieve it, reports show that over half of the sufferers receive no or inadequate medical counseling; many don't consult or fail to return to their physician for follow-up, instead trying to self-medicate with over-the-counter remedies. Some people endure headaches for many years before seeking medical help, even though there are now many effective medications.

An aura may precede the migraine

About one in seven migraineurs experiences a clear pre-headache stage known as an aura, which lasts about 10–30 minutes and typically includes visual disturbances such as jagged blind spots, zigzag flashes, shimmering sparks or size distortion. Some auras also feature a transient tingling or numbness on one side of the face and/or body, speech defects and fleeting incoherence. Normally the aura clears as the headache starts, but there can be some overlap. Many experience other pre-headache symptoms, such as elation, depression, unusual chattiness, voracious hunger, or specific food cravings.

During the aura of classic migraine, blood flow to the brain is decreased, but after about 20 minutes the blood flow rises to above-normal levels, and the increased circulation is associated with the headache phase. However, since the increased blood flow may outlast the headache by days, the headache cannot be due to the raised blood flow alone. Migraine is now seen as a central-brain problem, and the blood-flow changes are considered secondary to the initial events. Pain-causing chemicals such as bradykinin and inflammatory agents like prostaglandins are known to accumulate near the distended vessels and probably play some role.

In the most common forms of migraine there's no real aura, although many have some warning hints that may permit them to take evasive action in time to avert a full-fledged headache. Excitability and mood swings can occur a day or two before migraine appears.

Triggers may provoke migraine attacks

Despite popular misconception, most migraines have no obvious, provocative cause, although some people can cite specific triggers that bring on their headache. The triggers vary from person to person and may not be consistent for the same individual. Reported migraine triggers include weather changes, hunger, certain foods, perfumes, bright lights, intense noise, strong emotions, stress, allergies, menstrual

fluctuations and too little sleep. Extreme fatigue can be the reason, as can "sleeping in" on the weekend. While stress is a migraine-provoker, paradoxically relaxation is also a frequent trigger. The headache often appears *after* the week's stress, producing the weekend migraine typical among busy professionals.

Curiously, migraines tend to disappear temporarily in times of extreme stress or physical duress — during life-threatening illnesses or other crises and in wartime, for example. Migraine is common in general hospital patients but is seldom seen in intensive-care units.

Treatment to relieve migraine

Migraine treatment involves identifying and avoiding any triggers (if possible), and using suitable medication and strategies such as biofeedback and hypnosis. Black coffee or caffeine can help to offset a migraine headache in some people, provided it's taken as soon as the migraine is felt coming on.

Medications include:

Pain relievers such as ASA and acetaminophen, which can mute or abort the headache if taken early enough, in high enough doses, possibly together with an antinauseant such as dimenhydrinate or metoclopramide. (Adding codeine may help.)

Ergot alkaloids such as Cafergot and Migral, which help many if taken soon enough, but are not effective once the headache has taken hold. In excess, especially with poor timing, these medications may exacerbate rather than vanquish a headache.

Beta blockers such as propranolol (Inderal) — commonly used heart medications — which give relief in about 50 percent of cases (by their effect on cerebral blood vessels).

Pizotyline (Sandomigran), which blocks serotonin and histamine release and has had varying success rates.

Methysergide (Sansert), a potent anti-migraine drug which must be used with extreme caution, and only with strict medical supervision.

Calcium channel blockers, which alter narrowing and dilation of blood vessels.

Nonsteroidal anti-inflammatory drugs and low-dose antidepressants (such as amitriptyline), now under investigation.

DISTINGUISHING FEATURES OF A MIGRAINE HEADACHE:

- pulsating, throbbing pain;
- on one side of the head only;
- worsened by normal body movements;
- possibly accompanied by nausea, vomiting, sensitivity to light.

COMMONLY REPORTED MIGRAINE TRIGGERS:

- weather fluctuations — particularly low barometric pressure;
- certain drugs, caffeine and alcohol — particularly beer and red wine;
- certain foods, in a few people — especially preservatives in cured meats, chocolate and aged cheeses;
- allergies;
- anxiety, lack of sleep;
- hormonal changes (in women).

Sumatriptan (Imitrex), a new, rapidly effective remedy that works on the serotonin and 5-HT (5-hydroxytryptamine) neurotransmitter systems thought to be involved in migraine. The drug is available by prescription and can be used at any stage of a migraine, either as tablets or by self-injection, apparently bringing relief within half an hour — but it is expensive and may have adverse effects on those with cardiovascular and heart problems. Although claims for the drug suggest it affects *only* blood vessels in the head (constricting them), new evidence shows that it can produce chest pain or tightness and may pose a danger to people with any cardiac dysfunction.

To learn more about migraine, contact a neurologist or the Migraine Foundation.

HEART DISEASE

The heart is a fist-sized, hollow, muscular pump protected by the ribs and breastbone and covered by a thin, double-layered membrane, the pericardium. The heart normally contracts about 70–75 times a minute, pumping fresh oxygenated blood around the body, and its muscular wall, the myocardium, is strong enough to propel blood through the entire body. The heart's four chambers are the upper, thin-walled atria (which receive incoming blood) and the stronger-walled lower ventricles (which do the pumping). These four chambers are connected by valves that allow the blood to flow in one direction only. The heartbeat is divided into two main parts — the *diastole* (the relaxation phase) and the *systole* (the contraction or pumping phase).

STRUCTURE OF THE HEART AND ITS VESSELS

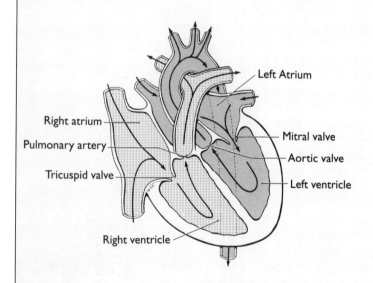

The heart is made up of four chambers: right atrium, left atrium, right ventricle, left ventricle. The right atrium receives blood (dark bluish, deoxygenated) from the body and passes it through the tricuspid valve to the right ventricle, which pumps blood out through the pulmonary valve to the lungs where it absorbs oxygen. The oxygenated blood returns to the heart's left atrium, then passes via the mitral valve into the left ventricle. The left ventricle pumps oxygenated (bright red) blood out through the aortic valve into the

aorta from which it is distributed to all parts of the body, delivering oxygen to the tissues.

The arteries carry oxygenated blood to the body's cells and the veins collect deoxygenated blood. A network of capillaries connects the veins and arteries and distributes blood to the body's tissues. Arteries, which carry blood under high pressure, have thicker walls than veins, which carry blood back to the heart and lungs for oxygenation. A system of valves in the blood vessels controls the direction of flow.

Because it works hard, the heart needs a good oxygen supply, and the coronary arteries, which encircle it like a web, continually supply it. If blood flow in the coronary arteries is impaired, blocked or obstructed in any way, heart tissue is deprived of oxygen, possibly damaging the myocardium (heart muscle). A temporarily blocked coronary artery can cause angina pectoris (chest pain). If the heart's blood flow is severely diminished, or stops altogether, oxygen lack (ischemia) results, perhaps causing a myocardial infarction — a heart attack.

What is atherosclerosis or "narrowing of the arteries"?

Arteries can become obstructed through the condition known as atherosclerosis, in which a fatty sludge or "plaque" coats the inner artery walls and obstructs blood flow, forcing the heart to work harder. Atherosclerosis in the heart's own arteries may deprive the heart muscle of oxygen and result in angina or a heart attack. In the legs, atherosclerosis can cause peripheral artery disease, which may lead to phlebitis (thrombosis or clot formation). In the brain, blood-vessel obstruction due to atherosclerosis can cause strokes. Thus atherosclerosis is bad news for all the body's blood vessels, and should be prevented if possible by steering clear of avoidable triggers — such as smoking, a fatty diet, obesity and lack of exercise.

Coronary artery disease

Coronary artery disease (CAD) is the forerunner and prime cause of heart attacks. The main risk factors are: advancing years, male gender, smoking tobacco, lack of exercise, obesity, high blood-cholesterol levels and atherosclerosis. Middle-aged males have the highest incidence of coronary heart disease, risks increasing with age. Being female is a protector up to menopause, after which (because of waning estrogen levels) women acquire heart-disease rates similar to men's.

Family history also counts, especially for those with relatives who died of CAD before age 50. However, heart disease is not limited to middle-aged men whose relatives died early of

---

SOME COMMON HEART AND CARDIOVASCULAR DISEASES

- **atherosclerosis (artery narrowing, popularly called "hardening" of the arteries);**
- **coronary artery disease (leading to angina and heart attack);**
- **congestive heart failure;**
- **heart-valve defects (such as mitral-valve stenosis);**
- **cardiomyopathies (due to a damaged myocardium, or heart muscle);**
- **arrhythmias (irregular heart rhythms);**
- **pericarditis (infection of the pericardium, the heart's outer covering).**

Known risk factors for atherosclerosis and heart disease:
- **male gender;**
- **age (risk increases as people get older);**
- **family history of heart disease;**
- **tobacco smoking;**
- **diabetes;**
- **high blood pressure;**
- **high blood-cholesterol levels;**
- **lack of exercise;**
- **obesity.**

---

heart disease; nor will such people necessarily have heart disease themselves.

Narrowing or blockage of the coronary arteries through atherosclerosis is the most frequent cause of CAD. It diminishes the heart's blood supply so that the heart receives too little oxygen; it may still be able to cope at rest or during minor activities, but with more exertion — shoveling snow, running for a bus, fighting a fever, enduring stress — the heart is unable to work hard enough.

Fortunately, the risk of CAD can be lowered. The most important modifiable activity is cigarette smoking; giving up smoking alone can ameliorate CAD and slash heart-attack risks by 50–70 percent. Lowering serum cholesterol levels can also reduce risks, although people with a total cholesterol level below 180 mg/dl should stop worrying and focus on something else, such as getting enough exercise. Regular exercise (done at the right heartrate) may offset heart disease. A lower-fat diet may help to reduce blood cholesterol, reduce weight and lower blood pressure.

Whether or not someone at risk of CAD should take medications (which have side effects) to reduce the dangers depends on individual risk profiles. Many physicians now promote an "Aspirin a day" to keep heart attacks at bay — but not for those with peptic ulcer, gastritis or a tendency to easy bleeding. (See also "Strokes," later in this chapter.)

POSSIBLE SYMPTOMS OF HEART DISEASE

- chest pain or discomfort, perhaps radiating to left arm or jaw;
- difficulty breathing, shortness of breath;
- palpitations;
- dizziness/fainting;
- swelling of the legs;
- excessive fatigue.

Diagnosing CAD

Exercise stress tests may be done to find out how efficiently someone's heart can cope with the stress of exertion. In this test, the subject is wired to a machine that records heart patterns as the person works a treadmill. Pulse and blood pressure are also recorded. Changes in an ECG heart tracing during exercise may reveal areas of poor coronary circulation that spell heart trouble ahead. ECG abnormalities, combined with chest pain during exercise, may indicate coronary problems that require preventive action.

Radio-isotope scanning (with thallium) may be done at the same time as exercise stress testing. A radioactive substance injected into a vein is scanned by a computerized camera that can distinguish normal from damaged cells. The scan can provide details of heart size, capacity, sites of poor blood flow or scars from previous heart attacks. It may help predict future areas of oxygen starvation.

Coronary angiography is a well-tried and informative test, done under local anesthetic, not painful (but momentarily uncomfortable). A dye-like chemical is infused into the body through an arm vessel and X-rays display its progress through the coronary artery network, outlining areas of narrowing that may need bypass graft surgery. (See "Bypass surgery," below.)

Heart attacks (myocardial infarction)

Heart attacks due to coronary-artery disease kill thousands of North Americans, mostly men over age 40, each year. Officially termed a myocardial infarction, a heart attack results from injury to the heart muscle when its blood (and oxygen) supply is cut off or reduced. If only a small amount of heart muscle is damaged, pumping ability may return virtually to normal once healing is complete. More severe injury may leave lasting damage.

Tragically, many heart-attack deaths occur within minutes or hours — often before the person reaches hospital — usually due to disturbance of the heart rhythm (ventricular fibrillation). A heart in ventricular fibrillation does not pump enough blood to keep brain cells alive, so the person may suffer brain death

although the original problem — the heart damage — need not have been fatal. Since ventricular fibrillation is highly responsive to electric shock treatment, ambulance crews are now trained and equipped to treat it *en route* to hospital, greatly increasing survival rates.

What often happens in a heart attack is that a "thrombus," or blood clot, lodges in one or more coronary arteries and further narrows the passage. Heart attacks may also be caused (less commonly) by sudden oxygen reduction due to a drop in blood pressure during surgery, or when there is a huge increase in oxygen demand, as during extreme exertion. (Cocaine abuse is increasingly implicated in heart attacks.)

The key to successful treatment of heart attacks is to get immediate medical aid and prevent further injury. Since many conditions mimic heart attacks, diagnosis can only be confirmed in hospital with an electrocardiogram. Electronic monitors allow quick diagnosis of the heart's condition, and biochemical tests measure cardiac enzymes released into the bloodstream from dying heart cells to aid in evaluating the damage. Heart catheters give minute-by-minute readings of pressure changes in the heart's chambers and monitor pumping ability. Today, immediate infusion of a clot-busting drug — such as streptokinase or tPA (a newer, genetically engineered product) can save lives and reduce the damage done by a heart attack.

The critical phase in recovery from heart attack is the first week after the attack. About 5–10 percent of those admitted die during this time, often while still in hospital. After this, the risk of death falls significantly, but a further 5–10 percent perish within the next six months to one year. Only after that does the risk truly drop. Consequently, current efforts concentrate on improving survival chances in three crisis periods: the first hours after the heart attack, the next week and the following year.

If you suspect a heart attack in yourself or someone else, *never* delay calling for help in the vain hope that the pain will vanish. Call an ambulance or dial emergency medical services and get to the nearest hospital or medical center at once, not only to avoid sudden death, but to minimize damage to the heart. (See chapter 17 for first aid for a heart attack.)

WARNINGS OF HEART ATTACK INCLUDE:

- persistent chest pain, possibly radiating to the neck, jaw, shoulder or left arm;
- tightness ("squeezing") in the chest;
- heaviness that may feel like indigestion;
- sweating, nausea and vomiting;
- pallor;
- shortness of breath;
- denial — a refusal to believe anything is seriously wrong.

TREATMENT OF CAD AND HEART ATTACKS

- *Beta-adrenergic blockers* (beta blockers, for short) such as propranolol (Inderal), and timolol (Blocadren) can reduce heart-attack risks by slowing the heartrate and allowing the heart to get along with less oxygen.
- *Blood-thinning medications* such as ASA or Anturan, a Canadian drug also used against gout, can decrease platelet clumping and blood stickiness (clotting).
- *Calcium-channel blockers*, a relatively recent class of drugs, can be used during the first stage of a heart attack, when oxygen-deprived heart cells lose their ability to block out calcium. (Calcium dissolved in the fluid surrounding the heart cells may move inward in excessive amounts and damage the cells.) These drugs block the channels through which calcium moves into the heart and may combat coronary-artery spasms.
- *Ballooning angioplasty*, increasingly used, involves inserting a thin plastic catheter with an inflatable balloon at its tip to squash any clots or other coronary-artery obstructions. In those deemed suitable, the ballooning works well, usually relieving angina and helping to prevent a heart attack. It has the great advantage of avoiding the need for surgery. Experts have now become so skilled, with such refined equipment, that they can guide a catheter right to the blockage within a coronary artery and squash it. But time is of the essence.
- *Chemical infusion with clot-buster chemicals* is a promising new procedure for clearing blocked heart arteries during, or right after, a heart attack with an enzyme called streptokinase, or newer agents, such as tPA. New studies show that tPA is more effective in preventing heart attacks, but more expensive than streptokinase.
- *Bypass surgery*, a dramatic and astonishingly successful method of alleviating CAD, replaces blocked coronary arteries with sections of vein — usually taken from the person's leg — reinstating the heart's oxygen supply. Bypass surgery is usually planned ahead but is occasionally tried on the spot as an emergency operation for life-threatening heart blockages — but success is uncertain under such acute conditions.

It is critical for survival that life-saving treatments be started within hours — preferably in the first hour. If only a small portion of the heart muscle is damaged, the heart can limp along, or even do quite well, afterward. Following initial recovery, mortality from a subsequent heart attack remains 6 to 10 percent in the first year. Thus, the goal during that year is to prevent a second attack without encouraging the recovering person to become a "cardiac cripple."

Angina

Angina pectoris — which can be "stable" or "unstable" — occurs when the heart's oxygen needs temporarily exceed its supply. A common forerunner of heart attacks, it has similar symptoms — chest pain or heaviness and shortness of breath — often brought on by exercise, emotional upheavals, anger, stress, cold exposure, a big meal or illness. Angina may be mistaken for indigestion. The symptoms are quickly relieved by rest and medication.

Stable angina crops up at predictable and regular intervals and is usually no cause for alarm. But anyone suddenly getting angina for the first time should seek medical advice.

In unstable angina, someone with ongoing, chronic angina may find the pain increasingly severe and frequent, or triggered by less and less physical exertion — perhaps just walking across a room, instead of, as previously, running or climbing stairs. Pain control may require more and more nitroglycerin or other medication. Unstable angina of increasing severity and changing pattern calls for immediate medical attention.

Angina is usually treated with drugs that reduce the heart's oxygen demand — for example, by lowering blood pressure and

WAYS TO REDUCE HEART-ATTACK RISKS

- **Quit smoking;** within five years of cessation, former smokers lower risks by 50–70% compared to those still smoking.
- **Reduce blood-cholesterol levels;** there is a 2–3% decline in risk for each 1% reduction in serum cholesterol (levels may drop an average of 10% with diet therapy and 20% with medication).
- **Exercise more.**
- **Achieve and maintain your desirable weight.**
- **Ask your physician** about the usefulness of regular low-dose ASA (e.g., coated Aspirin) — said to achieve a 33% lowering of risk.
- **Consume one alcoholic drink daily:** conservative drinkers have 25–45% lower heart attack risks than nondrinkers (but risk rises again with higher consumption).
- **Reduce hypertension** (high blood pressure); a decline in heart-attack risk accompanies a lowered diastolic (bottom number) pressure.
- **If menopausal,** consider estrogen-replacement hormone therapy.
- **If diabetic,** try to maintain normal blood-sugar levels, which may lower heart-attack risks.

heartrate — or with drugs (beta blockers or calcium channel blockers) that slow the heartrate, or by techniques to improve coronary blood flow (bypass grafts or angioplasty).

Congestive heart failure

In this disorder, the heart weakens — usually after a heart attack or other problems that damage the heart muscle — and the ventricles can no longer deliver enough blood to the body's tissues. Fluid may back up, causing edema (swelling of the lower extremities).

Symptoms include fatigue, dyspnea (breathlessness, especially on exertion), orthopnea (breathlessness when lying down), nighttime angina, paroxysmal nocturnal dyspnea (awaking at night short of breath). The most frightening symptom is acute pulmonary edema — coughing, breathlessness, wheezing and frothy sputum — which gives sufferers the sensation of drowning. Other symptoms of congestive heart failure are swollen neck veins and swollen ankles.

Treatment depends on the underlying cause, and may involve a pacemaker to normalize the heartbeat, valve surgery and withdrawal of drugs that exacerbate the problem. Typically those with congestive heart failure must be propped on pillows to obtain relief. Rest, not exercise, is best for this disease.

Drugs used to relieve heart failure include a combination of digitalis, diuretics and vasodilators. The ACE (angiotensin-converting enzyme) inhibitors, captopril, for example, are promising and are now started earlier in the course of the disease. In severe cases, heart transplants may be considered.

Arrhythmias

Arrhythmias are abnormal heart rhythms: the heart may speed up, miss a beat or slow down. They can cause a great deal of anxiety and worry, but are mostly benign. Some people with atrial or ventricular arrhythmias may have more severe palpitations, dizziness or syncope (fainting). Serious arrhythmias should be investigated and decisions made as to whether or not to treat them. (In some cases the condition places an individual at risk for sudden death — if, for example, a more serious heart condition already exists — in which case medications may be required.)

MAJOR HEART-SAVING MEDICATIONS

- Antiplatelet-clumping agents, e.g., ASA (Aspirin), reduce the "stickiness" of platelets, thereby decreasing blood clotting in arteries (not in veins). Low-dose ASA has been found effective in preventing myocardial infarction, but it also increases hemorrhage risks, so it should be taken regularly only on a physician's advice. Dipyridamole is a more expensive drug and no more effective than ASA alone.
- Cholesterol-lowering drugs lower LDL or "bad" cholesterol, and may raise HDL ("good") cholesterol, and are sometimes used if a cholesterol-lowering diet doesn't work. Some cholesterol-lowering drugs (cholestyramine, for example) have been shown to reduce heart-attack risks, but the drugs have side effects such as bloating and constipation.
- Thrombolytic ("clot-busting") agents, e.g., streptokinase and tPA (tissue plasminogen activator), are given by infusion right after a heart attack, and have revolutionized its management. They prevent widespread heart-muscle damage and possible death, by dissolving coronary blood clots. Since they are most effective before damage is done, it is important to get to the hospital as soon as a heart attack is suspected.
- Antiangina agents, including beta blockers (such as propranolol and timolol), nitrates, calcium-channel blockers (such as verapamil and nifedipine), relieve angina, palpitations and abnormal heartbeats and decrease the risk of heart attack in people with ischemic (oxygen-depriving) heart disease. Beta blockers are often given to patients who've already had a heart attack, to prevent further attacks. Since smoking decreases the efficacy of propranolol, smokers who cannot quit should take timolol instead.
- Antiarrhythmics to stabilize the heartbeat include amiodarone, quinidine, disopyramide, digitalis.
- Anti–heart-failure drugs include diuretics such as thiazides (to prevent water retention), inotropic agents (which influence muscle contractions) such as digitalis, digoxin (to increase the force of heart-pumping contractions) and vasodilators such as ACE inhibitors. These drugs relieve the symptoms of congestive heart failure: shortness of breath, and edema. Together they may prolong life in patients with heart failure.

Bypass surgery

Today, coronary-bypass surgery is the commonest single operation performed in North America. In the United States, surgeons seem ready to operate on almost anyone with coronary-artery disease — a practice now questioned by some cardiac specialists and critics. With low risks and phenomenal results, bypass surgery is now considered no more hazardous for some patients than a gallbladder or hernia operation, with a survival rate of about 98 percent.

Although the risks vary according to age, the severity and extent of cardiovascular disease and the technical success of the bypass grafts, the chances are high that people will leave hospital with their heart pain reduced or entirely banished, at least for the time being. Many find their quality of life immensely improved and rejoice at the renewed ability to do many activities.

How long does a bypass operation take?

A bypass operation usually lasts three to six hours. One surgical team opens up the chest and connects the patient to the heart-lung machine, which circulates and oxygenates the blood, while the surgeons are at work. (The body is cooled to 20°C (68°F) during surgery so that the tissues, especially the brain, need less oxygen. The heart is stopped so that surgeons can operate on it and sew up tiny vessels.) Meanwhile, another surgical team works on the leg, removing a piece of vein. Pieces of the leg vein are used to "bypass" the obstructed coronary vessels.

Once the bypass is completed, the body is warmed up, the heart restarted, the heart-lung machine disconnected and the patient taken to the intensive care unit (ICU). The stay in the ICU is usually one to two days, slightly more if it takes longer to stabilize the heart and lungs.

BYPASS SURGERY TO REPLACE BLOCKED CORONARY ARTERIES

Bypass surgery doesn't actually cut into the heart; it involves the coronary arteries which lie on the heart's surface and have several branches. Dye injection and X-ray tests (angiograms) prior to surgery show which coronary arteries are most badly blocked. Surgeons then construct a detour, bypassing the narrowed parts of the arteries with a piece of vein from the patient's leg. One end is attached to an opening made in the coronary artery beyond the blockage, and the other end is connected to the aorta, the body's main artery, bringing fresh blood to the heart. So far there's no reliable, artificial substitute for the use of human vessels in bypass surgery.

Sometimes surgeons circumvent the blocked artery by another technique — connecting the body's mammary artery (inside the ribcage) to a healthy vessel beyond the obstruction.

Someone with severe blockage of the coronary arteries may need three, four or as many as eight bypass grafts. But until surgeons actually assess conditions inside the body, they cannot decide in advance how many they will do.

The removal of a leg vein rarely presents any long-term problems because other veins take over its function after a few months. There may be some postoperative swelling, numbness and discomfort, which soon fade.

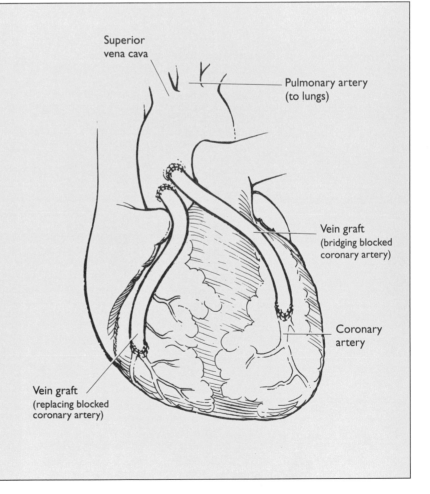

Superior vena cava

Pulmonary artery (to lungs)

Vein graft (bridging blocked coronary artery)

Coronary artery

Vein graft (replacing blocked coronary artery)

By the second day after surgery, improvement is usually sensational. Many tubes and lines are out, the patient can talk, sit up, move around and perhaps sip fluids. By about the fifth day, patients are back in their wards, taking walks along the corridor. During the rest of the hospital stay the staff try to get bypass patients onto an exercise program. By the time most go home they can take a shower, shampoo their hair, answer mail and attempt a few stairs.

Medications given to steady blood pressure and stabilize the heart rhythm are gradually tapered off. About six to ten weeks after surgery, most patients should get a thorough checkup, and perhaps an exercise stress test, before starting a cardiac rehabilitation program if they wish.

Many postbypass patients find a rehabilitation program aids adjustment after surgery. It helps diminish the postsurgical depression, lifts flagging spirits and teaches them how to exercise within safe limits.

Amazing improvement in the quality of life

Many people previously severely disabled by their angina, are amazed at their swift postsurgical improvement and the things they can do, including exercise, quite soon after a bypass operation. But for many, a heart operation still seems terrifying. The anxiety that accompanies most surgery is greater with the heart because of its symbolic significance and its image as the "center of life." Tampering with this organ seems worse than operating on other parts of the body, even though the actual risks may not be greater.

Who needs a bypass?

Those most likely to benefit from bypass surgery are individuals with disabling symptoms and severe angina unresponsive to medication; patients with left main coronary-artery blockage; those in whom atherosclerosis has narrowed three or more coronary vessels — particularly when there's an accompanying history of high blood pressure or previous heart attack; people unable to tolerate a restricted existence.

Many cardiologists believe that people with CAD who have mild symptoms or no symptoms should simply be treated with medication. Although properly controlled studies comparing surgery with medical (drug) therapy are difficult to conduct, most results suggest that bypass surgery outweighs medical therapy for some cardiac problems. However, very abnormal or defective left-ventricle (pumping) action bodes ill for the success of bypass surgery.

Bypass surgery is not a cure

Atherosclerosis is a condition that's built up over many years, aggravated by various lifestyle habits. Surgery can and often does remove the main symptom, but does not eradicate the disease itself.

Many (about two-thirds) can look forward to several years free of cardiac problems after their bypasses. Unfortunately, there are no guarantees. While about 76–90 percent have no angina one year after their bypasses, seven years later only about 40 percent remain symptom-free; angina returns owing to the unhalted progression of atherosclerotic disease in nonbypassed arteries and in the grafts.

Surgery cannot cure atherosclerosis. It's up to those who undergo bypass operations to adopt a lifestyle that helps fight their heart disease: to eat sensibly, exercise regularly, avoid stress and above all to quit smoking. Smoking is the one thing that will definitely cause artery hardening and clog up bypass grafts.

Does bypass surgery prolong life?

Surgeons from many centers maintain that the experience of over 15 years of bypass surgery indicates that patients' postsurgical lives are not only more comfortable but in some cases also prolonged. Some studies show a longer life expectancy after bypass surgery for patients who have main left-stem (coronary artery) disease, but not necessarily for other types of coronary disease. The evidence is still coming in.

For more information on heart disease, contact the Heart and Stroke Foundation.

HEART MURMURS

A heart murmur is a vibration or sound other than that of a normal heartbeat, due to unusual turbulence in the cardiac flow. Many heart murmurs are harmless variations from the norm. An estimated one in 20 people (especially women) has some kind of heart murmur, frequently of no consequence.

Distinguishing normal from abnormal heart sounds

Normal heart sounds arise from the opening and closing of the heart's four cardiac valves.

- *First heart sound* — closing of the mitral and tricuspid valves.
- *Second heart sound* — closure of the pulmonary and aortic valves.
- *Third heart sound* — early filling of blood into the right and left ventricles, which may be a normal sound in young people, but later in life may signify heart failure.
- *Fourth heart sound* — late ventricular filling, which may denote a non-compliant or "stiff" ventricle.
- *Ejection click* — opening of the aortic and pulmonary valves, often heard after the first heart sound.

Other heart sounds not directly linked to any particular valve include the *summation gallop* (in heart failure) and the *mid-systolic click* (in those with a floppy mitral valve).

The physician's task is to tell the difference between harmless or innocent murmurs that can be more or less ignored and those that signal some cardiac abnormality, such as a hole in the partition between the heart's two sides or a leaky, narrowed or otherwise malfunctioning valve. A careful checkup, taking age, character and lifestyle into account, can separate heart murmurs that need further medical investigation from those that can be ignored.

Heart murmurs in children, young adults and pregnant women are often innocent. Those that arise later in life may be serious, but many due to sclerosis (thickening) of the heart valve are also considered innocent. Many childhood murmurs fade with time, vanishing before the age of 30. Those that persist longer may warrant further investigation, such as an echocardiogram (ultrasound examination).

Some murmurs should be followed and checked every few years. For example, a murmur resulting from a congenitally defective heart valve may be faint in childhood but later become loud due to narrowing or calcification (hardening) of the valve. Athletes often have innocent heart murmurs because their rigorous training increases the heart's size and ability to pump blood with each heartbeat. The extra blood pumped may produce a harmless "flow" murmur that's heard when the athlete is lying down but tends to disappear when upright.

If some heart-valve malfunction shows up, additional tests may include chest X-rays and detailed electrocardiograms — heart-wave patterns obtained by placing electrodes on the chest. If there is any evidence of a significant murmur, the person is referred to a cardiologist for further assessment

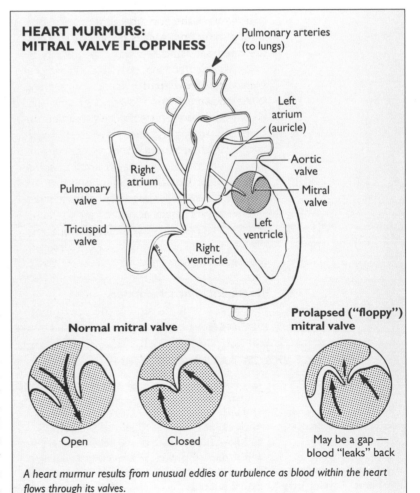

HEART MURMURS: MITRAL VALVE FLOPPINESS

Pulmonary arteries (to lungs)

Left atrium (auricle)

Aortic valve

Mitral valve

Right atrium

Pulmonary valve

Tricuspid valve

Left ventricle

Right ventricle

Normal mitral valve

Open

Closed

Prolapsed ("floppy") mitral valve

May be a gap — blood "leaks" back

A heart murmur results from unusual eddies or turbulence as blood within the heart flows through its valves.

REASONS FOR A HEART MURMUR INCLUDE:

- minor structural irregularities in the heart valves that cause innocent "flow" murmurs due to eddies in the flow of blood through the heart;
- a larger-than-usual amount of blood flowing through the heart, which may cause innocent flow murmurs in pregnant women and athletes;
- a narrowed (stenosed) valve that obstructs the normal amount of blood flowing through it — murmurs due to valvular stenosis can be serious;
- a regurgitant or leaky ("incompetent") valve that causes a murmur as blood backs up through it;
- a fistula (hole or small opening) in the partition between the heart's right and left sides;
- a floppy mitral valve — known as *mitral-valve prolapse* — where valve closure is imperfect and blood slips backward, giving a slight click, murmur or both.

When is a heart murmur serious?

Innocent heart murmurs usually stem from the systolic (pumping) phase of the heartbeat, due to a slight turbulence in the ejection of blood through the aortic and pulmonary valves. They are often not associated with any disability or medical problem and show no clinical, radiographic or electrocardiographic evidence of anything other than normal blood flow through the heart.

By contrast, diastolic and continuous murmurs are always due to some disease and/or faulty cardiac flow. Serious, noncongenital heart murmurs are usually caused by some degenerative disease or infection, such as rheumatic fever. The long-term consequences of an abnormal cardiac valve can be heart enlargement and eventual heart failure. Some damaged heart valves need to be surgically repaired or replaced.

Treatment of heart murmurs

Innocent murmurs require no treatment. Most organic or pathological murmurs need preventive antibiotics before dental work or surgery to prevent a possible heart infection (pericarditis) caused by a collection of stale blood.

A medically threatening heart murmur may call for medications and/or heart surgery, the urgency depending upon the severity of valve damage. Current medical opinion tends to favor valve repair rather than replacement because there are problems associated with mechanical valves. Nonetheless, artificial valves are needed when valve repair isn't feasible. Close monitoring is necessary for those with valve replacements. Blood-thinners may have to be taken, and artificial valves often develop structural flaws that necessitate repeat surgery.

HEARTBURN: NOT FROM THE HEART

Heartburn, a burning sensation felt beneath the breastbone — frequently after meals, especially large ones — stems *not* from the heart, but from irritation of the lower esophagus or gullet (foodpipe).

About half the world's Western population suffers occasional heartburn, known as reflux esophagitis, and it's particularly prevalent among the elderly. An irritated esophagus may cause not only heartburn, but also occasionally a sharp spasm or crushing pain beneath the breastbone that can be confused with angina or heart pain (see above).

It is obviously crucial to distinguish angina — which could require emergency aid — from a mere bout of esophageal irritation, but it's sometimes hard to tell the difference. Heartburn usually worsens when lying down or bending over, and lessens on standing, while angina frequently worsens with exercise. If in doubt, get medical assistance — better safe than sorry!

FACTORS THAT EXACERBATE HEARTBURN

- Too much stomach acid.
- Fatty and fried foods, chocolate, hot spices, citrus juices and tomato products.
- Tobacco, alcohol and caffeine — which may aggravate the stomach, increase acid production and cause esophageal backflow. (Caffeine and alcohol stimulate the production of gastric juices.)
- Eating large meals, especially at night.
- Gas in the stomach; almost everyone swallows some air, especially if gulping food.
- Certain drugs that reduce esophageal sphincter action, such as progesterone; antispasmodics (often taken to relieve indigestion and/or heartburn, they in fact aggravate it); a few antibiotics (especially tetracycline and erythromycin) that may irritate or "burn" the esophageal wall.
- Stress, nervous tension and anxiety.

MEDICATIONS TO RELIEVE HEARTBURN

- *Antacids* (e.g., Maalox, Gelusil, Mylanta, Amphojel, Tums, Pepto-Bismol or Rolaids) may help mild to moderate heartburn by neutralizing stomach acids — these are the traditional mainstay of heartburn therapy. Liquid forms give speedier relief but are messier and less portable than tablets. (N.B.: Some antacids contain magnesium and aluminum, which can be harmful in large doses. Those on salt-restricted diets must watch the sodium content of antacids.)
- *Alginic acid* (Algicon) and other mucilaginous or foaming agents — taken as tablets to suck, not chew — form a "raft" that floats on top of the stomach, coating its contents and preventing reflux.
- *H2-histamine receptor blockers* (e.g., cimetidine or ranitidine), taken as tablets, can ease severe heartburn by inhibiting gastric-acid secretion.
- *Dopamine agonists* (such as the older drug metoclopramide or Maxeran, and the newer domperidone or Motilium), which have minimal side effects on the central nervous system, increase gastric emptying, enhance LES muscle tone and allow the stomach contents to move more quickly through the digestive system.
- *Cholinergic drugs* (e.g., bethanechol) strengthen sphincter pressure.

Understanding heartburn

During normal swallowing, food moves down the digestive tract by involuntary smooth-muscle contractions known as peristalsis. At the lower end of the esophagus, the lower esophageal sphincter (LES) opens to let food pass into the stomach and then normally shuts tight once swallowing is finished. Between meals, this sphincter normally stays well closed, keeping down the stomach contents. However, for a variety of reasons, it can become lax and fail to shut tightly enough, allowing the stomach's acidic contents to escape back up (reflux) into the esophagus. This acidic reflux may irritate, inflame and perhaps damage the sensitive lining of the esophagus, producing the burning sensation known as heartburn. As the stomach empties, heartburn wanes.

Heartburn must be differentiated from pain due to stomach or duodenal ulcers, which worsens on an empty stomach, tends to awaken people at night and is often relieved by milk.

Tests for heartburn include a barium X-ray to inspect the lower esophagus and stomach, and direct endoscopic examination with a long fiber-optic viewing tube that can visualize the esophagus, stomach and duodenum.

The link to hiatus hernia

Hiatus hernia is one cause of heartburn. It occurs when part of the stomach protrudes past the diaphragm into the chest cavity. Over 10 percent of Canadians have unsuspected hiatus hernia, which may be totally without symptoms. But pressure from a hiatus hernia can weaken the LES, allowing gastric juices to back up and produce heartburn, causing sufferers to seek medical aid. (See also "Hernias," below.)

People prone to heartburn

The obese tend to have heartburn because a large part of the abdominal cavity is filled with fat, which pushes the stomach against the diaphragm. The increased abdominal pressure

MEASURES TO PREVENT HEARTBURN

- **Avoid dietary fat, which slows gastric emptying.**
- **Do not eat large meals that over-distend the stomach (especially within three hours of bedtime); it takes about four hours to empty a large meal from the stomach. Small ones are less burden-some.**
- **Chew food well and eat slowly to decrease swallowed air.**
- **Avoid suspected heartburn-inducing foods (e.g., coffee, fried items, citrus juices or tomato products).**
- **Avoid peppermint (which acts directly on the esophageal sphincter).**
- **Abstain from tobacco products, as nicotine lowers esophageal sphincter pressure and impairs stomach action.**
- **Lose weight if obese.**
- **Do not take post-prandial naps or lie down right after meals; a recumbent posture worsens the discomfort. Instead take a walk, exercise or move about following a large meal, staying upright for two to three hours.**
- **Remove tight-fitting belts and girdles.**
- **Prop up the head of the bed to raise the upper part of the body above the feet and minimize backup of stomach juices due to gravity.**
- **Eliminate or cut back on heartburn-aggravating medications (e.g., some antibiotics and anti-spasmodics — such as Buscopan);**
- **Minimize stress whenever possible.**

may force some acidic stomach contents back into the esophagus.

Pregnancy may also cause heartburn (in about 25 percent of expectant women). Progesterone, a hormone of pregnancy, tends to decrease sphincter muscle tone, allowing acidic stomach contents to regurgitate. Also, the growing uterus increases intra-abdominal pressure. Progesterone-containing birth-control pills cause heartburn in some women.

The elderly tend to get heartburn because their esophageal sphincters become weak and less efficient.

Surgery is a last resort for heartburn

When heartburn coexists with a hiatus hernia and symptoms resist all efforts at medical therapy, surgical repair of the hernia may relieve the discomfort. Fewer than 5 percent of those with reflux esophagitis qualify for an operation. Those who develop severe bleeding from esophageal ulcers or a critical narrowing of the esophagus are the most likely candidates. Aside from the cost, discomfort and risk, after-effects — such as "trapped gas" — can be more troublesome than the symptoms that prompted surgery. Seeking a second medical opinion about a proposed hiatus hernia operation makes good sense, especially if surgery is suggested before all nonoperative measures have been thoroughly exhausted.

HEMORRHOIDS

An estimated 50 percent of North American men and women have hemorrhoids — popularly known as "piles" — at some time in their lives. Hemorrhoids are rare before age 30, frequent over age 50. Although many people are reluctant to discuss anal problems, it is vital to report any rectal discomfort, bleeding or change in bowel habits to a physician as it may herald some more serious disorder.

The term "hemorrhoid" is often mistakenly applied to any minor anal or rectal problem, itching or irritation, but anal discomfort may arise from any number of other causes — such as *pruritis ani* (skin itchiness). Hemorrhoids are enlarged, blood-filled pads in the anal region. Humans are prone to them because their erect posture exerts a lot of pressure on

blood vessels around the anus. While some hemorrhoids give little or no discomfort, others cause burning during bowel movements, itchiness and a sense of incomplete emptying. The commonest symptom is bleeding from small vessels in the anal area.

Differentiating internal from external hemorrhoids

There are both "internal" and "external" hemorrhoids. Internal hemorrhoids are distended blood vessels in the moist bowel lining above the transition line. Visible only through a special viewing instrument, they usually produce no symptoms other than bleeding in their early stages and are generally painless unless thrombosed (clotted) or strangulated (causing muscle spasms at the anus). Spongy, swollen internal hemorrhoids sometimes prolapse — protrude through the anus — and can be difficult to ease back up, at which stage they often hurt. Although they usually go back spontaneously to their inner position, protruding internal hemorrhoids may need to be pushed back into the canal after defecating. As they develop further,

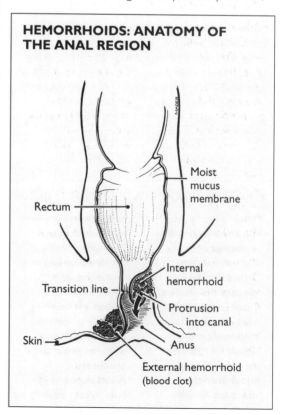

HEMORRHOIDS: ANATOMY OF THE ANAL REGION

Rectum

Moist mucus membrane

Transition line

Internal hemorrhoid

Protrusion into canal

Skin

Anus

External hemorrhoid (blood clot)

MAIN CAUSES OF HEMORRHOIDS

- Anything that increases intra-abdominal pressure, such as forcing or straining at stool, heavy physical effort, prolonged sitting or standing.

- Pregnancy — in the last trimester — as the enlarged uterus presses on anal blood vessels. Sometimes the strain of childbirth leads to postpartum hemorrhoids.

- Faulty diet — eating foods low in fiber (roughage) and fluid may produce hard stools that irritate the bowel. Hemorrhoids are less common in those who eat high-fiber diets.
- Poor bowel habits such as "holding back."
- Reading on the toilet may contribute, as sitting there too long exerts undue strain, without support for anal structures.
- Explosive diarrhea and chronic coughing may increase the risks.

ALERTING SIGNS AND SYMPTOMS

- An external hemorrhoid may be felt as a lump, perhaps due to a sizable blood clot.
- Itching, discomfort and difficulty in cleansing are most typical of external hemorrhoids.
- Bleeding from internal hemorrhoids may produce:
  - a smudge on the toilet tissue;
  - blood in the toilet bowl;

- streaks of blood on the stool;
- blood-stained underwear.
- Protrusion of internal hemorrhoids may be noticed after a bowel movement (they should be pushed back to avoid discomfort).

  N.B.: The first sight of rectal bleeding should trigger a prompt visit to the doctor. One cannot assume that rectal bleeding is due to hemorrhoids until other more serious causes (such as colitis or bowel cancer) have been ruled out. Any new rectal bleeding should be reported at once.

HOME HEMORRHOID REMEDIES

- Cold compresses to reduce the pain.
- Avoiding constipation. Relieve constipation with increased fiber and fluid intake, or gentle stool softeners such as Surfak or laxatives (such as milk of magnesia) if needed. (See also section in this chapter on constipation.)
- Witch hazel or other soothing lotions to alleviate the itching.
- Over-the-counter preparations such as Anusol ointment or suppositories, or Preparation H.
- Sitz (sitting) baths that soak the anal area in warm water two or three times a day.
- Anurex-R, an over-the-counter reusable device — a thin, short probe containing a gel that is cooled in the freezer before insertion into the anal canal. Used twice daily, it provides soothing relief and can stop bleeding from internal hemorrhoids.
- Good anal hygiene — best achieved by wiping with moist pads rather than dry toilet tissue.
- ASA or acetaminophen to relieve pain (but avoid codeine, which only increases constipation).
- Loose cotton underwear rather than tight synthetics.
- Avoiding prolonged sitting or standing when hemorrhoids act up.

Medical treatments
- Always seek medical advice about acute hemorrhoids that are large, hard, swollen and uncomfortable.
- Early excision and evacuation of a thrombosed (clotted) external hemorrhoid is a simple doctor's-office procedure done under a local anesthetic that sometimes gives immediate relief. Healing is speedy and helped along by warm sitz baths.
- Rubber-band ligation is a common treatment for eliminating internal hemorrhoids — done in the doctor's office with a high success rate. An elastic band is wrapped around the hemorrhoid with a special instrument that chokes off the blood supply, so that the rubber band and hemorrhoid slough off in two to 14 days. The procedure is performed without anesthetic since there are no pain endings in the mucosal tissue where internal hemorrhoids occur. It is quick, relatively painless and inexpensive.
- Rubber-banding is occasionally combined with cryotherapy (freezing). After the hemorrhoid is wrapped with an elastic band, the tissue is frozen. Since the rubber band is then snipped off, the patient may experience less discomfort than with rubber-banding alone.
- Injection sclerotherapy — injecting the hemorrhoid with certain solutions — is rarely used any more.
- Laser therapy is expensive and still experimental.
- Surgery in hospital is now rarely used, although occasionally needed for internal hemorrhoids that resist other therapy.

OTHER ANORECTAL PROBLEMS
(SOMETIMES MISTAKEN FOR HEMORRHOIDS)

- *Pruritus ani*: relatively common anal itching due to irritation from various causes, which responds well to hemorrhoidal ointments and scrupulous cleansing with moistened pads.
- *Anusitis*: inflammation of the lining in the anal canal — treated with steroidal anti-inflammatories or Anurex.
- *Anal fissures*: thin, slit-like tears in the anal tissue which cause itching, pain and bleeding during bowel movements. They usually respond to stool-softening agents, emollients or bulk laxatives and local application of a steroid cream. (Seek a physician's advice before proceeding with these measures.)
- *External skin tags*: not usually painful, they are leftover tissue from external hemorrhoids which may interfere with anal hygiene, a problem usually overcome by emollient cleansers.

they may bleed more and cause greater discomfort, especially if they protrude during bowel movements. In their late stages, internal hemorrhoids may permanently hang down (although they don't block defecation), be quite uncomfortable and bleed a lot.

External hemorrhoids (also called para-anal lesions) include a variety of bluish swellings, hematomas (small peasized lumps) and skin tags (loose skin flaps) that occur outside the anus or opening of the rectum below the transition line. The small bumps can be seen using a hand-held mirror. They are swollen skin-covered vessels which some experts do not regard as real hemorrhoids. External hemorrhoids may be itchy and tender, worsened by scratching and imperfect or overvigorous cleaning. Bleeding is rarely a sign of external lesions unless the area is injured or ulcerated.

Diagnosis and medical examination

Medical examination will include a visual and manual (gloved) inspection of the rectal area and use of viewing instruments — a rigid or flexible sigmoidoscope or the longer, farther-reaching colonoscope — to look varying distances up the colon. Some physicians suggest that all men and women over 45 should have a sigmoidoscopy every year or two and a more extensive bowel examination when indicated.

Treatment of hemorrhoids

Most hemorrhoids can be controlled by home treatment with warm sitz baths, soothing ointments and suppositories, as well as avoidance of constipation. Both internal and external hemorrhoids generally clear up within two weeks, but if not, medical treatment is needed. Office procedures (ligation, injection, freezing) can usually cure hemorrhoids, although persistent and/or particularly painful ones may require surgery in hospital.

HEPATITIS

Viral hepatitis is one of today's most threatening infections. Among the different forms of viral hepatitis, hepatitis B is the most serious. Those with the disease face serious risks of liver disease — cirrhosis (scarring) and hepatocellular (liver) cancer — perhaps 10 to 20 years down the road. Almost half of those chronically infected with hepatitis B ultimately die of liver cancer.

Chronic, unremitting hepatitis B currently affects about 5 percent of the world's population. The WHO estimates that there are over 300 million hepatitis-B carriers worldwide compared to only a tenth that number carrying the AIDS or HIV virus.

Hepatitis-B-carrier rates vary from place to place, averaging 0.3 percent of the population in Canada, Britain and the United States, 5 percent in some Mediterranean countries (such as Greece and Italy) and up to 15 percent in South East Asia, China and parts of Africa. A few isolated communities have even higher hepatitis-B-carrier rates — 45 percent among some Alaskan Eskimos and Native communities.

"Silent," symptomless hepatitis-B carriers, often unknowingly infected, can infect others even though they feel perfectly well themselves. Infected mothers can transmit hepatitis B to newborns. And many of the world's children, infected at birth, face a shortened lifespan. *The good news* is that there are now safe and effective vaccines against hepatitis B.

The hepatitis alphabet

Viral hepatitis is due to viruses A, B, C, D, E and perhaps other yet-to-be-identified forms — each causing a slightly different illness. Hepatitis

B was identified in Bremen, Germany, in 1883, but the virus (HBV) was not isolated until the mid-1960s, and the waterborne form, hepatitis A (HAV), 10 years later. Diligent medical detectives have now managed to ferret out non-A and non-B viruses. Over a quarter of the world's viral hepatitis and 90 percent of non-B blood-transfusion cases are now linked to hepatitis C. The D virus, isolated even more recently, is a virulent form that can cause disease only in collaboration with hepatitis B. Finally, the E virus, identified in the late 1980s, spreads primarily via contaminated water and food (like the A form).

There are few warning signs of viral hepatitis

When they produce symptoms at all, the viruses cause a flulike illness, typically with fever, nausea and pervasive tiredness, sometimes accompanied by jaundice (yellowed skin, mucous membranes and whites of eyes). The severity of viral hepatitis varies according to the virus involved and the age and immune defenses of the person infected. Many people have a subclinical infection that goes unnoticed except perhaps for some fatigue and lassitude lasting four to six weeks. The fact that someone has viral hepatitis is often discovered inadvertently by blood tests.

Different types of hepatitis spread differently

Hepatitis A and E are waterborne infections, spread mostly via the feces-to-mouth route, from contaminated water and food, dirty cooking utensils and poor hygiene.

Hepatitis B and D are spread mainly by sexual or intimate contact, via blood and other body fluids and also through household contact, tattoo or ear-piercing needles, drug injection and tribal rituals.

Hepatitis C spreads mainly via blood and blood products, particularly through blood transfusions, also via sex and intravenous drug abuse.

Hepatitis A (HAV) — the infectious, waterborne variety

The A virus, present in feces, can infect anyone who consumes sewage-polluted food or water

or anyone who touches a fecally contaminated object and transfers the virus from hand to mouth. Hepatitis A is also spread via shellfish such as mussels, clams and oysters. It can be sexually transmitted via anal intercourse. Its incubation period is about 28 days. Hepatitis A may be symptomless or produce fever, fatigue, nausea, diarrhea, appetite loss and jaundice. Young children infected by HAV, especially those under two years old, generally have no symptoms. Infected adults who never had the disease as children occasionally develop severe symptoms, and in about 0.1 percent of adults, hepatitis A produces a fulminating, rapidly progressing, potentially fatal illness. But once the illness is over, the hepatitis A virus always clears completely from the bloodstream, leaving the person immune to it.

Hepatitis B (HBV)

In over half of those infected, hepatitis B produces no symptoms. Any symptoms that do occur (such as fatigue, nausea and jaundice), usually disappear in a few weeks. While most adults with hepatitis B eliminate the virus and recover fully, 6 to 10 percent of adults — and 50 to 90 percent of infants — become chronic, lifelong carriers. Over the years, many HBV carriers experience active "flares" of their liver disease, which may also pass unnoticed. But the continuing infection will eventually lead to liver cirrhosis, and perhaps cancer (in about one-third of HBV carriers); the risks are highest for those infected in early childhood.

Hepatitis B poses a worldwide health problem sometimes compared to AIDS. But the overall global burden of hepatitis B far outweighs AIDS, because so many more millions carry it. Unlike the delicate HIV virus that causes AIDS, the hepatitis B virus is tough and can stay infective for days on blood-contaminated articles. Also unlike AIDS, hepatitis B can be transmitted by nonsexual contact, via saliva and contaminated razors, toothbrushes and other everyday objects, endangering family and household members.

Vaccination can prevent hepatitis B

Since there is no effective treatment for viral hepatitis, the best way is prevention. Although

THE ABC's OF VIRAL HEPATITIS AT A GLANCE

Virus Type	How it's spread (transmission routes)	Symptoms	Disease / illness features
Hepatitis A (HAV) (waterborne infectious type)	• From feces (fecal-oral route) in sewage-polluted water and food, cooking utensils, dirty hands, poor hygiene, soiled diapers (daycare centers); • via shellfish such as clams, mussels, oysters.	• Often none, especially in children under age two; • in adults, possibly flulike malaise, fever, nausea, fatigue, diarrhea, dull abdominal pain; • dark urine, jaundice (yellowed eye-whites and skin); • transaminase/enzyme levels in blood raised.	• Short incubation period, 28 days (most infectious at end of that period); • occasionally fulminant (rapidly progressing) in 0.1% — possibly fatal; • symptoms usually resolve and viruses clear completely in two to four months; • doesn't lead to chronic, persisting infection.
Hepatitis B (HBV) (infectious type)	• Via blood and blood products, blood transfusions; broken skin; • by intimate or sexual contact; via body fluids (semen, vaginal secretions, saliva); • via tattoo, ear-piercing needles, shared razors, toothbrushes, household items; • from mother to infant at birth, possibly through breastmilk.	• Usually few or no symptoms; • possibly flulike malaise, fever, nausea, fatigue typically lasting six weeks, perhaps jaundice/skin and eye white yellowing; • detected by blood tests for viral markers.	• 60–90% of infected children and about 10% of infected adults become persistent, chronic hepatitis-B carriers at risk of developing cirrhosis and liver cancer; • unsuspecting carriers harboring hepatitis B can unknowingly infect others; • fulminant, rapidly fatal course in one per 1,000 cases.
Hepatitis C (HCV) (newly discovered, previously called non-A, non-B form)	• Mainly via blood and blood products, blood transfusion; • responsible for 80% of post-transfusion hepatitis and 25% of all viral hepatitis; • by IV drug use; • less spread sexually than B (only 10% acquired through sex); • no mother-to-infant transmission yet documented.	• Often no or few signs of infection; • may produce flulike symptoms, fatigue, lassitude; • possibly jaundice/yellowed eye whites and skin; • if present, symptoms typically last six weeks.	• Long incubation period (50 days at least); • high rate of persistent chronicity (50% progress to long-term, possibly lifetime infection); • acute, fulminant form rare; • many develop cirrhosis (may also add to liver-cirrhosis risks in alcoholics); • liver-cancer risks high.
Hepatitis D (HDV)	• In blood, body fluids (much like HBV); • by blood and blood products; • by person-to-person intimate contact; • seemingly not spread by mother-to-infant route (at birth).	• In combination with B causes severe liver disease with greater chance of progression to cirrhosis, liver cancer, and higher fatality rates than B alone.	• Defective, weak virus — can usually only enter the liver and cause illness *together* with HBV; • needs B to flourish and cause infection; • superimposed on or as coinfection with B, can cause severe illness.
Hepatitis E (HEV) (waterborne)	• Through feces; • similar to A — waterborne transmission; • via sewage-contaminated water supplies, food and cookware, poor hygiene.	• Mild flulike malaise, fever, diarrhea, abdominal pain; jaundice, dark urine; • few or no symptoms in infants (like HAV).	• Despite mild symptoms, consequences possibly serious, especially in young adults; • very dangerous to pregnant women, especially in third trimester (with high fatality rate); • no blood test yet available.

Prevalence: where found and in whom	Treatment and/or prevention
• Worldwide, but commonest in poverty-stricken, crowded places, especially developing world — S.E. Asia, the Canadian north and some Native communities; • in some endemic areas (e.g., China), whole community exposed by age 10; • rare in Canada and U.S. but can be acquired by travel to developing countries, parts of S. Europe, Mexico, Africa; • in crowded daycare centers.	• No effective cure or treatment available, only supportive care; • handwashing and better hygiene may cut spread; boiling water and cleaner water supplies can stem epidemics; • immune globulin shots may prevent or mute symptoms; • if traveling abroad, take necessary precautions re: water and food intake; • vaccine being developed.
• Worldwide, 300 million carriers, commonest in Asia, sub-Saharan Africa, China, Hong Kong, Middle East, some Mediterranean countries (e.g., Italy, Greece); • groups at high risk include homosexuals; promiscuous heterosexuals; IV drug abusers; healthcare and emergency workers; police officers; embalmers; babies of infected mothers; travelers to endemic areas.	• No effective treatment; experimental therapy with alpha-interferon or other antivirals can make symptoms remit in 30% but recur if drug is stopped; • prostaglandin-E being tried; • liver transplants for selected cases; • vaccines available (safe and effective) — advised for all risk groups; • immunizing infected newborns urged to halt infection.
• Worldwide, most common in S.E. Asia, China, Italy and some other Mediterranean countries; • responsible for 90% of all transfusion-acquired cases (in U.S. 2% of blood transfusions cause hepatitis-C infection); • in North America, 1% show evidence of HCV exposure; • prevalent among IV drug abusers and hemophiliacs; in some dialysis patients; uncommon in homosexuals.	• No effective treatment; • experimental therapy with antivirals (e.g., alpha-interferon) helps 50% but ⅓ relapse if therapy stops; prostaglandins being tried; • liver transplants an option for some; • new test for C improves safety of blood supply and cuts transfusion risks; • no vaccine available yet.
• Found worldwide, especially in Mediterranean countries (e.g., Italy, Greece), Middle East, China, parts of Africa, S. America; • rare in Canada and U.S., except among IV drug abusers.	• No effective treatment to date; • poor response to antivirals, e.g., alpha-interferon therapy; • hepatitis-B vaccination prevents spread of D (because of its dependence on B for liver-damaging effect).
• Rare in Canada, but can be picked up by travel to endemic areas; • epidemics reported in India, S. America, S.E. Asia, Mexico, Commonwealth of Independent States (old U.S.S.R.).	• No good therapy available; • preventable by frequent hand-washing, good hygiene; • boiling drinking water can cut spread.

in Canada and the United States hepatitis B circulates primarily in high-risk groups — such as injection drug users, hemophiliacs and others receiving blood products, homosexuals and those with many sex partners — it can strike anyone. Since over one million people in Canada belong to high-risk groups, and immigration from endemic areas such as Africa and the Far East continues, hepatitis B is likely to become an ever more pressing Canadian health problem. Although there is no universal hepatitis vaccination in North America, many experts now promote *universal* immunization against this disease.

Effective vaccines against hepatitis B are widely available with very few side effects — at most a little soreness and swelling at the injection site. The current vaccine is administered in three doses over a six-month period, with a booster after five years. Public-health authorities urge all those at risk — especially healthcare workers and the relatives and household contacts of known hepatitis-B carriers — to be immunized. Many healthcare workers are accidentally infected and a few have died as a consequence. Yet, sadly, less than half of those at risk get their recommended antihepatitis shots. Each Canadian province has its own policy regarding eligibility for antihepatitis shots and insurance coverage.

It's crucial to protect newborns from hepatitis B

Hepatitis B is passed on to 30–60 percent of babies born to carrier mothers, usually at birth. But, unlike infants of mothers with AIDS, newborns exposed to hepatitis B can be vaccinated to prevent illness. The vaccination of all such newborns is a must.

The Canadian National Advisory Committee on Immunization and the Canadian Liver Foundation promote the screening of all pregnant women for hepatitis B, with an easy blood test, so that babies at risk can be immunized. Some authorities, such as the U.S. Centers for Disease Control, recommend universal vaccination of all infants, regardless of the mother's infective status. This means an immune globulin shot and vaccination within 24 hours of birth, followed by further vaccine shots at required intervals.

Few treatments for viral hepatitis — mostly experimental

As yet there is no really effective treatment for any form of viral hepatitis. Shots of immune globulin, a short-acting product derived from blood plasma, can prevent the spread of hepatitis A during outbreaks. Highly effective, safe vaccines for hepatitis B are available but are expensive unless covered by provincial or private drug plans — the rules vary. Hepatitis-B immune globulin (HBIg) is also provided, when circumstances warrant, for treating post–hepatitis-B exposure. There are as yet no vaccines for the other forms of hepatitis. The best way to combat this infection is prevention.

For more information contact the Canadian Liver Foundation.

HERNIAS

Theoretically any soft part of the body can herniate (bulge into or penetrate surrounding areas), but in fact hernias occur most commonly in the abdominal area — from the thorax to the groin.

Hiatus hernia

A hiatus, or diaphragmatic, hernia occurs when the abdominal contents protrude up through the hiatus — the space in the diaphragm through which the esophagus (food tube) passes into the stomach.

There are two main types of hiatus hernia: the more common "sliding" hiatus hernia and the less prevalent but more serious "para-esophageal" hernia. Pregnant women and the obese commonly suffer hiatus hernias from the extra load on the abdomen.

Although the majority of people with this abdominal defect have no symptoms, an estimated 10 percent of Canadians have hiatus hernia, climbing to 30 percent by age 60. When symptoms do arise, it's usually because the sphincter muscles around the lower end of the esophagus have become weakened. The esophagus runs from the mouth to the stomach, with a valve between the stomach and the gullet that remains tightly shut between swallows. If the valve's controlling muscles don't function properly, the valve won't stay closed, and stomach acids may spill into the esophagus.

Since the lining of the esophagus is sensitive to acid, unlike the tough lining of the stomach, heartburn, sharp pain, regurgitation, belching and sometimes bleeding may result. There may also be breathlessness and a choking sensation if regurgitated stomach contents are breathed in at night. Some people with symptomatic hiatus hernia have been wrongly diagnosed with asthma. About one-third of those with hiatus hernia eventually develop esophagitis, or heartburn, as the acids damage the esophageal lining, which may irritate the channel and make swallowing difficult. The gullet can even be perforated.

Diagnosis of a hiatus hernia depends on X-rays and diagnostic tests such as endoscopy (looking at the stomach via a fiber-optic tube); esophageal manometry (using a special instrument to measure sphincter pressure); and tests to measure esophageal acidity.

In the vast majority of cases (85–90 percent), therapy for hiatus hernia is simply treatment of heartburn. Losing weight may be recommended to relieve pressure. At night, sleeping with the upper part of the body propped up on pillows, or with the head of the bed raised 15–20 cm (6–8 in), relieves nocturnal acid reflux, and standing straight rather than slouching should also relieve the problem. (See the section on heartburn for drugs used to relieve it.)

Surgery to reinforce the malfunctioning sphincter muscle is now uncommon, but remains an option in severe cases if medical and dietary management don't succeed.

Paraesophageal hernia

A paraesophageal hernia, fortunately very rare, can be life-threatening because the hole enlarges and, in some cases, can allow the entire stomach (which may perforate) to slip into the chest cavity. Many sufferers have no symptoms, but if they do occur, the most common are pain, indigestion, nausea and retching. Heartburn and regurgitation are unusual with this problem. There is no medical treatment for paraesophageal hernia, and surgery is usually needed.

Inguinal hernia

A groin or "inguinal" hernia (or, less commonly, a *femoral* hernia) occurs when abdominal contents protrude into the groin area through a muscle tear or weakness in the abdominal wall, producing a groin bulge. Inguinal hernias can cause constant or intermittent pain on exertion. While they are not usually life-threatening, if the hernia hole closes and the bulge is squeezed off (strangulated or incarcerated), the blood circulation can become impaired and infection may set in (a rare emergency). Inguinal hernias affect 3 to 7 percent of the population, more commonly males than females. Inguinal hernias can occur at any age, but are most frequent in infancy (3 to 5 percent of full-term infants and 5 to 30 percent of premature babies) and after age 50.

Herniation may be caused by a congenital weakness or defect in the abdominal wall, which may be genetic, producing infant hernias. Alternatively, the abdominal or groin anomaly can go undetected for many years until, with aging, muscles and tissues sag and weaken, the abdominal wall becomes less able to sustain stress, and herniation occurs. Smoking and chronic coughing can contribute to inguinal hernia. Physical exertion such as lifting, although not a cause in itself, may suddenly cause weakened abdominal muscles to give way.

Treatment of inguinal hernias is almost always by surgical repair, or hernioplasty, which bundles the protruding mass back into the abdomen where it belongs, and then reinforces the weakened area so that the hernia does not recur.

HYPERTENSION (HIGH BLOOD PRESSURE)

A leading cause of heart attacks and strokes, hypertension afflicts one-tenth of North America's population. It may be linked to obesity, faulty diet and lack of exercise, but often arises for unknown reasons. High blood pressure weakens the walls of small arteries, which can lead to strokes, heart attacks, kidney damage and vision loss (due to injured blood vessels in the eyes). Because it is a "silent killer," usually symptomless until the blood vessels have suffered considerable damage and

THE SODIUM OR SALT CONNECTION

Many researchers feel that a lifelong over-consumption of sodium (salt) may contribute to hypertension. It appears that even people genetically predisposed to hypertension fail to develop it if they stick to a lifelong low-sodium regime. Statistically the link is clear, but there is still no absolute proof that excess sodium actually causes hypertension or that reducing sodium consumption can prevent it.

RISK FACTORS FOR HYPERTENSION

Although the underlying mechanism is not fully understood, known risk factors include:

- a genetic predisposition;
- obesity — weight loss alone often lowers blood pressure;
- smoking — a high-risk factor (nicotine both constricts blood vessels and speeds up the heartrate, raising blood pressure);
- pregnancy, which can temporarily elevate blood pressure;
- contraceptive drugs, especially in those prone to hypertension; women on the Pill should get regular medical checkups;
- lack of exercise (but while physical activity may lower blood pressure in some borderline cases, there is no guarantee of lasting effects);
- stress — long considered an accompaniment to hypertension — may activate the sympathetic nervous system and enhance adrenaline release, raising blood pressure;
- insufficient potassium or an imbalanced ratio of sodium to potassium — another possible cause that needs clarification. Researchers are investigating whether a potassium-rich diet can counteract high blood pressure;
- high alcohol consumption (three or more drinks per day), which seems to raise blood pressure, possibly by altering kidney function. Some experts consider this alcohol-related rise to be reversible if excess drinking ceases.

damage to the heart or other organs has already occurred, the only way to know if you've got high blood pressure is to have it checked regularly. Even after diagnosis, people often don't take their prescribed medication. It's a dangerous mistake, increasing the risk of unexpected death.

A decade or so ago, over half of those with hypertension were unaware of its presence, and of those who knew they had high blood pressure, only half got sufficient treatment. Today, many more people are aware of hypertension and the importance of getting proper treatment for it. Blood pressure should be measured every year or so, especially after the age of 30. This is one routine medical test that can really save lives, provided that those with unacceptably high readings take steps to redress the problem.

How high is high?

Blood pressure is measured using an inflatable cuff on the upper arm and a stethoscope to detect heart sounds. The cuff is inflated until the point where the pulse disappears, which gives the approximate systolic pressure in the arteries as the heart contracts and pumps blood. The cuff is then slowly deflated and, as the heart rests between beats and fills with blood, the diastolic pressure is measured. Blood pressure is recorded as systolic over diastolic, expressed in millimeters of mercury (Hg). Normal readings range from 100/60 to 130/80, and an average normal reading is 120/80 mmHg. When someone is thought to be hypertensive, physicians usually do several readings, maybe a few weeks, even months, apart, to get an accurate picture before initiating treatment; one high reading alone does not

BLOOD-PRESSURE DRUGS

The choice of blood-pressure drugs depends on the type and causes of hypertension and the person's individual health profile.

- *Diuretics* (such as thiazides), which flush water out of the body and reduce the blood volume pumped by the heart, are widely used, inexpensive and easy to tolerate. But because they tend to raise blood-lipid (cholesterol) levels and deplete the body's potassium and magnesium stores, they are sometimes replaced by other drugs such as beta blockers as the first line of attack.
- *Beta blockers* mute the heart's activity, dilate blood vessels, slow the heartbeat and reduce the pressure in blood vessels. Newer forms such as atenolol (Tenormin) and acebutolol (Monitan or Sectral) now complement older types such as propranolol.
- *Calcium-channel blockers* such as nifedipine (Adalat) lower blood pressure by dilating blood vessels and easing the heart's pumping action.
- *Angiotensin-converting enzyme (ACE) inhibitors* such as captopril (Capoten) or enalapril (Vasotec) block the pressure-raising action of the kidney's angiotensin hormone, preventing its conversion into the form that constricts blood vessels. ACE drugs are generally well tolerated, but possible side effects include a decreased white-cell count and a dry, hacking cough.

prove hypertension. External influences such as a heavy meal, exercise, anxiety — even the sight of a white lab coat — may alter readings.

The dividing line between normal and high blood pressure is somewhat arbitrary, with many divergent definitions. One standard, set by the World Health Organization, defines hypertension as 160/95, and designates normal blood pressure as less than 140/90. The area between normal and hypertensive, considered "borderline hypertension," is linked to increased risk of sickness and death, and still merits attention. About 10 to 15 percent of adults have blood pressures in the borderline area and could benefit from corrective lifestyle changes.

Hypertension can be lowered with exercise, weight loss, lowering excessive alcohol

---

TO LOWER BLOOD PRESSURE:

- keep weight down to a desirable level;
- exercise regularly (20 to 30 minutes at least three times weekly);
- limit alcohol intake to two (women) or three (men) daily drinks ;
- do not smoke;
- moderate salt
- (sodium) intake;
- eat a varied low-fat diet, rich in magnesium, potassium and calcium;
- continue taking any prescribed blood-pressure medication(s);
- get regular checkups.

---

intake, quitting smoking, and possibly limiting salt intake. In mild hypertension (90–95 mmHg diastolic) nonpharmacological lifestyle changes should be sufficient to get blood pressure down.

Treatment can control but not cure hypertension

The correct therapy for the 10 percent of the population with mild high blood pressure — a diastolic reading between 90 and 99 — remains a much-debated question. In the absence of other risk factors, this level of hypertension probably poses few health hazards. But accompanied by smoking, obesity, high blood cholesterol or a family history of heart disease, even slightly elevated blood pressure can be a health threat.

INFLUENZA

Influenza, a self-limiting viral infection, generally lasts from a few days to a couple of weeks, depending on the infecting strain, individual susceptibility, age and personal health. Currently, influenza leads infectious diseases as a cause of death among the elderly and debilitated (weak), often owing to secondary infections. Although influenza viruses usually cause a relatively mild illness, they constantly change their structure slightly — undergoing small alterations in the proteins on their surface membranes — and every 10 to 15 years there is a major reshuffling that produces a radically new strain. Since humans develop antibody defenses only against viruses they have already encountered, a large viral change leaves the population unprotected and produces severe epidemics. (Experts surmise that the reason 20 million died in the epidemic after World War I was that a particularly virulent strain struck populations malnourished and weakened by years of war.)

Of the three known types of influenza viruses, A, B and C, only type A has so far given rise to severe global outbreaks — recent examples being the 1958 Asian flu pandemic, which killed 70,000 in the United States alone, and the 1968 Hong Kong flu. Influenza-B strains, more stable than the A forms, can produce severe illness in children and the elderly, while type C usually causes only sporadic, local outbreaks of mild illness.

Influenza usually starts with a sore throat, fever, chills, headache, muscle and joint aches, dry cough and sometimes a runny nose. The nasal involvement is usually less pronounced than with a common cold, but with influenza — unlike a typical cold — the fever may be quite high. The cough may become irritating, with consequent chest soreness and interrupted sleep. Secondary infection of the lungs with *Pneumococci*, the bacteria responsible for pneumonia, can follow influenza, and requires prompt medical attention.

For a mild bout of influenza, bed rest, fluids and antipyretics (fever reducers) usually suffice. ASA (Aspirin) should not be used in children because of the possible danger of Reye's syndrome, which is linked to ASA-treated influenza B. Antibiotics do not help influenza since they're

WHO NEEDS FLU SHOTS?

- people over 65 (because of the risk of serious lung complications);
- adults with chronic heart or lung conditions (severe enough to merit frequent medical care), kidney disease, severe anemia, diabetes, immunosuppression and nonmalignant tumors;
- residents of nursing homes or chronic-care facilities (where close, confined quarters may enhance viral spread);
- children with recurrent (chronic) lung disorders, such as bronchopulmonary dysplasia (found in those who were premature babies with respiratory distress at birth); cystic fibrosis; asthma (bad enough to require frequent medical supervision); significant heart disease; cancer; immunodeficiency; sickle cell disease; and conditions requiring long-term ASA (e.g., Aspirin) therapy;
- those who might transmit influenza to high-risk individuals, e.g., healthcare personnel or others working in nursing homes, hospitals or some other institutions, or those caring for elderly relatives;
- possibly those who provide essential services, e.g., the military, firefighters, police (controversial).

ineffective against viral illnesses, but they may be required for a secondary bacterial infection, such as pneumonia.

New influenza vaccines created yearly

Vaccination is the best way to prevent or lessen the risk of influenza. Although it's never entirely certain which particular flu viruses are most likely to hit in a given season, vaccines can be prepared with a fair degree of accuracy. The decision as to which strains should be included in the year's vaccine is taken in the spring and the manufacturing process takes about six months, so batches are usually ready by late September. The new "split-virus" vaccines are now generally recommended, especially for children under 13 years, because they produce fewer side effects. Immunization is best done in September, before the start of the flu season in late October or early November; it takes roughly one month after vaccination to build adequate antibody defenses.

Flu shots do not protect against the multitude of other upper-respiratory infections, common colds, gastrointestinal upsets, sore throats and other ailments often wrongly labeled as influenza.

KIDNEY STONES

Anyone who has ever experienced it knows that passing a kidney stone — even one smaller than a grain of sand — through slender urinary channels can be excruciating. Although the passage of some stones causes little or no pain, most stones send people rushing in agony to the nearest hospital. The symptoms and severity depend on the location, type and size of the stones: whether they're smooth or spiky, whether they stay put, start moving or get stuck somewhere en route from kidney to bladder.

Urinary-tract stones are not recent afflictions; the earliest one recorded was found in some ancient Egyptian remains, and Galen, the renowned Roman physician, attributed them to factors such as race, heredity, climate, diet, drinking-water, gout, other diseases and alcohol intake — theories not so very far from those of today. Stones may form either in the bladder or inside the kidney, from where they can move down to the bladder and pass out through the urethra. In Western society, kidney stones are the common type and bladder stones are a rarity. But in developing countries, and in Europe up to the 1900s, bladder stones predominated, probably owing to inadequate diets — the increase in kidney stones may be due to a greater consumption of calcium-rich milk products.

About 70 percent of kidney stones (more precisely known as renal calculi) pass out spontaneously in the urine given enough time, often causing extreme pain while doing so. The remaining 30 percent create trouble by getting stuck inside the kidney or in the ureter leading from the kidney to the bladder. When they obstruct the flow of urine, stones must be removed, since blockage can damage the kidney.

Different stones afflict different folks

Stones are more prevalent in men than women and usually occur between the ages of 30 and 50. Certain races and ethnic populations are more prone to kidney stones than others, and more likely to have one kind of stone than another.

There are four main types of stones: calcium-containing; uric-acid; struvite; and cystine. About 40–70 percent of urinary-tract stones in Anglo-Saxon populations contain calcium (as calcium oxalate or as an insoluble phosphate salt, or a combination of both).

Uric-acid stones are found in 25–30 percent of some Mediterranean peoples and account for 75 percent of stones formed by the Portuguese. Apparently, uric-acid stones tend to form in Mediterranean races owing to a genetic propensity toward acidic urine, which favors uric-acid crystallization. Only 5 percent of kidney stones in Anglo-Saxons contain uric acid.

Struvite stones are large accretions accounting for about 10–20 percent of all renal stones. They involve the kidney's whole collecting system, accumulating in a branched structure known as a staghorn.

Cystine stones are relatively rare (about 2 percent of all stones). They form in people with cystinuria, a genetic defect in which an excess of cystine, an amino acid and normal body constituent, accumulates in the urine.

How do you know if you have kidney stones?

Symptoms of a kidney stone range from none at all, blood in the urine or a dull ache in the side or back, to intense pain radiating into the groin accompanied by nausea and vomiting. The worst pain usually occurs as a stone passes from the kidney along the ureter to the bladder. The presence of stones is confirmed by an intravenous pyelogram — X-rays taken with iodine-containing dye injected into the bloodstream to outline the kidney and its collecting system, revealing the size, number, shape and position of stones.

Treatment for kidney stones

Some uric-acid stones, and occasionally the cystine types inside the kidney, can be dissolved and then passed without difficulty. Small, uninfected stones in the kidney that cause no serious symptoms may be left alone.

Stones in the ureter normally pass out with time. Should they fail to pass within a reasonable period, or cause unbearable pain or endanger the kidney, they're removed by surgical or other means. Fortunately, there are new non-surgical ways to get some stones out.

- *Endoscopic basket extraction* is done under general or local anesthetic, for small stones stuck in the lower section of a ureter. Using a cystoscope, through which the surgeon can see, a fine tube is passed via the urethra and the bladder into the ureter, and a basket is then passed up the tube to ensnare and pull out the stones.
- *Ultrasound lithotripsy* is another way to avoid surgery. Under epidural (spinal) anesthesia an optical scope is used to "see" the stone, and then high-frequency ultrasound vibrations crumble it into pieces small enough to be passed out or removed with a basket.
- *Nephroscopy* allows the stone to be seen inside the kidney through a nephroscope passed through a small puncture in the side. The opening is gradually widened to allow entry of the scope and instruments that search for, grab and retrieve the stone. An ultrasound probe may be used through the same instrument to break up stones too large to be removed whole.
- *Extracorporeal lithotripsy*, another new method, blasts stones from outside the body and allows the fragments to pass out normally. Guided by X-ray technology, special "shock waves" shatter the kidney stones into fine sand. The procedure is done under epidural anesthesia while the patient is immersed in a water bath. Hard stones break up and pass without harming any tissues. Experts predict that half or more of all stones, except for the large staghorn types, could soon be treated by this method.

Surgery, involving a general anesthetic and abdominal incision, is still sometimes necessary for ureter stones caught in an awkward spot (high up in the ureter) or too large for basket removal or resistant to ultrasound crushing. Stones caught in the kidney that are infected, or cause bad pain or urine blockage, must come out and in some cases still require open surgery.

Preventing kidney stones — possible or not?

Chemical analysis of any stones passed and caught may improve the chances of finding out the underlying metabolic quirks that lead to stones, and possibly help to prevent their recurrence. Uric-acid and cystine stones can be dissolved by alkalinizing the urine, by either appropriate diet or taking chemicals — a strategy that may prevent recurrence of stones or stop existing ones from getting bigger.

In the days of Hippocrates, stone formers were urged to drink plenty of fluids to "flush out the pipes and dilute the salts." The advice still holds; stone formers should drink three or more liters or quarts a day.

Dietary means of reducing stone formation may work for stones resulting from underlying metabolic defects, particularly those due to elevated blood calcium. People with calcium-metabolizing problems, detectable by blood and urine tests, may reduce kidney-stone formation by going easy on calcium-rich foods such as dairy products, and reducing intake of items high in oxalate, such as rhubarb, spinach, tea, chocolate and colas.

People prone to high uric-acid levels (as in gout) may benefit by cutting down on foods high in purine — a precursor of uric acid found in meats, fish, organ meats, poultry and legumes.

Certain medications can help to prevent stones by controlling the levels of metabolites put out in the urine. Allopurinol reduces uric-acid levels; hydrochlorothiazide reduces the calcium level in the urine; and penicillamine can lower cystine levels.

For more information contact the Kidney Foundation of Canada.

KNEE PROBLEMS

Knees are remarkable mechanisms, able to absorb three times the body's weight with every step taken. But the rigor of sports added to everyday walking can make the knees extra vulnerable to damage. Anyone can have knee problems. Women are especially susceptible because their wider pelvis tends to make them knock-kneed.

Most knee complaints result from overuse and/or alignment problems, and many can be completely or partly prevented by following sensible guidelines. Diagnosing knee injuries can be tricky, but any sudden knee swelling usually signals trouble. Ice and anti-inflammatory drugs can help to bring down the swelling, but knee pain should never be ignored or masked with too much medication. If symptoms persist, consult a physician, sports clinic or exercise specialist. Avoid activities that hurt the knee. Orthotics (shoe inserts) and specific strengthening exercises may help to correct the problem.

Today's simpler arthroscopic knee surgery

Knee injuries can now often be diagnosed and surgically corrected at the same time with arthroscopy, reserving the older, open-knee operations for ligament and reconstructive problems. Arthroscopic surgery greatly reduces the recovery time after knee surgery, with far less trauma to the tissues. The arthroscope — a fiber-optic device — is useful for

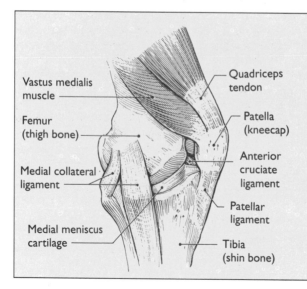

Vastus medialis muscle

Femur (thigh bone)

Medial collateral ligament

Medial meniscus cartilage

Quadriceps tendon

Patella (kneecap)

Anterior cruciate ligament

Patellar ligament

Tibia (shin bone)

ANATOMY OF THE KNEE

The knee's action is that of a complex screw. The two condyles (knuckles) at the lower end of the femur (thigh bone) rest on "plateaus" at the top of the tibia (shin bone). The patella (kneecap) protects the joint, also serving as a lever to straighten the knee. The back of the patella is covered with smooth cartilage. "Collateral" ligaments on the sides of the knee provide stability, and another group of ligaments supports the back of the knee. Other stabilizing structures include the anterior and posterior "cruciate" ligaments, which are unusually strong, and, inside the knee joint, semilunar cartilages, or "menisci," which form runners on which the femur can rotate and slide.

SOME COMMON KNEE INJURIES

- *Patellofemoral syndrome (chondromalacia patellae)* — one of the commonest of overuse knee injuries — is signaled by a noisy "clicking" when the knee is bent and straightened, pain and swelling after exercise or on climbing stairs, prolonged car driving or sitting too long. Bending the knee is difficult and causes pain across and on both sides of the knee. The condition occurs because of muscular imbalance due to a weaker inner than outer quadriceps muscle, if the kneecap rides outside its correct grooves or if the normally smooth inner surface of the kneecap becomes rough. The aim in treating patellofemoral syndrome is to reduce the swelling, avoid pressure and rest the knee while swollen and painful. Ice-packs can be applied twice daily and anti-inflammatory medications may ease the discomfort. The quadriceps muscles, which control movement of the kneecap, must later be strengthened to restore the patella's position, and orthotics (shoe inserts) help to realign the foot and improve its position. People with this problem should choose sports with a limited range of knee motion.
- *"Runner's knee,"* a less severe overuse problem, builds gradually, with pain around the kneecap during exercise, after sitting too long or when climbing stairs. Doing warm-ups to stretch the hamstrings and calf muscles before exercising helps to avoid runner's knee. If the feet pronate (turn or slope inwards), orthotics can help. When experiencing pain, runners should cover shorter distances and pay careful attention to running surfaces, opting for a more cushioned surface and avoiding hills.
- *Jumper's knee (patellar tendonitis)* is another overuse knee problem, resulting from excessive jumping as in basketball and volleyball. Pain is felt at the bottom of the kneecap (where the patellar tendon attaches to the bone). Small tears in the tendon's attachment to the patella cause swelling. The best treatment is to avoid jumping, and stretch and strengthen the quadriceps and calf muscles. Properly cushioned footwear and knee supports can help to prevent the condition.
- *Osgood-Schlatter's disease*, not strictly a knee disease, involves inflammation of the area where the patellar tendon joins the shinbone. It's a growth problem exclusive to adolescents, in which a painful little bump forms below the patella. Rest and occasionally leg splinting are the remedies. Limited activities can be resumed when pain subsides. Teenagers should avoid sports that require excessive squatting, bending or jumping, and do stretching exercises. Teenagers outgrow the pain but the bump remains.

- *Torn knee cartilage* involves the menisci — the cartilage between the femur and tibia. With a sudden, twisting knee movement (as in downhill skiing) or a blow to the knee, these cartilaginous shock absorbers may tear, sometimes with a "pop," bringing immediate and acute pain. Some meniscus tears respond well to bracing and quadriceps-strengthening exercises; usual sports may often be continued even though the knee still clicks and pops, swells up and is harder than usual to straighten. If symptoms persist, an MRI (magnetic resonance imaging) test may be ordered or arthroscopic investigation and surgery may be needed to remove the torn cartilage (which never heals).
- *Medial collateral ligament tears* (on the knee's inner side) can occur from a sudden wrenching. With mild tears, ice and strengthening exercises are enough; more severe tears need rest and possibly anti-inflammatory drugs. Sometimes a cast or long elastic knee supports are advisable. Very severe knee-ligament injuries (with complete rupture) can happen when the outside of the knee suffers a violent blow, causing extreme pain and usually an inability to walk. A pop may be heard at the time of injury, and the knee feels loose. Surgery may be necessary to reattach the torn ligament or reconstruct a new one from other leg tissues.
- *Anterior cruciate ligament tears*, although sometimes experienced alone, usually occur through violent knee twisting that also tears the medial collateral ligament and medial meniscus. The knee may not swell or seem particularly unstable, but surgical repair may be required.
- *Housemaid's knee (prepatellar bursa)*, with swelling in front of or on top of the kneecap, can be due to a blow on the kneecap, continual kneeling or repeated falls on the knees. Rest, ice, anti-inflammatory drugs and an elastic wrapping are usually sufficient treatment. Obviously, kneeling should be avoided.
- *Loose bodies and pieces of cartilage or bone chips* in the knee joint, common in athletes, are sometimes felt through the skin. They can become wedged between the knee bones, causing the knees to catch, lock or give way with accompanying pain and swelling. If the condition is serious or persistent enough, surgical removal is necessary.
- *Baker's cyst*, a protrusion of the knee joint lining due to fluid buildup, is felt as a lump at the back of the knee. The ankle or calf may also swell. While rest usually allows the knee to settle, if symptoms persist, surgery (arthroscopy) is an option.

removing torn cartilage and for ligament repairs. It contains a light and magnifying lenses that relay a clear view of the knee's interior through a TV monitor and eyepiece. Tiny incisions are made in the knee to insert the arthroscope and inject saline (salt) solution. An accurate diagnosis can often be made and surgical correction undertaken at the same time, under local or general anesthetic. An arthroscope can also be used to diagnose ligament tears and to plan open-knee surgery. After arthroscopic surgery, the small incisions are taped or stitched, the knee is bandaged and a few hours after surgery the person can usually go home. Crutches are usually supplied to keep weight off the knee for a few days, and physiotherapy may be advised to strengthen the knee. After arthroscopy the knee may feel slightly uncomfortable and a gurgling noise may be heard for a time when walking. After about four weeks or less of modified, mild exercise, regular sports can often be resumed.

Become knee-wise

Avoiding sudden jolting movements and rough walking or running surfaces can help to prevent knee injuries. Obesity adds pressure to the vulnerable knee joint, so weight reduction is a help. Learning the fundamentals of any chosen sport and being properly prepared, trained and equipped (with good footwear) can prevent taxing knee movements. Knee injuries can often be prevented or corrected by proper quadriceps (upper thigh) muscle strengthening, being sure to strengthen its counterpart (the hamstring muscle at the back of the thigh) to an equal degree. Exercises considered "good for the knees" include small (not deep) knee bends and straightening motions, walking and bicycling in low gear (to lessen the stress on the kneecap). The best sports for strengthening muscles in the weak-kneed are swimming, slow jogging, walking, skating, soccer, baseball, hockey, tennis and, depending upon the state of the knee, cycling (seat high, avoiding hills). Sports that are especially hard on the knees (as they entail deep knee bends) are: volleyball, basketball, downhill skiing, sprinting, football, racquetball and squash.

Common sense in knowing when to rest a hurt and fatigued knee will prevent overuse problems. Rest, ice and painkillers can relieve mild knee discomfort, but marked swelling or pain needs expert diagnosis.

LIVER CIRRHOSIS

Liver cirrhosis is a pressing global health problem and a major cause of death in men aged 25 to 64. It is twice as common in men as in women; however, *susceptibility* to alcohol-related liver injury appears to be greater in women than men, even though women drink less.

Cirrhosis is an insidious condition that often reaches an advanced stage without giving any hint of its presence. Among the causes of liver cirrhosis — such as some forms of viral hepatitis, inherited disorders of iron and copper metabolism, certain drugs and bile-duct obstruction — excess alcohol intake is by far the most frequent. Cirrhosis is about 30 times more common among heavy drinkers than among nondrinkers. Anyone who drinks heavily for many years will almost certainly end up with a damaged liver.

How alcohol harms the liver

There are three major types of liver injury related to alcohol: fatty liver, alcoholic hepatitis and cirrhosis. The first two are potentially reversible, but full-blown cirrhosis is not.

- *Fatty liver* is typical of those who drink heavily for a few years or who go on drinking binges for a few weeks. The liver is enlarged and full of fat droplets, but the condition usually has few overt symptoms, except perhaps some abdominal pain and possibly some jaundice.
- *Alcohol-induced hepatitis* may also go completely unnoticed. However, in severe alcoholic hepatitis the drinker has malaise (unwellness), perhaps also some vomiting, appetite loss, upper abdominal pain, sometimes jaundice and spider nevi (enlarged surface or skin blood vessels that look like a red spider's web). Approximately 30 percent of people who have alcoholic hepatitis go on to develop cirrhosis if alcohol intake does not cease.
- *Cirrhosis* is a form of liver damage whose main feature is breakdown of the liver's normal architecture, with the formation of scar (fibrous) tissue and nodules (the liver's attempt to regenerate its injured cells).

Extensive liver scarring develops over many years, generally giving little or no sign of its progress until the disease is advanced and complications occur — such as bleeding from enlarged veins (varices) that may burst and hemorrhage (the commonest cause of death in cirrhotics). In addition, ascites may form — corresponding to the biblical description of the dropsy — a huge accumulation of fluid in the abdomen that greatly expands its girth. Owing to the blockage and diversion of normal blood routes, nutrients may bypass the liver, resulting in malnutrition. Toxins from the gut that accumulate because liver cells can no longer detoxify them may disturb brain chemistry, creating apathy, confusion, drowsiness and ultimately coma.

There are no effective treatments for established liver cirrhosis, which is essentially irreversible. But impairment due to a fatty liver and "portal hypertension" (high blood pressure within the liver) can be greatly reduced by abstinence from alcohol. Various drugs for cirrhosis are currently under investigation. Colchicine is a chemical that seems to inhibit scar formation, and propylthiouracil — a drug that has been tested for several years at the Addiction Research Foundation in Toronto — shows some promise.

For more information contact the Canadian Liver Foundation.

LYME DISEASE

Lyme disease — now the number-one insect-borne disease in North America, exceeding Rocky Mountain spotted fever (a bacterial disease carried by dog ticks) — is caused by bacteria carried by tiny, wingless, eight-legged Ixodid ticks.

The U.S. Centers for Disease Control report some 1,500 new cases annually, and the numbers increase each year. Lyme disease is also prevalent in Northern and Central Europe. The real number of cases may be considerably higher, because many people know little about the disease and may be totally unaware of having been bitten by a tick. In addition, some health professionals still have trouble identifying this unfamiliar illness. It tends to remit and flare up, but gradually improves with time in most cases. It is identi-

---

THE THREE STAGES OF LYME DISEASE

- *Stage one*: a rash that appears within three days to three weeks (but usually within a week) of the tick bite, starting as a small red pimple at the bite site and gradually expanding to form a ring-shaped "bull's eye" — red at the edges, clear in the middle — which can get as large as a dime or a dinner plate. While the strange rash (which fades within three to four weeks) appears in only about half of those infected, other skin rashes may appear anywhere on the body (usually the chest, back, thigh, groin and armpit). The rash fades in a few weeks even if untreated. Some people never experience the rash and don't notice a tick bite, yet go on to develop more advanced stages, months, perhaps years, later. Other symptoms include a flu-like illness (with fever, chills, headache, malaise, stiff muscles, an aching neck), extreme fatigue and swollen lymph nodes.
- *Stage two*: Temporary neurological (nervous system) problems appear in about 8–10 percent of those with untreated Lyme disease — usually starting two to eleven weeks after the tick bite, signalled by violent headaches (similar to those experienced with meningitis), neuritis (inflammation of the neck nerves) and sensory disturbances (such as transient deafness). A condition similar to Bell's palsy (paralysis of the face muscles) is a common but temporary complication. In most cases the neurological symptoms vanish with appropriate treatment, or spontaneously in a few weeks to months. Heart problems, from blockage of the heart's electrical-conducting system, also develop in 5 to 8 percent of untreated people with Lyme disease, producing dizziness, palpitations, shortness of breath and irregular heartbeats. The cardiac difficulties may last from a week to a couple of months, and a temporary pacemaker may be needed.
- *Stage three*: Months or even years after the tick bite (but typically within six to 24 months), this stage strikes 60–80 percent of untreated patients, beginning with hot, painful joint swelling, especially in the knees, ankles, elbows, wrists and shoulders. If not promptly treated with antibiotics, this arthritic condition can lead to permanent disability. The third stage may also include demyelinating problems involving nerve-coat degeneration, limb numbness, memory lapses and overpowering fatigue.

---

fied by a skin rash, neurological (nerve) and heart disturbances, and if left untreated, can cause serious arthritis.

Lyme disease got its name from two small New England townships — Lyme and Old Lyme in Connecticut. Juvenile arthritis is very rare, and its incidence among children in the Lyme area in the mid-1970s was many times the national average: one in 100 compared to one in 100,000 nationwide. Also, parents noticed that children aged 5 to 16 developed a

---

HOW TO AVOID LYME DISEASE

- Find out whether any area you inhabit or plan to visit is known to harbor ticks. (In Canada, so far, only Long Point, Ontario, is a clearly defined risk area.)
- If in tick-infested areas, especially woodlands or fields, practice a daily skin inspection, not omitting hairy areas. Since a tick may take two or more days to attach and feed, the risk of infection can be reduced by frequent body checks and prompt tick removal.
- Immediately remove any ticks detected, brushing off those unattached and removing those already affixed by gently using tweezers to grasp head and mouth parts as close to skin level as possible, pulling slowly to detach the entire tick. Try not to squash them as this releases bacteria, which may enter the body.
- Avoid handling the ticks, as the infective spirochetes could pierce the body through a scratch or cut in the skin.
- Disinfect with soap and water (or with alcohol or Betadine) after tick removal.

- If gardening, hiking, playing or romping in a known tick-infested area, wear long-sleeved and long-legged clothing that fits tightly around wrists and ankles (tucking pants into socks or boots).
- Walk along the center of trail paths to reduce contact with underbrush.
- Favour light-colored clothes on which a black tick shows up.
- Use insect repellents containing diethyl m-toluamide (DEET).
- Apply the tick-repellent permethrin (Permanone) to clothing.
- Be sure to apply repellent to shoes, socks and pant-legs to protect the vulnerable feet and legs.
- Check pets and remove ticks before they enter the house.

N.B. Contrary to popular belief, getting rid of ticks with nailpolish, salt, mineral oil, matches or cigarettes is not as effective as removal with tweezers or forceps.

---

curious ring-shaped rash and severe headaches as well as swollen joints.

Many of the initial juvenile Connecticut sufferers lived near heavily wooded regions and caught the disease in summertime. At first, scientists suspected some environmental pollutant. But some children remembered having a tick bite, and all clues pointed to the small woodland biting tick, of the *Ixodes* genus. Yale University researchers ultimately confirmed the link to tick bites and to a similar condition already identified in Europe during the early 1900s.

A corkscrew-shaped bacterium (a spirochete) was extracted from the gut of one biting tick in 1982, and later identified in the blood, spinal fluid and inflamed skin of some humans. The spirochete was named *Borrelia burgdorferi* in 1982, for its discoverer, Dr. Willy Burgdorfer.

The ticks that transmit Lyme disease include *Ixodes dammini* in eastern areas of this continent, *Ixodes pacificus* in the west and *Ixodes ricinus* in Europe. The tick measures one to four millimeters across — not much larger than a sesame seed or small ant, and roughly half the size of the common dog tick. It is tiny enough to be overlooked or mistaken for a

freckle or a fleck of dirt. Many of those who develop Lyme disease don't remember having seen any such creature, nor do they recall being bitten.

Between hosts, the ticks usually inhabit tall grasslands and wooded areas. The likelihood of people becoming infected is greatest when the feet and legs come in contact with long grass or shrubs; the hungry ticks linger low down on the vegetation with their front legs up, poised in a "questing" position, ready to attach themselves to animals or humans that brush against them. While commonest in tall vegetation, they have been detected on well-trimmed suburban lawns and found crawling amid the foliage of England's famous parks. The ticks are especially numerous in places where deer thrive.

In their habitual hosts (mice and deer) the ticks cause no illness, but when infected ticks take a meal from other warm-blooded animals, they may cause disease. Ixodes ticks have been found on animals ranging from dogs, horses, sheep and cats to birds (e.g., wrens and yellowthroats). In Canada, Ixodes ticks infected with Lyme-disease spirochetes were first detected in Ontario's Long Point wildlife sanctuary and provincial park on Lake Erie, a popular tourist resort and stopover point for many migrating birds. (It is theorized that birds carrying infected ticks imported Lyme disease to this Ontario site, but the ticks may have been introduced when the area was purposely repopulated with deer during the early 1900s.) The number of cases reported in Canada since 1984 is under 200, almost all of these people having a history of travel outside Canada to places where Lyme disease is prevalent.

Diagnosis of Lyme disease remains tricky

Physicians sometimes have difficulty in identifying Lyme disease, which may become clear only when its later manifestations — the neurological complications and cardiovascular symptoms — emerge. The characteristic bull's-eye rash appears in only some of those infected, but "satellite" skin lesions away from the original bite site may be telltale clues. Confirmation of diagnosis depends on culturing the organism from the skin lesions, blood or cerebrospinal fluid. A high white-blood-cell count (denoting infection), muscle aches and general flulike malaise may be preliminary hints. A blood test for antibodies to the causative agent (present three to six weeks after the infecting tick bite) may help to confirm the disease. But serological (blood) tests lack specificity and many labs aren't set up to do them. Several different tests may have to be done for accurate diagnosis. Some people who experience no rash and no cardiac or nerve problems may become aware of having Lyme disease only when arthritis surfaces two or more years after the tick bite. New research is investigating the use of DNA probes for diagnosing Lyme disease.

Treatment of Lyme disease

Fortunately, Lyme disease responds well to antibiotic therapy. Treatment with antibiotics such as amoxicillin, ceftriaxone, penicillin, doxycycline or others prevents most serious complications of this bacterial illness. Even if Lyme disease has advanced to stage two or three, antibiotics are still effective in most cases, although intravenous administration and hospitalization for a few days may be needed.

PEPTIC ULCERS: DIGESTING MORE THAN FOOD

One of the world's most common maladies, and the subject of many a joke, ulcers are no laughing matter. Peptic ulcers make life miserable for 10 percent of North Americans at some point in their lives. While ulcers can also occur in other parts of the body, the popular term refers primarily to "peptic" ulcers in the duodenum (first part of the small intestine leading out of the stomach) or in the stomach itself.

A recent nationwide survey revealed how amazingly ill-informed many of us are about ulcers. Most people believe stress to be the main cause, and a survey showed that almost 90 percent of North Americans hold to the outmoded idea that milk and bland diets are good ulcer cures. Long-standing myths aside, new studies show *no* evidence that stress causes ulcers, although it may aggravate existing ones. Easygoing people are as likely to get ulcers as hard-driving workaholics. And bland milk diets are no longer considered effective cures.

Still more startling is the survey's discovery that half of those who'd already had an ulcer thought ASA was beneficial for the condition. "Incredible!" comments one University of Toronto expert, "because ASA (such as Aspirin), along with other nonsteroidal anti-inflammatory drugs, is a prime ulcer-provoker."

Ulcers are small pits or craters that develop in the mucous membrane that lines the stomach and duodenum — the top part of the small intestine. The word "peptic" comes from pepsin, the enzyme that normally helps to break down food and contributes to the erosion that produces an ulcer. Peptic ulcers occur most often in the duodenum — "duodenal ulcers" — and less commonly in the stomach itself — "gastric ulcers." Occasionally ulcers arise in the esophagus or in the small bowel ("Meckel's diverticulosis").

In the past, peptic-ulcer disease, especially duodenal ulcers, afflicted mainly men, but nowadays many women are also affected — particularly the elderly and those who take anti-inflammatory drugs to relieve conditions such as arthritis. Although ulcers vary in size from a pinhole to 2.5 cm (1 in) or larger, size has little to do with the intensity of pain. While some

COMPLICATIONS OF UNTREATED ULCERS CAN BE SEVERE

- *A bleeding ulcer* — found in 15–20 percent of ulcer patients — may be undetected until it signals its presence with bloody vomit and/or black, tarry stools. Slow-bleeding ulcers may cause anemia (with dizziness and fatigue) due to internal blood loss, but ulcer bleeding stops spontaneously in 90 percent of cases. The rest may need surgery, although injection therapy (see below) and laser treatment show promise in halting ulcer bleeds.
- *A perforated ulcer* — which eats into and penetrates the stomach or duodenal wall — affects 5 to 10
percent of ulcer sufferers, more commonly men than women.
- *An obstructive ulcer* — perhaps due to gastric-scar formation — blocks the passage of food through the stomach outlet and may cause sudden nausea and vomiting, typically late in the day.

ulcers heal spontaneously, others persist for months despite treatment. About three-quarters of those with duodenal ulcers have a relapse or repeat ulcer within a year of having one treated.

What causes ulcers?

The exact cause(s) of peptic-ulcer disease remains uncertain, but it's generally believed that it develops when aggressive forces in the digestive tract (the acid and pepsin) overwhelm its defensive elements (the mucosal lining and

its protective mechanism). While ulcers were formerly blamed on "too much acid," recent studies show that although duodenal-ulcer patients may have excess acid (up to double normal values), gastric ulcers develop in people with normal amounts of stomach acid. The collected scientific evidence suggests that ulcers form when something goes out of kilter, especially if the mucosal lining is weakened and strong digestive juices overpower its natural defenses and penetrate the surrounding gastrointestinal lining — literally eating it up.

Recent research implicates a spiral bacterium, *Helicobacter pylori*, as a factor in ulcer formation — a surprising connection since stomach acid is normally a bacterial killer! *H. pylori* bacteria appear to adapt well to the stomach's hostile acidic juices and are believed to promote ulcer formation by undermining defense mechanisms. Studies show that 84 percent of patients with duodenal ulcers harbor *H. pylori* infections, the incidence increasing with age. However, the causative role of *H. pylori* remains controversial. Some researchers suggest that overlapping risk factors (such as smoking and some diseases) may precipitate these infections. Treatment with bismuth salts and antibiotics may eliminate the *H. pylori* infection.

KNOWN RISK FACTORS FOR PEPTIC-ULCER DISEASE

- *Heredity* — close relatives of ulcer patients are three times more likely than others to develop peptic ulcers.
- *Smoking* — a prime contributor and one reason why women (now smoking in increasing numbers) are developing ulcers more often. Smoking doubles the chances of getting an ulcer, increases its severity, slows healing (perhaps because tobacco smoke stimulates
acid secretion) and enhances the risk of recurrence and complications. (Smokers have a 72 percent ulcer recurrence rate, compared to 21 percent in nonsmokers.)
- *Nonsteroidal anti-inflammatory drugs* or *NSAIDs* raise the chance of ulcers by 10 percent, and increase the risk of ulcer complications, especially bleeding and perforation.
- *Caffeine* — it stimulates gastric-acid
secretion. Ulcer-prone people should not drink coffee on an empty stomach.
- *Particular foods* — some foods that do not cause ulcers can aggravate or relieve ulcer pain, depending on the type of ulcer and the person who has it.
- *Eating frequent small meals* — far from being an ulcer cure, as previously believed, switches on the stomach's digestive secretions more
often, leading to greater destruction of the mucosal lining and a higher risk of ulcers.
- *Milk* — although it can temporarily soothe the discomfort of an ulcer, milk promotes the release of more gastric acid than it can counteract, and may aggravate the problem.
- *Alcohol* — while pure alcohol decreases gastric-acid production, the protein content of beers and wines may promote
acid secretion and increase ulcer risks.
- *Stress* — while hard-working, stressed-out "type A" people were once thought to be ulcer-prone, the link remains unproven. However, the inability to cope well with stress may play a role. While ulcer patients don't necessarily experience more stress than others, they may *perceive* more stress in their lives and handle it less well.

DRUGS FOR PEPTIC-ULCER DISEASE

Antacids

Useful mostly for duodenal ulcers, antacids neutralize acid, relieve pain and promote mucosal healing. They come in tablet or liquid form — liquids being the most effective — and are best taken one to three hours after meals and at bedtime. Aluminum hydroxide and magnesium hydroxide are the longest-acting forms. Calcium carbonate (found in Tums and Rolaids) gives rapid relief but is apt to trigger "acid rebound" — a surge of acid after two or three hours. One problem with antacids is failure to take the right amount: people often self-medicate without advice from a doctor or pharmacist and stop taking the medicine as soon as the pain vanishes, rather than continuing and allowing the ulcer to heal.

Antacids have side effects. Magnesium-containing antacids commonly cause diarrhea; aluminum compounds may produce constipation, and prolonged therapy can disrupt mineral metabolism; products rich in sodium should be avoided by anyone with high blood pressure and kidney or heart disease. Some antacids interfere with the action of other drugs — notably altering the effects of warfarin, digoxin, and some anticonvulsants, antibiotics and anti-inflammatories. (See appendix).

Gastric-acid suppressors (to reduce digestive acid levels)

- *Histamine H2-receptor blockers* (acid-reducing drugs) have transformed ulcer management. Taken as tablets, H2-blockers act on the stomach's surface receptors and prevent release of histamine, one of the substances that stimulates hydrochloric-acid secretion, inhibiting acid buildup. (Histamine is also involved in allergic reactions, but the receptors are different: ulcer drugs don't cure allergies.) The end result of H2-blocker treatment is less stomach acid, which permits healing. These drugs can reduce ulcer pain within hours of the first dose, allowing ulcers to heal in a few weeks. The first of the H2-blockers on the market, cimetidine, introduced in the early 1970s, revolutionized ulcer treatment. Besides cimetidine (Tagamet) and ranitidine (Zantac), acid-suppressing drugs include the more recent famotidine (Pepcid) and nizatidine (Axid) — a single bedtime dose healing a duodenal ulcer in four weeks and a gastric ulcer in six to eight weeks.

  Side effects of H2-blockers (especially cimetidine) include dizziness, mental confusion and drowsiness. They can also cause impotence in men and may interact with other drugs (such as warfarin, theophylline and Valium).

- *Proton-pump inhibitors.* The recently approved drug omeprazole is 10 times more powerful in suppressing stomach acid than the H2-blockers, able to promote duodenal ulcer healing in two to four weeks, though not necessarily as swift with gastric ulcers. This potent acid-inhibitor is especially useful for people whose ulcers fail to respond to H2-receptor blockers or other medications, and those with Zollinger-Ellison syndrome. (Side effects include diarrhea, cramps, indigestion and bloating in some.)

- *Anticholinergics* (to block acetylcholine neurotransmitter action). In wide use before the arrival of H2-receptor blockers (but now mainly of historical interest), these drugs are still occasionally used in conjunction with new medications for stubborn ulcers.

- *Gut-lining protectors or barrier shields.* These medications, such as sucralfate (Sulcrate or Carafate) — an aluminum salt of sucrose — don't alter stomach-acid levels, but coat the ulcer (crater), forming a barrier across which hydrochloric acid and pepsin cannot pass, promoting healing. Taken two to four times a day and at bedtime, sucralfate has fewer side effects than H2-blockers. However, about 5 percent report nausea, constipation or a metallic taste in the mouth.

- *Prostaglandin-like medications.* Misoprostol (Cytotec), a synthetic prostaglandin-E, is especially valuable for people such as arthritics who regularly take ASA or other NSAIDs that suppress natural prostaglandin production. Misoprostol decreases acid production and enhances gastric defenses. Healing rates parallel those with H2-receptor blockers, but one big advantage of this drug is its ability to combat the damaging effects of NSAIDs. Misoprostol is highly effective in healing ASA-induced ulcers, and studies suggest it can also protect against NSAID-induced kidney damage (a recently reported adverse effect of anti-inflammatories). Misoprostol may be prescribed along with anti-inflammatories for arthritis. However, its side effects, experienced by 9 to 13 percent of patients — especially diarrhea, abdominal cramps and menstrual disturbances — may limit its use. As it may cause uterine contractions, this drug shouldn't be prescribed for woman of childbearing age. (Other occasional adverse effects include headache, dizziness, fever and flushing.)

- *Antibacterials.* Colloidal bismuth suspensions such as Pepto-Bismol may promote ulcer healing — not by influencing gastric-acid levels, but by increasing prostaglandin secretion and suppressing *H. pylori* infections.

ASA and other nonsteroidal anti-inflammatory drugs (NSAIDs) — such as ibuprofen (Advil, Motrin), naproxen (Naprosyn), piroxicam (Feldene) and many others — have emerged as a powerful risk factor for peptic ulcers and are now considered major culprits in causing gastric ulcers. These medications injure the stomach lining and suppress its defense mechanisms, largely by blocking the production of protective prostaglandins. Ulcers due to NSAIDs pose a sizable health problem, as almost 50 percent of arthritics (two million in

Canada) regularly use them. Anyone taking NSAIDs should be alert to the danger of developing stomach ulcers, know the signs and get regular medical checkups.

Diagnosing your ulcer

Peptic ulcers generally herald their presence by abdominal pain — a dull, gnawing ache or hunger pain in the pit of the stomach, often described as "really bad indigestion." The discomfort may be relieved in short order by eating, drinking or taking an antacid.

Given symptoms suggestive of peptic ulcers, physicians may first prescribe medication, ordering diagnostic tests only if the pain persists. The barium X-ray, once the standard test, has now been largely supplanted by endoscopy — using a fiber-optic viewing tube, or endoscope, inserted via the mouth, to look inside the gastrointestinal tract and identify any abnormalities, collecting tissue for analysis at the same time.

If the examination reveals a duodenal ulcer, the usual treatment is medication. However, if a gastric ulcer is detected the person is generally sent for further tests — because about 4 percent of gastric ulcers have malignant potential. Endoscopy is usually recommended for gastric-ulcer patients (for biopsy and to test for cancer cells), and also for anyone with severe symptoms of ulcer disease — bleeding or scarring.

Differentiating duodenal from gastric ulcers

Gastric and duodenal ulcers have broadly overlapping symptoms, making it difficult to tell them apart without endoscopic tests. For example, while food often brings rapid relief for duodenal ulcers (in 20–65 percent of sufferers), it tends to worsen the gastric type. Yet a fair number (up to 50 percent) of those with gastric ulcers *also* find that food soothes the discomfort.

Nonetheless, there are clues to distinguish the two forms. Duodenal ulcers typically affect people under age 50, mostly men. And the pain generally hits when the stomach is empty, between meals (one to three hours after eating) and at night, often sending sufferers to the fridge for a "midnight" snack. Eating can stop the pain within minutes.

Gastric or stomach ulcers — less common than the duodenal variety — typically afflict the middle-aged and elderly of both sexes. Gastric ulcer pain tends to come and go unpredictably, sometimes being worst soon after eating (depending on the ulcer's location in the stomach). Sufferers may also have nausea and appetite loss.

"Silent ulcers" are also common; about 10 to 25 percent of peptic ulcers produce no pain or other symptoms until they bleed or perforate. Those particularly prone to silent ulcers include smokers, the elderly, those with a history of peptic ulcers, people on ulcer therapy who stop taking their medication too soon and those taking NSAIDs (90 percent remaining quiescent until serious complications occur).

Treatment of ulcers: what brings relief?

Before effective ulcer medications appeared on the scene, serious peptic ulcers were usually treated surgically. However, there have been dramatic advances in ulcer management. Used appropriately, new medications can stop ulcer symptoms within days and heal them in four to eight weeks, *and* prevent repeat attacks. The key lies in correct diagnosis and use of drugs *before* serious damage occurs. But even if symptoms abate, and the pain vanishes within days, the medication should *not* be stopped until the ulcer has fully healed. Occasionally, multiple drug courses are needed to complete the healing.

Bleeding ulcers are treated by adrenaline injections (via an endoscope), hypertonic saline or thermocoagulation — using heater-probes or lasers.

Surgery is now usually a last resort. Gastrectomy (removing part of the stomach) is generally performed only for severe complications or ulcers that refuse to heal.

Preventing repeat ulcers

Unfortunately, ulcers tend to recur, especially in smokers, and multiple drug courses may be necessary. People who have illnesses that call for NSAIDs therapy may require a maintenance or preventive dose of antiulcer drugs or, better still, might try alternative medication.

STROKES

A stroke typically strikes unexpectedly, out of the blue, with symptoms such as speech-slurring, unsteadiness, dimmed vision and perhaps one-sided paralysis. Strokes are not unavoidable, not restricted to the elderly and not a distinct disease but a symptom of many different disorders. The third leading killer disease in Canada, after heart attacks and cancer, stroke is also a leading cause of disability (ahead of car accidents).

The modern approach is early identification and prompt remedial steps to prevent worse trouble. Everyone should learn the warning signs of a stroke and seek medical advice if they occur, however fleeting they may seem.

A stroke damages brain cells

A stroke is a constellation of symptoms due to any of several possible disorders that disrupt blood flow to parts of the brain, cutting off its oxygen supply and impairing its function. The former medical term for stroke, "cerebrovascular accident," is now considered outdated and has been replaced by the World Health Organization definition, "a rapidly developing focal (localized) disturbance of cerebral (brain) function, lasting more than 24 hours or leading to death, with no apparent cause other than vascular." Sudden symptoms such as speech difficulties, visual loss, limb tingling and weakness are presumed to stem from a blood-supply problem unless other causes are found. In essence, a stroke arises because a blood clot or ruptured blood vessel limits blood flow to parts of the brain.

About 20 percent of the blood pumped by the heart goes to the brain, which is extremely sensitive to any disruption in its oxygen supplies. Even a few seconds of oxygen depletion can impair delicate neuron (brain cell) function. If the brain's blood (and oxygen) is cut off for two to eight minutes, some brain cells will inevitably die. The ischemia, or oxygen lack, causes different disabilities according to the location and severity of the brain injury. Those parts of the body controlled by the damaged parts of the brain can no longer operate properly.

STROKES VARY IN SEVERITY

- *Transient ischemic attack (TIA)*, a brief, sudden, fully reversible set of symptoms — such as limb numbness/weakness, slurring, hazy vision — lasts only minutes and clears completely within 24 hours, leaving no residual disabilities. A warning sign of possible stroke down the road, it merits medical attention.
- *Reversible ischemic neurological deficit (RIND)* is also fully reversible with transient symptoms similar to those in TIAs but lasting longer than 24 hours, disappearing completely within 72 hours to one week.
- *Completed stroke*, with symptoms lasting more than two weeks, leaves permanent disabilities of varying degrees.
- *Progressing or evolving stroke* involves neurological disabilities that worsen progressively over time.

Besides the oxygen lack, a cascade of chemical reactions triggered by the oxygen starvation contributes to the death of brain cells. An excess of glutamate and other nerve transmitters, released by the oxygen-deprived tissues, accelerates cell destruction. Impairment of nerve function appears before brain tissue is irreparably damaged, and if blood flow is swiftly restored, normal function may return.

Researchers are working on chemical antagonists that could slow down or stop the brain damage following oxygen depletion. Various substances, given immediately after a stroke, may preserve brain cells and allow clot-dissolvers such as tissue plasminogen activator (tPA) to stop the damage and aid the recovery of oxygen-starved tissues. Recent reports suggest that "clot-busters" such as tPA (also used for heart attacks) may reduce disability if given within an hour or two of stroke onset.

WHAT HAPPENS IN A STROKE

- *Hemorrhage* — the sudden rupture of a brain artery that bursts and bleeds into nearby tissues — may cut off oxygen-bearing blood to part of the brain. Brain hemorrhages account for about 20 percent of strokes and are often due to hypertension (high blood pressure).
- *Infarction or death of brain tissue* may be caused by a blood clot that originates in or travels to a blood vessel supplying part of the brain and blocks it. This event is called a *thrombosis* if the clot arises within a brain artery, an *embolism* if the clot forms elsewhere (perhaps in the heart or a neck artery) and is carried into the brain via the bloodstream. Infarcts are responsible for about 80 percent of strokes.

RISK FACTORS FOR STROKE

- *Increasing age* — stroke risks double for each decade after age 55. The incidence of stroke at ages 55–64 years is about 150 per 100,000 population per year, compared to 600 per 100,000 population per year in those over 80.
- *Male gender* — men are 30 percent more likely than women to suffer strokes, especially before age 65.

- *Race* — blacks are twice as likely as whites to suffer strokes, perhaps because they're more prone to high blood pressure.
- *Family history* — stroke is not inherited, but risk factors such as atherosclerosis and hypertension run in families.
- *Smoking* — an avoidable risk factor.
- *Hypertension* (high

blood pressure) — one of the main modifiable risk factors. Studies confirm that the higher the blood pressure is, the greater the chance of stroke.
- *Diabetes mellitus* — diabetics have stroke risks two to three times above average. Controlling diabetes can diminish the risk.
- *Certain drugs* — such as crack/cocaine and amphetamines

("speed") — can induce hemorrhagic strokes.
- *Cardioembolic heart problems* — blood clots originating in the heart — trigger 15 to 25 percent of strokes. One particular heart disorder, *atrial fibrillation* (AF) — a "quivering" upper heart chamber that produces an irregular heartbeat, which affects about

5 percent of those over 60 — greatly increases stroke risks. The Framingham Heart Study found a sixfold rise in strokes among those with AF compared to others. AF may arise from rheumatic heart-valve (e.g., mitral valve) flaws, coronary-artery disease, an enlarged heart, thyroid disorders and some lung diseases.

What are the signs and symptoms of stroke?

Stroke symptoms vary according to the causes (clots versus bleeding) and the location and severity of brain damage. They range from momentary slurring, brief visual loss and transient dizziness to complete paralysis. Since many functions, including movement, sight and sensation, are controlled by the *opposite* side of the brain, damage to the brain's left side will impair (perhaps paralyze) the body's right side and vice versa.

Specialized skills such as language, mathematical ability and space perception may be located on one or other side of the brain, so damage to the brain's left side will produce different disabilities from those of right-side injury. For example, language centers are usually situated in the brain's left hemisphere, so left-sided brain damage may abolish the ability to speak or understand speech. Right-sided brain (stroke) injury may leave speech untouched but ruin artistic or constructional capacities.

Heed the warning signs, however brief

Do not ignore the signs of stroke, however transient or seemingly insignificant, and even though the symptoms vanish completely. Symptoms may last only 10 to 15 minutes, but heeding even brief warning signals and

obtaining swift medical advice can prevent more devastating future consequences.

Transient ischemic attacks may be a warning

Transient ischemic attacks, or TIAs — popularly called incomplete, "mini" or "threatened" strokes — precede about 30 percent of all strokes. They involve a sudden, temporary loss of brain function, lasting less than 24 hours and leaving no residual ill effects. People who survive TIAs have a 10 to 20 percent higher-than-average risk of a repeat and worse attack within the next two years. Any unexplained fainting of an older person should be investigated as a possible TIA.

Those with TIAs due to severe carotid (neck) artery obstruction may consider surgery to prevent a subsequent stroke. Those at suspected risk due to blood clots can start on anti–platelet-clumping drugs such as ASA or the newer ticlopidine (Ticlid). People with cardiogenic (from the heart) stroke symptoms may be put on anticoagulants such as warfarin (Coumadin).

Sadly, the TIA danger signs can be so brief and faint that they are ignored. Yet those who experience TIAs have the good fortune to be warned; they have time to take preventive action and avoid lasting disability. Take the case of a 40-year-old advertising manager who, in the middle of a planning session, suddenly felt her right arm go inexplicably numb, her vision dim, her words — usually so crisp and clear — come out jumbled. Within half an hour the symptoms vanished, and she thought no more of them until the weekend, when she gave the perplexing episode a passing mention to her skiing companion. He advised her to tell her physician, and at her next checkup she was promptly sent for a full investigation. Her heart was thoroughly checked, the carotid artery in her neck was examined by ultrasound, a CAT (brain) X-ray scan was ordered, a battery of blood tests was done for her "clotting index" (platelet count, blood-fat profile) and her thyroid function was tested. A mild heart-valve condition seemed to have caused the fleeting symptoms and she was put on ASA therapy to avoid a possible future stroke.

Diagnosing the cause is essential

A stroke always originates from a vascular (blood supply) disorder. Conditions that mimic stroke and are commonly misdiagnosed as stroke include Bell's palsy (transient facial paralysis due to an inflamed nerve), seizures, psychiatric disorders (such as hysteria) and confusion due to previous strokes.

Where a true stroke is involved, modern practice tends to classify it not only by cause and location but also by why it arose. It's essential not to accept a stroke as an unavoidable happening from which to recover as well as possible, but to discover why and how it occurred, track down the causes and prevent any future, possibly worse, episode. *Prevention is the essence of today's therapy.*

Tests may include CAT scans (special brain X-rays), magnetic resonance imaging (MRI), carotid-artery soundings, echocardiograms (to visualize the heart's chambers), a spinal puncture to detect blood in the cerebrospinal fluid (from a brain bleed) and other investigations. The tests check for cardiac causes — for instance, a faulty heart valve or a heartbeat irregularity — and for atherosclerotic narrowing of the neck arteries that supply blood to the brain. Physicians listen for a special sound or "bruit" in the neck to show whether or how badly the carotid arteries are obstructed.

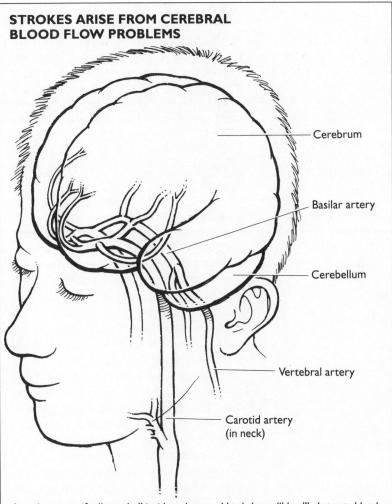

STROKES ARISE FROM CEREBRAL BLOOD FLOW PROBLEMS

Cerebrum

Basilar artery

Cerebellum

Vertebral artery

Carotid artery (in neck)

A stroke occurs if a "vascular" incident due to a blood clot or "bleed" obstructs blood flow in the brain and deprives it of oxygen.

THE MAIN WARNING SIGNS OF STROKE:

- sudden weakness or numbness, or even paralysis, on one side of the body (face, arm and/or leg);
- sudden speech loss, trouble speaking or difficulty in understanding spoken words or reading. The person may simply slur words, be unable to find the "right" word, experience a weakness in the jaw or a lack of tongue coordination;
- sudden blurring or partial visual loss, sometimes in one eye only;
- severe, unusual headache (the "worst ever experienced"), often accompanied by nausea and drowsiness;
- dizziness or vertigo ("room spinning");
- sudden falls, unsteadiness, clumsy movements;
- unexplained unconsciousness or falls (drop attacks);
- gait unsteadiness, imbalance;
- tingling on one side, one arm, one leg;
- difficulty swallowing;
- diminution in touch and feeling.

Hemorrhages (bleeds) into the brain may arise because of:

- the bursting of a small, deep brain artery due to longstanding hypertension (high blood pressure), accounting for 10 percent of strokes;
- a subarachnoid hemorrhage or ruptured aneurysm (outpouching) that spills blood into the space between the brain and skull. An aneurysm is a tiny sac or ballooning of a cerebral artery, more common in women than men. It may form because of a congenital (inherited) blood-vessel weakness, or due to head blows, atherosclerosis or inflammation. Responsible for 10 percent of all strokes, aneurysms account for half of all fatal strokes in people under age 45. An aneurysm rarely announces its presence until the bubble "bursts" and produces severe symptoms. Rupture can occur during sleep or if blood pressure suddenly increases (for instance during physical exertion, emotional stress, arguments, sex). If an aneurysm ruptures (not all do), blood rushes out at enormous pressure and can cause an excruciating headache ("as if hit on the back of the head"), nausea, vomiting, hallucinations, photophobia (light aversion), a stiff neck and perhaps confusion, lethargy and unconsciousness.

Serious consequences may be headed off by rapid diagnosis and treatment to stop the bleed. Neurosurgeons stress the importance of so-called warning leaks experienced by many people with aneurysms — producing symptoms such as double vision, a searing headache, pain at the base of the neck — in the days, weeks or months before a devastating attack. Treating the warning leak may avoid a full cerebral bleed — but the early signs are often confused with migraine, flu or sinus headaches.

Infarcts (clots that block blood flow) may arise because of:

- *atherosclerosis* — where arteries are narrowed by fatty deposits. Blood clots form easily in arteries scarred by atherosclerosis. Pieces of plaque may travel from wider to narrower brain blood vessels and obstruct blood flow. Blockages in small cerebral vessels account for 20 percent of strokes due to infarcts;
- *a narrowing or blockage* in one or more of the four large blood vessels supplying blood to the brain — the *carotids* in front of the neck and the *vertebral* arteries at the back — blamed for 20–25 percent of infarct-caused strokes;
- *cardiogenic embolisms* — breakaway clots from the heart— which account for another 25 percent of clot-caused strokes. A heart attack can trigger a stroke if a freshly damaged heart wall doesn't pump properly and forms a *mural thrombosis* (wall clot) that travels to the brain. Clots formed in malfunctioning heart valves may also break away and reach the brain; artificial replacement heart valves are especially prone to form clots;
- *atrial fibrillation* (a heart flutter) — described above;
- *blood coagulation problems* and rare blood disorders;
- *unknown causes.*

Surgery can unclog blocked carotid arteries

The operation known as *carotid endarterectomy*, which removes plaque from carotid (neck) arteries, has proved highly successful for preventing stroke in those with badly clogged carotid arteries. The American National Institutes of Health issued a 1991 medical alert suggesting that carotid endarterectomy be "considered standard treatment in those with severely blocked carotid arteries."

The presence of carotid-artery obstruction is suspected when a "bruit" or whooshing sound is heard in the neck. But surgery is advised only after extensive tests by ultrasound and angiography (X-rays after dye injection) confirm at least a 70 percent carotid narrowing. The surgery entails opening up the artery in the neck (under general anesthetic), scraping out the diseased portion, then sewing the artery up again; a piece of leg vein is sometimes inserted to patch the artery. Researchers stress that, although low, the surgical risks are not negligible: about 2 percent are disabled or suffer a stroke during or soon after carotid surgery. Thus it's wise to seek out a specialized center for the procedure.

For those with mildly (less than 30 percent) obstructed carotid arteries, surgery doesn't help. Patients who haven't had a TIA but have a carotid bruit are generally advised to take ASA (such as Aspirin) and "watch and wait."

The stroke-prevention message

It's estimated that half of all strokes could be avoided by correct preventive measures. Those who smoke should quit, those with high blood pressure can try to get it down. People who experience TIAs or minor strokes should be thoroughly examined to track down any underlying disorders that increase stroke risks. They may be advised to adopt a preventive program, which can avoid serious disability or death. Rapid, appropriate treatment promises good stroke recovery, particularly in younger people (under age 60–65) and — more crucially — can prevent subsequent and worse attacks.

Preventive steps
- Have blood pressure regularly measured and, if it's high, try to lower it.
- Check for and correct cardiac disorders such as heartbeat irregularities, mitral-valve and other heart abnormalities.
- Women (especially those with migraine headaches) who take contraceptive pills and also smoke may be at increased risk of stroke and should try to reduce the danger (e.g., stop smoking).
- Heed mild signs of stroke and get immediate medical advice.

Can an "Aspirin a day" keep strokes away?

Even after 100 years of use, we do not know exactly how acetylsalicylic acid or ASA (such as Aspirin) works. Nevertheless, the results of a U.S. Physicians' Health Study released in 1989 showed that regular ASA use almost halved the incidence of stroke and heart attacks, especially in men (allegedly less so in women). While ASA diminishes platelet stickiness, clumping and clot formation, not all medical trials show that it can prevent strokes.

Nonetheless, many clinicians now prescribe enteric-coated brands of Aspirin as standard therapy after a TIA or mini-stroke — in doses of about 650 mg per day. Recent research suggests that "baby Aspirins" (30–40 mg daily) may be just as effective in preventing clot formation, with less stomach irritation; a Dutch study showed that 30 mg alters platelet aggregation more favorably than the large doses currently used to prevent strokes.

How ASA reduces stroke risks isn't fully understood. One theory is that it blocks the release of thromboxane-A2 — a substance that promotes blood clotting. While the best dose for stroke prevention isn't conclusively known, it's important to remember that ASA is a powerful drug that should only be taken under medical supervision. In the Physicians' Health Study, Aspirin-takers were 33 percent more likely than average to suffer nosebleeds, bruising, vomited blood, bleeding ulcers, oozing from cuts and other anticoagulant effects.

As an alternative, the new antiplatelet drug ticlopidine (Ticlid), approved for use in Canada since September 1991, has shown itself equal to ASA in preventing strokes, with less gastric irritation. A multicenter Canadian-American study showed that in twice-daily doses of 250 mg, ticlopidine consistently reduced risks of stroke in women as well as in men — results superior to those for ASA. Ticlopidine is especially valuable for people who can't tolerate ASA. But ticlopidine has its own nuisance effects — diarrhea and a skin rash in some, and the slight risk (about 2 percent) of producing neutropenia (a fall in white-blood-cell numbers). Fortunately, neutropenia shows up within three months of starting ticlopidine, and is fully reversed if the drug is stopped.

Disabilities from stroke

The degree of recovery from stroke varies greatly: some people make a good recovery with little or no lasting impairment, others suffer minor but permanent handicaps and yet others are left virtually helpless. Although rehabilitation from stroke may take a long time — up to a year or more — full function may ultimately return.

The treatment and rehabilitation of stroke sufferers depends on the severity of the stroke and its effects. Nondamaged areas of the brain may continue to function efficiently, so that many intellectual and physical tasks can be

LEFT-BRAINED STROKES AND THEIR MANAGEMENT

Left-brain injury may produce:
- right-sided paralysis or weakness;
- slow, cautious manner and hesitant, anxious approach (perhaps in sharp contrast to former confident style);
- dysarthria — difficulty in clearly articulating words;
- swallowing problems;
- disorganized way of doing familiar actions;
- aphasia — language, reading and writing difficulties. Some people with left-brain damage may be unable to speak but still understand more than is apparent; others are better at saying things than understanding them. In a society so dependent on verbal communication, the inability to speak seems catastrophic. But just because people can't communicate verbally does not mean that they can't communicate at all. A lot of day-to-day communication can be carried on without speech — with hand gestures, body language, music, writing on a board, drawing pictures or using computers.

Tips for dealing with left-brain strokes:
- Never underestimate the ability to communicate, even if normal language modes cannot be used.
- Try other forms of communication — such as pantomime, drawing, demonstration and writing. Computers and "communication" boards can improve interaction. Use whatever works best for the individual situation.
- Don't over- or underestimate residual speech comprehension.
- Don't overload the person with too many words — use simple, brief statements.
- Don't shout — keep messages simple and short. (But watch for possible hearing problems.)
- Don't be patronizing or use "special" voices.
- Divide tasks into simple steps.
- Give plenty of feedback for tasks well done and applaud/reward progress.

RIGHT-BRAINED STROKES AND THEIR MANAGEMENT

Injury to the brain's right side may produce:
- difficulty with dressing, spatial tasks (throwing, catching, tooth-brushing), inability to judge distance, space, position, rate of movement;
- perceptual deficits (poor understanding of what's seen);
- quick, impulsive behavior (perhaps in sharp contrast to former deliberate manner);
- memory flaws, problems in remembering dates, appointments, difficulty learning new tasks, impaired performance of music, math, many motor skills;
- problems in positioning hands, feet (e.g., misses buttons, applies lipstick crookedly);
- frequent stumbling, inability to steer wheelchair through door;
- inability to tell whether leaning or standing upright;
- unsafe driving or crossing of streets;
- poor judgment about own actions; a sufferer may wildly overestimate remaining capacities, ignore defects, display overconfidence;
- understanding of oral commands but not visual cues;
- a need for feedback for success in relearning tasks — encouragement to "go slow," "take your time," "try again."

Tips for dealing with right-brain strokes:
- Anticipate poor spatial judgment, impulsiveness, clumsiness, over-rapid movements.
- Put good lighting in rooms, halls, stairwells.
- Don't overestimate abilities. Spatial-perceptual deficits are easy to miss.
- Use spoken cues if visual demonstrations seem hard to grasp.
- Break tasks into small steps and give much positive feedback.
- Make sure that tasks are done safely rather than taking safety for granted.
- Minimize clutter and remove obstacles to trip over.
- Avoid over-rapid movements.

For more information contact the Heart and Stroke Foundation; social workers from any large rehabilitation center or hospital rehabilitation department; speech-recovery clinics — e.g., the Ontario Speech Centre.

carried on as before, making the person appear as capable as ever. However, even minor brain injury may make it hard to perform other, seemingly comparable tasks. Damage to either side of the brain tends to affect the *opposite* side of the body, with severity ranging from weakness and/or clumsiness to complete paralysis.

Damage to the brain's left side often produces aphasia (language loss), one of the most devastating consequences. Different aspects of language — reading, writing, naming objects, word meaning, the ability to repeat words — can be affected. Aphasics may "get stuck" and repeat the same word (maybe a swearword) over and over, or use nonsense words and bizarre phrases to express desires. Caregivers must learn to respond to the new modes of communication and use simple, clear language in a normal tone of voice. Treating stroke sufferers as though they don't understand is a mistake.

Damage to the brain's right hemisphere may undermine the ability to convey emotions and to judge distance, space and time. People with right-sided cerebral damage may also have trouble finding their way, knock into things, or be unable to button up their clothes or recognize familiar faces and places. (In most left-handers and some right-handers, language function is situated in the brain's *right* hemisphere, so aphasia may also follow right-sided brain injury.)

Articulation and swallowing abnormalities are common in stroke sufferers, whichever side of the brain is injured. Strokes that affect nerve fibers controlling movement of the face, lips, mouth, throat and tongue can make speech sound different and hard to understand (dysarthria).

Hearing is rarely affected by a stroke, but if there was a prior hearing problem, the stroke may further diminish hearing ability as well as comprehension. Hearing aids can help.

Visual pathways may be affected and cause double vision or the sensation that objects are oscillating. With right-sided brain injury, left-sided vision may be impaired, and vice versa. Some stroke sufferers miss certain parts of the visual field; most learn to compensate for these cuts by turning their heads,

but some cannot make the adjustment. Such "neglect" can involve signals from all senses on one side, so the person may not recognize his or her own arm or leg as a part of the body. Neglect on one side may make someone divide things at the midline (viewing only half the field): for example, eating from one side of the plate and leaving the rest, unless the plate is then turned around. Sufferers may ignore those who speak to them from the impaired side and the speaker's appearance on the "good" side may elicit surprise — as if he or she had just arrived. Or they may become confused when traveling; if wheeled down and back an unfamiliar corridor, they may see one side going, the other coming back, as if there were two separate corridors.

While intellectual abilities often remain untouched or return within a few months, there may be startling alterations in behavior. The previously garrulous person may become uncommunicative, the meticulous become sloppy, the energetic become lazy or the lazy become hyperactive. Right-sided strokes may make people impulsive, while left-sided brain injury often leaves people passive. These behavior changes make enormous demands on caregivers.

It can take weeks or longer just to assess the full impact of a stroke. Although destroyed brain tissue cannot regenerate itself, other parts of the brain may develop new connecting pathways and take over the functions of damaged areas. Post-stroke management strategies must be individually tailored by rehabilitation experts for maximum results.

Rehabilitation is a multidisciplinary process

Therapy for stroke involves the joint help of physicians, occupational, physical and speech therapists, nurses, psychologists, social workers and other experts to help stroke victims adapt to their handicaps. The patient and caregivers must be "active" members of the rehab team and participate in the recovery process, not just accept advice. With good rehabilitation methods and time, many can return to near-normal activities.

THYROID DISORDERS

The thyroid gland can produce health problems through changes within its own tissues or changes in its hormone output. Severe thyroid disease can cause dramatic symptoms, but milder, more subtle thyroid problems may take years to develop. However, once thyroid disease is accurately diagnosed, treatment is generally simple and effective.

The thyroid gland is part of the body's endocrine system, which encompasses the lymph glands, which fight infection, and the endocrine glands, which make and release hormones — biochemical messengers that target specific organs and tissues.

What the thyroid does

A well-functioning thyroid is essential to normal growth and development. The gland stores and secretes two hormones — thyroxine (T4), and triiodothyronine (T3) — both of which circulate in the bloodstream and act on specific target cells or organs. T3 and T4 hormones are vital cell accelerators that speed up the metabolism. In order for the body to maintain a healthy metabolic rate, the thyroid must release the correct amount of hormones into the blood. Its balance is constantly adjusted by a feedback process similar to the thermostatic control of room temperature.

The rate at which the thyroid gland produces T3 and T4 hormones is regulated by yet another hormone — thyrotropin, or thyroid-stimulating hormone (TSH) — secreted by the *pituitary* gland in the floor of the brain. And TSH production is controlled by yet another hormone, thyrotropin-releasing-hormone (TRH), from the *hypothalamus*, within the brain.

Once a certain level of thyroxine in the blood is reached, TSH and TRH production drop, shutting off thyroid-hormone release, achieving just the right balance for the body's needs.

Too much or too little thyroid hormone can cause health problems. If the thyroid gland is low in hormone output, cellular processes slow down; "hypothyroidism" can reduce the basal metabolic rate — the body's rate of oxygen use and energy production — by as much as 40 percent. If, on the other hand, thyroid hormones are produced in excess, the basal metabolic rate may rise 60- to 100-fold, leading to "hyperthyroidism" — the target cells and tissues working too hard. For unknown reasons thyroid dysfunction affects more women than men.

Hyperthyroidism — too much thyroid hormone

Hyperthyroidism, due to an excess of T4 hormone or thyroxine, affects mainly women aged 20–45, with an estimated incidence of two per 1,000 men and 19 per 1,000 women. Thyroxine increases the rate at which fats and carbohydrates are used by the body's cells, also increasing rates of protein synthesis. Someone with T4 overproduction may have an accelerated metabolic rate and lose weight despite a normal or large food intake, may also have an increased respiration rate and is apt to pant or perspire with the least exertion.

Thyroxine also stimulates cardiovascular activity, so people with overactive thyroid glands may have an increased heartrate and experience palpitations. Robert Graves, the nineteenth-century Irish physician who originally described hyperthyroidism, was struck by its cardiac manifestations: "I could distinctly hear the heart beating when my ear was distant at least four feet from the chest," he said. In addition, an excess of thyroxine can affect the central nervous system, making

THE THYROID GLAND NEEDS IODINE

In order to form thyroxine (T4 hormone), the thyroid gland must obtain at least a trace of iodine — about 1 mg a week. Iodine deficiency during early childhood development can lead to goiter and possible mental retardation. Good natural sources of iodine are fish and other seafood, but some inland areas are low in iodine. Iodine-poor areas in North America include the Great Lakes region from the Appalachians to Washington — formerly called the "goiter belt" — where thyroid-deficiency problems used to be widespread.

To offset the possibility of iodine-deficiency, ordinary table salt is now iodized in North America. However, many developing countries don't iodize their salt, and international agencies still list iodine deficiency as one of the world's most pressing health problems. Millions in China, India, Africa, Latin America and other countries are at risk of thyroid disorders through iodine lack.

people anxious, jumpy, irritable and generally "hyper." Those with thyroid overproduction often sleep badly. In extreme cases, hyperthyroidism can result in mental illness and psychosis.

Graves' disease

Graves' disease is now regarded as an autoimmune disorder in which the body produces an antibody that attacks its own thyroid cells, tricking the thyroid gland into producing excess T3 and T4 hormones. Since the antibody is not subject to the normal feedback mechanisms that inhibit excess thyroid activity, even if the level of thyroid hormone in the bloodstream rises dramatically, T3 and T4 thyroid hormones continue to be overproduced. In Graves' disease, the thyroid gland can secrete as much as 15 times above-normal amounts of T4 hormone.

Although not invariably present, a goiter or painless thyroid enlargement — a lump in the lower front of the throat — is a classic sign of the disease. Graves' disease may also be associated with bulging eyes, retraction of the eyelids and a staring "pop-eyed" look known as exophthalmos. The eye complications in Graves' disease can be severe, with thickened eye muscles producing double vision. If the optic nerve is compressed, blindness may follow. Whether Graves' disease and exophthalmos are both manifestations of the same underlying autoimmune disease, or whether they are closely related but different disorders, remains debatable. Mild eye problems are dealt with symptomatically, using lubricating eyedrops, or eye patches at night, or raising the head of the bed to prevent fluid accumulation. Severe cases require corticosteroids or immunosuppressants to reduce inflammation. Very severe cases may require eye surgery.

Tests for hyperthyroidism

A suspicion of thyroid dysfunction is followed up by tests to measure thyroid-hormone levels in the blood. Thyroid function may also be assessed by a radioactive iodine scan, a test used to determine the underlying cause(s) of hyperthyroidism and look for possible triggers other than Graves' disease.

DIFFERENT FORMS OF HYPERTHYROIDISM

- *Graves' disease,* the commonest example of hyperthyroidism, especially in those under age 40.
- *Toxic multinodular goiter* — an enlarged, benign thyroid with hyperthyroidism, most common in people over age 50.
- *Pituitary or hypothalamic tumors,* which increase thyroid hormone production (rare).
- *Hyperthyroidism due to certain drugs* such as amiodarone (an antiarrhythmic heart drug containing iodine).
- *Transient hyperthyroidism* due to thyroiditis (see below) — possibly accompanied by the release of stored thyroid hormone.

"Thyroid storm" — a rare occurrence

Very occasionally, exacerbation of a preexisting thyroid problem gives rise to a "thyroid storm." A sudden excess of thyroid hormones leads to burning fever, racing heart, severe sweating and restlessness — a medical emergency. Thyroid storm can result in dehydration, shock and death. It sometimes arises in those with an untreated hyperthyroid problem, or after sudden withdrawal of an antithyroid drug, infection, surgery or trauma (damage) to the thyroid. A thyroid storm is generally treated with propylthiouracil, sodium iodide, propranolol and steroid drugs to halt the hormone overproduction.

Hypothyroidism

In contrast to the restless energy of people with excess thyroid activity, those with a low thyroxine output are generally slow, sluggish and perpetually fatigued. An estimated 0.5 percent of adults — mainly women — have hypothyroidism, its prevalence increasing to

---

SYMPTOMS OF GRAVES' DISEASE (THYROXINE OVERPRODUCTION)

- sweating;
- palpitations, racing heart;
- heat intolerance;
- fine tremor of outstretched hand;
- diarrhea, weight loss (despite good nutrition);
- extreme nervousness, irritability; if severe, the hyperthyroidism (rarely) causes mental illness and psychosis.
- *In children* — retarded sexual maturation. During pregnancy, Graves' disease tends to remit spontaneously — a result of the autoimmune suppression which often occurs in pregnancy so that a woman's body won't reject the fetus as "foreign." However, Graves' disease tends to recur following the birth.

TREATMENT OF HYPERTHYROIDISM

- *antithyroid drugs*, such as propylthiouracil and methimazole;
- *radioactive iodine*;
- *surgical removal* of part of the thyroid gland.

The most usual treatment is with antithyroid drugs to block the formation of thyroid hormones. These drugs are relatively safe and effective, although it may take several weeks before thyroid hormone levels revert to normal, as some hormone lingers in tissue stores. Methimazole is fairly cheap, administered only once a day and tastes better than propylthiouracil. (Propylthiouracil may be preferable for pregnant and lactating women.) Those who require antithyroid medication usually stay on it for about a year. About 20 percent go into permanent remission with drug therapy alone, requiring no further treatment. Those with mild hyperthyroidism and small goiters usually go into remission with drug therapy. (The antithyroid medication somehow tips the person's immune system back toward normal.) The remainder may suffer relapses once antithyroid medication is stopped. Adverse effects are rare, but about 1 to 5 percent of people on these drugs develop allergic reactions, and one serious side effect is a decreased white-blood-cell count, perhaps signaled by a severe sore throat. If this happens, the thyroid sufferer may need to stop the drug for a while.

Beta blockers such as propranolol may also be used, to manage accompanying heart palpitations and cardiac irritability. Although beta blockers don't affect thyroid hormone levels to a significant extent, they calm people awaiting the benefits of drug therapy.

Radioactive iodine therapy has been used since the mid-1940s for those who don't respond to drugs. The iodine is absorbed almost entirely by the thyroid gland, without harming other body tissues. It is administered after drugs have rendered the patient euthyroid (back to normal hormone outputs). Some studies suggest — but don't prove — that radioiodine may worsen eye disorders linked to hyperthyroidism unless antithyroid drugs are used first.

Radioiodine therapy means taking a tiny amount (about a millionth of a milligram) of radioactive iodine as a liquid or capsule. Over the years, this therapy has proven safe and effective; it alleviates Graves' disease in 90 percent of cases, and despite earlier fears, it does not produce birth defects or cancer. Its main drawback is that, as the years go by, the likelihood of *hypothyroidism* (lack of thyroid hormone) increases by about 3 percent per year to almost 100 percent in 10 years. Thus hyperthyroid patients treated with radioactive iodine may ultimately also require hormone replacement therapy.

Thyroid surgery — subtotal *thyroidectomy*, or partial removal of the thyroid gland — is not often done anymore, although it still has a place for those with very large, cosmetically unattractive goiters, in whom the amount of radioactive iodine needed to reduce the swelling would be dangerously high, or for those who prefer surgery to taking radioactive substances. Hypothyroidism following surgery is a risk, but less so than with radioactive iodine therapy.

about 5 percent among the elderly. Full-blown hypothyroidism, known as "myxedema," is characterized by symptoms opposite to those of Graves' disease: laziness, apathy, constant sleepiness and a bloated, puffy face. Some people with hypothyroidism gain weight, are constipated, have noticeably slow speech, can't stand the cold, lose their hair and develop coarse, dry skin, a hoarse voice and a goiter. Milder cases of hypothyroidism are more common than full-blown myxedema. Thyroid-hormone deficiency may also follow destruction of the gland by surgery or radioiodine therapy (for hyperthyroidism).

Treatment of hypothyroidism

Whatever its causes, the treatment of hypothyroidism is with hormone replacement. In Hashimoto's disease and hypothyroidism due to radioactive iodine treatment, or after surgery for Graves' disease, the gland can never function normally again, necessitating lifelong thyroxine replacement. In the elderly and those with heart problems, thyroxine doses must be kept low, as too much can trigger cardiac problems. Thyroid sufferers over age 60 should consult physicians about lowering their drug dosages.

Experts caution against overtreating

hypothyroidism, an error less likely to occur nowadays as hypothyroidism can be accurately detected by blood tests. (Before blood tests were widespread, many people with transient hypothyroidism or nonthyroid-related disorders were needlessly given thyroxine.)

There is considerable debate as to whether people with *subclinical* hypothyroidism — without symptoms, where the condition shows up only in blood tests — should be treated. Although taking thyroxine is relatively safe, treatment is usually lifelong. In addition, recent research suggests that even slightly too much thyroxine may predispose to loss of bone mass and osteoporosis. On the other hand, subclinical hypothyroidism may predispose to lipid abnormalities and coronary heart disease, therefore perhaps meriting correction.

Thyroid nodules and thyroid cancer

Sometimes the thyroid gland develops small, painless lumps or nodules — often discovered

---

THYROIDITIS

Thyroiditis is a term for inflammation of the thyroid gland, with consequent depletion of thyroid hormone. Infections or the formation of specific autoimmune antibodies can cause thyroiditis. Some types of thyroiditis involve both hyperthyroid (overactive) and hypothyroid (underactive) phases.

- *Hashimoto's thyroiditis*, an autoimmune condition that runs in families, affects 3 to 4 percent of the population. Treatment is with thyroxine.
  In fact, many patients and their physicians are highly relieved when a diagnosis of hypothyroidism is confirmed, since treatment is both easy and harmless.
- *Painful thyroiditis* is due to infective organisms that destroy thyroid tissue. Infectious thyroiditis usually causes an enlarged, tender thyroid, severe neck and ear pain and a high fever. Bacterial forms are called acute or bacterial thyroiditis, viral forms subacute thyroiditis or de Quervain's disease. Antibiotics are used to treat the bacterial forms.
  Viral thyroiditis occurs in sporadic epidemics, often preceded by upper-respiratory-tract infections, and possibly followed by hypothyroidism due to destruction of thyroid tissue. Treatment is with analgesics (such as ASA or acetaminophen), plus corticosteroids to reduce inflammation. Thyroid function almost always returns to normal after a few months.
- *Postpartum thyroiditis* — after pregnancy and childbirth — is more common than once imagined. Postpartum thyroiditis seems to occur if the stress of pregnancy uncovers a latent but transient autoimmune abnormality, most episodes resolving spontaneously. It affects 2 to 5 percent of pregnant women. Painless postpartum thyroiditis usually appears as a brief period of hyperthyroidism, followed by hypothyroidism. The condition may appear two to four months after delivery — with mothers feeling tired, anxious and irritable, experiencing palpitations and sweating. The hyperthyroidism phase may last for four months or so, followed by hypothyroid lethargy, fatigue, weight gain, depression and cold-intolerance. While the disorder usually resolves itself within months, a small goiter may remain. Women who have one bout of pregnancy thyroid trouble usually have repeat bouts after subsequent pregnancies. Treatment of postpartum thyroiditis is with propranolol during the hyperthyroid phase, followed by thyroid replacement during the temporary (6–12 months) of ensuing hypothyroidism.
- *"Hamburger" thyroiditis* (or epidemic thyroiditis) — due to consumption of thyroid tissue accidentally ground up in products such as hamburger meat and sausages — has been reported in both the United States and Europe as a very unusual form of thyroiditis.
- *Congenital hypothyroidism,* or "cretinism," occurs in about one birth per 4,000, resulting in permanent mental retardation and growth defects. The condition is not associated with maternal thyroid disease. In Canada all newborns are screened for hypothyroidism, and early thyroid replacement therapy has virtually eradicated the disorder. (In iodine-poor developing countries, cretinism remains a serious problem.)
  Hypothyroidism may also accompany irradiation of the head and neck (for cancer or some other disease); hypothalamic and pituitary tumors; and treatment with certain drugs (such as lithium, amiodarone and antithyroid drugs).

A THYROID NODULE MAY BE MALIGNANT IF:

- it's in a child, adolescent or male (thyroid nodules are less common in these groups, thus more likely to be malignant);
- there has been excessive head and neck irradiation (a formerly common

treatment for enlarged tonsils, adenoids or an enlarged newborn thymus, halted in the 1960s);
- a thyroid nodule is rapidly expanding;
- there is hoarseness (although this can also be associated

with nonmalignant thyroid nodules).

While many of the above factors increase the suspicion that a thyroid nodule is cancerous, full investigation is required before surgery is recommended.

incidentally during a medical examination. While under 1 percent of children have thyroid nodules, 6 percent of North American adults have palpable (easily felt) lumpy thyroids — and, as with other thyroid disorders, women are likelier to have them than men. Although the overwhelming majority of nodules are benign — often just a variant of normal — some 5 to 10 percent are malignant.

Owing to the possibility of cancer, doctors must differentiate between nodules that are premalignant or frankly malignant (requiring removal) and those that are benign and require conservative management. In the past, all nodules were removed, because there was no way to tell which were cancerous and which harmless. However, diagnostic advances make it far less likely that a malignant nodule will be missed, and somewhat less likely that a benign nodule will be needlessly treated with surgery. In some cases — for example, a very large goiter or one that impinges on the voicebox or windpipe — a benign nodule may also be surgically removed. Thyroxine treatment shuts off the growth-stimulating effect of thyrotropin and may be given to decrease the size of multinodular goiters before surgery.

In the last few years several new techniques have been developed to improve the diagnosis of thyroid cancer, including radioisotope imaging. This procedure measures iodine uptake to determine how well the nodular area of the gland is functioning, helping to confirm or allay the suspicion that a nodule may be malignant and indicating whether the patient needs more tests. Fine-needle-aspiration biopsy

(FNAB), another innovation pioneered by University of Toronto researchers, is now standard technique for diagnosing malignancy in thyroid nodules. The procedure involves insertion of a very thin needle into the suspicious nodule to obtain cells for direct examination. The combination of radioisotope imaging and FNAB has considerably improved thyroid-nodule diagnosis, so that it is less likely that a thyroid malignancy will be missed.

A final reassuring note: although certain types of thyroid cancer are highly lethal, death from cancer of the thyroid is extremely rare. Most people treated for thyroid cancer regain a normal life-expectancy.

For more information on the thyroid, contact the Thyroid Foundation of Canada.

URINARY TRACT INFECTIONS

As many as one in four adult women suffers at least one bout of cystitis, or bladder infection, at some time. A disorder particularly prevalent among elderly women, it can even affect young girls. Although heralded by alarming symptoms — pain when voiding and perhaps blood in the urine — a urinary-tract infection is not usually serious. Lasting complications in otherwise healthy people are rare.

A urinary tract infection (UTI) is a condition in which harmful organisms, usually bacteria, exceed a certain concentration in all or parts of the urinary tract. The infection can affect any of the structures responsible for collecting and voiding urine — including the kidney (collecting and sorting organ), ureter (tube leading from kidney to bladder), bladder (storage reservoir) and urethra (duct taking urine outside the body).

Uncomplicated urinary tract infections that don't involve anatomical abnormalities or obstructions are particularly prevalent in sexually active women aged 18 to 35. They often appear when women first start having sexual intercourse. Uncomplicated bladder infections tend to recur, but are usually simple to treat and generally clear up in a few days with a short course of antibiotics. Should the UTI fail to clear quickly, or recur time and again, physicians generally look for complicating factors, such as an infection focus elsewhere in the body, a permanent catheter (artificial urinary voiding tube), stones or other urinary-tract obstructions. A few groups are at increased risk of developing complications from UTIs — especially diabetics, pregnant women, those with kidney stones and anyone with congenital anomalies or urinary-tract obstructions.

About 1 percent of children under age four have some form of UTI, often due to an abnormal or narrowed urinary tract, or to *vesicoureteral reflux* — where urine is forced back to the kidneys via the ureter. The condition generally corrects itself as children mature. Should it fail to do so, the ureter may have to be surgically "reimplanted" to correct the fault and prevent possible injury to the kidneys. In infants, the incidence of UTI is slightly greater in males than females.

UTI patterns markedly different in men and women

Urinary tract infections are 10 times more frequent in women than men. A primary reason is anatomy: in women the urinary exit and bowel opening (anus) are close together, allowing easy transfer of bacteria from feces (stool) into the urinary tract. Women also have a shorter urethra than men, allowing infecting organisms easier access to the bladder. In addition, bacteria seem able to stick to the vaginal wall, acting as a concentrated source of infective organisms. Lastly, male prostate glands secrete a fluid that supposedly has bactericidal (bacteria-killing) properties. About 75 percent of UTI is caused by invasion of the urinary tract by normally harmless bowel-dwelling bacteria such as *E. coli, Klebsiella, Enterobacteria, Staphylococcus saprophyticus,* and *Pseudomonas.*

Candida albicans (yeast) can provoke a vaginal irritation in women that mimics and is often confused with a bladder infection. Yeast infections occur regularly in some women, but are most usual in the immunosuppressed, those with catheters inserted and people on long-term antibiotics. It is important to distinguish between vaginitis and a real bladder infection, as the two conditions require different treatment. In contrast to bladder infections, which cause burning only on urination, a vaginal infection tends to burn, itch and irritate constantly.

In men, urinary tract infections rarely

VARIOUS TYPES OF UTI

Urinary tract infections are named according to their location.

• *Cystitis* affects primarily the bladder.

• *Urethritis* is confined to the urethra, or urinary-outlet duct. Although the symptoms may resemble those of cystitis — i.e., frequency, urgency and burning — there's no suprapubic pain (over the bladder area) and the bladder is free of bacteria. Sexually transmitted microorganisms such as herpes, chlamydia and gonococci often cause urethritis in both men and women.

• *Prostatitis* (prostate-gland inflammation), prostatic enlargement or other male prostate problems can cause symptoms similar to UTI — frequency, urgency and burning — but may require altogether different treatment.

• *Pyelonephritis* — kidney infection and inflammation — can occur if an otherwise uncomplicated bladder infection extends to and affects the kidneys. Acute pyelonephritis — signaled by fever and flank pain — may permanently damage the kidneys if not promptly treated. UTI generally remains localized in the lower tract, only threatening the kidneys in about 2 to 5 percent of cases. However, the possibility of kidney involvement is greater in diabetics, pregnant women, people with indwelling catheters (plastic voiding tubes), those with stones or other urinary-tract obstructions and/or congenital anomalies and people with *ureteral reflux* (where a little urine flows back upward toward the kidneys). Other conditions can also give rise to pyelonephritis — such as septicemia (blood infection) or postsurgical complications.

• *Asymptomatic bacteriuria* is diagnosed when urine tests reveal the presence of bacteria in the bladder, even if there are no alerting signs. Asymptomatic bacteriuria poses an ever-present problem in the bedridden and incontinent. Catheters, initially sterile, tend to attract bacteria, and studies indicate that up to 80 percent of the catheterized elderly have infected urinary tracts. While some specialists promote treatment to eliminate the bacteria even when the condition gives little discomfort, others suggest treating bacteriuria only if it's bothersome, rather than risking the emergence of untreatable drug-resistant bacterial strains.

SYMPTOMS OF UTI:

- urgent need to urinate;
- frequent need to urinate;
- need to urinate at night;
- burning/painful sensation when urinating;
- cloudy or foul-smelling urine;

- bladder spasms;
- sense of incomplete bladder emptying;
- pain over bladder area;
- blood in the urine.

In addition (if the kidneys are also involved):
- lower back and/or

flank pain;
- fever and chills (rare with lower-tract UTI). While cystitis alone rarely elevates the temperature, a fever and flank pain may indicate kidney involvement;
- weakness, fatigue, nausea.

occur without accompanying prostate or other problems, such as kidney stones. Although the prevalence of UTI in young men is less than I percent, rates increase with advancing age — reaching 5 to 15 percent in men over age 65.

Some women are more prone than others

Many otherwise healthy women are particularly susceptible to UTI, possibly because of receptivity to the attachment of harmful bacteria. Lactobacilli — bacteria normally present in the vaginal flora (a natural mix of microorganisms living harmoniously in the female tract) — are believed to ward off harmful bacteria. But some women have unusually low amounts of lactobacilli, while others have less after a menstrual period. Studies suggest that a lack of lactobacilli allows overgrowth of harmful organisms, increasing the chances of UTI.

Sexual activity may also aggravate UTI problems. In some women, bacteria seem to

be easily swept up the urethra during intercourse, although postsex symptoms can simply be due to urethral irritation (not real infection). Urinating immediately after sex may help to dispel the bacteria! Some women seem to be most susceptible to UTI in the early phase of the menstrual cycle, when estrogen levels are higher than at the end of the cycle. Use of a diaphragm for contraception may increase the likelihood of UTIs in some women.

Pregnancy also increases risks of UTI. About 4 to 7 percent of pregnant women get a urinary-tract infection (75 percent in the first trimester), many without any alerting symptoms. The ureter expands during pregnancy and increases the risk of upper-tract infection. Pregnant women should be periodically tested for the presence of bacteria in the urine because infection may trigger premature birth.

"Holding in" can also be an aggravating factor for UTIs. Women who delay going to the bathroom and don't urinate frequently enough may allow bacteria to accumulate in urine. Experts recommend emptying the bladder at least every three to four hours, and drinking plenty of liquid.

Diagnosis and treatment of UTI

Physicians usually establish the presence of UTI by testing an uncontaminated midstream urine sample for bacteria. To collect the sample, the genitals are washed well with soap and water. The first third of the urine sample is discarded into the toilet and a sample of the remaining urine is collected into a sterile bottle.

SOME PRACTICAL ADVICE ON URINARY TRACT INFECTIONS

Once a UTI has set in, and for those prone to recurrences, try a few preventive measures:
- Drink lots of water, to encourage frequent urination and flush bacteria out of the urinary tract.
- Pay careful attention to personal hygiene.
- Always wipe from front to back after

going to the toilet, or use separate tissues for front and back — a practice that may curb the transfer of bacteria from rectum (anus) to urinary opening.
- Avoid tight underwear, pantyhose and jeans — which create a warm, damp environment ideal for

bacterial growth.
- Wear cotton undergarments that "breathe," to discourage bacteria from growing on undergarments. Panty liners should be frequently changed.
- Void promptly — at least every three to four hours; do not

delay urination until "time permits."
- Avoid douching, which tends to wash away beneficial bacterial strains that help to maintain a healthy urinary tract.

Those prone to post-sex cystitis can try:
- Cleaning the genitals before having sex —

which may remove harmful bacteria.
- Urinating after intercourse — to help flush bacteria out of the urinary tract.
- Temporarily halting use of spermicidals — recent research suggests that spermicides may disturb the vagina's normal balance.

New dipstick (Multistix) kits are available for home urine testing, but anyone with recurrent UTI should see a physician to make sure the problem is not something else. Long-term, stubbornly persistent cases may require further diagnostic tests such as ultrasound, X-rays, cystoscopy (bladder examination) and an intravenous pyelogram (dye test) to rule out underlying structural abnormalities.

Treatment with antibiotics usually brings swift relief

Many urinary tract infections vanish even without treatment, but today's approach is to treat symptomatic cases with antibiotics. Most cases clear up quickly with a short course of antibiotics such as amoxicillin, trimethoprim-sulfamethoxazole (Bactrim or Septra), nitrofurantoin (Furadantin) and/or the newer quinolone products, such as norfloxacin (Noroxin), and ciprofloxacin. The drugs are taken either as a single large dose, or as a three- to seven-day course. Treatment is ideally continued until all symptoms are gone and a midstream urine sample is free of bacteria. A repeat infection requires another course of antibiotics. If an infection persists, more of the same antibiotic or a different drug may be tried, as bacteria easily mutate and resistant forms may surface. If the UTI is associated with sexual activity, an antibiotic pill taken directly after intercourse may prevent cystitis.

Experimental treatments for UTI

One treatment sometimes tried is direct application to the vagina of preparations containing lactobacilli strains specifically designed to restore a normal vaginal balance. A recent small clinical trial found that special strains of lactobacilli could prevent UTI. A larger clinical trial is now underway at a University of Toronto hospital.

Yogurt or commercial lactobacilli products for douching are not medically approved and are of dubious help in combating UTI. Lactobacilli strains in various brands of yogurt differ markedly, and it is unwise to douche with those not known to prevent UTI. However, a few medical experts recommend eating yogurt between antibiotic doses when on therapy. Since antibiotics kill bacteria throughout the body, eating yogurt may restore some of the naturally protective gut bacteria.

Other experts promote cranberry juice and vitamin C as possible dietary aids that acidify urine and may help in preventing UTI. But once a urinary tract infection is established, these remedies are ineffective — an acidic urine only burns more!

ZOONOSES: DISEASE FROM PETS

Our pets provide comfort and amusement and may even promote good health by their friendly presence, which can alleviate stress and counter loneliness. The wag of a tail, a quiet purr or the song of a bird comforts many. But while pets provide unconditional love and companionship, they can also transmit diseases and provoke allergies in susceptible individuals.

Worldwide, there are more than 200 zoonoses (animal diseases transmissible to humans), of which at least 150 occur in Canada and the United States — including diseases caused by viruses, bacteria, fungi and parasites. Among city dwellers in industrialized countries, animal diseases are most likely to spread via house pets, usually dogs, cats, birds, mice, rabbits and hamsters. Cat-scratch fever, rabies and a variety of skin and stomach ailments are among the animal-transmitted illnesses that afflict millions of North Americans every year. Children who play in areas where animals have deposited infected feces are especially at risk.

The commonest zoonoses cause just mild discomforts, perhaps a skin irritation, upset stomach, headache or slight chill, but in a few cases they can be serious, even fatal. For instance, in 1992 a 31-year-old Colorado man died of pneumonic plague after rescuing a cat from under his house. The man picked up the disease agents by inhaling bacteria directly into his lungs from the cat, which was sneezing and coughing. Pneumonic plague is endemic among wild animals in several southwestern U.S. states, but not in Canada's cooler climate.

Untreated animal bites frequently cause trouble

Animal bites are the commonest way in which animal diseases are transmitted to humans, as the wounds are liable to become infected —

especially cat bites (or scratches). Thousands of people in North America are bitten or mauled each year by animals, particularly dogs. Health authorities view the bites as a preventable consequence of irresponsible pet ownership. Besides leaving permanent and disfiguring scars, the bites may spread rabies, tetanus and other infections. Nine out of ten animal bites are caused by dogs, male dogs being more dangerous than females, large dogs inflicting worse wounds than small ones. Men are evidently twice as likely as women to be bitten by a dog, but women are twice as likely to be bitten or scratched by cats. (For first aid for animal bites see "Animal bites" under "Bites and stings," in chapter 17.)

Some diseases from pets

• *Rabies*: Of the viral and bacterial diseases transmitted to humans from animals, rabies — although not the most common — is the most dreaded because, left untreated, it is virtually 100 percent fatal. Rabies, derived from the Latin *rabere,* "to rave or be mad," is spread by a virus transferred from the saliva of the biter that invades the nervous system and travels to the brain. Almost any warm-blooded animal can become rabid, but since the disease is transmitted through saliva it's usually spread by bites or licks, particularly those of carnivores (meat eaters). Animals living in the wild may bite pets, who pass on the disease to their owners. Southern Ontario has the highest reservoir of rabies in North America, carried mainly by foxes, bats, raccoons, dogs, skunks and cats.

The incubation period (time within which the disease may reach the brain and show itself) is ten days to eight months after the bite. The onset of the disease (in humans as well as animals) is heralded by pain around the wound, general malaise, behavior changes, a feeling of anxiety, perhaps a mild fever, unusual excitability (snapping and biting in a pet) or unusual docility (in a wolf or fox who approaches humans). Muscle spasms, especially in the throat, produce gagging and hydrophobia (fear of water), a dramatic aversion to fluids due to the inability to drink, followed by vomiting, salivation to the point of

drooling and ultimate paralysis and death. An animal with paralyzed limbs should be examined for the disease. Pet owners should make sure that their animals are annually inoculated against rabies.

The life of someone bitten by a rabid animal can be saved only by injecting rabies vaccine soon after exposure, *before* symptoms appear. The sooner the vaccine is given, the faster antibodies build up. Rabies vaccination, first developed by Louis Pasteur, the "father of immunology," previously consisted of 14 daily abdominal injections that were both painful and risky. A vaccine prepared from duck embryos superseded the Pasteur vaccine, although the injections were still painful. However, a new, safe vaccine grown in human diploid cells can now be administered as five (rather than fourteen) relatively painless injections.

• *Cat-scratch fever*: A mysterious malady, possibly due to the *Pasteurella* organism, this mild ailment afflicts many who are scratched or bitten by cats. Young children, liable to tease cats and get scratched, are more frequently affected than adults. The infected cats themselves show no signs of illness but carry the disease-causing pathogen on their claws or teeth. In its mild form it produces merely local swelling and soreness, but if full-blown it may lead to an abscess, swollen lymph nodes, appetite loss, fever, long-lasting malaise and other symptoms. Treatment is bed rest and fever antidotes. A team at the Centers for Disease Control in Atlanta has just isolated the bacterium that causes cat-scratch fever and is attempting to find an appropriate antibiotic.

• *Salmonellosis*: Due to *Salmonella* bacteria, a common cause of food poisoning, the disease can also be carried by many mammals, birds and reptiles, and infects about 50 percent of pet dogs. But the most notorious sources of pet-transmitted salmonellosis are imported baby turtles. During the heyday of the pet turtle business, cases of human salmonellosis acquired from touching these reptiles or their feces were a serious problem. In the United States, for instance, there were an estimated 280,000 cases of salmonellosis associated with pet turtles during the early 1970s. Although the Canadian government banned the importation of these creatures, some Montreal dealers circumvented the regulations in 1984 and imported and hatched turtle eggs, with a consequent salmonellosis outbreak.

The symptoms of salmonellosis include diarrhea, cramps, nausea, fever and septicemia (blood poisoning). The disease is seldom serious in healthy adults, but it can be life-threatening in young children or the elderly.

• *Psittacosis* (parrot fever or ornithosis): Previously viewed as a viral infection, this is now known to be due to a rickettsial microorganism that infects birds — especially parrots, canaries, parakeets, pigeons and others of the parrot variety, as well as some small mammals. Birds infected with psittacosis may seem droopy, off their food and unkempt and should be promptly treated by a vet. In humans the disease attacks the lungs, and symptoms often resemble influenza, with chills, coughing, headaches and fever. If severe, it can lead to chronic respiratory illness that requires antibiotic therapy.

• *Fish-tank disease:* This curious disorder, caused by a type of marine bacteria that occasionally grow in fish tanks, may spread to humans if the bacteria get into open cuts or lesions, triggering a local inflammation. The problem is easily avoided by wearing rubber gloves when cleaning fish tanks.

• *Ringworm*: Unsightly and disfiguring but not dangerous, ringworm infections stem not from worms but from a fungus that grows in a ring-shaped formation on the skin and scalp. Infected kittens, puppies, dogs, cats, and occasionally monkeys and horses, can transmit ringworm to humans. Children are at higher risk than adults, and boys more than girls. The disease is also contagious between humans. The fungal spores easily spread from person to person through inanimate objects such as toys, barber's instruments, towels and floor coverings.

Cats with ringworm often have round, sore, scaly, hairless patches on face and head. Humans who get the infection from their pets may develop small local sores and itchy swellings — especially on the hands, arms and abdomen. The condition is short-lived and readily treated with antifungal creams.

• *Roundworms*: Roundworm eggs from the intestines of puppies, dogs and cats can be swallowed by humans, causing toxocariasis. After ingestion, the roundworm embryos hatch and travel to various organs, including the lungs, liver, spleen, heart, muscles and intestines, causing inflammation, flulike symptoms, diarrhea, perhaps reddened eyes. Occasionally the larvae of these worms migrate through the body to the eyes, where they can cause blindness if left untreated.

Health authorities believe that human roundworm infections are more prevalent than previously believed, especially among toddlers. Roundworm eggs, passed out with feces, may survive for months, even a year, and infect children who play in sandboxes, gardens and playgrounds. Youngsters may ingest roundworm eggs when licking fingers or swallowing contaminated dirt or soil. Roundworm infections are particularly frequent in children with the disorder called pica (a behavioral aberration with compulsive ingestion of soil and grit).

• *Toxoplasmosis*: Caused by *Toxoplasma gondii*, a crescent-shaped microscopic parasite, this flu-like ailment goes unnoticed in most

TO PREVENT ANIMAL DISEASES, PRACTICE SENSIBLE HYGIENE

• **Keep pets' living quarters clean at all times and examine animals regularly for ticks and fleas.**
• **Wash your hands thoroughly after playing with your pets and teach your children to do likewise.**
• **If your pet is sick, take it to the veterinarian — don't wait.**
• **Be sure your animal is vaccinated properly against rabies**

and other diseases.
• **Get puppies and kittens dewormed as early as possible — some experts say two weeks old is not too soon.**
• **Never approach wild animals, especially in rabies-ridden areas such as southern Ontario; beware of any animal that seems to be behaving oddly, is excessively friendly or very aggressive.**

• **Teach children not to tease, overexcite or irritate animals, since it could provoke an attack, and tell them not to approach strange dogs, cats or other animals.**
• **Don't touch dead animals, as corpses can still pass on infections.**
• **Don't leave animals out alone overnight, as they may easily socialize with infected wild ones.**

people or is mistaken for another illness such as influenza. Toxoplasmosis can be contracted by consuming undercooked, contaminated meat (especially pork) or unpasteurized milk. Cat feces can also infect humans, but only for a short period, since the infective cysts are not infective when freshly excreted, but only three to five days later. Recent studies show that almost 50 percent of North Americans show some evidence (in blood tests) of previous toxoplasma infections.

Public interest in this animal-transferred disease arises from the fact that it may attack those with weakened immune systems, such as AIDS patients, and may also endanger unborn babies. An acute toxoplasma infection in pregnancy may produce fetal brain damage, seizures, eye and skin defects, jaundice and an impaired liver and spleen. As a precaution, pregnant women should wash their hands thoroughly after preparing raw meat, not eat undercooked meat or unpasteurized milk and avoid emptying the cat's litter box if possible.

Emergency first aid

How to help in an emergency • General principles of first aid • The ABC's of AR and CPR • Allergic shock (anaphylaxis) • Asphyxiation (suffocation) • Asthma • Bites and stings • Bleeding • Burns and scalds • Choking: the Heimlich maneuver • Choking infants • Convulsions • Dressings and bandages • Ear injuries • Electric shock • Eye injuries • Fainting • Fractures • Frostbite and freezing • Head injuries • Heart attack • Hyperthermia (heat illnesses) • Hypothermia (cold injury) • Mouth injuries • Nosebleeds • Poisonings • Seizures • Shock • Sports injuries • Teeth (knocked out) • Unconsciousness • Water accidents • Where to learn first aid and CPR

HOW TO HELP IN AN EMERGENCY

The prime necessity in helping injured people in an emergency is to *recognize* the situation as an emergency, and to know the local emergency phone number. Although the 9-1-1 number has been widely publicized, there are many areas where it is not yet operational. Know your emergency numbers at home, cottage and other regions you frequent. Post the emergency telephone number clearly on every phone in the house, and carry the appropriate emergency number with you if traveling away from home. Know how to reach your provincial police or RCMP in case of a highway accident.

When calling for emergency services, clearly state what the problem seems to be — for instance, whether it's a possible heart attack, drowning or broken bone — so that the dispatcher can estimate its urgency. Also provide precise information about your location, giving the address, and stating whether it is a house, apartment or office building, the floor and room number. Always put your home address on or near the telephone(s) so that strangers — such as babysitters, house-cleaners and workmen —

17

FIRST-AID PROVIDERS SHOULD:

- assess the situation, stay calm, take confident charge and ensure that no further harm befalls the casualty, rescuer, or bystanders; too often, a would-be rescuer becomes the next casualty;
- reassure the casualty, and urge him or her to accept necessary assistance (people sometimes deny real problems, out of embarrassment or fear);
- summon emergency medical services quickly — speed may be of the essence;
- keep the injured warm and at rest, if possible covered and on soft ground (clothes, blankets);
- check for consciousness, breathing, pulse and bleeding;
- look for injuries —

ask the casualty whether it hurts and where;
- try to find out what happened — it may give clues to possible injuries (ask the casualty and/or onlookers what went wrong);
- prevent the condition from worsening: cover wounds, try to immobilize possible fractures, handle gently.

Do not:
- attempt more than you are able or qualified to do;
- move the casualty unless you are *certain* the injuries are minor, or unless it is absolutely necessary;
- allow people to crowd around;
- touch the casualty's body or remove the casualty's clothing unnecessarily;
- give anything by

mouth to people with a suspected internal injury, those going unconscious or those who may need an anesthetic;
- administer any medications (although you may *assist* a conscious casualty to take necessary medications (heart pills, insulin, etc.);
- force first aid on anyone who refuses it.

FIRST AID IN THE AGE OF AIDS

Today's health-conscious good Samaritan may pause before attempting to render assistance to an injured person. The AIDS (HIV) and hepatitis B (HBV) viruses have been identified in the blood, breastmilk, sputum, tears and urine of infected people. Has first aid become risky? How can the risk be minimized?

Fortunately, there is a safe and effective vaccine against hepatitis B. All healthcare workers, those living with HBV carriers and others at risk should be immunized. For healthcare workers such as surgeons, dentists, nurses, emergency-care workers, ambulance drivers and laboratory staff who routinely come into contact with people carrying infectious diseases, there remains the risk — albeit slight — of becoming infected with HIV. The likeliest way to become infected is via a cut with an infected needle or scalpel that pierces the protective gloves. It is estimated that about one person in every 200 to 250 punctured by an HIV-contaminated needle or scalpel will develop HIV infection. However, so far in Canada only one healthcare worker has reportedly developed AIDS through an occupational mishap since the epidemic began.

All healthcare professionals are encouraged to "think AIDS" and protect themselves. Very precise guidelines have been laid out for those handling body fluids and looking after sick people. In its "Universal Precautions," published in 1988, the American Centers for Disease Control (CDC) set out precise rules to make the minimal risk of contracting AIDS or hepatitis B even smaller.

Professional emergency workers and trained volunteers, such as the St. John Ambulance personnel who give first aid to the injured, are equipped with "pocket masks" for mouth-to-mouth resuscitation, as well as gloves and other protective devices. However, casual first-aiders, teachers, daycare workers and bystanders at the scene — who may be called upon to give mouth-to-mouth resuscitation or to stem bleeding — do not usually carry protective equipment.

So what is the risk to an unmasked, ungloved layperson attempting to give mouth-to-mouth rescue breaths? It's estimated to be immeasurably small — zero or close to it. True, HIV and HBV viruses have been isolated from saliva, but neither HIV nor HBV infection has ever been documented following mouth-to-mouth resuscitation given by casual first-aiders. Similarly, the risk of contracting these infections by being splashed even with contaminated blood is minimal. No case of infection by this means has ever been reported in a first-aid provider — whereas the risk to a casualty of *not* receiving first aid may well be tragic. Still, it is up to the rescuer to assess the situation and make the decision.

Committees of the American Heart Association (AHA) and the World Health Organization (WHO) and, most recently, the 1992 Conference on Cardiopulmonary Resuscitation and Emergency Cardiac Care, have closely examined the risks of acquiring infectious diseases through giving first aid. The AHA concluded that "the average layperson who responds in an emergency should be guided by individual moral and ethical values." That is, you do what you think is right. The WHO is even less compromising, concluding that "mouth-to-mouth resuscitation is a life-saving procedure and should not be withheld through fear of contracting HIV or other infections." It adds that "people who are bleeding require immediate attention. The first-aider must not hesitate to help them as some wounds may be life-threatening." But ultimately it is the first-aider's decision. You are never *obliged* to begin first aid unless (like a police officer or an ambulance driver) you have a special responsibility to do so.

For those who are still anxious about administering first aid, especially in situations where there is a considerable likelihood that the casualty may harbor HBV or HIV infection, various national and international agencies recommend the following procedures:

- wipe blood and saliva from the casualty's mouth with a handkerchief before attempting mouth-to-mouth resuscitation;
- try to avoid touching blood by wearing latex gloves or using a thick cloth or clothing to prevent skin contact with the injured person;
- take particular care to prevent blood from coming in direct contact with your own broken skin, abrasions, a sore or mucous membranes (mouth, nose);
- wash the hands thoroughly with soap and water after giving first aid;
- if you are bleeding yourself while performing first aid (the most likely, indeed probably the only way of contacting a blood-borne disease), encourage the wound to bleed and then wash it well;
- if you believe you have been cut or splashed in the eye or mouth with the blood of an injured person, wash promptly and consult a physician.

can quickly find it. If you have helpers available, get someone to stay by the front door to open it and guide the emergency personnel to the injury scene.

GENERAL PRINCIPLES OF FIRST AID

First aid is defined as "things to do until medical help arrives," not ways to replace medical procedures. Its aims are:

- to sustain life;
- to relieve pain and distress;
- to prevent the condition from worsening;
- to promote recovery;
- to obtain medical care as fast as possible.

Stocking a first-aid kit

Your first-aid kit should be tailored to your family and your environment — a cottage kit will need more medications than a city kit, and a car kit should have ample dressings to stop bleeding on multiple casualties. But the following is a list of basics:

- absorbent cotton;
- adhesive strip plasters — assorted sizes;
- adhesive tape;
- calamine lotion;
- cotton-tipped swabs;
- painkillers such as acetaminophen or ASA (but do not give ASA products such as Aspirin to children — because of the risk of Reye's syndrome);
- disinfectant;
- rubbing alcohol;
- "triangular bandages" for tying splints and securing dressings;
- safety pins;
- sharp needles and tweezers to remove splinters (sterilize first);
- scissors;
- sterile eye pads;
- sterile gauze bandages — 25 mm and 50 mm;
- sterile gauze pads — 50 mm and 100 mm square;
- thermometer;
- tongue depressors — wooden;
- antihistamine tablets of choice;
- antibiotic cream;
- pad and pencil;
- latex gloves.

THE ABC'S OF AR AND CPR

The two processes of breathing and circulation (blood being pumped by the heart) combine to supply oxygen to the cells of the body. If breathing stops, either because the air passages are blocked by a foreign object (choking) or for some other reason, the heart will be pumping blood without adequate oxygen. Soon two things will happen — brain cells will begin to die, and the heart itself will stop.

Artificial respiration (AR) refers to first-aid techniques to replace breathing — the most common and effective method being mouth-to-mouth breathing. The principle is simple — first the rescuer checks whether the airway (air passages) are blocked by a foreign body, and clears them if they are (see "Choking" in this chapter for the Heimlich maneuver); then the rescuer breathes into the casualty's lungs, supplying enough residual oxygen to keep the brain cells alive and prevent the heart from stopping. Often AR will cause natural breathing to resume.

If the heart has stopped beating too — through a heart attack, drowning, poisoning, electrocution or any other cause — AR alone is not enough, because the oxygen put into the lungs will not be pumped to the cells that need it. In this case, the further step in cardiopulmonary resuscitation (CPR) — chest compressions — is required. This is a simple process of rhythmically squeezing the heart between the breastbone and the backbone to mimic the heart's natural pumping action. The combination of rescue breathing and chest compressions may not restart the heart, but it is designed to keep oxygenated blood flowing to the brain, preventing irreversible brain damage and death, until medical help can reach the scene.

The Heimlich maneuver, AR and CPR are vital techniques for laypeople, because brain damage can begin in as little as four to six minutes — often sooner than an ambulance can arrive, even in the best of circumstances. Too many people — the diner who chokes in a restaurant, the child who slips in a wading pool, the grandparent who climbs the stairs a little too quickly — die unnecessarily, just because no one on the scene knows how to bridge that gap of a few minutes!

AIRWAY

It's possible that the casualty's tongue is blocking the airway. Sometimes just tilting the head and dislodging the tongue allows the unconscious person to breathe again. Gently roll the person onto his or her back (supporting the head). Then tilt the casualty's head by simultaneously lifting up on the chin and pushing down on the forehead. With the airway open, place your ear close to the victim's mouth and again try to detect breathing:

- *look at the chest and stomach — for movement;*
- *listen — for sounds of breathing;*
- *feel — for exhaled breath on your cheek.*

If none of these signs is present, the victim is not breathing and AR is needed. If the person is breathing, and you have to go for help, first place him or her in the recovery position.

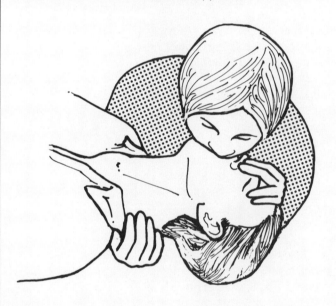

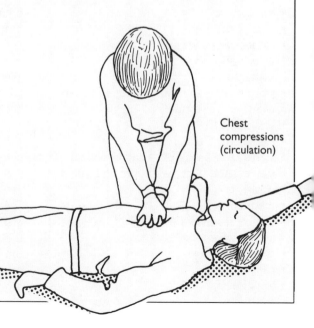

Airway passage (must be clear before doing mouth-to-mouth)

BREATHING

Place your mouth over the casualty's mouth, sealing well. Pinch the nostrils closed but continue to hold the head gently tilted. Breathe in two full breaths (each held for about 1–2 seconds), allowing time for the casualty to exhale in between. Watch the chest — if it does not rise, the air is not going in, and you should reposition the head and try again. If air still doesn't go in, the airway is obstructed — see "Choking." Then check for a pulse by putting two fingers gently over the carotid artery at the side of the neck for ten seconds. (The carotid is used because it's an accessible, strong pulse.) If there's a pulse but no breathing, continue rescue breathing at a rate of one mouth-to-mouth breath per five seconds (four seconds for a child). Keep watching the chest, to be sure that the breaths are going in. (If the casualty is an infant, place your mouth over the mouth and nose, and blow in light puffs only — one every three seconds. Check the brachial pulse — on the inside upper arm — as the carotid is hard to find on infants.)

CIRCULATION

If there is no pulse, and you are trained in CPR, begin external chest compressions for artificial circulation, kneeling beside the casualty, near the chest. The chest compressions should be a straight up-and-down movement, avoiding rocking while exerting rhythmic pressure on the breastbone with one hand atop the other (see diagram) and avoiding the xiphoid process (the posterior segment of the sternum). The arms are kept straight, with relaxation between the downward pushes. A solo rescuer with a pulseless, non-breathing casualty must alternate rescue breathing with chest compressions — giving two full mouth-to-mouth breaths and then 12–15 compressions per minute — until help arrives. CPR for a child is done with one hand only, alternating one breath and five compressions. CPR on an infant alternates one puff of air with five chest thrusts done with two fingers — see infant Heimlich, "Choking infants," in this chapter. Remember that CPR must never be done on a casualty with any detectable pulse.

Chest compressions (circulation)

RECOVERY POSITION

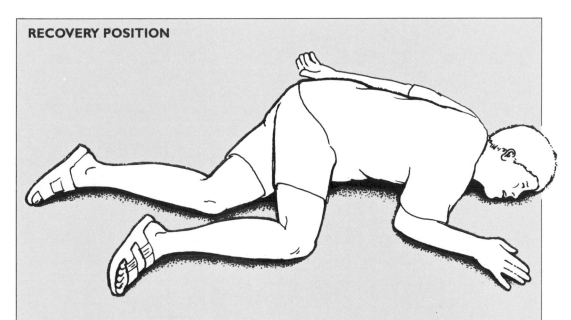

An unconscious casualty who is lying on his or her back may easily choke on the tongue or on inhaled vomit. If you are with a casualty you can watch for this and be prepared to act, but if you have to leave an unconscious person, or someone who may become unconscious — or if you have been injured yourself and are concerned about becoming unconscious — the safest position is the "recovery" position. The one knee forward and one arm back serve to prop the person securely, the bent arm should be forward near the face. The gently tilted head holds the airway open, with the mouth downward so any blood or vomit can drain out.

All these first-aid techniques are taught together in a single course under the general heading of "CPR." The methods for adult casualties can be learned in a few hours, and the techniques for children and infants take a few hours more. And the breathing and compressions are practiced on mannequins, not on strangers! (See "Where to learn first aid and CPR," at the end of this chapter.)

Although basic information on the Heimlich maneuver, AR and CPR is presented below, it is no substitute for an instructor and hands-on practice. **CPR (chest compressions) in particular should not be attempted without training.**

Before starting first aid on someone who has collapsed, the rescuer determines whether the casualty is conscious by gently shaking his or her shoulders, asking loudly, "Are you okay?" If there's no response, it is assumed that the casualty is unconscious. After shouting out for help, and sending anyone available to call for medical aid, the rescuer kneels over the casualty — placing the cheek above the casualty's mouth

and nose, and looking at the chest — and spends five seconds trying to feel or hear breathing, and to see the chest move. If there is no sign of breathing, the rescuer begins the sequence known as ABC — Airway, Breathing, Circulation.

ALLERGIC SHOCK (ANAPHYLAXIS)

Environmental pollutants, plant components, food ingredients, insect stings and other specific agents can occasionally provoke a drastic response in those allergic to them. Anaphylactic shock is an emergency indicated by one or more of the following:

- swelling of eyes, throat, tongue;
- face flushing;
- widespread hives (red weals or rash);
- difficulty breathing;
- vomiting, diarrhea;
- irregular heartbeat;
- faintness;
- loss of consciousness.

All or some symptoms can occur at the same time, often within minutes of exposure.

WHAT TO DO FOR ANAPHYLACTIC SHOCK

- **Help the casualty inject adrenalin (epinephrine) if available. Rub the site vigorously afterward to increase the absorption rate.**
- **If leaving an unconscious casualty to get help, place in recovery position.**
- **Call emergency medical services immediately.**
- **Be prepared to give artificial respiration or CPR (if qualified) if this becomes necessary.**

Death can result unless the person is immediately given a shot of adrenalin (epinephrine) and taken to the nearest medical facility. People who know they are severely allergic to certain substances should wear an identification bracelet. (For details on allergic reactions, see chapter 13, allergies section, and chapter 11, childhood allergies section.)

ASPHYXIATION (SUFFOCATION)

Asphyxiation occurs when the airway is blocked due to any number of causes, such as strangulation, smothering or near-drowning. Airway blockage may occur from choking on foreign bodies, food, teeth, vomit and even the tongue. It also follows other conditions that prevent oxygen from entering the body, such as airway spasms due to food, water, smoke, irritant gases, asthma and some chest infections. It may be caused by pillows and plastic bags that block breathing, smoke and gas fumes that displace the oxygen in the air.

Its symptoms are:
- heartbeat fast and faint, perhaps irregular;
- noisy labored breathing, with froth on the mouth;
- head, neck, face, lips and whites of eyes turning red, purple and then blue;
- drowsiness, person becoming unconscious.

ASTHMA

Asthma is a chronic breathing disorder marked by recurrent attacks of wheezing, coughing, shortness of breath, inflammation and thickened secretions (mucus). The symptoms may come on quickly or may slowly worsen over days.

Signs and symptoms of a severe asthma attack
- tight, difficult breathing;
- wheezing (whistling) sound;
- pale, clammy skin;
- rapid pulse;
- blueness around mouth, earlobes.

What to do for a severe asthma attack
- Call 9-1-1 or relevant number for emergency medical services. Never delay seeking help — most asthma deaths are preventable with prompt medical assistance.

WHAT TO DO FOR ASPHYXIATION
- **Move casualty to open, fresh air.**
- **Call emergency medical services.**
- **Clear airway — make sure that nothing is obstructing the air flow.**
- **Begin artificial respiration if casualty is not breathing.**
- **If no pulse can be felt, begin CPR, if qualified.**

- Stop any activities and remove any known triggers.
- Place person leaning forward comfortably, back upright.
- Calm and reassure the sufferer.
- Check if usual medication was taken — which and how much; help casualty take more if appropriate.
- Allow plenty of fresh air — no cigarette smoke, dust.
- Be prepared to give artificial respiration or CPR (if qualified) if necessary.

BITES AND STINGS

Animal bites
Animal bites, for instance by a bat, skunk, raccoon, fox, cat or dog, always carry some danger of infection, especially if the bite is deep. They may also carry some risks of rabies, and the animal should be kept under observation for signs of the affliction, such as agitation, viciousness, drooling, water-aversion, and paralysis.

What to do for animal bites
- Allow some bleeding, to help cleanse the wound.
- Wash wound site thoroughly with soap and water (preferably antiseptic soap) for several minutes to remove the animal's saliva.
- Rinse well with running water or salt solution.
- If wound is on arm or leg, apply a firm bandage.
- Get medical attention even for a small cat or dog bite to see if further care is warranted, and whether there is a need for tetanus and/or rabies vaccination.
- Try to catch and restrain the animal, while taking care no one else is bitten.
- Contact animal control or police to collect the animal for observation if necessary.

For human bites that cause bleeding:
- Wash wound thoroughly with soap and water.
- Seek medical care — human bites that bleed can easily become infected.
- Notify the local-public health agency (see sections on hepatitis B and HIV infections in this chapter and chapter 16).

Snake bites

A snake bite will show one or more puncture wounds, with swelling and discoloration in the area. Reactions may include pain and swelling, nausea, vomiting, weakness, vision blurring, sweating, difficulty breathing, speech slurring, paralysis and convulsions. But remember that the vast majority of snakes are harmless to people; unnecessary panic will only make matters worse.

Insect bites and stings

The venom of bees, wasps, hornets, yellow-jackets and fire ants produces a fierce burning, swelling and redness, as well as local swelling and itching around the sting.

What to do for bedbug, sand-fly and mosquito bites

- Wash affected area with soap and water; apply cold compresses or ice if swollen.
- Apply calamine lotion, eau de cologne or cheap perfume.
- Use antihistamine tablets if the bites are very itchy.
- For mosquito bites in malaria-infested areas, seek immediate medical advice if not protected by antimalarial tablets.

Tick bites

Wingless creatures about the size of a tiny ant, ticks range in color from brown to gray and are usually picked up in woodsy underbrush or tall grass or from the fur of free-ranging deer. The tick embeds its head in the skin to feed on animal blood. Tick bites are relatively painless, and the chief danger comes from the disease-causing organisms they may carry, such as Rocky Mountain spotted fever, Colorado tick fever, tularemia or Lyme disease, to name a few.

What to do for tick bites

- Remove ticks with care — don't detach with bare fingers as it may increase penetration by tick-borne microorganisms. Preferably remove tick with fine-tipped tweezers (or a gloved finger), grasping the tick near the head, as close to the skin as possible, and pulling away in a straight line. This may be painful, as the tick glues itself into the skin. Pull until tick releases its hold. Don't twist as you pull, and don't squeeze its bloated body — that may inject more bacteria into the skin. Ensure that the head of the tick is removed. (If the head stays in, seek immediate medical care.)
- Do not apply petroleum jelly, a burning cigarette or other popular methods touted for tick removal; these methods do not work.
- Thoroughly wash hands and bitten area with soap and water and apply antiseptic (such as rubbing alcohol). If you must touch the tick, cover fingers with tissue before doing so. Wash hands thoroughly.
- Save the tick in a small container labeled with the date, the bite site and where you think the tick came from. Tell the attending physician.

WHAT TO DO FOR SNAKE BITES

- **Stay calm, reassure the casualty and have him or her lie down.**
- **If the snake is known to be poisonous, seek immediate medical attention. *Do not attempt to suck out venom.***
- **Move affected part as little as possible.**
- **Do not apply ice.**
- **Firmly apply a bandage beginning at least 30 cm (12 in) above the bite and wind down over the bitten area, to finish about 30 cm below the bite.**
- **If bite is on a limb, splint to immobilize completely.**
- **Call the local poison control center.**
- **Be prepared to do artificial respiration or CPR (if qualified) if necessary.**
- **Transport the victim to the nearest medical center, moving the bitten part as little as possible. Bring the snake (dead); pick it up by the tail and place in a bag or sack.**

WHAT TO DO FOR STINGS BY BEES, WASPS, HORNETS, YELLOWJACKETS OR FIRE ANTS

- **If the sting is from a bee, remove the stinger. Don't pull at it with fingers because it has a sack that can pump in more venom. Instead, scrape away cleanly with a sharp blade or credit card held against the skin.**
- **Do not squeeze or rub the skin.**
- **Wash sting site with soap and water.**
- **Apply rubbing alcohol, ice, calamine lotion or a paste of water and baking soda, unless the sting is near the eyes; if nothing else is available, cover sting with a cold compress.**
- **If the sting is in the mouth, rinse well with mouthwash made up of 1 tsp (5 ml) of bicarbonate of soda in a tumbler of cold water.**
- **Call emergency medical services if there are any signs of a severe allergic reaction (hives, pallor, weakness, nausea, vomiting, breathing problems or collapse).**
- **For allergic shock see "Allergic shock," above.**

GENERAL EMERGENCY MEASURES FOR MARINE STINGS

- Get out of the water and try to identify the culprit so that you can apply appropriate first aid.
- Don't rub the affected area or rinse with fresh water — this can discharge more toxin.
- Get medical advice.

- If it is not readily available, try applying a paste made of talcum, baking soda or flour mixed with sea water. When the paste is scraped off, the marine creature's cells and toxins may come off with it.
- Some local gurus

suggest applying a papain-based meat tenderizer (in paste form), which may break down the toxins of marine creatures.
- If pain persists, apply a nonprescription topical anesthetic cream.

Stings from marine creatures

These need emergency medical assistance, as they are often very severe and some can be fatal. Adhere carefully to local guidelines for swimming and water safety as a preventive safeguard to avoid trouble. Get local advice on whether protective wear (such as a lightweight bodysuit) is advisable. Never harass marine creatures or touch underwater life.

Marine stingers include jellyfish, sea anemones, Portuguese men-of-war and some corals. On contact with the skin, they discharge a small barb and toxin. Some sea urchins, which live on the sea bottom but may show up in shallow water, have poisonous spines that can puncture the skin even through thongs or sneakers. If vacationing in places with exotic marine life, pack a small first-aid kit with needles and tweezers, rubbing alcohol, calamine lotion and baking soda.

What to do for specific marine creature attacks

- For stings by lionfish, catfish, stingrays and stonefish: place affected area in warm water (to deactivate the toxin).
- For jellyfish stings by translucent, bell-shaped creatures, of which about one in ten produces a severe reaction with burning and stinging, possibly long red weals that look like whip marks:
  - pull off the tentacles, protecting hands with cloth or gloves to keep the stingers off the skin;
  - deactivate the jellyfish sting by washing with seawater, then apply rubbing alcohol, vinegar or witch hazel.
- For Portuguese man-of-war stings (these are

bright blue or purplish-red creatures that are easy to spot but have tentacles that can trail invisibly for up to 18 m or 60 ft and can provoke red weals, a severe burning pain, shortness of breath, nausea, stomach cramps and shock):
- seek immediate medical aid;
- meanwhile, treat similarly to jellyfish stings — described above (you can also try ammonia).
- For injury from coral — which on contact may release toxins, or fragments that become embedded in the skin — seek immediate medical attention as it's a potentially life-threatening situation, but meanwhile:
  - apply calamine lotion or rubbing alcohol;
  - remove coral fragments with anything at hand — a handkerchief, tweezers or needle;
  - wash with soap and water;
  - splint if possible to immobilize limb.
- For sea-anemone stings — follow same measures as for jellyfish (do not rub and do not rinse with fresh water), seek medical advice.
- For sea-urchin barbs, where the toxic spines may cause infection if not promptly removed:
  - scrub with soap and water (gets rid of some barbs);
  - extract spines with sterilized needle or tweezers — ask a physician to pull out remainder;
  - apply hot compresses or immerse in hot seawater to increase blood flow, which helps remove toxins (since the punctured part may be numb, check the water temperature with your hand or uninjured foot).
- For attacks by blue-ringed octopus, which may cause weakness of the muscles, numbness and labored breathing: be prepared to give artificial respiration or CPR (if qualified) as necessary; this may have to be maintained until the paralysis wears off. Summon medical aid.
- For stingray attacks, which may cause sudden pain, swelling, redness around wound, nausea and vomiting, muscle spasms, convulsions and breathing difficulties:
  - carefully remove stinger if possible;
  - watch the breathing; if it stops, give artificial respiration or CPR as above;

- watch for signs of allergic shock and, if necessary, give appropriate treatment (see "Allergic shock").

BLEEDING

Any blood looks alarming, but most small wounds stop bleeding after a minute or so or with slight local pressure. Minor cuts, scrapes and abrasions do best if kept dry and open to some air. The loss of large amounts of blood causes pallor, weakness, possible collapse and unconsciousness, requiring swift medical aid.

What to do for external (visible) bleeding

For minor bleeding and small cuts:
- wash with soap and warm water; apply sterile gauze dressing.

For deeper cuts:
- apply firm, direct pressure with a gauze pad for 10 to 15 minutes (use disposable latex gloves if available, to reduce risks of picking up an infection from the casualty's blood). Apply more pressure if bleeding doesn't stop; maintain pressure and call for medical aid. (See "Dressings and bandages," below.)
- Elevate the part if possible, to drain blood back toward the heart.
- Keep person comfortable, lying down, reassure, give no drink or food.
- Call emergency medical services immediately if bleeding is severe, or if casualty vomits blood or passes blood through the rectum (blood by rectum may be black or tar-like in appearance).

BURNS AND SCALDS

For a minor burn, do not, as folklore suggests, apply butter — it won't relieve pain and may cause infection if blisters form and then break. Instead, use cold (not iced) water — by far the most effective first-aid burn treatment — which eases the pain as it cleanses.

What to do for minor (first-degree) burns

- Place the burned part in cold water, or cover with cold, wet cloths, for 10–15 minutes or until the pain subsides.
- Do not apply pressure over burned skin, or try to remove clothing which has become stuck to the skin.
- Try a local anesthetic cream if skin is not broken — to minimize the discomfort.
- Apply light, dry dressing for comfort (burn ointments are not necessary). See "Dressings and bandages," below.

Second-degree burns and what to do for them

Signs of a second-degree burn are blistering, pain and swelling. Sunburn that causes blisters, swelling and oozing is also a second-degree burn. For second-degree burns you should:
- Do the same as for minor burns.
- Don't put on creams or lotions, they may hamper medical treatment.
- Don't break blisters or peel damaged skin — you will only encourage infection.
- Seek physician care.

BLEEDING NEEDS MEDICAL AID IN THE FOLLOWING SITUATIONS:

- **if blood comes in spurts (an artery may have been cut);**
- **if bleeding won't stop with pressure. Cover the wound with a large soft cloth and, if possible, elevate above heart level. Press directly on the wound to stop blood flow; apply an additional compress on** *top* **of the first, if necessary (do not remove blood-soaked dressings, as clotting may be disturbed);**
- **if scrape is very large (for example, the whole length of an arm or leg);**
- **if the face is cut, which may need plastic surgery to avoid scarring;**
- **if a wound seems to have dirt or debris in it;**
- **if there are any signs of infection — redness, pus (meanwhile, soak the wound in salty water to encourage draining);**
- **for cuts that look deep, with gaping edges, or jagged cuts, particularly from broken glass. If a cut seems to need stitches, do not wait more than six hours to get them;**
- **for a deep puncture wound, especially one made with a dirty object (gardening tool, for example), if a tetanus booster shot hasn't been given within the past five years. Any puncture wound carries a potential threat of tetanus and calls for protective vaccination — not just clearly "dirty" ones. Arrange for a tetanus shot as soon as possible if unable to remember the date of the last one.**

Third-degree, or serious, burns need prompt medical attention

A deep or extensive burn, especially one caused by hot liquids or contact with fire, electricity or corrosive chemicals, requires immediate medical aid. Signs of a third-degree burn are lack of immediate pain (nerve endings have been destroyed), whiteness and or charring. These burns create severe shock, which can be life-threatening in itself. For serious burns you should:

- Call emergency medical services.
- Remove any tight clothing that is not stuck, such as rings, bangles, belts and shoes, before tissues swell. Do not try to remove damaged tissue or break blisters.
- Cover loosely with a clean dry dressing, such as gauze, handkerchief, pillowcase or strip of sheet; do not apply any home remedies such as ointments and antiseptics.
- Elevate and support injured arms or legs higher than the chest.
- Do not apply cold water.
- Be prepared to give artificial respiration or CPR (if qualified) if needed.
- Cover casualty with a clean sheet and blanket to keep casualty warm.
- If medical help is delayed, give frequent small cold drinks if burns are extensive to replace fluid loss.

CHOKING: THE HEIMLICH MANEUVER

Choking often occurs in the pleasantest of surroundings — enjoying Christmas dinner, talking with friends over coffee and cookies or cheering at a ball game while munching popcorn. Usually a good strong cough releases whatever has stuck in the throat and the person is left somewhat red-faced, teary-eyed, possibly with a sore throat and perhaps a trifle embarrassed. But respiratory distress and oxygen lack can quickly ensue if a small object, such as a piece of food or the tab of a pop can, becomes lodged in the throat (windpipe), partially or totally cutting off air to the lungs. If coughing can't dislodge the object, death can quickly follow. Within one or two minutes the choking person can become unconscious and suffer cardiac arrest.

A large proportion of choking deaths

occur because — prompted by good manners and social conditioning — the choking person seeks privacy while trying to clear the airway. Many people die locked in the bathroom. A choking person should never leave a room where others are present. If the person does leave, the potential rescuer should follow and offer to help if necessary.

Until 1976, there were two medically recommended ways to help a choking person — "washing down" the object stuck in the throat or slapping the back to dislodge it. Although today's experts consider both these older methods ineffective and even dangerous, many people still give choking persons a vigorous back blow or encourage them to take a drink or eat a piece of bread. These well-meaning techniques can push the object further down or create a bigger and more dangerous blockage.

The Heimlich maneuver, a quick, upward thrust below the diaphragm which simulates the effects of coughing, is now widely recognized as the safest and most effective way to help a choking adult or child over age one. A series of abdominal thrusts forces objects up and out of the airway. But proper training is necessary to perform the technique safely. Everyone should learn this life-saving measure.

Anyone who is choking but can still speak or cough with reasonable force should be encouraged and reassured (but *not* subjected to the Heimlich maneuver, which may do unnecessary damage). But anyone who has little or no ability to breathe needs help *immediately*. Lack of oxygen does damage to the brain within minutes, so it is *not safe* to wait for an ambulance. On children aged one to eight a modified version of the Heimlich maneuver is used (see below). On infants less than one, use back blows and chest thrusts (see below).

Call for emergency help as soon as any choking victim can't speak, becomes unconscious or begins to turn blue.

What to do for choking

- Ask the person, "Are you choking?" If the person can still breathe and make sounds, just reassure and stay with him or her and encourage vigorous coughing.

THE DISTRESS SIGNALS OF CHOKING

- a hand clutching the throat;
- a weak, ineffective cough;
- inability to speak or make sounds;
- increasing difficulty breathing — high-pitched wheeze;
- blue color of lips and earlobes;
- extreme efforts by the choking person to move air into the lungs, possibly with thrashing movements.

THE HEIMLICH MANEUVER

Before performing any lifesaving technique on a conscious person, the rescuer must obtain consent. Ask the victim: "Are you OK? Can I help you?" Once consent is received (a nod will do), the Heimlich maneuver can be performed.

The four basic Heimlich steps used to clear the airway in adults, and in children over age one, are:

• From behind, place your arms around the victim's waist.
• Make a fist with one hand (thumb outside, *not* tucked in) and place the thumb side of the fist against the choking person's abdomen, well below the rib cage and just above the navel.

• Grasp your fist with the other hand and press into the victim's abdomen (just above the navel) with quick upward thrusts. (Remember, you are simulating a forceful cough.)
• Repeat thrusts until the object is expelled.
  If the casualty becomes unconscious, try to make the person's fall to the ground as gentle as possible to prevent injury, especially to the head. An ambulance should be called at once, since brain and heart damage can quickly follow loss of consciousness.

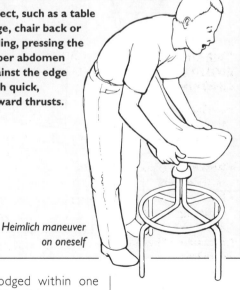

Heimlich maneuver on unconscious person

While awaiting emergency medical help, a trained rescuer can perform the Heimlich technique on an unconscious choking person, placed on his or her back. Although the principle is the same when the casualty is lying down, the technique varies slightly — the rescuer kneels astride the person, using body weight to produce upward thrusts — and several additional steps are required.

If the choker is seated, you may be able to save time by doing the maneuver in that position — depending on the chair. If the choker is a young child, you can kneel rather than stand behind. If the choker is so pregnant or obese that abdominal thrusts are impossible, pass your arms beneath the armpits and do the maneuver on the *upper* chest.

Any casualty who receives the Heimlich maneuver should seek medical attention as soon as possible, as the maneuver can cause unavoidable internal damage.

People who choke while alone can perform steps two to four of the standard Heimlich technique on themselves, applying upward thrusts with their hands, or they can lean over a fixed horizontal object, such as a table edge, chair back or railing, pressing the upper abdomen against the edge with quick, upward thrusts.

Basic Heimlich maneuver

Heimlich maneuver on oneself

• If the person has little or no ability to cough, speak or breathe, offer to perform the Heimlich maneuver. If consent is obtained (a nod will do), go ahead (see above).
• Summon immediate emergency help if the blockage can't be dislodged within one minute or by doing the Heimlich maneuver, or if the choker can't cough or speak or is losing consciousness. (Get someone else to call, while you stay with the choking person.)

CHOKING INFANTS NEED BACK BLOWS AND CHEST THRUSTS

The Heimlich method is not recommended for infants under one year old. Instead, Canada's Red Cross Society, Heart and Stroke Foundation and St. John Ambulance advise use of back blows and chest thrusts. Always call emergency medical services at once if a choking infant becomes limp or unconscious.

First aid for choking infants

- Test whether the infant is breathing by looking for chest movements, listening (placing ear near nose and mouth) and feeling for breath on the cheek. An infant who can still breathe and cry should be reassured and allowed to cough naturally. Do *not* pound the child on the back.
- Have someone call for emergency medical services if the infant has little or no ability to breathe, cough or cry, and/or if the child is turning blue or limp.
- Meanwhile try first aid: place the infant face down — hold by the legs or straddle over the arm with *head lower* than the trunk. Deliver four blows with the heel of the hand between the infant's shoulder blades. (A larger infant can be lain down across your lap.)
- If the blockage is not relieved, roll the infant face up on your arm or on a firm surface, still keeping the head lower than the trunk. Give four rapid chest compressions (thrusts) over the breastbone, using two fingers only. (The fingers should be centered between the nipples, and about one finger-width *below* the nipple-line.)
- If the blockage is still there after backslaps and chest thrusts, open the baby's mouth (place your thumb over the tongue and wrap your fingers around the lower jaw). If the foreign body can be seen, gently and carefully remove it with a sideways sweep of the finger. (For an infant, never poke a finger into the throat or do "blind" finger sweeps for an obstruction you can't see, as this may push the object farther down.)

CONVULSIONS

During a convulsion, people may fall to the ground, stiffen, arch backward, froth at the mouth, have uncontrollable jerking movements and become unconscious. There may be a high temperature.

What to do for convulsions

- Do not try to restrain the person, or put anything between the teeth.
- Offer nothing to drink during the attack.
- Clear the surroundings of hard or sharp objects.
- Loosen any tight clothing, especially around the neck, chest or waist.
- When the convulsion has stopped, place the person in the recovery position. Cover with a warm blanket or coat if cold.
- If hot, remove excess clothing or covers and sponge with tepid water.
- Be prepared to give artificial respiration or CPR (if qualified) if necessary.
- Call for emergency medical services.

DRESSINGS AND BANDAGES

A dressing should be germ-free (sterile) and act as a filter — restricting entry of germs but allowing air to reach the wound. If sweat cannot

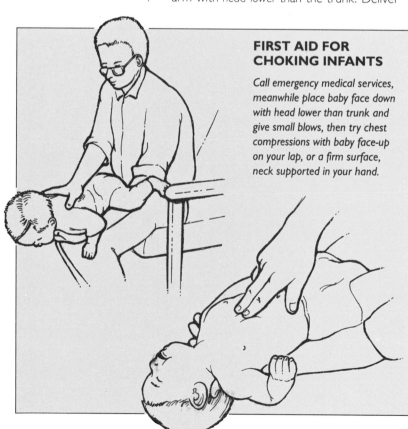

FIRST AID FOR CHOKING INFANTS

Call emergency medical services, meanwhile place baby face down with head lower than trunk and give small blows, then try chest compressions with baby face-up on your lap, or a firm surface, neck supported in your hand.

evaporate, an infection can set in. It should also be of nonadherent material so that it will not damage the repairing wound.

Adhesive dressings, often called "plasters" (e.g., Band-aids), consist of an absorbent pad of gauze or cellulose with an adhesive backing which, if perforated, allows sweat to evaporate. The surrounding skin should be dry before application.

Sterile dressings are layers of gauze covered by a pad of cotton wool. They come with a roller bandage to tie them in position.

Plain gauze dressings come in a variety of sizes. They tend to stick to wounds and assist clotting. There are specialized commercial dressings for burns, eye injuries and so on. But dressings may be improvised from clean hankies, freshly laundered towels or linen, or any other clean absorbent material.

Bandages are used to hold dressings and other protections in place, and to immobilize injured areas. It is not essential that they be clean as they do not touch the wound — ties, plastic bags or even used socks can be employed, in a pinch!

Wash the hands before handling dressings, and avoid touching wounds with fingers or breathing on them. In general, minor wounds are best cleaned with soap and water — creams and ointments should be avoided. Infected wounds need physician attention.

EAR INJURIES

Ear injuries are commonly due to cuts, foreign bodies and infection. If they are associated with possible head injuries, or if blood or clear fluid is escaping from *inside* the ear, seek immediate medical aid.

What to do for ear injuries
• Control bleeding from cuts by pressing gauze or a clean cloth directly over the wound and elevate the head.
• If bleeding is from *within* the ear, bandage loosely and keep head elevated but with injured side tilted slightly down, to encourage drainage. (Blocking the bleeding may cause pressure inside the ear.)
• Remove insects by gently flooding the ear with tepid water or olive oil. Beads, beans,

nuts and other solid objects should be removed by a doctor.
• Never stick sharp objects such as a Q-tip in the ear; if the ear feels blocked, see a doctor or instill a little warm mineral oil (a few drops) nightly and then flush well with warm water.

ELECTRIC SHOCK

Injuries due to low-voltage electrical contact are not usually severe, but can be serious for very young children or the elderly, who may go into shock. Higher-voltage shock is a major emergency causing severe burns and life-threatening shock, and requires immediate medical assistance. In *any* case of electrical shock, be careful not to touch the casualty until the source of the current has been removed.

What to do for electric shock
• Break the contact by switching off the current, removing the plug or wrenching the cable free.
• If the power is hard to disconnect, stand on something dry (blanket, rubber mat, newspapers) and break the contact by pushing the person free with a wooden pole or board, or pulling with a loop of rope around an arm or leg — or pull away a rug or carpet the person is lying on.
• Start artificial respiration or CPR (if qualified) if necessary.
• Give first aid for any burns (see "Burns and scalds," above).
• Summon emergency medical services.

EYE INJURIES

All eye injuries are potentially serious and require medical attention. Do not attempt to remove a foreign body which is on the pupil of the eye. Do not rub the eye.

What to do for eye injuries
For chemicals in the eye:
• Hold the eyelid open and flush with gently running tepid water for at least 15 minutes. (Make sure that the flow of water is away from the unhurt eye.)
• Don't press on the eye.
• Cover the eye with gauze loosely held in place with a bandage and seek medical aid.

SYMPTOMS OF FRACTURES AND DISLOCATIONS:

- pain at or near the site of injury, made worse by movement of the part;
- tenderness when gentle pressure is applied to affected part;
- swelling due to internal bleeding around fracture;
- loss of control of limb, deformity of limb, inability to move, unnatural movement of
- injured part;
- coarse, grating sound of broken ends of fractured bone;
- shock due to blood loss — internal or external.

For penetrating eye injuries:
- Lay the person down.
- Give comfort and reassurance.
- If the penetrating object is still embedded, *do not remove it*. Immobilize the head to prevent movement, and cover the eye and object with a paper cup or cone, secured with tape. Be sure there is no pressure on the eye or the object.
- Cover the eye with gauze padding held in place with a light bandage around the head.
- Transport to hospital immediately.

For foreign body on the eye:
- Remove from white of eye with the corner of a clean handkerchief or a moistened wisp of cotton wool.
- If under the lower lid, pull the lid down and remove foreign body.
- If this is unsuccessful or the object is under the upper lid, try blinking with the eye under water.
- If still not removed, seek medical help.

FAINTING

Fainting is caused by a temporary shortage of oxygen to the brain. It is often due to fatigue, long periods of standing still or such stresses as fear, pain or distress. But it may also signal a more serious condition, especially in older people. If the cause of fainting is not clear, a physician should be consulted.

What to do for unusual, single episodes of fainting
- Don't allow someone who feels faint to go off alone. Help the person into fresh air, if possible, and to lie down with feet up. If a standing person starts to faint, allow him or her to fall to the ground gently — do not keep sitting upright.
- Loosen tight clothing. Sponge face lightly with

cold water and keep person warm. If casualty does not respond in a short time, summon medical help.
- Once consciousness returns, the person should remain lying down quietly for ten or fifteen minutes.

FRACTURES

Anyone with a suspected fracture or joint dislocation needs prompt medical attention. Suspect a fracture if an injured part is very painful, swollen or deformed, or if movement causes pain. If in doubt, treat as a fracture. Try not to move until the injury is splinted. If a neck or back injury is suspected, do not move the casualty; summon emergency medical services. Moving someone with a spinal injury can cause paralysis or death.

What to do for fractures
- Attend to bleeding of severe wounds before dealing with fracture (see "Bleeding," above).
- Move the person as little as possible from the site of accident — only if life (the casualty's or your own) is endangered. Move by pulling the person along, holding underneath the armpits.
- Cover with blanket or clothes; give reassurance.
- Immobilize injured part as soon as possible, using other limbs and bandages as emergency support, or with makeshift splint and bandages. Raise the injured part after immobilization to reduce pain and swelling.
- Splints can be improvised from walking sticks, umbrellas, broom handles, pieces of wood, cardboard, firmly folded newspapers, folded pillows, magazines, etc.
- Splints should be sufficiently rigid, long enough to immobilize the joint above and the joint below fracture, well padded, wide enough to immobilize the part and applied over clothing.
- Bandages must be tight enough to immobilize the part but not so tight as to interfere with the circulation. Check the tightness of bandaging every ten minutes — if distal parts of limb such as fingers or toes become pale or blue, or feel cooler than on the other limb, bandages may be too tight — and in case of swelling (especially important in elbow injuries) loosen slightly.

FROSTBITE AND FREEZING

The body areas most vulnerable to frostbite are those most exposed — the toes, fingers, ears, cheeks, nose, neck. To avoid frostbite, use the old mountaineer's adage: "Keep warm, moving and dry." Most frostbite damage occurs during the freezing and thawing process, so people who are frostbitten should be left cold until they can be completely thawed out and remain so — a repeated thawing and freezing will only increase the damage. A few hours or an extra day of frostbite causes no further damage to already frozen human tissue.

FIRST AID FOR FREEZING TO METAL OBJECTS

If someone has frozen his or her tongue or hand to a metal object:

- **try to prevent pulling away from the metal;**
- **blow hot breath onto the stuck area or pour warm water onto the object. Then gently release the person;**
- **if bleeding occurs, as on the tongue, grasp with folded sterile gauze and apply direct pressure.**

What to do for frostbite

- Shelter from further cold exposure.
- Handle and rewarm the frostbitten area gradually, but only if there is *no* chance of refreezing.
- For mild frostbite (tingling, slight white patches), warm extremities by holding in own (or someone else's) armpits. Warm ears and nose with palm of hand.
- Give warm drinks, not hot and *no alcohol*.
- Remove constrictive clothes, rings, boots, bracelets.
- Do not rub the affected part. Do not apply snow, cold water or any kind of direct heat.
- Do not break any blisters formed.
- For deeper frostbite, put frozen part in warm (not hot) water (41 to 43°C or 106 to 110°F) for 20 minutes or more.
- Protect frozen part from further damage. Apply sterile gauze and elevate the injured area.

HEAD INJURIES

Any moderate to severe blow on the head will likely cause some concussion (temporary brain disturbance), even if there is no damage to the underlying bone. If the blow has been severe enough that spinal injury is possible, keep the person still, do not move, and call for emergency medical services. For lesser injuries that are anything more than a small superficial cut or knock to the head, remove the person to the nearest medical aid. Any tear or cut to the scalp or face tends to bleed heavily. Most are not serious, although they look bad. Severe injury to the head can cause fracture of the underlying bones and in some cases injury to the brain.

Emergency care for head injuries

- Keep casualty lying down.
- Give warmth and comfort.
- Do not give any drinks.
- Apply a cold compress to the location of the blow or injury, but do not put pressure on the skull.
- If bleeding, clean with soap and water, compress wound to stop bleeding. (Do not, however, put pressure on the skull if you suspect a fracture there, as this might put pressure on the brain.)
- If unconscious, place casualty in the recovery position (see "Recovery position," earlier in chapter) and call emergency medical services.
- Watch the casualty in case unconsciousness sets in later, even if this means half-waking the person once or twice during the night to check responsiveness (for the first 24 hours).

Call emergency medical aid if the person is:

- unconscious or drowsy;
- twitching or having convulsions;
- experiencing weakness or inability to move any body part;
- vomiting;
- oozing blood or fluid from ears or nose;
- complaining of persistent headache or double vision;
- less than one year old.

SIGNS OF FROSTBITE:

- **grayish color, or whitening of skin;**
- **heavy numbness;**
- **loss of touch, sensation;**
- **sharp pricking, stinging, itchiness.**

SYMPTOMS OF CONCUSSION:

- **"seeing stars";**
- **temporary, partial or complete loss of consciousness;**
- **shallow breathing;**
- **nausea and vomiting;**
- **pale, cold and clammy skin;**
- **later — loss of memory.**

  Any person with signs of concussion should see a physician or seek medical aid at a hospital emergency department.

HEART ATTACK

A heart attack, otherwise known as a myocardial infarction, results from a small clot in one of the coronary arteries that supply the heart muscle itself with oxygen. Some heart-attack deaths are instant and likely could not be prevented by first aid; others could be averted by quicker recognition of a life-threatening situation. All too many victims of a heart attack — or those who witness one — mistake it for something else, perhaps indigestion or a muscular twinge. Lacking a sense of urgency, or denying a suspicion they are afraid to accept, many wait too long before seeking help. Waiting to "see what happens next time" often has fatal consequences. It is crucial to understand that such denial is one of the signs of heart attack; if the casualty will not respond to the situation, someone else must take charge.

Recognizing the signals of heart attack, knowing the emergency telephone number, and applying CPR — an easily learned procedure — can save lives. (See "The ABC's of AR and CPR," above, and also chapter 16.)

What to do for a heart attack

- Recognize the signals. Expect denial. Take charge.
- Have the person stop all activity and sit or lie down (semi-sitting is usually most comfortable).
- Offer reassurance; loosen tight clothing.
- If the person has known heart disease, assist in taking the usual medication, if appropriate.
- Call emergency medical services *immediately*, or go to the nearest hospital emergency room. When calling for emergency help, identify the problem as a possible heart attack.
- Be prepared to begin CPR (if qualified) if cardiac arrest occurs.

HYPERTHERMIA (HEAT ILLNESSES)

The degree of heat-related illness ranges from mild to severe, and its onset often goes unnoticed — producing only irritability, confusion and slowed reactions. A severe rise in body heat impairs coordination, hindering the ability to focus or think clearly. Hot, confused people may further endanger themselves by failing to don hats, losing sunglasses, forgetting to take off excess clothes and not drinking enough fluids. Huge swings in blood volume and pressure may produce sudden collapse, even death.

General first aid for heat illness

- Cool down in the shade with legs and feet elevated.
- Apply wet towels or tepid water spray over the body.
- Put ice packs in groin, neck and underarms.
- Slowly sip cool (not ice-cold), noncaffeinated fluids.
- Summon medical help if serious.

Signs of different stages of heat illness

Heat cramps:
- pallor;
- sweaty skin;
- weakness and nausea;
- tingling in arms or legs.

What to do for heat cramps:
- Massage the cramped muscle.
- Cool the body with tepid water and wet towels.
- Sip plain, cool water (don't use salt tablets). Solutions such as Gatorade aren't as good as plain water.

Heat syncope (fainting):
Typically seen in outdoor summer workers, travelers unaccustomed to hot, humid conditions and those who stand a lot in one position (e.g., military personnel), its symptoms are dizziness fainting, light-headedness, clammy skin.

What to do for heat syncope:
- Get away from the heat.
- Lie down with legs raised.
- Apply wet towels all over.

Heat exhaustion:
This stage of heat illness may build slowly over several days or weeks. Its symptoms are profuse perspiration; vague flulike malaise; fatigue, extreme listlessness; rapid pulse; pale, clammy skin.

What to do for heat exhaustion:
- Stay in a cool place, lying down with feet elevated.
- Replace body fluids.
- Apply wet towels to the body.

Heatstroke

The most serious stage of heat illness, and a potentially fatal condition, heatstroke calls for emergency medical aid. In heatstroke, the sweat glands stop working, resulting in a dangerously high body temperature — possibly above 41°C (106°F) or, rectally, even as high as 44 °C (111°F).

The symptoms are:

- cessation of sweating;
- agitation, restlessness, bizarre behavior (the most telltale sign);
- rapid pulse;
- hot, dry, reddened look;
- drop in blood pressure, dizziness;
- headache;
- staggering gait;
- seizures, unconsciousness.

N.B.: A cool skin may hide a deceptively high core body temperature.

What to do for heatstroke (while awaiting medical aid):

- Remove casualty to a cool place.
- Remove as much clothing as possible.
- Cool the body by fanning, spraying or sponging with cool, not cold, water. (Even if clothes can't be removed, water-cool the casualty.)
- Give small amounts of fluids.
- Monitor the casualty. Be prepared to do artificial respiration or CPR (if qualified) if necessary.

HYPOTHERMIA (COLD INJURY)

Hypothermia is a dangerous cooling of the body's interior or "core." Mild hypothermia occurs with a body temperature drop to between 33 and 35°C (91–95°F); below 30°C (86°F), hypothermia is life-threatening. Hypothermia may result from cold weather, or from prolonged exposure to chilly water.

In *mild hypothermia*, shivering is intense (the body's effort to produce heat); the person has slow reactions, stumbles, has slurred speech and acts as if intoxicated.

In *moderate hypothermia*, shivering lessens; the person is very tired, seems withdrawn and irritable, may act strangely — even undress despite the cold — due to a deceptively warm sensation. The pulse is slow and weak. Breathing can be slow and shallow.

In *severe hypothermia* (core body temperature under 30°C or 86°F), shivering ceases, the pupils have a fixed stare, the person may hallucinate and lose consciousness; heartbeat and breathing become slow, almost undetectable.

What to do

For mild to moderate hypothermia (person still shivering and coherent):

- Prevent further heat loss, get to shelter.
- Put on extra clothes, replace wet clothing with dry.
- Gradually rewarm by placing between blankets, cuddling against others, sharing a sleeping bag.
- Give tepid water, sweets (sugar) if still conscious.
- Do not give alcohol; it dilates the blood vessels and gives a false sense of warmth.
- Check pulse — if slow, condition is worsening.
- If person doesn't recover within 30 minutes, summon emergency medical services.

For severe hypothermia:

- Get medical aid as fast as possible. Correct rewarming of someone with severe hypothermia can make the difference between life and death. (It's often safest to leave severely hypothermic people cold until reaching medical assistance.)
- Rewarming must not be fast, as it may harm the heart. Below 30°C (86°F) the heart is in danger of fibrillating (producing irregular beats) and needs constant monitoring.
- While transporting to hospital, keep the hypothermic person horizontal with as little jolting as possible. With a slowed metabolic rate, the body is in a "metabolic icebox" that may protect it from more damage.

MOUTH INJURIES

- Clear the mouth of any broken teeth. For first-aid action if whole teeth have been knocked out, see "Teeth (knocked out)," later in this chapter.
- Lean the casualty slightly forward. Provide a bowl for the person to spit into.
- Apply direct pressure to tooth socket or wound by placing thick gauze or cotton-wool pad firmly in position.

For tongue, cheek or lip:
- Compress the bleeding part between finger and thumb, using a clean handkerchief or gauze dressing until bleeding stops. Have the casualty bite on the pad for five to ten minutes, supporting the chin with the hand.
- Do not wash the mouth out, as this can disturb the clotting. Do not attempt to plug the sockets of lost teeth.

NOSEBLEEDS

Bleeding from the nose is very common and does not usually denote anything serious. It is generally due to a ruptured blood vessel in the septum, which divides the nostrils. However, severe head injuries may cause blood to trickle from the nose (see "Head injuries," above).

What to do for nosebleeds
- Sit up and do not lean forward — tilt the head slightly back.
- Loosen any tight clothing around the neck.
- Pinch the lower end of the nose to close the nostrils continuously for 5–10 minutes. (Do not press on the bony part of the nose because this does not work.)
- Apply cold compress to forehead and bridge of nose.
- Don't blow nose for several hours afterward.
- If bleeding doesn't stop within 15 to 20 minutes, seek prompt medical advice.

POISONINGS

There are nearly three million cases of poisonings each year in North America, almost 70 percent of them in children under age six. Poisons may enter the body by being swallowed, inhaled, absorbed through the skin or injected under the skin. Children mistake household cleaners for beverages, or medications for candy, sometimes playfully emulating adult drug-taking, with possibly serious, even fatal, results. Nearly half of all accidental poisonings are caused by ASA, acetaminophen (such as Tylenol), insecticides, household bleach, detergents, fragrances, cleaners, furniture polish, kerosene, iron and vitamin compounds, disinfectants, deodorizers, lye, other corrosives or laxatives. To be prepared for poisonings, post the number of the local Poison Control Center near every phone.

Poisoning can cause a variety of effects on breathing and the central nervous system, and may lead to collapse, unconsciousness and death. The following early signs may help to identify the nature of the poison.
- *Swallowed*: nausea, cramps, vomiting; burning or discoloration around mouth; odor of poison on breath.
- *Inhaled*: coughing, chest pain, disturbed breathing; some gases cause dizziness and headache.
- *Injected or absorbed through the skin*: irritation at point of entry. Injected poisons usually act more quickly than those absorbed through the skin, and have more widespread effects.

What to do for poisonings
- Call your local Poison Control Center. Give the age of the person, what was ingested, how much, when ingested, how the casualty is feeling or acting, your name and phone number. If you are directed to go to an emergency department, take the container of poison or a sample with you. Save any vomit for later analysis.
- Keep a bottle of syrup of ipecac (available over the counter at pharmacies) on hand to induce vomiting if needed. But *do not use it* unless instructed to do so by the Poison Control Center or a physician. Some corrosive chemicals and petroleum products cause even more harm if they are brought up. If in doubt, treat the poison as a corrosive substance.
- If using syrup of ipecac, give 5–10 ml (1-2 tsp) every 15 minutes.
- Never make someone vomit if he or she:
  - is drowsy, sleepy or unconscious;
  - has swallowed a petroleum product (such as furniture polish, Varsol, kerosene, gasoline) or corrosives (such as lye or bleach).

What to do for specific poisonings
- *For swallowed poisons*, give plenty of milk or water if so instructed by a physician or Poison Control Center; loosen clothes, allow plenty of fresh air.
- *For splashes in the eye*, flood the eye with

lukewarm water for at least 15 minutes. Encourage blinking while flushing the eye, but do not force the eyelid open. (See "Eye injuries," above.)

- *For liquid poisons on the skin*, remove contaminated clothing and flood the area with water, then follow with mild soap wash and a final rinse.
- *For corrosive powders on the skin,* brush off powder using a cloth or tissue (not the bare hand), then treat as for liquid poisons on the skin.
- *For inhaled poisons*, move casualty to fresh air immediately or open all doors and windows. Be prepared to do artificial respiration or CPR (if qualified) if necessary.
- *For injected poisons*, keep casualty at rest and keep limb at heart level to slow absorption. Seek medical aid immediately. Be prepared to do artificial respiration or CPR (if qualified) if necessary.
- *If the casualty is unconscious*, place in recovery position (see "Recovery position," above).
- *As a rescuer*, take care not to get contaminated while decontaminating someone else.

SEIZURES

Seizures, or convulsions, are characterized by a stiffening of the body, eyes rolling upwards and jerky movements of face and limbs. They are usually very brief, lasting one to two minutes, but occasionally up to 15 minutes. Most seizures, especially in young children, are due to high fever — known as febrile seizures, these occur in 2 to 5 percent of children aged five months to five years of age. Other seizures are due to epilepsy. (See "Childhood fever" in chapter 11, and "Epilepsy" in chapters 11 and 16.) But seizures can also indicate serious medical problems such as stroke.

What to do for seizures

- Remain calm.
- Protect the person from injury.
- Lie the casualty on the side, with head lower than hips, or on the stomach.
- Put nothing in the mouth.
- Summon emergency medical help if the seizure lasts more than five minutes, or if it is the person's first seizure.

SHOCK

The medical condition known as "shock" results from inadequate blood circulation to body tissues. It accompanies all injuries and illnesses, to some degree, and when severe it can lead to unconsciousness or death. It should certainly never be underestimated and dismissed as "just shock"!

Signs of shock are:
- pale or bluish complexion;
- cold, clammy, sweaty skin;
- possible giddiness, blurring of vision and vomiting;
- pulse at first rapid, perhaps later becoming very faint, almost undetectable;
- drowsiness and possibly unconsciousness;
- rapid and shallow breathing.

What to do for shock

- Sit or lay the person down and deal with the immediate causes of shock (bleeding, pain, despair, fear, etc.). Move as little as possible.
- Do not overheat, as warmth draws blood into skin and away from vital organs.
- Do not give drinks.
- Loosen any tight clothing and allow plenty of fresh air.
- If injuries permit, keep the person's head flat and support the legs in an elevated position — this encourages blood flow to the brain.
- If vomiting seems likely or the person is unconscious, place in the recovery position (see "Recovery position," early in this chapter).
- Summon medical aid as soon as possible.
- Be prepared to give artificial respiration or CPR (if qualified) if necessary.

SPORTS INJURIES

Sports injuries range from simple bruises and strains to dislocated joints and broken bones. They can be sudden and acute or occur slowly due to overuse. A few, such as spine or skull fractures, hyperthermia (heat stress), abdominal bleeds or organ rupture can threaten life. Given the importance now placed on physical fitness, the management of sports injuries has become a prime sphere of emergency medicine.

Main types of sports injury

Acute sports injuries can happen in several ways:

- by a hard force, blow or jolt — including overstretching (such as a pulled hamstring muscle);
- through friction or repetitive mechanical irritation (such as friction tenosynovitis — inflammation of the sheath around the tendon);
- by twisting (such as ligament or tendon tears and fractures);
- via shearing/sliding forces (such as abrasions, cuts, fractures);
- from consistent overuse — repeated, long-term abuse of the musculoskeletal system — through intrinsic factors (such as muscle imbalance or malalignment of the leg/foot during activity) or extrinsic factors (such as faulty training techniques, improper equipment or poor surfaces).

Key steps in managing sports injuries

- Use the RICE principle: rest, ice, compression and elevation, plus limited motion as soon as possible after injury. The primary goal is to reduce the inflammation that follows injury in the first 72 hours as blood and tissue fluids accumulate at the injured site.
- Rapid swelling suggests damage to blood vessels. Once the swelling goes down, gentle controlled movement should begin, with gradual return of the injured area to full function. Experts strongly promote prudent, limited movement during recovery.
- Consult a physician about any but the mildest of sprains, strains or other injuries.
- Never disregard pain.
- Wrap the injured part in well-crushed ice or a package of frozen peas (wrapped in a towel or old woolen sock to prevent frostbite) and apply for 15 to 20 minutes every two hours for severe injuries, every six hours for less severe injuries. Deep-seated injuries will require the full 20 minutes, one to four times daily. Apply ice for briefer periods if the injury is close to the skin. (Do not use ice if you have circulatory problems.)
- Apply pressure (compression) with an elastic bandage that's moderately tight but does not press on nerves or reduce blood circulation. Always wrap from the point farthest away from the heart toward the heart (e.g., wrist to elbow). The tensor bandage should not usually be worn at night, to prevent circulation problems. Tip: if the far end of the injured limb turns blue, the bandage is too tight!
- Elevate the injured part to prevent pooling of the fluid accumulated by inflamed tissues. The goal is to let gravity direct blood back to the heart. Injured legs should be propped at rest above hip level. Injured hands and forearms can be supported in a sling with hands at shoulder level. For upper-arm injuries, raise the arm above the head at regular intervals.
- To combat pain, use painkillers.
- To reduce swelling/inflammation, take ASA or other nonsteroidal anti-inflammatories — such as naproxen (Naprosyn or Aputex) or ibuprofen (Advil) — as advised by a physician.
- Beware of prolonged inactivity — begin limited gentle exercise during recovery to regain strength and flexibility, preferably guided by a trained physiotherapist.
- Return to full activity only when well healed and pain-free — usually ten days to eight weeks for a sprain or fracture, depending on severity.
- Beware of heat, often improperly used to treat exercise-induced injuries. Never apply heat to any bruise, strain or soft-tissue injury. (That means no hot baths and no heating pads following such injuries.) It's generally best to opt for ice. Heat may make the injury feel better, but will also increase local inflammation and worsen the swelling. Heat should only be used, if at all, once the swelling has gone down. Contrast baths — alternating cold with hot water — may be useful for stimulating blood circulation to the injury, but only several days after the acute injury phase.

When to seek medical advice for sports injuries

One person's ache is another's agony. Pain is an individual matter, but even minor delays in consulting a physician can allow serious, long-standing problems to develop. Never hesitate to seek expert help if the injury is more than a

COMMON SPORTS INJURIES AND THEIR TREATMENT

- **Skeletal injuries** are fractures that involve the breaking of bone(s) and are potentially serious. If the skin remains intact, the broken bone is a simple or closed fracture. If the skin is pierced by the broken bone, the break is an open fracture. Skeletal injuries result mainly from falls and blows in cycling and contact sports such as football, hockey, soccer and rugby. Consequently, sport authorities ban potential sources of severe fracture injuries, such as "boarding" in hockey and "collapsing the scrum" in rugby. Bicycling accidents and careless diving into shallow or rocky waters are common causes of severe head and spinal injuries.

Treatment of bone fractures involves:
- consultation with a trained physician;
- cleaning and covering up any open wound(s) to avoid infection;
- elevating the limb/part at first if possible;
- immobilizing the affected limb by splinting;
- applying a supportive cast, and sometimes surgery to fix the bone by a plate or nail.

- **Soft-tissue injuries/bruises** usually include blood-vessel damage, muscle spasm, pain and swelling.

Treatment of soft-tissue injuries aims to reduce swelling, relieve pain and prevent further damage (allowing a return to activity as swiftly as possible) by applying ice and compression (pressure), elevating the damaged part and ensuring limited motion only, until healed. (Heat is not the best treatment for acute bruises or other soft-tissue damage in the first 72 hours.)

- **Muscle strains** — among the mildest and commonest of sports injuries — usually arise from a direct or indirect blow, or from overuse when muscle fibers are overstretched or torn, causing bleeding and an acute inflammatory response with pain, tenderness, swelling and reduced mobility.

The basic treatment for strains is:
- application of ice or cooling packs;
- elevation of the affected area;
- an elastic support bandage (between ice treatments);
- alleviating the load on the affected part while it heals with crutches, canes, walkers or slings;
- rest — but usually not total disuse. Limited movement is often best during recovery.

- **Sprains** are joint injuries involving the partial or complete tearing of ligaments (which join bone to bone), such as ankle, knee, shoulder and elbow sprains. They occur when a joint is forced beyond its normal range of motion. Quick diagnosis and speedy treatment hasten recovery.

Treatment for sprains includes a thorough examination by a physician to diagnose the severity of the ligament tear, plus prompt measures to reduce the swelling with ice, compression and elevation. The sooner ice is applied, the more it diminishes swelling due to fluid accumulation. Ice also acts as a local anesthetic and may relieve muscle spasm. Apply ice three to four times a day to the injured area, for 20 minutes each time. A flexible elastic bandage will stabilize the joint, help to reduce swelling and aid recovery. Depending on their severity, sprains require complete rest (and sometimes immobilization in a cast) for 72 hours or

longer, and perhaps also temporary use of crutches for ankle and knee sprains. Controlled motion is usually advocated (to avoid prolonged joint immobility) after the first 72 hours, avoiding twisting or full weight-bearing, slowly progressing to more movement — using pain as the guide. The return to full activity should be gradual, with only limited movement until the sprain is completely healed. Serious sprains may need surgical repair.

- **Joint dislocation** occurs if the joint capsule and its surrounding ligaments are torn by an extreme movement exceeding the joint's normal range of motion. Dislocations can be total (joint parts no longer in contact with each other) or partial (bone ends still partly in contact).

Treatment of dislocations is by application of cooling packs and immediate transportation to a physician or hospital for assessment and treatment to reposition the dislocated bones. *Do not try to replace a dislocated joint by home methods.*

- **Tendon injuries** involve the complete or partial rupture of a tendon (which attaches bone to muscle). Tendon tears may be acute (sudden) or chronic (from continual overuse), and are especially frequent in people who take up a new sport, in those who exercise after a sedentary life and in athletes who increase their training volume too quickly.

Treatment of tendon injuries requires the usual — rest, ice, elevation — and perhaps also a supportive bandage or immobilizing cast, a mild exercise regime during recovery (especially stretching exercises) and anti-inflammatory drugs. Complete tendon tears need the attention of an orthopedic surgeon, immobilization in a brace, sling or cast, and occasionally surgical repair. Athletes should not return to full training until complete tendon strength is regained. Stretching exercises and gentle movement aid recovery.

- **Nerve or neurological injuries** involving the brain and spinal cord are mostly due to the impact of the head, neck or back against a solid structure (such as the boards in hockey, the cement bottom of a swimming pool or an icy surface) — even at a slow pace. Head and spine injuries — most frequent in young males — can be catastrophic, producing lifelong disability or death. Sport and recreational activities are the second-commonest cause of spine and head injuries in Canada (following auto crashes).

Treatment of head and spinal injuries requires extreme caution. The spine must be completely immobilized to prevent additional damage from the movement of an unstable vertebral column. Return to some sports may be impossible after severe injuries; even mild spinal injury may hamper the resumption of usual sporting activities.

- **Eye injuries** are particularly common in racquet sports such as squash, tennis and badminton (among adults) and in hockey, baseball, football and soccer (among children). Many can be prevented by enforcing game rules, better supervision, wearing suitable eye protectors endorsed by the Canadian Standards Association — types with polycarbonate lenses mounted in a sturdy frame. Lensless eye protectors are no longer recommended for racquet sports and hockey. (See "Eye injuries," above.)

simple bump or bruise. Consult a physician or sports-medicine specialist within 48 hours if the injury does not seem to be getting better, to check for fractures and other damage. Sports-medicine specialists can discuss the right shoes and equipment, and the safest training techniques.

TEETH (KNOCKED OUT)

Baby (primary) teeth are not usually replaced if knocked out or broken, but adult (permanent) teeth may recover if carefully replanted.

What to do for knocked-out teeth

- Rinse mouth gently in running water.
- Do not rub or scrub mouth.
- Do not handle the tooth by its roots.
- Gently insert the tooth into its socket and hold it there.
- If it's not possible to reinsert the tooth, place it in cool water or milk or in damp gauze. Do *not* store the tooth in antiseptic.
- Get to dentist as fast as possible — preferably within 30 minutes.

UNCONSCIOUSNESS

The first stage of unconsciousness is often drowsiness, from which the casualty may be easily aroused; the next stage may be stupor, from which arousal is difficult; the most serious and advanced stage is coma, from which the person cannot be aroused. Unless the person is fully alert, or can be roused, treat as if unconscious.

What to do for unconsciousness

- Ensure that the airway is open and that the person is breathing.
- Summon emergency medical services immediately.
- Loosen clothing around neck, chest and waist.
- Ensure that plenty of fresh air is available.
- If injuries permit, lay in recovery position — preferably with the lower part of the body slightly raised above the head. This will ensure that vomit or saliva does not flow into the lungs. (See "Recovery position," early in this chapter.)
- Cover with a blanket and stay with casualty until medical help arrives. Never leave an unconscious person unattended for even a moment unless it is absolutely necessary.
- Speak reassuringly even while the casualty appears to be unconscious.
- If consciousness returns, moisten the lips and keep the person calm and quiet. Never try to give a drink to an unconscious person.

WATER ACCIDENTS

Personal flotation devices (PFDs) should be worn at all times when boating — not just in rough or cold weather. The type to choose is a CSA-approved one. Standard kapok and loose foam vests give little protection; close-fitting foam vests or garment-type, insulated plastic flotation jackets or suits are better. The newer survival body suits — hooded and with shorts — are best for extending survival time.

What to do in a water accident

- If submerged in water or fallen overboard, don't remove clothes (except large, loose boots). Although clothing feels heavy, it retards body-cooling by over 50 percent. The heavier the clothing, the better the insulation.
- Given a choice in a boating mishap, don't dive but jump feet first into water. Lower yourself in gently if possible.
- Keep as much of the body as possible above

WATER SAFETY TIPS (ESPECIALLY FOR CHILDREN)

- **Teach children to swim as soon as possible.**
- **Don't leave unsupervised young children near water deeper than 5 cm (2 in). Never leave a baby alone near water or in the bathtub even for a moment — drowning can happen in seconds.**
- **If the telephone rings while bathing baby, wrap in towel and carry with you to the telephone — also when answering the doorbell.**
- **Never let young children play around cesspools, puddles, ditches or wells.**
- **Keep swimming pools covered with a hardtop during months when not in use.**
- **Forbid young children to enter neighbors' swimming pools without permission.**
- **Never let a toddler run loose near a pool.**
- **Know the depth of a pool before letting a child enter the water.**
- **Encourage children to use inflated tubes, rafts or armbands under supervision.**
- **Never let your child go swimming alone.**
- **Never allow a child to get out of his or her depth unless well able to swim.**
- **Keep all children out of boats unless supervised.**
- **Supervise all fishing expeditions — never let a child go fishing alone.**
- **Insist that everyone wear life-jackets or PFDs when boating or canoeing.**

"HELP" POSITION IN WATER

A "tucked-up" position lessens heat loss in cold water, increasing survival time.

water and hang on to any available floating object, such as an overturned boat or log.

- Reduce movement to a minimum. Exercise increases core heat loss — by over 30 percent — compared to holding still and shivering in cold water.
- Treading water is best (if not wearing a PFD), keeping the head above water.
- Adopt the HELP (Heat Escape Lessening Posture — see diagram), a tucked-up or fetal position, with arms tight against chest, elbows bent, knees tucked up to protect the groin. This posture lessens heat loss and increases survival time.
- Unless in warm water, never adopt the "drownproofing" position (floating with arms wide open, face down, coming up occasionally for air). Although "drownproofing" uses less energy than treading waters, much heat is lost from the open arms and immersed head. In cold Canadian waters, drownproofing is a fast route to hypothermia, exhaustion and drowning.
- Several people who are immersed can preserve body heat by huddling together, pressing their chests together.
- Sandwich children between adults or place them on top of a flotation device.
- After the rescue, wrap up in warm, dry blankets topped by a waterproof cover (even a plastic garbage bag). Later, get into a warm bath. Have hot, nonalcoholic drinks and calorie-rich snacks.

Scuba-diving complications

Scuba divers learn to recognize dive-related disorders (barotrauma) in their training, but often react to their symptoms with denial; also, some people dive without proper training. Dive-related disorders require intensive oxygen administration and frequently need treatment in a hyperbaric (pressure) chamber as well.

Anyone who shows any of the following signs of barotrauma after scuba diving — *regardless of the length or depth of the dive* — should contact a physician knowledgeable about diving without delay:

- dizziness, visual blurring;
- pain in chest or limbs;
- disorientation or personality change;
- numbness, tingling;
- unusual fatigue, weakness or paralysis;
- bloody froth from nose or mouth;
- skin itching or blotchy rash;
- shortness of breath or coughing spasms;
- staggering;
- convulsions or collapse.

If a "diving doctor" is not available, call the Divers Alert Network (DAN) 24-hour emergency hotline: (919) 684-8111.

WHERE TO LEARN FIRST AID AND CPR

You can learn first aid — including the Heimlich maneuver and most of the other topics in this chapter, except (at present) artificial respiration and CPR — in a weekend or a few evenings. Courses are run regularly by local branches of the Red Cross and the St. John Ambulance Society.

Courses in artificial respiration and CPR (as well as the Heimlich maneuver) are also taught by the Red Cross and St. John Ambulance, as well as the Heart and Stroke Foundation, the Royal Life Saving Society, and many other educational and community organizations. Courses range from a few hours to a full weekend or several evenings.

Specially tailored courses are available for people with particular needs and interests — such as babysitters, new parents and those giving extended healthcare in the home. Courses in first aid and CPR for children are also offered by the Canadian Pediatric Society.

IN CASE OF DROWNING

- **Once on land, immediately hold children hanging over the knee for five to ten seconds to encourage free drainage of water from lungs.**
- **Summon emergency services.**
- **If necessary, commence artificial respiration or CPR (if qualified).**
- **Be sure *anyone* who has aspirated (breathed in) water — fresh or salt — gets medical attention. Even someone who feels fine may have suffered lung damage which, if not treated immediately, can lead to acute respiratory distress within hours.**

Sensible use of medications

Use and abuse of prescribed drugs • Use nonprescriptions medications wisely

A

Medications are an essential part of modern healthcare, but they can bring harm if used unwisely. Today's medications fall under two broad headings: prescribed drugs available only with a physician's prescription, and nonprescription or over-the-counter (OTC) medications. Prescription medications are usually dispensed for more serious illnesses and include those most likely to be misused or to cause dangerous side effects. Some products available as over-the-counter preparations in one form need a prescription in another. The amount of active drug in the medication usually determines whether a prescription is required. Examples: "222s" (containing 8 mg codeine) can be purchased over-the-counter *without* a prescription, but "Tylenol No. 3s" (containing 30 mg codeine) need a prescription; Advil (containing 200 mg ibuprofen) is available OTC, while Motrin (tablets, containing 300 mg ibuprofen) needs a prescription.

When and how to take medications

Always follow instructions about how and when to take medications. To aid absorption, some drugs should be taken on an empty stomach (one hour before or two hours after meals) with a full glass of *cold* water. It is sometimes unwise to take medications with acidic juices, milk, fizzy pop or food unless advised by a pharmacist or doctor that it's okay to do so. For example, the (prescription) antibiotic tetracycline does not work nearly as well when accompanied by milk products, antacids or calcium supplements, as they bind to the drug and reduce its effectiveness. Laxatives containing bisacodyl (found in Dulcolax) may cause severe cramping if taken with milk or antacids. On the other hand, some medications should be consumed with food. For example, ASA (e.g., Aspirin) commonly causes some stomach bleeding and is best consumed with light food, milk or a full glass of water.

Watch for adverse drug reactions with alcohol

Alcohol interacts with many medications. Itself a potent drug, alcohol reduces coordination, depresses central-nervous-system function, diminishes alertness and impairs judgment. These effects are easily potentiated by various prescription and OTC drugs, which increase central nervous system depression, perhaps leading to respiratory failure. For instance, with antihistamines, tranquilizers or sedatives, alcohol greatly increases drowsiness, compounds brain depression and may cause dizziness, also impairing coordination and driving ability. Medications that should *not* be taken with alcohol include: muscle relaxants, codeine, antihistamines, tranquilizers, blood-pressure-lowering drugs and sleep-aids. The caution against using drugs with alcohol is usually marked on the label and should be heeded. (Note that some OTC products themselves also contain alcohol.)

Know about and watch
for drug interactions

Different drugs interact with each other and can intensify or decrease, perhaps block, efficacy. Whenever two medications are taken at the same time, there's a possibility of adverse interaction. For instance, some sedatives (such as Sleep-Eze) may render blood-thinners (anticoagulants) less effective or, on the other hand, they could increase the sedating effect of antihistamines. ASA/Aspirin and the blood-thinner, warfarin — both of which act on blood platelets — can cause excessive bleeding. According to one estimate, people taking more than five medications have a 7 percent chance of developing a serious problem; the probability rises to 24 percent in those on more than 10 medications. The additive effect of two drugs can sometimes be beneficial, as when ASA/Aspirin and codeine together increase painkilling efficacy. But their joint action can also produce unwanted side effects — such as confusion and impaired coordination. Cough and cold medications often contain antihistamines which increase drowsiness if used together with other antihistamines, antidepressants or anti-Parkinsonian drugs. By contrast, some drugs block the absorption of another. For example, antacids block the absorption of many drugs (such as tetracycline and propanolol) and can lead to phosphate depletion and vitamin-D deficiency. Mineral-oil laxatives hinder absorption of the oil-soluble vitamins (A, D, E, K) and of certain elements such as calcium.

USE AND ABUSE OF
PRESCRIBED DRUGS

Prescription-drug misuse results in more North American injuries and deaths than *all* illegal drugs combined. Adverse drug reactions account for 15 percent of hospital admissions in those over age 50. Hypnotics (sleep medications) result in almost 60 percent of drug-related emergency-room visits and 70 percent of all drug-related deaths. Prescription drugs

may be misused even if taken in moderate amounts for the wrong reason — for example, codeine taken to solve psychological distress rather than to suppress a cough or mute pain.

There is no exact dividing line between moderate and excessive drug use. If drug use begins to disrupt social and family life, damages the user's health, reduces work performance or causes financial burdens, use becomes "abuse." The Addiction Research Foundation (ARF) states that "addiction or dependence exists when a drug is so central to someone's thoughts, emotions and activities that there's a compulsive need to obtain and use it." Physical dependence can occur without the addictive component, as happens with pain patients who hardly ever become addicted to their narcotic (opiate) medications and readily give them up once the pain goes away.

According to one University of Toronto expert, "many substances are overprescribed, especially antibiotics, blood pressure medications, hypnotics (sleep-inducers) and narcotic analgesics (painkillers)." Among today's most misused medications are the opiates, such as codeine. The 1989 National Alcohol and Other Drugs Survey, conducted by Health and Welfare Canada, reported that one in 20 adult Canadians regularly uses opiate painkillers. When correctly used these medications are invaluable pain relievers, but they're sometimes inappropriately used in wrong doses and for too long.

Opiate misuse widespread

The opiates include natural poppy derivatives such as codeine and morphine and related synthetics such as oxycodone, and meperidine (Demerol). Some are contained in combination products, for instance: Percocet (a mixture of oxycodone and acetaminophen), Percodan (with oxycodone and ASA), Tylenol No. 3 (containing codeine, acetaminophen and caffeine) and Fiorinal-C (containing codeine, ASA, caffeine and barbiturates).

Canada is currently the world's top codeine consumer, with a per-capita consumption twice that of the United States. Codeine is *not* an innocuous substance. Those who habitually use it are apt to have impaired concentration and

REASONS FOR MEDICATION MISUSE

- *Strong social expectation of "a pill for every ill," a prescription to alleviate every little discomfort — even minor aches and pains due to normal everyday life!*
- *Misprescribing by physicians, perhaps because of insufficient knowledge about medications, inability to keep up with new products, overreliance on drug-* company promotion and sometimes because a prescription is easier (given little time) than unraveling the root of problems (such as anxiety disorders).
- *Too little joint decision-making by physicians and medication consumers, inadequate explanation given about what a drug does, how it should be taken, side* effects to watch for, addictive potential, possible interactions with alcohol and other substances. (Pharmacists are often better sources of information about medications.)
- *Lack of consumer knowledge about what prescribed medications are for — to allay symptoms or cure disease.*
- *Noncompliance by* consumers, who don't take the medications as prescribed and fail to report adverse effects.
- *Exaggerated publicity about "drug wonders."*
- *Pharmaceutical company advertising that persuades physicians and consumers to try new products that may be no better or cheaper than older "trusted and tried" remedies.*
- *Failure to take account of self-medication with OTC products and drug interactions. Physicians may not ask, and patients often don't tell the doctor, about OTC products being taken.*
- *Diversion of prescription drugs from physicians' offices, hospitals and pharmacies through illegal channels to the street.*

diminished performance skills — risky when on the job, operating machinery or driving a car. Studies show that drivers who take codeine have more collisions in simulated tests than those who took tranquilizers (e.g., diazepam) or alcohol (0.5 mg per kg body weight).

Physician misprescribing

The prescription pad has become as much a part of the modern physician's paraphernalia as the stethoscope. A 1987 Canadian literature review, entitled *Drug Utilization*, concluded that prescribers (physicians) and consumers are both to blame for prescription-drug misuse. The report states that "physicians know too little about the correct use of the medications they prescribe, and what they do know comes primarily from biased sources: the pharmaceutical companies." Practicing physicians are often inadequately prepared for good medicine prescribing. They may prescribe the wrong drug or faulty doses because of failure to keep up with medical advances, unfamiliarity with new medications and overreliance on the promotional material of pharmaceutical companies. It may seem easier (but is not safer) to rely on material put out by pharmaceutical companies instead of consulting scientific and pharmacological journals.

To improve matters, more ongoing physician education in applied pharmacology (how to utilize drugs to best advantage) might help. Pharmacology courses in modern medical schools often pay too little attention to the *clinical* (practical) aspect of prescribing. There's an ongoing need to update physicians' knowledge about new products, whether genuine breakthroughs or copy drugs. Some new drugs offer few or no advantages over established products. There's an equal call for consumers to become more knowledgeable medication-takers.

Consumer expectations compound drug misuse

In a society that believes "there's a pill for every ill," some people seek a remedy for every little twinge, expecting every doctor visit to terminate with a prescription, whether or not they need one. Having got the prescription, some may not properly follow directions, discontinue the medication too soon, take wrong amounts, skip or forget a pill and then take two or three to "make up." Some go on the mistaken theory that "if one dose is good, two or three must be better." Conversely, some carry a treasured prescription around without ever getting it filled, as a talisman or symbol of recovery. Not knowing (or checking) the patient's failure to follow drug-taking instructions, physicians may be misled into believing that the medication didn't work and prescribe more or other drugs.

Physicians like to appear "actively helpful,"

and sometimes handing out a prescription seems a satisfactory way to end the visit. "The act of transmitting a prescription from doctor to patient," comments one University of Toronto expert, "has nonpharmacological dimensions. It symbolizes an act of healing and the psychological reaction can facilitate recovery." In many cases, the mere anticipation of relief, the sense of "help on the way," exerts a neurohormonal effect on the mind. Up to one-third of patients respond with a placebo effect by feeling better, even if no medication is taken. But if used as a coping mechanism for unresolved or everyday problems, medications may expose people to needless risks. The dangers may arise not only from the drugs (chemicals) themselves but because reliance upon them undermines coping skills.

Doctors may feel pressured to prescribe drugs even when nondrug interventions without adverse side effects — such as a diet change, relaxation therapy, biofeedback, exercise or counseling — might be as good or better. Trying to find out what's causing a problem and discussing both medication and nondrug alternatives can help people decide which to choose. For example, while some might opt for sedatives to combat insomnia, others may decide to try relaxation therapy.

Who are the chief prescription-drug misusers?

It's a common misconception that medication misusers are fringe people, unemployed dropouts or stressed-out professionals. It may be true, for example, that the job stress of stock-market traders, intensive-care nurses or businessmen encourages a few to overuse tranquilizers or become addicted to painkillers, but not most. Anyone can develop a drug overuse problem, although there are no good "markers" to identify those likely to do so. Some fall into the trap following legitimate use of prescription medication(s) for conditions such as migraine or arthritis. They may become dependent on the medication, seek multiple prescriptions and use too much for too long. Others likely to overuse prescribed medicines are the inveterate worriers, people with chronic anxiety or those who demand instant relief of the slightest distress.

It's hard to obtain accurate figures on prescription-drug misuse because of widespread underreporting. Statistics depict only those who have been caught as abusers. But surveys conducted by Health and Welfare Canada and Toronto's Addiction Research Foundation give a rough picture. Such as they are, studies show that those convicted of prescription-drug abuse average 35 years of age, three-quarters are employed and women account for almost half the cases.

"Multiple doctoring"

Popularly called "double doctoring," the practice of visiting several physicians to obtain multiple prescriptions for the same product is quite widespread. Yet people are legally obligated to inform physicians of any controlled narcotic (opiate drug, such as codeine) obtained from another doctor within the same month. Getting a prescription for a narcotic or controlled substance from more than one physician within a 30-day period is a criminal offense under the Narcotic Control Act. It can lead to a fine or jail sentence. Health and Welfare Canada reports that nearly 90 percent of prescription-drug abuse convictions in the past decade were for opiates — codeine accounting for most of it, followed by oxycodone, Percocet and Percodan.

The elderly are particularly "endangered" by drug misuse

Adverse drug reactions among the elderly account for many hospital admissions, especially as they often take several different medications, sometimes prescribed by different physicians. Older people are at special risk of harmful drug reactions because doses suitable for younger adults may be too high for aging bodies that absorb, metabolize and eliminate drugs differently. The elderly require specialized prescribing tactics, better supervision and accurate records of all drugs taken. On medical visits they're encouraged to "brown bag" it — to put *all* medications (including over-the-counter products) in a bag to show the physician everything being taken. Older people should beware of taking drugs that are only marginally useful. They can ask their doctor(s) what the medication is for and whether there's any nondrug alternative or a substitute with fewer side effects.

Ways to improve prescription-drug use

Responsible use of prescribed medication ideally involves a partnership between the consumer with a problem (bodily discomfort, pain, stress, anxiety or illness) and the physician who diagnoses and treats the disorder. In the Hippocratic tradition and to the best of their ability, physicians follow the tenet of *primum non nocere* — "above all, do no harm." But the safe administration of substances considered too dangerous for over-the-counter availability is no easy matter. Prescribing today's vast array of medications requires considerable pharmacological knowledge. What's needed is more continuing education for physicians about new products and better-educated consumers who follow drug-taking instructions.

Consumers need to ask about their medicines — whether they are supposed to *relieve* symptoms (e.g., remove pain) or *cure* disease (e.g., kill the bacteria causing infection). Informed consumers use their medication correctly, know when and how to take it, for how long and possible side effects to watch for. The key is to weigh the benefits against possible risks.

USE NONPRESCRIPTION MEDICATIONS WISELY

Nonprescription medications, available without a doctor's prescription, are generally considered safe, with little potential for damaging health at recommended doses. Some are "public access" products that can be sold in grocery stores as well as pharmacies. Others — considered potentially harmful — are obtainable only "behind the counter" by asking the pharmacist. They include, for example, products containing the narcotic codeine — such as 222s or Tylenol No. 1. Because they contain codeine — a potent and addictive substance — these medications must be specifically requested. Similarly, the antihistamines Hismanal and Seldane have recently been placed behind the counter, because they may cause problems in people with heart ailments or because of possible adverse reactions when combined with certain drugs, such as the antibiotic erythromycin and ketoconazole, an antifungal remedy.

Interestingly, some scientists feel that if ordinary acetylsalicylic acid (ASA, such as in Aspirin) — long ago classed as an OTC substance — were to be reclassified under today's more stringent rules, it might be considered too dangerous to be a nonprescription drug (mainly because of side effects, such as stomach bleeding, which increase peptic-ulcer risks).

With such a variety of drugs on the pharmacy shelves, how does one choose which to buy? Cost is one factor: choose the cheapest generic brands. For instance, "Swiss Herbal" vitamins are the same chemicals as other, cheaper brands. Once inside your body the cells don't discriminate about the name, origin or cost of a vitamin. Similarly, one type of acetaminophen is like any other of the same

USE YOUR PRESCRIBED MEDICATIONS WISELY

- Be sure to tell the prescribing physician about all other medications being taken, including OTC products and those prescribed by other doctors.
- Write down both the generic and brand names of each medicine prescribed.
- Ask the doctor about the purpose of each medication ordered — is it for symptom relief or disease-cure? How soon will improvement occur?
- Ask the physician or pharmacist exactly how, when and for how long to take each medicine. Should the medication be taken with or between meals?
- Discard unused and outdated medications — they can deteriorate over time.
- Keep all medicines correctly labeled in original containers.
- Ask about possible side effects from a particular medication (e.g., drowsiness, difficulty in concentrating, mood, appetite or sex-drive alterations).
- Find out what to do if unpleasant or seemingly dangerous side effects occur.
- Store medicines properly. A bathroom medicine chest may be a poor location because of high humidity. Likewise, unless directed to do so, don't put medication in the refrigerator, as the cold may affect it and household members can take it by mistake. A locked cabinet in the bedroom is a good place to store medications, well beyond the reach and sight of children.

TIPS FOR SENSIBLE USE OF NONPRESCRIPTION OVER-THE-COUNTER MEDICATIONS

- When buying an OTC medication ask yourself: Why am I taking it? What type of drug is it? How soon will it work? What's the right dose? How and when should it be taken? Are there any restrictions on who should use it, or with what?
- Remember that OTC medications are meant for brief, intermittent use, not for extended periods (except under physician guidance). If symptoms increase even when using a medication — if a headache becomes worse despite use of painkillers, or a stomachache doesn't get better with antacids — seek medical advice.
- Don't take OTC preparations for continuing or worsening pain, which usually signals something wrong. Taking pills to mask symptoms will not cure a serious illness. For instance, habitually taking painkillers or antacids for a stomachache can mask an underlying condition that needs medical attention.
- Keep track of what you're taking and how much.
- Always take single-ingredient medications rather than combination products.
- Those with diabetes, epilepsy, heart conditions, bleeding disorders, high blood pressure or asthma should consult a physician before taking any OTC products.
- Always read the label and/or package insert — noting when and for how long the medicine should be taken and which drugs or foods it may interact with. (Ideally, read the inserts while in the pharmacy and ask the pharmacist about whatever is unclear.)
- Follow package instructions. People often do not comply with them. It is a common mistake to think that if one dose is good, two will be better. With many nonprescription medications (e.g., acetaminophen, ASA) there is a "ceiling" beyond which more is not only useless but possibly harmful.
- Always store medications well out of the reach of children.
- Don't reach for medicines in the dark: you may take the wrong thing.
- Tell the physician about any medications you're taking — especially before lab tests are done — as some can interfere with the results.
- If pregnant, do not use any medication without consulting your physician.
- Consult the pharmacist about medications — the pharmacist is a trained professional who can be very helpful, sometimes more so than a physician. Asking the advice of both may be a good idea.
- Make the pharmacist your ally. Choose a pharmacy close to home with a pharmacist who is helpful, especially as you get older and may need several medications or have a chronic health problem.
- Home delivery of medications is a definite plus if your mobility is restricted. To attract and keep customers, some pharmacies also offer private areas for counseling about medications.

strength. When possible, choose longer-acting medications that need to be taken only once a day (to increase compliance and reduce the possibility of forgetting to take a pill). People with digestive problems can try coated pills. Check whether the medication will make you sleepy; look for nondrowsy forms. Drugs have different effects on different people: if one drug doesn't work for you, consult a health professional or a pharmacist for advice about choosing another. Pharmacists are knowledgeable, know how drugs interact and can help you to use OTC products wisely. Try to avoid combination products: choose a different medicine for each symptom.

Generic versus brand-name medications

When a drug is first developed, it's given a generic name and a patent granting the discovering company the sole right to sell the drug while the patent remains in effect. Once the patent has expired, the drug becomes public property and other companies are free to manufacture and market it under either its generic or a brand name. Generic drugs cost 30 to 50 percent less than brand-name products, and buying generics is one way to reduce medication costs. Generic products must contain precisely the same active ingredients, in the same form and strength, as the brand-name drug. Ask the pharmacist for advice when deciding between generic versus brand-name products.

Not all nonprescription medicines are entirely safe

Today's most popular over-the-counter medications include analgesics (painkillers), laxatives, cough and cold products and allergy remedies. Since it wastes everybody's time and money to

GUIDE TO SOME COMMONLY USED NONPRESCRIPTION MEDICATIONS

Drug name	Uses	When or why to choose	Warning: Don't choose	Adverse interaction with:
ANALGESICS (Painkillers) • acetylsalicylic acid (ASA) — e.g., Aspirin, Anacin, Midol; • acetaminophen — e.g., Tylenol, Panadol, Tempra; • ibuprofen — e.g., Motrin, Advil; • products with codeine — e.g., 222s, Tylenol #1, some cough syrups.	• fever-reduction; to ease minor pains (e.g., headache, menstrual cramps, muscle aches).	• for pain relief; • for reducing fever; • to reduce inflammation — ASA (but not acetaminophen).	• if pain/problem is persistent — in which case seek medical advice.	• other painkillers; • sedatives; • alcohol; • antihistamines.
Acetylsalicylic acid (ASA) (e.g., Aspirin, Arthrisin, Entrophen, Percodan)	• to reduce fever, ease pain, lessen inflammation; • blood-thinning (anti-clotting) properties may help to prevent cardiovascular (heart) disease (but also increase wound-bleeding).	• cheap, well tolerated by most; • very effective anti-inflammatory (e.g., for arthritis); • preventive for cardiovascular disease, heart attack, stroke; ask about right dose and safety.	• if you have asthma (ASA can trigger attack); • if you have ulcers (ASA can worsen them); • in children or teens (because of link to Reye's syndrome — a deadly liver/brain condition); • if diabetic (ASA may lower blood sugar and alter insulin needs); • if on anticoagulants (unless medically advised); • before surgery.	• zidovudine; • oral antidiabetic agents, e.g., sulfonylureas (ASA prolongs action); • acetazolamide, methotrexate, valproic acid, alcohol; • anticoagulants (ASA increases risks); • other painkillers (excess may dampen breathing); • other NSAIDs (ASA decreases their efficacy).
Acetaminophen (e.g., Tylenol, Panadol, 222s).	• reduce fever, ease pain.	• if allergic to ASA (allergic reactions rare with acetaminophen); • in children (who shouldn't use ASA).	• if liver problems or alcohol abuser (as may increase liver damage).	• alcohol; • phenobarbital, other sleep-aids; • other painkillers.
Ibuprofen (e.g., Advil, Motrin, Apotex)	• painkiller.	• if effective, although relatively expensive.	• don't use if allergic to ASA.	• oral anticoagulants, diuretics, lithium, methotrexate.
Codeine-containing products (e.g., Tylenol # 1, Coryphen)	• narcotic painkillers; • cough suppressants.	• for severe pain (stronger than ASA); • for nighttime cough (codeine suppresses cough).	• if need to stay alert (it is very sedating, disturbs coordination); • if pregnant; • if constipated (it is constipating); • overuse causes pinpoint pupils, respiratory distress.	• oral anticoagulants; • alcohol (avoid combination); • other sedating products.

Drug name	Uses	When or why to choose	Warning: Don't choose	Adverse interaction with
LAXATIVES	• to alleviate constipation, facilitate passage and elimination of stool, to stimulate bowel action.	• never use for too long — if no relief after 10–14 days, consult a doctor.	• if severe cramps, diarrhea, electrolyte losses, calcium loss (osteoporosis), fatty stools, liver disease.	• other laxatives; • overuse can produce lazy, flaccid, nonfunctioning colon/bowel.
Bulk-forming laxatives e.g., Metamucil, Prodiem, psyllium, Fibyrax.	• absorb water; good for initial constipation relief, also for elderly, those with irritable bowels, postpartum; • facilitate passage of stool, stimulate bowel action — may take 2–3 days.	• inexpensive, more "natural," mild; • not absorbed into bloodstream, few side effects (although some allergies); • take with full glass of water.	• with intestinal ulcers (because can cause fecal impaction/obstruction); • for fast relief, because take some days to work; • unless you follow product instructions exactly.	• other bulk-formers.
Stimulant laxatives e.g., phenolphthalein (Ex-Lax, Feen-A-Mint), bisacodyl (Dulcolax), senna glycosides (Senokot, Glysenid), cascara, castor oil.	• speed intestinal movements; • powerful purgatives, act quicker than bulk formers (3–8 hours).	• for fast relief, occasional use; • work quickly (but unpredictably); • can cause severe cramps, diarrhea, fluid loss, electrolyte imbalance.	• when pregnant or breastfeeding (can cause diarrhea in babies); • castor oil not generally recommended (can lead to excess fluid and electrolyte losses).	• antacids; • some blood pressure medications; • cimetidine, ranitidine (stomach ulcer remedies).
Stool-softening laxatives e.g., docusate sodium (Colace, Doss), docusate calcium (Surfak).	• short-term occasional relief for constipation; • increase stool wetness, take 24–48 hours to work.	• only on physician recommendation; • for elderly, infirm, postsurgery, or if have very hard stools.	• don't use if have abdominal pain, cramps, diarrhea.	• danthron, digoxin; • mineral oil; • phenolphthalein.
Osmotic and saline laxatives e.g., magnesium hydroxide (Milk of Magnesia), magnesium citrate (Citro-Mag), magnesium sulfate, sodium phosphate (Fleet-enemas).	• powerful forms used to evacuate bowel before medical tests/surgery; • use with care; • draw water into gut and increase intestinal motility.	• with physician advice as they are potent agents; • not in the infirm, heart patients.	• without medical advice; • don't use if have kidney disorders, heart disease, high blood pressure; • risk of dehydration, electrolyte imbalance, cramps, gas.	• digoxin; • tetracycline; • diuretics.
Lubricant laxatives e.g., liquid petrolatum (Mineral oil), olive oil, Agarol.	• coat and soften stools; • take 6–8 hours to work; • emulsified oils more effective than nonemulsified forms; • only for occasional use.	• best to use on doctor's recommendation; • after surgery or hemorrhoid treatment to avoid danger of "straining" (e.g., with hernia, aneurysm, postsurgery).	• if elderly, debilitated, very young (inhalation of oil may cause pneumonia); may delay gastric (stomach) emptying; • in pregnancy (may decrease absorption of vitamin K by fetus).	• possibly decrease effect of anticoagulants; • hinder absorption of fat-soluble vitamins (A, D, E, K).

GUIDE TO SOME COMMONLY USED NONPRESCRIPTION MEDICATIONS (continued)

Drug name	Uses	When or why to choose	Warning: Don't choose	Adverse interaction with:
ANTACIDS (e.g., Tums, Rolaids, Amphojel)	• to neutralize stomach acidity, heartburn, gastritis, indigestion; • liquid forms act better than tablets (chew well, with full glass of water); • contain various ingredients — e.g., calcium carbonate, magnesium, aluminum; • promote healing of gastric mucosa (lining).	• choose types least likely to disturb electrolyte balance; • for mild heartburn, indigestion; • best taken 1–3 hours after meals to prolong effects — up to three hours; • if no relief after 2 weeks or if problem recurs — see doctor; • select most suitable type — not indiscriminately.	• interchangeably — differ in action; • avoid calcium-rich types for long-term use (upset bone turnover); • aluminum and magnesium products offer best results with least toxicity; • if on low-salt diet, choose forms without sodium; • if have persistent stomach pain or indigestion — need medical investigation.	• may enhance action of ephedrine and some antidepressants; • decrease absorption of tetracyclines, digoxin, corticosteroids, levodopa, diazepam, valproic acid, ketoconazole (Nizoral), ranitidine (Zantac); • increase clearance of ASA and phenobarbital (Luminal); • interfere with warfarin, anticonvulsants.
Sodium bicarbonate e.g., Alka Seltzer, Eno.	• good for fast, short-term relief of overeating, indigestion, heartburn, gastritis (acid stomach); • not for too long — may produce sodium overload.	• for most transient digestive upsets (N.B.: baking soda and water — cheaper than Alka Seltzer and equally effective).	• if have peptic ulcer or gastric bleeding; • if pregnant; • if on low-sodium diet or diuretics; • not with milk or calcium — can cause milk-alkali syndrome (nausea, vomiting, mental confusion).	• iron supplements; • ketoconazole (antifungal); • levodopa; • lithium; • some antibiotics; • salicylates (e.g., ASA).
Calcium carbonate e.g., Tums, Os-Cal, Caltrate.	• potent acid neutralizer.	• for occasional heartburn, gastritis; • for gas or bloating.	• for prolonged time, as may cause hypercalcemia (which may lead to kidney stones).	• anticoagulants, corticosteroids, diuretics, iron supplements.
Aluminum e.g., Amphojel, Basaljel.	• good acid-neutralizing ability (but less than calcium carbonate).	• choose for occasional use; • avoid if have kidney problems.	• if constipated (as is constipating); • if family history of Alzheimer's.	• can bind to and prevent absorption of phosphate.
VITAMINS Popular OTC drugs — many people believe vitamins give extra energy, ward off colds and make one "smarter" — but no scientific validity.	• needed for all body functions but well-balanced diets supply plenty; • most don't need supplements, but preschoolers, pregnant or breastfeeding women, the elderly, alcoholic and malnourished may need extra vitamins; also vegetarians lacking vitamin B_2 (riboflavin) and B_{12}.	• choose only products with DIN numbers (federal drug permits); • never take in excess of recommended daily allowances.	• never take megadoses; • keep out of children's reach (excess can be toxic).	

VITAMINS (continued)

Drug name	Uses	When or why to choose	Warning: Don't choose	Adverse interaction with:
Vitamin C	• some people take megadoses in mistaken belief vitamin C will prevent colds or other ills.	• remarkably safe even at high doses, but megadoses can decrease vitamin B_{12} absorption; side effects include diarrhea, nausea, urinary-tract stones.	• in pregnancy — large doses may cause "rebound" scurvy in newborns; • if prone to kidney stones.	• amphetamines; • some antidepressants; • ASA.
Vitamin A, Vitamin D (Fat-soluble vitamins)	• for health of bones, skin, teeth and eyes.	• with calcium (1000 mg per day) for prevention of osteoporosis — after menopause, in women (vitamin D).	• high doses can lead to hypervitaminosis A (fatigue, malaise, lethargy, scaly skin, loss of hair or hyper-vitaminosis D (anorexia, nausea, wakefulness, weight loss, kidney damage).	• cholestyramine; • mineral oil (decreases vitamin absorption); • isotretinoin (for skin problems).
Iron	• if iron-deficient (e.g., anemic).	• use if anemic (low iron stores); • if on vegetarian diets low in iron; • watch for toxicity (even 15 tablets of ferrous sulfate may be lethal).	• in children or elderly for long time as may develop iron poisoning which can cause acute illness; • not if have fever (iron alters body reaction to fever).	• interacts with ASA, may cause excess bleeding; • don't take with antacids (which decrease iron absorption); • tetracycline reduces absorption.
COLD MEDICATIONS	• to relieve runny nose, nasal congestion; • often sold in combination, perhaps with vitamin C, antihistamines; • single-ingredient types best.	• select single-ingredient medicines — e.g., pseudoephedrine for decongestion; ASA (Aspirin) for muscle aches and fever; DM or codeine for cough; antihistamine for allergy symptoms.	• not in pregnancy without medical advice (especially forms containing pseudoephedrine); • if have asthma, diabetes, heart condition.	• may alter effect of oral antidiabetic pills (e.g., DiaBeta).
Oral decongestants e.g., pseudoephedrine (e.g., Actifed, Novahistex, Sinutab, Benylin, Sudafed), phenylpropanolamine, phenylephrine (Neo-Synephrine, Novahistine).	• to reduce congestion, nasal stuffiness, shrink nasal tissues; • peak effect 3–4 hours after taken.	• if don't need sleep (decongestants are stimulating, perk one up), may transiently raise blood pressure.	• if need sleep; • if have hypertension, thyroid or heart condition, diabetes, glaucoma; • if taking MOAI anti-depressants.	• certain blood-pressure pills.
Nasal decongestant sprays e.g., naphazoline (Privine, Rhino-Mex-N), xylometazoline (Otrivin), oxymetazoline (Afrin, Dristan Mist).	• for temporary relief of nasal stuffiness; • shrink nasal tissues.	• if desire fast local relief rather than slower systemic effect; • impair ciliary action in clearing mucus.	• for long periods of time — more than 3–5 days — as causes rebound congestion if overused; • if have diabetes, thyroid trouble, heart disease, glaucoma.	• may irritate nasal tissues; • interact with CNS stimulants (cause jitteriness).

GUIDE TO SOME COMMONLY USED NONPRESCRIPTION MEDICATIONS (continued)

Drug name	Uses	When or why to choose	Warning: Don't choose	Adverse interaction with:
COUGH MEDICINES **DM/dextromethorphan** e.g., Balminil DM syrup, Delsym, Benylin.	• DM is nondrowsy, doesn't cause jitteriness; best choice for children; • nonaddictive (in contrast to codeine).	• for dry cough or if cough prevents sleep.	• for too long, if need to expel phlegm, mucus.	• MAOI antidepressants.
Codeine (e.g., Benylin-codeine, D.E.)	• acts on brain's cough center and is sedating (with abuse potential — can be addictive).	• for those nonresponsive to DM, e.g., for whooping cough; • effect lasts 3–6 hours.	• for long periods, if tendency to addiction — not without medical advice; • not in children under age 12.	• alcohol, other painkillers, sedatives, antihistamines (enhanced depression of brain and breathing).
ANTIHISTAMINES e.g., ethanolamines (such as Benadryl, Tavist), ethylenediamines (e.g., Pyribenzamine), alkylamines (e.g., Chlor-Tripolon, Dimetane, Actifed), piperazines (e.g., Atarax).	• for hay fever, hives, skin rashes and other allergies; • very sedating, can have other side effects.	• ethanalomines most sedating but give least gastrointestinal side effects; • alkylamine, piperazines (less sedating); • phenothiazines and piperazines for motion sickness, skin allergies, rashes.	• for stuffy nose; • if must stay awake, drive a car, operate machinery; • if have narrow-angle glaucoma; • during pregnancy (without medical advice); • if have prostate trouble (may worsen it).	• MAOI antidepressants; • narcotics (e.g., codeine); • sedatives; • alcohol (bad mix); • muscle relaxants.
New (nondrowsy) antihistamines terfenadine (Seldane), astemizole (Hismanal), loratadine (Claritin).	• nonsedating, longer-acting.	• useful if other antihistamines put you to sleep; some find them good, but adverse cardiovascular effects reported if taken in excess.	• if have heart, blood-pressure, liver problems; • without medical advice — too much can produce health-harming cardiovascular effects.	• sleep-aids, alcohol, barbiturates; • erythromycin; • ketoconazole (but not loratadine).

dash off to the doctor for every bellyache or muscle twinge, OTC drugs are useful for minor ailments. However, successful self-medication depends on good judgment, common sense and reading the labels. Self-medicating with OTC products should never delay or deter you from seeking medical advice for a persistent or serious problem. It is foolish to mask a severe headache (that may signal a stroke) with ASA or to treat the symptoms of bowel cancer with Milk of Magnesia.

Since nonprescription medications — for example, painkillers (such as acetaminophen or Tylenol), antihistamines (such as chlorpheniramine or Chlor-Tripolon) and laxatives (such as phenolphthalein or Ex-Lax) — are sold in supermarkets alongside cat food and soap, many assume that they and other OTC medications are harmless. While over-the-counter drugs are used by millions of people and generally considered safe, they are still chemicals that affect the body's metabolism. Even nonprescription drugs can be toxic and cause adverse side effects in some people. All medications, even those bought at the corner variety store, must be treated with cautious respect. Consumers should make it their business to be "informed" medication users, read labels carefully and ask their pharmacist about what it is they're taking.

Read the labels!

When selecting OTC medications, look for the following information: the name of the medication, directions for use, special precautions, the suggested dosage and the list of possible (main) adverse effects. The package inserts and labels usually contain information about the purpose of the medication, its proper dosage, precautions, warnings about when not to take it and a mention of possible drug interactions. As the print may be small, you can ask the pharmacist to read or explain it to you.

A recent survey revealed that many people don't read labels or seek medical advice before popping pills. Most OTC drug users consult neither a physician or pharmacist about the medications they're taking, nor about mixing them with each other. Yet it can be potentially risky to mix a combination of drugs — either OTC or prescription types. For instance, the survey found that one-third of allergy sufferers take their allergy medication along with several other products, perhaps causing drug interactions that compound drowsiness. In addition, 70 percent of allergy sufferers wrongly thought that the allergy drugs lose their effectiveness after a while, 40 percent mistakenly believing that all allergy drugs are much the same. Adding OTC to prescription medications can make a dangerous cocktail. U.S. statistics show that almost 10 percent of emergency-room poisonings involve OTC drugs, mostly analgesics (painkillers) and sedatives.

To obtain maximum benefits while minimizing harmful effects, people should find out as much as possible about their medicines. Don't hesitate to question your physician and/or pharmacist. While some OTC drug side effects are mild and relatively harmless — such as feeling slightly "hyper" or restless (as with some decongestants) or somewhat constipated (as with codeine-containing products) — other side effects may be serious and warrant a call or visit to the physician. Examples of potentially hazardous side effects are dizziness (e.g., from decongestants), allergies, excessive drowsiness (e.g., from antihistamines) and stomach bleeds (e.g., from ASA). Also, someone with a specific disease may not realize the possibly risky effects

---

AVOID LAXATIVE MISUSE

Laxatives help to soften, add bulk and lubricate bowel contents, or to stimulate and facilitate the passage and elimination of stools. They can be very effective if used occasionally, but they are frequently abused, especially by the elderly and by people with eating disorders such as anorexics and bulimics. Constipation has different meanings for different people and as a result some people misuse laxatives to alleviate their so-called irregularity. The most sensible and cheapest way to relieve constipation is to increase the intake of dietary fiber and water and to exercise more. In general, a laxative should not be used for more than one week. If symptoms persist for more than two weeks, see a physician. Excessive use of laxatives can lead to severe cramps, diarrhea or vomiting, which results in fluid and salt losses. Long-term use over many years can permanently weaken bowel function, producing lazy, flaccid intestines that increase the problem of constipation and lead to still more laxative abuse.

---

of an OTC medication. For example, diabetics may be unaware of the high sugar content of some cough syrups or the alcohol in other medicines and get into trouble from it.

"Dependence" an occasional problem with OTC drugs

Although most people know that street drugs are addicting, few link dependence to OTC products. Yet some over-the-counter medicines can produce dependence, the two main culprits being laxatives and nasal-decongestant sprays. When taken for prolonged periods, these drugs can produce withdrawal or rebound symptoms. The net result may be a paradoxical situation in which the symptoms that initially led to drug use become worse, necessitating still more medicine. For example, nasal-decongestant sprays constrict the swollen nasal tissues, shrink blood vessels and temporarily ease congestion. But if taken too often and repeatedly, the tissues no longer react, leading to a vicious cycle with greater congestion and an increased need for nasal spray.

Psychological addiction is less common with OTC than prescription medications but can occur, especially with phenypropanolamine (sometimes called "pseudospeed"), a central-nervous-system stimulant found in many cough and cold remedies. There are occasional reports of people becoming addicted to cough syrups, and repeated administration or overuse of these agents has led to drug-induced psychosis.

Index